Medicine, Ethics
and
the Law

Second Edition

This book is dedicated to my mother Clare with all my love

Medicine, Ethics and the Law

Second Edition

by

DEIRDRE MADDEN

BCL, LLM, PhD, BL
Senior Lecturer in Law, University College Cork

Bloomsbury Professional

Published by
Bloomsbury Professional
Maxwelton House
41–43 Boltro Road
Haywards Heath
West Sussex
RH16 1BJ

Bloomsbury Professional
The Fitzwilliam Business Centre
26 Upper Pembroke Street
Dublin 2

ISBN: 9781847666703

© Bloomsbury Professional Limited 2011
Bloomsbury Professional, an imprint of Bloomsbury Publishing Plc

British Library Cataloguing-in-Publication Data
A catalogue record for this book is available from the British Library

Typeset by Marlex Editorial Services Ltd, Dublin, Ireland
Printed and bound in Great Britain by
Martins the Printers, Berwick-upon-Tweed, Northumberland

Preface

In the second edition of this book I hope to provide students, researchers and practitioners of medical law and ethics with a text which will enable them to understand and enjoy learning about the fascinating and complex issues that arise in this subject area. The topics covered by this book offer a great opportunity to reflect on and analyse many diverse legal and ethical concepts and their application to medical practice in a constantly changing environment of new medical treatments, surgical techniques and innovative research.

As well as updating all of the chapters contained in the previous edition published in 2002 I have also chosen to add two new chapters to this edition. Chapter Ten deals with property rights in the human body including issues relating to the retention of organs following post-mortem examinations and the legal and ethical concerns that arise in relation to the storage of human tissue for research. Chapter Thirteen deals with medical research and clinical trials, the ethical questions that arise in this context and the regulatory mechanisms currently in operation in Ireland. I have chosen not to include organ donation/ transplantation in this edition as there is currently no legislation in Ireland on this matter and there have not been any relevant judicial decisions in Ireland. It is expected that this area will be the subject of legislation in the near future and will hopefully feature in further editions of this text. Nor have I included medical negligence in this edition as there are many excellent tort law texts already in existence which cover this area, in particular those written by my former colleague John Healy.

In updating previous chapters and researching new topics for this edition I have been very fortunate in learning a great deal from discussions with friends and colleagues in UCC, in particular Dr Mary Donnelly whose expertise and writings on healthcare decision-making I greatly admire, Professor Maeve McDonagh who helped my understanding of freedom of information and data protection law, and Professor David Gwynn Morgan who is always available to clarify questions about administrative law. I am indebted to Mr William Kennedy, Head of Professional Standards at the Medical Council for reading and commenting on Chapter Two of this book, and to Professor Andrew Green (UCD) who provided helpful comments on Chapter Eight. I am also grateful to colleagues in other universities, in particular Professor David Smith (RCSI) who has always been very generous in sharing knowledge and literature on medical ethics.

I am very lucky to work in an energetic and research-active academic department in UCC and throughout my career here I have enjoyed the support and friendship of my colleagues in the law department as well as those in other faculties and colleges in UCC; I am grateful to all of them. My understanding of medical law and ethics has also been enhanced by periods of time spent teaching at the law school in St Louis University, Missouri, where the warm welcome and interest of faculty and students in this area of law made my visits an academic and personal pleasure. I am very grateful to colleagues and friends there and I look forward to more visits in coming years.

In recent years I have been very fortunate to have had the opportunity to work with people from diverse academic and professional backgrounds in other colleges and universities, government departments, state agencies, regulatory bodies, and on many multi-disciplinary commissions and working groups. Though they are too numerous to mention individually, I greatly appreciate the expertise of all those I have worked with in these organisations as well as the individuals whose personal accounts of their interactions with the health service have taught me far more than I can express in this book. I would also like to sincerely thank the members and staff at the Medical Council for teaching me so much about medical practice and professional regulation and, in particular, Professor Kieran Murphy, President of the Medical Council, for his support for my crusade about the importance of medical ethics.

The staff at Bloomsbury Professional, in particular Sandra Mulvey, have been a pleasure to work with, and have never crossed the delicate line between encouragement and pressure. It is not an easy task to keep authors enthusiastic during the writing process, and I very much appreciate the patience, professionalism and courtesy shown to me throughout this time.

I would also like to sincerely thank my close friends, in particular Anne Marie Linehan, Margo Topham, Geraldine Luddy, Anthony Cunningham, Jennifer Dowler and Gayle Hantak, for their friendship and support over the last few years.

Finally, I would like to thank my family, in particular my wonderful parents Alf and Clare who continue to inspire me with their courage, strength and wisdom, and my lovely children Ali, Jess, Kate and James of whom I am immensely proud. I would also like to thank my partner Denis for his endless patience, good humour and encouragement while I was writing this book and for his incredible personal support in recent months.

Deirdre Madden
21 July 2011

Contents

Chapter 4   Assisted Reproduction

Chapter 5   Artificial Insemination and Egg Donation

Chapter 6   In Vitro Fertilisation

Chapter 7   Surrogate Motherhood

Chapter 8   Genetics

Chapter 9   Capacity, Consent and Refusal of Treatment

Chapter 13 Medical Research

Table of Cases

Table of Legislation

Bunreacht na hÉireann

European Legislation

Statutory Instruments

Other Jurisdictions

Chapter 1

Provision of Health Care in Ireland

INTRODUCTION

[1.01] The provision of health care in Ireland is based on a mixture of public and private funding. The State has been involved in the funding and allocation of health care resources since the 19th century, with many of the principles upon which the present health care system is founded informed by that historical context. This chapter will examine the development of the role of the State in health care provision from the 19th century and the structure of the modern system. It will examine the legal rights of citizens to health care and whether such rights may be enforced against the State either under the provisions of the Constitution, or by virtue of international obligations. The involvement of the government in the decision-making process as it relates to allocation of health care resources at a national level is also examined.

THE ROLE OF THE STATE IN HEALTH CARE PROVISION

The historical context

[1.02] The provision of medical relief services and public health in the 19th century was the basis upon which the modern health service was founded. At the turn of the 20th century few people worried about the State's role in ensuring access to high-quality health care because the limitations then placed on medicine's ability to conquer disease were such that hospitals remained places of last resort for those with untreatable illness, and for those with insufficient means to access even minimum medical care.[1]

> People did not expect the state to provide for more than a minimum level of medical care for the population. Government in these islands had not yet accepted a general responsibility for the health of the population, nor a duty to make medical facilities available to all at little or no cost to the patient...Only the medical care of the very poor and the control of infections associated with poverty were considered to warrant public intervention. These responsibilities were known to contemporaries as 'medical relief' and 'public health' respectively.[2]

[1.03] Medical relief was the provision of infirmaries for the care of the sick and diseased poor in each county, financed by public and charitable efforts. A dispensary service operated which divided the country into districts with medical officers and

---

[1] For a more detailed discussion of medicine and Irish society in the 20th century, see Barrington, *Health, Medicine & Politics in Ireland 1900–1970* (Institute of Public Administration, 1987).

[2] Barrington, *Health, Medicine & Politics in Ireland 1900–1970* (Institute of Public Administration, 1987) p 4.

1

sometimes midwives to attend to the poor. These medical officers, whose recruitment and educational qualifications were assessed under criteria laid down by the Poor Law Commission, had to attend every sick person in the district possessing a ticket entitling them to attendance at home or at the dispensary. These officers were often the medical doctors for the workhouses and soon became responsible for other duties, such as vaccination and birth registration, leading to the emergence of the 'general' practitioner and calls for further development in the health service.[3] At the same time, these doctors were free to devote the time not spent on these duties to private practice. These private patients were normally seen at the doctor's house. "It was taken for granted that private and public patients should be seen in separate premises, since 'respectable' people feared catching infections from the poor."[4]

[1.04] The public health movement developed with the aim of preventing the spread of infectious disease in Ireland and Great Britain. Legislation was enacted to protect water supplies, appoint sanitary inspectors, destroy unsound food, isolate those suffering from infectious disease and supervise slaughterhouses. However, the apathy with which many local authorities approached their tasks, the poverty of the majority of Irish people and the opposition to increases in taxation with which to fund these improvements, made sure that progress was very slow in this context.

[1.05] Pressure for reform of the system began to grow around the early 1900s as access to medical care began to be viewed as a social right of all citizens, mirrored by an increased role and responsibility for government. Health insurance was introduced in Britain in 1911 to give people some protection against medical costs and loss of income due to ill health and unemployment. Compulsory contributors to the scheme included most wage earners, whose contribution would be boosted by contributions from employers and the State. Others could join on a voluntary basis. This insurance was to entitle the contributor to free attendance by a medical practitioner and free medicines. They would be entitled to maternity and sick benefits as well as disability and sanatorium benefits. The difficulty in the Irish context was its practical applicability here in very different social circumstances. Due to the intervention of many factors – socio-political issues, religious hierarchical opinion, the resistance of sections of the medical profession and the financial implications – insurance-based medical benefit was not introduced to Ireland, and the development of the health systems in Ireland and Britain thereafter continued along different lines.

[1.06] A national health insurance scheme for Ireland was again put forward in the 1930s, although with a different emphasis. Around this time, a more modern hospital service was put into place and the National Health Insurance Act 1941 was designed to extend hospital benefits rather than medical benefit. It suffered from problems relating to funding, extensions to the insured person's family, and applicability to those outside the system, such as the self-employed. The consequent lack of attention given to the dispensary service, together with the prevalence of tuberculosis, led to many problems in the early 1940s.

---

3   Hensey, *The Health Services of Ireland* (2nd edn, Institute of Public Administration 1972) p 8.
4   Barrington, *Health, Medicine & Politics in Ireland 1900–1970* (Institute of Public Administration, 1987) p 11.

[1.07] Ironically, 'the Emergency' during World War II advanced the health service in a number of ways due to a widening of access to the service and a focus on strategic plans for the development of a comprehensive system. Deprivation and poverty during these years increased concentration on the control of infectious diseases and pressure for the establishment of a separate Department of Health, which was set in motion in 1944. The Department of Local Government and Public Health had, by the end of 1945, a strategy for the provision of a free health service and other short-term objectives such as the improved treatment of tuberculosis and other conditions, as well as the protection of the health of mothers and children. "The challenge was to persuade the government and the medical profession to follow the road charted by the Department."[5]

[1.08] The Public Health Bill was drafted in 1945 primarily to deal with infectious diseases (which proved controversial in its methodology), but also dealt with the provision of maternity services, and the compulsory medical inspection of school children. Although much opposition was voiced to the Bill's provision of powers of detention and inspection, along the lines of State interference with individual liberty and increasing control over citizens' lives, there was nonetheless a good deal of support for the aim of improvement of the health of mothers and children. However, due to the inevitable interference of personal political ambitions and rumblings within the medical profession about intervention in its practices, the sponsor of the Bill was forced to resign in 1946 when the Bill was at its final stage. Despite this setback, a separate Department of Health was set up in 1946, with the first Minister for Health appointed in 1947. Many of the provisions of the doomed 1945 Bill were restated with some amendments to remove its more controversial provisions. The two most controversial issues remained the impact that a free mother-and-child health service would have on the medical profession, and the interference with family authority and privacy imposed by compulsory medical inspection in schools. The Catholic hierarchy was also extremely concerned at the direction of 'State medicine' and its interference with the Church's position on contraception, abortion and sex education. This led to an alliance between the Church and the medical profession in opposition to the provisions of the Act and the more wide-ranging ambitions for reform of the health services to which the government of the day seemed committed.

[1.09] When pressure was put on the subsequent Minister for Health, Dr Noel Browne, to introduce a mother-and-child scheme as provided for by the Act, much opposition came his way, both political and religious. Although the Minister was heavily committed to other issues, such as hospital building programmes and the eradication of tuberculosis, he was obliged to make good on the scheme set out in the Act. His proposals for the introduction of such a scheme emphasised that the services (which provided for children up to 16 years and maternity care for expectant mothers) would be free and voluntary. The Minister also wanted to introduce a medical card, as a substitute for the dispensary tickets that entitled the holder to once-off care. These issues, together with a hostile relationship with the medical profession, led to vociferous opposition to the scheme, both from the profession itself and the Catholic hierarchy, that eventually caused the Minister to resign, having failed to secure the support of his government

---

[5]   Barrington, *Health, Medicine & Politics in Ireland 1900–1970* (Institute of Public Administration, 1987) p 167.

colleagues for the introduction of his scheme. The influence of the Catholic Church on politics was clear to all when correspondence between the Church, the Minister and the Taoiseach was released to the press after the Minister's resignation.

[1.10] In the aftermath of this debacle the Government fell, and the general election that followed concentrated on health issues as never before. The new Minister for Health tactically decided to introduce a weakened version of the mother-and-child scheme as part of a wider extension of health services enabled by the hospital building programme and other improvements brought about by his predecessor. Despite resistance to the idea of a free health service, an uneasy compromise was reached with the profession and the Church, and the Health Act 1953 became law. "The government conceded nothing on the principle that the state had a responsibility for the medical care of the majority of the population and for the welfare of all mothers and infants…".[6] However, while the Act introduced many improvements on the system as it existed prior to 1950, the notion of a free health service for all sectors of the population and across all services remained unrealistic in the face of such opposition as existed. For example, general practice was left unchanged by the Act, except for the ability to provide a mother-and-infant service to lower- and middle-class mothers free of charge. However, in hindsight it did provide a stepping stone to other changes that followed and showed the profession that, in many ways, it had less to fear from a free service than it imagined.

[1.11] Controversy and political disagreement continued to dog the debate surrounding any extensions of the mother-and-infant scheme to other groups and services. Proposals were put forward and rejected in the 1960s, and eventually in 1970 the Health Act was introduced which, inter alia, provided for a scheme to compensate persons of lower income for expenditure on prescribed drugs, and for those suffering from certain diseases, regardless of income. The dispensary system was replaced with a choice-of-doctor scheme, which allowed all general practitioners to treat public patients and which took control from the department over the organisation of general practice. Changes were made to health service administration, with the setting up of eight regional health boards. Despite a general election during the time when the Bill was being discussed, government policy remained unchanged and the Bill became law in 1970. The profession became reconciled to working within a system that was publicly funded and centrally planned.

[1.12] In summary, the main factors that give Irish medical services their character are "the legacy of the nineteenth century, the role of the state as the chief mediating force between the medical profession and the patient … the aspiration for a health service comparable to Britain's and the limits set by the formidable alliance of the Catholic Church and the medical profession."[7] These characteristics, also shaped by economic factors such as severe cutbacks on health spending in the 1980s followed by increased availability of funding with the birth of the Celtic Tiger in the 1990s, have led to sharp criticism in recent years of the disparity in levels of services available to public and private patients, the growth of private health insurance and concerns over lengthy

---

6   Barrington, *Health, Medicine & Politics in Ireland 1900–1970* (Institute of Public Administration, 1987) p 241.

7   Barrington, *Health, Medicine & Politics in Ireland 1900–1970* (Institute of Public Administration, 1987) p 286.

waiting lists for treatment. The foundation in 1957 of the Voluntary Health Insurance (VHI) scheme may have been motivated in part by a desire to provide private income for the medical profession who had, with the help of the Catholic Church as outlined above, opposed a comprehensive public health system such as existed in Britain. Private health insurance generally provides preferential access to health care at rates less than the full economic cost, the balance of the costs being provided by the State. The opening of the market to foreign competitors by the Health Insurance Act in 1994 led to the entry to the Irish market of other health insurers, all of whom are required to provide community rating, open access and lifetime cover to members. Health insurance companies must offer a minimum level of benefits to patients in respect of in-patient and out-patient treatment, maternity benefits, convalescence and psychiatric treatment. The minimum accommodation level is semi-private in a public hospital. Health insurance companies must accept anyone who wishes to join, subject to any applicable waiting periods before coverage takes effect, regardless of age, sex or health status. This is known as 'open enrolment'.

[1.13] The Health Insurance Authority is the independent statutory regulator for the private health insurance market in Ireland. The Authority monitors the operation of health insurance businesses and advises the Minister for Health and Children in this regard, including assessing the effect of any regulations or new legislation on consumers. The Authority aims to ensure that consumers are aware of their rights, that policies and publicity material describe coverage in a fair and comparable way and that community rating, open enrolment and lifetime coverage are protected and maintained. The Authority also reviews the appropriateness of the procedures used by insurers in their dealings with consumers. One of the Authority's functions relates to the operation of a Risk Equalisation Scheme. Risk equalisation is a process that aims to equitably neutralise differences in insurers' costs that arise due to variations in the health status of their members. The Minister for Health and Children determined that risk equalisation would commence from 1 January 2006.

The current structure of the Irish health service

[1.14] Ireland's health system is characterised by a mix of public and private health service funding and provision. The public system is predominantly tax-funded and is determined annually in negotiations between the Departments of Finance and Health. Funding is provided by the Department of Health to the Health Service Executive (HSE) as well as voluntary hospitals and other service delivery agencies in the voluntary sector.

[1.15] In Ireland, those without private health insurance are either covered by the General Medical Scheme (GMS) or have no cover. The GMS provides free hospital and general practitioner care to holders of medical cards, which accounts for approximately 30 per cent of the population. It is designed primarily for the elderly and social welfare recipients, and does not assist those on low incomes who fall just outside the threshold but cannot afford to pay the premiums for private insurance. From 2000, all patients over the age of 70 years became entitled to a medical card, irrespective of their financial means. For those under 70 years, cards are issued on the basis of financial need or chronic disease requiring frequent medical assistance/prescription. Since 2005, there are two categories of medical cards – the first is the traditional card, which entitles the person to free GP care and prescription medicine while the second covers GP care only.

Of the remaining 70 per cent of the population, just under 50 per cent have private health insurance and the others are not covered by either the GMS or by private insurance.

[1.16] Other State services include mother-and-infant services during and immediately after birth, childhood vaccinations, free or subsidised care for those with Hepatitis C contracted from the use of blood products within Ireland, medication and appliances for patients with certain long-term illnesses. Since 1991 all persons, regardless of income, are entitled to free in-patient services in public hospitals and out-patient clinics. Patients who do not have medical cards must pay a nominal amount for in-patient hospital care. Non-medical card holders attending Accident and Emergency services must also pay a fee unless referred to A & E by their general practitioner. There is also a Drug Payment Scheme in operation which limits the maximum monthly payment by an individual or family for prescription medicines, with the remainder of the costs being paid by the State.

[1.17] The State's role in the provision of health services has changed in character from provider of services to the poor to overall regulation of standards and an increase in management of targets and objectives within the system. The Minister for Health and Children is responsible for the development and operation of the health services in accordance with legislation and public policy. This includes making statutory regulations, supervising the activities of the health boards and controlling the methods of appointment and conditions of employment of health personnel. The Department, which was set up in 1947, supports the Minister in the formulation, development and evaluation of health policy. Its stated objectives include the strategic development of services; the encouragement of the highest standards of effectiveness, efficiency, equity, quality and value for money in the health system; the improvement of accountability at all levels of the health services; the encouragement of a customer-service ethos in the health service; the optimisation of staff performance; and the representation of Irish interests in international forums relating to health issues.[8]

[1.18] Health services in Ireland are provided by a number of different bodies, namely the HSE, the voluntary hospitals and agencies; specialist bodies; bodies established under the Health (Corporate Bodies) Act; and registration bodies. Prior to the establishment of the HSE, local health boards had a statutory responsibility under the Health Act 1970 (as amended by the Health (Amendment) (No 3) Act, 1996) to administer the services provided for in health legislation and by the Minister. Health boards existed to manage services across geographical areas and were based on population size, local planning and development advice. The Boards were made up of elected county councillors, health and other professionals and Ministerial nominees, who often represented user groups. The Boards' functions included resource allocation, co-operation with voluntary bodies providing services in the area and implementing government policy. Public hospitals, which include regional and county hospitals, and district, fever and orthopaedic hospitals, were managed by the Health Boards and funding was sought from the budget allocated to each board by the Department of Health. The Hospitals Board (*Comhairle na hOispideal*) was established by the 1970 Act to advise the Minister for Health in relation to the work of hospitals and to regulate the role, number and qualifications of consultants appointed to hospitals. The Health

---

[8] *Statement of Strategy* (Department of Health and Children, 1997).

Board structure has been fundamentally changed by the establishment of the HSE, which is discussed below.

[1.19] The voluntary health sector has long been recognised by the Department of Health as playing an integral role in the provision of health services in Ireland, through identification of community needs and development of appropriate responses. This sector is the major provider of services to those suffering from mental disabilities in the country. Voluntary hospitals, first instigated in the early 18th century to cater for the sick poor, are funded by the Department of Health but run by boards comprised of religious and lay members. Private hospitals and clinics also exist in the health care system, some of which are managed by religious orders; others are managed by commercial enterprises and largely financed by direct payment for services from patients or indirectly through health insurers and private investors. At the current time, such private enterprises exist without any State regulation or licensing, although it is intended that this will change with the introduction of legislation in 2012. This is discussed further below.

[1.20] Specialist bodies have also been established under specific Acts, such as the Food Safety Authority of Ireland and the Irish Medicines Board. These bodies provide an advisory service to the Department of Health on a range of issues, such as food safety and the licensing of medicinal products for human use. Other bodies set up under the Health (Corporate Bodies) Act 1961 for the purpose of advising on health policy and the provision of health services on a national basis, include the Health Research Board (which promotes, commissions and conducts medical research); the Irish Blood Transfusion Service Board (which organises the national blood transfusion service); and the National Rehabilitation Board (which provides guidance, training, information and public awareness services for people with physical disabilities). There are a number of professional regulatory bodies such as the Medical Council, the Dental Council and An Bord Altranais (the Nursing Board), which maintain a register of health practitioners, monitor standards of education and training and provide a disciplinary process to inquire into alleged unprofessional conduct and unfitness to practise.

Reform of the health service

[1.21] The modern reform of the Irish health services began with the publication by the Department of Health in 1994 of the strategy document called *Shaping a Healthier Future: A Strategy for Effective Healthcare in the 1990s*. It was based on three principles: equity, quality and accountability. On equity, the strategy proposed that access to health care should be based on need rather than ability to pay. On quality, it recommended a more modern approach using audit as a tool to ensure the best outcomes. On accountability, it required service providers to take responsibility for achieving agreed objectives.[9]

[1.22] A new National Health Strategy, *Quality and Fairness: A Health System for You*, was published in 2001. Following its publication and the associated strategy for Primary Care, *Primary Care: A New Direction*, (2001) the 10-year Health Reform Programme

---

[9]   See generally O'Shea, *Clinical Directorates in the Irish Health Service* (Blackhall Publishing, 2009) Ch 4.

was developed to implement the actions set out in the Strategy. This also added a fourth principle, namely 'people-centeredness', to the three principles set out in the earlier strategy document. In 2003, an independent Audit of Structures and Functions of the Health System, and the Commission on Financial Management and Controls in the Health Service were also published with broadly similar conclusions and recommendations for the system which provided the background for government decisions on the Health Service Reform Programme.

[1.23] The main findings and recommendations of these reports were, inter alia, that the multiplicity of health boards and specialist agencies operating in the public health sector had resulted in a complex and fragmented system. There was a need for rationalisation, standardisation and much improved coordination within the system, greater clarity of roles, accountability and responsibility, including the roles of the Department and the delivery system. As a consequence of these and other reports, the main elements of the Reform Programme focussed on structural reform, legislation, modernisation and improvement coupled with increased investment and enhanced governance and accountability.

[1.24] The structural aspects of the reform programme led to rationalisation of health service agencies to reduce fragmentation, including abolition of the health board/health authority structure. This resulted in the establishment of the HSE as a single national entity to manage the health services, as well as some restructuring of the Department of Health and Children and the establishment of the Health Information and Quality Authority (HIQA). The HSE was established on 1 January 2005 under the Health Act 2004. HIQA was established on 15 May 2007 under the Health Act 2007. The Department of Health and Children was restructured to take account of these changes, and now reflects its current core roles of national policy development and oversight of the operations of the State bodies under its aegis. This separation of policy and executive functions is in keeping with overall government policy at the time, which was to divest Ministers of executive functions and enable them to focus on policy and planning.

[1.25] The HSE has responsibility for the management and delivery of health and personal social services in the Republic of Ireland. Its objective, according to the Act, is 'to use the resources available to it in the most beneficial, effective and efficient manner to improve, promote and protect the health and welfare of the public.' It was given responsibility for the integration of the delivery of services and in so doing, it replaced the previous structure of the regional health boards, the Eastern Regional Health Authority and other agencies and organisations. The HSE is the largest organisation in the State, employing over 130,000 people. Its stated mission is to ensure uniform high-quality, safe services across the public system, efficient management of health care resources and accountability for their use.

[1.26] In addition to the establishment of the HSE, HIQA was established to underpin patient safety and quality in the new restructured health service. A core function of the Authority is to set standards on safety and quality of services and to monitor enforcement of these standards in an open and transparent way. Other functions of the Authority include: undertaking investigations into the safety, quality and standards of services where it is believed that there is a serious risk to the health or welfare of a person receiving services; carrying out reviews to ensure best outcomes/value for money for the resources available to the HSE; inspecting and registering designated residential care services for older people (eg nursing homes), for children and for people with disabilities; monitoring of foster care services, day facilities and children's detention centres; undertaking Health Technology Assessments to inform decision-making for safety and quality; adopting a central role in health information development and implementation of the recommendations set out in the National Health Information Strategy; evaluating information available on services provided by the HSE and other service providers and on the health and welfare of the population, identifying information deficiencies and advising the HSE and Minister accordingly.

[1.27] The Health Act 2004 also established a statutory complaints framework to help ensure a high standard of complaints management within the health service. The Health Act 2007 provided for protected disclosures or 'whistleblowing' safeguards. Under the Act, employees making protected disclosures in good faith and on reasonable grounds about issues of patient safety or patient welfare are protected from penalisation in the workplace and from civil liability.

[1.28] Other important pieces of legislation introduced to support the reform programme included the Health and Social Care Professionals Act 2005, the Pharmacy Act 2007 and the Medical Practitioners Act 2007. The Health and Social Care Professionals Act 2005 provides for a system of statutory registration for 12 health and social care professions to ensure that members of the public can be confident that health and social care professionals providing services are properly qualified, competent and fit to practise. There is an overarching Health and Social Care Professionals Council, with separate registration boards for each profession. The first Council was established on 26 March 2007. The Pharmacy Act 2007 reforms the regulation of pharmacy practice by setting new standards of governance, fitness to practise and registration for pharmacy. It also lifts restrictions on qualified EU pharmacists setting up practice in Ireland.

[1.29] The Medical Practitioners Act 2007 provides for an enhanced system of regulation of the medical profession in Ireland. Some of the important changes introduced by the Act (as discussed in Chapter 2) include increased non-medical membership on the Medical Council and the statutory obligation on medical practitioners to maintain their professional competence throughout their careers by participation in competence assurance schemes which include peer review and clinical audit.

[1.30] The Clinical Indemnity Scheme (CIS) was established in 2001 following enactment of the National Treasury Management Agency (Amendment) Act in 2000 with a dual remit to manage all claims relating to professional clinical services in the Irish public health sector and to lead and support the development of clinical risk management in this sector.

PATIENT SAFETY AND QUALITY ASSURANCE

[1.31] In the years from 2002–2007 a number of investigations were carried out in Ireland following adverse clinical events. These events, in particular the Report of Judge Maureen Harding Clark SC following the inquiry into peripartum hysterectomy at Our

Lady of Lourdes Hospital, Drogheda, 2006[10] and a number of reports into the management of breast cancer, caused significant public and political concern about the level of safety in Irish hospitals and other health services. The general findings from these reports highlighted a long list of failings, such as:

- lack of appropriately skilled senior personnel in acute care specialties;
- lack of senior clinical leadership within hospitals or on a national level;
- poor team working within hospitals and lack of integration of primary care professionals in the medical team;
- lack of protocols within hospital departments to deal with referrals between departments;
- insufficient communication with general practitioners following hospital discharge;
- poor communication processes with patients and their families following adverse events;
- lack of structured adverse event reporting, or monitoring systems;
- inconsistent system of root cause analysis of adverse events and complaints;
- poor management skills;
- deficits in staff knowledge of hospital policy;
- insufficient induction of health-care staff;
- dysfunctional processes and interpersonal relationships and management structures within hospitals;
- lack of engagement and poor working relations between management and clinicians;
- poor communication and protocols within and between hospitals regarding transfer of patients;
- lack of clerical support for consultants with clinical leadership and educational roles;
- difficulties in relation to availability of medical records in emergency cases
- under-developed or absence of leadership of or responsibility for clinical governance programmes;
- lack of or failure to implement formal risk management policies;
- lack of clarity in relation to accountability and reporting relationships within hospitals;
- failure to develop or implement clinical audit processes, and;
- failure to participate in continuous professional development programmes.

As a result of these failures in the health system, in January 2007 the Commission on Patient Safety and Quality Assurance was established to propose a system-wide response to these issues.[11] This was in keeping with increased international emphasis on patient safety and quality assurance. The Commission reported to the Minister in 2008

---

[10] *Report of the Lourdes Hospital Inquiry* (Dept of Health and Children, 2006), available at www.dohc.ie (accessed 16 May 2011).

[11] Chaired by Dr Deirdre Madden and comprised of members representing medical, nursing and pharmacy professions, hospital management, patients, HIQA, HSE, CIS and other stakeholders. Available at www.cpsqa.ie/publications/pdf/patientsafety.pdf (accessed 11 July 2011).

with a series of recommendations in relation to the need for effective governance and leadership to ensure that the environment in which health care takes place is supportive of safe and good-quality care, greater accountability of institutions and their management for institutional performance, greater accountability in the different bodies that regulate clinical practice, a strengthened system of information on adverse clinical events and complaints and patient reporting to be formalised, thereby providing a stronger role for patients and carers in providing feedback on care received.

[1.32] The Report of the Commission, entitled *Building a Culture of Patient Safety,* was accepted by the Government in 2009 and is currently in the process of being implemented by the Department of Health and Children in partnership with other relevant bodies such as the HSE, HIQA, professional regulatory bodies and educators. Implementation of the report will require significant legislative action in relation to the introduction of licensing of all health-care providers, structural changes in relation to governance and accountability mechanisms, professional changes in terms of clinical audit and adverse event reporting, and investment in IT infrastructure to support patient safety initiatives such as a unique health identifier and an electronic health record. It will also require structural and organisational changes in health-care providers, and legislative exemptions from Freedom of Information legislation for certain categories of information, such as adverse event reports and clinical audit.

LEGAL RIGHTS TO HEALTH CARE

The enforcement of rights against States

[1.33] In the context of rights and their enforcement generally, there is a distinction drawn between negative rights and positive rights. This distinction is seen particularly in international human rights law, where a significant emphasis is placed on equality, autonomy and anti-discrimination. There is an awareness found in many bills of rights and political writings of the need to protect the individual against the power of the State. The rights given to citizens limit the State's power in certain respects, for example the right to privacy limits the State's power to interfere in the private lives of its citizens. These rights are often classified as 'negative' in the sense of non-interference rights, which is conducive to the idea of limited government. By contrast, 'positive' rights are seen as giving an entitlement to individuals that the State act in a particular way to the benefit of the individual, such as through the provision of education. In this way, duties are imposed on the State to provide the necessary resources to vindicate these positive rights of the citizen.[12]

[1.34] The enforcement of rights against States in international human rights law has often been seen from the perspective of the types of obligations imposed in fulfilment of individual rights.[13] These obligations may be described as an obligation to respect (preventing the State from encroaching on recognised rights or freedoms), an obligation

---

[12] See further, Steiner and Alston, *International Human Rights in Context* (3rd edn, OUP, 2008).
[13] Van Hoof, 'The Legal Nature of Economic, Social and Cultural Rights: A Rebuttal of Some Traditional Views' in Alston and Tomasevski (eds) *The Right to Food,* (Martinus Nijhoff, 1984) 97–119 at 106.

to protect (obliging the State to take steps to prevent others from violating rights or freedoms), an obligation to ensure (the active creation of conditions within which the realisation of rights can take place) and an obligation to promote (the long-term realisation of goals). Positive obligations are generally associated with economic, social and cultural rights and commonly entail financial obligations for the State. For example, if an enforceable positive right to health (the obligation to ensure, under the preceding classification) were imposed on a State, the State would be obliged to provide hospitals and medical treatment in realisation of this right. However, it has been argued that these economic, social and cultural rights do not have a binding force in law and are thus legally inferior.[14] This argument is premised on the classification of rights as those that are justiciable, ie enforceable in a court of law or other comparable tribunal, and that social rights are not directed at government action that can be described in legal terms. Therefore, in the absence of an effective enforcement mechanism in international law in respect of economic, social and cultural rights, these are not legal rights at all.

[1.35] It is argued against this premise that this argument insists on a false comparison between national and international law. The former system encompasses institutional law-making processes, an executive branch of government and a law enforcement mechanism. In international law, these functions are generally performed by the States themselves in a non-institutionalised way. It is the exception rather than the rule that norms of international law can be enforced through courts of law, but this is an insufficient reason to deny such norms the status of binding rules. The enforcement of such rules through methods that differ from those available at national level does not detract from their efficacy.

[1.36] It is also argued against the legal nature of economic, social and cultural rights that the realisation of these rights entails financial effort on the part of the State that is not required in the realisation of civil and political rights. It is also argued that the latter rights do not require active intervention by the State and are more in the nature of non-interference rights. However, such distinctions are difficult to adhere to in relation to some civil and political rights, such as the right to a fair trial and the right to free elections, both of which involve the State in their active fulfilment and require financial expenditure. In fact, national and international courts are increasingly interpreting civil and political rights in such a way that they not only imply State abstention but also State intervention or action.[15] This is demonstrated by case law under the European Convention on Human Rights, in particular the right to respect for private and family life under Article 8, considered later.

The right to health in international law

[1.37] The importance of good health is something that is uncontroversial amongst policy-makers; however, the action to be taken in furtherance of good health at the expense of the State is a topic that has exercised many governments, activists, academics and medical practitioners alike. The legal and moral responsibility of the State to

---

14   Vierdag, 'The Legal Nature of the Rights Granted by the International Covenant on Economic, Social and Cultural Rights' (1978) 9 Netherlands Yearbook of International Law, 69–105.

15   Toebes, *The Right to Health as a Human Right in International Law* (Hart/Intersentia, 1999) p 232.

prevent disease as well as to promote good health amongst its citizens is the subject of longstanding debate.[16]

[1.38] Claims to health rights have generally taken two forms: 'a right to health' and 'a right to health care'. On an international level, the right to health first began to be claimed during the rise of public health programmes, when people began to be aware of the effects of industrialisation on sanitation, pollution and health. Demands began to be placed on governments to guard against the ill-effects of these developments. Similarly, with increased knowledge regarding the spread of disease, demands were placed on governments to instigate programs of vaccination. These rights evolved in the same era that other social rights were being translated into legal rights, such as rights to education and reasonable working conditions.[17] The claim of a right to health care was asserted when objections arose to various economic, social or geographic obstacles in the paths of many people who sought adequate health care. Underlying the response to these obstacles was the assumption that everyone ought to have equal access to needed health care.[18]

[1.39] It is important to stress that the right to health, if it exists, is not a right to be healthy.[19] This is something that would be impossible to guarantee in any event. It is, however, a right to certain health services and a right to be safeguarded from certain threats to health for which the State can be held responsible.[20] It concerns situations in which, if the State denies its responsibility, infringements of people's well-being and dignity are at stake. It is a right to see a doctor when necessary and to be able to afford

---

[16] Montgomery, 'Recognising a Right to Health' in Beddard and Hill (eds) *Economic, Social and Cultural Rights, Progress and Achievements,* (MacMillan, 1992).

[17] Harron, Burnside and Beauchamp, *Health and Human Values, A Guide to Making your Own Decisions* (Yale University Press, 1983), p 116–117.

[18] Harron, Burnside and Beauchamp, *Health and Human Values, A Guide to Making your Own Decisions* (Yale University Press, 1983), p 116.

[19] Disagreement exists as to the correct terminology to use in this context. The term 'right to health' is most commonly used in international treaties and seems to envisage not only a right to health-care services but also a right to underlying preconditions for health. It is argued that a 'right to health' is awkward, as it suggests that people have an enforceable right to something that is highly subjective and impossible to guarantee:

 "Health is a state of being, not something that can be given, and only in indirect ways something that can be taken away or undermined by other human beings. It no more makes sense to claim a right to health than a right to wisdom or courage. These excellences of soul and of body require natural gift, attention, effort, and discipline on the part of each person who desires them. To make my health someone else's duty is not only unfair: it is to impose a duty impossible to fulfil."

 Kass, 'Regarding the End of Medicine and the Pursuit of Health' (1975) The Public Interest, 40 (1975), p 39.

[20] For example, the Dutch Constitution contains, in Article 22(1), the stipulation that 'the authorities shall take steps to promote the health of the population', which is generally referred to as a right to health care. Health promotion is interpreted as including protection against threats to health. In cases heard under this section, the Dutch government has been obliged to ensure access to particular necessary treatments and to ensure that patients are not on unacceptably long waiting lists for treatment. See further Toebes, *The Right to Health as a Human Right in International Law* (Hart/Intersentia, 1999) p 203.

the bill afterwards. It is also a right to have access to safe drinking water and to be free from exposure to environmental health threats.

[1.40] The recognition of economic, social and cultural rights on the international level is often seen as having begun in 1941 with Franklin Roosevelt's Four Freedoms Speech in which he referred, inter alia, to 'freedom from want'.[21] He went on to explain this freedom as 'economic understandings which will secure to every nation a healthy peacetime life for its inhabitants – everywhere in the world.' In 1944 he advocated the adoption in the US of an economic Bill of Rights which would include 'the right to adequate medical care and the opportunity to achieve and enjoy good health.'[22] After the Second World War, these economic, social and cultural rights were included in various international treaties and national constitutions that were drafted around this time.[23]

[1.41] In 1946, representatives of 61 States signed the Constitution of the World Health Organisation (WHO) during the International Health Conference in New York. Its preamble formulates a right to health for the individual as a right to the highest attainable standard of physical, mental and social well-being and not only the absence of infirmity and disease. The WHO Constitution is binding on States that are a party to the WHO, including Ireland.[24] However, the WHO has been criticised for failing to enforce the right to health through the adoption of legislation clarifying the obligations on States in relation to the right to health.[25]

[1.42] A number of other international treaties and declarations also make reference to the right to health. For example, after much discussion, debate and redrafting, the European Social Charter 1961 refers to the right to protection of health whereby the Contracting Parties undertake to remove, as far as possible, the causes of ill-health, to provide educational and advisory facilities for the promotion of health and the encouragement of individual responsibility in health matters, and to prevent, as far as possible, epidemic, endemic and other diseases.[26] Since revision in 1996 the latter now also includes the prevention of accidents.

[1.43] Article 25.1 of the Universal Declaration of Human Rights states that "everyone has the right to a standard of living adequate for the health and well-being of himself and his family, including food, clothing, housing and medical care and necessary social services." Article 12 of the International Covenant on Economic, Social and Cultural Rights 1976 refers to the 'right to the highest attainable standard of physical and mental well-being'. It is recognised that the right to health is closely related to and dependent on the realisation of other human rights, such as the right to food, housing, work, education,

---

[21] Address to Congress, 6 January 1941.
[22] Address to Congress, 11 January 1944.
[23] Toebes, *The Right to Health as a Human Right in International Law* (Hart/Intersentia, 1999) p 14–15.
[24] For further information on the structure, powers and functions of the WHO, see Toebes, *Right to Health as a Human Right in International Law* (Hart/Intersentia, 1999) p 33.
[25] See generally Taylor, 'Making the World Health Organisation Work: A Legal Framework for Universal Access to the Conditions for Health' (1992) American Journal of Law and Medicine, Vol 18, No 4, 301–346.
[26] See Roscam Abbing, *International Organisations in Europe and the Right to Health Care* (Deventer, 1979).

human dignity, life, non-discrimination, equality and so on. In adopting article 12 of the Covenant, the Third Committee of the UN General Assembly therefore did not confine the right to health to the delivery of health care. While recognising that the right to health does not mean a right to be healthy, it does contain both freedoms and entitlements such as the (negative) right to be free from interference in relation to sexual and reproductive choices, and freedom from non-consensual medical treatment. Positive entitlements include the right to a system of health protection that provides equal opportunity to people to attain the highest level of health. The latter must take into account the individual's biological and socio-economic preconditions and the State's available resources.[27]

Rights to health and the EU

[1.44] Although health is not an area which is generally regarded as falling within the remit of EU law, it may nonetheless have an effect on national health law and policy. This is illustrated by cases such as *R v Human Fertilisation and Embryology Authority (ex parte Blood)*, where an application by a woman to the Human Fertilisation and Embryology Authority to export the sperm of her late husband was prohibited by UK law but subsequently granted by the Court of Appeal on the basis of her right under EU law to receive medical treatment in another Member State.[28]

[1.45] In addition to this example of direct effect, there is also an effect on national health policy through changing international norms and political pressures. Each EU Member State has its own national health policy, which in turn lends itself to differences in approach across the EU in relation to regulatory mechanisms and interpretation of legal measures. However, as Hervey and McHale argue, 'at least at a level of abstraction, "fundamental values" such as the sanctity of life, dignity, autonomy, privacy, justice and solidarity may be said to underpin all health regimes within the EU although the interpretation of those values may differ considerably in practice.'[29]

[1.46] The concept of a right to health or health law is a relatively fluid or even ambiguous one. What constitutes 'health' may be considered in the light of international statements such as those outlined above but these, in particular that of the WHO, tend to describe health in terms of well-being, which, unfortunately, may be impossible to achieve in a large part of the world where living standards are extremely poor. In legal terms it is difficult to conceptualise the content of the 'right to health' which could in any sense be justiciable if health is defined as broadly as 'a state of complete physical, mental and social well-being'. Therefore there are inherent dangers in a broad definition of a right to health because it is less likely to have clearly defined content than a

---

[27] For details of the substantive issues arising in the implementation of this covenant, see General Comment No 14 (2000), Committee on Economic, Social and Cultural Rights, available at www.unhchr.ch under the link to treaties. See also the Irish national report under the covenant and criticism thereof at www.irlgov.ie in the Department of Foreign Affairs human rights unit. [Both accessed 16 May 2011].

[28] *R v Human Fertilisation and Embryology Authority (ex parte Blood)* [1999] Fam 151, [1997] 2 WLR 807.

[29] Hervey and McHale, *Health Law and the European Union* (Cambridge University Press, 2004) p 5.

narrower definition, and this may severely limit its practical impact.[30] It has been suggested that the WHO standard is not achievable and, even if it were limited to a reasonable rather than an absolute standard, there would be considerable practical difficulties with implementation.

[1.47] Gostin and Lazzarini propose an alternative approach, namely that the right to health may be regarded as 'the duty of the state within the limits of its available resources to ensure the conditions necessary for the health of individuals and populations.' They argue that many factors which have an impact on an individual's right to health, such as genetics, behaviour and climate, are beyond governmental control. However, the State has the power to ensure conditions under which people are healthy, and therefore it has a responsibility, within the limits of available resources, to intervene to prevent or reduce serious threats to the health of individuals and populations. Thus, the obligations of States to protect human health apply not only to the protection of the health of individuals but also to the health of populations.[31]

[1.48] The evolution of the discipline of 'medical law' towards that of 'health law' in recent years demonstrates an increasing expansion of the field of academic commentary and research beyond the traditional engagement with the doctor-patient relationship. 'Health law' now occupies itself with other issues, including the financing of health care, the rules regarding the relationship between health-care providers and patients, health care insurance and public health measures aimed at promoting good health of populations. Health law has also been affected by ethical principles as new technological developments have raised new or different questions about regulation.

[1.49] In the EU, the most prominent human rights statements came from the Council of Europe, in particular the European Convention on Human Rights and Fundamental Freedoms in 1950 (ECHR) rather than the EU itself. This has led to a number of significant challenges to national policy on matters affecting health, in particular mental health. The Convention on Human Rights and Biomedicine was drafted by the Council of Europe in 1996.[32] It contains provisions relating to, inter alia, consent, privacy, genetics, research, organ transplantation and disposal of body parts. The Convention also stipulates that States are obliged to take appropriate measures to provide equitable access to health care of appropriate quality, taking health needs and available resources into account. The latter phrase allows States a certain leniency in the provision of health-care facilities. A number of EU Member States have either not signed or not ratified the Convention, including Ireland.[33]

---

[30] Gostin and Lazzarini, *Human Rights and Public Health in the AIDS Pandemic* (OUP,1997), quoted in Hervey and McHale, *Health Law and the European Union* (Cambridge University Press, 2004) p 9.

[31] Hervey and McHale, *Health Law and the European Union* (Cambridge University Press, 2004) p 10.

[32] Also known as the Oviedo Convention, its full title is the *Convention for the Protection of Human Rights and Dignity of the Human Being with Regard to the Application of Biology and Medicine*, adopted by the Committee of Ministers on 19 November 1996 (DIR/JUR (96) 14). Opened for signature 4 April 1997.

[33] See http://conventions.coe.int/ (accessed 16 May 2011).

[1.50] In 1994, the WHO (Europe) issued the Amsterdam Declaration on patients' rights in Europe. A number of EU Member States have subsequently adopted legislation on patients' rights, such as Finland, Denmark, the Netherlands, France, Belgium and Austria. In some countries, such as the UK, such rights may be seen as encompassed within human rights law through the incorporation into national law of the ECHR. Hervey and McHale argue that while human rights discourse is clearly influential at a rhetorical level and human rights undoubtedly underpin legal engagement with health, there are a number of difficulties with application of a human rights analysis, such as problems of interpretation due to the breadth of human rights provisions, and the problems associated with conflict of rights. Nonetheless, they argue that despite these problems, the application of human rights analysis will continue to play a crucial role in health law in the future.[34] They refer to the Charter of Fundamental Rights of the European Union (2000), which includes articles on human dignity, integrity of the person, the right to life, privacy, right to marry and found a family, and other rights which may directly or indirectly have relevance to health law. In particular, art 35 provides that 'everyone has the right of access to preventive health care and the right to benefit from medical treatment under the conditions established by national laws and practices.' However, Hervey and McHale acknowledge that the human rights approach may have both positive and negative effects. In a positive sense, the application of human rights theories and instruments to health law brings with it a 'conceptualisation of health law that includes legal provision for individual patients' entitlements, in the manner of their treatment, for instance, on rights to informed consent and bodily integrity.' However, human rights have 'limitations as drivers of law and policy. Human rights provisions may be of rhetorical significance, particularly in policy-making debates and, in some circumstances may assist in construction of specific legal instruments, or the determination of their legality. In other cases, however, their practical impacts are likely to be limited …'[35]

[1.51] Despite the reservations expressed above, case law on civil and political rights shows that several health-related issues have been addressed within this framework of human rights. Such cases concerned the obligation to provide access to health-care facilities, the obligation not to deprive people of medical treatment, and the obligation to offer protection against environmental health threats.[36] In some of these cases, claims were made that expulsion from a Member State would inevitably have a deleterious effect on the claimant's health, bearing in mind the lack of suitable medical facilities in the claimant's own state. It was claimed that the deprivation of medical treatment was inhuman treatment within the meaning of art 3 of the ECHR. For example, in *D v the UK*[37] the European Court held that expulsion from St Kitts of the claimant, who was in the last stage of HIV, would violate art 3. However, the Court pointed out that, in

---

[34] Hervey and McHale, *Health Law and the European Union* (Cambridge University Press, 2004) p 25.

[35] Hervey and McHale, *Health Law and the European Union* (Cambridge University Press, 2004) p 27.

[36] Toebes, *Right to Health as a Human Right in International Law* (Hart/Intersentia, 1999) p 233.

[37] *D v the UK* (2 May 1997), 1997–III, No 37. See also European Commission, No 30240/96, 26 June 1996.

principle, a person subject to expulsion cannot claim any entitlement to remain within the territory of a particular state in order to benefit from medical assistance. In a comparable case, *Tanko v Finland*[38], the expulsion of the applicant from Finland to Ghana was challenged on the basis that it would subject him to the risk of losing his eyesight in view of the lack of suitable medical facilities and treatments for him in Ghana. The Commission held the claim to be inadmissible but said that 'a lack of proper care in a case where someone is suffering from a serious illness could in certain circumstances amount to treatment contrary to Article 3.'

[1.52] Other cases have examined the issue of environmental health and the information to be given to residents in a locality in which their health could be affected by pollutants. These cases have decided that the failure to take steps to prevent severe environmental pollution that might affect health and to inform of the risks to health is a violation of the right to respect for private and family life under art 8 of the ECHR.[39]

In the context of the discrepancy between public and private health-care provision by states, the reporting mechanisms imposed by, for example, the European Social Charter[40] and the International Covenant on Economic, Social and Cultural Rights, mean that international expert committees assess the provision by the contracting states of hospital beds, accessible services, highly qualified personnel and so on. States are obliged to reduce infant mortality, to ensure that privatisation does not disadvantage the elderly or other vulnerable groups, provide accessible services in geographically remote areas, ensure that no discrimination exists in the provision of health care to socially disadvantaged groups as well as to pursue other important policies in this context. However, whether states organise their health care systems publicly or privately is essentially a matter for each state to decide for itself. International treaty provisions do not require states to organise their health-care system publicly in order to guarantee equality of access and quality of services.[41] In some states there is a strong public national health system, as in the United Kingdom and Canada, whereas in others the health-care system is privately organised, as in the United States.

Although states are not required to provide a free national health service, they cannot abdicate their responsibilities by pointing to the fact that the requisite services are available privately. The international committees, to which states report under international obligations, are concerned about the increasing tendency of states to privatise health care. 'They request State representatives to indicate whether disparities exist between the standard of health services offered in the private and public sectors and whether access to health care services is the same in both sectors.'[42]

---

38 *Tanko v Finland*, European Commission, No 23634/94, 19 May 1994.

39 *Lopez Ostra v Spain* 9 December 1994, A.303C (1995); *Anna Guerra v Italy* (Application No 14967/89) 19 February 1998. See also *McGinley and Egan v the UK* (9 June 1998) App No 10/1997/794/995–996 and *LCB v the UK* (9 June 1998). App No 14/1997/798/1001.

40 Each state that has ratified the Charter (including Ireland) must submit reports for examination every two years (from June 1997) under the headings of removal of causes of ill-health, advisory and educational facilities and prevention of diseases. See www.coe.int/t/dghl/monitoring/socialcharter/reporting/statereports/reports_EN.asp (accessed 27 June 2011).

41 Toebes, *Right to Health as a Human Right in International Law* (Hart/Intersentia, 1999) p 248.

42 Toebes, *Right to Health as a Human Right in International Law* (Hart/Intersentia, 1999) p 249.

[1.53] Under European law[43] a Member State may be obliged to fund medical treatment in another Member State in certain circumstances. Citizens may make an application to their local Health Authority for authorisation to travel to another Member State of the European Union to receive medical treatment there. For example, it is possible for a citizen resident in Ireland to obtain authorisation to receive medical treatment in Germany or Austria or any other Member State of the European Union. Authorisation is generally required from the Health Authority in the home state where the treatment is not available in the home Member State or where the treatment cannot be provided in the home state without undue delay. If the authorisation to obtain treatment in a hospital or institution in another Member State is granted, the cost of the treatment will be paid for by the Health Authority in the citizen's home state. This means that where a citizen who is resident in Ireland obtains authorisation to receive medical treatment in Germany, the cost of the treatment will be paid by the Irish HSE.

[1.54] The criteria for such funding may be summarised as follows: the treatment is not available in this country; there is an *urgent medical necessity* for the treatment; there is a reasonable medical prognosis; the treatment is a proven form of treatment; and the treatment is in a recognised hospital.[44] Based on the *Watts* case,[45] where the treatment is available in the home state but the treatment cannot be provided without undue delay, the Health Authority should also consider whether the waiting time for the treatment in the home state exceeds the period which is acceptable in the light of a medical assessment of the following: the clinical needs of the citizen in the light of his/her medical condition; the history and probable cause of illness; the degree of pain, and the nature of the disability at the time when the authorisation is sought.

[1.55] In *Pierik (No 1)*[46] the European Court of Justice (ECJ) applied these rules in the context of physiotherapeutic treatment for a rheumatic ailment, where the individual concerned had already received treatment in Germany, and a medical expert in the Netherlands was of the opinion that no treatment available in the Netherlands would be as effective as the treatment sought. 'This ruling suggests that an individual seeking reproductive treatment according to a procedure which is not available in her own Member State, for instance, an Austrian seeking IVF with gametes donated by someone who is not her husband or cohabitee, could require her Member State's national health insurance to meet the cost.'[47] However, a subsequent ruling on the same issue suggests that the Court is unlikely to interpret the regulation to this effect. In *Pierik (No 2)*[48] the

---

43   Regulation (EEC) No 1408/71 of the Council of 14 June 1971 on the application of social security schemes to employed persons and their families moving within the Community, contained in the Official Journal of the EEC No L230 dated 22 August 1983, and Council Regulation (EEC) No 2001/83, which amends No 574/72 contained in the Official Journal as above.

44   The EC Regulations in question are Council Regulation (EEC) No 2000/83 which amends No 1408/71 contained in the Official Journal of the EEC No L 230 dated 22 August 1983 and Council Regulation (EEC) No 2001/83 which amends No 574/72 contained in the Official Journal as above.

45   *Watts v Bedford Primary Care Trust and Secretary of State for Health*, Case C-372/04.

46   *Pierik (No1)*, Case 117/77 [1978] ECR 825.

47   Hervey, 'Buy Baby: The European Union and Regulation of Human Reproduction' (1998) 18 Oxford Journal of Legal Studies 207–233 at 216.

48   *Pierik (No2)*, Case 182/78 [1979] ECR 1977.

ECJ was asked to deal with the question of whether the regulation applied where the Member State deliberately excluded a medical treatment from its national health service, inter alia, on ethical grounds. Although the facts of the case did not require the Court to consider this issue, 'the submissions of the Commission suggest that Member States are permitted to refuse authorisation for treatments "seriously contrary to the ethical rules prevailing" in its jurisdiction, on the grounds that Member States retain competence to regulate public morality'.[49]

Rights to health under the Irish Constitution

[1.56] Article 40.3.1° of the Irish Constitution 1937 provides that 'the State guarantees in its laws to respect, and, as far as practicable, by its laws to defend and vindicate the personal rights of the citizen.' Subsection 2 of that section provides protection 'in particular' for the 'life, person, good name, and property rights of every citizen'. Other subsections relate to the inviolability of the dwelling, freedom of expression, right to peaceful assembly and the right of association. As the other provisions of Art 40 do not specifically protect the citizen's right to life or a good name, the inference has been drawn that those provisions are not an exhaustive enumeration of the rights guaranteed.[50] This has led to the development of a category of unenumerated rights by the Irish courts which, although not expressly provided for in the text of the Constitution, are nonetheless constitutionally protected by Art 40.3 as coming within the 'personal rights' of the citizen. For example, rights to privacy,[51] to dissociation,[52] to access to the courts[53], to travel,[54] to legal representation[55] and to fair procedures have been recognised within this category. The development of the law in this way has been criticised by some who view the rights thus far granted constitutional protection within this category as coming from a subjective interpretation by judges who have upper-middle-class fundamental values rather than any objective determination of personal rights.[56]

[1.57] The right to protect one's health was the subject of *Ryan v Attorney General*[57] in which the plaintiff claimed that legislation providing for the compulsory fluoridation of public water supplies violated her constitutional rights and those of her family. The main argument in this case was that fluoridation was dangerous to health and therefore compulsory fluoridation violated her constitutional right to bodily integrity. Kenny J in the High Court found that the plaintiff had failed to demonstrate that fluoridation was

---

49   Hervey, 'Buy Baby: The European Union and Regulation of Human Reproduction' (1998) 18 Oxford Journal of Legal Studies 207–233 at 216, quoting Watson, *Social Security Law of the European Communities* (Mansell Publishers, 1980), p 258.
50   Casey, *Constitutional Law in Ireland* (Round Hall, Dublin, 2000),p 394.
51   For example, *McGee v Attorney General* [1974] IR 284; *Norris v Attorney General* [1984] IR 36; *Kennedy v Ireland* [1987] IR 587; *In Re a Ward of Court (No 2)* [1996] 2 IR 79.
52   *Educational Co Ltd v Fitzpatrick (No2)* [1961] IR 345.
53   *Macauley v Minister for Posts and Telegraphs* [1966] IR 345.
54   *State(M) v Minister for Foreign Affairs* [1979] IR 73.
55   State (Healy) v Donoghue [1976] IR 325.
56   See Hogan, 'Unenumerated Personal Rights: *Ryan's* Case Re-evaluated' (1990–92) The Irish Jurist Vols. XXV–XXVII, 95–116. Also Ely, *Democracy and Distrust: A Theory of Judicial Review* (Cambridge: Harvard University Press, 1980).
57   *Ryan v Attorney General* [1965] IR 294.

dangerous to health, and that in fact it was beneficial in the reduction of the incidence of dental disease, a finding upheld by the Supreme Court. In its judgment, the Supreme Court concluded that one of the unenumerated rights protected by Art 40.3 of the Constitution was the right to bodily integrity. In the High Court, Kenny J had held that this right meant that:

> [N]o mutilation of the body or any of its members may be carried out on any citizen under the authority of the law except for the good of the whole body and that no process which is or may, as a matter of probability, be dangerous or harmful to the life or health of the citizen or any of them may be imposed (in the sense of being made compulsory) by an Act of the Oireachtas.[58]

However, although the Supreme Court upheld Kenny J's decision, the Court declined to define the right to bodily integrity or comment on Kenny J's definition of it.

[1.58] Ó Dálaigh J observed that the State has an obligation to take the necessary steps to protect persons' health; that the State 'has the duty of protecting the citizens from dangers to health in a manner not incompatible or inconsistent with the rights of these citizens as human persons.'[59] However, 'it was not indicated in what circumstances the Court would order the State to adopt measures necessary to protect health. For instance, if there was no Fluoridation Act on the statute book, in the light of the evidence given in the *Ryan* case, would the Court order that such an Act be introduced?'[60] This case also demonstrates that in some instances public health efforts will conflict with an individual's rights or civil liberties, particularly in the context of compulsory vaccinations and infectious disease control.[61]

[1.59] In the later Supreme Court case *In re a Ward of Court (No 2)*,[62] the Court emphasised that no one may be compelled to accept medical treatment, even though the consequences of such a refusal may be death. Any obligation to the contrary would conflict with the right to bodily integrity as well as privacy.

[1.60] The rights of the citizen in this context are not restricted to the operation of legislation. They also extend to acts or omissions of the executive that could expose the health of the person to risk.[63] However, as with all the unenumerated rights, they are not unqualified. In *State (C) v Frawley*[64] the plaintiff argued that the State was failing to vindicate his constitutional rights by not providing him with a very specialised secure unit during which he could serve his prison sentence. He suffered from psychological disturbances, which resulted in the self-infliction of physical harm. The plaintiff argued

---

58 *Ryan v Attorney General* [1965] IR 294 at 313–14.
59 *Ryan v Attorney General* [1965] IR 294 at 348.
60 Forde, *Constitutional Law of Ireland* (Cork and Dublin: The Mercier Press, 1987) p 541.
61 Brazier and Harris, 'Public Health and Private Lives' (1996) 4 Medical Law Review 165; Old and Montgomery, 'Law, Coercion and the Public Health' (1992) 304 BMJ 891.
62 *In re a Ward of Court* [1996] 2 IR 79.
63 Where an individual health board or hospital makes a decision that has negative consequences for the individual, it is more likely that such action or omission would be challenged through a negligence action, as in *Healy v North Western Health Board* (31 January 1996, unreported) HC, where a health board was found liable in negligence for discharging from a mental institution a man suffering from depression who subsequently committed suicide.
64 *State (C) v Frawley* [1976] IR 365.

that, by failing to provide him with a specialised unit, the State was in breach of its duty to vindicate his right to bodily integrity. Also, it was argued that the restrictions placed on him, such as deprivation of items that could be used by him for self-harm, solitary confinement for certain periods, and the use of handcuffs to restrain the plaintiff, were contrary to his personal right to be free from torture and inhuman and degrading treatment. The Court held that the restrictions imposed on the plaintiff were imposed to prevent self-injury or self-destruction, and were not imposed for any evil purpose. While acknowledging that the right to bodily integrity applied to acts of the executive as much as to the application of legislation and that this right included the right not to have one's health endangered, the Court held that the executive's duty to the plaintiff was not an absolute one, and had not been breached in this case. Finlay J stated, 'I see no reason why the principle [ie the right of bodily integrity as an unspecified constitutional right] should not operate to prevent an act or omission of the Executive which, without justification, would expose the health of a person to risk or danger.'

[1.61] There have been a number of such cases dealing with the lack of provision by the State of secure institutional facilities for young people and prisoners with psychological difficulties where they may be detained and treated. These cases have been brought on the basis of the failure of the State to vindicate the constitutional rights of those in question. While not founded exclusively on the right to protect one's health, these cases may nonetheless be seen as linked to such a right. The courts have taken the view that this right is not exercisable only against the legislature but also extends to acts of the executive which violate the personal rights of citizens. For example, in *D.B. (A Minor suing by his mother and next friend S.B.) v Minister for Justice, Minister for Health, Minister for Education, A.G. and the Eastern Health Board,*[65] Kelly J, in granting an injunction obliging the State to provide suitable places for detention of troubled minors, affirmed that the courts are as entitled to invoke these rights on behalf of a citizen against the executive, as against the legislature, although the courts would not do so lightly. He adopted the position taken by Finlay CJ in *Crotty v An Taoiseach*[66] where he said,

> [W]ith regard to the executive, the position would appear to be as follows:- This Court has on appeal from the High Court a right and duty to interfere with the activities of the executive in order to protect or secure the constitutional rights of individual litigants where such rights have been or are being invaded by those activities or where activities of the executive threaten an invasion of such rights.

[1.62] Other cases relevant in this context have focused on the obligations on the State to provide necessary educational and medical services to those with intellectual disabilities. These cases have not concentrated primarily on the right to protect one's health but have examined the rights of the citizen to education without limitation of age or intellectual ability. Such cases are relevant in the context of the imposition of positive duties on the State within the economic, social and cultural rights categorisation.

65 *DB (A Minor suing by his mother and next friend S.B.) v Minister for Justice, Minister for Health, Minister for Education, AG and the Eastern Health Board* [1999] 1 IR 29. Other similar cases include *TD v Minister for Education* [2000] 3 IR 62; *F (N) v Minister for Education* [1995] IR 29.
66 *Crotty v An Taoiseach* [1987] IR 713 at 773.

O'Donoghue v Minister for Health[67] involved an application for judicial review to oblige the State to provide for free primary education for the applicant, an eight-year-old boy suffering from severe mental disability. In a lengthy judgment exploring the issue of education for people with disabilities in Ireland, O'Hanlon J concluded that "there is a constitutional obligation imposed on the State by the provisions of Article 42.4 of the Constitution to provide for free elementary education of all children." This was affirmed by the Supreme Court. The Court accepted that the plaintiff's rights had been violated and ordered the State to provide primary education as appropriate. However, this case was firmly grounded on the obligations imposed by Art 42 to provide education, and could not be extended to other fundamental rights not specifically imposed on the State.

[1.63] In *Sinnott v Minister for Education*[68] the plaintiff, through his mother, claimed that the State had failed to provide him with free education and had thereby breached its duty to vindicate the plaintiff's constitutional rights in this regard. In the Supreme Court the State conceded the right to free primary education to the age of 18. On the plaintiff's behalf it was argued that the right to primary education endured as long as the student could benefit from it, which in this case would be the remainder of his life. However, it was argued on behalf of the State that although a person such as the plaintiff who suffers from intellectual disability needs education for life, the State is not obliged by the Constitution to provide education after the age of 18. The Supreme Court took the view that the Constitution obliges the State to provide free primary education, the word 'primary' being interpreted as basic or fundamental. This is an absolute duty. However, the plaintiff's right to education did not extend after the age of 18 years, as this would be extending the interpretation of 'primary', which was historically and logically linked with the definition of 'child', such definition applying to persons up to the age of 18 years. Interestingly in the context of health care, in his judgment Murphy J also pointed out that the Constitution imposes no obligation on the State to provide health care of any description for its citizens.

[1.64] Based on the foregoing, it is unlikely that an action taken against the State on constitutional grounds for failing to provide necessary health-care services would succeed.[69] Despite the lack of jurisprudence on the point, the courts would doubtless be slow to oblige the government to expend huge financial resources on specific health-care facilities, as this would substantially interfere with the policy-making functions of the executive. The courts have taken the view in other areas of law that it would be a violation of the separation of powers doctrine if the courts were to be concerned with the distribution of national resources.[70] In order for the courts to equip themselves with the ability to make such decisions, it would be necessary to examine the many competing

---

[67]   *O'Donoghue v Minister for Health* [1996] 2 IR 20.

[68]   *Sinnott v Minister for Education* [2001] IESC 39.

[69]   In relation to the non- recognition generally of economic and socio-economic rights under the Constitution, see Murphy, 'Economic Inequality and the Constitution', in Murphy and Twomey (eds), *Ireland's Evolving Constitution 1937–1997* (Hart Publishing, 1998), pp 163–181. Also Hogan, 'Unenumerated Personal Rights: *Ryan's* Case Re-evaluated' *The Irish Jurist* Vols XXV–XXVII, 95–116, and Humphreys,. 'Interpreting Natural Rights' (1993–95) 28–30 *Irish Jurist* 221.

[70]   See Morgan, *A Judgement Too Far, Judicial Activism and the Constitution* (Cork University Press, 2001) p 62–71.

claims on national funds and arguments as to the correct priority to be accorded to those claims. Individual judges have expressed the opinion that matters of national policy are outside of the judicial function and it would be wholly inappropriate for the courts to resolve disputes in this context on a case-by-case basis. However, that is not to say that the judiciary wash their hands of claims that the State has failed to vindicate personal rights where such vindication would involve the State in financial expenditure.

[1.65] In *O'Reilly v Limerick Corporation, Minister for the Environment, Minister for Health, Minister for Education, Ireland and the Attorney General*,[71] the plaintiff, who was a member of the travelling community, claimed that the State had violated his constitutional right to be provided with certain resources, specifically a halting site. He claimed that he had a right under the Constitution to basic material conditions to foster his dignity and freedom as a human person, and the authority of the family with which he lived. His argument essentially was that there had been a failure on the part of the State to distribute adequately in the plaintiff's favour a portion of the community's wealth. Costello J reiterated the distinction between negative and positive rights explained above and stated that usually a claim in relation to unspecified rights under the Constitution related to a wrongful interference in some activity which the plaintiff seeks to protect. In this case the claim was entirely different, as the plaintiff was asserting that the State had a duty to provide him with the resources and services he lacked. Although he did not use the floodgates argument as the basis for his decision, he adverted to it in pointing to the homeless and other deprived people in the community to which the State may similarly owe obligations if the plaintiff's case succeeded. He distinguished distributive justice, which is the distribution of common goods and burdens, and commutative justice, which is fixing what is due to one individual from another individual.[72] He classified this claim as involving distributive justice, which does not fall within the administration of justice function given to the courts.

> I am sure that the concept of justice which is to be found in the Constitution embraces the concept that the nation's wealth should be justly distributed (that is the concept of distributive justice), but I am equally sure that a claim that this has not occurred should, to comply with the Constitution, be advanced in Leinster House rather than in the Four Courts.[73]

The learned judge felt that if the court adopted the suggested supervisory role, it would have to make an assessment of the validity of the many competing claims on those resources, the correct priority to be given to them and the financial implications of the plaintiff's claim. This would involve adjudication on the fairness of the manner in which the State administered public resources. He continued:

> Apart from the fact that members of the judiciary have no special qualification to undertake such a function, the manner in which justice is administered in the courts, that is on a case

---

[71] *O'Reilly v Limerick Corporation, Minister for the Environment, Minister for Health, Minister for Education, Ireland and the Attorney General* [1989]ILRM 181.

[72] Morgan, *A Judgment Too Far? Judicial Activism and the Constitution* (Cork University Press, 2001) p 67.

[73] *O'Reilly v Limerick Corporation, Minister for the Environment, Minister for Health, Minister for Education, Ireland and the Attorney General* [1989] ILRM 181 at 195.

by case basis, make them a wholly inappropriate institution for the fulfilment of the suggested role. I cannot construe the Constitution as conferring it on them.

[1.66] In *Brady v Cavan County Council*[74] the applicant asked the Court to make an order requiring the local authority for the area in which he lived to keep the roads in the area in good condition. The local authority argued that to do so would leave insufficient funds to discharge some of its other functions such as public housing provision, and water and sewerage facilities. The Supreme Court held, in rejecting the application, that the local authority did not have the means to comply with such an order and it was not known whether central government would assist in this regard. While this case may be confined to the facts which turned on the relative poverty of this particular local authority and the length of time it would have taken to bring the roads into a satisfactory condition, nonetheless the case is also important in that it shows judicial 'sensitivity to the general financial implications of colossal expenditure for public bodies'[75], as it also explored the notion that the Oireachtas was not and could not be a party to these proceedings on the basis of the doctrine of separation of powers.

[1.67] On one view it could be said that these cases, *O'Reilly* and *Brady*, are in conflict with the *DB*, *O'Donoghue* and *Sinnott* line of authority in which the State has been obliged to provide certain educational and treatment facilities, irrespective of the cost. According to Morgan, there are three distinctions between these cases. The first is that the latter cases were held to concern education, which is dealt with specifically in the Constitution. Secondly, at least in *DB*, the Department of Health had already drawn up a plan for the treatment of disturbed children on which the court could rely to counter arguments that it did not have the expertise necessary to draft such a scheme. Thirdly, the decision protected a minority interest that was seen to be otherwise neglected.[76]

[1.68] In the context of the imposition of specific obligations on the State regarding the provision of health care, it may be argued that the executive should be bound by the Constitution in the same way as any other citizen. If there is a right to health included in the unspecified personal rights protected by Art 40.3, the executive as well as the legislature should be bound by the terms of the Constitution.[77] However, it has been suggested that a more sophisticated approach to understanding our political system indicates that this was not intended by the drafters of the Constitution. On the contrary, it was feared that putting socio-economic guarantees into the fundamental rights provisions of the Constitution would open the floodgates for the imposition of many difficult and costly obligations on the State. Therefore, these rights were instead inserted into a clause headed Directive Principles of Social Policy, contained in Art 45 and devolved exclusively to the Oireachtas by that article. The intention was to ensure that, unlike all the other constitutional rights, they would not be justiciable or cognisable by

---

[74] *Brady v Cavan County Council* [2000] 1 ILRM 81.

[75] Morgan, *A Judgement Too Far, Judicial Activism and the Constitution* (Cork University Press, 2001) p 67.

[76] Morgan, *A Judgement Too Far, Judicial Activism and the Constitution* (Cork University Press, 2001) p 68–69.

[77] As Morgan notes from Kelly J in *DB,* "the Minister for Health is not immune from a court order vindicating the personal rights of a citizen." Morgan, *A Judgement Too Far, Judicial Activism and the Constitution* (Cork University Press, 2001) p 69.

the courts, a fact that has led to the marginalisation of their impact in constitutional terms. The only exception was the free primary education provisions in Art 42.4, the only enforceable socio-economic right in the Constitution.[78]

[1.69] The Report of the Constitution Review Group[79] examined the issue of whether specific socio-economic rights should be included in the Constitution and recommended against such a step. One of the arguments adopted by the Group centred on the fact that the development of fundamental rights is a matter for political decision rather than a judicial function:

> These are essentially political matters which in a democracy it should be the responsibility of the elected representatives of the people to address and determine. It would be a distortion of democracy to transfer decisions on major issues of policy and practicality from the Government and the Oireachtas, elected to represent the people and do their will, to an unelected judiciary.[80]

While favouring the identification of fundamental rights in the Constitution as far as possible, the Group also felt that the concept of unenumerated rights had considerable merit, as it allowed for the evolution of social attitudes and approaches to justice over time. However, the Group was reluctant to entrust the further development of socio-economic rights to 'subjective judicial appraisal' bearing in mind that judges can never be completely independent of the social class, gender, professional background and religion that has shaped their individual attitudes to such issues.

[1.70] The Review Group also stressed the financial cost objection to the inclusion of socio-economic rights in the Constitution. It argued that 'It would not accord with democratic principles to confer absolute personal rights in the Constitution in relation to economic or social objectives, however desirable in themselves, and leave the Oireachtas with no option but to discharge the cost, whatever it might be, as determined by the judiciary.'[81] However, this has been criticised by the Irish Commission for Justice and Peace, which points out that the Group expressly recommends the inclusion of the specific right of access to the courts, acknowledging that such a positive right would involve financial expenditure and without clarifying exactly how the State is to implement such a right.[82]

---

[78] This point is taken from Hogan, 'Unelected Judges Cannot Remedy Some Wrongs', (2001) The Irish Times, 14 July.

[79] The Report of the Constitution Review Group (Government Stationery Office, 1996).

[80] The Report of the Constitution Review Group (Government Stationery Office, 1996) p 235.

[81] The Report of the Constitution Review Group (Government Stationery Office, 1996) p 236.

[82] Irish Commission for Justice and Peace, *Re-Righting the Constitution, The Case for New Social and Economic Rights: Housing, Health, Nutrition, Adequate Standard of Living.* (Genprint, 1998) p 11–12. This report calls for specific inclusion in the Constitution of specific rights such as the right to health in the following terms:
'Each person has the right to health including the right to emergency medical assistance. The enjoyment of this right should in the first place be ensured by the initiative and efforts of each person. Where individual persons or their dependants are unable adequately to exercise or enjoy the right to health, the State shall ensure that this right is respected and protected. As guardian of the common good the State shall take reasonable steps to promote the general and progressive enjoyment of this right, in view of actual conditions, resources and standards', p 27.
See useful discussion of this proposal at pp 60–75.

[1.71] In summary, it is unlikely that the Supreme Court would decide that the Constitution gives the judiciary power to investigate and allocate public expenditure.[83] At the present time this would be seen as unjustifiable interference with the power of the executive and a violation of the separation of powers doctrine.[84] Arguably, the cases that have indicated that such a power might be available to the courts do not recognise the dangers of such an approach as fully as they might have done. 'It seems inappropriate for an unelected body to assert the power… to increase public expenditure.'[85] However, although the separation of powers doctrine has stood the test of time and the public/private divide may become fragile if too many openings are created for State action and interference, it may in the future be possible to view economic, social and cultural rights in a way that brings them into closer alignment with the separation of powers doctrine.[86]

ALLOCATION OF HEALTH-CARE RESOURCES

National policy-making

[1.72] The principle of equality of access to health-care resources and treatments is stated in many international documents, as discussed in previous sections of this chapter. The provision of the highest-quality services to all those who may benefit from them would obviously entail a huge, if not impossible, financial commitment on a relatively small state such as Ireland where resources, personnel and patient demand for specialised treatments are less than might be the case in larger states. The debate between those who favour a wholly public or free health-care service, and those who prefer a privatised system or a combination of the two, as is currently the case in Ireland, is likely to continue and is not the subject of this text.

---

[83]   Mason and Laurie take the view that although it may seem surprising that there have not been more actions brought by patients who feel that the State has failed in its duty to provide health-care services, this is probably due to the 'extreme improbability of a successful outcome.' Mason and Laurie, *Law and Medical Ethics* (8th edn, OUP, 2010), p 385.

[84]   The classic case in England is *R v Secretary of State for Social Services, ex parte Hincks* (1979) 123 Sol Jo 436, in which patients in an orthopaedic hospital sought a declaration that the health authorities were in breach of their duty in that the patients had been forced to wait for an unreasonable time for treatment due to a shortage of facilities arising in part from a decision not to add a new block to the hospital on cost grounds. Wien J said it was not the court's function to direct Parliament as to what funds to make available to the health service nor how to allocate such resources as had been made available. The court could only intervene if the Minister acted unreasonably or in frustration of the Act. Similar decisions were made in *R v Central Birmingham Health Authority, ex parte Walker* (1987) 3 BMLR 32, and *R v Central Birmingham Health Authority, ex parte Collier* (6 Jan 1988, unreported) See Newdick, 'Rights to NHS Resources After the 1990 Act' (1993) 1 Med L Rev 53, and Miller, 'Denial of Health Care and Informed Consent in English and American Law' (1992) 18 Am J Law Med 37.

[85]   Morgan, *A Judgement Too Far, Judicial Activism and the Constitution* (Cork University Press, 2001) p 70.

[86]   Quinn, 'Rethinking the Nature of Economic, Social and Cultural Rights', in Costello (ed) *Fundamental Social Rights, Current European Legal Protection and the Challenge of the EU Charter on Fundamental Rights* (Irish Centre for European Law, 2001) No 28 pp 35–54.

[1.73] There are issues too in relation to national strategies dealing with prioritisation of different programmes or treatments. 'No resources are infinite... It is clear that it is impossible to provide every form of therapy for everyone – some sort of selective distribution must be made.'[87] The wide spectrum of decisions that must be made on a national level in the context of resource allocation in health care is well described by Kass as follows:

> Personnel and facilities for medical research and treatment are scarce resources. Is the development of a new technology the best use of scarce resources, given current circumstances? How should we balance efforts aimed at prevention against those aimed at cure, or either of these against efforts to redesign the species? How should we balance the delivery of available levels of care against further basic research? More fundamentally, how should we balance efforts in biology and medicine against efforts to eliminate poverty, pollution, urban decay, discrimination, and poor education? This last question about distribution is perhaps the most profound.[88]

The development of any national strategy to deal with these questions must first decide what resources are available nationally to deal with health care. That is essentially a political question. Then it must be determined how the resources are to be divided between all of those who need them. The latter problem is that of distributive justice and involves a determination or prioritisation of needs in the community as between basic necessities and luxuries.

[1.74] There are four major theories of justice: utilitarianism, egalitarianism, libertarianism and contractarianism. When applied to health care, each of these theories provides guidance on a just system of health-care distribution. Although this section can only give general indications of how each system might work in practical settings, it is nonetheless useful to examine the different methods briefly.

Utilitarianism

[1.75] The most well-known proponent of this theory of justice, John Stuart Mill, argued that a just allocation provides the greatest good to the greatest number of people.[89] In applying this theory to health-care allocation, utilitarians would seek to promote the maximum benefit for the greatest number. Therefore, they would seek to prevent or cure the most common illnesses, adopt programmes that help many rather than few persons, and generally use funds where they will have the greatest impact for most people. Thus, expensive treatments for few people would not be provided at the expense of programmes to help provide basic care for larger numbers.[90] Utilitarianism would justify preferential treatment of children on the basis that such treatment will offer the most years of benefit.[91] On this basis, funding of routine care, screening, immunisations, and other prevention programmes would be more beneficial than the development of a few

---

87   Mason and Laurie, *Law and Medical Ethics*, (8th edn, OUP, 2010), p 376.

88   Kass, 'The New Biology: What Price Relieving Man's Estate?' (1971) Science 174; 779.

89   Mill, *Utilitarianism*, (Parker, Son, and Bourn, 1957, edn) (1863). See in particular Chapter 2, 'What Utilitarianism Is'.

90   Kopelman and Palumbo, 'The US Health Delivery System: Inefficient and Unfair to Children' (1997) 23 Am J L and Med 319.

91   Callahan, 'Terminating Treatment: Age As a Standard"' Hastings Center Report Oct./Nov. 1987, at 21.

specialised therapies that might save relatively few children. Problems arise in the application of this theory in the sense that it is sometimes difficult to calculate what is best for the greatest number, and whole groups could be excluded or discriminated against if they have rare or expensive conditions, in the interests of the common good.

Egalitarianism

[1.76] This theory attempts to resolve allocation problems by giving similar benefits, goods and services to all on the same basis. It directs us to equalise, as much as possible, in terms of everyone's well-being up to a certain level. Therefore, all similarly situated persons should be able to receive similar goods and services. In relation to expensive treatments or scarce resources, egalitarians might argue that lotteries are the most just way of allocating such finite resources amongst people similarly situated.[92] This would acknowledge the right of each person to gain fair access to the benefits of the treatment in question.[93] However, problems exist in trying to determine what kind of equality is important, ie age, life expectancy with/without treatment, family circumstances and so on. Again, here certain groups could be excluded if they fall within certain prejudices.

Libertarianism

[1.77] This theory argues that the State should not limit the liberty of competent adults except to prevent harm to third parties.[94] On this basis, market forces and choices about how to use one's own money should shape the kind of health care people get. However, concern may be expressed here for the protection of vulnerable groups such as the elderly, the poor, children or incompetent adults, as libertarianism seems to disproportionately favour the wealthy.

Contractarianism

[1.78] According to this theory, fair distributions of social goods occur when informed and impartial people agree on the procedures used for distribution. The most well-known proponent of this theory is John Rawls, who contends that people should form a consensus as to allocation of resources within their society.[95] Although he did not specifically address health-care resources in his writings, his theory has been built on by Daniels, who argues that a just society should provide basic health care to all, but redistribute goods and services more favourably to children to provide them with fair equality of opportunity to compete with their peers.[96] Critics argue that it is difficult to apply the equality of opportunity rule fairly and that it seems unsatisfactory to fund expensive treatment of a few disadvantaged people to the detriment of the fulfilment of the needs of many others.

---

[92] Childress, 'Who Shall Live When Not All Can Live?' (1970) 53 *Soundings* 339, at 347–54.

[93] Kopelman and Palumbo, 'The US Health Delivery System: Inefficient and Unfair to Children' (1997) 23 Am J L and Med 319, p 325.

[94] The most well-known proponent of this theory was Locke, *Treatise of Civil Government* 18–33 (Blackwell, 1956) (1689). Also see Nozick, *Anarchy, State and Utopia* (Basic Books, 1974) pp 120–46.

[95] Rawls, *A Theory of Justice* (1971) (Revised edn, OUP, 1999) and *Political Liberalism* (Columbia University Press, 1996).

[96] Daniels, *Just Health Care* (Cambridge University Press, 1985) pp 111–12.

[1.79] It can be seen, therefore, that the application of various theories of justice while useful in stimulating discussion about priorities and objectives of the health-care system, nevertheless are not perfect. Each theory ranks values differently, from equality to liberty and so on. The difficulty is how to choose between these theories in determining how to prioritise scarce resources, and who is to be the decision-maker in these situations: doctor, patient or politician? Ideally the State should provide equal access to comprehensive high-quality health care for all those in need but the vast amount of literature on this subject acknowledges the near impossibility of a just system. Decisions at a national level require priority setting between different types of service, which in turn depends on professional medical assessment and advice, public opinion and economic evaluation. Mason and Laurie point out that public opinion is a 'fickle measuring instrument' as 'not only can polls be grossly distorted by the way in which questions are put but also opinion is very subject to political and other extraneous influences – particularly that of the media whose circulations depend on maintaining an aggressive and partisan attitude.' They say that the importance of transparency in decision-making in rationing resources has become increasingly important in recent years.[97]

Although the politician's duty is to make the sort of macro decisions that must be made regarding the provision and funding of expensive treatments generally[98], at a micro level the medical practitioner's ultimate duty is to his patient, and he must also be conscious of the resource implications of his decision-making. This is considered below.

Decisions as between individuals

[1.80] As well as the issues that arise on a national and international level regarding the health rights enjoyed by citizens in Ireland, there is also the problem of the allocation of scarce resources as between individual citizens, all of whom may have reasonable claims to the medical resource. How is an individual medical practitioner to decide as between these competing claims? 'Resources have never been infinite and unenviable decisions between patients have always been made, though in a manner less visible in the past. Doctors care for groups of patients and know very well that the use of a bed or operating theatre for one patient may mean that the treatment of another will be delayed or denied altogether.'[99] Those with responsibility for allocation of health resources face difficult dilemmas in deciding whether or not to fund particular treatments for patients.

[1.81] For example, in *R v Cambridge Health Authority, ex parte B*[100] a 10-year-old child who was suffering from lymphoma had received chemotherapy, radiotherapy and a bone marrow transplant before she relapsed. The medical team were of the view that no other treatment would be beneficial and that her life expectancy was between six and eight weeks. Her father sought a second opinion from doctors in the United States which estimated that further treatment carried an 18% chance of cure. B's doctors in the UK were of the opinion that this was overly optimistic and estimated the chances of success

---

[97] Mason and Laurie, *Law and Medical Ethics*, (8th edn, OUP, 2010), p 380.

[98] See generally, Hon. Justice Kirby, 'Bioethical Decisions and Opportunity Costs' (1986) *Journal of Contemporary Health Law and Policy* Vol 2:7–21.

[99] Newdick, *Who Should We Treat?* (OUP, 1995) p 277.

[100] *R v Cambridge Health Authority, ex parte B*, (1995) 25 BMLR 5; reversed (1995) 23 BMLR 1 CA.

at between 2 and 10%. The cost of the treatment for the local health authority would be £75,000. They refused to fund the treatment on the grounds that it would not be in B's best interests and that the expenditure of so much money with such a low prospect of success was an inefficient use of their limited resources, bearing in mind the needs of other patients. B's father sought judicial review of this decision.

[1.82] In the High Court, Laws J determined that the decision of the health authority conflicted with B's right to life and with her father's right to determine her health care. He considered that where there was even a slim chance that the child might be saved the authority must do more than consider the financial implications involved. He ordered that the authority's decision be reconsidered. However, the Court of Appeal reversed this decision, emphasising that its role was not to judge the merits of the medical judgment made but to examine the lawfulness of the decision of the authority. The Court felt that the authority had adequately considered the parents' wishes, that the proposed treatment was innovative and that it was unrealistic to proceed on the basis that any treatments needed by a patient would be provided, irrespective of the cost. The Court said it could not make a judgment as to how the limited budget of the authority should best be spent, and it was open to the authority to reach the decision it had in fact reached.[101] Sir Thomas Bingham MR said:

> I have no doubt that in a perfect world any treatment which a patient…sought would be provided if doctors were willing to give it, no matter how much it cost…It would, however, be shutting one's eyes to the real world if the court were to proceed on the basis that we do live in such a world.[102]

[1.83] From the perspective of the individual doctor, they are expected not only to treat their patients to the best of their ability, but also to be aware of the economic costs of their treatment decisions. For example, the most recent edition of the Medical Council's Ethical Guide[103] advises doctors that:

> 49.1 Subject to your duty to act in the best interests of patients, you have a responsibility to engage and advocate with the relevant authorities to promote the provision of appropriate healthcare resources and facilities.

> 49.2 You have a duty to assist in the efficient and effective use of healthcare resources and to give advice on their appropriate allocation. While balancing a duty of care to the individual patient, you should be aware of the wider need to use limited healthcare resources efficiently and responsibly. Such awareness should inform decision making in your clinical practice. For example, you are encouraged to prescribe bio-equivalent generic medicines where they are safe and effective and only commission investigations if they are clinically indicated.

[1.84] The inherent danger in this kind of dilemma is that subjective value judgments may be brought to bear on the decision-making process. In the UK, the National

---

[101] As a result of a sympathetic media campaign, B's treatment was funded privately but she died 14 months after the hearing. See Entwistle, Watt, Bradbury and Pehl 'Media Coverage of the Child B Case' (1996) 312 BMJ 1587.

[102] *R v Cambridge Health Authority, ex parte B* (1995) 23 MBLR 1 at 8–9.

[103] Medical Council, *Guide to Professional Conduct and Ethics* (7th edn, 2009) www.medicalcouncil.ie/Professional-Standards/Professional-Conduct-Ethics/ (accessed 27 June 2011).

Institute for Clinical Excellence (NICE) recommends that neither age nor income group should be primary criteria regulating choice. They take the view that health should not be valued more highly in some age groups rather than others (unless age is an indicator of benefit or risk in the particular circumstances) and that individual's social roles should not influence considerations of cost effectiveness.[104]

[1.85] What are the criteria that should be used to make decisions of this kind? The first and most obvious one is the probability of successful medical outcome. In itself this appears unproblematic and, indeed, ethically mandatory. However, it is argued that many predictions of successful medical outcome might also be covert value judgments[105] and might in fact be basing decision-making on a second criterion, ie the patient's value or disvalue to society, or where patients have somehow, by their lifestyle or other choices, caused their own illness. This has been debated, for example, in the context of the exclusion of smokers from cardiac surgery[106], although the potential for such a policy is also evident in relation to persistent drug or alcohol abusers. The question here is whether quality of life considerations should be relevant in deciding how to allocate scarce resources.[107] While it is generally agreed that individuals have responsibilities as well as rights in relation to their own health care, it would be impossible to maintain an exclusionary policy that did not transgress equal status principles of non-discrimination on the basis of disability, age, class or social background.

[1.86] While the courts would generally be reluctant to interfere with clinical decisions made by a responsible practitioner, it would not necessarily be sufficient to answer an allegation of negligence that there were not enough resources to provide the requisite care. There are a number of different problems involved in decision-making in this context. These range from the distinction between basic and luxury care to ageism, 'undeserving' patients and the meaning of futile care.[108] In the context of the NHS in the United Kingdom, cases have been decided on the basis of the reasonableness or otherwise of the clinical decision not to offer treatment in individual circumstances. For example, in *R v Sheffield Health Authority, ex parte Seale*,[109] the plaintiff was refused in vitro fertilisation treatment because she was deemed to be too old, at 37 years of age. She argued that the setting of a blanket upper age limit failed to take into account her own clinical circumstances and was therefore illegal. The Court of Appeal held that this was not so; the age limit was neither irrational nor absurd for failing to consider individual case merits.

A clinical decision on a case by case basis is clearly desirable and, in cases of critical illness, a necessary approach. However, it is reasonable, or at least not *Wednesbury*[110]

104 NICE, *Social Value Judgements* (2005) recommendation 6.
105 Stauch, Tingle & Wheat, *Sourcebook on Medical Law* (2nd edn, Cavendish, 1998) p 48.
106 Underwood and Bailey, 'Coronary Bypass Surgery Should Not Be Offered to Smokers" (1993) 306 BMJ 1047.
107 For further discussion of this issue see *The Report of the Independent Inquiries into Paediatric Cardiac Services at the Royal Brompton Hospital and Harefield Hospital* (April 2001) available at www.rbh.nthames.nhs.uk (accessed 20 May 2011).
108 See Newdick, 'Resource Allocation in the National Health Service'. (1997) 23 Am. JL and Med 291.
109 *R v Sheffield Health Authority, ex parte Seale* (1994) 25 BMLR 1.
110 *Associated Provincial Picture Houses Ltd v Wednesbury Corp* [1947] 2 All ER 680.

unreasonable…of an authority to look at the matter in the context of the financial resources available to it and the many other services for which it is responsible. I cannot say that it is absurd for this authority …to take thirty-five as an appropriate criterion when balancing the need for such provision against its ability to provide it.

The anti-ageist argument is well put by Harris, who claims that:

[A]ll of us who wish to go on living have something that each of us values equally, although for each it is different in character, for some a much richer prize than for others, and we none of us know its true extent. The thing is of course 'the rest of our lives'. So long as we do not know the date of our deaths then for each of us the 'rest of our lives' is of indefinite duration.[111]

[1.87] Therefore, we each suffer the same injustice if our wish to live the rest of our lives, however long or short a time that might be, is taken from us. Why should something we each value equally be taken from some based on their date of birth? However implausible it might thus seem to distinguish between people on the basis of age, when the boundaries of the argument are pushed to their logical extremes, the ageist argument creeps back in. For example, no one may suggest that a 20-year-old should be treated ahead of a 30-year-old simply on the basis of age, but should a 5-year-old not be treated ahead of an 85-year-old? Harris suggests in reply that one strategy for dealing with this situation would be the 'fair innings' argument, which takes the view that there is some span of years that is considered to be a reasonable life. If a fair share of life is taken at, say, 70 years, then anyone who reaches that age should be relatively satisfied that they have had a fair innings, and that anything beyond that is a bonus rather than an entitlement.

The attraction of the fair innings argument is that it preserves and incorporates many of the features that made the anti-ageist argument plausible, but allows us to preserve our feeling that the old who have had a good run for their money should not be endlessly propped up at the expense of those who have not had the same chance.[112]

The difficulty with this seemingly easy solution to resource allocation problems is that the setting of a reasonable lifespan is subjective and when generalised will always become an argument in favour of saving the life of the person furthest away from that cut-off point, ie the younger person. This brings us back again to ageist distinctions with which we may feel uncomfortable.

Quality adjusted life years

[1.88] Another solution is that of Quality Adjusted Life Years (QALYs).[113] This approach attempts to evaluate health-care outcomes according to a generic scale. It asks for how long a proposed treatment will improve the quality of a patient's life and how much the treatment costs. Each full year of health counts as one, and each year of declining health counts as less than one. Thus, if the patient's improvement is likely to be long-lasting and significant, then the patient accumulates a high score on the quality of life measure. If the cost of the treatment is relatively low, then the cost per unit of

---

111 Harris, *The Value of Life* (Routledge, 1985) p 89.

112 Harris, *The Value of Life* (Routledge, 1985).

113 See Williams, 'The Value of QALYs' (1985) *Health and Social Services Journal*; Harris. 'QALYfying the Value of Life' (1987) 13 *JME* 117; Newdick, *Who Should We Treat?* (OUP, 1995) p 22.

quality is also low. 'The theory favours treatments which achieve the greatest increase in the quality of life, over the longest period, for the least cost.'[114]

[1.89] Newdick gives the example of the treatment of premature babies in neonatal intensive care. The number of babies that survive very low birthweight difficulties has grown significantly in the last 20 years but there is still the fact that some will not survive despite best medical efforts, others will survive with varying degrees of disability, while others will survive and live a normal, healthy life. It is sometimes difficult to distinguish between these groups at the outset. Economists point to the fact that the cost per QALY for this group of patients is extremely high because of their short life expectancy. Does this mean that we should not treat them if the money can be better expended elsewhere? Although a health economist may argue that strictly speaking this should be the case, and although it may be strictly egalitarian in not favouring one patient over another, it is nonetheless instinctively difficult to accept, as it might result in the withdrawal of pain relief from a cancer patient who is likely to die in any event, non-treatment of a child with cerebral palsy and other decisions that would conflict with the values and objectives in most health-care systems.

[1.90] In the context of medical futility, conflict may also arise here between the legal duty on doctors to prioritise the health of their patients, and the ethical duty to allow the patient to die with dignity. When may treatment be withdrawn from a patient on the basis that it is futile to continue? For example, in the House of Lords decision in *Airedale NHS Trust v Bland*[115] in which the Court held that it was lawful to discontinue artificial feeding and other treatment from the patient, who was in a persistent vegetative state, the Court held that there is no absolute obligation to keep patients alive regardless of their prospects of recovery. In extreme cases it is not in the patient's interests to continue with treatment, even though the withdrawal of treatment may result in the patient's death. 'It is the futility of the treatment which justifies its termination.'[116]

[1.91] Critics of the QALYs system point to the difficulty in scoring the degree of likely improvement of a patient after treatment and point to its subjectivity, something that the system is supposed to avoid. While one patient may be content to live with physical limitations for 10 years after surgery, another patient may prefer to die than be confined to a wheelchair. The system works on the assumption that most rational people would prefer a shorter, healthier life to a longer period of survival in discomfort or disability. However, this would discriminate against disabled and elderly persons from the outset, as they would never be able to achieve the optimum score on an objective assessment of their quality of life. Economists say that such decisions are made every day, they are inevitable and the inherent value of the QALYs system is that it tries to make such decisions on a more rational and transparent basis.

[1.92] It is also argued that rather than treating all needy patients equally, the QALYs system would prefer one person's life over the other's, even if the difference in life expectation was very small, such as two days. Proponents of QALYs rebut this by pointing to the fact that if all needy patients were to be treated equally, then one whose

---

[114] Newdick, *Who Should We Treat?* (OUP, 1995) p 22.
[115] *Airedale NHS Trust v Bland* [1993] 1 All ER 821.
[116] *Airedale NHS Trust v Bland* [1993] 1 All ER 821 at 896.

life expectancy was 30 years after treatment would be treated the same as one whose life expectancy was 2 days after treatment.[117]

[1.93] There are conflicting and arguably unrealistic obligations placed on doctors in this context to act as gatekeepers in the management of scarce resources. To what extent can, or should, a doctor serve simultaneously the needs of his patients, his own interests and those of society?[118] As well as having obligations to promote their patient's welfare, doctors are under constraints to restrict the use of expensive medical services, which raises dilemmas in cutting corners and exposing themselves to later allegations of negligence. Harris proposes, as an alternative to QALYs, a random selection of patients or lottery method.[119] Such a method has the advantage of apparent objectivity and could be defended as the morally desirable choice but, as Mason and Laurie point out, it is a bad medical option because it takes no account of the gravity of the patient's condition and no account of medical benefit – it concentrates on justice and ignores welfare. 'Nevertheless it may be the way of allocating scarce resources that the public prefer and it is, in fact, practised in the form of, say, waiting lists for transplantable organs.'[120]

[1.94] A public consensus model was attempted in Oregon, USA, where a policy was devised which tried to compile a list of health services ranked by priority, from the most important to the least important, representing the comparative benefits of each service to the population.[121] This was so as to enable the funding received from central government under the Medicaid scheme (designed to cover those unable to afford health insurance) to be administered according to the net benefit to be obtained and the priorities generally set by the relevant community. Services were listed by reference to specific treatments and conditions, distinguishing in 17 categories as between acute and chronic illness, preventative and curative treatments, illnesses causing death and those causing disability and so on. A separate ranking process took place within each category and only those ranked high on the lists would be funded.

[1.95] Although praise-worthy in its attempt to involve the community in the prioritisation of resources, a number of problems became apparent with this option, too. For example, the results of one list placed obstetrical care low and infertility treatment high in the priority ranking, causing concern from those administering the scheme. Many conditions were not listed, and problems could arise for patients presenting with more than one condition, some of which were not fundable. Many of those within the population most likely to be affected did not participate in the exercise and the results may indicate that the difficult ethical issues arising in some medical conditions could not be appreciated by those who did not understand the resource implications inherent in

---

[117] See series of articles by Harris and McKie each arguing opposite sides of the QALY debate in (1996) 22 JME 204–21.

[118] Pellegrino, 'Rationing Health Care: The Ethics of Medical Gatekeeping' [1986] Journal of Contemporary Health Law and Policy Vol 2: 23–45.

[119] Harris, *The Value of Life* (Routledge, 1985).

[120] Mason and Laurie, *Law and Medical Ethics*, (8th edn, OUP, 2010), p 395.

[121] US Congress, Office of Technology Assessment, Evaluation of the Oregon Medicard Proposal, OTA-H-531 (Washington DC: US Government Printing Office, May 1992) available at www.fas.org.ota/reports/9213.pdf (accessed 11 July 2011); Honigsbaum, *Who Shall live? Who Shall Die? – Oregon's Health Financing Proposals* (King's Fund, 1993).

their choices. "As the experiment in Oregon showed, it is difficult to involve a representative cross-section of people in the exercise. Often, particular groups will be involved and some will effectively lobby for funds, but one wonders who will speak up for the less articulate groups such as the mentally handicapped, the elderly, and those with 'unpopular' diseases."[122]

Health technology assessment (HTA)

[1.96] Health Technology Assessment has been introduced in a number of countries in recent years as a means by which health resources are assessed to ensure that they are being used in a way that maximises the best outcome for patients. It involves an assessment of the clinical and cost effectiveness of the medicines, devices, diagnostics, and health promotion used across the health system. It also includes the evaluation of social and ethical issues, quality of life and quality of end of life and cost effectiveness in relation to health technology. In Ireland, the Health Information and Quality Authority (HIQA) currently carries out HTAs in order to enable the Minister for Health and Children to make informed decisions on the desirability and effectiveness of investing in new therapies, drugs, equipment or health-promotion activities. For example, some of the HTAs already carried out by HIQA include an assessment of the role of vaccination against human papillomavirus (HPV) in reducing the risk of cervical cancer in Ireland and an assessment of a population-based colorectal cancer screening programme.[123] The HSE is also developing an internal HTA process.[124]

[1.97] The objective of HTAs is to support decision-makers such as the Minister for Health to develop policies in relation to health technology which are socially and medically acceptable in the community. There is no national or international consensus on the correct approach to this exercise. The emphasis in the literature on this issue is on ensuring that the decision-making process itself is fair, open and inclusive of all perspectives.[125] It is important that the decision-maker is as transparent as possible in relation to the ethical stance taken and the values underpinning the decision. Provided the bases for decision-making are flexible in relation to the times, then the underlying system is probably just and likely to produce just results.[126]

---

122   Newdick, *Who Should We Treat?* (OUP, 1995) p 36.
123   See http://www.hiqa.ie/healthcare/health-technology-assessment (accessed 27 June 2011).
124   Available at http://www.hse.ie/eng/about/who/population_health/health_intelligence/ health_intelligence_work/health_technology_assessment/ (accessed 27 June 2011].
125   Drummond *et al*, 'Key Principles for the Improved Conduct of Health Technology Assessments for Resource Allocation Decisions' (2008) Intl J of Technology Assessment in Health Care 24:3.
126   Gillon 'Justice and Allocation of Medical Resources' (1995) 291 BMJ 266.

Chapter 2

Regulation of Medical Practice in Ireland

THE PRACTICE OF MODERN MEDICINE

[2.01] Until the middle of the last century the medical profession was largely, though not always, harmless and essentially ineffective: comfort more than cure. The doctor's primary duty was to diagnose an illness and then track its natural course. Doctors did all they could to help the sick, but they did not have either the tools or the understanding of the body's workings they needed to consistently succeed. It was not until after World War II that biomedical research provided the profession with the weapons it needed. 'Doctors were widely hailed as miracle workers, and "quality" care became synonymous with "more" care. More doctors. More nurses. More hospitals. More drugs. More diagnostic equipment.'[1] Doctors are now expected to provide safe, high-quality care, participate in research, be effective and compassionate communicators and often to run their own businesses as well. Medicine has become hugely more effective in the last few decades, but this has brought its own challenges, with increasing expectations of the public, use of high-end expensive technology, changes in the dynamic of the doctor-patient relationship and pressure on health-care resources.

[2.02] The tradition in the medical profession was, for much of the last two hundred years, that the patient was the passive recipient of medical care and doctors took it upon themselves to decide what treatment and information should be provided. Doctors were encouraged to protect their patients from information about their own health, in case it made them sicker. This tradition of strong paternalism is particularly evident in the Irish and English legal systems where, in matters of civil liability, the courts allowed doctors to broadly set their own standards.

[2.03] Criticism of medical paternalism is often seen in the context of calls for recognition of patients' rights, whereby the moral agency of the individual and the value of respect for the patient as person is proclaimed. Suppression of the patient's voice is considered incompatible with legitimate expectations about individual choice and freedom to decide what is done to one's body. These expectations argue a right to the kind of disclosure and dialogue that will permit informed decision-making.[2] In recent years there has been a movement in the education and training of doctors, as well as professional guidelines to practitioners, towards encouragement of greater patient participation and a more collaborative approach to medical decision-making. Despite much improvement, however, the traditional approach has not yet completely

---

[1] Millenson, *Demanding Medical Excellence, Doctors and Accountability in the Information Age* (University of Chicago, 1997) p 4.
[2] See generally Teff, *Reasonable Care, Legal Perspectives on the Doctor-Patient Relationship* (Clarendon Press, 1994).

disappeared, particularly in the hospital environment, where the busy context and hierarchical nature of the organisation can hinder the development of such a partnership model.

> The nature of medical practice may have changed considerably in recent times but the hospital setting still bears the stamp of the Hippocratic tradition. The more impersonal and hierarchical hospital regime still reflects a time-honoured ethos that remains a potent force in medical schools. There are signs that its hold is weakening, in the face of new managerial policies and financial constraints dictated by governmental drive for cost containment and greater accountability. But such developments do not argue a professional conversion to the primacy of patient choice and patient's rights.[3]

[2.04] In the context of general practice, although the traditional paternalistic model was based in part on the belief that keeping negative information from the patient was good for his health, this too has come under attack in recent years. Studies show how failure to involve patients can lead to error in diagnosis and treatment, delay recovery and adversely affect long-term outcomes. To experience a measure of control over one's illness can itself be therapeutic and can reduce levels of anxiety and depression. This has been reflected in more recent literature on medical ethics that stress the doctor-patient relationship as a partnership or a collaborative effort. Patients are unlikely to want to dictate to their doctor or to determine their own treatment. They are more likely to want co-determination and genuine communication.[4]

[2.05] Principles of autonomy and empowerment of the individual have been brought to medical practice with far-reaching consequences for the relationship between medicine and law. Medicine is certainly not alone in feeling the effects of social and cultural changes brought about by increased public education and access to information at the touch of a button. Freedom of information policies and legislation dealing with access to personal records have added to 'the unease of doctors keeping such records and to increased defensiveness in the practice of medicine in Ireland because the documentation of clinical standards and of consent procedures is now readily scrutinised.'[5]

[2.06] Another issue of importance in the changing medical-legal relationship is the growing recognition and awareness of rights as a precursor to any medical treatment. This has become evident not only in the increase in medical litigation, but also in the ways in which doctors approach the issues of capacity and informed consent. Whereas in the past doctors may have been prepared to treat patients without fully informing them of possible risks and complications where they were of the opinion that the patient did not want the information or would be distressed by it, this approach would generally not be seen as acceptable today. There has also been a move towards patient charters and national guidelines on what patients can expect from their doctor and hospital.[6] While such documents may provide useful benchmarks against which health service providers

---

3   Teff, *Reasonable Care, Legal Perspectives on the Doctor-Patient Relationship* (Clarendon Press, 1994) at xxv.
4   Donnelly, *Consent: Bridging the Gap Between Doctor and Patient*, (Cork University Press, 2002).
5   Cusack, 'Ireland: Breakdown of Trust Between Doctor and Patient' (2000) The Lancet 356:1431 at 1432.

can measure themselves and be assessed, the language of rights sometimes used in such documents is not necessarily accurate or conducive to a collaborative relationship.

[2.07] The common use of the internet has also led to a radical change in the way in which patients come to their doctors for treatment. Whereas the patient traditionally came to the doctor in need of an explanation, a diagnosis and a reassurance that a means could be found to cure the ailment, now patients often search for information on the internet prior to attending the doctor, so they can easily find an explanation for their symptoms and the preferable method of treatment. They then present themselves to the doctor already self-diagnosed from a perusal of a vast array of medical information and advice on treatment. While the increase and accessibility of information may be considered a huge advance in educating the public on illness and its management, a note of caution must also be sounded in respect of the accuracy and reliability of some of the websites that may be accessed by the public, which are not based on sound objective facts and may be sponsored by agencies or commercial enterprises with financial interests at stake. Internet advice is often given by people without medical training, is unconventional and may be inappropriate. Therefore, electronic resources should always carry a warning about adherence to their advice.

[2.08] From the perspective of its effect on the doctor-patient relationship, the challenge may be for the doctor to explain and justify any disagreement with this internet diagnosis to which the patient may be wedded, and any deviation from the treatment the patient has come to the doctor expecting to receive. The shift in the balance of information and power has, without doubt, added to the empowerment of the patient, and perhaps the defensiveness of the profession, which feels under more scrutiny than ever before. 'Empowered patients are challenging the professional's medical advice and choices of treatment, sometimes by finding alternative sources or providers of treatment on the Internet.'[7]

[2.09] For doctors, too, the internet has provided a rich source of learning. The technical evolution in the field of therapeutic medicine has been impressive. Although the bases for making a diagnosis today remain the same as 20 years ago, collaboration with colleagues nationally and internationally, medical information retrieval and case discussion now takes place faster and with higher degrees of speciality.[8] Telemedicine or telehealth[9] is used to more advantage now and, in particular, for remote diagnosis in sparsely populated areas.[10] Robotic surgery may be carried out even where the doctor

---

[6]   Health Service Executive, *The HSE and You*, (2010), available at www.hse.ie (accessed 23 May 2011).

[7]   Cox, *The Impact of the Internet on the Doctor-Patient Relationship*, (Imperial College Management School, 2000). A preliminary study carried out by Cox on the impact of the information revolution reported that 40 per cent of obstetricians interviewed said that use of the internet 'could damage the traditional doctor-patient relationship.'

[8]   'Medical Diagnosis in the Internet Age.' (1999) The Lancet Vol 354, supplement 4.

[9]   'Telemedicine' means medicine across distance. X-rays were probably the first documented medical visual communication across distance, being transmitted over telephone lines in 1948. It is now being replaced by 'telehealth', which is the systematic application of telecommunication technology to the field of health care.

[10]   For an historical overview see Barrett and Brecht, 'Historical Context of Telemedicine' in Viegas and Dunn, *Telemedicine: Practising in the Information Age* (Lippincott Williams & Wilkins, 1998).

and patient are not physically present in the same room.[11] However, computer-based technologies could be seen as a double-edged sword, as they also provide the opportunity for the commission of illegal and unprofessional conduct. 'The loss and damage which could result from the improper use of on-line technologies are formidable, both in financial and human terms.'[12] The risks inherent through interception of communications, computer hacking, copyright infringement and breach of confidentiality are just some of the dangers lurking in this form of practice. There are also concerns arising in the area of medical negligence claims that could become even more complicated where medical practice transcends jurisdictional lines, and where the very existence of the doctor-patient relationship may be brought into question.[13]

[2.10] In recent years there has also been an increased focus on health information technology as a means of ensuring patient safety. There have been numerous calls for the introduction of information communication technology in the health-care system, such as electronic health records, electronic prescribing, disease surveillance databases, electronic adverse-event-reporting systems, digital imaging and transmission of radiological images, GP electronic booking for referrals and hospital appointments, discharge summaries, reporting of laboratory results and so on. National strategy and policy documents all support these measures and the government has accepted the necessity to introduce such technology as part of a patient safety framework proposed by the Commission on Patient Safety and Quality Assurance.[14] The proposed Health Information Bill will put in place the necessary legislative framework to support the introduction of many of these ICT measures. This is discussed further in Chapter 3.

[2.11] Apart from the internet, other new technologies also generate dramatic responses. Medical practice has changed almost beyond recognition in 50 years. Patients with congestive heart failure can now live longer, laparoscopy can be used to perform surgery, anaesthetic techniques enable lengthy and complicated operations to take place and immunisations are available that were not dreamt of then.[15] Technology is expensive

---

11   The world's first transoceanic operation on humans was recently conducted over high-speed fibreoptic connections. Surgeons in New York successfully used remotely controlled robots to laparoscopically remove a gall bladder from a woman in France. The operation lasted less than an hour, no intraoperative complications occurred and the 68-year-old-patient was discharged within 48 hours after an uneventful hospital stay. BMJ 2001; 323:713 (29 Sept.).

12   Smith Russell, 'Medicine, Crime and Unprofessional Conduct in the Online World' *Medico-Legal Journal* 65/3.

13   It may, for example, be argued that in the absence of any direct contact between the doctor and patient in the practice of telemedicine, that no such relationship is formed, and therefore no duty of care arises. However, if the doctor has participated in the diagnosis of the patient, or prescribed a course of treatment for him, a professional relationship is established. 'All professionals who engage in telemedicine practice should assume that their telemedicine encounters impose on them at least the same obligations arising from a professional relationship as do their non telemedicine encounters.' Blair, Bambas and Stone, 'Legal and Ethical Issues', in Viegas and Dunn, *Telemedicine: Practising in the Information Age* (Lippincott Williams & Wilkins, 1998).

14   *Building a Culture of Patient Safety*. Section 7.7, available at www.cpsqa.ie/publications/pdf/patientsafety.pdf (accessed 23 May 2011).

15   Herman, 'The Good Old Days', (1998) The Lancet, Vol 353 No 9144.

but promises more hope than ever before, as does the increasing array of new drugs, devices and procedures launched every year. The increasingly effective use of medical technologies, however, also leads to higher patient expectations and sometimes ethical concerns as to misuse. Difficulties arise regarding the funding of such technology and how scarce resources will be allocated if the technology does become available. Issues arise in relation to reproductive technology, genetic diagnosis and the use of stem cells that were unimaginable 50 years ago and pose huge ethical and legal problems now. The hope held out for the future is set in promising terms – 'Once science enables us to know our own genome, we will be able to anticipate future health problems, change any risk-taking behaviour, and have personalised treatments designed for us.'[16] Yet, this knowledge too may have inherent disadvantages, as it forces individuals to confront their own health and mortality, at perhaps psychological detriment to themselves and their families, and perhaps without holding out any cure for the predicted disease.

MEDICAL ETHICS

[2.12] Medical ethics are vital to the practice of medicine and thus to any understanding of medical law for a number of reasons. Firstly, many practitioners look for guidance in their decision-making to ethics rather than law. Most practitioners will have had the benefit of a module on ethics during their training and may also look to the Medical Council and other sources for guidance on ethics. Secondly some legal principles have been influenced by the evolution of ethical principles – for example, the law of consent to medical treatment is based on respect for autonomy, and attempts to legislate in the area of medical practice are sometimes resisted on grounds of ethical principles such as respect for autonomy and freedom of choice.[17] Thirdly, in Ireland many areas of medical law are as yet undeveloped, with relatively sparse legislation and few judicial precedents. Although the courts are quick to point out that the judicial function is not to be an arbiter of different ethical perspectives, such perspectives nonetheless inform public debate and academic literature on medical law, and undoubtedly influence legal thinking. Thus Jackson says, 'it is impossible to study medical law without confronting complex ethical dilemmas.'[18] She gives examples, such as when is it acceptable for doctors to withhold treatment from a profoundly disabled baby? Should parents be allowed to choose the sex of their children? Is it wrong to pay someone to donate a kidney? Should voluntary euthanasia be legalised? 'It would be difficult to work out the appropriate *legal* response to such questions without also considering their ethical implications.' For this reason, this section will briefly outline some of the main ethical theories that might be used in discussing and resolving such ethical dilemmas.

[2.13] The word 'ethics' comes from the Greek *ethos*, which means 'custom or practice, a characteristic manner of acting, a more or less constant mode of behaviour in the deliberate actions of men.' Broadly speaking, ethics is the science or study of the morality of human acts though the medium of natural reason.[19] There are a number of

---

[16] Berger and Smith, 'New Technologies in Medicine and Medical Journals' (1999) BMJ: 319: 7220.

[17] McHale & Fox, *Health Care Law, Text and Materials* (Sweet & Maxwell, 1997) at 71.

[18] Jackson, *Medical Law, Text, Cases and Materials* (2nd edn, OUP, 2010) p 2.

[19] McFadden, *Medical Ethics* (6th edn, FA Davis Co, 1967), p 1.

approaches to the study of ethics that may be explained briefly. *Normative ethics* generally tries to evaluate what general norms for the guidance of conduct are morally acceptable and why. It is a 20th century idea that, in theory, satisfies a set of criteria for inquiry into moral concepts and principles. *Practical or applied ethics* are an attempt to work out the implications of general theories for specific forms of conduct, or for specific professions or public policy. These theories are invoked to help develop guides for action in those contexts. *Non-normative ethics* are categorised as, firstly, *descriptive ethics,* which is a factual investigation of how moral attitudes are expressed in practice, codes and policies, and, secondly, *metaethics,* which involves analysis of the language, concepts and methods of reasoning in ethics. Both of these have as their objective to establish what factually or conceptually is the case, not what ought to be the case.[20]

[2.14] *Medical ethics* is an application of general ethical principles to the solution of the moral problems of the medical profession and is principally concerned with what it means to be a good doctor. It involves an analysis of the concepts, assumptions, beliefs, attitudes, emotions, reasons and arguments underlying medico-moral decisions[21]. There are many different approaches to medical ethics and the methodologies that may be used when confronted by difficult moral problems. To assist doctors, ethical guidelines are produced by medical professional regulatory bodies to impose rules on doctors to ensure that their conduct towards their patients and colleagues meets certain agreed standards. Some have argued that the focus of medical ethics has been too narrow – in emphasising the duties of doctors, the obligations of patients have been ignored. Draper and Sorrell argue that medical ethics makes very few demands of patients and that 'little is said about the kinds of decisions patients *ought* to make. Nor is much said about their responsibilities for making good rather than bad decisions. Indeed… mainstream medical ethics implies that a competent patient's decision is good simply by virtue of having been made by the patient. At times it seems as though patients never make, or cannot make, bad decisions…'.[22]

[2.15] Of all the professions, medicine raises the most complex and difficult moral problems, concerned as it is with the intricacies of the beginning and ending of life. *Biomedical ethics* or *bioethics* is the application of ethical principles to the biological sciences, medicine and health care. It emerged as a discipline in the 1960s in response to technological developments and challenges to medical paternalism, with a corresponding rise in the principle of patient autonomy.[23]

---

20 Beauchamp and Childress, *Principles of Biomedical Ethics* (4th edn, New York: OUPOUP, 1994) p 4. Chapter 1, 'Morality and Moral Justification', provides a very useful explanation of the terminology used in the study of ethics and the methodologies that may be employed in problem-solving.

21 Gillon, *Philosophical Medical Ethics* (Wiley, Medical Publications, 1986) p 2. Gillon begins his book with an interesting example of how ethical issues arise in medical situations, and he uses this example as a backdrop for his later discussion of medical ethics. The case is that of Dr Leonard Arthur, who was acquitted of the attempted murder of a newborn infant with Down's syndrome. Dr Arthur had prescribed dihydrocodeine and 'nursing care only' after the baby had been rejected by his mother.

22 Draper and Sorrell, 'Patients' Responsibilities in Medical Ethics' (2002) 16 Bioethics 335–51.

23 Kuhse and Singer, 'What is Bioethics? A Historical Introduction' in *A Companion to Bioethics* (Blackwell, 1998) 3–11.

Traditionally, medical ethics has focussed primarily on the doctor-patient relationship and on the virtues possessed by the good doctor. It has also been very much concerned with relations between colleagues within the profession…Bioethics, on the other hand, is a more overtly critical and reflective enterprise. Not limited to questioning the ethical dimensions of doctor-patient and doctor-doctor relationships, it goes well beyond the scope of traditional medical ethics in several ways. First, its goal is not the development of, or adherence to, a code or set of precepts, but a better understanding of the issues. Second, it is prepared to ask deep philosophical questions about the nature of ethics, the value of life, what it is to be a person, the significance of being human. Third, it embraces issues of public policy and the direction and control of science.[24]

[2.16] There are a number of theories or traditions which inform bioethical debates. Firstly, teleological (derived from the Greek *telos,* meaning consequences) or consequentialist ethics judges the rightness or wrongness of an action based on its consequences. The most well-known theory in this tradition is utilitarianism, which is based on the maximisation of pleasure or happiness for the greatest number of people in society. It emerged as an alternative to Christian ethics in the late 18th and early 19th centuries through the work of Jeremy Bentham and John Stuart Mill. Consequentialists will examine an action not in terms of its intrinsic rightness but rather on the basis of what consequences it may bring for society. For example, in examining arguments for active euthanasia, they may argue that legalising such an activity would have negative consequences for society, as it may damage the doctor-patient relationship. This approach looks at the total welfare of the community rather than that of an individual and may necessitate some ranking or prioritisation of values.

[2.17] Another ethical tradition is deontological ethics (derived from the Greek *deontos* meaning duty), which looks not at the consequences of actions but rather at whether they conform to basic moral principles. For example, in relation to voluntary euthanasia, one might argue that it should be legalised so as to conform to the ethical principle of respecting the autonomous decisions of adults. The best-known example of this ethical tradition is known as Kantianism, named after the famous philosopher Immanuel Kant. His writings, and in particular his 'Categorical Imperative' which he described as an unconditional obligation, have been applied in support of autonomy, independence and rationality. Categorical imperatives are principles that are intrinsically valid; they are good in and of themselves; they must be obeyed in all, and by all, situations and circumstances if behaviour is to observe the moral law. It is from the Categorical Imperative that all other moral obligations are generated, and by which all moral obligations can be tested. Kant believed that if an action is not done with the motive of duty, then it is without moral value. He thought that every action should have pure intention behind it; otherwise it was meaningless. He did not necessarily believe that the final result was the most important aspect of an action, but that how the person felt while carrying out the action was the time at which value was set to the result. He gave four formulations of the Categorical Imperative, two of which are particularly relevant to bioethics. The First Formulation requires that the maxims be chosen as though they should hold as universal laws of nature, in other words we should act according to consistent and just rules. The Second Formulation requires us to act with reference to

---

[24] Kuhse and Singer, 'What is Bioethics? A Historical Introduction' in *A Companion to Bioethics* (Blackwell, 1998) 3–11.

every rational being so that it is an end in itself, meaning that the rational being is the basis of all maxims of action and must be treated never as a mere means but as an end at the same time. This means we must not treat other persons (or allow ourselves to be treated) solely to serve another's purpose, or as a means to an end. Kantian ethics place a primacy on rationality and individuality as a basis for qualification as autonomous beings, which may be argued to ask too much of patients. 'This idealistic concept is of little practical relevance in health contexts where patients, on the whole, bear little resemblance to the Kantian free, independent, exclusively rational individual.'[25]

[2.18] A third ethical tradition is virtue ethics, which is derived from Ancient Greek moral philosophy, in particular the work of Aristotle, and which emphasises not only good outcomes but also the character or motivation of the individual carrying out the actions. Virtue ethicists argue that people should always do the right thing for the right reason. They do not hold with the view that patient autonomy trumps all other ethical values. Thus, in relation to euthanasia, the fact that the patient chooses to die does not in itself make euthanasia the right thing to do. Causing a patient to die might only be right if the patient's quality of life lacked basic human goods.

[2.19] While examination of the theories above may help our understanding of ethical dilemmas, it rarely yields a clear solution for doctors faced with the practical difficulty of deciding what to do. The prime question for many doctors is how to make decisions for and with their patients that respects their wishes and at the same time safeguards their well-being. Many different authors who put forward various theories based on moral principles have given answers to this question. For example, Beauchamp and Childress put forward the principle of 'respect for autonomy, beneficence, non-maleficence, and justice'.[26] Downie and Calman indicated the principles of 'utility, justice, non-maleficence, compassion (benevolence) and self-development', governed by the principle of 'respect for the autonomous individual' as the consensus principles[27]. Engelhardt suggested the principles of 'permission' and 'beneficence' as the principles of bioethics.[28] Veatch identified 'utility, veracity, fidelity to promises, avoid killing, justice and autonomy' as principles of right actions.[29] Macer argued that love should be foundation of bioethics in the form of 'self-live (autonomy), love of others (justice), loving life (do no harm), and loving good (beneficence).'[30]

[2.20] The 'four principles' approach put forward by Beauchamp and Childress is generally regarded as the origin of the principles-orientated bioethics method in Western societies. Many professional bodies and associations have thus used these principles as a

[25] Secker 'The Appearance of Kant's Deontology in Contemporary Kantianism: Concepts of Patient Autonomy in Bioethics' (1999) 24 Journal of Medicine and Philosophy 43–66.
[26] Beauchamp and Childress, *Principles of Biomedical Ethics* (4th edn, OUP, 1994).
[27] Downie and Calman, *Healthy Respect* (2nd edn, OUP, 1994).
[28] Engelhardt, *The Foundation of Bioethics,* (2nd edn, OUP, 1996).
[29] Veatch, 'Theories of Bioethics' in *Global Bioethics: the 4th World Congress of Bioethics Program Book.* Proceedings of a conference presented by the International Association of Bioethics in conjunction with the Asian Bioethics Association, Nov. 1998, Japan.
[30] Macer, *Bioethics Is Love of Life: An Alternative Textbook* (Christchurch New Zealand: Eubios Ethics Institute, 1998).

framework within which to develop their own ethical guidelines and codes of conduct, adding to or elaborating on these principles where appropriate in a given speciality. This approach has also been expanded, particularly in the United States, by a concern for the scope of application of these principles. The 'four principles plus scope' approach claims that the four principles alone do not provide a method for choosing between moral principles in the event that they are in conflict. This may be a source of dissatisfaction for those who want ethics to be a neat set of rules that will provide an exact and complete answer to any ethical problem. However, by looking at the scope of the principles, a common set of moral commitments and a common moral language can be discovered by which to confront moral issues.[31]

[2.21] Each of the four principles will be considered briefly in turn – first, respect for autonomy.[32] Autonomy literally means self-rule, in other words making one's own deliberate decisions. Respect for autonomy therefore is 'the moral obligation to respect the autonomy of others in so far as such respect is compatible with equal respect for the autonomy of all potentially affected.'[33] Respect for autonomy is also sometimes described as treating others as ends in themselves rather than as means to an end. In the medical arena, respect for autonomy is of vital significance in relation to consulting with and informing patients about their health care and their choices and respecting the right of competent adults to make decisions about their treatment. It requires doctors to obtain informed consent from patients before any treatment or intervention (except in cases of incapacity or medical emergency). It also requires patient confidentiality to be maintained, appropriate behaviour to be practised and good communication methods to be used.

[2.22] Beneficence and non-maleficence are sometimes considered together as two sides of the same coin, although in some situations one of these duties may exist without the other. The ultimate aim in health care is to produce net benefit over harm, while recognising that, inevitably, some risk of harm may exist when any medical intervention takes place. Beneficence is the traditional Hippocratic duty to do good, while non-maleficence is the duty not to harm. These duties mean that those who treat patients must be appropriately qualified to do so, otherwise the risk of causing harm becomes disproportionate. The medical profession undertakes to provide extensive training and education to prospective and current practitioners to ensure adequate protection of patients.

[2.23] The duty of justice is generally synonymous with fairness and may thus be described as the moral obligation to act on the basis of fair adjudication between competing claims. This may be subdivided into three categories of obligations: distributive justice, which involves the fair distribution of resources;[34] rights-based

---

31   Gillon, 'Medical Ethics: Four Principles Plus Attention to Scope' (1994) BMJ 309:184.
32   For a discussion of the history of the concept, see Faden and Beauchamp *A History and Theory of Informed Consent* (OUP, 1986).
33   Gillon, 'Medical Ethics: Four Principles Plus Attention to Scope" (1994) BMJ; 309:184, p185.
34   See further Rawls, *A Theory of Justice* (Harvard University Press, 1971); Beauchamp and Walters (eds) *Contemporary Issues in Bioethics* (Wadsworth Publishing Co, 1989) at 25–34.

justice, which involves respect for people's rights;[35] and legal justice, which involves respect for morally acceptable laws.[36] There are many moral conflicts that can arise in this context, for example how to decide between a number of deserving patients as to provision of a scarce resource[37]. There are also issues in regard to the wider use of resources, conscious that payment must be made for those resources either by the patient, an insurer or the State. For example, one controversial issue here might be whether a doctor may decide to withhold a heart bypass operation from a patient who refuses to give up smoking, or a liver transplant from a patient who refuses to give up alcohol. It may be argued that it is the doctor's responsibility to ensure that scarce resources are allocated not only on the basis of need but also on the basis of maximising the benefit to be obtained from the use of those resources. However, the counter argument is that the doctor's role is not to punish patients for personal habits or lifestyle choices, even though those choices may have contributed to the person's illness and need of those resources.

[2.24] It is important to recognise that these four duties do not and cannot exist separately from each other and, of course, may come into conflict with each other. This requires consideration of the 'scope' of the principles. While ensuring that doctors must do good, it is also necessary to realise that the 'good' may be subjective and may not, in fact, coincide with respect for the choice made by the patient. In such a case, which duty is paramount – beneficence or respect for autonomy? This may arise in relation to treatment which may offer the patient a good chance of survival or recovery from their illness, but may impair their quality of life so much that, in that patient's eyes, life would no longer be worth living. In such a case respect for autonomy must take priority, as otherwise the patient would be treated without having given a truly voluntary consent, which would be unethical and illegal.[38] This decision becomes more difficult in cases where the choice appears irrational and may cause harm to another person, such as in cases of refusal to undergo a caesarean section delivery in order to save the fetus's life.[39] Although the decision to refuse treatment may be unpalatable (which in itself is a subjective judgment on the doctor's part), nonetheless it may be argued that it is the patient's right to make it.[40]

---

[35] This may be seen, for example, in the context of the abortion debate in Ireland where much debate takes place around the issue of the woman's right to choose an abortion, and the fetus's right to life. For further discussion of the influence of the language of legal rights in the health care context, see Montgomery, 'Patients First: The Role of Rights' in Fulford et al (eds) *Essential Practice in Patient-Centred Care,* (Wiley-Blackwell, 1996); Brazier 'Rights and Health Care' in Blackburn (ed) *Rights of Citizenship,* (London: Mansell Publishing Ltd, 1993); Raz, *The Morality of Freedom* (Oxford: Clarendon Press, 1986).

[36] Gillon 'Medical Ethics: Four Principles Plus Attention to Scope' (1994) BMJ; 309:184 at 186.

[37] For reflections on this argument in the UK health-care system, see Newdick, *Who Should We Treat? Law, Patients and Resources in the NHS* (OUP, USA, 1995).

[38] This follows John Stuart Mill's argument that restrictions on liberty may only be permissible in the interests of other people, and then only to a strictly limited extent. Restrictions on liberty imposed on a person for his own good may never be justified. JS Mill, *On Liberty,* originally published in 1859, reprinted in 1956.

[39] For example, *Re S (Adult: Refusal of Medical Treatment)* [1992] 4 All E R 649.

[40] See Chapter 12 for further discussion of this point in relation to end-of-life decisions.

[2.25] Traditional medical paternalism as described by the Hippocratic Oath says only that doctors must work for the benefit of their patients, and says nothing about consulting patients, describing alternatives or even doing what the patient wants. The old (and, in some instances, current) view is that the doctor knows best. Some doctors may argue that, although the explanation of the Oath in such terms seems blatantly outdated, in many cases patients would be best served by not having the information explained to them or choices given to them in circumstances in which they are already terrified by their illness, in severe pain, confused and distressed. Adding to that distress, it is said, would not be in their best interests. Although it is necessary to recognise that some patients do not want to hear bad news, it would, however, be wrong to make such an assumption without clear statements to that effect by the patient. Concealing such information from the patient also sometimes takes place at the request of the patient's family, who would prefer to shelter their parent, sibling or child from such trauma. However, in such a difficult situation, the doctor has to decide whether the subjective decision of a family member on the basis of the patient's welfare takes priority over the individual's right to respect for autonomy. Deceiving the patient in this way breaches the normal rules of medical confidentiality, may cause distress to the family in trying to conceal the truth, engender further alarm and fear in the patient who suspects the truth and cause resentment or anger if the patient later discovers the deceit.[41]

[2.26] An illustration of this difficult balancing act is provided by the controversy that arose as a result of the retention of human organs following post-mortem examination. In the past, in Ireland and elsewhere, organs and tissue were removed and retained from the bodies of persons undergoing post-mortem examination in order to complete a thorough examination and comprehensive diagnosis of the cause of death. Organs were sometimes retained for long periods of time for teaching and research purposes without the knowledge of the deceased's family. It was not hospital or professional policy to inform parents about this practice. The shock, anger and betrayal felt by families at the revelation of these long-standing practices highlighted the existence of a significant communication gap between the medical establishment and the general public. Doctors argued that their reluctance to inform families of the details surrounding the post-mortem examination and retention of organs was to protect rather than insult, that they had a different professional perspective of the body, that the information was likely to cause more grief and pain than it alleviated and that therefore they were behaving ethically. In Ireland, the Report on Post Mortem Practice and Procedures (the Madden Report) found that 'this argument has a clear and reasonable humanitarian appeal but rests on a paternalistic basis that patients, parents, and the general public now interpret as unnecessarily secretive and disrespectful. Medical paternalism is unacceptable by modern standards whereby doctor and patient now stand in a different relationship to each other, one that is based on mutual trust and shared understanding.'[42]

---

[41] See generally Gillon, *Philosophical Medical Ethics* (Wiley Medical Publications, 1986) 60–106.

[42] Report of Dr Deirdre Madden on Post Mortem Practice and Procedures (Government Stationery Office, Dublin, 2005) para 2.4.

THE RELATIONSHIP BETWEEN LAW AND MEDICINE

[2.27] The relationship between law and medicine has not been an easy one. Both have traditionally been regarded as powerful and elite professions and have been at once honoured and attacked on this ground. Both professions have traditionally been self-regulating and have resisted any attempts at State intervention, although this resistance has not proved successful in the face of demands for greater accountability and lay involvement in recent years. The medical profession has tended to resent the interference or encroachment of lawyers into their professional lives and practices, and the interference brought about by spiralling medical litigation. Many blame the legal profession for encouragement of such claims against doctors with little regard for the long-term consequences for medical practice. To doctors, the law constitutes 'a symbolic representation of the limits of medicine's authority' and, commonly armed with only a hazy understanding of medical law, doctors are 'fighting a battle of symbols...to defend their jurisdiction.' [43] The legal profession are perhaps a little sceptical too of the medical profession's ability to find expertise to support wildly differing medical facts and to vouch for medical injuries and ailments that are exaggerated by their clients.

[2.28] The description of law's relationship with medicine has been characterised by the famous quote of Windeyer J in *Mount Isa Mines v Pusey*, where he said that law is seen as 'marching with medicine but in the rear and limping a little'.[44] With the rapid advances witnessed in medicine over the last few decades, the changing structure of the health services and increased medical knowledge in the community, a new conceptualisation of the medical relationship not only between doctor and patient, but also between law and medicine more generally is necessary. Those who criticise the traditional formulation of the medical relationship argue that what is needed is more focus on patients' rights. Others argue that more account needs to be taken of patient welfare. The two approaches are not altogether complementary. 'Should the emphasis be on the accountability of doctors or on their responsiveness, on the legal entitlements of the "purchaser" of health care, or on the therapeutic benefits of being involved in one's treatment?'[45]

[2.29] Medical litigation is naturally concerned with the resolution of disputes, and therefore the court must make a decision in relation to the rights and duties of the parties involved. Liability for negligence is essentially a form of public ordering, a standardised mechanism for regulating doctors' conduct, because what is in issue is whether the doctor has fallen below the requisite standard of care. Their professional calling is to ensure the well-being of patients, to safeguard their welfare rather than their rights. However, medical litigation should accommodate a medical model of 'therapeutic alliance' which both acknowledges the doctor's responsibility for patient welfare as well as respecting patients' rights. This would have advantageous consequences for both patient and doctor in terms of decision-making and consent to treatment.

---

[43] Zussman, *Intensive Care* (University of Chicago Press, 1992) 183–185.
[44] *Mount Isa Mines v Pusey* [1970] 125 CLR 383 at 395.
[45] Teff, *Reasonable Care, Legal Perspectives on the Doctor-Patient Relationship* (Clarendon Press, 1994) at xxvii.

The therapeutic case for a collaborative approach, being medically inspired, rooted in patient welfare, and non-confrontational in nature, is far more likely than an appeal to 'patients' rights' to elicit the sympathy and co-operation of the medical profession, a key practical consideration which is too often neglected. The law obviously cannot determine the nature of medical relationships, but it could have a positive influence on them by proclaiming more responsive standards as norms for medical practice.[46]

[2.30] The negative attitude of the medical profession to the law is perhaps shaped in part by the traditional lack of education on legal issues in medical training schools. Such education as is given has traditionally focused on forensic medicine, death certification, giving expert evidence and compliance with other relevant statutory provisions. As for the broader legal responsibilities of doctors: 'consent, professional confidence, drug legislation, failure to communicate and the whole expanding field of negligence and malpractice form a minefield into which many new graduates now seem to wander unprotected by little if any knowledge, or even awareness of the problem.'[47] Although the tide is certainly turning in recent years in favour of the teaching of specialised legal subjects dealing with the wider areas of medical jurisprudence, the vast array of medical courses to be digested by medical students tends to swamp any such attempts.

[2.31] The most prominent legal concern of any doctor is inevitably the avoidance of litigation. The natural fear and resentment felt by many doctors towards the prospect of being sued leads to a hostile beginning to the relationship between law and medicine. There are concerns that the law is unduly intrusive and threatening, that it distracts the doctor from his real work of treating patients and that the maze of legal rules and procedures are designed to trip up those who are unfamiliar with the system. Their opinions are often misinterpreted or distorted by opposing legal teams, their answers led by clever advocacy. 'The physician, normally masterful and self-confident in the setting of medicine, becomes infantilised in the setting of adversarial litigation.'[48] The adversarial approach to which our legal system subscribes is not designed to investigate without confrontation. The system tends to encourage hostility and distress and parties are forced into a trial by battle. Doctors are not alone in finding such an approach to the resolution of complicated medical disputes incomprehensible, as patients too are dispirited by the system.

[2.32] In recent years there has been an increased emphasis on consumer awareness and consumer rights in many areas of society, not least in relation to health care. Higher public expectations of doctors, greater levels of understanding of illness and medicine and a corresponding ease of access to information and travel has led to a demand for patient charters of rights to which hospitals and doctors may be held to account. However, it has been claimed that a reliance on rights in medical law would lead not only to increased medical litigation but also to an increase in the practice of defensive medicine. Such practices, which encourage doctors to order every possible test or

---

[46]   Teff, *Reasonable Care, Legal Perspectives on the Doctor-Patient Relationship* (Clarendon Press, 1994) at xxxi.

[47]   Knight and McKim Thompson, 'The Teaching of Legal Medicine in British Medical Schools' (1986) 20 *Medical Education* 246, 247.

[48]   Dickens, 'The Effects of Legal Liability on Physicians' Services' (1991) 41 University of Toronto Law Journal 168, 180.

procedure in circumstances in which they are not clinically justifiable, in order to defend themselves against possible future litigation, is seen as potentially damaging to patients, and certainly to the health-care system in general. If doctors feel that they have to change their medical practices in order to ward off potential claimants, as has been argued in the context of increased rates of caesarean sections and episiotomies, patients, health insurers and the State will ultimately be the losers, as the costs of excessive and unjustifiable tests have to be paid for by someone.

REGULATION OF MEDICAL PRACTICE IN IRELAND

[2.33] Health care is commonly delivered by a range of professionals acting individually or as a team. This can include general practitioners, specialists, nurses, therapists, pharmacists and many health and social care professionals. The common feature shared by these professions is that they are special kinds of knowledge-based occupations. The type of knowledge, the social and cultural value attributed to it and the way in which each occupation handles that knowledge are seen as central to both the process of professionalism and maintaining or extending professional positions. Another factor that commonly distinguishes health professional groups in particular is the requirement to obtain a licence to practice from the State. In this way, health professionals draw a boundary around their knowledge which excludes outsiders. This boundary is usually underpinned by legislation which brings about market control for health professionals in the supply of health care.[49]

[2.34] The medical profession in every country in the world has always been held in special esteem. Doctors are respected, trusted and admired as healers, protectors and confidants. Doctors in most communities are regarded as persons with unquestionable authority and with special skills and intellect. Their opinions have therefore traditionally been deemed of the utmost importance, both in terms of clinical advice and psychological support and empathy given to those in distress. Doctors are also scientists who help to develop new technologies and treatments through clinical research and trials, thus improving diagnoses and outcomes for the patients. The medical profession may also be seen as having a political function through involvement in public policy debates about health care, lobbying for change on various health-care provision and patient safety issues and negotiating with the government for better conditions of employment for doctors in the public health-care system.

[2.35] In more recent times, the relationship between the doctor and the community has gone through many changes as the layperson has steadily become more informed about health-care issues and more inquisitive about his choices. This is reflected in the expectations that patients have of their doctors in relation to diagnoses and prescribing practices. The old adage of 'doctor knows best' has almost been consigned to the realms of the history books. These changes have had a huge impact not only on the day-to-day practice of the medical profession, but also on their ethical and legal responsibilities. The medical profession in Ireland, as elsewhere, traditionally jealously guarded their

---

[49]   Report of the Commission on Patient Safety (2008) para 6.3. *Building a Culture of Patient Safety.* Section 7.7, available at www.cpsqa.ie/publications/pdf/patientsafety.pdf (accessed 23 May 2011).

professionalism and ability to self-regulate. Proponents of self-regulation argue that it offers the advantages of bringing insider knowledge to bear on a problem and is more acceptable to those being regulated, thereby encouraging compliance. It is also said to be more responsive, as self-regulating bodies can move faster without the necessity to change legislation, and it is cheaper, as it requires less monitoring. However, in recent years public confidence in the profession in Ireland was shaken by a number of medical scandals which led to a perception that the profession was failing to regulate the small number of aberrant doctors who caused harm to patients. It was argued that self-regulating bodies lack legitimacy, are open to accusations of self-protection, fail to provide public accountability and may be dependent on support from members of the profession.

[2.36] Internationally, the role of health professions in society and their self-regulatory status has also changed in recent years. This change is driven by a number of trends, such as the decline in public trust in health professions, change in regulatory structures for other professions, challenges to traditional hierarchical structures in the health-care delivery system through the increase in multi-disciplinary care teams, changes in working arrangements and globalisation of the workforce with increased mobility and diverse expectations. The combination of these factors led to a substantial change in the way in which the medical profession is regulated in Ireland, with the passing of the Medical Practitioners Act in 2007, discussed in more detail below.

[2.37] There are a number of professional regulatory bodies in Ireland governing the practice of medicine.

- The Medical Council regulates registered medical practitioners under the Medical Practitioners Acts 1978–2007. Its functions include assuring the quality of undergraduate education of doctors; assuring the quality of postgraduate training of specialists; registration of doctors; disciplinary functions; and providing guidance on professional standards/ethical conduct.
- The Dental Council regulates dental practitioners under the Dentists Act 1985. Its roles include the maintenance of a register of dentists and dental specialists; assessment of the adequacy and suitability of dental education and training in the dental schools in the State; disciplinary functions; and advising the dental profession and the public on matters relating to dental ethics and professional behaviour.
- The Nursing Board (*An Bord Altranais*) regulates nurses under the Nurses Act 1985. A new Nurses and Midwives Bill 2010 has been published and is now going through the Dáil and Seanad. The Board's functions include the registration of nurses; provision of education and training; disciplinary functions; giving guidance to the profession; managing a careers centre to provide a centralised system of processing and selection of applicants wishing to enter nursing and provision of careers advice to nurses and midwives.
- The Pharmaceutical Society of Ireland is the regulator of pharmacies under the Pharmacy Act 2007. Its roles include the maintenance of a register of pharmacists and pharmacies; inspection of pharmacy premises; development of codes of conduct for pharmacists; promotion of high standards of education and training; disciplinary functions; and recognition of qualifications of pharmacists from other jurisdictions.

- The Opticians Board regulates optometrists and dispensing opticians under the Opticians Act 2003. It has functions in relation to registration and education and training.

- The Health and Social Care Professionals Council regulates 12 health and social care professions under the Health and Social Care Professionals Act 2005. These cover clinical biochemists, dieticians, medical scientists, occupational therapists, orthoptists, physiotherapists, podiatrists, psychologists, radiographers, social care workers, social workers and speech and language therapists. The functions of the Council include coordination of the activities of the 12 registration boards established for each of the foregoing professions; the enforcement of standards of practice for registrants; disciplinary functions; and promotion of collaboration between the registration boards including in relation to education and training.

This chapter deals primarily with the functions of the Medical Council in relation to education and training, and the maintenance of standards of professional conduct by registered medical practitioners.

THE MEDICAL COUNCIL

[2.38] The Medical Council of Ireland was established by the Medical Practitioners Act 1978 and commenced operation in April 1979. It has been amended a number of times since 1978, most substantially by the Medical Practitioners Act 2007 (hereafter 'the Act'). It has 25 members, comprised of elected and appointed members. Historically, the Medical Council had a majority of medical members (21 out of a total membership of 25 were doctors) but the 2007 Act substantially changed the composition of the Council by requiring that 10 of the 25 members must be doctors, 11 must not be doctors and the remaining 4 may/may not be doctors, depending on the nominations made by the Health Service Executive (HSE) and approved bodies delivering undergraduate medical education. Therefore the Act facilitates the appointment of a lay majority though it does not guarantee it, as this will depend on the qualifications of those appointed by the latter groups. Members of the Council hold office for five years, renewable up to a maximum of two terms.

[2.39] The Council is a statutory body entrusted with important functions to be performed in the public interest. Section 6 of the Act states that the object of the Council is to 'protect the public by promoting and better ensuring high standards of professional conduct and professional education, training and competence among registered medical practitioners.' The Council is 'not a body established to manage the affairs of the medical profession or to protect its interests.'[50]

[2.40] The principal functions of the Council are set out by the 1978 Act as amended by the 2007 Act, as: the maintenance of a register of medical practitioners, the supervision of the standards of medical education and training of doctors, the control of postgraduate training of specialists, the imposition of disciplinary procedures and the development of professional standards of ethical conduct. The Council has committees

---

[50] *Philips v The Medical Council, the Minister for Health, Ireland and the Attorney General* [1991] 2 IR 115, per Costello J.

dealing with, inter alia, education and training, registration, health of medical practitioners, competence assurance, fitness to practise, standards in practise and ethics. The committees generally meet on a monthly to quarterly basis. The Minister for Health has the power to make certain orders relating to the training of doctors or the implementation of European Directives and Regulations and may also give directions to the Council on matters other than professional conduct and ethics or disciplinary matters.

Registration

[2.41] A person cannot practise medicine in Ireland unless he is registered with the Medical Council. Section 41 of the Medical Practitioners Act 2007 provides that certain designated titles may only be used by doctors and that breach of this provision is a criminal offence. The Medical Council is obliged to maintain a General Register of Medical Practitioners. Those entitled to be registered include:

- those registered by the Medical Registration Council pursuant to the Medical Practitioners Acts 1927–1961, and those entitled to be so registered;
- persons awarded any of the primary qualifications specified by the Act[51];
- citizens of any European Member State who have been awarded a qualification in medicine by a competent body or designated authority pursuant to any Directive adopted by the Council of the European Communities;
- or any person who satisfies the Council that he has undergone specified courses of training and passed specified examinations as set out by the Council;[52]
- or any person entitled to be registered pursuant to an order under the Medical Practitioners Act 1927.

[2.42] Applicants who fulfil these conditions are entitled to be registered on submission of a registration fee to the Council.[53] However, the Council is empowered to refuse registration on the grounds of the unfitness to practise medicine of any applicant. Under the 2007 Medical Practitioners Act the register is divided into:

---

[51] Medical Practitioners Act 2007, s 27 refers to the Fourth Schedule to the Act which specifies those primary qualifications as Bachelor of Medicine and Bachelor of Surgery of the National University of Ireland and the University of Dublin, and Licentiates of the Royal College of Physicians of Ireland and of the Royal College of Surgeons in Ireland. This has been amended by the 2002 Act, s 6 which allows for graduates of colleges in EU Member states to become interns in Ireland.

[52] See *Bakht v Medical Council* [1990] 1 IR 515 in which the Supreme Court dealt with the case of a doctor who qualified in Bangladesh, was temporarily registered in Ireland for various periods of time, obtained postgraduate qualifications in the State, became an Irish citizen and was nonetheless unable to receive full registration. The judgment discusses the rule-making functions of the Council under the Act and its powers in relation to registration. Rules made by the Council must be of general application and not merely rules under which a restricted class of doctors can apply.

[53] Refusal to register a person who is entitled to registration will be actionable. See *Philips v The Medical Council, the Minister for Health, Ireland and the Attorney General* [1991] 2 IR 115.

- The General Division – this is open to those who have completed medical training in Ireland, the EU or elsewhere and who have completed any required examinations or have satisfactory evidence of experience sufficient to permit registration.
- The Specialist Division – this is open to those who have completed specialist medical training in a speciality recognised by the Council and who can provide evidence from an appropriate body that satisfies the Medical Council.
- The Trainee Specialist Division – this is open to qualified doctors who are practising medicine in an individual identifiable specialist training post, and interns.
- The Visiting EEA Practitioners Division – this is for practitioners who are practising medicine in an EU Member State and who wish to practise in Ireland only on a temporary or occasional basis. The practitioner must notify the Council of intended periods and scope of practice in Ireland and make declarations as to good standing in their native country.

[2.43] Under the 2007 Act, doctors who entered the General Division of the register could take up any post in Ireland including unsupervised locum general practice positions and could work wholly in private practice. In July 2011, an amendment to the 2007 Act was passed to establish a new Supervised Division of the medical register which ensures that doctors registered in this division will be restricted to working under supervision, only in Council-approved posts, for a period of two years or less.[54] Registration in this division is contingent on doctors satisfying the Council that their education and training in their country of qualification meet required standards and that they have not been subject to disciplinary actions in any country where they previously practised medicine. They will also be required to undertake an examination here related to their chosen specialty which will assess their competence in areas of clinical judgement, communication and data interpretation.[55]

[2.44] Registration of medical practitioners serves many important functions, not least of which is the maintenance of public confidence in the supervision of educational standards imposed by the Council and adherence to codes of professional conduct. The classic characteristics of a profession would usually include an agreed ethical code, discipline rules and control of entry and training standards. There is also an expectation among members of the public that doctors will be members of their relevant professional organisation.

[2.45] The Council is obliged by the Act to publish copies of the Register (and supplements to it) at specified intervals and to keep available for inspection at Council offices the most recently published copy of the Register.[56] Only a person registered under the Act may sign a certificate that is required to be signed by a medical practitioner. It is a criminal offence to make any false declaration or misrepresentation to the Council in order to obtain registration. The practitioner must state his registration number on all medical documents, such as prescriptions or other records.

---

[54] Medical Practitioners (Amendment) Act 2011.
[55] See statement of the Medical Council in relation to the new Act at www.medicalcouncil.ie/media-centre/press-release/2011.
[56] Medical Practitioners Act 2007, s 57.

Medical education and training

[2.46] Under the Medical Practitioners Acts 1978–2007, the Medical Council is statutorily responsible for the accreditation of medical schools in Ireland, for the assessment of the quality of educational programmes and for the registration of graduates as medical practitioners.[57]   Section 35 of the 1978 Act, as amended, states that:

It shall be the duty of the Council from time to time to satisfy itself

(a)   as to the suitability of the medical education and training provided by any body in the state recognised by the Council for such purposes,

(b)   as to the standards of theoretical and practical knowledge required for primary qualifications,

(c)   as to the clinical training and experience required for the granting of a certificate of experience.

[2.47] The Medical Council is obliged to ensure that the minimum standards required by any Directive of the European Community relating to education and training are met by the formal qualifications in the State. The Council must satisfy itself as to the suitability of undergraduate medical education and training provided by recognised medical schools and the standard of theoretical and practical knowledge required at the examinations for primary qualification. It must also satisfy itself as to the clinical training and experience required for the granting of a certificate of experience, and the adequacy and suitability of postgraduate education and training. The Council has a Professional Development Committee which implements the Council's policy for medical education in Ireland by:

• visiting the medical schools in relation to undergraduate medical education;
• ongoing assessment of the intern year;
• visiting the hospitals approved for the purposes of internship training and temporary registration, and;
• liaising with the recognised postgraduate training bodies.

[2.48] Each medical school is responsible for devising and delivering its own curriculum, which is then assessed by the Medical Council using national and international best practice, such as the World Federation of Medical Education, as a benchmark. Each medical school has a broadly similar curriculum, usually five years pre-clinical and clinical education, and a year spent as an intern acquiring further clinical experience. It is regarded as a fundamental part of medical education that students receive a significant part of their education in a clinical environment. Approximately one-half of undergraduate training is delivered in clinical settings, usually in a hospital, but also in some primary and community care facilities. It is usually in the last two to three years of their medical education that students attend clinical settings for lectures, 'bedside' tutorials and attachment to health-service teams in which students follow a variety of team activities including ward rounds, attendance at outpatient clinics and theatre and case conferences. This learning method is largely observational, as students are not generally expected to interact with patients other than

[57]   Review of Medical Schools in Ireland, Medical Council 2007.

in minor ways. Most of the clinical education is provided by consultant and non-consultant doctors who do not have a specific academic contract and who provide teaching services in a voluntary capacity. The Fottrell Report[58] noted that:

> While there is a weak contractual basis for the training carried out by health professionals, it should be noted that there has traditionally been a strong ethic among doctors to train their successors, and indeed involvement in training is perceived to be integral to professional development.

[2.49] Following graduation, graduates receive internship registration with the Medical Council and must then complete an intern year, during which they are employed and paid by the health service and expected to fulfil relevant clinical activities. The intern year is therefore the first year of postgraduate training. The vast majority of intern posts are in hospitals, though it is also possible to do an internship in general practice. It is the Medical Council's responsibility to approve intern posts, based on approval of the hospital's programme of education and training for the interns. During the 12-month period, graduates must spend at least 3 months in an internship in medicine and 3 months in surgery. The Medical Council will also approve suitable posts in obstetrics and gynaecology, emergency medicine, paediatrics, psychiatry, general practice and perioperative medicine (which includes anaesthesia and pain management).

[2.50] Upon successful completion of this intern year, all graduates are then fully registered by the Medical Council and may choose to progress through a number of postgraduate education streams, for example surgery, anaesthesia, radiology, pathology and general practice, which are coordinated by recognised postgraduate training bodies. The Medical Council also has functions in relation to the determination of recognised medical specialities and the recognition of bodies granting evidence of satisfactory completion of specialist training.

[2.51] In recent years there has been much discussion on the topic of continuing education and professional development of health-care professionals. As a result, the Medical Council devised a competence assurance programme to enable doctors to participate in learning activities throughout their careers. This involves participation in competence assurance schemes run by the postgraduate training bodies and is in keeping with the Report of the Commission on Patient Safety in 2008 which stated:

> It is clear that a health professional can no longer be regarded as trained for life upon qualification. Instead what is required are systems of lifelong learning and professional development, with regular competence assurance to ensure that there is a workforce of skilled professionals who are fit for purpose, competent in managing patients' needs, aware of the limits of their own competency and adaptable and capable of responding to changing needs. Continuing Professional Development (CPD) is a key responsibility of individual practitioners, a core function of training bodies and a crucial component of the professional regulatory reforms e.g. the Medical Council's Competence Assurance Scheme.[59]

[2.52] At a practical level it is also a key issue for employers, who should have systems in place to ensure that all professional staff participate in CPD and are provided with

---

[58] Department of Health (2006) *Medical Education in Ireland: a New Direction.*
[59] *Building a Culture of Patient Safety* (2008), p 99 available at www.cpsqa.ie/publications/pdf/patientsafety.pdf (accessed 23 May 2011), p 99.

adequate time and resources to do so. CPD involves not only the continuous upgrading of clinical skills but also the development of the necessary skills of accessing and appraising evidence, clinical audit and reflective practice, the application of standards and the monitoring of performance against standards.

[2.53] The Medical Practitioners Act 2007, s 94 introduced for the first time a legal obligation on registered medical practitioners to maintain their professional competence throughout their working lives. Part 11 of the Medical Practitioners Act provides a statutory basis for the development of Professional Competence Schemes in Ireland. Section 91(1) of the Act provides that 'It shall be the duty of the Council to satisfy itself as to the ongoing maintenance of professional competence of registered medical practitioners.' If a registered medical practitioner refuses or ceases to cooperate with the Scheme, the Council may make a complaint to the disciplinary or Fitness to Practise section of the Council. Health-care employers are obliged by s 93 of the Act to facilitate the maintenance by the practitioner of his professional competence. Section 93 provides as follows:

> (1) The Health Service Executive shall facilitate the maintenance of professional competence of registered medical practitioners pursuant to a professional competence scheme applicable to the practitioners concerned.

> (2) An employer of a registered medical practitioner, not being the Health Service Executive, shall facilitate the maintenance of professional competence of registered medical practitioners pursuant to a professional competence scheme applicable to the practitioners concerned.

Freedom of establishment

[2.54] Under European law, citizens are entitled to freedom of movement, which means that the presence of national borders should not be an impediment to the free market. Therefore, a doctor who is qualified in one EU state should, in principle, be free to travel to and work in another EU Member State. Issues that have caused some difficulties in recent years centre on the recognition of qualifications from other countries and language proficiency tests. A number of EU Directives were introduced to deal with free movement of persons and freedom of establishment. These were consolidated in 2005 in Directive 2005/36/EC. A person who wishes to carry on a regulated profession in another Member State is obliged to fulfil certain minimum criteria set out in the Directive and provide evidence that he has obtained equivalent professional and educational qualifications and training in an EU Member State. If these conditions are met, permission may not be refused to an EU citizen to practise in another Member State. If the training is not deemed equivalent, the host state may offer an aptitude test and period of adaptation in the host country.

Illegal practice of medicine

[2.55] The Medical Practitioners Act 2007 provides in s 37 that an unregistered medical practitioner shall not practise medicine or advertise his services as a medical practitioner. The expression 'practise medicine' is not clearly defined in the Act; it is simply stated to mean 'to engage in the practice of medicine'. This phrase in turn is defined as including 'the practice of surgery and other disciplines of medicine.' Section 38 of the Act provides that a medical practitioner does not contravene s 37 if:

(a)   the practitioner is a dentist registered under the Dentists Act 1985 who only practises medicine in the course of, and for the purpose of, the lawful practise of dentistry,

(b)   the practitioner is a person registered under the Nurses Act 1985 who only practises medicine in the course of, and for the purposes of, the lawful practise of nursing or midwifery,

(c)   the practitioner is a registered pharmaceutical chemist or a registered dispensing chemist and druggist, under the Pharmacy Acts 1875 to 1977, who only practises medicine in the course of, and for the purposes of, the lawful practise of pharmacy in accordance with those Acts,

(d)   the practitioner is a person registered under the Health and Social Care Professionals Act 2005 to practise a profession designated under that Act who only practises medicine in the course of, and for the purposes of, the lawful practise of that profession,

(e)   the practitioner only practises medicine in the course of rendering first aid to a person,

(f)   the practitioner only practises medicine in the State pursuant to the provisions of section 50 (this section provides that, subject to the conditions set out in the Act, a medical practitioner who is a national of a Member State and lawfully established in medical practice in a Member State may, on visiting the State, practise medicine on a temporary and occasional basis without first being registered, and advertise the practitioner's services as a medical practitioner for this purpose.)

(g)   the practitioner only practises medicine in any combination of any of the circumstances specified in paragraphs (a) to (f).

[2.56] Section 39 of the Act provides that the Minister for Health may make regulations to designate for the purposes of this Act any title or variants thereof to be used by any registered medical practitioner. This power will only be exercised following consultation with interested parties and organisations, and where the designation of title is deemed to be in the public interest. The Minister will consider the extent to which any class of medical practitioners has a defined scope of practise and applies a distinct and recognised body of knowledge, as well as the degree of risk to the health, safety or welfare of the public from the incompetent, unethical or impaired practise of any class of medical practitioners. If the Minister exercises the power under this Act, s 40 provides that a registered medical practitioner shall not use a designated title other than in accordance with such regulations.

[2.57] Section 41 of the Act provides that a person is guilty of an offence if they practise medicine while unregistered or use a designated title without being so entitled, falsely represent themselves to be a registered medical practitioner, or represent themselves to be registered in a division of the register other than that in which they are so registered. Section 42 provides that an unregistered medical practitioner shall not be entitled to recover fees or expenses incurred in providing services in the course of practising medicine.

Fitness to Practice

[2.58] As part of its statutory functions, the Medical Council is obliged to hear inquiries into the conduct of registered medical practitioners. An application for an inquiry may be made to the Preliminary Proceedings Committee of the Council either by the Council itself or by any other person. Under s 57 of the 2007 Act, an application for an inquiry may be brought on the following grounds:

a)   professional misconduct;

b)   poor professional performance;

c)   a relevant medical disability;

d)   a failure to comply with a relevant condition;

e)   a failure to comply with an undertaking or to take any action specified in a consent given in response to a request made under s 67(1)[60];

f)   a contravention of a provision of the Medical Practitioners Act 2007, and;

g)   a conviction in the State for an offence triable on indictment or a conviction outside the State for an offence consisting of acts or omissions that, if done or made in the State, would constitute an offence triable on indictment.

Section 57(2) provides that a complaint may be made on the grounds of professional misconduct or poor professional performance notwithstanding that the matter to which the complaint relates occurred outside the State.

[2.59] In recent years there has been discussion about the retention of the disciplinary function by professional regulatory bodies. At the present time, Fitness to Practise inquiries held by the Medical Council are generally heard by a small panel of medical and non-medical members of the regulatory bodies and co-opted members. Such members may sit on inquiries for a number of days per year and each team may be comprised of different members. The Fifth Shipman Inquiry Report in the UK[61] raised a number of concerns in relation to the operation of the Fitness to Practise (FTP) process in the General Medical Council (GMC). One of those concerns was that those adjudicating on FTP panels may each sit for only a few days per year. They will therefore have little opportunity to develop real expertise and there are likely to be problems in ensuring consistency of decision-making. This Report states that since all health-care regulatory bodies are obliged to appoint and train panellists for the FTP procedures, it would be preferable to appoint a body of full-time or nearly full-time panellists who could sit on panels of all such bodies. This would ensure greater consistency of decision-making as well as clear separation between the power to investigate and the power to adjudicate concerns about health professionals.

---

[60]   Medical Practitioners Act 2007, s 67 (1) provides that the Fitness to Practise committee may, at any time after a complaint is referred to it, request the doctor to give an undertaking to not repeat the conduct complained of, or to undertake to be referred to a professional competence scheme and comply with any requirements imposed in that regard, consent to undergo medical treatment, or consent to being censured by the Council.

[61]   Safeguarding Patients: Lessons from the Past – Proposals for the Future (9 December 2004) Cmnd Paper Cm 6394: www.shipman-inquiry.org.us/reports.asp (accessed 27 June 2011).

[2.60] In Ireland similar recommendations were made in the Report of the Commission on Patient Safety and Quality Assurance in 2008.[62] The Report considered the findings and recommendations of the Shipman Report above and stated that although some changes had been introduced in Ireland in the Medical Practitioners Act 2007, it remained concerned that the members of the Fitness to Practise Committee who will hear the evidence and submissions in the Inquiry and reach conclusions on the allegation of professional misconduct will be members of the same body that will make the final decision as to professional misconduct, although they will not be part of the final decision-making process. The Commission was of the view that 'the appearance of separation of function must be matched by the reality of the processes and procedures.' The Commission was concerned that the current system does not facilitate the development of expertise in relation to the disciplinary process and may result in inconsistencies in the application of standards. In addition, the increase in multi-disciplinary team care and treatment of patients may result in complaints being made against a team rather than an individual practitioner. For example, skills extension for nurses has led to the assumption of specifically defined clinical decision-making, drug-prescribing and the performance of medical procedures such as bronchoscopy and colonoscopy. The Commission was of the view that the current disciplinary structures in the professional regulatory bodies do not facilitate an investigation and hearing of such a complaint, which may therefore fall between the regulatory bodies.

[2.61] The Commission therefore recommended that there should be greater separation between the investigation and adjudication functions performed by the professional regulatory bodies so that the public might have greater confidence that the disciplinary functions exercised by those bodies are independent and robust. Although there are arguments for removing the entire disciplinary process from the regulatory bodies, the model preferred by the Commission would maintain the involvement of the regulatory body as arbiter of the first stage of the disciplinary process, ie the regulatory body would make the decision as to whether the professional against whom the allegation was made had a case to answer. The regulatory body would then investigate and prepare a case to be heard by an independent panel of health-care professionals and lay members. Under the model proposed by the Commission, the regulatory bodies would also have a role in the development of standards, criteria and thresholds for all stages of the process, including the adjudication stage. They would be able to monitor the outcomes of cases and thereby inform themselves of the need for any adjustment in the standards, criteria and thresholds. With this model, a body of full-time or nearly full-time panellists should be appointed who could sit on joint panels of all the health-care regulatory bodies. This would provide a measure of independence from any one particular regulatory body and would also ensure that panellists developed experience and expertise. A full-time legal assessor would be appointed to sit with all adjudicating panels so as to ensure consistency of standards and to address all legal issues arising. It remains to be seen how these recommendations will be implemented.[63]

---

[62] *Building a Culture of Patient Safety*, p 13, available at www.cpsqa.ie/publications/pdf/patientsafety.pdf (accessed 23 May 2011).

[63] The Report of the Commission was accepted by the Government as providing the framework for patient safety and quality assurance in Ireland and is currently in the process of being implemented. See further www.patientsafetyfirst.ie (accessed 27 June 2011).

Professional misconduct

[2.62] The complaints received in relation to professional misconduct are mainly in relation to clinical care such as incompetence, misdiagnosis or lack of diagnosis, adverse outcomes or lack of hygiene. There is also a high rate of complaints in relation to communication such as rudeness, lack of consideration for patients, poor or lack of communication and prejudicial remarks. There are only a relatively small number of complaints in relation to professional behaviour and these tend to relate to issues such refusal to treat or refusal to refer patients.[64]

[2.63] Under the 1978 Act, s 46 provided that where a registered medical practitioner has been found guilty of professional misconduct or to be unfit to engage in the practice of medicine because of physical or mental disability, or has failed to pay the appropriate retention fee, the Council may decide that the name of that person should be erased from the register, or that during a specified period registration of his name in the register should not have effect. A person to whom such a decision applies may apply to the High Court within 21 days for cancellation of the decision. If such an application is not made, the Council may apply *ex parte* to the High Court for confirmation of the decision. The High Court shall, unless it sees good reason to the contrary, confirm the Council's decision.

[2.64] The meaning of professional misconduct is defined in the Medical Council's Guide to Professional Conduct and Ethics (2009) as:

> [C]onduct which doctors of experience, competence and good repute consider disgraceful or dishonourable; and/or conduct connected with his or her profession in which the doctor concerned has seriously fallen short by omission or commission of the standards of conduct expected among doctors.[65]

[2.65] There have been a number of judicial decisions heard under the 1978 Act in relation to the meaning of professional misconduct in this context, the most important of which is *O'Laoire v The Medical Council*[66] in which the Court defined professional misconduct as follows:

(1)   Conduct which is 'infamous' or 'disgraceful' in a professional respect is 'professional misconduct'…;

(2)   Conduct which would not be 'infamous' or 'disgraceful' in any other person, if done by a medical practitioner in relation to his profession, that is, with regard either to his patients or to his colleagues, may be considered as 'infamous' or 'disgraceful' conduct in a professional respect;

(3)   'Infamous' or 'disgraceful' conduct in turn is conduct involving some degree of moral turpitude, fraud or dishonesty;

(4)   The fact that a person wrongly but honestly forms a particular opinion cannot of itself amount to infamous or disgraceful conduct in a professional sense;

(5)   Conduct which could not properly be characterised as 'infamous' or 'disgraceful' and which does not involve any degree of moral turpitude, fraud

---

64   2009 statistics are available at http://www.medicalcouncil.ie/Professional-Standards/Statistics/Statistics-2009/ (accessed 23 May 2011).

65   Irish Medical Council, *Guide to Ethical Conduct and Behaviour* (7th edn, 2009).

66   *O'Laoire v The Medical Council* (27 January 1995, unreported).

or dishonesty may still constitute 'professional misconduct' if it is conduct connected with his profession in which the medical practitioner concerned has seriously fallen short, by omission or commission, of the standards of conduct expected among medical practitioners.

[2.66] Keane J also said that the tests must be read in the context of the definition of professional misconduct set out in the Medical Council's Guide to Ethical Conduct and Behaviour. Tests (1) to (4) are commonly referred to as the 'moral turpitude test' and test (5) is referred to as 'the expected standards test'. These tests have been followed in subsequent cases including: *An Bord Altranais v O'Ceallaigh*;[67] *Millett-Johnson v Medical Council*[68]; and *Cahill v Dental Council*.[69]

[2.67] In the UK the term 'professional misconduct' was considered in a number of cases, including *McCandless v GMC*[70] in which it was argued on behalf of the doctor that his poor treatment of patients was not enough to constitute professional misconduct, as the doctor had been doing his best and may have simply been overworked or not very good at his job. The Court found that seriously negligent treatment can amount to professional misconduct and upheld the finding against the doctor in question. The Court took the view that the public has higher expectations of doctors and that their regulatory bodies are under a duty to protect the public against the genially incompetent as well as the deliberate wrongdoers.

[2.68] In *Prendiville and Murphy v The Medical Council*,[71] the applicants sought an order by way of judicial review against the Council to quash a finding of professional misconduct imposed on them following an FTP Inquiry. The applicants complained that the Council misdirected itself as to its jurisdiction and acted ultra vires in following the legal advice tendered to it to the effect that it was obliged to confirm the findings of the FTPC and confine itself solely to the question of penalty. It was also contended that the Council was wrong in law in permitting members of the FTPC who adjudicated upon the complaint against the applicants to sit as members of the Council which considered the findings of that FTPC. It was also alleged that the Council was guilty of an illegality in failing to provide any reasons for its decision and that an incorrect standard of professional misconduct was applied by the FTPC and the Council. The applicants also argued that the findings of both the FTPC and the Council were unreasonable and irrational having regard to the lack of evidence to support such findings. They also criticised the paucity of reasoning given for the Council's decision.

[2.69] Kelly J took the view that the Council was incorrect in its interpretation of the law to mean that it was bound to confirm the report of the FTPC in relation to its findings of professional misconduct. The learned judge favoured an alternative construction which would result in a report of the FTPC being capable of review by the Council. This means that a doctor charged and found guilty of professional misconduct by the FTPC would not be deprived of having his case and that decision considered by the Council. Kelly J

67 *An Bord Altranais v O'Ceallaigh* [2000] IESC 21, [2000] 4 IR 54 & 102 (17th May, 2000).
68 *Millett-Johnson v Medical Council* (12 January 2001, unreported) HC.
69 *Cahill v Dental Council* [2001] IEHC 97.
70 *McCandless v GMC* [1995] 1 WLR 169.
71 *Prendiville and Murphy v The Medical Council* [2007] IEHC 427.

said that 'given the huge importance to any doctor's career of a finding of professional misconduct, the alternative construction is, in my view, much more conducive to enjoyment of the rights conferred under the Constitution and the Convention.' As a result, Kelly J held that the Council had acted ultra vires in behaving as it did and its decision was quashed.

[2.70] On the second ground put forward by the applicants, the Court held that it was wrong that members of the FTPC should have participated in the work of the Council on the occasion of its consideration of the FTPC report. The involvement involved a breach of the *nemo iudex in causa sua* rule. In relation to the legal advice tendered to the Council the Court held that it was inappropriate that such advice was given by the Registrar, who is also the officer who presented the case against the applicants before the FTPC. Kelly J said that there was a perception of bias arising from the role played by the advice giver when the cases were before the FTPC. It was also wrong that the legal advice was tendered only to the President and Vice President of the Council rather than the whole Council. Given that the advice was tendered in the absence of the applicants and their lawyers, this was a denial of the *audi alteram* rule because it enabled the Council to rely upon information obtained outside the hearing and not disclosed to the applicants who were adversely affected by it.

[2.71] The applicants also argued that the FTPC had applied the wrong test of professional misconduct, in that it had used the 'expected standards' test rather than the 'moral turpitude' test. The former test was first contained in the 2004 edition of the Ethical Guide, although Keane J had adverted to it in *O'Laoire v the Medical Council* in 1998. Kelly J said in the present case that the FTPC applied the expected standards test in circumstances where the alleged misconduct took place in 1998. Therefore the judge said the FTPC was not entitled to apply this test, as it was unreasonable and unfair to expect medical practitioners to be subjected to a test of professional misconduct, which the Council had not promulgated or notified to the profession until years after the event.

[2.72] Finally, Kelly J also held that the applicants were entitled to at least a general explanation of the basis for the majority decision of the FTPC. 'Reasons are necessary in order to ensure that the superior courts may exercise their jurisdiction to enquire into, and if necessary, correct such decisions.' The Court quashed the decision of the FTPC and the Council and declined to remit the matter to the Council for further consideration. Kelly J said that he was satisfied that having regard to the passage of time since the events complained of, the number of years that disciplinary proceedings had been hanging over the applicants and the undoubted damage which had been done to them, it would be quite inequitable and unfair to remit the case. The case was not appealed to the Supreme Court.

[2.73] Part 7 of the 2007 Act has made a number of changes to the FTP procedure, and the Council in recent years has introduced new procedures in line with the Act as well as the judgment in the *Prendiville and Murphy* case. These are outlined in the next section. In addition to complaints of alleged professional misconduct, the Council may also hear a complaint in relation to an alleged poor professional performance and/or relevant medical disability on the part of a medical practitioner. Poor professional performance is defined in the Act as 'a failure by the practitioner to meet the standards of competence (whether in knowledge and skill or the application of knowledge and skill or both) that can reasonably be expected of medical practitioners practising medicine of the kind practised by the practitioner.' Relevant medical disability is defined as 'a physical or mental disability of the practitioner (including addiction to alcohol or drugs) which may impair the practitioner's ability to practise medicine or a particular aspect thereof.'

Fitness to Practice procedure

[2.74] Under the Medical Practitioners Act 2007 the Council has two committees pertaining to disciplinary matters: the Preliminary Proceedings Committee (PPC), and the Fitness to Practise Committee (FTPC). Under the Act, the PPC must have a medical majority and the FTPC must have a non-medical majority. Both committees may co-opt medical and non-medical members who are not members of the Council. The PPC considers all applications for inquiries. Although the Act does envisage the possibility of oral evidence being heard by the PPC, in practice the PPC makes its decision on the basis of an examination of the written complaint received, any additional material obtained by the Council and the observations and comments submitted by the medical practitioner.

[2.75] The function of the PPC is to investigate the complaint and determine as expeditiously as possible whether there is sufficient cause to warrant the holding of an inquiry by the Council.[72] This decision is passed on to the Council, which may then consider that no further action is required, or that the Committee should hold an inquiry into the matter. The Council may follow the view of the PPC in this regard or alternatively may refer the complaint to a professional competence scheme, or refer it for resolution by mediation. It must duly inform the Committee and the applicant. If the Committee is of the opinion that there is a prima facie case for holding the inquiry or has been so directed by the Council, the Committee will refer the complaint to the FTPC to hear the Inquiry. The medical practitioner who is the subject of the complaint must be notified by the Chief Executive Officer of the referral to the FTPC, the nature of the complaint, the evidence supporting the complaint, the right to be legally represented and the right to apply for the inquiry to be held in private.

[2.76] The Chief Executive Officer (CEO) (formerly known as the Registrar under the 1978 Act) of the Council collects evidence in the case for presentation to the FTPC.[73] The person against whom the complaint has been made is given notice of the evidence in the case and has the opportunity to be present at the hearing of the case, or be legally represented. In practice, both the doctor and the CEO of the Council are usually legally represented and the procedure is inevitably relatively formal, though perhaps not to the same degree as court proceedings. The Committee has the powers, rights and privileges of the High Court in relation to the calling and examination of witnesses and the production of documents. Refusal to attend a hearing following a summons by the Committee to do so, or failure to produce documents called for by the Committee, or any other conduct which would constitute a contempt of court, is an offence.[74] Witnesses

---

[72]   Medical Practitioners Act 2007, s 57(3).
[73]   The relationship between the Committee and the Registrar was described by Costello P in *Barry v The Medical Council* [1998] 3 IR 368 as analogous to that between the chairman of a tribunal and solicitor and counsel employed by him to present the evidence, rather than that which exists between prosecutor and the judge in a criminal trial.
[74]   Medical Practitioners Act 2007, s 45(7).

have the same immunities and privileges as in the High Court. The inquiry team also has the assistance of a legal assessor who is not a member of the Committee but who is present to give legal advice if requested, and to ensure that fair procedures are observed. Any such advice by the legal assessor is given in the presence of all parties to the inquiry and an opportunity is given to the parties or their legal advisors to make representations to the FTPC in respect of any such advice.

[2.77] Given the significant impact that a finding of professional misconduct or poor professional performance may have on a medical practitioner's career and reputation, strict adherence to fair procedures in the conduct of an inquiry is required.[75] This means that the medical practitioner must receive a copy of the evidence to be presented at the inquiry, must be given an opportunity to cross examine witnesses and give evidence in rebuttal and in his own defence. There is no corresponding obligation on the medical practitioner to notify the Council in advance of the evidence he proposes to call in his defence in the inquiry. As Keane CJ said in *Borges v The Fitness to Practice Committee*[76]

> It is also not in dispute that the practitioner concerned is entitled to have the hearing conducted in accordance with fair procedures and natural justice. That is not to say that a body of this nature may not depart from procedures which would be essential in a court of law, as was made clear by this court in *Kiely v Minister for Social Welfare* [1977] IR 267: in particular, they may act on the basis of unsworn or hearsay evidence. But, as was also made clear in that case, their freedom from the constraints to which courts of law are subject does not permit them to act in a way which is inconsistent with the basic fairness of procedures guaranteed by implication by Article 40.3 of the Constitution.

> It is beyond argument that, where a tribunal such as the Committee is inquiring into an allegation of conduct which reflects on a person's good name or reputation, basic fairness of procedure requires that he or she should be allowed to cross-examine, by counsel, his accuser or accusers. That has been the law since the decision of this court in *In re Haughey* and the importance of observing that requirement is manifestly all the greater where, as here, the consequence of the tribunal's finding may not simply reflect on his reputation but may also prevent him from practising as a doctor, either for a specified period or indefinitely.

[2.78] The facts of that case involved an inquiry into the conduct of an obstetrician and gynaecologist who was registered in Ireland and had been erased from the corresponding register in the United Kingdom following allegations of inappropriate and indecent examination of female patients. The witnesses who had given evidence before the inquiry held by the General Medical Council (equivalent body in UK) were not willing to travel to Ireland to give evidence or give evidence by way of video-link. The FTPC therefore sought to rely on the transcripts of evidence given before the GMC as well as the decision of the GMC as ratified by the English court. This was challenged by the medical practitioner as a breach of fair procedures, namely the lack of opportunity to cross-examine witnesses. Keane CJ said:

> [O]ne must bear in mind the reasons which have led courts in this jurisdiction to hold that, in some cases at least, the right of a person to have the evidence against him given orally

---

[75]   In keeping with *In re Haughey* [1971] IR 217.
[76]   *Borges v The Fitness to Practice Committee* [2004] 1 IR 103.

and tested by cross-examination before the tribunal in question may be of such importance in a particular case that to deprive the person concerned of that right would amount to a breach of the basic fairness of procedure to which he is entitled by virtue of Article 40.1 of the Constitution. It is not simply because the tribunal is in greater danger of arriving at an unfair conclusion, absent the safeguard of material evidence being given orally and tested by cross-examination. Such a departure from the normal rules of evidence might well be justifiable, as I have already noted, in the case of a tribunal of this nature. It is because, depending on the nature of the evidence, its admission in that form may offend against fundamental concepts of fairness, which are not simply rooted in the law of evidence, either in its statutory or common law vesture.

Although the Court was cognisant of the important statutory function to be discharged by the Council in protecting the public, it took the view that such consideration could not relieve the court of the obligation of ensuring that the right of the doctor concerned to a fair hearing is, so far as practicable, upheld.

[2.79] At the conclusion of the inquiry, the FTPC makes its decision in relation to the allegations of professional misconduct and/or poor professional performance and submits a report to the Council on the inquiry, including recommendations in respect of sanction. Reasons are given for each finding of misconduct or poor professional performance. Members of the inquiry team are not present for the Council's discussion of the report. Under s 70, if the Committee finds that no allegation against the registered medical practitioner the subject of the complaint is proved, the Council shall dismiss the complaint. If the Committee finds that any allegation against the practitioner is proved, the Council shall decide on the sanction to be imposed on the practitioner. Therefore, the Council is obliged to accept the findings of the FTPC in relation to professional misconduct or poor professional performance but has discretion in relation to the sanction to be imposed, if any.

Burden and standard of proof

[2.80] The evidential burden of proof in cases brought before the Committee is on the person making the allegations. Irish health professional regulatory bodies generally apply the criminal standard to their disciplinary hearings, including the Nursing Board (*an Bord Altranais*) and the Dental Council. Other professional bodies such as the Chartered Accountancy Regulatory Board apply the civil standard. Internationally the civil standard of proof is applied by a number of regulatory bodies, including the GMC in the UK since 2008. This followed criticism in the Fifth Report of the Shipman Inquiry,[77] a report from the Chief Medical Officer called *Good Doctors, Safer Patients*,[78] and a Government White Paper called *Trust, Assurance and Safety*,[79] all of which questioned the retention of the civil standard. The Health and Social Care Act 2008 implemented the civil standard for all health-care regulators in the UK.

[2.81] The law in Ireland on this point was set out in *O'Laoire v Medical Council*,[80] in which the Supreme Court discussed whether the standard of proof was the civil or

---

[77]   Safeguarding Patients: Lessons from the Past-Proposals for the Future (9 December 2004) Cmnd Paper Cm 6394: www.shipman-inquiry.org.us/reports.asp (accessed 27 June 2011).
[78]   Dept of Health (UK) 14 July 2006.
[79]   Dept of Health (UK) 21 February 2007.
[80]   *O'Laoire v Medical Council* (25 July 1997, unreported) SC.

criminal standard. The FTPC had decided the case in question on the basis of proof beyond a reasonable doubt. O'Flaherty J took the view that, although the criminal standard of proof ought to be confined to criminal trials to which that standard is particularly suited, in civil hearings such as this one the evidential burden must be commensurate with the gravity of the matter at hand. He said:

> The essence of a disciplinary enquiry into alleged professional misconduct, such as concerned the Committee and the trial judge here, is to find out by clear evidence the pith and substance of the misdeed being investigated and decide whether the case has been established against the person, always bearing in mind the grave consequences that such a finding will, in general, have for the person whose conduct is called in question but also remembering that the public has an interest in making sure that proper standards of professional conduct are upheld. The graver the allegation the greater will be the care which the tribunal or court will take to make sure that the case has been brought home against the person whose conduct is impugned.

[2.82] He went on to discuss cases from the UK,[81] Canada,[82] Australia[83] and New Zealand[84] with which he was satisfied that the Irish decisions on the point concurred. Murphy J referred to his own previous decision in *Grant v Garda Síochána Complaints Board* (12 June 1996) in which he said:

> Whilst I am concerned as to the basis on which the criminal standard of proof has come to be applied to professional bodies in the exercise of their disciplinary functions I accept that this is the position and will remain so unless and until the Supreme Court should otherwise direct.

[2.83] Since the decision in *O'Laoire*, the application of the criminal standard of proof has been confirmed in a number of other cases including *Millett-Johnson v Medical Council*,[85] *O'Connor v Medical Council*[86] and *Barry v Medical Council*.[87] However, there is no requirement to apply the criminal standard set out in the Act and it may be that the Council may decide to apply the civil standard in an appropriate case in the future. Such a case would undoubtedly result in a legal challenge but may ultimately provide useful clarity for professional regulators.

Private or public hearings

[2.84] An issue which has in the past exercised both the Medical Council and the courts is whether the FTPC should hold its inquiry in public or in private. This was at the heart of *Barry v The Medical Council*[88] in which the practitioner, who was the subject of an inquiry by the FTPC, wished to have the hearing in public in order to vindicate his character, in circumstances in which the complaints against him had received much damaging advance publicity. The Committee refused on the basis that it had discretion

---

81 *Reg v Home Secretary, Ex-p Khawaja* [1984] AC 74; *R v Wolverhampton Coroner* [1990] 2 All ER 759.

82 *Rizzo et al v Hanover Insurance Co* (1990) 68 DLR (4th) 420.

83 *Neat Holdings PTY Ltd v Karajan Holdings PTY Ltd* 1992 67 ALJR 170.

84 *Back v National Insurance Company of New Zealand Ltd* [1996] 3 NZLR 363.

85 *Millett-Johnson v Medical Council* (12 January, unreported) HC, Morris J.

86 *O'Connor v Medical Council* [2007] IEHC 304.

87 *Barry v Medical Council* [1997] IEHC 204, [1998] 3 IR 368 (11 February 1997).

88 *Barry v Medical Council* [1998] 3 IR 368.

under the scheme of the Act in any case and in this case had exercised its discretion in favour of a private hearing. This was grounded on the nature of the allegations against the practitioner, in this case being of an intimate personal nature, a fact that may deter those making the complaints from giving evidence in public.

[2.85] In the High Court the applicant claimed that he had a constitutional right to fair procedure and that this required a public hearing of the allegations made against him. He relied on the provisions of art 6(1) of the European Convention on Human Rights (ECHR), which provides as follows:

> In the determination of his civil rights and obligations or of any criminal charge against him, everyone is entitled to a fair and public hearing within a reasonable time by an independent and impartial tribunal established by law. Judgement shall be pronounced publicly but the press and public may be excluded from all or part of the trial in the interests of morals, public order or national security in a democratic society, where the interests of juveniles or the protection of the private life of the parties so require, or to the extent strictly necessary in the opinion of the court in special circumstances where publicity would prejudice the interests of justice.

[2.86] The applicant accepted that the Convention was not part of Irish law but argued that in giving effect to the notion of fair procedures under Art 40.3 of the Constitution, the Court should be guided by internationally accepted norms enshrined in the Convention.[89] He also pointed out that Art 34 of the Constitution provides that justice is to be administered in public, save in limited cases prescribed by law. However, the applicant did not argue that the Committee infringed this Article, as it was accepted that the Committee does not administer justice. In order to have any legal effect, the Council must accept the Committee's decision and apply for confirmation to the High Court which, sitting in public, *determines* the dispute. Costello P accepted the Committee's argument that it had a statutory discretion as to whether to hold its hearings in public or in private. In light of the intimate private details of the case and the reluctance of some witnesses to proceed with giving evidence in public, he held that the Committee had correctly applied the principles contained in art 6(1) of the Convention in this case. This was on the basis of the right to privacy of others and the interests of justice.[90]

[2.87] The Supreme Court unanimously agreed that the Committee has discretion under the Act to conduct its proceedings in public. Barrington J said:

---

[89] The applicant relied on the decision of the European Court of Human Rights in *Diennet v France* (1995) 21 EHRR 554 where, in similar circumstances, a French doctor successfully argued that art 6(1) of the Convention was breached by the fact that he did not receive a public hearing before the disciplinary section of the National Council of the French Medical Association. However, Barrington J in the Supreme Court pointed out that in this case the applicant had appealed the decision of the Disciplinary Committee to the French *Conseil d'Etat* on a point of law only. There was no rehearing of the case and therefore it was possible for the Court to agree that there had been no public hearing of an issue which touched on the doctor's civil rights, contrary to the Convention. In the instant case the applicant had the right to appeal the decision of the Medical Council to the High Court where he would be entitled to a full rehearing and possibly rehearing in public.

[90] Arguments made on the basis that there was no objective separation of the functions of prosecutor and adjudicating tribunal in this case were also rejected by the Court.

While the Act contemplates that proceedings before the Fitness to Practise Committee shall be in private it does not require it. I can see no reason why the Committee should not hold its proceedings in public if all parties were agreed and if the Committee itself thought it was the proper thing to do.

The Supreme Court also agreed that the Committee had properly exercised its discretion on the facts of this case. The above case has lost its significance somewhat given that s 65 of the Medical Practitioners Act 2007 now provides that a hearing before the FTPC shall be held in public unless the medical practitioner or a witness who will be required to give evidence at the hearing requests that it be held in private and the Committee is satisfied that it would be appropriate in the circumstances to hold the hearing (or part of it) in private. Inquiries are now regularly held in public.

Sanctions

[2.88] Under s 46 of the 1978 Act, the Council could impose sanctions including erasure or suspension from the medical register, provision of advice, admonishment or censure or the attachment of conditions to the retention of the name of a medical practitioner on the medical register. This section was considered in *M. v The Medical Council and the Attorney General.*[91] The plaintiff applied to the High Court under s 46 for an order cancelling the decision of the Council to remove his name from the register. The plaintiff claimed, inter alia, that ss 45 and 46 of the Act were unconstitutional[92], and that the Council's decision was therefore null and void. He alleged that the powers vested in the FTPC or in the Medical Council by the 1978 Act were powers to administer justice which, due to the fact that their effect would be to deprive him of his livelihood by striking him from the register of medical practitioners, could not be considered to be limited powers under Art 37 of the Constitution.[93] He also alleged that the procedures set out by the Act were unfair and inconsistent with Art 40 of the Constitution[94] in that his case came before the Court with a predetermination of guilt from the Council. He claimed that there was no prohibition on the Council from publishing its findings that the practitioner was guilty of misconduct, which was a failure to vindicate and defend the practitioner's good name under Art 40.

The Council argued that its functions did not constitute the administration of justice as it lacked the finality or enforceability necessary to that function by virtue of the fact that the decision of the Council was not effective unless confirmed by the Court. It was also argued that it was in the public interest that publication be made of the fact that his colleagues had found the doctor guilty of misconduct.

---

[91] *M v The Medical Council and the Attorney General* [1984] IR 485.

[92] Article 34, s 1 of the Constitution provides 'Justice shall be administered in courts established by law by judges appointed in the manner provided by this Constitution, and, save, in such special and limited cases as may be prescribed by law, shall be administered in public.'

[93] Article 37 of the Constitution provides 'Nothing in this Constitution shall operate to invalidate the exercise of limited functions and powers of a judicial nature, in matters other than criminal matters, by any person or body of persons duly authorised by law to exercise such functions and powers, notwithstanding that such person or such body of persons is not a judge or a court appointed or established as such under this Constitution.'

[94] Article 40.3.2° provides 'The State shall, in particular, by its laws protect as best it may from unjust attack and, in the case of injustice done, vindicate the life, person, good name, and property rights of every citizen.'

[2.89] Finlay P distinguished the facts of *In re the Solicitors Act 1954*,[95] in which the disciplinary committee of the Law Society had the power to determine complaints of professional misconduct against solicitors, strike their names off the register and award restitution and costs. He said that there was 'a very striking difference between the extent and nature of the powers there conferred on the disciplinary committee and the powers conferred by the Act of 1978 on the Committee and the Council.' He went on to explain that the only power the Committee or the Council had was to initiate proceedings in the High Court which may lead to an order suspending the practitioner from his practice, erasing his name from the register or the other sanctions provided by the Act. He adopted the test laid down in the *Solicitors Act* case that the essential question here was whether the tribunal in question had power by its determination to impose liability or affect rights. In this case the only powers of the Council that could be said to be final were the publication of a finding of misconduct or unfitness to practise, and the Council's power to advise, admonish or censure a practitioner. Even if these powers could be said to affect the rights of the practitioner in the present context, these functions would be so clearly limited in their effect and consequence as to come within the exception provided by Art 37 of the Constitution.[96]

[2.90] The plaintiff also argued that there was a lack of fair procedure in the manner by which his application came before the High Court, with a badge of guilt arising from a finding of the Committee. In rejecting this contention, Costello P equated any such implication or imputation that might arise from such a finding by a professional body with the implication or imputation which arises from a decision on the part of the Director of Public Prosecutions to prosecute an accused person. Accordingly this ground also failed. However, it may be questioned whether this is in fact a correct interpretation of the position in relation to the Director of Public Prosecutions where it would be inconsistent with the constitutional right to fair procedures to have any implication of guilt arising in a criminal prosecution prior to a court hearing. Despite the seriousness of the decision to strike a practitioner from the Register, it is not a criminal prosecution and the two situations are not directly comparable.

[2.91] The plaintiff also challenged the constitutionality of the Council's power to publish the fact that the Committee had reached a decision as to the practitioner's conduct. Costello P held that Art 40.3.2° does not guarantee to protect a person from every statement which may damage his good name. The common good may require, as in these circumstances, that a decision reached as to the conduct of a person carrying out a profession affecting the public be made known to the public.

> In the case of a person practising medicine, the public have a clear and identifiable interest to be informed of a responsible view reached by his colleagues with regard to his standard of conduct or fitness. I cannot see that the absence from the statute of a prohibition on the publication of an adverse finding of the Committee [where they have made a finding of misconduct or of unfitness] can be a failure to protect the good name of the practitioner from an unjust attack.[97]

---

95   *In re the Solicitors Act 1954* [1960] IR 239.
96   *M v The Medical Council and the Attorney General* [1984] IR 485 at 497.
97   *M v The Medical Council and the Attorney General* [1984] IR 485 at 500.

[2.92] According to the Court, the practitioner's right to have a full public hearing before the High Court during which he may completely vindicate his good name and reputation constituted a sufficient protection of his good name so as to make the scheme of the Act consistent with Art 40. This would seem to be a sensible approach bearing in mind the clear necessity of protecting the public from unfit practitioners. Once appropriate safeguards have been observed from a procedural point of view and the Committee has reached a decision on the practitioner's conduct, it would not be inappropriate for the Committee to publish its findings in that regard.

[2.93] In *Casey v The Medical Council*,[98] the plaintiff argued that the Council's power to attach conditions to the retention of his name in the register was ultra vires the Council. The plaintiff complained that although the Committee considered that there was insufficient evidence to find him guilty of misconduct, the Council advised him to avail of continuing medical education and professional development courses in his field, keep more comprehensive clinical notes, attend a course in communication skills, and, where appropriate, consider the presence of a chaperone when dealing with patients. These conditions were attached to the retention of his name in the register and were to be reviewed after one year. The plaintiff argued that the Council had no power to make such a decision and had therefore acted ultra vires.

[2.94] The plaintiff's argument was grounded on the contention that in the absence of a finding of misconduct by the Committee, the Council had no power under the Act to do any of the things it purported to do. By imposing conditions on the retention of his name on the register the Council was in effect reversing the findings of the Committee, which had heard all the evidence and the witnesses in the case. The plaintiff relied on the judgment of Finlay P in *Re M, a Doctor*,[99] in which the judge was said to have demonstrated the correctness of the plaintiff's case that before a power could be exercised under s 47 of the Act, there must have been a finding of guilt by the Committee. The Council argued that not only was it entitled to invoke the powers in question, but it ought to do so having regard to the public interest and the care of patients. The Council sought to rely on *M v The Medical Council and the Attorney General*[100] in which Finlay P had considered the provisions of s 47. However, in that case he had taken the opposite view, namely that the Council could exercise its powers under the section irrespective of the precise findings of that enquiry by the Committee.

[2.95] Kelly J held that there was nothing in the words of ss 47 or 48 that would require as a condition precedent to their being acted upon by the Council a finding of guilt on the part of the practitioner who has been the subject of an inquiry by the Committee. 'Under the express terms of each section all that is required in order to trigger the entitlement of the Council to utilise them is that there should have been an inquiry held and a report made by the Committee pursuant to Section 45 of the Act.' He disagreed with Finlay P in *Re M, a Doctor*, taking the view that the learned judge had not accurately described the statutory provisions in that case. There was, he held, no basis for indicating that the Council's powers could only be exercised where the practitioner

98   *Casey v The Medical Council* [1999] 2 IR 534.
99   *Re M, a Doctor* [1984] IR 479.
100 *M v The Medical Council and the Attorney General* [1984] IR 485. Both this and *Re M, a Doctor* [1984] IR 479, discussed above, relate to the same doctor.

had been found guilty of misconduct. Such a view was inconsistent with the express provisions of the Act and also with his own views in the later decision, *M v The Medical Council and the Attorney General*, with which Kelly J agreed.

[2.96] As regards the issue of where the public interest lies in such cases, it had been contended by the plaintiff that s 51 of the Act, which enables the Council to apply to the High Court to suspend a practitioner's registration for a specified period, was sufficient protection for the public. Kelly J took the view that, although it was quite clear from the wording of that section that the Council had a role to play in the protection of the public interest, s 51 was not the only way in which this might be achieved. On the contrary, that section was reserved for exceptional cases in which a doctor ought to be suspended in the public interest.

> There must be cases where the Council would, from the point of view of protecting the public, wish to bring about an improvement in the standards of an individual practitioner. It would be absurd that in every such case where the Council desired so to do it would have to invoke the provisions of Section 51. To contend that this is the only mechanism that the Council is given by the Legislature in order to address the public interest is, in effect, to advocate the use of the proverbial sledge hammer to crack a nut with consequent hardship being suffered by the unfortunate medical practitioner who would be the recipient of such force.

[2.97] Accordingly, the Medical Council was held not to have acted ultra vires in its decision to attach conditions to the plaintiff's registration. In reaching this decision, the Court recognised the complexity of the medical relationship and the seriousness of any finding of misconduct. On examination of the doctor's conduct in this case the Committee was of the opinion that, although certain aspects of his practice needed improvement, such as communication and note taking, there was not the level of misconduct involved as to justify a recommendation that he be struck off the register. The plaintiff's argument that it was essentially *all or nothing* so far as the imposition of any sanctions was concerned does not take account of the pragmatic approach taken by the Council in fulfilment of its function in protecting the public.

[2.98] Another power of the Council following a hearing by the FTPC is to 'advise, admonish or censure' a practitioner in relation to his professional conduct. It was argued in *Ogochukwu Anachebe v The Medical Council*[101] that the sanctions that the Council could impose by way of recommended erasure from the register had such grave consequences for a practitioner that they constituted an administration of justice, a function reserved for the courts by the Constitution. It was for this reason that the confirmation of the High Court was required for such an action and that the practitioner had the right to appeal to the High Court to set such a decision aside. The power of the Council to refuse to renew temporary registration and to censure the practitioner in relation to his conduct were no less serious sanctions for the practitioner, and yet no right of appeal to the High Court was given by the Act to the practitioner in such instances. Morris P held that the power that was exercised in this case was to censure the plaintiff in relation to his professional conduct and that no right is given to the practitioner to apply to the court to set that decision aside. 'This is because the sanction of advice, admonishing and censuring is not of sufficient gravity.' This further

---

[101] *Ogochukwu Anachebe v The Medical Council* [2000] IEHC 193.

recognises the point that a gradation of misconduct exists in relation to medical professionals and that, while serious sanctions may be imposed at one end of the scale, it is also necessary to acknowledge that, in keeping with the Council's role in protection of the public interest, less serious penalties may also be appropriate in certain circumstances. It is seen as being impractical to give a right of appeal in such cases where the livelihood of the practitioner is not threatened.

[2.99] Section 71 of the Medical Practitioners Act 2007 provides for the power of the Council to impose the following sanctions:

a) an advice or admonishment, or a censure, in writing;
b) a censure in writing and a fine not exceeding €5,000;
c) the attachment of conditions to the practitioner's registration, including restrictions on the practice of medicine that may be engaged in by the practitioner;
d) the transfer of the practitioner's registration to another division of the register;
e) the suspension of the practitioner's registration for a specified period;
f) the cancellation of the practitioner's registration, or;
g) a prohibition from applying for a specified period for the restoration of the practitioner's registration.

[2.100] A decision to impose a sanction (other than that referred to in s 71 (a)) must be confirmed by the Court before it will become effective. A doctor may appeal the Council's decision (other than a decision to impose a sanction under s 71 (a)) to the Court within 21 days of receipt of notification of the imposition of a sanction by the Council. The Court may, on appeal, consider any evidence adduced or argument made, whether or not adduced or made to the FTPC (s 75(2)). The Court may either confirm or cancel the decision, substitute a different/no sanction, and give directions to the Council. Where a doctor does not appeal the Council's decision within the stated time period, the Council must make an application to the Court for confirmation of the decision. This is done on an *ex parte* basis and the Court will confirm the decision unless the Court considers there is good reason not to do so.

[2.101] The Council also has an important power under s 60 to make an *ex parte* application (without notice to the doctor) to the Court for an order to suspend a doctor's registration, whether or not the doctor is the subject of a complaint, if the Council considers that the suspension is necessary to protect the public until further steps are taken. Such applications will be heard in private unless the Court considers it appropriate to hear the application in public. The Court may make any order it thinks appropriate on foot of such an application, including suspension of the doctor's registration and may give the Council any further directions it thinks appropriate.

Delay

[2.102] The investigation and completion of the disciplinary process can sometimes take a substantial amount of time. This may be because the disciplinary inquiry may be adjourned pending a criminal prosecution, or a coroner's inquest, or there may be difficulty in getting patients to provide evidence. There is also the practical complication of recruiting expert witnesses and scheduling an inquiry to be heard by members of the FTPC who also have other professional commitments outside of the Council. The issue of delay may give rise to a challenge on behalf of the doctor in that art 6 of the ECHR provides that persons have a right to be 'tried' within a reasonable time and violation of this right may be an abuse of process. This is an issue that has also arisen not infrequently in the prosecution of criminal offences. If the complaint relates to incidents that are alleged to have occurred years previously, the Committee may have to consider why the complainant did not come forward sooner, is the recollection of events reliable and is the practitioner prejudiced in any way by the passage of time and the inability to provide a substantial defence due to lack of records or recollection. In criminal cases it is not usually sufficient to prevent the hearing of a case to say that the passage of time renders the process contrary to fair procedure unless some specific prejudice can be proven. Similarly, it is unlikely to be successful in relation to disciplinary hearings unless there is a real risk that an inquiry could not be conducted fairly.

GUIDE TO PROFESSIONAL CONDUCT AND ETHICS

[2.103] Section 69(2) of the Medical Practitioners Act 1978 provides that 'it shall be a function of the Council to give guidance to the medical profession generally on all matters relating to ethical conduct and behaviour.' In this context the Medical Council has traditionally published an ethical guide on a five-yearly basis that are designed to be applied by doctors in various situations. Although the Ethical Guide of the Council does not have any binding force in law, it is important for the internal regulation of the profession and it lays down what is ethical medical practice in Ireland. These guidelines are not rules that will provide the doctor with an answer to every difficult issue. Rather, they are principles that ought to be used by doctors together with their judgment, experience, knowledge and skills in each situation. The Guide therefore does not generally catalogue behaviour which may be deemed to be unprofessional but sets out broad principles against which doctors may judge the situation in which they find themselves.

[2.104] It is possible that the Guide may be indirectly incorporated into law through case law in the same way as the guidelines of other professional bodies, such as accountancy bodies in tax and accountancy cases. In the case of the latter, the guidelines are seen as a body of professionally desirable standards for the accountancy profession, departure from which would be strictly scrutinised. Although the Medical Council's current Guide is not as detailed and specific, it could be argued that the principles set out therein should be regarded in a similar fashion. In the absence of legislation, a court may therefore decide that although not of binding legal force, departures from the Guide may constitute a breach of professional duty for the purposes of establishing negligence unless justified by the specific circumstances of the case. A patient may also argue that he had a legitimate expectation that the guide would be adhered to by the doctor and that this formed an implied term of the contract with the doctor.

[2.105] The Medical Practitioners Act 2007, s 7(2)(i) provides that the Council shall:

> Specify standards of practice for registered medical practitioners, including the establishment, publication and maintenance and review of appropriate guidance on all matters related to professional conduct and ethics for registered medical practitioners.

Section 7(3) provides that this function referred to at subs (2)(i) shall include:

Standards of practice relating to advertising by registered medical practitioners, or classes of registered medical practitioners, and in connection therewith, the disclosure of appropriate information relating to the fees to be charged for the medical services the subject of such advertising.

These parts were commenced by SI 231/2008, on 3 July 2008.

[2.106] The current Guide[102] is divided into five sections dealing with professional conduct; responsibilities to patients; medical records and confidentiality; consent to medical treatment; and professional practice. The new Guide expands on the previous edition in relation to areas such as confidentiality, consent and advertising. It also contains new provisions on dealing with adverse events, open communication to patients, reporting of alleged abuse and how to deal with concerns in relation to a colleague's competence. Its provisions are mentioned throughout this book where relevant.

---

[102] *Guide to Professional Conduct and Ethics for Registered Medical Practitioners* (7th edn, 2009) available at www.medicalcouncil.ie/professional-standards/professional-conduct-ethics/ (accessed 24 May 2011).

Chapter 3

Protection of Personal Health Information

INTRODUCTION

[3.01] Personal health information is information collected from and on behalf of a patient which is retained for the benefit of the patient in his current or future treatment. It generally includes clinical information such as blood type, allergies, test results, diagnoses, previous surgeries and medications. Such information is usually entrusted by a patient to his doctor on the strict understanding that it will remain confidential and will not be disclosed to others without the patient's consent. This implicit understanding of confidentiality is central to the trust between patient and doctor.

[3.02] The information which is collected as part of a patient's medical records may be sought by the patient himself or by others who may have a financial or social interest in the information. The first part of this chapter will explore the issue of access to personal health information by the patient himself and by others and, in particular, the framework of access governed by the Freedom of Information Acts.

[3.03] Where information is being stored, either manually or electronically, there are duties imposed on those who have control over the information, to ensure that the information is not misused or inappropriately accessed. Part Two of this chapter will examine the duty of confidentiality and the circumstances in which information may be disclosed even in the absence of the patient's consent. This part will also discuss the provisions of the Data Protection Acts, which give very detailed guidance in terms of collection, retention, use and destruction of personal data.

Due to advances in information technology in recent years, some jurisdictions have moved towards the storage of health information on electronic records using unique patient identifiers. Health information technology will be discussed in Part Three of the chapter.

Part One

ACCESS TO MEDICAL RECORDS

[3.04] Doctors are ethically obliged to maintain records of their care of patients and many doctors also have a legal obligation to do so under the terms of their General Medical Scheme (GMS) contract[1] with the Health Service Executive (HSE) as well as under the common law duty of care to patients. The length of time for which records should be retained is not set by law and will depend on what kind of record it is and what the nature of the relationship between the doctor and patient is, as well as other issues

---

[1]   The GMS is operated by the HSE, whereby general practitioners provide free primary care to patients with a medical card.

such as the occurrence of an adverse event or patient dissatisfaction with the outcome of treatment. Section 7 of the Civil Liability and Courts Act 2004 provides that in the case of medical negligence causing personal injuries, the patient has either two years from the date of the injury or two years from the date on which the patient discovers that he has suffered an injury through negligence in which to institute legal proceedings. This becomes more complicated in relation to children, as the two-year period does not begin until the child turns 18 years of age. In *Toal v Duignan*[2] the plaintiff discovered he was infertile when he was 22 years old and alleged negligence on the part of the doctor in failing to diagnose an undescended testicle after birth. His action was taken within the technical time limit of three years after discovery of the alleged negligence (as noted above, the time limit is now two years). However, his action was unsuccessful due to the time lapse between the alleged negligence and the taking of the action (26 years), despite the fact that the plaintiff could not have reasonably discovered the infertility at any earlier time.

> Where there is a clear and patent unfairness in asking a defendant to defend a case after a very long lapse of time between the acts complained of and the trial, then if that defendant has not himself contributed to the delay, irrespective of whether the plaintiff has contributed to it or not, the court may as a matter of justice have to dismiss the action.

[3.05] The Court did not address the common law right of access to medical records but indicated that it was unreasonable to expect that medical records would be retained for 26 years. In the absence of statutory provisions setting out retention periods, doctors are generally advised by indemnity and regulatory bodies to retain records at least for the following periods:

- Eight years following last treatment or death of an adult patient
- Children and young people – until the patient's 25th birthday, or 26th if the young person was 17 at the conclusion of treatment, or 8 years after the patient's death. Records should be kept for longer periods if the contents have relevance to adult conditions or have genetic implications
- Maternity records – 25 years after the birth of the last child

[3.06] There are a number of ways in which the doctor may store this information, and at common law the legal provisions dealing with access differed depending on the method of storage. For example, a doctor may keep written manual records locked in a filing cabinet in his office or he may store the information on a computer database. In either case, the doctor is in control of the information given to him by the patient and this control traditionally caused difficulties to patients in trying to get access to their medical records.

[3.07] At common law the question of control of the record turned on the question of ownership of the record. This, in turn, was dependent on who owned the paper on which the records were written. If the patient was a private patient and he had a contract with his doctor, then the contract would determine who owned the records. It would not be common practice to include express contractual terms dealing with this issue and the courts were reluctant to imply terms that were not considered necessary for the efficacy

---

[2] *Toal v Duignan* [1991] ILRM 135.

of the contract. If he was a public patient, again he could not claim ownership of the physical records that were provided and paid for by the State.

[3.08] In theory, the patient could try to assert ownership of the records on the basis that the information contained in records 'belonged' to him.[3] Alternatively he could claim that it was an implied term of the contract between himself and his doctor that he be given access to his records. He could claim that the doctor was in a fiduciary relationship with his patient and was obliged by that relationship to hold the information for the benefit of the patient, which included a right of access by that patient. These arguments were considered by Canadian and Australian courts with markedly different judicial views in each.

[3.09] In *McInerney v McDonald*[4] the Canadian Supreme Court considered the fiduciary relationship between doctor and patient. Mrs McDonald had been treated over a number of years by various physicians before she came to be treated by Dr McInerney. On Dr McInerney's advice she stopped taking medication that had been prescribed to her by a previous physician but became concerned at the care she had received before attending Dr McInerney. She requested Dr McInerney to give her copies of her complete medical file, including reports and correspondence from other doctors that had treated her in the past. Dr McInerney gave her all the notes and reports she had prepared herself but refused to give reports prepared by other doctors as, in Dr McInerney's opinion, these were the property of those doctors and it would be unethical for her to release them.

[3.10] La Forest J identified the central issue in this case as whether, in the absence of legislation, a patient is entitled to inspect and obtain copies of his medical records upon request. He was prepared to accept that the doctor, institution or clinic that compiles the records owns the physical records but the patient has a vital interest in the information contained therein. He said:

> Medical records include information about the patient revealed by the patient, and information that is acquired and recorded on behalf of the patient. Of primary significance is the fact that the records consist of information that is highly private and personal to the individual. It is information that goes to the personal integrity and autonomy of the patient.

[3.11] The judge also examined the nature of the relationship within which such personal information was entrusted to the doctor and found it to be similar in character to that between a priest and confessor, or a lawyer and client. In describing it as a fiduciary relationship, however, La Forest J also made it clear that he did not wish to apply fixed rules and principles to all circumstances of this kind – the rules are shaped by the demands of the situation. Nevertheless some duties do arise from the special relationship of trust and confidence that exists in a fiduciary relationship. 'Among these are the duties of the doctor to act with utmost good faith and loyalty, and to hold

---

[3]   For arguments that patients should be allowed to look after their own records, see Gilhooly and McGhee, 'Medical Records: Practicalities and Principles of Patient Possession' (1991) J Med Ethics, 17, 138–143; Gillon, 'Should Patients Be Allowed to Look After Their Own Records?' (1991) J Med Ethics, 17, 115–116; Coleman 'Why Patients Should Keep Their Own Records' (1984) J Med Ethics, 1, 27–28.

[4]   *McInerney v McDonald* [1992] 93 DLR (4th) 415.

information received from or about a patient in confidence.' Information given by a patient in the context of that relationship remains the patient's own and the doctor holds that information in a fashion akin to a trust. While the doctor owns the record, the information contained therein is to be used by the doctor for the benefit of the patient. The beneficial interest of the patient means that, as a general rule, he should have a right of access to it and the doctor should be obliged to provide such access. This means that the patient is entitled to examine and copy the records but not to remove them from the doctor's premises, as this would disrupt the doctor's ability to provide future care for the patient.

[3.12] This case is useful because it recognises the fundamental importance of privacy on the one hand, but also stresses that disclosure to the patient reinforces the trust placed in the doctor. The trust given by the patient to the doctor mandates that the flow of information works both ways. It improves patient understanding, cooperation and compliance, which, in turn, promote the well being of the patient.

> The personal privacy of the patient which he entrusts to a certain extent to the physician must be met with a corresponding openness and full disclosure…Personal privacy and access to medical information are not incompatible partners but interchangeable rights.[5]

The judge rebutted arguments that disclosure may facilitate unfounded litigation by pointing out that in fact denial of access may actually encourage unfounded litigation, as in many cases taking legal action is the only means by which the patient fulfils a strong need to discover information about his medical treatment. Arguments were also put to the Court that the information may be meaningless or may be misinterpreted by the patient but the judge was of the view that this did not justify non-disclosure, as the patient could obtain assistance in understanding the file, and that a more general regime of access might also encourage doctors not to use medical jargon and technical terminology in the patient's file.

[3.13] Another argument frequently used in the debate around access to records is that doctors would be less complete and frank in their note keeping if the patient might get access to them. This was also addressed by La Forest J, who doubted the practical significance of this argument, bearing in mind the ethical and legal obligations on doctors to keep accurate records. Although he recognised that doctors may indeed become more cautious in what they record, this did not necessarily imply that such caution would operate to the detriment of the patient, as any information relevant to the patient's medical care would have to be included on the record in any event.[6]

[3.14] The only argument for non-disclosure in which the judge found merit was if there was a real potential for harm to the patient as a result of the disclosure. However, this

---

5 Knoppers, 'Confidentiality and Accessibility of Medical Information: A Comparative Analysis' (1982) 12 RDUS 395, at 431, quoted by La Forest J in *McInerney v McDonald* [1992] 93 DLR (4th) 415.

6 In fact, a more open system of access to notes may help to encourage doctors not to use 'offensive surgical witticisms' in medical records such as FLK (funny looking kid) or FTM (first-time mum), or the use of terms such as 'hysterical', 'neurotic', 'senile' or 'geriatric', which have pejorative, even abusive, connotations. See Gillon, 'Should Patients Be Allowed to Look After Their Own Records?' (1991) J Med Ethics, 17 at 116.

should be limited to the most compelling cases, as non-disclosure too can cause harm to the patient, who may speculate as to far worse difficulties than might actually exist. The paternalism evident in such an argument, which relies on the doctor's perception of the patient's best interests, conflicts sharply with the patient's right to self-determination. Both interests are worthy of protection, but as a general rule records should be disclosed to the patient 'unless there is a significant likelihood of a substantial adverse effect on the physical, mental or emotional health of the patient or harm to a third party.' This reinforcement of the 'therapeutic privilege' is also significant, as it does allow for exceptional situations in which the doctor's duty to protect the patient outweighs the patient's right to access. However, it is likely that these situations will arise in fewer numbers than before, as patients are now more informed and educated regarding health issues, and also as their contact with any one individual doctor becomes more fragmented in larger clinics and across other health-care environments.

[3.15] In the Australian case of *Breen v Williams*[7] Ms Breen, a former patient of Dr Williams, claimed a legal right of access to records kept by the doctor as to her treatment. She based her claim on, inter alia, a proprietary right and interest in the actual information in the records, an implied contractual obligation and a fiduciary duty. All of these grounds were rejected by the High Court of Australia.[8] On the first argument based on proprietary interests it was conceded that the doctor owns the paper on which the records are written but it was argued that the records themselves were not owned by anybody, not having been abandoned. The Court held this argument to be ill-founded and contrary to common law. It was held that, in the absence of statutory or contractual provision to the contrary, medical records prepared by a doctor are the property of the doctor and, accordingly, he has the right to refuse access to those records.

[3.16] The Court stated that the doctor-patient relationship was contractual in origin whereby the doctor offers a patient diagnosis, advice and treatment.[9] However, due to the informal nature of the relationship, the terms of this contract are rarely expressly made. Therefore, it was the role of the Court to imply the terms of such a contract according to established legal principles. One of the arguments made by Ms Breen was that it was an implied term of the contract with her doctor that he would act in her best interests, and that this meant that she should be given access to her records should she request it. The Court said that there was no such implied obligation on the doctor, whose duty is rather to exercise reasonable care and skill in the provision of medical care and treatment. Somewhat strangely the Court said, 'the doctor does not warrant that he or she will act in the patient's best interests'. This was not a term that it was necessary to imply to give the contract efficacy, and it was not consistent with tortious duties which obliged the doctor to exercise reasonable care.

[3.17] As for fiduciary duties, the Court did not recognise the doctor-patient relationship as implying fiduciary obligations as might be found in the relationship between trustee and beneficiary, lawyer and client, agent and principal. Although a patient is dependant

---

[7]   *Breen v Williams* [1996] 70 ALJR 772 , Australian HC.

[8]   For comment on the case, see Swanton and McDonald 'Patients' Right of Access to Medical Records – a Claim Without a Category' (1997) 71 Aust LJ 413–417.

[9]   The court cited with approval *Sidaway v Governors of Bethlem Royal Hospital* [1985] AC 871 at 904.

on the doctor for advice and treatment, and confides intimate personal details to the doctor in the course of that treatment, that does not mean that the relationship is a fiduciary one for all purposes, although it may imply fiduciary obligations for some purposes.

> If Dr. Williams owed a fiduciary duty to Ms. Breen, the duties and obligations which arose from their fiduciary relationship could only come from those aspects of the relationship which exhibited the characteristics of trust, confidence and vulnerability that typify the fiduciary relationship. They could only attach in respect of matters that relate to diagnosis, advice and treatment.

[3.18] The Court went on to say that a consideration of the fundamental obligations of a fiduciary relationship showed that Dr Williams owed no fiduciary duty to Ms Breen to give her access to the records he had created. The judgment of La Forest J in *McInerney* was robustly criticised on the basis that the law in Australia does not characterise the doctor-patient relationship as fiduciary and that it is not accurate to describe information in the records as property. The records themselves are the only property in question, and these belong to the doctor. This does not mean that he may misuse the information contained in the records to make a profit for himself at the expense of the patient, but otherwise he may save or destroy them as he wishes. 'The idea that a doctor who shreds the records of treatment of living patients is necessarily in breach of fiduciary duties owed to those patients is untenable.' The Court went on to describe the differences between Australia and Canada in the imposition of fiduciary duties and held that in Australia no such fiduciary relationship would be recognised in this case.

There have been no cases in Ireland which have explored the nature of the relationship between doctor and patient in this context and the issue of access to records is now dealt with by the Freedom of Information Acts and the Data Protection Acts, considered below.

THE FREEDOM OF INFORMATION ACTS 1997–2003

[3.19] The Freedom of Information Acts 1997 to 2003 (the FOI Act) covers official information which an individual may seek to have access to and to have amended if inaccurate. The legislation establishes a presumption in favour of access to information in visual, written or electronic forms. The Act gives individuals rights to access personal and non-personal information, have personal records amended or deleted where the information is incorrect, incomplete or misleading and to seek reasons for decisions affecting them.

[3.20] Personal information is defined in the Act as 'information about an identifiable individual that (a) would, in the ordinary course of events, be known only to the individual or members of the family, or friends, of the individual, or (b) is held by a public body on the understanding that it would be treated by it as confidential.' Such definition is clearly applicable to personal health information and indeed the Act gives illustrative examples of such information, including 'information relating to the educational, medical, psychiatric or psychological history of the individual.'

[3.21] It is important to note that the Act applies only to public bodies.[10] This means that medical records held by private hospitals or clinics, or records created on a private basis between doctor and patient are not accessible under the Act. However, the Act does apply to records created by a doctor in the carrying out of duties as part of his employment by the State, for example in the treatment of a patient with a medical card, or within a public hospital. Decisions on access to such records are made by designated decision-makers or FOI officers within the public body.

[3.22] There are exemptions provided for in the Act outlining circumstances in which the requested information may not be released, for example to protect the confidentiality of another person. Reasons for refusals of access must be given, and the Office of Information Commissioner has been set up to review decisions by and practices of public bodies as well as the operation of the Act generally.[11] Section 28(3) provides that access may be denied where release of the record might be prejudicial to the person's physical or mental health, well-being or emotional condition.[12] Where access is denied, s 28 (4) states that the information may be provided through a nominated health professional, such as the patient's general practitioner.

[3.23] There are two broad categories of exemptions:

- class exemptions where all records in that class or category are exempt, eg records to which legal professional privilege attaches and;
- harm-based exemptions where records which might damage a particular public interest are exempt, eg records which reveal the negotiating positions of public bodies.

[3.24] Examples of exemptions include circumstances in which disclosure of the record would prejudice the privacy of another person, the request is frivolous, vexatious or voluminous or the record would disclose deliberations of a public body that it would be against the public interest to disclose. Many but not all exemptions may contain what is often referred to as a public interest override, that is, even though a record is exempt under the FOI Act a public body or the Information Commissioner may decide, on balance, that the overall public interest justifies its release. Some exemptions may provide that a public body may refuse to disclose the very existence of a particular record where to do so might disclose exempt information. Some classes of records may also be excluded from the scope of the FOI Act, for example records created by the Attorney General, records relating to the President and the private papers of TDs and Senators.

Parental access to records in relation to children

[3.25] A issue which sometimes causes difficulty in practice is in relation to a parent's right of access to the health records of their children. In 1999 regulations were made under the 1997 Act to enable parents and next of kin to access records on behalf of

---

[10] For a list of public bodies under the Act, see www.oic.gov.ie/en/PrescribedPublicBodies/ (accessed 24 May 2011).

[11] See generally McDonagh, *Freedom of Information Law in Ireland* (2nd edn, Round Hall Sweet & Maxwell, 2006).

[12] This is similar to an exemption contained in Data Protection law except that refusal of access is discretionary under FOI but mandatory under Data Protection law in such circumstances. There is also a difference in the degree of potential harm to the person seeking access, with FOI law setting a lower threshold than Data Protection.

relatives who were unable to exercise their own rights of access themselves.[13] In *McK v The Information Commissioner*[14] the issue to be decided by the Court was whether a father, a widower who had been separated from his late wife, and who was joint guardian of his children, was entitled under the Freedom of Information Act, 1997 to information, in the form of hospital notes, about an illness of his daughter. The circumstances were that there had been an unproven allegation of sexual abuse by the man of his daughter prior to the couple's separation. As part of the separation agreement, the man had supervised access to his children and the parties were working towards a position of unsupervised access at the time of the wife's death. By agreement, the children went to live with the wife's brother. The father, his brother-in-law and his wife were joint guardians of the children. Following admission of the man's daughter to hospital for an unspecified viral infection, the man sought further information from the hospital, which was not forthcoming. The other joint guardian refused permission for release of the records. On appeal to the Information Commissioner, the Commissioner decided that in any situation in which there is disagreement between parents/guardians regarding the release of records relating to a minor, release will only be directed where there is tangible evidence that such release would actually serve the best interests of the minor.

[3.26] On appeal to the High Court and subsequently to the Supreme Court it was held that:

> As a matter of Constitutional and family law a parent has rights and duties. In general a parent would expect to be given and would be given medical information about his or her child. It would only be in exceptional circumstances that medical information about a child would not be given to a parent/guardian.

[3.27] The Supreme Court held that the Commissioner erred in determining that release of the medical information would only be directed where there is tangible evidence that such release would actually serve the best interests of the minor. The Court held that a parent has rights and duties in relation to a child. It is presumed that his or her actions are in accordance with the best interests of the child. This presumption, while not absolute, is fundamental. The 'tangible evidence' test of the Commissioner reversed the onus of proof. The obverse is the correct approach. The presumption is that the release of such medical information would best serve the interests of the minor. However, evidence may be produced that it would not serve her interests, and, in considering the circumstances, her welfare is paramount.

Access to records of deceased person

[3.28] Another issue which has caused some concern is in relation to access to medical records after death. From an ethical perspective, most professional codes of conduct, including the Medical Council's Guide to Professional Conduct and Ethics for Registered Medical Practitioners (7th edn) stipulate that the duty to maintain confidentiality extends after death. However, confidentiality is not absolute and is usually qualified by the need to protect third parties or society. (This is discussed in Part Two of this chapter). The rights of individuals to confidentiality after death can be a

---

13   Freedom of Information Act 1997 (Section 28(6) Regulations 1999 (SI 47/1999).
14   *McK v The Information Commissioner* [2006] IESC 2.

difficult and sensitive issue, as views range from those who assert that the deceased have no rights and that therefore information can be disclosed to the deceased's family after death, to those who argue that the principle of confidentiality must be maintained even after death so as not to damage the relationship of trust between doctor and patient.

Robinson and O'Neill discuss the issue of whether disclosure of information after death can cause harm.[15] They argue that there are several possible areas of concern that may arise, such as the patient's own expectations, the protection of others and the preservation of societal expectations of confidentiality. They are of the view that for some patients, posthumous disclosure of sensitive information may cause as much fear as contemporaneous disclosure.

[3.29] Such fears affect patient behaviour and candour, which may result in suboptimal care during life. Individuals frequently withhold information from loved ones to protect them, and there is no reason to assume that this should be different after a person's death. An expectation among the living that their private medical information may be released after death may inhibit the patient-clinician relationship.

[3.30] However, there are circumstances in which it may be in the family's interests to access information relating to the deceased after death, such as where they may be concerned about the care the person received prior to death, or inherited diseases, or their testamentary capacity. In some of these situations, the family may seek a court order for discovery of the medical records such as to confirm the validity of a will. Robinson and O'Neill argue that it might be preferable to consider the possibility of controlled release of information in a clinical manner as part of a bereavement care programme involving the patient's doctor. Support could also be given by expert clinicians independent of the particular health-care institution involved in the deceased patient's care.

This solution may be considered a balance between the rights of the deceased to privacy (by avoiding indiscriminate release of their health care records) and of the living to access information pertinent to their own health and peace of mind (by providing a clinically informed response to their concerns).[16]

[3.31] Section 28(5) of the FOI Act provides that:

'Where, as respects a request …the grant of which would, but for this subsection, fall to be refused under *subsection (1)*, in the opinion of the head concerned, on balance—

(a) the public interest that the request should be granted outweighs the public interest that the right to privacy of the individual to whom the information relates should be upheld, or

(b) the grant of the request would benefit the individual aforesaid, the head may… grant the request.'

---

15 Robinson and O'Neill, 'Access to Health Care Records After Death, Balancing Confidentiality with Appropriate Disclosure' (2007) JAMA Vol 297 No 6, 634–636.

16 Robinson and O Neill, 'Access to Health Care Records After Death, Balancing Confidentiality with Appropriate Disclosure' (2007) JAMA Vol 297 No 6, at 635.

[3.32] McDonagh and Donnelly[17] pose the question as to whether the public interest override provided for in s 28(5) can be applied in cases where requests for access to records of deceased persons do not meet the conditions for the granting of such access provided for in the Regulations, discussed below. 'A positive response to this question would permit the granting of FOI requests concerning records of deceased persons in circumstances other than those provided for in the Regulations, for example where the requester does not fall into any of the three categories of requester to which the access rights in the regulations apply.'

[3.33] Under the FOI Regulations of 1999, as superseded by the 2009 Regulations, access to health records of the deceased may be given to three categories of people with specific interests. These are: the deceased person's personal representative acting in the course of the administration of his estate or someone acting with the consent of the personal representative; a person on whom a function is conferred by law in relation to the deceased person or his estate acting in the course of the performance of this function; and, finally, the spouse or a next of kin of the individual where, in the opinion of the head of the public body concerned, the public interest would, on balance, be better served by granting than by refusing to grant the request.[18]

[3.34] The first two of these categories are easily identifiable and uncontroversial in their scope, but the third category was one which was the subject of amendment as between the 1999 and 2009 Regulations. 'Persons coming within the scope of this category are, in the first place, defined primarily on the basis of their familial relationship to the deceased, as opposed to their performance of particular legal functions.'[19] This category can also be contrasted with the preceding two in so far as it imports a public interest requirement as a condition of access. The original 1999 Regulations had provided an automatic and unlimited right of access to spouses and next of kin.[20] Under the 2009 Regulations, spouses and next of kin will only have a right of access to information about deceased persons where the public interest, including the public interest in the confidentiality of personal information, would on balance be better served by granting than by refusing to grant the request.

[3.35] Another significant change brought about by the 2009 Regulations is that while the 1999 Regulations had applied the right of access, in addition to spouses and next of kin, to such other person or persons as the head considers appropriate having regard to all the circumstances and to relevant guidelines drawn up and published by the Minister, the amended Regulations confine the scope of this category of eligible requester to spouses and next of kin only. 'Thus persons who are neither spouses nor next of kin of the deceased person are now ineligible to apply for access to records of deceased persons on the basis of the Regulations. This limitation would affect, for example,

---

[17] McDonagh and Donnelly, 'Access to Health Information in respect of deceased persons: The Law in Ireland' (2010) 16(1) MLJI 7–15.

[18] Reg 4(1)(b)(iii).

[19] McDonagh and Donnelly, 'Access to Health Information in respect of deceased persons: The Law in Ireland' (2010) 16(1) MLJI 7–15.

[20] This was confirmed by the High Court (McCarthy J) in *Rotunda Hospital v Information Commissioner* [2009] IEHC 315.

relatives of the deceased other than next of kin, as well as friends and other interested parties'.[21]

[3.36] As noted above, s 28(5) provides for the granting of access to records which would disclose personal information where, on balance, in the opinion of the head of the public body concerned, either the public interest that the request should be granted outweighs the public interest that the right to privacy of the individual to whom the information relates should be upheld, or the grant of the request would benefit the individual aforesaid. McDonagh and Donnelly state that the applicability of each of these conditions to requests for information relating to the dead raises interesting questions.

[3.37] In the case of the first condition, it raises issues about the extent to which, if at all, a dead person can be said to enjoy a right to privacy. It also requires an exploration of the public interest factors favouring the granting of requests for access to health information about the dead. These matters will be considered below in the context of the discussion of the public interest test contained in the Regulations. The second condition raises the question of whether the granting of an FOI request could ever be said to benefit a deceased person. In the same way that the existence of posthumous harm gives rise to significant conceptual challenges,[22] it is difficult to see how recognition could be afforded to the notion of a dead person's enjoyment of a benefit.

[3.38] The introduction of the public interest test by the 2009 Regulations is of central importance to the operation of the access rights of spouses and next of kin.[23] The Minister for Finance has drawn up detailed Guidance Notes in relation to the interpretation of 'public interest' in this context. These advise that the following matters should be taken into consideration –

- The confidentiality of personal information as set out in s 28(1) of the Act.
- Whether the deceased would have consented to the release of the records to the requester when living?
- Has the person outlined arrangements in his will or other instrument in writing consenting to release of personal records?
- Would the release damage the good name and character of the deceased?

---

[21] McDonagh and Donnelly, 'Access to Health Information in respect of deceased persons: The Law in Ireland' (2010) 16(1) MLJI 7–15.

[22] As described by Sperling, *Posthumous Interests: Legal and Ethical Perspectives* (Cambridge University Press, 2008), p15, the difficulty with a concept of posthumous harm is first, how a person can be harmed if they cannot experience the 'evil of harm' and secondly, if a deceased person no longer exists for legal purposes, who is the subject of posthumous harm? Although several commentators have tried to develop theories justifying the conceptual possibility of posthumous harm, (see, for example, Feinberg, *The Moral Limits of the Criminal Law: Harm to Others* (OUP, 1984), pp 89–91; Sperling, *Posthumous Interests*), the issue remains conceptually problematic. For further discussion of the conceptual issues involved, see McDonagh and Donnelly, 'Keeping the Secrets of the Dead: An Evaluation of the Statutory Framework for Access to Information About Deceased Persons' 31(1) *Legal Studies* (2011) 42–70.

[23] Reg 4(1)(b)(iii).

- The nature of the relationship of the requester to the deceased and the circumstances of the relationship prior to the death of the deceased.
- The nature of the records to be released.
- Can the requester obtain the information they seek without accessing the records of the deceased, for example from another family source?
- Any other circumstances relevant to the request as set out by the requester.

In relation to medical records, the Guidance Notes indicate that 'due regard should be had to the confidentiality of medical records in accordance with the Irish Medical Council Guide to Ethical Conduct and Behaviour'. The Medical Council's Guide is discussed further below.

[3.39] In *Rotunda Hospital v Information Commissioner*[24] the Court had to consider an appeal from the Rotunda Hospital against the decision of the Information Commissioner to grant access to information in a Labour Ward Book and a Porter's Lodge Book in the hospital. This information was sought by Ms W on behalf of her elderly father Mr W (deceased at the date of the judgment), who had been given up for adoption in 1922. The information sought related to the age of the woman believed to be registered in the hospital records as Mr W's mother. This was sought by the family in order to assist Mr W in tracing his family roots. The hospital refused access to the information on the grounds that it had a policy of ensuring that women who came to the hospital have an absolute guarantee of confidentiality, whether it was information required for therapeutic purposes or not. The Information Commissioner overturned the hospital's refusal to grant access to the information sought. The hospital appealed the decision to the High Court.

[3.40] McCarthy J in describing the substance of the appeal said, 'Needless to say there is not now and was never at any time in our law absolute confidentiality in respect of information passed between, say, a patient and doctor or a patient and the servants or agents of a hospital (which amounts to the same thing) so one should proceed, of course, on the basis that what is advanced here is a claim for confidentiality in terms of the Acts, without prejudice to any other circumstance where disclosure could be compelled.'

[3.41] One of the issues in contention was whether the age of the woman who had given birth was 'personal information'. Section 28(2)(a) of the Act removes the ban on access to a record where it would involve disclosure of personal information where the information concerned relates to the requester. However, one may not obtain, as of right, personal information pertaining to oneself if it also relates to another person. It is only if the information is in the public domain or the subject of regulation that disclosure arises as of right. McCarthy J took the view that the mother's age was personal information relating to the requester and therefore subject to the Act.

[3.42] The second issue was whether this information was confidential and therefore subject to a prohibition on disclosure. The Commissioner took the view that since information on age is available through birth, marriage and death certificates, this is information already in the public domain and thus not properly regarded as confidential. The judge considered definitions of confidential information in other jurisdictions as well as Irish authorities, including *House of Spring Gardens Limited and Others v Point*

---

24   *Rotunda Hospital v Information Commissioner* [2009] IEHC 315.

Blank Ltd and Others[25] in which the Supreme Court said that the issue was to be decided by looking at the relationship between the parties and the nature of the information. McCarthy J also examined case law surrounding the nature of the duty of confidentiality, including *W v Egdell*[26] and *X v Y*[27](discussed below). The judge considered whether the mother in this case, presumably now deceased given the passage of time since giving birth in 1922, could enjoy constitutional rights or whether such rights might be exercised on her behalf by her personal representatives.

> She could have no right to life or surely anything of the nature of a right going to the nature of the human personality or freedom of expression or liberty nor a right against self incrimination or to marry…I find it hard to accept any such right could ever arise. Privacy is a highly personal right and surely it must be the case that such a right could not arise.

The learned judge later went on to say that he was of the opinion that 'no right to privacy exists in deceased persons.' He held that the record did not enjoy the necessary quality of confidentiality for the purpose of prima facie prohibiting disclosure under s 26. On appeal to the Supreme Court,[28] the court (Denham J dissenting) allowed the appeal and held that the FOI Act did apply to the relevant hospital records, that personal information about the man's mother would have been given to the hospital in confidence and on the understanding that it would be kept confidential, and that the public interest did not justify its release.

[3.43] In *National Maternity Hospital v Information Commissioner*[29] the Parents for Justice Group sought access to documents submitted by the National Maternity Hospital to the Inquiry on Post Mortem Practice and correspondence between the hospital and the Inquiry in relation to the matters under consideration by the Inquiry. The Commissioner was highly critical of the behaviour of the hospital in refusing access to the documents and described it as 'obstruction of my office in the performance of its functions.' The Inquiry had concluded by the time the matter came before the Information Commissioner, and the Commissioner decided to direct release certain of the records. This was upheld by the High Court.

[3.44] In *ACF v the North Eastern Health Board*,[30] a woman who had spent some of her childhood in the care of the health authorities sought the records relating to her care. The request was refused on the basis that the records also contained information relating to members of her family. The Information Commissioner decided that the confidentiality of individuals who may be affected by another person's request for information must be protected. Access was refused to all records other than the minutes of meetings which the requester herself had attended.

[3.45] Access to medical records may be refused if it is prejudicial to the physical or mental well-being of the individual concerned although access through a nominated

---

[25] *House of Spring Gardens Limited and Others v Point Blank Ltd and Others* [1984] IR 611.
[26] *W v Egdell* [1990] 1 All ER 835.
[27] *X v Y* [1988] 2 All ER 648.
[28] *Rotunda Hospital v Information Commissioner* [2011] IESC 26.
[29] *National Maternity Hospital v Information Commissioner* [2007] IEHC 113.
[30] *ACF v the North Eastern Health Board* [2001] IEIC 4.

health professional may be possible.[31] This serves to reinforce the position that rights of access to medical records are more restricted than other records, dependent on the decision of either the executive of the public body in question (who may not have any medical qualifications with which to assess the request for access) or a nominated health professional who will exercise his own medical judgment. Although such refusals are subject to the right of appeal, the individual does not have a broad right to records of his health care, which seems to be in conflict with the overall aim of the Act.

FOI and data protection

[3.46] There are some similarities and differences in substance and perspective between freedom of information and data protection. As Lennon states, 'the essential principle of data protection is the protection of individual privacy and the putting in place of safeguards where personal information is collected, used, disclosed or transferred to other persons and/or other countries. It imposes obligations on all individuals, agencies or organisations that keep personal information, and not just public bodies.'[32] The essential principle of FOI is that there should be access to records held by or under the control of public bodies 'to the greatest extent possible consistent with the public interest and the right to privacy'[33]. There is a clear overlap between the two frameworks and the protection that they provide. However, there are also differences in terms of the definitions of personal data or information and in relation to the release of information on grounds of public interest.

[3.47] Although the Data Protection Act 1988 applied only to data retained in electronic form, the amending Act of 2003 extended the provisions to personal information in both manual and electronic forms. Not all personal information is covered by data protection law due to the definition used in the Act and, similarly, not all personal information is classed as sensitive information within the freedom of information provisions.

[3.48] The Data Protection Act provides in s1 (5) (a) that a right conferred by this Act shall not prejudice the exercise of a right conferred by the Freedom of Information Act 1997. This means that if a request for access to records under the FOI Act is refused, the applicant may nonetheless be able to seek access under Data Protection law. The relevant provisions of the Data Protection Acts are described below.

THE DATA PROTECTION ACTS 1988–2003

[3.49] The Data Protection Act was first introduced in 1988 to address concerns regarding the protection of data stored on computer.[34] The concerns centred on the ease

---

[31] FOI Act 1997, s 26(4). The aim of the provision is to give the individual to whom the information relates indirect access to the information and, as it has been expressed in an Australian report, 'to ensure that people receive 'disturbing' information in a supportive environment.' McDonagh, *Freedom of Information Law in Ireland* (2nd edn, Round Hall Sweet & Maxwell, 2006) p 284.

[32] Lennon, *Protecting Personal Health Information in Ireland, Law and Practice* (Oak Tree Press, 2005), p 323.

[33] Long Title to the FOI Act 1997.

[34] See Kelleher and Murray, *Information Technology Law in Ireland* (2nd edn, Bloomsbury Professional, 2007).

with which computerised data could be retrieved and transferred without the knowledge of the individuals to whom the data related. This led to fears that the State would have the ability to access sensitive information about every individual and that the information could be stolen or otherwise misused by others who were able to break into the system.[35] The Act does not preclude an action at common law in relation to the mishandling of data, such as defamation, negligence or breach of privacy. In fact, the Act actually facilitates actions for negligence by providing under s 7 that the data controller owes a duty of care to the data subject for the purpose of the law of torts.

[3.50] The aims of data protection are outlined in the Data Protection Principles set out in the Acts as follows:

1. Obtain and process information fairly.
2. Keep it only for one or more specified, explicit and lawful purposes.
3. Use and disclose it only in ways compatible with these purposes.
4. Keep it safe and secure.
5. Keep it accurate, complete and up to date.
6. Ensure that it is adequate, relevant and not excessive.
7. Retain it for no longer than is necessary for the purpose or purposes.
8. Give a copy of his/her personal data to that individual, on request.

[3.51] The Data Protection Act 2003 was introduced to implement the EU Data Protection Directive 1995. One of the most important features of the 2003 Act in the health-care context is that manual or paper files also became subject to data protection provisions where they form part of a filing system. A filing system for these purposes is any structured set of personal data which is accessible according to specific criteria, whether centralised, decentralised or dispersed on a functional or geographical basis.[36]

[3.52] The Act provides that personal data may only be processed if certain conditions are met. Processing includes almost any use of the data, including collection and storing it, altering, transmitting it to others and deleting it. In relation to the processing of sensitive personal data, such as medical records, the Act sets out detailed conditions, one of which must be met before processing such data. These include:

- obtaining the consent of the data subject;
- the processing is necessary for the discharge of a legal obligation;
- the processing is necessary in order to protect the vital interests of the data subject;
- the processing is necessary for the legitimate interests of the data controller or a third party to whom the data is disclosed;
- the processing is necessary in order to obtain legal advice, and;
- the processing is necessary for medical purposes and is carried out by a health professional or a person who would owe a similar duty of confidentiality.

[3.53] The term 'health professional' includes a registered medical practitioner, within the meaning of the Medical Practitioners Act 1978, a registered dentist, within the meaning of the Dentists Act 1985 or a member of any other class of health worker or

---

[35] 375 Dáil Debates, Cols. 2846–7, Mr G Collins TD, then Minister for Justice.
[36] Article 2(c) of the Directive, defined in the Data Protection Act 2003, s 2.

social worker standing specified by regulations made by the Minister. 'Medical purposes' includes the purposes of preventive medicine, medical diagnosis, medical research, the provision of care and treatment and the management of health-care services.

[3.54] This indicates that patient consent is only one of a set of conditions which must be met prior to processing, and is not a necessary pre-condition in itself. Consent may be expressly given in writing by signing a consent form or hospital admission form in which the processing of personal data is indicated, or consent may be implied by the actions of the patient in attending the doctor's clinic or hospital. In such circumstances, however, patients should be made aware by notices or otherwise on display that their personal data will be processed. The Data Protection Commissioner has indicated that the adequacy of such notices will depend on the circumstances and it may not be sufficient to display such a notice in an Accident and Emergency waiting area, as persons attending such areas are likely to be in pain, anxious, and distressed and thus not in a position to properly take note of such notices.[37] Implied consent would generally cover the sharing of information within a clinical team where this is in the interests of providing care to a patient. It would also cover administrative uses of the information, for example sharing certain information with the billing department of a hospital. However, the amount of information and the nature of the data shared should be carefully kept to a minimum and only shared to the extent necessary. It does not cover sharing of information for other purposes such as teaching or research, for which explicit consent is required.

[3.55] Lennon argues that it is reasonable for a health-care service provider to rely on implied consent by individuals in certain circumstances. He cites the example of a patient attending a medical practitioner for medical consultation or treatment during which the practitioner writes down certain information.

> Generally, this will be regarded as giving implied consent to the practitioner to collect the information for certain purposes. The extent of these purposes should usually be evident from the discussion during the consultation. Similarly, if a medical practitioner collects a specimen to send to a pathology laboratory for testing, it would be reasonable to consider that the individual is giving implied consent to the passing of necessary information to that laboratory.[38]

Part Two

CONFIDENTIALITY

[3.56] Confidentiality is one of the most important elements of the relationship between doctors and patients and is a well-accepted principle of medical law. Patients presume when they attend a doctor for diagnosis and treatment that all aspects of their personal information will be kept confidential by the doctor. This aspect of the relationship is fundamental to the trust which patients place in their doctors and has been regarded as a

---

[37] Case study 1/97 of the Data Protection Commissioner, available at www.dataprotection.ie (accessed 24 May 2011).

[38] Lennon, *Protecting Personal Health Information in Ireland, Law and Practice* (Oak Tree Press, 2005), p 140.

crucial aspect of medical professionalism since the Hippocratic Oath, which stated 'whatsoever I shall see or hear concerning the life of men, in my attendance on the sick, or even apart therefrom, which ought not to be noised abroad, I will keep silence thereon, counting such things to be as sacred secrets'. Although the Hippocratic Oath is no longer commonly sworn by doctors, all professional codes of ethics and international declarations on medical ethics advocate strict adherence to the principle of confidentiality, subject to certain exceptions considered below.[39]

[3.57] Confidentiality is crucial not only to respect the sense of privacy of a patient but also to preserve his or her confidence in the medical profession...Without such protection, those in need of medical assistance may be deterred from revealing such information of a personal and intimate nature as may be necessary in order to receive appropriate treatment and, even, from seeking such assistance, thereby endangering their own health and, in the case of transmissible diseases, that of the community.[40]

[3.58] In Ireland the duty of medical confidentiality arises from a number of sources, including the constitutional right to privacy, the protection of privacy under art 8 of the European Convention on Human Rights (ECHR), the ethical duties imposed on doctors, possible contractual obligations arising from the doctor-patient relationship and equitable duties imposed by virtue of the relationship and nature of the information disclosed.

[3.59] The right to privacy has been recognised by the Irish courts as an unenumerated constitutional right.[41] In *Kennedy v Ireland*[42] Hamilton P said:

> Though not specifically guaranteed by the Constitution, the right of privacy is one of the fundamental personal rights of the citizen which flow from the Christian and democratic nature of the State...The nature of the right to privacy must be such as to ensure the dignity and freedom of an individual in the type of society envisaged by the Constitution, namely, a sovereign, independent and democratic society.

[3.60] However, the right to privacy is not absolute. Its exercise may be restricted by the constitutional rights of others or by the requirements of the common good and it is subject to the requirements of public order and morality. The doctor-patient relationship does not come within the relationships typically afforded the right to privacy under the constitution, such as marriage. 'However, in few other relationships is the conflict between the public interest in freedom of information and the need to protect personal privacy more poignantly marked and the boundaries more ambiguous.'[43] It is likely that personal medical information would thus be protected by the right to privacy, although this may be overridden by the public interest in certain circumstances.

---

[39] For example, the Declaration of Geneva and the Irish Medical Council's Guide to Professional Conduct and Ethics for Registered Medical Practitioners (7th edn, 2009) considered below at para **3.65**.

[40] *Z v Finland* (1997) BMLR 107.

[41] See *McGee v Attorney General* [1974] IR 284; *Norris v Attorney General* [1982] IR 241; *Madigan v Attorney General* [1986] ILRM 136; *Attorney General (SPUC Ireland Ltd) v Open Door Counselling Ltd* [1987] ILRM 477.

[42] *Kennedy & Arnold v Ireland* [1987] IR 587.

[43] O'Neill, 'Matters of Discretion – The Parameters of Doctor/Patient Confidentiality' (1995) MLJI, 94–104.

[3.61] If an express contract exists between doctor and patient, the obligation of confidentiality may, of course, be specifically included as a term of that contract. The extent of the obligation will depend on the terms used and the interpretation put on the contract. However, it would not be usual for a doctor to have a written contract with his patient and therefore the existence of duty of confidentiality may be implied into the contract. It may be argued by the patient that he had a legitimate expectation that the relationship with the doctor would be governed by the ethical guidelines of the profession and that this encompassed the duty of confidentiality. In this way, the doctor's ethical duties become part of his legal obligations *vis-à-vis* his patient.

[3.62] In the English case *Hunter v Mann*,[44] Boreham J said:

> Medical practitioners and others in a similar position, such as bankers, accountants, priests and journalists are bound by a duty which the law respects and enforces from disclosing without the consent of the patient or client communications or information obtained in a professional capacity, save in exceptional situations in the public interest.

[3.63] The existence of an equitable remedy for breach of confidence was recognised in the English case of *Attorney General v Guardian Newspapers (No 2)*[45] and in the Irish case of *House of Spring Gardens v Point Blank Limited*[46] where Costello J said that an action for breach of confidence must consist of the following elements: (i) There must exist from the relationship between the parties an obligation of confidence regarding the information which had been imparted; (ii) the information which had been communicated must properly be regarded as confidential; (iii) The recipient of the information must have breached his duty to act in good faith, ie he must have used the information for a purpose for which it was not imparted to him and to the detriment of the informant.

[3.64] It is also important to recognise the ever-widening circle of health professionals who may legitimately have access to a patient's medical records. This is increased even further in the case of a hospital admission where technical and ancillary staff may also have access.[47] Patient data are generated in many locations in a hospital and handled by a range of different parties. As Jackson says:

---

[44] *Hunter v Mann* [1974] QB 767, [1974] 2 All ER 414.
[45] *Attorney General v Guardian Newspapers (No 2)* [1988] 3 All ER 545, also known as the *Spycatcher* case where Lord Goff accepted 'the broad general principle ...that a duty of confidence arises when confidential information comes to the knowledge of a person in circumstances where he has notice, or is held to have agreed, that the information is confidential, with the effect that it would be just in all the circumstances that he should be precluded from disclosing the information to others.'
[46] *House of Spring Gardens v Point Blank Limited* [1984] IR 611; see also *Cook v Carroll* [1945] IR 515.
[47] See Siegler, 'Confidentiality in Medicine – A Decrepit Concept.' (1982) New Eng J Med, Vol 307 (24) 1518–1521, where it is argued that confidentiality no longer exists, it is old, worn out and useless. Siegler gives one example of a fairly straightforward hospital admission which prompted at least 75 health professionals at the hospital to access the patient's medical records, including doctors, residents, nurses, pharmacists, secretaries, financial officers and medical students, many of whom changed on shift relief. (contd.../)

The provision of appropriate diagnostic and therapeutic care is often dependent upon a number of health care professionals having access to a patient's records. Medical care is generally provided by teams of doctors and nurses. Patients may be referred to specialist consultants, or for additional diagnostic procedures, such as blood tests, x-rays, and scans. If information about the patient's condition could never be shared with others, the provision of health care would grind to a halt.[48]

The Medical Council's Guide to Professional Conduct and Ethics

[3.65] In Ireland the Medical Council, which regulates the medical profession, publishes a Guide to Professional Conduct and Ethics which sets out the standards of behaviour expected of registered medical practitioners. In every edition since its inception, the Guide has contained strong advice to doctors in relation to the maintenance of confidentiality. The most recent, seventh edition of the Guide was published in 2009 and contains a section on medical records and confidentiality which states that 'confidentiality is a fundamental principle of medical ethics and is central to the trust between patients and doctors.' Doctors are advised to be vigilant to ensure that accidental disclosures of patient information do not occur and that such information is maintained securely and in compliance with data protection legislation.

[3.66] The Guide recognises that confidentiality is not absolute and that there may be circumstances in which it is necessary or justifiable to share patient information with others. It advises doctors not to share information with the patient's family members or carers without their consent, or unless disclosure is necessary to protect others from a risk of serious harm. Doctors may also be obliged by law to disclose patient information such as in the context of court proceedings or by virtue of infectious disease regulations under which notification is mandated in the public interest to prevent the spread of disease.

[3.67] The Guide also states that in exceptional circumstances disclosure of patient information without their consent may be justifiable when it is necessary to protect the patient or others from serious risk of death or serious harm. Doctors are advised to seek patient consent to such disclosure where possible. Where disclosure is justifiable, doctors should anonymise the information as far as possible, thereby protecting the patient's identity. Doctors should only disclose as little information as possible and take care to disclose to an appropriate person or body who understands that the information must be kept confidential. In all such instances, the patient should be informed about the disclosure unless this would cause them serious harm.

[3.68] Disclosure of patient information may also be necessary in the public interest, such as in a public health emergency, such as that which occurred in 2009 with the emergence of swine flu. The public interest exception also covers the reporting of serious adverse events to an appropriate health authority or relevant statutory agency.

---

[47] (\...contd) He claims that 'as medicine expands from a narrow, disease-based model to a model that encompasses psychological, social, and economic problems, not only will the size of the health-care team and medical costs increase, but more sensitive information (such as one's personal habits and financial condition) will now be included in the medical records and will no longer be confidential.'

[48] Jackson, *Medical Law: Text, Cases and Materials* (2nd edn, OUP, 2010) p 352.

[3.69] In relation to the disclosure of patient information to other health-care professionals, the Guide points out that most patients understand the need for such disclosure, which is done in order to provide the most appropriate care to the patient, and readily accept it. Information may also be shared with other staff, particularly in a hospital environment, as part of clinical audit and quality assurance systems which are designed to ensure that patient care is provided in a safe and effective manner and environment. Such information should be anonymised where possible and, if this is not possible, the patient should be informed and any objection should be respected. Similar advice is given to doctors in respect of sharing information as part of education and training activities.

Exceptions to confidentiality

Consent

[3.70] There will be no breach of the duty of confidentiality when a patient expressly consents to disclosure.[49] Consent should be fully informed and freely given, and the subsequent disclosure should not exceed the terms of the consent given. In relation to mentally ill patients, special caution is needed to ensure that the patient has the capacity to understand the nature and implications of the disclosure and is not under undue influence from any third party in giving consent.

[3.71] In the case of minors, again the question of competence arises.[50] If the minor is regarded as the patient, does this status of itself infer the obligation of confidence, or does it depend on the perceived capacity of the minor? The common law does not have a fixed age at which a child is held to have capacity to consent to the disclosure of confidential medical information. However, in *Gillick v West Norfolk and Wisbeck Area Health Authority*[51] it was held that a child is competent to consent to the medical treatment if he fully comprehends the nature of the treatment and the consequences involved of treatment and non-treatment. By analogy to the question of disclosure it would seem that the child may consent to disclosure if he understands the nature of secrecy and the consequences of disclosure. However, the Gillick case has never been judicially considered in Ireland and may be decided differently in light of the Constitutional provisions in relation to the family. This is discussed further in Chapter 11.

Court Order

[3.72] In the context of personal injury litigation it is usual for the defendant to request disclosure of the medical records pertaining to the plaintiff's case. If the plaintiff refuses to consent to such disclosure, an order for discovery may be sought by the defendant. This will compel production of the relevant documents. Where the patient consents to disclosure of his records, doctors have an ethical responsibility to supply medical reports to solicitors or insurers on behalf of such patients they have seen or treated. These reports must be factual and true and are not to be influenced by the fee involved or by pressure from anyone to omit or embellish details. If the case results in a court

---

[49] *C v C* [1946] 1 All ER 562.
[50] See Donnelly, 'Capacity of Minors to Consent to Medical and Contraceptive Treatment' (1995) Medico-Legal J of Ireland 18.
[51] *Gillick v West Norfolk and Wisbeck Area Health Authority* [1985] 3 All ER 402.

appearance by the doctor, all notes, records and conversations with the patient may be disclosed by the doctor without incurring responsibility for breach of duty. He will be entitled to legal professional privilege in relation to the information he discloses in the medical report and in the witness box. The report must have been drawn up for the purpose of litigation in order for the privilege to apply.

The doctor may well be uncomfortable when asked questions in the witness box which would involve the disclosure of confidential information about the patient, and a judge may try to clarify whether the disclosure is necessary in the circumstances.[52] However, if pressed to do so, the doctor is obliged to answer any question put to him and a refusal may leave the doctor open to a charge of contempt of court.

The patient's best interests

[3.73] Although the patient's consent is always preferable where the doctor wishes to disclose confidential information, it may be possible in certain circumstances for the doctor to justify disclosure on the grounds that it was necessary to protect the interests of the patient. A doctor may believe it is in the best interests of his patient to disclose certain information regarding the patient's health to a relative or carer. The doctor may presume that the patient impliedly consents to such disclosure and that it is in the patient's best interests for close relatives to share this information so as to provide optimum care and support for the patient. However, unless the patient is not capable of giving consent, the patient's consent should be obtained prior to any disclosure, and if the patient expressly refuses to give consent, the doctor must respect the patient's wishes, even if the doctor is of the opinion that this is contrary to the patient's best interests. In exceptional circumstances where non-disclosure might result in serious harm to the patient or others, the doctor may disclose information but only on a strict need-to-know basis and with minimal sharing of information.

[3.74] In *W v Watters & Mental Health Commission*[53] the Court had to consider whether the release of medical records to a legal representative of a person detained involuntarily under the Mental Health Act 2001 was in that person's best interests. The applicant was a 70-year-old woman suffering from early-onset Alzheimer's disease, who was detained involuntarily in a psychiatric hospitals of which the defendant was the clinical director. Under the Mental Health Act 2001 the applicant was entitled to have the admission order reviewed by a mental health tribunal within 21 days of admission. The Mental Health Commission is required to ensure that certain procedures are complied with following the making of an admission order, including the appointment of a legal representative to represent the patient. The Commission appointed a solicitor who sought to interview the applicant and review her medical records. Due to her incapacity,

---

52 In *Hunter v Mann* [1974] QB 767, Lord Widgery stated: 'If a doctor is asked in court a question which he finds embarrassing because it involves him in talking about things which he would normally regard as confidential he can seek protection from the judge and ask if answering is necessary. The judge, by virtue of the overriding discretion to control his court which all …judges have, could tell the doctor that he does not need to answer the question. Whether or not the judge would take that line depends largely on the importance of the potential answer to the issue being tried.' Such judicial discretion may be exercised following a private examination by the judge of the evidence in question.

53 *W v Watters & Mental Health Commission* (2008) IEHC 462.

the applicant was unable to give consent to the review of her records or to give instructions to the solicitor. The hospital took the view that it was not authorised to release the medical records in the absence of consent from the patient unless obliged to do so by the Mental Health Tribunal. All parties agreed that it was in the best interests of the patient that her legal representative had access to medical records as early as possible in order to best represent and protect the patient's best interests. The Court heard arguments from counsel in relation to the wording and role of the Medical Council's Guide in relation to confidentiality and the exceptions thereto. Peart J took the view that the disclosure of a patient's medical records to her legal representative, where the patient lacked the capacity to consent to such disclosure, was necessary to protect the interests of the patient and did not contravene the duty of confidentiality.[54]

Protection of another individual:

[3.75] The issue has also arisen whether a doctor is justified in disclosing, and indeed has a duty to disclose, confidential information where another individual may be at risk. This has arisen in the context of the treatment of patients diagnosed with HIV infection, and also in psychiatric care where a patient exhibits a threat of violence to an identifiable person.[55]

[3.76] In the context of HIV, infected persons pose a risk to their sexual partners, depending on the nature of the sexual activity and the level of precautions taken. Patients would generally be counselled as to the risks of transmission and would be advised to inform their partners. 'It is unsurprising that there will be some patients who are not prepared to do so nor, indeed, to inform their general practitioners; the doctor is then faced with the problem of whether or not he, himself, should inform those with a need to know'.[56]

[3.77] The Medical Council's Guide provides that in exceptional circumstances disclosure of patient information without their consent may be justifiable when it is necessary to protect the patient or others from serious risk of death or serious harm. Doctors are advised to seek patient consent to such disclosure where possible. Therefore, in the context of HIV transmission, it may be ethically justifiable to disclose to the patient's partner in order to enable that person to seek testing for themselves and so as to ensure that appropriate protection is put in place Although an action for breach of confidence may be taken by a patient whose spouse or partner was informed in such circumstances, it is likely that the court, in balancing the interests of both parties involved, would be of the view that disclosure was justifiable in the interests of protecting others from a possibly fatal risk.[57]

---

54 See further Whelan, *Mental Health Law and Practice* (Round Hall, 2009) at paras 7–55.
55 For discussion of other issues such as marital violence, contraceptive treatment of minors and sterilisation, see O'Neill, p 99–100.
56 Mason and Laurie, *Law and Medical Ethics* (8th edn, OUP, 2009) p 200.
57 For further reading on this point see Neave, 'AIDS: Confidentiality and the Duty to Warn' (1987) 9 Univ. of Tasmania L Rev 1; Gostin and Hodge, 'Piercing the Veil of Secrecy in HIV/ AIDS and Other Sexually Transmitted Diseases: Theories of Privacy and Disclosure in Partner Notification' (1998) 5 Duke J of Gender L & Pol 9; Caswell, 'Disclosure by a Physician of AIDS-Related Patient Information: An Ethical and Legal Dilemma' (1989) 68 Can Bar Rev 225; Patterson, 'AIDS, HIV Testing and Medical Confidentiality' (1991) 7 Otago L Rev 379.

[3.78] In relation to psychiatric care, changes in emphasis in treatment have increased the 'open door' approach, which enables patients to continue to live within the community as much as possible, while being treated as voluntary out-patients with drugs and psychotherapy. In some circumstances it has been argued that it is justifiable, and perhaps obligatory, for a medical practitioner who is aware of psychiatric difficulties which may give rise to violence, to disclose such a risk to those who may be in direct contact with the patient. The idea that psychiatrists can predict dangerousness in such a person has meant that in some jurisdictions, most notably the United States, a duty has been imposed on doctors to breach the patient's confidentiality in the interests of protecting another person from a predicted violent attack.

[3.79] The psychiatric profession generally objects to the imposition of such a duty on it on the grounds that (i) not all psychiatric patients are dangerous, (ii) there is no reliable means for predicting danger, (iii) trust in the relationship is damaged by disclosure, and (iv) disclosure provides a disincentive to discussion of violent fantasies. Some examples from case law are illustrative of this dilemma.

[3.80] The most well-known case in this area is *Tarasoff v Regents of the University of California*.[58] The facts were that a student, Poddar, who was studying at Berkeley, had undergone psychotherapy at the university, during which he had reported to his therapist, Dr Moore, that he intended to kill a girl who was identifiable to Dr Moore as Tatiana Tarasoff, with whom Poddar had a previous short romantic relationship. The doctor concluded that Poddar should be placed under observation in a psychiatric hospital. The doctor notified the campus police and Poddar was taken into custody. However, the police became satisfied that Poddar was rational and released him from custody. Some weeks later Poddar went to Ms Tarasoff's apartment and killed her. Ms Tarasoff's parents sued Dr Moore, the campus police and the university on the basis that they had failed to detain a dangerous patient, and had failed to warn others, and in particular Ms Tarasoff herself, regarding the danger presented.

[3.81] The California Supreme Court upheld the action on the basis that there was a breach of the duty to warn Ms Tarasoff of the danger to herself, despite the fact that she was not a patient of Dr Moore. The Court held that:

> When a therapist determines, or pursuant to the standard of his profession should determine, that his patient presents a serious danger of violence to another, he incurs an obligation to use reasonable care to protect the intended victim against such danger…[This] may call for him to warn the intended victim or others likely to apprise the victim of the danger, to notify the police or to take whatever other steps are reasonably necessary under the circumstances.[59]

---

[58] *Tarasoff v Regents of the University of California* 529 P 2d 55 (Cal, 1974); on appeal 551 P 2d 334 (Cal, 1976). For discussion see Kermani and Drob, '*Tarasoff* Decision: A Decade Later Dilemma Still Faces Psychotherapists' (1987) Am J of Psychotherapy, Vol XLI, No 2, 271; Wulsin et al, 'Unexpected Clinical Feature of the *Tarasoff* Decision: The Therapeutic Alliance and the Duty to Warn' (1983) Am J Psychiatry 140:5, 601; deHaan, 'My Patient's Keeper? The Liability of Medical Practitioners for Negligent Injury to Third Parties.' (1986) Professional Negligence, May/June, 86–91.

[59] *Tarasoff v Regents of the University of California* 529 P 2d 55 (Cal, 1974), per Tobriner J.

Although there was no special relationship in this case between Dr Moore and Ms Tarasoff, the Court imposed liability on the basis that its most important consideration in establishing a duty to warn was forseeability. The Court was of the opinion that a therapist becomes sufficiently involved with his patient that he assumes some responsibility for the safety, not only of the patient, but also of those who are threatened by the patient. It stated that the public policy favouring protection of the confidential nature of patient-psychotherapist communications must yield to the extent to which disclosure is necessary to avoid danger to others. In other words, as the Court put it: 'the protection privilege ends where the public peril begins.'

[3.82] Dissenting judgments in the case were based on the argument that a diagnosis of mental illness is not a prediction of dangerousness and that psychiatrists do not possess a crystal ball with respect to the future actions of their patients. The dissents also concentrated on the relationship between the patient and the therapist, which will only work successfully if the patient trusts the therapist sufficiently to divulge his fantasies. Critics of the majority decision have argued likewise:

> The imposition of a duty to protect, which may take the form of a duty to warn threatened third parties, will imperil the therapeutic alliance and destroy the patient's expectation of confidentiality, thereby thwarting effective treatment and ultimately reducing public safety.[60]

[3.83] Following *Tarasoff*, there have been other cases in the US which have further explored this issue. Some cases place a duty to warn of danger in circumstances only where there is a specific threat to a specific individual, as was the case in Tarasoff. *Brady v Hopper*[61] provides a celebrated and dramatic illustration. In that case, a psychiatric patient, Hinckley, tried to assassinate President Ronald Reagan in an attempt to impress the actress Jodie Foster. The plaintiff was a presidential aide who was wounded in the attack. He claimed that the psychiatrist treating Hinckley should have known that he had a gun and that he identified with a political assassin in a film in which Ms Foster had appeared. The plaintiff alleged that the doctor was negligent in failing to warn law enforcement officials and Hinckley's parents. The Court rejected the claim on the basis that the plaintiff's injuries were not foreseeable. Hinckley had not made any specific threats against any individual, and had no predisposition to violence. Therefore, the possibility of his injuring someone was 'vague, speculative and a matter of conjecture.'[62]

This seems to generally be regarded as a sensible decision not only on the basis of proximity principles in tort law, but also on the basis of medical confidentiality.[63] If the patient's confidences are to be disclosed, then this should only be in clearly exceptional cases. The 'specific threats to specific individuals' test seems a reasonable boundary in this regard.

---

[60] Stone, 'The *Tarasoff* Decision: Suing Psychotherapists to Safeguard Society' (1976) Harvard Law Review 90: 358–378.
[61] *Brady v Hopper* 570 F Supp 1333 (1983).
[62] See also *Thompson v County of Alameda,* 167 Cal Rep 70 (1980); *People v Murtishaw* 175 Cal Rep 738 (1981); *Mavroudis v Superior Court of County of San Mateo* 161 Cal Rep 724 (1980); *Leedy v Hartnett* 510 F Supp 1125 (MD PA 1981).

[3.84] On the other hand, some cases have extended the duty to the prediction of dangerousness generally.[64] In *Lipari v Sears*[65] the patient was under the care of a psychiatrist as an outpatient. He had not displayed any signs of dangerousness and had never threatened anyone. He purchased a shotgun from the defendants and fired it into a crowded nightclub, killing a man and blinding the man's wife. The woman sued Sears for negligence in selling a gun to a mentally ill individual. Sears in turn sued the hospital at which the patient was being treated for not having recognised the danger. The Court upheld the claim, holding that psychotherapists have a duty to third parties if the patient presents an unreasonable risk of harm. The Court rejected the limitation of this duty to identifiable individuals. In doing so, 'the court essentially imposed a duty on therapists to predict dangerousness in general terms and to protect society at large from all "dangerous" individuals whom they have occasion to treat.'[66]

[3.85] The extension of the *Tarasoff* case in this way may be argued to be unreasonable, as it obliges doctors to do something which they argue is impossible, that is, to predict dangerousness. It also involves disclosure of confidential information in circumstances which, arguably, falls outside of the ethical principles under which doctors work, as the disclosure is not necessary to protect a particular individual. However, it could conceivably be argued that disclosure to police authorities in circumstances such as occurred in *Lipari* would be in the public interest.[67] It has been claimed, however, that this would turn psychotherapists into law enforcement agents and subject psychiatric patients to indirect police surveillance.[68]

[3.86] In the English case *Palmer v Tees Health Authority*[69] the patient, Mr Armstrong, had been diagnosed as suffering from personality disorder or psychopathic personality. He had been admitted to hospital on a number of occasions. While being treated as an out-patient, he killed a four-year-old child who lived in a neighbouring house. The girl's mother sued the hospital for negligence in discharging Mr Armstrong and for the consequent nervous shock she suffered as a result of her daughter's death. Stuart-Smith J

---

[63] See also *Home Office v Dorset Yacht Company Ltd* [1970] AC 1004 where the House of Lords held that although there was no general duty to control the actions of another, the existence in this case of a special relationship between seven Borstal trainees and the three officers supervising their training provided a source for such a duty. As the wrongdoers in this case were under the control of the defendants, and control imports responsibility, the defendants owed a duty to take reasonable care in the exercise of their supervision and control.

[64] See further Mullen, 'Mental Disorder and Dangerousness' (1984) 18 Aust NZ J of Psych. 8; Grisso and Applebaum, 'Is it Unethical to Offer Predictions of Future Violence?' (1992) 16 Law and Hum. Behvr. 621; Rudegeair and Applebaum, 'On the Duty to Protect: An Evolutionary Perspective' (1992) 20 Bull Amer Acad Psych Law 419.

[65] *Lipari v Sears* 497 F Supp 185 (Neb 1980).

[66] Kermani and Drob, '*Tarasoff* Decision: A Decade Later Dilemma Still Faces Psychotherapists' (1987) Am J of Psychotherapy, Vol XLI, No 2, at 278. See also *McIntosh v Milano* 403 A 2d 500 (1979); *Durflinger v Artiles* 673 P 2d 86 (Kan 1983); *Perreira v State* 768 P 2d 1198 (Colo 1989); and *Estates of Morgan v Fairfield Family Counselling Center* 673 NE 2d 1311 (Ohio 1997).

[67] See Jones, *Medical Negligence* (Sweet & Maxwell, 1992) at para 2.62–2.68.

[68] Kermani and Drob, '*Tarasoff* Decision: A Decade Later Dilemma Still Faces Psychotherapists' (1987) Am J of Psychotherapy, Vol XLI, No 2, 271 at 281.

[69] *Palmer v Tees Health Authority* [1999] EWCA Civ 1533.

held that there was insufficient proximity between the hospital and the child and that for a duty of care to be established, the victim would have to be identified or identifiable, as in the *Tarasoff* case. He went on to say:

> An additional reason why in my judgement in this case it is at least necessary for the victim to be identifiable…to establish proximity, is that it seems to me that the most effective way of providing protection would be to give warning to the victim, his or her parents or social services so that some protective measure can be made.

The judge also suggested that to impose liability could lead to the practise of defensive medicine. It is argued that this would negatively affect the introduction of new treatments, lead to the confinement of patients exhibiting anti-social behaviour and would generally be a retrograde step for the profession. In the Irish case *C v North Western Health Board*[70] it was held that a health board owed a duty of care to a man who was attacked by a patient who had escaped from a psychiatric hospital, but on the facts it was held that the duty of care had not been breached. White J held that if the patient was known to be dangerous, every step possible would have to be taken to prevent him from doing damage.

[3.87] Under the ECHR, breaches of confidentiality may also be justified in certain circumstances. For example in *Andersson v Sweden*[71] where a psychiatrist disclosed concerns regarding the health of a patient's son, the European Commission held there was no case to answer under art 8 of the Convention, as the disclosure of the information pursued the legitimate aims of protecting 'health or morals' and the 'rights and freedoms of others'. Also in *TV v Finland*[72] where prison staff were notified of the health status of a prisoner with HIV. These cases are reconcilable with the *Egdell* case discussed below.

The protection of society/public interest

[3.88] This is the most general and controversial exception to the rule of medical confidentiality, due to its possible diversity. A straightforward example of the kind of circumstances in which the public interest may justify disclosure of health information is the statutory obligations imposed on doctors to disclose certain information. The Health Act 1947 entitles the Minister for Health and Children to specify by regulation the diseases that are infectious diseases which require notification to public health authorities. The current regulations are contained in the 1981 Infectious Diseases Regulations, which were revised on nine occasions between 1985 and 2007. On 1 July 2000, the Infectious Diseases (Amendment) Regulations, 2000 (SI 151/2000) came into force. Under these regulations, as amended by SI 865/2004, the Health Protection Surveillance Centre (HPSC) was assigned responsibility for the collation and analysis of weekly notifications of infectious diseases, taking over from the Department of Health and Children.

[3.89] On 1 January 2004 a major revision to the regulations came into operation. SI 707/2003 established a revised list of notifiable diseases and introduced a requirement for laboratory directors to report infectious diseases. As soon as a medical practitioner

---

[70]   *C v North Western Health Board* [1997] Irish Law Log Weekly 133. (Circuit Court).
[71]   *Andersson v Sweden* Application No 20022/92, 7 August 1997.
[72]   *TV v Finland* [1994] 18 EHRR CD 179.

becomes aware of or suspects that a person on whom he is in professional attendance is suffering from or is the carrier of an infectious disease, he is required to transmit a written or electronic notification to a Medical Officer of Health. A clinical director of a diagnostic laboratory is subject to the same requirement as soon as an infectious disease is identified in that laboratory. The notifiable diseases include meningitis, measles, tuberculosis, hepatitis and syphilis.[73] HIV is not currently a notifiable disease, although proposals have been made in the past few years to amend the list of notifiable diseases to include this condition.[74] The legal duty to report such disease is reinforced by the ethical guidelines issued by the Medical Council discussed above and is justified on the grounds of public health protection. Disclosure of patient information to the HPSC is on the basis that no patient-identifiable information is published by the HPSC.

Apart from specific statutory obligations, the doctor may be justified in disclosing confidential information in order to safeguard the public interest. Some of the issues which have been judicially considered in this context have centred on the disclosure of criminal offences committed or likely to be committed by a patient, the disclosure of a patient's HIV status, the patient's capacity to drive and suspected child abuse.

[3.90] In relation to the commission of a criminal offence, it would appear to be the case that it may be justifiable (though not obligatory) for a medical practitioner to provide information to the police if he becomes aware that his patient has committed or is likely to commit a criminal offence and if he forms the view that, on balance, to do so is in the public interest.[75] In making this decision, account should be taken of the seriousness of the offence and the potential damage to the public arising from non-disclosure.

[3.91] In the case of patients who present a serious risk of violence, is the doctor ethically and legally justified in breaching the patient's confidence in the public interest? In *W v Egdell*[76] a consultant psychiatrist, Dr Egdell, was asked to examine a prisoner, W, in a secure hospital for the purposes of a review of his case with a view to transferring W to another unit. Dr Egdell strongly opposed the transfer and recommended that further tests and treatment were advisable. He drew attention to W's interest in firearms and explosives, which was probably of particular relevance in this case as W had been convicted of shooting and killing five people and wounding two others. Dr Egdell subsequently learned that as a consequence of his report W withdrew his application for a transfer and that therefore the medical report had not been seen by anyone other than W's legal team. Dr Egdell contacted the medical director of the hospital where W was housed and agreed to forward a copy of his medical report to the hospital. The hospital, with the doctor's permission, also sent a copy of the report to the Secretary for State who, in turn, forwarded it to the tribunal dealing with applications for transfer.

---

[73] See http://www.ndsc.ie/hpsc/NotifiableDiseases/NotificationLegislationandProcess/ (accessed 25 May 2011).

[74] Notifiable Diseases Sub-Committee of the Scientific Advisory Committee, National Disease Surveillance Centre, Feb 2001 http://www.hpsc.ie/hpsc/NotifiableDiseases/ NotificationLegislationandProcess/ (accessed 25 May 2011).

[75] See the classic statement by Avory J: 'There are cases where the desire to preserve the confidential relation which exists between the medical man and his patient must be subordinated to the duty which is cast on every good citizen to assist in the investigation of serious crime.' Birmingham Assizes, 1 December 1914. Reported in (1914) 78 JP 604.

[76] *W v Egdell* [1990] 1 All ER 835.

[3.92] W sought an injunction against the recipients of the report to prevent them from using or disclosing it further and damages for breach of the duty of confidentiality. The Court was of the opinion that the circumstances of the medical examination did import a duty of confidentiality on Dr Egdell so that, for example, he could not have sold the contents of his report to a newspaper. Stephen Brown P referred to Lord Goff's judgment in the *Spycatcher* case[77] where he said that:

> [A]lthough the basis of the law's protection of confidence is that there is a public interest that confidences should be preserved and protected by the law, nevertheless that public interest may be outweighed by some other countervailing public interest which favours disclosure…It is this limiting principle which may require a court to carry out a balancing operation weighing the public interest in maintaining confidence against a countervailing public interest favouring disclosure.

[3.93] He also referred to the General Medical Council's advice on professional conduct and discipline, contained in what is known as the 'Blue Book'. He said that while the rules themselves do not have statutory authority, they were valuable in showing the approach of the General Medical Council to the breadth of the duty of confidence. In the circumstances of the present case Dr Egdell was within the scope of the exception in relation to communicating confidential information to other health professionals involved in W's treatment. Stephen Brown P held that there were also broader considerations involved. Although the doctor had been engaged on behalf of W his duty was not to W alone. Dr Egdell also owed a duty to the public which 'would require him…to place before the proper authorities the result of his examination if, in his opinion, the public interest so required.' Therefore, Dr Egdell was justified in making the disclosure to those responsible for W's treatment and to the Secretary of State, who was responsible for securing public safety. Bingham J Concurred, saying:

> Where a man has committed multiple killings under the disability of serious mental illness, decisions which may lead directly or indirectly to his release from hospital should not be made unless a responsible authority is properly able to make an informed judgement that the risk of repetition is so small as to be acceptable. A consultant psychiatrist who becomes aware, even in the course of a confidential relationship, of information which leads him, in the exercise of what the court considers a sound professional judgement, to fear that such decisions may be made on the basis of inadequate information and with a real risk of consequent danger to the public is entitled to take such steps as are reasonable in all the circumstances to communicate the grounds of his concern to the responsible authorities.

[3.94] This case demonstrates that it would be unrealistic to suggest that confidentiality must be maintained where there is a risk of danger to public safety, and the disclosure is measured in terms of those to whom it is made. Disclosure in such circumstances must be only to those to whom it is necessary to tell and only if the risk is a real rather than fanciful one. In a more recent case, *Stone v South East Strategic Health Authority*[78] it was held that the publication of a report into two homicides carried out by Mr Stone was lawful, even though it included details relating to Mr Stone's medical history. David J held that there was a public interest in knowing the treatment provided, or not, to Mr

---

[77]   *Attorney General v Guardian Newspapers (No 2)* [1988] 3 All ER 545.
[78]   *Stone v South East Strategic Health Authority* [2006] EWHC 1668. See Munro, 'Privacy v Publication: Homicide Inquiries in the Balance' (2007) 15 Med L Rev 109.

Stone in order to correctly identify any failures in such treatment and the appropriate steps to be taken to address any deficiencies.

[3.95] Also in the context of the public interest as a justification for disclosure of medical information, the English case *X v Y*[79] provides further authority. In this case some employees of a health authority supplied information to a newspaper which identified two doctors in general practice as having AIDS. The health authority sought an injunction to prevent publication of the names of the doctors. The question arose as to whether the newspaper was justified in publishing this information in the public interest.

[3.96] It was clearly recognised that in the particular case of AIDS it was of vital importance that those affected by the disease would not be inhibited from coming forward for treatment by fears that their confidentiality might be breached. If treatment was not provided to those suffering from the disease not only would the individual patient suffer but also there would be a consequent increase in the spread of the disease. Therefore, the preservation of confidentiality was in the public interest. The newspaper argued strongly in favour of the public interest in freedom of the press and the necessity to foster debate about the issues involved in AIDS, both of which were accepted as valid by the Court. However, the Court nonetheless held that when balanced against the public interest in confidentiality, the latter was the stronger right generally and particularly in the context of AIDS patients. As for the second point, the Court held that the debate sought by the newspaper in the public interest could take place without identifying the individual doctors involved.

[3.97] In relation to the point made in *Egdell* that disclosure is only justified if made on a need-to-know basis to the appropriate authority, the New Zealand case of *Duncan v Medical Practitioner's Disciplinary Committee*[80] is instructive. In that case a bus driver, Mr Henry, was required under the terms of his licence to furnish a medical certificate on an annual basis for renewal of the licence. In one year he suffered two heart attacks and other problems and underwent a triple bypass operation. A few months later he returned to the doctor in whose care he had been admitted to hospital for an outpatient visit. He asked her to furnish a medical certificate for him to renew his driving licence. The doctor declined, as in her opinion he was not fit to drive passenger vehicles, but referred him to the surgeon who had performed the operation. The latter supplied the necessary certificate. On the night before a scheduled bus trip Mr Henry received a telephone call from a Dr Duncan, who informed him that his licence was invalid and that therefore he could not undertake the trip. The doctor had at that stage already contacted one of the intended passengers and informed her that Mr Henry was not fit to drive and could have a heart attack at any time. Dr Duncan went on to organise a petition to have Mr Henry barred from driving.

[3.98] Mr Henry complained to the Medical Practitioner's Disciplinary Committee on the basis that there had been a breach of patient confidentiality. That committee found Dr Duncan guilty of professional misconduct in informing members of the public (as opposed to the licensing authority) of Mr Henry's medical condition. Dr Duncan

---

[79]   *X v Y* [1988] 2 All ER 648.
[80]   *Duncan v Medical Practitioner's Disciplinary Committee* [1986] 1 NZLR 513.

brought an action for judicial review of the Committee's decision. In rejecting Dr Duncan's action, the High Court described medical confidence in the following terms:

> The platform support of a description of medical confidence is to identify the doctor/patient relationship as a fiduciary one. Without trust it would not function properly so as to allow freedom for the patient to disclose all manner of confidences and secrets in the practical certainty they would repose with the doctor. There rests with a doctor a strong ethical obligation to observe strict confidentiality by holding inviolate the confidences and secrets he receives in the course of his professional ministerings. If he adheres to that ethical principle then the full scope of his ability to administer medical assistance to his patient will develop.

[3.99] The Court also set out the grounds upon which disclosure could be justified,[81] along the lines already discussed above, and was of the view that the Disciplinary Committee correctly confined such disclosure to exceptional circumstances, and even then, to be exercised in a careful way to ensure that the recipient of the information is a responsible authority. If the patient refuses to report his disability and refuses consent for the doctor to do so, it is likely following the *Egdell* line of authority, that protection of the public would justify the doctor in informing the licensing authorities.[82] It has been mooted whether a doctor who knew that an unsafe patient of his (for example, someone suffering from epilepsy) was continuing to drive and who then failed to take any action on the point might be liable in damages for negligence to anyone harmed by his patient on the road.[83] In the US case, *Crosby v Sultz*[84] an action against a doctor who allowed a diabetic patient to drive was rejected on the grounds that injuries inflicted on a person who could not be notified of the driver's condition were not foreseeable.

[3.100] Although there have not been any cases on breach of confidence in this context in Ireland, it is likely that an interpretation similar to that made in *Egdell* would be made by an Irish court, based on the exception given in favour of the disclosure in the public interest by the Medical Council's Guide, and the recognition that constitutional rights to privacy are limited in favour of the common good.

Part Three

HEALTH INFORMATION TECHNOLOGY

[3.101] It is fundamental for a country to have accurate, meaningful and accessible information to assist patients, the public, healthcare professionals, planners and politicians in improving the safety and quality of the healthcare provided at all levels of the system. Consequently, it is impossible to think about improvements in safety and

---

[81] 'There may be occasions when a doctor receives information involving a patient that another's life is immediately endangered and urgent action is required. The doctor must then exercise his private judgement based on the circumstances and if he fairly and honestly believes such a danger exists, he must act unhesitatingly to prevent injury or loss of life.' *Duncan v Medical Practitioner's Disciplinary Committee* [1986] 1 NZLR 513.

[82] See O'Neill, 'Matters of Discretion – The Parameters of Doctor/Patient Confidentiality' (1995) MLJI, 94–104, p 98.

[83] See 'Doctors, Drivers and Confidentiality' (1974) 1 BMJ 399.

[84] *Crosby v Sultz* 592 A 2d 1337 (Pa, 1991).

quality in healthcare, and the development of a high reliability healthcare system, without also considering the health information and health information technology (HIT) developments that are required to enable and sustain these improvements and further the understanding and knowledge of the health system.[85]

[3.102] With increased emphasis in Ireland in recent years on patient safety and the delivery of safe, high-quality care, there has been a recognition that in addition to other quality initiatives, it is necessary to also ensure that high-quality information is at the core of decision-making concerning health at all levels, from individual patient care to the planning and management of services at local and national levels. However, it is also recognised that access to information in health care is frequently limited and fragmented, as patient records in many areas of care are paper-based or, if computerised, are in formats that cannot be shared easily between providers.

[3.103] Health information technology (HIT) is commonly regarded as critical to the transformation of healthcare. However, the sector has lagged behind other sectors in the adoption of technology, and the underpinning foundations of an effective ICT infrastructure in healthcare are often seen as a low priority, particularly when decisions to invest in ICT to improve patient safety are competing with other service delivery priorities. The implications of the delays in building these foundations often result in increasing cost requirements and risks to the implementation of new information systems when the existing legacy systems are out of date and inoperable with new technology.

[3.104] The *eHealth for Safety: Impact of ICT on Patient Safety and Risk Management Report*,[86] undertaken on behalf of the European Commission, identified that in many European countries, one of the most important developments in eHealth in recent years has been the implementation of electronic health records at national, regional and local levels. In the Irish context, the Commission on Patient Safety reported in 2008 that the effective use of quality-based information systems, modern communications technology and the effective use of health information has the potential to make a major contribution to improved patient safety and quality through the following means:

- reducing errors in drug prescribing by flagging allergies and contra-indications and in the dispensing and administration of medications;

- providing more evidence-based care and seamless integrated care across all healthcare sectors and environments because information will accompany the patient through the system and be available where it is needed and when it is needed;

- empowering patients and other healthcare service-users by opening up health related knowledge bases to assist choice thereby facilitating a new information based relationship between patients and healthcare professionals and health agencies;

---

[85] *Building a Culture of Patient Safety* (www.cpsqa.ie/publications/pdf/patientsafety.pdf (accessed 11 July 2011)) Chapter 7, section 7, p 185.

[86] *eHealth for Safety: Impact of ICT on Patient Safety and Risk Management Report* (European Commission 2007), available at:http://ec.europa.eu/information_society/activities/health/ (accessed 25 May 2011).

- improving planning, management and the delivery of health services and health projects through better information management, enhanced business planning and control and greater risk management;

- better research and disease management outcomes which benefit both individuals and society, due to total population studies rather than limited sample ones;

- establishing new data collections and data sets that will help identify and manage the specific health needs of defined population groups across different care settings;

- mitigating public health and other population threats by improving our ability to detect and respond quickly, for example to disease outbreaks;

- extending the scope of healthcare beyond its current boundaries through, for example, telemedicine and home-based care, especially for patients with chronic conditions, which has particular relevance for rural and island communities;

- more accessible continuing education for healthcare professionals through online training models, and;

- enhancing the privacy, confidentiality, integrity and security of patient information through the computerised tracking and auditing of access to patient records.[87]

The importance of health information and HIT to underpin the wider health reform programme, including the safety and quality agenda, has been set out in a number of key national strategy documents in Ireland, including *Quality and Fairness – A Health*

[3.105] *System for You*, the *National Health Information Strategy* and *Primary Care: A New Direction* (2004). The main actions of the National Health Information Strategy (NHIS) were to establish a legislative and information governance framework to underpin health information; to adopt an integrated, national approach to the development and expansion of information sources and systems; to establish processes and structures that ensure the fuller use of health information in policy-making, service planning and care provision and to underpin quality assurance and accountability; to improve access to health information for all stakeholder groups to be promoted through the development of a health portal for the public; to establish health information standards that ensure the quality and comparability of health information and enable sharing; to develop and implement an electronic health record supported by unique identification and information governance, and to exploit the enabling technologies in the collection, processing, analysis and dissemination of health information and its application in the delivery of health services.

[3.106] The NHIS was published in 2004 prior to major structural changes involving the establishment of the HSE and Health Information and Quality Authority (HIQA). This work is currently being advanced by the Health Information Inter-Agency Group, which was established in 2008 and includes representatives from each of the three bodies in question.

---

[87] *Discussion Paper on Proposed Health Information Bill* (Department of Health and Children, 2008).

[3.107] One example of successful health information and HIT developments in the Irish health system in recent years is *Healthlink,* which is a HSE-funded national ICT project.[88] The objective of the *Healthlink* project is to implement a prototype health-care communications network with specific reference to GPs and acute hospital relationships through data exchange. The service is available free of charge to all GPs, although some initial investment is required by hospitals to become involved. Some key initiatives at *Healthlink* revolve around supporting ICT links between primary and secondary care to allow the secure transfer of patient information over the internet to GPs including:

- laboratory and radiology results;
- accident and emergency attendance;
- death notifications;
- discharge notifications and discharge summaries;
- out-patient clinic appointment updates, and;
- waiting list updates as well as allowing GPs to order tests and make referrals.

[3.108] The Patient Safety Commission was of the view that:

> [T]he ability to reliably and rapidly share the right information in the right way and at the right time is an essential component of ensuring safety in the care of patients. Achieving this requires more than simply the development and implementation of electronic health record systems. It requires common standards for information, the ability to correctly match records to the individual patient, appropriate arrangements which govern the handling and use of the information, the necessary legal enablement to share information across institutional boundaries, including the interface between public and private healthcare, and providing healthcare professionals with the business change skills required to adapt to an information-rich environment. Complex healthcare processes, missing information, regular interruptions of ongoing activities, and at times chaotic communications, all contribute to medical errors and adverse events. The development and implementation of effective health information and HIT solutions are essential in order to address these challenges.

It recommended, inter alia, that rapid progress must be made on the development and implementation of a unique identifier for the health system and that there should be a commitment to the full implementation of an appropriate standards-based electronic health record, with appropriate sharing of information within and between providers so that critical information about the care of patients is available at the point of care. This is currently being progressed through the Health Information Bill.

[3.109] The main objectives of the Bill are to support safe patient care and health research, bring consistency and clarity to the rules on the processing of personal health information, strengthen the rules on security of personal health information and provide an enabling legal framework for initiatives such as a Unique Health Identifier, Population Health Registries and an Electronic Health Record. The Bill has a wide scope and will apply to private, public and voluntary health sectors providing primary, secondary and tertiary care. It will apply to all health-care professionals in every service activity, anyone conducting research or genetic testing, management and planning of health services, health insurance and life assurance companies, sports clubs, gyms, etc. Everyone who collects, uses, shares or discloses personal health information will be affected by the Bill.

---

[88] www.healthlink.ie (accessed 27 June 2011).

[3.110] Discussions on unique patient identifiers and electronic health records have been ongoing in this country for some time. The benefits of both ICT initiatives in terms of patient safety have been well documented in relation to ease and speed of access to accurate patient information at the point of care. However, the financial cost and administrative burden of introducing such a system, as well as possible lack of enthusiasm from health-care professionals may impede the successful realisation of some of these objectives. [89]

---

[89]   Greenhalgh et al, 'Adoption and Non-Adoption of a Shared Electronic Summary Record in England: A Mixed-Method Case Study' (2010) BMJ; 340: 3111.

Chapter 4

Assisted Reproduction

INTRODUCTION

[4.01] The World Health Organisation (WHO) defines infertility as the failure to conceive after at least one year of unprotected intercourse. Between 10 per cent and 15 per cent of couples are thought to be infertile and this is predicted to increase in the coming years. Much research has been done, and is continuing, in the area of reproductive medicine to enable the physical causes of childlessness to be treated.

[4.02] Assisted reproduction technologies are a phenomenon of relatively recent origin in the context of medical practice, although the first reported insemination procedures are thought to have been performed in the late 18th century. The Feversham Report in 1960 reported that while there had been isolated cases on insemination in the 19th century, donor insemination was hardly practised at all until the 1920s. Donor insemination appears to have been carried out from the '30s and '40s in the United States, the United Kingdom, Australia, Canada, Belgium, Switzerland, Denmark, Italy, Spain and Israel.[1] The second half of the 20th century witnessed stunning changes in the available methods for building families and yet many societies still struggle to find adequate structural mechanisms to deal with the legal, cultural, religious and ethical dimensions of what this progress may mean to individuals, the concept of family and society.[2] Some of the new reproductive technologies that have been developed, and their application in unusual circumstances, have caused heated debates around the ethical, philosophical and legal implications of such advances in medical science.

[4.03] The 1970s brought a dramatic development in reproductive technologies with the birth of the first baby conceived through in vitro fertilisation (IVF). This development was greeted with mixed reactions ranging from delight on the part of infertile couples and many medical practitioners, to horror from those who saw it as a gross interference with nature. Some criticised the development on resource allocation grounds, arguing that medical funds should be spent instead on reducing overpopulation in the world and enhancing the adoption of children with special needs, or on other pressing medical and social problems.[3] Another argument was that since infertility was not a disease in the ordinary sense of the word, treating infertility through IVF was non-therapeutic and artificial since it did not treat the underlying cause of the infertility.[4] Another attack

---

[1] Cusine, *New Reproductive Techniques, A Legal Perspective* (Dartmouth Publishing, 1990) Ch 3.
[2] Andrews, 'Regulating Reproductive Technologies' J Legal Med (2000) 21:1 at 1.
[3] See for example, Hellegers and McCormick, 'Unanswered Questions on Test Tube Life' (1978)139 America 74.
[4] See Kass, '"Making Babies" Revisited' (1979) 54 Public Interest 32.

criticised the technique as unnatural because it separates the physical aspects of conception from the emotional and spiritual aspects, and procreation thereby becomes a mechanical process.[5] Finally, another major concern was that it represented an unprecedented opportunity for people to apply technology to their own shaping, an inappropriate attempt to 'play God'. Some of these concerns are considered further in Chapter 6.

[4.04] Eventually, IVF gained fairly widespread acceptance, though there remain controversies surrounding the legal repercussions of some associated procedures such as embryo storage, research and destruction, the use of donated gametes and genetic screening of embryos to avoid transmission of disease and for sex and trait selection. The 1980s also brought a further controversial reproductive technology to public attention with the advent of surrogate motherhood in the public domain, which was criticised as facilitating the commodification of children and the exploitation of women. Surrogacy is considered in more detail in Chapter 7.

[4.05] In the 1990s reproductive technologies went one step further and created worldwide concern when the first cloned mammal was created. Controversy erupted surrounding the possibility that this technology could be used to clone a human. Legislation banning cloning was introduced almost immediately in a number of countries. This is considered in Chapter 8.

[4.06] Lee and Morgan argue that we must locate the emergence of reproductive technologies in their modern form at the time that established social boundaries were decomposing. They point to the waning in the nature and stability of the family and marriage, the increasing acceptability of heterosexual partnerships without marriage and homosexual relationships, and the changing roles and expectations of women in the family and community.[6] The development of reproductive technologies enabled humans 'to access their very genesis and it caused a wave which still impacts on our understanding of ourselves'.[7] Assisted reproduction affects and challenges assumptions about family, kinship, parentage and personal identity with the result that:

> Any change in custom or practice in this emotionally charged area has always elicited a response from established custom and law of horrified negation at first; then negation without horror; then slow and gradual curiosity, study, evaluation, and finally a very slow but steady acceptance.[8]

EFFECTS OF INFERTILITY

[4.07] For those who want to have children, infertility can be a devastatingly traumatic experience. They may experience guilt, low self-esteem, depression and isolation, and consequently some couples may suffer marital conflict and sexual dysfunction. Some

---

[5]   Kerby Anderson, *Genetic Engineering* (Zandervan Publishing House, 1982).
[6]   Lee and Morgan, *Human Fertilisation and Embryology, Regulating the Reproductive Revolution* (Blackstone Press Ltd, 2001) at p 2.
[7]   Winston, *The IVF Revolution: The Definitive Guide to Assisted Reproductive Techniques* (Vermillion, 1999) at 137.
[8]   Kleegman and Kaufman, *Infertility in Women, Diagnosis and Treatment* (FA Davis Co, 1966) at 178.

couples feel that they have nothing to contribute to society and that they do not have a common bond with their friends and the wider community. The treatments may involve physical, emotional and financial hardship, which can continue for several years. Assisted reproduction clinics generally recognise the need for appropriate counselling at all stages of diagnosis and treatment of infertility to help the infertile individual to adjust to and mourn their inability to have a child naturally, and to face the possibility of childlessness if treatments are unsuccessful.

[4.08] Many couples who are infertile desire to have a child with a genetic or biological link to them.[9] Their reasons are no different from those of fertile couples: some believe that having a biological child will give them a sense of immortality while others believe their biological child will be an expression of themselves or their relationship. Other couples stress the importance of child-bearing or child-rearing as an important life experience, with some women expressing the view that they would feel less fulfilled without children. Although adoption may fulfil some of these desires, many people want to see their own features and characteristics expressed in their children.

[4.09] Those who have not experienced infertility may take genetic and biological parenthood for granted. Some might question the motives of infertile individuals and couples who seek treatment. Yet why should we question the motives of an infertile couple seeking to have a child any more than we examine the motives of those who do not have a fertility problem? The fertile do not usually find themselves in the position of having to explain their desire to conceive and bear a child. Considering that genetic and biological parenthood is highly valued in our society, it seems unfair to demand that the infertile provide greater justification for their desire to reproduce than we require of the fertile population.[10]

TREATMENTS FOR INFERTILITY

[4.10] The choice of procedure employed in the treatment of infertility depends on the cause of the inability to conceive or carry a pregnancy to term. If the cause of the infertility is due to male factors such as poor-quality sperm or absence of sperm, then the male partner's sperm may be used to attempt a pregnancy using ICSI (Intra-cytoplasmic sperm injection) combined with the techniques of fertilisation of the egg in vitro and embryo transfer. If the male partner is lacking sperm, then donor sperm (DI) may be used to attempt a pregnancy.

[4.11] If the infertility is caused by female factors, IVF could be used. This would be the case, for example, in trying to circumvent blocked fallopian tubes. By this method, in its simplest form, the woman's egg is removed from the ovary and fertilised with the man's sperm in a petri dish in the laboratory. If fertilisation occurs the resulting embryo is then

---

[9]   The cost of infertility treatment is often a major obstacle to couples seeking to have a child. In the UK in July 2011, a charity called 'To Hatch' launched a lottery with online £20 tickets giving a chance of winning £35,000 worth of infertility treatments. This move was branded 'totally unacceptable' by critics and 'entirely inappropriate' by the UK regulatory body, the Human Fertilisation and Embryology Authority. http://to-hatch.co.uk.

[10]   Andrews and Douglass, 'Alternative Reproduction' (1991) Southern California Law Review Vol 65: 623–682, at 628.

transferred back to the woman's uterus and it is hoped that a pregnancy will then ensue. This method of procreation (simple IVF) is not possible where one or both partners cannot provide the gamete (egg/sperm) to create the embryo. Nor will it be successful where the woman's uterus is not receptive to the embryo, as this would prevent implantation of the embryo in the lining of the uterus, thus leading to a miscarriage. In such circumstances as these, a third party may become involved to donate the eggs, sperm, embryo or use of her uterus to enable the couple to have a child. Gamete donation could also be sought by couples who, though not necessarily infertile, carry a genetic abnormality that they do not want to risk passing on to their children.

THE RIGHT TO REPRODUCE

[4.12] One of the issues which has caused debate amongst policy makers in the context of assisted reproduction is the extent to which the State should prohibit or regulate the exercise of reproductive choice by infertile individuals or couples. Western societies generally place a high priority on private choice and decision-making in reproductive matters, for example in relation to the control of fertility and avoidance of pregnancy through the use of contraceptives. However, the right to reproduce – to bear, beget and rear children – has received less explicit recognition.

[4.13] One of the most prominent legal writers in this area is John A Robertson, who argues in favour of the presumptive priority of procreative liberty, which he describes as the freedom to decide whether or not to have children and to control the use of one's reproductive capacity.[11] He says that while this value is widely acknowledged when reproduction occurs naturally, 'it should be equally honoured when reproduction requires technological assistance.'[12] If there is a moral right to reproduce for those who are fertile then, based on principles of equality and non-discrimination, the same right should apply to those who are infertile. Whether one is born with reproductive potential or not, or whether one loses the potential in the course of one's life, if there is a right to reproduce, the same principles should apply to the fulfillment of that reproductive potential.[13] 'Their infertility should no more disqualify them from reproductive

---

[11] Robertson, *Children of Choice, Freedom and the New Reproductive Technologies* (Princeton University Press, 1994) p 16.

[12] Robertson, *Children of Choice, Freedom and the New Reproductive Technologies* (Princeton University Press, 1994) p 16.

[13] There are however those who argue that such a principle, if it were to become enshrined as a matter of Constitutional law, would be too broad and would not necessarily be in the interests of the child. See Bartholet, *Family Bonds: Adoption and the Politics of Parenting* (Houghton Mifflin, 1993) p 229, 'If we really care about children, we should question why there is so much talk of the adult's right to procreate, right to control his or her body, and right to parent, but so little talk of the child's right to anything.' Also Maclean Massie, 'Regulating Choice: A Constitutional Law Response to Professor John A Robertson's Children of Choice' (1995) 52 Wash & Lee L Rev 133. Massie questions Robertson's assertion that procreative liberty could not be interfered with by claims that the welfare of the child would be in jeopardy. While he admits that the welfare of the child is important, he claims that in all instances existence for the child is better than non-existence. Massie cites the example of a HIV-positive applicant for IVF services who, under the presumption of procreative liberty, would be entitled to access to that treatment. (contd.../)

experiences than physical disability should disqualify persons from walking with mechanical assistance.'[14]

[4.14] On this basis Robertson argues that procreative liberty should be given presumptive priority in all conflicts due to its central importance to individual meaning, dignity and identity and that there should be a burden on opponents of any particular technique to show that harmful effects from its use justify limiting procreative choice. This means that in cases of conflict involving such a right it should be presumed to take precedence. Procreation is thus regarded as a Constitutional right in the same category as liberty and freedom of expression which, though of fundamental importance to each individual in society, similarly do not have a guarantee of absolute protection. This is by virtue of the nature of societies as requiring some safeguarding of the common good, which may require imposition of restrictions on those fundamental rights, such as deprivation of liberty for those who are a danger to society. Reproduction may not be thought of by many as being of as vital importance to liberty, but to those who suffer the trauma and devastation of infertility, it is the centre of their lives.

[4.15] The moral right to reproduce is respected because of the centrality of reproduction to personal identity, meaning and dignity. This importance makes the liberty to procreate an important moral right, both for an ethic of individual autonomy and for ethics of community or family that view the purpose of marriage and sexual union as the reproduction and rearing of offspring. Because of this importance, the right to reproduce is widely recognised as a prima facie moral right that cannot be limited except for very good reason.[15]

[4.16] Thus far procreative liberty has been considered as a negative right which means that other persons have a duty not to interfere with the exercise of a procreative choice. It would seem that a more positive interpretation of the right to exercise procreative choices has not found favour with the US judiciary 'despite plausible moral arguments for governmental assistance'.[16] This is more a question of social justice than law. It is also a question relating to the proper allocation of resources in any given society. Many would feel that the world is over-populated already and that money should not be spent

---

[13] (\...contd) Her fundamental constitutional right to reproduce would override any interest the State might have in restricting her right (because the resulting child might be HIV-positive and might not have the care of its parent(s) for very long after its birth) on the basis that it would be better for the child to be born than not to be born. Massie says of this principle that it is too broad and that it forecloses important discussions relating to social values and concerns for the future of our society:

'His glib recitation of the rubric that, from the perspective of any individual, it is invariably better to have been born than not to have been born makes too short a shrift of a concern central to the reproductive technologies debate – namely, what we should do to ensure the physical, mental, and psychological well-being of the children whom we are deliberately bringing into existence.' 145.

[14] Robertson, *Children of Choice, Freedom and the New Reproductive Technologies* (Princeton University Press, 1994) p 32.

[15] Robertson, *Children of Choice, Freedom and the New Reproductive Technologies* (Princeton University Press, 1994) p 30.

[16] Robertson, *Children of Choice, Freedom and the New Reproductive Technologies* (Princeton University Press, 1994) p 23.

on bringing more children into existence when their education and employment prospects may be low. Others may feel that the ethical aspects of these techniques for society sufficiently outweigh any one individual's 'need' to have a child as compared to funding for, say, treatment of those suffering from cancer. Those holding such views would argue that reproduction should not even be viewed as a negative right, let alone a right to oblige the State to provide financial assistance.

[4.17] It is argued that the principle of procreative liberty proposed by Robertson does not take account of differences in class and wealth which, for some, may make the exercise of procreative choices impossible. The distribution of wealth acts as a prime determinant of who exercises reproductive rights, particularly in access to reproductive technology. However, it is argued by proponents of this principle that questions of social justice are not compelling reasons for limiting the procreative choice of those who can pay for treatment: '[Y]et it does not follow that society's failure to assure access to reproductive technologies for all who would benefit justifies denying access to those who have the means to pay.'[17] This reasoning has been criticised on the basis that such an approach cannot become the dominant framework for addressing issues if it fails to consider seriously its costs for women and society.[18]

[4.18] If reproduction is to be given the status of a right then this must be because it is an interest worthy of special protection, exceptions to which must require particular justification. The use of the language of rights emanates from the history of the debate on reproductive freedom, which began in the late 19th century. At that time the feminist movement demanded voluntary motherhood and the right to birth control as validating the procreational right of women to choose whether and when to reproduce. This was more of a right *not* to reproduce or control reproduction rather than a right to reproduce in itself but it did prove to be a starting point in the debate on procreational autonomy.

[4.19] In the early years of the 20th century concern began to be expressed in the United States about the ability of another party such as the State to intervene in an individual's right to bodily integrity and right to self-determination. This was evidenced by the condemnation of the eugenics movement, which had been seen in the case of *Buck* v *Bell* in 1927,[19] in which a statute providing for compulsory sterilisation of inmates in a

---

[17] Robertson, *Children of Choice, Freedom and the New Reproductive Technologies* (Princeton University Press, 1994) p 226.

[18] Sherwin, 'The Ethics of Babymaking' (1995) March-April, Hastings Center Report, 34. Sherwin argues that Robertson's claim that reproduction is central to individual meaning and dignity is overstating its importance in the light of practices of sexual promiscuity and some uncaring and irresponsible parental attitudes amongst other interests pursued by many individuals. 'There is simply no argument offered for assuming that genetic connection (or its absence) is so central to the goals of (all) human beings as to merit its being granted pride of place within the generally libertarian schema Robertson supports.' She also criticises the lack of accounting for the effects of such a policy on women in a world in which women are 'systematically oppressed' and 'coercively controlled' in relation to many aspects of reproduction. She claims that although Robertson does deal with the objections of many feminist writers he does not appreciate the gravity of the harm which concerns those writers and is unwilling to consider the impact of his proposed policy on vulnerable groups, such as disadvantaged women, in society.

[19] *Buck v Bell* 274 US 200.

mental hospital was upheld. Eugenics was seen as a means of protecting society from the burden of having to cope with individuals who were considered to be unfit. It was argued that compulsory reproductive control was essential if societies were not to be swamped by the unfit, the disabled, the poor and the shiftless. This argument found favour by drawing on the fears at that time that America would become 'black' and the belief that certain non-white immigrant races were inferior. These theories, which were incorporated into legislation in most American States, were 'surely the clearest example of the non-recognition at that time of a universal right to reproduce.'[20] Reproduction was seen as a duty for those deemed to be biologically superior, and a capacity which could be controlled by State interference for those who did not fall within that elite group. The oft-cited judgment of Holmes J in *Buck* v *Bell* clearly demonstrates the thinking at that time:

> The right to reproduce was not perceived to be a right and it was more as a privilege. We have seen more than once that the public welfare may call upon the best citizens for their lives. It could be strange if it could not call upon those who already sap the strength of the State for these lesser sacrifices, often not felt to be such by those concerned, in order to avoid our being swamped with incompetence. It is better for all the world if instead of waiting to execute degenerated offspring for crime or let them starve for their imbecility, society can prevent those who are manifestly unfit from continuing their kind. The principle that sustains compulsory vaccination is broad enough to cover cutting the Fallopian tubes. Three generations of imbeciles is enough.[21]

[4.20] At the time it was made, this statement reflected the concerns and fears of American society. If nothing else it demonstrates how issues concerning public morality and policy statements are clear indicators of the era in which they are made and should not automatically be presumed to be applicable to every other time and place in the future. However, in *Skinner v Oklahoma*[22] the United States Supreme Court moved away from the position discussed above and held unconstitutional a statute which provided for the involuntary sterilisation of certain classes of offenders. The case was decided

---

[20] McLean, 'The Right to Reproduce', in Campbell, Goldberg, McLean and Mullen (eds) *Human Rights: From Rhetoric to Reality*, (Blackwell Publishing, 1986) 105. McLean discusses the use of the language of rights in the debate about reproduction and how it has elevated reproduction from a mere capacity that may not be interfered with, to a kind of right which depends on an element of choice. This debate is also linked with the right to self-determination and concern about State intervention in choices made by individuals relating to their reproductive capacities. It is also important to recognise that the use of rights terminology in reproduction does not imply an obligation or duty but rather a choice. McLean examines the social history of the right to reproduce from the right to access to birth-control methods, to compulsory sterilisation cases, to abortion. She also discusses the legal approach to the existence of a right to reproduce, which has been shaped to some extent by the public debates raised by demands for reproductive services. She concludes that although there can be identified the core and scope of a right to reproduce which is deserving of respect, it is unlikely that this guarantees to citizens the ability to insist on provision of services by the State to facilitate the exercise of the right in circumstances such as those relating to the provision in infertility treatments. 'The reality is that the rhetoric of rights has limited practical value in this as in other areas.' p 120.

[21] *Buck v Bell* 274 US 200, 207.

[22] *Skinner v Oklahoma* 316 US 535 (1942).

principally on equal protection grounds but the court also stressed the importance of marriage and procreation as among 'the basic civil rights of man' and noted that 'marriage and procreation are fundamental to the very existence and survival of the race.'[23]

[4.21] On a slightly different point, the substantive content of the right to reproduce was not clarified by the Court in *Skinner v Oklahoma* in terms of eligibility for the right and whether it applied to social as well as biological parenting: that is to say, does the right apply to those who intend to bring up the child after, for example, a surrogate birth? These issues were not directly relevant to the facts of the aforementioned cases, as the concepts of surrogate motherhood and egg donation had not been brought to judicial attention at this stage. The issue turns on whether the right to reproduce is simply a biological right or whether it also encompasses the right to rear a child. In most instances the right to reproduce would include both aspects of parenting but this will not always be the case. It may be, for example, that a woman wishes to conceive and give birth to a child without ever having the intention to raise it, as in surrogacy. Would she have a right to the first while renouncing any duty under the second?

[4.22] *In re Baby M*[24] is an infamous example of a case in which the two aspects – the rights to reproduce and to rear – were seen as separate. The case involved a surrogacy arrangement in which a couple, the Sterns, commissioned a surrogate, Mary Beth Whitehead, to be artificially inseminated with Mr Stern's sperm and carry the child to term, upon which it would be given up to the Sterns. When the child was born, Mrs Whitehead changed her mind and attempted to retain custody of the child. In examining the right to procreation, the New Jersey Supreme Court said:

> The right to procreate very simply is the right to have natural children, whether through sexual intercourse or artificial insemination. It is no more than that ... The custody, care, companionship, and nurturing that follow birth are not parts of the right to procreation.[25]

[4.23] Thus in this case the Court held that the biological and social aspects of parenting are divisible and that the right to procreate necessarily only encompasses the former. Although Mrs Whitehead was given 'parental rights', this did not entitle her to custody of the child, rather she was only given visitation rights. The biological contributors to

---

23   The case is not as strong as it may appear at first instance – the right to reproduce was not seen so much as a right deserving of protection but rather a means of resisting unwarranted State interference in decisions involving procreational choices. It is doubtful therefore that this case could be used to found a case against the State to compel the provision of infertility treatments. Although the issue was not specifically addressed by the Court in *Skinner* it is thought that the applicability of the right to reproduce put forward in that case to treatments such as artificial insemination, in vitro fertilisation and surrogacy is open to question. It was concerned with State interference with a civil right to reproduce naturally, not the application by a citizen to enforce his/her procreational choices against the State so as to insist upon the provision of artificial methods of reproduction.

24   *In re Baby M* 109 NJ 396, 537 A 2d 1227 (1988) This case caused a public outcry in the United States, as it was perceived as a tug-of-love between an impoverished woman who desperately wanted to keep custody of her baby and a cold-hearted professional woman who chose not to take time out of her busy career to become pregnant.

25   *In re Baby M* 109 NJ at 448, 537 A 2d at 1253 (1988).

Baby M's life, Mr Stern and Mrs Whitehead, were both recognised as the child's parents, but due to the circumstances and the conflict involved in the custody dispute, only Mr Stern was given the right to social parenthood, ie the right to rear the child.

[4.24] In the modern era, the classic statement of privacy in the context of reproduction is *Griswold v Connecticut*,[26] which dealt with the constitutionality of statutes prohibiting contraceptive devices. The Court said:

> Would we allow the police to search the sacred precincts of marital bedrooms for tell-tale signs of the use of contraceptives? The very idea is repulsive to the notions of privacy surrounding the marriage relationship. We deal with a right of privacy older than the Bill of Rights. Marriage is a coming together for better or for worse, hopefully enduring, and intimate to the degree of being sacred.

Goldberg J agreed with Marlan J's dissenting judgment in *Poe v Ullman*,[27] in which he said:

> The home derives its pre-eminence as the seat of family life. And the integrity of that life is something so fundamental that it has been found to draw to its protection the principles of more than one explicitly granted constitutional right. Of this whole private realm of family life it is difficult to imagine what is more private or more intimate than a husband and wife's marital relations.

Goldberg J continued: 'The entire fabric of the Constitution and the purposes that clearly underlie its specific guarantees demonstrate that the rights to marital privacy and to marry and raise a family are of similar order and magnitude as the fundamental rights specifically protected'.

[4.25] In the later case of *Eisenstadt v Baird*[28] in which the Court extended the right to obtain contraceptives to unmarried persons, Brennan J said: 'If the right of privacy means anything, it is the right of the individual, married or single, to be free from unwarranted governmental intrusion into matters so fundamentally affecting a person as the decision whether to bear or beget a child'.

[4.26] The importance of these two cases in the context of the recognition of a right to reproduce is that they provide a clear judicial statement that procreational choices made by a husband and wife (or by unmarried individuals) are so personal to them that they must, by necessity, be protected by the constitutional right to privacy. The sacred nature of such private and intimate decisions reached within a relationship must be protected by law.

[4.27] In *Roe v Wade*,[29] which involved a challenge to State criminal abortion legislation, the Court recognised that although not specifically mentioned in the Constitution, a right to privacy does exist and that this extended to activities relating to marriage – procreation, contraception, family relationships and child rearing and education. This case was, and is, of fundamental importance in the context of abortion law, as it sets out the parameters for permissible abortion in the United States, which

---

[26] *Griswold v Connecticut* 381 US 479, 85 S Ct 1678, 14 L Ed 2d 510 (1965).
[27] *Poe v Ullman* 367 US 497, 551–552 (1952).
[28] *Eisenstadt v Baird* 495 US 438 (1972).
[29] *Roe v Wade* 410 US 113 (1973).

remain in force today. It recognised that although the right to privacy came under the umbrella of fundamental rights protected by the Constitution and that it included activities relating to procreation and contraception, it was not an absolute right, as some State regulation of these areas must also be acknowledged. The Court was of the opinion that a State may properly assert important interests in, inter alia, safeguarding health, maintaining medical standards and protecting potential life.

[4.28] These cases[30] indicate that there is a Constitutional right, in a married couple at least, (and probably unmarried individuals) to resist State interference with the restriction of coital reproduction unless the State can show that great harm would result from the reproduction in question. The law has not yet dealt with the legal claim of a married infertile couple to procreate although, as has been stated earlier in connection with the presumption in favour of procreative liberty, the same underlying principles should apply. If this is so, they would have a constitutional right to access to a wide variety of non-coital technologies to have children. This right, by analogy with the right to procreate given to fertile couples, should only be interfered with if justified by the State on the same standard as applicable to fertile couples. 'Noncoital reproduction should thus be constitutionally protected to the same extent as is coital reproduction, with the state having the burden of showing severe harm if the practice is unrestricted'.[31]

[4.29] The only cases that directly consider the extension of married couples' procreational rights into the realm of non-coital reproduction involve surrogate mother contracts. In *Doe v Kelley*[32] a married couple sought a declaratory judgment establishing their right to contract with a woman who was to be inseminated with the husband's sperm, carry the child and then relinquish it to the couple at birth. The Court of Appeal in Michigan found that the fundamental right to bear or beget a child was not infringed by the State law which prohibited the payment of fees for adoption. The Court noted that the couple was not prevented from having the child, but only from using the State process to effectuate the adoption.

[4.30] It has been suggested[33] that the Court should have recognised that by denying the couple access to State adoption procedures, the State was burdening their exercise of the right to bear and beget, and then should have scrutinised the weight of the State interests allegedly served by the prohibition. However, based on the language of rights heretofore

---

[30] In another case dealing with abortion, *Casey v Planned Parenthood* 112 S Ct 2791 (1992), the Court stated:
       Our law affords constitutional protection to personal decisions relating to marriage, procreation, contraception, family relationships, childrearing and education. These matters, involving the most intimate and personal choices a person may make in a lifetime, choices central to personal dignity and autonomy, are central to the liberty protected by the Fourteenth Amendment.

[31] Robertson, *Children of Choice, Freedom and the New Reproductive Technologies* (Princeton University Press, 1994) p 39.

[32] *Doe v Kelley* 106 Mich App 169, 307 NW 2d (1981) The couple had argued that by prohibiting the payment of money in connection with adoption, the legislature was also effectively prohibiting surrogacy, which necessitated recourse to formal adoption procedures. This, the couple argued, denied them their fundamental right to have a child.

[33] Robertson, 'Procreative Liberty and the Control of Conception, Pregnancy, and Childbirth' (1983) 69 Virginia Law Review 428.

used by the courts, this decision is in keeping with the case law in relation to privacy and reproduction. The cases indicate a willingness on the part of the judiciary to resist interference by the State in personal freedoms but a hesitation to enforce positive (perhaps costly) duties against the State. In this case, the State did not choose to interfere directly with the surrogacy arrangement, as this would have been tantamount to an interference with reproductive choices. However, the State did not consider itself bound to change its laws and policies in relation to adoption in order to effectuate such an arrangement.

[4.31] It may be argued that other cases on surrogate mother contracts such as *Syrkowski v Appleyard*[34] and *In re Baby Girl*[35] are also examples of situations in which the courts, by refusing to recognise surrogate contracts, are unduly restricting the right to reproduce without due regard being had for the need for strict scrutiny of the justification for the infringement of the Constitutional rights in question.

[4.32] By contrast, in *Cameron v Board of Education*[36] an Ohio court declared that a woman had a Constitutional privacy right to become pregnant by artificial insemination, while in *JR v Utah*[37] the genetic parents of a child born to a surrogate mother successfully argued that the State's mandated determination of parentage in such cases violated their constitutional right to procreative liberty by forcing them to adopt their own genetic child.

[4.33] Even though the courts have found the right to privacy to exist under the Constitution, they still reserve for the legislature the power to intervene for the protection of compelling State interests, although this term is neither defined nor explained. Legislative obstacles to the use of assisted reproduction may be seen as excessive even though in some cases, such as prohibition of the use of adoption procedures in surrogate motherhood, they may be indirect. It seems that the broad nature of public morality and the common good is something which the courts will use in order to defend an infringement of the right to privacy, and as these justifications may be of particular relevance to assisted reproduction, it is likely that any supposed interference with the individual's right to have a child through such techniques might be exonerated on these grounds.

> At the very least, state interference which effectively prohibits procreation by the initiating parents must be subject to strict scrutiny. The fundamental interest of begetting a child should not be abrogated without proof that preservation of a compelling state interest justifies the denial of the right and can be achieved by no less restrictive means.[38]

[4.34] The two most likely justifications for denying access to reproductive technology are the State's interest in public morals and its interest in health and safety. In relation to the first, the State might argue that the existence of families created with the aid of reproductive technology would disrupt traditional family values by bringing a third party

---

[34]   *Syrkowski v Appleyard* 9 Fam L Rep (BNA) 2260 Mich Ct App, 19 January 1983.

[35]   *In re Baby Girl* 9 Fam L Rep (BNA) 2348 (Ky Cir Ct 8 March 1983).

[36]   *Cameron v Board of Education* 795 F Supp 228, 237.

[37]   *JR v Utah* 261 F Supp 2d 1268.

[38]   Stumpf, 'Redefining Mother: A Legal Matrix For New Reproductive Technologies' 96 Yale LJ 187 (1986) at 199.

into the conception of the child and moving away from natural methods of conception. However, the counter argument might be made that most applications of reproductive technology take place within a stable heterosexual relationship, married or unmarried. The 'family' unit thus remains the same irrespective of the method of conception of the child. This can be seen in relation to families with adopted children – the State could not argue that bringing an adopted child into a family would somehow threaten traditional family values.

[4.35] The second argument which might be made within the context of the 'common good' justification for State interference concerns the State's interest in health and safety – 'If a particular reproductive procedure were found to pose a substantial health risk to either children or parents, the State could probably restrict the technique.'[39] However, to date, the technologies do not appear to have raised any such problems. The children born of these techniques appear to have no greater risk of abnormality than children conceived through normal methods of conception. A major federal study of IVF in the United States found that the health threat to children conceived by those methods is insufficient to justify banning the procedures.[40]

[4.36] In practice the issue of whether assisted reproduction is a procreative liberty is really a question about who society allows to become a parent. Where a genetic tie exists between the parent and the child, the law often associates the recognition and promotion of parental rights as a benefit to the child. In this way, the best interests of the child can be promoted through the law's deference to parental rights. But where this genetic relationship is absent, as where sperm or eggs are donated, the best interests of the child becomes more controversial.[41] This is considered further below.

The right to reproduce in Ireland

[4.37] In Ireland, despite the onus placed on the courts to uphold and vindicate the personal rights of the citizen, the position is not much clearer than the US position outlined above. One of the issues which has arisen in the context of assisted reproduction is the extent to which, if any, the State has an obligation to respect and vindicate a right to reproduce. There are different contexts in which such a right might arise, for example, it might be argued that the State has a positive duty to provide assisted reproduction such as IVF treatments to citizens or to facilitate the use of pre-implantation genetic diagnosis for families who are carriers of serious genetic diseases. There might also be a counter-argument that might support the view that the State has the right to restrict the use of assisted reproduction to married couples in keeping with the primacy accorded to the marital family under the Irish Constitution. The right to reproduce has been recognised by the Supreme Court as falling within the ambit of personal rights protected by Article 40.3.1° of the Constitution 1937, which states:

> The State guarantees in its laws to respect, and, as far as practicable, by its laws to defend and vindicate the personal rights of the citizen.

---

39   'Reproductive Technology and the Procreation Rights of the Unmarried' (1985)98 *Harvard Law Review* 669–685 at p 682.
40   Protection of Human Subjects – HEW Support of Human In Vitro Fertilisation and Embryo Transfer: *Report of the Ethics Advisory Board*, 44 Fed. Reg. 35,033 (June 18, 1979) at 35057.
41   Storrow, 'The Bioethics of Prospective Parenthood: In Pursuit of the Proper Standard for Gatekeeping in Infertility Clinics' (2007) Vol 28 (5) Cardozo Law Review 101, at 117.

[4.38] In *Murray v Ireland*[42] the plaintiffs, a married couple, were convicted of the capital murder of a member of *an Garda Síochána*. They claimed that their Constitutional rights to privacy and procreation were violated by the failure of the State to facilitate conjugal visits. The Court acknowledged the existence of these Constitutional rights but held that they were not absolute and must be qualified by the exigencies of the common good, in this case prison security. In *Roche v Roche*[43] Denham J stated that

> The right to procreate was recognised in *Murray v. Ireland*. There is an equal and opposite right not to procreate. In the circumstances of this case, while the plaintiff and her husband have family rights, the exercise of a right not to procreate by the husband is a proportionate interference in all the circumstances of the case to the right of the plaintiff to procreate[44].

[4.39] It is not clear from this statement whether the right to reproduce as it exists under the Constitution is a negative or a positive right. The use of the terms 'positive' and 'negative' in relation to rights is seen particularly in the context of international human rights law where contemporary liberal theory places a large emphasis on the equality of the individual, respect for the autonomy of the individual and the protection of minorities against discrimination. The 'rights' language which is found in constitutions, bills of rights, legislation and various political writing is conscious of and addresses the need to protect the individual against the State. The rights which are given to the individual citizen limit the power of the State, for example the right to private property and the right to equality guard against undue interference by the State and unlawful discrimination. Some of these rights are 'negative' in the sense of: 'the hands-off or non-interference rights (don't touch), or the right to be interfered with (as by arrest, imprisonment) only pursuant to stated processes.'[45] This idea of negative rights and negative freedom as the absence of constraints helped in the development of the liberalist school of thought in relation to limited government. On the other hand, the term 'positive rights' may be described as:

> [E]ntitlements of individuals that the state not simply respect the 'private' sphere of inviolability of the individual (the negative rights), but also 'act' in particular ways to benefit the individual, perhaps by providing education or health care. In this sense, the 'positive rights' of individuals such as the right to education or health care impose duties on the state to provide the necessary institutions or resources.[46]

The relevance of the distinction between negative and positive rights to reproduce may be on the one hand resisting interference by the State in personal choices, and on the other hand obliging the State to provide the necessary clinics and health-care assistance to enable a couple to reproduce by means of IVF or other reproductive technologies.

[4.40] The imposition of positive duties on the State has not been a strong feature of the case law on constitutional rights to date. Although there have been cases in which the State has been attacked for its failure to provide educational services or housing the

---

[42]   *Murray v Ireland* [1991] 1 ILRM 465.
[43]   *Roche v Roche* [2009] IESC 82.
[44]   *Roche v Roche* [2009] IESC 82, para 39 per Denham J.
[45]   Steiner and Alston, *International Human Rights in Context* (OUP, 1996) p 189.
[46]   Steiner and Alston, *International Human Rights in Context* (OUP, 1996).

decisions of the courts have unfortunately not placed much emphasis on the imposition of positive obligations on the State in this regard.

A case which may be seen as imposing a positive obligation on the State in the context of personal rights is *O'Donoghue v the Minister for Health*.[47] This case involved an application for judicial review to oblige the State to provide for free primary education for the Applicant, an eight-year-old boy suffering from severe mental disability. In a lengthy judgment exploring the issue of education for people with disabilities in Ireland, O'Hanlon J concluded that 'there is a constitutional obligation imposed on the State by the provisions of Article 42.4 of the Constitution to provide for free elementary education of all children…'[48] This principle was subsequently affirmed by the Supreme Court. This case perhaps may not be as strong as it may appear, as it is grounded on the particular obligation imposed on the State by Art 42 to provide free primary education for children and the financial outlay that this entails. *Sinnott v the Minister for Education*[49] confirmed that the State's obligation exists only until the individual reaches 18 years of age.

Other cases concerning the possibility of the imposition of positive duties on the State have declined this opportunity by stating that it was not for the courts to fulfil such a role in adjudicating the fairness or otherwise of the administration of public resources. For example, in *O'Reilly and Others v Limerick Corporation, Minister for the Environment, Minister for Health, Minister for Education, Ireland and the Attorney General*,[50] members of the traveller community claimed that they had a constitutional right to be provided by the State with certain physical resources and services. They claimed that they had a right under the Constitution to basic material conditions to foster their dignity and freedom as human persons and the authority of the family within which each of them lived. Costello J stated that usually a claim in relation to unspecified rights under the Constitution relates to a wrongful interference in some activity which the plaintiff seeks to protect. In this case the claim was entirely different, as the plaintiffs asserted that the State had a duty to provide them with the resources and services they lacked. Although Costello J did not use the floodgates argument as the mainstay of his decision, he certainly adverted to it in pointing to the homeless and other deprived people in the community to which the State may similarly owe obligations if the plaintiffs' case succeeded. The learned judge instead concluded that issues relating to the distribution of national resources did not fall within the administration of justice function given to the courts by the Constitution. If it adopted the suggested supervisory role, the court would have to make an assessment of the validity of the many competing claims on those resources, the correct priority to be given to them and the financial implications of the plaintiffs' claim. This would involve adjudication on the fairness of the manner in which the State administered public resources. He continued:

> Apart from the fact that members of the judiciary have no special qualification to undertake such a function, the manner in which justice is administered in the courts, that is on a case

---

[47]   *O'Donoghue v the Minister for Health* [1996] 2 IR 20.
[48]   *O'Donoghue v the Minister for Health* [1996] 2 IR 20 at 94.
[49]   *Sinnott v the Minister for Education* [2001] IESC 39.
[50]   *O'Reilly and Others v Limerick Corporation, Minister for the Environment, Minister for Health, Minister for Education, Ireland and the Attorney General* [1989] ILRM 181.

by case basis, make them a wholly inappropriate institution for the fulfilment of the suggested role. I cannot construe the Constitution as conferring it on them.[51]

[4.41] Although the right to privacy may include reproduction within the realms of Constitutional protection, this has most commonly been seen in relation to the availability of contraceptives, which is the enforcement of a negative right against State interference with reproductive choices. As such, it does not easily extend to the enforcement of a positive right to insist upon the State making provision for assisted reproduction. Marital privacy was the first area to be significantly considered as part of the right to privacy. In *McGee v Attorney General*,[52] which considered the constitutionality of a statutory provision which effectively deprived the plaintiff, a married woman, of access to contraceptives, the Court recognised the necessity of the marital relationship having the protection of a right to privacy.[53] Walsh J said:

> The sexual life of a husband and wife is of necessity and by its nature, an area of particular privacy. If the husband and wife decide to limit their family, or to avoid having children, by use of contraceptives, it is a matter peculiarly within the joint decision of the husband and wife and one into which the State cannot intrude unless its intrusion can be justified by the exigencies of the common good.

[4.42] This is familiar language when one looks at the jurisprudence from the United States and reports from bodies such as the Wolfenden Committee in the UK, which felt that there must remain 'a realm of private morality which in brief and crude terms is not

---

[51] In relation to the non-recognition generally of economic and socio-economic rights under the Constitution see Murphy, 'Economic Inequality and the Constitution' in Murphy and Twomey (eds) *Ireland's Evolving Constitution 1937–1997*, (Hart Publishing, 1998) 163–181. Murphy refers to various academic arguments as to why such rights have not been recognised, such as Hogan's three reasons, namely: class bias on the part of the judiciary; the reluctance to introduce directive principles of social policy into judicial review by the back door; and the feeling that if courts were to recognise such rights they would be acting as little more than a third House of the Oireachtas. See Hogan, 'Unenumerated Personal Rights: *Ryan's* Case Re-Evaluated' (1990–1992) 25–27 Irish Jurist 95 at 108. For a criticism of these arguments, see Humphreys, 'Interpreting Natural Rights' (1993–95) 28–30 Irish Jurist 221 at 230.

[52] *McGee v Attorney General* [1974] IR 284.

[53] During the 1970s there was an apparent tension between Church leaders and politicians. The Church was anxious that the liberal moral trends they perceived in other jurisdictions would not take hold in Ireland through rights decisions in the courts. Contraception proved to be a contentious issue at this time with bills being raised by backbenchers to relax the prohibition on contraceptives, Church leaders opposed to any such move and party leaders not wanting to hold the 'hot potato'. After *McGee v Attorney General* in 1974, a number of measures were attempted to provide for access to contraceptives, some restrictive and unworkable measures which tried to yield a little to pressure from the Church. Eventually in 1985 the Family Planning (Amendment) Act was passed, which was seen as 'the triumph of pluralist politicians over the Church. Although the hostility of the Church was made very clear, the official stance of the Hierarchy conformed to the 1973 principles: it was for the clergy to give guidance to Catholics and for the politicians to decide. However, some bishops and many other clergy did not adhere to that line, and by adopting a harder and more traditional stance heightened the impression of a confrontation between the Church and the state which the Church lost.' Chubb, *The Politics of the Irish Constitution* (Dublin: Institute of Public Administration, 1991) 53.

the law's business.'[54] Walsh J went on to explain that public morality does not of itself justify State intervention, as this would be seeking to impose on a married couple a code of private morality which they did not desire. However, unlike the other judges in the Supreme Court, Walsh J did not base the right to marital privacy on Art 40.3.1°, but on Art 41 of the Constitution, which seeks to protect the family. Since it is 'a matter exclusively for the husband and wife to decide how many children they wish to have' and since the State cannot dictate that they shall have a certain number of children, 'the husband and wife had a correlative right to have no children.'[55] While the Court agreed that, wherever the right was based, the intimacy of married life was possibly the most fundamental situation in which the right to privacy necessarily operated, Budd J took the view that if the State is entitled to prevent people from determining the number of children they shall have, then the Constitutional guarantees are virtually meaningless. 'The State guarantees as far as practicable by its laws to vindicate the personal rights of the citizen. What more important personal right could there be in a citizen than the right to determine in marriage his attitude and resolve his mode of life concerning the procreation of children?'[56]

[4.43] Henchy J was of the opinion that the violation by the State of Mrs McGee's right to privacy lay in frustrating and making criminal any efforts by her to effectuate a decision taken, on medical advice, by herself and her husband, to use contraceptives so as to ensure her health and the security of her family. Thus, in this decision, the Supreme Court recognised that a right to privacy was Constitutionally guaranteed, whether through Art 40.3.1° or Art 41. This applied to the broad area of personal marital relations and control of reproduction within the marital relationship. In this sense then it might be used to establish a right of a married couple to make positive decisions regarding the medical treatment of their infertility. That is to say, if a particular infertility treatment were available in Ireland, such as IVF using donated gametes, a married couple would have a Constitutional right of access to this treatment, (within the limits set down by the medical profession regarding medical indications and so on), without interference from the State.

[4.44] Despite a judgment in favour of the existence of the right to privacy, the Court in *McGee* agreed that there remained the possibility of State intervention in the interests of the common good, although no such State interest existed in the circumstances of this particular case. Such reliance on the 'common good' might enable the State to resist attempts to make public funding available, for example, for egg donation services for post-menopausal women, or for surrogacy arrangements. Unfortunately, very little useful definition of this expression 'the common good' may be taken from the judgment, as the judges tended to refrain from any general discussion of the law and morality question. Walsh J did draw a distinction between public and private morality, although he did not clarify how public morality was to ascertained: 'It is undoubtedly true that among those persons who are subject to a particular moral code no one has a right to be in breach of that moral code. But when this is a code governing private

---

54 *Report of the Committee on Homosexual Offences and Prostitution*, (1957) London, Cmnd 247.
55 *McGee v Attorney General* [1974] IR 284 at 311.
56 *McGee v Attorney General* [1974] IR 284 at 322.

morality and where the breach of it is not one which injures the common good then it is not the State's business to intervene'.[57]

[4.45] In *Norris v Attorney General*,[58] which challenged the Constitutionality of laws penalising homosexual acts between males, the plaintiff asserted that the State had no business in the area of private morality and for the State to legislate in relation to private sexual conduct between consenting adults was, as O'Higgins CJ put it, 'to shatter that area of privacy which the dignity and liberty of human persons require to be kept apart as the haven for each citizen.' The Court accepted, however, that, as a general proposition concerning the purpose of law and with particular reference to the Constitutional right to privacy, the State must have an interest in the general moral well-being of society and must be entitled to discourage conduct which is contrary to the values of society. O'Higgins CJ was of the view that there are certain acts which may take place in private which, although they do not harm any other individual, must be condemned by the State on the basis that they are morally wrong. He gave the examples of abortion, incest, suicide attempts, suicide pacts, euthanasia or mercy killing, though saying nothing directly relevant to the present context. A right of privacy, the Court held, can never be absolute. McCarthy J (dissenting), said 'the right to privacy is not in issue – it is the extent of that right – the extent of the right to be let alone.' He referred to the compelling State interest which is necessary in order to justify intrusion into areas within the realm of the right and stated that a 'very great burden lies upon those who would question such personal rights'. The examples of justifiable interference which he gave included the protection of minors or incapacitated persons, and public decency. If none of these obvious justifications exist, then he was of the view that State interference would be of a most grievous kind. Henchy J (also dissenting) recognised that there were many aspects to the right to privacy which are as yet judicially undeveloped and that they all seemed to fall 'within a secluded area of activity or non-activity, which may be claimed as necessary for the expression of an individual personality, for purposes not always necessarily moral or commendable, but meriting recognition in circumstances which do not endanger considerations such as State security, public order or morality, or other essential components of the common good'.

[4.46] He therefore recognised that there are activities which may be carried out in private, and which do not contravene policy considerations of the State, which are neither moral nor commendable, but yet should not be condemned by law. The extent of the justification of State policy, particularly in the area of morality, was unfortunately not elaborated on here.

[4.47] On the basis of the consideration of the right to privacy by the Irish Courts[59] it can be said that the development of the right has taken place along similar lines to that taken

---

[57]   *McGee v Attorney General* [1974] IR 284 at 313.
[58]   *Norris v Attorney General* [1984] IR 36.
[59]   See also *Kennedy & Arnold v Ireland* [1987] IR 587, which involved the interception of telephone conversations of two journalists by order of the Minister for Justice. Hamilton P recognised the general right of privacy and held that the plaintiffs' Constitutional rights had been violated. He also held that the right to privacy was not absolute and was open to exceptions such as the common good, public order and morality, and the Constitutional rights of others. (contd.../)

in the United States.[60] The right is seen as worthy of Constitutional protection but not in any absolute form. It is seen as necessarily subject to State interference in the interests of the common good, which is itself a general and undefined term. As Walsh J stated in an academic article:[61]

> Various justifications are offered for invasions of privacy such as the public interest and these are to some extent recognised by the European Convention of Human Rights in Art.8 ... The State's rights as such, can only be upheld if they can be equated with the common good and again a delicate balance has to be preserved between the power of the Oireachtas to decide what is in the common good and the powers of the judge to so decide ... What is, I think, universally acceptable is that the requirements of the public good must depend upon the needs and conditions which exist at any given moment.

[4.48] The case might be made that the right to procreate, which it is thought would come within the realms of the right to privacy, would also be similarly susceptible to State interference along those principles.[62] The phrase 'common good' seems to import notions of public morality, social justice and perhaps good government. It has been said that social justice cannot be considered to be the old standard of 'the greatest good of the greatest number, for, at the present day, it may be considered proper that the claim of a minority be made paramount on some topic.'[63] It is thought that the 'common good' or 'social justice' cannot be regarded as being of a constant quality, as what is good for citizens of one state may not be considered good in another state.

> In a court of law it seems to me to be a nebulous phrase, involving no question of law for the courts, but questions of ethics, morals, economics, and sociology, which are, in my opinion, beyond the determination of a court of law, but which may be, in their various aspects, within the consideration of the Oireachtas, as representing the people, when framing the law.[64]

59 (\...contd) In *Attorney-General (Society for the Protection of the Unborn Child) v Open-Door Counselling Ltd* [1987] ILRM 477, Hamilton P held that the right to privacy could not be invoked to interfere with such a fundamental right as the right to life of the unborn. Although this was because of the express protection of the unborn under Art 40.3.3°, the case broadly demonstrates again the limited development and use of the right to privacy in Ireland when faced with competing claims.

60 Indeed, this similarity has given some commentators cause for concern, as it was thought that the development of individual privacy from the marital privacy protection in *McGee* could provide the opportunity to derive a right to abortion in Ireland, in the same way as in *Roe v Wade*. See Binchy, 'Ethical Issues in Reproductive Medicine: A Legal Perspective' in Reidy (ed), *Ethical Issues in Reproductive Medicine* (Gill & McMillan, 1982) 95–117, at 104.

61 Walsh, 'The Judicial Power and the Protection of the Right to Privacy' (1977) Dublin University Law Journal 3.

62 So, in *Murray v Ireland* [1991] 1 ILRM 465, the right to reproduce was seen as necessarily subject to the exigencies of the provision of State security, in the context of a refusal to grant conjugal rights to prisoners in order that they might conceive a child. This was a case in which the Court arguably gave insufficient weight to the couple's reproductive rights and too much weight to the State's claims of administrative inconvenience but, it is submitted that due to the special circumstances of the case, that is to say, the special setting of a prison, it is not a strong precedent for limiting procreative freedom in non-prison settings.

63 *Pigs Marketing Board v Donnelly (Dublin) Ltd* [1939] IR 413, per Hanna J.

64 *Pigs Marketing Board v Donnelly (Dublin) Ltd* [1939] IR 413, per Hanna J.

[4.49] The promotion of the common good is specifically referred to in the Preamble to the Constitution as one of its objectives. The Preamble has been adverted to in a number of cases but no case has been decided solely on the strength of it. For example, it has been said that 'the justice or otherwise of any legislative interference with the right ... [in regard to guarantees for property]... has to be considered in relation, *inter alia*, to the proclaimed objects with which the Constitution was enacted, including the promotion of the common good.'[65] Although the precise meaning of this phrase has not been elaborated upon, the courts have taken the view that judicial activism may be sanctioned by reference to the changing values to be accorded to the common good. In *McGee*, Walsh J said:

> According to the Preamble, the people gave themselves the Constitution to promote the common good with due observance of prudence, justice and charity so that the dignity and freedom of the individual might be assured. The judges must, therefore, as best they can from their training and their experience interpret these rights in accordance with their ideas of prudence, justice and charity. It is but natural that from time to time the prevailing ideas of these virtues may be conditioned by the passage of time, no interpretation of the Constitution is intended to be final for all time.[66]

The 'exigencies of the common good' has also been referred to in the context of the right to private property, which is specifically protected by the Constitution. The courts have taken the view that despite the existence of the right as a natural right which is antecedent to all positive law, the State has the right to regulate the exercise of such rights in accordance with the common good.

[4.50] To return to privacy and procreation rights under the Constitution – these rights, if they exist at all, are not absolute and would seem to be subject to the vagaries of the courts' interpretation of social justice. The courts have not expressed clearly what is intended by the use of the phrase 'the common good' and seem to use it as an all-encompassing formula for principles of public morality and social justice. But, in the particular context of procreational choices, it is difficult to see how the 'common good' could be used in any way other than imposing a set of *moral* principles on a private individual or couple without having to demonstrate harm to any specified person/group of persons. The State should have to show a pressing and substantial concern which must be of such sufficient importance to justify overriding a Constitutional right, and the infringement on the right ought to be proportionate to the concern to be safeguarded.[67] There are very few circumstances in which such a substantial concern

---

[65] *Attorney General v Southern Industrial Trust* [1960] 94 ILTR 161 per Davitt P.

[66] *McGee v Attorney General* [1974] IR 284. This approach was endorsed by O'Higgins CJ in *The State (Healy) v Donoghue* [1976] IR 325; and by McWilliam J in the High Court in *Norris v Attorney General* [1984] IR 36. In the latter case McWilliam J considered whether 'the Legislature could now, under current social conditions, having regard to the prevailing ideas and concepts of morality and the current knowledge of matters affecting public health, reasonably come to the conclusion that the homosexual acts declared unlawful by the statutes under challenge were such as ought to be prohibited for the attainment of true social order as mentioned in the Preamble to the Constitution'.

[67] This is similar to the proportionality requirement in the Canadian Charter of Rights and Freedoms as interpreted in *R v Edwards Books and Art Ltd* (1986) 35 DLR (4th) 1 per Dickson CJ.

might be demonstrated to be sufficiently weighty so as to justify State intervention here. It might occur, for example, in a situation in which the conception of the child was sought for some criminal purpose such as child prostitution or if the child's conception was to serve another purpose such as to harvest bone marrow to save the life of an existing sibling. These are issues in which the State might be justified in having an interest, for the *direct* safety and protection of the child to be conceived. Any other vague societal interests claimed by the State under the auspices of the 'common good' would require detailed and substantial proof of harm directly caused by the reproductive technology proposed.

[4.51] In conclusion, therefore, the use of the familiar expression 'common good' in any justification of State interference with procreational choices or indeed any defence of the failure of the State to respect or promote the right to procreate must be open to question, due to the fundamental importance of private procreational choices and the unsatisfactorily vague notions of what constitutes protection of the common good.

An international right to reproduce

[4.52] In international law, the existence of negative and positive rights may also be seen in the language and jurisprudence of human rights conventions. Positive obligations are generally associated with economic, social and cultural rights and commonly have financial obligations. An argument exists, however, which holds that these economic, social and cultural rights do not have a legally binding character and are thus legally inferior.[68] The thrust of this argument is that the term 'right' ought to be reserved for rights which may be enforced in a court of law or in a comparable manner and also that social rights are not directed at government action that can be described in terms of law: 'The creation of social and economic conditions under which social rights can be enjoyed is – as yet – not describable in terms of law. In order to be a legal right, a right must be legally definable; only then can it be legally enforced, only then can it be said to be justiciable'.[69] In the absence of any effective enforcement mechanism in international law in respect of economic, social and cultural rights, these are not legal rights at all. However, it may be argued that the realities of international law are not taken into account in this false comparison between national and international law. There are wide-ranging differences between national communities and the international community based on the vertical structure and central organisation of the one and the horizontal structure and decentralised organisation of the other. National legal systems are usually equipped with an institutionalised law-making process, an executive branch of government and law-enforcement mechanism. In the international context these functions are largely performed in a non-institutionalised way by the states themselves.

[4.53] It is the exception rather than the rule that norms of international law can be enforced through courts of law, or in a comparable manner. However, this is generally considered an insufficient reason to deny to such norms the status of binding rules of

---

68 Vierdag, 'The Legal Nature of the Rights Granted by the International Covenant on Economic, Social and Cultural Rights.' (1978) 9 Netherlands Yearbook of International Law 69–105.

69 Vierdag, 'The Legal Nature of the Rights Granted by the International Covenant on Economic, Social and Cultural Rights.' (1978) 9 Netherlands Yearbook of International Law 69–105, at 93.

international law. Similarly, it does not mean that there is no way to enforce, or rather to implement, such rules of international law. All that it implies is that rules of international law usually have to be enforced or implemented through methods different from those available in municipal legal systems. So even if the availability of enforcement through courts of law constitutes a pre-condition for according a legally binding status to a norm in national legal systems, this does not justify the same conclusion with respect to international law.[70]

[4.54] Article 16(3) of the Universal Declaration of Human Rights in 1948 provides that the family is 'the natural and fundamental group unit of society' and is therefore entitled to State protection. Article 12 of the European Convention on Human Rights (ECHR) provides that men and women have the right to marry and to found a family according to the national laws governing the exercise of that right. While the ideas behind these provisions are laudable, the scope of the provisions themselves is uncertain. It is thought that the limitations intended by the expression used in the Convention must relate to legitimate purposes such as to prevent incest or bigamy and do not sanction a complete and arbitrary deprivation of rights by national laws. If this were not the case the Convention would be meaningless, as it would entitle national legislatures to ignore its provisions without legitimate justification.[71]

[4.55] The wording of the provision appears to link marriage and the right to found a family, which implies that unmarried couples or individuals may not avail of the right. In the *Van Oosterwijck* case[72] the complainant argued that the Belgian authorities were violating his right to marry and found a family by not permitting him to change his birth certificate to reflect the fact that he had undergone a sex change operation. The Commission agreed with this contention but the Court did not consider this point, holding that there had been a failure to exhaust domestic remedies. The Commission said that the right to found a family was attached indissolubly to the right to marry in art 12. The Commission gave the view that a marriage could be valid despite the lack of an intention or capacity to procreate, as the latter is not a prerequisite for marriage but it did not mention the other side of the argument, that is to say whether marriage was a prerequisite for procreation: 'Although marriage and the family are in fact associated in the Convention and in domestic legal systems, there is nothing to support the conclusion that the capacity to procreate is an essential condition of marriage or even that procreation is an essential purpose of marriage'.[73]

[4.56] This inextricable link between the two rights contained in art 12 was also adverted to in another case concerning the right to adopt,[74] where the Commission said 'the provision [art 12] does not guarantee the right to have children born out of wedlock. Article 12, in fact, foresees the right to marry and to found a family as one simple right.'

---

[70] Van Hoof, 'The Legal Nature of Economic, Social and Cultural Rights: A Rebuttal of Some Traditional Views' in Alston and Tomasevski (eds) *The Right to Food*, 97–110, at 101.

[71] Liu, *Artificial Reproduction and Reproductive Rights* (Dartmouth Publishing Ltd, 1991) at 27–31, and Harris, O'Boyle, Warbrick, *Law of the European Convention on Human Rights* (Butterworths, 1995) 435.

[72] Report of 1 March 1979, B 36 (1983) 28–29.

[73] Report of 1 March 1979, B 36 (1983) 28–29 at 28.

[74] Dec Adm Com Ap 6482/74, 10 July 1975, D and R7, at 55 (77).

It further said that, even if it may be assumed that the right to found a family may be considered irrespective of marriage, art 13 recognises that the existence of a couple is fundamental to the exercise of this right. Therefore, it is doubtful whether a single individual right to reproduce can be found under art 12 of the Convention.[75]

[4.57] As changes continue to take place within society and its perception of the institution of marriage and family, this link between marriage and procreation may be abolished, however. This may result in demands for reproductive services as rights of the individual rather than the couple. Although the right to reproduce using assisted conception has yet to be recognised in international law, as demands continue to be made in this area the pressure on states to provide such services, (probably initially at least without the provision of financial assistance) will increase. 'Technological developments have, however, created demands that a right to parenthood be recognised: the availability of effective treatments of infertility, embryo transfer, and surrogate motherhood, have created a host of demands for entitlements concerning procreation'.[76]

[4.58] Even within the marital relationship, there is no right to adopt or found a family by alternative means. The possibility of artificial reproductive techniques being used to create a family was certainly not in the minds of those who drafted the Convention. However, the Commission would probably take the view that as societal attitudes change and reproductive technologies become more widely available, the substance of an existing relationship should be looked at and its effective enjoyment provided for, rather than confining the protection of 'family life' to formal relationships. This would expand the obligation to perhaps an obligation to protect from discrimination on the basis of marital status or sexual orientation.

> It does not seem likely that the Convention imposes any limits on what choices a state may make and it is probably premature to decide that the Convention imposes a[n]… obligation on a state to legislate to allow any particular technique. However, as the acceptability of those measures which are closest to natural reproduction (e.g. IVF) increases, states may find themselves having an increasingly heavy burden to explain why married persons may not avail themselves of them. It is much less likely that a positive duty will be placed on the state to provide the appropriate treatment.[77]

[4.59] Even if a positive right to respect for family life (and within this, the right to procreate) were to be established under the Convention, it is possible that individual states would be given a wide 'margin of appreciation' to decide what 'respect' required in the particular circumstances of an individual applicant.[78] What this means in effect is that the State has to have regard 'to the fair balance that has to be struck between the general interest of the community and the interests of the individual, the search for

---

[75]   Liu, *Artificial Reproduction and Reproductive Rights* (Dartmouth Publishing Ltd, 1991) at 30.

[76]   Tomasevski, 'Women', in Eide, Krause and Rosas (eds) *Economic, Social and Cultural Rights* (Martinus Nijhoff Publishers, Dordrecht, 1995) 273–288, at 281.

[77]   Harris, O'Boyle, Warbrick, *Law of the European Convention on Human Rights* (Butterworths, 1995), at 441.

[78]   In *Cabales and Balkandali v UK*, A 94 para 67 [1985], the Court said: '…especially as far as those positive obligations are concerned, the notion of 'respect' is not clear-cut: having regard to the diversity of practices followed and the situations obtaining in the Contracting states, the notion's requirements will vary considerably from case to case.'

which balance is inherent in the whole Convention.'[79] In balancing the interests of an infertile couple in receiving treatment, eg IVF and embryo freezing, against the general interest of the community in protecting its traditional respect for and Constitutional protection of the unborn child, it may well be that, even if the couple was seen by the Commission as having a right to financial assistance from the State in pursuance of a family, the State may come within this margin of appreciation and avoid obligation.

[4.60] Eijkholt argues that examination of the recent case law of the European Court of Human Rights suggests that art 12 is no longer the vehicle within which to assert the sorts of claims that tend to be made under arguments for a right to procreate. Claims related to assisted reproduction, and access thereto, have been submitted under art 8. References to art 12 have been ignored or, possibly, avoided, and art 12 hardly plays any role in cases concerning reproduction. Hence, it seems that art 12 no longer offers the legal basis for a right to procreate, if it ever did.[80]

[4.61] She states that the article's restrictive interpretation is, 'first, a result of its wording.' Eijkholt continues:

> Article 12 refers to 'men and women of a marriageable age'. This wording has constrained the Court in its application to, for example, single individuals. Furthermore, the wording obviously refers to heterosexual couples and seems not necessarily to encompass reproductive desires expressed by homosexual couples. Second, Article 12 is limited by a narrow understanding of the notion of 'family'. It extends only fully to cases that concern natural and genetic children, and, by analogy, to 'acts' by which they are reproduced. Where there is no genetic bond, for example, in issues about non-genetically related children or extra-marital children, protection lies in Article 8 instead. Third, the Article seems to have been applied in a conservative way. The Court remains hesitant to go outside the prescribed application.

[4.62] Two recent cases in particular illustrate the approach taken by the Court in recent years – *SH and others v Austria*[81] and *Sijakova v the Former Yugoslav Republic of Macedonia*,[82] in which the Court explicitly held that 'Article 12 of the Convention does not guarantee a right to procreation'. In *S.H and others v Austria,* two couples appealed against the Austrian Artificial Procreation Act. The Act excluded them from fertility treatment, as it did not allow the use of donor gametes. One couple required donor sperm for IVF treatment because the husband was infertile. The other couple required implantation of an embryo created with a donor ovum, since the woman did not produce any ova herself. While the two couples and the Government both relied, to a significant extent, on arguments under art 12, the Court dismissed these arguments. The Court declared that the interpretation of art 12 was incompatible with the *ratione materiae* of the provisions in the Convention. It held that art 12 would not guarantee 'a right to procreation', and relied on the second case, *Sijakova.*

---

[79]   *Cossey v UK*, A 184 para 37 [1990].
[80]   Eijkholt, 'The Right to Found a Family as a Stillborn Right to Procreate?' (2010) Med L Rev 18(2), 127–151.
[81]   *S.H. and others v Austria* (Application No 57813/00, 15 November 2007).
[82]   *Sijakova and Others v The Former Yugoslav Republic* (Application No 67914/01, 6 March 2003).

[4.63] In the *Sijakova* case, a group of parents had applied to the Court on the basis that their right to found a family was violated. Their children had taken holy orders and a vow of celibacy in the Macedonian Orthodox Church, and as a result, the applicants could 'not found a larger family and have grandchildren'. The group of parents argued that the Church's rules were unconstitutional and against their Convention rights. Yet, while declaring the case inadmissible, the Court stated that 'the right to have grandchildren ...', and '...the right to procreation is not covered by Article 12 or any other Article of the Convention'. Hence, despite the fact that procreation was central to both cases, the Court did not take any steps to protect the claims to have a child under art 12, and dismissed any claim to a right to procreate under art 12. These judgments reject any argument that the core of art 12, the right to found a family, could be phrased as a right to procreate.[83]

[4.64] By contrast, article 8 may provide a more fruitful means to establishing a right to procreate, despite the ambiguous nature of the obligation to 'respect' which is contained in the wording of the article. In the case of *Natalie Evans v UK* the judgment of the Grand Chamber explicitly declared that the right to respect private life included, among other things, 'the right to respect for both the decisions to become and not to become a parent'.[84] In *Dickson v UK* a prisoner and his wife requested that the Secretary of State provide them with facilities for artificial insemination. The wife would be too old to conceive naturally when her husband would be released from detention. The European Court of Human Rights held that the individual's interests in the right to become a genetic parent were more important than the public interests advanced by the Secretary of State.[85] In *SH v Austria,* considered above, the Court said that legislation which made it impossible to use certain techniques for medically assisted conception would raise 'serious issues of law and fact under Article 8 of the Convention'.[86] Further judicial development of the art 8 right might thus prove to be more successful in the recognition of a positive right to procreate.

Regulation of assisted reproduction in Ireland

[4.65] The provision of assisted reproduction services in Ireland is not currently dealt with by any primary legislation and is subject only to regulations which transpose the European Commission Directive 2004/23/EC which lays down standards of quality and safety for the donation, procurement, testing, processing, preservation, storage and distribution of human tissues and cells. An associated Commission Directive, 2006/17/EC, sets out technical requirements for the activities of donation, procurement and testing of human tissues and cells and came into force on 1 November 2006. Both of these Directives were transposed into Irish legislation via the European Communities (Quality and Safety of Human Tissues and Cells) Regulations 2006.[87] The Irish Medicines Board (IMB) is designated as the competent authority for the implementation of this legislation.

---

83 Eijkholt, 'The Right to Found a Family as a Stillborn Right to Procreate?' (2010) Med L Rev 18(2), p 137.
84 *Evans v The United Kingdom* [2007] EHRR 728 [71].
85 *Dickson v The United Kingdom* [2007] 46 EHHR 927 [76].
86 *SH and others v Austria* (Application No 57813/00, November 15 2007).
87 SI 158/2006.

[4.66] The original intention of Directive 2004/23/EC was to regulate the transplantation of cells and tissues in order to prevent transmission of disease and to ensure biological traceability of transplanted cells and tissues. Not until close to the end of the drafting process was the transmission of gametes and embryos, inside the family, included in the transplantation concept. Because of this, most of the experts who participated in forming the Directive were from medical fields other than Assisted Reproduction Technology (ART). Consequently, it has been argued that the Directive is strongly influenced by a lack of understanding of what ART actually is and how it is performed.[88]

[4.67] Under these regulations, any entity involved in the procurement (and also in the testing, processing, preservation, storage and distribution) of human tissues or cells intended for human use is required to apply to the IMB for an authorisation to perform such activities. The IMB must ensure that tissue and cell procurement is carried out by persons with appropriate training and experience and that it takes place in conditions authorised for that purpose. The IMB must ensure that appropriate control measures are in place for the procurement of human tissues and cells.[89]

[4.68] It is estimated that in Ireland approximately 3,500 IVF/ICSI treatments are performed each year with about 500–800 frozen embryo replacement cycles and 1,000–1,500 intra uterine insemination treatments.[90] For registered medical practitioners working in the area of assisted reproduction, the Medical Council's Guide to Professional Conduct and Ethics is also of significance. The Medical Council is a statutory body established by the Medical Practitioners Act 1978, as amended in 2007, to protect the public by promoting and better ensuring high standards of professional conduct and professional education, training and competence among registered medical practitioners. One of the functions of the Council is to specify standards of practice for registered medical practitioners, including providing guidance on all matters related to professional conduct and ethics.[91] The Council achieves this objective by publishing a Guide to Professional Conduct and Ethics, which doctors are expected to comply with in their professional practice. The current, seventh edition of the Guide was published in 2009 and contains the following guidance in relation to assisted reproduction.

20.1 Assisted human reproduction treatments, such as In Vitro Fertilisation (IVF), should only be used after thorough investigation has shown that no other treatment is likely to be effective. You should ensure that appropriate counselling has been offered to the patient and that the patient has given informed consent before receiving any treatment.

20.2 Assisted reproduction services should only be provided by suitably qualified professionals, in appropriate facilities, and according to international best practice. Regular clinical audit and follow-up of outcomes should be the norm.

---

[88]   Presentation by Aonghus Nolan, embryologist, to the Department of Health Steering Committee on Tissue and Cells Directive 2005. www.dohc.ie/working-groups/Concluded/tissues-cells/nolan.pdf?direct=1 (accessed 11 July 2011).

[89]   See www.imb.ie (accessed 26 May 2011).

[90]   Presentation by Aonghus Nolan, embryologist, to the Department of Health Steering Committee on Tissue and Cells Directive 2005. www.dohc.ie/working-groups/Concluded/tissues-cells/noan.pdf?direct=1 (accessed 11 July 2011).

[91]   See http://www.medicalcouncil.ie/Professional-Standards/Professional-Conduct-Ethics/ (accessed 26 May 2011).

20.3 If you offer donor programmes to patients, you must consider the biological difficulties involved and pay particular attention to the source of the donated material. Such donations should be altruistic and non-commercial. You should keep accurate records for future reference.

20.4 You should not participate in creating new forms of life solely for experimental purposes. You should not engage in human reproductive cloning.

[4.69] In relation to compliance with the Guide, the Medical Council obliges doctors on their annual registration form to confirm that they have read and comply with the Guide. If the Council receives a complaint in respect of non-compliance with any aspect of the Guide, the Preliminary Proceedings Committee of the Medical Council must decide whether the case should proceed to become an inquiry before the Fitness to Practise Committee. Consideration of complaints against registered medical practitioners is provided for under Part 7 of the Medical Practitioners Act, 2007. This is further discussed in Chapter 2.

[4.70] In 2000, the Minister for Health established the Commission on Assisted Human Reproduction (CAHR) to prepare a report on the possible approaches to the regulation of all aspects of assisted human reproduction and the social, ethical and legal factors to be taken into account in determining public policy in this area. The membership of the Commission was comprised of medical, scientific, social and legal expertise and additional workgroups with additional experts were also established to explore particular aspects of AHR. A public consultation exercise was carried out by the Commission as well as a survey of service users, and consultation with medical practitioners working in the area of AHR in Ireland. The Commission also took account of the position in other jurisdictions in relation to the regulation of AHR services.

[4.71] The CAHR reported to the Minister in March 2005.[92] It made 40 recommendations to the Minister in relation to the regulation of AHR, many of which are referred to in subsequent chapters of this text. The Commission recommended that a new Act of the Oireachtas should be passed to establish a regulatory body to regulate AHR services in Ireland. Among the body's executive functions would be the issuing of licences to services providers. It would be mandatory for any provider of AHR services to obtain a licence from the statutory body in respect of the provision of any of the clinical and laboratory services specified in the legislation. The Report was referred by the Minister to the Oireachtas Joint Committee on Health and Children in 2005 but no further action has yet been taken at a legislative level in relation to implementation of the Report.

Regulation of assisted reproduction in other jurisdictions

[4.72] Internationally, there is wide divergence in relation to the regulation of AHR. The development of IVF and its subsequent variations and extensions appears to have generated more interest and concern among religious leaders, bioethicists and the general public than any other medical procedure. This widespread interest and concern has attracted the attention of the political process in many countries. As a result of these events, many expert committees have examined the ethical, legal, religious, medical,

---

92   Report of the Commission on Assisted Human Reproduction (Government Publications Office, 2005), http://www.dohc.ie/publications/cahr.html (accessed 26 May 2011).

and public policy aspects of AHR, resulting in the establishment of unofficial guidelines and/or government regulations in many states where AHR is practised. There are several states which have adopted guidelines, described as sets of rules to be followed voluntarily, generally proposed by unofficial organisations such as an infertility society or a society of obstetrics and gynaecology. Other states have passed regulations, that is, sets of rules adopted by legislative action, with assigned penalties for violations. Other states have neither regulations nor guidelines.

[4.73] The International Federation of Fertility Societies (IFFS) is an international organization representing the national fertility societies of approximately 70 states, including Ireland. It has conducted international surveys of the regulatory landscape and, in its most recent publication in 2007, it states that:

> Guidelines or regulations have taken various forms. They often not only express a particular medical perspective but sometimes reflect the social and religious mores of the particular sovereign state. Some of the guidelines or regulations have been formulated to accommodate special-interest groups. Furthermore, surveillance of compliance with guidelines or regulations ranges from none at all to the issuance of a license by a governing body after designated requirements are fulfilled, often including periodic follow-up inspections.[93]

[4.74] In 2007 countries with specific statutes dealing with AHR included Austria, Belgium, Bulgaria, Canada, Czech Republic, Denmark, France, Germany, Greece, Hong Kong, Hungary, Israel, Italy, Korea, Latvia, Netherlands, New Zealand, Norway, Russia, Saudi Arabia, Slovenia, Spain, Sweden, Switzerland, Taiwan, Tunisia, Turkey, United Kingdom and Vietnam. Those countries which rely on guidelines include Argentina, Australia, Brazil, Chile, China, Croatia, Egypt, India, Ireland, Japan, Lithuania, Mexico, Morocco, Philippines, Singapore, South Africa, Thailand and the USA.[94]

[4.75] A commonly cited example of statutory regulation in the form of licensing is that in operation in the United Kingdom. The provision of AHR services in the UK is regulated by the Human Fertilisation and Embryology Act 1990, as amended in 2008. Clinics must be licensed by the Human Fertilisation and Embryology Authority[95] (HFEA) and must comply with both the Act and the Codes of Practice issued by the Authority. The HFEA has 22 members, more than half of whom must be lay members, that is, not scientists or clinicians. The Authority regulates the provision of fertility treatment and the carrying out of embryo research by an inspection and licensing regime. It also maintains a register of information about the provision and outcome of fertility treatments. It publishes a Code of Practice and Directions which gives guidance to clinics about the conduct of activities regulated by the Authority. This is seen as an advantageous model rather than primary legislation, as it allows flexibility in changing rules to adapt to emerging technologies and clinical practice. Jackson notes that:

---

[93] http://www.iffs-reproduction.org/documents/Surveillance_07.pdf (accessed 26 May 2011).

[94] http://www.iffs-reproduction.org/documents/Surveillance_07.pdf (accessed 26 May 2011).

[95] See http://www.hfea.gov.uk/ (accessed 26 May 2011). Recent reports in the UK suggest that the HFEA is to be abolished, with its functions being divided between other entities such as the Human Tissue Authority and the Care Quality Commission. See http://www.bionews.org.uk/page_68168.asp (accessed 26 May 2011).

The Code thus has the advantage of being able to respond fairly promptly to a continually shifting evidence base. The legal status of the Code of Practice is, however, a little unclear. A breach of the Code is not a criminal offence, unlike many breaches of the Act itself. Nevertheless, breaches of the Code can be taken into account by a licence committee when deciding whether to vary or revoke a licence.[96]

[4.76] Despite the comprehensive nature of the licensing regime in the United Kingdom, the HFEA is unable to exercise control over the market in fertility services or so-called 'reproductive tourism', where people seeking fertility services travel to other countries which they perceive to offer better, faster, cheaper or less restrictive services, or where fertility services such as gamete donation are purchased online. Brazier argues that the most profound change in regulating reproductive medicine since the 1980s is the dramatically increased role of commerce which was not fully foreseen at the time of the Warnock Report in 1984, which was the precursor for the introduction of the regulatory regime in the UK.[97] She notes that a fertility industry has developed to provide treatment on a profit-making basis both to British citizens and procreative tourists escaping more prohibitive regimes elsewhere in Europe.

[4.77] Another nightmare awaits the HFEA and its counterparts in Continental Europe. Each national jurisdiction has sought to fashion a scheme of regulation acceptable to its own culture and community. However those wealthy enough to participate in reproduction markets can readily evade their domestic constraints. Brazier asks if sperm can be ordered on the internet, or a surrogate mother can be hired from Bolivia, are national regulators wasting their time? 'The international ramifications of the reproductive business may prove to be a more stringent test of the strength of British law than all of the difficult ethical dilemmas that have gone before'.[98]

[4.78] Another recent phenomenon is the provision of anonymous sperm donation in foreign ships moored in UK waters, which are governed by the laws of the country whose flag they fly and can therefore evade UK legislation in relation to the prohibition of anonymous sperm donation. Hunter and Oultram note that the key concern is that such enterprises would allow a person to live in one country but live by the rules of another. 'While sperm ships don't technically challenge a nation's sovereignty they do challenge its ability to effectively regulate the healthcare technologies available to its citizens. And this challenge makes a mockery of the notion that states can regulate these technologies'.[99] These jurisdictional issues are undoubtedly challenges that will also face legislators in Ireland in the future.

Access to AHR services and the welfare of the child

[4.79] The restriction of AHR services based on marital status, sexual orientation or considerations of the welfare of the future child is one of the most controversial issues in this area of medical practice. The issue confronts societal prejudices about different

---

[96] Jackson, *Medical Law: Text, Cases and Materials,* (2nd edn, OUP, 2010), p 766.
[97] Department of Health and Social Security, *Report of the Committee of Inquiry into Human Fertilisation and Embryology* ('The Warnock Report'), July 1984, Cmnd 9314.
[98] Brazier, 'Regulating the Reproduction Business?' (1999) 7 Medical Law Review 166–93.
[99] Hunter and Oultram, 'The Challenge of "Sperm Ships": The Need For the Global Regulation of Medical Technology' (2008) 34 Journal of Medical Ethics 552–6.

lifestyle choices and forms of parenting, and from a legal perspective it questions whether a refusal to provide AHR services to a person on the basis of marital status or sexuality would be regarded as an interference with reproductive choice and would constitute unlawful discrimination. As discussed above, the Irish courts have recognised a right to privacy and a right to reproduce, both of which are qualified by considerations of the common good. In the context of AHR clinics deciding whether or not to provide services for an individual or couple, the welfare of the child is seen as an important guiding principle.

[4.80] Child welfare is a multi-faceted concept ranging from narrow inquiries about protecting children from physical harm and abusive parents on the one end of the spectrum to expansive questions about what promotes a child's best interests on the other.[100] Lee and Morgan describe the concept of the welfare of the child as 'broad and all-embracing.' They say that a very wide range of factors must be taken into account when considering the future lives of children who may be born as a result of the treatment.[101]

[4.81] Parents who have conceived their children naturally generally enjoy a presumption of fitness that frees them to exercise their parental prerogatives without State interference. The courts do not intervene to safeguard the child's welfare unless this is necessary for the protection of the child. However, for those who seek to adopt children, no parental rights attach until the fitness to parent and the best interests of the child tests have been assessed and the State's standards satisfied. The fitness assessment takes place prior to placement of the child with the prospective adopters in order to assure the State that the parents are not likely to harm a child placed in their care and that they have the capacity to provide for the child's basic needs. If this test is satisfied and a child is placed with them, the adoption authorities must also be satisfied that the child's best interests will be safeguarded by placement with this family. The two tests measure different issues – the first measures the parents' competency while the second measures the specific needs of the particular child and how those needs will be met by placement in a particular home. The best interests test is prominent in case law about custody and access rights, medical treatment of children, child support, adoption and guardianship. It also underpins the UN Convention on the Rights of the Child.

[4.82] Assisted reproduction legislation in many states mandates consideration of child welfare in advance of the child's conception. This is generally couched in very general terms and has often been criticised for its inconsistent and often biased application. Some commentators believe that such provisions are inherently speculative given the lack of evidence regarding parenting ability.[102] For example, Jackson states that 'unless we are concerned to prevent reproduction in anyone who may offer a suboptimal environment for their children's upbringing, then restricting the reproductive options of

---

[100] Storrow, 'The Bioethics of Prospective Parenthood: In Pursuit of the Proper Standard for Gatekeeping in Infertility Clinics' (2007) Vol 28 (5) Cardozo Law Review 101 at 118 referring to Robertson, 'Procreative Liberty and Harm to Offspring in Assisted Reproduction', (2004) 30 Am J L & Med 7.

[101] Lee and Morgan, *Human Fertilisation and Embryology, Regulating the Reproductive Revolution* (Blackstone Press Ltd, 2001) at p 161.

[102] Jackson, *Regulating Reproduction: Law, Technology and Autonomy* 192 (2001).

infertile people on the basis of some vague appeal to child welfare may be both disingenuous and discriminatory.'[103] In practice it appears to be used as an indirect means of preferring certain kinds of families that fit a particular idealised stereotype.

[4.83] In Ireland, the Equal Status Acts 2000–2004 prohibits direct or indirect discrimination on grounds of, inter alia, disability, sexual orientation, marital status, age, gender, or religion, in relation to the provision of services.[104] 'Service' here includes 'a service or facility of any nature which is available to the public generally or a section of the public'[105] and therefore, in the absence of any future contrary legislative provision, would cover clinics providing assisted reproduction treatments. In the context of the provision of AHR services to a single person or gay couple, a refusal by a clinic to treat such a person/couple on grounds of marital status or sexual orientation would clearly come under the prohibitions in the Act. However, a refusal on grounds of age may be defended by a clinic on clinical grounds in relation to that particular patient,[106] or, where the refusal is on grounds of disability, that such treatment may result in harm to any child that could be conceived by the treatment.[107]

[4.84] The Commission on Assisted Human Reproduction considered this issue in its Report in 2005.[108] It recommended that services should be available without discrimination on the grounds of gender, marital status or sexual orientation, subject to consideration of the best interests of any children that may be born. Any relevant legislation on the provision of AHR services should reflect the general principles of the Equal Status Acts 2000–2004, subject to certain qualifications as set out in –section 4.8 of the Report. These qualifications would support the introduction of an upper age limit on persons seeking treatment in order to confer some protection on the future child in respect of its need to have a parent into his or her maturity and also in respect of protection of the health of the person seeking treatment which might be contra-indicated for older persons. The second qualification recommended by the Commission was that legislation may confer on AHR clinics discretion to deny services to a person where there are serious concerns supported by objective evidence that the welfare of any resultant child could otherwise be at risk.

[4.85] The Commission considered the best interests of the child in Appendix VII of its Report. It acknowledged that this issue would undoubtedly play a large part in any debate on how to regulate AHR in Ireland and that societal consensus was difficult. It discussed different ways of evaluating welfare, such as the maximum and minimum welfare principles.[109] The maximum welfare principle implies that one should not knowingly and intentionally bring a child into the world in less-than-ideal circumstances. Research shows that children need a stable home with mature, caring adults who themselves have a sound relationship. However, it is also important to

---

[103] Jackson, *Regulating Reproduction: Law, Technology and Autonomy* 192 (2001) at 174.
[104] The prohibited grounds or discrimination are set out in the Equal Status Acts 2000–2004, ss 2 and 3.
[105] Defined in the Equal Status Acts 2000–2004, s 2.
[106] Section 16(2)(a).
[107] Section 4(4).
[108] See http://www.dohc.ie/publications/cahr.html (accessed 26 May 2011).
[109] See http://www.dohc.ie/publications/cahr.html, page 116 (accessed 26 May 2011).

remember that fertile couples often have children in less than ideal circumstances, and it is not possible or even desirable to try to control natural reproduction. 'The difficulty with the use of this principle is that every characteristic of those who request medical assistance that does not conform to the stereotypical family based on heterosexual married parents and their genetically related children' is assumed to result in negative consequences for the child.[110]

[4.86] The second measure of evaluation of welfare is described as the minimum threshold principle. As it may be impossible to reach consensus on what it means to be a good parent, society instead agrees a minimum threshold below which prospective parents must not fall in order to be given access to reproductive technologies. It is likely that a reasonable consensus could be reached on which circumstances would be considered unacceptable, such as previous criminal convictions for child abuse, serious mental illness, history of drug abuse and perhaps severe marital strife. This standard takes the view that child should not be brought into the world only if it would have been better for that child never to have been born.

[4.87] A middle ground between these two alternatives may be considered the reasonable welfare principle, which does not aim to ensure that the child is perfectly happy, but is reasonably happy. Given that no parents are perfect and no one is completely happy, parents may make decisions that might negatively impact upon their children, such as moving house or changing schools. The State generally only interferes in very exceptional circumstances when parental decisions have disastrous consequences for their children. So this test would apply to render AHR acceptable when the child conceived as a result of treatment will have a reasonably happy life. This would include having a normal range of opportunities, and the abilities to realise goals which in general make human lives happy. The true determining factors for the child's well-being (strong desire for parenthood, warm and supportive relationships) do not coincide with and are not (mainly) determined by the sexual orientation, the number of parents or the genetic relatedness.[111] Pennings argues that if we are seeking to prioritise the welfare of the child, we should focus on characteristics and conditions which have a proven influence on the well-being and happiness of children, and not on ideologically or religiously based features. [112]

[4.88] In the United Kingdom much is left to the discretion of the centres licensed to perform such procedures. The centres are obliged to have an ethics committee to supervise the treatments and research programmes, and they must comply with the Code of Practice of the Human Fertilisation and Embryology Authority (HFEA). Section 13(5) of the 1990 Act provided that one of the conditions of the licences given to centres was that consideration had to be given by the centre to the welfare of the child who may be born as a result of the treatment, including the child's need for a father.[113] Although

---

[110] Golombok, 'New Families, Old Values: Considerations Regarding the Welfare of the Child' (1998) Human Reproduction, Vol 13 No 9: 2342–2347.

[111] Golombok, 'New Families, Old Values: Considerations Regarding the Welfare of the Child' (1998) Human Reproduction, Vol 13 No 9: 2342–2347.

[112] Pennings, 'Measuring the Welfare of the Child: In Search of the Appropriate Evaluation Principle' (1999) Human Reproduction, Vol 14, No 5, 1146–1150.

[113] Human Fertilisation and Embryology Act 1990 (UK), s 13(5).

this condition could be interpreted as including a social as well as biological father, (that is to say someone in the immediate family circle who will take on the role of father to the child), nevertheless the condition apparently made some clinics reluctant to give treatment to single persons and gay couples.

[4.89] In *R v Ethical Committee of St. Mary's Hospital: ex parte Harriott*,[114] a woman was refused IVF treatment because she had a criminal record for prostitution. Her application for judicial review failed on the basis that this was not a decision to which no reasonable consultant could have come. However, the door to judicial review was left slightly ajar in that Schiemann J indicated that a policy by a centre, for example to refuse treatment on the grounds of colour or religion, might be declared illegal.[115]

[4.90] Section 13(5) was the subject of much debate[116] as to how a clinician could base his decision as to whether to provide AHR services to a particular person in part by a consideration of the future child's welfare. Since the policy of the law generally is to assume a position that existence is better than non-existence, it was difficult to argue that in given circumstances, a child would not be benefited by being brought into existence. Clinicians do not have access to all the relevant information or the specialist training required to make such decisions and it was argued that it would impose an unfair burden on infertile parents to prove their fitness to parent despite the fact that those who are fertile do not have to pass any such test. There are counter arguments to the effect that there is an inherent difference with AHR where medical intervention is necessary to assist in the creation of new life and such intervention brings with it a responsibility towards any future children who may be born. In 2005 the House of Commons Science and Technology Committee strongly criticised s 13(5) as follows:

> The welfare of the child provision discriminates against the infertile and some sections of society, is impossible to implement and is of questionable practical value in protecting the interests of children born as a result of assisted reproduction. …The welfare of the child provision has enabled the HFEA and clinics to make judgments that are more properly made by patients in consultation with their doctor. It should be abolished in its current form. The minimum threshold principle should apply but should specify that this threshold should be the risk of unpreventable and significant harm.[117]

[4.91] The amendment of the 1990 Act in 2008 resulted in the replacement of the consideration of the child's 'need for a father', with the need for 'supportive parenting'.[118] The HFEA Code of Practice states in para 8.2 that the centre should have documented procedures to ensure that proper account is taken of the welfare of any child who may be born as a result of treatment services, and any other child who may be affected by the birth. Paragraph 8.3 provides that the centre should assess each patient

---

[114] *R v Ethical Committee of St Mary's Hospital: ex parte Harriott* (1987) 137 NLJ Reps 1038.

[115] *R v Ethical Committee of St Mary's Hospital: ex parte Harriott* (1987) 137 NLJ Reps 1038, p1039.

[116] See for example,Jackson, 'Conception and the Irrelevance of the Welfare Principle' (2002) 65 Mod Law Rev 176–203.

[117] Human Reproductive Technologies and the Law, Fifth Report (2005) para 107, available at http://www.publications.parliament.uk/pa/cm200405/cmselect/cmsctech/7/706.htm#a18 (accessed 26 May 2010).

[118] Human Fertilisation and Embryology Act 2008, s 14(2).

and their partner (if they have one) before providing any treatment, and should use this assessment to decide whether there is a risk of significant harm or neglect to any child referred to in 8.2. The centre is expected to consider the wishes of all those involved, and the assessment must be done in a non-discriminatory way. In particular, patients should not be discriminated against on grounds of gender, race, disability, sexual orientation, religious belief or age. (8.7)

[4.92] Centres are advised that they should consider factors that are likely to cause a risk of significant harm or neglect to any child who may be born or to any existing child of the family. These factors include any aspects of the patient's or (if they have one) their partner's:

    a)   past or current circumstances that may lead to any child mentioned above experiencing serious physical or psychological harm or neglect, for example:

        i)   previous convictions relating to harming children

        ii)   child protection measures taken regarding existing children, or

        iii)   violence or serious discord in the family environment

    b)   past or current circumstances that are likely to lead to an inability to care throughout childhood for any child who may be born, or that are already seriously impairing the care of any existing child of the family, for example:

        i)   mental or physical conditions

        ii)   drug or alcohol abuse

        iii)   medical history, where the medical history indicates that any child who may be born is likely to suffer from a serious medical condition, or

        iv)   circumstances that the centre considers likely to cause serious harm to any child mentioned above.

[4.93] When considering a child's need for supportive parenting, centres should consider the following definition: 'Supportive parenting is a commitment to the health, well being and development of the child. It is presumed that all prospective parents will be supportive parents, in the absence of any reasonable cause for concern that any child who may be born, or any other child, may be at risk of significant harm or neglect. Where centres have concern as to whether this commitment exists, they may wish to take account of wider family and social networks within which the child will be raised.'[119]

[4.94] If similar legislative provisions were introduced in Ireland it is possible that a Constitutional challenge could be brought in relation to the provision of AHR services to non-marital families under art 41 of the Constitution, although the success of such an action is doubtful. It may be argued that, by obliging clinics to provide assisted reproduction treatments without reference to the marital status of the patients, the State would be failing to 'guard with special care the institution of Marriage, on which the family is founded' under Art 41.3.1°.

[4.95] In an Appendix to the Report of the Commission on Assisted Human Reproduction, it is noted that this constitutional duty is imposed only on the State and so

---

[119]   HFEA Code of Practice (8th edn) para 8.11.

would not apply in the context of private clinics or hospitals offering services to non-marital families. The success of a constitutional challenge would require the acceptance of the argument that a legislative requirement obliging clinics to treat non-marital families amounted to an inducement not to marry. 'It remains to be seen whether the courts would agree that a statutory requirement that AHR services be provided to non-marital families satisfied such a test so as to render the requirement unconstitutional.' [120]

[4.96] The ECHR might also be called into service in aid of single persons or gay couples who seek access to assisted reproductive technologies and the subsequent recognition of their family as deserving respect under the Convention. In *Kerkhoven, Hinke and Hinke v The Netherlands*[121] two women lived together as a family and shared parental authority over a child born to one of them through use of DI. The Commission refused to recognise this as a legal relationship and to grant parental authority to the mother's partner, despite the existence of the factors on which they had denied the right of an unmarried man to seek paternity rights, namely the existence of a stable relationship, the planned birth of the child and the bond between the child and the person seeking to assert parental authority.[122]

[4.97] In *G v The Netherlands*,[123] the Commission noted that cohabitation is only one of the factors to be taken into account in determining the existence of family life under the Convention. In this case, the applicant had donated sperm to a lesbian couple who were known to him. Subsequent to the birth, and having visited the child and the couple on a number of occasions, the applicant wished to establish regular access to the child, whereupon the couple broke off all contact with the applicant. The judge declared that donation of sperm was, in itself, an insufficient basis for the establishment of parental

---

[120] See http://www.dohc.ie/publications/cahr.html, page 138 (accessed 26 May 2011).

[121] *Hinke and Hinke v The Netherlands* 15666/89, (decision of 19 May 1992, unreported).

[122] Other cases in point include the English case in *Re W (a minor) (Homosexual adopter)* [1997] 2 FLR 406; the Irish case *MacD v L* [2009] IESC 81 (discussed in Ch 5 at para **5.63**); and the 2010 judgment of the ECtHR in *Schalk and Kopf v Austria* (Application No 30141/04) in which the Court noted that:

'there is an emerging European consensus towards legal recognition of same-sex couples. Moreover, this tendency has developed rapidly over the past decade. Nevertheless, there is not yet a majority of States providing for legal recognition of same-sex couples. The area in question must therefore still be regarded as one of evolving rights with no established consensus, where States must also enjoy a margin of appreciation in the timing of the introduction of legislative changes.'

However, in *obiter* comments, the Court also went on to recognise that stable relationships of cohabiting same-sex couples fall with the notion of family life:

'The Court notes that (...) a rapid evolution of social attitudes towards same-sex couples has taken place in many member States. Since then a considerable number of member States have afforded legal recognition to same-sex couples (...). Certain provisions of EU law also reflect a growing tendency of include same-sex couples in the notion of 'family' (...). In view of this evolution the Court considers it artificial to maintain the view that, in contrast to a different-sex couple, a same-sex couple cannot enjoy 'family life' for the purposes of Article 8. Consequently the relationship of the applicants, a cohabiting same-sex couple living in a stable de facto partnership, falls with the notion of 'family life', just as the relationship of a different-sex couple in the same situation would.'

[123] *G v The Netherlands* 16 EHRR CD 38, January 1993 (16944/90).

rights and duties, and for the creation of family life under art 8 of the Convention. Before the Commission, the applicant argued that the latter point had not been adequately or properly considered by the judge, as he did have a biological link to the child and had regular contact with her until the couple broke the arrangement. The Commission considered that the situation in which a man donates sperm only to enable DI to take place, does not give the donor a right of respect for family life with the child. The Commission considered that the contacts between the applicant and the child had been limited both in time and intensity. The applicant had also not considered making any contribution to the child's upbringing.

[4.98] In *X, Y and Z v UK*,[124] the Commission had to deal with the recognition, for birth certification purposes, of the legal relationship between a child born through DI and its social father, who was in fact a female-to-male transsexual who had been living in a permanent and stable union with the mother of the child. The inability of the partners to marry also led to the inability to adopt the child, and the status of illegitimacy being conferred on the child, which although of little effect in reality, also meant the inability to register the applicant as father. It is worthwhile to note the position taken by a majority within the Commission, despite the fact that the Court later disagreed with this position.

[4.99] The Commission considered that whether de facto family ties are deemed sufficient to fall within the scope of family life under the Convention will depend on the circumstances of the case, including the existence of blood ties, cohabitation, the nature of the relationships involved and the demonstrable interest, commitment and dependency between them. The Commission recognised that it had yet to find a case for family life that did not involve a blood link or a legal relationship through marriage or adoption. It noted that on the facts of this case, to all appearances, the applicant was the child's father. It distinguished the *Kerkhoven* case on the basis of the medical condition of a transsexual called gender dysphoria by which the person may receive medical treatment to enable the transsexual to become the gender to which he or she has the conviction of belonging.

[4.100] The Commission was of the opinion that the relationships between the applicants had the appearance and substance of family life. The only factor detracting from this was the fact that the first applicant had been registered at birth as a female, with the consequence that he was unable to marry the child's mother or be registered on the birth certificate as the father. Accordingly:

> The Commission is of the opinion that this element, whether seen as biological or historical cannot outweigh the reality of the applicant's situation which is otherwise undistinguished from the traditional notion of family life. It would note that the UK, in the context of children born by artificial insemination by donor has itself for the purposes of the 1990 Human Fertilisation and Embryology Act accepted that there are circumstances where a 'father' need not be linked to a child either by blood or by marriage to its mother and that it was by virtue of UK law in force that the relationships between the three applicants were created.[125]

---

124 Com Rep of 27 June 1995, unreported (21830/93).
125 Com Rep of 27 June 1995, unreported (21830/93) at para 58.

[4.101] Consequently, the Commission found that the applicants were entitled to enjoy respect for their family life under art 8 of the Convention. The next issue for the Commission to decide was whether respect for family life implies a positive obligation on the State to change its legal system in respect of transsexuals. The Commission noted that, despite the assertion on behalf of the State that the use of a birth certificate is uncommon in the UK now, there were circumstances in which it may be required for official or educational purposes. The inability to have the applicant registered as the child's father may cause trauma and upset to the child and to others. Also, due to the inability of the applicant to be regarded as the father of the child, the child had no rights to participate in the distribution of the applicants' estate on intestacy. The Commission regarded the granting of a residence order in favour of the applicant as insufficient recognition of the parental authority of the applicant.

[4.102] As a consequence of the lack of respect for the family life of the applicants, the Commission was satisfied that the family unit could suffer a lack of security and value and that the child could be affected in her personal development and sense of identity. The Commission found that there had been a violation of art 8 by the UK which had not been sufficiently outweighed by the public interest. Nor was it within the margin of appreciation afforded to States in situations where the issue was controversial, novel and sensitive. 'Having regard therefore in particular to the welfare of the third applicant and her security within the family unit, the Commission finds that the absence of an appropriate legal regime reflecting the applicant's family ties discloses a failure to respect their family life.'[126]

[4.103] However, despite the adoption of the above opinion by the majority of the Commission, the Court disagreed, finding that there had been no violation of art 8.[127] The basis for the Court's decision was the lack of consensus in Europe in relation to parental rights to be granted to transsexuals and the legal relationship between a DI child and its 'social' father. This allowed the UK to have a wide margin of appreciation which it had not breached in the circumstances of the case. Although the Court admitted that de facto family ties did exist between the applicants, the community also had an interest in a coherent system of family law which gave priority to the best interests of the child. The Court felt that the disadvantages which might be sustained by the applicant and the child by the failure to recognise the former as the legal father would not cause undue hardship. Further, it was not certain that the registration of the applicant would benefit this child or DI children in general.[128]

---

[126] Com Rep of 27 June 1995, unreported (21830/93) at para 69.
[127] *X, Y and Z v UK*, judgment of 22 April 1997.
[128] Com Rep of 27 June 1995, unreported (21830/93) at para 37. Court decision is reported at (1997) 24 EHRR 143.

Chapter 5

Artificial Insemination and Egg Donation

ARTIFICIAL INSEMINATION

[5.01] Artificial or assisted insemination may provide a solution to male infertility in some circumstances. Semen is injected into the female genital tract to time with ovulation in an attempt to induce pregnancy.[1] Generally the procedure is performed by a medical practitioner, although this is not necessary to its success, with some women preferring to self-inseminate in the privacy of their own homes.[2] The sperm may be obtained either from the husband/partner of the woman upon whom the procedure is performed (hereafter referred to as Artificial Insemination by Husband (AIH)) or from a third-party donor (Donor Insemination (DI)). A more recent development used in the treatment of male sub-fertility is ICSI (intra-cytoplasmic sperm injection), which enables couples in which the man has a very low sperm count to conceive. This procedure takes a single sperm from a semen sample from the male partner and injects it directly into the cytoplasm of the female egg, thereby rendering it more likely to fertilise. The resulting embryo is then transferred to the uterus of the female partner, where it is hoped that a pregnancy will result. The success of this procedure in recent years has led to a decline in the use of sperm donation for couples where male sub-fertility is identified as the cause of the couple's inability to conceive.

[5.02] The concern in relation to declining sperm counts which has been publicised in medical and scientific journals in recent years has led to an increased awareness of the possibilities and opportunities offered by artificial insemination through storage of sperm for the future. The increase in knowledge relating to the effect of environmental pollutants on the male reproductive system gives us the opportunity to be vigilant on behalf of future generations, who will almost certainly be affected by the declining sperm counts which now appear to be evident from recent studies.[3]

---

[1] The procedure involved in artificial insemination is not a new technological development, the first reported case occurring in 1799 for AIH and 1884 for DI. See Klayman, 'Therapeutic Impregnation: Prognosis of a Lawyer – Diagnosis of a Legislature' (1970) 39 U Cin L Rev 291.

[2] Indeed, the privacy of this procedure makes it difficult to monitor or regulate.

[3] See de Kretser, 'Declining Sperm Counts – Environmental Chemicals May Be to Blame' (1996) 312 British Medical Journal 457; Irvine S et al, 'Evidence of Deteriorating Semen Quality in the United Kingdom: Birth Cohort Study in 577 Men in Scotland Over 11 Years' (1996) 312 British Medical Journal 467–70; de Kretser, 'Male Infertility' (1997) Lancet 349 (9054): 787–790.

[5.03] This chapter examines the legal and ethical issues arising from artificial insemination, posthumous reproduction, donor insemination and egg donation. Issues relating to embryo donation are also referred to where relevant.

ARTIFICIAL INSEMINATION BY HUSBAND (AIH) OR PARTNER

[5.04] The sperm used to inseminate the woman may be taken from her husband or partner. Where the couple are married, the procedure does not give rise to any major ethical or legal difficulties per se, as it is seen simply as a method of conception which bypasses normal intercourse. The main ethical objection is one which applies to all forms of reproductive technologies, that is that it interferes with nature. There are also objections from some religions such as the Catholic Church, which is opposed to all forms of reproductive technologies on the grounds that such technologies separate the procreative process from the conjugal act within marriage.[4] The main legal issues considered in the context of AIH relate to the legal status and parentage of the child in the context of posthumous conception, where the husband has predeceased the conception of the child. Where the couple are not married, there are difficulties in relation to legal parentage of the child.

Parentage

[5.05] The question of parentage in AIH is relatively simple due to the absence of any donation of genetic material. A child born to a married woman as a result of artificial insemination in which her husband's sperm is used is a marital child of that couple.[5] The child will be recognised legally as his, in the same way as if the child had been conceived through sexual intercourse between the spouses. Therefore, this form of AIH does not pose any legal difficulties for the parties or the resulting child. It clearly does not apply to an unmarried man whose sperm is used to inseminate his partner.

[5.06] An English case has questioned the applicability of the presumption of paternity in certain circumstances. In *Re H and A (children)*[6] an application was made by a man to have blood tests carried out on twins born to a married woman with whom he had a sexual relationship, in order to establish that he was their biological father. At first instance, the judge balanced the advantage of scientific truth against uncertainty and dismissed the application on the basis that the best interests of the family as a unit were

---

[4]   Vatican's Congregation for the Doctrine of the Faith, *Instruction on Respect for Human Life in its Origin and on the Dignity of Procreation,* (1987), published in English by the Catholic Truth Society. The *Instruction* states: 'Homologous artificial fertilisation, in seeking a procreation which is not the fruit of a specific act of conjugal union, objectively effects an analogous separation between the goods and the meanings of marriage.' Ch II, sect 4 at 27. As Coughlan points out '… [H]omologous artificial insemination is accepted as licit only under stringent conditions, viz, only if it serves to facilitate the conjugal act and is not a substitute therefor, or if it does not involve a dissociation of the unitive and procreative meanings of this act. The last point means, for example, that the obtaining of sperm by masturbation, even for the purposes of homologous artificial fertilisation, is not permissible.' Coughlan, *The Vatican, the Law and the Human Embryo* (Iowa City: University of Iowa Press, 1990) at 5.

[5]   Status of Children Act 1987, s 46.

[6]   *Re H and A (children)* LTL 21/3/2002.

that the woman's husband would continue as the father of the twins. On appeal, the Court held that the interests of justice were best served by the ascertainment of truth. The Court should be furnished with the best available science and should not be confined to unsatisfactory alternatives such as presumptions and inferences. The Court questioned the relevance of the presumption of paternity of children born within marriage and the justification for its application. The presumption was a necessary tool in the 19th century but because science had progressed and children were increasingly born out of marriage, the paternity of a child should now be established by science and not by legal presumption or inference.

[5.07] In Ireland if a child is born outside of marriage, the mother is the sole legal guardian. The position of the unmarried father of the child is not so certain. If the mother agrees, the father can become a joint guardian if both parents sign a statutory declaration. However, if the mother does not agree to sign the statutory declaration or agree that the father be appointed as joint guardian, the father must apply to the court to be appointed as a joint guardian. While the mother's views are taken into account, the fact that she does not consent to the guardianship application does not automatically mean that the court will refuse the order sought by the father. Instead, the court will decide what is in the best interests of the child. In situations where the father has been appointed joint guardian of a child, then his consent is required for certain matters relating to the child's general welfare and other items including any proposed adoption of the child.

[5.08] Many commentators have advocated in recent years for reform of this situation on grounds that it is in the best interests of the child to know and enjoy a legal relationship with its father, and also to rectify the discrimination against unmarried fathers which it currently reflects. The United Nations Declaration on the Rights of the Child, Article 7, Paragraph 1 states:

> The child shall be registered immediately after birth and shall have the right from birth to a name, the right to acquire a nationality and, as far as possible, the right to know and be cared for by his or her parents. Commenting on this situation, the UN Committee on the Rights of the Child, whose function is to oversee implementation of the UN Declaration on the Rights of the Child, has expressed its concern about the disadvantaged situation of children born of unmarried parents due to the lack of appropriate procedures to name the father in the birth registration of the child.[7]

[5.09] In 1986 the *Johnston case* came before the European Court of Human Rights.[8] This case involved, amongst other things, the legal status in Ireland of an illegitimate child. The Court held that an illegitimate child 'should be placed, legally and socially, in a position akin to that of a legitimate child".[9] The Court considered Ireland's failure to establish an appropriate legal regime reflecting the illegitimate child's natural ties, a violation of art 8.1 of the European Convention on Human Rights (ECHR). Article 8.1 states: '1) Every one has the right to respect for his private and family life, his home and his correspondence.' Dissenting judge De Meyer went further in saying that in his view it was not sufficient to state that the illegitimate child's position should be akin to a

---

[7]   United Nations Committee on the Rights of the Child, 1998, para 17, p 7.
[8]   *Johnston and Others*, 01/24/1986, Series A, n 112.
[9]   *Johnston and Others*, 01/24/1986, Series A, para 74.

legitimate child, and that the Court should have been more unequivocal in stating that 'the legal situation of a child born out of wedlock must be identical to that of a child of a married couple'.[10] However, as is pointed out by Meeusen,[11]

> [B]y its refusal to accept the De Meyer rule, the majority made clear that, in spite of its rejection of the restriction of illegitimate's patrimonial rights on the mere basis of their status, States can adopt certain specific regulations concerning children born out of wedlock. The status of illegitimacy as such is not condemned by the Court.

[5.10] In response to this case, the Status of Children Act was introduced in Ireland in 1987 to abolish the presumption of legitimacy[12] and replace it with a presumption of paternity[13]. The Act significantly improved the legal situation of children born out of wedlock by providing that where a married woman gives birth to a child, her husband will be presumed to be the father of the child. This is rebuttable on the balance of probabilities.[14] However, the Act did not go far enough in recognising the rights of unmarried fathers in respect of their children, and the rights of children to have access to the identity of their genetic fathers. The Act does not deal with the position of a child born through DI.

[5.11] In relation to birth registration, the Civil Registration Act 2004 contains the details to be recorded in the register of births. These include the name, address and occupation of the mother and the father, and any former surname(s) of both parents. It also requires that the Personal Public Service (PPS) numbers of the child, the mother and the father be recorded. While the details of both parents are listed in the schedule as information to be recorded, the mother's details come first in the list and there is no legal requirement to record the details of both parents. If a woman who is not married wishes to register the birth of her child and chooses not to provide information in relation to the father, there is no requirement for her to do so. In these circumstances it appears that a woman is asked no questions in relation to the father of the child, on the basis that to do so would be an invasion of her privacy.[15]

---

[10] Opinion of Judge De Meyer, III,1, p.39.

[11] Meeusen, 'Judicial Disapproval of Discrimination Against Illegitimate Children – A Comparative Study of Developments in Europe and the United States' (1995) 43 The American Journal of Comparative Law 119 at 141. Meeusen discusses the case law emanating from the US Supreme Court concerning the rights of children born outside of marriage. These cases form the basis of the principle that *substantive* discrimination between children born within marriage and those born outside marriage is unconstitutional, but that *procedural* discrimination may be permitted in certain circumstances. He also examines the cases which have come before the European Court of Human Rights and forms the conclusion that the European Court has formulated a similar principle in rejecting discrimination against the illegitimate child but nonetheless falling short of striking down the concept of illegitimacy per se.

[12] Status of Children Act 1987, s 44.

[13] Status of Children Act 1987, s 46.

[14] See further discussion at **5.55**.

[15] Law Reform Commission report 'Legal Aspect of Family Relationships' at 2.03: http://www.lawreform.ie (accessed 26 May 2010).

[5.12] If a person wishes to be registered on the birth certificate of a child as the father there are four options available:

(a) The mother and the person may jointly register the birth. The request for joint registration must be made to the Registrar in writing and the person must sign a declaration that he is the father of the child.

(b) The mother may request in writing that the person be registered. This must be accompanied by a written declaration of the mother that the person is the father of the child and a statutory declaration by the person that he is the father of the child.

(c) The person can make an application in writing to the Registrar, accompanied by a declaration that he is the father and a statutory declaration from the mother stating that he is the father of the child.

(d) The mother or the person requests in writing that the person be registered as the father of the child on foot of a court order finding that the person is the father, in which the person will be registered as such. This provision states that the court order must relate to proceedings referred to in section 45 of the Status of Children Act 1987. This primarily relates to applications for guardianship or maintenance. The party making the application must produce a certified copy of the court order to the Registrar. In these circumstances the Registrar is required to notify the other party of the application.

The effect of these provisions is that it is complicated to register a birth to include the names of both parents in circumstances where the parents are not married. Either both parents must be available to attend at the Registrar's office, or both must to be in a position to write and sign the necessary declarations.[16]

[5.13] Irish courts have traditionally been reluctant to accord natural unmarried fathers any rights in respect of their children. The Supreme Court in *State (Nicolaou) v An Bord Uchtála*[17] held that there is a significant difference in moral capacity and social function between the mothers and fathers of children born outside of marriage. The parents of the child were a couple who had lived together for a time and conceived a child together. The mother of the child decided to give the child up for adoption without informing the father. The father subsequently applied to have the adoption declared invalid on the basis that the Adoption Act 1952 was discriminatory in requiring consent to adoption from the child's mother and not the child's father. The Supreme Court felt that such discrimination was justified on the basis that in most cases of this kind the fathers do not have a relationship with the mother and do not have any interest in the child born out of that relationship.

[5.14] In *Keegan v Ireland*,[18] the applicant had met his girlfriend in May 1986, and they began living together in February 1987. In February 1988, it was confirmed that she was pregnant. The conception was the result of a deliberate decision, and the couple had planned to marry. Shortly afterwards, however, the relationship broke down and they ceased to cohabit. After the child was born, it was placed for adoption by the mother

---

[16] Law Reform Commission Report para 2.08.

[17] *State (Nicolaou) v An Bord Uchtála* [1966] IR 1.

[18] *Keegan v Ireland* 18 EHRR 342 1994.

without the applicant's knowledge or consent. The relevant provisions of the Adoption Act 1952 permitted the adoption of a child born outside marriage without the consent of the natural father. The applicant applied to the Circuit Court, under the Guardianship of Infants Act 1964, to be appointed as the child's guardian, which would have enabled him to challenge the proposed adoption. He was appointed guardian and awarded custody of the child. The decision of the Circuit Court was upheld by the High Court, but on appeal by way of case stated the Supreme Court ruled that the wishes of the natural father should not be considered if the prospective adopters could achieve a quality of welfare which was to an important degree better. The case was remitted to the High Court. On the rehearing a consultant psychiatrist gave evidence that if the placement with the prospective adopters was disturbed after a period of over a year, the child was likely to suffer trauma and to have difficulty in forming relationships of trust. The High Court therefore declined to appoint the applicant as guardian. An adoption order was subsequently made.

[5.15] On appeal to the European Court of Human Rights, the Court held that the notion of the 'family' in art 8 is not confined solely to marriage-based relationships and may encompass other de facto 'family' ties, where the parties are living together outside marriage. 'A child born out of such a relationship is ipso facto part of that family unit from the moment of his or her birth, and by the very fact of it. There thus exists between the child and the parents a bond amounting to family life even if at the time of the child's birth the parents are no longer co-habiting or if their relationship has then ended.' The relationship between the applicant and the child's mother lasted more than two years, during one of which they cohabited. The conception was the result of a deliberate decision, and the couple had planned to get married. The Court held that the relationship between the applicant and the child's mother had the hallmark of family life for the purposes of art 8, and accordingly from the moment of the birth a bond amounting to family life existed between the applicant and the child.

[5.16] As regards the alleged violation of art 8 of the Convention (respect for private and family life) the Court held that the fact that Irish law permitted the secret placement of the child for adoption without the applicant's knowledge or consent, leading to the bonding of the child with the proposed adopters and to the subsequent making of an adoption order, amounted to an interference with the applicant's right to respect for family life. The decision to place the child for adoption without the father's knowledge or consent, and the decisions taken by the courts concerning the child's welfare, were in accordance with Irish law, and pursued the legitimate aim of protecting the rights and freedoms of the child. However, the interference was not necessary in a democratic society. The essential problem was that Irish law permitted the child to be placed for adoption shortly after her birth without the applicant's knowledge or consent. The placement not only jeopardised the applicant's ties with the child, but also set in motion a process which was likely to prove irreversible, thereby putting the applicant at a significant disadvantage in his contest with the prospective adopters for the custody of the child. The government had advanced no reasons relevant to the welfare of the child to justify this.

[5.17] The Court also held that the adoption process had to be distinguished from the guardianship and custody proceedings. The applicant had no rights under Irish law to challenge the decision to place the child for adoption, and indeed had no standing in the adoption procedure generally. His only recourse to impede the adoption was to bring guardianship and custody proceedings. By the time these proceedings had terminated, the scales concerning the child's welfare had tilted inevitably in favour of the prospective adopters. His right to a hearing under art 6(1) of the Convention had accordingly been violated.

[5.18] As a result of this case Ireland became obliged to give natural fathers to whom children are born in the context of 'family life', as interpreted by the European Court of Human Rights, a legal opportunity to establish a relationship with that child. This was interpreted as requiring a legal entitlement to be consulted before the child is placed for adoption, and also possibly rights of access to the child and joint guardianship or joint custody with the natural mother.

[5.19] The Constitution Review Group in its consideration of the constitutional provisions in relation to the family and the unmarried father recognised the difficulties involved in an extension of the definition of 'family' to those not based on marriage.[19] It recommended that the Constitution should retain its pledge to safeguard the institution of marriage but that the legislature should not thereby be prohibited from legislating for families not based on marriage. This might entail a recognition of the de facto family, consistent with the European jurisprudence.

> There has been much criticism of the continued constitutional ostracism of natural fathers. This can be readily understood in relation to those natural fathers who either live in a stable relationship with the natural mother, or have established a relationship with the child. However, there does not appear to be justification for giving constitutional rights to every natural father simply by reason of biological links and thus include fatherhood resulting from rape, incest or sperm donorship.[20]

The Review Group considered that the solution lay in following the approach of art 8 of the ECHR in guaranteeing to every person respect for 'family life', which has been interpreted to include non-marital family life but yet requiring the existence of family ties between the mother and the father.

> This may be a way of granting constitutional rights to those fathers who have, or had, a stable relationship with the mother prior to birth, or subsequent to birth with the child, while excluding persons from having such rights who are only biological fathers without any such relationship.[21]

[5.20] In *WO'R v EH & An Bord Uchtála*,[22] the Supreme Court considered the alteration of the relationship between two children and their unmarried father, through the marriage of their mother to another man. The natural father wished to be appointed guardian to the children, with whom he had a relationship through having lived together as a family for a number of years, and thereafter through liberal access arrangements by agreement. The new husband wished to formalise his relationship with his wife's children through adoption, which the natural father would have been opposed to.

---

19 Available at http://www.constitution.ie/reports/crg.pdf (accessed 26 May 2011).
20 Available at http://www.constitution.ie/reports/crg.pdf (accessed 26 May 2011).
21 Available at http://www.constitution.ie/reports/crg.pdf (accessed 26 May 2011).
22 *WO'R v EH & An Bord Uchtála* (23 July 1996, unreported) SC.

[5.21] The Court considered the right of the natural father in this case, as in others of similar facts, to be a right to apply for guardianship under the 1987 Act, rather than a right to be appointed guardian. Hamilton CJ accepted a statement made in *JK v VW*, by Finlay CJ in which he stated that 'no constitutional right to guardianship in the father exists.[23] However, he did accept that there may be circumstances in which it may be in the interests of the child's welfare to enjoy the 'society, protection and guardianship of its father'.[24] The Court felt that in circumstances where the child had been born into a stable relationship between a couple and had been cared for initially by both parents, the rights of the natural father would be very extensive. However, the Court also had to take into account the interests of the children in this case in the context of the proposed adoption by their mother's husband, particularly when the parties agreed that such an order would not alter the existing arrangements with regard to access to the children.

[5.22] Interestingly, Murphy J, tentatively, and obiter, broached the subject of sperm donors and egg donors in his judgment. He considered that such biological fathers, in circumstances of sperm donation, would not have any natural or constitutional parental rights, along the same lines as the decision in *Nicolaou*, mentioned above:

> In more recent times one has to recognise a category of biological parenthood within which the male contributes sperm which is provided by means of artificial insemination in a female recipient unknown to the donor. This must be the case by which can be tested the basic proposition whether the mere donation of sperm confers on the donor any natural or constitutional right over the child that may subsequently be identified as having been conceived as a result of such a procedure. In my view that cold and clinical scenario would do much to strengthen the view expressed in the *Nicolaou* case that the mere fact of fatherhood does not give rise to natural; or constitutional rights.[25]

[5.23] Although Murphy J recognised that social and moral attitudes towards children outside marriage had changed significantly in the intervening period since that case, he nevertheless appeared to endorse that decision. In the context of the sperm donor it was very far removed from the facts of the case before the Court (which involved a relatively long-term relationship with the mother and children, regular access to the children and emotional and financial support being given). It was presumed by Murphy J, without very much analysis, that the fact of mere biological parentage would not entitle the father to any parental rights whatsoever.[26]

[5.24] Although Barrington J's judgment may be lauded by advocates of rights for natural fathers, he also felt that a blood tie was insufficient to give parental rights to the father. He was the only judge who criticised the *Nicolaou* case on the basis that the reasoning in the case was fundamentally flawed and inadequate. He was of the view that

---

[23]   *JK v VW* [1990] 2 IR 437.

[24]   *WO'R v EH & An Bord Uchtála* (23 July 1996, unreported) SC at 32.

[25]   *WO'R v EH & An Bord Uchtála* (23 July 1996, unreported) SC, per Murphy J.

[26]   Murphy J also went on to raise the issue of motherhood in the context of gestational surrogacy and asked, 'Who is the mother for the purposes of Article 40 of the Constitution? The woman who provided the ovum or the woman who gave birth to the child? These very questions illustrate the fundamental distinction between the line which may have to be drawn between the provision of the genetic material on which life depends and the nurturing of the being not merely from the time of birth but from the moment of conception.'

in circumstances such as those before the Court, a denial of the relationship between the parent and the child may be a cruel injustice.[27] He felt that a dispute between unmarried parents in such cases should be decided on the same basis as if they were married parents.

[5.25] The case is disappointing because it failed to avail of the opportunity to extend the rights of natural fathers in line with even the most conservative decisions of the European Court of Human Rights. The dismissal of the concept of the de facto family as not being within the framework of the Constitution, despite the recognition of such families by the European Court, which recognised their existence if nothing else, is unrealistic and unduly entrenched bearing in mind societal changes since the days of *Nicolaou,* changes in the legal status of children born outside of marriage, the introduction of divorce to recognise the increase in breakdown of the traditional Constitutional family unit and the importance attached by modern commentators to the actuality of family care and support, irrespective of legal marital ties. This was further discussed by the Supreme Court in *McD v L*, para **5.63** below.

[5.26] The Adoption Act 1998 now makes provision for consultation with unmarried fathers in respect of the proposed adoption of their child. The Act amends the Adoption Act of 1952 by the insertion of additional provisions to Section 7. Section 7D provides that the father of a child may give notice to the Adoption Board that he wishes to be consulted in relation to the adoption of his child. Section 7E (2) provides that where an adoption agency proposes to place a child for adoption and the identity of the father is known to the agency, the agency shall, before placing the child for adoption, take such steps as are reasonably practicable to consult the father for the purpose of informing of the proposed placement, explaining to him the implications of, and the procedures related to, adoption, and ascertaining whether or not he objects to the proposed placement. If the man has no objection, the adoption of the child may proceed. If the man does have an objection, the adoption will be deferred to enable the man to make an application to court to be appointed a joint guardian of the child.

[5.27] Section 7F provides that in certain circumstances, having regard to the nature of the relationship between the father and mother or the circumstances of the conception of the child, it would be inappropriate for the agency to contact the father. In such cases, the Adoption Board may authorise the placement of the child for adoption. If the mother refuses to disclose the identity of the father or the identity of the father is unknown, subs 3 provides that the agency shall counsel the mother to attempt to obtain her cooperation, indicating to her:

(i)   that the adoption may be delayed;

(ii)   the possibility of the father contesting the adoption at some later date;

(iii)   that the absence of information about the medical, genetic and social background of the father may be detrimental to the health, development or welfare of the child, and;

(iv)   such other matters as the agency deems are appropriate.

[5.28] Where the Board receives a report pursuant to subsection (3) (b) and is satisfied that the adoption agency (*a*) has taken such steps as are reasonably practicable to obtain

---

[27]   (23 July 1996, unreported) SC at 37, 38.

the cooperation of the mother, and (*b*) has no other practical way of ascertaining the father's identity, the Board may authorise the agency to, and the agency may, at any time thereafter at which it has not ascertained the father's identity, place the child for adoption. Subsection (5) provides that where the mother of a child provides an adoption agency with a statutory declaration stating that she is unable to identify the father, the agency may, at any time thereafter, place the child for adoption if it has no other practical way of ascertaining the father's identity.

The position of sperm donors is considered below.

Law Reform Commission proposals

[5.29] In Ireland, the Law Reform Commission published a consultation paper and subsequent report on Legal Aspects of Family Relationships which considers a statutory presumption in favour of granting unmarried fathers an order for guardianship unless this is not in the best interests of the child.[28] The Commission considers that a child has a right to know his or her identity and part of this is being aware of who his or her parents are. In practice, the courts operate a presumption that a non-marital father who makes an application for a guardianship order should be successful, unless there are strong reasons why he should not be in the position of a guardian. The Commission suggests that it would be helpful to place this operational presumption on a statutory footing.[29]

[5.30] The Law Reform Commission states that one of the reasons given for not extending automatic guardianship/parental responsibility to non-marital fathers is a concern that this would guarantee rights to genetic fathers who play no role in the child's life following conception. The existence of automatic rights would ensure that the genetic father had an effective veto on decisions that the mother might wish to make with regard to the child in the future. The Commission notes the distinction between non-marital fathers who have no connection with the child from conception or birth and who play no role in the child's upbringing, and fathers who, although not married to the mother, are in a committed relationship with the mother of the child and play a significant role in raising the child. It states that in the former situation the extension of automatic rights and responsibilities might be seen as not being in the best interests of the child.[30]

European Convention on Human Rights (ECHR)

[5.31] The ECHR came into force in Ireland at the end of 2003. The European Convention on Human Rights Act 2003 requires the Irish courts to interpret Irish law in a manner compatible with the Convention. While states are afforded a wide margin of appreciation, especially in relation to custody cases, the European Court in its recent judgments has also emphasised the changing European context and culture as well as the increasing number of unmarried parents. Kilkelly states that the case law of the European Court of Human Rights has long viewed contact between parent and child as integral to the maintenance of their family life relationship.[31]

---

[28] Available at http://www.lawreform.ie (accessed 26 May 2010).
[29] Law Reform Commission Report, para 3.08.
[30] Law Reform Commission Report, para 3.20.
[31] Kilkelly, *Children's Rights in Ireland* (Bloomsbury Professional, 2008) at 150. See *Andersson v Sweden* [1992] 14 EHRR 615, para 72.

[5.32] In *Zaunegger v Germany*[32] the European Court of Human Rights held that the denial of a fathers' right to custody of a child born out of wedlock violated his right to respect for family life under art 8, in conjunction with discriminatory treatment under art 14 of the European Convention. The appellant had a child out of wedlock in 1995 that was raised by both parents until their separation in August 1998. Pursuant to art 1626a § 2 of the German Civil Code, the mother held sole custody for the child upon their separation. Article 1626a § 2 of the Civil Code only grants joint custody to parents of children born out of wedlock by consent of both parents. In the absence of mutual agreement between the parents, custody is automatically granted to the mother in the child's best interest. The applicant was given visitation of the child that amounted to four months per year following the separation but a minimum agreement for a declaration of custody was not reached by the parties.

[5.33] The applicant made a complaint on the grounds that he had no possibility of obtaining joint custody against the will of the mother and that he was excluded by force of law from seeking judicial review. His application for joint custody was dismissed by the Cologne District Court, and this decision was upheld by the Cologne Court of Appeal in October 2003. The Federal Constitutional Court declined to hear the appellants' constitutional complaint. In a previous challenge, the Constitutional Court upheld the constitutionality of art 1626a § 2 of the Civil Code on the basis that, in the event of a serious dispute between parents, courts could not be expected to consider joint custody to be in a child's best interests. Accordingly, the Constitutional Court did not consider art 1626a § 2 to be incompatible with the right to respect for the family life of fathers.

[5.34] For the purpose of art 8, the European Court of Human Rights reiterated that 'the notion of family … is not confined to marriage-based relationships and may encompass other *de facto* "family" ties where the parties are living together out of wedlock'. The Court further noted that 'the mutual enjoyment by a parent and child of each other's company constitutes a fundamental element of family life, even if the relationship between the parents has broken down, and domestic measures which hinder such enjoyment amount to an interference with the right protected by art 8'. Having determined that the facts of the case engaged art 8 of the Convention, the Court then turned to consider whether there was a violation of art 14, which 'affords protection against different treatment, without an objective and reasonable justification of persons in similar situations'. The Government argued that art 1626a § 2 of the Civil Code and the vesting of custody in the mother is designed to ensure that, from birth, there is certainty as to the legal custodian of the child. The Government further argued that the presumption against joint custody without consent is 'based on the notion that parents who could not agree to make a custody declaration were highly likely to come into conflict when specific questions relating to the exercise of parental custody were at stake, which could cause painful disputes which would be detrimental to the child's interests'.

[5.35] The European Court explained that while it is hesitant to examine domestic legislation in the abstract, an examination of the application of the legislation to this case revealed an unjustified and different treatment of the applicant in comparison with

---

[32] *Zaunegger v Germany* [2009] ECHR 22028/04 (3 December 2009).

the mother and divorced fathers. The Court reasoned that dismissing the father's application without evaluating the child's best interests was discriminatory. This was especially so in the present case, given that the father had been a consistent presence in the child's life from birth until the child reached the age of three and a half. Further, even after the separation, the father continued to have close contact and involvement with the child, 'providing for his daily needs'.

[5.36] In finding a violation of art 14 when read in conjunction with art 8, the Court stated that it could not share the Government's assumption that joint custody against the will of the mother is prima facie not to be in the child's interests. The Court determined that there was no reasonable relationship of proportionality between the general exclusion of judicial review of the initial attribution of sole custody to the mother and the aim pursued, namely the protection of the best interests of a child born out of wedlock. The Court found the Government's arguments insufficient to allow for less judicial scrutiny or for the appellant, who had been acknowledged as a father and acted in that capacity, to be treated differently from a father who originally held parental authority and later separated from the mother or divorced.

[5.37] Ireland has yet to incorporate the UN 1989 Convention on the Rights of the Child into domestic law, although Ireland has signed and ratified the Convention. Article 5 provides that 'States Parties shall respect the responsibilities, rights and duties of parents ... to provide, in a manner consistent with the evolving capacities of the child, appropriate direction and guidance in the exercise by the child of the rights recognised in the present Convention'. Article 9 of the Convention refers to the need to respect the right of the child to ongoing contact with both parents. In 2002, the Council of Europe adopted a Convention on Contact Concerning Children. The aim of the 2002 Convention is to improve the right of children to maintain regular contact with both parents. Ireland is not a state party to the Convention and has not signed or ratified it.

For discussion of the parentage rights of known sperm donors, see para **5.60** below.

Posthumous conception

[5.38] Problems may arise in situations where a widow wishes to use her husband's sperm after his death.[33] This would usually occur where the sperm had been stored in a sperm bank for various reasons such as where the husband was undergoing treatment for cancer which might leave him sterile,[34] or if he was employed in a dangerous job or hazardous pursuit.[35] There is no legislative prohibition in Ireland on a widow gaining

---

[33] The same issues would arise where a man wished to have eggs removed from his wife prior to her death for use after her death. This situation is less common and would necessitate the participation of a gestational surrogate.

[34] Deterioration of sperm quality occurs as a result of the damaging effect of chemotherapy. This may be permanent or temporary. Men with cancer should be given the opportunity to freeze semen samples for possible future use. Knowledge that their fertility potential is secured may also help in the emotional battle against the cancer. Such a facility was opened in the Rotunda Hospital in Dublin in 1998.

See Lass, 'Cancer Patients Should Be Offered Semen Cryopreservation' (1999) 318 British Medical Journal 1556.

[35] It is common for soldiers who are being deployed to active service areas such as Iraq or Afghanistan to store sperm in the event that they sustain serious injury.

access to her deceased husband's frozen sperm in an attempt to become pregnant. Some Irish clinics require couples seeking treatment to sign a consent form which stipulates that if the man dies the sperm will be thawed without transfer. It is unclear whether such a provision would be upheld by a court faced with a testamentary provision to the opposite effect and a claim by a widow to have constitutional rights to inherit under her husband's will. As such a case has not yet arisen in Ireland, the legal status of a child born in such circumstances is also uncertain. The court may take the view that the deceased man had ownership rights in relation to his body and its tissue and that therefore he was entitled to bequeath it to his partner. Alternatively, the court could decide that this issue should not be decided on property grounds and should instead be decided on the basis of autonomy and the proven intent of the deceased to become a father after his death. The issue of property rights in the human body generally, and specifically in relation to gametes, is considered in detail in Chapter 10.

Parentage issues in posthumous reproduction

[5.39] The development of cryopreservation (the technology of freezing used to preserve gametes and embryos) has created the potential for posthumous conception of children.[36] It is increasingly common for men, such as soldiers and athletes, to store sperm for potential use by a wife or partner in the event of their injury or death. Sperm harvesting, the process by which sperm is extracted following a man's death, has also been the subject of a number of requests from spouses or partners of men who have been hospitalised following road traffic and other accidents. More infrequently, requests have been made for retrieval of oocytes or eggs from women hospitalised following accidents or sudden brain injuries.[37] Courts in other jurisdictions have been asked to resolve disputes relating to the status of children and parents in these circumstances, and it is likely that such a case will come before an Irish court in the coming years.

[5.40] Until the advent of assisted reproductive technology, a child born to a woman after the death of its genetic father was necessarily born within about nine months of its father's death. Legislation in many countries recognises this situation by protecting such children's rights to inherit as a lawful heir of the deceased. However, inheritance issues are more complicated where assisted reproduction is involved, as posthumous children

---

[36] It is estimated that hundreds of thousands of cryopreserved embryos exist in the United States and the number is climbing as the practice of American soldiers storing their sperm increases, as the practice of harvesting sperm from newly deceased spouses becomes more common and as the technology of cryopreserving ova advances. See The President's Council on Bioethics, *Reproduction and Responsibility: The Regulation of New Biotechnologies* (March 2004), chapter 2, page 17. http://bioethics.georgetown.edu/pcbe/reports/ reproductionandresponsibility/index.html (accessed 26 May 2011).

[37] For example, see case report in the New England Journal of Medicine 15 July 2010. 'Case 21–2010 A request for retrieval of oocytes from a 36-year-old woman with anoxic brain injury' NEJM Vol 363: 276–283 Number 3. The case involved a married woman who had a cardiac arrest after a massive pulmonary embolism resulting from venous thrombosis that occurred while she slept in a sitting position on a long airplane flight. Her husband and parents wished to have her oocytes retrieved (which could then be fertilised with the husband's sperm and carried by a surrogate mother on behalf of the husband) but there was no clear evidence of the patient's own wishes. The request was refused.

can now be born years after the death of the parent and may therefore fall outside of the legislative provisions.

[5.41] In the United States, the National Conference of Commissioners on Uniform State Law studies and reviews the law of the states to determine which areas of law should be uniform.[38]The commissioners promote the principle of uniformity by drafting and proposing specific statutes in areas of the law where uniformity between the states is desirable. No uniform law is effective until a state legislature adopts it.[39] In the area of assisted reproduction, there are a number of relevant uniform acts, such as the Uniform Parentage Act 2000, which incorporates the Uniform Status of Children of Assisted Conception Act of 1988 and the Uniform Probate Code 1993. The 2000 Act provides that if a couple consents to any sort of assisted conception, and the woman gives birth to the resultant child, they are the legal parents. A donor of either sperm or eggs used in an assisted conception may not be a legal parent under any circumstances. The Uniform Probate Code does not provide for posthumously conceived children to inherit but neither does it prohibit it. It provides that 'for purposes of intestate succession…an individual is the child of his or her natural parents, regardless of their marital status.' A finding of heirship of a child conceived using the gametes of a genetic parent who consented to the gametes being used after his or her death to conceive that person's child would seem to be consistent with this provision.[40] The Uniform Parentage Act provides that if an individual who consented in writing to be a parent by assisted reproduction dies before the child's conception, the deceased is not to be regarded as the parent of the child unless he/she consented in writing to being a parent after death.[41] This requirement for written consent, both to the posthumous use of gametes and the assignment of parentage, is also imposed by the Human Fertilisation and Embryology Act 2008 in England. The requirement for written consent clearly precludes the use of gametes in circumstances where the person dies an untimely death, such as following an accident.

[5.42] Courts in the United States have considered the issue of parental recognition and inheritance in a number of cases dealing with social security and pension entitlements. In 1993, the absence of express statutory provision dealing with the status of a child born to a widow came up for consideration in the context of a social security claim in Louisiana. The circumstances of this case, *Hart v Charter*,[42] were that Mr Hart had deposited sperm in a sperm bank prior to undergoing chemotherapy for a tumour which led to his death a short time later. Before undergoing surgery to remove the tumour, Mr Hart told his wife that he wanted her to carry out their plans to have a child even if he should die. Three months after his death, his widow became pregnant using the stored sperm and gave birth to a baby girl in June 1991, 355 days after her husband's death.

---

38 http://www.nccusl.org/ (accessed 26 May 2011).
39 For updated information on uniform acts and their adoption in all states see http://www.nccusl.org/Legislation.aspx (accessed 26 May 2011).
40 Kindegran and McBrien, 'Posthumous Reproduction', (2005) 39 Family Law Quarterly 579.
41 Similar provisions have been enacted in Colorado, Delaware, Texas, Washington and Wyoming. Other states, such as North Dakota, have taken a prohibitory approach which prevents the child from inheriting even if the deceased consented. The Californian statute allows the child to inherit if the deceased consented in writing and the child is in utero within two years of the deceased's death – Cal Probate Code §248.5 (2005).
42 *Hart v Charter* no 04–3944 (ED La Dismissed 18 March 1996).

Mrs Hart applied for social security Survivor's Benefit for her daughter but this was denied on the basis that Mr Hart was not the child's father. Counsel argued that excluding the child from being able to obtain benefits was unconstitutional. The Social Security Administration declined to defend against that argument and agreed to pay benefits.

[5.43] In *Estate of Kolacy*,[43] a New Jersey court decided that twins born 18 months after the death of their father were his legal heirs. The Court took the view that posthumously conceived children should be able to inherit as long as there is evidence of consent from the deceased and unless doing so would unfairly intrude on the rights of other heirs or seriously disrupt the orderly administration of the deceased's estate. Similarly, in *Woodward v Commissioner of Social Security*,[44] a Massachusetts court addressed whether twins conceived from frozen sperm and born two years after the father's death from leukemia had specific inheritance rights under state law and were consequently eligible for certain federal survivor benefits. After the Social Security Administration (SSA) denied benefits to Mrs Woodward's daughters on the grounds that 'she had not established that the twins were the husband's "children" within the meaning of the [US Social Security] Act,' Mrs Woodward brought suit in federal court against the agency. In this case, eligibility for SSA benefits turned on whether the children would be treated as the husband's natural children for the disposition of his personal property under the Massachusetts law of intestate succession. The Supreme Judicial Court ruled that under limited circumstances, posthumously conceived children do have inheritance rights under state intestacy laws. First, the child's surviving parent or legal representative must establish a genetic relationship between the child and the deceased. Second, the parent or representative must demonstrate that the deceased 'affirmatively consented' to posthumous conception and the support of any resulting child. The Court noted further that even should such circumstances exist, time limitations as mandated by the Massachusetts intestacy statute might preclude the claim. Finally, the Court required that notice be given to all interested parties in any action brought to establish such inheritance rights.

[5.44] The *Woodward* Court noted that no American court of last resort had previously considered in a published opinion the question of posthumously conceived genetic children's inheritance rights under other states' intestacy laws. The Court considered three important issues in its decision. First, under the 'best interests of the child' consideration, the Court concluded that posthumously conceived children should be, as far as possible, entitled to the same legal rights and protections as children conceived before death. The Court provided a number of factors supporting this conclusion, including the fact that the legislature had expressed its will that all children be entitled to the same legal rights and protections 'regardless of the accidents of their birth' and that intestacy statute provisions had been regularly amended to expand the class of non-marital children eligible to succeed from an intestate estate. It also pointed to the fact that some reproductive technologies, such as sperm preservation, had been performed for a number of years, and in that time the legislature had not acted to preclude posthumously conceived children from inheriting on intestacy.

---

43   *In re Estate of Kolacy* 753 A 2d 1257 (NJ Super Ct Ch Div 2000).
44   *Woodward v Commissioner of Social Security*, 435 Mass 536 (2002).

[5.45] In relation to the need for efficient administration of estates, the Court considered a second important legislative purpose of providing certainty to heirs by effecting the prompt and accurate administration of intestate estates. The Court noted that two issues are critical to these goals, certainty of relationship between the deceased and his 'issue', and limitation periods for the commencement of claims against the estate. The Court addressed the first issue in its requirement of proof of genetic relationship (seen as particularly necessary in light of the possibility of different 'legal' and 'genetic' parentage), and noted that while the second issue of time limitation was highly relevant, it was outside the scope of the facts of this particular case.

[5.46] Finally, the Court considered a third important state interest in honouring the reproductive choices of individuals. The Court found that consent by the deceased to posthumous reproduction as well as to the support of the children was necessary to satisfy the goal of fraud prevention. The Court provided a number of reasons supporting this requirement, including that an individual has a protected right to control the use of his or her gametes, silence should not be construed as consent and that gametes are preserved for a variety of reasons beyond posthumous reproduction. Accordingly, the Court stated, 'where conception results from a third-party medical procedure using a deceased person's gametes, it is entirely consistent with our laws on children, parentage, and reproductive freedom to place the burden on the surviving parent ... to demonstrate the genetic relationship of the child to the decedent and that the decedent consented to reproduce posthumously and to support any resulting child.'

[5.47] In a similar case in Arizona, *Gillett-Netting v Barnhart*,[45] the mother of twins conceived 10 months after their father's death claimed social security survivor benefits. The children had been conceived using sperm their father stored before undergoing chemotherapy treatment for cancer. The Court noted that parentage was not in dispute, as the children were unquestionably the biological children of the deceased and were deemed dependent under the wording of the Social Security Act. In general, it seems that in social security cases in the US, the courts tend to favour the rights of the child wherever possible.

[5.48] In the United Kingdom in the Human Fertilisation and Embryology Act 1990, as amended in 2008, the posthumous use of gametes is not prohibited, as can be seen from the discussion of the *Blood* case above. Under the 1990 Act the child was not recognised as the child of the deceased. Section 28(6)(b) of the 1990 Act provided that where 'the sperm of a man, or any embryo the creation of which was brought about with his sperm, was used after his death, he is not to be treated as the father of the child.' This provision was inserted according to the recommendations of the Warnock report, to ensure that estates could be administered with some degree of finality and to actively discourage such practices in effect. This was apparently due to the feared potential psychological problems which could ensue for a child and its mother as a result of such procedures. However, as pointed out by Morgan and Lee:

> The instrument which is used is that of punishing the child for what are seen as 'the sins of its mother.' This is an odd, not to say indefensible, way of proceeding ... It seems inconsistent with the general legislative mood of recent years which has sought to minimise

---

[45]   *Gillett-Netting v Barnhart* 371 F 3d 593 (9th Cir, Ariz 2004).

or mitigate the differential statuses of children (and the adults they will become) based solely on the conduct of their parents.

The 1990 Act was amended in 2008. Section 39(1) of the 2008 Act provides that:

— if a child has been carried by a woman as a result of the placing in her of an embryo or of sperm and eggs or her artificial insemination after the death of the man, and

— the man consented in writing to the use of his sperm after his death, and

— to being treated for the purpose mentioned in subsection (3) as the father of any resulting child, and

— the woman has elected in writing not later than 42 days from the day on which the child was born for the man to be as the father of the child, and

— no-one else is to be treated as the father of the child,

— then the man is to be treated for the purpose mentioned in subsection (3) as the father of the child.

Subsection (3) states that the purpose referred to in subsection (1) is that of enabling the man's particulars to be entered as the particulars of the child's father in a relevant register of births. This means that posthumous conception using the sperm of a deceased man is dependent upon his written consent (as was the case under the 1990 Act). This consent must also confirm the man's intent to be considered as the father of the child for birth registration purposes. These provisions confer parenthood for birth registration purposes only.

[5.49] In relation to succession rights, there are two main approaches that may be taken to the resolution of the difficulties posed by inheritance provisions and the administration of estates in the case of posthumously conceived children. Firstly, the law might allow the child to be registered as having a father for administration purposes, for example birth certification, but simply prohibit succession to his estate. Secondly, it might allow the child to inherit only if he or she was born within a stipulated time period after the death of the deceased man. The most commonly suggested time period within which such a child might be eligible is birth within two years of the deceased's death. This time period is taken as reflecting the usual time period within which estates are settled and within which the child might retain a sense of connection to the parent. A longer period might interfere with the administration of the estate while a shorter period might interfere with procreative liberty.[46] This balancing of procreative liberty against an adminstratively workable fixed time period results in an admittedly arbitrary time frame, as it may very easily take longer than two years to conceive and give birth to a child in these circumstances but it seems to offer the best compromise. It offers recognition to procreational autonomy of the individual and legal connection between the child and its father with the attendant financial responsibilities which this entails, while at the same time respecting the right of the State and other interested parties to a relatively normal administration period for the settlement of the estate for the deceased.

---

[46] Chester, 'Freezing the Heir Apparent: A Dialogue on Postmortem Conception, Parental Responsibility and Inheritance' (1996) 33 HLR 967, 995–996.

[5.50] In the Australian case, *Estate of K*, in 1996[47] the deceased, who died intestate, was survived by a wife, four children and two frozen embryos. His widow wished to have the embryos implanted in her. The question for the administrator of the estate, and ultimately the Court, was whether the frozen embryos were issue of the deceased so as to give them inheritance rights in relation to the estate. Slicer J decided that, once born, the frozen embryo could be regarded as the child of the deceased in the same way as the common law had done for children *en ventre sa mere* born within a defined time of the deceased father's death. He saw no logical distinction between the in vitro child born posthumously who was at birth the biological child of the father and mother, irrespective of the time of implantation, and the child *en ventre sa mere* who had a contingent interest dependent on birth. The conclusion reached in this case has been criticised on the basis that, as a matter of law, the deceased could not be the father of the child, as the legislation in question applies the presumption of paternity to married women only.[48] The death of the child's father terminates the marriage and therefore when the implantation occurs, she is not a married woman and does not come within the terms of the legislation. However, it could be argued that it is the provision of the semen rather than the embryo implantation which is the relevant time to consider the question of paternity. At the time of the provision of the semen used to create the embryo, the marriage was still in subsistence and therefore the statutory presumption of paternity should apply.

[5.51] These cases indicate that the issues raised by reproductive technology are 'neither academic nor avoidable'.[49] The social context in which decisions may be made in relation to the child's status must also be considered:

> If a child is born to a man's widow which is genetically his child – and he was a willing participant in the process – then it should be considered his child if indeed the child is born alive. *Not* to reach such a conclusion is historically regressive: placing the children back in the era of bastards, with all their disabilities, if not necessarily the same social stigmas.[50]

[5.52] Consent is not the only consideration to be taken into account here – the best interests of the future child must also be a significant factor in determination of this issue.[51] The European Society of Human Reproduction and Embryology (ESHRE) acknowledges that there is no consensus among the different religions on posthumous conception and that there are different ethical considerations to be taken into account.[52] These include the principle of respect for the autonomy of the individual to decide about reproduction, and the principle of beneficence or concern for the welfare of the future

---

[47]   *Estate of K* [1996] 5 Tas R 365. For further discussion see Chalmers, 'Frozen Embryos: Rights of Inheritance. *In Re the Estate of the late K*' [1997] Med L Rev 121.

[48]   Atherton, 'En Ventre sa Frigidaire: Posthumous Children in the Succession Context' (1999) 19(2) Legal Studies 139–164 at 159.

[49]   Atherton, 'En Ventre sa Frigidaire: Posthumous Children in the Succession Context' (1999) 19(2) Legal Studies 139–164 p 159.

[50]   Atherton, 'En Ventre sa Frigidaire: Posthumous Children in the Succession Context' (1999) 19(2) Legal Studies 139–164 p 159.

[51]   Jones and Gillett, 'Posthumous Reproduction: Consent and Its Limitations' (2008) J Med Law Oct 16(2): 279–87.

[52]   ESHRE Task Force on Ethics and Law 11: Posthumous Assisted Reproduction (2006) Human Reproduction Vol 21, No 12 pp 3050–3053.

child. No research has been conducted to study the consequences for the child who has been conceived posthumously and it is speculated that a number of factors may be influential here, including being raised in a one-parent family and possible stigmatisation, although there is no empirical evidence about serious harmful effects on the child. On the positive side, the child will have knowledge of its genetic parentage and will see its conception as a story of a much-desired gift from a loving relationship. ESHRE advises an evaluation of the surviving parent's motives and expectations, as there is a danger for the autonomy of the child if the parent sees the child as a commemoration or symbolic replacement of the deceased partner. The society also recommends written consent from the deceased and a minimum waiting period of one year after death before treatment should be commenced.

[5.53] It remains to be seen what approach the Irish legislature or judiciary will take to this complex area. In the absence of legislation, a property approach to this issue could result in an Irish court being asked to decide on the validity of a testamentary disposition of gametes, most usually sperm, to the deceased's partner. Respect for reproductive autonomy might demand that the deceased man's wishes in relation to the posthumous use of his sperm be observed but this may cause problems for the law. The two main difficulties in Ireland, as elsewhere, relate to the status of the child and his/her inheritance rights to the estate of his/her parent. The status of a child born through the posthumous use of sperm is uncertain in Ireland, even where the woman who wishes to use the sperm is the widow of the deceased and his intent to reproduce in this way in clearly evident from a will or other legal document. The marriage of the parties is no longer in existence due to the husband's death and, therefore, in essence the child is born to a single parent and will be a non-marital child. This is curious, as the intent to reproduce is clear and the sperm was donated at a time when the parties were legally married. Perhaps it is due to the focus on the child's right to inherit from its father's estate which at common law was dependant on the child's legitimate status[53]. However, in Ireland, due to the Status of Children Act 1987, distinctions between children on the basis of the marital status of their parents are no longer valid for succession purposes. The difficulty here, however, is that the child would not be recognised as a child of its deceased 'father' at all and would therefore be regarded as legally fatherless rather than simply a non-marital child. This would effectively prohibit the child's inheritance rights and claims to succession. In such circumstances, where the child's genetic parentage is clear, it is inconsistent with the best interests of the child. This classification, if used at all, should be reserved for situations in which paternity is unknown or unclear, such as in situations where a single woman gives birth to a child through donor insemination. The problem is a reflection of the common law position under which a child would only be regarded as legitimate if born within the usual period of gestation (child *en ventre sa mere*) after its married father's death.[54] In this way the court could be satisfied that conception took place within the legitimate bounds of a valid marriage.

---

[53] Shatter, *Family Law* (4th edn, Bloomsbury Professional, 1997) at 427–443.

[54] The Succession Act 1965, s 3(2) provides 'Descendants and relatives of a deceased person begotten before his death but born alive thereafter shall, for the purposes of this Act, be regarded as having been born in the lifetime of the deceased and as having survived him'.

DONOR INSEMINATION

[5.54] In this procedure (hereafter referred to as DI[55]) the sperm used to inseminate the woman is that of a donor. There is no sperm bank facility currently in operation in Ireland, although men who are undergoing chemotherapy are advised to store sperm in advance of treatment. Sperm can be imported from other jurisdictions for those who seek sperm donation in order to conceive. These activities currently occur in a legislative lacuna regarding the status of any resulting child. Couples who choose to undergo this treatment usually choose to keep this fact a secret. Due to matching of physical characteristics of the donor with those of the husband (ie blond hair, blue eyes, etc.) and the confidentiality of relationship between the couple and the medical practitioner, it was easy for couples to believe that 'no-one need ever know' and couples traditionally were advised not to tell anyone about the circumstances of the child's conception. This advice has changed in recent years with the increasing recognition of the negative effects of secrecy within families and the child's moral right to know the circumstances of its conception and the identity of its genetic parents.

Parentage where child is born within marital family using DI

[5.55] Under the common law, the presumption of legitimacy provided that a child born to a married woman was legitimate, her husband being the father of the child. It was based on a two-fold premise – namely, the presumption of sexual intercourse between the spouses and the presumption that the child was born as a result of that intercourse. To rebut the presumption, it would have been necessary to prove that the couple had not had sexual intercourse during the period when the child must have been conceived. In Ireland the giving of such evidence was complicated by the rule in *Russell v Russell*[56] which effectively prohibited either spouse giving evidence which would have the effect of 'bastardising' a child born in wedlock. It was not until 1982 that this rule was held to be unconstitutional as a violation of the guarantee of fair procedures.[57] The Status of Children Act 1987 abolished the presumption of legitimacy.[58] Section 46 of that Act provides that where a woman gives birth to a child (a) during a subsisting marriage to which she is a party, or (b) within the period of ten months after the termination, by death or otherwise, of a marriage to which she is a party, then the husband of the marriage shall be presumed to be the father of the child unless the contrary is proved on the balance of probabilities.

---

[55]   AID (Artificial Insemination by Donor) was the usual acronym for this procedure until the advent of the AIDS, virus which led to unnecessary confusion in terminology. The term Donor Insemination (DI) is therefore now more commonly used in practice and will be used here unless quoting directly from another source.

[56]   *Russell v Russell* [1924] AC 687 (HL).

[57]   In 1982 the Law Reform Commission in its *Report on Illegitimacy* stated that it was 'unjust for the law to distinguish between children on the basis of the marital status of their parents' and it recommended the introduction of legislation to 'remove the concept of illegitimacy from the law and equalise the rights of children born outside marriage with those of children born within marriage'. LRC Report No 4 at 85. This recommendation was further strengthened by *S v S* [1983] IR 68 in which the Court held that the rule in *Russell v Russell* [1924] AC 687 was unconstitutional.

[58]   Status of Children Act 1987, s 44.

[5.56] If the child's paternity is challenged (although this has not happened to date in Ireland in the context of children born through use of donor sperm) the presumption that the husband is the father may be overturned. In theory such a child could then be regarded as a non-marital child, which is inconsistent with child law and policy, which prioritises the best interests of the child. In other jurisdictions, the courts and/or the legislature have dealt with this issue on the basis that the consent of the husband to the DI procedure carried out on his wife results in the imposition of parental responsibility on him. For example, in the American case, *People v Sorenson*[59] where a married woman had DI with her husband's consent, her husband was deemed the legal father for the purposes of child maintenance payments after the couple divorced. The anonymous donor of sperm could not be considered the natural father, as he was no more responsible for the use of his sperm than the donor of blood. As a result, the Court held that the child had no 'natural father' and it had to look instead for a lawful or consenting father. Sorenson, having 'consent[ed] to the production of a child', and having thereby made it 'safe to assume that without [his] active participation and consent the child would not have been procreated', became the child's father and as a result became responsible for supporting the child.[60]

[5.57] A number of draft laws have been promulgated in the US under Uniform Laws provisions but have either been adopted by only a handful of states or none at all. They are the Uniform Act on Paternity 1960, the Uniform Parentage Act 1973, the Uniform Putative and Unknown Fathers Act 1988 and the Uniform Status of Children of Assisted Conception Act 1988. The latter, which has been adopted in a small number of US states, provides that a husband who gave consent in assisted conception is the father of the child and donors are not regarded as parents. If the identity of the sperm donor is known it also raises the question of whether that man has any parental rights in the child. The US Uniform Parentage Act 1973 provides that the donor is treated in law as if he were not the natural father of a child conceived through the use of his sperm.[61] This is also the case in the UK where the Human Fertilisation and Embryology Act 1990, s 28 (6), as amended by s 41(1) of the 2008 Act, provides that where donor sperm is used in accordance with a consent given by him under the schedule to the Act then the donor is not to be treated as the father of the child.[62] This is considered further below.

---

[59] *People v Sorenson* 437 P 2d 495 (1968). The case was brought by way of criminal prosecution for failure to support a child. Sorenson argued that he had no duty of support, p 497.

[60] *People v Sorenson* 437 P 2d 495 (1968) at 499. *Sorenson* is one of a number of cases in the 1960s and 1970s in which the court determined paternity on the 'intent' or 'consent' of the mother's husband or partner. See, for example, *In Re Adoption of Anonymous* 345 NYS 2d 430 (NY Sup Ct1973) in which a man who had consented to the conception and pregnancy of his wife by DI was enabled to veto the adoption of the child by his (now) ex-wife's new husband. Also *Gursky v Gursky* 242 NYS 2d 406 (NY Sup Ct 1963), in which a man who consented to DI of his wife was obliged to support the child despite the annulment of his marriage on grounds of non-consummation.

[61] Uniform Parentage Act, s 5.

[62] Human Fertilisation and Embryology Act 1900, s 28(6) provides, as far as is relevant here, as follows:

'Where ... the sperm of a man who had given such consent as is required by... this Act was used for a purpose for which such consent was required ... he is not to be treated as the father of the child.'

[5.58] In relation to embryo donation, the legal position in Ireland is unclear due to the absence of legislation. If the woman giving birth to the child is treated as the legal mother (as is the case in the UK and other jurisdictions), then her husband would also benefit from the presumption of paternity. Thus both parties would be acknowledged as the parents of the child despite the lack of a biological link.

Parentage of child born outside of marriage using DI

[5.59] In the context of an unmarried couple who have a child through DI or embryo donation, although the male partner is clearly not the biological father, he could be registered as the legal father with the mother's consent. If she does not consent, such as where the relationship has ended during the pregnancy, he does not have any parental rights in respect of the child, as he is neither the genetic father, nor is he married to the birth mother. This is discussed above at para **5.07**.

Paternity rights of known sperm donors

[5.60] In most cases of DI the sperm donor will not be known to the mother, nor will he wish to have a parental relationship with the child. However, in some circumstances children may be conceived using donor sperm where the identity of the donor is known. This primarily occurs in situations where the mother is a single woman or in a lesbian partnership and although not necessarily infertile, she seeks the assistance of a male friend in order to have a child. A similar situation could arise through embryo donation if the donating couple is known to the woman seeking the pregnancy. In many cases of this kind, it is agreed that the man will not have any financial responsibilities to the child but will play a role in the child's life such as that of an uncle or godfather. However, where the arrangement breaks down, the sperm donor may seek to formalise his access to the child by applying for recognition as the biological father.

[5.61] In one of the first reported cases on this issue, the American case *CM v CC*, in 1977[63] a sperm donor sought parental rights to the child conceived as a result of donor insemination using his sperm. The donor was known to the mother at all times and claimed that he believed that he would be treated as, and wished to be treated as, the child's father. The question for the Court was whether a sperm donor should be treated as the natural father of the child, thereby entitling him to visitation rights, etc. Based on family law principles in relation to parentage, the New Jersey Appeal Court found the case to be analogous to Artificial Insemination by Husband in that the donor was known to the mother and intended to have a parental role in relation to the child. The Court held that 'if an unmarried woman conceives a child through artificial insemination from a known man, that man cannot be considered to be less a father because he is not married to the woman.'

[5.62] The Court also relied on policy considerations in deciding that it was in a child's interests to have two parents wherever possible. This case is important because it refuses to distinguish, for the purposes of visitation and custody rights, between a child conceived by natural means and a child conceived by artificial insemination. It also refuses to cast any aspersions on the morality of unmarried persons seeking artificial insemination.

---

63   *CM v CC* 152 NJ Super 160, 377 A 2d 821.

[5.63] In an Irish case involving a known sperm donor, *McD v L & Another*,[64] a gay man donated sperm to a lesbian couple on the understanding that he would have a role in the child's life such as that of a godfather or favourite uncle. The relationship between the man and the couple, particularly the birth mother, deteriorated after the child's birth due to disagreements regarding the extent of the relationship between the man and the child. The man sought the right to be appointed legal guardian of the child and access. The High Court dismissed the action on the basis that it was not in the best interests of the child. Hedigan J held that the lesbian couple and the child constituted a de facto family and that there was nothing in Irish law to suggest that a family of two women and a child has any lesser right to be recognised than a de facto family comprised of a man and woman unmarried to each other and a child. The case was appealed to the Supreme Court which held that the man was entitled to access to the child but not guardianship at the present time. The Court unanimously held that the agreement between the parties prior to the conception of the child was unenforceable but nonetheless relevant as a factual background and context to the case. All judges were also unanimous in stating that the welfare of the child, as the first and paramount consideration, was central to the determination of the issues in this case as provided by s 3 of the Guardianship of Infants Act 1964.

[5.64] The issue of the recognition of the de facto family in the context of the application of art 8 of the ECHR was also discussed by the Court. The Court held that the High Court had no jurisdiction to apply directly the provisions of the Convention to the lesbian couple and the child. Denham J stated that there is no institution in Ireland of a de facto family and that the family in Ireland is defined as that based on marriage.[65] She held that the man had rights as a natural father to apply to be appointed guardian and the Court had to consider such an application using the best interests of the child as its paramount consideration. She also held that there is benefit to a child in having the society of its father and that it was unfortunate that the parties had not been able to agree between them on what form of contact the child should have with his father. Geoghegan J held that:

> Even within the narrow confines of a sperm donor situation, as in this particular case, there may be wholly different sets of circumstances. There may be the anonymous donor who afterwards purports to claim such rights. There may be the known donor, as in this case, but with quite different types of side agreements (whether binding or not). In either of those situations, the donee may be married or unmarried and may be living in a heterosexual or homosexual relationship or none. In all these cases, the judge dealing with the application, must stand back and consider what is the just and common sense solution, always bearing in mind that the child's welfare is the first and paramount consideration.

[5.65] He also recognised that it was well-known from adoption situations that a child not brought up by and out of contact with his or her natural parents will frequently have a real interest at some stage in making such contact. Therefore, the blood link is always a factor to be taken into account in considering the child's best interests but any conclusions will vary enormously depending on the circumstances of the particular

---

[64]   *McD v L & Another* [2009] IESC 81.
[65]   Note the recent decision of the European Court of Human Rights in *Schalk and Kopf v Austria* (Application No 30141/04) mentioned in Ch 4, fn 121.

case. He was of the view that if there was to be any contact between a sperm donor father and the child, the only viable role was that originally agreed by the parties, that is of a 'favourite uncle'. The learned judge felt that 'any connection closer than that, at least in the absence of complete agreement, would be bound to be wholly disruptive and against the child's interests'.

[5.66] The Court allowed the appeal on the issue of access and remitted the matter to the High Court for determination. Despite the decision not to grant guardianship in this case based on the application of the best interests of the child test in light of the poor relationship between the mother and father of the child, the decision is a positive step in the direction of the recognition of the rights of natural fathers and the acknowledgement that it is generally in the best interests of children to know who their fathers are and to have a relationship with them where possible.

[5.67] There have also been cases brought under the ECHR in an attempt to establish a legal relationship between the father/donor and the child. For example, in *M v the Netherlands,* an application was brought under art 8 of the ECHR (though held to be inadmissible) by a man who had agreed to be a sperm donor for a lesbian couple.[66] The man had kept in regular contact with the couple during the pregnancy and with the resulting child. He did not make any financial contribution to the child's upbringing. Disagreements arose as to his visitation rights to the child and he instituted court proceedings in the Netherlands claiming an entitlement to contact with the child. The Dutch Supreme Court denied his application on the basis that biological fatherhood alone was not sufficient to establish 'family life' within the meaning of art 8. The applicant complained to the Commission, which also required close personal ties such as cohabitation to establish a relationship within art 8. It found that donation of sperm by itself could not found a claim to family life. Although he had some limited contact with the child, this again was insufficient to form the close personal ties required.

There is further discussion of the rights of unmarried fathers above at para **5.07** et seq.

Parentage provisions in the UK

[5.68] In the UK under s 35 of the Human Fertilisation and Embryology Act 2008, the husband of a woman receiving DI treatment will be recognised as the father of the child unless it is shown that he did not consent to the treatment. In the case of unmarried couples, under s 36 a man will be treated as the father of a child where he has given written notice that he consents to being treated as the father of any child resulting from treatment provided to a woman. This provision replaces the previous provision in s 28 (5) of the 1990 Act, which granted parenthood to unmarried couples only on the basis that they were 'treated together'. Difficulties in interpretation of this provision can be seen in *Re D (a child)*[67] where a woman who had previously received unsuccessful treatment with donor gametes together with her partner, returned to the clinic for further treatment after the relationship had ended. She did not inform the clinic that she was no longer being treated together with her ex-partner and the clinic relied on the consent forms previously signed by her ex-partner. After she gave birth to a child, her ex-partner

---

[66] *M v Netherlands* (1993) 74 DR 120.
[67] *Re D (a child)* [2005] UKHL 33.

applied for parental responsibility and contact orders in respect of the child but the Court held that they had not been treated together at the relevant time and so he could not be regarded as the child's father. The House of Lords confirmed that the relevant time is the time of embryo transfer or donor insemination, not the time when the couple are accepted for treatment.

[5.69] In *Leeds Teaching Hospital NHS Trust v A*[68] Mr and Mrs A (a white couple) were being treated at the same time by the same clinic as Mr and Mrs B (a black couple). By mistake, Mr B's sperm was used to fertilise Mrs A's eggs and she subsequently gave birth to mixed-race twins. The Court held that Mr A was unable to acquire paternity under s 28(2), as he had not consented to the treatment his wife had actually received. However, all the parties were agreed that the children should remain in the custody of Mr and Mrs A, and that Mr A should be able to acquire fatherhood by adoption.

[5.70] These cases and others[69] led to the replacement of s 28 (5) with a series of formal consent requirements called the 'agreed parenthood conditions'. Section 37 provides, inter alia, that the agreed fatherhood provisions apply only where the man has given notice that he consents to being treated as the father of the child and that the woman has given notice that she consents to him being so treated. The only restriction in the Act is that the man and woman may not be within prohibited degrees of relationship to each other (for the purposes of incest). This means that a woman may consent to a male friend, but not her brother, becoming her child's father. Section 38 of the Act states explicitly that a child may have only one father and that the common law marital presumption of paternity continues in existence. Section 41 provides that men who donate sperm under the relevant consent provisions of the Act are not the legal fathers of children born from the use of such sperm.

[5.71] The Act also clarifies the position in relation to lesbian couples. For couples who are in a civil partnership, s 42 provides that a woman's Civil Partner will be the 'presumed female parent' of any child born to her partner unless it can be shown that she did not consent. This equates to the position of husbands in relation to the acquisition of parenthood. For same-sex couples who are not in a civil partnership, s 44 is in direct parallel to the fatherhood provisions in s 36, in that it enables the same-sex partner to acquire the status of second legal parent by giving notice of her agreement to being so recognised. There is a slight difference in terminology in the Act, which has the effect that while a mother's male partner can be recognised as the child's legal father from birth, the same-sex partner of the woman who gives birth is not regarded as the child's second mother, but rather as the 'second legal parent'.[70]

[5.72] The wording of the Act also means that the presumption of legal parenthood applies to husbands and civil partners whether the DI takes place in a clinic or otherwise. By contrast, the agreed parenthood provisions only apply where the DI takes place in a licensed clinic.

---

[68] *Leeds Teaching Hospital NHS Trust v A* [2003] EWHC 259.
[69] For example, *Re Q (Parental Order)* [1996] 1 FLR 369; *U v W* [1996] 1 FLR 569.
[70] Jackson, *Medical Law: Text, Cases and Materials* (OUP, 2006) p 794.

The right to know one's origins

[5.73] Donor insemination and egg or embryo donation raise a fundamental difficulty for the child born as a result of the procedure, namely the absence of information about his or her biological parents. It is argued that with the development of a sense of personal identity during adolescence comes an identification with one's past. This necessitates a connection with those to whom the person is genetically related. If the child or young adult is separated from genetic relatives this can disrupt the development of the individual leading to identity confusion.

> The first generation of donor-conceived offspring is now becoming young adults who are beginning to share their unique perspectives. Many are telling a story of psychological distress. They describe a strong need to know "where they came from;" to know their genetic origins as an essential part of constructing their identities.[71]

[5.74] Secrecy used to be thought of as the best way to protect families using this technique from social disapproval and stigmatisation. With donation of gametes and embryos, in contrast to adoption, the family could produce a pregnancy and therefore potentially no one outside the immediate family need ever know.[72] However, there is a growing acknowledgment that this is not in the best interests of the donor-conceived child.[73] It is argued that the maintenance of secrecy demonstrates that the paramount concern here is for the parents and not the child.[74] The debate surrounding disclosure of donor identity is typically framed as a tension between the rights of donors and parents on one hand, and those of donor-conceived offspring on the other. Donors, it is argued, have a right to maintain anonymity in order to avoid potential future liabilities, and

---

[71] Ravitsky, '"Knowing Where You Come From": The Rights of Donor-Conceived Individuals and the Meaning of Genetic Relatedness' (2010) Minnesota Journal of Law, Science & Technology; 11(2):655–84.

[72] Haimes, 'Secrecy: What Can Artificial Reproduction Learn From Adoption?' (1988) 2 Int J of Law and the Family, 46–61. Haimes cites unpublished work by Humphrey and Humphrey who report being disconcerted by the number of couples they had counselled for DI who proposed not to tell their children, but intended telling, or had told, others in the family. p 51.

[73] 'The young child's partial overhearing of mysterious allusions, and his sense of parental lies, half-truths and evasions may incur confusion, suspicion and anxiety for which he needs his parents' help – instead he feels cut off from them by a conspiracy of silence.' Holland, 'Adoption and Artificial Insemination: Some Social Implications.' (1971) 50(4) *Soundings: An Interdisciplinary Journal* 302 at 305. Similarly, Triseliotis argues: 'It can now be claimed with some confidence from the available evidence that there is a psychological need in all people, manifest principally among those who grow up away from their original families, to know about their background, their genealogy, and their personal history if they are to grow up feeling complete and whole'. Triseliotis, 'Obtaining Birth Certificates' in Bean, (ed) *Adoption* (Tavistock Publication, 1984) at 38. Also see Macklin, who remarks that: 'Donor offspring ... rarely find out the truth of their origins. But, some of them do, and we must listen to them when they speak of their anguish, of not knowing who fathered them; we must listen when they tell us how destructive it is to their self-esteem to find out their father sold the essence of his lineage for $40 or so, without ever intending to love or take responsibility for them.' Macklin, 'Artificial Means of Reproduction and Our Understanding of the Family' (1991) 21 Hastings Center Report 5, 11.

[74] Snowden and Mitchell, *The Artificial Family* (Allen & Unwin, 1981) 79.

parents have a right to keep the circumstances of conception private. On the other hand, it is argued, offspring have a right to know their genetic origins.[75]

[5.75] Ravitsky argues that there are four aspects to the right to know one's origins. The *medical* aspect points towards the right to know one's full medical history and to know medically relevant genetic information about the donor.[76] 'Not only is it helpful in diagnosing medical problems to know of family history, but certain hereditary diseases such as haemophilia or Huntington's Chorea, must be of concern to persons planning to have children of their own.'[77] The *identity* aspect points towards the right to personal information about the donor as a person (narrative information) that would assist offspring in overcoming identity issues. The *relational* aspect points towards the right to know the full identity of the donor in order to contact him or her and attempt to establish a relationship. Finally, the *parental disclosure* aspect relates to the right to know the truth about the circumstances of one's conception as trumping parents' right to privacy.

[5.76] The notion of a right to know one's genetic origins may be premised on a human rights approach or a consequentialist ethics argument that lack of such knowledge harms those who are born through donor conception. Warnock stated in 1987: 'I cannot argue that children who are told of their origins are necessarily happier or better off in any way that can be estimated. But I do believe that if they are not told, they are being wrongly treated.'[78] The consequentialist argument is that knowledge of one's origins is essential for psychological well-being and the establishment of healthy family relationships.

---

[75] Ravitsky, '"Knowing Where You Come From": The Rights of Donor-Conceived Individuals and the Meaning of Genetic Relatedness' (2010) Minnesota Journal of Law, Science & Technology; 11(2): at 667.

[76] There are many reasons why a person might need to know his/her genetic background, such as the ability to preserve one's health by altering behaviour to prevent problems; cautioning proper diet if there is a history of heart disease in the family; avoiding alcohol if there may be a predisposition to alcoholism; advising regular mammograms if there is a history of breast cancer; or by enabling kidney or bone marrow transplants to be made between compatible relatives if necessary. It also helps parents to avoid passing on certain genetic defects to their children. Obviously, this does not necessitate the identity, as opposed to genetic health, of the donor being made available. Swanson, 'Donor Anonymity in Artificial Insemination: Is It Still Necessary?' (1993) 27 Columbia J of Law and Social Problems, 151 at 174.

[77] O'Donovan, 'A Right to Know One's Parentage' (1988) 2 I J of Law and the Family 27–45 at 30. O'Donovan questions the existence of a general right to access information regarding one's parentage and claims that there are three interests which may be benefited by such information – medical, legal and psychological. She argues that if access to genetic and identifying information is regarded as an important interest in the case of those who have been adopted, then there is no legitimate distinction which may be drawn between those children and children born as a result of reproductive technology. She also points to the inconsistency in the position of the medical profession who, on the one hand encourage a person to be aware of his/her medical history but, on the other hand, make no attempt to record it in the case of adopted children or those born through donor insemination. The arguments for and against openness in this context are examined by O'Donovan, who concludes that there is a strong and powerful case to be made out in favour of telling a child of its genetic origins, but that there are wider issues which should be confronted in society such as why we put such an emphasis on genes at all when we allow children to be brought up on a separate, social basis.

[78] Warnock, 'The Good of the Child', (1987) 1 Bioethics 141, 151.

Although the collection of data on donor-conceived adults is difficult due to the fact that many have not been told about the circumstances of their conception, such research as does exist, as well as powerful personal accounts available on online support networks,[79] provide a basis for substantiation of the ethical argument in favour of disclosure.

[5.77] Despite strong arguments in favour of disclosure, studies conclude that many couples do not tell their children of their true biological origins.[80] Donor-conceived adults advocate openness from an early age so that there is never a time in the child's life when disclosure comes as a shock to them. For example, as one donor-conceived young woman puts it:

> The way to manage DI in a family is to be open and unashamed about your decision. Parents have to let go of their own feelings and focus on the needs of their children – my parents managed to do this and I respect them for it. I can trust my parents totally, feel wanted and loved by them. I have respect for them for 'telling' me, unlike, if I was to find out now, the lack of respect shown to me would affect my relationship with them in the most detrimental of ways. Hiding DI seems to imply that it is something bad, to be ashamed about, that their children are something to be ashamed about.[81]

[5.78] The main reason generally given for the reluctance to give identifying information to children born through sperm donation is the belief that the supply of sperm donors would cease. It is thought that the sperm donor may have a strong interest in remaining anonymous and may not welcome a potentially traumatic disruption of his family life by the appearance of a child of whose existence he was not aware. He may not have a developed perception of the needs of the child and may simply see it as an unwanted intrusion.[82] He may fear the imposition of legal responsibility on him for the child and maintenance obligations. However, this may also depend on social or cultural

---

[79]   Eg Donor Conception Network UK, http://www.donor-conception-network.org/ (accessed 27 May 2011).

[80]   The rates vary with different studies, for example: Brewaeys et al 'Anonymous or Identity-Registered Sperm Donors? A Study of Dutch Recipients' Choices' (2004) 20 Human Reproduction 820, finding that only 17% of parents intended to disclose; Klock et al 'A Prospective Study of Donor Insemination Recipients: Secrecy, Privacy and Disclosure' (1994) 62 *Fertility and Sterility* 477 finding that 27% of couples planned to disclose.

[81]   http://www.donor-conception-network.org/zannah.htm (accessed 27 May 2011).

[82]   Some studies, however, show the contrary, that is, that the donor *does* have an interest in his potential children. In a study in New Zealand, 80 per cent of donors wanted to know if children were conceived. See Purdie, Peek, Irwin, Ellis, Graham & Fisher, 'Identifiable Semen Donors – Attitudes of Donors and Recipient Couples' (1992) New Zealand Med J 27–28. This is similar to previous studies in Australia, New Zealand and USA. See Kovacs, Clayton & McGowan, 'The Attitudes of Semen Donors' (1983) 2 Clin Reprod Fertil 73–5; Rowland, 'Attitudes and Opinions of Donors on an Artificial Insemination by Donor (AID) Programme' (1983) 2 Clin Reprod Fertil 249–59; Daniels, 'Semen Donors in New Zealand: Their Characteristics and Attitudes' (1987) 5 Clin Reprod Fertil 177–90; Daniels, 'Semen Donors: Their Motivations and Attitudes to Their Offspring' (1989) 7 J Reprod Infant Psychology 121–7; Handelsman, Dunn, Conway, Boyland & Jansen, 'Psychological and Attitudinal Profiles in Donors for Artificial Insemination' (1985) 43 Fertil Steril 95–101; Sauer, Gorrill, Zeffer & Bustillo, 'Attitudinal Survey of Sperm Donors to an Artificial Insemination Clinic' (1989) 34 J Reprod Med 362–4. Some of these studies show that many donors often think about their DI children.

factors. Surveys suggest that most donors have serious misgivings about their legal responsibility for offspring that might cause them to stop donating if their identities were revealed without legal protection. Even in the absence of such legal risks, anonymity remains important to some donors due to the risk that a donor offspring would appear in their later lives. But these reservations might be minimised if social and professional attitudes changed overall.[83]

[5.79] The social parents similarly may fear the disruption of their family life if the donor's identity were made known, as the child may attempt to establish a relationship with the donor, which might result in a sense of loss to the parents.[84] They may also fear interference from the law in granting the donor parental rights in respect of the child at some point in the future.[85] Such concerns may be exacerbated in the Irish context following the *McD v L* case discussed at para **5.63** above.

[5.80] In the United States, disclosure is not regulated and donor anonymity is still the norm. However, practice varies between states and between various clinics. Some clinics offer a double-track policy, which offers recipients of DI treatment the option of choosing a traditional anonymous treatment or an open donation/identity release treatment in which they agree that identifying information will be shared with offspring years later. In other jurisdictions the practice also varies with a number of European countries introducing legislation in recent years prohibiting anonymity, for example Norway, Sweden, Austria, Switzerland, the Netherlands, the UK and Finland. New Zealand and three Australian states similarly prohibit anonymity.[86] In a recent interesting development, in *Prattan v British Columbia (Attorney General)*[87] the Supreme Court of British Columbia held that anonymous donation discriminates against offspring, because, unlike adopted people, they have no right to know their origins or prevent the destruction of records that would help identify their biological parents. The court has given the province 15 months to devise a new law to provide for the rights of people conceived via donation. However, the problem remains that even with the prohibition of anonymity, the right of the child to know its genetic origins is dependent on the openness of its parents in disclosing the truth about the child's conception.

[5.81] None of the countries which have prohibited anonymity have introduced a system for ensuring that the child is informed; that decision is left to the parents.[88] Although

---

[83] Gibson, 'Artificial Insemination by Donor: Information, Communication and Regulation' (1991–2) 30(1) J of Fam Law 1 at 32.

[84] They may also fear that the child will suffer negative reactions in society and they may wish to hide their infertility. See Kirkman, 'Parents' Contributions to the Narrative Identity of Offspring of Donor-Assisted Conception' 57 Social Science and Medicine 2229 (2003); R Nachtigall et al 'The Disclosure Decision: Concerns and Issues of Parents of Children Conceived Through Donor Insemination' (1998) 178 American Journal of Obstetrics and Gynaecology 1165.

[85] For example, *Jhordan C v Mary K,* 179 Cal App 3d 586 (1986) in which the donor was granted legal rights to visitation, as well as a legal responsibility to support the child.

[86] New South Wales, South Australia and Western Australia.

[87] *Prattan v British Columbia (Attorney General)* [2011] BCSC 656.

[88] Frith, 'Beneath the Rhetoric: The Role of Rights in the Practice of Non-Anonymous Gamete Donation', (2001) 15 Bioethics 473 at 477.

there are strong arguments in favour of the creation of a legal mechanism, which would ensure that the child is told of its origins such as through the issuing of a donor conception certificate which would be attached to a child's birth certificate, or the insertion of the words 'by donation' on the birth certificate, this remains a highly controversial proposition.[89] A policy which forces parents to disclose is in keeping with a true understanding of genetic relatedness and also obliges the State not to collude in the deception of the child. It may be argued that genetic relatedness is of such importance to the child as to warrant such intrusion into the family. On the other hand, such a policy would infringe upon the parents' right to privacy as well as their fundamental Constitutional right to make decisions regarding their children's welfare. The middle ground currently adopted in most jurisdictions in which anonymity is prohibited is through education and public awareness campaigns aimed at social change.

[5.82] In the United Kingdom, the Human Fertilisation and Embryology Act 1990 provided that children conceived using donated gametes could apply to the Human Fertilisation and Embryology Authority for certain information when they reached the age of 18 years, or 16 years if they were getting married and wanted to find out if their spouse could be related to them. The information that could be disclosed under the Act was restricted to non-identifying information such as physical description (height, weight, eye and hair colour), year and country of birth, ethnicity, whether the donor had any children at the time of donation and any additional information the donor chose to supply such as occupation, religion, interests and a brief self description.

[5.83] Regulations were introduced in 2004 which allowed details about egg donors and sperm donors registered after 1 April 2005 to be passed on to the offspring, including the name and last address of the donor. Section 31ZA of the 2008 Human Fertilisation and Embryology Act further amended the position by providing that a person may request the Authority to give notice as to whether or not the person was conceived using donated gametes, and if so, must give the person information relating to the donor (including identifying information such as name, date of birth and last known address) and any half-siblings (non-identifying information only unless the half-siblings consent otherwise). The applicant must be given a suitable opportunity to receive proper counselling about the implications of compliance with the request. If the applicant is under the age of 18 years, the Authority cannot be required to release identifying information. Donors can be told the number, age, sex of any children born from their donation but not the children's identity.

[5.84] The applicant may apply under section 31ZB for information as to an intended spouse. This information may show whether the applicant might be related to a specified person whom they propose to marry, enter into a civil partnership with or with whom they are in an intimate physical relationship. The applicant must be over the age of 16 years to avail of this provision. Donors can be informed that a person conceived using their gametes has made a request for identifying information, though the identity of the applicant for information will not be disclosed to the donor.

---

89   Blyth, 'The Role of Birth Certificates in Relation to Access to Biographical and Genetic History in Donor Conception' (2009) 17 International Journal of Child Rights 207.

[5.85] There was widespread concern that the change in the law in the UK would lead to a consequent shortage of sperm donors. However, the evidence so far is that this has not occurred. The Human Fertilisation and Embryology Authority (HFEA) reported an increase in the number of donors following the change in 2005[90] and also noted a change in the profile of sperm donors. In 1994–95 sperm donors were most commonly men between 18 and 24 years, only 1 in 5 of whom already had children of their own. In 2004–2005 the most common age group for sperm donors was 36–40 and more than 40 per cent of them already had children of their own.

[5.86] In the international arena, the law of human rights may be considered as providing a means through which a child could claim a right to information as to its parentage. Beeson says that the child's right to know his or her origins is now broadly recognised and respected.[91] It has also been guaranteed by international human rights law and in particular the case law of the European Court of Human Rights since 1989 based on the ECHR (1950), the Convention on the Rights of the Child (1989) and the Hague Convention on the Protection of Children and Co-operation in Respect of Intercountry Adoption (1993).

[5.87] Article 8 of the ECHR provides that:

(1) Everyone has the right to respect for his private and family life, his home and his correspondence.

(2) There shall be no interference by a public authority with the exercise of this right except such as is in accordance with the law and is necessary in a democratic society in the interests of national security, public safety or the economic well-being of the country, for the prevention of disorder or crime, for the protection of health or morals, or for the protection of the rights and freedoms of others.

[5.88] Although it does not contain any express reference to any aspects of the child's identity, art 8 (1) has been interpreted by the European Court of Human Rights in *Gaskin v UK*[92] as requiring that everyone should be able to establish details of their identity as individual human beings. However, this right has not been very clearly defined by the Court. It is said to cover the right of an adult placed in care as a child to consult his personal file (*Gaskin v UK*[93]), the right of a child to identify her father

---

[90] See http://www.hfea.gov.uk/3411.html (accessed 27 May 2010).

[91] Beeson, 'Enforcing the Child's Right to Know Her Origins: Contrasting Approaches Under the Convention on the Rights of the Child and the European Convention on Human Rights' (2007) International Journal of Law, Policy and the Family, 21, 137–15. She cites as examples Triselotis, *In Search of Origins: The Experiences of Adopted People* (Routledge, 1973); O'Donovan, 'A Right to Know One's Genetic Parentage?' (1988) International Journal of Law Policy and the Family, 2, 27 – 45; Stewart, 'Interpreting the Child's Right to Identity in the UN Convention on the Rights of the Child' (1992) *Family Law Quarterly,* 26, 221 – 33; Hodgson, 'The International Legal Protection of the Child's Right to a Legal Identity and the Problem of Statelessness' (1993) International Journal of Law, Policy and the Family 7, 255 – 70; Freeman, 'The New Birth Right?: Identity and the Child of the Reproductive Revolution' (1996) 4 International Journal of Children's Rights, 3, 273–97; Frith, 'Gamete Donation and Anonymity: The Ethical and Legal Debate' (2001) 16 *Human Reproduction,* 5, 818 – 24.

[92] *Gaskin v UK* [1990] 1 FLR 167, 10454/83 [1989] ECHR 13 (7 July 1989).

[93] *Gaskin v UK* [1990] 1 FLR 167, 10454/83 [1989] ECHR 13 (7 July 1989).

through DNA testing (*Mikulic v Croatia*[94] and *Ebrü v Turkey*[95]), and the right of an adult to obtain a post-mortem DNA sample of his presumed father (*Jäggi v Switzerland*[96]). However, the Court in *Odièvre v France* rejected the claim that the absolute birth secrecy granted in France violates art 8.[97]

[5.89] Article 7 of the Convention on the Rights of the Child (CRC) provides that 'The child shall be registered immediately after birth and shall have the right from birth to a name, the right to acquire a nationality and, as far as possible, the right to know and be cared for by his or her parents.' The term 'parents' has been argued to include not only social or legal parents, but also biological or genetic parents.[98] Article 8 provides:

> 1) States Parties undertake to respect the right of the child to preserve his or her identity, including nationality, name and family relations as recognized by law without unlawful interference.

> 2) Where a child is illegally deprived of some or all of the elements of his or her identity, States Parties shall provide appropriate assistance and protection, with a view to re-establishing speedily his or her identity.

[5.90] The right is both a negative and a positive right, meaning that it protects a person from active violations by State authorities but also protects against a passive omission by the State. This is important in the imposition of obligations on states to establish and maintain registers of birth data to which the child can have later access in fulfilment of the right to know his or her origins. Beeson claims that this is a 'truly innovative provision. It is the first time an international instrument guarantees identity rights, and to children.'[99] However, despite its apparently innovative nature, she points out that it does not define the concept of identity. She also argues that although states are the main duty-bearers in respect of this right, perhaps individuals, for example mothers, should also be imposed with direct duties pertaining to the right.

[5.91] Difficulties may arise in this context where the fundamental rights and values of various parties involved are in conflict. For example, the rights and interests of the genetic parents and the legal parents may often be very different. The genetic parent(s) may wish to keep their identity secret and the legal parents may not wish to have their social ties to the child affected by revelations regarding the circumstances of the child's conception. Balancing of rights is therefore necessary at a policy level. Articles 7 and 8 of the CRC do not adjudicate on the issue of how this balance should be struck. It may be argued that since art 7 grants the child the right to know 'as far as possible' this may be interpreted as conditional on granting respect for other legal rights and duties.

---

[94] *Mikulic v Croatia* 53176/99 [2002] ECHR 27 (7 February 2002).

[95] *Ebrü vTurkey* 60176/00 [2006] ECHR (30 May 2006).

[96] *Jäggi v Switzerland* 58757/00 [2006] ECHR (13 July 2006).

[97] *Odièvre v France* 42326/98 [2003] ECHR 86 (13 February 2003).

[98] Freeman, 'The New Birth Right?: Identity and the Child of the Reproductive Revolution' (1996) 4 International Journal of Children's Rights, 3, 273–97.

[99] Beeson, 'Enforcing the Child's Right to Know Her Origins: Contrasting Approaches Under the Convention on the Rights of the Child and the European Convention on Human Rights' (2007) International Journal of Law, Policy and the Family, 21, at 143. She notes that it was introduced following an Argentinean proposal due to the disappearance of many children in Argentina during the 1970s and 1980s.

Beeson argues that this interpretation is too limited, however. 'A more complete interpretation is that the right to know is granted only as far as this is possible within the limits of the legal order and that illegal restrictions to the right to know are prohibited.'[100] There is no mechanism for individual petition under the CRC, and therefore it is difficult to draw from the CRC any criteria by which such conflicts might be resolved. As a result, states are given a wide margin of appreciation in relation to their compliance with arts 7 and 8.

[5.92] In relation to the ECHR, art 8 (2) acknowledges the possible restriction of the right to know in circumstances when it conflicts with the rights of others. The case law of the Commission and the European Court of Human Rights also confirms its interpretation of art 8 as not intending to grant an absolute right to know one's origins. In balancing this right with the rights of others, the Court also grants states a wide margin of appreciation. For example, in *MB v UK*,[101] the Commission decided that the national authorities' refusal to order blood tests to enable an unmarried man to discover whether he was the father of a child born to a married woman was reasonable in the circumstances. The Commission was influenced by the fact that the alleged father had never lived with the mother, had not planned for the child and did not see the child or form any bond with her. The authorities had defended their refusal to order blood tests on the basis of the best interests of the child being the maintenance of a stable private life in the family unit within which she was being brought up. The Commission found that this approach was justifiable in giving greater weight to the child's interests than to the ascertainment of a biological fact which may be to the detriment of the child and the family.

[5.93] In *Odièvre v France*[102] the applicant argued that the French practice of anonymous birth ('under X') by which her mother was allowed to retain her anonymity from the applicant, who was her daughter, infringed art 8. The French authorities were prepared to give the applicant non-identifying information, and legislation in 2002 would enable an independent council to waive anonymity, but only with the mother's consent. The Court said:

> Article 8 protects a right to identity and personal development and the right to establish and develop relationships with other human beings and the outside world...The preservation of mental stability is in that context indispensable precondition to effective enjoyment of the right to respect for private life. Matters of relevance to personal development include details of that person's identity as a human being and the vital interest protected by the Convention in obtaining information necessary to discover the truth concerning important aspects of one's personal identity, such as the identity of one's parents. Birth, and in particular the circumstances in which a child is born, forms part of a child's, and subsequently the adult's

---

[100] Beeson, 'Enforcing the Child's Right to Know Her Origins: Contrasting Approaches Under the Convention on the Rights of the Child and the European Convention on Human Rights' (2007) International Journal of Law, Policy and the Family, 21, at 150.

[101] *MB v UK*, dec of 6 April 1994, DR 77A, p 108 (22920/93). Although the applicant attempted to bring an action also in the child's name, this was refused, as he did not have any responsibility for the child under national law.

[102] *Odièvre v France* 42326/98 [2003] ECHR 86 (13 February 2003).

private life guaranteed by Article 8 of the Convention. That provision is therefore applicable in the instant case.

[5.94] The Court went on to say that the child's vital interest in its personal development is also widely recognised in the general scheme of the Convention. On the other hand, a woman's interest in remaining anonymous in order to protect her health by giving birth in appropriate medical conditions cannot be denied. The two private interests with which the Court was confronted in the present case are not easily reconciled. The Court took the view that the State had provided evidence that it had made an effort to balance competing interests and that its decision came within the margin of appreciation given to individual states. The case has been criticised, however, as according too much weight to the margin of appreciation and for effectively giving the birth mother an absolute veto in respect of the release of information, thereby negating any real balancing of rights.[103]

[5.95] The two later cases of *Ebrü v Turkey*,[104] and *Jäggi v Switzerland*[105] may demonstrate a different approach by the Court. In *Ebrü*, the applicant brought a paternity suit in Istanbul against a well-known Turkish folk-singer, Emrah Ipek, claiming that he was her child's biological father. The Court attributed paternity to Ipek, on the basis of the blood and genetic test results, and all the other evidence before it. It ordered the registrar-general to amend the child's birth certificate accordingly. The Appeal Court later quashed this judgment and remitted the case for further consideration on the basis of additional forensic tests. Ipek did not attend any of the appointments made for forensic testing and the Court decided to lodge a complaint for abuse of authority with the public prosecutor against the police officers responsible for executing an arrest warrant. It also decided to notify Ipek that failure on his part to submit to DNA tests would be construed as an admission of paternity. On the basis of further tests the court later ruled that Ipek was the father. The various stages of the proceedings, which lasted over eight years, received wide media coverage because of Ipek's national celebrity status.[106]

[5.96] The Court found that the civil proceedings had failed to strike a fair balance between the applicants' right to establish the truth as to the boy's paternity without undue delay, and the right of the alleged father not to have to undergo DNA tests. In conclusion, the inability of the domestic courts to settle the paternity issue in a timely manner had left the applicants in a prolonged state of uncertainty as to the child's

---

[103] Beeson, 'Enforcing the Child's Right to Know Her Origins: Contrasting Approaches Under the Convention on the Rights of the Child and the European Convention on Human Rights' (2007) International Journal of Law, Policy and the Family, 21, at 151.

[104] *Ebrü v Turkey* 60176/00 [2006] ECHR (30 May 2006).

[105] *Jäggi v Switzerland* 58757/00 [2006] ECHR (13 July 2006).

[106] The applicants complained of the excessive length of the proceedings and of the lack of a judicial forum to which a complaint might be submitted. They argued that, throughout that period, they had been in the media spotlight because Ipek was a celebrity, and that if they had received maintenance, the child would have had a better life and education. They relied on art 6 § 1 (right to a fair hearing within a reasonable time), art 13 (right to an effective remedy) and art 8 (right to respect for private and family life).

individual identity.[107] The applicants' right to respect for their private life had thus been breached and the Court held that there had been a violation of art 8.[108]

[5.97] In *Jäggi,* the Swiss authorities refused an adult man the right to obtain a post-mortem DNA sample from his dead father. Shortly before the applicant's birth in 1939, his mother brought an action against AH, his putative father, seeking a declaration of paternity and the payment of a contribution towards his maintenance. The action was dismissed by the Geneva Court of First Instance in 1948. On registering the applicant's birth, his mother declared that his father was AH The applicant was placed with a foster family. He was informed by his mother in 1958 that AH was his father.

[5.98] The applicant asserted that he had had regular contacts with AH and had received presents from him and money every month until he came of age. AH's family rejected those allegations, and AH always refused to submit to tests to establish his paternity. In 1999 the applicant applied for revision of the judgment of 1948, requesting a DNA test on the remains of AH. His application was refused by the trial courts. The Federal Court dismissed an appeal by the applicant on the ground that at the age of 60 he had been able to develop his personality even in the absence of certainty as to the identity of his biological father. The applicant brought an action to the European Court of Human Rights alleging violation of art 8.[109]

[5.99] The Court considered that persons trying to establish their ancestry had a vital interest, protected by the Convention, in obtaining the information they needed in order to discover the truth about an important aspect of their personal identity. However, the need to protect third parties might exclude the possibility of compelling them to submit to any kind of medical analysis, particularly DNA tests. The Court would therefore weigh against each other the conflicting interests, namely the applicant's right to discover his parentage against the right of third parties to the inviolability of the deceased's body, the right to respect for the dead and the public interest in the protection of legal certainty.

[5.100] The Court considered that an individual's interest in discovering his parentage did not disappear with age and that the applicant had always shown a real interest in discovering his father's identity, since he had tried throughout his life to obtain reliable information on the point. Such conduct implied moral and mental suffering, even though this had not been medically attested.

[5.101] The Court noted that in opposing the DNA test, which was a relatively unintrusive measure, AH's family had not cited any religious or philosophical reasons.

---

[107] The Court noted that a period of over eight years and nine months was excessive, particularly in view of the applicants' interest in the dispute, and did not meet the reasonable-time requirement. Accordingly, the Court held unanimously that there had been a violation of art 6 § 1.

[108] The Government had failed to indicate the existence of any specific remedy by which the applicants might have complained about the length of the proceedings. Accordingly, the Court held unanimously that there had been a violation of art 13 because of the lack in domestic law of a remedy allowing the applicants to assert their right to a ruling on their case within a reasonable time.

[109] He also alleged violation of art 14 (prohibition of discrimination).

The Court observed that the private life of the deceased person from whom it was proposed to take a DNA sample could not be impaired by such a request since it was made after his death. The Court considered that Switzerland had not secured to Jäggi the right to respect for his private life and held that there had been a violation of art 8.

[5.102] These cases illustrate a different approach taken in recent years to the interpretation of art 8 and, in particular, the balancing of conflicting rights at national level. The Court seeks to ensure that States do not grant absolute protection to either the child's right to know or the parents' right to privacy but rather examines the specific context in which the conflict has arisen and the interests to be protected. Beeson argues that this demonstrates that the Court considers some interests to be more fundamental than others and that those interests, such as the right to know one's origins, form part of the inner core of the right to respect for private life and must be respected as such.[110]

Ireland

[5.103] In Ireland the only analogous legislation pertaining to the right to know one's origins is in relation to adoption. Most adoptions are arranged through adoption agencies which seek to preserve the anonymity of the parties involved. A voluntary contact register exists which contains details in relation to the birth of every adopted child. This enables adopted people, natural parents and any natural relative of an adopted person to sign up to facilitate contact and meetings.[111] A statutory provision exists under the Adoption Acts[112] which would enable an adopted person to gain access to the information appearing on his or her birth certificate if this is in his or her best interests. In *CR v An Bord Uchtála*[113] the High Court held that the Adoption Board is required to consider each application for information on its own merits and not to simply decide the matter on the basis of traditional practice. Morris J was of the opinion that the applicant should be screened by the relevant adoption society, who have trained personnel available to deal with such applications, and that the application should be considered with care and sensitivity.

[5.104] In *IO'T v B and the Rotunda Girls' Aid Society*[114] it was held that the right to be told the identity of a natural mother is not absolute, and must be balanced against the natural mother's right to privacy. This was a case stated from the Circuit Court pursuant to the provisions of s 16 of the Courts of Justice Act 1947, and the plaintiffs were children born before the enactment of the Adoption Act 1952 (and were 'informally adopted' in 1941 and 1951 respectively). It is clear from the report that they were born out of wedlock. By a majority (Keane J dissenting), and as appears from the judgment of Hamilton CJ, it was held that the right to know the identity of one's natural mother is a basic right flowing from the natural and special relationship which exists between a

---

110 Beeson, 'Enforcing the Child's Right to Know Her Origins: Contrasting Approaches Under the Convention on the Rights of the Child and the European Convention on Human Rights' (2007) International Journal of Law, Policy and the Family, 21 at 152.
111 In total, 5,916 adopted people and 2,628 relatives have signed up to the contact register since its launch in 2005. As of 2011 there have been 429 matches.
112 Adoption Act 1952, s 22; Adoption Act 1976, s 8.
113 *CR v An Bord Uchtála* [1993] 3 IR 535.
114 *IO'T v B and the Rotunda Girls' Aid Society* [1998] 2 IR 321.

mother and her child, which relationship is clearly acknowledged in passages quoted from the judgments of the Supreme Court in *The State (Nicolaou) v An Bord Uchtála*[115] and *G v An Bord Uchtála*.[116] He further said that:

> The existence of such right is not dependent on the obligation to protect the child's right to bodily integrity or such rights as the child might enjoy in relation to the property of his or her natural mother but stems directly from the aforesaid relationship. It is not, however, an absolute or qualified right: its exercise may be restricted by the constitutional rights of others, and by the requirement of the common good. Its exercise is restricted in the case of children who have been lawfully adopted in accordance with the provisions of the Adoption Act, 1952 as the effect of an adoption order is that all parental rights and duties of the natural parents are ended, while the child becomes a member of the family of the adoptive parents as if he or she had been their natural child.

[5.105] As to the rights of the natural mother (giving rise to a restriction on such right of the child), Hamilton CJ said:

> While they enjoy the constitutional right to know the identity of their respective natural mothers, the exercise of such right may be restricted by the constitutional right to privacy and confidentiality of the natural mothers in respect of their dealings with … [a society which had provided for an "informal" adoption] … whether they are so restricted depends on the circumstances of the case and whether they, or either of them, wish to exercise this right to privacy.

And further:

> [Where] there is a conflict of constitutional rights, the obligation on the courts is to attempt to harmonise such rights having regard to the provisions of the Constitution and in the event of a failure to so harmonise, to determine which right is the superior having regard to all the circumstances of the case. So far as the applicant and the plaintiff are concerned, the court must decide whether their constitutional rights outweigh the constitutional and legal status of their natural mothers.

[5.106] In the case of *Rotunda Hospital v Information Commissioner*[117] a request was made under the Freedom of Information Act by Ms W on behalf of her elderly father Mr W (deceased at the date of the judgment), who had been given up for adoption in 1922. The information sought related to the age of the woman believed to be registered in the hospital records as Mr W's mother. This was sought by the family in order to assist Mr W in tracing his family roots. The hospital refused access to the information on the grounds that it had a policy of ensuring that women who came to the hospital have an absolute guarantee of confidentiality, whether it was information required for therapeutic purposes or not. The Information Commissioner overturned the hospital's refusal to grant access to the information sought. The hospital appealed the decision to the High Court. In dismissing the appeal, McCarthy J said:

> The proposition has been advanced that the rights of more remote parties such as prospective or putative siblings or perhaps a widowed spouse of a mother might be infringed, (in particular a right to privacy) by disclosure of information, say, about the fact of motherhood of which such persons knew nothing. I would have to question whether or

---

[115] *The State (Nicolaou) v An Bord Uchtála* [1966] IR 567.
[116] *G v An Bord Uchtála* [1980] IR 32.
[117] *Rotunda Hospital v Information Commissioner* [2009] IEHC 315.

not the right extends that far. It might extend to some more immediate intrusion or some more egregious impingement but, at bottom, it would be necessary to say that the right to privacy enjoyed by such persons extends to a right not to have made known to another member of one's family (at least in the case of siblings about them) information about one. Even if the rights of third parties (whether under the heading of rights to privacy or otherwise) extend to limitations on the provision of information which might allow such persons to be identified (the natural mother, say, being dead) it seems hard to see that there would be circumstances in which their rights could not but be outweighed by the constitutional right to know the identity of one's natural mother.[118]

[5.107] In the absence of legislation in Ireland clarifying the position of donor-conceived persons who seek access to the identity of the gamete donor, the position is far from satisfactory. At present, sperm donation is facilitated by the importation of sperm from other jurisdictions, including the UK and Denmark. Centres in the UK are permitted to export sperm under certain conditions. If the importing country is within the EEA (European Economic Area) the person responsible must obtain and retain (for three years) written evidence that the receiving or sending centre is accredited, designated, authorised or licensed in accordance with the requirements of the 2004 European Tissues and Cells Directive.[119] In all cases, all the requirements in the relevant HFEA Directions on import and export of gametes and embryos relating to identification, consent, parenthood, payment of the donor, use of the gametes and embryos and screening must be met.[120] So, if a child is born in Ireland using sperm that was imported from the UK, the question arises as to whether the child would be entitled to seek information from the HFEA on reaching the relevant age.

[5.108] As discussed above, s 31 of The Human Fertilisation and Embryology Act 1990 (as amended in 2008), requires the HFEA to maintain a Register of licensed fertility treatment carried out in the UK, and to respond to requests for information from persons entitled to information held on the Register, such as persons who are donor-conceived. The Act requires HFEA-licensed centres to supply the HFEA with the necessary information which then enables the HFEA to respond to individual requests from the register. The HFEA, however, is not permitted to hold data about treatment cycles held outside of a UK licensed centre. As a result, it would not be able to provide register information to persons who were conceived following treatment outside of a UK licensed centre, such as in Ireland.[121] Thus, as the law currently stands, a child born in Ireland following importation of sperm is not in the same position as a child born in the UK, and would not be able to access the identity of the donor.

[5.109] The Commission on Assisted Human Reproduction recommended that gamete and embryo donation should be permitted in Ireland, subject to regulation by a licensing body. It considered at length the issues relating to donor anonymity and concluded that the best interests of children born through AHR required that they be facilitated in accessing information relating to their genetic parentage. The Commission therefore

---

118   *Rotunda Hospital v Information Commissioner* [2009] IEHC 315 at para 108.
119   Directive 2004/23/EC of the European Parliament and of the Council of 31 March 2004.
120   http://www.hfea.gov.uk/ (accessed 27 May 2011).
121   http://www.hfea.gov.uk/535.html (accessed 27 May 2011).

recommended that 'any child born through the use of donated gametes or embryos should, on maturity, be able to identify the donor(s) involved in his/her conception.'[122]

[5.110] It also recommended that donors should not be regarded as the legal parents of any children born from their donation. In relation to assignment of parentage, the Commission recommended that in the context of treatments using donor gametes, the woman who gives birth to a child should be regarded as the child's legal parent and that there should be a requirement that her partner, if any, should give a legal commitment to be recognised as the child's second parent.

Egg Donation

[5.111] In some circumstances egg donation may be sought if, for example, the woman's ovaries were damaged during treatment for cancer[123] or if she suffered from Turner's syndrome in which she was born without ovaries, or she had non-functioning ovaries due to premature ovarian failure or premature menopause. The procedure itself is time-consuming and invasive, as the donor must undergo medical and genetic screening, blood tests, the administration of fertility drugs and hormone injections, and ultrasound-guided retrieval of the eggs. Risks to the donor include ovarian cysts, caused by stimulation of the ovaries, and possible bleeding, injury, or infection of internal organs during the process of egg retrieval. For the recipient, too, the procedure involves physical risk and intrusion. Synchronisation of the recipient's ovulatory cycle with the donor's ovulatory cycle requires close monitoring and, in the case of recipients with ovarian failure, estrogen and progesterone replacement to achieve endometrial maturation.

[5.112] The donation may be followed by fertilisation of the egg in vitro with the recipient's husband's sperm, (or donor sperm), and then transferred to the uterus of the recipient. Alternatively it may be transferred together with the sperm to the fallopian tube where it is hoped that fertilisation will occur (Gamete Intra Fallopian Transfer).

[5.113] Egg donors generally tend to be women who are undergoing surgical procedures which would allow access to the eggs, women who specifically want to become egg donors, such as sisters or friends of an infertile woman, or women who are undergoing IVF and who produce more eggs than they require for their own treatment, although this 'egg sharing' facility is not widely available. Some clinics believe that egg sharing compromises the preferred altruistic nature of donation, as the donor receives a discount on her own IVF treatment in return for the donation. In the UK and most European countries, egg donors must be under the age of 35. In some countries some of these women would be paid expenses under governing legislation,[124] while others may be

---

[122] http://www.dohc.ie/publications/pdf/cahr.pdf?direct=1 at 46 (accessed 27 May 2011).

[123] Some of these difficulties might be avoided in future years due to recent reported successes in freezing ovarian tissue. The ovarian transplant technique has been pioneered primarily to help women facing early menopause or sterility caused by chemotherapy treatment. In such cases the ovaries would be removed before treatment, frozen and later reimplanted to give the woman back the ability to produce eggs.

[124] In the United States, in the absence of regulation, eggs may be sold in many states. Mead claims that in 1999 through agencies and advertisements, almost 5,000 women sold them. (contd.../)

offered their own medical procedure (such as sterilisation) free in return for the eggs. The question arises in the latter case, as in egg sharing, whether discounted medical treatment should be regarded as a financial inducement in the same way as direct payment.

[5.114] One of the most interesting legal questions to arise from egg donation is well expressed by an English judge, Scott Baker J:

> Until recently, when the advance of medical science created the possibility of *In Vitro* Fertilisation, it was not envisaged that the genetic mother and the carrying mother could be other than one and the same person. The advent of *In Vitro* Fertilisation presented the law with a dilemma: who should the law regard as the mother?[125]

[5.115] To ask the question another way: is the legal mother to be the genetic mother who donated her eggs or the gestational mother who carried the child to term and gave birth to it?[126] Many definitions of motherhood have been put forward, some of which emphasise the importance of the nine-month gestation period during which the mother's body supplies physical and emotional protection to the developing child. Others argue that gestation is 'an experience of identity or, more precisely, of undifferentiation' and that pregnancy is experienced 'not so much as presence of a separate entity in the womb, but as an alteration of the entire body.'[127]

[5.116] The Warnock Report in the UK in 1984 concluded 'where a woman donates an egg for transfer to another the donation should be treated as absolute and that, like a male donor, she should have no rights or duties with regard to any resulting child.'[128] Section 33 of the Human Fertilisation and Embryology Act 2008, (as also provided by

---

[124] (\...contd) Mead, 'Eggs for Sale' The New Yorker, August 9, 1999. Mead discusses at length details relating to a young student who decided to become an egg donor, the medical procedure she had to go to, her motives and her payment (up to $5,000 per donation) as well as the market for egg donation generally. She reports details of 'coercive' advertisements offering up to $50,000 and other agency eye-catching ploys to induce students to donate. Mead says that there is a concern that high prices attract women who may not be mature enough to make the kind of philosophical decision implicit in donating eggs, but also about infertile patients who cannot afford these prices. 'Egg donation is generally not covered by insurance, and the price for one retrieval ... in New York City, including donor fees and medications for both participants, is currently twenty thousand dollars, with the chances of success being around fifty per cent. Some patients undergo as many as three cycles in their efforts to become parents.' p 59. Reports in the media in 1999 relating to an 'egg auction' of model's eggs for anything from $15,000 to $150,000, also sparked angry responses about the commercialisation and depersonalisation of reproduction. See reports in Herald Tribune 25/10/99; The Guardian 25/10/99; The Independent 25/10/99; The Sunday Business Post 31/10/99; Weidman Schnieder, 'Jewish Women's Eggs: A Hot Commodity in the IVF Marketplace' (2001) 26(3) Lilith 22.

[125] *Re W (Minors)(Surrogacy)* [1991] 1 FLR 385.

[126] This same question was posed in Ireland, obiter, by Murphy J in *WO'R v EH & An Bord Uchtála* [1996] 2 IR 248.

[127] Ashe, 'Law-Language of Maternity: Discourse Holding Nature in Contempt' (1988) 22 New Eng L Rev 521–549.

[128] *Report of the Committee of Inquiry into Human Fertilisation and Embryology* (1984) Cmnd. 9314, HMSO, London.

the preceding 1990 Act s 27(1)) provides that a woman who carries a child as a result of the placing in her of an embryo or of sperm and eggs, and no other woman, is to be treated as the mother of the child. This emphasises the social, psychological and nurturing aspect of motherhood and gives these elements priority over the genetic link. Section 35 of the 2008 Act provides that where the woman to whom the sperm, eggs or embryo is donated is married and her husband's sperm is not used in the procedure, then he is to be treated as the father of any resulting child unless it is shown that he did not consent to the procedure. Section 36 provides that where the woman is not married and her partner consented to the procedure and agreed to be recognised as the father of the child, he will be considered the legal father.

[5.117] In keeping with arguments made above in relation to the child's right to know his or her origins, it may be suggested that birth records in egg donation cases should reflect genetic parentage as well as gestational parentage. However, this raises similar arguments as those discussed above in the context of sperm donation in relation to the balancing of the rights of the child, the gestational parents and the gamete providers.

[5.118] In relation to the issue of the sale of gametes and embryos, the question becomes largely one of public policy. Most societies would regard some values as impossible to put a price on, such as personal relationships, justice, health and children. The problem here, however, is to decide where to draw the line between what is necessary in the public good and therefore ought to be encouraged at whatever price and that which is considered to be too valuable to be priced, despite the cost to those who need it. A regime whereby gametes could be bought and sold, for many, encourages the correlation of procreation and commerce that undermines the dignity of the child and the parents. 'Certain things should be above the hustle and bustle of the market-place so as to preserve their dignity.'[129]

[5.119] Another much-voiced concern here is the possibility for exploitation of impoverished women by offering them financial inducements to enter into a procedure, which, as outlined earlier, is invasive and risky. The prospect of payment may therefore have a coercive effect for some of these women, thereby negativing their free consent to the procedure. The counter-argument to this is that by prohibiting payment, society is being unduly paternalistic[130] as regards women who may exercise their autonomy to utilise their bodies in any way they so wish. In other words, it deprives the woman of the ability to sell her product without offering her any alternative solution to her desperate financial plight. However, 'while it is true that a legal system which discourages or

---

[129] Prichard, 'A Market for Babies?' (1984) 34 U Toronto LJ 341, 352.

[130] Mead, 'Eggs for Sale' (1999) August 9, The New Yorker, discusses the views of a US lawyer, Thomas Pinkerton, who has placed advertisements looking for egg donors for clients, offering fees of $50,000 per donation, if the donors fit the bill of requirements. His view, in defence of such high fees, was that there was nothing wrong with a client paying premium rates for hard-to-come-by goods. He said: 'People have asked, "How can a donor make an informed choice about undertaking the risk of going through a medical procedure when there is so much money at stake?" – as if she weren't going to be able to use her mind any more. But put it in the context of what we are offering other youngsters, such as football players – is that unethical? It is almost an assault on womanhood to say that this woman can't make a decision because there's fifty thousand dollars at stake.' p 65.

prohibits sales will reduce opportunities for the poor, such a system does not increase social injustice – it merely highlights it."[131]

[5.120] The predominant negative effect of the prohibition of payment for eggs is that the supply of an already scarce commodity will diminish even more, thereby perhaps costing the infertile couple the chance to conceive. Although the evidence suggests that not all women donate their eggs for the payment involved, with some women donating to help a friend or relative, it is thought that most would not donate without financial compensation. The compromise position that has been adopted in many countries is to allow for the payment of expenses to the donor to compensate her for the risk, discomfort and inconvenience involved in the procedure.

LEGAL RESPONSIBILITY FOR CONGENITAL ABNORMALITY

[5.121] Where a child is born with an abnormality or genetic defect may he or she sue the sperm donor and the medical practitioner who carried out the procedure? The safety of sperm donation is of crucial importance in any responsible institution. In the US the screening of sperm donors is not done under any compulsory guidelines. Recommended standards are available from private groups but compliance with them is voluntary.[132] Although donors may generally give all necessary information to the clinic prior to donation they may, of course, be carriers of a genetic defect of which they are unaware.[133]

[5.122] Centres must follow certain guidelines as a minimum, such as procedures set out for the testing of semen for the HIV virus.[134] Current medical practice in this regard would demand that only frozen sperm be used in the insemination programme. The reason for not using fresh sperm is to help to prevent the transmission of the AIDS virus

---

[131] Reichman Schiff, 'Solomonic Decisions in Egg Donation: Unscrambling the Conundrum of Legal Maternity', 80 Iowa L Rev (1995) 265 at 294.

[132] McIntyre, 'The Potential for Products Liability Actions When Artificial Insemination by an Anonymous Donor Produces Children With Genetic Defects' (1994) 98 Dickinson L Rev 519 at 522.

[133] HFEA Code of Practice (8th edn) provides a list of screening requirements that clinics must comply with in the provision of donor services, such as HIV, hepatitis and syphilis. www.hfea.gov.uk/498.html (accessed 11 July 2011).

[134] Timmons et al, 'Genetic Screening of Donors for Artificial Insemination' (1981) 35(4) Fertility and Sterility 451–456. The authors state that it is insufficient to ask donors themselves whether there were any genetic or hereditary problems in the family history, even where the donor had formal medical training. They concluded as follows:
  'Since the purpose of AID is to provide the patient with as healthy a child as possible, and one-half of that child's genetic material will come from the donor, it is appropriate that AID programs have a carefully planned routine for genetic screening of donors. The fact that a donor has fathered a normal child does not exclude the possibility of genetically related birth defects, fetal wastage, or diseases in his future offspring, and should not be used as the sole criterion for his participation as a donor in an AID program. Asking whether or not a donor has genetic disorders in himself or his family is not accurate. Only careful investigation of the donor and his extended family will permit the recipient couple to be confident that, within the means possible, their future child will not be at increased risk for a genetic condition transmitted by the biologic father.' p 456.

by use of sperm which has not undergone an incubation period of usually three months and rigorous double checking procedures.

> The major risk of the transmission of AIDS with fresh semen is a 'window' of up to 120 days, or possibly longer, during which time the AIDS virus can be transmitted after the donor becomes infected and before seroconvertion ... The only effective way to close this 'window' in an insemination program is to use frozen semen, have the donor re-tested and found to be seronegative for HIV at least 120 days before using the semen.[135]

[5.123] In the absence of compulsory testing procedures, is it possible that a child born with a genetic defect, or the child's mother, may have a reasonable claim for damages against the clinician/doctor and/or the donor? This discussion presupposes that causation, ie the evidential link between the donor's genes and the defect or disease sustained by the child, will be proved, which is a medical and legal minefield. There are also enormous public policy considerations involved in allowing such actions to proceed.[136]

[5.124] If a defect or disease would have been reasonably foreseeable or detectable by a medical practitioner performing his duties along professional guidelines, and if the defect was not detected or warned about, then the medical practitioner might be liable in negligence. The doctor may have a defence on the basis of following current medical practice in the screening or testing of the sperm but perhaps the common practice is also inadequate. This comes back to the necessity for complex genetic testing and compulsory testing standards. This raises the unfortunate question of the costs of the procedure but 'most prospective recipients would be willing to pay for the increased likelihood, albeit not certainty, of giving birth to a normal, healthy child.'[137]

[5.125] A sperm donor might also be liable for non-disclosure of a genetic abnormality of which he knows or could know on reasonable enquiry (for example, if he knew of a family history of a particular defect or disease but did not know if he was a carrier). He might be negligent in failing to warn the doctor of the possibility of a genetic defect or in supplying his sperm for use by a doctor when he knew or suspected it to be carrying a genetic disease. Although he has no direct contract with the recipient of his sperm 'since the sperm donor knows that his semen will be used by someone other than the person to whom he delivers it and because the donor's negligence in failing to reasonably identify

---

135 Peterson, Alexander, Moghissi, 'A.I.D. and AIDS – Too Close for Comfort" (1988) 49(2) Fertility and Sterility 209.

136 Donnelly, 'The Injury of Parenthood: the Tort of Wrongful Conception' (1997) 48(1) NILQ 10–23. Donnelly discusses the tort of wrongful conception, an action which has yet to come before the courts in the Republic, examining the policy implications of allowing such an action to succeed, the approaches taken in other jurisdictions and the damages which may be awarded and the assessment thereof. She concludes that the action should not be prohibited by public policy and should be recognised as an economic one rather than one which tries to place a value on the life or worth of a child. Such an approach would fulfil 'the most basic function of the law of tort by putting the "victim" as far as possible in the financial position he or she would have been in had the negligence not occurred.' p 23.

137 McIntyre, 'The Potential for Products Liability Actions When Artificial Insemination by an Anonymous Donor Produces Children With Genetic Defects' (1994) 98 Dickinson L Rev 519 at 527.

his genetic risk factors could cause foreseeable harm to that person, he may be liable in negligence without privity.'[138]

[5.126] Identifying the donor, of course, may be problematical as his anonymity is usually protected. However, in the US in some states the donor's identity may be made known on showing 'good cause'. Good cause may be found in such circumstances as these where the donor withheld vital information which has resulted in a child being born with a genetic abnormality. In the UK, a donor-conceived person born with an abnormality could sue their donor for damages if it is proven that the donor had not told the clinic relevant facts about their or their families' medical history when they donated.[139]

Product liability

[5.127] Apart from negligence, is there also the possibility of an action under product liability law or consumer protection law? This would involve consideration of the sperm as a product or substance capable of being owned and therefore sold or supplied within the meaning of the relevant legislation. The ownership of gametes is discussed in Chapter 10. In the US at common law there have been cases where liability has been imposed on the medical providers of contaminated blood for transfusions, even where the contamination was unknown or undiscoverable.[140] This was in line with the strict liability nature of the sale (meaning that it was the defect in the quality of the product that was relevant for liability to be imposed, not whether any precautions has been taken by the seller). Other cases classified the provision of blood as a 'service' rather than a 'sale' thereby avoiding the imposition of liability on medical personnel who were unaware of any defect in the blood.[141] It remains to be seen whether sperm will be treated in the same way as blood.

[5.128] In Ireland, the Sale of Goods and Supply of Services Act 1980 provides a remedy against the seller of unmerchantable goods. Merchantability may be defined as the fitness of the goods for the purpose(s) for which they were bought. Whether sperm donation comes within the meaning of sale is as yet undecided. The Act's provisions apply to the sale of goods 'in the course of a business', which presumably would not generally apply to the sperm donor, as there would not usually be any contract between the sperm donor and the recipient of the sperm. However, it may apply to sperm banks who store donated sperm until required for use by a medical practitioner or clinic.[142]

---

138 McIntyre, 'The Potential for Products Liability Actions When Artificial Insemination by an Anonymous Donor Produces Children With Genetic Defects' (1994) 98 Dickinson L Rev 519 p 525.
139 http://www.hfea.gov.uk/1972.html (accessed 27 May 2010).
140 *Hekeler v St Margaret's Memorial Hospital*, 74 Pa D & C 2d 568 (1976).
141 *Perlmutter v Beth David Hospital* 123 NE 2d 792 (NYCA 1954).
142 It may be argued that the sperm bank is operating a charity rather than a business if it supplies the sperm for less than the market rate. Who decides what the market rate for sperm should be? Is it decided on the characteristics of the donor or should there be a flat fee charged, irrespective of the donor's physical attributes? It is possible now to order sperm through the Internet with web pages of a number of US based fertility clinics advertising their services for those who wish to avail of this no-questions-asked facility. (contd.../)

[5.129] In relation to the supply of sperm by the sperm bank it may be that this could be considered to be the provision of a service under s 39 of the 1980 Act. If the supplier is acting in the course of a business then terms are implied into the contract with the consumer of the service. The supplier must have the necessary skill to render the service. He must supply the service with due skill, care and diligence. Where materials are used they must be sound and reasonably fit for the purpose for which they are required. Where goods are supplied under the contract, they must be of merchantable quality within the meaning of the Act.

[5.130] As regards the provision of the service, including in this case the screening procedures in relation to the sperm, liability is fault based and imposed on the proven negligence of the supplier. If the supplier is supplying goods (if sperm may be considered 'goods') then liability is strict, as the goods must be of merchantable quality, ie fit for the purpose for which they were supplied. Therefore, whether the supply of sperm is considered to be a service or a sale, liability may be imposed for defective quality under the terms of the Act. However, if the supply is deemed to be a service (and not a sale) then exclusion clauses may be inserted in the contract which may be upheld by the court if considered to be fair and reasonable. For example, the sperm bank could insert a provision to the effect that it will test the sperm for HIV, hepatitis and syphilis but that no liability would be accepted for communication of any other virus. Such a term, within accepted testing procedures, would probably be considered 'fair and reasonable', and so within the exception allowed by the Act, once it was brought to the attention of the recipient of the donor sperm before the procedure took place.

[5.131] The European Community Products Liability Directive 1985 implemented by the Liability for Defective Products Act 1991 in Ireland imposes strict liability on the producer of a defective product for damage caused. The definition of 'products' is very wide and includes 'all movables'. It is thought that, as the product does not have to be the result of some form of manufacturing process, the term would include blood and, by analogy, it may also include semen. This could potentially leave the sperm donor, if he could be identified, open to the imposition of liability for damage caused by the use of his defective sperm.

---

[142] (\...contd) On some of these web pages, the donors are listed only by first name or number but other attributes are also given such as: hair and eye colour; ethnic ancestry; physical build; weight and height; complexion and tanning ability; predominant hand; teeth, hearing and vision; distinguishing marks such as dimples or cleft chin; sexual orientation and marital status; educational qualifications and hobbies.

Despite the attraction for some people of having no questions asked regarding their marital status or sexual orientation, the disadvantages are there are no guarantees regarding the testing done on such sperm; that the sperm is of good enough quality to achieve fertilisation; or even that it came from the man advertised.

Chapter 6

In Vitro Fertilisation

INTRODUCTION

[6.01] One of the main treatments for female infertility is IVF (in vitro fertilisation). This may help women who have been diagnosed with conditions such as blockage of the fallopian tubes or endometriosis. The procedure usually requires the woman to take ovarian stimulation drugs for a period of time to stimulate the ovaries to produce a number of eggs (optimally six to eight) which are retrieved vaginally or by laparoscopy. The eggs are then incubated with sperm in a petri dish in a laboratory. Approximately 18 hours after insemination visible changes can be seen under microscopic examination with pronuclear development of the embryo. On the second day after egg collection and insemination, the embryos (if any) will be transferred to the woman's uterus, or may be stored for future use.

[6.02] If the woman does not have eggs or they cannot be used due to poor quality, she may become pregnant using egg or embryo donation. Eggs are scarcer and more difficult to handle than sperm, but egg donation is a regular procedure now in many countries. The legal and ethical issues associated with gamete and embryo donation are discussed in Chapter 5. Since the first IVF baby, Louise Brown, was born in 1978 over four million children have been born worldwide through this technique. Although IVF has largely become more acceptable in society, there are still controversies surrounding its use or misuse in certain circumstances.

[6.03] Multiple gestations are recognised as a major problem associated with assisted reproduction. The rate of twin, triplet and higher-order pregnancies as a result of IVF practices is a huge concern to IVF practitioners, as these pregnancies carry higher risks for the mother's health, and higher risk of premature deliveries with possible negative long-term consequences for the children such as bleeding in the brain, intestinal problems, developmental delays and lifelong learning disabilities. Much international work in recent years has focused on reducing the incidence of such pregnancies, and it is now standard practice in many countries, including Denmark, Norway and the United Kingdom, to transfer a maximum of two embryos to the uterus at any one time. Other countries, such as Italy, Germany and Spain, allow for a maximum of three embryos. Others, such as Greece, Hong Kong, Japan and the United States, allow for the transfer of more than three embryos but usually this is done only in older women or those who have had repeated IVF failures. Single-embryo transfer is preferred in some countries, particularly where the woman is less than 36 years of age.[1] The International Federation of Fertility Societies (IFFS) recommends that a responsible attitude to embryo transfer

---

[1]   IFFS Surveillance 2007 Chapter 5, http://www.iffs-reproduction.org/documents/ Surveillance_07.pdf (accessed 30 June 2011).

should be taken which would include the transfer of no more than two embryos, and only under exceptional conditions; and the improvement of results with cryopreservation in all centres.[2]

Development of the early embryo

[6.04] The process of formation of an embryo begins with the production of the gamete, that is, the eggs and sperm, within the bodies of the woman and the man. The fertilisation process begins with the sperm making its way through the cumulus cells surrounding the egg. The sperm then reaches the zona pellucida, or shell of the egg, with which it binds. It passes through the zona into the perivitelline space (that is, the space between the zona and the egg) by releasing special enzymes, which help dissolve the area of the zona immediately in front of the sperm head. The sperm is then drawn into the egg cytoplasm (the ooplasm) by pseudopodal-like processes from the egg. The chromosome sets of the egg and sperm forming the female and male pro-nucleus come together in a process called syngamy about 28–30 hours after the beginning of the process. The fertilisation process is only completed, by formation of the single celled diploid zygote, 26–32 hours after the first contact between egg and sperm.

[6.05] After the formation of the single pluri-potent and toti-potent cell[3] with its complement of 46 chromosomes, the process of cell division continues. After 5 days, when there are between 64 and 128 cells present, the blastocyst begins to form in which cells begin to differentiate as the future embryo, the placenta and other membranes. In normal reproduction it appears that up to 80 per cent of blastocysts are shed spontaneously and unnoticed around this stage. This may be due to abnormalities in these blastocysts or to other factors such as the uterus not being fully receptive, which would actively inhibit implantation. At about the fifth or sixth day after fertilisation the blastocyst sheds its zona pellucida and begins to attach to the lining of the uterus. This is a crucial point in the development of the embryo.

> Implantation is a vital step in the development of the fetus, and the pre-embryo is now safer than it has been so far in its short life. Some would date conception from this point, and both legal and medical opinions now regard it as the starting-point for the law of "unlawfully procuring a miscarriage".[4]

---

2   Controversy erupted in 2009 in the United States when a woman called Nadya Suleman gave birth to octuplets following the transfer of multiple embryos by an IVF practitioner. She was already the mother of six other children. It was reported that the doctor agreed to transfer six embryos, two of which subsequently split to form two sets of identical twins. This was only the second set of octuplets to be born worldwide, and the only set to survive. Six embryos far exceeds the American Society for Reproductive Medicine's (ASRM) guidelines for women Suleman's age. The guidelines, based mainly on patient age and embryo quality, recommend transferring only one or two embryos in patients under age 35 to reduce the risk of multiple births. The doctor was subsequently expelled from the ASRM.

3   Totipotency means the cell can develop into any other cell or even into an entire new embryo; pluripotency means the cell may develop into many different cell types, but not all. The cells of the early embryos are totipotent, in that they have the ability to form all the different cell types of the body, including the stem cell of the next stage, the blastocyst. Stem cells are said to be pluripotent in that they have the ability to form multiple cell types.

4   Williams, 'The Fetus and the "Right to Life"' (1994) Cambridge Law Journal, 71–80 at 76.

[6.06] At around the 14th day after fertilisation, a line known as the primitive streak is identifiable on the surface of the embryonic disc. It is this primitive streak that was identified by the Warnock Committee in the United Kingdom as the point at which the boundary is crossed between molecular matter and the potential human being. It is also at this point that twinning will become evident, as the number of embryos will be determined by the number of primitive streaks that develop. Some commentators and scientists argue that this is the most important stage in the development of the new human being:

> To me the point at which I began as a total whole individual human being was at the primitive streak stage … If one tries to trace back further than that there is no longer a coherent entity. Instead there is a larger collection of cells, some of which are going to take part in the subsequent development of the embryo and some of which aren't.[5]

[6.07] After the development of the primitive streak, the pre-embryonic phase is over and the embryonic phase begins.[6] Thus, fertilisation is a process which takes place over many hours and has two important consequences, namely that the egg is activated to continue development and that a single set of chromosomes from each parent combines to produce a new unique double set in the zygote. The egg and sperm have an earlier history as specialised cells of the female and male:

> The sperm is specialised for transport of the condensed chromosomes and for penetration of the egg. The egg is specialised to cooperate in its own penetration and for almost everything else necessary to develop into an individual of a new generation. These gametes are as alive and human as any other cell in the parental bodies; what they acquire at fertilisation is no more or less (but still very much) than a new impetus to develop with a new and unique chromosomal set. These consequences are realised not in an instant but over hours of continuous change.[7]

Cryopreservation of embryos

[6.08] In 'simple' IVF, where a married couples' own gametes are used (without the complication of embryo storage), the process corresponds with that of Artificial Insemination by Husband and, as such, presents no major legal problems. 'The genetic and natural parentage of the resulting infant is not disputed. All that has occurred is that a technique has been substituted for a natural process; if any would protest that this is in some way immoral, they would, at the same time, have to contend that the surgical

---

[5] McLaren, 'Prelude to Embryogenesis' in Bock and O'Connor (eds), *Human Embryo Research* (Tavistock Publications, 1986) p 22.

[6] In coming to an understanding of the status of the early embryo, it is important to recognise that conception is a process or series of phases of development rather than one single moment. 'The idea of a moment of conception when a new human being is miraculously created is over-dramatised, and results from ignorance of modern biology. The "moment" when two gametes (the sperm and the ovum) fuse resolves itself under the microscope into a succession of clearly discernible stages, which may take 24 hours or more to complete. No one of these stages identifies itself as obviously the "moment of conception". However you date man's beginning, it is, like his ending, a process.' Williams, 'The Fetus and the "Right to Life"' (1994) Cambridge Law Journal, 71–80 at 76.

[7] Grobstein, 'The Early Development of Human Embryos' (1985) 10 Journal of Medicine and Philosophy, 213 at 214.

treatment of any disease is similarly immoral'.[8] The main legal issues that arise in the context of IVF occur due to the cryopreservation or storage of embryos as recommended by the best-practice guidelines discussed above. In the absence of legislation, this leads to uncertainty and disputes in relation to the legal status of the embryo and the locus of decision-making authority in respect of the embryos.

[6.09] Due to the stimulation of the ovaries for the purposes of IVF, it is often the case that a number of eggs are retrieved. This averages about 6 but may be as high as 10 or more. Egg freezing is not very successful though the techniques have improved in recent years[9] but in common practice all eggs are usually incubated with sperm in order to create embryos which can be stored more successfully. As discussed above, medical practice indicates that no more than three embryos[10] (and preferably only two) should be transferred. In most countries in which IVF is practiced, the remaining embryos may be cryopreserved or frozen for future use. The first successful birth from a frozen and thawed embryo was in 1983.

> It would now be considered dangerous for an IVF clinic not to have an embryo freezing programme available to cope with instances where a 'freeze-all' is indicated on safety grounds, such as where ovarian hyperstimulation syndrome – OHSS – is very likely. If there are additional embryos available surplus to requirement for immediate transfer, these can be stored for future cycle usage, sparing the couple the full procedure should the present one not succeed or they wish to try to procreate again if it does. Importantly, freezing allows the number of embryos transferred in one cycle to be reduced and with that, the chances of multiple pregnancy.[11]

[6.10] It is technically possible to successfully freeze the pre-embryo at the pronuclear stage in its development before syngamy begins at about 16–20 hours after the sperm has penetrated the outer membrane of the egg. It may be that this procedure would be less objectionable than freezing at a later stage in the embryo's development.[12] If it is felt

---

[8] Mason and Laurie, *Mason and McCall Smith's Law and Medical Ethics* (7th edn, OUP, 2010) para 8.50.

[9] Until recent years it had been thought that the composition of ova and the formation of ice crystals within the cytoplasm in the freezing process would negate the possibility of thawing them successfully, damaging their potential to be used in IVF.

[10] Some doctors argue that it should be a matter for clinical discretion whether, in exceptional cases, more than three embryos should be transferred. In *R (on the application of Assisted Reproduction and Gynaecology Centre) v Human Fertilisation and Embryology Authority* [2002] EWCA Civ 20, a clinic wished to treat a 47-year-old woman, who had undergone 8 failed IVF attempts previously, by using more than 3 embryos (at that time, 3 was the maximum number approved by the Human Fertilisation and Embryology Authority (HFEA)). The clinic argued that it should, as an exception, be able to use its discretion to transfer five embryos to this particular patient in this situation. The HFEA disagreed on the basis that, although the chances of this woman becoming pregnant at all were slight, there was nonetheless an accompanying risk of multiple pregnancy, which would be increased if the number of embryos to be transferred was five instead of three. On an application for judicial review of the Authority's decision, the Court, in dismissing the application, held that the Authority had taken its decision rationally, carefully and thoroughly and the fact that the clinic disagreed with the Authority's advice was 'neither here nor there.'

[11] Harrison, *The Smart Guide to Infertility* (Hammersmith Press, 2009) at p 230.

[12] The Assisted Reproduction Sub-Committee of the Institute of Gynaecologists and Obstetricians was divided on the time at which the fertilised egg should be frozen.

that human life does not begin until the first point at which the chromosomes from the male and female meet and the cell division process begins, then pronuclear freezing may provide a solution to some of the difficulties here. However, embryologists disagree as to the effectiveness of pronuclear freezing for technical reasons and would generally be more in favour of freezing at the four- or eight-cell stage.[13] It is thought by many of those involved in IVF that pronuclear freezing is an unsatisfactory compromise for the following reasons: the impracticability of successfully transferring three healthy pronuclear embryos and freezing the others (without knowing at this stage which is healthy or normal); the costs for the couple in paying for the storage of what they consider embryos but which may be abnormally fertilised eggs; the costs for the clinic in having round-the-clock supervision of the fertilised eggs so as to ensure that they do not get beyond the pronuclear stage before being frozen; and the need for inspections to ensure that this is *in fact* what is taking place.

[6.11] The history of embryo freezing in Ireland has been complicated by lack of clarity in relation to the constitutional status of the embryo and the ethical guidelines of the Medical Council, which is the regulatory body for registered medical practitioners in Ireland. The 4th edition of the *Ethical Guide of the Medical Council* obliged medical practitioners to transfer all fertilised eggs to the woman's body. The 5th (1998) and 6th

---

[13]   It is felt by some embryologists that pronucleur freezing is not as effective as embryo freezing for a number of reasons:

(i)   The male and female pronuclei, which ought to be visible in order to identify the egg as being on the way to being fertilised and to therefore enable the embryologist to proceed with freezing, are not always visible at this stage, as they actually disappear prior to the first cell division. If the eggs are viewed at this stage they may be considered unfertilised. This leads to confusion, as the exact number of fertilised eggs cannot be determined at this stage.

(ii) Some embryos begin to degenerate following cell division and would be inappropriate for freezing, as they will not survive the freeze/thaw process. If they are frozen at the pronucleur stage it would not be possible to determine viability and everything would be frozen. This leads to distress for the patients in the future when they are thawed and are found to be nonviable, and also has resource implications in terms of the costs involved in storage.

(iii) The impossibility of determining viability in the pronucleur embryos   also has other implications for the patients and clinics in that patients may not be willing to undergo the expense and trauma of thawing embryos which may not be viable, and the clinic is then faced with the dilemma of what to do with them.

Embryo freezing expenses can be minimised if embryo viability can be determined prior to freezing. If embryos are frozen at the pronucleur stage, thousands of embryos are available for freezing, thus requiring numerous expensive storage tanks and two or three scientists to perform such freezing alone. Embryo freezing has proven most successful when embryo viability has been determined prior to freezing, thus providing the patient with accurate success rates.

In a small number of cases the appearance of two pronuclei may not necessarily guarantee fertilisation. Occasionally, an egg fails to extrude a polar body, thus the egg only contains maternal chromosomal material. Such eggs appear to have fertilised when in fact they have not. If parthogenesis occurs (cell division without fertilisation) cell degeneration usually results.

(2004) editions of the Guide both stated that 'all fertilised eggs must be used for normal implantation and must not be deliberately destroyed'. The absence of any indication as to when the implantation had to take place facilitated IVF practitioners freezing 'fertilised eggs' or embryos. The most recent, seventh edition of the Guide, now called the Guide to Professional Conduct and Ethics for Registered Medical Practitioners, in 2009 does not specifically mention embryo freezing. Paragraph 20.2 states that 'assisted reproduction services should only be provided by suitably qualified professionals, in appropriate facilities and according to international best practice'.[14]

ETHICAL ISSUES IN IVF

[6.12] Before discussing the legal issues arising in relation to the status of the embryo, this section will briefly examine some of the ethical issues in IVF. Any debate about the regulation of assisted reproduction in Ireland will inevitably involve arguments relating to the moral status of the embryo as well as other ethical objections.

Personhood

[6.13] The moral issue that has perplexed many philosophers in relation to IVF revolves around the question of 'when does life begin?' It has been argued, however, that this question is unanswerable and indeterminate and that the question should be 'when does life begin to matter morally?' or 'when does life begin to have that special value we believe attaches to human life?'[15] 'The question is not whether the conceptus is human but whether it should be given the same legal protection as you and me.'[16] By defining what significance the embryo has, we are laying down the parameters within which we may be able to accord it rights and privileges in the legal context. However, in an attempt to clarify the issue, perhaps this argument ought to be reversed. It might well be that it is by discovering what we are prepared to do with the embryo that we can determine what its status is, as opposed to the other way around.[17]

[6.14] If life begins at the point at which the sperm penetrates the egg then this would, for many, prohibit the storage or freezing of or experimentation on such a human life. However, if human life does not begin until some later point, such as: syngamy (when

---

[14] Guide to Professional Conduct and Ethics (7th edn, 2009). Para 20.2 http://www.medicalcouncil.ie/Professional-Standards/Professional-Conduct-Ethics/ (accessed 30 May 2011). In light of the recommendations of the IFFS discussed above, Irish IVF practitioners who might be challenged in relation to embryo freezing could argue that adherence to international best practice requires responsible embryo transfer and cryopreservation policies.

[15] Harris, *The Value of Life* (1985) p 8.

[16] Williams, 'The fetus and the "right to life"' (1994) Cambridge Law Journal p 78.

[17] Evans, 'Pro-Attitudes to Pre-Embryos', in Evans (ed) *Conceiving the Embryo* (Martinus Nijhoff Publishers, 1996) 27. Evans considers the character of, what he terms, 'pro-attitudes to pre-embryos', in attempting to come to a conclusion on the status of the embryo. He argues that science alone cannot determine the issue, as scientists too are divided on when life begins. He asks whether philosophical reflection can assist in the discussion and demonstrates that here too the debates are split. In the face of such division and disagreement he queries whether regulation would be proper and concludes that a minimalist programme of regulation which would broadly give respect for human life would be the most we could hope for in this debate.

the chromosomes from the male and female begin to come together); or at the point when the blastocyst implants in the uterine wall commencing a pregnancy; or at the emergence of the primitive streak when individuality is certain – then, before these various stages, the mass of cells could be stored for future use, or used for beneficial research purposes, without transgressing the principle of dignity and respect for human life. After human life has been established the application of this principle of respect and dignity would ensure that no medical intervention could be made which would harm the developing embryo.[18]

[6.15] There are many different approaches to the question of when life begins to matter.[19] Some of these arguments look at whether one can describe the embryo as 'a life', while still recognising that it is human and alive. Thus the issue for consideration is whether the cell mass that is the embryo constitutes a human life in its own right, thereby according to it moral and legal rights and placing corresponding duties on others. This is not to say that if it does not constitute a human life that it is worthy of *no* protection or *no* respect, but rather that it is deserving of less respect and protection than a human life.

Is the human embryo a person?

[6.16] In Catholic philosophy, the definition of person is usually derived from Boethius, a philosopher and theologian from the 5th century, who defined 'person' as 'an individual substance of a rational nature'.[20] Aquinas later indicated that this definition applies to human beings because they are separate from each other, thus they are individuals, and because they are rational, that is 'they have control over their own actions and are not only acted upon as are all other beings, but act of their own initiative'.[21] He considered the term *person* to be a special name differentiating substances of a rational nature from other substances based on their intrinsic nature, not decisions based on social acceptance or law. As Aquinas uses the term, 'the mere presence of the intellective soul is sufficient for personhood.'[22] In more modern times, Locke further defined a person as:

> '[A] conscious thinking thing (whatever substance made up of, whether spiritual or material, simple or compounded, it matters not) which is sensible, or conscious of pleasure and pain, capable of happiness or misery, and so is concerned for itself, as far as that consciousness extends.'[23]

---

[18] Madden, '*In Vitro* Fertilisation: the Moral and Legal Status of the Human Pre-Embryo' (1997) 3(1) Medico-Legal Journal of Ireland, 12–20 at 13.

[19] Harris argues that there are only two types of answer which might be given to when does the embryo begin to matter morally. One is in terms of what the embryo *is*, the other is in terms of what it will *become*, that is to say, its *potential*. See Dyson and Harris, *Experiments on Embryos* (Routledge, 1990) p 67.

[20] Boethius, 'De Duabis Naturis' 3 in Migne, *Patrologia Latina*, vol 64, 1343. Quoted in O'Rourke, 'The Embryo as Person' (2006) Essays, National Catholic Bioethics Center, 241–251 at 243.

[21] St Thomas Aquinas, *Summa Theologiae*, I, Q 29.1

[22] O'Rourke, 'The Embryo as Person' (2006) Essays, National Catholic Bioethics Center, 241–251 at 243.

[23] Locke, *An Essay Concerning Human Understanding* (OUP, 1975) 62, quoted in O'Rourke.

[6.17] Many modern bioethicists have focused on the issue of consciousness as the necessary component of personhood. According to this definition, it is possible to be a human being in the sense of being a member of the *homo sapiens* species, but yet not be a person. Engelhardt claims:

> Not all humans are persons...Fetuses, infants, the profoundly mentally retarded, and the hopelessly comatose provide examples of human nonpersons. Such entities are members of the human species but they do not in and of themselves have standing in the moral community. They cannot blame or praise or be worthy of blame or praise...For this reason, it is nonsensical to speak of respecting the autonomy of fetuses, infants, or profoundly retarded adults, who have never been rational.[24]

[6.18] On the other hand, many Catholic bioethicists do not exclude from personhood human beings who have lost or never attained consciousness. Pope John Paul II said in 2004 'a man, even if seriously ill or disabled in the exercise of his highest functions, is and always will be a man, and he will never become a vegetable or an animal.'[25] O'Rourke concludes that there is a 'considerable gulf' between the meaning of the word *person* in the Catholic tradition and its meaning among contemporary bioethicists, though he is of the view that the latter admit that there is a continuity observable in the conscious person, that is to say, the conscious adult was at one time a child, an infant and even a fetus with the capacity to develop consciousness.

[6.19] O'Rourke and other Catholic theologians claim unequivocally that the embryo is a person from fertilisation and that society has a responsibility to protect unborn children. This approach, that what matters morally is being a member of the human species and that membership begins at fertilisation, has been described by Harris as 'the hedgehog's approach to the moral status of the embryo.'[26] It suffers from the difficulty that, fertilisation is a continuous process which would not be possible without a process of development and maturation of the egg that begins at a much earlier stage.[27] So, too, the sperm is alive before it penetrates the egg.[28] So if the egg and sperm are alive before

---

24 Engelhardt Jr, *The Foundations of Bioethics*, (OUP, 1986) 107; Also Lizza 'Persons and Death' (1993) Journal of Medicine and Philosophy 18.4: 351–374.

25 John Paul II, "On Life-Sustaining Treatments and the Vegetative State" (March 20, 2004) National Catholic Bioethics Quarterly 4.3.

26 Harris takes this description from a famous essay on Leo Tolstoy, called *The Hedgehog and the Fox,* by Isaiah Berlin. 'Berlin takes a fragment of Greek poetry and uses it to create a celebrated typology of human thought. "The fox knows many things, but the hedgehog knows one big thing." There are those, according to Berlin, who pursue many ideas and those who like to bring everything under one central vision or organising principle. The latter are hedgehogs, the former are foxes.' Harris describes the fox's approach to this problem as being more sophisticated. The fox will attempt to identify morally relevant features of the embryo or fetus (such as its form, development of functioning organs, sentience and so on), and argue that in virtue of its possession of these characteristics, it is worthy of protection. Harris, *Experiments on Embryos* (Routledge, 1990) pp 67–68.

27 Harris, *The Value of Life* (Routledge, 1985) p 10.

28 The argument, between the spermatozoists and the ovists, as to the relative significance of the sperm and the ovum in reproduction was seen in the 17th Century, with each group of the opinion that preformed human life was in the preferred gamete and the corresponding dormant partner gamete either sparked off the growth of the preformed embryo (contd.../)

conception, it is difficult to state that life begins at that moment when the sperm successfully penetrates the egg.[29]

[6.20] Another argument sometimes used in favour of conferring personhood on the embryo from the earliest possible time stems from the fact that there is no stage of early development as significant as this point in time. Everything that occurs after conception is simply a development of the potential attributes with which the embryo was bestowed at that time.

> The embryo or fetus possesses its fundamental right to life from the moment of conception. From that moment the fetus is already provided with all the genetic elements that will shape its future development as an adult human person. To use the language of genetics, the embryo, from the instant of the meeting of the mother and father cells, is already equipped with the entire 'programme' of its future physical characteristics, right down to the minutest detail...as well as of its basic mental capacity and personality traits. Everything that education and environment will later have to work on is already present in the embryo.[30]

[6.21] In 1987, the Catholic Church concluded from findings of biological science that the zygote constitutes the biological identity of a new human individual. Although not issued with papal authority, the Instruction does have the express approval of the Pope as an instruction for the teaching of the faith. While not intended as an infallible statement or a final pronouncement on the matter, it does nevertheless constitute the current official response of the Catholic Church to the moral issues raised by reproductive technology. It states: 'Certainly no experimental datum can be in itself sufficient to bring us to the recognition of a spiritual soul; nevertheless, the conclusions of science regarding the human embryo provide a valuable indication for discerning by the use of reason a personal presence at the moment of this first appearance of a human life. How could a human individual not be a human person?'[31] One response to this question is that the embryo is not yet a human individual since it is not developmentally single. This does not mean that it can be treated simply as disposable tissue. On this view, the potentiality argument is weighty – under favourable conditions the fertilised egg will move through developmental individuality then progressively through functional, behavioural, psychic and social individuality. This potential entitles the embryo to profound respect and any interference with the potential of the embryo to develop through these pre-ordained stages must be taken seriously. Steps that destroy the embryo

---

[28] (\...contd) (the role of the sperm according to the ovists), or provided the necessary context for the growth of the preformed embryo (the role of the ovum according to the spermatozoists). See Evans, 'Pro-Attitudes to Pre-Embryos', in Evans (ed) *Conceiving the Embryo* (Martinus Nijhoff Publishers, 1996) 27, p 32.

[29] It has been known for some time that sperm entry is not the only stimulus for cleavage to begin. Parthogenic activation of early development can be achieved in some mammalian species including humans. Braude and Johnson ask 'how should we regard, in philosophical terms, these unfertilised but cleaving "pre-embryos"?' 'The Embryo in Contemporary Medical Science' in Dunstan, *The Human Embryo: Aristotle and the Arabic and European Traditions* (University of Exeter Press, 1990) 208–221, p 218.

[30] Bishops of Ireland, 'Yes to Life', Extract From the Pastoral Letter 'Human Life is Sacred', in 'Abortion, Law and Conscience' (May/June 1992) 42(5) Doctrine and Life 326–335 at 328.

[31] Congregation for the Doctrine of the Faith, 'Instruction on Respect for Human Life in its Origin and on the Dignity of Procreation'" (1987) 16 Origins at 706 701–2.

cannot be undertaken 'for any but the most serious reasons, going far beyond considerations of convenience or scientific curiosity, and affecting either that being's own prospects for the future as in cases of genetic abnormality, or the life and welfare of others, as in cases of rape and incapacity in a woman to carry a child to term without risk to herself.'[32]

[6.22] Other philosophers argue that certain criteria must be satisfied before personhood is possible. In other words, there should be at least a biological stability or organisation in the embryo before it will be granted the privilege of personhood. Some call it a 'spatially-defined entity', while others refer to the fact that preliminary developments in the fertilised egg are not the development of the embryo proper but rather the establishment of the trophoblast, or feeding layer, that is crucial to any future development. 'The first sign that primary organisation is underway is the appearance of what is called the primitive streak.'[33] No use has been made by the Church of the distinction between genetic individuation and developmental individuation. There is, in the document:

> [N]o awareness that in the embryo's early stages neighbouring cells are loosely associated, that the cells of the inner cell mass of the early blastocyst are…'little different in developmental capability from the zygote. Each can contribute to any part of the embryo, and separation of the mass into two parts can still yield two or more embryos.'[34] It shows no awareness that only with the process of implantation do we eventually attain primary embryonic organisation.[35]

[6.23] Others argue that seeking to identify the embryo as a person or non-person is irrelevant because in identifying the characteristics of personhood, we are inevitably coming to the debate with our own value-laden view of what characteristics are important. For some, brain function will be the most important aspect of personhood, for others individuality, ensoulment or moral capacity. These arguments may be based on emotion without any appeal to rational or scientific debate but at the end of the day, it does not matter on what premise the definition of personhood is based because each one will define it based on his own value system and this will miss something, which, for others, will be of vital importance. Perhaps therefore it is preferable not to try to define a person at all or try to fit the embryo into the mould of personhood and simply recognise that it is necessary to reach some form of minimum consensus as to the status of the embryo as such without thereby according the label of person to it.

Sanctity of life

[6.24] Another objection taken to IVF by the Catholic Church is based on the sanctity of human life from its beginning. Pope Paul VI in 1973 said the State's protection of human life should begin at conception, 'this being the beginning of a new human being.'[36] The Congregation for the Doctrine of the Faith issued a Statement on Procured Abortion in

---

32   Mahoney, *Bioethics and Belief* (Steel and Ward, 1984) p 85.
33   Grobstein, *Science and the Unborn* (Basic Books, 1988) p 27.
34   Quoting Grobstein, *Science and the Unborn* (Basic Books, 1988).
35   McCormick 'Who or What is the Preembryo?' (1991) 1 Kennedy Institute of Ethics Journal 1 p 8.
36   *Pourquois l'Eglise Ne Peut Accepter l'Avortement*' (1973) 70 Documentation Catholique, 4–5. English translation: (1973) 17 The Pope Speaks, 333–335.

1974, which also dealt with the status of the embryo. It states that 'From the time that the ovum is fertilised, a life is begun which is neither that of the father nor the mother, it is rather the life of a new human being with his own growth. He will never become human if he were not human already.'[37] The Catholic Church asserts that modern genetic science confirms this position because it shows that from the very beginning, the genetic package is in place. However, this refers only to genetic individuality and not developmental individuality.[38] The Declaration of the Congregation of the Faith also states that it is leaving aside the thorny question of when the moment of animation occurs. It expressly refrains from stating that the soul is present from the beginning but yet human life must be protected from the time of fertilisation. It states: 'From a moral point of view this is certain: even if a doubt existed concerning whether the fruit of conception is already a human person, it is objectively a grave sin to dare to risk murder.'[39] The Declaration is admitting the presence of a doubt about personhood but claiming that it is immoral to act when such a doubt is present: 'It calls to mind the age-old chestnut: when the hunter is uncertain whether it is an animal or human moving in the underbush there is a certain obligation not to shoot.'[40]

---

[37] Congregation for the Doctrine of the Faith (1974) p 9. The final sentence of this statement has been troublesome for many theologians in terms of Christian teaching. This is due, in part, to its contradiction of the principle developed by St. Thomas Aquinas known as hylomorphism, which became the dominant theory in the theology of the Middle Ages from 600–1500 AD. The concept defines the human being as a unity of two elements: primary matter, which represents the potentiality of the body; and substantial form, which represents the actualising principle of the soul. 'It implies that hominisation is delayed to some point after the embryo has become a fully human body. Despite the body's potential as primary matter, there is no human person without the actualising principle of the substantial form, the soul. This substantial form, or soul, can only be present in a body capable of receiving it, one that has developed beyond the earliest stages of pregnancy.' Hurst, *The History of Abortion in the Catholic Church – The Untold Story,* (Washington DC Catholics for a Free Choice, 1989) p 13. This doctrine thus defines human beings as a unity of body and soul, not as a potential inherent in a developing body, which will eventually gain a human soul. In claiming that the fertilised egg 'would never be made human if it were not human already', the Church has changed the terms of arguments without confronting hylomorphism and the delayed hominisation principle. Hurst p 21.

[38] McCormick, 'Who or What is the Preembryo?' (1991) 1 Kennedy Institute of Ethics Journal 1, p 6. McCormick sees this as a fatal flaw in the reasoning behind the document, as it misunderstands the meaning of individuality and does not cater for the scientific knowledge, which clearly points to the conclusion that the embryo is not developmentally individual at this stage.

[39] McCormick, 'Who or What is the Preembryo?' (1991) 1 Kennedy Institute of Ethics Journal 1, p 10.

[40] McCormick, 'Who or What is the Preembryo?' (1991) 1 Kennedy Institute of Ethics Journal 1, p 7. However, as mentioned earlier, this tutiorist argument is only relevant in circumstances in which the doubt is a reasonable one. It has no place in modern discussions relating to the embryo due to the knowledge now available in relation to the development of the early embryo. Any doubt in respect of whether the embryo is a human individual at this stage in its development is, it may be argued, an unreasonable one and therefore should not be used in a tutiorist argument in favour of a prohibition on any action in relation to the embryo other than transfer to the uterus.

The position of the Roman Catholic Church

[6.25] Although Ireland has in recent years become a more multi-cultural and multi-denominational country, in the population census carried out in 2006, almost 87 per cent of the Republic's population described themselves as Roman Catholic, with other religious communities such as Protestant, Muslim, Jewish, Jehovah's Witnesses, and Orthodox faiths increasing steadily.[41] Article 44 of the Irish Constitution guarantees freedom of conscience and the free profession and practice of religion to all citizens. However, the Roman Catholic tradition has had a significant influence on the development of health policy in Ireland and the Irish Constitution bears the hallmarks of this in its natural law philosophy. Indeed, McDonnell and Allison claim that in relation to bioethical issues, the Catholic Church 'is not simply asserting its voice of dissent in the context of public debate as one voice amongst a plurality of other voices, but to shape the emerging debate as a powerful, institutional actor.'[42] They state that Ireland has been slow to debate or regulate bioethical issues, including assisted reproduction.

> The apparent reticence of policy makers to engage in the emerging international bioethical discourse on advances in biomedical science and biotechnology reflects, in large part, the legacy of...the 'moral monopoly' of the Catholic Church over questions of identity, ethics and public morality in Ireland.[43]

[6.26] The Catholic Church is opposed to IVF and other forms of assisted reproduction on the grounds that it is contrary to the teachings of the Church and the dignity of the human being. '[A]ll the teaching of the Church in regard to medical ethics results from the Christian understanding of the worth and activity of the human person.'[44] This understanding may be paraphrased as being based on the view that God creates the human person in his own image and likeness and possessing a spiritual intelligence and free will. According to traditional Catholic views, beginning at conception the embryo has moral status as a human being, and this means that most assisted reproductive technologies are forbidden. 'Although the human body is brought into being through the cooperation of human parents, the creation of the human soul is a direct act of God (Gn 2:7; 2 Mt 7:22–23)'.[45] The Catholic Church states that procreation must conform to the dignity of the person. The only possible way in which to procreate in such conformity is to respect the link between the meanings of the conjugal act and respect for the unity of human beings:

> In his unique and irrepeatable origin, the child must be respected and recognised as equal in personal dignity to those who give him life. The human person must be accepted in his

---

41 See http://beyond2020.cso.ie/Census/TableViewer/tableView.aspx?ReportId=74644 (accessed 30 May 2011).

42 McDonnell and Allison, 'From Biopolitics to Bioethics: Church, State, Medicine and Assisted Reproductive Technology in Ireland' (2006) Sociology of Health and Illness Vol 28 No 6 p 817–837.

43 McDonnell and Allison, 'From Biopolitics to Bioethics: Church, State, Medicine and Assisted Reproductive Technology in Ireland' (2006) Sociology of Health and Illness Vol 28 No 6 p 818.

44 Ashley and O'Rourke, *Health Care Ethics* (2nd edn, Catholic Health Association of the United States, 1982) p 162.

45 O'Rourke and Boyle, *Medical Ethics: Sources of Catholic Teachings* (2nd edn, Georgetown University Press, 1993) p 4.

parents' act of union and love; the generation of a child must therefore be the fruit of that mutual giving which is realised in the conjugal act …He cannot be desired or conceived as the product of an intervention of medical or biological techniques; that would be equivalent to reducing him to an object of scientific technology. No one may subject the coming of a child into the world to conditions of technical efficiency which are to be evaluated according to standards of control and dominion.[46]

[6.27] In modern times the Catholic Church has taken the view that the human being is in existence from the 'moment of conception' and that, therefore, contraceptives that may act as abortifacients, and abortion itself, is morally wrong. This position is a relatively new one, being a creation largely of the late 19th century:

[T]he claim to absolute protection for the human embryo 'from the beginning' is a novelty in the western, Christian and specifically Roman Catholic moral traditions. It is virtually a creation of the later nineteenth century, a little over a century ago; and that is a novelty indeed as traditions go.[47]

[6.28] Studies of theology in the old civilisations of the Levant, out of which some of the laws of the Old Testament were shaped, show that, for example, compensation for inducing a miscarriage depended not only on the woman's status but also on the gestational age of the fetus.[48] In the third century BC, the principle was developed that if the fetus was not yet sufficiently formed to be a copy or portrayal of the human form, the penalty was less than it would otherwise be.[49] This was based on the principle of animation, that is, the point at which the soul enters the body. It was thought that until

---

[46] Congregation for the Doctrine of the Faith, 'Instruction on Respect for Human Life in its Origin and on the Dignity of Procreation' (1987) 16 Origins at 706.

[47] Dunstan, 'The Human Embryo in the Western Moral Tradition' in Dunstan and Seller (eds) *The Status of the Human Embryo, Perspectives from Moral Tradition* (London: King Edwards Hospital Fund 1988) p 40. Dunstan discusses the moral tradition of according protection to the fetus depending on its developmental stage, a tradition which he claims has been ignored by those who try to claim protection for the fetus from conception. The evidence for such a tradition is found in the philosophical discussion of animation (the relation of the soul to the human person) and in the moral and legal sanctions for abortion. See earlier version in Dunstan, 'The Moral Status of the Human Embryo: A Tradition Recalled' (1984) 1 J of Medical Ethics 38–44. This is similarly acknowledged by Smith: '[t]he Catholic Church once assumed that the fetus did not become a human being until several weeks after conception.' 'What Is Christian Teaching on Abortion?' in Abortion, Law and Conscience (May/June 1992) 42(5) Doctrine & Life 305–317 at 306. He quotes Noonan, who maintains that '…this remained the practice until 1869 when Pope Pius IX in the constitution *Apostolicae Sedis* dropped the reference to the 'ensouled fetus' in the excommunication for abortion so that the excommunication now seemed to include the abortion of any embryo.' Noonan, 'An Almost Absolute Value in History' *(*1977) in The Morality of Abortion: Legal and Historical Perspectives p 39.

[48] Dunstan, 'The Human Embryo in the Western Moral Tradition' in Dunstan and Seller (eds) *The Status of the Human Embryo, Perspectives from Moral Tradition* (London: King Edwards Hospital Fund 1988) p p 41. Examples are given of the Babylonian Code of Hammurabi and the Hebrew law of Exodus.

[49] Dunstan, 'The Human Embryo in the Western Moral Tradition' in Dunstan and Seller (eds) *The Status of the Human Embryo, Perspectives from Moral Tradition* (London: King Edwards Hospital Fund 1988) p 42.

the fetus had taken a human form it was similar to an animal or even a monster and was not therefore worthy of receiving a soul. This tradition was followed in the Old Latin versions of *Exodus* before the end of the second century AD, and the language of these versions became the language of the moral tradition of the west as it coincided with current philosophical perceptions of the relation of soul and body and with the physiology developed in Hippocratic and Galenic medicine. This notion of animation became associated with the maternal observation of quickening (movement of the fetus in the womb at about 16 weeks) which then became an important point in the canon and, later, in the common law. For example, Pope Innocent III in 1211 issued a canon for suspension of a priest from his ministrations if he had been a party to a miscarriage: 'If the conceptus is not yet quickened he may minister; otherwise, he must abstain from the service of the altar.'[50] Major canonists who influenced the formation of the common law in England took up this point.[51] The canon law and English common law were thus, for their respective purposes, in step. Quickening became a determining point for various purposes in the common law. This is evident from a quotation from Blackstone's Commentaries in 1770:

> Life begins in contemplation of law as soon as an infant is able to stir in the mother's womb…[t]o be saved from the gallows a woman must be quick with child – for barely with child, unless he be alive in the womb, is not sufficient.[52]

[6.29] Until the 1800s, people generally believed that human life was not present until the stage of quickening had been reached. This gave women a great deal of freedom in dealing with early unwanted pregnancies. Almost all medical manuals at that time gave women the information necessary to procure a miscarriage.[53] Indeed the term 'abortion' was never applied to a married woman; it was reserved only for single women who were thought of as promiscuous. The methods employed by married women were tolerated because they were declared to be an attempt, not to procure an abortion, but to cure amenorrhoea (ie absence of menstruation). However, the problem of amenorrhoea was not as prevalent as the widespread use of these cures might suggest. A contribution to the Lancet in 1898 concludes, from a study of women attending at an outpatient clinic, that the vast majority of instances in which a period was missed was due to the commencement of a pregnancy, despite the records showing that a large number of them had amenorrhoea. Doctors and society tolerated this kind of behaviour in general due to the conviction that until the fetus began to move in the womb, no human life had begun.

[6.30] As a result of the perceived increase in the use of abortifacients for the cure of so-called amenorrhoea as well as for true abortions, which were at this time widely condemned, doctors began to become more wary of providing these cures without first ensuring that no pregnancy had commenced. Many doctors related how their patients

---

50   Dunstan, 'The Human Embryo in the Western Moral Tradition' in Dunstan and Seller (eds) *The Status of the Human Embryo, Perspectives from Moral Tradition* (London: King Edwards Hospital Fund 1988) p 43.

51   Dunstan, 'The Human Embryo in the Western Moral Tradition' in Dunstan and Seller (eds) *The Status of the Human Embryo, Perspectives from Moral Tradition* (University of Exeter Press, 1990, 1990) pp 45–46, for extracts from Raymond de Penafort (1185–1275) and Henry de Bracton *On the Laws and Customs of England*.

52   Blackstone's *Commentaries* (4th edn, 1770) p 129.

would trick them into providing these remedies to bring on an abortion. In 1803, abortion was made a statutory offence both before and after the stage of quickening. Up to this point, the law stated that an abortion prior to quickening was a crime, but as only the woman herself knew if the fetus had moved prior to her having taken an abortifacient, the law could not be enforced. It is thought that the Act of 1803 was introduced to deal both with the spectre of the unmarried woman attempting to hide evidence of her promiscuity and the problem of the death of many women through the use of poisons as abortifacients.

[6.31] The papacy concerned itself primarily with matters of penance with regard to abortion until Pius IX. It was only in 1869, in response to the increase in abortions, that Pope Pius IX declared that he would excommunicate anyone who procured an abortion.[54] This was without reference to the age of the fetus. Up to this point moral tradition had been to accord protection to the fetus according to the different stages of its development: 'The doctrine of delayed hominisation has been the majority opinion of both the papacy and moral theologians throughout most of Roman Catholic history.'[55] Although it is unclear as to what motivated such a change to take place in 1869 (this being the first implicit teaching on abortion by the papacy), it is thought that it was no more than an attempt to bring Church teaching into line with modern medical knowledge. However, some critics argue that if this was the main factor influencing the Church, then it would have been expected to have changed its views a lot sooner than it did, as the advances in science which exploded Aristotelian theories had taken place in

---

53   McLaren. 'Policing Pregnancies: Changes in Nineteenth-Century Criminal and Canon Law', in Dunstan, *The Human Embryo: Aristotle and the Arabic and European Traditions* (University of Exeter Press, 1990) pp 187–207. McLaren focuses on the prohibition of abortion through the ages and the importance of public opinion in influencing change in the law. In his view, one of the reasons why the notion of quickening was abandoned as a legitimate recognition of a stage of development of the fetus was not only due to advances in embryological knowledge but also due to attacks on it by medical men who wanted to resist interference in their practices by both lawyers who were trying to frame legislation and female patients who could themselves determine with authority whether a new human life had in fact begun. This latter notion was strenuously resisted by medical men who did not want to lose control over the determination of matters of physiology and vitality to others they perceived to be less qualified in this area. At the end of the 19th century, the priests, doctors and laity had all gone in a different direction – the priests stuck to the notion of ensoulment and the moment of conception, the doctors turned to developmental issues and the women held on to the importance of quickening as the first indication of the presence of human life. The concern by the medical profession to monopolise the grading and servicing of pregnancy and the carrying out of terminations led to their rejection of any other approach other than their own.

54   *Apostolicae Sedis* of 12 October 1869. This is repeated in the 1983 Edition of the *Codex Iuris Canonici*, Lib VI, Tit VI, can. 1398.

55   Hurst, *The History of Abortion in the Catholic Church – The Untold Story*, (Washington DC Catholics for a Free Choice, 1989) p 22. Hurst studies the complex history of the Catholic Church's teaching on abortion focusing on the principle of hominisation, the unity of mind and body in the nature of human beings and the relationship between the condemnation of abortion and the church's view of sexuality. Her study reveals 'inconsistencies and unresolved questions' in the history of the Church's attitude to abortion. It also highlights the fact that this teaching on abortion is 'not governed by papal infallibility'. p 1.

the early 18th century. While the motive ascribed to the Church may have played a role in the change brought about in 1869, this may not be the whole story.

> The Church was more alarmed than relieved by the reports of doctors' increased ability to not only observe but to intervene in the process of reproduction. Pius, in dropping the reference to the ensouled fetus and thereby condemning all abortions, was clearly launching the Church in a campaign against medical intervention in childbirth.[56]

[6.32] The Catholic Church takes the view that the combination of penitential punishment with what is taken as authoritative teaching has settled the matter in relation to abortion, 'despite the fact that this is not considered to be infallible teaching.'[57] Nevertheless, there are those among Catholics who believe that the immediate hominisation theory cannot be supported, and they regard the total ban on abortion as an anomaly.[58]

[6.33] The Catholic Church places heavy emphasis on the unitive and procreative purposes of the conjugal act within marriage. This also affects the Church's position in relation to donation of gametes for fertilisation purposes. For example in 1949, Pius XII stated that Artificial Insemination by Husband (AIH) must be absolutely rejected.[59] He continued this theme in 1951 by saying that AIH turns the home into a biological laboratory and that the Holy Scripture gave propriety to the conjugal act as a union in one flesh only – more than the union of two seeds which may be brought about even artificially.[60] Again in 1956, he spelled out in greater detail that the biological generation of a child should only take place within the unity of the conjugal union.[61] '...Pius XII was insisting that the child (for the good of the child and the marriage) must be the fruit of the *conjugal* union. But it is the fruit of the *conjugal* union only when it is conceived *in a conjugal way,* that is, by sexual intercourse.'[62]

[6.34] Pope Paul VI repeated this analysis of the conjugal act as having an inseparable unitive and procreative dimension in 1968 in *Humanae Vitae,* as did Pope John Paul II in 1982 in *Familiaris Consortio.* It preaches that the conjugal act signifies not only love but also potential fruitfulness, and that therefore it cannot be deprived of this significance by artificial means. The unitive and procreative aspects of the conjugal act

---

56 McLaren. 'Policing Pregnancies: Changes in Nineteenth-Century Criminal and Canon Law', in Dunstan, *The Human Embryo: Aristotle and the Arabic and European Traditions* (University of Exeter Press, 1990) p 197.
57 Hurst, *The History of Abortion in the Catholic Church – The Untold Story* (Washington DC Catholics for a Free Choice, 1989) p 2222.
58 Hurst also states that, in modern practice, the Church does not always hold to the doctrine of immediate hominisation. 'It does not practice fetal baptism in all cases of miscarriage. It rarely performs baptism, extreme unction or the funeral mass, even when a full-term baby is stillborn. It seems that the church makes a distinction, in every case except abortion, between the potential human being represented in the developing fetus and the actual human being which the fetus eventually becomes.' p 21.
59 Address to the Fourth International Congress of Catholic Doctors, AAS 41 (1949) 559–60.
60 Address to the Italian Catholic Union of Midwives, AAS 43 (1951) 835–54.
61 Address to the Second World Congress on Fertility and Sterility, AAS 48 (1956) 467–74.
62 McCormick, *The Critical Calling, Reflections on Moral Dilemmas since Vatican II*, Ch 19 'Therapy or Tampering: the Ethics of Reproductive Technology and the Development of Doctrine' (Georgetown University Press, 2006), p 335.

are inextricably linked and may not be separated. If the act is deprived of its intimate truth, to which both of these aspects pertain, it ceases to be an act of love and is instead simply a bodily union.

[6.35] However, there are those who argue that, on a technical point, the inseparability of the unitive and procreative is of the conjugal act, and not necessarily of the generative process. 'All we learn from this passage [of *Humanae Vitae*] however, is that *if the conjugal act is performed* it should have these qualities: it should not be falsified in either of its essential "significations". This does not necessarily imply that if there is to be procreation it should be by means of a unitive act.' [63] In other words, the inseparability of the unitive and procreative in the conjugal act does not rule out generative acts outside of it. It must be remembered that Paul VI and John Paul II, in making these assertions, were directly concerned with rejecting contraception in marriage. Artificial reproductive procedures were not of immediate concern to them at that time.[64] However, those official formulations viewed the procreative process in sweeping terms and any doubts were put to rest by the Instruction in 1987,[65] which sees IVF as an analogous separation of the unitive and procreative dimensions.[66]

Human dignity

[6.36] Objection is sometimes taken to IVF and associated practices on the basis that it is contrary to human dignity. The classical definition of human dignity comes from Greek and Roman antiquity, with the expressions *dignus* and *dignitas* expressing the

---

[63]   Daniel, 'In Vitro Fertilisation: Two Problem Areas' (1986) 63 Australasian Catholic Record 21–31 at 31.

[64]   Guzzetti, 'Debolezza Degli Argomenti Contro l'Embryo Transfer' Revista di Teologia Morale 17 (1985):71–79 at 72–73. Quoted in McCormick p 336.

[65]   Congregation for the Doctrine of the Faith, 'Instruction on Respect for Human Life in its Origin and on the Dignity of Procreation' (1987).

[66]   There are two senses in which the inseparability of the unitive and the procreative might be considered. One is the narrow sense, which refers only to the conjugal act. Therefore, if the conjugal act is performed, these dimensions may not be separated. In this way, nothing is implied about artificial reproduction beyond the marital act – it does not exclude IVF. The broad sense, in which inseparability may be considered, is that procreation ought not to occur in marriage except as the result of a sexual act – IVF is excluded. McCormick argues however that IVF may be viewed not as a substitution for sexual intimacy but as a kind of prolongation of it and therefore as not severing the unitive and the procreative. He quotes Verspieren: '[N]ot everything that is artificial is unnatural.' 'L'Aventure de la Fecondation in Vitro', Etudes (Nov.1982): 479–92. McCormick believes that this view has sufficient theological weight behind it to be a 'solidly probable opinion'. He concludes:
   …[t]he issue at stake should be clear. It is the meaning of the inseparability of the unitive and procreative. If this inseparability must be read *in the broad sense* in *Humanae Vitae* and *Familiaris Consortio* … then clearly, both contraception and IVF must be excluded. If, however, inseparability can be understood differently, then IVF would not necessarily be excluded. Specifically, it might be sufficient if the *spheres* of the unitive and procreative are held together so that there is no procreation apart from marriage, and no full sexual intimacy apart from a context of responsibility for procreation …'.
   McCormick, *The Critical Calling, Reflections on Moral Dilemmas since Vatican II*, Ch 19 'Therapy or Tampering: the Ethics of Reproductive Technology and the Development of Doctrine' (Georgetown Univ Press, 2006), pp 337–338.

notions of 'worthiness for honour and esteem'. This notion of dignity as something rare and exceptional retains some power in modern times in relation to our respect for those who are somehow distinctive and admirable due to their courage, heroism, athleticism, or selflessness in the service of others. But if we are to speak about 'human dignity' there must be something in the nature of human beings per se that makes them worthy of respect.[67] Schulman argues that the classical notion of dignity lends itself to invidious distinctions between human beings, and is not fully at home with democratic ideals of equality, freedom and tolerance. He says that 'to make the case for human dignity as a robust bioethical concept for our age, one would have to show that dignity can be something universal and accessible to all human beings as such.'

[6.37] Another source of the notion of dignity is the Bible, which talks about man made in the image of God, and thus possessing an inalienable dignity. In 2008 the Congregation for the Doctrine of the Faith published an 'Instruction *Dignitas Personae* on Certain Bioethical Questions' in which it states that 'the dignity of a person must be recognised in every human being from conception to natural death'. The Instruction goes on to say:

> The human embryo has...from the very beginning, the dignity proper to a person. Respect for that dignity is owed to every human being because each one carries in an indelible way his own dignity and value. *The origin of human life has its authentic context in marriage and in the family,* where it is generated through an act which expresses the reciprocal love between a man and a woman. Procreation which is truly responsible vis-à-vis the child to be born "must be the fruit of marriage".

However, the Biblical account of human dignity points in different directions and may be said to be inherently unreliable. Macklin argues that religious sources, especially writings of the Catholic Church, may explain why so many articles and reports appeal to human dignity 'as if it means something over and above respect for persons or for their autonomy'. Birnbacher suggests that human dignity is used as a camouflage for a theological tradition that sees the order of nature as divinely sanctioned.[68]

[6.38] Kantian philosophy states that dignity is the intrinsic worth that belongs to all human beings and to no other beings in the natural world. All men possess dignity because of their rational autonomy, ie their capacity for free obedience to the moral law of which they themselves are the authors. Kant's doctrine of human dignity demands equal respect for all persons and forbids the use of another person merely as a means to one's own ends. Yet there are problems with this theory, too. If dignity depends on rational will and the capacity to act autonomously, does this imply that those who do not have such capacity, eg intellectually disabled persons, infants or persons in a comatose state, are not worthy of human dignity?[69]

[6.39] Some commentators take the view that the vague and illusory nature of the concept of human dignity begs the question as to whether it has any place in bioethical

---

[67] Schulman, *Bioethics and Human Dignity*, The President's Council on Bioethics, Working Paper 2003.

[68] Birnbacher, 'Human Cloning and Human Dignity' (2005) Reproductive Biomedicine Online 10 (Suppl. 1) 50–55.

[69] Schulman, *Bioethics and Human Dignity*, The President's Council on Bioethics, Working Paper 2003.

discourse at all.[70] Examples of the use of the concept of human dignity in bioethics shows how it can be manipulated to serve opposing sides of the same issue, such as end-of-life decision-making. Where both proponents and opponents of voluntary euthanasia appeal to human dignity in their arguments. This is perhaps due to the fact that the idea of human dignity emanates from a number of different sources, each of which brings with it its own difficulties.

[6.40] Many international declarations, such as the Universal Declaration of Human Rights (1948), the Universal Declaration on Bioethics and Human Rights (2005), and various national constitutions refer to human dignity, yet its meaning and content is never expressly defined. Shultziner explains that this reflects a political consensus among groups that may well have different beliefs about what human dignity means and what it entails. In effect, it serves as a placeholder for whatever it is about human beings that entitles them to basic human rights and freedoms.[71] This made a lot of practical sense after World War II when the most important issue was to ensure that agreement was reached that the atrocities inflicted at concentration and death camps would never be repeated. The 'inviolability of human dignity' was thus enshrined in some of these international documents to prevent a second Holocaust. However, although a baseline of inviolable rights is undoubtedly welcome, some argue that the same objective could be achieved by invoking the concept of 'respect for persons' instead.[72]

[6.41] In the context of assisted reproduction, the simple case of IVF, that is the fertilisation of a single egg from a married woman by sperm taken from her husband, and then transferred to her uterus, may be more readily reconcilable with the concept of human dignity. As this practice does not create spare embryos which are either stored or destroyed, and takes place within a marital relationship, it does not necessarily suffer from the same moral condemnation as other uses of IVF procedures. For example, the Catholic Bishop's Joint Committee on Bioethical Issues declined to come to a conclusion about the morality of this case and left it an open question.[73] Others, however, dispute the acceptability of even the straightforward case of IVF and would argue that, IVF itself, as a technique, is flawed morally.[74]

[6.42] Iglesias argues that the technical procedures involved in IVF must be understood in the light of requirements deriving from the commitment to the principle of respect for the sacredness of human life. In IVF there are countless variables contributing to the success rates achieved. The gametes are handled with machines and instruments, and exposed to artificial environments such as light, heat and culture media.

> In practice all this carries with it, for the embryonic human being, either the risk of death, that is, of being killed during the process (for many more embryos die in the process than survive it), or the risk of serious and irreparable harm, that is, of being seriously damaged in

---

[70] Macklin, 'Dignity is a Useless Concept' (2003) BMJ 327:1419–1420.

[71] Shultziner 'Human Dignity – Functions and Meanings' (2003) Global Jurist Topics 3:3.

[72] For example, Macklin argues that this ensures voluntary informed consent, the protection of confidentiality, and the need to prevent discrimination and abusive practices. Macklin, 'Dignity is a Useless Concept' (2003) BMJ 327:1419–1420.

[73] O'Mahony, *A Question of Life, Its beginning and Transmission* (Christian Classics, 1990) 121, referring to reflections in The Tablet, 20 April 1985.

[74] O'Mahoney at 100 quoting from Iglesias, The Tablet, 14 July 1984.

the process or by the process (for many embryos begin to develop abnormally). These risks can never, in principle, be excluded.[75]

[6.43] On the other side of the argument, in natural reproduction many more embryos are lost than survive – around 80 per cent of blastocysts are shed spontaneously in the early stages after fertilisation.[76] It is also the case that embryos may equally begin to develop abnormally when conceived in vivo but, as most of these are expelled from the uterus soon after fertilisation, the likelihood of IVF being seen to have an increased rate of abnormal development is simply due to the fact that such abnormalities may be seen in the laboratory, rather than in the uterus. Seen in this light, IVF may perhaps be a more efficient method of reproduction than sexual intercourse. Haring, a respected Catholic theologian, writing in 1972 when IVF had not yet been successful, in considering the risks to fertilised eggs inherent in IVF says:

> We are not to forget, however, the high rate of loss after *in vivo* fertilisation. It may be that in the earlier experimental phases the loss will be higher, but with progress in procedural techniques, scientists might be able to reduce the risks to a minimum. Those who are convinced of 'ensoulment' at the moment of fertilisation will be forced to cry 'immorality' in reference to the procedure, especially if it must be interrupted at a certain stage. In their eyes, this is homicide. However, if at the present stage of embryological science we give high probability to the opinion that individualisation does not coincide with fertilisation – that hominisation in the full sense happens at a later stage – then experimentation at initial cell division stages cannot be called homicide.[77]

[6.44] Iglesias concludes that, by embarking on IVF, both doctors and parents choose to have any defective embryos discarded and choose to give life to a child in conditions which involve it in a serious risk of death or damage. Neither of these two choices is morally justifiable. She says:

> There really cannot be a 'simple case' of in vitro fertilisation. IVF is not a morally permissible mode of generation for those who are committed to cherishing and caring for every individual human being from conception to death; IVF is not a course open to those who want to give life and love to a child just for his own sake, as is appropriate and right in the case of a human person.[78]

---

[75] Iglesias, *IVF and Justice,* (Linacre Centre for Health Care Ethics in London, 1990) p 31.

[76] 'Not much more than 25 per cent of successfully fertilised eggs reach the blastocyst stage of development. Even once implanted the failure rate is prodigious.... 22 per cent of very early pregnancies which can be detected by raised blood levels of human chorionic gonadotrophin (hCG)...will fail. This group does not include those pregnancies that fail before the hCG can be produced and thus go undetected. In addition, a further 12–15 per cent of clinically recognised pregnancies fail within the first four months of pregnancy. In all, fewer than 15 per cent of fertilised eggs will result in a birth.' The reasons for these early losses are unclear but in some cases, although placental development can be detected, no embryonic or fetal parts are seen to have formed. 'Since embryonic precursor cells may never have differentiated from the initial cleavage stages in these cases, can we say legitimately that there ever was an embryo associated with this clinical pregnancy?' Braude and Johnson, "The Embryo in Contemporary Medical Science' in Dunstan, *The Human Embryo: Aristotle and the Arabic and European Traditions* (University of Exeter Press, 1990) 208–221, at 218–9.

[77] Bernard Haring, *Medical Ethics* (St Pauls, 1972) p 93.

[78] Iglesias, *IVF and Justice,* (Linacre Centre for Healthcare Ethics in London, 1990) p 35.

[6.45] If it is not life itself that begins at fertilisation, perhaps it can be said that it is the life of the new genetically unique, individual human being that begins at conception. However, the mortality rate for zygotes (embryos at the one-cell stage) may be as high as 80 per cent which causes some commentators to argue that it is ridiculous to claim that God creates a human soul for each zygote and then shortly afterward allows it to die.[79] O'Rourke admits this is a quandary and that clearly, many of the zygotes that do not survive are not human from the time of fusion of sperm and egg. Often the fusion is not successful due to chromosomal abnormalities.

> When the fusion does result in a human zygote that is never implanted in the uterus and dies shortly after fertilisation, there is no facile explanation. The Creator seems to provide in abundance "seeds" that never bear fruit. But are we to say that historically, when more than half of the infants born died during childbirth, they were never living human beings?[80]

Twinning

[6.46] Another argument commonly raised in relation to the proposition that personhood begins at fertilisation is that multiple births such as twinning can occur after formation of the zygote. In the case of identical or monozygotic twins, each of these twins, when born, will be accorded the status of individuals.[81] Thus, the question arises whether there was one person present or two people present at the formation of the zygote. If there was only one person, what happened to this person when the second person appeared, and if there were two people to begin with, did they inhabit the same body?

[6.47] One response to this argument[82] is what may be called the 'I'm in there somewhere' approach, which takes the view that because the embryo contains some cells which will later become the fetus, the entirety should be treated as if it had the potential to be human. However, this approach may be criticised on the basis that it does not advert to the lack of the 'spatially-defined entity'. Also the fact that some cells may form the later fetus does not mean that they are singled out at this early stage as having that destiny. This is a gradual process that takes place over time, each cell having the potential to develop into many different parts of the body as well as the potential to develop into extra-corporeal matter. So it becomes very difficult to identify the person who is said to be 'in there somewhere'. The taking of the time of fertilisation as the starting point for the granting of protection is not necessarily logical. "The pro-lifers think they solve the problem by admitting that the development of the fetus is continuous; they say that because no line can be drawn, the law must protect the human organism from the time of fertilisation. But what is the logic (never mind the practicality) of beginning with fertilisation? It is an essential stage in our development but so are all the others'.[83]

---

79   Rahner, 'The Problem of Genetic Manipulation' in Theological Investigations, Vol 9 trans Graham Harrison (Seabury Press, 1972) 225–252.
80   O'Rourke, 'The Embryo as Person' (2006) Essays, National Catholic Bioethics Center, p 248.
81   Dunstan states: 'It is axiomatic in Western philosophy that there can be no personality without discrete individuality'. Dunstan and Seller (eds) *The Status of the Human Embryo. Perspectives From Moral Tradition* (London: King Edwards Hospital Fund, 1988) p14.
82   See Holland, 'A Fortnight of My Life Is Missing: A Discussion of the Status of the Human Pre-Embryo' (1990) 7(1) Journal of Applied Philosophy 25.
83   Williams, 'The Fetus and the "Right to Life"' (1994) Cambridge Law Journal p 77.

Life is a continuum which semantics, ethics and the law force us to divide at arbitrary points … To pursue a less emotive parallel from postnatal life, we would not in a democracy give the vote to a child of 6 months or withhold it until an individual is 60, but whether the franchise is given at 18, 20 or 30 is an arbitrary decision.[84]

[6.48] Since twinning can occur prior to the emergence of the primitive streak, it is argued that individuality is not yet certain. 'Developmental individualisation is completed only when implantation has been completed, a period of time whose outside time-limits are around fourteen days'.[85] A human individual is not divisible, therefore an entity that *is* divisible, and therefore lacks continuity of existence, cannot be individual. Therefore, the answer to the question – how could a human individual not be a human person? – is, 'by not being, yet, a human individual.'[86] The Instruction[87] makes two different assertions in relation to the embryo. On the one hand it says that the embryo must be *treated as* a person, yet it also says that the embryo *is* a person. It is easier to defend the first of these assertions than the second. In its failure to take account of such scientific facts relating to developmental individualisation, and in its refusal to draw lines at anything other than at an 'enormous protective distance from the hellish center, many argue that the Instruction 'loses its power to persuade'.[88]

[6.49] Many critics, however, argue that developmental individualisation, or the phenomenon of twinning, is a special case and should be treated as the exception which proves the rule. In other words, they say that we can confer personhood on the embryo at the time of conception but, for twins, their personhood only begins at the 14-day stage when individuality becomes evident.[89] It is argued, in relation to the problem of twinning, that a living being as a whole does not turn into two or more living beings. But *parts* (such as cells or tissues) of the living being can be detached and added to other

---

[84] Potts, 'Postcoital contraception or abortion?' The Lancet Vol 322, Issue 8343, p 223, 23 July 1983.

[85] McCormick, 'Therapy or Tampering: the Ethics of Reproductive Technology and the Development of Doctrine' in *The Critical Calling, Reflections on Moral Dilemmas since Vatican II* (Georgetown University Press, 1989) Ch 19, 329–352 at 346.

[86] McCormick, 'Therapy or Tampering: the Ethics of Reproductive Technology and the Development of Doctrine' in *The Critical Calling, Reflections on Moral Dilemmas since Vatican II* (Georgetown University Press, 1989) Ch 19, 329–352, p 345.

[87] Congregation for the Doctrine of the Faith, 'Instruction on Respect for Human Life in its Origin and on the Dignity of Procreation' (1987) 16 Origins at 706.

[88] Krauthammer, New Republic, 4 May 1987, 18.

[89] Gardner, an ordained Protestant minister and consultant gynaecologist, in his justification of abortion, considers that the soul does not enter the body until the child takes its first breath. Three scientific points are made to support this argument: First, the question of monozygotic twins, where the embryo splits in two. Gardner says '[U]nless we are to agree with the suggestion that the soul splits likewise we are driven to conclude that in some cases at least its infusion is not before the fourth week of intrauterine life.' Secondly, drawing attention to the high rates of fetal wastage, or spontaneous miscarriage, he considers it inconceivable that God should fill his heaven with these young lives, and concludes that it is evidence of the absence of 'spiritual status' on the part of the fetus. Thirdly, to suggest that embryos created in vitro, experimented on, and disposed of possess a soul, would be to trivialise the 'meaning of the soul'. Gardner, *Abortion: The Personal Dilemma* (Exeter: The Paternoster Press, 1972) pp 123–131.

beings. This is not a division of the whole.[90] The biological picture which is given in relation to twinning has been criticised as being constructed out of what is seen through mechanistic or dualistic 'mental spectacles' – the early embryo, which is a conglomerate of undifferentiated cells, may enter or be brought into subsequent cellular divisions and aggregations of various kinds. It is only when such divisions and combinations can no longer be brought about, that we have a stable individual that is not capable of becoming two or more by twinning.

The potentiality argument

[6.50] Many commentators argue that although life itself may not begin at conception, nevertheless at least the potential for human life begins there. Since the fertilised egg is a *potential* human being it must be accorded the same rights and privileges as an *actual* human being. However, there are a number of difficulties with this argument. The first is the logical premise that even if something will become X, this does not mean that it has the right now to be treated as if it were X.[91] There is no certainty that the fertilised egg will ever become an embryo, or that the embryo will become a fetus, but even if this were an accepted scientific fact it would not of itself give the fertilised egg the rights and privileges accorded to human beings.[92]

> …[t]he fact that an entity can undergo changes that will make it significantly different does not constitute a reason for treating it as if it had already undergone those changes. We are all potentially dead, but no-one supposes that this fact constitutes a reason for treating us as if we were already dead.[93]

[6.51] Lizza argues that we must take into account the probabilities of whether a potentiality may be realised, as otherwise our notion of potentiality would be 'too promiscuous' to be of any use in our ethical deliberations.[94] An embryo requires many external factors, such as implantation in a hospitable womb and nutrition, in order for it to develop intellect, will and other characteristics of personhood.

[6.52] Another difficulty relates to the chronology of human development in that while the fertilised egg may have the potential to become a human being, it is also true to say that the unfertilised egg and sperm are equally potential human beings. A fertilised egg will only have the potential to become human if certain stages in its development are passed, such as cleavage, implantation, emergence of the primitive streak and other developmental milestones, and if some things do not happen to it, such as a miscarriage. The same can be said of the egg and sperm: 'if certain things happen to the egg (like meeting a sperm) and certain things happen to the sperm (like meeting an egg) and

---

[90] Iglesias, *IVF and Justice* (Linacre Centre for Health Care Ethics in London, 1990) p 11.

[91] Dyson and Harris, *Experiments on Embryos* (Routledge, 1990) p 70.

[92] Dunstan says that it is insufficient to rest a claim to the status and rights of a person on the 'potential' for personality in the embryo. 'Roger Bacon, among the Scholastic philosophers of his day, disposed of that argument seven centuries ago. The argument will not bear the weight put upon it.' Dunstan and Seller (eds) *The Status of the Human Embryo. Perspectives from Moral Tradition* (London: King Edwards Hospital Fund, 1988) 14.

[93] Dunstan and Seller (eds) *The Status of the Human Embryo. Perspectives from Moral Tradition* (London: King Edwards Hospital Fund, 1988) 14.

[94] Lizza, 'Potentiality and Human Embryos' (2007) Bioethics Vol 21 No 7 379–385 at 380.

thereafter certain other things do not (like meeting a contraceptive), then they will eventually become a new human being'.[95]

> Given the appropriate conditions, these entities have the potential to develop into persons and so we would have to accord them the same moral status as the embryo. Moreover, if every cell in our body could be used for reproductive cloning, every cell would then have the potential for personhood. If we wish to deny the potential for personhood to gametes and these other cells, we must deny it to the embryo. In all these cases, external factors must be added or assumed in order to attribute the potential for personhood to the entity.[96]

[6.53] So, the argument logically concludes with an assertion that the sperm and egg also have a right to life and any form of contraception is murder. As Lizza points out, this *extension* argument is a *reduction ad absurdum* criticism of the claim that the human embryo has the potential for personhood in a morally relevant sense. Evans illustrates the point thus:

> For example was the sperm which played a part in my generation potentially me? Was it also potentially a multiplicity of other people who never materialised (because my father happened to have had relations with different women from my mother)? Do all sperm have the potential to become people (given that they outnumber the oocytes in the world by a factor of millions in any given week)? Or again does the fact that I am potentially dust justify someone's treating me like dirt?[97]

[6.54] Most of those who argue for potentiality try to distinguish between the fertilised egg and the sperm so as to accord the former the status of a full human being, but not the latter. One way in which this argument is made is to point out that fertilisation is the beginning of a process, which, if left alone, will result in a baby. On the other hand, the sperm and egg unjoined, if left alone, will not develop into anything. However, even leaving apart the very poor rates accorded to natural reproduction, the argument cannot apply in the context of embryos conceived in vitro. A fertilised egg in vitro has no chance of becoming anything unless someone intervenes to transfer it to a receptive uterus. In this sense, it is the same as the unfertilised egg and sperm, in that something has to be done in order for it to achieve a pregnancy.

---

[95]   Harris, *The Value of Life* (Routledge, 1985) p 12.

[96]   Lizza, 'Potentiality and Human Embryos' (2007) Bioethics Vol 21 No 7 379–385 at 381.

[97]   Evans (ed), *Conceiving the Embryo, Ethics, Law and Practice in Human Embryology* (Martinus Nijhoff, 1996) 3 at 6. Although Evans recognises that for some people this sort of argument is absurd and illogical and therefore the whole principle should be discarded. However, he counters that such a discard would be mistaken without at least careful deliberation on this important question. Although absolute certainty is impossible and unrealisable here, it does not mean that it is not safe to act. We rarely in life enjoy absolute certainty in respect to the consequences of our actions, and our actions should be judged in light of this fact. Evans discusses the principle of moral theology called tutiorism, which bases itself on the understanding that we should be judged on the basis of what it is reasonable to believe in any given situation rather than on what is demonstrably certain. However, he says that this does not require us to err on the side of caution in relation to embryos, as the doubt in question in relation to whether they are persons is not a reasonable one. This does not mean they may be destroyed at will, as we may still have certain moral responsibilities to the embryos.

If it is claimed that gametes are not potential people, because they will not, on their own, develop into human beings, then it must be acknowledged that precisely the same is true of extra corporeal embryos. At least in the context of IVF, there does not seem to be an enormous moral difference between the zygote in the petri dish just after fertilisation has occurred and the sperm and the ovum in the petri dish just prior to fertilisation.[98]

Scientifically, the embryo has a dynamic structure of human cells with a wide range of potentialities. 'For example, it could develop into one or more human beings, or it could just form a troublesome mole or cyst in the womb. At its earliest stages, the embryo is no more the individual human being into which it may come to grow, than the clay on the potter's wheel is already a particular pot.'[99]

Independent moral status

[6.55] This approach is an intermediate or compromise position that has much merit. The position is adopted that the embryo is a living entity deserving some respect, though not the same protection as human persons.

> The embryo is at least potential humanity, and as such it elicits, or ought to elicit, our feelings of awe and respect. In the embryo ... we face a mysterious and awesome power, a power governed by an imminent plan that may produce an indisputably and fully human being. It deserves our respect not because it has rights or claims or sentience (which it does not have at this stage), but because of what it is, now and prospectively.[100]

[6.56] To the extent that the embryo 'is not nothing', this argument is a sensible one. The collection of cells that make up the conceptus is living and *may* have the potential for human life in the future. This is entirely different from saying that it is a new human

---

[98] Steinbock, 'The Moral Status of Extra-Corporeal Embryos: Pre-Born Children, Property or Something Else?' in Dyson and Harris (eds) *Ethics and Biotechnology* (Routledge, 1994) at 85. Steinbock cites an example from George Annas in 'A French Homunculus in a Tennessee Court' (Nov/Dec 1989) 19:6 Hastings Center Report 22, where he poses the question of who would be saved if a fire broke out in a laboratory in which seven embryos were stored and there also happened to be a two-month-old child. If only the embryos or the child could be saved, he argues, no one would hesitate before saving the child. This shows that no one really equates embryos and children and the 'absurdity of a best-interests analysis applied to blastocysts.'

[99] Coughlan, 'From the Moment of Conception ... The Vatican Instruction on Artificial Procreation Techniques' (1988) 2 Bioethics No 4, 194 at 213. Coughlan wonders why the Vatican's Instruction does not injunct civil authorities to act on the basis of the moral weight of the principles outlined in the document. A clear demand for action from civil authorities is only made in relation to the prohibition of experimentation, mutilation or destruction of human beings, even at the embryonic stage. He claims that if civil authorities are to be expected to act in relation to this principle there should be a convincing exposition by the Vatican, which could stand independently of religious persuasion, as to the justification of this view. His article is an examination of the defence offered in the Instruction for this principle. He concludes that the lack of persuasive revelation-independent justification given by the Instruction forfeits the authority to press the case on legislators for the inclusion of the moral principles espoused by the document.

[100] Kass, 'Ethical Issues in Human In Vitro Fertilisation, Embryo Culture and Research, and Embryo Transfer.' This was a submission to the Ethics Advisory Board, US Dept of Health, Educ. & Welfare, in Appendix (No 2) (May 4, 1979): *HEW Support of Research Involving Human In Vitro Fertilisation and Embryo Transfer.*

life or that consequently it is deserving of the same rights as the fetus in vivo. For the embryo in vitro there is no potential to become a human life unless and until it is transferred to the uterus and implants in the uterine wall. Nevertheless the fertilised egg is alive, it is human in origin and it therefore is deserving of some protection. This argument is not based on the grounds of its potential to become a person, for this is not sufficient to distinguish it from the unfertilised egg, which also has the potential to become a person, but is based on its independent moral status.

> All preembryos have moral status due to their potential to become persons and due to their symbolic significance in society. That is not to say, however, that the preembryo therefore has all the rights accorded to human persons.[101]

[6.57] This intermediate approach is taken in many official and professional reports, such as the Ethics Advisory Board in the United States, which found that 'the human embryo is entitled to profound respect; but this respect does not necessarily encompass the full legal and moral rights attributed to persons.'[102] This position was also adopted by the Warnock Committee in the United Kingdom: 'The human preembryo ... is not under the present law of the United Kingdom accorded the same status as a living child or adult, nor do we necessarily wish it to be accorded the same status. Nevertheless, we were agreed that the preembryo of the human species ought to have a special status.'[103]

[6.58] The biology of the early embryo supports the view that the pre-implantation embryo is not a person or a rights-bearing entity but, despite this, it may yet be the subject of duties created to demonstrate a commitment to human life and persons generally. Once this basis for valuation is clear then it may be acceptable to accord the embryo a higher value than accorded to other human tissue in order to symbolise respect for human life. However, such symbolic valuation must be balanced against the procreative liberty of the couple involved and the restriction of activities with the embryos that could be of benefit to society through the advancement of medical knowledge in the treatment of disease and disabilities.[104]

---

[101] Robertson, *Children of Choice: Freedom and the New Reproductive Technologies* (Princeton Press, 1994) 102. See also Robertson, 'Embryos, Families, and Procreative Liberty: the Legal Structure of the New Reproduction' (1986) 59 Southern California Law Review 939 at 972. Robertson argues that justice does not require us to treat the embryo as a full human being but that we may wish nevertheless to treat it differently from other human tissue as a sign of respect. Since it is living and has the potential to become a human person if transferred to a uterus, it evokes feelings in us in the same way that dead persons do. We would consider certain actions in relation to cadavers offensive even though we do not consider them to have the status of the living. In the same way we may choose, for it is a choice, to symbolise our respect for human life by prohibiting certain actions in relation to embryos.

[102] Department of Health and Human Services, the Ethics Advisory Board in the United States, US Department of Health, Education and Welfare, Ethics Advisory Board, *HEW Support of Research Involving Human In Vitro Fertilisation and Embryo Transfer*, 44 Fed Reg 35,033 (1979).

[103] *Report of the Committee of Inquiry into Human Fertilisation and Embryology* (1984) United Kingdom, Department of Health and Social Security.

[104] See also Robertson, 'In the Beginning: the Legal Status of Early Embryos' (1990) 76 Virginia Law Review 437 at 444–450. (contd.../)

Welfare of children

[6.59] Apart from those objections to IVF considered above, which are based on theological or philosophical grounds, there are also a number of fundamental objections to IVF based on the claim that the procedure commodifies children and treats them as a means to an end rather than an end in themselves. This view, which is also shared by the Catholic Church, is based on the belief that by translating the wish to have children into a moral or legal right to reproduce, the child's human dignity is instrumentalised from the start – the child is being conceived to satisfy the couple's ego. Practices which presently allow couples to select the sex of their child (primarily for medical reasons) may in the future enable couples to 'design' traits (such as intelligence, personality, appearance) in the children they conceive through IVF. This contradicts the principle of unconditional acceptance by which parents should love their children as equals, and instead treats them as objects to be designed according to specifications and susceptible to rejection if they fall short of expectations.[105]

> Parents are naturally proud of their children, and sometimes disappointed in their children. In the final analysis, however, children are not for their parents. Their value is in themselves, and in their vocation as the sons and daughters of God who created them. There is a risk, in all our relationships, that we seek to possess the one we love. It is arguable that this risk is increased when technology becomes dominant, because the child who is born has been carefully planned, with the outlay of considerable emotional energy and economic resources. What if the end result doesn't measure up to our hopes and expectations?[106]

---

[104] (\...contd) Robertson expounds his theory in relation to the principle of according respect to the embryo as a matter of choice. However, he goes on to say that the notion of respect here must mean something – that it is not just empty rhetoric. It must at some point confront the situations in which the content of respect must be constituted. There must be some limits on the actions which may be taken in relation to embryos if respect for them is to mean anything. Such conflicts involve a trade-off between the differing interests at stake and the competing values which they encompass rather than a consideration of whether the embryo is a prenatal subject of rights.

[105] O'Donovan, *Begotten or Made?* (OUP, 1984). O'Donovan distinguishes the child-as-object from the child-as-equal as follows: 'That which we beget is like ourselves. Our offspring are human beings, who share with us one common nature, one common human experience and one common human destiny...But that which we make is unlike ourselves...it is the produce of our own free determination. We have stamped the decisions of our will upon the material, which the world has offered us, to form it in this way and not in that. What we 'make', then, is alien from our humanity. In that it has a human maker, it has come into existence as a human project, its being at the disposal of mankind...That which we beget can be, and should be, our companion; but the product of our art...can never have the independence to be that 'other I', equal to us and differentiated from us which we acknowledge in those who are begotten...A being who is the maker of any other being is alienated from that which he has made, transcending it by his will and acting as the law of its being. To speak of 'begetting' is to speak of quite another possibility than this: the possibility that one may form another human being who will share one's own nature, and with whom one will enjoy a fellowship based on radical equality.'

[106] *Towards a Creative Response to Infertility*, Response of the Irish Catholic Bishops Conference to the Report of the Commission on Assisted Human Reproduction.

[6.60] Although the Catholic Church is concerned to demonstrate its understanding of the suffering of infertile couples, it is firm in its view that this does not entitle the couple to have a right to a child. This would be contrary to the child's dignity and nature:

> The child is not an object to which one has a right, nor can he be considered as an object of ownership: rather, a child is a gift, "the supreme gift" and the most gratuitous gift of marriage, and is a living testimony to the mutual giving of his parents. For this reason, the child has a right... to be the fruit of the specific act of the conjugal love of his parents, and he also has the right to be respected as a person from the moment of his conception.[107]

[6.61] It is argued that a basic demand of all human beings is to be loved and respected for our own sakes and not for any instrumental gains that others may seek from us. 'In our society a child tends to be thought of merely as an object that satisfies a need. If desired, anything will be done to have it; if not desired it will be rejected, even to the point of being destroyed. This attitude of regarding children as commodities will be fostered by IVF programmes.'[108] However, it may be counter-argued that children born through IVF are not, and should not be regarded as, any different from children conceived naturally. Mary Warnock, Chairman of the Committee of Inquiry into Human Fertilisation and Embryology in the UK, stated that with improvements in the success rates for IVF, she believed that it would come to be regarded as a more or less routine procedure. She went on: '[C]hildren born by IVF will, I believe, be no more remarkable than children born by caesarean section. It is impossible to see that they could suffer in any way from the technical method of their birth.'[109]

[6.62] Welfare of the child issues were considered in a report from the Victorian Law Reform Commission in Australia in 2004.[110] The report concluded that the concerns that Assisted Reproductive Technology (ART) parents may have dysfunctional parenting styles due to the intensive and interventionist nature of conception are not borne out in research. 'ART parents are found not to be over-protective, not to have unrealistic expectations of the child, nor to have increased marital problems following fertility treatment. The non-biological parent of a donor-conceived child is found to accept the child as his or her own, and to be just as effective as the biological parent.' In common with studies in the UK[111], the report also found that a number of positive differences have been found in the quality of parenting within ART families when compared with natural conception families – mothers express more warmth toward their child; mothers and fathers are more emotionally involved and interact more with their child; mothers and fathers are less stressed by parenting; fathers who have children through ART are less authoritarian than fathers of naturally conceived children, regardless of whether they are biologically related to them or not; and children report less parental criticism than natural or adoptive children. In addition it found that the psychological development of children in ART families is no different to that of children in naturally conceived families.

---

[107] O'Donovan, *Begotten or Made?* (OUP, 1984).
[108] Iglesias, *IVF and Justice: Moral, Social and Legal Issues Related to Human In Vitro Fertilisation* (Linacre Centre for Health Care Ethics in London, 1990) p 53.
[109] Warnock, 'The Good of the Child' (1987) 1 (2) Bioethics 141–155 at 147.
[110] Victorian Law Reform Commission (2004) Outcomes for Children Born of ART in a Diverse Range of Families.

THE LEGAL STATUS OF THE HUMAN EMBRYO

[6.63] Of all the controversies surrounding the creation and use of IVF embryos, disputes over the fate of the embryos which sometimes arise between the parties concerned are particularly difficult.[112] In law it is usual to categorise things into property, which can be owned and controlled, and persons, which cannot. It is difficult to decide which of these categories is most appropriate for the embryo. On the one hand, if the embryo were property then this would signify that the providers of the genetic material from which it is developed could own it. This, in the absence of regulation, would enable the couple to dispose of it in any way they wished, subject to legislative policy. On the other hand, it is difficult to apply the notion of personhood to the early embryo for biological and moral reasons as outlined earlier. To say that the pre-implantation embryo is a person is to accord it the full rights and protections accorded to a living human person. This position entails the obligation to provide an opportunity for implantation to occur and to prohibit any action that might harm the embryo, such as freezing.

Embryo custody disputes in the US

[6.64] This question of whether the embryos are property or persons was considered in the US case *Davis v Davis*,[113] during a divorce settlement where a dispute arose as to who should have custody of seven frozen embryos stored in a fertility clinic at the

---

[111] MacCallum, 'Embryo Donation Parents' Attitudes Towards Donors: Comparison With Adoption' (2009) Human Reproduction, 25, 517–523; MacCallum & Keeley, 'Embryo Donation Families: A Follow-Up in Middle Childhood' (2008) Journal of Family Psychology, 22, 799–808; MacCallum, Golombok & Brinsden, 'Parenting and Child Development in Families With a Child Conceived Through Embryo Donation' (2007) Journal of Family Psychology, 21 (2), 278–287; Golombok, 'Parenting and the Psychological Development of the Child in ART Families' in Vayena, Rowe & Griffin, (eds) *Current Practice and Controversies in Assisted Reproduction: Report of a Meeting on Medical, Ethical and Social Aspects of Assisted Reproduction* (Report of a Meeting on 'Medical, Ethical and Social Aspects of Assisted Reproduction', 2002) World Health Organization, Geneva; Golombok, 'Preface' in D. Singer & M. Hunter (eds) *Assisted Human Reproduction: Psychological and Ethical Dilemmas.* (Wiley, 2003); Golombok, 'The Potential Impact of Removing Donor Anonymity on Donors, Parents, Offspring and Service Provision' (2003) Report commissioned by the Department of Health UK; Golombok, 'Reproductive Technology and its Impact on Child Psychosocial and Emotional Development' (2003) in Tremblay, Barr & Peters (eds) *Encyclopedia on Early Childhood Development*, 1–7 [online]. Centre of Excellence for Early Childhood Development. Canadian Institute of Child Health, Montreal; Golombok, 'Assisted Reproduction Families: Key Policy Issues. Report to House of Commons Science and Technology Committee Review of Human Reproductive Technologies and the Law' (2004); Golombok, 'Unusual Families' in Edwards (ed) 'Ethics, Science and Moral Philosophy of Assisted Human Reproduction' (2005) Vol 10, Supplement 1; Middelburg et al, 'Neuromotor, Cognitive, Language and Behavioural Outcome in Children Born Following IVF or ICSI – A Systematic Review' (2008) Hum. Reprod. Update 14 (3): 219–231.

[112] Chan and Quigley, 'Frozen Embryos, Genetic Information and Reproductive Rights' (2007) Bioethics Vol 21(8) p 439.

[113] *Davis v Davis* 842 SW 2d 588 (Tenn 1992).

couple's request. At first instance the wife wished to use the embryos herself in an attempt to become pregnant after the divorce, a plan to which the ex-husband was opposed. By the time the case was finally decided by the Tennessee Supreme Court she had remarried and no longer wished to use the embryos herself but to donate them to an infertile couple. The ex-husband maintained throughout the case that he did not want the embryos to be used at all, as it would be an interference with his procreational autonomy in forcing him to become a parent against his wishes. He argued that whether his ex-wife used them or an anonymous couple were given them as a donation, he would consider himself to have fathered a child somewhere in the world. He would feel a responsibility to seek the child out and maintain it even if it was born to someone else. Therefore, he preferred to see the embryos kept in storage until he decided whether or not he wanted to become a parent outside of marriage.

[6.65] At first instance the trial court decided that the embryos were human beings from the moment of fertilisation and awarded custody to the wife on the basis that she should be given the opportunity to bring them to term through implantation. The Court of Appeals reversed this decision, holding that the husband had a constitutionally protected right *not* to beget a child where no pregnancy had taken place. The Court gave joint control to the couple. This was, in effect, giving a veto to each party in respect of decisions the other might make in relation to the embryos.

[6.66] Before the Supreme Court, the parties' positions had altered in that the ex-wife no longer wished to use the embryos herself, and the ex-husband preferred to have them discarded rather than donated to another couple. This change in positions meant that the Court, in weighing each party's procreational rights against the other's, was able to conclude that the ex-husband's rights in seeking to avoid the burden of parenthood were greater than the ex-wife's right to know that her genetic material contributed to the bringing into existence of children somewhere by another couple. The Court admitted that the case would have been more difficult to decide if the wife wanted to use the embryos herself in circumstances in which she was unable to achieve a pregnancy by attempting IVF again. On the question of ownership of genetic material, the Court held that the embryos occupied an interim category between persons and property, which entitled them to special respect because of their potential for human life. The Court said:

> Pre-embryos are not, strictly speaking, either "persons" or "property", but occupy an interim category that entitles them to special request because of their potential for human life. It follows that any interest that …[the couple] have in the pre-embryos in this case is not a true property interest. However, they do have an interest in the nature of ownership, to the extent that they have decision-making authority concerning disposition of the pre-embryos, with the scope of policy set by law.

[6.67] Even though the bundle of rights over the embryo has been judicially described as 'dispositional control' rather than as ownership, it may be argued that the rights given are, in effect, a property right akin to ownership. It gives the individuals who provided that genetic material the right to decide which of several options may be legally taken in respect to the embryo. Two cases in the US seem to support the right of ownership of embryos. In *Del Zio v Columbia Presbyterian Hospital*[114] a jury awarded $50,000 to a couple whose embryos had been destroyed by a doctor who objected to their attempts to

---

[114]   *Del Zio v Columbia Presbyterian Hospital* No 71–3588 (SDNY 1978).

have IVF done without obtaining review board approval. This decision recognises that negligent or intentional destruction of pre-embryos would also be actionable due to the significant financial, emotional and physical loss involved for the couple. 'Only difficulties in calculating damages, and not doubts about the ownership rights of the couple, would stand in the way of tort remedies for negligent destruction of preembryos.'[115] In *York v Jones*[116] a couple who moved from Virginia to California wished to have 'their' embryos, which were stored at a clinic in Virginia, released and transported to California to be transferred to the wife's uterus by a doctor there. The clinic refused to release the embryos for transportation on various grounds, including the demeaning effect of shipping human embryos by air in the same way as cattle. The Court found that the Virginia clinic was merely a temporary custodian of the embryos and had no right to keep them against the couple's wishes. This case is significant because the court 'assumes without question that embryos are the property of the gamete providers, and finds that any transfer of their dispositional authority must be explicitly stated in the documents of participation provided by the program.'[117]

[6.68] In other embryo custody cases in the United States, the issue has not been centred on ownership per se, but rather on the interpretation of contractual provisions between the couples and the clinics involved, and the question of whether one party should be facilitated in a change of mind subsequent to marital separation or divorce. In *Kass v Kass*,[118] Mrs Kass had undergone 10 unsuccessful IVF attempts over a 3-year period prior to the final attempt which, for the first time, included cryopreservation or freezing of the surplus embryos. The couple signed four consent forms drafted by the hospital, one of which stated that in the event of divorce all surplus embryos would be used for scientific research and destroyed. A number of embryos were transferred to Mrs Kass' sister, who had volunteered to be a surrogate mother, but this was unsuccessful. The remaining embryos were frozen. The couple applied for a divorce shortly after the last unsuccessful attempt. Mrs Kass applied for sole custody of the embryos, an application which was opposed by Mr Kass. The Court decided that the parties' prior statement of intent with regard to the embryos, as demonstrated by the signed consent forms, should be given a clear and unambiguous reading. The Court therefore granted Mr Kass's application for specific performance of the consent form. It stated as follows:

> We find that the decision to attempt to have children through IVF procedures and the determination of the fate of cryopreserved pre-zygotes resulting therefrom are intensely personal and essentially private matters which are appropriately resolved by the prospective parents rather than the courts. Accordingly, where the parties have indicated their mutual intent regarding the disposition of the pre-zygotes in the event of the occurrence of a contingency, that position must be scrupulously honoured and the courts must refrain from any interference with the parties' expressed wishes. The documentary evidence overwhelmingly demonstrates that the parties in this case made such a clear and

---

[115] Robertson, *Children of Choice* (Princeton University Press, 1994) p 105.
[116] *York v Jones* 717 F.Supp. 421 (ED Va 1989).
[117] Robertson, *Children of Choice* (Princeton University Press, 1994) p 106.
[118] *Kass v Kass* 663 NYS 2d 581 (1997).

unequivocal choice, and the plaintiff's subsequent change of heart cannot be permitted to unilaterally alter their mutual decision.[119]

[6.69] In *A.Z. v B.Z.*[120] a couple underwent IVF treatment for a number of years and had twins following IVF in 1991. During that attempt surplus embryos were formed and two vials containing embryos were stored on behalf of the couple for possible future transfer. In 1995, the wife had one of these embryos transferred without her husband's knowledge. Her husband received a letter from his health insurance company informing him of the treatment. Relations between the couple subsequently deteriorated and the husband sought a divorce. At the time of the divorce there was one vial containing four embryos in storage at the clinic.

[6.70] At each stage during the couple's treatment by the clinic, the couple had signed a consent form. The consent forms contained a blank line to permit couples to insert their preferred option in the event of separation, divorce or death. The first form was filled out by the wife to the effect that in the event of separation, they agreed that their embryos would be returned to the wife for implantation. The husband signed this first form after it was completed. Six further consent forms were signed over the years of treatment but these were all signed in blank by the husband for convenience, and later filled in by the wife to the same effect as the first form. When the couple divorced, the husband sought to avoid enforcement of the consent form.

[6.71] This was the first reported case in the US concerning the disposition of frozen embryos in which a consent form signed between the couple and the clinic provided that, on the couple's separation, the embryos were to be given to one of the parties for implantation. The Court took the view that given the purpose of the form (which was drafted by and to give assistance to the clinic) and the circumstances of its execution, it could not be said with certainty to represent the intent of the husband and wife as to the disposition of the embryos. Therefore, the Court concluded that it should not be enforced in the circumstances of this case.

[6.72] The basis for the Court's decision rested on a number of grounds. Firstly, the Court said that the consent form's primary purpose was to explain to the couple the benefits and risks of freezing, and to record their desire for disposition of the frozen embryos *at the time the form was executed* in order to provide the clinic with guidance if the couple later decided they did not wish to use the embryos. The form did not indicate that the couple intended the consent form to act as a binding agreement between them in the event of a later dispute. Secondly, the form did not contain a duration provision and the Court was of the opinion that there was no evidence from which it could be assumed that the parties intended it to govern the disposition of the embryos four years after it was signed, especially in light of the fundamental change in their relationship.

---

[119] Although sympathetic to the physical and emotional strain endured, particularly by Mrs Kass, the Court dismissed the notion that the disposition of the embryos involved reproductive liberty or privacy concerns. The court reasoned that because the embryos were not yet implanted, the fundamental rights that arise with a traditional pregnancy were not implicated. For criticism of this approach see Daar, 'Assisted Reproductive Technologies and the Pregnancy Process: Developing an Equality Model to Protect Reproductive Liberties' (1999) 25 Am JL and Med 455.

[120] *AZ v BZ* 725 NE 2d 1051 (2000).

[6.73] Thirdly, the form used the term 'should we become separated' in reference to the disposition of the embryos. Because this dispute arose in the context of a divorce, the Court said it could not conclude that the consent form was intended to govern in these circumstances as separation and divorce have different meanings in law. Fourthly, the Court took into account the circumstances in which the husband had signed the consent forms in blank before the wife had filled in the form, indicating that the embryos would be returned to her following separation. The Court said it was unable to conclude that the consent form represented the true intention of the husband. The Court also said that the consent form was not a separation agreement and was legally insufficient in a number of respects to be considered as an enforceable contract.

[6.74] In addition to the points mentioned above, the Court also stated that even if the husband and wife *had* signed an unambiguous agreement, it would not be enforceable in the circumstances where this would force one person to become a parent against their will. It stated that:

> As a matter of public policy, we conclude that forced procreation is not an area amenable to judicial enforcement. It is well-established that courts will not enforce contracts that violate public policy. While courts are hesitant to invalidate contracts on these public policy grounds, the public interest in freedom of contract is sometimes outweighed by other public policy considerations; in those cases the contract will not be enforced.

[6.75] In *JB v MB*[121] the couple had signed a consent form provided by the clinic prior to undergoing IVF. The form described the IVF procedure and contained provisions discussing the control and disposition of the embryos, which indicated that the embryos 'belonged' to the patient and her partner. JB gave birth to a daughter but the couple divorced a short time later. She sought an order for destruction of the embryos on the ground that she had intended only to use the embryos during her marriage to MB and that they had never discussed the disposition of the embryos in the event that the marriage were to end. MB disputed this on the basis that, after having long discussions with JB about his Catholic beliefs, they had agreed to donate any surplus embryos to other infertile couples. The Supreme Court of New Jersey held that the consent form did not manifest a clear intent regarding disposition of the embryos in the event of divorce. It also accepted that where the procreational interests of both parties are in conflict, the right not to procreate outweighs the right to procreate. Therefore, the Court suggested that since JB did not oppose continued storage, MB could continue storage if he paid the storage fees, but that otherwise the embryos would be destroyed.[122]

Thus the position in the US seems to favour upholding the terms of the written agreement between the couple and the clinic, but nonetheless facilitating a change of mind by one of the parties in circumstances where upholding the contract would impose unwanted parenthood.

---

[121] *JB v MB* WL 909294 (NJ 2001).

[122] 'Although the court suggested it was willing to enforce embryo disposition contracts, its rule ultimately renders all such contracts unenforceable. Because mere disagreement by either party vitiates the contract in favour of balancing the procreative rights of the parties, there is really no contract.' Glenn Cohen, *Case Comment on JB v MB* [2001] Harvard L Rev Vol 115 p 701. See also *Litowitz v Litowitz* 146 Wash 2d 514 (2002) and *Roman v Roman* 193 SW 3d 40 (Tex App-Hous (1 Dist) 2006).

Embryo custody disputes in the UK

[6.76] In the UK, the Human Fertilisation and Embryology Act 1990, as amended in 2008, recognises that the gamete providers have decision-making authority in relation to what may be done with the embryos created from their eggs and sperm. The couple must sign a consent form indicating to what use the embryos may be put and what is to happen to the embryos in the event of the death or separation of the couple. The Act does not provide a permanent resolution for the situation which is most likely to arise and cause difficulty, namely the sorts of 'custody' disputes discussed above in the US case law.

[6.77] In *Evans v Amicus Healthcare Ltd, Hadley v Midland Fertility Services Ltd*,[123] the Court was asked to consider whether consent to storage and use of the embryos given at the time of their creation, was capable of being withdrawn following a change of mind by the male partners in each case. The two women, Ms Evans and Mrs Hadley, each sought injunctions to restore their former partner's consent, declarations that they could be treated lawfully under the terms of the 1990 Act, and a declaration that the restrictions imposed by the 1990 Act were incompatible with the Human Rights Act 1998, which gave effect to the European Convention on Human Rights (ECHR).

[6.78] Under the 1990 Act, clinics which provide IVF treatment services must do so pursuant to the terms of a licence provided by the Human Fertilisation and Embryology Authority established under the Act. One of the conditions imposed on every licence is that the provisions of Sch 3 of the Act must be complied with. Schedule 3 sets out provisions in relation to necessary consents to be obtained prior to the storage or use of gametes or embryos. Paragraph 2 provides that effective consent must specify the purposes for which the embryo may be put, the maximum storage period agreed and what is to be done with the gametes or embryos in the event of death or incapacity of the person giving consent. Paragraph 4 provides that the consent may be varied or withdrawn by the person who gave the consent by giving notice at any time to the clinic, unless the embryo has already been used in the provision of treatment services or for research purposes. Paragraph 5 provides that a person's gametes must not be used for the purposes of treatment other than in accordance with an effective consent given by that person. Paragraph 6 provides that an embryo must not be used for any purpose unless there is an effective consent by each person whose gametes were used to bring about the creation of the embryo.

[6.79] Having heard that the male partners in each of these cases had withdrawn their consent to the use of the embryos by their former partners, the Court refused to grant the injunctions and declarations sought on the grounds that there was no 'effective consent' as required by the provisions of the Act. In the absence of consent, the clinics were not authorised to store or use the embryos. The Court recognised that the two pillars of the

---

[123] *Evans v Amicus Healthcare Ltd, Hadley v Midland Fertility Services Ltd* [2003] 4 All ER 903. See Mason, 'Discord and Disposal of Embryos' (2004) 8 Edin L Rev 84; Alghrani, 'Deciding the Fate of Human Embryos' (2005) 13 Med L Rev 244; Annett, 'Balancing Competing Interests Over Frozen Embryos: The Judgment of Solomon' (2006) 14 Med L Rev 425; Enright, 'Justice, Convention and Anecdote: *Evans* and the Right to Become a Mother' [2006] 4 Irish Journal of Family Law 11.

statutory scheme embodied in the Act were consent and the welfare of the child. The clear policy of the Act is to ensure continuing consent from the commencement of treatment to the point of implantation. The Court said it would be 'extremely slow to recognise or to create a principle of waiver that would conflict with the Parliamentary scheme.'

[6.80] In relation to the application for a direction that the restrictions imposed by the Act were incompatible with human rights, the Court principally addressed arts 8 and 14 in respect of the women's rights, and arts 2 and 8 in relation to the embryos. Article 8(1) of the ECHR provides that 'everyone has the right to respect for his private and family life, his home and his correspondence.' Article 8 (2) provides that there shall be no interference with the exercise of this right except such as is in accordance with the law and is necessary in a democratic society in the interests of national security, public safety or the economic well-being of the country, the prevention of disorder or crime, the protection of health or morals, or for the protection of the rights and freedoms of others.

[6.81] It was accepted that the refusal of treatment to the women at the centre of these cases was an interference with, and therefore a failure to respect, their private life. The question for the Court was therefore whether such interference was prescribed by law and necessary for the protection of the rights and freedoms of others, namely the male gamete providers. In *Evans*, the Court of Appeal said that 'while legislation modifying private law liabilities can be expected not to infringe their Convention rights without clear justification, legislation directed to the implementation and management of social policy may well have to infringe some individuals' Convention rights in the interests of consistency.' The Court stressed that the question was whether a less drastic means could be used to achieve the same end without infringing the rights of the claimant. The less drastic means argued for in this case would be a rule that would make the withdrawal of consent by her former partner, Mr Johnston, non-conclusive. This would enable Ms Evans to continue treatment due to her inability to conceive by any other means. However, the Court said that unless it gave weight to Mr Johnston's firm wish not to be a father to a child born to Ms Evans, such a rule would diminish his right to respect for private life in direct proportion as it enhanced the respect accorded to hers. Arden LJ said that if Ms Evans' argument succeeded, 'it would amount to an interference with the genetic father's right to decide not to become a parent. Motherhood could surely not be forced on Ms Evans and likewise fatherhood cannot be forced on Mr Johnston.' The Court therefore concluded that 'the sympathy and concern which anyone must feel for Ms Evans is not enough to render the legislative scheme of Schedule 3 disproportionate.'

[6.82] Another ground for Ms Evans' appeal was based on unlawful discrimination contrary to art 14 of the Convention. Article 14 provides that the enjoyment of the rights and freedoms set out in the Convention shall be secured without discrimination on any ground such as sex, race, colour, language, religion, political opinion, origin and so on. Ms Evans claimed that she was being discriminated against in that she was treated differently to fertile women in that the consent of a male partner could not be withdrawn in natural reproduction at any time following the fertilisation of the egg. Under the scheme of the Act, in the case of IVF the male partner was permitted to withdraw his consent subsequent to fertilisation at any time prior to implantation. Therefore, Ms

Evans argued that this differential treatment of infertile women was unjustifiably discriminatory. Although Arden LJ agreed that, seen from this perspective, there was discrimination in that the genetic father was allowed to withdraw his consent in IVF later than he could so in normal sexual intercourse, she was of the view that the conditions imposed by the Act were objectively justified for the reasons given above in relation to art 8.

[6.83] An argument was also made under art 2 of the Convention, which provides that 'everyone's right to life shall be protected by law'. Ms Evans argued that although the embryo has no right to life in the sense that a human being has such a right, an embryo does have a qualified right to life which is consistent with its mother's wishes. Arden LJ acknowledged that neither the Convention nor English law provided a clear-cut answer to the question as to what point human life attained the right to legal protection. She took the view that while an embryo has the potential to become a person, it is not itself a person since further changes must take place. She was of the view that an embryo does not have a qualified right to life given that the Act provided that embryos must be destroyed after the expiration of the maximum statutory storage period or if either party withdrew consent to storage. She therefore concluded that 'the embryo has no right to life which trumps the right to choose of a person whose ongoing consent to its use or storage is required under the 1990 Act.'

[6.84] Ms Evans' appeal was declined on all grounds by the Court of Appeal and she subsequently challenged the legislation at the European Court of Human Rights.[124] The appeal failed on the grounds that the UK's policy lay within a national jurisdiction's margin of appreciation when determining the balance to be struck between the rights of both parties.

[6.85] Enright suggests that the 'conflict of rights' model is the basic foundation for the decided embryo custody cases.[125] In America, these disputes have set the right to avoid parenthood (usually on the part of the male partner) against the right to become a parent. The *Evans* decision suggests an equality theory, namely that male and female rights are absolutely equivalent and therefore decisions regarding the embryo must be made on an equal basis – a mutual consent requirement must be adhered to. Enright states that in America and Israel, the courts have adopted a clear hierarchy of rights. 'In the American courts the "right not to procreate" has become the default rule; it trumps the "right to parenthood" even in the most difficult circumstances and no matter whether the court decides on the basis of contractual or constitutional principle.' In Israel, it appears that the female right takes precedence over the male.[126]

---

[124] Application 6339/05, Fourth Section Judgment of 7 March 2006: *Evans v United Kingdom* (2006) 43 EHRR 21.

[125] Enright, 'Justice, Convention and Anecdote: *Evans* and the Right to Become a Mother' [2006] 4 Ir J Fam Law 11.

[126] *Nachmani v Nachmani* AH 2401/95, 50(4) PD 661. The Israeli Supreme Court decided by a seven-to-four majority that the ex-wife's right to have a child trumped her ex-husband's right not to have one, in particular since she had no more eggs and therefore had no other means of having a genetic child of her own. See Chen, 'The Right to Her Embryos: An Analysis of *Nachmani v Nachmani* and its Impact on Israeli In Vitro Fertilisation Law' (1999) 7 Cardozo J I & Comp L 325.

[6.86] It has been suggested that these cases 'push men's procreative rights far beyond their expected boundaries.'[127] Where the man's refusal to consent will result in the destruction of the embryo, it is argued that the right claimed is not the right 'not to procreate' but the right to stop the procreative process once it has begun. Traditionally, that it is a right available to women in countries where abortion is permitted, but which is not afforded to men. Enright argues that in circumstances where the use of the embryos represent the woman's last chance to have a genetic child (as in *Evans*), the man's refusal is not merely a cancelling out, or a restoration of the position that existed prior to the IVF attempt. In such cases the woman is not restored to her previous position, as the man, in many ways, is.

> Her important expectation interests in becoming a mother are irretrievably breached. She is further harmed because she cannot recoup her emotional and material investments in the reproductive process. He, on the other hand, gains or is healed by his refusal; he obviates a future harm and relieves himself of present stress and worry.[128]

[6.87] She concludes that the Court in *Evans* used the principle of equality in order to put distance between the law and the emotive facts of the case. However, in doing so it 'eschewed individualised decision-making in favour of essentialist dogmatic presumption'. She argues that a case-by-case analysis is preferable, which reflects the differences between men and women, but also the argument between the individual man and woman in dispute. This would enable the court to consider the effect of the decision on the individuals concerned; for example, the burden that unwanted paternity would impose on the man, and the deprivation of the last opportunity for genetic maternity for the woman. 'Such an approach accords meaningfully and readily with the law's stated concern for reproductive autonomy and the interests of the warring couple.'

[6.88] Chan and Quigley are of the view that the *Evans* case demonstrates the tremendous importance that is placed on genetic relationship by many people in modern society, particularly when it comes to reproduction:[129] 'The extensive use of artificial reproductive technologies and the attention devoted to extending the limits of these methods in order to allow more people to reproduce genetically illustrate the value that is placed on genetic relatedness as a part of parenthood, in addition to birth parentage and upbringing.' They advocate a different approach to embryo disputes based on a property framework in respect of genetic information. They acknowledge that the law governing genetics is confusing in that it is drawn from a multitude of sources, both common law and statutory, some of which contain conflicting ideals. However, they say that nonetheless the law does recognise some rights of confidentiality, privacy and control in both our genetic material and genetic information. Property rights might be accorded to genetic information in the context of, for example, locating a previously unknown gene, determining its function and making it accessible for further

---

[127] Enright, 'Justice, Convention and Anecdote: *Evans* and the Right to Become a Mother' [2006] 4 Ir J Fam Law 11, p 13.

[128] Enright, 'Justice, Convention and Anecdote: *Evans* and the Right to Become a Mother' [2006] 4 Ir J Fam Law 11, p16.

[129] Chan and Quigley, 'Frozen Embryos, Genetic Information and Reproductive Rights' (2007) Bioethics Vol 21(8) p 439–448.

exploitation.[130] Such rights can be transferred or ceded, for example when sperm is donated to a sperm bank for the purpose of transfer to another person for reproductive purposes.

> When gametes fuse to form an embryo in the process of in vitro fertilisation, the individual rights which the gametic progenitors have over the separate gametes are altered. There can be no property or rights claims over those gametes because the two separate gametes no longer exist. In their place there is an embryo. Embryos can also be viewed as a type of genetic material containing physical and informational property, but both the physical and informational components are contributed to by both parents.[131]

[6.89] Chan and Quigley argue that when the partners agree to attempt IVF in order to have a child, they cede any rights they might have had not to become a parent as soon as the egg is fertilised with the sperm. Therefore, once the embryo is created, the male partner no longer has the right to prevent its birth on the grounds of not wanting a genetically related child.

> The implication of this is plain and simple: once you have given up your genetic informational rights in this manner you cannot take them back. The creation of IVF embryos involves both parents giving up some rights over their genetic information in pursuit of the creation of the embryos. Once this has occurred, any right of the parents not to have those embryos created (as new genetic entities from their genetic information) is lost, and only the physical rights to the embryos persist.

[6.90] They do not claim that there are no circumstances under which embryo transfer can be stopped once the embryo has been created, as they do acknowledge that, for example, there may be some exceptional child-welfare issues which might be of such significance as to alter the situation. However, this does not detract from their central argument that there can be no right not to have a child once the embryos have been created. As seen above, however, the English and American courts do not appear to have accepted this argument, and have generally given priority to the party who does not want to have a genetically related child.

Reproductive blunders

[6.91] In recent years there have been a small number of cases in which mistakes have been made in the course of egg fertilisation or embryo transfer which have resulted in women giving birth to children who are genetically related to another couple being treated at the same clinic at the same time. These cases give rise to 'very interesting and complex questions about genetic origins, genetic identity and the desirability or undesirability of full knowledge disclosure and access to all the types of relatedness that can exist between human beings.'[132]

[6.92] Prior to the advent of IVF and associated technologies, laws determining parentage and parental rights flowed directly from the laws of nature. Under common

---

[130] Laurie, 'Patenting and the Human Body', in *Principles of Medical Law,* Grubb (ed) (2nd edn, OUP, 2004) 1079–1102 at 1085.

[131] Chan and Quigley, 'Frozen Embryos, Genetic Information and Reproductive Rights' (2007) Bioethics Vol 21(8) p 445.

[132] Harris, 'Assisted Reproductive Technological Blunders (ARTBs) (2003) J Med Ethics; 29:205–206 doi:10.1136/jme.29.4.205.

law, maternity was easily established by the biological fact that pregnancy occurred as a result of natural sexual intercourse, a fetus was carried to term by the woman and maternity was thus established from the moment of birth.[133] Paternity was less easily established and courts relied on certain presumptions or social policy to assign paternity on the basis of the man's relationship with the birth mother. Thus the presumption of paternity applies to a married man to ensure that he is recognised as the legal father of a child born to his wife. Establishing paternity for men outside marriage was more problematic at common law and relied on the testimony of the woman. Advances in medical technology, blood and DNA tests have now made it easier to establish a biological link between father and child.

[6.93] In assisted reproduction disputes, the courts in other jurisdictions have taken diverse approaches based on property law, contract law, causation, public policy, constitutional rights, intent, and the best interests of the child. Some commentators argue that a 'bright-line test' ought to be agreed in order to establish certainty and avoid disputes. This could be, for example, a presumption that placement with the gestational mother is always in the child's best interests, or conversely, that the child's interests are best served by being with its genetic mother. Others argue for a multi-factorial best interests analysis, such as that used in custody disputes in a divorce setting.[134] The former has appeal, as it allows parentage to be established with certainty from the moment of birth whereas the latter would hold parental status in limbo pending a judicial determination.

[6.94] There is considerable disagreement between those who favour the genetic mother and those who favour the gestational mother in such disputes. Those who favour the genetic mother focus on the bonds of nature, ie the concept of genetic identity. Those who favour the gestational mother prioritise the social bonding that occurs between the mother and child during the pre-natal and post-natal nurturing. This is resonant of the well-rehearsed nature versus nurture debates in human psychology, to which there is no clear answer.

[6.95] A best interests approach combined with an analysis of the intent of the parties has been suggested as the most appropriate solution in cases where genetic material has been mistakenly switched. The first step of such a test would be to establish who had the intent to parent the child, starting from the presumption that the birth mother is the legal mother. Her intent to procreate and raise the child may be implied from her participation in the IVF process. On this basis she has an exclusive claim to parental rights in the absence of a claim from the genetic mother, who may establish her genetic link to the child, that her genetic material was used without her consent and that she has not abandoned her parental rights to her child. Thus, both women have sufficient *locus*

---

[133] This is recognized by the ancient maxim *mater est quam gestation demonstrat* (by gestation the mother is demonstrated).

[134] Noble-Allgire, 'Switched at the Fertility Clinic: Determining Maternal Rights When a Child is Born From Stolen or Misdelivered Genetic Material' (1999) Vol 64(3) Missouri Law Review 517 at 577.

standi to claim parental rights to the child and the outcome should be determined by application of the best-interests-of-the-child test.[135]

[6.96] In *Perry-Rogers v Fasono*,[136] two couples, the Fasanos and the Perry-Rogers, went for treatment to an IVF clinic in New York on the same day. Due to a clinical error that caused an embryo mix-up that day, six of the Perry-Rogers' embryos were transferred to Mrs Fasano along with at least one of the Fasano's embryos. She became pregnant and gave birth to twin boys, one of whom was Caucasian like the Fasanos and the other of whom was African-American like the Perry-Rogers couple. The Fasanos were happy to raise both boys but once the Perry-Rogers couple discovered the mistake and the birth of the twins, they insisted on genetic tests being undertaken, which revealed that one of the twins was their genetic child. They applied for a declaration of parentage and custody. The case was settled on the basis that the Fasanos agreed to relinquish custody to the Perry-Rogers couple on the understanding that they would have visitation rights. The baby was handed over when he was almost five months old. However, two weeks later the Perry-Rogers couple sued for exclusive custody in contravention of their written agreement. The Court initially granted the Fasanos extensive visitation but on appeal by the Perry-Rogers couple, the Appeal Court held that the Fasanos had no standing to claim visitation rights to the child and had no parental rights to ask the Court to enforce the visitation agreement. They did not have the opportunity to petition the Court in relation to the child's best interest, nor was the other twin granted any visitation rights as a sibling. The decision was based on the wording of the New York statute, which provided that only parents could be accorded visitation and in the circumstances of this case the Fasanos did not qualify under the statutory provisions. The Court held that where a child is properly in the custody of its parents, those parents are accorded extremely broad rights to exclude any visitation, even by a person who has raised and nurtured the child as his or her own.

[6.97] The Court stressed that it was not making its decision based solely on a prioritisation of genetics over other biological or social factors. However, its decision in favour of the genetic parents without providing the gestational mother an opportunity to make a contrary argument seems to suggest otherwise. The Court also said that once the Fasanos became aware of the mistake during pregnancy it was incumbent on them to have the mistake rectified as soon as possible after birth rather than allow a bond to develop with the child and subsequently use this bond as a basis upon which to deny custody to the genetic parents. It has been argued that the application of this equitable 'dirty hands' argument is deeply flawed both in principle and in fact, as denial of the right to visitation seems a disproportionately harsh punishment for forming a bond with the child, and also the Perry-Rogers couple could be said to have acted badly in agreeing to visitation in order to regain custody of the child and then immediately violating the terms of the agreement.[137]

---

[135] Noble-Allgire, 'Switched at the Fertility Clinic: Determining Maternal Rights When a Child is Born From Stolen or Misdelivered Genetic Material' (1999) Vol 64(3) Missouri Law Review 517 at 589.

[136] *Perry-Rogers v Fasono* 715 NYS 2d 19 (App Div 2000).

[137] Bender, 'Genes, Parents and Assisted Reproductive Technologies: ARTs, Mistakes, Sex, Race and Law' (2003) 12 Columbia Journal of Gender and Law 1.

[6.98] Bender states that mistakes such as that which occurred in this case force us to confront the underlying assumptions in our legal notions of kinship and the values we want to reflect in our applications of law. She says that society cannot expect to use technologies without mistakes, whether negligent, reckless or intentional. Although tort actions may serve important social justice goals in these cases, they do not resolve who will be the parents of the child. All too often, courts are expected to resolve these cases without legislative guidance and are bound to get it wrong in some cases.[138]

[6.99] In an English case, *Leeds Teaching Hospital NHS Trust* v *Mr & Mrs A & Others*[139] two couples, the As and the Bs, were attending the same hospital for infertility treatment. Mr and Mrs A, a white couple, consented to Mrs A's eggs being fertilised with Mr A's sperm and any resulting embryos to be transferred to Mrs A. Mr and Mrs B, a black couple, gave consent to similar IVF procedures for themselves but Mr B also expressly refused to allow his sperm to be used for research purposes. Following a mix-up at the clinic, Mr B's sperm was used to fertilise Mrs A's eggs. She became pregnant and later gave birth to twins. The mistake only became apparent when the twins were delivered, as they were of mixed race. It was confirmed that Mr B was the father of the twins but they continued to live with the As and he had no contact with them. All of the parties agreed that it was best for the children to reside with the As but the High Court was asked to resolve the issue of paternity of the children.

[6.100] The Human Fertilisation and Embryology Act 1990 (subsequently amended in 2008) provides in s 28 that where a woman is married, her husband is the father of any child born to her unless he did not consent to the treatment she received. Although Mr A gave his consent to the IVF procedure, his consent was limited to the creation of an embryo using his sperm, not that of Mr B. Therefore the Court said 'Mr A did not consent to the placing in his wife of the embryo which was actually placed. Accordingly, section 28(2) does not apply.' The only possible outcome was to revert to the common law assumption that Mr B, who had been shown to be the genetic father, was also the legal father. Butler-Sloss J held that he had the same legal status as an unmarried father, ie he had no automatic rights to the children.[140]

[6.101] Ford and Morgan take the view that rather than prioritising a social view of parenthood, the case favours a biological accident by declaring the gamete provider rather than the man with whom the children have a familial bond to be their legal father. The judge considered the impact of art 8 of the Human Rights Act 1998 in connection with the right of the children to know the identity of their biological father. She said:

> To refuse to recognise Mr B as their biological father is to distort the truth about which some day the twins will have to learn through knowledge of their paternal identity. The requirement to preserve the truth will not adversely affect their immediate welfare nor their welfare throughout their childhood. It does not impede the cementing of the permanent relationship of each with Mr A who will act as their father throughout their childhood.

---

[138] Bender, 'Genes, Parents and Assisted Reproductive Technologies: ARTs, Mistakes, Sex, Race and Law' (2003) 12 Columbia Journal of Gender and Law 1 at 26.

[139] *Leeds Teaching Hospital NHS Trust v Mr & Mrs A & Others* [2003] EWHC 259.

[140] All parties were agreed that the children should remain in the A's custody and that Mr A should be able to acquire fatherhood by adoption.

Embryo disputes in Ireland

[6.102] The first Irish case to deal with a dispute in relation to the disposition of frozen embryos arose in 2006 in *MR v TR & Ors*[141] (also known as *Roche v Roche)*. The facts of this case were that MR and TR were married in 1992 and sought fertility advice from their general practitioner in 1994. They were referred to the National Maternity Hospital for specialist treatment and subsequently had a son in 1997. Shortly after the birth of the child, MR underwent ovarian surgery as a result of which she sought fertility treatment at an IVF clinic in 2001. In January 2002, the couple attended the clinic and signed a number of documents covering consent to treatment and the cryopreservation of the embryos.

[6.103] TR signed a form in which he acknowledged that he was MR's husband and consented to the fertilisation of her eggs and the transfer of three embryos to her uterus. He also acknowledged that he would become the legal father of any resulting child. As a result of the treatment, six viable embryos were created. Three were transferred to MR's uterus and the remaining three were frozen. MR became pregnant and gave birth to a daughter in October 2002. Marital difficulties arose between the couple and they subsequently separated. The case arose as a result of the fact that MR wished to have the three frozen embryos transferred to her uterus whereas TR did not wish this to happen nor to become the father of any child that might be born as a result of such a treatment.

[6.104] There were a number of issues before McGovern J in the High Court. The first related to the extent to which TR could be held to have agreed to the transfer of the embryos to MR and whether such an agreement was binding on the parties in the circumstances of their marital separation. The second issue related to whether the embryos enjoyed the protection of Art 40.3.3° of the Constitution. This second issue is considered in **6.121**.

[6.105] On the first issue, McGovern J held that there was no agreement between the parties as to what would happen to the frozen embryos if the first embryo transfer was successful and resulted in pregnancy. The Court held that TR did not give his consent, either express or implied, to the transfer of the frozen embryos and acknowledged that the clinic was unwilling to release the embryos into the custody of MR in the absence of such consent. On appeal to the Supreme Court, the Court unanimously upheld the decision of the High Court that the husband had not given consent, either expressly or impliedly to the transfer of embryos to his wife. The Court held that the forms signed by the husband were not contractually binding and were simply medical consent forms. There was no question of an offer or acceptance or consideration, or an intention to create a legal contract, nor was the man bound by the application of equitable principles to permit the frozen embryos to be implanted.

[6.106] Consent is a crucial aspect of all medical treatment and, in the case of IVF, would appear to be required from both partners at all stages of the process from fertilisation until embryo transfer. There is an argument to the effect that an implied consent arises by virtue of the couple presenting for IVF treatment together and that any subsequent dispute should be resolved in favour of the party seeking to procreate, as that

---

[141] *MR v TR & Ors* [2006] IEHC 359.

was the original intention of the treatment.[142] On this basis 'voluntary participation in the IVF process could be regarded as conduct reasonably leading to the assumption that both parties have committed to reproduction. In the event of changed circumstances, the doctrine of promissory estoppel becomes essential, as the party who subsequently seeks to use any non-transferred embryos relies, to his or her detriment, on the other party's commitment to reproduce jointly.'[143] Therefore, the partner who opposes implantation of the embryos should be estoped from asserting his or her right not to reproduce. This argument was put to the Court in the present case, to the effect that the husband was estopped from withholding consent to embryo transfer after the creation of the embryos and the use of some of them in an earlier, successful IVF cycle, was not upheld by the Court. Denham J stated that even if the husband had entered an agreement on this issue, it would not necessarily be irrevocable and that the Court would have to take all the circumstances into account, including whether the use of the embryos at issue represented the last opportunity for either party to have a biological child of their own. In acknowledging the existence of a right to procreate, which was recognised in *Murray v Ireland*,[144] she said that:

> There is an equal and opposite right not to procreate. In the circumstances of this case, while the plaintiff and her husband have family rights, the exercise of a right not to procreate by the husband is a proportionate interference in all the circumstances of the case to the right of the plaintiff to procreate.

[6.107] The forms used by the clinic in this case did not deal with the position of the parties in respect of any frozen embryos. It did not stipulate, therefore, what the parties intended should happen to such embryos in the event that a pregnancy was achieved on the first attempt, or that the couple separated, divorced or died. The legal insufficiencies of the forms used in this case provide a clear illustration of the need for clarification and guidance in Ireland on legal issues relating to IVF. The Commission on Assisted Human Reproduction recommended in 2005 that appropriate guidelines should be put in place by the regulatory body proposed by the Commission, to govern the options available for excess frozen embryos. These would include voluntary donation to other recipients, donation to research or allowing the embryos to perish. It also recommended that 'the regulatory body should, in accordance with statutory guidelines, have power to address cases where embryos are abandoned, where the commissioning couple cannot agree on a course of action, where the couple separates or where one or both partners dies or becomes incapacitated.'[145]

---

[142] Waldman, 'The Parent Trap: Uncovering the Myth of Coerced Parenthood in Frozen Embryo Dispute' (2004) Am Univ Law Rev 53:1021; Apel, 'Cryopreserved Embryos: A Response to "Forced Parenthood" and the Role of Intent' (2005) Fam Law Q 39: 663.

[143] Sills and Murphy, 'Determining the Status of Non-Transferred Embryos in Ireland: A Conspectus of Case Law and Implications for Clinical IVF Practice' (2009) Philosophy, Ethics and Humanities in Medicine 4:8.

[144] *Murray v Ireland* [1991] 1 ILRM 465.

[145] Report of the Commission on Assisted Human Reproduction (Government Publications Office, 2005) p 17.

Constitutional issues

[6.108] Article 40.3.3° of the Irish Constitution 1937 states:

> The State acknowledges the right to life of the unborn and, with due regard to the equal right of life of the mother, guarantees in its laws to respect, and, as far as practicable, by its laws to defend and vindicate that right.[146]

[6.109] The most important word, from the perspective of IVF, is the word 'unborn'. For the purposes of IVF if the 'unborn' includes the pre-implantation embryo, then the application of the constitutional protection in Art 40.3.3° would have implications for IVF practices insofar as embryo freezing may not be permissible, at least unless there was a guarantee that the embryo would subsequently be transferred to a receptive uterus. This would be necessary due to the interpretation of the 'right to life' as meaning the right to have the opportunity to grow and develop in the uterus and be born. This is evident from *G v An Bord Uchtála*[147] in which Walsh J stated:

> [A child] has the right to life itself and the right to be guarded against all threats directed to its existence whether before or after birth … The right to life necessarily implies the right to be born, the right to preserve and defend, and to have preserved and defended, that life ….

[6.110] The use of the word 'unborn' in the Constitution is unfortunate because it introduces uncertainty into the law regarding the presumed intention of the People that is reflected in that document. If the 'unborn' means 'not yet born' or 'with the potential to be born' then, in the light of the biological development of the early embryo and the absence of potential in the pre-implantation embryo, it is likely that the embryo in the laboratory does not qualify for this Constitutional protection.

[6.111] In its report the Constitutional Review Committee said in relation to Art 40.3.3°:

> There is no definition of "unborn" which, used as a noun, is at least odd. One would expect "unborn human" or "unborn human being". Presumably the term "unborn child" was not chosen because of uncertainty as to when a fetus might properly be so described. Definition is needed as to when the "unborn" acquires the protection of the law. Philosophers and scientists may continue to debate when human life begins but the law must define what it intends to protect. "Unborn" seems to imply "on the way to being born" or "capable of being born". Whether this condition obtains from fertilisation of the ovum, implantation of the fertilised ovum in the womb, or some other point, has not been defined.[148]

[6.112] This expression 'on the way to being born' reinforces the view that the pre-implantation embryo is not covered by the Constitutional provision as it stands. The embryo at this stage, without implantation, is neither on the way to being born nor capable of being born. It may not even be human nor individual unless it is transferred to the uterus, implants in the uterine wall and develops a primitive streak. Whereas arguments may continue in relation to the embryo in the womb and whether and at what stage it is 'on the way to being born' so as to prohibit abortion, these arguments do not apply to the embryo outside the body, which will only qualify for the same protection if it is transferred to the uterus.

---

146 Inserted by the Eighth Amendment of the Constitution in 1983.
147 *G v An Bord Uchtála* [1980] IR 32.
148 Report of the Constitution Review Group (1996) at 275.

[6.113] Williams dismisses claims that the embryo is an 'unborn child' as follows:

In the early stages of fetal development some people, not only lawyers, would incline to think the phrase "unborn child" out of place. It would certainly be odd to refer thus to a microscopic fertilised ovum, or to the mass of cells into which it shortly develops – cells nearly all of which will be shed as part of the afterbirth. To call this an "unborn child" would be a flight of fancy.[149]

[6.114] In the case of *Attorney General v X.* in 1992,[150] the Supreme Court considered Art 40.3.3° in the context of whether a young girl who was at risk of suicide could travel abroad to obtain an abortion. The Court held that the interpretation of the provision required that the termination of pregnancy was permissible only when it was established as a matter of probability that there was a real and substantial risk to the life of the mother if such termination were not affected.

[6.115] For the purposes of a consideration of the meaning of the provision in relation to the pre-implantation embryo, the judgment of the Court is not of great assistance. It must be borne in mind that the Court, in referring to the 'unborn' in the course of the judgment were doing so in light of the facts of the case, which involved a pregnancy already begun, an embryo 'on the way to being born'. For this reason, much of the judgment of the Court is not applicable to the pre-embryo outside the body, which is not 'on the way to being born' unless implantation takes place. In instances where the meaning of 'unborn' is indirectly adverted to, it is spoken of in relation to 'the life of the infant in the womb'. This has no application to the embryo *outside* the womb.[151]

[6.116] According to Hederman J (dissenting), the objective of the Constitutional provision is the protection of human life. He states:

The Eighth Amendment establishes beyond any dispute that the constitutional guarantee of the vindication and protection of life is not qualified by the condition that the life must be one which has achieved an independent existence after birth. The right of life is guaranteed

---

[149] Williams, 'The Fetus and the "Right to Life"' (1994) Cambridge Law Journal at 73.

[150] *Attorney General v X* [1992] 1 IR 1. This case appears to have been followed by the Court in a case in which a pregnant 13-year-old girl, who had allegedly been raped, was allowed to travel to the UK for an abortion on the grounds that she would commit suicide if she had to continue with the pregnancy. The facts were seen as coming within the precedent set by the *X* case and therefore it was unnecessary to go into the meaning of 'unborn' or the protection given by the Constitution. An unusual aspect of this case was the fact that this girl was in the care of the health board at the time of the application and subsequent journey to the UK and therefore the abortion was carried out at the expense of the State. See *A and B v Eastern Health Board* [1998]1 IR 464.

[151] In *Abortion and the Law* (Round Hall, 1997), Kingston and Whelan are of the view that the Supreme Court would have the ultimate say in determining when the right to life begins. They note that Hamilton P indicated obiter in *Attorney-General (Society for Protection of Unborn Children (Ireland) Ltd v Open Door Counselling Ltd and Dublin Well Woman Clinic Ltd* [1988] IR 593, that the right to life of the unborn was protected by the criminal law from the moment of conception and he appeared to 'assume that the protection afforded the unborn by the Constitution dates from the same moment. However, as the issue has not been squarely addressed, it cannot be said definitively that the Supreme Court would share Hamilton P's assumption.' p 31.

to every life born or unborn. One cannot make distinctions between individual phases of the unborn life before birth, or between unborn and born life.[152]

[6.117] This extract from the judgment of Hederman J is the closest the Court gets to discussing what is meant by the expression 'unborn' used in the Constitution, yet it does not go far enough. Even if it is accepted that distinctions cannot be made as between the fetus at 6 weeks (or earlier) and the fetus at 36 weeks for the purposes of the Constitutional protection they both may enjoy, it may be argued that this does not apply to the embryo outside the body. In this instance the embryo is not 'an autonomous human being'[153] (another phrase used by Hederman J) because it can never become human unless it is transferred to the uterus, (which depends on the actions of someone else), nor does it establish a pregnancy (in which the right to life of the mother may be given priority over the right to life of the embryo). It does not share any of the characteristics possessed by the fetus in the womb except that it is human in origin. It is not sentient, it has no 'potential' to become anything while it remains in the petri dish in the laboratory. Therefore, it may be argued that the Constitutional provision has no application to the pre-implantation embryo. This does not detract from its moral or symbolic value but it does allow medical procedures such as freezing to take place without contravention of the Constitution.

[6.118] In 2002 a Constitutional amendment was put before the Irish people which would have inserted a new provision, Art 40.3.4°, in the Constitution as follows: 'In particular, the life of the unborn in the womb shall be protected in accordance with the provisions of the Protection of Human Life in Pregnancy Act 2002.' It was also proposed to insert a new Art 40.3.5° that would have had the effect that the Human Life in Pregnancy Act could only be changed by another referendum.

[6.119] The Protection of Human Life in Pregnancy Bill intended to remove the threat of suicide as a ground for a legal termination of pregnancy, as provided by the Supreme Court's interpretation of Article 40.3.3° in the *X* case. It was also intended to give protection to medical practices carried out to save the life of the mother, other than in circumstances where the risk presented to the woman was that of self-destruction. There were many problems associated with the wording of the Bill but, for the purposes of the present discussion, it is significant that the proposed definition of abortion in the Bill was the 'intentional destruction by any means of unborn human life after implantation in the womb of a woman', excluding a medical procedure carried out to save the mother's life. Therefore, it might have been thought that, standing alone, the Bill did not protect the pre-implantation embryo.

[6.120] However, much confusion was caused by the method of insertion of the Bill into the Constitution, the exact wording used and the conflicting messages given to the public by campaigners on all sides. Due to the insertion of the words 'in particular' in the proposed Art 40.3.4° it was argued that the Bill was designed to deal only with the post-implantation embryo, and that the existing Article 40.3.3° therefore dealt with the pre-implantation embryo. This would mean that the existing Constitutional provision obliging the State to protect the right to life of the unborn applied to the pre-

---

[152] Williams, 'The Fetus and the "Right to Life"' (1994) Cambridge Law Journal, p 72.
[153] *Attorney General v X* [1992] 1 IR 1.

implantation embryo. This not only had connotations in the context of IVF and embryo freezing, but also in the context of emergency contraception, such as the morning-after pill, which impedes implantation of the fertilised egg. The Referendum Commission put it no stronger than that the present constitutional position of the latter was open to doubt whether or not the referendum was passed[154], but it is arguable that the passing of the referendum would have made it more likely than not that the morning-after pill would have been deemed unconstitutional, with consequent effect on IVF and embryo freezing. The referendum was ultimately rejected by a narrow margin.

[6.121] The first judicial consideration of the application of Art 40.3.3° to embryos took place in *MR v TR & Ors*[155] (also known as *Roche v Roche)*, the facts of which are outlined above at para **6.102** et seq. On the Constitutional issue, the Court was asked to consider whether Article 40.3.3° applied to the frozen embryos which were the subject of the dispute between the estranged couple in this case. The High Court heard from a number of witnesses who gave their view as to when life begins. Some argued that 'from the moment of fertilisation of the ovum by the sperm a new human life begins.' Others argued that 'it was only when the embryo became implanted in the uterus that the potential to be born existed and that human life began at that point'. Yet other witnesses stated that 'human life began at the formation of the primitive streak' and others took the view that it was impossible to say when human life begins. In this regard, McGovern J stated that:

> It is possible for scientists and embryologists to describe in detail the process of development from the ovum to the embryo and on to the stage when it becomes a foetus after implantation of the embryo in the wall of the uterus, but in my opinion, it is not possible for this Court to state when human life begins.

[6.122] The judge went on to acknowledge that the point at which people ascribe human characteristics to genetic material depends on other issues besides science and medicine, and is dependent upon one's own moral or religious beliefs. He stressed that it was not the function of the Court to choose between competing moral beliefs and that the only issue that he had to decide was whether the three frozen embryos in this case were 'unborn' within the meaning of Art 40.3.3° of the Constitution. In deciding upon this important point, McGovern J first stated that in considering the words in Art 40.3.3° the Court could have regard to the legislative history of the Constitutional amendment but not to debates in the Oireachtas in order to clarify what was in the contemplation of the People in passing the amendment. He referred to a number of cases mentioned above – *McGee v Attorney General, G v An Bord Uchtála, Attorney General v X*, as well as s 58 of the Civil Liability Act 1961, which provides that the law relating to wrongs 'shall apply to an unborn child for his protection in like manner as if the child were born, provided the child is subsequently born alive'.

[6.123] He also referred to the Medical Council's Guide to Ethical Conduct and Behaviour (in its previous edition dated 2004), the Report of the Constitution Review Group and the Report of the Commission on Assisted Human Reproduction, also mentioned above. McGovern J concluded that there had been

---

[154] See the explanatory booklet published by the Referendum Commission, available at www.refcom.ie (accessed 1 June 2011).

[155] *MR v TR & Ors* [2006] IEHC 359.

[N]o evidence adduced that it was ever in the mind of the people voting on the Eighth Amendment to the Constitution that "unborn" meant anything other than a foetus or child within the womb. To infer that it was in the mind of the people that "unborn" included embryos outside the womb or embryos in vitro would be to completely ignore the circumstances in which the amendment giving rise to Article 40.3.3 arose. While I accept that Article 40.3.3 is not to be taken in isolation from its historical background and should be considered as but one provision of the whole Constitution, this does not mean that the word 'unborn' can be given a meaning which was not contemplated by the people at the time of the passing of the Eighth Amendment and which takes it outside the scope and purpose of the amendment.

[6.124] Consequently, the Court held that the word 'unborn' within Art 40.3.3° does not include embryos in vitro and therefore did not include the three frozen embryos in this case. McGovern J stated that in the absence of any regulation in this country 'embryos outside the womb have a very precarious existence' and that 'until the law or the Constitution is changed this issue remains within the sphere of ethics and morality.'

[6.125] On appeal to the Supreme Court, the judges all took the view that decisions in relation to the definition of life or adjudications on matters of science, theology or ethics were not appropriately made by a court of law. The court's function was to make a legal decision on the interpretation of an article of the Constitution, and it was a matter for the legislature to make policy choices in relation to the regulation of assisted human reproduction and the protection of the embryo. The Court said that the provision had been inserted into the Constitution to deal with termination of pregnancy and the balancing of rights between the foetus and the mother. The language and intent of the article envisages a specific constitutional and legal relationship between the unborn and the mother which only exists by virtue of a physical connection between them. This only happens after implantation and therefore an 'unborn' under Art 40.3.3° is established when an embryo implants in the womb.

[6.126] Denham J also said that the concept of 'unborn' envisages a state of being born, the potential to be born or the capacity to be born, which occurs only after implantation. She said that if embryos were considered to be 'unborn' within the Constitution, the State would have an obligation to protect all embryos in the State in every clinic and hospital and would have to intervene to facilitate their implantation irrespective of the parents' wishes, and this would be inconsistent with the rights of the family. A similar point was made by Hardiman J who expressed concern that if respect for the embryo were carried to the point of equating it to a life in being, that view would lead to the outlawing of one of the most widely used methods of contraception, the morning-after pill, which operates by prevention of implantation.

[6.127] All five judges said that legislation should be introduced to deal with the legal issues arising in Assisted Human Reproduction (AHR) and that it was disturbing that four years after the report of the Commission on Assisted Human Reproduction the government had still not enacted legislation on these issues. Following the judgment of the Court, the Minister for Health stated that the government accepted that it had a responsibility to introduce legislation in relation to AHR and that a legislative proposal would be brought before the Cabinet as soon as possible.

The Report of the Commission on Assisted Human Reproduction

[6.128] In 2000, the Irish Government established the Commission on Assisted Human Reproduction to report on the possible approaches to the regulation of all aspects of assisted human reproduction and the social, ethical and legal factors to be taken into account in determining public policy in the area. The Commission reported in 2005.[156] For a number of reasons, including the welfare of the child, the Commission decided that a new Act of the Oireachtas should be passed to establish a regulatory body to regulate AHR services in Ireland. Among the body's executive functions would be the issuing of licences to service providers. It would be mandatory for any provider of AHR services to obtain a licence from the statutory body in respect of the provision of any of the clinical and laboratory services specified in the legislation. The recommendations of the Commission are extracted here in full:[157]

1. A regulatory body should be established by an Act of the Oireachtas to regulate AHR services in Ireland.

2. National statistics on the outcome of AHR techniques in Ireland should be compiled and made available to the public.

3. Longitudinal studies of children born as a result of AHR should be established, in accordance with standard ethical/legal requirements and with the consent of families, in order to facilitate long-term monitoring.

4. Appropriate guidelines should be put in place to govern the freezing and storage of gametes and the use of frozen gametes. The regulatory body should, in accordance with statutory guidelines, have power to address cases where gametes are abandoned, where the commissioning couple cannot agree on a course of action, where couples separate or where one or both partner(s) dies or becomes incapacitated.

5. Superovulation should be allowed according to well established clinical protocols. Appropriate guidelines should be put in place by the regulatory body to govern superovulation and the harvesting of ova following ovarian stimulation.

6. Service providers should facilitate users who wish to avoid any treatment that might result in the production of 'surplus' embryos.

7. Appropriate guidelines should be put in place by the regulatory body to govern the fertilisation of ova.

8. Appropriate guidelines should be put in place by the regulatory body to govern the number of embryos to be transferred in any one treatment cycle and when to transfer embryos.

9. Appropriate guidelines should be put in place by the regulatory body to govern the freezing of excess healthy embryos.

10. Appropriate guidelines should be put in place by the regulatory body to govern the options available for excess frozen embryos. These would include voluntary donation of excess healthy embryos to other recipients, voluntary donation for research or allowing them to perish.

---

[156] See http://www.dohc.ie/publications/pdf/cahr.pdf?direct=1 (accessed 1 June 2011).

[157] The recommendations of the Commission were unanimous except for numbers 10, 16, 30, 33, 34, 36, 40.

11. The regulatory body should, in accordance with statutory guidelines, have power to address cases where embryos are abandoned, where the commissioning couple cannot agree on a course of action, where the couple separates or where one or both partner(s) dies or becomes incapacitated.

12. Counselling should be provided before, during and after treatment to those considering AHR treatment so that they are adequately informed of the risks involved, the potential benefits that may be obtained, and the possibility of success in their particular situation. Suitably qualified professionals should adequately convey the complex medical and scientific ramifications of different treatment approaches in verbal and written form.

13. It should be obligatory for all recognised providers of AHR services in Ireland to obtain written informed consent for all the services they provide. Each stage of the AHR process should be covered by comprehensive consent procedures. A set of guidelines should be drawn up setting out the specific types of consent that need to be obtained and it should be obligatory for all service providers to observe the terms of these guidelines.

14. Best practice infertility treatment guidelines should be developed for general practitioners and gynaecologists working outside specialist clinics. These guidelines should be reviewed on a regular basis.

15. Centres that collect and store gametes and that generate and store embryos should be regulated and licensed by the regulatory body. The regulatory body should lay down quality assurance standards for such centres. Information on the range of services provided by the specialist clinics should be available to the general public.

16. The embryo formed by IVF should not attract legal protection until placed in the human body, at which stage it should attract the same level of protection as the embryo formed in vivo.

17. Services should be available without discrimination on the grounds of gender, marital status or sexual orientation subject to consideration of the best interests of any children that may be born. Any relevant legislation on the provision of AHR services should reflect the general principles of the Equal Status Acts 2000–4 subject to the qualifications set out in section 4.8.

18. Where there is objective evidence of a risk of harm to any child that may be conceived through AHR, there should be a presumption against treatment.

19. Donation of sperm, ova and embryos should be permitted and should be subject to regulation by the regulatory body.

20. Suitably qualified professionals should provide appropriate counselling in advance to all donors of gametes and embryos. Such counselling should be a pre-condition for informed consent by donors.

21. Appropriate guidelines should be put in place to govern the selection of donors; to screen for genetic disorders and infectious disease; to set age limits for donors and to set an appropriate limit on the number of children to be born by the use of sperm or ova from a single donor.

22. Any child born through use of donated gametes or embryos should, on maturity, be able to identify the donor(s) involved in his/her conception.

23. Donors should not be paid nor should recipients be charged for donations per se. This does not preclude payment of reasonable expenses and payment for AHR services.

24. In donor programmes, the intent of all parties involved – that the donor will not have any legal relationship with the child and that the woman who gives birth to the child will be the child's mother – should be used as the basis for the assignment of legal parentage.

25. In cases involving sperm donation, there should be a requirement that the partner, if any, of the sperm recipient also give a legal commitment to be recognised as the child's parent.

26. In the case of a child born through ovum donation and in the case of a child resulting from an embryo donation, the gestational mother should be recognised as the legal mother of the child and her partner, if any, should be recognised as the child's second legal parent.

27. Donors should not be able to access the identity of children born through use of their gametes or embryos.

28. Donors should, if they wish, be told if a child is born through use of their gametes.

29. In general, donors should not be permitted to attach conditions to donation, except in situations of intrafamilial donation or the use of donated gametes/ embryos for research.

30. Surrogacy should be permitted and should be subject to regulation by the regulatory body.

31. Women who decide to participate as surrogate mothers should be entitled to receive reimbursement of expenses directly related to such participation.

32. The child born through surrogacy, on reaching maturity, should be entitled to access the identity of the surrogate mother and, where relevant, the genetic parents.

33. The child born through surrogacy should be presumed to be that of the commissioning couple.

34. Embryo research, including embryonic stem cell research, for specific purposes only and under stringently controlled conditions, should be permitted on surplus embryos that are donated specifically for research. This should be permitted up to fourteen days following fertilisation. The regulatory body should stipulate under what conditions and for what purposes embryo research is permitted. Those donating embryos for research must receive pre-donation information and counselling and they must give informed consent for the use of donated embryos for research. No inducement, financial or otherwise, should be offered/accepted for the donation of embryos for research. Once embryos are used for research their subsequent use for reproductive purposes should be prohibited. The generation of embryos through IVF specifically for research purposes should be prohibited.

35. Human reproductive cloning should be prohibited.

36. Regenerative medicine should be permitted under regulation.

37. The generation and use of interspecies human embryos should be prohibited.

38. Preconception sex selection should be permitted only for the reliable prevention of serious sex linked genetic disorders but not for social reasons.

39. Research on gametes should be permitted provided it is governed by strict conditions set out by the regulatory body and subject to informed consent from donors. Specific consent should be required from the regulatory body for specific valid research.

40. Pre-implantation genetic diagnosis (PGD) should be allowed, under regulation, to reduce the risk of serious genetic disorders. PGD should also be allowed for tissue typing only for serious diseases that cannot otherwise be treated. Each licence issued for PGD should specify the proposed procedure. The regulatory body should oversee and monitor developments in PGD.

Chapter 7

Surrogate Motherhood

INTRODUCTION

[7.01] Surrogacy is not a modern development; indeed, in a simpler form, it has been in existence for centuries.[1] In modern practice, surrogate motherhood is an arrangement whereby a woman agrees to be artificially inseminated, or have an embryo transferred to her uterus in order to become pregnant and carry a child to term, with the intention of relinquishing custody of that child upon birth to the couple with whom she has made the agreement. In commercial surrogacy, the surrogate mother is paid a fee, which can range from €10,000 to €50,000 or more depending on the jurisdiction in which it takes place. In addition, medical and other expenses as well as a fee to the clinic which facilitates the arrangement may be payable. Sometimes surrogacy arrangements are made between family members or friends, in which case no money is usually paid other than reimbursement of medical and out-of-pocket expenses. The intended parents are usually referred to as 'the commissioning couple', although the arrangement could, of course, also be made by a single person using donated gametes.

[7.02] Surrogacy might be an option where a woman has severe pelvic disease which cannot be remedied surgically, or where she was born without ovaries, or has no uterus. It might also be used in situations where a woman has suffered repeated miscarriages and is unable to carry a pregnancy to term. Unlike in vitro fertilisation (IVF), traditional surrogacy, in which the surrogate mother's egg is fertilised by the commissioning man's sperm, can be performed without the assistance of a doctor or any modern technology. Impregnation can occur by intercourse or with the aid of a syringe. Due to the fact that no medical assistance is required, regulation of this form of surrogacy is very difficult, as it may occur without detection. Gestational (or IVF) surrogacy, on the other hand, demands medical assistance, as the surrogate is the carrier of the commissioning mother's egg, which has been fertilised in vitro by the commissioning father's sperm. If the commissioning couple is unable to provide the eggs and sperm themselves, then donor gametes may be used to create the embryo which is transferred to the surrogate's uterus.

---

[1]   Genesis, Chapter 16: 4–7, where Abraham's wife Sarah could not bear a child so Abraham lay with a slave-girl, Hagar, in order to found a family through her. Hagar duly bore Abraham a son, Ishmahel. Unfortunately, there was not a happy ending to this tale, as Sarah became bitter and jealous and cast out Hagar and Ishmahel, who later returned only to be again rejected by Abraham and Sarah. Ishmahel grew into a 'wild ass of a man, his hand against every man and every man's hand against him.' 16:12. See also *Briody v St. Helen's Knowsley Health Authority* [2000] EWHC QB 178, per Ebsworth J at 19; and Eriksson, *Reproductive Freedom in the Context of International Human Rights and Humanitarian Law* (Martinus Nijhoff Publishers, 2000) at 207.

[7.03] In the 1980s, surrogacy sparked off controversies unheard of before.[2] Issues such as the meaning of motherhood, the role of gestating a baby, the consequences for women, the importance of the mother-child bond, payment for gestational services and the valuation of parenthood were debated as the result of a small number of high-profile cases which caught the public's attention. Surrogacy became 'the whipping post for the moral backlash against the brave new world of technological rationality and scientific finality.'[3] The tug-of-love scenario usually conjured up when surrogacy was discussed also demonstrated the role of the media in focusing on the sensationalist angle of surrogacy, drawing attention to the very few cases in which the surrogate changes her mind and decides to keep the child.[4]

[7.04] In the cases in which surrogacy has come to judicial and public attention, much energy and public debate is expended on the ethical issues involved in this practice. However, when faced with a custody dispute in relation to the child, some judges have taken a pragmatic view and held that the morality of the practice is irrelevant now that the child has already been born. Others have entertained arguments on issues such as whether surrogacy is baby-selling, whether it is exploitative of women and whether such arrangements are inherently immoral, such that they should be held contrary to public policy. If and when an Irish court is faced with such a dilemma, it is likely that similar arguments will be raised. For this reason it is relevant to examine some of these ethical arguments here.

---

[2]   Perhaps the reason for the discomfort which usually characterises public reaction to surrogacy is the change which technology brings to familiar traditions and structures. 'We need not look too deeply into history to understand that technology consistently places old questions in new contexts. Technology usually unsettles settled expectations; it often jars and frightens; it has a way of disorienting us by wresting away our confident assumptions from a simpler past. Occasionally, it forces us to rethink our very moral fabric, or at least to explore our values anew to determine how they apply in wholly unprecedented contexts. So it is, in my judgement, with surrogacy.'
      Bezanson, 'Solomon Would Weep: A Comment on *In the Matter of Baby M* and the Limits of Judicial Authority' (1988) 16:1–2 Law, Medicine and Health Care 126–130 at 126.

[3]   Morgan and Lee, *Human Fertilisation and Embryology, Regulating the Reproductive Revolution* (Blackstone Press, 2001) at 191.

[4]   It is difficult to assess with accuracy the number of cases in which breaches of the arrangement take place, as it is impossible to know how many surrogacy cases occur at all. However, those involved in arranging surrogacy believe that the incidence is very low. See Schuck, 'Some Reflections on the *Baby M* Case' (1988) 76 Geo LJ 1793 at 1801 fn.30, recording an interview with a lawyer dealing in surrogacy transactions. It was claimed that there were 9 problem cases out of about 600, and 4 (including the infamous *Baby M* case, which is discussed later) that ended up in court. A report in the UK estimates that it is only in 4–5 per cent of cases that the surrogate refuses to hand over the child. Surrogacy: Review for Health Ministers of Current Arrangements for Payments and Regulation (Cm.4068) (Department of Health, 1998) at para 3.38. In the Republic of Ireland, no cases of this nature have been brought to judicial attention, although there have been children born to Irish couples through surrogacy arrangements made in the US, Ukraine, India, Romania and other jurisdictions.

ETHICAL ISSUES IN SURROGACY

Baby selling

[7.05] One of the widely used legal and moral arguments for total prohibition of surrogacy has been to consider it an example of baby selling.[5] It is argued that surrogacy is unethical because the payment of money commodifies the child and treats it as a product rather than a person. However, it may be counter argued that the term 'baby selling' is a misnomer, as the baby itself is not being sold as an object; rather, parental rights are being exchanged for a fee.[6] As Mason and Laurie point out, 'it is possible, however, to maintain that a baby is "sold" only if persons with no genetic association purchase an infant that is already in being.'[7] They suggest that it is more logical to regard the transaction as payment for gestational expertise or 'services rendered', with a crucial distinction being drawn between reasonable recompense and inducement to gestate.[8] Brazier argues that such a distinction is specious unless the usual consequences of paid employment ensue[9] and the contract is regarded as enforceable in the same way as other contracts for services. She says that the reproductive labour which commissioning couples are prepared to pay for is inevitably 'the labour of having a child *for them* – they are paying for their child.'[10] The only difference from a baby market is that the child is genetically related to one or both of the commissioning parents. She questions whether this is sufficient to distinguish surrogacy from adoption, where payments are explicitly prohibited.

---

[5] The idea of paying a price for a human being was the driving force behind the Surrogacy Arrangements Act 1985 in the UK. However, the Act merely prohibits payments to third parties or brokers in relation to surrogacy. It does not ban payments to the surrogate herself due to concerns about the effect on the child born to a woman who is subject to the taint of criminality. In the US case of *Baby M* (discussed at para **7.34**) the New Jersey Supreme Court stated: 'This is the sale of a child, or, at the very least, the sale of a mother's right to her child, the only mitigating factor being that one of the purchasers is the father. Almost every evil that prompted the prohibition of money in connection with adoptions exists here.'

[6] Shapiro argues that the child is not 'conceived in order to be given away', as this would imply that the child would be handed over to the first person who came along. He argues that: '[T]he child is not being conceived because the transfer of the child is itself the intrinsically valuable goal of the arrangement. The child is conceived as part of the formation of a nuclear family – with all the bonds, relationships and duties for which one hopes. That is the purpose of the overall transaction. The new family is, of course, not that of the birth mother, so transfer is a necessary mechanism. The transfer is not the purpose or goal, but the means.' Shapiro, 'How (Not) to Think About Surrogacy and Other Reproductive Innovations' (1994) 28 University of San Francisco Law Review 647 at 657.

[7] Mason and Laurie, *Law and Medical Ethics* (8th edn, OUP, 2010) page 291.

[8] See also Freeman 'Does Surrogacy Have a Future After Brazier?' (1999) 7 Med L Rev 1 at 9; Dickenson, *Property, Women and Politics* (Rutgers University Press, 1997) at 160–165; Purdy *Reproducing Persons*, (Cornell University Press, 1996) at 47.

[9] Brazier 'Can You Buy Children?' (1999) *Child and Fam Law Quarterly* Vol 11 No 4, 345–354.

[10] Brazier 'Can You Buy Children?' (1999) *Child and Fam Law Quarterly* Vol 11 No 4 at 351.

[7.06] The connotations of buying and selling infants are instinctively unpleasant to most people. This is especially true when economic or market language enters familial relationships. In 1979, Posner and Landes controversially explained how a market in babies should be regarded and regulated.[11] They began by pointing out the shortage of babies for adoption in the United States. This was due, largely, not to the increased availability of contraception and abortion, as might have been thought, but to the fact that a larger proportion of parents of illegitimate children were keeping them instead of giving them up for adoption:

> This trend may be due to inexplicable (on economic grounds) changes in moral standards; or it may be due to the fact that the increased opportunities for women in the job market have made them less dependent on the presence of a male in raising a child. An additional feature is that, given the increased availability of contraception and abortion, an illegitimate baby is more likely than formerly to be a desired baby.[12]

[7.07] The effect of the shortage is obvious – some couples have to wait for years to get a baby, others never get one and others are put off by the size of the queue from even applying. Where demand outstrips supply, and where there are restrictions on payment, as there are in connection with adoption, it is understandable that surrogacy, with clandestine payments or payments of only medical expenses, could be seen as providing a solution. This may lead to a black market situation in which surrogates use their genetic backgrounds to make the sale to prospective commissioning couples. The legal sanctions that may apply to such an arrangement may lead to the risks being overcome by an increase in the financial incentives involved. It may also be the case that these sanctions may lead to fraud, dishonesty, misrepresentation and blackmail on the part of the surrogate who is selling her services.

[7.08] It may be argued that all of the potential ill effects in relation to the market in babies are as a result of the fact that the market is an illegal one. Although these arguments are directed towards a legal market in adoptions, an analogy may be drawn with surrogacy. Landes and Posner argue that a legal market would allow: enforceability of contracts (which would decrease the risks involved for both parties); increase in consumer satisfaction (due to the higher-quality package of rights thereby obtained); decrease in the price to be paid (the net medical costs would be cancelled out by the fact that paying the surrogate's medical bills are comparable to the hypothetical costs of the commissioning couple's medical bills had they been able to conceive themselves); and allow more lower-income families to obtain a child (as the cost of acquiring a baby would often be small).

[7.09] Although the notion of a regulated market in babies seems far fetched and offensive to some, Brazier acknowledges that we may be closer to such a situation than we are prepared to countenance in that the Catholic Church in Scotland advertised the availability of payments to encourage pregnant women not to have abortions and to consider surrendering the child for adoption at birth,[13] and advertisements regularly

---

[11] Landes and Posner, 'The Economics of the Baby Shortage' (1979) 7 Journal of Legal Studies 323.

[12] Landes and Posner, 'The Economics of the Baby Shortage' (1979) 7 Journal of Legal Studies 323 at 325.

[13] The Times, 11 and 12 October 1999, quoted in Brazier, 'Can You Buy Children?' (1999) *Child and Fam Law Quarterly* Vol 11 No 4 at 349.

appear in the American press offering large sums of money to students to sell their eggs and sperm.[14] In the case of the payments made by the Church, these are to enable the woman to meet the costs of pregnancy, maternity clothes and so on, and there is no inducement to give the baby up for adoption, yet there is no continuation of such payments after the baby's birth, which renders it more difficult for an impoverished young woman to rear the child herself, thus perhaps leading to the conclusion that adoption is the best solution. If continuation of the pregnancy and surrendering of the child for adoption are linked, then it could be said that the payments come close to inducements to sell the child.

[7.10] Although there may be some attraction in the economic analysis, there are many obvious criticisms of a legal market in babies, most importantly the issue of protection of the child. A free market in adoptions does not necessarily coincide with the objective of the adoption process, which is to ensure that the child's best interests are safeguarded.[15] Usually a free market increases the satisfaction of those trading in it, but this does not take account of the fact that the product being sold in this instance is a child whose individual welfare and interests society is committed to protect. 'The question is whether the price system would do as good a job as, or a better job than, adoption agencies in finding homes for children that would maximise their satisfactions in life.'[16]

[7.11] In looking at the practice of adoption, one can see that the screening process is an obvious attempt to safeguard the welfare of the child by eliminating any unfit parents from consideration as adopters. However, once the couple makes it onto the waiting list, the allocation of children then usually works on a 'first-come, first-serve' basis, so that those who are best suited as parents do not necessarily get priority on the list. Also important is that the adoption agency does not know what the individual needs of the particular child will be in the future, apart from necessities such as love, warmth, food and shelter:

> One cannot read from the face of a new born whether he or she will be of above or below normal intelligence, or be naturally athletic, musical, or artistic. Hence agencies cannot be presumed to match these very real, if inaccessible, qualities of infants with the qualities of the adoptive parents any more effectively than a market would.[17]

Thus, once the commissioning couple is screened for suitability in the same way as prospective adopters, the newborn child's best interests may be as well served by placement with that couple as they would with an adoptive couple. The issue of payment arguably does not affect the child's welfare at all.

[7.12] Another concern in relation to the market in babies is the equation of property rights with human beings, with its resonances of slavery. The idea that one is purchasing

---

[14] The Guardian 15 Dec 1998, The Times 26 Oct 1999, quoted in Brazier, 'Can You Buy Children?' (1999) *Child and Fam Law Quarterly* Vol 11 No 4 at 345.

[15] Landes and Posner 'The Economics of the Baby Shortage' (1979) 7 Journal of Legal Studies 323 at 342.

[16] Landes and Posner, 'The Economics of the Baby Shortage' (1979) 7 Journal of Legal Studies 323 at 342.

[17] Landes and Posner, 'The Economics of the Baby Shortage' (1979) 7 Journal of Legal Studies 323 at 343.

a baby gives the impression that one is thereby free to do with one's property whatever one likes. However, this is untrue in relation to adoption and surrogacy because, *even if* one is said to buy a baby, this does not mean that the baby can be abused or neglected or mistreated,[18] as the laws forbidding such activities still apply to adoptive or commissioning parents. 'The laws against child abuse have never distinguished among different methods of acquiring custody of the child. Natural parents are not permitted to abuse a child because they are natural rather than adoptive parents.'[19]

[7.13] A problem often raised in this context is what happens when the child is born disabled. Although in an ordinary market scenario, the buyer could reject defective goods, parents (whether they are natural or adoptive parents) are not permitted to reject their baby simply because it does conform with their expectations. The welfare of the child must be considered along with that of the contracting parties, as: 'The child is an interested third party whose welfare would be disserved by a mechanical application of the remedies available to buyers in the market for inanimate goods.'[20]

[7.14] In a later article Posner deals specifically with the market engendered by surrogacy. He claims that the case for making surrogacy contracts legally enforceable from an economic perspective is straightforward. Such contracts are made by the parties in the belief that they will be mutually beneficial:

> The father and wife must believe that they will derive a benefit from having the baby that is greater than $10,000, or else they would not sign the contract. The surrogate must believe that she will derive a benefit from the $10,000 (more precisely, from what she will use the money for) that is greater than the cost to her of being pregnant and giving birth and then surrendering the baby. So *ex ante*, as an economist would say (i.e. before the fact), all the parties to the contract are made better off.[21]

[7.15] Of course, such an analysis fails to consider the effects of the contract on the non-party most closely affected by the contract, the child. However, Posner claims that it is more likely that the child is made better off by surrogacy than worse off. This is on the basis that without the contract the child would not be born at all, whereas with the contract the child becomes part of a family with at least one if not both genetic parents involved in its upbringing. Although studies on surrogate children are still at their early stages, there is no evidence thus far that such children grow up to regret that they were ever born or that they are any less stable or happy than natural children. The possibility that knowledge of the circumstances of his birth and the payment involved will have

---

18 There is no evidence to establish that children born of surrogacy arrangements are faced with any different problems than other children. Gostin states that there is 'no data to demonstrate that children born as the result of surrogacy contracts are worse off by any measure – that they suffer more neglect, abandonment, and physical abuse, or that they receive less nurturing and love.' Gostin, 'A Civil Liberties Analysis of Surrogacy Arrangements', in Gostin, (ed) *Surrogate Motherhood* (Indiana University Press, 1990) 3.

19 Posner, 'The Regulation of the Market in Adoptions' (1987) 67 Boston University Law Review 59 at 66.

20 Posner, 'The Regulation of the Market in Adoptions' (1987) 67 Boston University Law Review 59 at 67.

21 Posner, 'The Ethics and Economics of Enforcing Contracts of Surrogate Motherhood' (1989) 5 Journal of Contemporary Health Law and Policy 21 at 23.

detrimental effects on the child is no less than the possible effect on a child born through IVF or artificial insemination who will also at some point understand that his parents spent large sums of money to bring about his conception. Any such detriment remains unproven at present.

[7.16] In the Report of the Ethical Committee of the American Fertility Society,[22] the Committee rejected the buying and selling of infants as demeaning to all parties involved. However, they agreed that payment should be possible for a surrogate's time, risk and inconvenience.[23] This might include monetary compensation[24] for pre- and postpartum leave from a job, and could include the entire period from the woman's first involvement with the commissioning couple to the end of maternity leave:

> This policy respects the autonomous choices of adults who agree to become involved in reproduction, while at the same time attempting to avoid inappropriate commercialisation and to protect the welfare of children who may result from the new reproductive technologies and arrangements.

[7.17] In Ireland, the Report of the Commission on Assisted Human Reproduction also made a similar recommendation in 2005. The Commission was concerned with the possibility of commercial interests being involved in surrogacy and felt that participants in surrogacy should not profit from such arrangements. It said:

> The prohibition on commercialisation reflects a concern that by placing a monetary value on a woman's reproductive capacity, the inherent value of women and children is implicitly undermined. Surrogate mothers should not suffer financial loss, but there should be no element of profit involved in the arrangement.[25]

It therefore recommended that women who decide to participate as surrogate mothers should be entitled to receive reimbursement of expenses directly related to such participation.

Welfare of the surrogate mother

[7.18] Another common objection to surrogacy is the potential for the economic exploitation of women. It is argued that the women who become surrogates are

---

[22] 'Ethical Considerations of the New Reproductive Technologies' (1990) 53: 6 Fertility and Sterility at 20.

[23] This is also the position in New Zealand where payments to a surrogate mother referred to as maintenance, and containing no element of profit relating to the adoption of the child, do not contravene adoption laws. See *Re P (Adoption:Surrogacy)* [1990] NZFLR 385.

[24] Gostin argues that banning payment for gestational services (as opposed to termination of parental rights) would deprive the woman of the right to be paid for valued labour:
'They are entitled to economic gain for the physical changes in their bodies, the changes in lifestyle, the work of carrying a fetus, and the pain and medical risk of labour and parturition. Critics of surrogacy assert that it enslaves the woman. But performing personal services and labour in exchange for money is not equivalent to slavery. There is no slave-master relationship, no involuntary peonage, and no entitlement to control any human being.'
Gostin, 'A Civil Liberties Analysis of Surrogacy Arrangements' (1988) 16:1–2 Law, Medicine and Health Care 7–17 at 10.

[25] Report of the Commission on Assisted Human Reproduction (Government Publications Office, 2005), p 50.

financially impoverished and have few employment prospects. Thus, it is said they are women whose financial circumstances therefore may make them more likely to be influenced by the prospect of the monetary compensation offered by surrogacy and may be tempted to participate against their better judgment.

[7.19] Steinbock agrees that a practice that exploits people or violates human dignity is immoral, but she argues that surrogacy is not guilty on either of these counts.[26] She says that the mere fact that pregnancy is risky does not make surrogate agreements exploitative or morally wrong, as people often do risky things for money. There is a sense that surrogacy is morally wrong because of its potential for coercion and exploitation – a sense that no one would do it unless driven by poverty. However, most surrogates choose the surrogate role primarily because the fee provides a better economic opportunity than alternative occupations, but also because they enjoy being pregnant. Some derive a feeling of self-worth from an act they regard as highly altruistic: providing a couple with a child they could not otherwise have. 'If these motives are present, it is far from clear that the surrogate is being exploited. Indeed, it seems objectionably paternalistic to insist that she is.'[27]

[7.20] Surrogacy has been a divisive issue in the feminist academic community, as the issues involved focus on the potential exploitation of women, the paternalism of men, the stereotypical image of women as nurturers and the capability of women to enter into contracts involving their reproductive capacity for profit.[28] On one hand, concerns have been raised about exploitation, with images depicted of poor, uneducated women enlisted to produce babies for wealthy men and their wives, either because of fertility problems, or because pregnancy is simply too inconvenient for those women who can afford to hire someone to do it for them. On the other hand, there is the spectre of the State passing laws, once again, that tell women what they can and cannot do with their bodies. The traditional patriarchal allegations that 'biology is destiny' have always infuriated feminists, who claim rather that it is male domination and oppression that have cast women into the role of homemaker and mother. However, some feminists now argue against the insistence by men that surrogacy contracts should be enforced, on the grounds that women who enter into these arrangements are not giving a fully informed consent. They claim that the surrogate does not know, when she enters into the contract, how she will be affected by the hormonal changes brought about by pregnancy and the

---

[26] Steinbock, 'Surrogate Motherhood as Prenatal Adoption' (Law, Medicine and Ethics, 1988) 16: 1–2, p 47.

[27] Steinbock, 'Surrogate Motherhood as Prenatal Adoption' (Law, Medicine and Ethics, 1988) 16: 1–2, p 48.

[28] Seven different feminist positions on surrogacy may be detected, ranging from liberalist; through acceptance with strict regulation; acceptance of traditional though not gestational surrogacy; acceptance of familial surrogacy only; acceptance of same-race surrogacy only; acceptance of contract surrogacy on certain conditions; and acceptance on the fulfilment of certain medical prerequisites by the commissioning parents. Van Dyck, *Manufacturing Babies and Public Consent* (New York University Press, 1995) at 172–3. See also Mahoney, 'An Essay on Surrogacy and Feminist Thought' (1988) 16 Law, Medicine and Health Care 81.

bonding process which may take place with the growing foetus[29]. Therefore it is impossible for her to determine how she will feel about relinquishing the child.

[7.21] Some feminists argue that if surrogacy is prohibited by legislation, this will be unduly restrictive of women's reproductive choices. After all, men are free to donate or, in some countries, sell their sperm so women should also be able to donate or sell their reproductive potential. Any difference in treatment between the male and female roles might thus be argued to be discriminatory against women. However, if anti-surrogacy legislation was framed as prohibiting baby selling rather than as protecting women, and if it applied to prevent both men and women from entering into surrogacy contracts, it would be less likely to be viewed as discriminatory.[30]

[7.22] In relation to the motivation of surrogate mothers and the extent to which it might be argued that financial reward might influence their decision-making such as to negate their appreciation of the risks and consequences of their participation, research shows that the typical surrogate mother, at least in the Western World, does not appear to be so economically desperate that the promise of financial reward would coerce her into doing something she does not want to do. A study done in the 1980s in the United States indicates that surrogate mothers are largely drawn from the middle-class and have sufficient experience and education to understand the physical and emotional risks involved.[31] Parker found that there were several factors involved in the women's agreement to become a surrogate mother – the financial advantages, enjoyment of pregnancy and the perception that the advantages of relinquishment outweighed the disadvantages. This was based on two components – firstly, the wish to give the gift of a child to a couple who could not have one, and, secondly, for some of the women it enabled them to master unresolved feelings they had in relation to a previous voluntary loss of a child.

[7.23] Many women in fact volunteer to become surrogates for reasons other than financial ones. Some women choose surrogacy not only for the fee involved but also because they enjoy being pregnant and the respect and attention that it draws.[32] Generally, the concept of remuneration is de-emphasised by both the surrogate mothers and the intended parents, which fosters the sense of the pregnancy being a 'gift' from the surrogate to the couple, and also conforms to the culturally held belief that children are priceless. However, most surrogates feel that it would be unreasonable to expect them to give birth and relinquish the child with no compensation, even if this only covers reimbursement of expenses. In a study of women taking part in contract pregnancies in the US, it was noted that the women rarely spent the money on themselves, but used it to buy things for their families, perhaps as a reward for the disruption to their home and family life during the pregnancy.[33] Altruism, as a

---

29   Hassenthaler, 'Gestational Surrogacy: Legal Implications of Reproductive Technology' (1995) 21 North Carolina Central Law Journal 169 at 177.

30   Mahoney, 'An Essay on Surrogacy and Feminist Thought' (1988) 16 Law, Medicine and Health Care at 82.

31   Parker, 'Motivation of Surrogate Mothers: Initial Findings' (1983) 140 Am J Psychiatry 117.

32   Robertson, 'Surrogate Mothers: Not So Novel After All' (1983) 13 Hastings Center Report, No 5.

33   Ragone, *Surrogate Motherhood: Conception in the Heart* (Westview Press, 1994).

motivation for surrogates, can be seen from the applications of some surrogates as including enjoyment of pregnancy, a protest against abortion, having a perfect birth and a wish to give a baby to a couple who could not have one.[34] Some women applied who had previously had an abortion or given a baby up for adoption, surrogacy allowing them to assuage the guilt they may have felt. While this may seem strange to many, for behavioural scientists it is a well-known aspect of some gift relationships. It provides a means of redressing balances that have been upset.[35]

[7.24] In addition to the concerns about possible exploitation of the surrogate mother, there has also been unease about the potentially adverse effects of surrogacy on the surrogate mothers, particularly in relation to the distress of relinquishment of the baby. There is a concern that either the surrogate mother would bond with the baby during pregnancy and she would find it very difficult to hand over the child to the commissioning couple, or that she may distance herself from the pregnancy by reinforcing the belief that the child is not hers, thus making her more likely to put her health and that of the child at risk. The risk of post-natal depression and feelings of anger or guilt may all put a further strain on her psychological health. There may also be a negative impact on her partner and children, with the potential for ostracisation in the community.

[7.25] Very little research has been done on the experiences of surrogate mothers other than small studies exploring their motivation. However, the concerns outlined in the preceding paragraph were explored in the largest and most representative systematic study to date in the UK in 2003, in which it was found that surrogate mothers do not generally experience major problems in their relationship with the commissioning couple, in handing over the baby or from the reactions of those around them. The emotional problems experienced by some surrogate mothers in the weeks following the birth appeared to lessen over time.[36] The study found that 91% of women were motivated by wanting to help a childless couple, 15% were motivated by enjoyment of pregnancy while 3% were motivated by payment. In the weeks immediately following relinquishment of the baby, 32% of women experienced some difficulties but these were not severe, tended to be short-lived and resolved within a number of weeks or months. One year after the birth, all of the women were happy with their decision to relinquish custody of the child and none had any doubts about the decision. The degree of continuing contact with the child varied from case to case, with some (41%) of the women feeling a special bond with the child but none of the women feeling that the

---

[34]   In her study, Ragone noted that the majority of surrogates were either housewives and mothers or were in occupations with limited prospects. She hypothesised that a highly attractive aspect of surrogacy was the opportunity it gave them to transcend their everyday roles, and to participate in something where everybody treated them as special. This was also touched on by four of Blyth's subjects, who perceived surrogacy as doing something valuable and unusual. One woman said, 'I wanted to do something that was out of the ordinary and that made me a little bit special'. MacCallum points out that while there is no intrinsic harm in this motivation, problems may arise when the pregnancy is over, the child is relinquished and the surrogate mother is no longer receiving this special attention.

[35]   For example, see Schwartz, 'The Social Psychology of the Gift' (1967) Am J Soc 1.

[36]   Jadva et al, 'Surrogacy: The Experiences of Surrogate Mothers' (2003) Human Reproduction Vol 18, No 10 pp 2196–2204.

child was like their own. Surrogate mothers were generally open with family and friends about the arrangement and while some received initial negative reactions, these people later accepted the idea and the majority of surrogate mothers reported that their partners and children were positive and supportive. The authors conclude that:

> Overall, surrogacy appears to be a positive experience for surrogate mothers. Women who decide to embark upon surrogacy often have completed a family of their own and feel they wish to help a couple who would not otherwise be able to become parents. The present study lends little support to the commonly held expectation that surrogate mothers will experience psychological problems following the birth of the child.

[7.26] The experiences of commissioning couples were also studied by the same authors in a separate study in 2003.[37] This study found that couples had considered surrogacy only after a long period of infertility and when it was the only option available. Relationships with the surrogate mothers were generally good and continued after the birth. All couples had told family and friends about the surrogacy and were planning to tell the child. The authors conclude that commissioning couples generally perceived the surrogacy arrangement as a positive experience.

[7.27] From a public policy perspective, there are those who believe that surrogacy is inherently immoral, and it is irrelevant whether the surrogate mother has entered into the contract for altruistic reasons or has insisted on a fee. Some might believe that a woman might make a competent and fully informed legitimate decision to become a surrogate (such as one sister becoming a surrogate for another sister) but that, despite the clarity of her decision, she should not be allowed to make such an agreement, as it is a commodification of the child and a debasement of the mother-child relationship. It is argued that a court is entitled and perhaps obliged to act paternalistically to limit freedom of contract for the purpose of protecting potential surrogate mothers from class bias, inequality of bargaining power and infringement of individual rights.[38] On the other hand, as well as those who support regulated commercial surrogacy, there are those who would support the idea of surrogacy if there was no exchange of money involved. This is because they believe that the financial element to the arrangement must have a negative effect on the child. This is considered further below.

[7.28] The argument to prohibit surrogacy for money is based on the belief that only a woman under extreme financial hardship would agree to such a contract. Therefore, she must be protected by ensuring that she only enters into such an arrangement for

---

[37] MacCallum et al, 'Surrogacy: The Experiences of Commissioning Couples' (2003) Human Reproduction Vol 18 No 6, 1334–1342.

[38] Celeste Schejbal-Vossmeyer, 'What Money Cannot Buy: Commercial Surrogacy and the Doctrine of Illegal Contracts' (1988) 32 Saint Louis Univ LJ 1171 at 1199. The author disputes the claims by some feminists that surrogacy empowers women by enabling them to take their reproductive potential into the market-place, by taking the view that instead surrogacy enables women to sign away their rights, thereby providing men with a convenient means by which to go back in time to an era when women had no legal rights to custody of their children. She concludes that surrogacy contracts are illegal at common law and principles of freedom of contract are outweighed by the compelling interests of the children born under such arrangements. Therefore public policy considerations should justify the unenforcement of such contracts.

altruistic reasons. However, when the woman makes this agreement she never expects to keep the child, she intentionally conceives the child with the intention of giving it up.[39] This is sufficient to differentiate the surrogacy situation with the baby-selling contract which has often been used as an analogy to surrogacy. In the latter situation, the woman is usually already pregnant and is under financial strain when she is offered an escape from her problems through selling her unborn child.

[7.29] It may be argued that it is insufficient to say that women who enter into surrogacy are vulnerable to exploitation because they are poor. Their motivation for entering the agreement should not invalidate an otherwise valid arrangement. If the goal is to protect the surrogate mother who enters into the contract not fully appreciative of the consequences of her decision, milder forms of paternalistic intervention can be imposed to protect her. Traditional contract law protects anyone who lacks the mental capacity or is otherwise under duress or coercion from their bad decisions. To presuppose that a woman is incompetent to enter into such a contract for economic enrichment may be to label women, especially poor ones, as incompetent.

> We need to be careful that we do not rationalize the need for laws that restrict women's freedom on the basis that women need to be protected from their own mistakes in judgement. Because women historically are a disenfranchised group, such restrictive laws quickly move from being 'benignly' paternalistic to being viciously sexist and classist.[40]

Welfare of the child

[7.30] It is sometimes claimed that surrogacy may be harmful to the future child due to psychological problems it may suffer as a result of the method of its conception. Steinbock argues that although feelings of worthlessness are harmful and can prevent people from living happy, fulfilling lives, a surrogate child, even one whose life is miserable because of those feelings, cannot claim to have been harmed by the surrogate agreement.

> Without the agreement, the child would not have existed. Unless she is willing to say that her life is not worth living because of these feelings, that she would be better off never

---

[39] This concept is difficult for us to accept, as we have a notion of mothers being devoted, selfless, generous women who could not choose separation from their children. However, surrogates have said that they see themselves in a different light: they do not regard the child as theirs. It is reasonable to surmise that the surrogate may love the child partially, within boundaries that she has set for herself, knowing that the child is someone else's. Sanger says that surrogacy forces us to accept or acknowledge that motherhood is not an all-or-nothing proposition. Women sometimes elect to experience degrees of motherhood, such as in fostering where women perform an extraordinary social function in providing maternal care to children between two sets of mothers, natural and adoptive. These women are encouraged to feel the opposite of maternal love (unless they are going to adopt the foster child), as they know that separation from the foster child is inevitable. This form of partial mothering is applauded and financially compensated. Why is it so difficult then to accept a surrogate's decision to experience only part of motherhood? See Sanger, 'Separating From Children' (1996) 96 Columbia Law Review 375 at 494–5.

[40] Rush, 'Touchdowns, Toddlers, and Taboos: On Paying College Athletes and Surrogate Contract Mothers' 31 Ariz L Rev 549 (1989) pp 609–610.

having been born, she cannot claim to have been harmed by being born of a surrogate mother.[41]

[7.31] Although there have been only a small number of reliable studies carried out in relation to the impact of surrogacy on the children themselves, and the children studied have been very young, the evidence thus far suggests that any fears are unfounded. In a longitudinal study in the UK, which published reports in 2003 and 2006, the authors concluded that the commissioning mothers showed more positive parent-child relationships with the children, and the fathers reported lower levels of parenting stress, than their natural conception counterparts. They found that surrogacy does not appear to impact negatively on parenting or child development.[42] The authors found this to be consistent with previous studies of assisted reproduction families that showed greater warmth and emotional involvement between parents and children than in natural conception families. They are of the view that these couples who have gone to great lengths to have a child are thus more likely to be highly motivated and committed parents. The children themselves did not differ from naturally conceived children with respect to socio-emotional or cognitive development. The authors conclude that a gestational or genetic bond with the child is of less importance for positive maternal representations of the mother-child relationship than a strong desire for parenthood. They emphasise, however, that the children in this study were not yet aware of the nature of their birth and 'it is not until they grow older and acquire an understanding of their unusual family situation that the impact of surrogacy for parents and children can be fully understood.'

ENFORCEABILITY OF THE SURROGACY CONTRACT

[7.32] There are no cases on surrogacy to date in Ireland. In other jurisdictions surrogacy has received a mixed response, with some states refusing to enforce it on grounds of public policy, others dealing with it solely as a custody dispute between the birth mother and biological father and others enforcing it on contractual grounds. The cases that have come to judicial attention have largely been in the context of custody disputes between the commissioning couple and the surrogate mother.

[7.33] Where the surrogate mother changes her mind and refuses to relinquish the baby, a number of legal issues arise. Although surrogacy may be largely considered as a social or family law issue, it has its legal roots in the bargain made between the surrogate and the commissioning couple. 'A surrogate mother provides a strange blend of intimate services and products. She permits a doctor to artificially inseminate her, carries a child to term, and in nine months delivers a new born child to whoever hired her. She sells her ovum, her ability to nurture a single cell into an infant and all her future claims to rear

---

[41] Steinbock, 'Surrogate Motherhood as Prenatal Adoption' (Law, Medicine and Ethics, 1988) 16: 1–2, p 49.

[42] Golombok et al. 'Surrogacy Families: Parental Functioning, Parent-Child Relationships and Children's Psychological Development at Age 2' (2006) Journal of Child Psychology and Psychiatry 47:2 pp 213–222 at 213.

the child she bears.'[43] One of the main issues, therefore, is whether a surrogacy contract will be upheld as valid and enforceable.

[7.34] One of the first cases to come to judicial attention in the United States was the *Baby M* case.[44] In this well-known case, Mary Beth Whitehead, a married mother of two children, agreed to be inseminated with the sperm of William Stern and to relinquish the child to him for a fee of $10,000. Mr Stern was a biochemist and his wife, Elizabeth, was a paediatrician who had MS which, although it did not render her infertile, would have been exacerbated by pregnancy. When the baby was born, Mrs Whitehead handed her over to the Sterns as promised but, a few days later, changed her mind and asked the Sterns to let her have custody of the child for a short while. The Sterns reluctantly agreed to this course of action. Mrs Whitehead, however, subsequently refused to give the child back to the Sterns and fled the jurisdiction. After a period of some months the police seized the child and returned her to the Sterns, whereupon a lengthy custody battle ensued.

[7.35] At the trial, Judge Sorkow held that the surrogacy contract was valid and that specific performance of it was in the best interests of the child. He said the contract was not baby selling: 'The money to be paid to the surrogate is not being paid for the surrender of the child to the father ... he cannot purchase what is already his.' He felt the contract was merely a contract for services. Immediately following his decision he also enabled Mrs Stern to legally adopt the baby.

[7.36] The decision was appealed to the New Jersey Supreme Court, which reversed Judge Sorkow in relation to the validity of the contract. The Court held that a surrogacy contract, which provides for payment to the surrogate and for her irrevocable consent to the surrender of her child at birth, is invalid and unenforceable.[45] As a result, the adoption order granted by Judge Sorkow was improperly granted and Mrs Whitehead was the child's legal mother.[46] However, it was further decided that the sole determining

---

43 'Rumpeltstiltskin Revisited: The Inalienable Rights of Surrogate Mothers' 99 Harvard Law Review 1936.

44 *In re Baby M*, 525 A, 2d 1128, 217 NJ Super 313 (Superior Ct Chancery Div 1987), reversed on appeal, 1988 West Law 6251 (NJ Supreme Ct, 3 February 1988).

45 It has been argued that the application of existing legal precepts to this novel situation was misguided, as the courts are not equipped to deal with matters of social policy. Bezanson argues thus:
    'The surrogacy dispute in *Baby M* provided the court with an issue as to which there is no law. Existing statutory provisions and common law doctrines are relevant to the surrogacy question only as they are grounded on assumptions about parentage, family, and the reproductive process. But these assumptions are simply irrelevant to the dilemmas posed by surrogacy arrangements, and by many other reproductive technology issues as well. There was no right or wrong answer in the *Baby M* case, but there is a lesson to be learned. Courts are not equipped to create fundamental social policy. Our society's basic moral and ethical values must be shaped and expressed through the pluralistic legislative process, not in court. The *Baby M* court should have decided only the question of *Baby M*'s custody, based on its determination of the child's best interests.' Bezanson, 'Solomon Would Weep: A Comment on *In the Matter of Baby M* and the Limits of Judicial Authority' (1988)16:1–2 Law, Medicine and Health Care 126–130, at 126.

46 When Baby M (Melissa Stern) turned 18 years of age she initiated the process of allowing Elizabeth Stern to adopt her, terminating Whitehead's parental rights.

factor in a custody dispute was the child's best interests, and in the instant case this meant that the child should remain in the custody of the Sterns. It was also provided that the surrogate mother should have visitation rights in respect of the child. The result reached in this case – that Mr Stern was the child's legal father and Mrs Whitehead was her legal mother, was described by some as 'the worst result possible'.[47]

[7.37] The sensationalist facts of this case led to the kind of media attention and public outrage that one has come to expect from a custody battle of this nature.[48] The public were caught up in the intricacies of Mary Beth Whitehead's relationship with her husband and children; the financial details of both couples; the suitability of both women as mothers, and the psychological well-being of all of the parties. The case raised comments about the needs of children, such as whether they should focus on financial and educational benefits or emotional bonds. It conjured up fears that surrogacy would be used for the convenience of wealthy professional couples who could exploit an impoverished woman in order to avoid the bother of being pregnant.[49] Many commentators criticised the assessment made of Mrs Whitehead's ability to be a good mother as being based on middle-class prejudices and the evidence of mental health officials who testified at the hearing. Although the Court did not find her to be an unfit mother to her other children, 'she was portrayed as immature, untruthful, hysterical, overly identified with her children, and prone to smothering their independence.'[50] As

---

[47]   Bezanson, 'Solomon Would Weep: A Comment on *In the Matter of Baby M* and the Limits of Judicial Authority' (1988)16:1–2 Law, Medicine and Health Care 126–130, at 126.

[48]   There has also been a flood of academic writing on the case. See, for example: Brandel, 'Legislating Surrogacy: A Partial Answer to Feminist Criticism' (1995) 54 Maryland Law Review 488; Steinbock, 'Surrogate Motherhood as Prenatal Adoption' in Gostin (ed) *Surrogate Motherhood: Politics and Privacy* (Indiana University Press, 1990) 123–28.
   Carney, 'Where Do the Children Go? – Surrogate Mother Contracts and the Best Interests of the Child' (1988) XXII Suffolk Univ Law Review 1187; Dolgin, 'Status and Contract in Surrogate Motherhood: An Illumination of the Surrogacy Debate' (1990) 90 Daily Journal Report 2; Hey, 'Assisted Conception and Surrogacy – Unfinished Business' (1993) 26 The John Marshall Law Review 775; Klinke, 'The *Baby M* Controversy: A Class Distinction' (1993) 18 Oklahoma City Univ. Law Review 113; Johnson, 'The *Baby M* Decision: Specific Performance of a Contract for Specially Manufactured Goods' (1987) 11 Southern Illinois Univ LJ 1339; Recht, "M' is for Money: *Baby M* and the surrogate motherhood controversy'(1988) 37 The American Univ. Law Review 1013.

[49]   This was on the basis that it was disputed whether Mrs Stern was actually infertile or not. It seems that she was probably suffering from multiple sclerosis and could have risked paralysis by becoming pregnant. See 'Father Recalls Surrogate Was Perfect' (1987) Jan. 6, New York Times B2.

[50]   Steinbock, 'Surrogate Motherhood as Prenatal Adoption' (Law, Medicine and Ethics, 1988) 16: 44 at 46. Steinbock says that it is clear that Mrs Whitehead should not have been accepted as a suitable surrogate mother in the first place and that her uncertainty about giving up the child during the pregnancy should have alerted others to the potential problems which lay ahead. Also, it is unusual for the surrogate to be given the baby; rather, the adoptive parents are involved in the birthing process and are handed the child at birth, which serves to promote their bonding and lessen the surrogate mother's pain at the separation.

the New Jersey Supreme Court concluded, the application of the best-interests test boils down to a judgment call regarding the "likely future happiness of a human being.'[51]

[7.38] There have been many criticisms of this case on various levels, including the sense that if Mrs Whitehead had not fled the jurisdiction, which led Judge Sorkow to order the return of the baby to the Sterns, and which also influenced the subsequent decision that the child had been so long in the custody of the Sterns that it would be detrimental to the child to reverse that order, the decision may have been different. Nevertheless on the actual facts of the case, the issue of custody appears to have been correctly decided. The instability of the Whitehead's marriage, the educational concerns for the child and the period of time spent in the care of the Sterns, all combine to suggest that the child's best interests were correctly served by granting custody to the only parents she had known in her life at that stage. Commentators also criticised the granting of visitation rights to Mrs Whitehead on the grounds that this was not likely to be in Baby M's best interests and would serve to undermine the Stern's parental authority.

[7.39] On what grounds could a court decline to enforce a surrogacy contract? Contracts may be invalidated through the operation of the doctrines of mistake, misrepresentation, duress and undue influence, incapacity and illegality. In surrogacy the terms of the contract are not generally unduly complex or difficult to understand. The parties agree that the surrogate mother would be inseminated or have an embryo transferred to her uterus, would carry the child to term, and upon its birth would relinquish custody to the commissioning couple (usually) in exchange for a sum of money agreed between them. This does not leave very much scope for mistake or misrepresentation between the parties, unless on some minor matter. More important, here, are arguments that due to an inequality of bargaining power between the surrogate mother and the commissioning couple, the validity of the contract must be in doubt.

[7.40] In the debate over surrogate motherhood, different perspectives about the nature of human choice tend to become entangled with moral judgments about the mother's decision to surrender custody of her child. Those who view the mother's decision to surrender custody as unnatural or reprehensible explain her decision in terms of financial pressures 'overcoming' her free will. Those who emphasise the benefit to infertile couples from surrogacy arrangements are more likely to view the mother's choice as a rational decision in which the financial payment makes more attractive an option which could be justified on non-monetary grounds.[52] Whether contract principles

---

[51]   *In re Baby M* 217 NJ Super, 313, 525 A 2d 1128 (NJ Super Ct Ch Div 1987) at 2024. See also Goldstein, Freud and Solnit, *Beyond the Best Interests of the Child* (New York, Free Press, 1973).

[52]   Carbone, 'The Role of Contract Principles in Determining the Validity of Surrogacy Contracts' (1988) 28 Santa Clara Law Review 581 at 600. Carbone examines the validity of using contract principles in domestic arrangements and why they have not been so used traditionally. She analyses the different characteristics present in commercial and domestic arrangements, such as the difference in equality between the parties, the implications for those outside the contract and the willingness of the judiciary to interfere in any dispute which may arise. She finds that contract has not been seen as the governing principle in family relationships due to these differences where status is seen as more important in determining rights and obligations. (contd.../)

can offer any solutions to reconcile these opposite viewpoints is very much open to question.[53]

[7.41] Although there was a traditional reluctance to involve the law in domestic matters, Carbone argues that the role of contract in governing family relationships is growing. 'Family matters, and, indeed, intimate relationships generally, are no longer a separate world into which contract and the courts dare not tread.'[54] In relation to solving custody disputes in surrogacy, she says that apart from a symbolic affront to traditional values in ensuring mothers' commitment to their children, it is difficult to identify a societal interest that is in fact injured by surrogacy arrangements.[55] 'The pregnancy is not accidental. Indeed, the parents conceive the child with far more advance thought, care and commitment than attends the conception of most children. The mother is not abandoning the child. She is simply agreeing that the child's father, who can be screened for fitness, will have custody.'[56]

[7.42] It is often argued that a woman is not capable of knowing in advance whether she will be able to relinquish custody of the child she has carried. In an ordinary pregnancy many factors, biological, emotional and social, combine to reinforce a woman's bond with the unborn child. Do these factors suggest that no woman can give a truly informed consent to an agreement to surrender custody of a child until after she has experienced the birth of that child? Or does it mean that a decision made at a time prior to conception would be more likely to be more dispassionate and more presumptively valid?[57]

---

52   (\...contd) However, she also examines the increasing willingness to incorporate contract principles into family law on a case-by-case basis to overcome specific problems. Public policy is also of relevance here in the reinforcement of traditional morality and societal norms and presumptions. In *Re Baby M*, (discussed above at para **7.34**) the Court phrased much of its discussion, according to Carbone, on contract principles but interprets and applies those principles using a moral bias derived from normative standards. In the absence of legislative intervention, she concludes that the uncertainty inherent in such compromises is more dangerous to the children, the couples and society than the agreements themselves could ever be.

53   Freeman says that the law of contract is 'a blunt instrument which cannot adequately tackle the problems spawned by the issue of surrogacy.' He demonstrates this by examining the question of remedies. The enforcement of a surrogacy arrangement by specific performance of the contract, he says, would 'smack of a form of slavery' and would not be contemplated by any court. Freeman, 'Children's Rights in Surrogacy' 16 Childright 8. Similarly, Singer and Wells, 'The Reproduction Revolution: New Ways of Making Babies' (OUP, 1984) at 122 say: '[t]he compulsion involved would be of a uniquely odious form. The contract is not like an ordinary contract for services, since its fulfilment involves a physical invasion of the contractor's body. The surrogate could not, like any other contractor, walk out of the work-place. She is the work-place.'

54   Carbone, 'The Role of Contract Principles in Determining the Validity of Surrogacy Contracts' (1988) Vol 28 Santa Clara Law Rev 581 at 589.

55   Carbone, 'The Role of Contract Principles in Determining the Validity of Surrogacy Contracts' (1988) Vol 28 Santa Clara Law Rev 581 at p 594.

56   Carbone, 'The Role of Contract Principles in Determining the Validity of Surrogacy Contracts' (1988) Vol 28 Santa Clara Law Rev 581.

57   Carbone, 'The Role of Contract Principles in Determining the Validity of Surrogacy Contracts' (1988) Vol 28 Santa Clara Law Rev 581 at p 597.

Conclusions about the utility and morality of surrogacy will colour discussion of these questions, as those who object to surrogacy are more likely to argue that women who enter into such contracts underestimate the bonding process, and thus any subsequent change of mind on the surrogate mother's part is both valid and correct. Proponents of surrogacy will argue that changes of mind are precisely the type of changes the contract is designed to guard against and that the appropriate response is counselling, advice and support for the surrogate mother prior to making the commitment, and at the time of relinquishment of the child.

[7.43] In *Johnson v Calvert*[58] a black woman acted as a surrogate for a white couple for a fee of $10,000. The Court acknowledged that women of lower means typically served as surrogates but the Court said that there was no proof that surrogate contracts exploited these women to any greater degree than the general exploits of poorly paying and undesirable employment.[59] The Court pointed out that the wages being paid to surrogates are on a par with the wages being paid to the same category of women hired as childcarers and housekeepers, work which also takes them away from their own homes and families.

> Why is it "exploitation" to give these women the free choice of opting to earn money while remaining at home, or perhaps earning more money while performing their previous jobs and, at the same time, also serving as a gestator? Rather than exploiting women, commercial surrogacy will liberate many women by allowing them to engage in employment that is less distasteful and more remunerative than their present choices.[60]

[7.44] It has been argued, however, that the payment of $10,000 for nine months work is equivalent to a wage of $1.54 per hour, and that this is similar to the condemned 'sweat-shop' wages referred to by the Court and clearly exploitative.[61] However, although such

---

58   *Johnson v Calvert* (1993) 851 P.2d 776 (Cal Sup Ct).
59   *Johnson v Calvert* (1993) 851 P.2d 776 (Cal Sup Ct) at 785.
60   Ingram, 'Surrogate Gestator: A New and Honorable Profession' (1993) 76 Marquette Law Review 675 at 684. Ingram criticises the application of old legal codes and principles to new disputes as looking backward when science is looking forward. He examines the participants in gestational surrogacy arrangements, the reasons for their choices and the objections that have been taken thereto. He takes perhaps a rather simplistic view that because society generally does not consider it exploitative to expect people to perform difficult and dangerous tasks that they have freely undertaken, society should view gestational surrogacy in the same light. It must, however, be recognised that such an approach is naïve in its assumption that all dangerous tasks are equivalent in moral terms, as the potential for loss of life and limb which may be inherent in, say military combat, are very different considerations from the bringing into existence of a new life with all its inherent demands and possibilities, which occurs in surrogacy. In the former, one may make such a choice concerning one's own life but, in the latter, choices are being made about another person's life and very existence and therefore demand greater attention and consideration. He makes some admittedly facetious suggestions in the article (such as obliging all couples to adopt, as their third child, a hard-to-place child before being allowed to conceive again naturally) to draw attention to, what he considers, to be the unfairness of limiting potential opportunities available to infertile couples who have not chosen to be in the situation in which they find themselves.
61   Hessenthaler, 'Gestational Surrogacy: Legal Implications of Reproductive Technology' (1995) 21 North Carolina Central Law Journal 169 at 176. (contd.../)

low payments to employees may be considered to be morally unjust, they are nonetheless enforceable in law in the same way as any other contract.[62]

[7.45] It may be disputed whether the prospective surrogate mother has no choice but to enter into this agreement. It would appear that there are choices available to her but these are undesirable. She may want to use the contract fee to build an extension to her home, to get extra tuition for her children[63] or to re-furnish her house.[64] On the other hand, she may be *in extremis* and may need the money for specialist medical care or other non-luxury items. Usually a person who makes a voluntary choice from a set of available alternatives cannot revive a choice rejected under a claim of duress.[65] The fact that there was a way to avoid the threat or coercion weakens a party's right to complain later about the result. The consideration of alternatives also involves taking into account the alleged victim's personal circumstances and characteristics, which may include her reasonable beliefs about the alternatives open to her.[66] In the case of a surrogate mother she might claim, for example, that her financial hardship was such that unless she obtained a lump sum payment, a financial institution would foreclose on her mortgage, which was heavily in arrears, and she would be homeless.[67] The fact that there are alternatives open to her must be taken into account in deciding whether her will was coerced in entering this contract but her personal beliefs and characteristics must also be considered here.

---

[61] (\...contd) This article gives a detailed description of the facts of the Calvert case, the trial proceedings, and the concurring and dissenting judgments. The author disputes the Supreme Court's assertion that Constitutional rights were not implicated in the case because the surrogate was free to terminate the pregnancy at will. She says that the decision is lacking in substance and is patronising to women by paying mere lip-service to the importance of the gestator's role in bringing the child into existence. She takes the view that although surrogacy has enabled women to fulfil their maternal instincts in circumstances where the infertility would otherwise have prevented this, the masses of women who are physically and psychologically harmed by surrogacy far outweigh those who gain by it. The unanswered question resulting from the *Calvert case* is whether satisfaction of the strong desire to have one's own child is worth the social price of surrogacy.

[62] Freeman points out that a similar result would probably obtain were a matched sample of applications for a factory job to be considered: 'Is Surrogacy Exploitative?' in McLean (ed) *Legal Issues in Human Reproduction* (London: Gower, 1989) Ch 7.

[63] This was one of the reasons given by Mary Beth Whitehead, who was the surrogate mother in the *Baby M* Case, discussed at para **7.34**.

[64] 'Names and Faces' (1985) January 6, Boston Globe, A5, col 2.

[65] Bigwood, 'Coercion in Contract: The Theoretical Constructs of Duress' (1996) 46 University of Toronto LJ 201 at 263. Also see 'Duress and Undue Influence' 25 American Jurisprudence at 366.

[66] This is seen in cases where, for example, due to the existence of familial ties, a father is coerced into an improvident contract out of affection for his son who is in financial difficulties. See *Williams v Bayley* (1866) LR 1 HL 200.

[67] She might, for personal reasons, not wish to be dependant on the State for housing and welfare payments and, due to the fact that she has young children of her own, she may feel under pressure to avail of the opportunity presented by surrogacy.

FAMILY LAW ISSUES

[7.46] One of the central issues in dealing with surrogacy from a policy perspective is whether it should be regarded and treated simply as a contractual agreement, or a family law issue. 'The central policy issue is settling on the paradigm that should govern surrogate motherhood, a model of family relations (adoption) or of contractual relations (sale of a product or service). And the central legal issue is whether any restrictions on personal choice that follow from the policy selected – and especially from a rejection of the contractual model with its implication of free choice – are constitutionally permissible.'[68]

Surrogacy as a form of adoption

[7.47] Capron and Radin argue that surrogacy should be handled from the perspective of adoption, since existing law is inadequate to deal with surrogacy, and the emergence of surrogacy as a social practice does not require major law reform. Families in modern society have many different forms and, although certain core values are recognised by states as matters of legitimate concern for the state, nonetheless there is increasing latitude given to private ordering of families without State interference. The core values that are of relevance to surrogacy would include the protection of children's welfare and interests and the prevention of human exploitation. In light of concern for those values, states have adopted laws about parentage and adoption which aim to provide certainty and protection for children.

> These legal rules serve children's interest in having clearly identified people recognised from the moment of birth as their legal parents, with all the obligations and expectations consequent to this role. If the status of adult parties in relation to a newborn child is dependent on any contracts or other agreements they may have reached, then this status – and the rights and responsibilities that flow from it – may be thrown into doubt when contractual terms are unclear or when the contract is disavowed due to alleged breaches or other disagreements.[69]

[7.48] In many jurisdictions, agreements to relinquish parental rights are not permitted prior to the child's birth. Adoption statutes also typically provide for a period of time after relinquishment of the baby during which the birth mother may change her mind. Capron and Radin say that such provisions aim to balance several interests. On the one hand, the child needs unqualified acceptance and stability in its surroundings. This need is fostered by ensuring the people who are serving as caregivers are appropriate for that role and are confident that they will be able to keep the child. On the other hand, permitting the birth mother to change her mind reinforces a societal respect for biological ties and recognises that circumstances might force a woman to make a decision immediately after birth of a child that does not reflect her true wishes.

[7.49] It may be argued that the law should not differentiate between women who become pregnant pursuant to surrogacy contracts from those who become pregnant by

---

[68] Capron and Radin, 'Choosing Family Law Over Contract Law as a Paradigm for Surrogate Motherhood' (1988) Law Medicine & Health Care Vol 16:1–2 at 37.

[69] Capron and Radin, 'Choosing Family Law Over Contract Law as a Paradigm for Surrogate Motherhood' (1988) Law Medicine & Health Care Vol 16:1–2 at 35.

other means. Thus, the normal rules of adoption would apply to the transfer of parental status to the couple who will raise the child as their own. Any element of uncertainty created by restricting specific performance and allowing the surrogate to change her mind would simply serve to underline the need for caution by all parties involved. There is an obligation on the State to ensure the paramount importance of the child's best interests, whether the child is born to a surrogate mother or otherwise. One key advantage of bringing surrogacy within the ambit of adoption law is that it would involve the State in the process through assessment by social workers and the court procedure which is necessary to approve the adoption. This would mean that the child's best interests were protected by the rigorous screening procedures that exist prior to a couple being deemed suitable adopters. However, this may prove to be contentious in a case where the prospective adopters were deemed unsuitable, for example on age grounds or other criteria. In a case of gestational surrogacy where the prospective adopters are the genetic parents of the child, commitment to the principle that the child's best interests are paramount would presumably result in a refusal to allow the child to be adopted by its genetic parents, and the care of the child remaining with the surrogate mother if she was willing to take on that responsibility, or the child being adopted by an unrelated couple if she was not willing to do so.

[7.50] In some states, judicial pre-authorisation of the surrogacy arrangement is required by law in order to validate the arrangement.[70] For example, New Hampshire in the United States has a very extensive statutory scheme to regulate surrogacy arrangements.[71] Under that scheme, the intended parents must be married to each other and one of them must be genetically related to the child. The surrogacy arrangement must be judicially preauthorised. Evaluations and counselling of the parties must be conducted prior to impregnation of the surrogate. Such evaluations include home studies of all parties; the surrogate, the intended mother and the intended father. The agreement must be submitted in the form of a petition to Probate Court. At the hearing, the probate judge validates the surrogacy agreement after meeting with the parties, reviewing the agreement's terms and conditions, verifying that all the required counselling and appropriate evaluations have occurred and, finally, determines whether everything will be ultimately in the best interest of the resulting child.

[7.51] Under the law in New Hampshire the birth mother has the right to take all health-care decisions concerning the foetus, including any decision to abort. After the birth, the surrogate has 72 hours in which to decide whether to keep the child. Once parental rights are transferred to the intended parents, they have a duty to support the child. The child born under surrogacy is considered to be the legitimate child of the intended parent. Fees for surrogacy as negotiated between the parties are limited to medical expenses, lost wages, insurance, legal costs and home studies. New Hampshire laws prohibit fees for arranging a surrogacy contract. There are also provisions addressing issues of the contract being breached or terminated, termination and transfer of parental rights to intended parents, and intestate and testate succession in the context of children born in surrogacy.

---

[70] For details on legal provisions in all US states, see http://adoption.uslegal.com/surrogacy/ (accessed 2 June 2011).

[71] New Hampshire statute RSA §§ 168–B:1–B:32.

Custody disputes

[7.52] The most obvious conflict that can arise in a surrogate agreement involves both the surrogate and the couple seeking custody of the child.[72] In most jurisdictions the paramount consideration in such instances is that of the welfare and best interests of the child. This is necessarily determined on a case-by-case basis with an examination of the needs of the child and the ability of the parties to provide for those needs from a financial, psychological and emotional perspective.

[7.53] In surrogacy cases, unless a different approach is mandated by legislation, the judiciary has tended to adopt the same approach to the determination of custody disputes as in other cases. This can be seen in the classic US case *In Re Baby M* discussed earlier,[73] in which the New Jersey Supreme Court held that the sole determining factor in a custody dispute was the child's best interests.

[7.54] Reliance on the best interests of the child standard in these cases may yield the result that the child is adopted by the commissioning couple, who perhaps can afford to care for and educate the child to a higher standard than the surrogate mother. However, the welfare of the child depends not only on financial well-being but also, more importantly, on psychological security. In this sense, each party may be equally well placed to provide the care and nurturing necessary to rear a child. The court would no doubt be influenced by whether the surrogate mother had 'bonded' with the child or had relinquished custody at birth, although courts have in recent years accepted that ties of attachment have less to do with biological links and more to do with the psychological attachment that takes place after the child has reached the age of six months.

[7.55] A different approach, which has been taken in some jurisdictions, focuses on the intention of the parties when they deliberately chose to bring the child into existence. Thus, the contractual intent is enforced through recognition of legal parentage in the commissioning couple.[74] This can be seen in *Johnson v Calvert*,[75] in which the Supreme Court of California ruled that in a case of gestational surrogacy, the legal mother of the child is the genetic mother. The facts of this case involved a couple who agreed with a surrogate mother to pay her $10,000 in return for the surrogate bringing to term a child created from the gametes of the couple. During the course of the pregnancy the relationship between the couple and the surrogate mother deteriorated, and each party applied to court for a declaration of parentage. In relation to the contractual issue, the Court held there was no question of coercion or duress involved and it was unconvinced

---

[72] The numbers of cases in which this occurs is actually very small. In the US it is estimated at about 1 per cent – See Schuck, 'Some Reflections on the *Baby M* Case' (1988) 76 Geo LJ 1793 at 1801 fn 30, and in the UK about 4–5 per cent – see Surrogacy: Review for Health Ministers of Current Arrangements for Payments and Regulation (Cm 4068) (Department of Health, 1998) at para 3.38.

[73] See para **[7.34]**.

[74] This effectively allows the birth certificate of the child to record the commissioning couple as the legal parents. This may raise conflict of laws issues if the arrangement is entered into by non-US nationals who subsequently bring the child back to their own jurisdiction. This is discussed further below.

[75] *Johnson v Calvert* 851 P 2d 776 (Cal 1993). Also discussed above at para **7.43**.

that such contracts generally would exploit or dehumanise women of lower economic status.[76] It also dismissed any claim that by enforcing surrogacy contracts, the Court was recognising that children could be treated as mere commodities.[77]

[7.56] The Court held that each woman had a claim to be declared the legal mother of the child under existing Californian law: the surrogate by reason of having given birth to the child, and the commissioning mother on the basis of blood tests which showed her to be the genetic mother. An argument was put to the court by *amicus curiae* that in this situation the child should be recognised as having two legal mothers, but the Court rejected this approach. The Court preferred the claim of the genetic mother to be regarded as the legal mother, not, however, simply on the basis of the genetic link, but rather on the basis of the parties' intention when the surrogacy arrangement began. Panelli J, giving the majority judgment, said:

> The parties' aim was to bring Mark's and Crispina's [the commissioning couple] child into the world, not for them to donate a zygote to Anna [the surrogate]…Although the gestative function Anna performed was necessary to bring about the child's birth, it is safe to say that Anna would not have been given the opportunity to gestate or deliver the child had she, prior to implantation of the zygote, manifested her own intent to be the child's mother… she who intended to procreate the child – that is, she who intended to bring about the birth of a child that she intended to raise as her own – is the natural mother under California law.[78]

[7.57] The Court in this case concentrated on what has been described as the 'intellectual conception' of the child, and the 'but for' test in deciding the issue of parentage.[79] In other words, without the intention of the commissioning couple, this

---

[76] The Court said that 'there has been no proof that surrogacy contracts exploit poor women to any greater degree than economic necessity in general exploits them by inducing them to accept lower-paid or otherwise undesirable employment'. *Johnson v Calvert* 851 P 2d 776 (Cal 1993) at 785.

[77] The case has been criticised on many fronts. It has been argued that the facts of this case show how exploitative surrogacy can be in relation particularly to class and race distinctions, as the surrogate in this case was black, of African-American ancestry, had one child of her own and was on welfare. It may be argued that African-American and Hispanic women, who have fewer economic choices than Caucasian women, will be hired as gestators because they will accept lesser fees than Caucasian women. Russell-Brown describes the decision as 'a modern version of reproductive slavery.' Russell-Brown, 'Parental Rights and Gestational Surrogacy: An Argument Against the Genetic Standard' (1992) 23 Colum Hum Rts L Rev 525.

[78] Russell-Brown, 'Parental Rights and Gestational Surrogacy: An Argument Against the Genetic Standard' (1992) 23 Colum Hum Rts L Rev 525.

[79] Douglas, 'The Intention to Be a Parent and the Making of Mothers' (1994) 57 Modern Law Review 636. Douglas examines the focus in the *Johnson* case on intention and the consequences this may have for our attitudes to parenthood and family life generally. Due to men's physical incapacity to produce a child, is the reliance on intention to reproduce a convenient way to reinforce the male experience of reproduction and a concentration on the assertion of their parentage? If intention is to be the determining factor, how does this fit in with traditional norms of a two-parent heterosexual family? There would also be the difficulty of accommodating the welfare and interests of the child within this model, which itself is unpredictable and subjective. Proof of intention may not always be easy to find unless written evidence were forthcoming and it implies a willingness to consider children as forms of property that are freely alienable. (contd…/)

267

child would never have come into existence. The reliance on intention in family law matters is a relatively new trend, although it does have a weak precedent in relation to adoption and guardianship applications whereby an adult forms the intention to become a social parent and acts on that intention in order to legalise his/her relationship with the child. The law is perhaps becoming more cognisant of the idea of social or psychological parenting, which de-emphasises genetic or gestational parenting and concentrates on the rearing of the child.

[7.58] This reliance on intent may also be seen in a case which came before the California Supreme Court in 1998, *In Re Marriage of Buzzanca*.[80] The convoluted circumstances of this case are interesting, as they show just how complicated assisted reproduction may become. A married woman (Mrs X, who remained anonymous) decided to become an egg donor, on condition that she and her husband would have the opportunity to approve who was to get her eggs. One particular couple (Mr and Mrs Davidson) were approved for the donation. Seventeen eggs were harvested from Mrs X and fertilised with Mr Davidson's sperm. Four were implanted in Mrs Davidson, who gave birth to twins. The others were then available for further donation according to the consent form signed by Mr and Mrs Davidson (seemingly without the knowledge of the initial egg donor Mrs X or her husband). One of the embryos was implanted in the uterus of a surrogate, Mrs Snell, on behalf of another couple Mr and Mrs Buzzanca. A few weeks before the birth of the child, Mr and Mrs Buzzanca separated and divorce proceedings were instituted.

[7.59] In the divorce Mrs Buzzanca tried to get maintenance for the child but the Court ruled that Mr Buzzanca was not the child's legal father, as he had not contributed the sperm. Further, Mrs Buzzanca was held not to be the legal mother because she was neither the genetic nor the gestational mother. The surrogate was not the legal mother due to a contractual provision between the parties to that effect. The gamete donors and their spouses were unknown to the Court and not parties to the case. So the child, theoretically, had eight parents, but legally had none.

[7.60] The California Supreme Court eventually overturned this decision by relying on a principle that people should be held responsible for the reproductive outcomes of their actions. Therefore, Mr Buzzanca, who had consented to the surrogacy arrangement and intended to raise the resulting child, was imposed with legal fatherhood. Similarly, although Mrs Buzzanca was neither the genetic nor the gestational mother, she intended the child to be born, and she was held to be the legal mother. The case was simplified somewhat by the fact that the surrogate withdrew her claim for custody and the gamete providers were not involved.

[7.61] Other states in the US also hold that intent manifested in a surrogacy agreement offers another way, besides procreation and adoption, by which parentage can be

---

79   (\...contd) Underlying this article is the presumption that society retains its abhorrence of surrogacy and is still clinging on to traditional models of family life from which surrogacy radically departs. Douglas concludes that the *Johnson* case is a step closer to recognition of social as opposed to biological parenthood.

80   *In Re Marriage of Buzzanca* 61 Cal App 4th 1410, 72 Cal Reptr 2d 280 (1998).

established.[81] For example, Nevada law provides that a person identified as an intended parent in a surrogacy contract must be treated in law as a natural parent under all circumstances.[82] Similarly, Arkansas law provides that a child born to a surrogate mother is presumed to be the child of the biological father and the intended mother as long as the father is married.[83]

[7.62] A common criticism of the approach taken in these cases is that by concentrating on intent, the court is implicitly refusing to give the surrogate parental rights over the child she carried. This amounts to a denial of the fundamental importance of her role in nurturing the child for nine months in her womb. Essentially, the surrogate has complete control over the health and safety of the fetus, as it will be affected by her lifestyle, habits, diet and arguably her psychological and emotional health. Her choices as to consumption of alcohol, drugs, cigarettes, nutritional food, vitamin supplements and so on may, to a larger or lesser degree, have permanent effects on the developing child. The argument, therefore, is that if effects on the child are seen as sufficient to recognise the importance of the genetic input of the commissioning parents, then the surrogate should also be regarded as having made a vital contribution to the developing child. While this argument is a valid one, it does not, however, advance the question of who should have custody of the child in the event of a dispute.

[7.63] The use of intent in the determination of parenthood is significant, as it respects the understanding upon which the parties have relied in their arrangement. The parties rely on this understanding of their roles in their appreciation of the financial and emotional costs of becoming involved in surrogacy. Any rules which negative these commitments or create ambiguities where there were none in the minds of those who participated in the programme are, arguably, destructive of the autonomy of the individuals in shaping their reproductive futures. Since both the gestational and genetic mother play an essential role in the creation of the child, a legal determination of which of the two roles is more important is arbitrary.[84] There is no psychological evidence to support the proposition that a child is better or worse off being raised by a woman who is its genetic but not gestational mother and vice versa. There are objections to contract law being used in relation to parental status, such as in the inappropriateness of using commercial law doctrines in familial disputes, the failure of contract law to safeguard the best interests of the child, and the lack of appreciation of the emotional involvement of the parties. However, these objections may be countered by recognition that, while in sexual reproduction the intentions of the partners as to parenthood may be blurred, in cases of surrogacy the demarcation lines are firmly drawn in advance of the process taking place at all. It may thus be argued that the law should recognise the importance for the parties involved of being able to deliberately plan and negotiate their roles unhindered by traditional notions of parenthood that are inapplicable to their relationship.

---

[81] Spivack, 'The Law of Surrogate Motherhood in the United States' [2010] Am J of Comp Law Vol 58, 97–114.

[82] Nev Rev Stat 126.045 (2001).

[83] Ark Code Ann §9–10–201.

[84] Anne Reichman Schiff, 'Solomonic decisions in Egg Donation: Unscrambling the Conundrum of Legal Maternity', 80 Iowa L Rev (1995) 265 at 277.

[7.64] In reconciling the intent-based determination of parenthood with the need to secure the best interests of the child, adhering to the pre-conception agreement as articulated by the parties will generally coincide with the most positive outcome for the child. Those who are strongly motivated and act upon their intentions regarding parenthood are most likely to be motivated and fill those intentions consistently and well. It also reduces the necessity of litigation, as the predictability of the outcome will deter frivolous applications to court that would ultimately only serve to destabilise the child and its relations with others. There may well be situations in which the upholding of the parties' intentions may conflict with the child's best interest and in such circumstances the court must decide which interest is more important. There should, in such cases, be a presumption in favour of upholding the agreement made but this should not be conclusive in cases where it would be detrimental to the child.

[7.65] In other states in the US, courts have upheld surrogacy arrangements on contractprinciples,[85] or on the basis of the commissioning couple's genetic tie to the child.[86]

A different approach is evident in the first litigated surrogacy case in Australia, *Re Evelyn*.[87] The facts here were that two couples were friends for a number of years. Mr and Mrs Q were unable to conceive, Mrs Q having had a total hysterectomy arising from ovarian cancer. They had an adopted son who was aged three at the time of the trial. Dr and Mrs S had three children of their own aged between three and seven years. Mrs S offered to be inseminated with Mr Q's sperm and then to carry the child with a view to handing it over to the Qs after birth. The arrangement was entirely altruistically motivated.

[7.66] Baby Evelyn was born in December 1996 and was taken by the Qs to their home a week later. Mr Q was registered as the father on the birth certificate. It had been intended that the couples would remain in close contact, particularly between Mrs S and the baby. Mrs S became frustrated at the level of communication which she perceived as inadequate and she also began to attend grief counselling and a relinquishing mothers' support group. She decided that she could no longer abide by her decision to relinquish the baby and in July 1997 she travelled to the Qs home and took the baby from them. An initial hearing returned the baby to the Qs with a contact order in favour of the Ss. By the time the trial came to full hearing, the baby was one year old and had been living with the Qs for most of her young life. The judge refused to criticise the couples for having become involved in this arrangement and concentrated instead on the paramount

---

[85] *PGM v JMA*, 2997 WL 4304448 (Minnesota Court of Appeals) – the Court held that the parties had entered into a valid agreement that reflected their joint intention, was not coerced and did not contravene state policy.

[86] *Clark v Belsito* 644 N E 2d 760 (Ohio 1994) where the Court ruled that 'the law requires that those who provided the child with its genetics…must be designated as the legal and natural parents'. See also *Perry-Rogers v Fasano* 715 NYS 2d 19 (NY App Div 2000), in which two embryos were transferred to Ms Fasano, one of which was genetically related to Ms Fasano and her husband, but the other of which was unrelated and transferred to her by mistake. Ms Fasano gave birth to two children of different races. The Court appears to have relied in part on genetics in ruling that Ms Fasano was a mere gestational carrier for the child to whom she was not related.

[87] *Re Evelyn* [1998] Fam CA 103.

importance of the child's welfare. He took the view that the arrangement had been entered into with the noblest of motives and that all the adults involved were genuine and well intentioned.

[7.67] The trial judge took it that the agreement between the parties was void and unenforceable but nonetheless he said that 'whilst, of course, such considerations are secondary to an independent determination of what is in Evelyn's best interests, the circumstances surrounding her creation are pertinent to such an assessment.'[88] However, he held that public policy considerations prevailed over the expressed intention of the parties, and that Evelyn's best interests were the paramount consideration. He took the view that Evelyn should reside with the Ss (the surrogate mother and her husband) although contact was arranged with the Qs and they were to have shared long-term responsibility for her care, welfare and development. Although the judge said that he was satisfied that both couples would be capable of providing Evelyn with the highest standard of care, he focused on the long-term implications for Evelyn, having regard to the special circumstances of her conception. He found that Evelyn would be likely to suffer identity problems during her adolescence and that her biological mother, Mrs S, was better equipped to deal with those problems. Mrs S also had a more flexible attitude to future contact in the event her application was successful than did the Qs. Jordan J also found that the loss to Evelyn of not growing up with her half-siblings outweighed the loss to her of her relationship with her adopted brother.

[7.68] An appeal to the Full Court of the Family Court and ultimately to the High Court by the Qs was unsuccessful. The Full Court of the Family Court held that as a matter of principle, there was no presumption in favour of a biological parent and that although Jordan J had given a preferential position to the biological mother in this case, this was done on the basis of his evaluation of the personal qualities of the parties, their parenting capacities and the expert evidence before him. The Court concluded that the judge was entitled to place greater emphasis on the long-term rather than short-term issues for the child. Evelyn was ultimately handed over to the Ss in September 1998, when she was almost two years old.

[7.69] Legal provisions in force in Australia at the time of this case meant that Mrs S, as the birth mother, was deemed to be the legal mother and her husband was the legal father. The biological father, Mr Q, was characterised almost in the same way as a sperm donor and was presumed not to be the father. Thus, the legal provisions of parentage operated to deny the commissioning parents the possibility of establishing legal parentage through the use of their genetic material. This does not make any allowance for the existence of agreements between the parties and their joint intention that Mr Q would be the legal father, as evidenced by his registration on the birth certificate as such. Despite the conclusion reached in this case, it would be a mistake to overstate the significance of legal parentage rules, as Jordan J clearly stated that the parentage rules must be read as subject to the paramountcy principle. He said he would 'consider the case on its merits without being unduly fettered by legal fictions based on broad considerations of public policy'. The Full Court did not consider this issue further.[89]

---

[88]   *Re Evelyn* No BR 7321 of 1997 (unreported) at 29.
[89]   See further discussion of this case in Otlowski, '*Re Evelyn* – Reflections on Australia's First Litigated Surrogacy Case' Med Law Review (Spring 1999) 7, p 38–57.

SURROGACY IN THE UK

[7.70] The Warnock Report on Human Fertilisation and Embryology, which was published in 1984 in the UK, was one of the first reports worldwide to consider the implications of biotechnology for human reproduction. The committee gave its blessing to In Vitro Fertilisation, Artificial Insemination, Egg Donation and, to a more limited extent, Embryo Donation. It recommended that each of these practices be regulated by a new statutory licensing authority which would gather empirical data, issue guidelines and guard against potential abuses. Surrogacy is the only reproductive alternative to receive outright condemnation. The Committee said, 'It is inconsistent with human dignity that a woman should use her uterus for financial profit and treat it as an incubator for someone else's child.'[90]

[7.71] The Committee recommended that the commercialisation of surrogacy arrangements by an agency should be a criminal offence. This recommendation was enacted in the Surrogacy Arrangements Act 1985,[91] following the public debates brought about by the *Baby Cotton* case.[92] The Act was designed to catch anything that held the possibility of payment, but did not deal with altruistic or family arrangements or those that had been assisted by a charitable organisation. The Act was criticised by many as a stop-gap measure which would have the undesirable effect of driving some aspects of surrogacy underground rather than having them dealt with by professionally qualified advisors.[93] The Act renders surrogacy agreements unenforceable and there is a criminal sanction for commercial surrogacy arrangements.[94]

---

[90]   Report of the Committee of Inquiry into Human Fertilisation and Embryology (1984) Cmnd. 9314, para. 8.10.

[91]   The Parliamentary debates at the time the Bill was being passed are instructive. Surrogacy was condemned as: 'sick' (Peter Bruinvels HL Vol 77 Col.42); 'totally immoral' (Ian Paisley, Vol 68 Col 555); 'repugnant' (W Benyon, Vol 68 Col 582); 'the sale of children' (Jill Knight, Vol 68 Col 565); 'trafficking in human beings' (Patrick Cormack, Vol 74, Col 1193); an 'extremely distasteful matter' (Roger Sims, Vol 74 Col 1189); a 'well defined evil' (Norman Fowler, Vol 74 Col 1193); and 'sheer effrontery' (AJ Beith, Vol 77 Col 33).

[92]   *Re C (a minor)* [1985] FLR 846. The consequence of this first commercial surrogacy case, which occurred in January 1985, has been described as a 'moral panic', defined by Cohen as 'a condition, episode, person or group of persons which emerge to become identified as a threat to societal values or interests'. Cohen, *Folk Devils and Moral Panics* (MacGibbon and Kee Ltd, 1972) at 9. Kim Cotton, the surrogate mother involved, overnight became a 'folk devil', a 'visible reminder of what we should not be.' Dyer, 'Baby Cotton and the Birth of Moral Panic', The Guardian, 15 January 1985. 'The intermingling of commerce and the family, the public realm and the private sphere, prompted a government, committed to free enterprise on the one hand and valorisation of the family on the other, to take swift action.'

[93]   Eaton criticises the Act on the basis of a logical inconsistency between its objectives and methods. The Act clearly purports to combat the perceived evils of commercialism, but there is no prohibition against the couple paying a surrogate a substantial fee for her services. 'It is difficult to see how a fee is any less commercial, coercive or exploitative if offered by the couple rather than through their commercial agent'. The most serious danger posed by this 'piecemeal legislation' is its encouragement of amateurish agreements. The definition of the offence is broad enough to include legal, medical and psychological counsellors who, for a fee, might otherwise assist the parties. (contd.../)

[7.72] The Human Fertilisation and Embryology Act 1990 ('the HFE Act') did not expressly deal with surrogacy but provided that any medical treatment used as part of a surrogacy arrangement, such as the donation of eggs or sperm, or embryo transfer, must take place in a licensed treatment centre. Therefore, 'although the Authority [Human Fertilisation and Embryology Authority (HFEA)] does not directly regulate surrogacy, licensed treatment services provided to establish a surrogate pregnancy will be carried out under its auspices.'[95] In circumstances where the creation and transfer of embryos is involved, as in gestational surrogacy where the couple's own gametes are used, this can only be done in centres licensed by the HFEA. This means that clinical, scientific, counselling and legal services should be available to commissioning couples and surrogate mothers under the Code of Practice issued by the HFEA.[96]

[7.73] The Brazier Committee[97] was established to examine surrogacy arrangements from the perspective of public policy, the designation of parenthood and the meaning of 'reasonable expenses' which may be paid to the surrogate mothers. The Report of the Committee acknowledges a policy vacuum and an absence of a coherent policy in relation to surrogacy. The Report believes that it was anticipated that the Surrogacy

---

93   (\...contd) 'They are left to stumble through the process without advice. It is most unfortunate that a law that does not condemn the agreement itself does not permit the parties to pursue it in a professional manner.' Eaton, 'The British Response to Surrogate Motherhood: An American Critique' 19 The Law Teacher 163.
      See also Freeman, 'After Warnock: Whither the Law?' (1986) 39 Current Legal Problems 33. Freeman says the Act is 'short-sighted and ultimately self-defeating'. He believes that criminalisation of surrogacy will not prevent its occurrence and that regulation is the best solution. 'It is inevitable that we will have to recognise that surrogacy is a legitimate response to a felt need and that it requires regulation to ensure it is practised so as to promote the best interests of all involved.'

94   See comments of Ebsworth J in *Briody v St Helen's and Knowsley Health Authority* [2000] 2 FCR 13. This was quite an unusual case in that it involved a claim for damages for medical negligence that had allegedly resulted in the plaintiff being unable to bear children. The plaintiff claimed for the cost of commercial surrogacy entered into in California. This was dismissed by the Court, as such an award would enable an unenforceable and unlawful contract to be entered into, which was contrary to public policy and would not be allowed.

95   Morgan and Lee, *Human Fertilisation and Embryology, Regulating the Reproductive Revolution* (Blackstone Press, 2001) at 199.

96   See http://www.hfea.gov.uk (accessed 2 June 2011).

97   The review was prompted in part by a highly publicised dispute between a married surrogate, Karen Roche, and a Dutch couple who paid her £12,000, three days after she became pregnant with the man's sperm. The relationship deteriorated and the surrogate told the couple, falsely, that she had terminated the pregnancy. She had also contracted with another couple to give them custody of the child. She subsequently decided to keep the baby, who then became the subject of a custody battle. 'The Baby Market' (1997) The Lancet; 349:1487; The Independent, 20 January 1997. Freeman claims that the review was also sparked off by the arrival in the UK of an American, Bill Handel, 'who "advertised" his presence in the UK [without breaching the 1985 Act] and let it be known that payments of between £30,000 and £45,000 were available for willing surrogates.' Freeman, 'Does Surrogacy Have a Future After Brazier?' (1999) 7 Medical Law Review, 1–20 at 2, n.14, referring to *Surrogacy: Review for Health Ministers of Current Arrangements for Payments and Regulation* (Cm. 4068) (Department of Health, 1998).

Arrangements Act 1985 would be effective in deterring commercial surrogacy, which would then 'largely disappear'[98] or 'wither on the vine'.[99]This has not occurred, and it appears that, in Britain and the US at least, the number of surrogacy arrangements is on the increase.[100] The Report also estimates that, contrary to early fears, it is only in a handful of cases (4–5 per cent) that 'the nightmare scenario occurs and a surrogate refuses to hand over the child.'[101]

[7.74] The concerns in relation to surrogacy, as seen by the Committee are: '…whether the law and practice adequately safeguard the welfare of the child; whether it protects the interests of the surrogate, her family and the commissioning couple…and whether it should do so; and whether payment of the surrogate is acceptable.'[102] The ethical issues in surrogacy, therefore, remain largely the same as they were when considered by the Warnock Committee in 1984. The danger of exploitation of women, and the subjection of others as a means to an end, is always open to objection. Brazier takes the view that payment increases the risks of exploitation if it is an inducement to participate in an activity whose risks the surrogate cannot predict.[103]Although the Committee's remit did not include a consideration of whether to outlaw surrogacy, Brazier seems to take the view that surrogacy should not become an acceptable occupation, and that there is sufficient cause for concern to make regulation of the practice essential.

[7.75] The Report made recommendations in relation to payments to surrogates, the regulation of surrogacy and new legislation. It also proposed a new code of practice for dealing with surrogacy arrangements. In relation to the question of payments, the evidence before the Committee was that in only 3 per cent of cases was payment more than £10,000. Brazier recommends that payments should cover only genuine expenses associated with the pregnancy (a list is provided), and actual loss of earnings (the difference between the surrogate's usual earnings and State benefits). The reasons for this are as follows: firstly, children are not commodities to be bought and sold; secondly, it is in line with emerging policy in relation to gamete donors; thirdly, women should not be attracted to surrogacy by the lure of financial reward; and fourthly, it is not in the child's best interests to learn that their surrogate mother benefited financially from giving them up.[104]

[7.76] In relation to the regulation of surrogacy, Brazier is of the view that regulation might reduce the hazards to the child and the others involved. He rejects the idea of

---

98   Brazier Report at para 3.5.
99   Brazier Report at para 3.44.
100 Freeman 'Does Surrogacy Have a Future After Brazier?' (1999) 7 Medical Law Review, 1–20 at 3.
101 Freeman, 'Does Surrogacy Have a Future After Brazier?' (1999) 7 Medical Law Review, 1–20.
102 Freeman, 'Does Surrogacy Have a Future After Brazier?' (1999) 7 Medical Law Review, 1–20 at 4, quoting from the Brazier Report at para 4.6.
103 Freeman says of this point: '[t]he prospective surrogate's autonomy must, it seems, be protected by a healthy injection of paternalism.' 'Does Surrogacy Have a Future After Brazier?' (1999) 7 Medical Law Review, 1–20 at 5.
104 For a criticism of these reasons, see Freeman, 'Does Surrogacy Have a Future After Brazier?' (1999) 7 Medical Law Review, 1–20 at 9–10.

giving regulatory powers to infertility clinics,[105] preferring the option of having surrogacy agencies registered with the Department of Health, who would impose a statutory Code of Practice. Brazier recommends a new Surrogacy Act to deal with the main legal principles governing surrogacy arrangements and to offer a Code of Practice. This Act would continue existing prohibitions in relation to commercial activity in surrogacy arrangements; define and limit lawful payments to surrogates; and set out a Code of Practice for agencies with the child's interests of paramount concern. In terms of eligibility, Brazier argues that there should be a minimum and maximum age for commissioning parents, and for the surrogate mother. The surrogate should have had a child and have one still living with her; a period of two years between pregnancies; a maximum number of surrogate births (usually one); independent counselling; comprehensive information regarding risks; legal advice; and a period of reflection before conception is attempted. The relationship between the surrogate and the commissioning couple should be based on a memorandum of understanding which, though not legally binding, would clarify the expectations of the parties from the outset regarding contact, the welfare of the child and information to be given to the child regarding his/her origins.

[7.77] The HFE Act was amended in 2008 but the provisions in relation to surrogacy remained substantially unchanged. In relation to legal parentage, there is an important provision in the 2008 Act (similar to the provision under the 1990 Act) which would allow for the court to make a 'parental order' in favour of gamete donors, which would enable legal parentage to be assigned to a genetic mother who did not gestate the child, as in a surrogacy case. Section 54 of the Act provides that on an application made by two people (the applicants) the court may make an order providing for a child to be treated in law as the child of the applicants if, *inter alia*, (a) the child has been carried by a woman who is not one of the applicants, as a result of the placing in her of an embryo or sperm and eggs or her artificial insemination, (b) the gametes of at least one of the applicants were used to bring about the creation of the embryo.

[7.78] This provision is aimed at a situation such as surrogacy where, for example, a woman can donate eggs but cannot carry a child to term. She and her partner or husband may agree with a surrogate mother that the surrogate will carry to term an embryo created by the fertilisation of the wife's eggs and the husband's sperm. The Act allows the court to make an order providing for the child carried by the surrogate to be treated in law as the child of the commissioning couple, provided that the gametes of one or both have been used and they are adult and married, in a civil partnership or living as partners in an enduring family relationship. It is also subject to other conditions, including the consent of the surrogate, her husband and the genetic father where applicable and where they can be found. The application must be made within six months of the child's birth and no money or payment other than expenses must be involved in the agreement unless authorised by the court. The child must be living with the commissioning couple both at the time of the application and at the time of the making the order. Either or both of the partners in the commissioning couple must be

---

[105] Staff at infertility clinics have expertise in medical and scientific matters but such skills are not usually required in surrogacy. The skills required in surrogacy are more likely to be found in adoption-like agencies.

domiciled in the UK, the Channel Islands or the Isle of Man. The welfare of any child born as a result of treatment must be taken into account when considering licensed treatment.

SURROGACY IN THE US

[7.79] In the United States, there are few ground rules for surrogacy. It is a practice that occurs without regulation, with no authority deciding on the fitness of the commissioning couple to become parents, or no independent screening process to decide if the woman is suitable to act as surrogate. Surrogacy appears to be controlled mainly by doctors and agencies, some of which adhere strictly to voluntary guidelines, and some of which do not. In some states parents must go through a formal adoption process to gain legal custody but often this is done after the child has been born and is in the care of the commissioning couple, in effect leaving the courts with little option but to approve the adoption. Some states allow prebirth orders that place the parents' names on the birth certificate without any screening. If a custody dispute arises, states differ in relation to how such situations are handled. For example, Californian courts have upheld the validity of surrogacy contracts with the result that the commissioning couple is likely to get custody of the child in the event of a dispute other than in exceptional circumstances such as where this is not in the best interests of the child. Some other states, such as Michigan, hold that surrogacy is contrary to public policy and unenforceable, with the result that the surrogate mother is likely to retain custody.

[7.80] The American Bar Association has proposed a Model Act for surrogacy, one section of which provides that where the commissioning couple has no genetic link to the child, the surrogacy arrangement should get judicial pre-approval following a home study. The American College of Obstetricians and Gynaecologists has also published guidelines for surrogacy which recommends that surrogacy be handled by non-profit agencies.[106]

SURROGACY IN IRELAND

[7.81] There is no mention of surrogacy anywhere in enacted legislation in Ireland. However, anecdotal evidence suggests that Irish couples travel to other jurisdictions to avail of surrogacy arrangements, and there have been a small number of familial surrogacy cases reported in medical journals.[107] The legal issues that arise here stem from the potential application of the adoption legislation, conflict of laws difficulties for couples who travel abroad for surrogacy and Constitutional issues in the event of a custody dispute between the commissioning couple and a surrogate mother who changes her mind.

---

[106] Surrogacy can be very lucrative in the US. Between brokers, legal and medical expenses and surrogate fees, a successful surrogacy can cost prospective parents approximately $100,000. See further Saul, 'Building a Baby With Few Ground Rules' New York Times, December 13, 2009.
[107] Sills et al, 'First Irish Pregnancies After IVF With Gestational Carrier' (2009) Irish Medical Journal Vol 102 (2).

Adoption

[7.82] In surrogacy, in the absence of legislation to the contrary and in keeping with legal policy in the UK and other jurisdictions, it is likely that the birth mother of the child would be held to be the child's legal mother irrespective of whether or not she was the biological or genetic mother. If she is married, then by application of the presumption of paternity, her husband would be presumed to be the child's legal father. If she is unmarried, the commissioning man's name may be entered on the child's birth certificate as the biological father either with her consent or by court order as discussed in Ch 5 at para **5.12**. In order for the commissioning couple to establish a legal relationship with the child, they would have to avail of either guardianship or adoption procedures.[108] If the commissioning man is registered as the child's father, then he could apply for guardianship of the child. In order for the commissioning woman to establish a legal relationship with the child, she would have to apply for adoption. The court is obliged to consider the welfare of the child as the first and paramount consideration in any such application in relation to guardianship or adoption.

> The primary legal consequence of an adoption lies in the transformative effect it has on the respective parental rights of the parties. Notwithstanding the natural mother's or guardian's rights, the adoption acts to expunge all parental rights and obligations of that mother or guardian in respect of her child. Simultaneously, the effect of an adoption order is to vest full parental authority in the adoptive parent or parents, with full rights and duties residing in them as if the child was the child of the adopters, born to them within wedlock.[109]

[7.83] One of the first issues to consider here is the effect of the payment of money to the surrogate mother. In common with most other jurisdictions, the Irish Adoption Acts make it illegal to pay any money in connection with an adoption of a child. The Adoption Act 1952 provides in s 42(1) that 'an adopter, parent or guardian of a child shall not receive or agree to receive any payment or other reward in consideration of the adoption of the child under this Act.' Subsection (2) provides that 'No person shall make or give or agree to make or give any payment or reward the receipt of which is prohibited by subsection (1).' Contravention of these provisions is an offence. This provision is repeated in s 145 of the 2010 Act. The question arises, therefore, whether a payment made to a surrogate mother would be considered to fall foul of section 145 as being a payment in consideration of the adoption of a child. If the Adoption Authority took the view that an offence had been committed under the Act, this could render the adoption invalid. It is possible that the Adoption Authority might consider the payment to be recompense for pregnancy-related expenses only and therefore not to fall foul of the spirit and policy of the Act. However, this would turn on the facts of the individual

---

[108] This may follow the example of *Moschetta v Moschetta*, 30 Cal Rptr 2d 893 (Cal Ct App 1994), in which a California Court of Appeals held that a traditional surrogacy contract was unenforceable because the contract was incompatible with the parentage and adoption statutes of the state. The Court said that the surrogate had not consented to an adoption by the intended mother when she signed the surrogacy contract. (Under the relevant adoption statute law, birth parents were required to consent to an adoption before a social worker. This had not occurred.) The contract was therefore not an adoption agreement and the surrogate had not given her consent to give the child up to the intended parents.

[109] Shannon, *Child Law* (2nd edn, Round Hall, 2010) 9.07.

case and the amount of money paid, and is therefore difficult to predict with any certainty since any adoption applications that may have arisen in this context to date have not been reported.

[7.84] Another issue is the validity of the surrogate mother agreeing to place the child for adoption by the commissioning couple, one or both of whom may be the biological parents of the child. Private placements are dealt with in Part 13 of the 2010 Act which provides in s 125 that:

(1) A person shall not—

(a)   make or attempt to make an arrangement for the adoption of a child,

(b)   for the purpose of having a child adopted -

    (i)   retain the child in the person's custody, or

    (ii)   arrange to have the child retained in the custody of another person, or

(c)   take part in the management or control of a body of persons which exists wholly or partly for the purpose of making arrangements for adoption.

(2) A person shall not give a child, or cause a child to be given, to another person for the purpose of having the child adopted unless—

(a)   the first-mentioned person is a parent of the child, and

(b)   the person who intends to adopt the child is—

    (i)   a parent of the child,

    (ii)   a relative of the child, or

    (iii) the spouse of a parent of the child.

(3) A person shall not receive a child for the purpose of adopting the child unless the person is—

(a)   a parent of the child,

(b)   a relative of the child,

(c)   the spouse of a parent of the child, or

(d)   a person with whom a child is placed by an accredited body or the Health Service Executive.

[7.85] Subsection (4) provides that notwithstanding subsections (1) and (2), the Health Service Executive (HSE) may carry out any of the activities described in those subsections. Subsection (5) provides that notwithstanding subsections (1) and (2), an accredited body may carry out any of the activities described in those subsections in respect of which the accredited body is registered in the register of accredited bodies.

[7.86] The effect of this section is that a child cannot be placed for adoption other than by the HSE or an accredited body except in circumstances where the child is placed by one of its parents with the other parent, his or her spouse or a relative of the child. 'Relative' here means the child's grandparent, brother, sister, uncle or aunt, or the spouse of any such person. The relationship to the child can be on either the maternal or paternal side. In principle, then, the birth mother could place the child with the biological father and his wife, or a family member such as a sister for whom she has carried the pregnancy. Private placement of a child in any other circumstances is prohibited. Therefore, if the surrogacy arrangement is extrafamilial or if the commissioning man is not the biological father (eg where donor sperm or embryo has been used), such a private placement of the child would be prohibited.

[7.87] A further issue arises in relation to the marital status of the surrogate mother and whether a child born within marriage may be adopted. This issue arises due to the application of the presumption of paternity, which means that if the surrogate mother is married, then her husband is presumed to be the child's father. Under previous Adoption Acts, a child born within marriage was not eligible for adoption. The following children may now be adopted under the 2010 Act: a child whose parents are deceased; a child born outside marriage and not subsequently legitimated by its parents' marriage; a legitimated child whose birth has not been registered under the Legitimacy Act 1931; and an abandoned child, even where the parents were married to each other. The child must already be born (thus the pre-birth adoption orders in some US states would not be possible here) and the necessary consent shall not be valid unless the child is more than six weeks of age. Marital children may be eligible for adoption only if freed for adoption by the High Court in circumstances where the Court is satisfied that the parents of the child have, for physical or moral reasons, totally failed in their duty towards the child for a period of not less than 12 months. This abdication of duty must amount to an abandonment of all parental rights.[110] Therefore, if the child is born to a married woman through a surrogacy arrangement, it would not be possible for the commissioning couple to apply for adoption of the child unless the High Court took the view that the surrogate mother and her husband had abandoned the child for the previous 12 months.

International surrogacy arrangements

[7.88] Intercountry adoptions must comply with the provisions of the 2010 Act and the 1993 Hague Convention, or be pursuant to a bilateral agreement with the state of origin of the child. If a child is born outside the jurisdiction pursuant to a surrogacy arrangement, difficulties may arise in the context of securing re-entry to Ireland with the child. Foreign surrogacy raises problems also in relation to the sources and quality of the information available to couples searching internet resources, as these sources do not always highlight the difficult conflict of laws and immigration issues that may arise following the child's birth. Fertility tourism appears to have increased significantly in recent years due to ease of travel, more permissive legal environments, cost factors and so on. Although there have not been any reported legal cases in Ireland to date, anecdotal evidence and media reports suggest that many Irish couples have availed of this route in making surrogacy arrangements.

[7.89] The law in the EU varies considerably in relation to surrogacy. Surrogacy arrangements in the UK are lawful, although it is an offence for third parties to broker arrangements on a commercial basis. Non-profitmaking organisations provide introductory services between surrogates and commissioning parents and assist in the formation of arrangements between them. These agencies are not prosecuted, as they are non-commercial in nature. Surrogacy will not generally be enforced in UK courts so if the surrogate mother changes her mind about relinquishing the child, the courts will not generally intervene.[111] Other European countries such as France, Italy and Germany take a more restrictive approach than the UK. As a result, many of those seeking surrogacy

---

[110] Shannon, *Child Law* (2nd edn, Round Hall, 2010) 9–152.

have travelled to the UK in an attempt to avail of the legal position there. However, English law has been drafted specifically to prevent its use as a safe haven for surrogacy. One of the conditions for obtaining a parental order under the Human Fertilisation and Embryology Act is that at least one of the commissioning parents must be domiciled in a part of the UK, Channel Islands or Isle of Man.[112] In *Re G (Surrogacy: Foreign Domicile)*,[113] a Turkish couple travelled to the UK as part of an arrangement with a surrogate mother which had been facilitated by a surrogacy agency. The couple applied for a parental order but the Court held that such an order could not be given under the Act.[114] After protracted litigation the couple were finally granted an order under s 84 of the Adoption and Children Act 2002, granting them parental responsibility and allowing them to take child back to Turkey for adoption. McFarlane J warned that English law should not be used by foreign couples to evade more restrictive domestic legislation and that any similar cases in the future should expect to pay heavy costs orders.

[7.90] Irish couples tend to travel to other countries, such as the United States, Ukraine and India, for surrogacy, as some of these jurisdictions permit surrogacy without delay or restrictions, making them very attractive though not always cheap options for some couples. The difficulty with such arrangements lies in the conflict of laws problems that may ensue. These are clearly demonstrated in an English case, *Re X and Y (Foreign Surrogacy)*.[115] In this case, a British couple went to the Ukraine to avail of a surrogacy programme there. They conceived twins through use of an anonymous egg donor's eggs, which were fertilised by the commissioning father's sperm, and carried by a Ukrainian surrogate mother. In accordance with Ukrainian law, the couple agreed to pay the surrogate mother €27,000, which she intended to use to help her to buy a flat for her family. They were assured that the legalities were straightforward but this turned out not to be the case, despite the fact that Ukrainian law regarded the commissioning couple as parents of the twins and absolved the Ukrainian surrogate mother and her husband of any legal responsibility for them. However, this was directly contrary to the position under English law by virtue of which the legal parents of the twins were the surrogate mother and her husband, and the commissioning parents had no responsibility for them.

> The practical effect of this conflict over legal parenthood was that each system of law abdicated parental responsibility for each set of parents. The children were, therefore, born parentless, and, by extension, stateless (entitled to neither British nor Ukrainian citizenship).[116]

[7.91] The twins were thus stuck in a legal vacuum without parents and with no right to either enter the UK or remain in the Ukraine. The British parents took responsibility for them from birth but they had only a limited visa and would be forced to leave the

---

[111] However, see *in the Matter of N (a child)* [2007] EWCA Civ 1053, in which the Court held that custody of the child should be awarded to the commissioning couple, as this was in the best interests of the child due to the deceit of the surrogate mother as a result of her compulsive desire to bear children.

[112] The HFE Act 2008, s 54(4).

[113] *Re G (Surrogacy: Foreign Domicile)* [2008] 1 FLR 1047.

[114] The relevant provision in the 1990 Act was s 30(3).

[115] *Re X and Y (Foreign Surrogacy)* [2009] 1 FLR 733.

[116] Gamble and Ghevaert, '*Re X and Y (Foreign Surrogacy)*: A Trek Through a Thorn Forest' (2009) Fam Law 239.

children in a Ukrainian orphanage if the legal difficulties were not resolved. DNA tests were undertaken to establish that the commissioning man was the biological father of the twins and the children were given discretionary leave to enter the UK 'outside the rules' for 12 months to enable the couple to apply for a parental order.

[7.92] The main difficulty in this case arose from the fact that the surrogate mother was married and therefore, under English law, she and her husband were regarded as the legal parents of the twins. Had she not been married, the biological father could have been treated as their legal father and automatically been entitled to bring them into the country. The Court considered whether this statutory provision (s 28 of the 1990 Act) should apply in foreign surrogacy cases but held that a distinction should not be drawn between domestic and foreign cases. Thus, the couple had to apply for a parental order in respect of the twins.

[7.93] Section 30 of the HFE Act 1990 (s 54 of the 2008 Act) provides a mechanism whereby the commissioning parents of a surrogate-born child can apply for a parental order which acts like an adoption order in extinguishing the rights of the surrogate mother and her husband, if any. The court must be satisfied that no money (other than expenses reasonably incurred) has been given or received by the applicants in consideration of the making of the arrangement or handing over of the child, unless approved by the court. In this case, the surrogate mother received payment which was in excess of reasonable expenses and therefore the Court had to consider whether to authorise the commercial payment so that a parental order could be made.

[7.94] Hedley J considered that there were three issues involved in deciding whether or not to approve the payment. The first was whether the sum paid was disproportionate to reasonable expenses. He noted that reasonable expenses will vary from country to country and heard evidence about the cost of living in the Ukraine. He concluded that the sum was not so disproportionate that the granting of the order would be an 'unacceptable affront to public policy'. The second issue was whether the applicants were acting in good faith and without 'moral taint' in their dealings with the surrogate mother. On this point Hedley J held that there was no doubt that this was so, and was satisfied that no advantage was taken of the surrogate mother who was herself 'a woman of mature discretion'. The third issue was whether there had been any attempt to defraud the authorities and on this point Hedley J held that in fact the opposite was true in that the applicants had sought at all times to comply with the requirements of English and Ukrainian law.

[7.95] The Court also had, of course, to consider the welfare of the children in this case. Conscious of the fact that the children were stateless and parentless unless the order was granted, Hedley J said that this made the granting of the order 'most uncomfortable'. He recognised that what he was being asked to do was to balance two potentially irreconcilably conflicting conflicts in that Parliament expected the courts to implement its policy decision in relation to commercial surrogacy, but at the same time the rigour of such implementation must be mitigated by considerations of the welfare of the child. He added: 'The difficulty is that it is almost impossible to imagine a set of circumstances in which by the time the case comes to court the welfare of any child (particularly a foreign child) would not be gravely compromised (at the very least) by a refusal to make an order.' The effect of this judgment is, as Gamble and Ghevaert, point out that:

[T]he only sanction the court holds against commercial surrogacy (i.e. to refuse a parental order) has the effect of punishing an innocent child, and it would be difficult – even impossible – for an English family court to do this, no matter how badly the parents had infringed public policy. The case therefore goes a significant way to allowing fully commercial surrogacy in the UK, particularly where the court is in practice presented with a *fait accompli.*[117]

[7.96] It is possible that a similar situation could arise in the event that an Irish couple travelled to another jurisdiction to avail of more permissive legislation on surrogacy. If the surrogate mother was married then her husband would be the child's legal father and the child could not be placed for adoption without a High Court ruling that the child had been abandoned for at least a year by its parents. If the surrogate mother was unmarried, the commissioning man could establish paternity through DNA tests and be recognised as the legal father, and could apply for guardianship on that basis. Such an application would only be granted if this was in the best interests of the child. If the surrogate mother was paid, and in most of these international arrangements she would be, this may also fall foul of the Adoption Act 2010. If the child was legally registered in another jurisdiction as the child of the commissioning parents, the issue arises as to whether this birth certification would be recognised in granting Irish citizenship to the child. Under the Irish Nationality and Citizenship Acts, 1956 to 2004, a person who was born outside Ireland is automatically an Irish citizen by descent if one of that person's parents was an Irish citizen who was born in Ireland. It is likely that circumstances such as those which arose in *X and Y* will occur in Ireland in the near future with the result that a conflict of laws dispute will ensue in order to determine legal parentage of the child.

CONSTITUTIONAL ISSUES IN SURROGACY

[7.97] In Ireland the problems inherent in surrogacy arrangements are likely to be further complicated by the impact of the 1937 Irish Constitution. The Constitution both acknowledges the special status of the family as 'the natural primary and fundamental unit group of society' and recognises the natural rights of its members. In surrogacy, some particular Constitutional issues are likely to be raised. Firstly, do married couples have a right to privacy in the affairs of their marriage? If so, does it extend to methods of procreation within marriage? Secondly, could a surrogate mother be said to have a right of privacy (individual or marital, if she entered into the arrangement together with her husband) in conducting her private affairs? Thirdly, does the surrogate mother of a child conceived through such an arrangement have a right to its custody? Fourthly, does the natural father of a child born to a surrogate and therefore outside of the marital relationship, have any recognised Constitutional rights with regard to its care and custody? If the surrogate is married, what rights does her husband have in relation to the child? These are issues which have unfortunately not yet been clearly addressed, either in the Constitution itself or in the body of case law that has built up around the interpretation of its various provisions.

---

[117] Gamble and Ghevaert, '*Re X and Y (Foreign Surrogacy)*: A Trek Through a Thorn Forest' (2009) Fam Law 239.

The right to privacy

[7.98] Before looking at the Irish Constitutional provisions in relation to privacy in this context it is useful to look briefly at some of the earliest reported cases in the US on surrogacy in which arguments were made that state legislation which prohibited surrogacy directly or indirectly might be an unconstitutional infringement of reproductive liberty. Proponents of this argument asserted that the right to privacy, which included the right to make marital and procreational choices, the right to raise one's children as one sees fit and so on, encompassed the right to hire a surrogate mother to gestate a child.

[7.99] In the first American case on surrogacy, *Doe v Kelley* in 1981,[118] it was argued that legislation prohibiting payment of money in connection with adoption interfered with a couple's plan to pay $5,000 to a potential surrogate mother, and was unconstitutional, as it interfered with their right to privacy.[119] The Court said that the right to adopt a child upon the payment of money is not a fundamental personal right but even if it were, the state had an interest in preventing commercialism from affecting a mother's decision to surrender her child for adoption and therefore the statute was not unconstitutional. The Circuit Court judge said:

> The evils attendant to the mix of lucre and the adoption process are self-evident and the temptations of dealing in 'money market babies' exist whether the parties be strangers or friends. The statute seeks to prevent a money market for the adoption of babies. Mercenary considerations used to create a parent-child relationship and its impact on the family unit strikes at the very foundation of human society and is patently and necessarily injurious to the community.

The State of Michigan Court of Appeals affirmed the Court's decision and said that the statute did not interfere with the commissioning couple's right to autonomy in deciding to have a child, but rather prevented them 'from paying consideration in conjunction with their use of the state's adoption procedures'.

[7.100] In another Michigan case, *Syrkowski v Appleyard*,[120] a childless married man entered into an agreement with a married woman who agreed to become a surrogate mother for a fee of $10,000. They agreed that the man and his wife would take custody of the child after the birth and raise the child as their own. The parties later asked the Court to rule on the matter of paternity in order to enable Mr Syrkowski's name to be inserted on the birth certificate. At first instance the Court refused the application on the basis of the limited terms of the relevant legislation. This was affirmed by the Court of Appeals but reversed on appeal to the Michigan Supreme Court, which held that under the state's Paternity Act, the biological father was allowed to petition for an order declaring his paternity and adding his name to the child's birth certificate. The Court rejected the argument by the state's Attorney General that such petitions should only be allowed when the child in question was born out of wedlock.

---

[118] *Doe v Kelley* 106 Mich. App. 169, 307 N.W. 2d 438 [1981].
[119] *Doe v Kelley* 106 Mich. App. 169 at 174, 307 N.W. 2d at 441[1981].
[120] *Syrkowski v Appleyard* 362 N W 2d 211 (Mich. 1985).

[7.101] In Ireland, the special relationship involved in marriage is one area where the right to privacy has been judicially considered. These issues have already been discussed in the broader context in Chapter 4[121] but receive particular application here in the context of surrogacy. In *McGee v Attorney General*[122] which concerned the right of a married couple to use contraceptives, at that time illegal, Walsh J said:

> The sexual life of a husband and wife is of necessity and by its nature, an area of particular privacy. If the husband and wife decide to limit their family, or to avoid having children, by use of contraceptives, it is a matter peculiarly within the joint decision of the husband and wife and one into which the State cannot intrude unless its intrusion can be justified by the exigencies of the common good.[123]

[7.102] In limiting the area in which the State can justifiably concern itself, Walsh J may seem to be echoing the views of the Wolfenden Committee in England, who felt that there must remain 'a realm of private morality which in brief and crude terms is not the law's business.'[124] However, the Supreme Court refused to shut the door tightly on the possibility of State intervention – if the exigencies of the common good required the State to open the bedroom door, then the right to privacy could be displaced for this purpose.[125] Thus, in *Norris v Attorney General*[126] O'Higgins CJ said that the right to privacy can never be absolute and the State has an interest in 'the general moral well-being of the community' and is entitled 'to discourage conduct which is morally wrong and harmful to a way of life and to values which the State wishes to protect.' In *Murray v Ireland and the Attorney General*,[127] which concerned a claim by a married couple, who were both serving prison sentences, to have a right to beget children, the Court held that while the Constitution, by explicitly recognising and protecting the concept of the institution of marriage, implicitly recognised the right of each spouse to beget children (which came from Art 40 not Art 41 of the Constitution) this right might be validly restricted by the State in certain circumstances. In this case, the right was curtailed by the circumstances of imprisonment.[128]

---

[121] At para **4.42**.

[122] *McGee v Attorney General* [1974] IR 284.

[123] *McGee v Attorney General* [1974] IR 284 at 312.

[124] Wolfenden Report 1957, Cmnd. 247. This view was challenged by Lord Devlin, *The Enforcement of Morals* (OUP, 1965).

[125] *McGee v Attorney General* [1974] IR 284 at 312.

[126] *Norris v Attorney General* [1984] IR 36.

[127] *Murray v Ireland and the Attorney General* [1991] ILRM 465.

[128] Costello J stated: '[t]his is not a case in which the court should balance the so-called "right" of the State to imprison wrongdoers against the plaintiffs' right to beget children. The issue is whether the restrictions on the plaintiffs' rights caused by the exercise of the State's power to imprison the plaintiffs are constitutionally permissible.'
Similar cases in the US have also rejected such claims on the grounds of security, scarce resources and treating prisoners equally. For example, *Goodwin v Turner* 908 F 2d 1395, 1400 (8th Cir 1990) in which the Court said the prison's policy, in refusing the inmate's request that he be allowed to provide a container of semen for his wife for AIH, was 'reasonably related to the legitimate penological interest of treating all inmates equally.' See also *Percy v New Jersey*, 651 A.2d 1044 (NJ Super Ct App Div 1994); *Anderson v Vasquez*, 827 F Supp 617 (ND Cal 1992).

[7.103] Based on the foregoing cases, in which the courts have stated that it is outside the authority of the State to endeavour to intrude into the privacy of the husband and wife relationship for the sake of imposing a code of private morality upon that husband and wife which they do not desire, a case could be made out by a married couple who decide to participate in a surrogacy arrangement.[129] They might argue that they entered into a decision to beget a child conscientiously and responsibly (as Mrs McGee did in her decision not to have a child). The couple may have medical reasons for their inability to conceive a child in any other way (just as Mrs McGee had medical reasons for requiring contraceptives.) The couple desire the joy and happiness that a child can bring[130] and would argue that there is no compelling State interest that could interfere with this decision.[131] It may be argued that public policy does not support such an arrangement, but whether the Court would find this as a sufficient justification for intervention in the marital relationship is open to question.

[7.104] It may also be argued that the surrogate mother has a Constitutional right to privacy, either individually or together with her husband, which would encompass her choice to be artificially inseminated, regardless of who the legal parent of the child will be. In Ireland, a general right to individual privacy has been held worthy of Constitutional protection in *Kennedy and Arnold v Ireland and the Attorney General*[132] where it was held that the right to privacy is one of the fundamental personal rights of the citizen which flow from the Christian and democratic nature of the State. It may, however, be restricted by the Constitutional rights of others and by the requirements of the common good.

---

[129] In *Re Baby M*, Judge Sorkow put a high priority on a right of free self-determination, extending to the right to conceive a child and form a family. He said:
> …[I]f one has a right to procreate coitally, then one has the right to reproduce non-coitally. If it is the reproduction that is protected, then the means of reproduction are also to be protected. The value and interests underlying the creation of family are the same by whatever means obtained. This court holds that the protected means extends to the use of surrogates. The contract cannot fall because of the use of a third party.

In Re Baby M, 217 NJ Super 313 at 386.

[130] Robertson says: 'What then about married couples who cannot reproduce coitally? Their need and interest in forming a family may be as strong as fertile couples. Furthermore, coital infertility does not render a couple inadequate as child-rearers. The values and interests that undergird the right of coital reproduction clearly exist with the coitally infertile. Their interest in bearing, begetting, or parenting offspring is no less than that of the coitally fertile'. Robertson, 'Procreative Liberty and the State's Burden of Proof in Regulating Noncoital Reproduction' (1988) 16:1–2 Law, Medicine and Health Care 18 at 19.

[131] Robertson argues that restrictions on noncoital reproduction by an infertile married couple should be subject to rigorous scrutiny: 'Only serious harm to the interests of others, not avoidable by less restrictive means, should justify interference with such a fundamental choice, with the state having the burden of establishing the requisite degree of harm." Robertson, 'Procreative Liberty and the State's Burden of Proof in Regulating Noncoital Reproduction' (1988) 16:1–2 Law, Medicine and Health Care 18 at 19.

[132] *Kennedy and Arnold v Ireland and the Attorney General* [1988] ILRM 472.

The right to custody

[7.105] A woman who gives birth to a child is recognised as having a special relationship with that child and a strong claim to custody of a child in all but exceptional circumstances. In surrogacy arrangements the question arises as to whether a surrogate mother would have an absolute Constitutional right to the custody of a child borne by her for another couple, irrespective of whether she is genetically related to the child or her intention regarding relinquishment at the time the child was conceived.

[7.106] In Ireland, if the surrogate mother is unmarried, she would prima facie have a more favourable claim to custody of the child than the father of that child. For many years there was a presumption that children of tender years were better catered for by their mother, although it was possible to rebut this by evidence that the mother was an unfit person to have custody of the child. In all instances, the courts have always been consistent on the fact that the child's welfare is of primary and paramount concern. In relation to surrogacy, therefore, it would seem that the surrogate mother who wishes to keep the child and does not relinquish it at birth, would have the stronger case, especially with regard to a newborn baby.[133]

[7.107] If the surrogate mother is married, the presumption of paternity would operate to recognise the child as a child of the marriage. This would make it more difficult for the commissioning couple to claim custody of the child, as the surrogate's husband would also have a right to custody of the child.[134] In most instances where the surrogate mother is married, best practice requires a declaration from the surrogate's husband to the effect that he does not consent to the arrangement. This is an attempt to rebut the presumption of paternity operating to defeat the whole purpose of the contract being entered into. It then becomes a straightforward custody case between the surrogate and the couple to be decided in the best interests of the child based on fitness of both parties, material circumstance of each party, the opportunities which the child would receive, any bonding which has taken place and so on. However, in Ireland there would be additional obstacles due to the status of the child as a child born within marriage and therefore ineligible for adoption other than in exceptional circumstances.[135]

[7.108] As a general rule it could be said that, where the parties disagree as to custody of the child, an Irish court would be likely to favour the rights of the surrogate mother. This is so even if the commissioning couple is able to provide an economically more stable

---

[133] This is on the basis that she is likely to be held to be the legal mother of the child. However, if the court were to decide that the genetic mother was the legal mother, then the surrogate would arguably not have any Constitutional right to the child at all. In *Johnson v Calvert*, the Court discussed the Constitutional right of a mother to custody of her child but said that in this case, as the genetic mother was held to be the legal mother, the surrogate's Constitutional interests were 'something less than those of a mother'. The Court also concluded that a surrogate in this situation was not exercising her own procreative choices, but simply agreeing to provide a service.

[134] Ironically, the role of the biological father does not seem to be given much attention in any of the surrogacy cases which have come before the court. For example, in the Australian case *Re Evelyn*, [1998] Fam CA 103 there was very little discussion of the role of the child's biological father in the case.

[135] See para **7.87**.

home life and education. This is based on the traditional importance given, in adoption and custody disputes, to the bond between mother and child and the notion that young children, in particular, are better off in their mother's custody.[136] However, these principles were generally formulated in response to custody disputes between a married couple who were in the process of separating. It was seen as a preference for the traditional role of the mother in the home as opposed to the absent, working father. These stereotypical roles do not typify modern relationships where, very often, both parents are working outside the home. Neither does it apply to a typical surrogacy situation in which the dispute is between the surrogate (who may or may not be married and/or working outside the home) and the commissioning couple, who may in fact be the child's genetic parents.

[7.109] The courts may also choose to further develop the idea of the 'psychological parent' that has featured in some adoption cases.[137] This concept is based on the theory that 'whether any adult becomes the psychological parent of a child is based thus on day-to-day interaction, companionship and shared experiences. The role can be fulfilled either by a biological parent or by an adoptive parent or by any other caring adult – but never by an absent, inactive adult, whatever his biological or legal relationship to the child may be.'[138]

LEGISLATIVE APPROACHES TO SURROGACY

[7.110] In relation to reproductive technology generally, legislation has been slow to arrive in most jurisdictions. Many countries have chosen to deal with the problems thrown up by these techniques in a piecemeal fashion by adaptation of existing private law doctrines,[139] or through professional guidelines for medical practitioners. However, when it comes to surrogacy, at least in the United States and the United Kingdom, public

---

[136] It is likely that in the situation where the surrogate changes her mind about relinquishing the child, she will probably never have given the child to the couple since its birth. Therefore, the child will have bonded with her, rather than the commissioning couple. This may be strengthened further if there is a delay of a number of weeks or months in having the case heard by the court. However, both the delay factor and the bonding process should not be overstated. In the *Baby Cotton* case, the application to have the child registered as the child of the commissioning couple, for the purpose of enabling the American couple to remove the child from the jurisdiction, was heard and decided within three days of the child's birth. Also the facts of the Australian case, *Re Evelyn,* show that despite the bonding in that case between the child and the commissioning couple for almost the first two years of the child's life, the Court decided that the surrogate mother should have custody of her. This result is unlikely to be followed in the Irish context, based on cases dispensing with the birth mother's consent to adoption.

[137] For example, *S v the Eastern Health Board* (February 1979, unreported) HC; *JM & MM v An Bord Uchtála* (November 1984, unreported) HC; *State (MG) v AH &MH* [1984] 4 ILRM 237 (HC); *JK v VW* [1990] 2 IR 437.

[138] Goldstein, Freud and Solnit, *Beyond the Best Interests of the Child* (Free Press, 1973).

[139] It may be argued that sensitive adaptation of existing doctrines could go a substantial way toward confronting problems of exploitation in reproductive arrangements. Shultz argues that these rules should not be ignored: (contd.../)

fears and the 'moral panic'[140] engendered by surrogacy has ensured, in many jurisdictions, a speedy legislative reaction to the practice.

[7.111] The *Baby M* case in the US was 'a catalyst for many lawmakers to urge various legislative regulation of surrogacy, although there was a wide spectrum of views as to what kind of regime was called for, ranging from calls to criminalise the practice to urgings to protect such arrangements.'[141] A Uniform Law was proposed which offered two approaches – one banning surrogacy and the other regulating it.[142] Four different approaches appear to be taken in the US: prohibition, inaction, status regulation and contractual ordering.[143] Some states prohibit all forms of surrogacy and impose civil and criminal penalties on anyone taking part in such arrangements, for example Arizona, District of Columbia, Indiana, Michigan and North Dakota. Others refuse to ban surrogacy by statute but allow courts to nullify such arrangements on grounds of public policy. Some states differentiate between paid and altruistic surrogacy, for example Kentucky, Louisiana, Nebraska, New York, North Carolina and Washington refuse to enforce paid surrogacy. Others such as Florida, Nevada, New Hampshire, New Mexico and Virginia explicitly make only unpaid surrogacy legal, thereby effectively banning surrogacy contracts since paid surrogacy is by far the most prevalent form there. Some states focus on banning payments to intermediaries, for example New Hampshire, New York and Virginia. In other states the status of surrogacy is unclear, as no legislation has been passed and couples entering surrogacy arrangements do so with the risk that the court may later rule that it is unenforceable or illegal based on public policy grounds.

[7.112] It is also worth noting that, in most of the cases in which surrogacy has been dealt with by the courts, a plea has been made by the judges for legislative action to address the issues. The courts, it seems, are unhappy with the forced adaptation of existing laws to address the unique issues presented by surrogacy. For example, baby-selling legislation (which has been enacted in every state in the US and is prevalent in almost every jurisdiction, including Ireland) was drafted to prevent parents from selling their already existing children, or expected children, due to financial pressures upon them, in circumstances in which they would otherwise keep the child themselves. This does not apply to surrogacy, in which the surrogate decides, in a vacuum almost, to

---

[139]   (\...contd)

    'Their effective use seems preferable to making agreements for reproductive collaboration categorically illegal. The latter approach is ostrich-like and essentially pessimistic. It fails to guide and ameliorate technological development. It represents governance by nostalgia that is not only impractical but also punitive toward pluralist values. It imposes a standardised moral vision in a domain where personal values are crucial.'

    Shultz, 'Legislative Regulation of Surrogacy and Reproductive Technology' (1994) 28 University of San Francisco Law Review 613 at 619.

[140]   Morgan, 'Making Motherhood Male: Surrogacy and the Moral Economy of Women' (1985) 12 J L & Soc 219, 222 (citing Cohen, *Folk Devils and Moral Panic* (MacGibbon and Kee Ltd, 1972)).

[141]   Spivack, 'The Law of Surrogate Motherhood in the United States' [2010] Am J of Comp Law Vol 58, 97 at 101.

[142]   Uniform Status of Children of Assisted Conception Act 9C ULA 383 (2001).

[143]   Rao, 'Surrogacy Law in the United States: The Outcome of Ambivalence' in Surrogate Motherhood: International Perspectives 23 (Rachel Cook et al eds, Hart Publishing, 2003).

become pregnant with the specific intention of giving that child up. This would appear to reinforce the validity of her decision rather than undermine it. Similarly, legislation dealing with child custody has often been based on the premise that the unwed father is uninterested in his progeny, again a factor which is not present in surrogacy in which the father has gone to extreme lengths to bring this child into existence. The application of contract law is also problematic in the context of human relationships, dealing as it does with the sale or supply of goods or services, activities which are worlds apart from bringing a child into existence.

[7.113] Even if existing schemes could be adapted to surrogacy, which is doubtful, legislation would still be necessary to ensure that the parties' expectations could be enforced in a consistent manner as between different judges, each of whom may take a different interpretation of existing precedent based, in part, on his or her own moral view of the practice of surrogacy. In the American context, due to the federal system of government, each state has taken a different view on surrogacy,[144] leading to potential reproductive tourism in the US. 'Legislation is needed in order to resolve the inconsistencies and uncertainty created by this patchwork of judicial precedent and legislative activity.'[145]

CONCLUSION

[7.114] The Commission on Assisted Human Reproduction recommended the establishment of a statutory body to regulate assisted reproduction services in Ireland. In relation to surrogacy, such a body could ensure that appropriate screening procedures, such as those carried out by the HSE in relation to prospective adoptive parents could be provided to surrogate mothers and commissioning parents. Counselling as well as medical, legal and psychological supports could be provided prior to conception of the child in order to ensure voluntary and informed consent from all parties and to guard against any exploitation. Reviews of procedures and fees could be conducted periodically by professionals and the optimum conditions for a safe and successful outcome ensured as far as possible. The Commission also recommended that surrogate mothers should be entitled to receive reimbursement of pregnancy-related expenses, that surrogacy-born children should be able to access the identity of the surrogate mother and that the child should be presumed to be that of the commissioning parents. The Commission came to this conclusion because the word 'presumed' allows some flexibility in relation to the legal parentage of the child in the case of some fundamental

---

[144] See *RR v MH & Another* (1998) 689 NE 2d 790 where the Supreme Court of Massachusetts addressed the issue of payments to surrogates and the validity of surrogacy in the absence of legislative guidance. The Court very usefully reviewed the laws of other states in the US and noted that three approaches could be found, namely: a prohibition on enforcement (for example, Arizona, Indiana and New York); a prohibition on paid surrogacy only (for example, Kentucky, Nebraska and Washington); and the explicit legality of unpaid surrogacy (for example, Florida and Virginia).

[145] Brandel, 'Legislating Surrogacy: A Partial Answer to Feminist Criticism' (1995) 54 *Maryland Law Review* 488 at 515.

change in the circumstances under which the surrogate mother consented to the arrangement. [146]

[7.115] The solution adopted in some US states, which involves a pre-birth or pre-conception legal process so that all legal issues are resolved in advance, has much to commend it. Dealing with any legal issues at the earliest possible stage is preferable to litigation after the child's birth. Such an approach ensures fairness between the parties, supervision of payments and protection of the health and welfare of the surrogate mother and the child. Surrogacy tends to be a morally divisive issue but attempts in other countries to prohibit or ignore surrogacy generally have had the opposite effect and have driven it underground.[147] The risk inherent in such an outcome is that persons who might be acting less than professionally may get involved in order to make some money out of the arrangement. It would be preferable to acknowledge that surrogacy happens and that regulation rather than prohibition would best protect the interests of all those involved.

---

[146] CAHR Report page 53. The Commission acknowledged that implementation of some of these recommendations may require amendment of the Constitution. See also dissent to these recommendations by O'Rourke at pages 76–77 of the Report.

[147] See Hibbs, 'Surrogacy Legislation – Time for Change?' (1997) Fam Law 564, discussing the English surrogacy arrangement involving Karen Roche as surrogate who initially claimed to have aborted the pregnancy because she was not happy with the commissioning couple, and then two days later admitted that the story was a lie. Hibbs says that any attempt to prohibit surrogacy entirely would be unwise and unworkable and that surrogacy should instead be regulated by the HFEA in the UK, whereby the question of payment could be monitored, the surrogate could be professionally counselled and the commissioning couple could be made aware of the risks involved in the arrangement.

Chapter 8

Genetics

INTRODUCTION

[8.01] The last 60 years or so have seen unprecedented breakthroughs in the biological sciences. The so-called 'new genetics' has increased our capacity to test for genetic diseases and to develop cures as well as advancing our knowledge about the workings of the human body. However, although there is much excitement and optimism for the future potential application of this knowledge, there is also concurrent unease and fear about the dangers of unregulated developments leading to eugenic tendencies slipping into policy-making, and the manipulation of human genes for commercial purposes. Genetics is 'a science that elicits vastly different reactions: at one pole we find celebration and boundless optimism; at the other, we have profound suspicion and dire prediction; and, between these extremes, there is a broad spectrum of opinion in which a positive view of genetics is qualified by expressions of caution and concern.'[1]

[8.02] In 1953 Crick and Watson published an explanation of the spiral structure of DNA and the way in which the genes operated through coded messages and sequences of letters.[2] A gene may be defined as the fundamental physical and functional unit of heredity. It is an ordered sequence of nucleotides located in a particular position on a particular chromosome that encodes a specific functional product, a protein.[3] Proteins are therefore made according to a specific 'recipe' set out in that coded message. Gene expression is the process by which the gene's coded information is converted into the structures present and operating in the cell. The structure of DNA (deoxyribonucleic acid) consists of an estimated three billion pairs of nucleotides, called base pairs, fitted together like steps of a twisting ladder at regular intervals, held together by sugar molecules and phosphates. DNA has been described as 'the true chemical of life … the essential component from which our genes are made. In it is encoded the genetic language that controls our destinies.'[4] Numerous breakthroughs in biological techniques followed Crick and Watson's elucidation of DNA, and this explanation now forms the central thesis of molecular biology. In the 1970s, the genetic basis of some genetic conditions was acknowledged and the revolution began:

---

[1]   Brownsword, Cornish and Llewelyn, 'Human Genetics and the Law: Regulating a Revolution' (1998) 61(5) Mod. L Rev 593.

[2]   The story of the discovery of DNA is told in the autobiography of James D Watson, *The Double Helix* (New York: Atheneum, 1968). See also Judson, *The Eighth Day of Creation* (Simon & Schuster, 1979).

[3]   *A Primer on Molecular Genetics* (1992) US Dept of Energy, Office of Energy Research, Office of Health and Environmental Research, Washington, 36.

[4]   Bodmer and McKie, *The Book of Man: The Quest to Discover Our Genetic Heritage* (Little Brown and Company, 1994) p 10.

291

We are witnessing a revolution brought about by scientific and technological advances, one in which change occurs at an accelerated pace. By 1945 we had the ability to destroy life on a large scale. By 2045, only a hundred years later, we ought to be able to create life from scratch, both in real space and in cyberspace.[5]

[8.03] In 1990 it was decided to sequence the entire human genome, which is the complete set of genes and chromosomes of the human organism. The intention was to construct a high-resolution genetic, physical and transcript map of the human, with ultimately, a complete sequence. The Human Genome Project was the largest research project ever undertaken with the intention of analysing the structure of human DNA and determining the location of the estimated 25,000 human genes.[6] It was heralded as having three main advantages, namely improved diagnostics, new approaches to the prevention of disease and gene replacement therapy. As the President's Council on Bioethics in the United States put it:

> By all accounts we have entered upon a golden age for biology, medicine and biotechnology. With the completion of [the DNA sequencing phase of] the Human Genome Project and the emergence of stem cell research, we can look forward to major insights into human development, normal and abnormal, as well as novel and more precisely selected treatments for human disease…In myriad ways, the discoveries of biologists and the inventions of biotechnologists are steadily increasing our power ever more precisely to intervene into the workings of our bodies and minds and to alter them by rational design.[7]

[8.04] Gene defects are estimated to underlie approximately 4,000 different diseases, and this estimation does not include polygenic diseases where there is interaction between certain genes and the environment.[8] As Mason and Laurie point out, 'few diseases are unifactorial and the great majority result from multifactorial traits which are believed to be the result not only of the effects of one or several genes but also of a combination of genetic and environmental factors.'[9] Tests are already available for many genetic diseases, such as cystic fibrosis, which enables carriers to be identified and more accurate genetic counselling to be offered. Individuals who may be susceptible to diseases such as schizophrenia, where many genes interact with environmental factors, may be targeted with preventative regimes. Personalised medication may be developed according to the specific genetic profiles of individual patients. This is the objective of pharmacogenetics which aims at understanding how genetic variation contributes to variations in response to medicines. The variation that exists in all genes causes different people to express different forms of proteins, including those that metabolise drugs. This can lead to different responses to those drugs. Genetic databases which bring

---

5   Baldi, *The Shattered Self: The End of Natural Evolution* (MIT Press, 2002) at 163.

6   The new genetics has led to a 1,000-fold increase in capacity to read a DNA sequence and a 10,000-fold reduction in the cost of DNA sequencing. House of Lords Science and Technology Committee, *Human Genetics: The Science and its Consequences* (July 1995) para 71.

7   President's Council on Bioethics, *Beyond Therapy*, (2003) at 5–6, quoted by Brownsword in 'Human Dignity, Ethical Pluralism, and the Regulation of Modern Biotechnologies', Murphy (ed) *New Technologies and Human Rights* (OUP, 2009) 19–85 at 19.

8   Wexler, 'Disease Gene Identification: Ethical Considerations' (October 15 1991) Hospital Practice 145.

9   Mason and Laurie, *Law and Medical Ethics,* (8th edn, OUP, 2010) para 7.07.

together several streams of data about individuals – molecular genetic data, standardised clinical data, data on health lifestyle and environment and so on – will enable correlations to be made which will guide mechanistic, pharmaceutical and other investigations. Measuring the genetic differences in this way will help predict the variation in response to the medicine and enable doctors to identify patients with a greater chance of effective response and reduced risk of adverse reactions.[10] Drug development will become faster and more efficient.

[8.05] If the predictions prove to be correct, the new genetics could represent a major advance in general health.[11] Thus, embracing genomic medicine could be legitimately seen as an economic necessity in order to fast-track new forms of preventative medicine for both poor and rich countries. The development of effective vaccines at low cost, based on DNA or related genomic research, could offer assistance to poor countries which carry huge burdens of infectious disease.[12] However, some geneticists advise against being seduced by 'genohype' and are concerned that the clinical benefits that will accrue from the application of genetics for therapeutic purposes have been exaggerated. For example, they argue that it will be almost impossible to find the genes involved in polygenic forms of common diseases where the clinical outcome is determined by complex gene, environmental and behavioural interaction, and similarly it will be difficult to develop useful and reliable predictive tests for them. [13]

[8.06] The medical, as opposed to the scientific, view of the value of the new genetics is also noteworthy. Many medical practitioners feel that their knowledge of genetics is lacking and that genetic advances will have little effect on the management of common diseases. However, the likely increases in availability of DNA-based tests and demand by patients for genetic information and advice mean that general practitioners will need to become genetically literate.[14] They have an important role in recognising the features of common genetic conditions, providing basic genetic information to patients, recognising the psychosocial issues for a family affected by a genetic condition and other vitally important services. Issues in genetic medicine that may be relevant in primary care would include reproductive risk, adult-onset genetic disorders, genetic variations in immune response and drug metabolism. Family history is currently used in determining risk of some specific cancers and informing decisions about early screening or genetic testing.[15] However, for other genetic conditions some practitioners may feel

---

10 Roses, 'Pharmacogenetics and the Practice of Medicine' (2000) Nature; 405: 857–865.

11 McLean, 'Interventions in the Human Genome' (1998) 61(5) Mod L Rev 681 at 682.

12 Richards, 'Three Views of Geneticists: The Enthusiast, the Visionary, and the Sceptic' (2001) 322 BMJ 1016, quoting Gordon Duff, professor of molecular medicine in the UK. See also 'Genetics and Developing Countries' (2001) 322 BMJ 1006.

13 Richards, 'Three Views of Geneticists: The Enthusiast, the Visionary, and the Sceptic' (2001) 322 BMJ 1016, quoting Neil Holtzman, director of genetics and public policy in Baltimore, USA.

14 Emery and Hayflick, 'The Challenge of Integrating Genetics Medicine into Primary Care' (2001) 322 BMJ 1027.

15 For discussion of how giving patients information about their genetic risk of developing common disease will be helpful if they can be persuaded to adopt healthy lifestyles that reduce risk, see Marteau and Lerman, 'Genetic Risk and Behavioural Change' (2001) 322 BMJ 1056.

that it is unethical to inform patients that there may be a genetic risk in their family, in the absence of effective screening technologies and therapies to reduce that risk.

[8.07] In addition to the potential benefits of genetic testing, new treatments may also be developed to counteract diseases caused by a specific gene defect, such as Severe Combined Immune Deficiency, in which patients cannot deal with infection and have to live in sterile environments. It is possible to treat these patients by way of gene therapy, whereby normal genes are inserted into their blood cells which, along with other treatment, would enable these patients to live a normal life.[16]

[8.08] There are many issues raised by genetics, in particular how to assimilate the mass of new information and translate it into clinical practice which both fulfils scientific criteria and respects ethical and social concerns.[17] The importance of evaluating public attitudes toward genetic testing is critical in appreciating patient response to future screening and in developing public policy. The need for greater general public understanding of genetics is evident in reports from the Nuffield Council on Bioethics, the British Medical Association, the European Commission, the World Health Organisation and the National Institute of Health in the United States.

[8.09] From a legal perspective, the picture is not particularly clear or satisfactory. Tension exists between those who promote principles of scientific freedom and those who fear social engineering, invasions of privacy and a loss of control over the uses to which increased knowledge will be put.[18] As a result, there is a 'paucity of legal protection or acknowledgement of the commercial implications of scientific research. Legislators in many countries, including Ireland, seem reluctant to involve themselves in these issues and it may be argued that rapid developments in biotechnology appear to render it unsuitable to cumbersome legal machinery. Moreover, a legal response has the potential to frustrate and hinder scientific progress.'[19] It is argued that the legal community is not well equipped to deal with the revolution in biotechnology, particularly one of the proportions indicated by modern genetics. Law has traditionally been reactive rather than proactive, responding to specific developments rather than establishing structures within which flexibility is possible by monitoring advances on the one hand while accommodating changing knowledge and capacity on the other.[20] The pace of change in this area, the need for flexibility, and the importance of developing public understanding through education and debate, means that any legislative intervention should be passed with as full as possible an appreciation of the consequences, and kept under periodic review.[21]

---

[16] See Nevin, 'Advances in Genetics: Spiralling into Trouble?' (2001) 68(4) Medico-legal Journal 4–12.

[17] Duboule, 'The Evolution of Genomics' (1998) 278 Science 555.

[18] See Smith, 'Genetic Enhancement Technologies and the New Society' (2000) 4 Med Law I 85–95.

[19] Gannon, 'The Science of Biotechnology: Present, Past and Future Quagmires' in Petersen, *Intersections: Women on Law, Medicine and Technology* (Dartmouth Publishing, 1997) p 216.

[20] McLean, 'Interventions in the Human Genome' (1998) 61(5) Mod L Rev 681 at 695.

[21] See recommendations of the UK Select Committee on Science and Technology, Third Report, *Human Genetics: The Science and its Consequences*, HC 1994–95, HC Paper 41, paras 2 and 3.

[8.10] At a European level, there have been attempts to harmonise the response to developments in genetics through the Convention on Bioethics and Biomedicine (also known as the Oviedo Convention) which was agreed in 1996. Ireland is not a signatory to the Convention. This Convention acknowledges that progress in genetics will enable advances in disease prevention, diagnosis and treatment but also warns that the risks should not be ignored, as it is no longer the individual or society that may be at risk but the human species itself. The Convention marks a significant attempt to address the diverse dilemmas of bioethics through the use of a human rights framework. It was drafted in an attempt to keep pace with biomedical developments and to close legal loop-holes that might exist within Europe where scientists could exploit lack of regulation in order to evade the legal restrictions in force in their own countries. The underlying principles contained in the Convention are autonomy and informed consent, although McGleenan questions whether such a model would provide effective protection against powerful bodies such as employers and insurers.[22] Cloning is specifically prohibited in a Protocol to the Convention[23] and the granting of patents for cloning processes has been prohibited by the Directive on the Legal Protection of Biotechnological Inventions.[24]

[8.11] UNESCO has also played an important role in setting ethical standards internationally in the area of genetics. It stated that:

> Genetic data can be used for medical diagnosis, disease prevention and population genetics studies. As each person's genetic heritage is unique, forensic science and the judicial system also use them for identification purposes. The number of genetic databanks is rising, with some containing more than a million records. Some are maintained at a national level and contain samples from virtually entire national populations. In this rapidly developing field, many people fear that human genetic data will be used for purposes contrary to human rights and freedom. Governments, non-governmental organizations, the intellectual community and society in general are calling for guidelines at the international level.[25]

As a result, it published the International Declaration on Genetic Data in 2003.[26]

[8.12] In 2003 UNESCO also decided that it was opportune and desirable to set universal standards in the field of bioethics with due regard for human dignity and human rights and freedoms, in the spirit of cultural pluralism inherent in bioethics. It stated:

> A growing number of scientific practices have extended beyond national borders and the necessity of setting universal ethical guidelines covering all issues raised in the field of

---

[22] McGleenan, 'Legal Regulation of Genetic Technology' in *The Concise Encyclopaedia of the Ethics of New Technologies,* Chadwick (ed) (Academic Press, 2001) 199.

[23] Additional Protocol to the Convention for the Protection of Human Rights and Dignity of the Human Being with regard to the Application of Biology and Medicine, on the Prohibition of Cloning Human Beings (Paris, January 1998).

[24] Directive of the European Parliament and of the Council on the Legal Protection of Biotechnological Inventions, No 98/44/EC of 6 July 1998, OJ L213, 30/7/98, p 13.

[25] http://www.unesco.org/new/en/social-and-human-sciences/themes/bioethics/human-genetic-data/ (accessed 2 June 2011).

[26] http://www.unesco.org/new/en/social-and-human-sciences/themes/bioethics/human-genetic-data/ (accessed 2 June 2011).

bioethics and the need to promote the emergence of shared values have increasingly been a feature of the international debate. The need for standard-setting action in the field of bioethics is felt throughout the world, often expressed by scientists and practitioners themselves and by lawmakers and citizens. States have a special responsibility not only with respect to bioethical reflection but also in the drafting of any legislation that may follow.[27]

[8.13] It published its Universal Declaration on Bioethics and Human Rights in 2005, which attempts 'to balance the somewhat divergent claims of social solidarity with the protection of individual human rights'.[28] 'It protects the rights and liberties of individuals and also enshrines the role of science and knowledge in helping civilisation to progress. The declaration is also designed to remind the international community of its duty of solidarity towards poorer countries from the benefits of biomedical progress.'[29] Brownsword says that the key feature of the most recent declaration is 'the continuing commitment to ethically clean science coupled with a willingness to engage with cultural diversity.'[30] The UNESCO declarations promote the idea that while science and technology have the capacity to function as a positive force, they must be compatible with respect for human rights and human dignity.

[8.14] As well as concerns arising about the need for regulation, there are also many social concerns arising from the availability and use of genetic information.[31] These involve issues of fairness in the use of genetic information; ownership, privacy and confidentiality; psychological impact and possible stigmatisation; use of genetic information in reproductive decision-making; the ethics of testing for late-onset diseases or those for which no treatment is available; environmental issues; patenting of DNA sequences; and issues around the lines to be drawn between treatment and enhancement, acceptable diversity, freewill and genetic determinism.[32]

---

27   http://www.unesco.org/new/en/social-and-human-sciences/themes/bioethics/bioethics-and-human-rights/ (accessed 2 June 2011).

28   McGleenan, 'Legal Regulation of Genetic Technology' in *The Concise Encyclopaedia of the Ethics of New Technologies,* Chadwick (ed) (Academic Press, 2001), at 201.

29   Lenoir, 'UNESCO, Genetics and Human Rights' (1997) 7 Kennedy Inst. of Ethics Journal 31.

30   President's Council on Bioethics, *Beyond Therapy,* (2003) at 5–6, quoted by Brownsword in 'Human Dignity, Ethical Pluralism, and the Regulation of Modern Biotechnologies', Murphy (ed) *New Technologies and Human Rights* (OUP, 2009) 19–85 at 19.

31   It is important to avoid an approach labelled as 'geneticisation' whereby human beings are regarded essentially as gene carriers, and issues of nature, functioning, health and disease are all characterised in the language of genetics. This tendency would distract from explanations based on social, environmental or economic conditions and result in less resource allocation for social research and policy. It may also result in changes in reproductive decision-making as the traditional emphasis on parenting is replaced by the genetic quality in reproduction. Fatalistic attitudes may develop which avoid social and moral responsibility by referring to one's inability to avoid one's genetic heritage. See Nuffield Council on Bioethics, *Mental Disorders and Genetics: The Ethical Context*, at para 1.5–1.7, and Lippman, 'Led (Astray) by Genetic Maps: the Cartography of the Human Genome and Healthcare' (1992) 35 Social Science and Medicine 1469–76.

32   See www.ornl.gov/sci/techresources/Human_Genome/elsi/elsi.shtml for further discussion of some of these issues. (accessed 2 June 2011).

ETHICS AND GENETICS

[8.15] It has sometimes been argued that the development of the Human Genome Project raises no new ethical problems and few legal ones.[33] Such problems as there are come from the development of new therapeutic opportunities rather than the acquisition of the new knowledge itself.[34] On the other hand, Annas argues that what is unique about the new genetics is the advance realisation that serious ethical and policy issues are raised by the research and that pre-emptive steps must be taken to assure the maximisation of the benefits of the knowledge and the minimisation of the 'potential dark-side'.[35] Burley and Harris are of the view that no branch of science has created more acute or more subtle and interesting ethical dilemmas than genetics. Although other areas of science, such as nuclear physics, may create problems of greater moral importance, 'it is genetics that makes us recall, not simply our responsibilities to the world and to one another, but our responsibilities for how people will be in the future. For the first time we can begin to determine not simply who will live and who will die, but what all those who live in the future will be like.'[36]

[8.16] One of the features of the 'dark-side' referred to by Annas, is the fear of eugenics which has been defined as the 'conscious selection of humans by encouraging the production of those with desired inherited characteristics and for restricting those with undesirable inherited characteristics.'[37] The notion that humanity can and should be bettered by such conscious selection, and that science can be trusted with this task, forms the roots of eugenic policies. There are both negative and positive aspects to such policies on the wider population or societal level. On the one hand, negative eugenics policies would involve the imposition of restrictions on sexual freedom on those deemed 'unfit' to reproduce, whereas positive eugenics might, theoretically, promote the representation of certain genes in the gene pool of future generations.[38]

[8.17] The historical connotations associated with eugenic policies and programmes present obvious reminders of the dangers of abuse in the concept that humankind should be bettered.[39] In the United States in the 1920s it was thought that genetics provided evidence of the inferiority of certain minorities.[40] This was clearly the motivation behind the judgment of the Supreme Court in *Buck v Bell*[41] in 1927 where a law requiring the

---

[33] *Report of the Clothier Committee on the Ethics of Gene Therapy* (1992) Cm 1788.

[34] Maddox, 'New Genetics Means No New Ethics' (1993) 364 Nature 97.

[35] Annas, *Standard of Care* (OUP, 1993) 149–50. See also Morgan, *Issues in Medical Law and Ethics* (2001) Ch 9.

[36] Burley and Harris (eds) 'Introduction' in *A Companion to Genethics* (Blackwell Publishing, 2002) at 1.

[37] Rothley and Casini, 'Ethical and Legal Problems of Genetic Engineering and Human Artificial Insemination' (1990) EU Committee on Legal Affairs and Citizen's Rights.

[38] Kelves, *In the Name of Eugenics: Genetics and the Uses of Human Heredity* (Knopf, 1985).

[39] See Haker's discussion of the history of eugenic thought in the 20th century in 'Human Genome Analysis and Eugenics', Haker, Hearn and Steigler (eds) *Ethics of Human Genome Analysis, European Perspectives* (1993, Attempto Verlag Tubingen) p 293.

[40] Norton, 'Unnatural Selection: Non Therapeutic Pre-Implantation Genetic Screening and Proposed Regulation' (1994) 41 ICLA Law Rev 1586.

[41] *Buck v Bell* (1927) 274 US 200.

sterilisation of hospital inmates was upheld on the basis that 'three generations of imbeciles is enough.'[42] In European history, the horrors of the Nazi era provide the clearest context for discussion of the dangers of eugenics.[43] In the mid to late 1930s the idea of racial purity and a healthy population led to the policy that has subsequently been identified as the 'ultimate eugenic nightmare'.[44] The identification and elimination of those deemed responsible for the degeneration of human kind, such as those suffering from blindness and epilepsy[45] as well as those from 'inferior' races such as the Jews, was based on genetics. This also led to human experimentation carried out in order to attain the utopian dream of the perfect society.

[8.18] Germany's involvement in eugenic policies and negative population genetics, racist discrimination in the United States and sex selection in India and China has shaped international reaction to developments in genetics. While on the one hand science marches on regardless of moral values and concerns, on the other hand, calls for legal regulation of scientific developments continue to be made. The possibility for prospective parents to avoid passing on inherited diseases to their future children is extremely tempting, and some might say, coercive. There is a corresponding anxiety, however, that this will in time lead to the spectre of 'designer babies' and the search for the perfect child.[46] The elitism inherent in such a pursuit may seem to be dangerously close to the notion of the master race that successfully persuaded many followers of Hitler to the eugenic creed. The arguments used here are emotive and perhaps sensationalist as each side tries to capture the moral 'right'. The value of promoting 'genetic responsibility' or 'responsible parenting' so as to avoid increasing the transmission of deleterious genes in society, as opposed to the recognition of the intrinsic worth of every individual irrespective of their genes, raises an argument which it seems impossible to resolve. An example of the ethical issues that may arise in this context is given by the suggestion that there is a genetic basis to certain forms of criminal behaviour and that a predisposition to violence, or sexual deviance, could in some way excuse such behaviour on the grounds that the individual was compelled by his genetic make-up and thus had no free will. Whether such an argument could be

---

[42] *Buck v Bell* (1927) 274 US 200 at 207.

[43] See 'Eugenic Origins of Medical Genetics' in Paul, *The Politics of Heredity* (State University of New York Press, 1998) Ch 8.

[44] 'Justice and Eugenics' in Vollrath, Science and Moral Values (1990) at 107.

[45] Huntington's disease was listed as one of the disorders suitable for compulsory sterilisation in German law in 1933. It is thought that there were up to 5,000 sterilisations of those from families with the disease. See Muller-Hill, *Murderous Science* (Cold Spring Harbor Laboratory Press, 1998); Burleig, *Death and Deliverance, Euthanasia in Germany 1900–1945* (New York: Cambridge University Press, 1991); Harper, 'Huntington's Disease and the Abuse of Genetics' in Harper and Clarke, *Genetics, Society and Clinical Practice* (Garland Science, 1997) Ch 17.

[46] Negative interventions designed to avoid suffering seem to be less threatening and more acceptable than positive interventions designed to promote desirable characteristics. Harris argues that this is not necessarily plausible. He gives the example of an intervention designed to promote intelligence in children and says that to prohibit such an intervention is akin to 'inventing antibiotics but declining to put them into production'. See Harris, *The Value of Life* (Routledge, 1985) 150.

successfully used in the criminal justice system or whether it would reinforce the tendency to 'control, categorise and label people' is open to debate.[47]

[8.19] The concept of human dignity has been prioritised in all of the many international documents that have emerged since the recognition of the importance of the explosion of new information available. For example, the Preamble to the Council of Europe's Convention on Human Rights and Biomedicine states that States must take necessary measures 'to safeguard human dignity and the fundamental rights and freedoms of the individual with regard to the application of biology and medicine.'[48] Similarly, in the Preamble to UNESCO's Universal Declaration on the Human Genome and Human Rights[49] it is stated that research on the human genome 'should fully respect human dignity, freedom and human rights.' Some commentators argue that appeals to the concept of human dignity are 'comprehensively vague'[50] or that, though seemingly simple, it is an expression 'full of fragility'[51], as can be seen in the context of other debates such as that around euthanasia where both proponents and opponents use the concept to support their own values. This has also been discussed in Chapter 6.

[8.20] Beyleveld and Brownsword argue that dignity may be interpreted in two senses, the first, which is common in debates around instrumentalisation, is that dignity relates to the intrinsic value of persons and that therefore it is wrong to treat persons as mere things, or as means to an end. This is classically expressed by Kant's formulation of the Categorical Imperative: 'Act in such a way that you always treat humanity, whether in your own person or in the person of any other, never simply as a means, but always at the same time as an end.'[52] For Kant, every human being has a legitimate claim to respect from other human beings and, in turn, is bound to respect every other. Secondly, and less importantly in the context of human genetics, there is the idea that dignified conduct is a kind of virtue. In other words, the way in which a person presents himself socially, and the manner in which he handles adversity, is understood as a sign of a person's dignity.[53]

---

[47] See further Wells, '"I Blame the Parents": Fitting New Genes in Old Criminal Laws' (1998) 61(5) Mod L Rev 724–739.

[48] Council of Europe, *Convention for the Protection of Human Rights and Dignity of the Human Being with regard to the application of Biology and Medicine: Convention on Human Rights and Biomedicine* (DIR/JUR (96) 14) Strasbourg: Directorate of Legal Affairs, November 1996.

[49] Adopted by the General Conference on 11 November 1997.

[50] Harris, *Clones, Genes and Immortality* (OUP, 1998) 31.

[51] Bedjaoui, *Proceedings of the Third Session of the International Bioethics Committee of UNESCO*, Sept. 1995: Vol 1 at 144, quoted in Beyleveld and Brownsword, 'Human Dignity, Human Rights, and Human Genetics' (1998) 61(5) Mod L Rev 661.

[52] See Paton, *The Moral Law* (Kant's groundwork of the metaphysic of morals: first published 1785) (1948) at 91, quoted by Beyleveld and Brownsword, 'Human Dignity, Human Rights, and Human Genetics' (1998) 61(5) Mod L Rev 661 at 666.

[53] Beyleveld and Brownsword, 'Human Dignity, Human Rights, and Human Genetics' (1998) 61(5) Mod L Rev at 667, see also President's Council on Bioethics, *Beyond Therapy*, (2003) at 5–6, quoted by Brownsword in 'Human Dignity, Ethical Pluralism, and the Regulation of Modern Biotechnologies', Murphy (ed) *New Technologies and Human Rights* (OUP, 2009) 19–85 at 19.

[8.21] It is argued that it is an abuse of the concept of human dignity to operate it as a veto on any practice that is intuitively disliked. According to Gewirthian principles, it is rightly used to require that agents, that is, those who have the capacity freely to select and act for purposes, should be treated as ends and not mere things. Complementary to that is the principle that the freedom and well-being of agents should not be interfered with against their own will, so that if they choose to participate in genetic research or to sell their genes, it is argued that any interference with such actions on the grounds of human dignity would be misguided paternalism.[54] Therefore:

> [T]he concept of human dignity has a legitimate place in debates about human genetics. However, it is something of a loose cannon, open to abuse and misinterpretation; it can oversimplify complex questions; and it can encourage a paternalism that is incompatible with the spirit of self-determination that informs the mainstream of human rights thinking.[55]

GENETIC TESTING

[8.22] Genetic disorders are diseases and malformations caused entirely, or to a substantial extent, by a series of alterations in the genome. They are traditionally divided into three categories. First, disorders due to changes in single genes, such as Huntington's Chorea. These may be classified into dominant, recessive and x-linked inheritance patterns which reflect the probability of inheriting a genetic defect. Secondly, there are polygenic disorders which occur as a result of the absence or interaction of more than one gene. Information may be limited on these disorders due to a multiplicity of gene combinations and environmental factors. Many forms of cancer have an inherited genetic basis which may be triggered by environmental factors. Thirdly, there are chromosomal disorders caused by a rearrangement of chromosomes, such as Down's syndrome.[56]

[8.23] The National Centre for Medical Genetics was established in Dublin in 1994.[57] The clinic sees individuals and families affected by or at risk of a genetic disorder, both for diagnosis and after diagnosis. Once a diagnosis has been made, families are then advised on the interpretation of the test results and given non-directive counselling about related risks. Families may then seek further clinical care from their general practitioner or appropriate consultants. The clinic also maintains registers of families with specific conditions in order to maintain contact with the families to provide on-going information where relevant and offer further tests to other siblings where this

---

54   Beyleveld and Brownsword, 'Human Dignity, Human Rights, and Human Genetics' (1998) 61(5) Mod L Rev at 680, referring to the central contention in Gewirthian moral theory that agents are bound by the Principle of Generic Consistency under which agents have reciprocal rights and duties to respect one another's freedom and well-being. Gewirth, *Reason and Morality* (University of Chicago Press, 1978).

55   Beyleveld and Brownsword, 'Human Dignity, Human Rights, and Human Genetics' (1998) 61(5) Mod L Rev 661 at 662.

56   Brown and Gannon, 'Confidentiality and the Human Genome Project: A Prophecy for Conflict?' in McLean S (ed) *Contemporary Issues in Law, Medicine and Ethics* (Dartmouth, 1996) Ch 11.

57   See http://www.genetics.ie/ (accessed 2 June 2011). The Centre also has clinics in Cork, Galway and Limerick. It does not carry out genetic screening of healthy populations.

might be beneficial. The registers also act as a means of support for families who may have recently discovered their genetic condition. As well as the clinical services provided, the centre has a cytogenetics laboratory which analyses samples from individuals with suspected constitutional chromosome abnormalities, and a molecular genetics service which provides molecular diagnostic services for a range of inherited disorders.

[8.24] It is not currently possible to test for all genetic disorders. Genetic testing is not a single technology. It refers to a broad range of methods for gauging the presence, or absence of activity, of genes in cells. Individuals with a mutation or aberration affecting chromosomes or genes that cause disease later in life may not have any symptoms until early adulthood or later. However, the underlying mutation may be diagnosed by predictive genetic testing by way of chromosome and DNA analysis. This will provide information about the likelihood of the disorder appearing in the individual at some future time. Predictive genetic testing can be performed on individuals, members of a family at risk, specific sections of the population, or the general population as a whole. The systematic search for persons having particular genetic characteristics is called 'genetic screening'. In contrast to genetic diagnosis, screening is not usually sought by the person tested, but rather it is initiated by the provider of the test, such as public health authorities.

[8.25] A conventional medical diagnostic test provides information as to the patient's current state of health. By contrast, a predictive genetic test provides information about a future medical condition that may or may not develop. Although the identified risk might sometimes be high (as in Huntington's disease), there will always be an element of uncertainty about whether the condition will develop, when it will appear, and how severe the symptoms will be in this particular patient. The possible interventions for the condition may also be untested and recommendations may be based on presumed benefit rather than on observations of outcomes.[58] The notion of genetic 'report cards' that would successfully predict at birth the future health of the individual are, as yet, illusory and misrepresentative of the possibilities offered by predictive testing.[59] However, some argue that:

> It is not at all fanciful to foresee a day in which a single drop of blood from a newborn child provides the template upon which a completely automated system checks for the presence of a hundred different genetic conditions. A similar level of scrutiny will be available for the fetus, and, in time, premarital screening will routinely apprise couples of how they might fare in the genetic lottery occurring with each conception.[60]

[8.26] Another significant distinction between predictive testing and other diagnostic tests is that the latter do not usually have significance for other family members, except where the condition is communicable, such as an infectious disease. With predictive

---

[58] Evans et al, 'The Complexities of Predictive Genetic Testing' (2001) 322 BMJ 1052–1056; Burke W et al, 'Recommendations for Follow-Up Care of Individuals with an Inherited Predisposition to Cancer" (1997) 277 JAMA 997–1003 and 915–919.

[59] See Khoury et al, 'Challenges in Communicating Genetics: A Public Health Approach' (2000) 2 Genetics in Medicine 198–202.

[60] Reilly, 'Public Policy and Legal Issues Raised by Advances in Genetic Screening and Testing' (1993) XXVII Suffolk University Law Review 1327 at 1329.

testing there are usually direct implications for family members who share the same gene pool. The impact on individual autonomy, the possibility of making informed choices and the nature of the relationship between individuals and society are issues to be examined not only by the clinicians considering what tests to carry out, but also by those who choose to present for testing.[61]

[8.27] Voluntary and confidential predictive testing may be able to offer significant benefits to individuals carrying a particular genetic trait, in terms of improved duration and quality of life by early warning, and, in some cases, avoidance of exacerbating factors. However, the dangers of misuse are also clear, whether it be by virtue of inadequate methodology[62], lack of adequately trained test providers or lack of understanding of genetics by health care professionals and the public at large.[63] The psychological burden to the patient in knowing that he carries a predisposition to a specific disorder, the social pressures to act on that knowledge, the reduction in tolerance and discrimination in cases of genetic dysfunction,[64] as well as the possibility of misuse by third parties such as employers, insurers and the State,[65] all lead to the conclusion that a policy of caution is advisable in this context. This has been reflected in many recommendations of expert bodies that have considered the ethical issues involved in genetic testing and screening. For example, the Nuffield Council on Bioethics states that many of the ethical issues that arise in relation to genetic screening do so due to the inescapable involvement of families. It recommends that the factors to be taken into account in relation to any proposed screening programme should include: the predictive power and accuracy of the test; the benefits of informed personal choice; the psychological impact of the outcome for the individuals and families; therapeutic possibilities; possible social and economic disadvantage; and the resource implications of the programme.[66]

[8.28] It is likely that the duty to provide genetic information will become more commonplace as genetic research expands and as more patients become informed about genetics and seek testing for predisposition to chronic illnesses. The importance of providing accurate information is crucial both in psychological terms and also in the

---

[61] For a discussion on the relationship between genetics and behaviour, see Nuffield Council on Bioethics, *Genetics and Human Behaviour: The Ethical Context* (2002).

[62] The NIH Task Force on Genetic Testing recommends that 'the genotypes to be detected by a genetic test must be shown by scientifically valid methods to be associated with the occurrence of a disease. The observations must be independently replicated and subject to peer review.'

[63] Holtzman, *Proceed with Caution. Predicting Genetic Risks in the Recombinant DNA Era* (John Hopkins University Press, 1989).

[64] See Markel in Holtzman and Watson (eds) *Promoting Safe and Effective Genetic Testing in the United* States (1997) Task Force of the National Institutes of Health on Genetic Testing, Appendix 6.

[65] For consideration of whether pre-symptomatic individuals who have tested positive for a specific genetic disease, such as Huntington's, should come within the meaning of 'persons with disabilities' so as to prevent unlawful discrimination in employment opportunities, see Gin, 'Genetic Discrimination: Huntington's Disease and the Americans with Disabilities Act" (1997) 97 Columbia Law Review 1406–1434.

[66] Nuffield Council on Bioethics, *Genetic Screening: Ethics Issues* (1993).

context of seeking to avoid any legal fallout. Recent advances in direct-to-consumer (DTC) testing have led to concern in relation to consumer protection, assignment of legal responsibility, efficacy of national regulation in the face of worldwide internet access and so on. According to the European Society of Human Genetics, experience in relation to DTC advertising of prescription medicine has shown that this has created an inappropriate demand for medications. Moreover, it has shown that various advertisements for drugs have been misleading. 'Overstatement of effectiveness or minimization of risk has led to inadequate or inappropriate changes in medication, diet or lifestyle by consumers. DTC advertising of genetic tests for health related purposes runs the same risks as DTC advertising of prescription medicine in this regard. Aggressive marketing strategies and slogans for DTC genetic testing might overstate the potential for predictive information of such tests and overrate its future health implications.[67]

It is important that the technology is regulated to ensure that: information is accurate; individuals are provided with information about the identified problem in order to make informed choices; the implications for relatives of those tested are clearly understood by the individual undergoing the test; testing does not result in unfair discrimination at work or for life and health insurance; and priorities and resource allocation decisions are based on as sound evidence as possible taking account of the state of the art.[68]

[8.29] There are different types of genetic testing, ranging from requests from relatives of patients with a late-onset genetic disorder, to population screening, testing of symptomatic individuals, and susceptibility testing for common disorders.[69] In relation to population screening, in addition to helping patients to get the information they seek, there are also concerns about protecting people from information that they do not want to receive. For instance, from a public health perspective it might be beneficial to mandate blood tests in the general population in order to screen for carriers of a particular genetic disease.[70] However, there are concerns that not only might this lead to stigmatisation, particularly since certain genetic defects are more prevalent in particular ethnic groups, but that the concept itself 'smacks of the turn-of-the-century eugenics movement in the United States when laws were passed to sterilise people who were

---

[67] European Society of Human Genetics: 'Statement of the ESHG on Direct-to-Consumer Genetic Testing for Health-Related Purposes' (2010) European Journal of Human Genetics, 1–3. See also concerns expressed in February 2011 by the American Medical Association regarding the importance of medical supervision of genetic testing: www.ama-assn.org/resources/doc/washington/consumer-genetic-testing-letter.pdf (accessed 11 July 2011).

[68] Kinderlerer and Longley, 'Human Genetics: the New Panacea?' (1998) 61(5) Mod L Rev 603 at 613.

[69] For discussion, see Schwartz Cowan's *Heredity and Hope, The Case for Genetic Screening* (Harvard University Press, 2008) Ch 1.

[70] In the US in the 1960s and early 1970s, when the biochemical basis of Tay–Sachs disease (an autosomal recessive genetic disorder which causes deterioration of physical and mental capacity and commonly results in childhood death) was first becoming known, no mutations had been sequenced directly for any genetic diseases. Researchers of that era did not yet know how common polymorphism would prove to be and it was thought that a single mutation must have spread from one population into another. Subsequent research has proven that a large number of HEXA mutations can cause some form of the disease. Tay–Sachs disease was one of the first genetic disorders for which widespread genetic screening was possible.

thought to have the genes for feeblemindedness, epilepsy, prostitution, and pauperism.'[71] In the early days of large-scale genetic screening programmes, a lack of understanding of the complexities involved resulted in organizing efforts that were premature, poorly designed and had inadequate safeguards. Health officials, understandably wanting to bring the benefits of promising new technology to the public as rapidly as possible, frequently did not give adequate consideration to possible negative psychosocial and economic consequences. Thus carriers were sometimes denied employment and life insurance because genetic traits and genetic diseases were confused.[72]

[8.30] Carrier screening may generate anxieties and concerns in many people who will never benefit from being identified as such, because their partners are not carriers or they are not planning to have children or are not inclined to alter their life or reproductive plans as a result of their carrier status. Although carriers of genetic disease will not be affected themselves, studies have shown that many carriers suffer anxiety about their health, lower self-esteem and feelings of shame.[73] Such testing could therefore be seen as unduly burdensome to them, and the impact on their well-being must be brought into the balance in deciding whether to proceed with such screening. Another form of screening tries to identify susceptibility to a particular disease based on genetic profile but can only give relative risks due to the uncertainty of the impact of environmental factors and other variables.

[8.31] In relation to late-onset disorders, those who seek predictive testing usually perceive themselves to be at risk due to relevant family history. These kinds of tests are generally regarded as more problematic for ethical reasons. The benefits of testing in those cases would be the possibility of preventative measures or early treatment, although this is not always available; the ability to plan major life events and make decisions; and the awareness of passing on the risk to future family members.[74] However, the result of such a test rarely gives information on when the symptoms of the disorder will appear or how severe they may be, and a positive test result may lead to severe psychological problems.

[8.32] There have been many discussions in recent years about the extent to which genetic information is unique and requires a legal framework different from that which is applicable to other forms of medical information. This is referred to as 'genetic exceptionalism'.[75] However, genetic information covers 'a broad spectrum from highly monogenic disorders through susceptibility genes and on to a simple family history...Not every class of this information is predictive of future ill health – indeed, many examples of genetic information are no more predictive than is general health

---

[71]   Andrews, 'Genetic Fallout: New Technologies Are Changing the Legal Landscape' (1995) Trial 20 at 23.

[72]   Kenen and Schmidt, 'Stigmatization of Carrier Status: Social Implications of Heterozygote Genetic Screening Programs' (1978) American Journal of Public Health, Vol 68, No 11.

[73]   Clarke, 'Genetic Screening and Counselling' in Kuhse and Singer, *A Companion to Bioethics,* (Blackwell, 1998) at 221.

[74]   See detailed discussion in the UK Advisory Committee on Genetic Testing, *Report on Genetic Testing for Late Onset Disorders* (1998).

[75]   See Gostin and Hodge, 'Genetic Privacy and the Law: An End to Genetic Exceptionalism' (1999) 40 Jurimetrics 21.

information.'[76] Mason and Laurie argue that these factors militate against the argument that genetic data are in some way different from other forms of medical data. The Human Genetics Commission in the UK states that it does not take the view that all genetic information should be treated in the same way in every set of circumstances.[77] Nonetheless the legal response to genetics has tended to proceed on the basis that genetic information is different.

Privacy and the interests of family members

[8.33] The current revolution in genetic science has enabled us to examine our own genetic make-up for the first time. This has led to a greater understanding of known diseases, an improved ability to predict future health, an increased understanding of behaviour traits and a wider range of reproductive options. However, a genetic test result sometimes has implications not only for the proband (ie the person tested) but also for blood relatives who share a common gene pool. With this genetic revolution, and in particular the predictive power of genetic tests, have come ethical and legal problems, including the issues of privacy and confidentiality. The crucial issues here in relation to access to genetic information are: what are the rights of the individual, and what are the rights of third parties with a legitimate interest in the information? The presence of a genetic mutation within a family is significant for family members as well as the individual. 'Those individuals who are directly affected may suffer anxiety, fear, depression, guilt and the stress of being the bearer of bad news to the family.'[78] Genetic information may also yield unexpected details in relation to paternity or consanguinity.

[8.34] Any genetic information about a person may indicate that blood relatives should also be tested, particularly where there are interventions available to alleviate the condition. In relation to some genetic conditions it may also be necessary to test family members in order to refine the risk to one member. It is not difficult to imagine situations in which families may be split over the question of genetic testing. These might include situations where one family member will not provide a tissue sample necessary for a complete diagnosis within the family, or the refusal to inform relatives that they may be affected by a positive test result, or debates over whether to have a child tested for a late-onset disorder for which there is no effective intervention.[79] Where one family member refuses to undergo testing, this may effectively block other members' ability to discover their risk factor. The ethical and legal difficulties that may arise here centre on the value of the right to know one's genetic make-up and the right to refuse to be tested for genetic disorder. If the relative refuses to be tested due to a wish not to be informed of his/her own genetic risk, it may be possible to inform other relatives without informing the donor of the tissue, but this may not always be appropriate.[80]

---

[76] Mason and Laurie, *Law and Medical Ethics,* (8th edn, OUP, 2010) at para 7.25.

[77] Human Genetics Commission, *Inside Information: Balancing Interests in the Use of Personal Genetic Data* (2002). See also HGC, *Public Attitudes to Human Genetic Information* (2001).

[78] Skene, 'Legal Regulation of Genetic Testing, Balancing Privacy and Family Interests' in Iltis, Johnson and Hinze (eds) *Legal Perspectives in Bioethics* (Routledge, 2008) at 208.

[79] Reilly, 'Public Policy and Legal Issues Raised by Advances in Genetic Screening and Testing' (1993) XXVII Suffolk University Law Review 1327 at 1335.

[80] Obviously in a case of identical twins, any genetic diagnosis will affect both individuals.

[8.35] Another issue that may arise in practice is where test results indicate mispaternity. This may occur when a woman gives birth to a child with an autosomal recessive disorder (meaning that the disorder is inherited from both parents, who are usually themselves unaffected) and the husband is found not to be a carrier, or when linkage studies with other family members show that the child's genetic markers are incompatible with being the child of the presumed father.[81] This is certainly not a particularly novel problem and the practice in many laboratories is simply to answer the clinical question asked and avoid reporting information that is not medically relevant. Alternatively, the geneticist may meet the woman alone to report the finding, the husband is not directly informed and the biological facts are avoided. 'In such situations, the justification is that the geneticist owes a higher allegiance to the integrity of the family than to any one member. Disclosing the full truth to the husband might do more harm than good. Although it may be defensible ethically, the practice of deceiving the husband has shaky legal foundations.'[82]

[8.36] The availability of genetic tests has sometimes been accompanied by confusion in people's minds about what exactly will be achieved by the test. Genetic tests do not provide a cure for genetic disease, in fact in many cases in which genetic disease is indicated by the test result, no cure is possible. Although the futility of discovering that one is going to become ill with an incurable disease may mean that some people would rather not have that information, the reason that many do wish to have the test done is to prepare themselves for their future ill-health, both emotionally and financially. Those who may have intended to start a family may make a more informed decision about whether to take the risk of passing on the genetic disorder to future children. It has been argued, however, that this advance knowledge may not always be advantageous to the individual. There is evidence, for example, that the suicide rate among young Caucasians who know that they carry the gene for Huntington's disease (a late-onset neurological disease for which there is no cure) is at least four times higher than that of the national average for a comparable group of their peers.[83] Knowledge that one's health is going to deteriorate can cause psychological distress for many people, who then become self-obsessed and subject to feelings of victimisation. They may sometimes behave as though they already have the disease. The necessity of having counselling both prior to and after receiving genetic testing is self-evident so that individuals are given the necessary information upon which to base an informed choice and also the time for reflection before making that choice, as well as before receiving the

---

[81] Reilly, 'Public Policy and Legal Issues Raised by Advances in Genetic Screening and Testing' (1993) XXVII Suffolk University Law Review 1327 at 1335.

[82] Reilly 'Public Policy and Legal Issues Raised by Advances in Genetic Screening and Testing' (1993) XXVII Suffolk University Law Review 1327 at 1338.

[83] See Andrews, 'Legal Aspects of Genetic Information' (1990) 64 Yale J Biol Med 29. A more recent study states that the rate is up to 10 times higher: Almqvist et al, 'A Worldwide Assessment of the Frequency of Suicide, Suicide Attempts, or Psychiatric Hospitalisation After Predictive Testing for Huntington's Disease' (1999) 64 Amer J of Human Genetics 1293. See further Hayden, 'Predictive Testing for Huntington's Disease: Are We Ready for Widespread Community Implementation?' 40 Am J Med Gen 515; Brandt et al, 'Presymptomatic Diagnosis of Delayed-Onset with Linked DNA Markers: The Experience with Huntington's Disease" (1989) 216 J Amer Med Ass 3108.

results of the test. In Ireland, s 42 of the Disability Act 2005 provides that genetic testing shall not be carried out on a person unless (*a*) the testing is not prohibited by law, and (*b*) the consent of the person to the processing of any genetic data to be derived from the testing has been obtained in accordance with the Act.

[8.37] An important aspect of the dilemma posed by the existence of the competing interests here is: who is the patient, is it the individual or is it the family?[84] The importance of genetic testing for the person tested is that it gives him or her information about future health, some of which information may be utilised in behavioural change so as to delay the ill-health. It is argued that the same reasons point to disclosure to the relatives so that they can prepare themselves for what lies ahead. 'In many ways, therefore, the information is also theirs. The family has a claim as a collective, as does each of the individuals who make up that collective.'[85] This reinforces the view often expressed by clinicians who work in the area of genetics, that is, that the family is the patient. If that is the case, then the duty of confidentiality owed by the doctor is owed, not to the individual tested, but to each member of the family.[86] In that way, the doctor is justified, and indeed in some jurisdictions may be obliged, to inform affected relatives. This is often referred to as a 'communitarian' or 'family' approach.

[8.38] In 1997 the Anti-Cancer Council of Victoria, Australia, published a report in relation to the ethical implications of developments in familial cancer genetics.[87] This report stressed the need for a shift in focus away from the idea that the individual 'owns' his genetic material, towards the idea that patients should consider more than what will affect their own health. The report points out that generally patients seek genetic tests as a member of a family, because of a shared family history. This context adds to the responsibility to be placed on patients and doctors to inform other members of the family thus affected.[88] The report states that, in instances where the propensity to the disease is high and the symptoms serious, the doctor is justified in informing other

---

[84] Laurie, 'Genetics and Patient's Rights: Where Are the Limits?' (2000) Med L I Vol 5, 255–44. See also Bell and Bennett, 'Genetic Secrets and the Family' Med L Rev (2001) Vol 9:130–161; Skene, 'Genetic Secrets and the Family: A Response to Bell and Bennett' Med L Rev (2001) Vol 9: 162–169; Skene, 'Patient's Rights or Family Responsibilities? Two Approaches to Genetic Testing' (1998) 6 Med L Rev 1.

[85] Laurie, 'Genetics and Patient's Rights: Where are the Limits?' (2000) Med L I Vol 5, 25–44, p 29.

[86] There may be difficulties in determining where the duty on the doctor ends in this context in terms of contacting relatives. Questions arise as to how this communication is to take place, whether counselling is to be offered to each relative, at what level of dilution of the risk does the duty end, and so on.

[87] Anti-Cancer Council of Victoria, Cancer Genetics Ethics Committee, *Ethics and Familial Cancers: Including Guidelines on Ethical Aspects of Risk Assessment, Genetic Testing and Genetic Registers* (March 1997), discussed by Bell and Bennett, 'Genetic Secrets and the Family' Med L Rev (2001) Vol 9:130–161, p 133.

[88] For consideration of the issues in the US, see Parker, 'Camping Trips and Family Trees: Must Tennessee Physicians Warn Their Patients' Relatives of Genetic Risks?' (1998) 65 Tennessee Law Review 585; Deftos, 'Genomic Torts: The Law of the Future: The Duty of Physicians to Disclose the Presence of a Genetic Disease to the Relatives of Their Patients with the Disease' (1997) 32 Univ of San Fran L Rev 105.

relatives, despite objections from the proband. Disclosure may take place, if practicable, without identifying the particular person tested. Even if disclosure of the proband's identity is inevitable, the genetic status of that person need not and should not be revealed without specific consent. This would be in line with general principles regarding confidentiality in the context of clinical or surgical history.

[8.39] Despite the strong appeal of the notion of the family as patient in the context of genetics, others argue that genetic filiation is not enough in itself to warrant setting aside important legal and ethical protections.[89] It is argued that the existence of a cure or treatment for the condition, the likelihood of harm to relatives, and the degree of severity if the condition does occur, are all relevant factors that would need to be considered.[90]

> Knowledge of one's own genetic constitution and of possible future ill health can have profound effects on one's sense of 'self'. And, while an individual who seeks out genetic testing might have prepared himself for possible bad news, can the same be said of that person's relative who might suspect nothing as to the presence of genetic disease in their family?[91]

[8.40] Trust is a crucial element of the relationship between doctor and patient – the doctor trusts that the patient is disclosing all the facts relevant to his condition and the patient trusts that the doctor will respect his privacy and will not disclose confidential information about him to others. Doctors thus have legal, ethical and professional obligations to respect patient confidentiality. This is further discussed in Chapter 3. Genetics has a significant bearing on confidentiality as information concerning others may become apparent due to the fact that genes run in families. As Suter puts it, 'when genetic testing of one person can benefit another family member, privacy and autonomy interests of the former may collide with the relative's interests in protecting her health or planning her future.'[92] Thus the doctor has to reconcile his duty of confidentiality to his patient with his role in furthering the good of public health medicine.

> On the one hand, it is necessary to recognise individuals as autonomous moral agents, who should be free to make decisions regarding their own health care. However, when these autonomous agents make decisions that may prove detrimental to the health of others, problems arise. This is especially so when omitting to provide relatives with information interferes with their autonomy by restricting their present and future life choices and decisions.[93]

[8.41] Mason and Laurie state that a practitioner who is faced with a refusal by a proband to communicate test results to relatives when a cure or effective treatment is available would be justified in disrespecting the proband's wishes in order to protect

---

89 See Suter, 'Whose Genes Are These Anyway? Familial Conflicts Over Access to Genetic Information' (1993) 91 Mich L Rev 1854.

90 Laurie, 'The Most Personal Information of All: An Appraisal of Genetic Privacy in the Shadow of the Human Genome Project' (1996) 10 I J of Law, Pol & the Family 74 at 85.

91 Mason and Laurie, *Law and Medical Ethics* (8th edn, OUP, 2010) para 7.31.

92 Suter, 'Whose Genes Are These Anyway? Familial Conflicts Over Access to Genetic Information' Mich Law Rev 9, June 1993 at 1855.

93 Clarke, 'Genetic Screening and Counselling' in Kuhse and Singer, *A Companion to Bioethics*, (Blackwell Publishing, 1998) at 222.

other family members from harm. He might, however, be less inclined to disclose information about a condition for which nothing can be done and which has relatively mild symptoms.[94] In Ireland the Medical Council's Guide to Professional Conduct and Ethics (7th edn, 2009) states that there are some circumstances in which a doctor may justify a breach of confidentiality, such as in the interests of others. Paragraph 28.1 states:

> Disclosure of patient information without their consent may be justifiable in exceptional circumstances when it is necessary to protect the patient or others from serious risk of death or serious harm. You should obtain the consent of the patient to the disclosure if possible.

[8.42] Whenever a doctor exercises this discretion, he must be prepared to justify his decision and if he has exercised it incorrectly, he may be liable to sanction. In contrast, if a doctor is found to be under a duty to disclose information and he fails to do so, resulting in harm to a third party, he may be liable in negligence for any reasonably foreseeable harm that he failed to prevent. The question arises as to whether the court would accept in such cases that the public interest in warning an individual at risk of genetic disease outweighs the public interest in maintaining the confidentiality of his patient. In the UK, both the British Medical Association and the Nuffield Council on Bioethics take the view that a breach of confidentiality might be justified in exceptional circumstances, depending on the severity of the disorder and its implications for other family members. The International Declaration on Human Genetic Data in 2003 states that informed consent should be obtained for genetic testing although limitations on this principle might be prescribed by domestic law for compelling reasons. Article 14 (b) states that genetic data linked to an identifiable person should not be disclosed to third parties, including insurers, employers and the family, without the person's express consent except for an important public interest reason. Skene argues that those interests may include the health of close family members.[95] These recommendations, if accepted by the law, may provide a defence for a clinician who decides to divulge genetic information to a family member to enable that person to seek medical attention, but they do not go further in imposing a duty on the clinician to do so.

[8.43] In the US, the courts have considered whether there is a duty on clinicians to warn of genetic disease. For example in *Pate v Threlkel*,[96] Dr Threlkel had operated on Marianne New, the mother of Heidi Pate, for thyroid cancer three years before Pate's own thyroid cancer was diagnosed and treated, but had not warned Pate of the hereditary nature of her mother's condition. Pate and her husband alleged that the physicians knew or should have known of the likelihood that New's children would have inherited the condition genetically; that the physicians were under a duty to warn New that her children should be tested for the disease; that had New been warned in 1987, she would have had her children tested at that time; and if Pate had been tested in 1987, she would have taken preventative action, and her condition, more likely than not, would have been curable. Pate claimed that as a direct and proximate cause of the physicians' negligence, she suffered from advanced medullary thyroid carcinoma and its various damaging

---

[94] Mason and Laurie, *Law and Medical Ethics* (8th edn, OUP, 2010) para 7.38.
[95] Skene, 'Legal Regulation of Genetic Testing, Balancing Privacy and Family Interests' in Iltis, Johnson and Hinze (eds) *Legal Perspectives in Bioethics* (Routledge, 2008) at 209.
[96] *Pate v Threlkel* 661 So. 2d 278 (Fla 1995).

effects. The Court took the view that the duty to warn of the genetic nature of the disease was satisfied by informing the patient herself; there was no duty to inform the patient's children:

> If there is a duty to warn, to whom must the physician convey the warning? Our holding should not be read to require the physician to warn the patient's children of the disease. In most instances the physician is prohibited from disclosing the patient's medical condition to others except with the patient's permission ... Moreover, the patient ordinarily can be expected to pass on the warning. To require the physician to seek out and warn various members of the patient's family would often be difficult or impractical and would place too heavy a burden upon the physician. Thus, we emphasize that in any circumstances in which the physician has a duty to warn of a genetically transferable disease, that duty will be satisfied by warning the patient.

[8.44] However, in *Safer v the Estate of Pack*[97] this narrow approach was not followed. During the 1950s, Dr George Pack had treated Donna Safer's father for a cancerous blockage of the colon and multiple polyposis. In 1990, Safer was diagnosed with the same condition, which she claimed was inherited, and, if not diagnosed and treated, invariably would lead to metastic colorectal cancer. Safer alleged that Dr Pack knew the hereditary nature of the disease, yet failed to warn the immediate family, thus breaching his professional duty to warn. The Court said that although an overly broad and general application of the physician's duty to warn might lead to confusion, conflict or unfairness in many types of circumstances, the duty to warn of avertible risk from genetic causes, by definition a matter of familial concern, is sufficiently narrow to serve the interests of justice. This duty was owed not only to the patient himself but also 'extends beyond the interests of a patient to members of the immediate family of the patient who may be adversely affected by a breach of that duty.' The Court did not decide how precisely that duty is to be discharged, especially with respect to young children who may be at risk, except to require that reasonable steps be taken to assure that the information reaches those likely to be affected or is made available for their benefit. The Court further acknowledged the potential conflict between the physician's broader duty to warn and his fidelity to an expressed preference of the patient that nothing be said to family members about the details of the disease. The Court did not advise on how such a conflict could be resolved.

There have been no comparable reported cases in Ireland to date.

The right not to know

[8.45] In relation to the information to be provided to other family members who may be affected,[98] there is also the difficulty that some people may prefer not to have advance knowledge of future ill-health.[99] Knowledge can be useful and important where there is something that can be done with the knowledge in order to avoid future ill-health.

---

[97] *Safer v Estate of Pack* 677 A 2d 1188 (NJ 1996).
[98] Andrews, 'Gen-Etiquette: Genetic Information, Family Relationships and Adoption' in Rothstein, *Genetic Secrets: Protecting Privacy and Confidentiality in the Genetic Era* (Yale University Press, 1997) Ch. 14; Deech, 'Family Law and Genetics' (1998) 61 MLR 697.
[99] Ngwena and Chadwick, 'Genetic Diagnostic Information and the Duty of Confidentiality: Ethics and Law' (1993) 1 Med Law International 73.

However, in circumstances where individuals do not currently display symptoms of disease, have no knowledge that they might be affected by disease, and where there is no effective intervention available, the benefit of knowledge is less obvious. Laurie says that:

> To argue that this promotes preparedness for the onset of disease presupposes that people are able to prepare adequately for the harm to come. Moreover, it ignores the possibility of causing psychological harm by burdening people with information which forces them into a period of self-reflection and self-reassessment which they would not otherwise have experienced.[100]

[8.46] Knowledge of genetic disease can lead to what the Danish Council of Ethics called 'morbidification' which it says is the notion of falling victim to some inescapable fate through knowledge about risk of disease.[101] Laurie says this can affect the way people feel about themselves as well as how they treat their children, whether or not they are affected by the disease.[102]

[8.47] The right not to know has been recognised in the Convention for the Protection of Human Rights and Dignity of the Human Being with regard to the Application of Biology and Medicine (Oviedo Convention 1997)[103] and the UNESCO Universal Declaration on the Human Genome and Human Rights.[104] It is questionable, however, whether the grounding of a right not to know solely in terms of choice is effective. As Mason and Laurie put it:

> The principle of respect for autonomy requires that we see the individual as a 'moral chooser'. In order to choose meaningfully we require full information about the range of options available and the consequences of any particular choice. Unfortunately, this paradigm breaks down in the context of an interest in not knowing genetic information. Here, the choice is about knowledge itself. [105]

Interests of insurance companies and employers

[8.48] Other parties may also claim an interest in the information revealed by genetic tests. Much controversy has arisen in relation to the interest of insurance companies and employers, both of whom have financial interests in the information, and the State, which has an interest in the protection of public health and the reduction of financial

---

[100] Laurie, 'Genetics and Patient's Rights: Where Are the Limits?'(2000) Med Law International Vol 5 pp 25–44 at 34.

[101] Danish Council of Ethics, *Ethics and Mapping of the Human Genome*, (1993 Copenhagen) page 60.

[102] Laurie, 'Genetics and Patient's Rights: Where Are the Limits?'(2000) Med Law International Vol 5 pp 25–44 at 34.

[103] Council of Europe, *Convention for the Protection of Human Rights and Dignity of the Human Being with regard to the Application of Biology and Medicine,* Oviedo 1997, art 10 (2): 'Everyone is entitled to know any information collected about his or her health. However, the wishes of individuals not to be so informed shall be observed.'

[104] Adopted in Paris in 1997. Article 5c provides 'The right of every individual to decide whether or not to be informed of the results of genetic examination and the resulting consequences should be respected.'

[105] Mason and Laurie, *Law and Medical Ethics* (8th edn, OUP, 2010) para 7.36.

expenditure in this regard.[106] The overriding fear is that the information will be used in a way which will discriminate against those who may have inherited a genetic disease.

[8.49] Insurance is a way of mitigating the effects of harmful events of uncertain incidence by pooling modest premiums which provide the resources to make large payments selectively to those who suffer such events.[107] The types of policy for which it is argued that genetic information may have relevance, are health and life insurance. The latter would have significance in relation to a person's ability to purchase a house and apply for a mortgage, as a policy of life insurance is generally a requirement of any financial institution before any loan is given. Insurance contracts are contracts *uberrima fides*, ie of the utmost good faith, which means that full disclosure must be made by the applicant of all material facts relevant to the risk to be undertaken by the insurer. In life insurance, it is argued that the insured person is at an advantage in having all the information pertaining to his health and family background, information which would obviously be highly relevant to the insurer in deciding whether to insure and what premium to charge in recognition of the risk presented. To redress this 'imbalance', insurance contracts place a legal obligation on persons applying for insurance to disclose all material facts. This will include all relevant medical history and family background. If such information is not disclosed, the insurance contract could later be avoided by the insurers.

[8.50] In the context of genetic information there is a real fear that if insurers were to be entitled to gain access to the results of genetic tests, this information would be used to discriminate against the insured by either refusing to provide cover, or by charging excessive premiums. Studies in the US have shown, for example, that 85 per cent of the population are concerned about access to genetic test results by insurers and employers and would not take genetic tests if such access were permitted.[108] There are two different

---

[106] It is not proposed to deal with the mandatory screening of infants here. However, it is important to note the recent Supreme Court case of *North Western Health Board v HW and CW* [2001] 3 IR 622, [2001] 3 IR 635, [2001] IESC 90, where the issue of testing for phenylketonuria (PKU) was at issue. The parents of a young child refused permission for the test to be carried out by the 'heel test' method as, for them, this was the infliction of pain on their child. The Health Board stressed the importance for the child of this screening programme in order to make any necessary diagnosis early enough to be able to treat the serious disease that may result. The Supreme Court focused on the rights of the family under the Constitution to make such decisions in relation to the children of the family. It held that 'While there may inevitably be tensions between laws enacted by the State for the common good of society as a whole and the unique status of the family within that society, the Constitution firmly outlaws any attempt by the State in its laws or its executive actions to usurp the exclusive and privileged role of the family in the social order.' There is no mandatory obligation on parents to submit their child to this test, and if such was to be enforced by legislation, it would be open to review on grounds of interference with the jurisdiction of the family. Therefore, unless the State could clearly justify, in the interests of the common good, population screening for genetic diseases, it is likely that the privacy and authority of the family would usurp any such attempt to gain access to genetic information. Medical treatment decisions on behalf of children are dealt with in Chapter 11.

[107] O'Neill, 'Insurance and Genetics: the Current State of Play' (1998) 61:5 Modern Law Review at 716.

[108] Dept of Labour, Dept of Health and Human Services, Equal Employment Opportunity Commission, Dept of Justice *Genetic Information and the Workplace*, Washington DC 1998.

ways in which the insurer could seek such information. It could be made a term of the contract that the insured disclose the results of any genetic tests undertaken, or the insurer could oblige the insured to undertake certain genetic tests and disclose the results. In many instances, the insurers may argue that genetic information is no different from other medical information about which the insured has no difficulty in disclosing. If the insured is prepared to disclose a family history of heart disease or cancer, the disclosure of a genetic test result indicating the same information should not be treated any differently. However, one of the concerns here is that compulsory disclosure of test results would deter individuals being tested in the first place, which would have deleterious effects on health.[109] As regards insurers obliging individuals to be tested, there is concern that this would lead to the development and proliferation of predictive genetic testing,[110] (which may not be accompanied by necessary counselling) and that there would be a danger that the individual would not validly consent to such tests, due to the pressure of needing to get life assurance.

[8.51] The Disability Act 2005 provides that 'disability' in relation to a person means 'a substantial restriction in the capacity of the person to carry on a profession, business or occupation in the State or to participate in social or cultural life in the State by reason of an enduring physical, sensory, mental health or intellectual impairment'. It provides in s 42 that:

(2) A person shall not engage in the processing of genetic data in relation to:

(a) the employment of a person save in accordance with the provisions of section 12A of the Data Protection Act 1988 (as inserted by the Data Protection (Amendment) Act 2003),

(b) a policy of insurance or life assurance,

(c) a policy of health insurance or health-related insurance,

(d) an occupational pension, a retirement annuity contract or any other pension arrangement,

(e) the mortgaging of property.

[8.52] Therefore, insurers are not permitted to use genetic tests in relation to either health or life assurance policies. However, it is important to note that insurers still require patients to declare family history so if, for example, a woman's mother had young-onset breast cancer, that woman will have her insurance premium increased or loaded. Even if the woman's mother were found to have a BRCA mutation (a genetic mutation linked to an increased risk of breast and other cancers), and the woman herself did not have her mother's BRCA mutation, the woman could still be loaded by the insurer by virtue of family history alone. Insurers also now commonly ask if a person is having regular screening for a condition (without mentioning genetics), and if they are, their insurance premiums are loaded. Insurance companies argue that in the absence of such information, there is an imbalance in the insurance application process because an applicant for insurance may be aware of the results of a genetic test but the insurer will

---

[109] UK House of Commons Science and Technology Committee *Human Genetics: The Science and its Consequences*, Third Report, 6 July 1995.

[110] Chadwick and Ngwena, 'The Human Genome Project, Predictive Testing and Insurance Contracts: Ethical and Legal Responses' (1995) 1 Res Publica 115.

not be privy to such information. This is referred to as adverse selection. When this situation arises, it can be expected that high-risk people will purchase a disproportionate amount of insurance. The problem this creates is not simply a threat to insurers' profits. When insurers expect or experience adverse selection, they are forced to raise their rates across the board to anticipate it, because they are not able to identify those at higher risk whose rates they should selectively increase.[111] The Disability Act also allows the Minister for Justice to regulate the use of family history in assessment of insurance and/or employment, but no such regulations have yet been introduced.

[8.53] Also of relevance here is the Disability Discrimination Act 1998, s 6(1) (as inserted by s 4 of the Equality Act 2004), which provides that:

(1) For the purposes of this Act and without prejudice to its provisions relating to discrimination occurring in particular circumstances, discrimination shall be taken to occur where—

(a)   a person is treated less favourably than another person is, has been or would be treated in a comparable situation on any of the grounds specified in subsection (2) (in this Act referred to as the 'discriminatory grounds') which

   (i)   exists,

   (ii)   existed but no longer exists,

   (iii)   may exist in the future, or

   (iv)   is imputed to the person concerned.

[8.54] In relation to employment, the issues and concerns are similar in the sense that the employer has a financial interest in the health of the person he chooses to employ. If the employee is likely to become seriously ill, then his productivity will decrease, thus affecting the employer's profits. He may also fear that the work environment may exacerbate the symptoms of the employee's disease, thus causing ill-health earlier than perhaps might be expected. As well as the human concern that might be behind such fears, there is perhaps also the concern that the employer might be sued for compensation in such cases for failing to provide a safe workplace for the employee. Therefore, as with the insurer, the employer may argue that he is entitled to ask, before hiring, for results of any genetic tests undertaken, or perhaps to ask for those tests to be undertaken.

[8.55] The same concerns pertain here relating to the discriminatory effects of disclosure of genetic test results in the employment context. In a report by a number of government departments in the US in 1998, it was stated that genetic information could be used to unfairly discriminate against individuals in the workplace, for example by denying them jobs on the basis that they might be more likely to take sick leave, resign or retire early for health reasons, creating extra costs in recruiting and training new staff.[112] The Nuffield Council on Bioethics in the UK advised, in a report which was endorsed by the House of Commons Science and Technology Committee, that legislation should be introduced to protect the privacy of genetic information and that

---

[111] Hall and Rich, 'Laws Restricting Health Insurers' Use of Genetic Information: Impact on Genetic Discrimination' (2000) Am J Hum Genet; 66(1): 293–307.

[112] Dept of Labour, Dept of Health and Human Services, Equal Employment Opportunity Commission, Dept of Justice *Genetic Information and the Workplace*, Washington DC 1998.

employers should not be entitled to access the results of genetic tests, except where specifically relevant to the work environment within which the individual works.[113]

[8.56] In the United States, the Genetic Information Non-Discrimination Act 2008 (GINA) was introduced to provide federal protection from genetic discrimination in health insurance and employment. The law has two parts: Title I, which prohibits genetic discrimination in health insurance, and Title II, which prohibits genetic discrimination in employment. Title I makes it illegal for health insurance providers to use or require genetic information to make decisions about a person's insurance eligibility or coverage. This part of the law went into effect on May 21, 2009. Title II makes it illegal for employers to use a person's genetic information when making decisions about hiring, promotion and several other terms of employment. This part of the law went into effect on November 21, 2009.[114]

[8.57] In Ireland, the provisions of the Disability Act 2005 discussed above are also applicable in this context, as s 42 provides that genetic data may not be processed in relation to the employment of a person, thus allaying the concerns outlined.

Genetic testing of children

[8.58] Genetic testing of children raises particular difficulties. Controversies have arisen both in the context of screening newborns and testing infants and older children. Newborn screening is generally recommended only when there is a clear indication of benefit to the newborn, where there is a system in place to confirm the diagnosis and treatment is available for those affected.[115] Newborn screening is routinely carried out in many countries, including Ireland, within the first three days of birth for conditions such as PKU (phenylketonuria), which if detected early, may be effectively treated, and without which treatment may result in significant handicap. The benefits of such screening are generally considered so great as to obviate any need for detailed explanation or information for parents. 'Studies of parental knowledge of newborn screening have shown that few parents even know for what conditions their infants are screened.'[116] Screening for other conditions, such as muscular dystrophy[117] or chronic

---

[113] Nuffield Council on Bioethics *Genetic Screening: Ethical Issues* (1993), and House of Commons Science and Technology Committee, *Human Genetics: The Science and its Consequences*, Third Report, 6 July 1995 at 231–233. For a criticism of these recommendations see Rothstein, 'Genetic Discrimination in Employment: Ethics, Policy and Comparative Law' in Guillod and Widmer (eds) *Human Genetics Analysis and the Protection of Personality and Privacy* (Zurich: Schulthess Poylygraphischer Verlag, 1994). See also Olick, 'Genes in the Workplace, New Frontiers for ADA Law, Policy and Research' in Blanck (ed) *Employment, Disability and the Americans with Disabilities Act: Issues in Law, Public Policy and Research* (Northwestern University Press, 2000) 285.

[114] Senator Ted Kennedy called it 'the first major new civil rights bill of the new century'.

[115] Institute of Medicine, Andrews et al (eds) *Assessing Genetic Risks: Implications for Health and Social Policy* (1994) at 10.

[116] Clarke 'Genetic Screening and Counselling' in Kuhse and Singer, *A Companion to Bioethics* (Blackwell Publishing, 1998) at 220.

[117] Duchenne muscular dystrophy is a genetic disease which, in two out of three cases, is transmitted on the X chromosome to male offspring of female carriers; in the other cases the gene mutation happens as a sporadic event. (contd.../)

lung disease, has been seen as more questionable based on studies that have shown adverse impact on families and the emotional trauma of early diagnosis in some cases.[118] However, more recent studies have shown that there is medium- or long-term benefit to the child as a result of newborn screening for cystic fibrosis[119], and many centres world-wide are introducing this as a practice.[120] On the other hand, the avoidance of prolonged uncertainty during lengthy diagnostic processes, and the ability to plan for the future, may tip the balance in favour of screening in some situations.[121] It has been argued, however, that in requesting testing, parents typically think only of the benefits of a negative test result and not of the potentially damaging effects of a positive one.[122] Some

---

[117] (\...contd) Muscle wasting is one of the devastating symptoms of this disease, which usually manifests itself at around two years of age. It begins with developmental and motor delay, clumsiness and falling over. By the age of 11, 90 per cent of those suffering from the disease are wheelchair bound. Some live until their 20s, but the average age is about 17, with death resulting from respiratory infection or heart failure. Parsons and Bradley, 'Ethical Issues in Newborn Screening for Duchenne Muscular Dystrophy: the Question of Informed Consent' in Clarke (ed) *Genetic Counselling* (Taylor & Franus, 1994) at 99. This essay discusses the introduction of testing for DMD in Wales, which according to the authors, is a good example of the tension between the power of the technological imperative and the protection of the individual.

[118] In 1972 the Swedish government initiated national newborn screening for a condition known as alpha –1 antitrypsin deficiency, which is common in those with Scandinavian ancestry. For those infants who tested positive for the predisposition, preventative measures were recommended to avoid exposure to environmental antagonists. Follow-up studies demonstrated that more than half of the families suffered severe psychological consequences, some of which were still present five to seven years after testing. As a consequence of early feedback on these negative effects, the government discontinued the programme after just two years. See McNeil et al, 'Psychosocial Effects of Screening for Somatic Risk: The Swedish Alpha-1 Antitrypsin Experience' (1988) 43 Thorax 505–7; Clarke, 'Genetic Screening and Counselling' in Kuhse and Singer, *A Companion to Bioethics* (Blackwell Publishing, 1998) at 220.

[119] See Farrell et al, 'Nutritional Benefits of Neonatal Screening for Cystic Fibrosis' (1997) 337 (14) NEJM 963–967.

[120] Newborn screening for cystic fibrosis is due to start in Ireland in 2011.

[121] There has also been controversy surrounding the availability of the test for cystic fibrosis, which is a treatable but incurable autosomal recessive genetic disease that results in chronic pulmonary and digestive disease. Symptoms are generally seen in early childhood. Newborn screening tests for CF have been available for some time but studies of routine CF testing programmes in the US have shown that no clinical benefit accrued as a result of presymptomatic testing, and a number of ethical and psychological problems were encountered. See Holtzman, 'What Drives Neonatal Screening Programs?' (1991) 325 NEJM 802–4; Farrell and Mischler, 'Newborn Screening for Cystic Fibrosis' (1992) 39 Advances in Pediatrics 66. For similar studies in the area of muscular dystrophy see Bradley et al, 'Experience with Screening Newborns for Duchenne Muscular Dystrophy in Wales' (1993) 306 BMJ 357–61.

[122] Hoffman and Wulfsberg, 'Testing Children for Genetic Predispositions: Is It in Their Best Interest?' (1995) 23 Journal of Law, Medicine and Ethics 331–44 at 333. See also Wertz et al, 'Genetic Testing for Children and Adolescents: Who Decides?' (1994) 272 JAMA 875 at 878 and Fanos, *Developmental Consequences for Adulthood of Early Sibling Loss* (University of Michigan Microfilms, 1987).

studies have also shown evidence of a 'vulnerable child syndrome', where parents of a child with a genetic predisposition become over-protective, restricting the child's activities unnecessarily.[123]

[8.59] In relation to the young child, if he has a health problem whose management would be aided by accurate genetic diagnosis, it would seem to be in the best interests of the child to carry out genetic tests. A similar situation would apply if a healthy child is being tested for a late-onset disorder of which there is family history, and for which early intervention or treatment might be of benefit. However, the situation becomes more problematic where the test is for a late-onset disorder for which there is no medical benefit in early detection.[124] Very few geneticists would be prepared to carry out such testing at the request of parents on the basis that the information may be beneficial to the family, even though there may be little benefit to the child itself.[125] Various professional bodies and health organisations have developed guidelines in relation to predictive genetic testing of children, including the World Health Organisation (WHO), the Nuffield Council on Bioethics, the American Society of Human Genetics and the Human Genetics Society of Australasia. They have overwhelmingly concluded that predictive testing for adult-onset disease for which there is no known treatment or preventive strategy has no immediate benefits and should not be carried out on children but deferred until adulthood, or at least until the person is able to appreciate the relevant genetic facts, as well as the emotional and social consequences of what predictive genetic testing entails.[126]

[8.60] The ethical difficulties in predictive or presymptomatic testing are that firstly, it removes the right of the child to make an autonomous decision on reaching maturity whether to have the test or not; secondly, the confidentiality that would be accorded to an adult patient in such circumstances is not applicable to a young child; and thirdly, a positive test result may lead to deleterious social consequences, as the parents may relate to the child differently and may have different expectations of the child.[127] Sometimes

---

[123] Tluczek et al, 'Parents' Knowledge of Neonatal Screening and Response to False-Positive Cystic Fibrosis Screening' (1992) 13 Journal of Developmental and Behavioural Pediatrics 181–86.

[124] The Working Party of the Clinical Genetics Society in the UK has recommended that predictive testing not be carried out on children if the child is healthy and there are no effective medical interventions in the event of a positive test result. See 'The Genetic Testing of Children' (1994) 31 J of Med Genetics 785.

[125] See further Fost, 'Genetic Diagnosis and Treatment: Ethical Considerations' (1993) 147 Am J of Diseases of Children 1190–95; Wertz et al, 'Genetic Testing for Children and Adolescents: Who Decides?' (1994) 272 JAMA 875–82; Harper and Clarke, 'Viewpoint: Should We Test Children for 'Adult' Genetic Disease?' (1990) 335 Lancet 1205–06.

[126] WHO, *Proposed International Guidelines on Ethical Issues in Medical Genetics and Genetics Services,* 1997; Nuffield Council on Bioethics, *Mental Disorders and Genetics* 1998; ASHG/ACMG Report 'Points to Consider: Ethical, Legal and Psychological Implications of Genetic Testing in Children and Adolescents' (1995) 57 Am J Hum Gen 1233; Human Genetics Society of Australasia, *Predictive Testing in Children and Adolescents* (1999).

[127] 'Testing a child carries no medical advantage but puts the child at risk of harm, as a high-risk result may prejudice upbringing by either natural or adoptive parents, and may even result in stigmatisation. It also removes the child's future autonomy regarding the decision to be tested.' (contd...)

parents may request testing for their child for the parents' benefit rather than the child's, as the parents may want to reassure themselves that their 'genetic curse' was not passed on to their children or may want to prepare themselves emotionally or organise their home environment to cater for the future illness of their child. It may be argued that such a decision should focus exclusively on the child's best interests but Ross asserts that in actuality, parental well-being has a significant impact on children regardless of whether the child's well-being or best interest is at the core of the parent's desire to know. Therefore, an exclusive focus on the child's interest is too narrow, and clinicians should respect parental decisions that take into account familiar psychosocial factors, at least in relation to conditions that present in childhood.[128] In relation to adult-onset diseases such as Huntington's disease, many centres have refused to test children under the age of 18 for the gene, as it is perceived that the potential harms of testing in that age group are greater than the benefits. The International Huntington's Disease Association has also recommended that minors not be tested for Huntington's.

> Persons who learn that they are carriers are at risk for severe reactive depression, and it is known that among carriers the suicide rate is four-fold, higher than in the general population. In families with several children, survival guilt may be a serious problem as the child who learns that he or she does not have the gene, but that a sibling does, may have great difficulty resolving the issue of "why him and not me?" While learning early that one has *not* inherited the gene eliminates years of anxiety for the adolescent, it should be noted that half the time the hopes of both parent and child are dashed by a positive diagnosis.[129]

[8.61] In deciding whether to test for late-onset disorders, the geneticist should prioritise the best interests of the child, bearing in mind that 'best interests' are not limited to medical factors, but also include psychological health and relationships with other family members. If the symptoms of the disease running in the family are likely to manifest themselves in adolescence, it may be appropriate to prepare the child in advance. Malpas argues that children ought to be told about genetic conditions that are known to exist in the family on the basis that keeping secrets may result in more harm than good and that keeping information from children is an affront to their identity.[130] He goes on to argue that such at-risk children should also be tested for their genetic status, as knowing their genetic make-up may benefit them by offering them important choices that they would otherwise not have, and by allowing them to assimilate such knowledge into their identity so that the knowledge simply becomes a part of who they are. The UK Advisory Committee on Genetic Testing (later the Human Genetics Commission) recommends that careful consideration be given to the separate and potentially

---

[127] (\...contd) Ball, Tyler and Harper, 'Predictive Testing of Adults and Children: Lessons from Huntington's Disease' in Clarke (ed) *Genetic Counselling, Practice and Principles* (Routledge, 1994) at 74. See also Robertson and Savulescu, 'Is There a Case in Favour of Predictive Genetic Testing in Young Children?' (2001) Bioethics Vol 15(1) 26; Otlowski, 'An Exploration of the Legal and Socio-Ethical Implications of Predictive Genetic Testing of Children' (2004) Aus J Fam Law Vol 18.

[128] Friedman Ross, 'Predictive Genetic Testing for Conditions That Present in Childhood' (2002) Kennedy Inst of Ethics J 12.3: 225–244.

[129] Reilly, 'Public Policy and Legal Issues Raised by Advances in Genetic Screening and Testing' (1993) XXVII Suffolk University Law Review 1327 at 1340–41.

[130] Malpas, 'Why Tell Asymptomatic Children of the Risk of an Adult-Onset Disease in the Family But Not Test Them For It?' (2006) JME 32:639–642.

conflicting interests of children, parents and other family members in assessing the best interests of the child in this context. 'Where there is a particular concern over what is in the best interests of a child in certain circumstances, including where there is any dispute between those with parental responsibility for the child, it may first be necessary to seek an order from the court that the child be tested.'[131]

[8.62] Given the traditional deference shown by the courts to parental authority, it may be argued that the courts would permit the parents to make a decision in favour of testing the child, as long as the child's life would not be endangered by the test itself. However, genetic testing is not necessarily analogous to situations in which particular treatment or surgery is recommended for a child, and refused by a parent. If the geneticist is reluctant to perform the test for reasons such as those outlined above where no clinical benefit to the child would be obtained, and the parents insist upon it in order 'to satisfy their own curiosity', in light of the fact that the courts have traditionally taken the view that parents may not demand treatment for their children, particularly where this contravenes medical opinion, the decision would probably be to refuse testing until the child is mature enough to make his own decision.[132]

[8.63] In the guidelines published on this issue worldwide, there seems to be universal support for the view that the availability of medical benefit is the most important justification to perform predictive testing in minors, regardless of the onset of the disease. The absence of medical benefit is the most important reason to delay testing until the adolescent or adult is able to make a personal decision following full exploration of the issues.[133] Therefore, if a mature minor requests genetic tests, the geneticist should take into account the competence of the minor to understand the complex issues involved and, having explored them fully, may carry out the testing on the basis that it confers medical, psychological or emotional benefits on him.[134] If the request is made by a parent or other family member, the views of the minor should be obtained and consent given if he is competent. If there is disagreement between the minor and his parents as to whether testing should be carried out, although the geneticist should perhaps recommend delaying the tests until the age of majority is reached, the competent minor should be entitled to make a decision on this matter after full exploration of the issues and appropriate counselling.[135] Disclosure of the test results

---

[131] UK Advisory Committee on Genetic Testing, at 27. In the UK, the Children Act 1989, s 8 enables the court to make a 'specific issue order' for the purpose of resolving a specific question in connection with any aspect of parental responsibility for a child, such as consent for a genetic test.

[132] See discussion in Hoffman and Wulfsberg, 'Testing Children For Genetic Predispositions: Is It in Their Best Interest?' (1995) 23 Journal of Law, Medicine and Ethics 331 at 335–6. See also Clayton, 'Removing the Shadow of the Law From the Debate About Genetic Testing of Children' (1995) 57 Am J of Med Genetics at 630.

[133] See further Borry P et al, 'Presymptomatic and Predictive Genetic Testing in Minors: A Systematic Review of Guidelines and Position Papers' (2006) Clin Genet 70:374–381.

[134] The Nuffield Council recommends that caution be exercised before a child under the age of 16 be allowed to make a decision of this nature, as genetic testing may be seen to be in a novel category raising complex issues of benefit and possible harm, particularly if the testing is of no therapeutic benefit and cannot be categorised as treatment. Nuffield Council on Bioethics, Genetic Screening: Ethics Issues (1993) para 5.29.

[135] UK Advisory Committee on Genetic Testing, at 28.

will also necessitate a finding as to the minor's competence to understand and willingness to know the implications of the results. Whether the results of the test should remain confidential to the minor, unless he consents to disclosure to parents or other family members and the information is relevant to the current care of the minor, is also currently open to question. Under freedom of information legislation in Ireland, the parents of the child would have a presumptive entitlement to access the child's medical records. See para **3.25**.

Genetic testing and mental disorders

[8.64] 'The range of ethical issues raised by genetic information expands when the information concerns mental disorders. Some of these additional issues cluster around the notion of personal well-being, of how one views oneself and is viewed by others; others concern reproductive decisions and some arise from the fact that mental disorders are often stigmatised.'[136] In the treatment of persons suffering from mental disorder, the 'best interests' of the person is paramount.[137] This approach may permit interventions in the absence of consent, despite the fact that many of those suffering with mental disorders may not suffer comprehensive incapacity, but rather impaired or intermittently impaired capacity.[138] The term 'mental disorder' is explained by the WHO as implying 'the existence of a clinically recognisable set of symptoms or behaviour associated in most cases with distress and with interference with personal functions.'[139]

[8.65] In relation to single-gene disorders a genetic test may yield a high degree of certainty as to whether the individual will or will not develop a particular disorder. If the disorder has already been seen in the family, the individual member of the family already has information upon which to base a decision about whether to request testing or not. However, where the test is for a gene variant associated with relatively slight predispositions to a disorder, the issues are more difficult, as susceptibility is markedly different from certainty, although susceptibility may be relevant in making certain life-style choices. Most common disorders, both physical and mental, are influenced by variants in several or many genes, with each one having a relatively small effect. In addition, susceptibility may be affected by environmental factors.[140] This means that

---

[136] Nuffield Council on Bioethics, *Genetic Screening: Ethics Issues* (1993) at 1.19.

[137] See Chapter 9 for further discussion. See also UK Law Commission Report *Mental Incapacity* (1995), Law Com No 231, HMSO, London; Lord Chancellor's Department, *'Who Decides? Making Decisions on Behalf of Mentally Incapacitated Adults'* (1997) Cm. 3803, HMSO, London.

[138] Nuffield Council on Bioethics, *Genetic Screening: Ethics Issues* (1993) at 1.25.

[139] WHO, *The Classification of Mental and Behavioural Disorders: Clinical Descriptions and Diagnostic Guidelines* (1992) at 5. Most psychiatrists diagnose mental disorders only when an individual is unable to achieve realistic personal goals due to psychiatric symptoms. See Nuffield at para 2.1. For discussion about the difficulties of defining mental illness, and the distinction between illness and social deviance, see Nuffield Council on Bioethics, *Genetic Screening: Ethics Issues* (1993) at 2.1 – 2.11.

[140] Studies by the Institute of Psychiatry at King's College London have shown, for example, that males who have a 'low activity' version of a variation on the male X chromosome, are more likely to respond badly to childhood abuse, and may go on to develop criminal behaviour. (contd.../)

differences in individuals' genetic make-up may lead them to experience the same environment, such as traumatic life events, differently.[141]

[8.66] In relation to mental disorders, the genetic information obtained by way of testing might raise serious questions about the person's functional abilities and reproductive choices. In some cases, the acquisition of such knowledge might lead to extreme distress and anxiety, which might even precipitate the onset of the condition. The potential stigmatisation of mental disorder[142] for both the patient and family members must also be taken into account here, as the availability of genetic tests for such disorders may not necessarily serve to lessen this problem. Although it has been claimed that gene identification will be very valuable in personalising risks of mental disorder and that the increase in precision provided by the ability to calculate risks on an individual basis will be of enormous clinical benefit, this has been doubted by the Nuffield Council on Bioethics, which states that the evidence to support such claims is currently lacking.[143] As with all genetic tests, specialist counselling should be provided before such tests are undertaken, particularly as people with psychiatric problems have low self-esteem, and they may believe that positive test results confirm this opinion. This may cause fatalistic attitudes to develop towards their problem, and decrease their motivation to resolve it.[144]

[8.67] In order to give informed consent to be tested, the law requires that the patient is competent, is informed; understands the nature of the test and its benefits and risks; and voluntarily chooses to be tested. Understanding the complexities of genetics is not easy, particularly given the variety of scientific, psychological, familial and social issues involved. It has been argued that, from an ethical perspective, consent does not

---

[140] (\...contd) The gene in question is thought to be responsible for making the enzyme which breaks down brain chemicals which lead to aggressive behaviour. Indeed, 85 per cent of the group studied went on to develop anti-social behaviour. In this case, it seems that the combination of genetic factors and exposure to certain environmental factors influences the behaviour. See Williams, 'Innocent Until Proven Genetically' (August 7, 2002) The Guardian. In the case of anorexia nervosa, the Institute also studied the theory that although problems such as anorexia are often thought of as culturally driven, modern disorders, the illness could be as much as three-quarters genetic in origin. The theory is that people who are genetically vulnerable are more likely to develop eating disorder problems in response to stressful life events and the pressure of growing up. The Institute of Psychiatry team discovered that anorexic sufferers are more likely to have a genetic variant in one of the chemical messengers in the brain, called serotonin, which is involved with controlling mood and appetite. It is hoped that developing understanding about how this variant interacts with environmental factors in causing anorexia will lead to improved treatments.

[141] See further Rutherford et al, 'Genetic Influences on Eating Attitudes in a Normal Female Twin Population' (1993) 23(2) Psychological Medicine 425–36; Rutter and Plomin, 'Opportunities for Psychiatry from Genetic Findings' (1997) 171 British J of Psychiatry 209–19; Nuffield at 3.16–3.20.

[142] Stigmatisation results from ignorance and misconceptions about mental disorders. While less than 3% of mentally ill patients could be categorised as dangerous, 77% of mentally ill people depicted on prime-time television are presented as dangerous. See Dubin and Fink. 'Effects of Stigma on Psychiatric Treatment' in Fink and Tasman (eds) *Stigma and Mental Illness* (American Psychiatric Press Inc, 1992) at 3.

[143] Nuffield Council on Bioethics at 4.16.

[144] Nuffield Council on Bioethics at 5.5.

necessarily have to be complete once it is genuine.[145] Information should be given in a clear and balanced way, using non-technical language as far as possible, so as to facilitate the necessary level of understanding to be reached in order that the person would be competent to give or refuse consent to the testing. If the appropriate level of competence is not reached, a decision may be made in the patient's best interests. This may involve consultation with the family or carers so as to try to determine what the patient would have wished, but ultimately it will be a matter for the medical professional responsible for the patient (or a committee of the ward, or indeed the court, if the individual is a ward of court) to decide on therapeutic grounds.

PRENATAL DIAGNOSIS

[8.68] Approximately 8 million children are born worldwide with serious illnesses with a genetic cause every year. At least 3.3 million children less than 5 years of age die annually because of serious birth defects, defined as any serious abnormality of structure or function. An estimated 3.2 million of those who survive may be mentally and physically disabled for life.[146] For some couples, the birth of a child with a serious medical condition is the first indication that one or both of the parents carries a genetic mutation. Others may be aware of a family history of genetic disorder and may therefore know that they are at risk of conceiving a child with the particular disorder. Prenatal tests have been available for many decades which make it possible for parents to assess the severity of the risk that a child will be born with a genetic defect. If a genetic defect is identified in the fetus, the parents may nonetheless make a decision to continue with the pregnancy but there is psychological and practical value in being aware of the condition of the fetus at an early stage.

[8.69] Pre-natal diagnosis (PND) in the form of amniocentesis was first reported in 1930. This technique is relatively simple to perform. A small amount of amniotic fluid is removed from the pregnant woman at 16 weeks of pregnancy in order to identify specific genetic disorders. Chorionic villus sampling removes placental tissue at 11 weeks to detect fetal abnormalities. Both of these methods are invasive and carry some risks for the pregnancy. Non-invasive screening tests, such as nuchal thickness screening or serum screening, estimate the risks of a pregnancy giving rise to a baby with Down's syndrome, but these are only risk-based tests and not absolute diagnostic tests. A high risk on such a screening test would lead to an amniocentesis or chorionic villus sampling. Screening for neural tube defects is almost always done by way of antenatal ultrasound. In jurisdictions where abortion is permissible, couples face the dilemma of having to decide after diagnosis whether or not to terminate the pregnancy. In Ireland, the dilemma begins at an earlier stage, when the couple has to decide whether or not to have the test done, bearing in mind that a termination of the pregnancy in the event of a positive test result will not be possible in this jurisdiction. In the past Irish couples used

---

[145] Nuffield Council on Bioethics, *Human Tissue: Ethical and Legal Issues* (1995) at 6.20.

[146] Christianson, Howson and Modell, *The March of Dimes Global Report on Birth Defects: The Hidden Toll of Dying and Disabled Children* (2006). See http://www.modimes.org/aboutus/15796_18678.asp (accessed 3 June 2011).

to travel to Northern Ireland and the UK to avail of services there,[147] but termination for fetal abnormality is not now available in Northern Ireland to people from the Republic.

Ethical issues

[8.70] 'Any discussion of the ethical issues of genetic counselling and prenatal diagnosis is unavoidably haunted by a ghost called the morality of abortion.' This section will not discuss the money ethical issues involved in abortion – as Kass says, 'this ghost I shall not vex'. However, there are also particular ethical issues that arise in the case of PND leading to abortion for fetal indications, or as Kass calls it 'genetic abortion.' In public and political debates surrounding the availability of abortion in Ireland in the last two decades, the justification for abortion to save the life of the mother was much discussed, but the issue of abortion for genetic defect was also raised in the context of a fetus who was regarded as having disabilities incompatible with life. An abortion in those circumstances is not presently permissible under the provisions of the Irish Constitution, which have been interpreted as permitting abortion only in the rare situations where the life of the mother is in danger if she continues with the pregnancy.[148]

> Standing behind genetic abortion are serious and well-intentioned people, with reasonable ends in view: the prevention of genetic diseases, the elimination of suffering in families, the preservation of precious financial and medical resources, the protection of our genetic heritage.[149]

[8.71] Despite these admirable intentions, it must also be acknowledged that the decision to abort is based on an assessment of the quality of the fetus.[150] This strikes directly at the heart of issues around fundamental Constitutional rights to life irrespective of disability, the right to equality and non-discrimination policies enshrined in our laws and culture. This conflict should be addressed in a clear and conscious manner, with debate on the issues rather than any attempt to disguise or avoid dealing with them. Kass asks how the practice of genetic abortion will affect our view of and behaviour towards those 'abnormals' who escape detection and abortion. Such a person 'may be seen as a person who need not have been, and who would not have been, if only someone had gotten to him in time.'

---

[147] It is argued that availability of prenatal testing in Ireland would be a serious moral anomaly if the choice of abortion is not available here. For further discussion, see Dooley, 'Ethics and Genetic Screening in the Republic of Ireland' in Chadwick et al (eds) *The Ethics of Genetic Screening* (Springer, 1999) 95–104 at 103.

[148] *Attorney-General v X* [1992] 1 IR 1; *A, B and C v Ireland* (ECHR 2010) Application no. 25579/05.

[149] Kass, 'Implications of Prenatal Diagnosis for the Human Right to Life' in Hilton et al (eds) *Ethical Issues in Human Genetics: Genetic Counselling and the Use of Genetic Knowledge* (Springer, 1973) 185–199.

[150] 'Whatever else, prenatal diagnosis *is* a means of separating fetuses we wish to develop from those we wish to discontinue. Prenatal diagnosis does approach children as consumer objects subject to quality control.' Lippman, 'Prenatal Genetic Testing and Screening: Constructing Needs and Reinforcing Inequities' in Clarke (ed) *Genetic Counselling* (Taylor & Franus Ltd, 1994) at 146.

[8.72] Justification for genetic abortion rests on a few principles. Firstly, that society has a legitimate interest in the pursuit of genetic fitness of its members. It is argued that the financial implications of caring for people with disabilities could be more productively spent on caring for those who are likely to give something back to society.[151] Of course, this does not take account of the financial resources expended on public health, education and so on, of healthy citizens, nor does it take into account the immeasurable forms of social contribution that people with disabilities can make in the community, such as the provision of comfort and practical help to others living with disabilities, as well as teaching the value of patience, kindness and understanding to those with whom they come into contact.[152]

[8.73] Another justification might be that of the best interests of the parents or family. The argument is that parents should have a right to decide, based upon their own values of what is good for them, the number and health of their children if this is scientifically possible. If they believe that the birth of a child with a serious disease or disability would be psychologically, emotionally and financially harmful for themselves or their other children, they should be permitted to reach the decision to abort such a fetus. This argument is more likely to be understood and accepted than the argument on societal grounds, as appeals to possible harm to families and other children are perhaps more easy for us to relate to than the good of society. However, the elasticity of standards such as 'suffering' or 'harm' as well as the dangers of adopting the proposition of parental rights in relation to children shows how this justification too can be open to debate.

[8.74] The third justification could be described as 'the natural standard'. It is argued here that, due to our increasing knowledge of genetic diseases, it is known that those who suffer from certain diseases will never live the full life of a human being.[153] They will not be able to live independent lives, care for themselves, nor, in some cases, develop the distinctively human capacities for thought or self-consciousness. Nature has caused miscarriage to occur in many of these cases, or early death in others. Therefore, the altruistic argument is that we should not strive to keep alive people born with such conditions, and we should try to avoid their conception or birth if possible. By permitting prenatal screening or genetic abortions, we are thus 'saving potential future children from pain and harm.'[154] The logic of this argument is that standards in these

---

[151] See generally Kaplan, 'Prenatal Screening and its Impact on Persons with Disabilities' in Kuhse and Singer, *A Companion to Bioethics* (Blackwell Publishing, 1998) at 130–136.

[152] Buck, Foreword to *The Terrible Choice: The Abortion Dilemma* (Bantam Books, 1968).

[153] There is an assumption that there is a relationship between genetic conditions and a negative life experience. For less severe genetic conditions, this may not be a correct assumption. 'The disability rights movement certainly agrees that there are economic and social disadvantages that are associated with disability. However, the fact that so many persons with disabilities are engaging in ordinary lives with satisfying jobs, happy family situations, and a variety of community roles suggests that these disadvantages can be eliminated without eliminating persons with disabilities.' Kaplan, 'Prenatal Screening and its Impact on Persons with Disabilities' in Kuhse and Singer, *Bioethics* (Blackwell Publishing,1998) at 135.

[154] Kaplan, 'Prenatal Screening and its Impact on Persons with Disabilities' in Kuhse and Singer, *Bioethics* (Blackwell Publishing,1998) at 133.

cases are objective and of general application, thus avoiding the relativity and subjectivity of societal and parental interests.[155] However, the counter argument is that the boundaries between potentially human and potentially not human are ambiguous and lead to value judgments on the meaning of 'severe' and 'disability'. Even the notion that there is a norm of perfection to which nature strives is difficult to accept given that many of us would fall short of such a norm.

[8.75] There is also the argument that we should try to provide every child with a normal opportunity for health, even if this duty requires us to refrain from reproduction. Although this may again seem to incorporate unsatisfactory appeals to what may be considered 'normal', bearing in mind the worldwide differences in such measurements, another way of looking at it would be to say that parents ought to try to provide for their children health normal for that culture, although it may be inadequate if measured by other standards.[156] The argument is based on prospective views rather than retrospective ones, and therefore does not impinge on the value of those people already living with genetic disorders. It is based on the opinion that, for example, a world where nobody is at risk for Huntington's disease, must be preferable to the current situation where children are born with a 50 percent chance of suffering from this serious disease. It is thus regarded as defensible to prevent the birth of possible persons, who are not thereby deprived or injured if they do not exist. This is premised on the argument that possible persons do not exist, nor do they have any right to exist, and therefore they do not have any experiences or interests that might suffer if they are not brought into existence.[157]

[8.76] The slippery slope argument raises its head here too, in that a further extension of PND for 'minor' genetic abnormalities may become commonplace. Boyle and Savulescu state that the ethical objections to such an extension rest on grounds of irrationality, discrimination, rationing of resources, reduced genetic diversity, harm to the fetus, distinction between social terminations and terminations following PND, and harm to society.[158] Many of these would apply to Pre-implantation Genetic Diagnosis (PGD) also, as considered below. They say that before such objections are used as a basis for preventing access to genetic testing, they need to be backed up by evidence that such testing is harmful to society or that health-care resources would be better used elsewhere. Otherwise we may 'fall into the trap of interfering in individual liberty for no good reason.'

---

[155] Kass, 'Implications of Prenatal Diagnosis for the Human Right to Life' in Hilton et al (eds) *Ethical Issues in Human Genetics: Genetic Counselling and the Use of Genetic Knowledge* (New York: Plenum Press, 1973) 185–199.

[156] Purdy, 'Genetic Diseases: Can Having Children Be Immoral?' in Kuhse and Singer (eds) *Bioethics, An Anthology* (Blackwell Publishing, 1999) 123–129 at 126.

[157] Purdy, 'Genetic Diseases: Can Having Children Be Immoral?' in Kuhse and Singer (eds) *Bioethics, An Anthology* (Blackwell Publishing, 1999) 123–129 at 126.

[158] Boyle and Savulsecu, 'Prenatal Diagnosis for Minor Genetic Abnormalities is *Ethical*' (2003) Am J of Bioethics Vol 3 No 1.

PRE-IMPLANTATION GENETIC DIAGNOSIS

[8.77] Developments in in vitro fertilisation (IVF)[159] and embryo micromanipulation techniques led in 1989[160] to the ability to determine genetic diagnoses in early embryos prior to implantation of the embryo in the uterus.[161] Pre-implantation genetic diagnosis (known as PGD or PID) involves the removal of a single cell from an embryo created through IVF[162] which has been cultured in carefully controlled conditions until 6 to 12 discreet cells are present. This usually occurs about three days following fertilisation. Each of these cells contains the full genetic material of the baby that would develop if the embryo were to implant in the womb. The DNA contained in the cell is amplified and tested to determine whether or not the embryo from which the DNA was extracted carries a genetic mutation known to be carried by one or both parents. In this way, only unaffected embryos will be selected for transfer to the uterus.[163] The most common uses of PGD are for cystic fibrosis, sickle-cell disease, thalassaemia, Tay-Sachs mutations, X-linked diseases, Duchenne's muscular dystrophy and some chromosomal abnormalities. Tests for other genetic mutations may be possible depending on current knowledge of the genetic code underlying the disease.[164] PGD may also be used for sex selection and for HLA tissue typing but these uses are more controversial and will be discussed further below.

[8.78] The significance of PGD is that it offers high-risk couples the chance to have a child free from specific disorders without having to undergo invasive prenatal diagnostic procedures or terminations. Considerable differences in the regulatory oversight of PGD exist among countries, ranging from total bans on any embryo manipulation to the almost complete absence of any regulations or authority. Recommendations and regulations governing its use often draft the criteria for PGD broadly in line with the criteria for selective abortion, where such is permitted by law. PGD is becoming increasingly available throughout the world, although often in only limited circumstances. A survey carried out in 2010 by the International Federation of Fertility

---

[159] See Ch. 6 for further discussion of IVF.

[160] The first successful PGD was reported in 1990 when two sets of twin girls were produced where families were at high risk of passing on a serious X-linked disorder. See Handyside et al, 'Pregnancies From Biopsied Human Preimplantation Embryos Sexed by Y Specific DNA Amplification' (1990) 344 Nature 768–770. The first autosomal recessive disorder where PGD resulted in the birth of an unaffected child was cystic fibrosis. See Handyside et al, 'Birth of a Normal Girl After IVF and Preimplantation Diagnostic Testing for Cystic Fibrosis' (1992) 327 NEJM 905–909.

[161] See generally Hildt and Graumann, *Genetics in Human Reproduction* (Ashgate Publishing, 1999).

[162] The removal of one cell from an embryo does not seem to impair the viability of that embryo.

[163] For detailed discussion of the development of the technique, see Edwards and Schulman, 'History of and Opportunities for Preimplantation Diagnosis' in Edwards (ed) *Preconception and Preimplantation Diagnosis of Human Genetic Disease* (New York: Cambridge University Press, 1993) 3–40.

[164] For comment on the issues affecting couples who choose PGD, see Botkin, 'Ethical Issues and Practical Problems in Preimplantation Genetic Diagnosis' (1998) 26 JME 17.

Societies shows that it is prohibited in only six countries and is being used in 71 (59 per cent) of the 121 countries surveyed.[165]

[8.79] Those most likely to benefit from the technique include couples known to carry a genetic mutation who have a moral objection to termination of pregnancy following prenatal testing, women who are infertile and at risk of carrying a particular genetic disease and 'genetic disaster' families who have continued 'bad luck' in conceiving children with the disease.[166] Almost all genetically inherited conditions that are diagnosed in the prenatal period can also be diagnosed in the preimplantation period. As technology continues to develop it is argued that the temptation to subject embryos to a 'genetic check-up' prior to implantation will increase, although it will never ensure the birth of a completely 'normal' baby,[167] as it will be impossible to check for polygenic or multifactorial disorders or to rule out the possibility of the child being affected with diseases other than those already present in the family. It is also unlikely that PGD will ever be employed on as broad a basis as pre-natal testing as it is only available in conjunction with IVF, which is a complex and costly procedure[168], and also because of the very small number of viable offspring that result from its use.[169]

[8.80] In relation to the importance of genetic counselling[170] of couples seeking PGD it has been argued that, although the standard view is that non-directive counselling should be given, it is not possible, and may not be desirable, to do so in relation to PGD. This is due to the vulnerability of the couple, the social context and attitudes to disability and the structure of the genetic services offered.[171] Chadwick explains this firstly by the fact that in professional-client relations, there is typically an imbalance of power due to the difference in knowledge and, often, social status, between the parties. In reproductive counselling this is exacerbated by the extra vulnerability of pregnancy and in PGD, by the strains of the IVF process. Secondly, the significance of negative social attitudes towards disability will inevitably play a role in advancing the perception that PGD is

[165] See survey carried out by the International Federation of Fertility Societies at http://www.iffs-reproduction.org/documents/IFFS_Surveillance_2010.pdf (accessed 3 June 2011).

[166] Penketh, 'The Scope of Preimplantation Diagnosis' in Edwards (ed) *Preconception and Preimplantation Diagnosis of Human Genetic Disease* (New York: Cambridge University Press, 1993) at 82–84.

[167] The definition of 'normal' is obviously a matter of crucial debate in this context, as is any attempted definition of 'severe' or 'serious' disorder. Values differ amongst families, societies and ethnic groups and may change over time. It is difficult, therefore, to compile any list of disorders for which it would be ethical to test. The standard used in the context of PND in the UK is where there is a precise diagnosis and a 'substantial risk' of 'serious handicap.'

[168] PGD is not currently available in Ireland, but couples may travel to the UK, where a small number of clinics are licensed by the Human Fertilisation and Embryology Authority to carry out such testing. Alternatively, cells may be sent by Irish clinics to licensed clinics in other countries for diagnostic testing.

[169] Human Genetics Commission, *Response to the HFEA on the Consultation on PGD* (2001) para 4.

[170] For further explanation of the issues involved in genetic counselling, see Clarke 'Genetic Counselling' in Chadwick, *The Concise Encyclopedia of the Ethics of New Technologies* (Academic Press, 2001) at 131–146.

[171] Chadwick, 'Preimplantation Diagnosis – Implications for Genetic Counselling' in Hildt and Graumann, *Genetics in Human Reproduction* (Ashgate Publishing, 1999) at 253.

preferable to pre-natal diagnosis and that this will also affect the practice of genetic counselling. Thirdly, the fact that genetic counselling is available for certain conditions would seem to indicate that these conditions are more undesirable than others. So 'although there is explicit adherence to the ideal of choice, implicitly certain decisions are expected.'[172] Non-directive counselling may not be desirable in this context, as it may not be what couples want, being perceived as cold and unhelpful. Also it is argued that the principle of autonomy as the underpinning of such counselling may not be appropriate here as reproductive decisions should be made in the light of as much information as possible.[173] The suggestion of such a duty 'marks a move away from autonomous decision-making about reproduction to the suggestion that there are certain constraints on what decisions we ought to make.'[174]

[8.81] One of the issues that arises here is the extent to which the prospective parent's views about fetal disability should be taken into account. The rights-based approach to reproductive autonomy advocated by Robertson, Harris and others, discussed in Chapter 4, is relevant in deciding the extent to which a parent should have a say in the kind of child to be born. People vary in their reaction to the possibility of fetal abnormality: 'there are reasons to want to prevent the birth of a child affected by impairment which do not reflect discrimination against disabled people: for example, the desire to avoid the early death or suffering of a loved child, or a feeling that a family will be unable to cope with the strain of looking after a very impaired member.'[175] The difficulty is that moving to a rights-based system which accords full decision-making authority to the prospective parents, whether it be in relation to genetic abortion, PND or PGD, could lead to abortion on demand, whereas putting limits on decision-making authority interferes with reproductive autonomy.[176] While selection of an embryo to avoid serious impairment may be morally justifiable, the definition of 'serious' is problematic when we move beyond extreme conditions such as Tay-Sachs disease, which can include symptoms such as blindness, deafness, loss of intellectual and motor skills, feeding difficulties and seizures. Many reports and commentaries on this issue state that the task of defining 'serious' in this context is impossible. In cases where there is a reasonable disagreement between the prospective parents and the health professionals on whether a condition is 'serious', Scott argues that the parents' views should carry the most weight since they will have the responsibility of caring for and raising the child.

---

[172] Chadwick, 'Preimplantation Diagnosis – Implications for Genetic Counselling' in Hildt and Graumann, *Genetics in Human Reproduction* (Ashgate Publishing, 1999) at 254.

[173] Botkin suggests that 'it would make little sense to go through IVF procedures and genetic analyses only to be nondirective about which embryos to place in the uterus. The purpose of PGD is not simply to inform a couple about the genetic nature of their embryos. The explicit purpose is also to transfer healthy embryos and to discard those destined to be affected. Once a couple has chosen PGD, nondirectiveness is no longer relevant.' Botkin, 'Ethical Issues and Practical Problems in Preimplantation Genetic Diagnosis' (1998) 26 JME 17.

[174] Chadwick, 'Preimplantation Diagnosis – Implications for Genetic Counselling' in Hildt and Graumann, *Genetics in Human Reproduction* (Ashgate Publishing, 1999) at 254.

[175] Shakespeare, 'Choices and Rights: Eugenics, Genetics and Disability Equality' (1998) 13(5) Disability and Society 665, 672.

[176] See further discussion by Scott, 'The Uncertain Scope of Reproductive Autonomy in Preimplantation Genetic Diagnosis and Selective Abortion' (2005) Med Law Rev Vol 13: 291–327.

[8.82] In the UK, an embryo may be tested to establish whether it has a particular chromosomal abnormality only if a) that abnormality may affect its capacity to result in a live birth, or b) there is a particular risk that it has that abnormality, and where the Human Fertilisation and Embryology Authority (HFEA), which licenses centres to provide this service, is satisfied that there is a significant risk that a person with that abnormality will have or develop a serious medical condition.[177]

[8.83] Both PGD and PND can be used in an attempt to avoid the birth of a child with a genetically inherited condition or defect, although the use of genetic tests will never achieve perfection due to the fact that most people carry at least four or five recessive genes. When used for such a purpose, the chief moral advantage generally claimed for PGD over PND is that PGD does not involve terminating a life. 'This will not impress those who believe that a biologically human being has an inviolable 'right' to life from conception, but it does recommend PGD to those who believe that the embryo achieves this status only at the moment of implantation.'[178]

[8.84] There are many ethical issues associated with PGD, including whether moral status is accorded to the embryo from conception,[179] and the inherent 'selection' that PGD seems to offer.[180] PGD has sometimes been represented as the technique enabling parents to create 'designer babies' by selecting embryos with desired genes for intelligence, sporting ability, musical talent and so on.[181] Thus, it may be argued that 'once we decide to begin the process of human genetic engineering, there is really no logical place to stop. If diabetes, sickle cell anaemia, and cancer are cured by altering the genetic makeup of an individual, why not proceed to other "disorders": myopia, colour-blindness, left-handedness?'[182] Even if it is accepted that PGD should be available for serious or severe conditions, how may lines be drawn between severe conditions and non-severe conditions? 'Severity varies not only historically but according to the precise social context of each affected person.'[183] However, even if it

---

[177] See list of conditions for which licences may currently be given by the HFEA at http://www.hfea.gov.uk/cps/hfea/gen/pgd-screening.htm (accessed 3 June 2011).

[178] Beyleveld, 'Does PID Solve the Moral Problems of Prenatal Diagnosis? A Rights Analysis'. Beyleveld uses the acronym PID for preimplantation genetic diagnosis and PD for prenatal diagnosis.

[179] See Chapter 6 for detailed discussion of this issue.

[180] As Glover asks, 'how far should we go in choosing what kinds of people should be born?' Glover, 'Eugenics: Some Lessons from the Nazi Experience' in Harris and Holm (eds) *The Future of Human Reproduction* (Clarendon Press, 1998) 55 at 57. See also Krahn, 'Regulating Preimplantation Genetic Diagnosis: The Case of Down's Syndrome' (Spring 2011) 19, Medical Law Review, pp 157–191.

[181] For arguments that couples should be allowed to select embryos which are most likely to have the best life, based on available genetic information, including information about non-disease genes, see Savulescu, 'Procreative Beneficence: Why We Should Select the Best Children' (2001) 15 (5/6) Bioethics 413–426.

[182] This statement was made in the context of gene therapy but the sentiment applies equally here. Rifkin, cited in Holtug, 'Human Gene Therapy: Down the Slippery Slope?' (1993) 7(5) Bioethics 402–419.

[183] Holm, 'Ethical Issues in Pre-Implantation Genetic Diagnosis' in Harris and Holm (eds) *The Future of Human Reproduction* (Clarendon Press, 1998) at 184.

were technically possible to select embryos on the basis of desired genes, the ethical implications of using the procedure for non-disease genes or for social characteristics would be hard to overcome.[184]

[8.85] It may be argued that PGD, as a negative selection tool, meets the definition of eugenics, as it excludes the implantation of certain embryos after genetic defects are discovered, or prefers certain embryos on the basis of desired characteristics.[185] Article 3.2 of the EU Charter of Fundamental Rights 2000 proclaims the right to the integrity of the person and states that 'the prohibition of eugenic practices, in particular those aiming at the selection of persons' must be respected.[186] This provision may be interpreted as precluding PGD.[187] In addition to arguments that this comes close to eugenics, it may also be claimed that testing the embryo for specific genes interferes with the child's right to an open future.[188] Davis explains that 'good parenting requires a balance between having a child for our own sakes and being open to the moral reality that the child will exist for her own sake'.[189] For example, an embryo might be selected for its perfect musical pitch[190] yet the child has an interest in not having the way she is raised unduly affected by her parents' expectations consequent on their PGD decisions – she needs to be able to reject music if she wishes.[191]

---

[184] PGD 'could signify the reduction of human life to the sum of its genes'. Decisions based on quality of life criteria should be scrutinised on the basis of the distinction between illness and enhancement. See Mieth, 'In Vitro Fertilisation: From Medical Reproduction to Genetic Diagnosis' (1996) 1 (1) Biomedical Ethics 6–8.

[185] Advances in non-invasive prenatal testing may yield similar outcomes through testing of maternal plasma. Recent research shows that among high risk pregnancies clinically indicated for invasive prenatal diagnosis, non-invasive detection of fetal trisomy 21 (Down's syndrome) can be achieved with the use of sequencing of maternal plasma DNA. It is thought that the sequencing test could be used to rule out trisomy 21 among high-risk pregnancies before proceeding to invasive diagnostic testing to reduce the number of cases requiring amniocentesis or chorionic villus sampling. Chiu et al, 'Non-Invasive Prenatal Assessment of Trisomy 21 by Multiplexed Maternal Plasma DNA Sequencing: Large Scale Validity Study' BMJ 2011;342: c7401.

[186] See http://www.europarl.europa.eu/charter/pdf/text_en.pdf (accessed 3 June 2011).

[187] Somsen, 'Regulating Human Genetics in a Non-Eugenic Era' in Murphy (ed) *New Technologies and Human Rights* (OUP, 2009) 85–127.

[188] Feinburg, 'The Child's Right to an Open Future' in Aiken and LaFollette (eds) *Whose Child? Children's Rights, Parental Authority and State Power* (Rowman and Littlefield, 1980).

[189] Davis, 'Genetic Dilemmas and the Child's Right to an Open Future' (1997) Hastings Centre Report 27(2) 7 at 12.

[190] Robertson argues that selecting embryos for perfect pitch or other non-medical reasons may be justifiable, depending on the importance of the reproductive choice being asserted, the burdens of the selection procedure, its impact on offspring and its implications for deselected groups and society generally. Robertson, 'Extending Preimplantation Genetic Diagnosis: Medical and Non-Medical Uses' J Med Ethics (2003) 29: 213–216.

[191] Scott, 'Choosing Between Possible Lives: Legal and Ethical Issues in Preimplantation Genetic Diagnosis' (2006) 26(1) Ox J Leg Studies 153–178 at 170.

Disability discrimination

[8.86] It is argued that the use of PGD devalues people with disabilities, as it is akin to stating that they should not have been born. The purpose of PGD is not just to inform couples about the genetic conditions of their embryos but to enable them to avoid having a child with a disability. Perfection will thus become the norm in society, which will increase the stigmatisation of those who choose not to undergo such testing. The counter argument is that it is ethically acceptable to choose not to have a child with a particular disorder, while at the same time agreeing that any affected person would have the same rights and worth as any other member of society. Disability rights advocate Adrienne Asch acknowledges that although society can do a great deal to offer opportunities to people with disabilities, not all disabilities can be overcome – this is not a matter of social prejudice but of reality. She says:

> Not all problems of disability are socially created and, thus, theoretically remediable…The inability to move without mechanical aid, to see, to hear, or to learn is not inherently neutral. Disability itself limits some options. Listening to the radio for someone who is deaf, looking at paintings for someone who is blind, walking upstairs for someone who is quadriplegic, or reading abstract articles for someone who is intellectually disabled are precluded by impairment alone…It is not irrational to hope that children and adults will live as long as possible without health problems or diminished human capacities.[192]

[8.87] Steinbock asks whether PGD can be viewed as a form of prevention, comparable to recommending folic acid supplements to pregnant women to prevent the births of children with neural tube defects. Both measures are designed to reduce the number of individuals born with disabilities but no one claims that recommending folic acid constitutes discrimination against people with spina bifida. She says: 'there is no inconsistency in thinking, "if I have a child who has a disability or becomes ill, or has special needs, I will love and care for that child; but this is an outcome I would much prefer to avoid."'[193] Savulescu goes further in advocating a principle of procreative beneficence which states that couples should select the child, of the possible children they could have, who is expected to have the best life, or at least as good a life as the others, based on the relevant available information.[194]

[8.88] An early consultation paper published by the HFEA in the UK states:

> The vast majority of people hope that their children will be healthy and free from disability. This does not mean that they will not love and care for a child born with a disability. However, the impact on the quality of life of a child born with a disability, as well as their families will depend on a number of factors. These will include the seriousness of the disability, the circumstances of the family, as well as the emotional and material support available. Each family should be free to make their own choices in this respect and their

---

[192] Asch, 'Reproductive Technology and Disability' in Cohen and Taub (eds) *Reproductive Laws for the 1990s* (Humana Press, 1988) p 69–124. Quoted by Steinbock, 'Preimplantation Genetic Diagnosis and Embryo Selection' in Burley and Harris (eds) *A Companion to Genethics* (Blackwell Publishing, 2002) 175 at 180.

[193] Steinbock, 'Preimplantation Genetic Diagnosis and Embryo Selection' in Burley and Harris (eds) *A Companion to Genethics* (Blackwell Publishing, 2002) 175 at 182.

[194] Savulescu, 'Procreative Beneficence: Why We Should Select the Best Children' (2001) Bioethics 15(5/6) 414–425.

view will be one of the most important determining factors in assessing the justification for PGD.[195]

[8.89] Another issue is whether carrier or affected embryos should be transferred to the uterus in any circumstances. In some cases PGD will identify not only embryos directly affected by the genetic disorder but also those who may be carriers of recessive disorders. If there are not many embryos available for transfer the couple may choose to transfer a carrier embryo even though the child will face difficult reproductive decisions of its own at some future time. The Human Genetics Commission in the UK has advised that if it is possible to exclude affected embryos without discovering the carrier status of others, and without compromising the accuracy of the test, then this is to be preferred. 'This will result in an increased chance of the couple achieving an unaffected pregnancy. It will also protect the unborn child's subsequent right to decide for themselves whether or not to be tested for their carrier status.'[196]

[8.90] It is also possible that a couple may specifically wish to transfer an affected embryo, such as a deaf couple who may want to transfer an embryo carrying the gene for deafness because they are of the opinion that a hearing child born into their environment would be alienated and disadvantaged in the deaf community. Whether it is ethically acceptable to deliberately cause a child to be born with, what may be perceived as, a disability is open to question, given that the welfare of any resulting child should be considered before embarking on any IVF programme. However, it is also important to note the danger here of slipping down a slippery slope[197] where screening then becomes an obligation or inherent in responsible procreation.[198]

PGD and gender selection

[8.91] PGD allows for the chromosomal evaluation of embryos and therefore for the selection of embryos by gender prior to transfer to the uterus. Although sperm-sorting techniques had been available for this purpose for many years, PGD is a more effective and accurate method of gender selection. Many international bodies such as the United Nations,[199] the International Federation of Gynaecology and Obstetrics[200] and the

[195] Human Fertilisation and Embryology Authority and Advisory Commission on Genetic Testing, *Consultation Document on PGD* (1999).

[196] Human Genetics Commission, *Response to the HFEA on the Consultation on PGD* (2001) p 4.

[197] See further McGleenan, 'Reproductive Technology and the Slippery Slope Argument: A Message in Blood' in Hildt and Graumann (eds) *Genetics in Human Reproduction* (Ashgate Publishing, 1999) 273–283; and McGleenan, 'Human Gene Therapy and Slippery Slope Arguments' (1995) 21 JME 350–5.

[198] 'With the availability of genetic tests, bringing an affected child into the world could be construed by some as reproductive irresponsibility. This irresponsibility may be in respect of the child if born, or in respect of the community whose scarce resources will be used to support that child through its disability.' Whittaker, 'The Implications of the Human Genome Project for Family Practice' 35(3) J of Fam Practice 294 at 296.

[199] United Nations, 'Gender Equality, Equity and Empowerment of Women' in Population and Development: Programme of Action Adopted at the International Conference on Population and Development, Sept 1994, Cairo: New York UN 1995, 17–21.

[200] FIGO, Committee for the Ethical Aspects of Human Reproduction and Women's Health, 'Ethical Guidelines on Sex Selection for Non-Medical Purposes' I J Gyn Obst 2006; 92:329–330.

American College of Obstetricians and Gynaecologists[201] oppose gender selection for non-medical reasons on the basis that it is sexist and therefore discriminatory against women, and that it might lead to gender imbalances in the general population, as reported in India and China, where societies clearly favour male over female children. There is also a suggestion that evidence from evolutionary psychology and biology suggests that the sex of the offspring in mammals may not be a matter of chance. Instead, sex allocation may be the result of a finely tuned adaptive process involving the suitability of the mother to conceive a child of a particular sex. Therefore, more information needs to be obtained before a social policy is determined which could have disadvantageous consequences for children, their parents and society.[202]

[8.92] Although pre-conceptive sex and race selection enhance procreative liberty, the procedures are disturbing because they potentially reflect parental expectations of gender- appropriate stereotypical behaviour.[203] However, it may also be said that these arguments allow political correctness to abridge individual reproductive choice.[204] It is a presumption of liberal democracies that the freedom of citizens should not be interfered with unless good and sufficient justifications can be produced for so doing. As Dworkin puts it:

> The right of procreative autonomy has an important place…in Western political culture more generally. The most important feature of that culture is a belief in individual human dignity: that people have the moral right – and the moral responsibility – to confront the most fundamental questions about the meaning and value of their own lives for themselves, answering to their own consciences and convictions…The principle of procreative autonomy, in a broad sense, is embedded in any genuinely democratic culture.[205]

[8.93] However, Williamson argues that although personal freedom is important, 'it is an inadequate ethic if it effectively forecloses moral evaluation of any activity where harms have not yet been empirically demonstrated – especially where the nature of those possible harms makes them difficult to demonstrate'.[206] She says that advocates of an expansive concept of personal freedom have not shown that restricting some choices, such as selecting the traits of children, will have an adverse effect on the exercise of personal freedom in areas in which they are most significant or result in a slippery slope of ethical micro-management by an interfering State.

[8.94] It may also be argued that 'sex selection is intrinsically sexist in that it is based on assumptions about future individuals from differences that are socially constructed or at

---

[201] ACOG, Committee on Ethics. Sex Selection, Committee Opinion Number 360; Feb 2007; Obstet Gynecol 2007; 109:475–478.

[202] Grant, 'Sex Predetermination and the Ethics of Sex Selection' Hum Reprod Vol 21 No 7 pp 1659–1661, 2006.

[203] Berkowitz, 'Sexism and Racism in Preconceptive Trait Selection' (1999) 71(3) Fertility and Sterility 415–417.

[204] Paulson, 'Political Correctness and the Abridgement of Reproductive Choice' (1999) 71(3) Fertility and Sterility 418–419.

[205] Dworkin, *Life's Dominion* (Harper Collins, 1993). See also Harris, 'Sex Selection and Regulated Hatred' J Med Ethics 2005;31: 291–294 and Baldwin 'Reproductive Liberty and Elitist Contempt: Reply to John Harris' J Med Ethics 2005; 31:288–290.

[206] Williamson, 'Sex(ist) Selection?' Med Law I 2004, Vol 6 pp 185–206 at 194.

least mediated, rather than on experience of individual identity.'[207] Williamson says this may cause harm to the child that is selected because the parents may, consciously or unconsciously, express their expectations to the child. Failure to fulfil those expectations might result in parental disappointment, and discovery of the selection decision might result in a child perceiving parental love as conditional.

[8.95] Any social changes brought about by technologies such as PGD are likely to reflect the existing imbalance of power between males and females. Thus, it has been asserted that the widespread commercial availability of this technique would reduce the size of the female population – 'Given the well-documented societal preference for male children – and the fact that millions of women, as well as men, in the western world, not just third world countries, still react to the births of daughters with disappointment, sorrow, and even economic and social penalties – the potential widespread commercial availability of sex pre-selection techniques opens up ominous possibilities'.[208] Although it might be thought that a smaller female population might prove advantageous to women, studies of populations with sex-ratio imbalances have shown that such societies are characterised by 'bride-price and bride-service, great importance attached to virginity, emphasis on the sanctity of the family ... proscriptions against adultery ... marriage at an early age, and [prejudice against] women ... regarded as inferior to men ... [in] reasoned judgement, scholarship and political affairs.'[209] Thus, it is argued, technologies such as this would have the effect of furthering the imbalance of power and ultimately benefiting men to the cost of women.

[8.96] The importance of sex predetermination may be seen in the context of three population variables: first-child patterns, family size and the sex ratio.[210] In many countries, studies reflect a preference among both men and women for a boy for the first child and a consequent inclination to reduce family size if the desire for a particular sex is met with the first child or first two children. Possible reasons for the preference for a son are given as the tradition of carrying on the family name, the value they may have as adults in their chosen profession and a traditional wish among women to please their husbands. Girls would seem to be less valued, as their futures as wives and mothers may be less surprising and perhaps less financially valuable. Their birth is seen as less likely to please their fathers, as they are thought to be harder and more costly to raise. What is interesting about these studies is the fact of the societal preference itself, suggesting that if sex pre-determination were to become widely available, it would be taken advantage of by a large percentage of the population.

---

[207] Williamson, 'Sex(ist) Selection?' Med Law I. 2004, Vol 6 pp 185–206 at 193.

[208] Steinbacher, 'Sex Choice: Survival and Sisterhood' 5–6 (April 1984) (Paper presented at the Second International Interdisciplinary Congress on Women, Women's Worlds: Strategies for Empowerment, in Gronigen, Netherlands).

[209] Holmes and Hoskins, 'Prenatal and Preconception Sex Choice Technologies: A Path to Femicide?' April 1984 (paper presented at the Second International Interdisciplinary Congress on Women, Women's Worlds: Strategies for Empowerment, in Gronigen, Netherlands, quoting Guttentag and Secord, *Too Many Women? The Sex Ratio Question* (Sage Publications, 1983) p 79.

[210] Hanmer, 'Sex Predetermination and Male Dominance' in Roberts (ed) *Women, Health and Reproduction* (Routledge, Kegan & Paul, 1981) 163–190 at 166.

Sex predetermination is unlikely to change the patriarchal emphasis of our society but, adopted on a wide-scale, and this depends on the technique developed, it offers the possibility of strengthening son preference and daughter non-preference, of reinforcing sex roles by under-writing the conflation of sex and gender, of altering the sex ratio further in favour of males, of placing greater restriction on women's limited control over their reproductive capacities.[211]

[8.97] Although behaviour patterns in some countries suggest a societal preference for male offspring, this would not be the case in other countries such as the US, Australia and most European states, where in fact a preference for female children may be evident.[212] Thus, it may be argued that the technique is not inherently discriminatory towards women. Macklin says that although sex determination contributes to the devaluation of the female sex, this is a good reason for considering it to be undesirable but not a sufficient reason for legal prohibition. She points out that women and girl children may be worse off in other ways as a result of prohibiting sex determination than they would be if the practice were to be legally tolerated, such as that they are obliged to have more children than they want or than is healthy for them until they have the required number of sons; some go to private doctors for sex determination, which may be more costly and less safe than it would be in public hospitals; and those who do not bear sons are at risk of desertion by their husbands, leaving them with no financial means.[213] She argues that in countries such as India and China, social reforms rather than prohibition of sex determination are more likely to achieve the desirable effects of increasing respect for women and enhancing their status. Given the expense and inaccessibility of the technique for the vast majority of the population, it is also unlikely to be used so extensively as to contribute to societal sex-ratio imbalances.[214] However, it is important to note the increased availability of non-invasive prenatal diagnosis through genetic testing of maternal blood for free fetal DNA containing a Y chromosome at seven weeks of pregnancy.[215] This can be used for women who carry X-linked conditions, but is also now available worldwide via finger prick testing direct to the consumer at relatively inexpensive prices. These may replace poor-quality ultrasound in India and China for social sex selection.

[8.98] Another use of PGD for sex selection is where family balancing is sought by the couple. As Robertson explains, PGD for family balancing is where a couple seeks

---

[211] Hanmer, 'Sex Predetermination and Male Dominance' in Roberts (ed) *Women, Health and Reproduction* (Routledge, Kegan & Paul, 1981) 163–190 at 185. Hanmer agrees with other authors who see women's reproductive role in society as becoming more important as their proportionate numbers decrease, almost like the queen bees to be given as rewards to outstanding males.

[212] Gleicher and Barad, 'The Choice Of Gender: Is Elective Gender Selection Indeed Sexist?' Hum Reprod 2007; 22: 3038–3041.

[213] Macklin, 'The Ethics of Sex Selection' (1995) Indian J of Med Ethics 3: 61–64.

[214] Robertson, 'Extending Preimplantation Genetic Diagnosis: Medical and Non-Medical Uses' J Med Ethics 2003; 29: 213–216. See also Ashcroft, 'Back to the Future: Response to Extending Preimplantation Genetic Diagnosis: Medical and Non-Medical Uses' (2003) J Med Ethics; 29:217–219.

[215] Wright and Chitty, 'Cell-Free Fetal DNA and RNA in Maternal Blood: Implications for Safer Antenatal Testing' BMJ 2009; 339: b2451.

variety or balance in the gender of offspring because of the different rearing experiences that come with rearing children of different genders.[216] Although there is not yet strong evidence of a substantial need or desire for gender variety in children, it may be that if such evidence were presented, the use of PGD to choose a gender opposite to that of an existing child or children may be much less susceptible to a charge of sexism. However, it may be argued that any attention to the gender of offspring is inherently sexist. Robertson claims that the case is weak for allowing PGD for the first child, as this carries a risk of promoting sexist social mores, but may be acceptable for gender variety in a family as the risk of sexism is lessened.[217]

[8.99] Gender selection techniques may also be very important in the detection of serious heritable sex-linked diseases. The use of such techniques in these instances would mean predetermining the sex of the child but the selection itself is not a sexist act, as no gender-based stereotypical assumptions are made by the prospective parents who seek to avoid the heritable illness in their child.

Preimplantation tissue typing

[8.100] Preimplantation tissue typing is a technique which allows the selection of embryos in order to bring about the birth of a child who can provide a matched tissue donation to an existing sibling, either as the sole clinical objective or in combination with PGD to avoid a serious genetic condition in the resulting child.[218] The test involves taking a cell sample from the embryo at around the eight-cell stage. This cell can be tested to check if the embryo has the same genetic condition as the existing child. It also enables the clinician to establish whether the embryo would be a close enough tissue match for the existing child. The first baby, or 'saviour sibling', born following application of this technique was in the United States in 2001.

[8.101] The ethical issues raised by this procedure centre on the instrumentalisation of children, that is that the child becomes an instrument to cure another child. It is argued that this is contrary to the Kantian imperative which is one of the fundamental rules underlying Western moral thinking: 'Act in such a way that you always treat humanity, whether in your own person or the person of any other, never simply as a means, but always at the same time as an end.'[219] However, there are a number of difficulties with the application of this principle in this context. Firstly, Kant defines personhood with reference to rationality, which is a characteristic that embryos do not exhibit. Secondly, it is not always clear how it should be decided when someone is treated as a mere means and no longer as an end in himself. Kant's dictum says that an action should only be condemned when it treats a person *solely* as a means. Children are often conceived for a purpose or unconditional ends, such as to care for parents, to be a companion for a

---

[216] Robertson, 'Extending Preimplantation Genetic Diagnosis: Medical and Non-Medical Uses' J Med Ethics 2003; 29: 213–216.

[217] See also Savulescu and Dahl, 'Sex Selection and Preimplantation Diagnosis, A Response to the Ethics Committee of the American Society of Reproductive Medicine' Hum Reprod Vol 15 No 9, 1879–1880 (2000); and Pennings, 'Ethics of Sex Selection for Family Balancing' Hum Reprod Vol 11 No 11 pp 2339–2345 (1996).

[218] HFEA Report, Preimplantation Tissue Typing (2004).

[219] Kant, *Groundwork of the Metaphysics of Morals*, (Harper and Row, 1964).

sibling or to run the family business. This is not to say that such children are not also valued for themselves.[220] It may thus be asked, 'Who is harmed by allowing PGD to be performed solely for the benefit of a relative? Not the couple who wish to produce an embryo. Nor the child who would not otherwise have existed. Nor the person who receives the stem cell transplant that might save his or her life.'[221]

[8.102] What is the legal and ethical basis for the decision to carry out the stem cell transplant? The usual approach to the question of whether a medical intervention is acceptable is to seek the informed consent of the patient. If this is not possible due to age or mental incapacity, the decision is generally made following consideration of the best interests of that person. In the context of tissue typing, advocates argue that the child has an interest in growing up in an intact family and that the child will benefit if the older sibling survives. 'However vague, the underlying idea is that the social, emotional and psychological interests of a person depend on the happiness in the family in which he grows up'.[222] It may be argued that the child will feel diminished when informed about the reason for his existence or that it will give the child a sense of unworthiness or deficiency if the transplant fails, though the latter is unlikely given the age of the donor child. But it could be countered that being told that one was conceived to help a sibling may give the child a greater sense of self-esteem and self-worth, as there are few things that are as valuable as saving the life of another person.[223] It may also be claimed that the donor child will be at life-long risk of exploitation, of being a tissue source for the sibling, of being repeatedly subjected to testing and harvesting procedures, and of being pressurised despite protestations.[224] However, this ignores the purpose of tissue typing, which seeks only to use the stem cells available in the umbilical cord of the newly born child, a procedure which is not harmful to the child or its mother. Although it is true that the child might later in life become a candidate for bone marrow donation for its sibling, a child born in this way is no different from a naturally conceived child who is protected by law. 'Thus, just as no naturally conceived tissue matched child could legally function as a source of spare parts for its sibling, no child intentionally conceived as a tissue match could legally fill such a role.'[225]

[8.103] The question arises in this context as in many others in the area of reproductive choice whether the State is justified in interfering with a couple's free and informed

---

[220] Pennings, Schots and Liebaers, 'Ethical Considerations on Preimplantation Genetic Diagnosis for HLA Tissue Typing to Match a Future Child as a Donor Of Haematopoietic Stem Cells to a Sibling' (2002) Hum Reprod Vol 17 (3) 534–538.

[221] Boyle and Savulescu, 'Ethics of Using Preimplantation Genetic Diagnosis to Select a Stem Cell Donor for an Existing Person' (2001) 323 BMJ 1240–1243.

[222] Savulsecu, 'Substantial Harm but Substantial Benefit" (1996) BMJ 312, 241–242.

[223] Thomasna, 'Ethical Issues and Transplantation Technology' (1991) Cambr Quart Healthcare Ethics 4, 333–343. See also discussion of possible tort actions in circumstances where the treatment is unsuccessful by Chico, 'Saviour Siblings: Trauma and Tort Law' (2006) Med Law Rev 14: 180–218.

[224] Wolf et al, 'Using Preimplantation Genetic Diagnosis to Create a Stem Cell Donor: Issues, Guidelines and Limits' J Law Med Ethics 2003; 31: 327–39. See also a fictional depiction of such a scenario in Jodi Picoult's book *My Sister's Keeper* (Atria Books, 2004).

[225] Ram, 'Britain's New Preimplantation Tissue Typing Policy: An Ethical Defence' (2006) J Med Ethics 32: 278–282.

decision to avail of such a procedure. Brownsword says that in modern societies which are more pluralistic than in the past, the prospect of regulation that is both effective and judged to be legitimate must seem like an increasingly elusive concept.[226] He argues that in a community of rights, even allowing for a precautionary threshold for legitimate state intervention, the arguments for prohibiting a consenting couple's access to reliable reproductive technologies are weak.

[8.104] In 2001 in the UK the HFEA adopted a precautionary approach when considering this procedure and decided that it should only be permitted when it was combined with tests to enable parents to select embryos which are free from a serious genetic disorder. This was due to the invasive nature of the technique and the concern about a potential risk of damaging the embryo, so tissue typing was only allowed on cells which had already been taken from the embryo for genetic diagnosis. This policy was challenged by an interest group called CORE (Comment on Reproductive Ethics) which brought an application for judicial review, claiming that the policy was ultra vires the Human Fertilisation and Embryology Act 1990. In *Quintavalle (on behalf of Comment on Reproductive Ethics) v HFEA*[227] the facts involved a child called Zain Hashmi, who was six years of age and suffering from a serious genetic disorder called beta thalassaemia major. His bone marrow did not produce enough red blood cells and he needed daily drugs and regular blood transfusions to keep him alive but he could be restored to normal life by a transplant of stem cells from a tissue-compatible donor. His parents wanted to use PGD to select a suitable embryo which would be free of the disease and a compatible donor for their son. The Court had to consider whether HLA tissue typing fell within the list of approved purposes for which the HFEA was empowered to grant a licence. The 1990 Act provided that the Authority may license treatment services, including those designed to secure that embryos are in a suitable condition to be placed in a woman or to determine whether embryos are suitable for that purpose. The HFEA argued that tissue typing fell within that definition, as a woman would be entitled to regard an embryo as unsuitable unless it was free of abnormality and also a perfect tissue match for an existing child.[228] CORE argued for a narrower construction to the effect that 'suitable' must mean capable of becoming a healthy child free of abnormalities, not ensuring that the child would be a compatible donor. The House of Lords found that the HFEA was acting within its powers in providing a licence for tissue typing to enable the Hashmis to select an embryo which would be a good match for their son. Lord Hoffman stated that allowing the Hashmis greater control in their reproductive decision-making saved them from 'having to play dice with conception'.

[8.105] In 2004, following a detailed research and consultation process, the HFEA took the view that the risk to the resulting child associated with embryo biopsy is not enough

---

[226] Brownsword, 'Happy Families, Consenting Couples and Children with Dignity: Sex Selection and Saviour Siblings' (2005) Child and Fam Law Quarterly Vol 17 No 4 pp 435–473.

[227] *Quintavalle (on behalf of Comment on Reproductive Ethics) v HFEA* [2005] UKHL 28.

[228] Sheldon states that this is consistent with a healthy respect for women's or couple's autonomy in reproductive decision-making, as the embryo must not only be suitable in medical terms but also taking account of the wishes of Mrs Hashmi. See Sheldon. 'Saviour Siblings and the Discretionary Power of the HFEA' Med Law Rev (2005) 13: 403–411.

to warrant a policy which distinguishes between cases in which preimplantation tissue typing is used in combination with PGD for serious disease and where discovering tissue type is the sole treatment objective. The Authority found no evidence that adverse psychological effects would result from the procedure but recommended that further follow-up studies of these children and their families should be conducted. It concluded that the technique should be available subject to appropriate safeguards, in cases where there is a genuine need for potentially life-saving tissue and a likelihood of therapeutic benefit for an affected child.[229]

[8.106] PGD has not been available in Ireland due to concerns that the destruction of embryos with genetic abnormalities might be contrary to the provisions of the Irish Constitution which oblige the State to protect the right to life of the unborn. These fears have been allayed by the Supreme Court in *MR v TR*[230] in 2009, which held that the pre-implantation embryo is not within the definition of 'unborn' in Art 40.3.3° but no legislation has yet been introduced to provide a legal framework within which such services should be provided. The Commission on Assisted Human Reproduction recommended in its Report in 2005 that PGD should be permitted under licence to reduce the risk of serious genetic disorders in children born through IVF technology. It also recommended that PGD should be allowed for tissue typing but only for serious diseases that cannot otherwise be treated.[231]

GENE THERAPY

[8.107] As well as the advances in genetic testing and diagnosis brought about by increased knowledge of genetic disorders, it has become possible in recent years to manipulate the genes of existing and, possibly, future individuals by way of gene therapy.[232] 'Like most new developments in medicine and biotechnology, human gene therapy holds out the promise of substantial benefits to humanity while threatening both specific health hazards and fundamental damage to human dignity, and challenging us to consider the very limits of humanness.'[233] The main purpose behind gene therapy is to provide a patient with healthy copies of missing or flawed genes.[234] There are two types – somatic or germ-line gene therapy.[235] Somatic gene therapy attempts to remedy defects

---

[229] See http://www.hfea.gov.uk/763.html (accessed 3 June 2011).

[230] *MR v TR* [2009] IESC 82 discussed in Chapter 6 at para **6.121**.

[231] See http://www.dohc.ie/publications/pdf/cahr.pdf?direct=1 (accessed 3 June 2011).

[232] See generally Walters and Palmer, *The Ethics of Human Gene Therapy* (OUP, 1997).

[233] Dworkin, 'Law and Ignorance: Genetic Therapy and the Legal Process' (1996) Jahrbuch für Recht und Ethik, Annual Review of Law and Ethics, Volume 4.

[234] 'Gene therapy is the use of genetic information to intervene in the DNA of a human cell to relieve the symptoms and prevent the causes of diseases with a genetic component.' Hedgecoe, 'Gene Therapy' in Chadwick, (ed) *The Concise Encyclopedia of the Ethics of New Technologies* (Academic Press, 2001) 123.

[235] Other potential types of therapy could be described as enhancement genetic engineering, which would involve the insertion of a gene to enhance a known characteristic such as a growth hormone, and eugenic genetic engineering, which would be an attempt to alter or improve complex human traits coded by a large number of genes, such as intelligence, personality and character. See generally French Anderson, 'Human Gene Therapy: Scientific and Ethical Considerations' in Chadwick, (ed) *Ethics, Reproduction and Genetic Control* (Croom Helm Ltd, 1987) at 147; Torres, 'On the Limits of Enhancement in Human Gene Transfer: Drawing the Line' (1997) J Med & Phil Vol 22 No 1: 43–53.

within the patient by inserting genetic material to perform a function which the patient's own genetic material is not achieving.[236] Germ-line gene therapy involves either the insertion of genes into the germ cells of the patient, which will have no direct consequences for him but will have results in his children; or by insertion of genes into the early embryo. Both types of germ-line therapy are intended to cause children to be born with or without certain characteristics, and both are highly controversial.

[8.108] Somatic gene therapy is regarded as the simplest and least controversial form of gene therapy[237] as in many ways it is similar to other forms of medical treatment such as organ or tissue transplantation, drug therapy or surgical intervention. As somatic gene therapy generally affects only non-reproductive cells[238], none of the genetic changes produced by this form of therapy will be passed on to the patient's children.[239] Also, the products of the modified cells are, in some cases such as enzyme therapies, similar to mediations that the patient can take as an alternative.[240] The Clothier Committee in the UK, which reported in 1992, viewed the therapy as uncontroversial, though novel, and felt that it gave rise to no new ethical issues.[241] This view is shared by advisory bodies to the European Commission,[242] although it was advised that research be restricted to serious diseases at present,[243] and also by similar bodies in the US.[244]

---

[236] See further Walters and Palmer, *The Ethics of Human Gene Therapy* (OUP, 1997) Ch.2.

[237] This form of therapy is not scientifically unproblematic. For an overview of some of these difficulties, see Kinderlerer and Longley, 'Human Genetics: the New Panacea?' (1998) 61(5) Mod L Rev 603 at 615–618.

[238] Although it is possible that a gene delivered to one tissue may pass into the gonads, ie ovary or testis, and carry consequences for that person's offspring. All participants in gene therapy trials are advised to avoid pregnancy.

[239] For further information, see Friedmann, 'The Origins, Evolution, and Directions of Human Gene Therapy' in Friedmann (ed) *The Development of Human Gene Therapy* (CSHL, 1999).

[240] Walters and Palmer, *The Ethics of Human Gene Therapy* (OUP, 1997) at 36.

[241] *Report of the Committee on the Ethics of Gene Therapy* (1992).

[242] Opinion of the Group of Advisors on Ethical Implications of Biotechnology of the European Commission, *The Ethical Implications of Gene Therapy* (1994).

[243] In 1999 a young man, Jesse Gelsinger, died in the US during the course of a clinical trial on gene therapy run by the University of Pennsylvania. An investigation into his death carried out by the Food and Drug Administration found a number of breaches of rules such as the inclusion of Gelsinger as a substitute for another volunteer who dropped out, despite Gelsinger having high ammonia levels that should have led to his exclusion from the trial; failure by the university to report that two patients had experienced serious side effects from the gene therapy; and failure to mention the deaths of monkeys given a similar treatment in the informed consent documentation. See the useful discussion by Berry, 'Health Care and the Human Genome' in Iltis, Johnson and Hinze (eds) *Legal Perspectives in Bioethics* (Routledge, 2008) 95–125. For issues relating to how ethics committees should evaluate research protocols in this area, see Dettweiler and Simon, 'Points to Consider for Ethics Committees in Human Gene Therapy Trials' (2001) 15 (5/6) Bioethics 491–500.

[244] *Report and Recommendations of the Panel to Assess the National Institutes of Health Investment in Research on Gene Therapy* (1995).

[8.109] Germ-line gene therapy has raised a number of ethical issues due to its capacity to change future individuals.[245] 'The theory is that at a very early stage of an individual's development, perhaps even before conception, changes could be made to a person's genome that would have an effect on every single cell of their body (since all other cells would develop from those early ones) and upon children that they have (and upon all subsequent generations).'[246] The ethical issues here focus on human dignity, enhancement and eugenics[247], similar to the discussion above in relation to PGD.[248] In germ-line gene therapy, however, some of the changes that may theoretically be possible may turn out to be universally acceptable, such as the ability to ensure that carriers of serious genetic disorders will not pass on the disorder to their children.[249] An interesting concept raised in recent debates in this area is that of intergenerational justice[250], which suggests that current genetic knowledge *should* be used in ways which enhance the health and well-being of children yet to be born. It is thus argued that in considering the issues raised by the new genetics, there is a responsibility to take into account the implications for future generations, as it is their genome project also.[251] If research into germ-line gene therapy is prohibited, it may be that the obligation to protect future children from genetic compromise will not be fulfilled.

> The completion of the human genome project will provide a basis for acting on a moral obligation for *future* generations, a claim that has appeared weak in the past. A generation *with* such knowledge who neglected to use it to minimise the risks in reproduction could hardly be said to respect the requirements of intergenerational justice.[252]

[8.110] The concerns about risks and benefits to future children focus on the social and psychological consequences to engineered children arising out of the cure of a disease or the enhancement of a feature. However, advocates argue that such concerns are overblown and that we should embrace the possibility of future generations who might be engineered to be disease-free, long-lived, intelligent, strong, agile and free of hyper-

---

[245] For an interesting view on legal remedies that might be called into action in cases where gene therapy is unsuccessful for a particular patient, see Marshall, 'Medical Malpractice in the New Eugenics: Relying on Innovative Tort Doctrine to Provide Relief When Gene Therapy Fails' (2001) 35(4) Georgia L Rev 1277–1327.

[246] Hedgecoe, 'Gene Therapy' in Chadwick (ed) *The Concise Encyclopedia of the Ethics of New Technologies* (Academic Press, 2001) p124.

[247] For a summary of the issues, see Graumann, 'The Debate About the Moral Evaluation of Germ Line Therapy – A Critical Overview' (1997) 1 (2) Biomedical Ethics 12–16.

[248] See discussion of the arguments for and against germ-line gene therapy in Walters and Palmer, *The Ethics of Human Gene Therapy* (OUP, 1997) at 80–92.

[249] It may be asked why germ-line therapy should be condemned since it would spare future children the requirement of therapy for a gene defect, which perhaps could have been removed before birth.

[250] See further Lappe, 'Ethical Issues in Manipulating the Human Germ Line' in Kuhse and Singer (eds) *Bioethics, An Anthology* (2nd edn, Oxford: Blackwell, 2006), pp 198–208 at 155–164.

[251] Macer, 'Whose Genome Project?' (1991) 5 Bioethics 183 at 209.

[252] Fletcher and Wertz, 'An International Code of Ethics in Medical Genetics Before the Human Genome is Mapped' in Bankowski and Capron (eds) *Genetics, Ethics and Human Values: Human Genome Mapping, Genetic Screening and Therapy* (World Health Organisation, 1991) 97 at 103.

aggressiveness. While genetic engineering might be a novel technique, they argue that it is no different from parents vaccinating their children against disease, or undertaking other health-care or educational initiatives to increase their children's longevity, enrich their intellect, build their fitness and so on.[253]

[8.111] However, as is the case in much of the debates involving genetics, the danger of the slippery slope into eugenics[254] causes concern about this form of genetic engineering.[255] As Rifkin puts it, 'Once we decide to begin the process of human genetic engineering, there is really no logical place to stop. If diabetes, sickle cell anaemia, and cancer are to be cured by altering the genetic make-up of an individual, why not proceed to other 'disorders': myopia, colour-blindedness, left-handedness? Indeed, what is to preclude a society from deciding that a certain skin colour is a disorder?[256] Such slippery slope arguments have led a number of advisory and governmental bodies to ban the practice.[257] Legislation in Austria, Denmark, France, Germany and Sweden all prohibit the practice. The Council of Europe initially recommended a complete ban on this form of therapy on the grounds of human dignity, but later allowed germ cell manipulation for therapeutic purposes.[258] While many would support such a position, it remains difficult to draw fine lines between therapeutic purposes and enhancement objectives in some situations.[259] If it does become possible to draw such lines 'it should be necessary to forbid *all* work in this area only if it is felt that the demarcation line can never be held.'[260]

CLONING

[8.112] In July 1996 in Scotland, Dolly the sheep was born following the application of cloning techniques.[261] This involved taking a normal diploid[262] adult cell from the udder

---

[253] Berry, 'Health Care and the Human Genome' in Iltis, Johnson and Hinze (eds) *Legal Perspectives in Bioethics* (Routledge, 2008) 95–125.

[254] See Harris, 'Is Gene Therapy a Form of Eugenics?' in Kuhse and Singer (eds), *A Companion to Bioethics* (Blackwell Publishing, 1998) 165–170.

[255] For discussion of 'slippery slope' arguments in this context, see Pattinson, 'Regulating Germ-Line Gene Therapy to Avoid Sliding Down the Slippery Slope' (2000) 4 Med Law I 213–222.

[256] Rifkin *Algeny: A New Word – A New World*, in collaboration with Perlas, (Viking Press, 1983) p 232.

[257] For a critique of such arguments, see Pattinson, 'Regulating Germ-Line Gene Therapy to Avoid Sliding Down the Slippery Slope' (2000) 4 Med Law I 213–222.

[258] The Oviedo Convention provides in art 13 that 'an intervention seeking to modify the human genome may only be undertaken for preventative, diagnostic or therapeutic purposes and only if its aim is not to introduce any modification in the genome of any descendants.'

[259] 'For example, gene therapy might be used to increase the height of children with growth hormone deficiency to that of the norm in the population. This would count as therapy. But the same (or similar) techniques could be used to increase the height of a normal child so that they were of above average height. This would be enhancement of characteristics.' Hedgecoe, 'Gene Therapy' in Chadwick (ed) *The Concise Encyclopedia of the Ethics of New Technologies* (Academic Press, 2001) at 125. See also Smith, 'Genetic Enhancement Technologies and the New Society' (2000) Med Law I Vol 4 pp 85–95.

[260] Mason and McCall Smith, *Law and Medical Ethics* (5th edn, OUP, 1999) at 186.

[261] The team involved in Dolly's birth claim to have been motivated by the desire to produce transgenically modified animals which would contain valuable substances in their milk.

of a sheep, removing the genetic material from it and implanting that material within the membrane of an egg cell, which had already had its own genetic material removed. The resulting cell, which consisted of adult genetic material and the egg cell membrane, was transferred to the uterus of another sheep. The Dolly technique was regarded as an enormous development in medical science because her birth resulted from the transfer of the nucleus of a somatic (non-reproductive) cell into an enucleated egg cell. This showed that genetic material could be reprogrammed or reactivated well into the chronological life of the cell.[263] In 2001 American scientists announced that they had cloned the first human embryo for therapeutic purposes.[264]

[8.113] Human cloning might be suggested for four reasons: as a means for an infertile couple to have a child, to bring back a lost relative, to have a child as a copy of a person held in high esteem, or fourthly as a source of tissues for a sick person.[265] Robertson argues that if cloning was safe, it would add to the reproductive options already available and enhance procreative choice for the infertile.[266] For couples unable to take advantage of conventional fertility treatments, cloning one of the partners may be the only way of having a genetically related child.[267] It may also be a means of ensuring that a hereditary genetic disease is not transmitted from an adult to a future child. Use of the technique may also be sought to produce a replica of a dying child, or to produce a genetically identical child for tissue transplantation. Obviously, some of these uses may be seen as less meritorious than others.

[8.114] Those wishing to use cloning technology for any of the reasons mentioned above may assert a fundamental right to reproductive autonomy, including the right to produce a cloned child.[268] The importance of the right to procreative autonomy has been considered in detail in Chapter 4.[269] This right has generally been restricted to issues such as sterilisation, contraception and abortion, although it may be that future policies and judicial decisions will see an extension of the right to cover assisted reproduction.[270]

---

[262] Diploid means having two homologous sets of chromosomes, such as is found in adult cells.

[263] National Bioethics Advisory Commission, *Cloning Human Beings* (1997).

[264] Cibelli et al, 'Somatic Cell Nuclear Transfer in Humans: Pronuclear and Early Embryonic Development' (2001) Journal of Regenerative Medicine Vol 2 p 25.

[265] Ian Wilmut, 'Cloning in Biology and Medicine: Clinical Opportunities and Ethical Concerns' in Burley and Harris (eds), *A Companion to Genethics* (Blackwell Publishing, 2002) 33 at 36.

[266] Robertson, 'Liberty, Identity and Human Cloning' (1998) 76 Texas Law Review 1371 at 1372. See also Bell, 'Human Cloning and International Human Rights Law' (1999) 21 Sydney Law Review 202, and Beyleveld and Brownsword. 'Human Dignity, Human Rights and Human Genetics' (1998) 61(5) MLR 661.

[267] Robertson, 'Two Models of Human Cloning' (1999) 27 Hofstra Law Review 609 618–627.

[268] For detailed consideration, see Harris-Short, 'An Identity Crisis in the International Law of Human Rights? The Challenge of Reproductive Cloning', Conference paper given August 2002 at the 11th World Conference of the I Soc of Fam. Law: *Family Life and Human Rights*.

[269] At para **4.12** et seq.

[270] See Jackson, 'Conception and the Irrelevance of the Welfare Principle' (2002) 65(2) MLR 176; Harris, 'The Right to Found a Family' in Ladd (ed) *Children's Rights Re-visioned – Philosophical Readings* (Belmont: Wordsworth Knopf, 1996) 66; Liu, *Artificial Reproduction and Reproductive Rights* (Dartmouth, 1991).

It has been argued further that the principles of self-determination, autonomy and privacy would encompass the right to engage in reproductive cloning.[271]

> We have the right to make decisions on issues important to us – and have those decisions respected by the state and other persons (the right to moral integrity). The right to moral integrity, and to a lesser degree the right to physical integrity, affords us the opportunity to function freely, and the possibility of self-definition and 'self-creation'…A human rights regime which recognised the value of individual self-determination would not interfere in the right of persons to…clone themselves – unless there could be shown a good argument to the contrary.[272]

[8.115] Similarly, Robertson argues that the right to procreative liberty entails the right to choose which gametes and embryos to use.[273] This choice then extends naturally to negative selection of the embryos on the basis of genetic characteristics. The next important step in extending the right to cloning seems, to Robertson at least, to be perfectly natural, quite insignificant and thus convincing. When one looks at the most likely application of cloning techniques, to enable infertile couples to procreate genetically related children, he is of the view that cloning shares many features with assisted reproduction and genetic selection. Robertson argues that the motive behind the cloning should be considered as irrelevant, in the same way as motive is not considered when fertile couples reproduce. However, he does acknowledge that it is possible to take issue with one or more steps in his analysis, particularly in relation to the difference between cloning, or replication as he calls it, and reproduction which involves the union of DNA from two different sources.[274] He also sees the argument in favour of reproductive cloning as being much weaker where a fertile couple seeks, for narcissistic or eugenic reasons, to use the technique in order to have a child with a particular genome or relationship to the couple. In such cases, cloning in lieu of sexual reproduction would not seem to come within the meaning of procreative liberty as it is currently understood.[275]

[8.116] In relation to the question of whether a right to engage in human reproductive cloning might be protected by international human rights law, the basis upon which such a claim could be currently grounded is weak.[276] However, 'given the relatively recent interest in reproductive rights, there is a strong possibility of future significant expansion in this field. Any future developments are likely to move towards providing greater support for recognition of a right to access to artificial reproductive techniques, which will, in turn, open up the possibility of more far-reaching claims to engage in

---

[271] See Harris 'Goodbye Dolly? The Ethics of Human Cloning' in Kuhse and Singer, *A Companion to Bioethics* (Blackwell Publishing, 1998) at 149–50; Dworkin, *Life's Dominion* (Vintage Books, 1993) at 148 and *Freedom's Law* (OUP, 1996) at 237–8.

[272] Wheatley, 'Human Rights and Human Dignity in the Resolution of Certain Ethical Questions in Biomedicine' (2001) 3 EHRLR 312 at 313–4.

[273] See also Feuerberg Duffy, 'To Be or Not to Be: The Legal Ramifications of the Cloning of Human Embryos' (1995) 21 Rutgers Computer And Technology Law Journal 189–223.

[274] Robertson, 'Two Models of Human Cloning' (1999) 27 Hofstra Law Review 609.

[275] Robertson, 'Two Models of Human Cloning' (1999) 27 Hofstra Law Review 609 at 627–633.

[276] See Chapter 4 at para **4.53**.

genetic manipulation and cloning.'[277] Another, perhaps remote, possibility would be to claim that a total prohibition on cloning violates the right to 'respect for family life' under art 8 of the European Convention on Human Rights (ECHR).

[8.117] Cloning may also be of benefit in other ways. Ian Wilmut, the scientist who led the team which was responsible for Dolly's creation, says that although human cloning is ethically unacceptable, research stimulated by the birth of Dolly will lead to many new therapies in human medicine:

> It is a superficial paradox that the technique that could be used to make identical copies could, in principle, provide a means of introducing precise genetic change. This ability will generate the means to provide organs, such as kidneys or hearts, from animals for transplantation to human patients. In addition, cell therapy will provide more effective treatment of diseases associated with damage to cells that are not repaired or replaced: diseases such as Parkinson's disease, heart attack, blindness caused by macula degeneration or diabetes Type 1. This could be achieved with cells from animals, or by taking cells from the patient, growing them in the laboratory, treating them so as to obtain cells of the damages type, and returning these to the patient.[278]

[8.118] It is necessary in any discussion about cloning to distinguish between the different types theoretically possible. On the one hand there is reproductive cloning where a cell containing the donor's DNA is transferred to the enucleated egg. It is activated to begin cleavage and transferred to the uterus to grow into a fetus. The child will therefore be born with the same DNA as the DNA donor alone. Therefore, the clone is not the genetic *child* of the DNA donor but rather his/her 'identical' twin sister or brother, and the genetic child of the DNA donor's own genetic parents.[279] However, it is important to recognise that the child will not truly be identical due to differences in uterine environment, social environment and other factors. Clones would be less alike than genetically identical twins, because in most cases they would be derived from a different recipient egg, develop in a different womb, be fed by a different mother, brought up in a different era and subject to a different chapter of accidents and illnesses.[280]

[8.119] Alternatively, reproductive cloning could be achieved by cell mass division or embryo splitting, where the early embryo is divided or split into two or more parts, each of which will continue to cleave and develop into a child. This is similar to the process by which monozygotic or identical twins occur in natural reproduction.[281] Legal and

---

[277] Harris-Short, 'An Identity Crisis in the International Law of Human Rights? The Challenge of Reproductive Cloning', Conference paper given August 2002 at the 11th World Conference of the I Soc of Fam Law: *Family Life and Human Rights*.

[278] Wilmut, 'Cloning in Biology and Medicine: Clinical Opportunities and Ethical Concerns' in Burley and Harris (eds) *A Companion to Genethics* (Blackwell Publishing, 2002) 33.

[279] Harris, 'Goodbye Dolly? The Ethics of Human Cloning' in Kuhse and Singer, *A Companion to Bioethics* (Blackwell Publishing, 1998) at 148.

[280] Wilmut, 'Cloning in Biology and Medicine: Clinical Opportunities and Ethical Concerns' in Burley and Harris (eds) *A Companion to Genethics* (Blackwell Publishing, 2002) at 36.

[281] Harris argues that, as there are no ethical issues raised by the natural phenomenon of identical twins, why should there be apprehension when such twins are deliberately created? Harris, Goodbye Dolly? The Ethics of Human Cloning' in Kuhse and Singer, *A Companion to Bioethics* (Blackwell Publishing, 1998) at 144.

ethical issues in reproductive cloning include considerations of the scientific difficulties, such as the very high rates of miscarriage,[282] early postnatal death in animal cloning and the ethics of incurring those difficulties in humans. Other issues address the dignity of the human person, such as the argument that cloning instrumentalises the person by treating it solely as a means to an end, that it would be open to exploitation by the production of clones to be used as sources of spare parts and that it would severely disrupt family relationships. These issues are considered further below.

[8.120] Another use of the technique is in therapeutic cloning, referred to variously as somatic cell nuclear transfer (SCNT), or nuclear transplantation. As with reproductive cloning, a patient's DNA is transferred to an enucleated egg and activated. It behaves as an embryo and starts to split into cells which may be a source of stem cells for treatment of the patient. These cells are totipotent,[283] which means they may have huge potential for medical treatment in the future. The theory is that once the activated egg has subdivided sufficiently to yield over a hundred cells, it is broken open, the inner cells removed and the stem cells harvested. It is hoped that these stem cells may then be grown into a variety of cells for transplantation in human patients. The advantages of this procedure would be that, if used for transplantation in the person from whom the DNA was derived, the cell line would be free of contamination, would not be rejected by the patient's immune system, and would be capable of multiplying indefinitely in the laboratory, thus providing a wealth of transplant material.

[8.121] The ethical issues here revolve around the status of the human embryo, how it should be respected, and whether there is a difference between embryos that remain unused after IVF attempts, and embryos deliberately created for research purposes.[284] SCNT involves the deliberate creation and destruction of an embryo, which many people fear will lead to the instrumentalisation of human life and the erosion of other protections for participants in research. The validity of some of these objections presupposes that the embryo has the status of a human being so as to warrant prohibiting its use as a source of cells or tissues. Such an approach would be rejected by those who take a developmental approach, which accords lesser weight to the embryo in its earliest stages when there has been no differentiation yet between different tissues and organs. On this view, research on such embryos that could provide significant therapeutic benefit may be ethically justified.

[8.122] Whether it is possible to allow therapeutic cloning and prohibit reproductive cloning, is also a matter of debate, given that the techniques involved are the same in both cases. The fear is that once cloned embryos are created in the laboratory for any purpose, there will be no way of policing the use of that embryo to ensure that it is not transferred to a woman's uterus to produce a cloned child. On the one hand, it is argued that it is possible and important to avoid this particular slippery slope by criminalizing reproductive cloning while recognising the significant potential offered by continuing

---

[282] Dolly was born after 277 attempts.

[283] 'Totipotent' means that its potential is total, in the sense that it may develop into an embryo, or into other tissue or organs.

[284] See Lanza et al, 'The Ethical Validity of Using Nuclear Transfer in Human Transplantation' (2000) 284 (24) JAMA.

efforts in therapeutic cloning.[285] However, it must also be recognised that once the scientific feasibility of reproductive cloning exists, although reputable scientists will observe legal prohibitions, a small number of persons might be prepared to violate such a law.[286]

Ethical issues

[8.123] For many, Dolly was a shocking symbol of biotechnology raging out of control, warranting a swift and decisive halting of any further experimentation in the cloning arena before its inevitable spillover to the human race. For a smaller group, Dolly was a marvellous and long-awaited sign that a century-old inquiry into the possibility of asexual reproduction had yielded a tentative answer.[287]

The arguments most commonly raised against reproductive cloning are that it is not safe, it is contrary to human dignity, it would lead to identity confusion and consequent disruption of family relationships and that it would lead to a decrease in genetic diversity. Those who advocate cloning argue that there are people for whom cloning might offer the only plausible reproductive option if they wish to avoid the use of donated gametes or for those who wish to avoid the transmission of deleterious genes. A further benefit might be to assist single individuals and same-sex couples to reproduce or to aid parents who have suffered the loss of a child. There are also those for whom the duplication of their own genetic material holds a special appeal, usually for various dubious and narcissistic reasons.

[8.124] Animal cloning has not yet reached the minimum level of safety and efficacy that is needed before research on human cloning could even begin. In the research leading to the birth of Dolly the sheep, 62 per cent of fetuses were lost, many were born with serious abnormalities and many died soon after birth. It also appears that there may be other long-term deleterious effects in animals. It is unclear the extent to which the advanced age of the cloned adult cell affects the ageing process in the cloned animal. Given these concerns Ian Wilmut, one of the scientists involved in the creation of Dolly, has said that it would be obscene to even consider applying these techniques in humans.

[8.125] In international literature three views are generally put forward of the moral status of the embryo. The first is the right-to-life position, which maintains that embryos have the same moral status as human persons, irrespective of their stage of development. On this view, therapeutic cloning would be similar to creating a baby to harvest its organs, which would be clearly abhorrent. The second view is the person view, which maintains that moral status is not a matter of species membership but rather of psychological features, such as the ability to think and feel and experience. On this view, human embryos are not persons nor are they deserving of the same status as that

---

[285] Report of the Commission on Assisted Human Reproduction (Dublin, 2005) at 61.

[286] Robertson, 'Two Models of Human Cloning' in (1999) 27 Hofstra Law Review 609 at 614; also in Steinbock (ed) *Legal and Ethical Issues in Human Reproduction* (Ashgate Publishing, 2002) Ch. 11 at 352. Harris, 'Goodbye Dolly? The Ethics of Human Cloning' (1997) 23 Journal of Medical Ethics, pp 353–360.

[287] Daar, 'The Prospect Of Human Cloning: Improving Nature or Dooming The Species?' (2003) 33 Seton Hall L Rev 511.

conferred on human persons.[288] In between these two views is the position that even though embryos do not have moral status, they are a form of human life and, as such, deserving of respect.[289] Those who adopt this view may view therapeutic cloning as acceptable in exceptional and well-defined circumstances.

[8.126] Another of the arguments raised against cloning is that cloning will change our perception of personhood. While cloned human beings would be recognised as fully human and entitled to the same respect as any other, 'permitting and engaging in human cloning would intrinsically violate our conception of human dignity.'[290] Cloning would oblige us to regard people as repeatable, which would diminish the value of personhood.

> Deliberately cloning human beings is a threat to human identity, as it would give up the indispensable protection against the predetermination of the human genetic constitution by a third party. Further ethical reasoning for a prohibition to clone human beings is based first and foremost on human dignity which is endangered by instrumentalisation through artificial human cloning.[291]

[8.127] Human dignity is a 'very broad and fiercely contested concept. At its core, however, is the idea that every human being has an intrinsic value: that human life is beyond price.'[292] In its deliberations on stem cell research, the UK House of Lords Select Committee found the concept of human dignity to be ill-defined[293], but expressed concern that 'the range of ambiguities introduced into family relationship by cloning from a close relative would be large and the possibility for emotional confusion and uncertainty – not only on the part of the cloned child – considerable.'[294]

[8.128] The idea that cloning would involve a process similar to 'photocopying' an individual on an automated production line[295] seems to violate an inherent respect for human dignity. It is assumed that each one of us has a right to our own genetic uniqueness, which would somehow be denigrated by such a technique. However,

---

[288] Steinbock, *Life Before Birth: the Moral and Legal Status of Embryos and Fetuses* (1992) 51–8.

[289] The meaning of 'respect' is not clear and has been criticised as an empty phrase designed to make us feel better about killing embryos. Callahan, 'The Puzzle of Profound Respect' (1995) 25(1) Hastings Center Rep. 39–40. Callahan takes the view that it is not that we should not use embryos for research, but rather that the interests to be served by the research should be shown to be compelling and unreachable by other means.

[290] Kaebnick and Murray, 'Cloning' in Chadwick R (ed) *The Concise Encyclopedia of the Ethics of New Technologies* (Academic Press, 2001) 51 at 60.

[291] Council of Europe, *Additional Protocol to the Convention on Human Rights and Biomedicine on the Prohibition of Cloning Human Beings, Explanatory Report* (ETS No 168) Para 3.

[292] Harris-Short, 'An Identity Crisis in the International Law of Human Rights? The Challenge of Reproductive Cloning', Conference paper given August 2002 at the 11th World Conference of the I Soc of Fam Law: *Family Life and Human Rights*, quoting Beyleveld and Brownsword D and Brownsword R, 'Human Dignity, Human Rights and Human Genetics' (1998) 61(5) MLR 661 at 666.

[293] Harris also claims that appeals to the concept of human dignity are universally attractive, but comprehensively vague. Harris, 'Goodbye Dolly? The Ethics of Human Cloning' in Kuhse and Singer, *A Companion to Bioethics* (Blackwell Publishing, 1998) at 145.

[294] *Report from the Select Committee: Stem Cell Research,* HL 83(i), HMSO, 2002.App. 6, para 6.

[295] Wellcome Trust, *Report on Public Attitudes to Human Cloning* (1998) at 13.

geneticists have claimed that this is in fact an inaccurate representation of genetics.[296] The most usual way of demonstrating this is by use of the example of monozygotic or identical twins.[297] As the name suggests, the twins share the same DNA, but would clearly be regarded as separate individuals. As each twin grows and develops, its experiences and environment will shape its unique identity. In the case of a clone and its DNA source, the two will not share the same uterus, or mitochondrial DNA, and each will have a different childhood and environment.[298] Therefore, it is claimed that they will be less alike than identical twins in both character and appearance.[299] Thus, it is argued that:

> [T]o produce another Mozart, we would need not only Wolfgang's genome but mother Mozart's uterus, father Mozart's music lessons, their friends and his, the state of music in eighteenth century Austria, Haydn's patronage, and on and on, in ever-widening circles…we have no right to the…assumption that his genome, cultivated in another world at another time, would result in an equally creative musical genius.[300]

[8.129] Despite the refutation of this claim that the clone will be a replica of the DNA donor, nevertheless there is a planned similarity that cannot easily be achieved through current reproductive technology. As with germ-line gene therapy, this element of control is perhaps the most unsettling aspect of cloning as we speculate the future of the human gene pool. It is argued that the expectations placed on the cloned human to be similar to its twin, impairs that person's right to an individual identity and an open future.[301] If the child grows up in the shadow of such assumptions of its ability and has its future pre-determined, this will impair its own development and be contrary to its best interests. However, this does not take into account the expectations that most parents have of their children, for example, to follow their parents' or older siblings' footsteps in relation to career paths. The clone would not be identical to its twin; its health, appearance and personality would all be different, so in this sense it is difficult to accept this argument as a sound basis for rejection of cloning.

---

[296] The US National Bioethics Advisory Commission points out that the belief that a person's genes bear a simple relationship to the physical and psychological traits that compose that individual is based on misunderstanding. Such a belief is referred to as 'genetic determinism'. The Commission is of the view that the great lesson of modern molecular genetics is the profound complexity of both gene-gene interactions and gene-environment interactions in the determination of whether a specific trait or characteristic is expressed. 'In other words, there will never be another you'.

[297] The natural occurrence of monozygotic or identical twins is one in 270 pregnancies.

[298] Kaebnick and Murray, 'Cloning', in Chadwick (ed) *The Concise Encyclopedia of the Ethics of New Technologies* (Ashgate Publishing, 2001) 51 at 60.

[299] Cloned individuals will never be identical in the sense of looking identical at the same moment in time. The further separated in time the DNA source and clone are, the less likely they are to have similarities in character. Harris, 'Goodbye Dolly? The Ethics of Human Cloning' in Kuhse and Singer, *A Companion to Bioethics* (Blackwell Publishing, 1998) at 144.

[300] Eisenberg, 'Are Cloned Sheep Really Like Humans' (1999) 340 NEJM 471.

[301] Putnam, 'Cloning People' in Burley (ed) *The Genetic Revolution and Human Rights* (1999) at 11 suggests that cloning might give rise to a new human right – the right to be a complete surprise to one's parents.

[8.130] The concept of identity is one that has become the focus of much debate in recent years, particularly in relation to adoption and assisted reproduction. In relation to cloning the issue is not only whether the child should be told the truth about its parentage but also whether cloning itself violates the child's right to his/her own identity. Freeman describes the concept in the following way: 'Identity is what we know and what we feel is an organising framework for holding together our past and our present and it provides some anticipated shape to future life. It is an inner personal landscape, a "feeling of being at home in one's own body".'[302] Whereas in adoption and gamete donation the concern is that there will be gaps in the child's genetic story, in reproductive cloning the argument is that the story itself will be harmful to the child.[303] The knowledge of being profoundly different from other normal families as well as the huge problems of establishing parentage[304] may also increase the danger of identity confusion for the child. In conclusion on this point it would seem that 'given the strengths of the concerns raised about the effect of reproductive cloning on the fundamental rights and interests of the resulting child, there is a growing consensus among the international community that the risks posed to the child currently outweigh any competing rights and interests of the procreating adult (assuming they can be successfully established) and a total ban on reproductive cloning is thus fully justified.'[305]

[8.131] The slippery slope argument makes its appearance here again, with claims that cloning could be put to abusive uses. The idea that mad, uncontrollable scientists may clone replicas of dictators caught hold in the public imagination: 'scenarios of armies of Hitlers, clones used as organ farms for already existing individuals, and the imaginative portrayal in a Woody Allen movie of cloning the nose of a dictator, are only some of the images television news broadcasts presented to viewers…Science fiction stories that involve cloning have not portrayed the evils of producing human beings by this method but rather, the abuses of one application in the production of multiple clones of consummately evil people.'[306] Trust in the medical and scientific professions has

[302] Freeman, 'The New Birth Right? Identity and the Child of the Reproductive Revolution' (1996) 4 *I J of Children's Rights* 273 at 283.

[303] For critical comment on the possible 'right to have two parents' or the 'right to be the product of the mixture of the genes of two individuals' see Harris, 'Goodbye Dolly? The Ethics of Human Cloning' in Kuhse and Singer, *A Companion to Bioethics* (Blackwell Publishing, 1998) at 147–8.

[304] Harris-Short gives the example of 'the creation of a clone using the DNA of the intended child's social father: the social father would be the child's trans-generational identical twin sibling, the child's social grandparents would be the child's genetic parents and the child's social siblings would be in some sense his/her niece or nephew.' Harris-Short, 'An Identity Crisis in the International Law of Human Rights? The Challenge of Reproductive Cloning' Conference paper given August 2002 at the 11th World Conference of the I Soc of Fam Law: *Family Life and Human Rights*, p 16.

[305] Harris-Short, 'An Identity Crisis in the International Law of Human Rights? The Challenge of Reproductive Cloning' Conference paper given August 2002 at the 11th World Conference of the I Soc of Fam Law: *Family Life and Human Rights* at 27.

[306] Macklin, 'Cloning and Public Policy' in Burley and Harris (eds), *A Companion to Genethics* (Blackwell Publishing, 2002) 206 at 209.

decreased over the last few decades, and many people fear that it would be inevitable that illegal research would be impossible to patrol and prevent.[307]

The status of the 'cloned organism'

[8.132] When a human embryo is created through sexual reproduction or through assisted reproduction, the egg is fertilised by a sperm. The resulting entity is an embryo. With cloning, the egg is not fertilised by a sperm but by cells taken from a DNA source. Therefore, it is argued that this cloned organism is a new type of biological entity never before seen in nature, has none of the attributes normally seen in embryos, and will be disaggregated at the blastocyst stage[308] to form a cell line. Many would see this entity not as an embryo, but as an 'activated egg'. For those who believe that it is an embryo and that it has a right to life, then its deliberate creation in order to destroy it would be fundamentally wrong. Others argue that the benefits of the research and the possible therapies it might produce far outweigh the claims of the activated eggs.

[8.133] In the UK, s 1 of the Human Fertilisation and Embryology Act 1990 states that 'embryo' means a live human embryo where fertilisation is complete or in the process of completion. It was argued that as the cell that created Dolly was not a gamete (a sperm or egg cell) and it did not undergo fertilisation, it was not within the meaning of the term 'embryo' as defined in the Act. Section 3(3)(d) of the Act prohibits the replacement of a cell of an embryo with a nucleus taken from a cell of any person. However, it was argued that the Dolly technique did not involve the creation of an embryo and therefore did not come within this section either. This would mean that cloning was unregulated in the UK.[309] These arguments were tested at the end of 2001 in *R v Secretary of State for Health, ex parte Bruno Quintavalle (on behalf of pro-life alliance)*.[310] The claimant applied for judicial review of a Government opinion that the HFE Act covered the organisms produced by cell nuclear replacement (the Dolly technique). This opinion had been formulated as part of a response to the Donaldson Report, which had recommended that scientists should be allowed to use embryos created either through IVF or as a result of cloning cells in their research into human disease. Crane J held that s 1 of the Act could not be stretched to cover organisms produced by this technique, involving no fertilisation. This left such organisms outside the statutory and licensing framework. The case was appealed to the Court of Appeal. However, immediately following this case the Health Minister stated that emergency legislation would be introduced to change the law in the UK. The Human Reproductive Cloning Act 2001 was fast-tracked through Parliament to provide that a person who transfers 'an embryo that has been created otherwise than by fertilisation' into a woman will be guilty of an offence punishable by up to 10 years' imprisonment or a fine or both.

[8.134] On appeal it was held that it was essential to give the definition of 'embryo' in the 1990 Act a purposive construction so that an organism created by cell nuclear

---

[307] Wellcome Trust, *Report on Public Attitudes to Human Cloning* (1998).

[308] It is at this stage in reproduction that the embryo begins implantation in the uterine wall.

[309] Korek, 'Following Dolly' (1997) NLJ 428.

[310] *R v Secretary of State for Health, ex parte Bruno Quintavalle (on behalf of pro-life alliance)*. Decision of Crane J QBD 15/11/2001.

replacement came within the definition.[311] Such a construction was necessary to give effect to the legislative policy to bring the creation and use of embryos produced in vitro under strict regulatory control for ethical reasons. Lord Phillips MR, with whom the other judges agreed, held that there were no significant differences between an embryo created by cell nuclear replacement and the embryo created by fertilisation. He said 'the two are essentially identical as far as structure is concerned, and each is capable of developing into a full grown example of the relevant species. So far as the human embryo is concerned it is this capacity to develop into a human being that is the significant factor and it is one that is shared by both types of embryo.' He was of the view that a regulatory regime that excluded embryos created by cell nuclear replacement from its ambit would be contrary to the intention of Parliament, and would be both 'startling and alarming'. Therefore, the term 'embryo' in the legislation covers those created by cell nuclear replacement, as well as embryos created by fertilisation.

International responses

[8.135] After the birth of Dolly was announced in late February 1997, there was a worldwide rush to legislate for a ban on human cloning. On March 4 1997, US President Clinton issued an immediate moratorium on the use of federal funds for human cloning and requested scientists in the private sector to voluntarily comply with the ban. In the UK, the House of Commons Select Committee on Science and Technology issued a report on March 18 urging the Government to tighten existing law to ensure that human cloning did not take place in the UK. France, Italy, Norway and Germany all took similar steps. The European Parliament issued a resolution opposing human cloning, the Group of Advisors on the Ethical Implications of Biotechnology to the European Commission issued an opinion that cloning was unacceptable and the Council of Europe drafted an additional Protocol to the existing Convention for the Protection of Human Rights and Dignity with Regards to the Application of Biology and Medicine which stated that any intervention seeking to create a human being identical to another human being is unacceptable, although it left to domestic law the precise definition of 'human being'. UNESCO declared that cloning was unacceptable because it undermines genetic indeterminability, it overrates the biological link and it is contrary to human dignity. The World Health Assembly issued a statement in May 1997 which stated that cloning was contrary to human integrity and morality and requested the WHO to consult with other international organisations and governmental agencies on the matter.

[8.136] Macklin wonders at the speed of the response and asks why the prospect of cloning provokes such strong reactions. She says that it is open to question as to whether widespread revulsion, if it exists, provides good grounds for instituting legal prohibitions. Kass said that although revulsion is not an argument, it is 'the emotional expression of deep wisdom, beyond reason's power fully to articulate it'.[312] However, Macklin argues that to base public policy on 'what we intuit and feel' is questionable at

---

[311]   *R (Quintavalle) v Secretary of State for Health* [2002] 2 All ER 625, [2002] 2 WLR 550, [2002] 2 FCR 140. See commentary by Herring and Chau, 'Are Cloned Embryos Embryos?' (2002) 14(3) Child and Family Law Quarterly 315.

[312]   Kass 'The Wisdom of Repugnance' The New Republic, June 2 1997, p 20.

best, and irrational at worst.[313] She says that there is no evidence that human dignity, whatever it means, has been compromised by assisted reproduction, nor is it threatened by cloning.

> Rhetorical flourishes, even eloquent appeals, and vague references to human dignity are no substitute for reason and argument…Dignity is a fuzzy concept, and appeals to dignity are often used to substitute for empirical evidence that is lacking or sound arguments that cannot be mustered. If objectors to human cloning can identify no greater harm than a supposed affront to the dignity of the human species, that is a flimsy basis on which to erect barriers to scientific research and its applications, and to enact prohibitionist legislation.[314]

[8.137] Pattinson outlines the regulatory approaches taken in the EU, in particular the UK, as well as Canada and the US and concludes that although countries take divergent approaches to cloning, what legislation does exist tends to be prohibitive.[315] However, much of this legislation was drafted prior to the creation of Dolly the sheep, and needs to be interpreted very broadly in order to encompass the technique by which she was created. He considers the question of whether cloning can harm the resulting clone, thus perhaps rendering the technique immoral. 'The issue is whether merely allowing or causing the conception or birth of a child can ever constitute a wrong to that child.'[316] Many philosophers argue that a child cannot be harmed by conduct causing it to be conceived, where the only alternative is not to have been conceived at all. In other words, existence must be better than non-existence. Others agree in principle subject to the proviso that the child's condition must not be so severe as to render his life not worth living. Thus, Pattinson argues that unless the cloning technique itself causes the cloned embryo to be worse off relative to its alternatives, a cloned individual's rights cannot have been violated merely by its cloning.

Ireland

[8.138] In its Report to the Irish Government in 2005, the Commission on Assisted Human Reproduction discussed the scientific background to cloning as well as the arguments in favour and against the application of this technique to humans. It recommended that human reproductive cloning should be prohibited. In relation to therapeutic cloning, although the Commission recommended that the generation of embryos through IVF specifically for research purposes should be prohibited, it felt that an exception should be made for regenerative medicine. 'This exception is made on the basis that regenerative medicine is not actually IVF. The objective is to generate a stem cell line that in turn can be used to generate a particular tissue for treatment of a specific disease and one of the main potential advantages of this procedure is that the cloned embryonic stem cells are genetically identical to the host and will not generate an immune response following transplantation.' The majority of the Commission

---

313 Macklin, 'Cloning and Public Policy' in Burley and Harris (eds) *A Companion to Genethics* (Blackwell Publishing, 2002), at 212.
314 Macklin, 'Cloning and Public Policy' in Burley and Harris (eds) *A Companion to Genethics* (Blackwell Publishing, 2002), at 212.
315 Pattinson, 'Reproductive Cloning: Can Cloning Harm the Clone?' (2002) 10 Med Law Rev, 295–307.
316 Pattinson, 'Reproductive Cloning: Can Cloning Harm the Clone?' (2002) 10 Med Law Rev 295–307 at 303.

recommended that regenerative medicine (or therapeutic cloning) should be allowed under regulation.[317]

[8.139] The legal position in relation to cloning in Ireland in the current absence of legislation is the same as for embryos created through in vitro fertilisation. Irrespective of the method of its creation, it follows from the Supreme Court decision in *MR v TR* in 2009 that the embryo outside the womb does not qualify for the protection of Art 40.3.3°.[318] Thus, there is no current Constitutional or legislative impediment to therapeutic or reproductive human cloning in Ireland.

[8.140] For medical practitioners, the Guide to Professional Conduct and Ethics published by the Medical Council is of significance, as it provides in para 20.4 that doctors should not engage in reproductive cloning.[319] It is important to note, however, that the Guide is applicable to registered medical practitioners only and has no relevance to other health professionals or scientists working in the field of embryology research.

STEM CELL RESEARCH

[8.141] In human reproduction, the fertilised egg develops from a single totipotent[320] cell into a small, hollow ball of cells termed a blastocyst. The blastocyst has an outer layer of cells which will go on to form the placenta and other supporting tissues needed for fetal development, and an inner cell mass which will go on to form virtually all of the tissues of the human body. These cells are pluripotent, which means they can give rise to many types of cells but not all types of cells necessary for fetal development, so they do not have the capacity to develop into a fetus. These cells undergo further specialisation into stem cells that perform a particular function such as blood stem cells which form blood cells and platelets, or skin stem cells which give rise to skin cells. These specialised cells are multipotent and may also be found in children and adults, such as in bone marrow.

[8.142] Pluripotent stem cells may be derived from the inner cell mass of embryos at the blastocyst stage. This requires that the blastocyst is disaggregated or broken up into single cells which are then no longer able to make a whole organism. ES cells are capable of extensive self-renewal (where a cell makes an identical copy of itself) in the culture dish.[321] The embryos could be donated by couples following IVF or created by somatic cell nuclear transfer (cloning). In 2001 US scientists announced that they had cloned the first human embryo for therapeutic purposes. Using the Dolly technique, DNA from human skin cells was placed within enucleated human eggs and then exposed to chemical and growth factors. The most developed cloned embryo grew to six cells after being cultured for a week. Two others divided into just four cells. Volunteers who had provided their skin cells for the procedure had diseases such as diabetes or spinal

---

[317] See http://www.dohc.ie/publications/cahr.html (accessed 3 June 2011).

[318] *MR v TR* [2009] IESC 82, discussed in Chapter 6 at para **6.121**.

[319] The Medical Council, The Guide to Professional Conduct and Ethics (7th edn, 2009) available at http://www.medicalcouncil.ie (accessed 3 June 2011).

[320] Meaning that its potential is total, or that it has the potential to form an entire organism.

[321] Svendsen 'Stem Cells' in Burley and Harris (eds) *A Companion to Genethics* (Blackwell Publishing 2002) at 8.

cord injury. The scientists involved in the project intended to use the genetic material from these volunteers to generate pancreatic islets to treat the diabetes, or nerve cells to repair the damaged spinal cord. The potential applications of pluripotent stem cells include a better knowledge of cell specialisation, which could help understanding of diseases such as cancer and birth defects. It could also change the way drugs are developed and tested for safety by using cell lines to analyse the safety and efficacy of medication prior to animal and human testing. The National Institute of Health in the US says that the most far-reaching potential application of human pluripotent stem cells is the generation of cells and tissue that could be used for cell therapies.[322] Many diseases and disorders result from disruption of cellular function or destruction of tissue in the body. Pluripotent stem cells, stimulated to develop into specialised cells, offer the possibility of a renewable source of replacement cells and tissue to treat a myriad of diseases, conditions and disabilities including Parkinson's and Alzheimer's disease, spinal cord injury, burns, stroke, diabetes, arthritis and epilepsy, as well as provide heart muscle cells for congestive heart failure, arrhythmias and cardiac tissue scarred by heart attacks. Another important potential development would be to trigger stem cells to differentiate into cells of the blood and bone marrow in order to treat disorders such as multiple sclerosis, rheumatoid arthritis and other autoimmune diseases.[323]

[8.143] While ES cell research shows much promise, much work remains to be done before this potential might be realised, and the technologies incorporated into clinical practice. Basic research must be carried out to understand the cellular events leading to cell specialisation in the human so as to be able to direct the stem cells to become the type of tissue needed. Also the problem of immune rejection must be overcome. If the stem cells are taken from unrelated embryos or fetuses, their DNA would be different from that of the recipient. However, if the stem cells are derived by virtue of cell nuclear transfer (or therapeutic cloning) they would be genetically identical to the patient, there would be no rejection and no need for immuno-suppressants.

[8.144] It may be possible to derive multipotent stem cells from some types of adult tissue. Some scientists are of the view that adult stem cells, already committed to the development of one line of specialised cells, would not have the capacity to be reprogrammed into other types of specialised cells and therefore provide less therapeutic potential. However, research is continuing into ways in which the adult cells might be redirected. If successful, the adult stem cells could be taken from a patient, coaxed to divide and directed to specialisation. They could then be transplanted back to the same adult. The use of adult stem cells in this way would have medical advantages in not being rejected by the recipient, and would have ethical advantages in avoiding the use of cells from human embryos or fetal tissue. However, even if successful, there are limitations in that stem cells have not yet been isolated for all tissues of the body, such as cardiac or pancreatic stem cells. Also adult stem cells are often present in tiny quantities, are difficult to isolate and their numbers may decrease with age. If the patient has a genetic disorder, the genetic error may also be present in the patient's stem cells, and therefore would not be appropriate for transplantation. They may also contain more

---

[322] See http://stemcells.nih.gov/info/basics/basics6.asp (accessed 3 June 2011).

[323] The embryonic stem cell has been referred to as a 'factory-in-a-dish' by Regalado, 'The Troubled Hunt for the Ultimate Cell' (1998) Technology Review 35.

abnormalities caused by exposure to environmental factors such as toxins or sunlight. Adult stem cells are difficult to grow in a laboratory and their potential to reproduce diminishes with age so obtaining significant amounts of adult stem cells may prove difficult. There are no perceived ethical or legal difficulties associated with adult stem cells research, which should be governed by normal research criteria.

[8.145] The main arguments in relation to human embryology stem cell (hESC) research are in relation to the scientific evidence supporting claims made by both advocates and opponents, and ethical disagreement about the moral status of embryos and the cells derived from them. Solbackk and Holm say that these disagreements are unlikely to be resolved by philosophical argument and that there are no signs that the two heavily polarised sides in the debate are getting closer to compromise more than 10 years after hESC research was first introduced as a major topic of societal concern.[324] They take the view that if stem cell research leads to therapeutic breakthroughs, which they believe is fairly realistic, it is likely that human embryos will continue to be used in research but will only have a limited use in therapies. Many societies would be able to accommodate such a position while still maintaining an official claim that embryos deserve special respect.

[8.146] Since embryonic stem cells can only be taken from preimplantation embryos or aborted fetuses, the debates about their use turns on the moral status of the embryo and fetus.[325] 'While everyone has views about the moral status of the embryo and some of those who have views even have arguments to support their views, attempts to solve problems about issues which depend on the use of embryonic or fetal material by recourse to establishing the moral status of the embryo have proved intractable.'[326] These debates have been discussed earlier in Chapter 6.

[8.147] Advocates for hESC research argue that since there are numerous excess embryos stored in IVF clinics on behalf of couples who will never use them, nothing is lost by allowing couples to choose to donate these embryos for research purposes rather than have them destroyed or stored indefinitely. 'If one believes that human embryos are neither human persons nor beings deserving of respect that is incompatible with their destruction, then this reasoning provides strong support for use of surplus embryos for hESC research.'[327] The 'nothing is lost' principle will not justify such research for those who believe that embryos are human persons or beings deserving of respect that is incompatible with their destruction. However, Brock argues that few who hold this view

---

[324] Solbakk and Holm, 'The Ethics of Stem Cell Research: Can the Disagreements Be Resolved?' (2008) Vol 34 J Med Ethics 831.

[325] For further discussion of the ethical issues, see Holm 'Going to the Roots of the Stem Cell Controversy' (2002) Vol 16 (6) Bioethics 493; Savulescu, 'The Embryonic Stem Cell Lottery and the Cannibalization of Human Beings' (2002) Vol 16 (6) Bioethics 508; Green 'Benefiting From 'Evil': An Incipient Moral Problem in Human Stem Cell Research (2002) Vol 16 (6) Bioethics 544; and Agar 'Embryonic Potential and Stem Cells' (2007) Vol 21 (4) Bioethics 198.

[326] Harris, 'The Ethical Use of Human Embryonic Stem Cells in Research and Therapy' in Burley and Harris (eds), *A Companion to Genethics* (Blackwell Publishing) at 163.

[327] Brock, 'Is a Consensus Possible on Stem Cell Research? Moral and Legal Obstacles' (2006) J Med Ethics 32: 36–42.

accept its full implications. He says that embryos lost in natural reproduction are not grieved over in the same way as the death of a fetus or child.[328] He also quotes from Sandel's hypothetical example of a fire in a fertility laboratory where one could save a tray of ten surplus embryos or one eight-year-old child, but not both, virtually everyone would save the child.[329] This suggests that people do not view embryos as morally comparable to born human beings or persons.

[8.148] Those who do not believe that a human embryo is a full human person nevertheless believe it is not mere human tissue to be discarded at will. Instead it is a morally significant entity deserving of serious moral respect. There is concern that as a society we do not want to see embryos treated as products,[330] as this would cheapen reproduction and the value of parenting. As Robertson puts it:

> Although embryos do not themselves have rights, they are an occasion for expressing or symbolising one's views about the importance or value of human life, thereby constituting one's moral or national character in the process. People differ, however, over the degree and intensity of the symbolic associations that attach to non-rights-bearing entities such as embryos. The importance of signifying or constituting a highly protective attitude towards human life by objecting to certain kinds of embryo research is thus more determined by personal or public preferences than it is by the obligations of moral duty.[331]

[8.149] The President's Council on Bioethics in the US took the view that human embryos have some form of intermediate moral status between full human persons and morally insignificant things and said that it was incoherent and self contradictory to claim that embryos deserve special respect and yet to endorse research that requires the creation, use and destruction of those organisms.[332] However, Brock argues with this conclusion by drawing an analogy with the respect commonly shown to domestic pets or primates such as monkeys. He says that these animals are not mere things to be used for human purposes in any way we wish, as their capacity to suffer underpins their intermediate moral status. Yet these animals are bred and sometimes killed in the course of biomedical research aimed at treating serious human disease. Many people accept such a practice as morally permissible yet oppose the use of animals for other less significant purposes such as cosmetic research. The difference between these purposes lies clearly in the seriousness and importance of the two activities. Brock says it is

---

[328] Brock says that it is well known that for each embryo born alive from sexual reproduction, at least three are created who will die before birth. Brock, 'Is a Consensus Possible on Stem Cell Research? Moral and Legal Obstacles' (2006) J Med Ethics 32: 36–42.

[329] Brock, 'Is a Consensus Possible on Stem Cell Research? Moral and Legal Obstacles' (2006) J Med Ethics 32: 36–42.

[330] The use of embryos for commercial purposes is very controversial. The legal issues involved in patenting discoveries derived from stem cell research are not discussed in this book. However, readers may wish to note the EU Directive 98/44/EC on legal protection of biotechnological invention and the case of *Brüstle v Greenpeace eV* (Case C–34/10).

[331] Robertson: Presentation to Smithkline Beecham Ethics and Public Policy Board, Chewton Glen, July 11 1999; quoted by Harris, 'The Ethical Use of Human Embryonic Stem Cells in Research and Therapy' in Burley and Harris (eds), *A Companion to Genetics* (Blackwell Publishing) at 163.

[332] The President's Council on Bioethics, *Human Cloning and Human Dignity: An Ethical Inquiry* (US Government Printing Office, 2002) at 154.

incompatible with the intermediate moral status of the animals to destroy them for a trivial purpose and that by limiting their use to important valuable research aimed at treating serious illness, this shows them special respect. Likewise, human embryos could be shown the special respect that intermediate moral status requires by limiting their use to equally important human purposes that have reasonable promise of alleviating serious human disease.[333]

[8.150] In 2007 researchers announced that they had produced induced pluripotent cells (IP cells) from human adult somatic cells.[334] These cells are very similar to hES cells in that they are pluripotent and therefore have the capacity to differentiate into specific cell types. These findings have significant implications for stem cell ethics, as the production of these cells do not involve the contentious issue of embryo destruction as they are derived from skin cells not embryos. The ongoing research in relation to IP cells aims to produce the same ends as therapeutic cloning without destroying any embryos and therefore has attracted much attention as an ethical breakthrough. However, as Chan and Harris point out, the matter is not so straightforward.

> It has sometimes been argued that an embryo has the right to life by virtue of its interest in experiencing what has sometimes been called a 'future of value', because of its potential to be a person. Yet if skin cells and possibly other cells can be reprogrammed to embryonic status, are all of these now embryos *in potentio* in the same way as in some sense, an embryo is a person *in potentio*? Those who value the embryo for its potentiality might well feel obliged to value all cells that might be reprogrammable for the same reason.[335]

[8.151] They also argue that social acceptability of scientific progress should not be determinative of whether IP cells should be preferred to hES cells. 'It would be a bad day for scientific progress and for human welfare if priority-setting in science were dictated by the degree of opposition to a particular practice.' This does not mean that scientists should not be accountable by having to justify their research and obtain ethics committee approval but rather that they should not have to prioritise their research in terms of public approval ratings.

[8.152] Although the development of IP cells may be seen as a major breakthrough in stem cell research, it is also important to note that many scientists caution against abandoning hESC research at this stage for a number of reasons. Firstly, it is too early to know whether stem cells produced in this way will prove as effective as hES cells. Both IP cells and hESC research are directed towards similar goals and until there is evidence that one approach rather than the other is more effective in achieving those goals, many would argue that both should be pursued in tandem. Secondly, the use of hES cells is also essential in increasing scientists' understanding of IP cells; if an alternative to ES cells is to be produced, it is necessary to know everything about ES cells first. Thirdly, there is also concern that because IP cells are heavily manipulated to drive somatic cells

---

[333] Brock, 'Is a Consensus Possible on Stem Cell Research? Moral and Legal Obstacles' (2006) J Med Ethics 32: 36–42.

[334] Takahashe K et al, 'Induction of Pluripotent Stem Cells From Adult Human Fibroblasts by Defined Factors' (2007) Cell; Vogel and Holden 'Developmental Biology. Field Leaps Forward With New Stem Cell Advances' Science 2007; 318:1224.

[335] Chan and Harris. 'Adam's Fibroblast? The (Pluri) Potential of iPCs' (2008) J Med Ethics 34:64–66.

back in developmental time and then to drive them down a specialised pathway, they may end up losing their immune compatibility along the way, making them less beneficial for the patient from whom the skin cells have been derived.[336]

[8.153] The use of stem cells in medical treatment has also been controversial with reported success in China, India and elsewhere on spinal injuries and other disabilities. However, these treatments have not been validated in clinical trials and the International Society for Stem Cell Research is concerned about the safety of these procedures, which are offered without proper scientific validation to vulnerable patients, and the risk of maverick practitioners in an area of rapidly evolving technology. It has published guidelines for the clinical translation of stem cell research to ensure rigorous standards in the development of stem cell therapies, including stringent evaluation and oversight, a thorough informed consent process and transparency in operations and reporting.[337] The first clinical trial of ES cell therapy for acute spinal cord injury is being conducted in the US by a pharmaceutical company, Geron, with other trials to follow by other companies and in other jurisdictions.[338]

Regulation

[8.154] By comparison to the almost universal opposition to reproductive cloning, there is less consensus in relation to embryonic stem cell research. In Europe four different approaches might be described amongst those countries that have legislated on this issue.[339] Those with permissive legislation include Belgium, Sweden, Finland, Spain and the UK. These countries allow SCNT and stem cell research under certain conditions. A large group of countries pursue a compromise position which allows hESC research only on surplus IVF embryos and prohibits the use of SCNT or therapeutic cloning for this purpose. This group includes France, Denmark, the Netherlands, Norway, Portugal and Switzerland. Germany and Italy have a more restrictive compromise which allows hESC research only on cell lines created before a certain date. Countries with a prohibitive position include Poland, Austria and Slovakia. Similar groupings are evident in the United States, Asia and Oceania.

[8.155] In the United States, in addition to discussions about the ethics of stem cell research, there has also been much debate about the funding of hESC research since its inception. In 2001 President Bush decided that federal funding of research would be allowed only using existing stem cell lines of which he understood there were about 60. He banned federal funding for research using stem cells derived from frozen embryos, about 100,000 of which existed at fertility labs across the country. In 2005, the Stem

---

[336] In 2008 Doug Melton from Harvard University reported that he had been able to short-circuit the process of reprogramming an adult cell into a differentiated cell of another kind in mice through a process called 'lineage reprogramming.' However, it is unclear whether cells can be fully converted in this way. Zhou and Melton, 'Extreme Makeover: Converting One Cell Into Another' (2008) Cell Stem Cell 3(4): 382–8.

[337] See http://www.isscr.org/About_Stem_Cell_Treatment.htm (accessed 11 July 2011).

[338] For further discussion, see Skene, 'Recent Developments in Stem Cell Research: Social, Ethical and Legal Issues for the Future' Indiana Journal of Global Legal Studies, 2009; U of Melbourne Legal Studies Research Paper No 385.

[339] For up-to-date information on legislation and policy, see www.hinxtongroup.org (accessed 3 June 2011).

Cell Research Enhancement Act of 2005 was passed by the House of Representatives and in 2006 it was passed by the Senate. However, President Bush opposed embryonic stem cell research on ideological grounds and he exercised his first presidential veto on July 19, 2006 when he refused to allow the Act to become law. In April 2007, the Senate passed the Stem Cell Research Enhancement Act of 2007 and in June 2007, the House passed the legislation. President Bush vetoed the bill on June 20, 2007. On March 9, 2009, President Barack Obama lifted, by Executive Order, the Bush administration's eight-year ban on federal funding of embryonic stem research. [340]

[8.156] It has been debated whether regulatory harmonisation of stem cell research is possible and desirable. In principle, harmonisation is seen as having a number of important benefits by facilitating international trade, the avoidance of uncertainty about national regulation, and the elimination of expense and effort involved in monitoring compliance with the regulatory requirements of different countries.[341] In the context of stem cell research, harmonisation may be desirable also for ethical reasons so that researchers worldwide would be required to conform to the same ethical standards. It would also help increase public confidence in this area of science by highlighting the need to ensure that it is carefully monitored and regulated. Many countries have no legislation or policy in this area so 'the creation of international standards could fill this gap where it exists, and it might also prompt jurisdictions without any regulatory scheme to either directly adopt the standards or craft their own laws and policies in a manner consistent with the harmonised guidelines.'[342] One of the difficulties inherent in the harmonisation process where so many diverse views are present is the risk of reducing harmonised principles to 'the lowest common denominator'. For countries with rigorous regulations already in place, this could result in significant downgrading of domestic legal norms. Another difficulty exists in relation to cultural diversity, as the way in which countries respond to issues such as stem cell research is related to their cultural perceptions and values.

A country's historical experiences, religious values and its social and legal understandings of the human embryo all play a critical role in shaping its regulatory approach to stem cell

---

[340] In lifting the ban President Obama said, 'In recent years, when it comes to stem cell research, rather than furthering discovery, our government has forced what I believe is a false choice between sound science and moral values. In this case, I believe the two are not inconsistent. As a person of faith, I believe we are called to care for each other and work to ease human suffering. I believe we have been given the capacity and will to pursue this research – and the humanity and conscience to do so responsibly.... I can also promise that we will never undertake this research lightly. We will support it only when it is both scientifically worthy and responsibly conducted. We will develop strict guidelines, which we will rigorously enforce, because we cannot ever tolerate misuse or abuse. And we will ensure that our government never opens the door to the use of cloning for human reproduction. It is dangerous, profoundly wrong, and has no place in our society, or any society.' For more information see, http://stemcells.nih.gov/policy/defaultpage.asp (accessed 3 June 2011).

[341] Campbell and Mycum, 'Harmonising the International Regulation of Embryonic Stem Cell Research: Possibilities, Promises and Potential Pitfalls' (2005) Med Law International Vol 7, pp 113–148.

[342] Campbell and Mycum, 'Harmonising the International Regulation of Embryonic Stem Cell Research: Possibilities, Promises and Potential Pitfalls' (2005) Med Law International Vol 7 at 126.

research and cloning technology. Because these factors are so varied from one jurisdiction to the next, devising a single set of regulatory guidelines to which the entire international community must adhere would be a formidable task.[343]

[8.157] Campbell and Nycum advocate a harmonisation process developed by an independent non-political international agency marked by diversity in terms of culture and disciplinary expertise. The entity would strive for the creation of harmonised legal norms governing stem cell science which are clear enough to be implemented in all countries and could be revised as appropriate to consider new emerging knowledge and challenges. Although the enforceability of such norms would pose significant problems, they argue that by inclusion in the drafting of such norms, the scientific community would be persuaded to abide by the norms in their research. 'This model thus aims to reconcile the ongoing tension between the desire to create harmonised standards that are internationally perceived as desirable, legitimate and as having normative force, while at the same time ensuring that the harmonisation process does not negate local cultural values, norms and approaches to the governance of science.'

Ireland

[8.158] In Ireland there is no specific legislation governing the use of human embryos or stem cell research. The Commission on Assisted Human Reproduction recommended in 2005 that the embryo formed by IVF should not attract legal protection until placed in the human body and that embryonic stem cell research should be permitted on surplus embryos for specific purposes and under stringently controlled conditions.The Irish Council for Bioethics published a report on stem cell research in 2008 in which it also advocated in favour of permitting embryonic stem cell research within certain limits.[344] The Medical Council published its most recent edition of the Guide to Professional Conduct and Ethics in 2009 in which it stated in para 20.4 that doctors should not participate in creating new forms of life solely for experimental purposes. It also states that doctors should not engage in human reproductive cloning but there is no reference to embryonic stem cell research or regenerative medicine.[345]

[8.159] It had been speculated for some time that the destruction of embryos might be unconstitutional in Ireland in light of the provisions of Art 40.3.3°. However, in 2009 the Supreme Court delivered its long-awaited judgment in the case of *Roche v Roche*.[346] The facts of this case involved a dispute between a separated couple in relation to the disposition of frozen embryos which they had stored during a previous IVF attempt.[347] One of the issues arising before the Court was whether these frozen embryos qualified for Constitutional protection under the provisions of Art 40.3.3°, which acknowledges the right to life of the unborn. In a unanimous judgment of the Court, it was held that the

---

[343] Campbell and Mycum, 'Harmonising the International Regulation of Embryonic Stem Cell Research: Possibilities, Promises and Potential Pitfalls' (2005) Med Law International Vol 7 at 130.

[344] The Irish Council for Bioethics was disbanded in 2008 but its report on stem cell research is available at http://www.bioethics.ie/index.php/reports-and-opinions (accessed 3 June 2011).

[345] Medical Council, The Guide to Professional Conduct and Ethics (7th edn, 2009), available at http://www.medicalcouncil.ie/ (accessed 3 June 2011).

[346] *Roche v Roche* [2009] IESC 82.

[347] For further discussion, see Ch 6 at para **6.121**.

word 'unborn' did not extend to pre-implantation embryos and therefore the frozen embryos in this case did not qualify for Constitutional protection. As a result of this case, there is no Constitutional or legislative prohibition in Ireland at present on the use or destruction of human embryos for research purposes.

Chapter 9

Capacity, Consent and Refusal of Treatment

INTRODUCTION

'Over himself, over his own body and mind, the individual is sovereign'.[1]

[9.01] It has been said that non-disclosure and deference have been the hallmarks of the paternalistic tradition that has dominated orthodox medical practice over a period of some 2,500 years.[2] Traditional medical ethics were based on the Hippocratic Oath, which obliged the doctor to use his skill to the best of his ability and to abstain from harming the patient. These obligations did not require the doctor to consult with or seek permission from the patient for any medical intervention. The common understanding of the relationship between them was that since the doctor had more knowledge about the patient's condition, he would do what was best for the patient and the patient did not need to be informed. This form of decision-making is now known as paternalism, defined by Dworkin as 'interference with a person's liberty of action justified by reasons referring exclusively to the welfare, good, happiness, needs, interests, or values of the person being coerced.'[3]

[9.02] It was only in the 1960s that attitudes began to change, particularly in the United States, and questions began to be raised about whether in fact the doctor was in a better position to make health-care decisions for the patient than the patient himself. Donnelly says that the shift in emphasis occurred for a number of reasons. Firstly, challenges to medical authority were part of a broader picture of challenges to traditional authority, campaigns for civil rights and the rise of feminism which were prevalent at this time. Secondly, there were specific concerns about certain medical practices, in particular in relation to persons with a mental disorder, and abuses in medical research such as the infamous Tuskegee Syphilis Trial.[4] These factors led to a mistrust of the profession and reluctance to accept medical views unquestioningly.[5]

[9.03] Teff argues that the mounting criticism of the paternalistic approach has taken a variety of forms but a central theme is concern that the patient's voice is insufficiently heard.[6] 'The assertion of patients' rights is presented as a natural antithesis to medical

---

[1] Mill, *On Liberty* (John W Parker and Son, 1859).
[2] Pellegrino and Thomasma, *A Philosophical Basis of Medical Practice* (OUP, 1981).
[3] Dworkin, 'Paternalism' (1972) *The Monist* 56, p 65.
[4] For further information, see Final Report of the Tuskegee Syphilis Study Legacy Committee May 20, 1996; and Jones, *Bad Blood: The Tuskegee Syphilis Experiment* (Free Press, 1993).
[5] Donnelly, *Healthcare Decision-making and the Law, Autonomy, Capacity and the Limits of Liberalism* (Cambridge University Press, 2010) 14.
[6] Teff, *Reasonable Care, Legal Perspectives on the Doctor-Patient Relationship* (Oxford, Clarendon Press 1994) at xxiv.

paternalism, proclaiming the moral agency of the individual and the intrinsic value of respect for the patient as person.' The influential Belmont Report, which was published in the US in 1978, advocated a principles-based approach to medical research involving human participants.[7] Around the same time Beauchamp and Childress wrote one of most widely read and influential texts on medical ethics in which they proposed four governing principles for bioethics: autonomy, beneficence, non-maleficence and justice.[8] Although they did not prioritise amongst these four principles, autonomy quickly became regarded as the most important. Some ethicists, such as Gillon,[9] are of the view that this is the correct approach whereas others, such as Callahan,[10] feel that the failure to engage with the other principles results in an impoverished ethical framework.

[9.04] Despite the societal changes which led to the dominance of autonomy in healthcare ethics, paternalism has been remarkably resilient.[11] The medical profession has undoubtedly increased its emphasis on communication skills and ethics in medical education and training in recent years but some resistance remains. However, Teff argues that rights-based criticisms have originated mainly from outside the world of medicine and that within it patient welfare as traditionally conceived still takes pride of place, particularly in hospital settings where hierarchical and more impersonal regimes still often reflect a time-honoured ethos which has not converted to the primacy of patient choice and patients' rights.[12] On a practical level, some doctors claim that pressures of work and scarcity of time often constrain their ability to make a more conscious effort to involve the patient in his illness and treatment. Patients may also be reluctant to know the precise details of their condition and may prefer to leave the treatment in the doctor's expert hands. While this may also be seen as an exercise of autonomy in that the patient is making a choice not to know, there is a danger that the habit of decision-making on the patient's behalf may become a routine part of the doctor's management of all of his patients.[13] 'Practitioners are trained to make decisions for patients, and to put those decisions in the form of advice...The emphasis on giving advice rather than explanation has led practitioners (doctors, nurses and paramedics) to be more skilled at persuasion than at discussion, more dependent on authority than on rationale. And it has sometimes tempted them to take short cuts in gaining or assuming consent.[14]

---

7   National Commission for the Protection of Human Subjects of Biomedical and Behavioural Research, *Ethical Principles and Guidelines for the Protection of Human Subjects of Research* (Dept of Health, Education and Welfare, 1979).

8   Beauchamp and Childress, *Principles of Biomedical Ethics* (1st edn, OUP, 1979) (Now in its 6th edn, published in 2008).

9   Gillon, 'Ethics Needs Principles – Four Can Encompass the Rest – And Respect for Autonomy Should Be First Among Equals' (2003) 29 Journal of Med Ethics 307.

10   Callahan, 'Autonomy: A Moral Good, Not a Moral Obsession' (1984) 14 Hastings Center Report 40, quoted by Donnelly, *Healthcare Decision-making and the Law, Autonomy, Capacity and the Limits of Liberalism,* (Cambridge University Press, 2010) 15.

11   Teff, *Reasonable Care, Legal Perspectives on the Doctor-Patient Relationship* (Oxford, Clarendon Press 1994) at 69.

12   Teff, *Reasonable Care, Legal Perspectives on the Doctor-Patient Relationship* (Oxford, Clarendon Press 1994) at xxv.

13   See discussion by Brazier, 'Patient Autonomy and Consent to Treatment: The Role of the Law?' (1987) 7 Legal Studies at 169–193 at 174.

14   Williamson, *Whose standards? Consumer and professional standards in health care.* (Open University Press, 1992) p 110–111.

[9.05] Respect for the principle of individual autonomy is now regarded as central to healthcare decision-making.[15] This ethical principle has been reiterated by the law, as seen in the classic statement by Justice Cordozo: 'Every human being of adult years and sound mind has a right to determine what shall be done with his own body and a surgeon who performs an operation without his patient's consent commits an assault, for which he is liable in damages'.[16] Yet it is not entirely clear what autonomy means, what respect for it entails, and whether there are circumstances in which other ethical principles or values should take precedence over autonomy. Donnelly notes that 'the status of autonomy within ethical discourse has been challenged for almost as long as the principle has been revered, while in a legal context the degree of respect accorded to the principle of autonomy has varied depending on the circumstances in which the principle is called into action.'[17]

[9.06] The central idea of autonomy is that one's actions and decisions are one's own.[18] Some people regard it as a distinctively human ability to be able to reflect on and adopt attitudes towards one's desires, intentions and plans. Dworkin says that 'autonomy is a second-order capacity to reflect critically upon one's first-order preferences and desires, and the ability either to identify with these or to change them in light of higher-order preferences and values. By exercising such a capacity we define our nature, give meaning and coherence to our lives, and take responsibility for the kind of person we are.'[19] One gives meaning to one's life in any number of ways, and the equality that is accorded to every human person demands that recognition is given to the way that each person has chosen to value and define his or her life. Dworkin argues that there is something special about the role of autonomy in health care when the doctor's functions are examined in that context. A doctor cares for the health of the body, but the care of the body is intrinsically linked with our identity as persons. A doctor is not so much the preventer of death but rather the preserver of life capacities for the realisation of a reasonable, realistic life plan of the patient.[20] Beauchamp says that autonomy is associated with several ideas such as privacy, voluntariness, self-mastery, the freedom to choose and accepting responsibility for one's choices. 'To respect an autonomous agent is to recognise with due appreciation the person's capacities and perspective, including his or her right to hold certain views and to take certain actions based on personal values and beliefs.'[21]

---

[15] McCall Smith criticizes the prioritization of autonomy as the 'passive acceptance of a one-dimensional perspective' and questions the 'liberal individualist consensus' which dominates the debate. He says that 'the assertion that patient autonomy is a firm rule restricts discretion and places physicians in a straitjacket.' See McCall Smith, 'Beyond Autonomy' [1997] J of Contemp Health L & Policy Vol 14:23–39.

[16] *Schloendoff v Society of New York Hospital* 211 NY 125 (1914).

[17] Donnelly, *Healthcare Decision-making and the Law, Autonomy, Capacity and the Limits of Liberalism,* (Cambridge University Press, 2010) at 1.

[18] Dworkin, *The Theory and Practice of Autonomy* (Cambridge University Press, 1998) at 108.

[19] Dworkin, *The Theory and Practice of Autonomy* (Cambridge University Press, 1998) p 108.

[20] Fried, *Medical Experimentation: Personal Integrity and Social Policy* (American Elsevier, 1974) 98.

[21] Beauchamp 'Informed Consent' in Veatch (ed) *Medical Ethics* (2nd edn, Jones and Bartlett Publishers, 1997) 185 at 195.

[9.07] Decisions about what form of treatment to undergo, the probabilities of cure and of side effects, whether to spend one's last days at home or in hospital and so on, are not simply technical medical judgments to be made by medical professionals alone. 'To suppose that these are matters of expertise, decisions to be taken by experts, represents a denial of autonomy'.[22] Dworkin is of the view that such a denial of autonomy is particularly damaging because one's body is irreplaceable and inescapable. His argument is that as it is impossible for the patient to escape his body, and because he *is* his body, it is a particularly insulting denial of autonomy to fail to respect the patient's wishes in respect of his body. For others, autonomy is predicated on independence, individualism, and freedom from external influences. This view is well described by Berlin:

> I wish to be an instrument of my own, not of other men's, acts of will. I wish to be a subject, not an object; to be moved by reasons, by conscious purposes, which are my own, not by causes which affect me, as it were, from outside. I wish to be somebody, not nobody, a doer – deciding, not being decided for, self-directed and not acted upon by external nature or by other men as if I were a thing, or an animal, or a slave incapable of playing a human role, that is, of conceiving goals and policies of my own and realising them.[23]

[9.08] This definition of autonomy would not include the patient who lets the doctor make decisions for him, as he would then not be making an independent or self-sufficient judgment. This approach has been criticised as not reflecting the reality of medical practice in which patients may want to have the necessary information about their medical problem but may not want to be the one to make the important decisions about what treatment to take.[24] There is also evidence that patients given comprehensive information about their treatment fail to understand or even remember the information given to them[25] yet perhaps this is based in part on the adequacy and comprehensibility of the explanation given or due to lack of effective communication skills on the doctor's part. Epstein says that low socioeconomic status, poor education, old age, lengthy hospital stay, stress, language barriers, and misinterpretation of probabilistic data, as well as poor disclosure practices contribute to poor outcomes in terms of reflecting genuinely autonomous choices.[26] As a result of some of these difficulties, some bioethicists argue that the legal doctrine of informed consent is a 'cruel hoax'[27] or a myth, as it is unachievable and perhaps even undesirable.[28] However, although the ideal of informed consent may be aspirational rather than attainable, Faden and Beauchamp argue that it serves as an ideal benchmark against which the moral adequacy of legal and institutional practices should be evaluated.[29]

---

[22]   Dworkin, *The Theory and Practice of Autonomy* (Cambridge University Press, 1998) at 113.

[23]   Berlin, *Four Essays on Liberty* (OUP, 1969) 131.

[24]   Donnelly, *Consent: Bridging the Gap between Doctor and Patient* (Cork University Press, 2002) p 12. See also Jenkins, 'Consent: A Matter of Trust Not Tort' (1996) MLJI 83.

[25]   President's Commission for the Study of Ethical Problems in Medicine, *Making Health Care Decisions* (US Government Printing Office, 1982).

[26]   Epstein, 'Why Effective Consent Presupposes Autonomous Authorization: A Counterorthodox Argument' (2006) J Med Ethics 32:342–345.

[27]   Katz, 'Disclosure and Consent' in Milunsky and Annas (eds) *Genetics and the Law, Vol II* (Plenum Press, 1980) 122, 128.

[28]   Freedman, 'A Moral Theory of Informed Consent' Hastings Center Report (1975) 5:32–9.

[29]   Faden and Beauchamp, *A History and Theory of Informed Consent*, (OUP, 1986): 274–97.

[9.09] Respect for autonomy not only encompasses the right to consent to treatment, but also crucially, the right to refuse medical treatment. This aspect of autonomy has sometimes caused difficulty for health-care professionals and courts as they struggle to respect the rights of the individual without allowing harm to be caused to that person or another person as a consequence. This is considered further below at para **9.112** et seq. It is also important to note that there are circumstances in which it is justifiable for the doctor to proceed to provide treatment to a patient in the absence of consent, such as where the patient is unconscious and the treatment is clearly necessary in the patient's best interests. Decision-making for persons who lack mental capacity is also considered further below.

[9.10] In recent years there has been an increased emphasis on a model of collaborative autonomy or a patient-doctor partnership which balances the doctor's responsibility for the patient's welfare with due respect for patients' rights and choices. It is thought that such an approach, which is premised on genuine patient involvement and mutual trust, will also lead to therapeutic benefits for the patient.[30]

ASSESSMENT OF CAPACITY

[9.11] One of the constituent elements of a valid consent to treatment is that the decision-maker has capacity or the ability to make decisions for himself. The law has used the requirement for capacity as a means by which to determine difficult cases, enabling a distinction to be drawn between those whose decisions will be respected and those whose decisions will be set aside. In adopting any principles in respect of capacity, the law makes normative choices.[31] As the President's Commission in the US said: '[A] conclusion about a patient's decision-making capacity necessarily reflects a balancing of two important, sometimes competing objectives: to enhance the patient's well-being and to respect the person as a self-determining individual.'[32]

[9.12] In keeping with its respect for autonomy, the law presumes that all adults have capacity. In circumstances where this presumption is questioned, the individual's capacity must be assessed bearing in mind the gravity of the treatment or procedure proposed: 'The more serious the decision, the greater the capacity required'.[33] General

---

[30] Failure to involve patients can lead to error in diagnosis and treatment, delay recovery and adversely affect long-term outcomes. Patients who experience a measure of control over their illness may have reduced levels of anxiety and depression as a result. See Teff, *Reasonable Care, Legal Perspectives on the Doctor-Patient Relationship* (Oxford, Clarendon Press 1994) at xxvi.

[31] Donnelly, *Healthcare Decision-making and the Law, Autonomy, Capacity and the Limits of Liberalism,* (Cambridge University Press, 2010) at 90, referring to Buchanan and Brock, *Deciding For Others: The Ethics of Surrogate Decision-Making.* (Cambridge University Press, 1989) p 47.

[32] President's Commission for the Study of Ethical Problems in Medicine and Biomedical and Behavioural Research, *Making Health Care Decisions: A Report on the Ethical and Legal Implications of Informed Consent in the Patient-Practitioner Relationship.* (US Superintendent of Documents, 1982) p 57.

[33] *Re T (an adult: refusal of treatment)* [1993] Fam 95; *Re MB (An adult: medical treatment)* [1997] 2 FCR 541; *Fitzpatrick and another v K and another* [2008] IEHC 104.

capacity implies that most of the time the person can adequately do the things he needs to do in everyday life.[34] Specific capacity means that the person has capacity to do one specific thing, and perhaps may not have the capacity to do other things. In other words, a person may have capacity to make a health-care decision but may not generally have the capacity to manage other areas of his life.[35] Health-care professionals generally assume that if a person is able to manage their daily lives, they have capacity to make health-care decisions and, vice versa, if a person is not able to manage daily tasks, suspicion is raised as to that person's capacity to make a health-care decision. In terms of protecting the right to self-determination, the most important test is not whether the person can adequately manage daily tasks, but rather whether the person can understand and decide important health-care issues. Therefore, specific capacity is of more importance and should be assessed bearing in mind the seriousness of the medical procedure proposed.

[9.13] In recent years there has been much discussion in relation to whether a functional or status test should be adopted in relation to the assessment of capacity. The functional test assesses the person's ability to make a particular decision rather than focusing on the person's medical diagnosis. The status approach looks at the patient's condition in determining, by virtue of that condition, whether the person is capable of making the decision.[36] In recent years the functional test of capacity has been seen as preferable, as it is in keeping with respect for the autonomy of the individual. The functional test has been adopted in the Mental Capacity Act 2005 in England and Wales, which defines a person as being without capacity if at the relevant time, he is unable, by reason of mental disability, to make a decision for himself on the matter in question, or is unable to communicate that decision. A person is unable to make a decision if he is unable to understand or retain the information relevant to the decision or is unable to make a decision based on that information. Mental disability is defined as a disability or disorder of the mind or brain, permanent or temporary, which results in an impairment or disturbance of mental functioning. A person is not to be regarded as unable to understand if he can understand an explanation of the information in broad terms and in simple language. A person is not to be regarded as unable to make a decision just because he makes a decision which would not be made by a person of ordinary prudence. A person shall not be regarded as unable to communicate unless all practicable steps have been taken without success.

[9.14] In Ireland, although there are no legislative provisions in place to guide medical practice in this regard, the Medical Council advises doctors to use the functional test of capacity. The Guide to Professional Conduct and Ethics[37] states as follows:

---

[34] Abernethy describes it as appropriate functioning in 'an array of cognitive and interpersonal domains'. Abernethy, 'Compassion, Control, and Decisions About Competency' (1984) American Journal of Psychiatry 141:53–60 at 57.

[35] See discussion in Cox White, *Competence to Consent* (Georgetown University Press, 1994) 59 *et seq.*

[36] Law Reform Commission, *Vulnerable Adults and the Law* (LRC 83–2006).

[37] Medical Council, The Guide to Professional Conduct and Ethics (7th edn, 2009), available at: http://www.medicalcouncil.ie (accessed 4 June 2011).

34.1 Every adult patient is presumed to have the capacity to make decisions about their own healthcare. As their doctor, you have a duty to help your patients to make decisions for themselves by giving them information in a clear and comprehensible manner and by ensuring that they have appropriate help and support. The patient is also entitled to be accompanied during any such discussion by an advocate of their own choice.

34.2 Sometimes a person's capacity to give consent can be affected by infirmity. People who are considered not to have the capacity to give their consent are still entitled to the same respect for their human dignity and personal integrity as any person with full capacity.

34.3 A functional approach should be taken when assessing an individual's capacity. This approach assesses the individual's ability to make the relevant choice depending on:

➤ their level of understanding and retention of the information they have been given, and

➤ their ability to apply the information to their own personal circumstances and come to a decision.

34.4 If a patient is unable to understand, retain, use or weigh up the information they have been given to make the relevant decision, or if they are unable to communicate their decision, they may be regarded as lacking the capacity to give consent to the proposed investigation or treatment. A judgment that a patient lacks the capacity to make a particular decision does not imply that they are unable to make other decisions or will be unable to make this or other decisions in the future.

[9.15] The Law Reform Commission (LRC) recommends the inclusion of a statutory statement of the applicability of a functional approach in any new capacity legislation.[38] It states that capacity is to be understood in terms of the 'ability to understand the nature and consequences of a decision in the context of available choices at the time the decision is to be made.' However, the LRC's endorsement of the functional approach to capacity is tempered somewhat by the Report's recommendation that a 'common sense' approach should be applied in 'determining when a separate functional assessment of capacity is merited'. The LRC recognised that in certain situations a person is unlikely to recover lost capacity and in such circumstances, in practice 'some leeway is needed.' Therefore, in individual situations, where an adult 'profoundly lacks or has lost decision-making capacity in a particular sphere, or generally, and is unlikely to regain it, the need to carry out a capacity assessment every time a decision requires to be made may be reduced.'[39] Donnelly says the difficulty with the LRC suggestion is that it could be all too easy to allow 'common sense' to dictate a wholesale overriding of the functional approach to capacity. 'While it might be clearly unnecessary to require a new assessment of capacity every time medical treatment is provided to a patient in a persistent vegetative state, for example, a loose understanding that capacity assessment may be dispensed with on the amorphous basis of "common sense" could expand well beyond this category.'[40]

---

[38] Law Reform Commission Consultation Paper on *Vulnerable Adults and the Law: Capacity* (LRC CP 37–2005) para 2.30.

[39] Law Reform Commission Consultation Paper on *Vulnerable Adults and the Law: Capacity* (LRC CP 37–2005) para 2.69.

[40] Donnelly, 'Assessing Legal Capacity: Process and the Operation of the Functional Test' (2007) 2 Judicial Studies Institute Journal 141 at 149.

[9.16] In practice, the most common situation in which a person may have their capacity questioned is where the patient refuses a recommended or conventional treatment.[41] It is often therefore the disagreement with the doctor's view that causes the doctor to wonder whether the person can make a decision that is valid in process terms. However, it does not follow that decisions which are the same as those that would be reached by the doctor are made by someone who is competent.[42] A person may make a decision in favour or against treatment for a wide variety of reasons, some of which may appear to others to be unreasonable or irresponsible. According to John Stuart Mill, all such decisions must be respected as an exercise of autonomy, as it is only through liberty that individuality can develop.[43] However, there does arguably come a point where the rationale behind the decision is so bizarre as to lead to suspicions as to the person's mental state. Whether this is a clash of individual value systems or an imposition on individual freedom by claims of societal interests, is a matter for debate. What is crucial is that the decision is not overridden on the basis of instinctive beliefs that no one in their right mind would have made such a decision, and that therefore the patient must be lacking capacity. If the patient is rational enough to understand and process the information given regarding the diagnosis and treatment options, then the patient must be respected in the decision he makes as a result of that understanding. According a role to the nature of the decision reached is inappropriate because it 'penalises individuality and demands conformity at the expense of personal autonomy.'[44] There may be concern that a person might be sufficiently capable to comprehend the information but may be so influenced by factors such as fear, pain, distress and so on, that their capacity to actually make the decision is impaired. It is important here to examine the decision-making process itself and not the result of the decision when capacity is being examined. Section 1(4) of the Mental Capacity Act (UK) states that a person is 'not to be treated as unable to make a decision merely because he makes an unwise decision'.

[9.17] In an English case, *Re C (Adult: refusal of treatment)*,[45] a patient suffering from chronic paranoid schizophrenia was diagnosed as having gangrene of the foot. The doctor recommended amputation in order to save the man's life. The man refused to consent and a less invasive treatment was carried out successfully. However, the man applied for an injunction to prevent an amputation taking place in the future without his consent. The Court was satisfied that, despite his mental illness as demonstrated by delusional evidence being given in court by the patient himself, the man understood and retained the information about the medical treatment and that he had arrived at a clear choice. He understood that the consequences of his refusal might be death, but

---

41   See generally Cox White, *Competence to Consent* (Georgetown University Press, 1994).

42   Gunn, Wong, Clare and Holland, 'Decision-Making Capacity' (1999) 7 Medical Law Review 269–306 at 296.

43   Mill, *On Liberty*, p 70; see also Dworkin, *Life's Dominion*, (Vintage Books, 1994) p 239, in which he argues that recourse to objective standards, whether on the basis of objective conceptions of 'the good' or on any other basis, would appear to be inconsistent with the liberal acknowledgement of the individual's 'right to a life structured by his own values.' Quoted by Donnelly, *Healthcare Decision-making and the Law, Autonomy, Capacity and the Limits of Liberalism*, (Cambridge University Press, 2010) at 96.

44   UK Law Commission, *Report on Mental Incapacity* p 33.

45   *Re C (Adult: refusal of treatment)* [1994] 1 All ER 819.

continued to refuse the operation. Thorpe J held that the relevant question in such cases is whether the patient's capacity is so reduced by his mental illness that he does not sufficiently understand the nature, purpose and effects of the treatment. He said that a patient is competent to give consent if he can understand and retain the relevant information, believe it, and weigh it in the balance to arrive at a choice.

[9.18] This case is important because it affirms the fundamental principle of respect for autonomy, which can only be overridden in particular circumstances.[46] It also demonstrates the fallacy of the status approach to competence, as in this case such an approach would have automatically determined that the man was unable to consent to or refuse treatment. However, the decision is vague in terms of the standard imposed on health-care professionals to not only assess competence but also to assess the patient's actual understanding of the relevant information. Also, it is not clear exactly what that relevant information entails, as the judgment was broadly stated in terms of the 'nature, purpose and effects' of the treatment.[47] Nonetheless, the test set out in *Re C* has been very influential in determining the appropriate test for the assessment of capacity in both England and Ireland in subsequent cases.

[9.19] In the Irish context the first case to consider the issue of capacity was *Fitzpatrick and Another v K and Another*.[48] The facts of this case were that K, a 23-year-old African woman from the Congo, gave birth to a baby in an Irish hospital in 2006. Shortly thereafter she suffered a massive post-partum haemorrhage resulting in cardiovascular collapse. As blood was being prepared for immediate transfusion, the medical team was informed that K would not accept blood for religious reasons. The medical team was concerned that K would die without a blood transfusion and called the Master of the hospital.[49] Following discussions with K, during which she repeated her refusal of blood, the Master had doubts regarding her capacity to make such a decision and decided to apply to the High Court for an emergency order giving the hospital authority to transfuse K.

[9.20] Although the judge was of the view that K's capacity was not impaired, he considered that the rights of her newborn child must be taken into consideration in his decision. He made the order authorising the hospital to administer blood to K, including all appropriate steps by way of restraint as necessary. The Master informed K of the court order and she was transfused following the administration of a sedative. She subsequently made a full recovery. She later claimed that the court order should not have been given, that the transfusion was unlawful and therefore constituted an assault and trespass to her person, and that she was entitled to refuse all or any medical treatment by

---

[46] See Stauch, 'Rationality and the Refusal of Medical Treatment: A Critique of the Recent Approach of the English Courts' (1995) 21 J Med Ethics 162.

[47] Grubb argues that requiring excessive amounts of medical information to be understood in fact limits the category of autonomous persons to only 'the most comprehending' individuals. Grubb, 'Commentary' (1994) *2* Med L Rev 92 at 95.

[48] *Fitzpatrick and Another v K and Another* [2008] IEHC 104.

[49] The most senior obstetrician in the maternity hospital with responsibility for clinical governance.

virtue of her Constitutional rights and under Arts 8 and 9 of the European Convention on Human Rights (ECHR). In the High Court, Judge Laffoy was of the view that it could not be argued that a competent adult is not free to decline medical treatment. Thus, the question that arose on the facts of this case was whether K had capacity to refuse the blood transfusion. This question had not been determined by an Irish court up to this point and therefore Laffoy J examined relevant case law from other jurisdictions in her judgment. She also referred to the Law Reform Commission's Report on *Vulnerable Adults and the Law* in which the Commission recommends that 'capacity will be understood in terms of an adult's cognitive ability to understand the nature and consequences of a decision in the context of available choices at the time the decision is made'.

[9.21] Laffoy J held that the principles applicable to the determination of capacity are as follows:

- There is a presumption that an adult patient has the capacity, that is to say, the cognitive ability, to make a decision to refuse medical treatment, but that presumption can be rebutted.

- In determining whether a patient is deprived of capacity to make a decision to refuse medical treatment whether (a) by reason of permanent cognitive impairment, or (b) temporary factors..., the test is whether the patient's cognitive ability has been impaired to the extent that he or she does not sufficiently understand the nature, purpose and effect of the proffered treatment and the consequences of accepting or rejecting it in the context of the choices available (including any alternative treatment) at the time the decision is made.

- The patient's cognitive ability will have been impaired to the extent that he or she is incapable of making the decision to refuse the proffered treatment if the patient –

  (a)   has not comprehended and retained the treatment information and, in particular, has not assimilated the information as to the consequences likely to ensue from not accepting the treatment,

  (b)   has not believed the treatment information and, in particular, if it is the case that not accepting the treatment is likely to result in the patient's death, has not believed that outcome is likely, and

  (c)   has not weighed the treatment information, in particular, the alternative choices and the likely outcomes, in the balance in arriving at the decision.

- The treatment information by reference to which the patient's capacity is to be assessed is the information which the clinician is under a duty to impart – information as to what is the appropriate treatment, that is to say, what treatment is medically indicated, at the time of the decision and the risks and consequences likely to flow from the choices available to the patient in making the decision.

- In assessing capacity it is necessary to distinguish between misunderstanding or misperception of the treatment information in the decision-making process....on the one hand, and an irrational decision or a decision made for irrational reasons, on the other hand. The former may be evidence of lack of capacity. The latter is irrelevant to the assessment.

- In assessing capacity, whether at the bedside in a high dependency unit or in court, the assessment must have regard to the gravity of the decision, in terms of the consequences which are likely to ensue from the acceptance or rejection of the proffered treatment....

[9.22] Having regard to the nature of the evidence presented in relation to K's capacity, the Court was satisfied that K had been given the information necessary, in layman's terms, to enable her to make an informed decision in relation to the blood transfusion. The relevant factors to be taken into account in this case were that K's medical status was seriously compromised following a long labour, a difficult delivery and a massive haemorrhage. There were communication difficulties due to the fact the K's first language was not English, and the hospital believed that K had no family members in the country to support her at that time. Laffoy J concluded that K's capacity at the relevant time was impaired to the extent that she did not have the ability to make a valid refusal to accept the appropriate medical treatment which was proffered to her, a blood transfusion. Therefore, the administration of the transfusion was not unlawful or in breach of her Constitutional rights.

[9.23] This decision is important in setting out clearly the test for the assessment of capacity in the health-care context in Ireland. It closely follows the approach set out in *Re C*, described above, in relation to the three issues that must be considered, ie whether the patient has understood the information provided, has weighed it in the balance and applied it to his or her own situation in reaching a decision. As this is the first case on this issue in Ireland, its value in emphasizing the presumption of capacity and the right of a competent adult to refuse medical treatment cannot be understated. On the particular facts of this case the judge took the view that K lacked capacity to make her own decision, although at the interlocutory stage this had not been the view of the Master of the High Court on the evidence before him at that point in time. Although the factors taken into account by Laffoy J in assessing capacity were significant, it may be tempting to deduce that other women might similarly be assessed as lacking capacity during or following delivery, with the consequent overriding of their decisions made in those circumstances. Due to the finding of incapacity, Laffoy J did not consider the issue of whether the rights and interests of K's newborn child ought properly to have been taken into account in reaching the decision to override K's wishes. Thus, any consideration of a hierarchy of Constitutional rights in such contexts will have to await further judicial consideration.

Further consideration of the right of a competent adult to refuse treatment is considered below at para **9.112**.

ALTERNATIVES TO PERSONAL CONSENT

[9.24] As stated above, every adult is presumed to have decision-making capacity and is entitled to make a decision regarding medical treatment without recourse being had to family members or others. If the individual is assessed and deemed not to have capacity then there are a number of alternatives that may be applicable. Donnelly sets out clearly the consequences of an assessment that a person lacks capacity to make his or her own decisions:[50]

> A designation of incapacity has enormous practical, legal and psychological significance for the individual involved. Following the designation, she loses the freedom to make decisions for herself, at least in relation to the matter(s) to which the incapacity relates. Instead, others will decide for her on the basis of what they believe to be in her best interests. Depending on the circumstances, she may be told where to live, what medical treatment to have, what contracts she may enter, whether she may bequeath her property and whether or not she may marry or have a sexual relationship. Thus, her fundamental rights to liberty, to autonomy and to privacy will be significantly undermined by the designation of incapacity. Psychologically, too, a designation of incapacity may have an adverse impact on the individual who has to contend with both the practical limitations on her freedom and the stigmatising effect of being labelled "incapable". For these reasons, the way in which capacity is assessed must be monitored carefully in order to ensure that a designation of incapacity is made only where it is necessary and appropriate.

The defence of necessity is available if the medical procedure is medically necessary and the patient lacks capacity to make a decision for himself. This defence is always available in the context of emergency care as, without it, for example, a comatose patient who is rushed to casualty following an accident could not be treated. In non-emergency situations, it is necessary to seek consent from a proxy decision-maker who gives consent in place of the patient.

[9.25] Most commonly in circumstances where the person is assessed as lacking decision-making capacity an application is made to establish the individual as a ward of court.[51] This establishes the President of the High Court or the Circuit Court as the person's legal guardian.[52] This has the effect that no important decision in relation to that individual may be taken without the permission of the court, and any court decision must be taken with the individual's welfare as the paramount concern.[53] The court will appoint a wardship committee to secure the day-to-day welfare of the individual. This committee can give consent to medical treatment on behalf of the ward if the procedure is for the ward's benefit[54] although if the treatment is regarded as serious, the Committee

---

[50]   For a comprehensive discussion of the issues involved in assessing legal capacity, see Donnelly, 'Assessing Legal Capacity: Process and the Operation of the Functional Test' (2007) 2 Judicial Studies Institute Journal 141.

[51]   Lunacy Regulations (Ireland) Act 1871, s 68. There has been much criticism from families as well as medical and legal professionals of the language and procedures set out in this Act, which require the assessment of the ward as a person of 'unsound mind'. See, for example *In the Matter of Wards of Court and In the Matter of Francis Dolan* [2007] IESC 26 where Geogeghan J described it as more than understandable that parents would take umbrage at the terminology used in the Act.

[52]   For a more detailed discussion of procedural issues in the wardship context, see O'Neill, 'Wardship Law and Procedure' in O'Dell (ed) *Older People in Modern Ireland: Essays on Law and Policy* (First Law, 2006).

[53]   See generally Donnelly, 'Best Interests, Patient Participation and the Mental Capacity Act 2005' (2009) 17 Med Law Review 1; O'Keefe, 'A Clinician's Perspective: Issues of Capacity in Care' (2008) 14 Medico-Legal Journal of Ireland 41.

[54]   See *Re an Application by the Midland Health Board* [1988] ILRM 251 for confirmation that the power of the wardship committee to give consent is not confined to decisions in relation to property.

will seek the consent of the court. What is regarded as 'serious' enough to require court consent is unfortunately undefined. Donnelly is of the view that Irish courts would certainly follow the English example of requiring court approval in relation to sterilisation for contraceptive purposes, donation of tissue or organs and the withdrawal of hydration and nutrition. She also states that it is possible that court approval might be required in Ireland in a much wider range of circumstances.[55]

[9.26] An order of the court may also be made under its *parens patriae* jurisdiction. This comes from an old jurisdiction whereby the King, as feudal lord, had an obligation to protect those who could not protect themselves. This sovereign power was later transferred to the Lord Chancellor and subsequently the courts. It is now exercisable by the High Court[56] and is unlimited in scope. The Court must, however, exercise its discretion in favour of the best interests of the individual who is the subject of its jurisdiction.

[9.27] In relation to medical treatment, if all attempts have been made to improve the individual's ability to understand and communicate a decision in relation to the proposed treatment without success, then treatment may be authorised by the wardship committee, the court or by the doctor in emergency situations.[57] For example, in *Re F (Mental Patient: Sterilisation)*[58] a 36-year-old mentally handicapped woman formed a sexual

---

[55] Donnelly, *Consent: Bridging the Gap Between Doctor and Patient* (Cork University Press, 2002) p 45.

[56] Courts (Supplemental Provisions) Act 1961, s 9(1). The history of the jurisdiction given to the court is traced by Hamilton CJ in *In re a matter of a ward of court* [1995] 2 ILRM 401, 407–8. See also Hoggett, 'The Royal Prerogative in Relation to the Mentally Disordered: Resurrection, Resuscitation, or Rejection?' in Freeman (ed), *Medicine, Ethics and the Law* (Stevens Publishing, 1988); Seymour, 'Parens Patriae and Wardship Powers: Their Nature and Origins' (1994) 14 OJLS 159.

[57] In relation to capacity to marry, if the individual has the capacity to understand the duties and obligations of marriage, then the marriage contract will be valid. A challenge to the marriage (before it takes place) would have to be made by applying for an injunction to prevent the Registrar of Marriages from authorising the marriage. After the marriage, the law of nullity could be used to annul the marriage on grounds of lack of capacity to understand the meaning of marriage, for example due to developmental immaturity, or lack of consummation. However such an application would have to be brought by one of the partners themselves. In relation to embarking on a sexual relationship, the Criminal Law Amendment Act 1935 provides that it is an offence to have intercourse with a mentally disabled woman (described in the Act as an idiot, an imbecile or feeble-minded). It has been said that this restriction may be too broad, as it may constitute an unacceptable invasion of the woman's right to privacy and sexual fulfillment. The Law Reform Commission has described this archaic language as offensive and has recommended its replacement with an offence of having unlawful sexual intercourse with a mentally disabled person if that person was incapable of protecting him or herself against exploitation. It also recommended that such acts should not constitute a criminal offence if both participants were mentally disabled. In relation to the formation of contracts, if the individual is unable to maintain a fully independent life, he may (as, for example, under family law statutes) be termed a 'dependant'. As such, he would not strictly have the capacity to form contracts on his own behalf.

[58] *Re F (Mental Patient: Sterilisation)* [1990] 2 AC 1, *sub nom F v West Berkshire Health Authority* [1989] 2 All ER 545.

relationship with a male patient, also mentally handicapped, in the hospital in which they were both patients. The hospital authorities felt that she would be unable to cope with pregnancy and motherhood and, as all other contraceptive measures were considered unsuitable, they recommended that she be sterilised. The Court felt that, as this was a case where the incapacity to consent to the treatment was a permanent one, it was futile to wait for consent to be given. As the need for the procedure was obvious, the doctor was obliged to act in his patient's best interests, in the same way as if she had given consent.

[9.28] In *Re Y*[59] a mentally handicapped 25-year-old woman who had been institutionalised at the age of 10, donated bone marrow to her sister, who suffered from non-Hodgkin's lymphoma. The donor, due to her disabilities, was unaware of her sister's illness and of the surgical operation she herself would have to undergo in order to be a donor. Given that this was regarded as a minimally invasive procedure, the Court found that it was in her best interests to donate the bone marrow on the basis that if her sister died, her mother would be too distressed to visit her and she would lose the only family contact she really had. This case clearly demonstrates the difficulties with which individuals, families and authorities can be faced. However, it also shows an unsatisfactory application of a best-interests test in a case in which there was no obvious tangible benefit to the woman in undergoing a medical procedure to which she did not consent. The procedure was justified on the basis that although it would have no medical benefit for her, it would be for her 'emotional, psychological and social benefit.' This conclusion is somewhat difficult to support on the evidence before the Court, as Y did not live with her sister, nor did she have a particularly close relationship with her. It appears from some of the case law in this area that the patient's best interests may have been confused with the needs and desires of the carers. The test itself has been criticised as 'vague and [it] leaves considerable control and power in the hands of the health care professionals.'[60]

Non-consensual sterilisation

[9.29] An example of an area in which the best-interests test has been used in England and elsewhere in relation to patients lacking capacity is sterilisation decisions.[61] For a woman under the age of 18, court approval for sterilisation may be sought by the parents or guardians through the application of the *parens patriae* jurisdiction. For a woman over the age of 18, the issue becomes more complicated, as the power to consent on behalf of minors ends when the patient reaches 18. Due to the lack of legislation on this question in most jurisdictions, courts have sometimes used the doctrine of necessity to approve the carrying out of the procedure. Under this doctrine, treatment may be carried out in the best interests of the patient, which will be the case where the patient's life is in danger, or to ensure improvement or prevent deterioration in physical or mental health. The doctrine is used not only in situations of temporary incapacity, but also in relation to persons regarded as permanently incompetent, such as those with learning disabilities.

---

[59]   *Re Y* [1997] Fam 110, [1997] 2 WLR 556.

[60]   Mason and McCall Smith, *Law and Medical Ethics* (5th edn, OUP, 2005) p 264, (now in its 8th edn, 2010).

[61]   For a detailed examination of this topic, see Donnelly, 'Non-Consensual Sterilisation of Mentally Disabled People.' (1997) Irish Jurist, Vol 32, 297–322.

One of the difficulties here is that sterilisations are sometimes carried out for non-therapeutic reasons, such as to prevent pregnancy or to relieve the burden of preventing pregnancy from the carers, as opposed to medical reasons such as the alleviation of severe menstrual problems. Given that sterilisation involves the deprivation of the capacity to reproduce, it is important to consider whether the best interests test provides adequate protection to women with learning difficulties.[62]

[9.30] Under the best-interests test, each case turns on its own facts without the general application of explicit legal precedents. However, the case law in other jurisdictions suggests that the factors taken into account in relation to sterilisation decisions are perhaps inappropriate and the judgments show undue deference to medical opinion in this area. 'In cases of sterilisation, the views of the medical profession by and large have been accepted without challenge. In many cases there has been no medical objection to the proposed sterilisation, and the court has simply been called in to confirm the legality of the decision to sterilise. This appears to have been little more than a process of rubber-stamping the doctor's decision without undertaking any independent scrutiny.'[63]

[9.31] One of the problems in the sterilisation cases is the emphasis put on the pathology of learning difficulties, in other words, what is abnormal about the woman in question. The measurement of the woman in terms of her intellectual capacity denies the practical experience and behavioural skills built up by these women over many years, which in fact would be more relevant to parenting than intelligence.[64] By viewing learning difficulty as a medical problem, it enables a medical or surgical solution to be sought. The cases also show a concern with the extent to which the woman understands the link between sexual intercourse and pregnancy, but do not consider whether this link had ever been explained to her in a way she might hope to understand. Neither do they consider the risks of sexually transmitted disease or sexual exploitation in their concern for the woman with learning difficulties – the main concern is to avoid pregnancy. Whether this is an avoidance of confronting the sexuality of a woman with learning difficulties, or an erroneous belief that the child of such a woman will also have learning disabilities,[65] is difficult to know.

> The courts' failure to recognise the potential contraceptive responsibilities of male partners; the assumption that the woman will be promiscuous; the failure to consider the risk of pregnancy in isolation from risks of sexual abuse and sexually transmitted diseases, suggest that the courts are seeking not to protect women from unwanted sexual advances from male

---

[62]   For discussion, see Keywood, 'Sterilising the Woman with Learning Disabilities' in Millns and Bridgeman (eds) *Law and Body Politics: Regulating the Female Body* (Dartmouth, 1995).

[63]   Keywood, 'Sterilising the Woman with Learning Disabilities' in Millns and Bridgeman (eds) *Law and Body Politics: Regulating the Female Body* (Dartmouth, 1995) p 128, referring in particular to *Re M (a minor) (wardship: sterilisation)* [1988] 2 FLR 497.

[64]   Carson, 'The Sexuality of People with Learning Difficulties' [1989] 6 JSWL, 354.

[65]   This was the main justification for the eugenic policies of the early 20th century, as demonstrated by the famous judgment in *Buck v Bell* (1927) 274 US 200, Sup Ct where Holmes J upheld the legality of compulsory sterilisation of inmates by saying 'three generations of imbeciles are enough.'

residents, relatives or staff, but rather to protect women from the consequences of their own capricious sexuality.[66]

[9.32] The conflict that arises between the best interests of the incapacitated adult and his/her human right to reproduce has been raised in a number of cases, beginning with the English case of *Re D (a minor)*[67] where the girl in question was 11 years old and suffering from a condition that impacted upon her mental capacity but nonetheless did not make it impossible for her to manage her own life. Heilbron J was of the view that as this girl was so young, where her condition was shown to be improving, and where the evidence was that in the future she may have the capacity to understand the implications of the operation such that she could give her own consent, it would be a violation of her 'basic human right to reproduce' if she were sterilised without her consent for non-therapeutic reasons.

[9.33] This case was quoted with approval in the Canadian decision in *Re Eve*[68], in which it was sought to sterilise an intellectually disabled woman for contraceptive purposes, on the basis that neither Eve nor her mother would be able to look after a baby should Eve become pregnant.[69] In rejecting the application, La Forest J concluded that 'the grave intrusion on a person's rights and the certain physical damage that ensues from non-therapeutic sterilisation without consent, when compared to the highly questionable advantages that can result from it' meant that 'non-therapeutic sterilisation should never be authorised under the *parens patriae* jurisdiction.'[70] He also gave indications as to how to distinguish therapeutic from non-therapeutic circumstances. The former would include the protection of mental as well as physical health but should not be used as a 'subterfuge or for treatment of a marginal medical problem.'[71] The decision is noteworthy for its departure from the traditional reliance on the best interests test in these circumstances. The Court was of the view that it was not capable of determining what Eve's best interests were, and therefore the test was not sufficiently precise or workable to be applied in this case.

[9.34] This departure from best interests as determined by a court of law has, at least in theory, the advantage of avoiding the dangers which arise from judicial subjectivity in the application of a 'best interests' test. Once an individual right, such as the right not to be subjected to non-therapeutic medical interventions without consent, is considered to exist, then interference with that right will require justification. Thus, the Canadian approach to the issue starts from a perspective of protection of the individual thereby reducing the risk of the judiciary and other professionals imposing their own prejudices

---

66 Keywood, 'Sterilising the Woman with Learning Disabilities' in Millns and Bridgeman (eds) *Law and Body Politics: Regulating the Female Body* (Dartmouth, 1995) p 135.

67 *Re D (a minor)* [1976] 1 All ER 326.

68 *Re Eve* [1986] 31 DLR (4) 1.

69 For further discussion of this case, see Peppin, 'Justice and Care: Mental Disability and Sterilisation Decisions' (1989/90) 6 Canadian Human Rights Yearbook 65; Freeman, 'Sterilising the Mentally Handicapped' in *Medicine, Ethics and the Law: Current Legal Problems* (Stevens & Sons Ltd, 1988).

70 *Re Eve* [1986] 31 DLR (4) 1 at 32.

71 *Re Eve* [1986] 31 DLR (4) 1 at 34.

on the situation. The importance of this in an area fraught with preconceptions should not be under-estimated.[72]

[9.35] However, the decision is also open to criticism due to the lack of focus on the broader rights of the individual, other than the right not to be sterilised without consent, and the limitation placed on the Court's approach to the issue by avoiding discussion of the facts on a best-interests analysis. This, in effect, means that each case is pre-judged, which, together with the lack of analysis of other rights of the individual, may result in a one-sided perspective being taken of a very complex issue.[73]

[9.36] Coincidentally, at around the same time as the Canadian Supreme Court was deciding *Re Eve*, the House of Lords in the UK was also deciding a similar case, *Re B*.[74] The facts of this case concerned an intellectually disabled epileptic girl, Jeanette, aged 17, who was thought to be in danger of becoming pregnant. It was accepted by the Court that Jeanette would not be capable of understanding or supporting the inconveniences and pains of pregnancy. There was also the possibility that, if she became pregnant, the baby would have to be delivered by caesarean section and that there was a danger that she might interfere with the resulting wound. In granting the application for sterilisation, the House of Lords based its decision firmly on the welfare of the girl. The Court rejected as 'meaningless' the distinction between therapeutic and non-therapeutic sterilisation which had been seen as important in the Canadian decision. Lord Oliver stressed that there was no question of eugenic motivation, nor was there an issue of suiting the girl's carers. The Court found the decision in *Re Eve* to be 'totally unconvincing and in startling contradiction to the welfare principle.'[75] In relation to the argument that non-consensual sterilisation would be an infringement of Jeanette's basic right to reproduce, Lord Hailsham was particularly scathing. He was of the view that to suggest that there is a right to reproduce in a person who is incapable of understanding the connection between intercourse and pregnancy, the process of childbirth and the demands of caring for a child, was 'wholly to part company with reality.' The other judgments are based on the best-interests test although they do not elaborate on its application.

[9.37] In *Re F (mental patient: sterilisation)*[76] similar facts arose, though here with a 36-year-old intellectually disabled woman, and the Court again authorised the sterilisation, accepting that this was in the 'best interests' of the patient. Lord Brandon pointed out that treatment would be considered to be in a person's best interests only if it was carried out 'either to save their lives, or to ensure improvement or prevent deterioration in their

---

72 Donnelly, 'Non-Consensual Sterilisation of Mentally Disabled People' (1997) Irish Jurist, Vol 32, p 302.

73 Donnelly, 'Non-Consensual Sterilisation of Mentally Disabled People' (1997) Irish Jurist, Vol 32, p 303.

74 *Re B (a minor) (wardship: sterilisation)* [1988] AC 199, [1987] 2 All ER 206.

75 See criticism of *Re B* in Freeman, 'For Her Own Good' (1987) 84 LS Gaz 949; Lee and Morgan, 'Sterilisation and Mental Handicap: Sapping the Strength of the State' (1988) 15 J Law & Soc. 229; and Montgomery, 'Rhetoric and Welfare' (1989) 9 OJL Stud 395.

76 *Re F (mental patient: sterilisation)* [1990] 2 AC 1, *sub nom F v West Berkshire Health Authority* [1989] 2 All ER 545.

physical or mental health.'[77] This narrow definition of best interests does not seem to have been followed in later decisions, which have been decided on their own facts without laying down principles under which the best interests test should be applied. The determination of this issue on the basis of best interests is 'potentially devoid of legal or ethical analysis and therefore vulnerable to judicial and professional subjectivity.'[78]

[9.38] In *Re S (adult: sterilisation)*[79] the Court considered whether to authorise the sterilisation of a 29-year-old woman with severe learning difficulties. S's mother was concerned that S might become pregnant when she moved into a local authority home and also was concerned to alleviate the heavy menstrual bleeding suffered by S, with which she had difficulty coping. The trial judge held that either a hysterectomy or the fitting of an intra-uterine device would be in her best interests. However, the Court of Appeal held that the judge erred in providing a range of possible alternatives and should have decided which option was better for S, rather than leaving the decision to the medical profession. The correct decision was that the insertion of the intra-uterine device was in S's best interest, as it was the least invasive option, was not irreversible and left room for surgical procedures if it were ineffective.[80]

[9.39] Most of the cases on this issue have dealt with the question of female sterilisation, a fact that has been criticised by some, who see it as affirming that the avoidance or reproduction or the responsibility for pregnancy is predominantly that of the woman. However, in *Re A (Mental Patient: Sterilisation)*[81] the Court had to address the same issue in the context of a 28-year-old man with Down's syndrome who was on the borderline of significant and severe impairment of intelligence. His mother cared for and supervised him but she was concerned that when he moved into local authority care he might have a sexual relationship without understanding the consequences. She applied for a declaration that a vasectomy should be carried out on him in his best interests. The Court held that male sterilisation on non-therapeutic grounds could only be carried out if it was in the best interests of the patient, taking into account not just medical but emotional and all welfare issues. The Court found that the birth of a child or the disapproval of his conduct by others was not likely to impinge on a mentally incapacitated man very much, although his freedom of movement might be restricted as a result. It was clear that as long as A was in the care of his mother, he would be under her strict supervision, irrespective of whether the operation was carried out or not.

---

[77] *Re F (mental patient: sterilisation)* [1990] 2 AC 1 at 55.

[78] Donnelly, *Consent: Bridging the Gap Between Doctor and Patient* (Cork University Press, 2002) at 305.

[79] *Re S (adult: sterilisation)* [2001] Fam. 15; [2000] 3 WLR 1288; [2000] 2 FLR 389.

[80] See by contrast *Re ZM and OS (Sterilisation: Patient's Best interests)* [2000] 1 FLR 523, dealing with a 19-year-old girl with Down's syndrome who also suffered from heavy, painful and irregular menstruation. Due to the belief that a sexual relationship with her boyfriend was possible, it was sought to perform a hysterectomy on her. Expert evidence was conflicted as to whether this was more appropriate than the fitting of an intra-uterine device as a method of reducing the difficulties she experienced with menstruation but the decision was ultimately one for the Court. In granting the declaration sought, the Court decided that it was in her best interests to have a complete cessation of her periods and complete protection from pregnancy.

[81] *Re A (Mental Patient: Sterilisation)* [2000] 1 FLR 549.

Similarly, if he was to go into day care, the level of supervision there would not depend on his fertility but rather on the fact that it was a public place, so again this would be the case irrespective of whether he had the operation or not. Therefore, as the operation would be invasive and have minimal effect on A, the declaration was refused.

[9.40] There have not been any cases dealing with non-consensual sterilisation in the Irish context. However, statements made in other cases such as *In Re a Ward of Court* [82] demonstrate that the Constitutional protection of personal rights does not diminish due to the loss of mental capacity in the individual. The personal right that most obviously comes into play here is that of bodily integrity, although the right to reproduce may also be relied upon in argument.[83] It has been suggested by the Law Reform Commission that, although the problem was unlikely to come before an Irish court, the Canadian decision in *Re Eve* would most likely be followed here.[84] However, it may be argued that in some circumstances, sterilisation 'as a last resort' may well be a more appropriate vindication of the individual's right to protection of her life and health. The danger is that 'the Irish courts will adopt a best interests test, dress it up in constitutional garb and apply it without any understanding of the risks of judicial subjectivity or awareness that "judges are generally ill-informed about many of the factors relevant to a wise decision in this difficult area."'[85]

Proposals for reform

[9.41] The numbers of adults in Ireland who are unable to make decisions for themselves is already significant and these numbers are predicted to steadily increase. The main categories of persons who may be unable to make decisions for themselves are (a) the elderly (b) persons with acquired brain injuries (c) persons with mental illness and (d) persons with intellectual disabilities. It is estimated that each of these categories will grow as the Irish population continues to expand.[86] Many, though not all, of these persons will be unable to make decisions for themselves even for a short period of time.

---

[82] *In Re a Ward of Court* [1995] 2 ILRM 401.

[83] It is unlikely that the right to reproduce would be applicable in such a case as the right has been held, in *Murray v Ireland* [1991] ILRM 465, to apply to married persons. In most cases of the kind discussed above the individual would not have the capacity to marry and therefore would not have the right to reproduce. If the person did have the capacity to marry, then it is likely that they would also have the capacity to give or refuse consent to the operation. See further Donnelly, 'Non-Consensual Sterilisation of Mentally Disabled People' (1997) Irish Jurist, Vol 32, at 310–311.

[84] *Report on Sexual Offences Against the Mentally Handicapped,* LRC 33–1990 p 25.

[85] Donnelly, 'Non-Consensual Sterilisation of Mentally Disabled People' (1997) Irish Jurist, Vol 32, at 319, also quoting from *Re Eve* (1986) 31 DLR (4) 1 at 32.

[86] In 2001 there were 430,000 persons over the age of 65. It is projected that this figure will rise to 840,000 by 2031: LRC Report, (LRC 83–2006), Para 1.05. It is estimated that currently approximately 35,000 people in Ireland have dementia – The Alzheimer Society of Ireland, 'Your Guide to Understanding Alzheimer's Disease and Other Dementias', p 2. It is estimated that more than 10,000 people sustain a brain injury annually and more than 7,000 suffer a stroke – LRC Report, (LRC 83–2006), Para 1.16. There were 25,557 people registered in the National Intellectual Disability Database in 2003, representing a prevalence rate of intellectual disability of 6.52 per 1,000 population – LRC Consultation Paper on Capacity, Para 1.07.

[9.42] In contrast to decision-making by courts on the unsatisfactory best-interests formula, a different approach may be seen in other jurisdictions where legislation has been introduced to give individuals the right to appoint a medical treatment attorney[87] or, in some states, the use of a statutory health attorney. This is an attorney appointed by statute to make health-care decisions on behalf of a mentally incapacitated adult subject to the provisions of the statute. Such an approach may be quicker and therefore more useful in the Irish context in place of a court application under the present system as discussed earlier. 'If consent is indeed the key principle in health care ethics and law, then the person being provided with treatment is, and must be, centre stage. His or her views must be of paramount importance.'[88] Of course, this approach is only useful if the individual has had capacity at some time so as to enable him to appoint and instruct such an attorney.

[9.43] In Ireland in 2006 the Law Reform Commission (LRC) published a report on 'Vulnerable Adults and the Law' and the Government has proposed to introduce a new Mental Capacity Bill which will incorporate many of the recommendations in that report to protect adults who, due to illness, accident or intellectual disability, are unable to make decisions for themselves or exercise their legal capacity. (The provisions contained in the current draft of the Bill are outlined below). In advocating for the introduction of a new system of protection for vulnerable adults, it may be argued that current laws in this area may be in violation of Constitutional and human rights law.[89] The Irish Constitution 1937 and the ECHR provide for the protection of property rights, and any restriction of a property right must be subject to rigorous procedural safeguards. Given that wardship proceedings currently tend to be instigated in relation to the property of persons considered to be lacking decision-making capacity, the LRC suggests that some elements of the wardship procedures may conflict with the guarantee of a fair hearing required under art 6 of the ECHR.[90] Ireland has signed the UN Convention on the Rights of Persons with Disabilities. The next step towards ratification of the Convention is to ensure that Ireland complies with obligations under the Convention.

[9.44] There is currently considerable concern and frustration on the part of practitioners who practice in this area and who face families with such difficulties on a regular basis.[91] As Donnelly notes: 'the problems with the current legislative approach extend well beyond terminology. The current position is clearly untenable...' She argues that it is essential that the legislature engages with the reform process initiated by the Law Reform Commission. A suitable assessment process must be developed which includes 'a rigorous application of the functional test, the provision of independent

---

87 Woolard, 'The Appointment of Medical Treatment Attorneys: Some Lessons From Australia' (1998) 6 Medical Law Review 297–321.

88 Gunn, Wong, Clare and Holland, 'Decision-Making Capacity' (1999) 7 Medical Law Review 269–306 at 289.

89 See www.justice.ie (accessed 4 June 2011).

90 LRC Consultation Paper on Capacity, Para 4.12 on notice requirements and Para 4.15 concerning the inquiry process, see also Para 2.07 of the LRC Report on Vulnerable Adults and the Law (LRC 83–2006), on the ECHR.

91 O'Keefe, 'A Clinician's Perspective: Issues of Capacity in Care' (2008) 14 Medico-Legal Journal of Ireland 41.

representation for the individual involved, a careful review of medical evidence and the development of a participative element to involve the individual in the process insofar as this is possible.'[92]

[9.45] The proposed Mental Capacity Bill 2008 provides in Head 1 that the following principles apply for the purposes of this Act and every person (including the court) concerned in the implementation of the Act or in making any decision, declaration or order or giving any direction under the Act shall have regard to them:

(a) it shall be presumed unless the contrary is established that a person has capacity,

(b) no intervention is to take place unless it is necessary having regard to the needs and individual circumstances of the person, including whether the person is likely to increase or regain capacity,

(c) a person shall not be treated as unable to make a decision unless all practicable steps to help him or her to do so have been taken without success,

(d) a person is not to be treated as unable to make a decision merely because he or she makes an unwise decision,

(e) any act done or decision made under this Act must be done or made in the way which is least restrictive of the person's rights and freedom of action,

(f) due regard must be given to the need to respect the right of a person to his or her dignity, bodily integrity, privacy and autonomy,

(g) account must be taken of a person's past and present wishes, where ascertainable,

(h) account must be taken of the views of any person with an interest in the welfare of a person who lacks capacity, where these views have been made known, and

(i) any act done or decision made under this Act for or on behalf of a person who lacks capacity must be done or made in his or her best interests.

The Bill as currently framed also establishes a presumption of capacity. Capacity is defined as 'the ability to understand the nature and consequences of a decision in the context of available choices at the time the decision is to be made'. The test of capacity strongly reflects the test in *Re C*, outlined above. It states that a person lacks the capacity to make a decision if he is unable to:

(a) understand the information relevant to the decision;

(b) retain that information;

(c) use or weigh that information as part of the process of making the decision; or

(d) communicate his decision.

[9.46] Any question as to whether a person has capacity is to be decided on the balance of probabilities. The Bill also provides that a person is entitled to supported decision-making. The person must, so far as is reasonably practicable, be permitted to participate, or to improve his ability to participate, as fully as possible in any act done for him and any decision affecting him. Where it is not possible to support a person in this way, the court or a court-appointed personal guardian will act as the substitute decision-maker.

---

[92] Donnelly, 'Assessing Legal Capacity: Process and the Operation of the Functional Test' (2007) 2 Judicial Studies Institute Journal 141 at 168.

[9.47] In relation to medical decision-making, the Bill provides that before a medical practitioner performs any act in connection with the personal care, health care or treatment of another person whose decision-making capacity is in doubt, he must have regard to the general principles outlined above and take reasonable steps to establish whether the person lacks capacity in relation to the matter in question. He must also reasonably believe that the other person lacks capacity in relation to the matter in question, and it is in the other person's best interests that the act be done. The Bill gives medical practitioners immunity from liability if they follow these steps when treating patients.

[9.48] Where a person has been found to lack capacity, the Bill provides for the appointment of a personal guardian by the High Court or the Circuit Court to make decisions concerning his personal welfare or property and affairs. Decisions on certain matters such as non-therapeutic sterilisation, withdrawal of artificial life-sustaining treatment or organ donation will only be made in the High Court. The Bill will also establish an independent Office of Public Guardian to supervise persons appointed by the courts to perform guardianship or decision-making functions on behalf of incapacitated persons. In situations where there is no person willing or able to act as a personal guardian, the Office will act as a guardian of last resort. It remains to be seen whether the Bill will be enacted in its current form or whether substantial changes will be made during the legislative process.

INFORMED CONSENT

[9.49] The Hippocratic tradition in medicine did not discuss any obligations of disclosure on the physician, nor did any of the ancient or even early modern medical ethics literature, although concern did exist about how to make disclosures to the patient without harming him. Benevolent deception was the main practice in the 19th century, with the patient's right to be informed being overruled by the duty to benefit the patient in cases where the information may harm the patient. Up to the 1950s, permission for surgery was sought from patients in a fairly rudimentary way that absolved the physician of responsibility in cases of malpractice. The concept of 'informed consent' to medical treatment only emerged around the 1960s although perhaps one of the most influential cases, *Schloendorff v Society of New York Hospitals*[93] had come in the United States in 1914. This case was important because it developed the use of rights language in relation to the obligation to obtain the consent of the patient. Self-determination began to be recognised as the primary justification for legal requirements of consent. As Cardozo J famously said:

> Every human being of adult years and sound mind has a right to determine what shall be done with his own body; and a surgeon who performs an operation without his patient's consent commits an assault for which he is liable in damages.[94]

[9.50] In the middle of the 20th century other societal changes began also to impact upon the culture of consent such as a growing concern for issues of equality and civil rights, consumerism and an increasingly technologically driven health-care system.

---

93   *Schloendorff v Society of New York Hospitals* (1914) 211 N.Y. 125.
94   *Schloendorff v Society of New York Hospitals* (1914) 211 N.Y. at 128.

Knowledge became the fundamental constituent of self-determination. However, although the courts were clear on the link between respect for autonomy and the requirement for consent, in fact many of the cases which came to judicial attention related to the right to refuse treatment rather than give consent to it.

[9.51] The term 'informed consent' is often used to describe the process whereby a health-care professional discloses all necessary information to a patient prior to obtaining consent to go ahead with a procedure. It is an expression which has been imported into England and Ireland from the United States in a manner often criticised as a lazy, undiscriminating repetition of an easy formula.[95] In many of the English cases in which it has been used, it has invited judicial disapproval of the term, and Kennedy and Grubb refer to it as an 'unfortunate phrase and one prone to mislead.'[96] This has also been seen in Canadian[97] and Australian[98] decisions. It is a useful term, however, to remind those involved in health-care decision making that an uninformed consent may not be valid in law. Despite its wide usage in practice to cover all aspects of consent, it has no application to aspects of consent such as competence or voluntariness, as its sole purpose is to ensure that sufficient information has been provided to the patient prior to giving consent to medical treatment. The Australian judge Kirby J, writing extra-judicially, defined informed consent as 'that consent which is obtained after the patient has been adequately instructed about the ratio of risk and benefit involved in the procedure as compared to alternative procedures or no treatment at all.'[99] Although useful, the definition should perhaps also have included the necessity of giving basic information about the procedure itself and who will perform it.[100]

[9.52] One of the difficulties in the area of consent is that there may be a substantial difference between the ethical ideal of informed consent and the reality of what happens in daily medical practice. Patients are often simply required to sign a consent form which may be written in medical jargon that is incomprehensible to the average person. Seeking informed consent then loses all significance, as it becomes an undemanding formality that must be complied with for legal purposes.[101] Heywood says 'it may be relatively straightforward for a medical practitioner to escape liability if all that is required is a regimented disclosure of all risks, followed by a subsequent signature on a form. This may be a legally valid consent; it is not informed consent, and for all intents

---

[95] Skegg, 'English Medical Law and "Informed Consent": An Antipodean Assessment and Alternative"(1999) Med L Rev at 142.

[96] Kennedy and Grubb, (eds) *Principles of Medical Law* (OUP, 1998) at para 3.86.

[97] The Canadian Supreme Court said that it would be better to abandon the term, in *Reibl v Hughes* [1980] 2 SCR 880,889.

[98] The High Court of Australia said that the phrase is apt to mislead, as it suggests a test of the validity of a patient's consent, in *Rogers v Whitaker* (1992) 175 CLR 479,490.

[99] Kirby, 'Informed Consent: What Does It Mean?' (1983) 9 Journal of Medical Ethics 69.

[100] Skegg, 'English Medical Law and "Informed Consent": An Antipodean Assessment and Alternative' (1999) Med L Rev at 142.

[101] 'For those who consider that informed consent is merely a medico-legal requirement which must be endured in order to protect the doctor, there is a danger that they will engage in a formulaic process which does little to inform the patient, and, ironically, just as little to protect the doctor.' Jones, 'Informed Consent and Other Fairy Stories' (1999) 7 Med L Rev 103–134 at 126.

and purposes it never will be.'[102] It is argued, however, that if the process of seeking informed consent becomes too demanding in terms of what is to be disclosed to and understood by the patient, then it will never be achievable. Many doctors misinterpret the obligation to obtain consent as a simple requirement to disclose facts and receive a signature rather than a process of discussion of facts and getting permission.[103] In that sense, then, there are two ways of defining 'informed consent'.

> In one sense, an informed consent is an autonomous authorization by individual patients or subjects. In the second sense, informed consent is analyzable in terms of institutional and policy rules of consent that collectively form the social practice of informed consent in institutional contexts.'[104] In the first meaning a person gives an informed consent only if s/he voluntarily gives permission having had disclosure of the medical facts and options, and having understood that information. In the second meaning a person gives consent if s/he signs an approval that complies with the institution's rules, policies and guidelines. The difference between these two meanings of consent may be described as the difference between the ideal and the reality.[105]

[9.53] As leading ethicists Faden and Beauchamp point out, the fundamental characteristics of the ideal of informed consent are that the patient substantially understands both the nature of the procedure he is authorising and the fact that he is authorising it, in other words, that he has a choice in the matter. Many patients seem to feel that they are simply being informed as to what is about to happen to them and that their signature is an acknowledgement of their having been informed.[106] It is important that those who criticise the ideal of informed consent on the basis of its impossibility or at least impracticability, realise that the ideal situation is not necessarily that the patient have *full* understanding of the medical facts, but rather a *substantial* understanding. Complicated medical information that may be difficult to comprehend may be explained in lay language, using common everyday analogies and numerical explanations of risk factors. The core information relevant to the medical procedure to be carried out would be that which patients usually regard as relevant, such as the success rates, risks,

---

[102] Heywood, 'Excessive Risk Disclosure: The Effect of the Law on Medical Practice' (2005) *Med Law I* 93–112 at 105.

[103] In many instances, the most inexperienced member of the surgical team is sent 'to consent' the patient, a term which itself suggests that something is done to the patient, usually for the purposes of avoiding legal liability, not a process that the patient participates in, or indeed controls. Junior medical staff may not be able to answer reasonable questions from patients, and may have an understandable difficulty in explaining operative procedures to patients that they have never even witnessed, let alone performed. Jones, 'Informed Consent and Other Fairy Stories' (1999) 7 Med L Rev 103–134 at 125. See also *Learning from Bristol: the Report of the Public Inquiry into Children's Heart Surgery at the Bristol Royal Infirmary 1984–1995* (2001, Cm 5297(1)), available at www.bristol-inquiryorg.uk/final_report/ (accessed 4 June 2011).

[104] Faden and Beauchamp, *A History and Theory of Informed Consent* (OUP, 1986).

[105] Donnelly, *Consent: Bridging the Gap Between Doctor and Patient* (Cork University Press, 2002) p 15.

[106] See Cassileth et al, 'Informed Consent – Why Are Its Goals Imperfectly Realized?' (1980) NEJM 896; Boisaubin and Dresser, 'Informed Consent in Emergency Care: Illusion and Reform' (1987) 16 Annals of Emergency Medicine 62, quoted in Donnelly, *Consent: Bridging the Gap Between Doctor and Patient* (Cork University Press, 2002) p 16.

alternatives, costs, experience of the doctor and the doctor's recommendation. Faden and Beauchamp also require additional information to be given, dependant upon the patient's own concerns and wishes. As Donnelly says, how are doctors to know what information that patient deems worthy of consideration?

> The deceptively simple answer is that a doctor will only find out what information is relevant to the patient by listening to the patient. This focus on the individual patient regards communication of information as a two-way process. Achieving the ethical ideal of informed consent is therefore not just about imparting information but also about listening to the patient.

[9.54] In fact, as Healy points out, the legal action for failing to obtain informed consent is designed to encourage doctors to enquire more of a patient before the patient commits to a choice. In this way it benefits doctors, as it absolves them of the legal complications that may ensue when a patient submits to a particular treatment which ultimately proves unsuccessful.[107] By ensuring that the patient was sufficiently informed before giving consent, the patient thereby shares responsibility for the decision.[108]

[9.55] Five elements are deemed crucial in the concept of consent to medical treatment: disclosure, comprehension, voluntariness, competence and consent. 'One can confidently presume that an act is an informed consent if a patient or subject agrees to an intervention on the basis of an understanding of relevant information, the consent is not controlled by influences that engineer the outcome, and the consent given was intended to be a consent and therefore qualified as a permission for an intervention.'[109] Communication is regarded as crucial to the informed consent process, as it enables the context, background knowledge and commitments and competences of patient and doctor to be discussed.[110] However, Donnelly quotes studies which indicate that good communication is lacking to a significant degree in health-care decision-making. She says that 'in study after study, patients have indicated that they do not understand the consent form they are signing and that they quickly forget even the most basic information relating to the procedures consented to.'[111] The law has traditionally not

---

[107] When a medical accident occurs, patients generally seek answers and information regarding what went wrong and why. The failure to provide such information is perhaps an understandable reaction on the part of the doctor, due to the fear of litigation that may ensue. However, ironically, the failure to provide information itself is a factor leading to a complaint or claim for negligence. See Vincent, Young and Phillips, 'Why Do People Sue Doctors?' (1994) 343 Lancet 1609; also the Wilson Report in the UK – *Being Heard – Report of the Review Committee on NHS Complaints Procedures* NHSE, 1994.

[108] Healy, 'Duties of Disclosure and the Elective Patient: A Case for Informed Consent' (1998) MLJI 25 –29 at 26.

[109] Beauchamp, 'Informed Consent' in Veatch (ed) *Medical Ethics* (2nd edn, Jones and Bartlett, 1997) at 185.

[110] Manson and O'Neill, *Rethinking Informed Consent In Bioethics* (Cambridge University Press, 2007) p 56.

[111] Donnelly, *Healthcare Decision-making and the Law*, at 85, referring to Bergler et al, 'Informed Consent: How Much Does the Patient Understand?' (1980) 27 Clinical Pharmacology and Therapeutics 435; Cassileth et al, 'Informed Consent – Why Are Its Goals Imperfectly Realised?' (1980) 302 New Eng J Med 896; Jones, 'Informed Consent and Other Fairy Stories'(1999) 7 Medical Law Review 103.

been concerned with communication but in recent years there has been increased emphasis on the development of relevant communication skills in medical schools in Ireland and elsewhere. The Medical Council states in its Guide to Professional Conduct and Ethics that 'effective communication is the key to achieving informed consent.'[112]

Disclosure of risk

[9.56] The tort of battery involves touching another person without consent or other lawful reason. It might therefore be thought that this might provide a potential breeding ground for cases involving medical procedures where valid consent had not been given due to failure to disclose risks inherent in the procedure. However, the tort of battery has not generally been employed in such circumstances by the courts, and it is thought that it would only be of use where there was a fundamental mistake on the patient's part in giving consent, such as where the patient consented to touching on the basis that it was therapeutic, when in fact it was for a research paper, financial gain or sexual gratification of the doctor.[113] Another possibility would be if the patient claimed to have consented to a specific surgeon carrying out the procedure, and a different surgeon performs the operation instead.[114] However, it would be difficult for the patient to make such a case if all that he could show was that he consented to the procedure being performed by a person with the requisite skill and experience, as opposed to an identifiable person.[115] If the patient consented to the medical procedure, and later complained that he would not have consented had the true facts been disclosed, this is unlikely to be treated as a battery, given that the treatment was provided in good faith believing the patient to have consented. Allegations of failure to obtain informed consent are more usually dealt with by the tort of negligence.

[9.57] The tort of negligence is generally concerned with breaches of doctors' duties which caused harm rather than vindication of patients' rights to respect for autonomy.[116] Therefore, it might be difficult to see why and how this form of action is employed in cases where it is alleged that there was a failure to obtain consent from the patient prior to treatment. Jones suggests that there is an inherent imbalance of power in the relationship between doctor and patient, which is remedied by the legal requirement to

---

[112] Medical Council, *Guide to Professional Conduct and Ethics* (7th edn, 2009), para 36.1. Available at http://www.medicalcouncil.ie (accessed 3 June 2011).

[113] Skegg, 'English Medical Law and "Informed Consent": An Antipodean Assessment And Alternative'(1999) Med L Rev at 142.

[114] In *Walsh v Family Planning Services* [1992] 1 IR 496, a vasectomy operation was extensively assisted by a third party under the close supervision of the performing surgeon. The patient was operated on under local anaesthetic and was therefore aware of this, although he had not given his prior consent. McKenzie J in the High Court held that a 'technical assault' had been committed. However, the majority of the Supreme Court disagreed on the basis that the patient had given his consent to the procedure on the basis that it would be carried out by a person with the requisite skill and competence, and that this in fact had been done. He had not specifically consented on the basis that only a particular surgeon would carry out the procedure.

[115] Donnelly, 'Confusion and Uncertainty: The Irish Approach to the Duty to Disclose Risks in Medical Treatment' (1996) MLJI 3.

[116] Maclean, 'The Doctrine of Informed Consent: Does It Exist and Has It Crossed the Atlantic?' (2004) 24 Legal Studies 386, 404–6.

provide the patient with adequate information.[117] However, since litigation for medical negligence is founded upon the establishment that harm was caused to the patient, doctors are primarily concerned with the disclosure to the patient of information relating to the risk of harm. This reinforces the view that although the ethical concept of consent is concerned with respect for the autonomous choice of patients, in legal terms 'informed consent' has more to do with the liability of professionals as agents of disclosure.

[9.58] Failure to provide certain information in advance of obtaining consent to medical treatment may lead to the imposition of liability in the law of tort. In relation to what information must be disclosed, however, there is a divergence of opinion. The test which has been traditionally been adopted until recently in England is that of the 'reasonable doctor' or the professional standard, whereas the test which has been adopted in Ireland and elsewhere is that of the 'reasonable patient', or the patient standard. The former test has been associated with a judicial deference to the tradition of medical paternalism which enables doctors to decide what is appropriate to disclose to patients whereas the latter is seen as more in keeping with respect for patient autonomy. These tests and the relevant case law are discussed below.

[9.59] One of the landmark cases in the development of the doctrine of informed consent is the American case of *Canterbury v Spence*[118] where a 19-year-old plaintiff had been suffering shoulder pains, the cause of which the doctor suspected was a ruptured disc. He recommended surgical removal of the bony arches of the patient's vertebrae to expose his spinal cord. The patient was told that the procedure was not any more serious than any other operation and consent was given to proceed with the surgery. Shortly after the surgery, the patient fell from his bed and experienced paralysis from the waist down. At the trial the doctor argued that disclosure of minute risks of complication (in this case, a 1 per cent risk of paralysis) was not sound medical practice, as it could deter patients from undergoing necessary surgery. In essence, he was arguing that the doctor himself should decide how much to tell his patient. The judge rejected the argument that the standard of disclosure should be assessed in the light of professional custom and instead proposed that the court should assess whether the patient had been given enough information to enable him to make an intelligent choice between alternative courses of treatment. To this end, a doctor must disclose all risks that might materially affect the patient's decision. The court should assess materiality by how a reasonable person, in what the physician knows or should know to be the patient's position, would be likely to attach significance to the risk or cluster of risks in deciding whether or not to forego the proposed therapy.[119] In this case, the patient's right to self-determination was affirmed as the primary motivation behind the Court's decision: 'The patient's right of self-decision shapes the boundaries of the duty to reveal'. However, there were other factors that led to the Court's rejection of the professional standard of disclosure, such as the difficulty in achieving a meaningful consensus within the medical community as to communication of risk information and the inevitable

---

[117] Jones, 'Informed Consent and Other Fairy Stories' (1999) 7 Med L Rev 103–134 at 129.

[118] *Canterbury v Spence* (1972) 464 F 2d 772.

[119] See generally Healy, *Medical Negligence: Common Law Perspectives* (Sweet and Maxwell, 1999) 91 *et seq.*

conclusion that a professional standard would leave the decision to the individual physician. In replacing the professional standard of disclosure, the Court opted for an objective reasonable patient standard. This was so as not to expose doctors to an unreasonably high standard whereby they would have to know exactly what each of their patients would consider important to his decision. The Court said that materiality was not a static concept to be decided once and for all, and for all categories of patient. It was for the doctor, on the basis of his medical training and expertise, to assess the severity of the risk by reference to the patient's own circumstances.

[9.60] Later decisions have further elucidated this important theory by shifting the focus away from disclosure as an isolated right, to a duty which is rooted in the doctor's own vocation.[120] An example of this is *Truman v Thomas*[121] where the judge emphasised the inequality of the doctor-patient relationship, the patient's reliance on the doctor for information and the obligation on the doctor to ensure that clinical decision-making is not made at arm's length. In this case a gynaecologist was found liable for the death of a woman who had refused to give consent for a cervical smear, which would have revealed her cancer at a treatable stage. The judge felt that disclosure of risks also includes disclosure of the risk of not being treated, and that the standard is higher where the consequences for the patient are fatal.

[9.61] As a general rule, the greater the risks to the patient which the doctor knows or should know, but which the patient cannot be expected to know, the greater is the duty on the doctor to give the necessary information. A doctor must warn of likely or probable side effects but there is less clarity as regards warning about remote possibilities. The demarcation line between these categories is sometimes difficult to draw. In the Australian decision, *Chappel v Hart*[122] a patient who was suffering with a persistent sore throat and difficulties in swallowing, attended an ear, nose and throat specialist. He recommended surgery but failed to advise the patient that there was a small but known risk that her vocal cords could be damaged as a result of the surgery. The operation was performed with due care but the risk materialised nonetheless and the patient suffered serious voice loss. It was accepted by the Court that the patient had expressed concern to the doctor regarding the possibility of voice loss. Gummow J followed *Rogers v Whitaker*[123] stating that a doctor has a duty to warn a patient of a 'material risk' inherent in a proposed treatment and that a 'risk is material if, in the circumstances of the particular case, a reasonable person in the patient's position, if warned of the risk, would be likely to attach significance to it or if the medical practitioner is or should be reasonably aware that the particular patient, if warned of the risk, would be likely to attach significance to it.'

[9.62] This case also adopts a subjective approach where the courts will consider what the particular patient's response would have been if the proper information had been given. This approach 'accords maximum weight to the patient's interest in making their

---

120 Healy, *Medical Negligence: Common Law Perspectives* (Sweet and Maxwell, 1999) p 108. For an excellent analysis of medical negligence generally, see Healy, *Medical Malpractice Law,* (Round Hall, 2009).
121 *Truman v Thomas* 611 P 2d 902 (1980).
122 *Chappel v Hart* (1998) 72 ALJR 1344.
123 *Rogers v Whitaker* (1992) 175 CLR 479.

own decision about whether or not to have a given treatment.'[124] Kirby J noted that a more objective approach had been adopted in Canada and the US where the courts looked at what the response of a reasonable person in the patient's position would have been, rather than at the particular patient. He acknowledged the possibility that patients may use the subjective approach to bring claims with the benefit of hindsight, but felt that these dangers should not be overstated: 'Tribunals of fact can be trusted to reject absurd, self-interested assertions.'[125]

[9.63] One of the important features of this case is that, although the patient would probably have consented to the operation even if the risk had been disclosed to her, she would have taken more time over her decision, would have sought a second opinion, would have sought the most experienced surgeon and would have chosen the time of the operation. Thus, the High Court held that 'in all likelihood she would not have suffered the random chance of injury to her vocal cord.' This represented 'nothing more than an acceptance that such injury was an extremely rare occurrence.'[126]

[9.64] Stauch points out that the principal reason for imposing a duty to warn of risks is not to reduce the likelihood of the risks materialising, as that is, to some extent, unavoidable in the medical context.

> Rather, it is to promote the patient's decision-making autonomy: the latter's right 'to decide for himself whether or not to submit to the treatment in question'. Making one's own choice in this context necessarily includes assessing the various risks and benefits presented by the available treatment options (including non-treatment) and deciding, in the light of one's general goals and values, which of those risks one is prepared to run. The doctor, who, even with the best of intentions, offers an incomplete picture of the therapy he proposes by withholding information as to risks, usurps this right of choice.[127]

The inquisitive patient

[9.65] The courts have recognised that patients vary in their desire for knowledge and that some will therefore be more inquisitive than others. In *Sidaway v Bethlem Royal Hospital*[128] the majority of the judges took the view that where the patient asked questions, the doctor should answer them honestly and, per Lords Bridge and Keith, as fully as possible. However, the Court of Appeal subsequently interpreted these judicial opinions in a restrictive fashion in *Blyth v Bloomsbury HA*.[129] At first instance it had been held that in the context of the inquisitive patient who makes a specific enquiry, it would be right to give the whole picture. However, on appeal, Kerr LJ held that *Sidaway* meant that the professional standard test was 'all-pervasive' in this context and that the question of what a plaintiff should be told in answer to a query cannot be divorced from this test any more than when no query is made.

---

124 Stauch, 'Taking the Consequences for Failure to Warn of Medical Risks' (2000) 63 MLR 261 at 262.

125 *Rogers v Whitaker* (1992) 175 CLR 479 at para 93.7.

126 *Rogers v Whitaker* (1992) 175 CLR 479 per Kirby J at para 91.

127 Stauch, 'Taking the Consequences for Failure to Warn of Medical Risks' (2000) 63 MLR 261 at 267.

128 *Sidaway v Bethlem Royal Hospital* [1985] 1 AC 871.

129 *Blyth v Bloomsbury HA* [1993] 4 Med L Rev 151 (CA).

[9.66] In Australia, the case of *Rogers v Whitaker*[130] also raised the issue of the information to be given to the inquiring patient. In this case the patient became almost totally blind after surgery conducted by an ophthalmic surgeon. The surgery was performed with the required skill and care but the patient complained that the surgeon had failed to warn her that, as a result of surgery on her right eye, she might develop a condition known as sympathetic ophthalmia in her left eye. The development of this condition and the consequent loss of sight in her left eye were particularly devastating for the patient, who had lost sight in her right eye as a child due to an injury. When she went for an eye examination in relation to getting reading glasses she was referred to a consultant surgeon for possible surgery on her right eye. She was advised that surgery would improve the appearance of her eye and would probably restore significant sight to it. Not only did the surgery not improve the sight in her right eye, but it also led to loss of sight in her left eye (a 1 in 14,000 chance). As a result, the patient was left almost totally blind. Except for death under anaesthetic, it was the worst possible outcome for the patient.

[9.67] This patient had incessantly questioned the doctor as to possible complications and was keenly interested in the outcome of the proposed surgery, including the danger of accidental interference with her good left eye. On the day before the surgery she asked whether something could be put over her good eye to ensure that nothing happened to it and an entry was made in the hospital notes to the effect that she was very worried that the wrong eye would be operated upon. She did not ask the specific question as to whether an operation on her right eye could affect her left eye. There was a body of medical opinion to the effect that only if she had asked that specific question should she have been told about the danger of sympathetic ophthalmia. However, the judge was satisfied that although she may not have asked the right question, she made it clear that her great concern was that no injury would befall her good eye. This was reasonable in the circumstances of an elective procedure.[131]

[9.68] In a general sense it may be difficult to draw hard and fast distinctions between the inquisitive patient and one who may desire the same knowledge, but who is too intimidated by the medical experience to make the necessary enquiries. Patients are

---

[130] *Rogers v Whitaker* [1992] 67 ALJR 47 (Australian High Court).

[131] Skegg argues that in cases such as this it might be possible to bring an action for deceit as well as negligence on the basis that the doctor has made a false representation of fact, by omitting a vital piece of information, with the intention that the patient should rely on it. Although the patient may experience difficulty in establishing that the doctor knew that the representation was false, the patient could also claim that the doctor was negligent in not knowing. If the doctor claimed that he did know, then his only defence would be to claim that non-disclosure was in the interests of the patient, which would be extremely difficult in the case of a patient who makes specific enquiries and has shown herself to be extremely worried about the risk which subsequently transpires, as in the *Rogers* case. See Skegg, 'Informed Consent to Medical Procedures' (1974) 15 Medical Science Law 124 at 131. Healy admits that such an action would not be likely to float in the Irish or English jurisdiction, as the tort of deceit has not been seen to arise in the medical context where half-truths and therapeutic lies have been implicitly accepted by the courts. See Healy, 'Duties of Disclosure and the Inquisitive Patient: A Case for Informed Consent' (1998) MLJI 69–73 at 71.

expected to conform to their doctor's recommended treatments and not to disrupt the doctor's busy schedule.

> Illness disrupts one's natural equilibrium, one's perspective on life, and one's customary ability to translate will to action. It renders the person vulnerable; the temptation to exalt the one who potentially can help grows accordingly. In a hospital ward, the patient is sartorially and behaviorally exposed. Bed-bound and bed-clothes, encompassed by sickness, the distinct scents of the hospital, and the dominant colour of white, the patient is very much a person in alien surroundings, "a 'captive' who cannot leave the hospital without serious consequences to himself".[132]

[9.69] In their report *Informed Decisions about Medical Procedures* (1989) the Victorian, New South Wales and Australian Law Reform Commissions identify useful factors relevant to a court's determination of the central issue of the reasonable patient test, that is, whether a particular risk is material:

(i)   The personality and temperament of the patient – this includes an appraisal of the patient's intelligence and apparent understanding, in light of the simplicity or complexity of the recommendation the doctor is making.

(ii) Whether the patient wants information – if the patient wants information rather than reassurance, then the doctor is obliged to give it. If the patient does not want information, then the doctor is not obliged to force it upon her. In deciding whether the patient wants information or not, the doctor must exercise reasonable care and judgment.

(iii) Whether the patient asks questions – American courts have recognised that many patients will be unable to ask the relevant questions due to lack of knowledge, fear, illness or being overawed by their situation. Doctors should be required to give relevant information whether it is asked for or not. However, the Australian courts have said that more information should be given if the patient asks questions as this indicates what information is "material" for that patient.

(iv) The patients' level of understanding – the patient need not be cross-examined by the doctor but the doctor should give information which the patient can understand after an appraisal of her intelligence and understanding.

(v)   The nature of the treatment – more drastic treatment requires more information. However if the treatment is necessary to save the patient's life it may require less explanation than less urgent treatment, even if it is relatively serious.

(vi) The magnitude of the possible harm – there is a greater duty to provide information about the possibility of serious harm, even where the possibility is slight.

(vii) The likelihood of the risk – there is a greater obligation to discuss risks that are more likely to occur than those that are rare, even if the harm is relatively slight. However, it is probably not necessary to discuss risks which are inherent

---

[132] Healy, 'Duties of Disclosure and the Inquisitive Patient: A Case for Informed Consent' (1998) MLJI 69–73 at 71, quoting from Tagliacozzo and Mauksch, 'The Patient's View of the Patient's Role' in *Patients, Physicians, and Illness: A Sourcebook In Behavioral Science* (3rd edn, New York: Free Press, 1979) p196.

in any operation, such as the risks of anesthesia or infection after surgery, as the patient would be assumed to know these. It is also important to be aware that knowledge of alternative treatments may be as important to the patient as disclosure of the risks of the proposed treatment.[133]

(viii) The general surrounding circumstances – the duty may be affected by emergency conditions, or the absence of an opportunity for calm reflection or alternative source of advice.

Elective treatment

[9.70] In the context of disclosure it is also important to look at the distinction often drawn between elective and non-elective procedures. Where a treatment is immediately therapeutic, there may be little choice for the patient but to give consent to the treatment, particularly in an emergency. However, where the procedure is elective, the patient has more time to consider the information, weigh the risks and benefits, examine the alternatives and reflect on the decision. The difference between the two broad treatment types also impacts upon information disclosure as, in the case of the elective patient, the decision is much more of a choice to be made on the basis of substantial understanding of the procedure and its consequences, rather than a medical necessity which the patient cannot afford to refuse in any event.

[9.71] The majority of cases that have raised this distinction have concerned sterilisation procedures. This kind of procedure is usually perceived as an elective treatment to enable the patient to later enjoy sexual intercourse without concerns regarding reproduction. However, it is also possible that sterilisation could be, for some, a therapeutic treatment on the basis that further pregnancy might be dangerous for the woman in question. It is due to this unsatisfactory line-drawing that the distinction between elective and therapeutic treatment has sometimes been criticised as unworkable and artificial.[134] Healy argues, on the contrary, that such distinctions are possible if the doctor communicates with his patient in relation to the patient's demands, needs, circumstances and expectations. He argues that in cases involving non-disclosure of risks, the defence is often that the information would have harmed the patient by deterring him from consenting to the necessary procedure. In elective procedures, it will not harm the patient if he elects not to proceed with a treatment that he can afford not to undergo. Indeed 'where the treatment carries high risks, alarming the patient by discussing its full possible implications tends very much to be in that patient's best interests.'[135] Therefore, the justification for non-disclosure here is very weak.

[9.72] The distinction between elective and non-elective (or therapeutic) treatment is sometimes difficult but has been an important feature of some of the cases. 'The most basic difference between the two in obvious cases is that an elective treatment is opted for by a patient *more* freely and *less* for reasons of medical necessity. It is a treatment

---

[133] *Haughian v Paine* [1987] 37 DLR (4) 624 (Sask CA).

[134] Brazier, 'Patient Autonomy and Consent to Treatment: The Role of the Law?' (1987) 7 LS 169 at 183.

[135] Healy, 'Duties of Disclosure and the Elective Patient: A Case for Informed Consent' (1998) MLJI 25–29 at 29.

which comparatively the patient can afford *not* to undergo.'[136] The motives involved in a decision to undergo treatment may often be a mixture of medical necessity and social reasons. In such cases, is the distinction meaningful? It may be argued that doctors should not be expected to place such treatments into legalistic pigeon-holes in advance of every instance of disclosure. However, the extent to which any treatment may be therapeutic or elective for any particular person should become clear to any doctor following basic communication with his patient as to what he expects or hopes for from the treatment.

Causation

[9.73] Another important aspect of the legal doctrine of informed consent relates to causation. The traditional approach has been to assess whether the patient would have undergone the relevant procedure even if the risks had been disclosed to him. If the court is satisfied that the patient would have proceeded in any event, then the failure to disclose risks to the patient has not caused the injury complained of by the patient. As Lord Bingham put it in *Chester v Afshar*:

> [A] claimant is not entitled to be compensated, and a defendant is not bound to compensate the claimant for damage not caused by the negligence complained of. The patient's right to be appropriately warned is an important right, which few doctors in the current legal and social climate would consciously or deliberately violate. I do not for my part think that the law should seek to reinforce that right by providing for the payment of potentially large damages by a defendant whose violation of that right is not shown to have worsened the physical condition of the claimant.[137]

[9.74] However, the majority of the House of Lords in *Chester* held that although the patient in that case could not say that she would not have had the surgery had she been warned of the risks involved, she should nonetheless be awarded compensation for the injuries sustained. This decision represents a departure from the principles of causation which had previously been employed by the courts. The House of Lords was prepared to depart from these principles in the interests of justice, as otherwise the patient would have been left without a remedy. The Court held that if she had been warned, the plaintiff would not have gone ahead when she did, that she would have discussed the matter with others and explored other options. Although the inherent risk would have been precisely the same if she had had the surgery at another time or with another surgeon, and therefore the doctor's breach of duty did not cause or increase the risk of injury to the plaintiff, the issue of causation could not be separated from the issue of policy. Lord Hope started with the proposition that the law which imposed the duty to warn on the doctor has at its heart the right of the patient to make an informed choice as to whether, and if so when and by whom, to be operated on. Some patients will find such a choice difficult and will require time to think, take advice and weigh up the alternatives, whereas others will find the decision easy. The same duty to warn is owed to both, so to leave the patient who would find the decision difficult without a remedy would render the duty useless and would discriminate against those who cannot honestly say they would have declined the operation had they been warned. He went on to say:

---

[136] Healy, *Medical Negligence: Common Law Perspectives* (Sweet and Maxwell, 1999) p 149–150.

[137] *Chester v Afshar* [2004] UKHL 41 para 9.

The function of the law is to enable rights to be vindicated and to provide remedies when duties have been breached. Unless this is done the duty is a hollow one, stripped of all practical force and devoid of all content. It will have lost its ability to protect the patient and thus to fulfil the only purpose which brought it into existence.

[9.75] The Court referred to the Australian High Court decision in *Chappel v Hart*,[138] discussed earlier, in which a patient complained that she had not been warned of the risk that an operation on her oesophagus might result in perforation of the oesophagus which could damage her vocal chords. The plaintiff claimed that if she had been informed, she would have deferred the operation and had it performed instead by the most experienced surgeon in the field then available. The majority of the Court held in favour of the plaintiff, with Kirby J stating that:

> The 'commonsense' which guides courts in this area of disclosure supports Mrs Hart's recovery. So does the setting of standards which uphold the importance of the legal duty that was breached here. This is the duty which all health care professionals in the position of Dr Chappel must observe: the duty of informing patients about risks, answering their questions candidly and respecting their rights, including (where they so choose) to postpone medical procedures and to go elsewhere for treatment.

Donnelly says that the speeches of the majority in *Chester* are 'striking in the number of times they refer to autonomy.' As a result of this case, she says 'on both sides of the Atlantic, it may now be said that there is a positive obligation derived from respect for autonomy that certain information must be given to patients in advance of treatment.'[139]

English case law on risk disclosure

[9.76] In terms of the content of the information to be provided to the patient, the first important English case was *Bolam v Friern Hospital Management Committee*[140] where it was alleged that the plaintiff had not been warned of the risks involved in the treatment, thereby negating the possibility that he might have the opportunity to decide whether he wanted to take those risks. McNair J directed the jury that they had to consider whether the doctor had fallen 'below a proper standard of competent professional opinion on this question of whether or not it is right to warn'. This instruction has come to be known as the '*Bolam* test' and has been applied in many cases in the UK since the 1980s.[141] 'According to this test, practitioners are not negligent if they act in accordance with a practice accepted at the time as proper by a responsible body of medical practitioners.'[142]

[9.77] The landmark case of *Sidaway v Board of Governors of Bethlem Royal Hospital*[143] provided a good opportunity for the House of Lords to consider the

---

138 *Chappel v Hart* [1998] 195 CLR 232.

139 Donnelly, *Healthcare Decision-making and the Law, Autonomy, Capacity and the Limits of Liberalism,* (Cambridge University Press, 2010) at 82.

140 *Bolam v Friern Hospital Management Committee* [1957] 1 WLR 582

141 The House of Lords affirmed the Bolam test in the context of treatment in *Whitehouse v Jordan* [1981] 1 WLR 246, and in relation to diagnosis in *Maynard v West Midlands Regional Health Authority* [1984] 1 WLR 634.

142 Skegg, 'English Medical Law and "Informed Consent": An Antipodean Assessment and Alternative'(1999) Med L Rev 142.

143 *Sidaway v Board of Governors of Bethlem Royal Hospital* [1985] AC 871.

application of the *Bolam* test to the duty to disclose. In this case, the plaintiff, who had suffered recurrent pain in her neck, shoulder and arms underwent an operation performed by a senior neuro-surgeon at the defendant's hospital. The operation carried an inherent risk (1–2 per cent) of damage to the spinal column and nerve roots. As a consequence of the operation the plaintiff was severely disabled. The judge found that the surgeon did not tell the plaintiff that this was an operation of choice rather than necessity and did not tell her of the risk of damage to the spinal cord. This appeared to be consistent with medical practice in that speciality at the time. The majority of the House of Lords took the view that sufficient information had been given to the patient for her to make an informed decision as to the operation and therefore the doctor had not breached his duty to her.

[9.78] In the judgments of the House of Lords it was pointed out that there are two extreme positions that may be adopted in relation to the disclosure of information to patients. One is to tell the patient of all risks involved in the treatment. The Court said that this did not seem to have been accepted in any jurisdiction, as patients are expected to be aware of the general risks inherent in surgery under anaesthesia and some risks are too remote to justify disclosure. The second position is that once the doctor has decided what treatment is in the patient's best interests, he should not alarm the patient by volunteering a warning of any risk involved, however grave and substantial, unless asked by the patient. This paternalistic approach of 'doctor knows best', according to the Court, did not appear to have the support of the contemporary medical profession, as it would effectively exclude the patient's right to decide his/her own treatment, or seek a second opinion before submitting to treatment or surgery.

[9.79] The judges ranged in their views from adopting a strict line on *Bolam* to recommending a watered-down version of it. Lord Diplock was the only judge to wholeheartedly take on the *Bolam* test. He was satisfied that the decision as to what information to disclose was that of the doctor in the exercise of his professional skill and judgment in the same way as any other aspect of the doctor's duty of care towards his patient. Lord Bridge agreed that the issue of disclosure was to be decided on the basis of expert medical evidence but that there were some risks (such as a 10 per cent risk of a stroke) that were so obviously necessary to disclose that no reasonable doctor would fail to disclose them. Lord Templeman did not believe that the patient was entitled to know everything, nor that the doctor was entitled to decide everything. He said, 'the duty of the doctor in these circumstances, subject to his overriding duty to have regard to the best interests of the patient, is to provide the patient with information which will enable the patient to make a balanced judgment if the patient chooses to make a balanced judgment.' Lord Scarman took the view that full disclosure should be made of all material risks incident to the proposed treatment so that the patient, not the doctor, could make the decision whether to undergo treatment or not.

[9.80] The Court examined the test of the reasonable patient put forward in the US case of *Canterbury v Spence*,[144] but regarded it as impractical in application for a number of reasons. First, it was thought unrealistic to expect the doctor to seek to educate the patient to his own standard of medical knowledge of all the relevant factors that may be involved in the decision to be made by the patient. Secondly, the test was so imprecise as

---

[144]   *Canterbury v Spence* (1972) 464 F 2d 772.

to be meaningless in the sense that if it were to be left to individual judges to decide for themselves what a reasonable patient in this particular person's position would want to know, the outcome of litigation in this area would be unpredictable. The Court also noted that there seemed to have been a move away from this concept in the United States with many states enacting legislation curtailing the operation of the doctrine. The Court therefore rejected this approach as a solution to the problem of safeguarding the patient's right to decide whether to undergo a treatment proposed by his/her doctor. The preferred approach was to leave it to the clinical judgment of the doctor. The doctor must decide what is to be said and how it is to be said, bearing in mind the patient's right to information upon which to make a balanced judgment.

[9.81] In relation to the risks to be disclosed to the patient, Lord Bridge said that a doctor might be considered negligent if he failed to disclose information that was so obviously necessary to an informed choice on the part of the patient that no reasonably prudent medical man would fail to disclose it. He gave an example of a 10 per cent risk of a stroke, as being a substantial risk of grave adverse consequences. However, this formulation of risks as a percentage has the drawback that it may reduce the law's approach to an arithmetical one, which is concerned with experts' views of percentages. It also presumes that there is a level of harmonisation of views within the profession in relation to the level of risk that ought to be disclosed, whereas in reality experts will inevitably disagree as to what is the precise level of risk in any given case.

[9.82] To a certain extent it might be said that the guidelines of the profession itself might be read as an indication of the level of risk to be disclosed to patients. The General Medical Council (GMC) states that the information that patients want or ought to know before treatment may include details of the diagnosis and prognosis, uncertainties about the diagnosis, options for alternative treatment or non-treatment, the purpose of the proposed intervention, explanations as to the likely benefits and any serious or frequently occurring risks, and details of the experience of the doctor responsible for the treatment.[145] It goes on to advise doctors on the best time to discuss treatment with patients, to be part of a continuing dialogue with patients regarding changes in their condition, to provide clear explanations and answers to questions, to provide information in a considerate way, to allow time for reflection, and to involve other members of the team in discussions. These guidelines may be an admirable attempt to deal with the issues raised by the 'right' of patients to informed consent but whether they will be incorporated into legal doctrine through case law remains to be seen.[146]

[9.83] 'Despite the fact that Lord Diplock was in a minority of one in relation to the applicability of the '*Bolam* test' to disclosure, his view was the one accepted in the first Court of Appeal decision to consider the applicability of *Sidaway*.'[147] In *Gold v*

---

145 General Medical Council (UK) Guidance on Consent. Available at http://www.gmc-uk.org (accessed 3 June 2011).

146 Jones, 'Informed Consent and Other Fairy Stories' (1999) 7 Med L Rev 103–134 suggests that 'the iterative process between case law and professional guidance may, in time, create a more substantive "right" to truly informed consent for patients.' p 134.

147 Donnelly, 'Confusion and Uncertainty: The Irish Approach to the Duty to Disclose Risks in Medical Treatment' (1996) MLJI 3–8 at 4.

Haringey Health Authority[148] the Court of Appeal adopted the *Bolam* test as set out by Lord Diplock in *Sidaway* in holding that although all the expert witnesses (including those called on behalf of the defendant) stated that they would have disclosed the risk of a sterilisation operation failing to achieve complete sterility, there was nonetheless a responsible body of opinion within the profession at the time the procedure was carried out who would not have disclosed the risk.

[9.84] Mason and Laurie point out that there has been a movement away from *Bolam* in recent years and that 'rigid adherence to the *Bolam* standard in disputes over information disclosure is no longer the approach of the UK courts.'[149] For example, in *Pearce v United Bristol Healthcare NHS Trust*[150] a couple whose child had died in utero almost three weeks overdue, sued their doctor for failing to disclose the risks of fetal death in the womb as a result of a delay in delivery. Although the Court endorsed *Sidaway* and accepted *Bolam* as the relevant test, it also held that significant risks must be disclosed to enable the patient to make a balanced decision. Lord Woolf said:

> In a case where it is being alleged that a plaintiff has been deprived of the opportunity to make a proper decision as to what course of action he or she should take in relation to treatment, it seems to me to be the law…that if there is a significant risk which would affect the judgment of a reasonable patient, then in the normal course it is the responsibility of the doctor to inform the patient of that risk, if the information is needed so that the patient can determine for him or herself as to what course he or she would adopt.

[9.85] The Court did not clarify what it meant by 'significant' risks, although Lord Bridge's example of a 10 per cent risk in *Sidaway* was cited with approval by Lord Woolfe. Mason and Laurie say that this case provides little evidence that significance would be decided by patient-orientated criteria but the language used by the Court of Appeal is nonetheless 'suggestive of a movement away from the precedents of the past', as doctors now have to take into account all the relevant considerations.[151] Where there is a high statistical risk of serious harm which no reasonable person would withhold, the doctor must disclose it. In *Birch v University College London Hospital NHS Foundation Trust*[152] where the plaintiff suffered a stroke as a result of a cerebral catheter angiogram, liability was imposed for failure to discuss with the patient the different imaging methods of an MRI scan and an angiogram and the comparative risks and benefits associated with each. Lord Cranston said that a patient should be informed not only of the objectively significant risks of the proposed procedure but also how this risk compared to the risks associated with other procedures which might be relevant to the patient. He said:

---

[148] *Gold v Haringey Health Authority* [1988] QB 481.

[149] Mason and Laurie, *Law and Medical Ethics* (8th edn, OUP, 2010) para 4.129 referring to illustrative cases such as *Smith v Tunbridge Wells Health Authority* [1994] 5 Med L Rev 334; *McAllister v Lewisham and North Southwark Health Authority* [1994] 5 Med L Rev 343; *Newell v Goldenberg* [1995] 6 Med L Rev 371; and *Lybert v Warrington Health Authority* [1996] 7 Med Rev 71.

[150] *Pearce v United Bristol Healthcare NHS Trust* (1999) 48 BMLR 118.

[151] Mason and Laurie, *Law and Medical Ethics* (8th edn, OUP, 2010) para 4.133.

[152] *Birch v University College London Hospital NHS Foundation Trust* [2008] EWHC 2237.

[T]he duty to inform a patient of the significant risks will not be discharged unless she is made aware that fewer, or no risks, are associated with another procedure. In other words, unless the patient is informed of the comparative risks of different procedures, she will not be in a position to give her fully informed consent to one procedure rather than another.[153]

[9.86] A more recent Scottish case, *Montgomery v Lanarkshire Health Board*[154] has raised further questions in relation to antenatal risk disclosure. In this case the plaintiff (referred to in the Scottish legal system as the pursuer) brought an action against a consultant obstetrician who had delivered her son. During the labour the baby's head was delivered and he showed signs of shoulder dystocia.[155] The rest of his body was delivered approximately 12 minutes later, during which time he sustained acute hypoxia resulting in renal damage, epileptic seizures and cerebral palsy, as well as other injuries. In addition to a claim for negligence in the management of her labour, the plaintiff, who was diabetic and of short stature, also alleged that no ordinary competent obstetrician acting with reasonable skill and care would have failed to advise her of the risks of shoulder dystocia during vaginal delivery and failed to offer her the option of a caesarean delivery. The risk of shoulder dystocia in diabetics whose babies weigh over 4 kg was about 9–10 per cent but in the majority of cases this could be dealt with by a simple procedure, with the result that the risk of an adverse outcome was about 1–2 per cent. Lord Bannatyne focused on the risk of adverse outcome rather than the risk of occurrence, which meant that the plaintiff's case was weaker and her claim was unsuccessful. It has been argued that, in line with the *Chester, Pearce,* and *Birch* cases, Lord Bannatyne should have considered 'what the reasonable person, pregnant, diabetic, short in stature, and anxious about giving birth by vaginal delivery, would have found significant. The likely answer to this line of inquiry is that a 1–2 per cent risk of cerebral palsy would be significant and therefore there ought to be a duty on the doctor to disclose it."[156] Heywood says that this case is indicative of a historical approach from the courts which was thought to be in decline in recent years. He acknowledges that a certain amount of risk taking is an inescapable consequence of medicine, but if risks are to be taken, they must be taken in the full knowledge and with the consent of the patient.

Defence of therapeutic privilege

[9.87] It seems relatively clear that there is no obligation to inform patients about the risk of death from general anaesthetic, as this is something that patients are presumed to know. There is no obligation to inform patients about the risk of bleeding, pain, scars, and infection following surgery, for the same reason.[157] The question of whether the doctor must disclose information which he believes to be potentially harmful to the patient or of which the patient has declined to know, remains open. If the doctor can

---

[153] See Heywood, 'Medical Disclosure of Alternative Treatments' (2009) 68 CLJ 30.

[154] *Montgomery v Lanarkshire Health Board* [2010] CSOH 104.

[155] This can occur after the delivery of the head when the baby's shoulder cannot pass below the pubic bone, or requires significant manipulation to do so. Shoulder dystocia is an obstetrical emergency, and fetal demise can occur if the infant is not delivered, due to compression of the umbilical cord within the birth canal.

[156] Heywood, 'Negligent Antenatal Disclosure and Management Of Labour' (2011) 19 Med L Review 140–149 at 147.

[157] Jones, 'Informed Consent and Other Fairy Stories' (1999) 7 Med L Rev at 112.

explain his failure to warn of risks on the basis that such a warning would cause undue distress and anxiety that would somehow harm the patient, then it may be that he can bring himself within a responsible body of medical opinion that would not make such disclosure, and escape liability under the *Bolam* test. Heywood says the resolution of such a dilemma involves the balancing of professional moral duties against patients' rights.[158] He cites a hypothetical example of an elderly patient with a life-threatening condition who is informed about a 1 per cent risk of trivial harm and is sufficiently frightened by the prospect that he refuses the surgery and subsequently dies. Heywood asks whether this is excessive disclosure sparked by a fear of litigation which is against the patient's best interests. It brings into conflict the principle of respect for autonomy of the patient and the principle of non-maleficence, which proclaims that the doctor must do no harm. He submits that the only practical way to address this issue is for doctors to use their clinical discretion in assessing the circumstances of the individual patient in deciding what to disclose. In Sidaway, Lord Scarman said that even if the risk was material, the doctor would not be liable for non-disclosure if, having made a reasonable assessment of the patient's condition, he took the view that a warning would be detrimental to the patient's health. The defence of 'therapeutic privilege' thus allows doctors to withhold information from patients on the basis that it might cause them harm. Critics would undoubtedly argue that such an approach is a reflection of the paternalism of the past, and a refutation of the right to patient autonomy. However, where the defence is used only in situations where the patient suffers from serious anxiety disorders or other psychological conditions which would render it likely that the information would cause actual or physical harm to the patient, or make him so emotionally distressed that he would be rendered incapable of making a decision, it may arguably have an appropriate place in good medical practice.

Waiver of information

[9.88] A further issue arises in the suggestion that patients might be allowed to waive their right to make an informed decision. In this way the patient's autonomy remains intact in that the patient, as ultimate decision-maker, decides that he does not want any or detailed information about the treatment. However, there are no legal precedents in England or Ireland to suggest that such a waiver would excuse a doctor for treating patients who suffer a risk inherent in the procedure which they chose not to receive information about. Heywood argues that the courts would be likely to recognise the waiver in terms of information about risks and alternatives, providing there was strong evidence that the original intention of the doctor was one of disclosure. He also says that from an ethical point of view, doctors ought to recognise waivers as an exercise of autonomy, as forcing information on patients who have made it clear that they do not wish to know certain things may be said to represent bad medical practice.[159]

---

158 Heywood, 'Excessive Risk Disclosure: The Effect of the Law on Medical Practice' (2005) Medical Law International Vol 7, 93–112.

159 Heywood, 'Excessive Risk Disclosure: The Effect of the Law on Medical Practice' (2005) Medical Law International Vol 7, at 101. See also Kihlbom, 'Autonomy and Negatively Informed Consent' (2008) J Med Ethics 34: 146–149.

[9.89] This issue was also explored in the Irish Report on Post Mortem Practice and Procedure published in 2006.[160] The context of this Report was the removal and retention of the organs of deceased children without the knowledge or consent of the parents in some instances. One of the difficulties inherent in the post mortem procedure relates to communication with bereaved families. Many, though not all, parents feel that they must be informed of the details of each organ to be retained and the purpose for which it will be used. However, other parents prefer not to know the details of the procedure but are nonetheless satisfied to allow the examination to proceed. The Report discussed the use of the word 'authorisation' rather than 'consent' in these circumstances.

> Authorisation meets the concerns of those parents who do not wish to receive information about post-mortem examination and/or organ retention, but who nonetheless do not object to these procedures being carried out. 'Consent' requires the provision and comprehension of information, whereas 'authorisation' does not impose this requirement. Parents may thus authorise procedures without having information forced upon them.

[9.90] The Report stated that whereas 'consent' may be seen as a passive acceptance of a proposal put to the parents by someone else, 'authorisation' is a more active participation – the parents can choose, with the benefit of as much information as they require, whether to give someone power to do something in relation to their child. Without the exercise of their authority, the procedure will not take place.

> *Authorisation* allows those who do not wish to be given details about organ removal to nonetheless make a valid decision. It therefore empowers parents to remain in control of the post-mortem process while at the same time respecting their right not to be told the distressing details of it. Information is not being withheld from them, rather they are exercising their choice not to access such information and yet remain involved in the decision-making process.

Following the publication of this Report, the Department of Health undertook to introduce a new Human Tissue Bill and to that end a public consultation exercise took place in 2009.[161] It is unclear at the time of writing whether the model of authorisation recommended in the report will be adopted in legislation on this issue.

Irish case law on risk disclosure

[9.91] The law relating to medical negligence in Ireland emanates from a test put forward by the Supreme Court in *Dunne v National Maternity Hospital*.[162] The Court held that to establish negligence the plaintiff would have to prove that the defendant doctor had been 'guilty of such failure as no medical practitioner of equal specialist or general status and skill would be guilty of if acting with ordinary care.'[163] This is clearly an endorsement of the professional standard, or 'reasonable doctor' test of negligence. The Court, however, did not adopt the *Bolam* test completely, as the Court also held that

---

[160] Report of Dr Deirdre Madden on Post Mortem Practice and Procedure (Government Publications Office, 2006).
[161] http://www.dohc.ie/consultations/closed/human_tissue_bill/ (accessed 16 February 2011).
[162] *Dunne v National Maternity Hospital* [1989] IR 91.
[163] *Dunne v National Maternity Hospital* [1989] IR 91 at 109.

the doctor would not be protected by general and approved practice if this practice has inherent defects that would be obvious to anyone giving it due consideration.

[9.92] The Supreme Court decision in *Daniels v Heskin*[164] was the only one to consider the issue of disclosure prior to 1992. In this case, the Court considered the duty of a doctor to tell his patient that a broken part of a needle had been left in her body during stitching after childbirth. The doctor had left instructions that the patient should be x-rayed within six weeks if the needle had not been found. When this was done and an examination carried out by a different doctor, an operation was performed to remove the needle. The majority of the Supreme Court held that there was no obligation on the doctor to inform the plaintiff or her husband of the presence of the needle. Lavery J, with whom Murnaghan and O'Byrne JJ agreed, was of the view that if a dangerous operation was planned, then the doctor must disclose the risks involved. However, in other situations, the doctor could decide for himself whether or not to make disclosure. The decision is of limited value in the sense that it is unclear to what Lavery J was referring as a 'dangerous' operation, and it has not been referred to by many later judgments on the issue.

[9.93] In *Walsh v Family Planning Services*[165] the plaintiff had a vasectomy operation for contraceptive purposes. Prior to the operation he had been told that the operation would not disimprove his sex life and may possibly improve it. He was told that there might be some discomfort and swelling after the operation and that, very rarely, some patients experience pain for some years later. The patient suffered a variety of problems after the operation which included severe groin pain, impotence and eventual removal of his left testicle. Expert evidence showed that he suffered from a rare, but known, possible consequence of vasectomy, called orchialgia. At the time of the operation there was no known practice regarding disclosure of the risk of this possible condition. Finlay CJ was the only judge to adopt the reasonable doctor test put forward in *Dunne*, with the caveat that if the nature of the warning given was inherently defective, the court might be more prepared to judge that the doctor had not fulfilled the duty of disclosure prior to obtaining consent. He also accepted that when the procedure was elective, the courts might more readily decide that there were inherent defects in a standard medical procedure, such that the patient should have been warned about them. The Chief Justice said that he was satisfied that:

> [T]here is, of course, where it is possible to do so, a clear obligation on a medical practitioner carrying out or arranging for the carrying out of an operation, to inform the patient of any possible harmful consequence arising from the operation, so as to permit the patient to give an informed consent to subjecting himself to the operation concerned. I am also satisfied that the extent of this obligation must, as a matter of common sense, vary with what might be described as the elective nature of the surgery concerned. The obligation to give a warning of the possible harmful consequences of a surgical procedure which could be said to be elective may be more stringent and onerous.

[9.94] In fact, for all the judges, the fact that this was an elective procedure was of importance in deciding the extent of disclosure required. The element of choice involved meant that the doctor did not have to weigh up on the risks of not performing the surgery

---

[164] *Daniels v Heskin* [1954] IR 73.
[165] *Walsh v Family Planning Services* [1992] IR 496.

against the risks involved in the procedure.[166] O'Flaherty J took a clear approach to the issue in determining that it should be a matter for the trial judge to decide on general negligence principles. He said: '... [in the case of elective surgery] if there is a risk – however exceptional or remote – of grave consequences involving severe pain stretching for an appreciable time into the future and involving the possibility of further operative procedures, the exercise of the duty of care owed by the defendants requires that such possible consequences should be explained in the clearest language to the plaintiff.'

[9.95] In subsequent cases the Court has unfortunately not made any detailed analysis of the judgments in *Walsh*. In *Farrell v Varian*[167] O'Hanlon J was concerned with whether the plaintiff should have been warned that an operation aimed at curing a particular hand condition, could actually make the condition worse. The judge did not refer to *Walsh* but rather to the *Sidaway* case and in particular where Lord Bridge referred to the issue of disclosure as coming within the realms of clinical judgment unless the matter was so obviously necessary to disclose, that no medical professional would fail to disclose it. On that basis the warning given in this case was sufficient, as the risk was a slight one.

[9.96] In *Bolton v the Blackrock Clinic, Wood and Cumiskey*[168] the plaintiff sought treatment for a pulmonary condition for which surgery was recommended. She later complained that she had not been given sufficient information regarding the risks involved in this surgery. Geoghegan J in the High Court found that the defendants had not been negligent in their diagnosis and treatment of the plaintiff, which finding was later affirmed by the Supreme Court. In relation to the question of disclosure, Geoghegan was of the view that this was to be determined on ordinary principles of negligence and that in this case the risks had been properly disclosed. The Supreme Court upheld this finding of fact but held that the matter should be determined on the basis of the principles in *Dunne*.

[9.97] In more recent years the High Court judgment in *Geoghegan v Harris*[169] is of considerable importance in setting out clearly that the standard of risk disclosure is that of the 'reasonable patient'. In this case the plaintiff alleged negligence in the carrying out of a dental implant by the defendant dentist, during the course of which a bone graft was taken from the plaintiff's chin. This was alleged to have damaged a nerve in the front of the chin and left the patient with chronic neuropathic pain. It was alleged that the dentist failed to disclose in advance of the operation the risk that such pain might be a consequence of the procedure. The defendant accepted that he did not disclose this risk, as he was of the view that he had a duty to give information about rare complications where the risk exceeded 1%. He did not consider that this pain was associated with the proposed procedure. The plaintiff said that he would not have undergone the procedure even if the risk was 0.1%. Kearns J, having reviewed the cases in this area, observed that whichever approach was taken to determining the standard of disclosure, the same conclusion was reached as regards the most critical elements, namely: (i) the requirement to give a warning of any material risk which is a known

166 Donnelly, 'Confusion and Uncertainty: The Irish Approach to the Duty to Disclose Risks in Medical Treatment' (1996) MLJI 3 at 6.
167 *Farrell v Varian* (1995) MLJI 29.
168 *Bolton v the Blackrock Clinic, Wood and Cumiskey* (December 20 1994, unreported) HC.
169 *Geoghegan v Harris* [2000] 3 IR 536 (Kearns J).

complication of a procedure properly carried out, and (ii) the test of materiality in elective surgery is to enquire only is there is any risk, however exceptional or remote, of grave consequences involving pain for an appreciable time into the future; statistical frequency is irrelevant.

[9.98] The judge adopted the reasonable patient standard in relation to causation, in other words, that the negligence of the doctor caused the harm to the patient. This involves the patient convincing the court that he or she would not have proceeded with the procedure had the information been disclosed. 'The problem for claimants is that, because in the vast majority of cases the risks in a procedure are quite small and the potential benefits are quite large, most claimants cannot convincingly argue that they would have acted any differently even if they had been provided with a full picture.'[170] In this case, Kearns J considered whether a reasonable person in the plaintiff's position would have consented to the operation even if informed of the remote risk. The judge noted that the patient had been very keen to proceed with the surgery and held that a reasonable person in his position would have consented. The patient therefore failed to show that his injury was caused by the failure to disclose the risks and was unsuccessful in his claim against the dentist.

[9.99] The importance of this case comes from the requirement that the doctor must give a warning of material risk which, in elective treatment, is any risk of grave consequences no matter how remote the doctor deems the possibility of the risk materialising. This clearly and definitively upholds the right of the patient to choose his/her treatment with full knowledge of all material facts. Although rooted in elective treatment, it nevertheless represented an important indication of judicial willingness to move in the direction of greater recognition of patient autonomy generally.

[9.100] The patient's signature on a consent form does not always necessarily relieve the doctor from liability in the event of negligence on the doctor's part. In *Byrne v Ryan*,[171] the High Court was asked to award damages to a woman whose tubal ligation procedure had failed, with the result that she bore two subsequent children. Although Kelly J denied the plaintiff's claim for the costs of rearing the two children in question on policy grounds[172], he did award damages for personal injury in relation to the necessity for the plaintiff to undergo a second sterilisation procedure some years later. In relation to the issue of consent, the plaintiff had signed a consent form which acknowledged the possibility that it might not render her sterile. The defendant argued that by signing this document the plaintiff consented to that risk of failure, thus relieving the doctor of any liability. Kelly J did not accept this proposition. He said that the document in its terms was a consent to the operation being carried out and the administration of an anaesthetic. 'It is not a consent to the carrying out of a failure; still less is it a consent to the carrying out of the operation in a negligent fashion. It merely records the plaintiff's understanding that there is a possibility of failure. It might be possible to draft a form of

---

[170] Donnelly, *Consent: Bridging the Gap Between Doctor and Patient,* (Cork University Press, 2002) p 31.

[171] *Byrne v Ryan* [2007] IEHC 207.

[172] 'The value which the Constitution places upon the family, the dignity and protection which it affords to human life are matters which are, in my view, better served by a decision to deny rather than allow damages of the type claimed.' Per Kelly J.

consent which would exclude liability on the part of a doctor for negligent treatment but there is no attempt to do so here.'

[9.101] The most recent Irish judgment in relation to risk disclosure is *Fitzpatrick v White*.[173] The facts involved an alleged failure to give a warning to a patient prior to eye surgery. Kearns J reaffirmed the position adopted in Walsh that a warning must in every case be given of a risk, however remote, of grave consequences involving severe pain continuing into the future and involving further operative intervention. He went on to say:

> [T]he argument that the giving of an adequate warning, far from being a source of nuisance for doctors, should be seen as an opportunity to ensure they are protected from subsequent litigation at the suit of disappointed patients. I am thus fortified to express in rather more vigorous terms than I did in *Goeghegan v Harris* my view that the patient centred test is preferable, and ultimately more satisfactory from the point of view of both doctor and patient alike, than any 'doctor centred' approach favoured by part of this Court in *Walsh v Family Planning Services*.

[9.102] The judge held that a risk may be seen as material if, in the circumstances of the particular case, a reasonable person in the patient's position, if warned of the risk, would be likely to attach significance to it. Another noteworthy point from the judgment is in relation to the timing of seeking informed consent. In this case the plaintiff accepted that a warning had in fact been given but alleged that a warning which was given only shortly before the procedure was carried out was insufficient to discharge the duty of care on the doctor. In this case, the plaintiff had his eyesight fully tested and evaluated four months before his operation and the options for surgical intervention were plain from the orthoptist's report from that time. The plaintiff was seen on three occasions prior to his operation. The judge took the view that the risks associated with squint surgery could have easily been explained to the plaintiff at any of these meetings, or certainly well in advance of the time when they were explained – a mere 30 minutes before his operation. The judge said:

> There are obvious reasons why, in the context of elective surgery, a warning given only shortly before an operation is undesirable. A patient may be stressed, medicated or in pain in this period and may be less likely for one or more of these reasons to make a calm and reasoned decision in such circumstances.

[9.103] In this case, the plaintiff gave no evidence of being unduly stressed or anxious on the day of his operation, he was not in pain and had not been sedated prior to his operation. He was facing into what could fairly be described as a minor operation only. His evidence suggested he was in a clear and lucid mental state on the day of the operation and well capable of making a decision. He described how his conversation with the doctor was both cordial and relaxed. While the plaintiff said he would have 'walked straight out of the hospital' had he been warned on the day, he did not say he could not deal with a warning given at that point in time. In fact he said the opposite. In the absence of clear evidence that the plaintiff was actually disadvantaged in some material way by the lateness of the warning, the judge held that he would not declare or find the warning given to be invalid because it was given at a late stage. He went on to say that there was nothing in the evidence to suggest the plaintiff could not assimilate or

---

[173] *Fitzpatrick v White* [2007] IESC 51.

properly understand what he was being told. He said, 'I would make the point strongly however that in other cases where a warning is given late in the day, particularly where the surgery is elective surgery, the outcome might well be different.'[174]

Professional guidelines

[9.104] The Medical Council is the regulatory body for the medical profession in Ireland. As part of its functions, the Council publishes guidance for the profession in relation to professional conduct and ethics. The most recent edition of the Guide, published in 2009, gives detailed guidance in relation to informed consent.[175] Its guidance is based on the principle that:

> Consent given by the patient is the exercise of a voluntary choice; it is the giving of permission for the intervention to be carried out by competent professionals, where possible in an appropriate environment. You should explain the process in such a way as to ensure that patients do not feel that their consent is simply a formality or a signature on a page. As part of the informed consent process patients must be given sufficient information, in a way that they can understand, to enable them to exercise their right to make informed decisions about their care. This refers to the disclosure of all significant risks, or substantial risks of grave adverse consequences.

[9.105] The Council takes the view that effective communication is the key to achieving informed consent and advises doctors to take appropriate steps to find out what patients want to know about their condition and what they ought to know about their condition, its investigation and treatment. It acknowledges that the amount of information given to individual patients will vary, according to factors such as the nature of the condition, the mode of investigation, the complexity of the treatment, the risks associated with the treatment or procedure, and the patient's own wishes. For example, patients may need more information to make an informed decision about a procedure which carries a high risk of failure or adverse side effects; or about an investigation for a condition which, if found to be present, could have serious implications for the patient's employment, social or personal life.[176] When providing information, doctors are advised to consider patients' individual needs and priorities. For example, patients' beliefs, culture, occupation or other factors may have a bearing on the information they need in order to reach a decision. Any questions asked by the patient must be answered as fully as the patient wishes. Information necessary for decision-making must not be withheld from a patient unless disclosure would cause the patient serious harm. In this context 'serious harm' does not mean the patient would become upset, or decide to refuse treatment. The Council stresses that:

---

[174] On this point, the Medical Council states that 'it is not recommended to seek consent when a patient may be stressed, sedated or in pain and therefore less likely to make a calm and reasoned decision. Where possible, risks should be explained well in advance of an intervention.' Medical Council, *The Guide to Professional Conduct and Ethics* (7th edn, 2009), Section D. Available at http://www.medicalcouncil.ie (accessed 3 June 2011).

[175] Medical Council, *The Guide to Professional Conduct and Ethics* (7th edn, 2009), Section D. Available at http://www.medicalcouncil.ie (accessed 3 June 2011).

[176] Appendix A lists information which patients want or ought to know prior to giving consent. Medical Council, *The Guide to Professional Conduct and Ethics* (7th edn, 2009). Available at http://www.medicalcouncil.ie (accessed 3 June 2011).

Obtaining informed consent cannot be an isolated event. It involves a continuing process of keeping patients up-to-date with any changes in their condition and the treatments or investigation proposed. Whenever possible, treatment options should be discussed at a time when the patient is best able to understand and retain the information.

Voluntariness

[9.106] Another fundamental aspect of the ideal of informed consent is that of voluntariness. This concentrates on the absence of control or manipulative influence by others in the patient's decision. That is not to say that others, such as family members or friends, should not be involved in the decision-making, but that the decision is that of the patient. The law has long recognised that a consent coerced by threats or manipulated by misrepresentation is invalid. In the context of vulnerable patients, such as those in residential care, choices are made for those patients on a daily basis in order to promote the efficient running of the facility. These may be in relation to the timing and content of meals, the taking of baths, the administration of medicine and so on.

[9.107] The liberty of competent residents to live their lives in accord with their preferences and life plans must often be balanced against protecting their health, protecting the interests of others, promoting safety and efficiency in the facility, and allocating limited financial and other resources. Although respect for autonomy suggests individualized care in the nursing home setting, such care can rarely be individualized in the ways we expect outside such institutions.[177]

[9.108] To say that decision-making in an institutional setting is coercive is probably an exaggeration, indeed it could be said that by entering the institution the person consented to its rules and regulations. Whether the person entered the facility voluntarily or under some persuasion from family is another matter. The term coercion is best used to describe a situation where a person intentionally uses a threat of harm to control another. It is not immediately relevant to the health-care context, although it could be used in a prison or psychiatric hospital where patients are involuntarily detained. Persuasion is where a person is convinced by another's reasoning to adopt a certain course of action. Manipulation takes place in health-care decision-making when a person makes a decision on the basis of information given to him in such a way as to alter the person's understanding of the decision to be made and its consequences. This may be in relation to the use of 'routine' tests, or the alternatives to a procedure deemed to be medically desirable.

> [C]lients are more often bullied than informed into consent, their resistance weakened in part by their desire for the general service if not the specific procedure, in part by the oppressive setting they find themselves in, and in part by the calculated intimidation, restriction of information, and covert threats of rejection by the professional staff itself.'[178]

[9.109] The most important question here then is whether the person is sufficiently free to perform his or her own actions. In cases of deception, exaggeration, misleading management and withholding of information, the patient's autonomy is overridden and any consent given does not qualify as an informed choice. The same is true of the more

---

[177] Beauchamp and Childress, *Principles of Biomedical Ethics* (4th edn, OUP, 1994).

[178] Freidson, *The Profession of Medicine* (Harper and Row, 1970) p 376.

subtle form of manipulation where offers and rewards are used to influence a decision. The example commonly given of this kind of scenario is the Tuskegee syphilis experiments, where various methods were used to sustain the interest of participants in a study. The subjects, who were socio-economically deprived, were offered free burial assistance and insurance, free transportation, free medicines and a hot meal on the day of the examination, offers not easily refused by those particular individuals.[179]

[9.110] The underlying principle behind informed consent is that patients have sufficient information to be able to substantially understand the choice offered to them. This presupposes that whatever decision is made by the patient will be accepted by the doctor as an exercise of the patient's right of self-determination. However, very often the language used by doctors indicates that the only possible option for the patient is to consent to the treatment offered. For example, doctors sometimes speak of 'getting a consent' or 'consenting' the patient, which suggest that patients are expected to agree rather than disagree. One doctor writes:

> What matters is that the patient consents to that course of action which best serves her total interests. If that course of action is clear to her doctor then his/her duty is to get her to consent to it.[180]

[9.111] While doctors may, of course, recommend certain courses of action to their patients, it may be questioned how far the doctor may go in persuading the patient to choose a certain option without transgressing the necessary voluntariness of informed consent. The doctor must be able to accept the patient's choice even if he or she does not agree with it, otherwise the whole rationale for informed consent is lost.

> There are no neat answers to the dilemma of how to persuade without taking control. Each situation needs a judgment which can only be made if the professional has experience, knowledge of the situation and of the patient and, most crucially, an inherent respect for the patient's right to make his own decision.[181]

REFUSAL OF TREATMENT BY A COMPETENT ADULT

[9.112] The right of a patient to refuse medical treatment brings into conflict two ethical principles: respect for autonomy and non-maleficence. Apart from cases involving terminally ill patients or patients in a persistent vegetative state, there have also been a number of difficult cases before the courts in relation to refusal of blood transfusions by Jehovah's Witnesses, amputation of limbs, force feeding of an adult anorexic patient, refusal by parents of treatment for their children for religious and non-religious reasons[182] and refusal of caesarean sections by pregnant women. In some of these cases, the doctors and the courts took the view that no reasonable person in the patient's position would refuse the proposed medical treatment, and that therefore the patient must be regarded as temporarily lacking capacity. Refusal of consent is seen 'not as an assertion of will, but rather as a symptom of unsoundness of mind.'[183] A decision could

---

[179] Veatch, *Medical Ethics* (2nd edn, Jones and Bartlett, 1997) p 201.

[180] Jenkins, 'Consent: A Matter of Trust Not Tort' (1996) MLJI 83 at 85.

[181] Donnelly, *Consent: Bridging the Gap Between Doctor and Patient* (Cork University Press, 2002) p 21.

[182] See Chapter 11 for further discussion of parental authority in the treatment of sick children.

then be made to proceed with treatment in the 'best interests' of the patient. The difficulty for the courts in cases of refusal of treatment is that there is a stark decision to be made between the fundamental values of choice and health, or in some instances, life itself. Courts have commonly in such situations acknowledged the right of autonomy, but have expressly provided that such rights are not and cannot be absolute in any society. The preservation of life then comes within one of the exceptional situations in which societal interests override the value of self-determination. As will be seen in the discussion of the case law below, this attitude has changed in recent years with an increasing recognition that refusal of treatment is within the decision-making authority of the individual patient, even where the consequences of the refusal may be death or serious harm.

Sources of the right

[9.113] In addition to locating the right to refuse treatment in the respect for autonomy enshrined in Art 40.3.1° of the Irish Constitution 1937, it is also important to note the relevance of the ECHR in this regard. Wicks argues that individual autonomy under the Convention, though important, is balanced against the interests of society.[184] In the case of refusal of treatment, one significant interest of society is the sanctity of life. This potential conflict was addressed by Hoffmann LJ in *Bland*.[185] The principle articles of relevance in the ECHR are arts 2, 3, 8, 9 and 12.

[9.114] Under art 2 'everyone's right to life shall be protected by law…'. This has relevance for the area of euthanasia and refusal of life-sustaining treatment. Article 3 prohibits inhuman or degrading treatment, which may encompass non-consensual medical treatment. Degrading treatment has been defined as treatment or punishment of an individual which 'grossly humiliates him before others or drives him to act against his will or conscience.'[186] Although in one case an intention to humiliate was held to be necessary under art 3, the court has generally not imposed such a requirement.[187] Such a requirement would certainly make it almost impossible to succeed in relation to the imposition of medical treatment, as the doctor's intentions would be unlikely to include humiliation of the patient.[188] The emphasis on humiliation, however, seems to indicate a leaning towards the protection of human dignity as opposed to the concept of autonomy and therefore it may be argued that it excludes non-consensual medical treatment from its ambit. However, it is also clear that non-consensual medical treatment deprives a

---

[183] Kennedy, *Treat Me Right: Essays in Medical Law and Ethics* (Clarendon Press, 1991) at 337.

[184] See detailed discussion by Wicks, 'The right to refuse medical treatment under the European Convention on Human Rights' (2001) 9 Med L Rev 17–40.

[185] 'There is no morally correct solution which can be deduced from a single ethical principle like the sanctity of life or the right of self-determination. There must be an accommodation between principles, both of which seem rational and good, but which have come into conflict with each other.' *Airedale NHS Trust Ltd v Bland* [1993] AC 789 at 827 per Hoffmann LJ.

[186] *Denmark, Norway, Sweden and the Netherlands v Greece* [1969] 12 YB 1 at 186.

[187] *Abdulaziz, Cabales and Balkandali v UK* [1985] Series A. No 94, para 91.

[188] Wicks, 'The right to refuse medical treatment under the European Convention on Human Rights' (2001) 9 Med L Rev 17–40 at 21, fn16.

person of the freedom of choice over his own body, which is a fundamental part of individual dignity.[189]

[9.115] In *X v Denmark*[190] the Commission held that 'medical treatment of an experimental character and without the consent of the person involved may under certain circumstances be regarded as prohibited by Article 3.' The issue of experimentation is, of course, a particularly sensitive one, given the context within which the Convention was drafted and the response to the atrocities that took place in Germany and elsewhere during and after the Second World War. However, it is unlikely that medical treatment designed and intended to benefit the patient, albeit without the patient's consent, could be held to come within the term 'experimentation.' In the *Herczegfalvy* case,[191] the Court held that 'a measure which is a therapeutic necessity cannot be regarded as inhuman or degrading.' The Court must be satisfied of the medical necessity of the treatment, but once this is established, the imposition of the treatment without consent will not violate Article 3.[192]

[9.116] Article 8 provides that 'everyone has the right to respect for his private life.' This has been interpreted as including the 'physical integrity' of the person.[193] Although limitations to this right are possible on the basis of societal interests, such as the protection of health through compulsory vaccination against disease, such limitations are not likely to apply to an individual case of non-consensual medical treatment. In *X v Austria*[194] the Commission specifically stated that a 'compulsory medical intervention, even if it is of minor importance, must be considered as an interference with this right.' However, the protection of the right probably only applies where the adult is competent to make decisions and has been informed of the consequences of the decision. 'Where consent is normally required, as in the case of medical treatment, action without consent will not be an interference if the state can show that the individual was not in a position to give informed consent.'[195] The European Court of Human Rights stated in *Pretty v the UK*[196] that the right of autonomy comes within the protection of art 8 and that this permitted the refusal of medical treatment, even if this would lead to the patient's death. The Court said that the imposition of treatment on a capable adult patient without consent 'would clearly interfere with a person's physical integrity in a manner capable of engaging the rights protected under Art 8(1) of the Convention.'[197] This was also affirmed in *Tysiac v Poland*.[198]

---

[189] Wicks, 'The right to refuse medical treatment under the European Convention on Human Rights' (2001) 9 Med L Rev 17–40 at 22.

[190] *X v Denmark* [1983] 32 DR 282.

[191] *Herczegfalvy* [1992] Series A, No 244, para 82.

[192] See Wicks, 'The right to refuse medical treatment under the European Convention on Human Rights' (2001) 9 Med L Rev 17–40 at 24 for further discussion of the meaning of 'medical necessity' in light of the possibility of differing bodies of profession opinion on a particular treatment.

[193] *X and Y v Netherlands* [1986] 8 EHRR 235 at para.22

[194] *X v Austria* [1980] 18 DR 154.

[195] Harris, O'Boyle and Warbrick, *Law of the European Convention on Human Rights* (1995) at 337–8.

[196] *Pretty v the UK* [2002] 35 EHRR 1.

[197] *Pretty v the UK* [2002] 35 EHRR 1, para 63.

[198] *Tysiac v Poland* [2007] 45 EHRR 42, para 107.

[9.117] Article 9 provides protection of freedom of thought, conscience and religion. In many cases, discussed below, medical treatment may be refused on religious grounds. The most striking example of this occurs in the Jehovah's Witness faith, which is opposed to blood transfusions. In *Hoffmann v Austria*[199] the Austrian courts had refused to award custody of children to a woman, in part because she was a Jehovah's Witness and would have refused blood transfusions for her children. Although the European Court concentrated on violations of arts 8 (interference with private life) and 14 (prevention of discrimination) in the circumstances of this case, it also accepted that her opposition to transfusions was a manifestation of her religious beliefs. 'In doing so, the Court seems to have accepted that Article 9(1) may prima facie protect a refusal by Jehovah's Witnesses to consent to blood transfusions.'[200]

[9.118] Article 12 provides the 'right to found a family' subject to 'national laws governing the exercise of this right'. This may be of relevance in the non-consensual sterilisation cases where patients incapable of giving consent are sterilised in their best interests. These cases are considered below. In relation to Convention rights, the right to found a family is not an absolute one, as is clear from the express limitation in favour of national laws. However, it has been held that such restrictions as may be imposed by national authorities must not be such as to restrict the right in such a way or to such an extent 'that the very essence of the right is impaired.'[201] In most non-consensual sterilisation situations where the patient is incompetent to give or refuse consent, it would be incumbent on the hospital, in the UK at least, to seek court approval of the procedure. This may be perceived by the European Court as sufficient to provide protection of the rights of the individual patient, given the limitations on the right as previously noted.

[9.119] In conclusion, the Convention may be seen as protecting the ability to choose or refuse medical treatment in a number of ways discussed above. 'The key articles are 3 and 8 which, taken together, will ensure that treatment is consensual or, if the patient is genuinely incapable of consent, therapeutically necessary.' The test of capacity is crucial to any protection provided. Thus, there is a danger that decisions which are deemed unreasonable, irrational, or unorthodox, may be overridden on the basis of incapacity, and will not be protected by the Convention. However, as society becomes more rights-conscious and more concerned about individual autonomy, the courts may find more incompatibility between such interests and the traditional perception of the duties of the medical profession.

English case law on refusal of treatment

[9.120] The classic statement on the right to refuse treatment is found in the judgment of Lord Donaldson MR:

> An adult patient who...suffers from no mental incapacity has an absolute right to choose whether to consent to medical treatment, to refuse it or to choose one rather than another of

---

[199] *Hoffmann v Austria* [1993] Series A, No 255.
[200] Wicks E. 'The Right to Refuse Medical Treatment Under the European Convention on Human Rights' (2001) 9 Med L Rev 17–40 at 31.
[201] *Rees v UK* [1986] Series A, No 106, para 50.

the treatments being offered. This right exists notwithstanding that the reasons for making the choice are rational, irrational, unknown or even non-existent.[202]

Lord Goff further strengthened this in *Airedale NHS Trust v Bland*:

> It is established that the principle of self-determination requires that respect must be given to the wishes of the patient, so that if an adult patient of sound mind refuses, however unreasonably, to consent to treatment or care by which his life would or might be prolonged, the doctors responsible for his care must give effect to his wishes, even though they do not consider it to be in his best interests to do so.[203]

[9.121] These statements provide very powerful affirmation of the right to self-determination even where the exercise of such right is contrary to medical and non-medical recommendations. The courts have clearly stated that a competent patient may decide for himself whether to accept or refuse medical advice. However, when it comes to applying this principle in hard cases, the courts have sometimes used the determination of competence as a way of avoiding the implementation of this principle.

> While recognising a right to refuse treatment, courts have been careful as regards how this right has been applied in practice...[T]he most common reasons that the right has been held not to apply is because of the patient's lack of capacity. This capacity has acted as a safety-valve, allowing courts to endorse the right to refuse treatment while, at the same time, avoid applying it in practice.[204]

[9.122] For example, in *Re T (an adult: refusal of treatment)*[205] T was a 34-week pregnant woman who refused blood transfusions. Although she had been brought up by her mother who was a Jehovah's Witness, she was not practising this religion at the time of her hospitalisation and had a partner who was not of the same faith. Her condition worsened and a caesarean section was recommended to deliver the baby. While she was in intensive care following the section, it was considered medically advisable to administer a blood transfusion, but the hospital felt constrained by T's prior refusal. T's father and partner sought a declaration that the transfusion would be lawful despite T's refusal of consent. This was granted and upheld by the Court of Appeal which was of the opinion that T's own adherence to the Jehovah's Witness faith was no longer as strong as when she had resided with her mother. In addition, she had not been fully informed by the medical team regarding the consequences of her refusal. Given her pregnancy, medication, after-effects of the accident, and severe pneumonia, the Court was prepared to hold that she was incompetent at the time of her refusal. The Court was of the view that T had also been unduly influenced by her mother, as her refusals had come after time spent alone with her mother on each occasion and her mother declined to give evidence of the content of the conversations. As the critical medical situation in which she later found herself constituted an emergency, treatment could take place without her consent in her best interests. The significance of the case is in the unanimous recognition by the Court of Appeal of the right to refuse treatment, which was described by Lord Donaldson MR as 'absolute'.

---

[202] *Re T (an adult: refusal of treatment)* [1993] Fam 95 at 102
[203] *Airedale NHS Trust v Bland* [1993] 1 All ER 821 at 864.
[204] Donnelly, *Healthcare Decision-making and the Law, Autonomy, Capacity and the Limits of Liberalism,* (Cambridge University Press, 2010) at 57.
[205] *Re T (an adult: refusal of treatment)* [1993] Fam 95.

[9.123] A case in which it might have appeared at first glance that the Court might have decided that the patient lacked capacity due to his psychiatric condition and which demonstrates the dangers of a status approach to capacity is *Re C (adult: refusal of medical treatment)*[206] in which a 68-year-old man suffering from paranoid schizophrenia developed gangrene in his foot. He was told that there was a significant chance that he would die unless the leg was amputated. C refused to consent to the operation and sought an injunction preventing the hospital from carrying out such a procedure without his consent in the future. The medical evidence was, perhaps unusually, divided on the question of C's capacity but the judge decided that C had the capacity to refuse the treatment.[207] It was held that the test of capacity is that the patient understands or at least is capable of understanding the nature and effects of the proposed treatment in broad terms, to believe the information concerning this, and to weigh the information so as to make a choice.

[9.124] In cases where it is clear from the evidence before the court that the patient has full capacity to make the decision in question, the English courts have upheld the importance of respect for the autonomy of the patient and stated that the right to refuse treatment is absolute. For example, in *Re AK*[208] a 19 year-old with motor neurone disease, which is a progressive, incurable and fatal condition, had lost all limb movements, speech and the ability to swallow. He was unable to initiate communication or show any emotion and his only means of communication was a tiny movement of one eye which was soon to be lost. When this happened he would be 'locked-in' in the sense that he would hear, see and feel but have no means of communication whatsoever. Motor neurone disease does not affect intellectual capacity and therefore AK had full decision-making capacity as a competent adult. He informed his medical team that he wished his ventilator to be switched off in the event that he lost the ability to communicate. The health authority applied for a declaration that it would be lawful to act on AK's wishes to discontinue treatment two weeks after he lost all ability to communicate. The Court held, in granting the declaration, that doctors are not entitled to treat a person who, being of sound mind and full capacity, has let it be known that such treatment is against his wishes. The case thus reinforces the principle that a competent adult has an unassailable right to refuse all treatment at common law, even if it will lead to death. Hughes J said that in situations such as this, where communication is very difficult, doctors must exercise great caution, as there is a danger that the patient's wishes might not be properly understood and that external factors such as pain, stress or medication may affect his ability to exercise rational judgment. He said, however, that in this case AK was not influenced by external factors, was fully aware of his situation and demonstrated immense courage and maturity in reaching his decision.

[9.125] A similarly strong example of judicial support for the right to refuse treatment where there was no evidence of incapacity on the part of the patient is *Re B (Adult: Refusal of medical treatment)*.[209] In this case a 43-year-old paralysed woman was held

---

[206] *Re C (adult: refusal of medical treatment)* [1994] 1 All ER 819.

[207] It is worth noting that, despite his refusal of the amputation, C survived without any deterioration in his health, as a less invasive procedure was carried out successfully.

[208] *Re AK* [2001] 1 FLR 129.

[209] *Re B (Adult: Refusal of medical treatment)* [2002] 2 All ER 449.

entitled to have artificial ventilation removed notwithstanding that this would result in her death. She was found to be a well-informed woman with a high degree of mental competence. Dame Butler-Sloss P held that the physically disabled patient enjoys the same right to personal autonomy as the able-bodied patient and that where capacity is not an issue, the wishes of the patient have to be respected by doctors irrespective of outcome; clinical views as to the patient's best interests are therefore irrelevant. She was also entitled to damages for the prior interference with her right to refuse the treatment.[210]

[9.126] The courts have taken the view that in cases of doubt regarding the capacity of the patient to understand the consequences of their refusal, or whether an advance refusal continued to be valid despite a change in the patient's circumstances, the court will resolve the doubt in favour of the preservation of life. In *HE v A Hospital NHS Trust*[211] the father of AE, a 24-year-old woman who was a Jehovah's Witness, applied for a declaration that a blood transfusion should be administered to her despite her prior refusal. AE had recently become engaged to a Turkish man and it had been a condition of her marriage that she would reject her Jehovah's Witness faith and become a Muslim. She had not attended any religious services in the two months prior to her illness. Munby J said that in cases of doubt, there must be clear and convincing evidence of the continued validity of the advance refusal. He also said that such a refusal would not be valid in the event of a material change in circumstances, as had occurred here. Donnelly says this case leaves genuine doubts about what AE would have wished to happen due to the social context in which AE lived, her desire to please her fiancé and the fact that she had not destroyed the treatment refusal form.[212]

[9.127] Although English law has firmly taken the position that a competent adult can refuse medical treatment for whatever (or no) reason, where a pregnant woman refuses medical treatment with potentially fatal consequences for the fetus, this position has been more difficult for the courts to adhere to. 'Rather than subscribing to the established law on this issue, the courts have interpreted the law in such a way as to create an imbalance between the interests of the fetus and the woman. In doing so, pregnant women have become a new category of incompetent adults.'[213] In *Re S (Adult: refusal of medical treatment)*[214] a 30-year-old woman was admitted to hospital in spontaneous labour. The woman and her husband refused to consent to a caesarean section on religious grounds. The hospital applied to court for an order compelling the patient to undergo the procedure against her wishes. Sir Stephen Brown did not discuss the issue of the woman's competency, and dealt with the matter on the basis that the life of the fetus took precedence to the right to self-determination of the mother.[215] Despite

---

[210] She sought and was awarded nominal damages only.

[211] *HE v A Hospital NHS Trust* [2003] EWHC 1017 (Fam.).

[212] Donnelly, *Healthcare Decision-making and the Law, Autonomy, Capacity and the Limits of Liberalism,* (Cambridge University Press, 2010) at 65.

[213] Fovargue and Miola, 'Policing Pregnancy: Implications of the *Attorney General's Reference (no. 3 of 1994)*' (1998) 6 Med L Rev 265–296 at 281.

[214] *Re S (Adult: refusal of medical treatment)* [1992] 4 All ER 671.

[215] See Thomson, 'After *Re S*' (1994) 2 Med L Rev 127–148; Stern, 'Court-Ordered Caesarean Sections: In Whose Interests?' (1993) 56 Med L Rev 238–243.

heavy criticism,[216] this seems to have been followed in *Rochdale Healthcare (NHS) Trust v C*[217] where the Court ordered the procedure 'in the best interests of the patient'. The fetus seems to have been regarded by the judge as the 'patient' in this case, not the pregnant woman.[218] The patient was deemed incompetent to make a treatment decision, due in part to the fact that 'she was in the throes of labour with all that is involved in terms of pain and emotional stress.'

[9.128] The opportunity arose for the Court to consider the balance struck in this 'maternal-fetal conflict' in *Re MB (adult: medical treatment)*.[219] In this case MB was admitted to hospital and found to be in immediate need of a caesarean section, to which she consented. However, when she became aware of the necessity of the administration of an anaesthetic, she refused consent for the procedure to be performed. A consultant psychiatrist met MB and formed the view that she was suffering from an 'abnormal mental condition' of needle phobia which meant that 'at the actual point she was not capable of making a decision at all, in the sense of being able to hold information in the balance and make a choice.'[220] Butler-Sloss LJ, for the Court, held that there was a distinction between fear of an operation that may be a rational reason for refusing medical treatment, and therefore not impugning the person's competence, and fear that paralyses the will and therefore voids the patient's competence.[221] The Court held that the anaesthetic could be administered if this was in the patient's best interests, including her medical interests, but also taking into account relevant information about her circumstances and background. This appears to contradict the judge's own confirmation that a competent adult may 'for religious reasons, other reasons, for rational or irrational reasons, or for no reason at all, choose not to have medical intervention.' This position might be taken to imply that 'a competent adult may refuse to consent to a caesarean

---

[216] Harrington argues that Stephen Brown favoured the medically and socially orthodox way of proceeding to the point where he was prepared to allow the forced subjection of the patient to invasive treatment. 'The repugnance of *Re S* to many commentators is perhaps due to the fact that it represents an open endorsement of medically sanctioned standards of behaviour which also occurs in other, less controversial cases, though behind a veil of incompetence.' Harrington, 'Privileging the Medical Norm: Liberalism, Self-Determination and Refusal of Treatment.' (1996) Legal Studies, Vol 16 No 3 348–367 at 360.

[217] *Rochdale Healthcare (NHS) Trust v C* [1997] 1 FCR 274.

[218] Fovargue and Miola, 'Policing Pregnancy: Implications of the *Attorney General's Reference (no. 3 of 1994)*' (1998) 6 Med L Rev 265–296 at 282.

[219] *Re MB (adult: medical treatment)* [1997] 2 FLR 426, [1997] 8 Med L Rev 217.

[220] *Re MB (adult: medical treatment)* [1997] 2 FLR 426, [1997] 8 Med L Rev 217 at 221.

[221] Michalowski argues that the rationality of the patient's fear should be of no more significance than the rationality of other reasons of the patient to refuse treatment. 'While it is perfectly true that fear can exclude capacity if it overrides the patient's ability to understand and weigh treatment information, the Court should not betray its own principles, as irrational fear does not necessarily negate the patient's ability to consent to medical treatment. The only criterion should therefore be whether or not the patient's fear resulted in an inability to understand, retain, believe and weigh the treatment information presented, and not whether or not the patient's fear was rational or irrational.' Michaloski, 'Court-Order Caesarean Sections – The End of a Trend?' (1999) 62 *Modern Lr* 115 at 118. See also Morris, 'Once Upon a Time in a Hospital…The Cautionary Tale of *St. George's Health Care NHS Trust v S*' (1999) 7 Feminist Legal Studies 75–84.

section *provided* that she does not do so because of any form of phobia, rather it is better for her to refuse to give a reason for her lack of consent, and then there will be no attempt to deem her incapable to provide such consent.'[222] The case is important because it gives strong statements regarding the protection of the right of self-determination, but when it comes to applying those principles, the Court appears to have spent little time on the case in hand.

[9.129] A later English case seems to have put an end to the practice of using temporary incompetence in relation to pregnant women. *St. George's Healthcare NHS Trust, R v Collins and others, ex parte S*[223] concerned S, a 28-year-old woman with a long-standing aversion to medical intervention. She consulted a doctor when she was 36-weeks pregnant and was diagnosed as having severe pre-eclampsia. She was told that this condition posed a serious risk to her life and the life of the fetus. S declined the recommended treatment, which included an early induced delivery, believing that nature should take its course. She was interviewed by a social worker and two doctors but continued to refuse treatment. S was then admitted against her will to hospital under the Mental Health Act 1983, and subsequently transferred to another. Despite consulting solicitors and repeating her refusal orally and in writing, the hospital applied *ex parte* for a declaration that treatment, including caesarean section, was lawful. The judge was under the mistaken impression that S had been in labour already for some time, and authorised the procedure. S was delivered of a daughter and two days later her detention was terminated and she discharged herself. She later sought to challenge her admission, detention and treatment, as well as appealing the granting of the declaration authorising the operation.

[9.130] The Court of Appeal held that the caesarean section and accompanying medical procedures performed on S amounted to a trespass, and that in the extraordinary circumstances of the case the court declaration provided no defence to a claim for damages against the hospital. The Court held that the detention of the patient under the Mental Health Act was unlawful, as the mental disorder must be such as to warrant detention for assessment, and treatment must be integral to the mental disorder. S had only been detained in order to treat her pregnancy, (had she not been pregnant, her mental condition would not have warranted any medical interest) and was discharged shortly after the baby had been delivered. The Court also issued detailed guidelines to prevent problems in future cases where questions of capacity are raised in connection with any surgical or invasive treatment, although the guidelines have been described as procedural only and as putting the ball firmly back in the health carer's court once they play by the rules.[224]

[9.131] The Court went to great lengths to affirm the right of autonomy, even where the patient's own life is at stake. It resolved the conflict as between the exercise of individual autonomy and the paternalism of the medical profession very firmly in favour of the individual. In relation to the conflict between the right of the competent patient to refuse medical treatment and the right to life of the unborn child, the Court upheld previous

---

[222] Fovargue and Miola, 'Policing Pregnancy: Implications of the *Attorney General's Reference (no. 3 of 1994)*' (1998) 6 Med L Rev 265–296 at 283, emphasis in original.

[223] *St. George's Healthcare NHS Trust, R v Collins and others, ex parte S* [1998] 2 FLR 728.

[224] Mason and McCall Smith, *Law and Medical Ethics* (5th edn, OUP, 2005) at 269.

decisions[225] in stating that the unborn child only acquires legal personality at birth, although at 36 weeks it is certainly 'not nothing'. The Court refrained from commenting further on the status of the fetus at this stage, as the conflict, as the Court saw it, was not between the mother and child, but between the woman and the paternalism of the medical profession. While the unborn child was recognised as having interests, as opposed to rights, these must necessarily be subordinated to the woman's absolute right to self-determination.

> In our judgment while pregnancy increases the personal responsibilities of a woman it does not diminish her entitlement to decide whether or not to undergo medical treatment. Although human, and protected by the law in a number of ways...an unborn child is not a separate person from its mother. Its need for medical assistance does not prevail over her rights. She is entitled not to be forced to submit to an invasion of her body against her will, whether her own life or that of her unborn child depends on it. Her right is not reduced or diminished merely because her decision to exercise it may appear morally repugnant.[226]

This important case clearly states the law to be firmly opposed to non-consensual medical interventions in pregnancy, irrespective of the rationale for the woman's decision and irrespective of the consequences for the fetus. The Court did not address the moral justification of the pregnant woman's choice to exercise her legal right to refuse medical treatment.[227]

The right to refuse treatment in Ireland

[9.132] The cases on refusal of treatment in Ireland to date have focused on the right of Jehovah's Witnesses to refuse blood transfusions. In *JM v The Board of Management of St Vincent's Hospital*[228]an application was made by the husband of an African woman who was unconscious, that she should be given a blood transfusion despite the fact that she had refused this treatment while conscious. The woman had become a Jehovah's Witness on marriage and according to Finnegan P had refused treatment 'because of her cultural background and her desire to please her husband and not offend his sensibilities.' He said that if the woman was capable of making her own decision she would agree with her husband and be comforted by his attitude. Yet, this case is not easy to reconcile with legal principle. Donnelly says the decision shows both the dangers of taking a social or relational approach to agency and the dangers of not doing so.[229] The woman had indicated her refusal of treatment in advance of loss of capacity and there was no suggestion that her husband had pressurised her into doing so. Therefore, it might be questioned as to what basis existed to subject her autonomous decision to the

---

225 *Paton v British Pregnancy Advisory Service Trustees* [1979] QB 276; *Re F (in utero)* [1988] Fam. 122; *Attorney-General's reference (No 3 of 1994)* [1997] 3 WLR 421; *Re MB (medical treatment)* [1997] 2 FLR 426.

226 *St. George's Healthcare NHS Trust, R v Collins and others, ex parte S* [1998] 2 FLR 728 at 746 per Judge LJ.

227 For further discussion of the woman's moral duty to the fetus, see Scott, 'The Pregnant Woman and the Good Samaritan: Can a Woman Have a Duty to Undergo a Caesarean Section?' (2000) Oxford J of Legal Studies Vol 20, No 3, 407–436.

228 *JM v The Board of Management of St Vincent's Hospital* [2003] 1 IR 321.

229 Donnelly, *Healthcare Decision-making and the Law, Autonomy, Capacity and the Limits of Liberalism,* (Cambridge University Press, 2010) at 62.

wishes of her husband. On the other hand, there was also clearly a cultural element to this case in which the woman's primary motivation appeared to be to please her husband and therefore she would have agreed with his wish for her to have the transfusion. Perhaps it would be preferable in such situations to appoint independent representation to advocate on the patient's behalf in such circumstances.

[9.133] In relation to the refusal of caesarean sections, as can be seen from the case law above, the English courts have examined the conflict between the woman's right to autonomy and the right of the medical profession to make decisions in her interests. The weighing of rights as between the woman and the fetus has been avoided where possible on the grounds that the fetus is not an independent legal person. This also holds true in other jurisdictions such as the United States where differing judgments on the issue have been given at different times.[230] In the Irish context the position is complicated by the provisions of the Constitution which oblige the State to protect the right to life of the unborn, as well as granting rights to privacy and bodily integrity. The right to bodily integrity under the unenumerated rights in Art 40.3.1° might appear to be the most obvious place within which to locate a right of a pregnant woman to refuse to submit to a caesarean section. Art 40.3.1° provides that 'the State guarantees in its laws to respect, and, as far as practicable, by its laws to defend and vindicate the personal rights of the citizen.' In *Ryan v Attorney General*[231] Kenny J in the High Court said that this right means that 'no mutilation of the body or any of its members may be carried out on any citizen under the authority of the law except for the good of the whole body...' The Supreme Court agreed that a right to bodily integrity existed, but did not comment further on the definition given by Kenny J.

[9.134] In the case of *In Re a Ward of Court*,[232] which dealt with the cessation of artificial nutrition and hydration of a woman in a near persistent vegetative state, the Supreme Court recognised that competent adults had the right to refuse medical treatment, even though such refusal may lead to death. Loss of capacity does not result in the loss of the personal rights protected by the Constitution, including 'the right to life, the right to bodily integrity, the right to privacy, including self-determination, and the right to refuse medical care or treatment.' O'Flaherty J agreed that 'there is an absolute right in a competent person to refuse medical treatment even if it leads to death.' Denham J pointed out that medical treatment may be refused for a variety of reasons, some of which may not be regarded as 'good' or rational decisions, but they must be respected nonetheless. She also said that there were a few rare exceptions to the principle that treatment may not be given to a competent adult without his consent, such as in relation to contagious disease control. In relation to the right to life, Denham J stated that while respect for the right to life is absolute, the right to life itself is not absolute, as the State is required to defend and vindicate life 'as far as practicable'. She said that the State's respect for the life of the individual encompasses the right of the

---

230 For example, *Jefferson v Griffin Spalding County Hospital Authority* (1981) Ga 274 SE 2d 457 (caesarean ordered); *Re A.C.* 573 A 2d 1235 (DC App 1990) (reversing an earlier decision ordering caesarean); and *Baby Boy Doe* 632 NE 2d 326 (Ill App 1 Dist 1994) (caesarean not ordered)
231 *Ryan v Attorney General* [1965] IR 294.
232 *In Re a Ward of Court* [1996] 2 IR 79.

individual to refuse a blood transfusion for religious reasons. In relation to the right to privacy under Art 40.3.1°, the Supreme Court held that this right includes a right to refuse medical treatment even where this would lead to death. The case is crucially important due to the court's focus on the right to self-determination despite the consequences of the exercise of that right. However, the facts and decision may not be directly applicable to the caesarean section debate in that there was no conflict here between different Constitutional rights, only the meaning and extent of the individual's own rights.

[9.135] In relation to the maternal-fetal conflict inherent in the refusal of a caesarean section, the right to life of the unborn is of primary importance. Article 40.3.3° of the Constitution states: 'The State acknowledges the right to life of the unborn and, with due regard for the equal right to life of the mother, guarantees in its laws to respect, and as far as practicable, by its laws to defend and vindicate that right.' This 'very unique private right' is also 'a human right which there is a public interest in preserving.'[233] In *Attorney General v X*[234] the Court considered for the first time a conflict between the rights of the mother and the fetus and certainly seems to indicate 'a less absolutist approach to Article 40.3.3's guarantee of unborn life than the prior Supreme Court decisions.'[235] The Court held that a termination of pregnancy was permissible under the Constitution if it is established as a matter of probability that there is a real and substantial risk to the life, as distinct from the health, of the mother and that that risk can only be avoided by the termination of her pregnancy.

[9.136] The importance of the decision here is in relation to the question of whether or not all Constitutional rights are equal, or whether there is a hierarchy of rights in cases where it is impossible to harmonise interacting rights. Finlay CJ was of the view that although the Court's first objective should always be to interpret the Constitution harmoniously, where this is not possible there may be 'a necessity to apply a priority of rights.' He said that where there was a stark conflict between the right to travel and the right to life, 'the right to life would necessarily have to take precedence over the right to travel.' Egan J agreed on this point referring to *People v Shaw*[236] where Kenny J stated that there was a hierarchy of Constitutional rights and, when a conflict arises between them, that which ranks higher must prevail:

> This cannot be taken to mean that an immutable list of precedence of rights can be formulated. The right to life of one person (as in Shaw's case) was held to be superior to the right to liberty of another but, quite clearly, the right to life might not be the paramount right in every circumstance. If, for instance, it were necessary for a father to kill a man engaged in the rape of his daughter in order to prevent its continuance, I have no doubt but that the right of the girl to bodily integrity would rank higher than the right to life of the rapist.

[9.137] Egan J went on to say that in cases where the right to travel was explicitly stated to be with the intent to have a termination of pregnancy, the right to life of the unborn must take precedence: 'In the face of a positive obligation to defend and vindicate such a right (the right to life of the unborn) it cannot reasonably be argued that a right to travel

---

233 *Society for the Protection of Unborn Children v Coogan* (1989) IR 734 per Walsh J.
234 *Attorney General v X* [1992] 1 IR 1.
235 Casey, *Constitutional Law in Ireland*, (3rd edn, Round Hall, 2000) at 400.
236 *People v Shaw* [1982] IR 1.

simpliciter can take precedence over such a right.' Given that Egan J considered that the termination of pregnancy in the circumstances of this case would not be unlawful, the young girl could not be prevented from exercising her right to travel. McCarthy J sought to find a harmonious interpretation of the various Constitutional rights, stating that 'the guarantee to the unborn was qualified by the requirement of due regard to the right to life of the mother and made less than absolute by recognising that the right could only be vindicated as far as practicable.' He went on to extract Walsh J's judgment in *SPUC v Grogan*,[237] where he asked whether the right to bodily integrity involves the right to control one's own body:

> When a woman becomes pregnant she acquires rights which cannot be taken from her, namely, the right to protect the life of her unborn child and the right to protect her own bodily integrity against any effort to compel her by law or by persuasion to submit herself to an abortion. Such rights also carry obligations the foremost of which is not to endanger or to submit to or bring about the destruction of that unborn life.

[9.138] However, McCarthy J (with whom O'Flaherty J agreed on this point) disagreed with the Chief Justice in relation to the curtailment of the right to travel, stating that as between the right to life of the unborn and the woman's right to travel, 'if it were a matter of a balancing exercise, the scales could only tilt in one direction, the right to life of the unborn, assuming no threat to the life of the mother. In my view, it is not a question of balancing the right to travel against the right to life; it is a question as to whether or not an individual has a right to travel – which she has. It cannot, in my view, be curtailed because of a particular intent.' In discussing the relationship between the rights of the mother and the unborn, Hederman J, who was the only dissenting judge, said:

> The State's duty to protect life also extends to the mother. The natural connection between the unborn child and the mother's life constitutes a special relationship. But one cannot consider the unborn life only as part of the maternal organism. The extinction of unborn life is not confined to the sphere of private life of the mother or family because the unborn life is an autonomous human being protected by the Constitution. Therefore the termination of pregnancy other than a natural one has a legal and social dimension and requires a special responsibility on the part of the State. There cannot be a freedom to extinguish life side by side with a guarantee of protection of that life because the termination of pregnancy always means the destruction of an unborn life. Therefore no recognition of a mother's right of self-determination can be given priority over the protection of the unborn life. The creation of a new life, involving as it does pregnancy, birth and raising the child, necessarily involves some restriction of a mother's freedom but the alternative is the destruction of the unborn life.

[9.139] The final two sentences of this extract from Hederman J's dissenting judgment, although made in the context of a termination of pregnancy as opposed to a refusal of a caesarean section with the death of the fetus as a probable consequence, are very firm in their refutation of the possibility that a woman's right to self-determination could outweigh the right to life of the unborn.[238] The case 'graphically illustrates one potential shortcoming of the hierarchy of rights approach, since such *a priori* ranking of such

---

[237] *SPUC v Grogan* [1989] IR 753 at p 767.
[238] This view has also been expressed in Sheikh and Cusack, 'Maternal Brain Death, Pregnancy and the Foetus: The Medico-Legal Implications' (2001) 7(2) MLJI 75 at 78.

rights (e.g. life over liberty, liberty over free speech etc.) focuses on philosophical abstractions which, if inflexibly employed, would tend to lead to the pre-determination of the outcome of particular litigation, at the expense of the flexibility which is desirable in any judicial appraisal of the relevant facts of each case and the competing merits of particular arguments.'[239]

[9.140] Thus, although the case law around Art 40.3.3° has been concerned with the direct termination of the unborn life, as opposed to the death of the fetus as an indirect consequence of the woman's decision to refuse medical treatment, there are indications in some of the majority judgments in the Supreme Court that may be useful here. When read in conjunction with the robust statements in *Re a Ward of Court*[240] as to the importance of the right to self-determination, it is not clear whether the right to refuse treatment (in this case a caesarean section) would take precedence over the right to life of the unborn.

[9.141] Also of interest in this context is the decision of the Supreme Court in *North Western Health Board v HW and CW*[241] dealing with parental authority to refuse consent for a test (known as 'the PKU test') to be carried out on their child in order to detect certain biochemical or metabolic disorders. The facts of the case are discussed in more detail in Chapter 11.[242] In holding that the Court should not intervene to order the screening test on the child, some of the judgments demonstrate again a firm commitment to the values of autonomy and privacy. Denham J repeated her position in *Re a Ward of Court*[243] where she stated that 'medical treatment may not be given to an adult person of full capacity without his or her consent.' Although there are some exceptions, these are rare and only applicable in the interests of public health, such as control of contagious disease. In any other case where medical treatment is given without consent, 'it may be trespass against the person in civil law, a battery in criminal law, and a breach of the individual's constitutional rights.' A refusal of consent by a competent adult may be made for various reasons, including non-medical reasons or reasons that others may not regard as rational, but the choice is theirs. Denham J saw it as important to consider the effect that the granting of an order obliging the parents to allow this test to be carried out on their child would have on other medical tests and vaccinations. 'If the responsibility for making this decision is transferred from the parents to the State then it would herald in a new era where there would be considerably more State intervention and decision making for children than has occurred to date.' She also said that in exceptional circumstances, such as where an emergency order was sought to treat a child in a way that had been refused by its parents, it may be 'within the range of responsible decisions' that may be taken by the parents. 'This may occur where a child is suffering a terminal illness and parents decide responsibly that he or she has suffered enough medical intervention and should receive only palliative care.' Denham J was concerned that by making the order sought by the Health Board in this case, the Court would effectively be making the test compulsory for children, without the analysis

---

[239] Kelly, *The Irish Constitution* (3rd edn, Butterworths, 1994) at cvii.

[240] *Re a Ward of Court* [1996] 2 IR 79.

[241] *North Western Health Board v HW and CW* [2001] IESC 90.

[242] At para **11.46**.

[243] *Re a Ward of Court* [1996] 2 IR 79.

and policy framework that usually precedes legislation. 'Such an outcome would be at odds with the approach previously taken in Ireland that medical tests or procedures not be compulsory.' It would mean that parents have no right to refuse, which would have a far-reaching effect.

[9.142] Hardiman J examined the few statutory provisions in Ireland dealing with consent, such as the Health Act 1953, which states in s 4 that nothing in the Act imposes an obligation on any person 'to avail himself of any service provided under this Act or to submit himself or any person for whom he is responsible to health examination or treatment.' The history of this and other pieces of legislation demonstrate the legislature's commitment to the principle of voluntarism.[244] 'It appears to me that the principle of voluntarism in respect of medical treatment is plainly established in so far as public medical services are concerned. This extends to a patient himself or to a person making decisions as to medical treatment for another person for whom he is responsible.' Hardiman J also referred to exceptions relating to infectious or communicable disease. He, too, went on to consider medical treatment at common law where consent is the basis of any lawful medical treatment, and he endorsed the statement of Denham J referred to above regarding consent. He said that the order sought by the Health Board was to deny the child's parents their right not to consent to the test being carried out on their child, to compel them to consent to it and to compel them to present their child for a test which was contrary to their religious beliefs. If the Court compelled the parents to present their child for a public health service against their will, this would be contrary to, at the least, the spirit of s 4 of the 1953 Act. Such an order would have a 'chilling effect' on other persons sharing the views of these parents. However, he also said that this did not preclude the courts from acting to enforce the rights of a plaintiff, or infant, in a situation of emergency. He agreed with the trial judge when he said:

> If the State were entitled to intervene in every case where professional opinion differed from that of the parents, or where the State considered that the parents were wrong in their decision, we would be stepping rapidly towards the Brave New World in which the State always knows best. In my view that situation would be totally at variance with both the spirit and the word of the Constitution.

[9.143] Hardiman J took the view that if it were thought necessary to compel parents to submit their children for screening, this would be something for the legislature to consider, bearing in mind whether such compulsion was proportionate or desirable in the circumstances. 'Compulsory medical diagnosis or treatment in any form is…a topic regarded with some unease throughout the civilized world.' Whether such unease should be recognised and legitimate fears allayed, and whether the benefits of the medical test were sufficient to justify coercion, were matters to be addressed legislatively. It would then be for the court to decide whether such legislation was consistent with the provisions of the Constitution.

[9.144] This case reinforces the strongly held views previously expressed in *Re a Ward of Court* in relation to self-determination and consent to treatment. It also clearly resists

---

[244] He later said that a salient feature of this claim was that there was no legislation on this topic, other than that mentioned in his judgment, whose effect is to enshrine voluntarism and parental responsibility.

State interest or intervention in what the Court regarded as parental decision-making. Concerns were expressed regarding the nature of any state in which medical choices could be overridden by a paternalistic interpretation of 'best interests'. In that sense, the case provides further indications that if a competent adult woman were to refuse to submit herself to a caesarean section, particularly if such could be shown to present a serious risk to the woman's own life,[245] the court would not compel her to do so, notwithstanding the rights of the fetus.

[9.145] In *Fitzpatrick and Another v K and Another*[246] the High Court was asked to consider the right of an adult to refuse a blood transfusion. The facts of this case, also discussed above in relation to the assessment of capacity, were that K, a 23-year-old African woman from the Congo, gave birth to a baby in an Irish hospital in 2006. Shortly thereafter she suffered a massive post-partum haemorrhage resulting in cardiovascular collapse. As blood was being prepared for immediate transfusion, the medical team was informed that K would not accept blood for religious reasons. The medical team was concerned that K would die without a blood transfusion and called the Master of the hospital (the most senior obstetrician in the maternity hospital with responsibility for clinical governance). Following discussions with K, during which she repeated her refusal of blood, the Master had doubts regarding her capacity to make such a decision and decided to apply to the High Court for an emergency order giving the hospital authority to transfuse K.

[9.146] The judge made the order authorising the hospital to administer blood to K, including all appropriate steps by way of restraint. The Master informed K of the court order and she was transfused following the administration of a sedative. She subsequently made a full recovery. She later claimed that the court order should not have been given, that the transfusion was unlawful and therefore constituted an assault and trespass to her person, and that she was entitled to refuse all or any medical treatment by virtue of her Constitutional rights and under arts 8 and 9 of the ECHR. In the High Court, Laffoy J was of the view that it could not be argued that a competent adult is not free to decline medical treatment. She referred to the *Ward of Court* case cited above in support of this conclusion. Thus the question that arose on the facts of this case was whether K had capacity to refuse the blood transfusion. She decided that on the facts of this case K did not have such capacity and therefore the hospital had lawfully administered the transfusion.

[9.147] It is noteworthy that in relation to refusal of treatment the most recent, seventh edition of the Medical Council's Ethical Guide[247] states:

---

245 A caesarean section is major surgery, and, as with other surgical procedures, there are risks involved. The estimated risk of a woman dying after a caesarean birth is less than one in 2,500 (the risk of death after a vaginal birth is less than one in 10,000). Other risks for the mother include the following: infection, increased blood loss, decreased bowel function, respiratory complications, longer hospital stay and recovery time, reactions to anaesthesia and risk of additional surgeries.
246 *Fitzpatrick and Another v K and Another* [2008] IEHC 104.
247 Medical Council, The Guide to Professional Conduct and Ethics (7th edn, 2009), available at: http://www.medicalcouncil.ie (accessed 4 June 2011).

40.1 Every adult with capacity is entitled to refuse medical treatment. You must respect a patient's decision to refuse treatment, even if you disagree with that decision. In these circumstances, you should clearly explain to the patient the possible consequences of refusing treatment and a second medical opinion should be offered to the patient if possible.

40.2 The explanation you give the patient and the patient's refusal of treatment should be clearly documented in the patient's medical records.

[9.148] In its Opinion on Advance Directives in 2007, the Irish Council for Bioethics also acknowledged the right of individuals to refuse any form of medical treatment, including Artificial Nutrition and Hydration or any other form of life-sustaining treatment, in an advance directive if they so wish.[248] Advance directives are considered further in Chapter 12.[249]

---

[248] The Council was disbanded in 2010 but its publications remain available on http://www.bioethics.ie/uploads/docs/Advance_Directives_HighRes.pdf, (accessed 16 February 2011).

[249] At para **12.18** et seq.

Chapter 10

Property in the Human Body

INTRODUCTION

[10.01] The centrality of autonomy to discussions of medical law and ethics has been emphasised throughout this book. Respect for autonomy entails the acknowledgement and acceptance that the patient has the right to control what happens to his own body. In many instances, respect for autonomy is demonstrated through the concept of informed consent and/or refusal of treatment. However, another way in which respect for the right of the individual to control his own body might be through the property framework, which would give individuals decision-making control but may also raise complex questions regarding the limits of ownership and commercialisation of body parts and tissue.

> Property is a powerful control device for the bundle of rights that it confers. It also carries a particular message – one of the potential for commerce and trade; of market advantage and disadvantage. To recognise a 'quasi-property' claim to material is to support a normatively strong connection to that material and, accordingly, to establish a strong, justiciable legal interest...[1]

At common law the issue of property rights in the human body arose only in relation to dead bodies but with developments in medical science in more recent years, judicial attention has turned to ownership of human tissue taken from living persons. This has received particular attention in the context of biobanking, which offers huge potential benefits to public health but also raises complex issues in relation to respect for the rights of those whose tissue is stored for research purposes. These questions will be examined in turn below.

DEAD BODIES AND ORGANS

[10.02] Property rights do not appear to provide any procedural advantage to claimants in the post-mortem context, and Sperling argues that cases that deal with interferences with dead bodies can be perfectly well decided and remedied without the fictional and unnecessary appeal to the right to property in the body of the deceased.[2] In any event, the common law traditionally took the view that corpses and their parts are not capable of being owned, although those charged with their disposal have certain powers and responsibilities in respect of them. The exact origins of this position are unclear but it is often attributed to Coke, who wrote in 1644 that 'the burial of the cadaver (that is, *caro data vermibus*) is *nullis in bonis*[3] and belongs to Ecclesiastical cognizance'.[4] Cases

---

1   Mason and Laurie, *Law and Medical Ethics* (8th edn, OUP, 2010) at 14.13.
2   Sperling, *Posthumous Interests: Legal and Ethical Perspectives* (Cambridge University Press, 2008) at 142.
3   Translation – belonging to nobody.
4   3 Co Inst 203.

dating from the 17th and 18th centuries provide further authority for the principle that there is no property in a dead body.[5] For example, in *Hayne's case* the defendant was charged with stealing the sheets that bound four bodies, and upon conviction, he was whipped for petty larceny. At this time, grave robbing was punishable as a theft of coffins and burial shrouds rather than theft of the bodies themselves. When it became known that corpses could also have value for medical research and training purposes, graves began to be robbed for that purpose also in an activity known as 'burking', so-called after its infamous originators Burke and Hare.[6] However, academic commentators dispute the exact provenance of the rule, with some claiming that it has been based on a misunderstanding of the older cases.[7] Regardless of its exact origins, by the 19th century the principle was entrenched in English law and is cited in cases such as *R v Lynn* (1788),[8] *R v Sharpe* (1857),[9] *Foster v Dodd* (1866),[10] *R v Price* (1884)[11] and *Williams v Williams* (1881–85).[12] These cases posed difficulties for the courts, as the 'no property' rule meant that since there was no property, there could be no prosecution for theft. Thus, the cases were decided on the basis of offences against public health and decency.[13] Legislation was later introduced in many jurisdictions, including Ireland,[14] to regulate access to the non-owned corpse in order to enable medical schools to obtain and retain corpses donated for education and training purposes.

[10.03] In *Dobson v North Tyneside Health Authority*[15] the deceased's next of kin brought an action for medical negligence against the defendant for failing to diagnose tumours in the deceased's brain at a time when early diagnosis might have saved her life or at least lessened her pain with radiotherapy. The family required the brain of the deceased in order to have an independent post-mortem examination carried out, which

---

5   For example *Hayne's case* [1614] 12 Co Rep 113 and *Handyside's case* [1749] 2 East PC 652.
6   For detailed discussion, see Rodgers, 'Human Bodies, Inhuman Uses: Public Reactions and Legislative Responses to the Scandals of Bodysnatching' (2003) Vol 12(2) Nottingham Law Journal 1–17.
7   For example, Mason and Laurie maintain that the ruling in *Hayne's case* was not that the corpse was not property but that it could not own property. See Mason and Laurie, 'Consent or Property? Dealing with the Body and its Parts in the Shadow of Bristol and Alder Hey' (2001) 64(5) MLR 710 at 714. Also Magnusson, 'The Recognition of Proprietary Rights in Human Tissue in Common Law Jurisdictions' (1992) 18 Melbourne University Law Review 601 at 603.
8   *R v Lynn* [1788] 2 TR 394. This was the first reported conviction for disinterment of a corpse without authority. The defendant was charged with entering a burial ground and taking a coffin out of the earth, from which he took a dead body and carried it away for the purpose of dissecting it. It was argued that the offence was limited to stealing the shroud and trespass in disturbing the soil but the Court held that 'common decency required that the practice should be put a stop to' and that 'the offence was cognizable in a criminal court as being highly indecent and contra bonos mores: at the bare idea alone of which nature revolted.'
9   *R v Sharpe* [1857] 169 ER 959.
10   *Foster v Dodd* [1866] LQ 1 QB 475, (1867) LR 3 QB 67.
11   *R v Price* [1884] 12 QBD 247.
12   *Williams v Williams* All ER 840.
13   See Matthews, 'The Man of Property' (1995) 3 Med L Rev 251.
14   Anatomy Act 1832, repealed by Medical Practitioners Act 2007, s 106.
15   *Dobson v North Tyneside Health Authority* [1996] 4 All ER 474.

they claimed would substantiate the allegation of negligence. However, the brain had been disposed of by the hospital following the post-mortem examination and inquest, as was standard practice at that time. The family brought an action for conversion (a tort which protects against interference with possessory and ownership interests in personal property) in respect of the disposal of brain on the basis that the defendant owed a duty to preserve it. The action failed on the grounds that the hospital did not owe a duty to preserve body parts indefinitely and the family was unable to show actual possession of the brain at the time it was disposed of. The Court of Appeal confirmed the principle that there was no legal right to possession of the deceased's brain because the plaintiff administratrix, who had the legal duty to dispose of the body, had not been appointed until after the burial of the remainder of the deceased's body.

[10.04] The courts later began to recognise the need to carve out exceptions to the 'no property' rule in certain circumstances. One of these exceptions relates to the situation where the person in possession of the body applies 'work and skill' to it in such a way as to transform the body into property. For example, in the Australian case of *Doodeward v Spence*[16] the facts concerned an action for conversion and detinue of the body of a two-headed baby preserved by the mother's doctor in a bottle of spirits. The child had been kept as a medical curiosity by the doctor for 40 years and finally sold as part of the doctor's estate after his death. It passed into the possession of the plaintiff who exhibited it for profit. The defendant, who was the Inspector of Police, seized it and prosecuted him for indecent exhibition of a corpse, to which Doodeward pleaded guilty. At the conclusion of the case the judge refused to order that the baby be handed back to Doodeward so he took a private action to recover it. At first instance the matter was dismissed but Doodeward successfully appealed to the High Court. The three-judge court unanimously held that immediately after death, a corpse could not be the subject of property. However, they expressed different views as to whether there could *ever* be property in a dead body. Griffith CJ said that:

> When a person has by the lawful exercise of work or skill so dealt with a human body or part of a human body in his lawful possession that it has acquired some attributes differentiating it from a mere corpse awaiting burial, he acquires a right to retain possession of it.[17]

Higgins J agreed, saying that the corpse had been turned into something very different by the skill of the embalmer. Barton J agreed with the general proposition that there could be no property in an unburied corpse but did not consider that the stillborn baby came within this general rule, as it had acquired value 'not as a corpse but as something so unlike an ordinary corpse as to be a curiosity.'[18] On balance, therefore, the plaintiff was held to be entitled to the return of the body.

[10.05] In further illustration of the 'work and skill' exception, the facts of *R v Kelly and Lindsay*[19] are of interest. This case involved the prosecution of a sculptor who crafted casts for an art exhibition from human body parts stolen by a technician from the Royal College of Surgeons. The accused argued that theft could not have taken place, as there

---

[16] *Doodeward v Spence* [1908] 6 CLR 406.
[17] *Doodeward v Spence* [1908] 6 CLR at 414.
[18] *Doodeward v Spence* [1908] 6 CLR at 416.
[19] *R v Kelly and Lindsay* [1998] 3 All ER 741.

were no property rights attached to the objects that had been taken. Although the Court did not recognise full ownership, they did identify a proprietary interest in the body parts. The Court held that the common law rule that body parts do not constitute property is subject to an exception where those parts have acquired different attributes by virtue of the application of skill, such as dissection or preservation techniques, for exhibition or teaching purposes. Following this case it was thought that this may, in fact, avoid the perceived necessity for change to the general rule, as the exceptions may allow for solutions to be found to the particular problems posed by the rule, in particular in relation to transplantation procedures.[20] However, it was also argued that the 'work and skill' exception was an example of forcing the law.[21] In future cases it was thought that the exception may be extended to include body parts with a use or significance beyond their mere existence, even without the acquisition of different attributes. Examples of this might include organs or body parts intended for use in transplantation, or the extraction of DNA as exhibits in a trial.

[10.06] In recent years, it has been argued that property law should apply to grant rights to the relatives of deceased persons in circumstances where the deceased's organs were retained following post-mortem examination. Following a number of high-profile governmental inquiries in the UK,[22] claims were brought by bereaved parents in respect of post-mortem examinations carried out on the bodies of their deceased children in *AB v Leeds Teaching Hospital NHS Trust*.[23] In this case the parents sued the hospital for psychiatric injury sustained on learning that organs had been retained without the parents' knowledge. A claim was also made for wrongful interference with the body, which was a previously unrecognised form of legal action. Gage J followed the previous line of authority in confirming the 'no property in a human body' rule but held that parts of a body may acquire the character of property if skill and work were applied to it. In the circumstances of this case, the Court held that the post mortems had been lawfully carried out and the pathologist had applied work and skill in dissecting and 'fixing' the organ in order to produce blocks and slides for microscopic examination. This gave the pathologists possessory rights to the retained samples. Gage J held that there was no tort of wrongful interference with a body or conversion but he also held that a doctor is obliged to pass on any instructions received from parents to the pathologist. The pathologist is bound to adhere to any such lawful instruction within his duty of care. The Court also stated that unauthorised retention of organs for research purposes may engage the right to respect for private and family life under art 8 of the European Convention on Human Rights (ECHR) and that the circumstances in which this could be justified by the public authorities under art 8 (2) would be rare.

---

[20] Grubb Andrew, 'I, Me, Mine: Bodies, Parts and Property' (1998) 3 Medical Law International 299–317 at 308.

[21] White, 'The law relating to dealing with dead bodies" (2000) 4 *Med Law International* 145; Rosalind Atherton. 'Who owns your body?' (2003) 77 *Australian Law Journal* 178

[22] Bristol Royal Infirmary Inquiry, *Interim Report: Removal and Retention of Human Material* (May 2000); Report of the Royal Liverpool Children's Hospital (Alder Hey) Inquiry, House of Commons (Jan 2001) (Redfern Report); Advice from the Chief Medical Officer, *The removal, retention and use of human organs and tissue from post-mortem examination* (London: Dept of Health 2001)

[23] *AB v Leeds Teaching Hospital NHS Trust* [2004] 2 FLR 365.

[10.07] The UK Human Tissue Act 2004 now covers the storage, use and, for deceased persons, removal of organs and tissue. It established a Human Tissue Authority, which provides guidance about the Act, ensures best practice and licenses organisations that store human tissue for research.[24] The removal, storage and use of tissue from living individuals as part of their diagnosis or treatment does not fall within the scope of the Act and is covered by the usual ethical rules on consent to treatment. Consent is the central tenet of the legislation, and carrying out certain activities (referred to as scheduled purposes) without the necessary consent is a criminal offence. A person may give consent for their tissue to be used for research after their death and if there is no record of the deceased person's wishes, consent for research can be obtained from someone nominated by them to act on his or her behalf; or, if no one has been nominated, from a person in a 'qualifying relationship' – such as a partner, relative or friend.

[10.08] In a similar case to *AB* in Scotland, *Stevens v Yorkhill NHS Trust and another*,[25] the pursuer (plaintiff) claimed that it was never explained to her that the post mortem which she authorised to be carried out on her daughter would involve removal and retention of organs. She argued that there was a duty of care owed to inform her and seek her separate authorisation to the organ retention. She also argued that Scots law provided that wrongful interference with a corpse was actionable as an affront to human dignity. The Court found authority for the claim in the ancient *action injuriarum* which allowed the pursuer to recover damages for *solatium* (which is injury to feelings rather than psychiatric injury). The Court followed Gage J in relation to the acknowledgement of a duty of care owed to inform the mother about organ retention. The Court did not discuss issues relating to property rights.[26]

[10.09] In Ireland in 2000 a controversy arose surrounding the retention of organs following post-mortem examinations without the knowledge or consent of the families of the deceased. This mirrored similar controversies in England, Scotland and Northern Ireland and gave rise to a public outcry regarding the breach of trust and lack of communication on the part of hospitals and medical staff to the families of deceased persons. The Madden Report on Post Mortem Practice and Procedure (2006), which was established to examine paediatric post-mortem practices, concluded that:

> [P]ost-mortem examinations were carried out in Ireland according to best professional and international standards and that no intentional disrespect was shown to the child's body. The root causes of this controversy have been a lack of communication with parents as to why organs were retained, the difference in perspective as to their symbolic significance, and the legislative vacuum on the role of consent in postmortem practice.[27]

The Report discussed the legal position in relation to property rights in the human body and acknowledged the lack of a legislative framework or judicial authority to support the

---

24 See http://www.hta.gov.uk/ (accessed 4 June 2011).
25 *Stevens v Yorkhill NHS Trust and another* [2007] SCLR 606. See also *Report of the Independent Review Group on the Retention of Organs at Post-Mortem* (Jan 2001) (McLean Report).
26 See discussion in Mason and Laurie, *Law and Medical Ethics* (8th edn, 2010) para 14.47.
27 The Madden Report on Post Mortem Practice and Procedure (2006), at para 7.1. Available at http://www.dohc.ie/publications/pdf/madden.pdf. (accessed 4 June 2011).

recognition of such rights on the part of the parents of the deceased child. It acknowledged that one of the options for the recognition of the authority of parents in relation to the bodies of their deceased children was the property model.

> This argument would follow the line of thought sometimes expressed by bereaved parents to the effect that their children's bodies 'belong' to them, and that any removal or retention of organs was akin to 'stealing' what rightfully belongs to the parents. Other families find the language of ownership insensitive and abhorrent, as they prefer to identify with a sense of continuing parenthood, and see the child as a continuing member of the family.[28]

[10.10] The Report acknowledges that common law has rejected a property approach to the human body and that although many commentators have argued that the foundation of this principle rests on flimsy evidence from misreported cases, the principle of 'no property in the human body' has long stood the test of time and is likely to be accepted by the Irish courts. The differing views expressed by the English courts, discussed above, indicate the lack of clarity that exists in relation to whether or not the pathologist's act of fixing the organ transforms it into an item of property. It is similarly unclear whether or not the 'work and skill' exception would be applied in these circumstances in Irish courts, but, as with the 'no property' rule itself, it is likely to be followed unless affected by legislative change. The interpretation of the rule in the context of pathology practice and organ retention remains undecided. The Report recommended that the best resolution of this issue for bereaved parents was to enact clear and unambiguous legislation to ensure that organ retention practices could not happen again in the future without the knowledge and authorisation of the parents. The Government accepted the recommendations of the Report and undertook to introduce human tissue legislation to deal with post-mortem practice. Proposals for a Human Tissue Bill were published for consultation in 2009 but have not yet been enacted.[29]

[10.11] Cases arising out of organ retention practices were also brought by bereaved parents in Ireland for personal injuries, anxiety, distress and annoyance, loss and damage, misrepresentation, breach of contract, negligence, breach of duty, breach of bailment, conversion, detinue and trespass to the person. However, the issue of property rights in respect of the retained organs was not discussed in the judgments. In *O'Connor & Tormey v Lenihan*[30] the plaintiffs had two children who had died in 1996 and 1998. They first learned in 2000 that organs removed following post-mortem examinations carried out on their children had been retained. They sought damages for personal injuries arising from the distress suffered at the time they received this information and their subsequent retrieval and burial of the retained organs. Although very sympathetic to the plaintiffs' distress, Peart J held that no expert evidence of psychiatric illness or injury had been adduced by them to substantiate a personal injuries claim. For that reason, the claims were dismissed.

[10.12] In a case of broadly similar facts, *Devlin v the National Maternity Hospital*,[31] the Supreme Court upheld the judgment of the High Court that the accepted practice of the

---

[28]   The Madden Report on Post Mortem Practice and Procedure (2006) at para 12.1.
[29]   See http://www.dohc.ie/issues/human_tissue_bill/ (accessed 4 June 2011).
[30]   *O'Connor & Tormey v Lenihan* [2005] IEHC 176.
[31]   *Devlin v the National Maternity Hospital* [2007] IESC 50.

1980s was that when there had been consent to the post mortem, it was implicit that the pathologist had permission to remove or retain organs.

> This practice, and implicit acceptance, stemmed from Victorian times. Probably with the best of motives parents were not "troubled" with the grim reality of a post-mortem and the need to retain organs and samples of tissue. This practice was exercised with a complete lack of understanding as to the rights of parents in relation to their children, and the retention of organs indefinitely and without consultation. The position of parents, their rights, and family rights, and the dignity of the child, are now acknowledged. However, this case stems from a time when a paternalistic attitude to parents was endemic in hospitals. In this case the parents did not consent to the removal of their child's organs at post-mortem, and the court is required to consider the consequences.

[10.13] The plaintiff claimed that on learning about the retention of her child's organs she suffered shock and post-traumatic stress, a psychiatric illness. The Court held that grief and sorrow are not a basis on which to award damages and that the test for nervous shock had not been satisfied, specifically in relation to the requirement that the nervous shock sustained by a plaintiff must be by reason of actual or apprehended physical injury to the plaintiff or a person other than the plaintiff. In upholding the High Court's dismissal of the action, Denham J said

> The hospital's practice in relation to post-mortems of children in the 1980s was rooted in times long past. Probably with the best of motives, the policies were paternalistic and inappropriate. While it may have been thought kind not to trouble or disturb the parents, the decision to be made as to a post-mortem and their child's body is theirs to make…This was a misunderstanding, by the medical profession, of the rights of the parents. While parents may choose not to receive full information at the time, they must be given that choice when they are requested to authorise a post-mortem of a child. In the tragic and stressful situation of the death of a child parents may not wish to receive all the information at that time, but they are entitled to receive it specifically in relation to their child then, or later, or to receive it generally from printed information.

There are no other cases in Ireland which clarify whether human bodies or their parts might be considered to be the subject of property rights and therefore the matter must be regarded as undecided in this jurisdiction, although it is likely that Irish courts would follow the common law approach of 'no property in a human body'.

TISSUE FROM LIVING BODIES

[10.14] In relation to the removal of tissue from a living person the common law generally took the position, similar to that which applied to dead bodies, that such tissue had been abandoned by its original 'owner' or was '*res nullius*', ie belonging to no one.[32] This principle was developed at a time when the tissue was removed because it was diseased and therefore of no value to anyone. In more modern times, the courts appear to have become more willing to consider deviating from the common law rule, for example in the prosecution of cases involving theft of urine or blood in the context of driving under the influence of prohibited substances. In *R v Welsh*[33] the judge made passing reference to the tipping out of a urine sample as a 'technical property offence'. In *R v Rothery*[34] the defendant was charged with the theft of the container in which a

---

[32] McHale 'Waste, Ownership and Bodily Products' (2000) 8(2) Health Care Analysis 123–35.
[33] *R v Welsh* [1974] RTR 478.
[34] *R v Rothery* [1976] RTR 550.

blood sample was stored but it is not clear whether the container and the blood were regarded as one entity.

[10.15] Dickenson asks why it matters whether we own our bodies or not. She says that a large part of the concern is that commodification transforms us into objects of property-holding, rather than active human subjects and that this is inconsistent with respect for human dignity.[35] She argues that the distinction between persons and things is as much a philosophical question as a legal one, and that it draws its origins from Kant who said:

> Man cannot dispose over himself because he is not a thing; he is not his own property; to say that he is would be self-contradictory; for insofar as he is a person he is a Subject in whom the ownership of things can be vested, and if he were his own property he would be a thing over which he could have ownership. But a person cannot be a property and so cannot be a thing which can be owned, for it is impossible to be a person and a thing, the proprietor and the property.[36]

Dickenson says that human tissue and human genetic material, however, fall between two stools, containing elements of both person and thing, subject and object, and that perhaps societal discomfort with commodification is based on the realisation that recent developments take us closer to the object end of the spectrum. According to Kantian philosophy, this radically undermines our humanity. The extent to which such discomfort may influence the legal framework around human tissue remains to be seen.[37]

[10.16] In an important case called *Moore v Regents of California*,[38] the plaintiff was receiving treatment for hairy cell leukemia at the University of California Medical Centre. As a result of Moore's condition it was necessary to remove his spleen. His treating physician, Dr Golde, recognised the potential commercial advantage of Moore's cells due to their unique qualities. He was subsequently encouraged to return to the medical centre for ongoing treatment where blood, serum, skin, bone marrow and sperm were harvested from him and used for research purposes without his knowledge or consent. Throughout the period of time that Moore was under Dr Golde's care, Dr Golde and his colleagues were actively involved in a number of activities which were concealed from Moore. Specifically, the defendants were conducting research on Moore's cells and planned to benefit financially and competitively by exploiting the cells and their exclusive access to the cells by virtue of Golde's on-going doctor-patient

---

35   Dickenson, *Property in the Body: Feminist Perspectives* (Cambridge University Press, 2007) at p 4.

36   Kant, *Lectures on Ethics* (Indianapolis, Bobbs-Merrill) 1963, p 4, cited in Dickenson *Property in the Body: Feminist Perspectives* (Cambridge University Press, 2007) at 5.

37   See further Matthews, 'Whose Body? People As Property' (1983) Current Legal Problems 193 at 208; Mortimer, 'Property Rights in Body Parts: The Relevance of Moore's Case in Australia', (1993) 19 Monash University Law Review 217 at 245; Herring and Chau, 'My Body, Your Body, Our Bodies' Med Law Review 15, Spring 2007, pp 34–61.

38   *Moore v Regents of California* [1990] 271 Cal Reptr 146 (Cal Sup Ct). For discussion see Dickens, 'Living Tissue and Organ Donors and Property Law: More on Moore' (1992) 8 Journal of Contemporary Health Law and Policy 73; Alta Charo, 'Body of Research – Ownership and Use of Human Tissue' (2006) NEJM Vol 355 No 15: 1517–1519; Creagh, 'Property in the Living Body' (2001) Bar Review 209.

relationship with Moore. Golde established a cell-line from Moore's T-cells and the University applied for a patent on the cell-line. In his claim against the University, Moore claimed that although the true value of the cell-line was difficult to predict, it was estimated at approximately three billion dollars. He took an action for conversion, and as a result, he claimed a proprietary interest in each of the products that might be created from his cells or the patented cell-line. The Supreme Court stated that in effect what Moore was asking it to do was in effect 'to impose a tort duty on scientists to investigate the consensual pedigree of each human cell sample used in research.' The Court was of the view that the imposition of such a duty raised policy issues which would affect medical research of importance to all of society. The Court rejected Moore's claim for conversion on the grounds that there was no reported judicial decision to support his contention that he had retained an ownership interest in his cells following their removal, and Californian statute law also drastically limited the right of a patient to exercise control over excised cells. The Court rejected the argument that the unusual circumstances of Moore's claim should be used as a basis to extend the theory of conversion. It said:

> There are three reasons why it is inappropriate to impose liability for conversion based upon the allegations of Moore's complaint. First, a fair balancing of the relevant policy considerations counsels against extending the tort. Second, problems in this area are better suited to legislative resolution. Third, the tort of conversion is not necessary to protect patients' rights. For these reasons, we conclude that the use of excised human cells in medical research does not amount to a conversion.

[10.17] The Court went on to say that the extension of conversion law into this area would hinder research by restricting access to the necessary raw materials and that the exchange of scientific materials would be compromised if each cell sample were to become the potential subject matter of a lawsuit. Mosk J filed a powerful dissent from the majority opinion and said the fact that a patent had been granted in respect of the cell-line did not necessarily prohibit recognition of Moore's rights to share in the commercial exploitation of the cell-line derived from his own body tissue. He said that this was an unfair result which was not compelled by the law of patents. He went on to say 'a patent is not a license to defraud', and he suggested that a better approach might be to recognise Golde and Moore as joint inventors in order to ensure that each contributor is fairly compensated. Mosk J also opposed the policy considerations which found favour with the majority and argued that these were outweighed by two contrary considerations. The first consideration is that 'our society acknowledges a profound ethical imperative to respect the human body as the physical and temporal expression of the unique human persona.' He quoted Danforth as follows:

> Research with human cells that results in significant economic gain for the researcher and no gain for the patient offends the traditional mores of our society in a manner impossible to quantify. Such research tends to treat the human body as a commodity – a means to a profitable end. The dignity and sanctity with which we regard the human whole, body as well as mind and soul, are absent when we allow researchers to further their own interests without the patient's participation by using a patient's cells as the basis for a marketable product.[39]

---

[39] Danforth 'Cells, Sales and Royalties: The Patient's Right to a Portion of the Profits' (1985) 6 Yale Law and Policy Review 179 at 190.

[10.18] The second consideration was that of equity. 'Our society values fundamental fairness in dealing between its members, and condemns the unjust enrichment of any member at the expense of another. This is particularly true when, as here, the parties are not in equal bargaining positions.' Mosk J said that the university's denial of Moore's claim to a share in the proceeds of the cell-line was 'inequitable and immoral'. He quoted Murray as follows:

> The person who furnishes the tissue should be justly compensated...If biotechnologists fail to make provision for a just sharing of profits with the person whose gift made it possible, the public's sense of justice will be offended and no one will be the winner.[40]

[10.19] In relation to the issue of non-disclosure, the Court also took the view that a doctor who intends to treat a patient in whom he has either a research interest or an economic interest is under a fiduciary duty to disclose such interest to the patient before treatment and that Golde's failure to do so in this case gave rise to a cause of action. Mosk J also agreed with this decision but was of the view that a nondisclosure action was an inadequate remedy for three reasons. Firstly, he said the majority's reasoning was that the threat of litigation for non-disclosure would have a prophylactic effect and would give physician-researchers the incentive to disclose any conflicts of interest before treatment, thereby protecting patients' rights to make an informed choice. Mosk J was of the view that this remedy was illusory, as it fell within the realms of an action for medical negligence, which would therefore require the patient to prove a causal connection between the non-disclosure and an injury sustained by the patient. The patient would have to prove that if he had been fully informed, he would have refused consent to the relevant procedure, and that any reasonable person would have done likewise. Mosk J said that few judges would believe that disclosure of the possibility of research would dissuade a reasonably prudent person from consenting to the treatment and that therefore the threat of such litigation is 'largely a paper tiger'.

[10.20] Secondly, Mosk J said that the nondisclosure action was inadequate because it fails to solve half of the problem in that it gives the patient only the right to refuse consent, it does not allow him to give consent on the basis that he can share in the proceeds despite sound reasons for recognising the patient's right to participate in such benefits. Thirdly, he said that the non-disclosure action failed to reach a major class of potential defendants, namely researchers who fall outside of the doctor-patient relationship. In this case, the imposition of a duty of disclosure could only be placed on Dr Golde by virtue of the doctor-patient relationship he had with Moore. No such duty could be imposed on the other researchers involved in these activities, as they were not doctors and they did not have a fiduciary relationship with Moore. Yet some of these parties may well have participated more in, and profited more from, such exploitation than the doctor involved. Thus, the true exploiters may escape liability.

[10.21] The main significance of the *Moore* case is in denying the ownership claim of a patient in respect of cells taken from his body and used by doctors and researchers to invent a cell-line which they patented. The case protects the concept of ownership of tissue in the hands of the researchers, but not the person from whom it emanated.

---

[40]   Murray, 'Who Owns the Body? On the Ethics of Using Human Tissue for Commercial Purposes' (1986) IRB: A Review of Human Subjects Research 5.

Similar circumstances arose in *Greenberg v Miami Children's Hospital Research Institute Inc* in 2003 in which a law suit was brought by parents of children with a rare and incurable genetic disorder called Canavan disease against researchers who patented a test for the disease using samples donated by the families.[41] The families were concerned that by patenting the test, the researchers could limit access to information and research about the disease as well as the test itself, whereas the families wanted to ensure that information and testing were freely available. They therefore claimed a property interest in their samples and the genetic information contained in them. A preliminary ruling rejected the property claim argued by the families but suggested that an argument on grounds of unjust enrichment might be successful.

[10.22] Under Florida law, the elements of a claim for unjust enrichment are (1) that the plaintiff conferred a benefit on the defendant, who had knowledge of the benefit; (2) the defendant voluntarily accepted and retained the benefit; and (3) under the circumstances it would be inequitable for the defendant to retain the benefit without paying for it. It was not contested that the families conferred a benefit on the researchers, including, among other things, blood and tissue samples and soliciting financial contributions. However, the defendants contended that the plaintiffs had not suffered any detriment, and that no plaintiff had been denied access to Canavan testing. Furthermore, the plaintiffs received what they sought – the successful isolation of the Canavan gene and the development of a screening test. The plaintiffs argued, however, that when the defendants applied the benefits for unauthorised purposes, they suffered a detriment. Had they known that the defendants intended to commercialise their genetic material through patenting and restrictive licensing, the families would not have provided their samples to the researchers under those terms. The Court held that the families had alleged more than just a donor-donee relationship and that the facts painted 'a picture of a continuing research collaboration that involved Plaintiffs also investing time and significant resources in the race to isolate the Canavan gene'. Therefore, the Court held that the families had sufficiently established the requisite elements of an unjust enrichment claim and refused to dismiss the claim on that ground. The case was ultimately settled on the basis that the plaintiffs agreed not to further challenge Miami Children's Hospital's ownership and licensing of the Canavan gene patent; the hospital would continue to license and collect royalty fees for clinical testing for the Canavan gene mutation; and there would be licence-free use of the Canavan gene in research to cure Canavan disease.

[10.23] A further case arose in 2006 in *Washington University v Catalona*.[42] Professor William Catalona, a surgeon and researcher employed at Washington University in St Louis, Missouri, collected thousands of research samples from excised cancerous tissues of his patients and stored them in a biobank operated by the university and used strictly for research purposes. Patients were asked to sign consent forms which stated that they did not assert any ownership rights in respect of any products arising from the research and that the donations were a gift to research at Washington University. In 2003 Catalona left the university to work elsewhere and wrote to the research participants

---

[41]   *Greenberg v Miami Children's Hospital Research Institute Inc* 264 F Supp 2d 1064 (SS Fla 2003).
[42]   *Washington University v Catalona* 437 F Supp 2d 985 (ED Mo 2006).

inviting them to sign an authorisation form which would allow their samples to be released from the biobank into his custody. The university brought an action to clarify the ownership of these samples.

[10.24] In Missouri, where this case occurred, property ownership is determined by proof of exclusive possession and control of the property. The Court concluded that the university had been in exclusive possession of the samples and bore all legal and compliance risks in relation to them, as well as having control over them. The Court also considered whether the samples constituted a gift from the research participants or a bailment, which is a contractual obligation to retain possession of property on the expectation that the property will be returned to the owner in the future. It was held that the informed consent forms signed by the participants constituted clear and convincing evidence that they intended to make a gift to the university and that this intention could not later be revoked following a change of heart by the participants. The Court held that it was not a bailment, as the research participants did not have any expectation of having the samples returned to them at a future date. The Court followed the principle established in *Moore* that a research participant does not retain any ownership rights in the samples after the donation of the biological materials.

[10.25] In the UK, the Nuffield Council on Bioethics published a report in 1995 in which this issue was discussed at length.[43] The Council recommended that English law should take the view that tissue removed in the course of treatment (for which consent had been given) would be regarded as having been abandoned by the patient and that tissue removed in circumstances other than treatment, which is voluntarily donated, should be regarded as a gift. Legislative intervention has taken place in the UK in relation to some practical aspects of body parts to allow the individual concerned to exercise some control over the use of his body parts. The Human Tissue Act 2004 makes consent the fundamental principle underpinning the lawful storage and use of body parts, organs and tissue from the living or the deceased for specified health-related purposes and public display.[44] Consent is not required for the research use of 'existing holdings' (human tissue already in storage for a scheduled purpose when the Act came into force), or for the use of residual tissue from living individuals for research on an anonymous basis where the research has been approved by a research ethics committee. The Act does not apply to gametes, which are dealt with by the Human Fertilisation and Embryology Act 2008.

[10.26] Mason and Laurie argue that the time has come to recognise a modified form of property rights for individuals in their own body parts.[45] They say we should not assume that consent is the sole or best solution to the dilemmas thrown up by modern medicine and that consent actually disempowers individuals in that the only right it gives is the right to agree or refuse. It does not help those who are willing to participate in medical research subject to certain limitations in relation to the subsequent use of their samples for purposes which the individual finds objectionable. In such circumstances the

---

43 Nuffield Council on Bioethics, *Human Tissue: Ethical and Legal Issues* (1995).
44 See generally Mason and Laurie, *Law and Medical Ethics* (8th edn, OUP, 2010), Ch 14.
45 Mason and Laurie 'Consent or Property? Dealing with the Body and its Parts in the Shadow of Bristol and Alder Hey' (2001) 64 MLR 711. See generally Mason and Laurie, *Law and Medical Ethics* (8th edn, OUP, 2010), Ch 14.

individual may only choose not to participate, whereas if he had a property right in his sample he could continue to exert some control over its use.

[10.27] In the Irish context, the law is currently silent on these issues and therefore the legal status of human tissue is uncertain. Good clinical practice normally dictates over-collection of tissue at surgery so as to ensure sufficient material for sampling and diagnosis. This tissue is commonly archived and may be made available, usually strictly on an anonymous basis, for research, medical training, audit of laboratory procedures and scholarship. The large scale collection of such tissue, either archival samples or tissue specifically donated by patients or donors for research purposes, is referred to as biobanking, which is considered in more detail in the next section. Whether such tissue would be regarded as personal property in Ireland is a moot question, the answer to which may depend on the context in which the issue arises. Were the facts of *Moore* to come before a court in this jurisdiction, 'the court would undoubtedly be cognisant not only of patients' rights to autonomy, privacy and dignity, but also the substantial public interest in the activities of treatment, archiving, research and teaching.'[46] The application of patent law to advances in biotechnology and human genetics may also create further ambiguities and legal problems.[47]

BIOBANKING

Introduction

[10.28] As discussed in Chapter 13, medical progress is based on research and the human body and its tissue are indispensable for that purpose. The use of tissue in research is not new but the modern focus on genetic characteristics and the large-scale nature of such research which may extend across many generations and groups of individuals has changed the design of such research and the legal and ethical issues it raises. 'As a consequence of the developments in human tissue research, the status of the human tissue has changed from a *res derelicta* into a substance which has personal (informational) value; because of the commercial prospects the research offers, human tissue has also become a commodity.'[48] Tissue collections, sometimes called biobanks, are assembled for use in patient-care and research activities.[49] According to OECD Guidelines, human biobanks and genetic research databases are structured resources

---

[46] Madden, 'Legal Status of Archived Human Tissue'. (2004) 10, 2 Medico-Legal Journal of Ireland 76.

[47] See Sheikh, '"Owning" Life: New Frontiers in Patent Law, Genetics and Biotechnology?' (1999) MLJI 23; Mills O. 'Biotechnology and the Ethical Moral Concerns of European Patent Law' (2000) Eurowatch 46.

[48] Roscam-Abbing, 'Human Tissue Research, Individual Rights and Bio-Banks' in Gunning and Holm (eds) *Ethics, Law and Society, Vol II* (Ashgate, 2006) 7–16, at 7.

[49] Biobanks used in patient care include umbilical cord blood banks, which comprise collections of umbilical cord blood retained after delivery of a child to enable storage of stem cells for possible autologous transfusion (transfusion to the same donor) in the future. Such collections may also be used for unrelated transfusion, subject to matching with the recipient. For further details and discussion see European Group on Ethics in Science and New Technologies to the European Commission, Opinion No 19 *Ethical Aspects of Umbilical Cord Blood Banking* (2004).

that can be used for the purpose of genetic research which include: a) human biological materials and/or information generated from the analysis of same; and b) extensive associated information.[50] They have a high impact potential for public health and medicine, as new drug discovery and the development of so-called personalised medicine depend on the study of large collections of epidemiological, clinical and biological samples and information from large numbers of patients and healthy persons.[51] These databases may be disease-specific or unspecified collections of tissue that is donated or left over after surgery (population-based biobanks) and they may be established on a commercial basis or in the public sector. When combined with personal information about the donor/patient, they create a valuable virtual database as a source for research. The practice of biobanking raises profound ethical and legal questions about the circumstances under which such banks are established and how the benefits of the banks are harnessed.[52] The scope of variations between biobanks is growing and there are fundamental questions about how best to govern and regulate them given the differences between the characteristics of collections. Policymakers and lawmakers have struggled with these issues, and existing regulatory frameworks in the UK and elsewhere have come under sustained criticism.[53] Gibbons says that:

> Without any specifically tailored, comprehensive provision for biobanks, a highly complex, confusing, inconsistent, uncoordinated, duplicative yet incomplete governance patchwork has evolved. It is characterized by an excessive number of legal, ethical, and other guidance instruments; an array of competing regulatory authorities and actors, whose roles, remits, and responsibilities often are unclear; a *de facto* over-dependence on informal systems, self-regulation, and 'soft' regulatory techniques; and a worrying legitimacy deficit.[54]

[10.29] In addition to these important concerns about regulation and governance, there are also other issues that relate perhaps more personally to the person from whom the tissue is taken. Unlike other forms of medical research discussed in Chapter 13, the focus of concern here is not the physical integrity of the research participant, but rather on the control he has over his biological material. The concept of battery protects living people from physical interventions, but there is no overriding legal concept to govern the relationship between the tissue source and the biobank. Questions which arise here include what type of information should the tissue source be given about the purposes to which the tissue will be put; what form of consent is appropriate; what should be done with genetic information obtained from a biobank; under what circumstances is

[50] OECD 2009. *Guidelines for Human Biobanks and Genetic Research Databases* (00 2009 3B 1 P) no 89497. For more detail on trends in biobanking in Europe, see Schulte in den Baumen et al, 'Data Protection and Sample Management in Biobanking – A Legal Dichotomy' (2010) *Genomics, Society and Policy* Vol 6 No 1 pp 33–46.

[51] Zika et al, *Pharmacogenetics and Pharmacogenomics: State-of-the-Art and Potential Socio-Economic Impact in the EU* (2006) Euro Commission DG JRC/IPTS, EUR 22214.

[52] Andrews, 'Harnessing the Benefits of Biobanks' (Spring 2005) Journal of Law, Medicine & Ethics 22–30 at 23.

[53] Gibbons, 'Regulating Biobanks: A Twelve-Point Typological Tool' (2009) Med Law Rev 17, pp 313–346.

[54] Gibbons, 'Regulating Biobanks: A Twelve-Point Typological Tool' (2009) Med Law Rev 17, at 314 quoting from Kaye and Gibbons, 'Mapping the Regulatory Space for Genetic Databases and Biobanks in England and Wales' (2008) 9 Med Law I 111 at 126.

commercialisation of samples and information in biobanks acceptable; how can people protect themselves from the unauthorised use of or commercialisation of their tissue samples; and how should the benefits of biobanking be shared?[55]

[10.30] Confidentiality and data protection principles will also apply here due to the informational value of human tissue, and therefore safeguards must be built into the biobank relating to the quality of data, data security and other protections, which will be discussed below. A great variability exists in the identification of the samples used, depending on the source of the material and the purpose of the research. In some studies where individuals just serve as the sources of the samples, identifying them is not necessary. For other studies in which extensive information on diagnosis, family history and demographics is crucial, the ability to identify the source of the sample is essential.[56] The terminology used in this context depends on whether the tissue is anonymous or identifiable and many different models exist. At its simplest, tissue can be categorised in four categories, as described by the American Society of Human Genetics as follows:

- Anonymous – biological materials that were originally collected without identifiers and are impossible to link with their sources
- Anonymised[57] – biological materials that were originally identified but have been irreversibly stripped of all identifiers and are impossible to link to their sources
- Identifiable[58] – biological materials that are unidentified for research purposes but can be linked to their sources through the use of a code. Decoding can only be done by the investigator or another member of the research team.
- Identified – biological materials to which identifiers, such as a name, patient number, or clear pedigree location, are attached and available to the researchers.[59]

Consent

[10.31] The issue of informed consent is of prime importance in relation to biobanking, as elsewhere in health care. The doctrine and meaning of informed consent has been discussed in Chapter 9. In relation to research it is also a fundamental prerequisite that research should not be undertaken without the subject/participant's consent. 'The research goals of advancing scientific understanding and curing diseases are laudable, but research is not a matter of conscription. People can refuse to participate in research,

---

[55] Derived from Andrews, 'Harnessing the Benefits of Biobanks' (Spring 2005) Journal of Law, Medicine & Ethics 22–30 at 24.

[56] Godard et al, 'Data Storage and DNA Banking for Biomedical Research: Informed Consent, Confidentiality, Quality Issues, Ownership, Return Of Benefits. A Professional Perspective' Eur J of Hum Gen (2003) 11, Suppl 2, S88–S122.

[57] Also referred to as 'unlinked'.

[58] Also referred to as 'coded'.

[59] American Society of Human Genetics, Statement on Informed Consent for Genetic Research: Am J Hum Genet 1996; 59:471–474. See also Recommendation Rec (2006) 4 of the Committee of Ministers to member states on research on biological materials of human origin, https://wcd.coe.int/wcd/ViewDoc.jsp?id=977859 (accessed 4 June 2011).

even if it involves no risk to them and enormous potential benefit to the community.'[60] However, in recent years there have been calls for the reconceptualisation of participation in health research as a moral obligation. For example, Harris argues that seriously debilitating diseases give rise to important needs and since medical research is necessary to relieve those needs in many circumstances, people are morally obliged to act as research subjects.[61] Similarly, Rhodes says that research participation is a moral obligation for reasons of justice, beneficence and self-development: because we all benefit significantly from modern medicine, we are all required to do our part in advancing the state of medical knowledge.[62] However, if research participation is considered as a duty, then it may not make sense to seek informed consent at all since the freedom to decline to participate is restricted by the blameworthiness that would attach to such an action. People may thus choose to participate in research to avoid blame rather than based on their understanding of the risks and benefits of participation. Despite these arguments in favour of a moral duty to participate in research, informed consent currently remains the gold standard.

[10.32] In seeking informed consent to donate tissue to a biobank, it is generally agreed that the following information should be provided to donors:[63]

- the voluntary nature of participation;
- the type of consent used (specific or general);
- the circumstances of sampling, including risks of the procedure;
- the purposes, nature, extent and duration of the proposed use of the tissue;
- the possibility of transfer of samples and data to third parties;
- the possibility of communication of research results to the donor;
- information on the possible consequences of the communication of results for the donor and his family;
- storage and security/protection of personal data;
- the identifiability or anonymity of the samples and/or data;
- the right to withdraw at any time, and the consequences of withdrawal;
- any commercialisation prospects for the proposed research, and;
- any payments for donors or other form of benefit sharing.

[10.33] One of the most interesting issues in relation to informed consent in this context is the question of whether consent may be given in advance for future unspecified research uses to which the samples may be put, variously known as general, broad or

---

60 L Andrews, 'Harnessing the Benefits of Biobanks' (Spring 2005) Journal of Law, Medicine & Ethics 22–30, at 24.

61 Harris, 'Scientific Research is a Moral Duty' (2005) Journal of Medical Ethics 31, No 4,242–48.

62 Rhodes, 'Rethinking Research Ethics' (2005) Am J Of Bioethics 5, No 1; Rhodes, 'In Defense of the Duty to Participate in Biomedical Research' Am J Of Bioethics 8, No 10 (2008): 37–38. See also Schaefer et al, 'The Obligation to Participate in Biomedical Research' (2009) *JAMA* 302, 67–72; and Rennie, 'Viewing Research Participation as a Moral Obligation: In Whose Interests?' (2011) Hastings Centre Report 41, No 2: 40–47.

63 Watson, Kay and Smith, 'Integrating Biobanks: Addressing the Practical and Ethical Issues to Deliver a Valuable Tool for Cancer Research' (2010) Nature Reviews Cancer, Vol 10: 646–651.

blanket consent. Some argue that individuals cannot consent to a variety of uses which are not known at the point at which consent is given, as this cannot be accurately described as informed consent.[64] For example, Árnason says that 'There is no such thing as "general informed consent." The more general the consent is, the less informed it becomes. It is misleading to use the notion of informed consent for participation in research that is unforeseen and has not been specified in a research protocol.'[65] He takes the view that there are two options in relation to informed consent in this context. The first option is to obtain informed consent from participants before their health-care information is placed in the database. But at this point no specific research plans exist, so it is impossible to explain any of the ingredients of informed consent to the prospective participants. There are no specific objectives to be explained, no determinate risks or benefits to be assessed. Informed consent for research before entering the database would, therefore, be 'empty and senseless'. The only specific ingredient that would be possible to explain is the right to withdraw information from the database at any time. The second option would be to obtain informed consent from individual participants for each particular research after entering the database. But because of the heavy emphasis on coding and privacy this would be extremely complicated and cumbersome. Not only would it jeopardise individual privacy but also, according to many scientists, it would severely limit the research possibilities that the database is intended to provide.

[10.34] The classical ethical approach would insist that where it is impossible to specify in advance all future uses of the samples, it is necessary to get fresh consent for each use as it arises. Although laudable in its strict adherence to the ethical values enshrined in the doctrine of informed consent, this approach is perceived as problematic in practical terms, as the individual tissue source may have died in the intervening period, or may be uncontactable. Re-contacting donors some time after the initial donation also runs the risk of insufficient positive responses, which may undermine the value of the research.[66] From the perspective of researchers, 'the cry is widely heard that informed consent documents have become almost unintelligible, that individual's fears are unfounded, their desires for control unwarranted, and that research is being dramatically slowed and even brought to a halt'.[67] To overcome these difficulties, it has been proposed that a general or broad form of consent might be used which acknowledges that the samples might be put to other, unspecified uses in the future and dispenses with the requirement for further consent from the tissue source. This may be referred to as the 'right to take a risk', which allows donors to waive further information and consent as long as they are

---

[64] See Annas, 'Rules for Research on Human Genetic Variation – Lessons from Iceland' (2000) NEJM 342: 1830–33; Chadwick and Berg, 'Solidarity and Equity: New Ethical Frameworks for Genetic Databases' (2001) Nature Reviews Genetics, 2:318–21; O'Neill, 'Informed Consent and Genetic Information' *Studies in History and Philosophy of Biological and Biomedical Sciences* (Elsevier Science, 2001) 32(4): 689–704.

[65] Árnason, 'Coding and Consent: Moral Challenges of the Database Project in Iceland' (2004) Bioethics, Vol 18 No 1.

[66] Roscam-Abbing, 'Human Tissue Research, Individual Rights and Bio-Banks' in Gunning and Holm (eds) *Ethics, Law and Society, Vol II* (Ashgate, 2006) 7–16, at 13.

[67] Wright Clayton, 'Informed Consent and Biobanks' (2005) Journal Of Law, Medicine And Ethics, Spring 15.

fully informed at the time of initial consent about the incomplete degree of information to be provided to them in the future.[68] Opponents of general consent argue that the impracticality of re-contacting donors does not justify departure from important ethical principles and that it 'implies an erosion of the informed consent requirement that is neither necessary, nor proportional, and therefore not legally justified.'[69]

[10.35] One solution to the difficulty of re-contacting donors for fresh consent is to allow for a waiver of consent if the samples are anonymised and the research receives ethical approval from a research ethics committee, both of which are thought to provide sufficient safeguards against any potential harm to tissue donors. For example, under the UK Human Tissue Act 2004, tissue from living patients, for example biopsy or blood samples, can ordinarily be used for research only with the person's consent. However, consent is not required for research on tissue from living patients if the samples are anonymised (or coded to make sure patient or participant information is not identifiable) and the project has recognised ethics committee approval; or if the tissue samples were obtained before 1 September 2006 (when the Human Tissue Act came into force).[70]

[10.36] Another solution, according to Árnason, is not to 'stubbornly insist' on informed consent in circumstances in which it clearly does not fit, as in relation to biobanks where full information regarding future research projects cannot be given, but rather to find another way in which individuals may express their willingness to participate. This might be called 'permission' or 'authorisation' in order to avoid confusion with the traditional model of informed consent. Authorisation might be said to be in the spirit of informed consent, but it is far more general and open and should, therefore, not be confused with it. Authorisation does not imply a consent to any particular research project but implies that an individual permits in writing that health-care data will be processed from his medical records and moved in a coded form into the database. The authorisation also implies that the individual has been informed about, and that he claims to have understood at least the following: what information about him will be placed into the database; how privacy will be secured; how the information will be connected to other data; who will have access to the information; in what context the information will be used and for what purposes;[71] how consent for genetic research will be obtained; what are the foreseeable risks and benefits of participation; how research

---

[68] Discussed in Schulte in den Baumen et al, 'Data Protection and Sample Management in Biobanking – A Legal Dichotomy' (2010) *Genomics, Society and Policy* Vol 6 No 1 pp 33–46 at 39. The authors acknowledge that the 'right to take a risk' is a highly individualistic approach and is not yet a widely accepted concept in the biobanking community or among data protection experts.

[69] Roscam-Abbing, 'Human Tissue Research, Individual Rights and Bio-Banks' in Gunning and Holm (eds) *Ethics, Law and Society, Vol II* (Ashgate, 2006) 7–16, at 13.

[70] http://www.hta.gov.uk/boyorganandtissuedonation/howtodonateyourtissueforresearch.cfm (accessed 4 June 2011).

[71] For example, in Iceland these purposes are stated in the Act on a Health Sector Database no. 139/1998, art 10: 'Data recorded or acquired by processing on the health-sector database may be used to develop new or improved methods of achieving better health, prediction, diagnosis and treatment of disease, to seek the most economic ways of operating health services, and for making reports in the health sector.'

on the data will be regulated; and that the individual has the right to withdraw the health-care data at any time.[72]

[10.37] The establishment of population-based genetic databases is extensively covered in European and international regulations.[73] For example, in 2003 the World Health Organisation (WHO) stated that archived material removed in the course of medical care should be capable of being used for research once anonymised and subject to strong ethical justification to deviate from traditional consent requirements.[74] The Human Genome Organisation (HUGO),[75] the Council for International Organisations of Medical Sciences (CIOMS)[76] and UNESCO[77] have recommended that human biological samples may be used for research in either anonymised or coded form without re-consent, provided certain conditions have been met. These include notification of such a policy to patients, no objection by patients, approval by an ethics committee, minimal risk, potential significant benefits and the impracticability of obtaining consent in the circumstances.[78] In relation to samples specifically collected for research use, the question arises as to whether the samples may be used for further research for which consent was not initially obtained.[79] Although it is commonly accepted that future uses should be specifically disclosed to the donor at the outset if possible, in recent years there has also been discussion of a concept of general or broad consent (also called authorisation) which is particularly suited to large-scale longitudinal studies or research databases. Although not universally accepted yet, 'eventually it may constitute an acceptable exception for certain types of biobanking research provided it is justified both scientifically and ethically and certain criteria are met.'[80]

---

[72] Árnason, 'Coding and Consent: Moral Challenges of the Database Project in Iceland' (2004) Bioethics, Vol 18 No 1, at 45.

[73] For example, Council of Europe (1997) *Convention for the Protection of Human Rights and Dignity of the Human Being with regard to the Application of Biology and Medicine: Convention on Human Rights and Biomedicine,* Oviedo, 4. IV.1997; European Group on Ethics (EGE) in Science and New Technologies to the European Commission (1998) *Ethical Aspects of Human Tissue Banking;* World Medical Association (2002) Declaration on Ethical Considerations regarding Health Databases.

[74] WHO (European Partnership on Patients Rights and Citizens Empowerment) (2003) *Genetic Databases – Assessing the Benefits and the Impact on Human Rights and Patient Rights,* Geneva. Section 4.4.

[75] Human Genome Organisation (1998) *Statement on DNA Sampling: Control and Access,* para 6.1 – referring to general consent as 'blanket consent'.

[76] CIOMS (2002) *International Ethical Guidelines for Biomedical Research Involving Human Subjects,* Geneva, Guideline 4.

[77] UNESCO (2003) International Declaration on Human Genetic Data, Geneva, arts 16 & 17.

[78] See discussion by Knoppers, 'Biobanking: International Norms' (2005) Journal of Law, Medicine and Ethics, Spring 7.

[79] Recommendation Rec (2006) 4 of the Committee of Ministers to member states on research on biological materials of human origin, https://wcd.coe.int/wcd/ViewDoc.jsp?id=977859 (accessed 4 June 2011).

[80] Knoppers, 'Biobanking: International Norms' (2005) Journal of Law, Medicine and Ethics, Spring 7, at 9.

[10.38] Some European jurisdictions permit general or broad consent for unspecified future research use, for example Germany,[81] Sweden,[82] Iceland and Estonia.[83] General consent is seen as acceptable in these jurisdictions if two conditions are met, namely research ethics review and the right of the participant to withdraw at any time.[84] This is a relaxation of the classical research ethics position in relation to biobanks and a less strict standard of consent.[85] The first condition does not appear to pose significant problems, at least if research ethics committees apply consistent standards. Research ethics review is familiar to researchers working in biomedical research although some may argue that it slows the progress of their research and imposes an unnecessary bureaucracy on them. The second condition is perhaps more difficult as the withdrawal of samples in any significant number from the database conflicts with the scientific imperative of maintaining the statistical integrity of the population based databases, particularly given the ambition to use them as the vehicle for longitudinal studies. All biobanks incorporate the right of tissue sources to withdraw their samples but the interpretation of the right varies. For example, in Iceland the samples will not be withdrawn or destroyed but will be noted on a coded list of persons who have opted out so their data will not be used by biobanks.[86] The UK Biobank offers a set of graded options for withdrawal, ranging from complete withdrawal to discontinued participation and no further contact requested[87], which attempts to balance the interest of the donor in the removal of the data with the interest of the scientist in some form of continued access to the data if possible. In Estonia, donors have the right to have their data deleted from the database on request, with any violation of this right being punishable as a criminal offence.[88] The German Ethics Council says that donors must have the right to withdraw their consent at any time and that this right cannot be waived. However, there should be provision for

---

[81]   Nationaler Ethikrat (2004) *Biobanken fur die Forschung* Berlin, Germany.

[82]   Biobanks Act 2003.

[83]   Kaye et al, 'Population Genetic Databases: A Comparative Analysis of the Law in Iceland, Sweden, Estonia and the UK', *TRAMES* 8:15–33.

[84]   Roscam-Abbing says that this is incompatible with the right to private life under the ECHR, which, in the medical context, implies the obligation to provide sufficient information to allow the donor to make a well-founded decision. Roscam-Abbing, 'Human Tissue Research, Individual Rights and Bio-Banks' in Gunning and Holm (eds) *Ethics, Law and Society, Vol II* (Ashgate, 2006) 7–16, at 13.

[85]   Elger and Caplan, 'Consent and Anonymisation in Research Involving Biobanks' (2006) EMBO Reports Vol 7 No 7 1–6 at 3.

[86]   Regulations issued by the Icelandic Ministry of Health and Social Security on the Keeping and Utilisation of Biological Samples in Biobanks No 134/2001. This is described by some ethicists as a somewhat diluted version of withdrawal.

[87]   http://www.ukbiobank.ac.uk/docs/BIOINFOBK14920410.pdf. (Accessed 11 July 2011). For further discussion of guidance available in the UK, see Medical Research Council, *Human Tissue and Biological Samples for Use in Research, Operational and Ethical Guidelines* 2001; House of Lords Select Committee on Science and Technology, *Human Genetic Databases: Challenges and Opportunities* 2001; Human Genetics Commission, *Inside Information: Balancing Interests in the Use of Personal Genetic Data* 2002. For details about the Scottish biobank, Generation Scotland, see http://www.generationscotland.org/ (accessed 4 June 2011).

[88]   Human Genes Research Act 2000.

donors to allow samples and data to continue to be used if their identity cannot be disclosed.[89]

[10.39] The Council of Europe's Committee of Ministers recommended in 2006 that information and consent or authorisation to obtain biological materials for research should be as specific as possible with regard to any foreseen research uses and the choices available in that respect.[90] It provides that residual biological materials removed from persons for purposes other than research, should only be made available for research activities with appropriate consent or authorisation. Article 22 provides that if the proposed use of identifiable biological material is not within the scope of prior consent given by the person, reasonable efforts should be made to obtain fresh consent. However, if this is not possible with reasonable efforts, the material can be used for research subject to independent evaluation that the research addresses an important scientific interest; the aims of the research could not reasonably be achieved using biological materials for which consent can be obtained; and there is no evidence that the person concerned expressly objected to such research use. Unlinked anonymised samples may be used for research, provided such use does not violate any restrictions placed by the person concerned.

[10.40] In the United States the prevailing opinion for some time was in favour of the classical standard of informed consent. In dealing with the difficulties of obtaining consent for future unspecified uses, multi-layered consent was seen as the most acceptable means of ensuring that participants were informed of the relevant information and choices. This form of consent allowed for different choices to be presented on a detailed form, enabling participants to choose to limit their consent to use for research into a specific disease or a specific research project if they wished. This was seen by some as imposing a burden on research.[91] In 1999 the National Bioethics Advisory Committee proposed a strategy of waivers in which informed consent would not be necessary where the research involved no more than minimal risk, it would not adversely affect the rights or welfare of the subjects, the research could not practicably be carried out without the waiver, and whenever appropriate, the subjects would be provided with additional information following their participation. It was also recommended that, despite the granting of the waiver, consent should be sought unless it was impracticable to locate the subjects in question.[92]

[10.41] The US Office for Human Research Participation (OHRP)[93] has proposed a different solution. It takes the view that research on unidentifiable specimens should not be described as research involving human subjects and therefore it is not necessary to obtain informed consent or research ethics review. This is based on the interpretation of 'research involving human subjects' as involving an interaction with a living person.

---

[89] Nationaler Ethikrat, *Biobanks for Research OPINION* (2004).

[90] Recommendation Rec (2006) 4 of the Committee of Ministers to member states on research on biological materials of human origin, https://wcd.coe.int/wcd/ViewDoc.jsp?id=977859 (accessed 4 June 2011).

[91] Elger and Caplan, 'Consent and Anonymisation in Research Involving Biobanks' (2006) EMBO Reports Vol 7 No 7 1–6 at 3.

[92] NBAC (1999) *Research Involving Human Biological Materials: Ethical Issues and Policy Guidance,* Vol 1, Rockville MD, USA.

The OHRP considers private information or specimens not to be individually identifiable when they cannot be linked to specific individuals by the investigator(s) either directly or indirectly through coding systems.[94] To come within this definition, the following conditions must be met: the private information or specimens were not collected specifically for the currently proposed research project through an interaction or intervention with living individuals; and the investigator(s) cannot readily ascertain the identity of the individual(s) to whom the coded private information or specimens pertain because, for example, the investigators and the holder of the key enter into an agreement prohibiting the release of the key to the investigators under any circumstances, until the individuals are deceased; there are IRB-approved written policies and operating procedures for a repository or data management centre that prohibit the release of the key to the investigators under any circumstances, until the individuals are deceased; or there are other legal requirements prohibiting the release of the key to the investigators, until the individuals are deceased. The advantage of this approach is clearly that it facilitates research by avoiding the requirement for informed consent and ethics review simply by entering into an agreement prohibiting the researchers accessing the code by which the tissue sources might be identified.

[10.42] Studies indicate that a majority of patients favour the requirement of consent to the use of their tissue even where the samples are anonymised, particularly where the research involves genetic testing of the samples.[95] A substantial majority also find general consent adequate, largely because they do not wish to be burdened by repeated re-contact for fresh consent. A survey in Ireland in 2005 indicates that 86 per cent of the population would be willing to allow the use of their excised tissue for research purposes.[96] There is no legislation currently in place in Ireland dealing with the use of human tissue for research. The Tissue and Cells Regulations (2006) apply only where the tissues and cells are used for human application, not research.[97] The Irish Council for Bioethics published an opinion on the storage and use of human biological material in 2005 in which it recommended a form of layered consent which would provide

---

[93] OHRP is part of the Office of the Assistant Secretary for Health (OASH) in the Office of the Secretary (OS), US Department of Health and Human Services. It provides clarification and guidance, develops educational programmes and materials, maintains regulatory oversight, and provides advice on ethical and regulatory issues in biomedical and behavioral research. See http://www.hhs.gov/ohrp/index.html (accessed 4 June 2011).

[94] See http://www.hhs.gov/ohrp/policy/cdebiol.html (accessed 4 June 2011).

[95] Wendler, 'One-Time General Consent for Research on Biological Samples' (2006) BMJ 332:544–547; Wendler and Emanuel, 'The Debate Over Research on Stored Biological Samples: What Do Sources Think?' (2002) Arch Intern Med 162:1457–1462.

[96] Cousins, McGee et al, *Public Perceptions of Biomedical Research – A Survey of the General Population in Ireland* (2005) Health Research Board, para 3.7. The primary motivation for their willingness to donate was that it could be potentially beneficial for members of their own family (96%), or their own future health (92%) or to society generally (80%). In relation to consent, 36% preferred specific consent, 44% chose general consent, and 16% opted for the personal choice model, which leaves it up to the individual to choose specific or general consent for themselves.

[97] European Communities (Quality and Safety of Human Tissues and Cells) Regulations 2006, (SI 158/2006). The Irish Medicines Board is designated as the competent authority for the implementation of this legislation.

participants with options relating to future unspecified use of their biological material. It recommended that these options might include refusal of such future use; limitation of future use for research related to the condition for which the sample was originally collected; request for further contact and fresh consent for any future use; or permission for future use without the requirement for fresh consent but subject to approval by a research ethics committee.[98] Proposals for human tissue legislation were published by the Department of Health and Children in 2009 but have not yet been enacted.[99]

Data protection

[10.43] EC Directive 95/46/EC provides for the protection of individuals with regard to the processing of personal data and in relation to the free movement of such data. It was transposed into national law in Ireland by the Data Protection Act 2003. Its objective is to secure the free flow of personal data within the internal market while ensuring a high level of protection for citizens. Health data have a special position in the Directive but the protections offered therein are not absolute and may be overridden by considerations of the public interest where required. Biobanks were not common at the time when the Directive was drawn up and thus are not explicitly mentioned in the Directive. However, art 8 provides that the general prohibition on processing of sensitive data (which includes health data) does not apply where the data subject has given his explicit consent to the processing (para 2 (a)); where the processing is required for the purpose of preventive medicine, medical diagnosis, the provision of care or treatment or the management of health-care services (para 3); or where Member States have, for reasons of substantial public interest, laid down additional exemptions by national law or by decision of the supervisory authority subject to the provision of suitable safeguards (para 4). Recital 34 to the Directive which relates to art 8(4) provides that public health is a legitimate ground for Member States to derogate from the prohibition on the processing of sensitive data. These appear to be the only legal basis for biobanks in the Directive.[100] However, art 8(4) is not harmonising, as it enables rather than obliges Member States to lay down exemptions for reasons of public interest.[101]

> While the Directive enables Member States to set up regulations which enable biobanks to achieve their goals, there is no harmonized legal situation in Europe. Member States are not obliged to use Art 8(4) for biobanking purposes and if they do, they still have discretion how and to what extent they use it. The Directive also empowers Member States to define divergent safeguards which may force biobanking networks and multi-centre research studies using biobanks to follow a 'gold standard' (in this case the strictest regulatory environment) approach whenever they want to transfer data.[102]

---

[98] Irish Council for Bioethics, *Human Biological Material: Recommendations For Collection, Use and Storage in Research* (2005). The Council is no longer in existence but the Opinion is available at www.bioethics.ie (accessed 4 June 2011).

[99] http://www.dohc.ie/consultations/closed/human_tissue_bill/ (accessed 4 June 2011).

[100] See Schulte in den Baumen et al, 'Data Protection and Sample Management in Biobanking – A Legal Dichotomy' (2010) *Genomics, Society and Policy* Vol 6 No 1 pp 33–46 at 38.

[101] Article 8(4) of the Directive 95/46/EC provides that: "Subject to the provision of suitable safeguards, Member States *may*, for reasons of substantial public interest, lay down exemptions in addition to those laid down in para 2…" (emphasis added).

[102] See Schulte in den Baumen et al, 'Data Protection and Sample Management in Biobanking – A Legal Dichotomy' (2010) *Genomics, Society and Policy* Vol 6 No 1 pp 33–46 at 38.

[10.44] It is unclear whether biological samples themselves constitute data for the purposes of the Directive. Under art 2(a) of the Directive, personal data is 'any *information* relating to an identified or identifiable natural person' (emphasis added). Therefore, biological material may not be seen as data, as it is not information itself. 'Like a hard drive, it contains data but another technical step is required to extract the data'.[103] The Directive applies if data are extracted from biological material in a way which could identify a person. Therefore, a biobank may not encounter data protection issues if it stores and transfers information to a third party without any collection of secondary processing of personal information. However, the separation of data and samples seems artificial to most researchers and there is a growing tendency to apply the legal framework of data protection to both samples and data.[104] For example, in *S and Marper v the UK*,[105] the applicants complained under art 8 of the ECHR that authorities in the UK continued to retain their fingerprints, biological samples and DNA profiles after criminal proceedings against them had ended with an acquittal or been discontinued. The Court held that all three categories of personal information constituted personal data within the meaning of the Data Protection Directive. It considered that the systematic retention of such material was sufficiently intrusive to constitute interference with the right to respect for private life. An individual's concern about the possible future use of private information is legitimate and the Court could not discount the possibility that in the future the private-life interests bound up with genetic information may be adversely affected in novel or unanticipated ways. Although interference with private life may be justified 'where necessary in a democratic society', the margin of appreciation to be accorded to States in this regard must be narrower where the right at stake is crucial to the individual's enjoyment of intimate or key rights. The blanket and indiscriminate nature of the retention in this case of persons suspected but not convicted of criminal offences failed to strike a fair balance between the competing public and private interests involved, and thus the State had overstepped any acceptable margin of appreciation in this regard. The Court therefore held that there had been a violation of art 8 of the ECHR.

[10.45] Although there is potential for greater harmonisation of protection of personal data in relation to biobanks by application of the Data Protection Directive, there is no competence for the EU to govern the exchange of biological samples themselves, as this falls under the field of property law in many Member States.[106] Thus the problems appear to arise under data protection while samples are shipped routinely amongst EU Member States and beyond. Schulte in den Baumen et al argue that this situation arises from the fact that public health is not harmonised in the Data Protection Directive as

---

[103] See Schulte in den Baumen et al, 'Data Protection and Sample Management in Biobanking – A Legal Dichotomy' (2010) *Genomics, Society and Policy* Vol 6 No 1 pp 33–46 at 40.

[104] ECtHR Application Nos. 30562/04 and 30566/04.

[105] *Marper v the UK* 30562/04 [2008] ECHR 1581.

[106] For example, in Germany the donor retains property rights even after the biological material is permanently extracted from the body. See Schulte in den Baumen et al, 'Data Protection and Sample Management in Biobanking – A Legal Dichotomy' (2010) *Genomics, Society and Policy* Vol 6 No 1 pp 33–46 at 40. See also De Faria, 'Ownership Rights in Research Biobanks: Do We Need a New Kind of "Biological Property"?' (2009) in Solbakk et al (eds) *The Ethics of Research Biobanking*, (Springer, 2009) 263–276.

well as the perception that data protection principles are interpreted differently in Member States and their ethics committees.[107]

OWNERSHIP OF GAMETES

[10.46] The question arises as to whether there are fundamentally different and distinct issues applicable to gametes which render it necessary to apply a different framework entirely and whether a property analysis is appropriate in this context. It is generally considered ethically unacceptable that sperm or ova taken from a man or woman could be used for any purpose other than that for which it was donated. The reason for this is that with a donation of gametes there is a donation of genetic information which is readily usable to produce a new individual. Although we generally do not worry about the natural loss of sperm and ova, we are very anxious about their storage and subsequent use. The reason for this seems to come within the issue of privacy and bodily integrity as 'once down the drain the information they contain, in practical terms, is not usable: it will never find genetic expression: it will never mix with another germ cell's information to produce a new individual: we can forget about it.'[108] However, if not 'down the drain', it may be used to fertilise an egg, and may develop into a new individual who will forever have a genetic connection with the sperm donor.

[10.47] Therefore, it is the potential of the ova or sperm to become a new, unique individual which makes it different from donations of other body parts.[109] 'The germ cells differ from other human tissues that can be donated because they carry readily utilisable genetic information.'[110] It is this fact that makes gametes the subject of so

---

[107] See Schulte in den Baumen et al, 'Data Protection and Sample Management in Biobanking – A Legal Dichotomy' (2010) *Genomics, Society and Policy* Vol 6 No 1 pp 33–46 at 44.

[108] Jansen, 'Sperm and Ova as Property' (1985) 11 Journal of Medical Ethics 123. Jansen considers the reasons why so much emotion is expended in relation to the use of stored gametes in comparison to situations in which gametes are lost every day naturally without any controversy. He examines the quantitative arguments in relation to the number of eggs a woman might release during her lifetime and the opportunities for those to become babies through sexual reproduction. He concludes that there is not the time for more than about 15 or 20 of the 7 million eggs with which a woman is born (of which only about 300,000 are left by the time of fertilisation due to the process of atresia in which eggs degenerate and are lost naturally) to become babies (69 if multiple ovulations are included). The other 299,000 are destined for oblivion. The comparison for males is 'even more spectacular' as only as an infinitesimal fraction of the spermatozoa which he may have produced during his lifetime are likely to fertilise an egg. Jansen argues that no one cares about these sperm and eggs that are wasted, as long as they are wasted in nature.

[109] Jansen claims that the courts of common law countries have held that once organs or tissues are separated from a person, the person has little or no right of ownership over those separated parts. 'Human body parts in law appear simply to be incapable of being owned.' He asks whether this lack of dominion over body parts could be applicable to frozen sperm. However, he acknowledges that the idea that sperm stored on behalf of a man, who might, for example, be undergoing chemotherapy treatment for cancer, might be used for any purpose other than the purpose for which it was stored, that is to impregnate the man's wife in the future, would be unthinkable. Jansen, 'Sperm and Ova as Property' (1985) 11 Journal of Medical Ethics 123.

[110] Jansen, 'Sperm and Ova as Property' (1985) 11 Journal of Medical Ethics 123 at 124.

much concern and emotional debate, that is, their ability to find genetic expression in a new living human being. By comparison, the donation of a kidney, while it may indeed be life-saving, does not have the potential to *create* a new existence carrying forward the genetic inheritance of the donor. This valuable and important potential is rightly a matter of personal responsibility for the donor of the gametes. Jansen argues that it should also be considered his property to deal with as he wishes. 'This potential should always remain the responsibility, the provenance, the dominion, perhaps the property, of the donor.'[111]

[10.48] If the person from whom the gametes are taken is alive, then following the common law cases in respect of which theft actions were successful in relation to urine and blood, it could be argued that sperm could similarly be the subject matter of a prosecution for theft[112] and, in that sense at least, could be regarded as 'property'.[113] The moral connotations of enabling a person to then sell their genetic material, ie, their 'property', would be similar to those in relation to sale of blood or human organs and could be resolved by legislation.[114]

[10.49] In relation to the ownership of body parts or genetic material of a person who is now deceased, the common law rule is that there is no such right of ownership. However, as discussed above, there is an exception in relation to situations in which work or skill has been employed on the parts/material, in which case there would be a right of possession in the person who had applied the skill. This would enable him to exclude others from possession of the parts. It is unclear to what extent preservation (particularly relevant in the context of gametes) without application of any other specific skill would

---

[111] Jansen, 'Sperm and Ova as Property' (1985) 11 Journal of Medical Ethics 123 at 125.

[112] In England, a case was settled out of court in early 2000 involving a claim by an Austrian businessman that a fertility clinic used his semen without his consent. He sued the clinic for unauthorised use of his semen after learning that his former girlfriend had given birth to a daughter using his frozen semen without telling him. He sued for breach of contract and breach of duty rather than for theft of his semen but the case opens up previously unexplored possibilities in the context of property rights in gametes. See brief description of the case in British Medical Journal (2000) 320: 464.

[113] See also 'birth control fraud' cases where it has been alleged that women have 'stolen' sperm in order to become pregnant. These cases have usually come about through consensual sexual intercourse where the man has been deceived as to the contraceptive protection taken by the woman. His genetic parentage thus gives rise to liability for maintenance of the child, irrespective of his lack of knowledge or consent to such paternity. Claims have been brought in this context for breach of contract, deceit and trespass to the person. More interestingly here, claims have also been brought for conversion (where a person deliberately deals with the property of another in such a way as to be an unjustifiable denial of that person's rights to the property). See further Madden, 'Recent Developments in Assisted Human Reproduction: Legal and Ethical Issues' (2001) MLJI Vol 7 No 2 53 –61; Sheldon, 'Sperm Bandits, Birth Control Fraud and the Battle of the Sexes' (2001) 21 Legal Studies 460–480.

[114] The world-wide shortage of transplant organs has led to the legalisation by some developing countries of transplant a trade by offering payment to live donors. The unethical means by which these organs may sometimes be donated and the concerns about cross-border traffic in such organs have led to calls for legislative action in this area. See Bulletin of the World Health Organisation Vol 85 No 12 December 2007, Shimazono Y, 'The State of the international organ trade: a provisional picture based on integration of available information'.

satisfy this test. The exception was developed to in some sense reward the creator of a new 'thing' for his efforts, so that mere storage/freezing of gametes (without application of any other specific skill which might change its characteristics) would not necessarily entitle the clinic to legal possession.

[10.50] Robertson takes the view that decision-making authority implies a property right or interest. He says that 'a property interest in gametes must exist, regardless of whether an action for conversion will lie. The term "property" merely designates the locus of dispositional control over the object or matter in question. The scope of that control is a separate matter and will depend upon what bundle of dispositional rights exist with regard to that object.[115]' Robertson's argument is based on the right of a person to decide what is to be done with stored sperm and, logically, this must be the person who made the deposit of the sperm. This right, he says, implies a property right or ownership in the sperm, which means the sperm donor has the right to decide what happens to it. However, it is argued that this conclusion is drawn from a circuitous process of deriving ownership from dispositional control and then dispositional control from ownership.[116]

> Parents have the right to control virtually every aspect of their children's lives, from the medical care they will receive to where they will live to the kind of education they get. Yet parents do not own their children, and children are not property. Doctors and hospitals often rely on family members to make decisions about what should be done with incompetent patients, including whether the patients should be kept on life-support, yet these surrogate decision-makers do not own their incompetent relatives, and incompetent patients are not property. These are situations in which individuals have dispositional authority, but not a property interest.

[10.51] To put this premise at its simplest – since the abolition of slavery, people cannot be bought or sold and therefore cannot be regarded as property. Property is essentially something which can be bought and sold in a market, therefore simply having decision-making authority over something is not sufficient to regard it as property.

> Whether sperm is property depends on what we think may permissibly be done with it. If there is a strong moral, legal, or policy argument against allowing individuals to store sperm for the purpose of posthumous reproduction, then sperm should not be considered property for that purpose. In the absence of a compelling argument against posthumous reproduction,

---

[115] Robertson, 'Posthumous Reproduction' (1994) 69 Ind LJ 1027 at 1038. This article follows Robertson's general proposition in favour of procreative liberty, as discussed in his book, *Children of Choice: Freedom and the New Reproductive Technologies* (Princeton University Press, 1994). He admits that no right can be absolute but that the right to reproduce should only be interfered with in instances when the State can show such great harm resulting from the exercise of the right, that the fundamental interest in having children is justifiably limited.

[116] Steinbock, 'Sperm as Property' (1995) 6(2) Stanford Law and Policy Review 57 at 60. Steinbock's arguments are based on the premise that individual autonomy should prevail in instances of posthumous reproduction unless there are convincing arguments to the contrary. She considers in detail the *Hecht* and *Davis* cases and concludes that these cases represent judicial decisions 'to eschew a categorical approach to the ownership issues raised by disputes over bodily parts and gametes.' p 60. See also Tober, 'Semen as Gift, Semen as Goods: Reproductive Workers and the Market in Altruism' (2001) 7 Body and Society 137–60.

individual autonomy should prevail, and sperm is correctly regarded as property that can be bequeathed by will.[117]

[10.52] A number of cases have arisen in relation to ownership of gametes in the context of legal challenges to deny surviving spouses the right to access sperm stored prior to their husband's death. In the earliest of these reported cases in 1984, *Paraplaix v CECOS*,[118] the widow of a man who had died from cancer requested the release of her husband's frozen sperm to her[119]. Her husband had not made any specific disposition of the sperm in the event of his death. The deceased's widow and parents argued that the sperm formed part of the movable property of the deceased's estate and was therefore capable of being inherited. As they were the natural heirs of the deceased, they became the owners of the sperm and CECOS[120] was a bailee obliged to deliver the sperm to them. CECOS argued firstly on privity of contract grounds, that it was obligated only to

---

[117] Steinbock, 'Sperm as Property' (1995) 6(2) Stanford Law and Policy Review 57 at 66. She argues that it is relevant to consider the quality of life of the child who may be born as a result of posthumous conception and whether it is a serious disadvantage to a child to be born without a father. She discusses Robertson's premise that it is always better for a child to be born than not to be born but she says that this justification for posthumous reproduction is to confuse two very different situations. One is whether existing lives are worth living due to serious handicaps and whether stopping treatment on such a child can be justified. The other situation is whether or not to bring a child into existence at all in circumstances in which it is likely to have a substandard life. She states: 'Refraining from procreating is not the moral equivalent of killing. Causing the death of an existing child deprives that child of its life, a life that may well be of value to the child, despite its limits, burdens, and difficulties. By contrast, no one is harmed by not being brought into existence. The child who is never conceived is not frustrated or miserable or unhappy. To be sure, if one is not conceived, one is deprived of the opportunity to exist. But this is not a harm to *anyone*. It is not as if there are potential children waiting in the wings, so to speak, longing for the chance to be born. The decision not to procreate makes no one worse off, and so the decision not to procreate does not require a justification. A responsible decision to procreate, however, requires thoughtful consideration of the welfare of the children one brings into the world.' At 63.

[118] *Paraplaix v CECOS*, Trib.gr.inst. Creteil, 16–17 Sept 1984, Gazette du Palais (2e sem.) 560. For further discussion, see Jones, 'Artificial Procreation, Societal Reconceptions: Legal Insight from France' [1988] 36 Am J of Comparative Law 525–545. Also Shapiro and Sonnenblick, 'The Widow and the Sperm: The Law of Post-Mortem Insemination' (1986–7) 1 J Law and Health 229; Kerr, 'Post-Mortem Sperm Procurement: Is it Legal?' (1999) 3 DePaul J Health Care 39.

[119] Posthumous conception is now prohibited in France by legislation which provides that assisted conception may only take place where the man and woman are both alive. Law 94–654 of 29 July 1994, art 8. Where one partner dies, the other partner may be asked to consent to donating stored embryos to another couple. The position in other European countries is varied. For example, the Spanish legislation permits posthumous conception where the woman's partner has expressly consented to such conception to take place within six months of his death. If a child is born, the deceased man is considered the child's legal father. Posthumous conception is prohibited in Sweden (Regulations and General Recommendations No 35 of 30 November 1989, rubric 4), Denmark (Law No 460 of 10 June 1997, ss 15(2) (3) and 19), Germany (Law of 13 December 1990, s 4 (1) (3), and Switzerland (Federal Law of 18 December 1998, art 3(4)). Other countries, such as Norway, Austria, and Belgium do not have any specific measures dealing with posthumous conception.

[120] *Centre d'Étude et de Conservation du Sperme* – a French federation of 20 sperm banks.

the deceased donor himself in contract, and secondly that sperm, being an indivisible part of the body in the same way as a limb or organ, was not inheritable. The deceased's widow was ultimately successful although not on the property argument.[121] The Court seemed to have been more influenced by privacy arguments and procreational autonomy. It held that Mr Paraplaix's intent to preserve his opportunity to procreate, by entering into an agreement with CECOS for sperm preservation, obligated CECOS to return the sperm to the person for whom it was intended – namely, his wife. It defined sperm as 'the seed of life; it is connected to the fundamental liberty of a person to conceive or not to conceive.' As such it should not be the subject of legal rules or contracts but should be governed by 'the intent of the man from whom it emanates.' The Court was satisfied, despite the absence of any clear statement left on the matter by the man in question, that his intent was to make his wife the mother of a common child either before or after his death.[122] The Court found this evidence from the unusual circumstances of the marriage (the couple married two days before Mr Paraplaix died from cancer) and the testimony of his surviving widow and parents to that effect. Although the Court did not discuss the specific source of the 'right to give life' or procreative liberty, the effect of its decision was to expand the right of procreative autonomy.[123]

> The case expands the procreative rights of both sperm donors and unmarried, non-medically sterile women…In effect, the decision authorised a "single" heterosexual woman to become inseminated through the services of CECOS. Presented with the choice between maintaining one's procreative means in a repository subject to state control or returning the same to an individual with whom the donor had been intimately related, the court chose the private sphere.[124]

[10.53] In the United States a different approach was taken in *Hecht v Superior Court of Los Angeles County*, where a legal dispute began as a result of a bequest by William Kane of 15 vials of his sperm to his long-time companion, Deborah Hecht, for the purpose of conceiving a child after his death. Kane had expressly authorised the sperm bank to release the sperm to his executor. He had bequeathed the sperm to Hecht in his will and appointed her his executor. One month later he committed suicide. Kane's two adult children from a previous marriage wished to have the sperm destroyed 'to prevent the birth of a fatherless child, disruption of their existing family, and additional emotional, psychological and financial stress.' They characterised the desire to father children after one's death as 'egotistic and irresponsible.' Hecht argued that the destruction of the sperm bequeathed to her would violate her Constitutional rights to

---

[121] The Court specifically rejected the applicability of the Civil Code by finding that sperm does not constitute a 'thing in commerce but secretion containing the seed of life destined for human procreation.' *Paraplaix v CECOS*, Trib.gr.inst. Creteil, 16–17 Sept 1984, Gazette du Palais (2e sem.) at 562.

[122] It may be argued that the Court, in investigating and deciding on the basis of the deceased's intent, was using the substituted judgment standard as used in the law of medical treatment decision-making for the incompetent patient. In this way, the Court examined the deceased's expressed intentions in order to pursue the decision which he would have made had he survived.

[123] Jones, 'Artificial Procreation, Societal Reconceptions: Legal Insight from France' (1988) 36 Am J of Comparative Law 525–545 at 530.

[124] Jones, 'Artificial Procreation, Societal Reconceptions: Legal Insight from France' (1988) 36 Am J of Comparative Law 525–545 at 539–540.

privacy and liberty in procreation. At first instance, the Court ordered the sperm destroyed. However, the Californian Court of Appeal held that at the time of his death

> [Kane] had an interest, in the nature of ownership, to the extent that he had decision-making authority as to the use of his sperm within the scope of policy set by law. Thus, the decedent had an interest in his sperm which falls within the broad definition of property ... as anything that may be subject of ownership and includes real and personal property and any interest therein.[125]

[10.54] Further, the Court held that there were no legislative provisions existing in California which could justify infringement of this authority. Therefore Kane had the right to bequeath the right to the sperm by will. However, the Court limited its decision by concluding that because of the unique nature of sperm as property, the ownership interest may be affected by factual circumstances and public policy. The Court was unable to decide, due to genuine issues of material fact as to Kane's testamentary capacity, what Kane's intention was in relation to the sperm and adjourned the case until this, and other issues, were adjudicated. In March 1994 a probate judge in Los Angeles ruled, on the facts, that Hecht was entitled to at least 3 of the 15 vials of sperm left by Kane under an agreement signed by the parties after his death.

[10.55] This case demonstrates a willingness to consider sperm as property in some sense – to the extent at least that it may be considered part of the deceased's estate[126]. The case was lauded by some as respecting the right of a man to do what he wishes with his sperm while others warned of 'sperm bank orphans'[127] (in other words, sperm left in a sperm bank without any decision as to its future use or any person competent to make such decisions), and it was opposed by others as the pursuit of immortality by storage of gametes for use decades after one's death.

[10.56] In the UK, the issue of control and disposition of gametes is determined by the provisions of the Human Fertilisation and Embryology Authority Acts 1990–2008. In *R v Human Fertilisation and Embryology Authority (ex parte Blood)*[128] Stephen Blood was hospitalised with meningitis and while he was in a coma, his wife, Diane, asked doctors to remove sperm from him so that it might be stored for future use. Mr Blood subsequently died and Mrs Blood sought access to the sperm in order to conceive a child.[129] The Human Fertilisation and Embryology Authority took the view that the

---

[125] 20 Cal Reptr 2d 275 at 281.

[126] Atherton, 'En Ventre sa Frigidaire: Posthumous Children in the Succession Context' (1999) 19(2) Legal Studies 139–164, at 152.

[127] This is also referred to by Steinbock, who argues that, on the fact of *Hecht*, it *must* be detrimental to a child to learn that its parent committed suicide before its conception. The assurance given in Kane's letter to his children, and expressly extended to any children yet to be conceived, that he loved them in his dreams, might not be enough to alleviate their feelings of rejection and abandonment. However, she says that this is different from the situation in which, say, the widow of a man who died of natural causes wants to conceive a child through use of his sperm, as the child in this case should not feel rejected by its father. Steinbock, 'Sperm as Property' (1995) 6(2) Stanford Law and Policy Review, 57 at 64.

[128] *R v Human Fertilisation and Embryology Authority (ex parte Blood)* [1999] Fam 151.

[129] Morgan and Lee, 'In the Name of the Father? *Ex parte* Blood: Dealing with Novelty and Anomaly' (1997) Modern Law Review 841–856 at 841.

storage was unlawful and that the intended use of the sperm would be illegal. This was based on the wording of the 1990 Act (repeated in the 2008 Act) which in Schedule 3 makes written consent to the posthumous use of sperm mandatory.[130] The case was brought by way of judicial review of the Authority's decision to refuse to deliver up the sperm to Mrs Blood for use in the UK and, alternatively, its refusal of a request to allow Mrs Blood to export the sperm to another European country for treatment there. The Court of Appeal considered three issues – the storage and use of the sperm in the UK, the export of sperm (including EU law), and the decision of the Human Fertilisation and Embryology Authority (HFEA). In relation to storage and use in the United Kingdom, the Court held that the Act was clear that no storage of gametes could lawfully take place without written consent. Therefore, the storage of Mr Blood's sperm was prohibited in the absence of written consent and the Authority had no discretion to authorise treatment in the UK. In relation to the export issue, the Court was of the opinion that it was unrealistic of the Authority to argue that its refusal of permission to export the sperm was not withholding the provision of fertilisation treatment in another European State under arts 59 and 60 of the EC Treaty:

> From a functional point of view the ability to provide those services is not only substantially impeded but made impossible ... However, the fact that there is interference with the freedom to provide services does not mean that Art 59 is infringed. It means no more than that ... the interference has to be justified in accordance with the well established principles if it is not to contravene art 59. Those principles are ... that the decision must be non-discriminatory, it must be justified by some imperative requirement in the general interest, it must be suitable for securing the attainments of the objects which it pursues and it must not go beyond what is necessary to attain that objective ...[131]

[10.57] The decision of the HFEA in this case, according to the Court, was made without due consideration having been taken of the cross-border rights to which Mrs Blood was entitled to under EC law. If the Authority had taken into account that Mrs Blood was entitled to receive treatment in another Member State unless there was some good reason why she should not be allowed to receive that treatment, and if the Authority had also taken into account the fact that this case did not set a precedent (it being made clear by the Court that the taking of sperm in these circumstances was technically an offence), their decision may well have been different. The Court therefore allowed the appeal and remitted the matter to the HFEA, which subsequently permitted

---

[130] The relevant provisions of the 1990 Act are as follows. Section 4(1) provides:

'No person shall – (a) store any gametes, or (b) in the course of providing treatment services for any woman, use the sperm of any man unless the services are being provided for the woman and the man together ... except in pursuance of a licence.'

It is also provided that certain conditions must be complied with by the licence holder under the terms of the Act. Those conditions, which were directly relevant to Mrs Blood, were set out in Schedule 3 of the Act which, inter alia, sets out the conditions in relation to the storage of gametes. Paragraph 8 (1) states 'A person's gametes must not be kept in storage unless there is an effective consent by that person to their storage and they are stored in accordance with that consent.' Paragraph 1 requires that any consent given in pursuance of the Acts must be written.

[131] *R v Human Fertilisation and Embryology Authority, ex p Blood*, Court of Appeal, 6 February 1997.

457

Mrs Blood's application to export the sperm to Belgium. The Court did not consider the issue of the best interests of Mr Blood, stating only that:

> The question of the lawfulness of the storage is quite separate from the lawfulness of the taking of the sperm from Mr. Blood as he lay unconscious. The Act does not deal with this and the propriety of the treatment involved in taking the sperm in this case is governed by common law principles relating to the patient's consent to the electro-ejaculation which have not been argued before us. It is therefore not necessary to make any comment about this.[132]

[10.58] The Human Fertilisation and Embryology Act 2008 gives dispositional control to gamete providers, although it does not specify the issue of ownership. By requiring the gamete providers to give an effective written consent to the use to which the gametes may be put '…an aspect of a "property" interest in a "thing" is present – dispositional control – but it is difficult to see a set of "rights" over embryos that come close to anything other than a quasi-property interest in embryos and sperm'.[133] In the first case of its kind in England, *Yearworth v North Bristol NHS Trust* in 2009,[134] the Court of Appeal considered the question of ownership of sperm. The facts of the case were that six men were diagnosed with cancer for which they received treatment at a hospital in Bristol for which the defendant was responsible. The men accepted the advice of doctors at the hospital that they should undergo chemotherapy. They were also advised that the treatment might damage their fertility and they were asked whether they wished to produce semen samples prior to the start of the treatment on the basis that the hospital, which had a fertility unit licensed by the HFEA, would freeze their samples for their possible future use. The men all responded that they wished to do so.

[10.59] The men all signed consent forms for the storage and use of their sperm in accordance with the Human Fertilisation and Embryology Act.[135] They were informed that their sperm would be stored in liquid nitrogen and that the hospital would look after the sperm with all possible care. The sperm provided by the men was duly stored by the hospital but in June 2003 the amount of liquid nitrogen in the tanks in which the sperm was stored fell below the requisite level and the men's sperm thawed and perished irretrievably. The men were told about the loss of their sperm and five of them alleged that they suffered consequent psychiatric injury, namely a mild or moderate depressive disorder. Three of the five men subsequently recovered their natural fertility so their claims were limited to the period during which they believed their fertility had been irretrievably lost, the fourth man's sperm count was too low to have given rise to paternity in any event, the fifth man had died in the intervening period, and the sixth man alleged continuing mental distress in that it was unclear whether his fertility potential would recover in the future. The men claimed in negligence for compensation for personal injury. The Court took the view that damage to, and consequent loss of, the sperm did not constitute 'personal injury'. Lord Judge CJ said:

---

132 [1997] 2 WLR at 815.

133 Grubb, 'I, Me, Mine: Bodies, Parts and Property' (1998) 3 Medical Law International 299–317 at 304.

134 *Jonathan Yearworth and others v North Bristol NHS Trust* [2009] EWCA Civ 37.

135 The events in this case took place under the provisions of the Human Fertilisation and Embryology Act 1990 but the amendments introduced by the 2008 Act would not have altered the outcome even if they had been in force at the time.

[I]t would be a fiction to hold that damage to a substance generated by a person's body, inflicted after its removal for storage purposes, constituted a bodily or "personal injury" to him....We must deal in realities. To do otherwise would generate paradoxes, and yield ramifications, productive of substantial uncertainty, expensive debate and nice distinctions in an area of law which should be simple and the principles clear.[136]

[10.60] The men also claimed compensation in respect of the damage or loss of their property, ie their sperm. Therefore the Court had to consider the novel claim that the men had legal ownership or possession of the sperm at the time when the loss occurred. The issue was considered by the court in the context firstly of whether a bodily substance such as sperm was capable of being owned, and secondly whether the circumscription of rights imposed by the HFEA was such as to remove the men's ownership of the sperm. The Court of Appeal held that the question of whether something is capable of being owned cannot be decided in a vacuum and must be reached in context. Lord Judge CJ said 'the concept of ownership is no more than a convenient global description of different collections of rights held by persons over physical and other things.' He reflected upon the historical position in relation to the human corpse as well as the common law rule that a living human body is incapable of being owned. He discussed the case law above, both in the UK and US, as well as the Human Tissue Act 2004 and the Human Fertilisation and Embryology Act 2008. The latter imposes limitations on the ability of the gamete provider to deal with their gametes as they might wish by obliging licensed clinics to comply with the provisions of the Act in respect of storage and use of gametes. Thus, it was argued on behalf of the Trust that since the men could only have requested, as opposed to *directed,* the Trust to deal with their sperm in a particular way, within the scheme of the Act, this equated to a denial of the men's ownership of the sperm.

[10.61] The Court concluded that there needed to be a re-analysis of the common law's treatment of and approach to the issue of ownership of parts or products of a living human body. It acknowledged that the easiest course would be to uphold the men's claim by reference to the exception to the 'no property' rule set out in the *Doodeward* and *Kelly* cases discussed above, namely on the basis of the 'work and skill' applied in the freezing of the sperm which conferred on it a substantially different attribute, ie the arrest of swift perishability. However, the Court declined to take this approach, as it was of the view that the 'no property' rule itself did not have a solid foundation and the distinctions drawn on the basis of the 'work and skill' exception were not entirely logical. Instead, the Court took a broader approach and held that the men had ownership of the sperm.

[10.62] The basis for the Court's decision was that the men had generated the sperm and had requested that it be stored for their later use. Although their rights to its use had been restricted by the Act, this did not derogate from their ownership of it. The Court drew an analogy with statutes which limit a person's ability to use his land, such as building regulations and tenancy law, without eliminating his ownership of the land. It also took the view that the provisions of the Act in prioritising the requirement for consent from gamete providers preserved the right of the men to direct that the sperm *not* be used in a certain way and therefore 'their negative control over its use remains

---

[136] *Jonathan Yearworth and others v North Bristol NHS Trust* [2009] EWCA Civ 37, para 23.

absolute'. Although the licence holder, namely the clinic, has duties under the Act which may conflict with the wishes of the men, for example in relation to continued storage past the expiration of the maximum statutory storage period, the Court held that 'no person, whether human or corporate, other than each man has any *rights* in relation to the sperm which he has produced.'[137]

[10.63] The Court also considered whether the men had a distinct cause of action against the Trust under the law of bailment. It held that there was a bailment of the sperm by the men and the unit was liable under the law of bailment as well as the law of tort. This provided them with a remedy under which, in principle, they were entitled to compensation for any psychiatric injury or distress reasonably foreseeable as a consequence of the breach of duty and breach of promise. Assessment of the amount of compensation to be awarded was referred for determination to the county court.

[10.64] This case is significant because it is the first major departure from previous judicial reasoning on the issue of property in the body and separated body parts. Mason and Laurie say that although the Court was emphatic to point out that its decision was context-specific and should therefore be confined to the facts of the case, the decision is 'an important turning point in medical jurisprudence' and that it 'signals a sea change in judicial attitude towards patients' rights.'[138] It is also noteworthy because 'it is the first time that a case involving human tissue has been considered under the law of bailment.'[139] Quigley is of the view that this is particularly beneficial in cases such as this, where damages for psychiatric injury and mental distress are notoriously difficult to recover in tort so this ruling creates another option for plaintiffs. It is unclear whether the reasoning in this case would apply to cases involving other forms of tissue, as great emphasis was placed in this case on the mental distress suffered by the men due to the implication of the loss of the sperm for their future chances of fatherhood. Cases involving other forms of tissue are unlikely to attract the same level of damages. The basis for the Court's decision is of interest in this jurisdiction also, bearing in mind the lack of legislation here and the uncertainty regarding the application of the common law 'no property' rule. It remains to be seen whether and to what extent the case will be followed in Ireland.

---

[137] *Jonathan Yearworth and others v North Bristol NHS Trust* [2009] EWCA Civ 37 Para 45(f)(v).

[138] Mason and Laurie, *Law and Medical Ethics* (8th edn, OUP, 2010) para 14.35 and discussion 14.31 et seq.

[139] Quigley, 'Property: The Future of Human Tissue?' (2009) 17 Medical Law Review 457 at 464.

Chapter 11

Medical Treatment of Children and Minors

INTRODUCTION

[11.01] The medical treatment of children and minors raises unique issues in law and ethics. The interaction of rights and interests between the child, its parents or guardians and the medical profession, often poses difficult questions for the courts. As discussed in Chapter 9, in general the law accords central importance to the individual's right to autonomy or self-determination, and consent is required for any form of medical treatment other than in limited emergency circumstances. Many of the legal authorities in this area have been decided in the context of patients who have full capacity to give consent. However, when the patient is a young child who does not have the legal capacity to make such decisions, someone else, usually a parent, must give consent on his behalf. This does not detract from the value of respecting the autonomy of the child and ensuring that they participate as much as possible in decision-making about their own health. Communication to and with children, parents or guardians and the medical profession is vital if meaningful collaboration is to take place in making such decisions.

[11.02] Children also sometimes undergo medical procedures that are not intended to improve their own health but might help another person such as a sibling through, for example, a bone marrow or organ transplantation. One of the bases on which such procedures are authorised is that the child has an obligation to its family and that the best interests of the donor child are broader than just medical interests and must be taken to include emotional, psychological and social interests also. It appears in this context that children may be treated differently from adults in that non-consenting adults would not be obliged to act as a donor, whereas children may be so obliged.[1] It may be disputed whether such differential treatment is ethical and in keeping with the protection of the child.

[11.03] The treatment of very young children or infants who have been born with significant disabilities demonstrates the importance of collaboration between medical and parental interests, both of whom are presumed to act in the child's best interests. Non-treatment of severely disabled infants raises ethical and legal issues as to the subjectivity of determinations as to the value of life, and how best to safeguard the best interests of such a child. The difference in perception between parents and doctors as to where those best interests lie have posed problems in a number of cases discussed below. The limits of parental decision-making authority is an issue not yet definitively decided in Ireland, although it is expected that the Constitutional rights of the family would play a vital role in setting any limit in this regard. This chapter also examines case law from

---

1   See comprehensive discussion of this issue by Lyons, 'Obliging Children' (2011) Med Law Review 19, pp 55–85.

461

other jurisdictions in assessing to what extent parental consent to, or refusal of consent for, treatment of children has influenced judicial decisions here, or may in the future.

[11.04] As the child develops towards maturity, its understanding and independence from its parents grows. Treatment decisions may be taken on behalf of a minor child by its parents or legal guardians, although the child may be deemed competent to also give consent. This may be relatively unproblematic unless a decision is made by the child that does not coincide with parental views or professional advice, for example when an adolescent suffering from anorexia nervosa refuses food or other medical treatment. The assessment of capacity is important here, as the Court may struggle to find a way to save the person's life while still respecting the right to self-determination. These issues are considered in detail below.

SELECTIVE NON-TREATMENT OF INFANTS WITH SEVERE DISABILITIES

[11.05] The treatment of critically ill newborns who may develop serious disabilities is a matter of extreme concern for doctors and parents. While on the one hand decisions in relation to treatment of such a child are profoundly personal and private, there are also questions about law and public policy that should be addressed. The overriding concern of the medical team caring for and treating the infant is the best interests of the child. This is true whether or not they are born with serious disabilities or are likely to develop such disabilities as they grow. However, as medicine becomes more advanced and more technologically capable of keeping such infants alive, the issue arises as to whether prolongation of life in such situations is always in the best interests of the child.[2] There may be situations where an exception exists to the general duty to provide life-sustaining treatment, for example where there is an irreversible progression to imminent death, where treatment would clearly be ineffective or harmful, where life would be severely shortened regardless of treatment, where non-treatment would allow a greater degree of caring and comfort than treatment, or where the child's life would be one of intolerable pain and suffering.[3] In many of these situations, the best interests of the child are uncertain because medicine is not an exact science and it may not be possible to predict whether a particular treatment will work or, if it does work, what the outcome for the child will be in the long term. As a result, questions arise in relation to the wisdom or utility of trying to save all babies in this situation, particularly when they are born extremely prematurely. It is in these situations that the law has sometimes been asked to intervene to provide an objective determination of where the balance lies in protecting the child's best interests.

[11.06] Discussion of this issue sometimes raises the argument of medical futility, or the likelihood of benefit to the child from the proposed treatment. It is important that this issue is not linked or confused with the question of rationing of health-care resources, as these are entirely separate issues.[4] Respect for the dignity of all patients demands that

---

[2]   Bioethics Committee, Canadian Paediatric Society 'Treatment Decisions for Infants and Children' (2000).

[3]   Bioethics Committee, Canadian Paediatric Society 'Treatment Decisions for Infants and Children' (2000).

[4]   See *R v Cambridge Health Authority, ex parte B* (1995) 25 BMLR 5, rev'd [1995] 2 All ER 129.

consideration be taken only of their medical and emotional needs and interests, and that decisions be taken only on that basis. Although perhaps more commonly arising in the context of end-of-life care, 'futility is hardly a novel idea in medicine. Its roots in ancient medicine go back at least to the fifth-century BC physician Hippocrates. Yet debates over its meaning and ethical implications are surfacing with growing frequency. Increasingly, physicians seek to limit the lengths to which they must go to sustain the lives of patients who have lost the ability for conscious, interactive, and meaningful functioning.'[5]

[11.07] The concept of futility should be regarded within the medical rather than the economic sphere and may be described as a treatment 'which cannot give a minimum likelihood or quality of benefit'.[6] It may be argued that the term 'futility' is not always useful in the context of severely disabled infants for whom the question may not be one of life or death, but rather the possibility of sustaining an unacceptable quality of life. Pelligrino says that the term 'futility' suffers from 'vagueness in definition, clinically unpleasant connotations, and intense criticisms by credible bioethicists' but that there is nevertheless a role for the idea of futility where treatment cannot achieve anything and therefore 'futility is the inevitable corollary of the fact of human mortality.'[7] However, there are 'positive dangers of abuse if the term "futile treatment" is adopted uncritically within the medical vocabulary. These include the resurgence of inappropriate paternalism, the erosion of patient autonomy, the unjustified avoidance of the duty to treat – or the creation of an ephemeral duty not to treat – and the introduction of disguised and arbitrary rationing of resources.'[8] It may be that the term 'non-productive treatment' better serves to place the problem firmly in the medical field and also clarifies the intention of the decision-makers.[9] As can be seen from the case law below, the English courts have tended not to use the language of 'futility' or 'non-productive treatment' but have focused on 'intolerability' in an adjudication of the best interests of the child.

[11.08] The issue of selective non-treatment of neonates or young babies is one that is fraught with difficulty. While deliberate non-treatment at any age is problematic, the newborn baby born with seemingly insurmountable difficulties raises emotive ethical and legal issues around disability and the protection of the dignity of all human life. Parents who are faced with this dilemma are shocked, vulnerable, and probably inexperienced in medical language and decision-making of this kind. Therefore, in the majority of situations, the parents of the child will agree with the medical advice regarding their child and it is only in the rare instances where the family and the medical team have disagreed regarding treatment that the question has reached the courts. In 1970 Friedson wrote of the medical profession that its status reflects a societal belief that the job has attributes such as superior skill, theoretical learning, ethical behaviour

---

5   Jecker and Pearlman, 'Medical Futility: Who Decides?' (1992) 152(6) Arch Intern Med 1140.
6   Schneiderman and Jecker, 'Futility in Practice' (1993) 153 Arch Intern Med 437.
7   Pelligrino, 'Futility in Medical Decisions: The Word and the Concept' (2005) 17 HEC Forum 308 at 309.
8   M Wreen, 'Medical Futility and Physician Discretion' (2004) 30 J Med Ethics 275.
9   Mason and Laurie, *Law and Medical Ethics* (8th edn, OUP, 2010) para 15.06.

and belief in the importance and value of its work.[10] He argued that a profession claims autonomy over the content of its work 'by virtue of the objective and reliable character of its expertise which it claims is so complex and esoteric that only properly trained men can know and evaluate it.'[11] Doctors who work in the neonatal intensive care unit are highly qualified, technically skilful and motivated by the desire to do good.[12] Although the traditional model of deference to the profession has been challenged in recent years by a decline in trust, a focus on autonomy and patient-centred care and a rise in consumerism,[13] nonetheless it appears that conflicts between doctors and parents in the neonatal care unit are rare and most parents are content to comply with medical advice.[14] Some disagreements, however, can arise from parental adherence to a particular religious belief or from an inability to comprehend the severity of the problems or an unwillingness to accept the prognosis despite unanimous medical evidence. Where this occurs, the relationship between the parents and clinicians can deteriorate and the hospital may seek judicial sanction for the proposed treatment decisions, as seen in the cases discussed below. As Mason and Laurie put it:

> Treatment decisions taken immediately after birth concern human beings who are at the most vulnerable period of their lives – human beings, moreover, who cannot express their feelings for the present or the future and who clearly cannot have indicated their references to their surrogates. Parents faced with decision making at this point may agree with their medical advisors simply because they have no evidence on which to *disagree*. It is only when the bonds of adversity have been cemented between the parents and the disabled infant that the former are likely to have developed strong independent opinions as to which treatments are appropriate.[15]

[11.09] Another facet of the dilemma facing doctors in this area is the risk of contravening the criminal law by facilitating the death of the severely disabled infant. Killing a child or any other person is murder and even where the actions of the doctor were those of omission rather than commission, he might still be charged with manslaughter.[16] This risk is illustrated by *R v Arthur*[17] in which a doctor was prosecuted for the attempted murder of a newborn child. The facts of this case involved a baby born with Down's syndrome who was otherwise believed to be healthy but whose parents did not want him to survive. Dr Arthur noted the parents' wishes on the baby's chart and

---

[10]   Friedson, *Profession of Medicine: A Study of the Sociology of Applied Knowledge* (Harper & Row, 1970) 187, quoted by Morris, 'Selective Treatment of Irreversibly Impaired Infants: Decision-Making at the Threshold' (2009) 17 Med Law Review pp 347–376 at 363.

[11]   Friedson, *Profession of Medicine: A Study of the Sociology of Applied Knowledge* (Harper & Row, 1970) at 360.

[12]   Morris, 'Selective Treatment of Irreversibly Impaired Infants: Decision-Making at the Threshold' (2009) 17 Med Law Review pp 347–376, at 363.

[13]   See Ch 2, para **2.01–2.11**.

[14]   McHaffie et al, 'Deciding for Imperilled Newborns: Medical Authority or Parental Autonomy?' (2001) 27 JME 104.

[15]   Mason and Laurie, *Law and Medical Ethics* (8th edn, OUP, 2010) at para 15.09.

[16]   See Cuttini, 'End of Life Decisions in Neonatal Intensive Care: Physicians' Self-Reported Practices in Seven European Countries' (2000) 355 Lancet 2112; Barton and Hodgman, 'The Contribution of Withholding or Withdrawing Care to Newborn Mortality' (2005) 116 Pediatrics 1487.

[17]   *R v Arthur* [1981] 12 BMLR 1.

prescribed 'nursing care only' in addition to prescribing medication to be administered at regular intervals to keep the baby sedated. The baby did not receive nourishment or sustenance and died within a few days of birth. It was alleged against the doctor that by prescribing nursing care only, he took steps to bring about the baby's death and intended that the baby should die. In his defence, Dr Arthur argued that his actions constituted acceptable medical practice and not murder. The doctor was initially charged with murder, but it transpired through the forensic evidence that the baby was not physically healthy in any event and therefore the doctor's actions may not in fact have caused the child's death, so the charge was reduced to attempted murder, and Dr Arthur was acquitted.

[11.10] In Farquharson J's summing up to the jury he discussed the careful and agonising consideration that had to be given in relation to the best interests of a child born with Down's syndrome, bearing in mind the 'most appalling' handicap facing the child, and in this case the rejection of the child by the parents. At the centre of the case was the fact that although doctors do not have the right to kill children who are handicapped or seriously disadvantaged, it is sometimes difficult to decide whether a doctor is carrying out a positive act or allowing a course of events to ensue. Evidence was given to the effect that allowing a newborn baby with serious handicap to die was not rare and that Dr Arthur's treatment of the baby was within responsible medical practice. One expert called to give evidence said 'There is an important difference between allowing a child to die and taking action to kill it. Withholding food is, I think, a negative, not a positive act. It is not a positive step to cause the child's death. The doctor indeed has a duty to order feeding, but if he orders food to be withheld, and he does it with the knowledge and wish of the parents, then that is permissible.' The President of the Royal College of Physicians at the time said:

> Where there is an uncomplicated Down's case and the parents do not want the child to live...I think there are circumstances where it would be ethical to put it upon a course of management that would end in its death ...I say that with a child suffering from Down's and with a parental wish that it should not survive, it is ethical to terminate life.[18]

[11.11] The prosecution of Dr Arthur for his management of this baby led to a storm of protest from the medical profession, largely on the basis of the passive-active distinction.[19] It was argued that Dr Arthur should not have been prosecuted at all for treating a patient in a manner that most paediatricians would have seen as acceptable medical practice at that time. The reason the doctor was prosecuted may have been because the baby was 'treatable', in that he was in no physical pain and required no intervention as far as the doctors knew at the time. 'Death in such circumstances depends on the withholding of nourishment and to take away such a life is to make a social rather than a medical decision – the fact that it was taken by a doctor rather than a member of the public should be irrelevant.'[20] The case would seem to be of limited value now by virtue of the cases that have been decided in recent years in the UK and its

---

18 *R v Arthur* [1981] 12 BMLR 1 at 21–2, quoted in Mason and Laurie *Law and Medical Ethics* (8th edn, OUP, 2010), at para 15.18.

19 See 'Paediatricians and the Law' (1981) 283 BMJ 1280; 'After the Trial at Leicester' (1981) 2 Lancet 1085.

20 Mason and Laurie, *Law and Medical Ethics* (8th edn, OUP, 2010) para 15.18

significance is largely confined to acting as an example of 'the dangers of extrapolating the concept of 'futility' to one of an obligation not to treat in the face of parental pressure.'[21]

[11.12] Interestingly, another case decided at around the same time in the UK also dealt with the question of treatment or non-treatment of a baby with Down's syndrome and seems to be in conflict with the *Arthur* case. In *Re B (a minor)*[22], described as the first neonatal euthanasia case in the UK, B was an infant whose Down's syndrome condition was complicated by intestinal obstruction, which would be fatal in the absence of surgical intervention. The parents took the decision that it would be in B's best interests not to have the surgery and for her to die, a decision described by the Court as 'entirely responsible'. The baby was made a ward of court and the question thus came before the Court as to whether she should be treated. Dunn LJ said that B 'should be put in the position of any other mongol[23] child and given the opportunity to live an existence.' Templeman LJ was concerned that the judge at first instance in refusing the operation had placed too much emphasis on the wishes of the parents and not enough on the interests of the child. The issue was simply whether to allow an operation to take place which may result in the child living for 20 or 30 years as a mongoloid or whether to terminate the life of a mongoloid child because she also had an intestinal complaint.

> It devolves on this court...to decide whether the life of this child is demonstrably going to be so awful that in effect the child must be condemned to die or whether the life of this child is still so imponderable that it would be wrong for her to be condemned to die....Faced with the choice, I have no doubt that it is the duty of this court to decide that the child must live.[24]

[11.13] Templeman LJ did, however, concede that there may be situations in which the damage to the child is so severe and the child's future so certain to be full of pain and suffering, that the court may come to a different conclusion. In this case the Court of Appeal found no evidence that B's life would be 'intolerable' and held therefore that it was in her interests to have the operation. This case lays the foundation for 'a quality of life therapeutic standard rather than one based on a rigid adherence to the principle of the sanctity of human life.'[25] These quality of life arguments must be based not on economic or social worth but on the infant's capacity for future contentment.[26]

[11.14] In *Re C (A minor) (wardship: medical treatment)*[27] C was a newborn baby suffering from congenital hydrocephalus. She was also a ward of court for other reasons. The local authority sought the determination of the Court as to how she should be treated in the event of a serious infection or in the event of her feeding regimes becoming unviable. C's prognosis was very poor, she was severely brain-damaged, blind, probably deaf, had spastic cerebral palsy of all four limbs and was not absorbing food.

---

[21] Mason and Laurie, *Law and Medical Ethics* (8th edn, OUP, 2010) para 15.19.

[22] *Re B (a minor)* [1990] 3 All ER 927, [1981] 1 WLR 1421, CA.

[23] A term sometimes used in the past as a synonym for persons with Down's syndrome.

[24] *Re B (a minor)* [1990] 3 All ER 927 at 929, [1981] 1 WLR 1421 at 1424. See Raphael, 'Handicapped Infants: Medical Ethics and the Law' (1988) 14 J Med Ethics 5.

[25] Mason and Laurie, *Law and Medical Ethics* (8th edn, OUP, 2010) para 15.23.

[26] Freeman, 'Can We Leave the Best Interests of Very Sick Children to Their Parents?' in Freeman and Lewis (eds) *Law and Medicine* (OUP, 2000).

[27] *Re C (A minor) (wardship: medical treatment)* [1990] Fam 26.

By contrast with *Re B,* the evidence here was that C was dying and there was nothing that the medical team could do to alter that fact. The Court held that C should be treated in a manner appropriate to her condition and that measures should be taken to ease her suffering rather than prolong her life. *Re B* was distinguished on the basis that in this case there was no option for the child to have a normal life span and that the child's life would be demonstrably awful and intolerable with no capacity to interact on any level, seemingly coming within the kind of exceptional situation envisaged by Templeman LJ in *Re B.*

[11.15] *Re J (a minor) (wardship: medical treatment)*[28] also concerned the question of whether treatment should be withheld from a baby with severe disabilities. J was a ward of court who had been born prematurely, had suffered very severe and permanent brain damage, was epileptic, and would be quadriplegic, blind and deaf. His life expectancy was uncertain but he was expected to die before late adolescence. He had been ventilated twice for long periods but it was the opinion of the medical team treating J that any further collapse requiring ventilation would be fatal. The question for the Court was whether if he suffered a further collapse the medical staff should re-ventilate him. The Court held that even though J was not dying, life-sustaining treatment need not be given where the physical disabilities were so grave that the infant's life would be intolerable. However, the Court could never sanction positive steps to terminate the life of a person. The Court had to perform a balancing exercise between J's right to survive and the pain and suffering he would continue to experience for as long as he did survive. It was held that having regard to the invasive and hazardous nature of re-ventilation, the risk of further deterioration, and the extremely unfavourable prognosis, it would be in J's best interests that he not be re-ventilated.

[11.16] Lord Donaldson MR stated that no one could dictate the treatment to be given to a child, neither court, parents nor doctors. There must be checks and balances in the system such that doctors may recommend one treatment or refuse to adopt another treatment on medical grounds. The court or parents can refuse to consent to treatment but cannot insist on any particular treatment in its place. 'The inevitable and desirable result in that choice of treatment is in some measure a joint decision of the doctors and the court or parents.' Issues of resource allocation do not come into this balancing exercise for the court. He said that what was at issue here was not the imposition of death, but the right to choose a course of action that will fail to avert death. 'The choice is that of the patient if of full age and capacity, the choice is that of the parents or court if by reason of his age, the child cannot make the choice and it is a choice which must be made solely on behalf of the child and in what the court or parents conscientiously believe to be his best interests.' The Court rejected submissions that respect for the sanctity of life means that there should be no instance in which life-saving treatment should be withheld, irrespective of the side effects of treatment and the quality of life of the child thereafter. It held that there was no authority on principle or precedent for such an absolute position and that there was only one test, namely, the paramount nature of the child's best interests. Consideration of those interests might involve the court determining that deliberate steps should not be taken to artificially prolong the miserable life of a child doomed to incurable pain and suffering.

---

[28]   *Re J (a minor) (wardship: medical treatment)* [1991] Fam 33, [1990] 3 All ER 930.

[11.17] These cases show a firm commitment to the welfare of the child as the paramount concern for the court, as well as strong opposition to any notion that the court could sanction any measures designed to end life. The issue was less about the quality of life of the infant in terms of social value, but rather about the pain, distress and suffering likely to be suffered by continuation of the child's life. In another case, also called *Re J (a minor) (child in care: medical treatment)*[29] a mother attempted to insist on treatment for her son, who was profoundly mentally and physically handicapped as a result of a fall when he was one month old. He suffered from microcephaly, cerebral palsy, blindness, and severe epilepsy. He was fed by nasogastric tube and was unlikely to progress beyond his present state. His life expectancy was uncertain but likely to be shortened. His convulsions required him to be resuscitated in hospital. The paediatrician considered that it would be medically inappropriate to use mechanical ventilation in any future resuscitation. The health authority, which shared parental responsibility for J, sought the Court's direction as to whether life-saving measures should be administered to J in the future if he suffered a life-threatening event. The Court held that the Court could not order a medical practitioner to treat a patient contrary to his clinical judgment and professional duty. The proper approach was for the Court to consider the options available to it in light of the paramountcy of the child's best interests and to authorise or refuse to authorise a proposed treatment in light of that consideration. The Court was of the view that this was largely a matter of clinical judgment and was not prepared to direct that any particular treatment should be given that might conflict with such judgment.

[11.18] These cases taken together demonstrate the reluctance of the courts to stray into the area of clinical autonomy or judgment. The courts have stated on many occasions that a doctor could not be forced to provide a treatment to which he was professionally and ethically opposed on the grounds that it was not in his patient's best interests. Therefore, parents can never have a right to treatment for their child where this is considered medically inappropriate. The courts seem to support a wide-ranging clinical discretion whereby the *clinical* judgment of the doctor is applied to the 'best interests' of the patient, even though those interests involve issues beyond diagnosis and prognosis.[30] It is not clear what the courts would decide in less clear-cut cases than those discussed above where the medical evidence is less than unanimously in favour of non-treatment of the child, although the general tenor of the judgments of the courts suggests that it would be more likely to opt for the salvaging of life.

[11.19] In *Re C (a minor) (medical treatment)*[31] the Court again had to consider whether to authorise non-treatment of a young child. In this case C was 16 months old and suffered from spinal muscular atrophy, as a result of which she suffered occasional respiratory arrest for which she had to be ventilated. At the date of the hearing she was on ventilation in hospital, which delayed her death but did not alleviate her suffering. The doctors were of the opinion that ventilation should not be continued indefinitely and that it should not be reintroduced in the event of further respiratory arrests. The parents

---

29 *Re J (a minor) (child in care: medical treatment)* [1993] Fam 15.
30 Morris, 'Selective Treatment of Irreversibly Impaired Infants: Decision-Making at the Threshold' (2009) 17 Med Law Review, pp 347–376 at 354.
31 *Re C (a minor) (medical treatment)* [1998] 1 FLR 384.

felt unable to consent to this course of action on the basis of firmly held religious views. The Court reiterated the statement expressed in previous cases that a doctor should not be required to treat a child contrary to his clinical judgment and that the parents' insistence on ventilation in the event of further respiratory arrests would oblige the doctors to undertake a course of treatment that they were unwilling to do. The Court held that on the evidence, it was in C's best interests to be taken off ventilation and that she should not be re-ventilated in the event of further respiratory failures. This case demonstrates again how parent and child interests might come into conflict. C's parents were unable to face losing their daughter yet the Court determined that their assessment of her best interests should be overruled. Although they wanted her to live as long as possible, the Court held that it was not in her interests to continue to suffer. It is interesting to note that the parents' opposition in this case stemmed from religious beliefs, similar to the Jehovah's Witness cases. They believed in the sanctity of life at all costs, a principle to which the courts have not ascribed, holding that it may not always be in a child's best interests to be kept alive, especially where the child will have a life full of suffering and distress.

[11.20] In *A NHS Trust v D*,[32] the Court was asked to consider the treatment of a 19-month-old child who had been born prematurely with serious disabilities, in particular a severe, chronic, irreversible and worsening lung disease, giving him a very short life expectancy. He also had heart failure, hepatic and renal dysfunction and severe developmental delay. The NHS Trust involved in his care applied for a declaration that in the event of any future respiratory or cardiac failure, it was in his best interests not to resuscitate him but to apply palliative measures to permit him to die peacefully. The medical evidence was that the child's condition could not improve and that invasive treatment would cause distress, discomfort and pain. His parents strongly opposed the application on the grounds that it was premature.

[11.21] Cazelet J outlined four legal principles applicable to this case as follows: firstly, the Court's paramount consideration must be the best interests of the child. This involves consideration of the parent's views, but such views cannot override the Court's views of the child's best interests. Secondly, the Court must respect the sanctity of human life and is obliged to take all steps to preserve life, save in exceptional circumstances. Thirdly, the Court could never approve a course designed to terminate life or accelerate death. It should only be concerned with whether to prolong life. Fourthly, the Court should not direct a doctor to provide treatment that he is unwilling to give according to that doctor's clinical judgment. Having regard to these principles and the minimal quality of life that the child had in the short life span left to him in any event, the judge weighed any possible short-term extension to his life against the increasing pain and suffering caused by further ventilation. A declaration was granted that withholding ventilation would be lawful but, in essence, the decision would be that of the paediatrician in charge of the child's care. This re-affirms previous decisions on the principle that the best interests of the child do not demand heroic measures to be performed in order to prolong life where the child's life expectancy is short and the quality of life is poor. The Court appears to have preferred the opinion of the consultant in charge of the baby's care, who said he had 'minimal awareness' despite the views of his parents and community health workers

---

[32] *A NHS Trust v D* [2000] Fam Law 803; [2000] 2 FLR 677.

who had noted improvements in his condition in preceding months. Parental wishes are taken into consideration but are not determinative of the issue, which must be decided on clinical grounds.[33]

[11.22] In *Re Wyatt (A child) (Medical Treatment: parent's consent),*[34] baby Charlotte had been born prematurely at 26 weeks gestation, and suffered from severe and repeated respiratory failure with associated heart and renal failure. She was blind, deaf and could make no voluntary movements. Medical evidence was unanimously of the view that she would have minimal cognitive function but would be able to experience the pain of any future medical treatment. Her treating doctors were of the view that further ventilation was not in her best interests, as it would require a tracheotomy and subject Charlotte to pain and distress without any chance of restoring her to health or prolonging her life significantly. Her parents, who were devout Christians, disagreed. Hedley J held that artificial ventilation not recommended by the medical team would not be in Charlotte's best interests. The judge was influenced by the medical views that even if she were to survive re-ventilation, her condition was likely to deteriorate and the experience of intensive care treatment would imperil a peaceful death. On appeal, an argument was put to the Court that the proper test to apply was whether Charlotte's life was 'intolerable' and the parents were of the view that her condition had improved to the extent that it could not be described as intolerable. However, the Court said that 'intolerability' was only a potentially valuable guide towards the determination of best interests and that any improvement in her condition was minimal. In refusing the appeal, the Court of Appeal held that:

> The intellectual milestones for the judge in a case such as the present are, therefore, simple, although the ultimate decision will frequently be extremely difficult. The judge must decide what is in the child's best interests. In making that decision, the welfare of the child is paramount, and the judge must look at the question from the assumed point of view of the patient. There is a strong presumption in favour of a course of action which will prolong life, but that presumption is not irrebuttable. The term "best interests" encompasses medical, emotional, and all other welfare issues. The court must conduct a balancing exercise in which all the relevant factors are weighed and a helpful way of undertaking this exercise is to draw up a balance sheet.

[11.23] The media and public attention surrounding the case led to Charlotte's case becoming something of a 'battleground in the defence of the sanctity of life', with Brazier referring to the transformation of private tragedy to public spectacle as disturbing.[35] 'There is no right answer to the dilemma in *Re Wyatt*. Resolution in the courts may indeed exacerbate a tragedy nature created. But is there any alternative?' Brazier also questions how the initial decision to treat Charlotte was taken, given that the longer the child lives, the more agonising the decision of the parents becomes. Although the principles applied in this case were by and large those used previously,

---

[33] For analysis of the position in the Netherlands, see Brownstein, 'Neonatal Euthanasia Case Law in the Netherlands' (1997) 71 Aus LJ 54. See also Moor S 'Euthanasia in Relation to Newborn Babies – A Comparative Study of the Legal and Ethical Issues' (1996) 15 Med Law 295.

[34] *Re Wyatt (A child) (Medical Treatment: parent's consent)* [2004] EWHC 2247.

[35] Brazier, 'An Intractable Dispute: When Parents and Professionals Disagree' 13 Med Law Rev (2005) 412–418 at 413–414.

nevertheless 'the furore surrounding the case indicates a deep-seated unease about any decision that suggests a life is not worth living.'[36] It may also be questioned why only relatively few cases of conflict arise between doctors and parents, how they arise and whether the courts are the best place to resolve them.

> There are, also, wider considerations of the role of the medical profession, the 'rights' of parents and – underlying it all – the ultimate question of the value of life, including lives affected by physical or mental impairments. Changing attitudes to disability have been due in part to an increasing determination by those with impairments to have their voices heard, and some vociferously oppose the notion that anyone should, as they see it, decide that another person's impaired life is not worth living. Others, who accept that sometimes difficult decisions have to be made, are concerned to establish a transparent ethical and legal framework. The dilemmas raised by these babies encompass the limits of medical technology, professional ethics, parental responsibility, and the role of law in setting standards for society.[37]

[11.24] The balance sheet approach referred to above is illustrated by *An NHS Trust v M*,[38] where M had a severe form of spinal muscular atrophy. Such conditions are fatal without artificial ventilation. The unanimous medical opinion was that M's quality of life was so low and the burden of living was so great that it was unethical to continue treatment. Holman J said that he was being asked to approve, against parental wishes, the removal of life support from a conscious child with sensory awareness and assumed normal cognition. Taking the balance sheet approach, he noted M's inability to move or communicate as well as his pleasure in his family and his soft toys. He said M's life was helpless and sad but he had a relationship of value with his family as well as other pleasures from sight, touch and sound. He held that the burdens of treatment did not outweigh the benefits and he did not grant the declaration sought by the hospital to discontinue ventilation and provide palliative care only. The case is significant in that it shows that courts *can* sometimes direct doctors to treat even where doctors are of the view that it would be unethical, and this can itself create practical dilemmas for the daily care and treatment of the patient.[39]

[11.25] The Royal College of Paediatrics and Child Health in England in its Framework for Practice[40] stated that there are five situations in which it is ethical and legal to consider withholding or withdrawing treatment from a child. In the first two, where the child is either brain dead or in a permanent vegetative state, an accurate diagnosis means that there is no curative treatment. The other three situations are described as 'no chance', 'no purpose', and 'unbearable.' 'No chance' refers to situations in which the

---

36   Morris, 'Selective Treatment of Irreversibly Impaired Infants: Decision-Making at the Threshold' (2009) 17 Med Law Review, pp 347–376 at 347.

37   Morris, 'Selective Treatment of Irreversibly Impaired Infants: Decision-Making at the Threshold' (2009) 17 Med Law Review, at 347–348.

38   *An NHS Trust v M* [2006] EWHC 507.

39   Morris, 'Selective Treatment of Irreversibly Impaired Infants: Decision-Making at the Threshold' (2009) 17 Med Law Review, at 369.

40   *Withholding or Withdrawing Life Sustaining Treatment in Children: A Framework for Practice*, (2nd edn, RCPCH, 2004). See also BMA guidelines, *Withholding and Withdrawing Life-Prolonging Medical Treatment: Guidelines for Decision-Making* (3rd edn, BMJ Books, 2007).

child has such severe disease that life-sustaining treatment simply delays death without significant alleviation of suffering. This is a fairly straightforward category, since the child will die no matter what is done, for example anencephaly and severe spinal muscular atrophy where life expectancy is short.[41] 'No purpose' refers to situations in which although the patient may be able to survive with treatment, the degree of physical or mental impairment will be so great that it is unreasonable to expect them to bear it.' 'Unbearable' is where the child and/or family feel that in the face of progressive and irreversible illness, further treatment is more than can be borne. They wish to have treatment withdrawn even though medical opinion is that it may be of some benefit. Both of these latter categories are more controversial, as the child is capable of living for at least a short time but with a very poor quality of life.

[11.26] In 2006 the Nuffield Council on Bioethics published its Report on *Critical Care Decisions in Fetal and Neonatal Medicine*,[42] which proposed guidelines based on gestational age for deciding on the initiation and continuation of intensive care. At 25 weeks gestation and above, it recommended that intensive care should be initiated unless the baby is affected by some severe abnormality incompatible with any significant period of survival. Between 24 and 25 weeks it recommended that a baby should normally be offered intensive care unless parents and clinicians are agreed that in light of the baby's condition, or likely condition, it is not in his best interests to start intensive care. Between 23 and 24 weeks, it is recommended that precedence should be given to the wishes of the parents regarding resuscitation and intensive care but that 'when the condition of the baby indicates that he or she will not survive for long, clinicians are not legally obliged to proceed with treatment wholly contrary to their clinical judgment, if they judge that treatment would be futile.' Parents may decline intensive care because, the Report recognises, 'it will be the parents who will live with the consequences.'[43] Between 22 and 23 weeks, standard practice should be not to resuscitate unless parents request it and the clinicians agree that it is an exceptional case and the resuscitation is in the baby's best interests. Below 22 weeks it is recommended that resuscitation should not be attempted unless it is within an approved research study.

[11.27] The Report received a mixed response, with some commenting that the guidelines are to be 'commended for striving for transparency' and for taking account of factors other than purely medical considerations such as the child's capacity to experience pleasure and form relationships.[44] Others such as the British Medical Association called them 'blanket rules' smothering clinical discretion. The Chair of the Working Party which produced the report, Margaret Brazier, defended charges that the report treated newborn life as of lesser value than the lives of older children by pointing to the fact that few people insist that when life can be prolonged for however short a time, it must be. She says "What the baby, older child or adult is entitled to, morally and

---

41 Morris, 'Selective Treatment of Irreversibly Impaired Infants: Decision-Making at the Threshold' (2009) 17 Med Law Review, at 356.

42 Nuffield Council on Bioethics, Report on *Critical Care Decisions in Fetal and Neonatal Medicine*. Available at www.nuffieldbioethics.org (accessed 4 June 2011).

43 Nuffield Council on Bioethics, Report on *Critical Care Decisions in Fetal and Neonatal Medicine,* para 9.17.

44 Morris, 'Selective Treatment of Irreversibly Impaired Infants: Decision-Making at the Threshold' (2009) 17 Med Law Review, at 350–351.

legally, is appropriate care. Neonatal intensive care is invasive and burdensome. A baby may be subjected to 200 or so intrusive and painful procedures in one fortnight. He or she is isolated from the love and warmth of their family, and deprived of the care that should be the birthright of any newborn. When insisting on treatment imposes an intolerable burden on the baby, such treatment becomes inhumane.'[45]

[11.28] One of the important features of the Report is the emphasis on listening to parents' views, and it recommends a partnership model between clinicians and parents. The question arises, however, to what extent parents' views will be considered in reality, as there is a vast difference between parents being informed as to what will happen and, on the other hand, parents being asked to make the final choice. McHaffie wonders whether parents are really sharing decision-making or 'are neonatologists practising a form of benevolent paternalism?'[46] Although parents may perceive that they have been involved in decision-making, in many instances they will simply have been agreeing with the clinical recommendation. McHaffie believes that parents have 'an impressive ability to understand the issues and weigh up the consequences for their own child' and where the child spends a lengthy period of time in intensive care, the parents will become very familiar with procedures and medical terminology and can participate effectively in decision-making. The Nuffield Report also recognises that in some cases consensus between clinicians and parents will not be achieved, and in most of these situations the parents' views should take priority. It recommended that every effort should be made to resolve disputes without judicial intervention, such as mediation and the use of clinical ethics committees, which are more prevalent in the United States, to assist in providing advice in individual cases.

[11.29] The Report does not accept the distinction between not commencing intensive care and withdrawing such care after it has begun. Neither does it accept the approach taken in the Netherlands, which allows doctors to take active steps to end newborn life. Brazier acknowledges that some people argue that there is no moral difference between deliberately ending a life and allowing it to end but she says that doctors and parents see a 'real and huge difference between ending treatment that only prolongs a terrible life, and giving a lethal injection.' The Report seeks to 'respect the feelings of those most intimately involved in decisions about premature babies and who may want the opportunity to spend time caring for a dying baby.'[47]

[11.30] In the Netherlands the Coroners Act was amended in 1993 to provide that doctors who carried out euthanasia upon request, or actively terminated a patient's life without request, should report the case to the coroner who would inform the District Attorney. No judicial inquiry would be started if the circumstances indicated that the doctors acted with due conscientious care.[48] The requirements of good medical practice were not explicitly mentioned in the Act. During 1995 two test cases concerning

---

[45]   Brazier and Archard, 'Letting Babies Die' (2007) JME 33:125–126; See also April and Parker, 'End of Life Decision-Making in Neonatal Care' (2007) JME 33:126–127.

[46]   HA McHaffie et al, 'Deciding for Imperilled Newborns: Medical Authority or Parental Autonomy?' (2001) 27 JME 104.

[47]   Brazier and Archard, 'Letting Babies Die' (2007) JME 33:125–126.

[48]   Fenigsen, 'The Netherlands: New Regulations Concerning Euthanasia Issues' (1993) 9 (2) Law Med 167.

neonatal euthanasia came before the Dutch courts. In the first case, Dr Kadijk administered a combination of lethal drugs to a 25-day-old neonatal girl at the request of the parents.[49] He was charged with murder under the Penal Code. The baby had been born with Patau Syndrome, or Trisomy 13, which caused her to have a cleft lip and palate, skull defects, overlapping fingers and microphthalmia. Ninety per cent of children born with this condition died within the first year of life with serious mental retardation, multiple neurological defects, convulsions and motor retardation. She had a cardio-respiratory arrest shortly after birth and was resuscitated, subsequently evidence of renal failure was also noted. It was decided that should another arrest occur, no further resuscitation would be attempted and she was discharged home. One of her scalp defects became infected and she experienced convulsions, spinal fluid leakage and other difficulties. Analgesics and sedatives were considered unsuitable, as they would have caused her death due to her other medical problems. The doctors and parents took the view that no other option was available than ending of her life. The doctor complied with the necessary regulations and notified the coroner before the death of the child. Dr Kadijk was acquitted, with the Court noting that he had acted with scientific responsible medical insight and in accordance with accepted norms of medical ethics.

[11.31] The second case heard on the same day in 1995 involved Dr Prins, who was charged with murder for administering lethal medication to a three-day-old neonate suffering from hydrocephalus and spina bifida.[50] The baby was in severe pain with grossly deformed and paralysed limbs and a poorly developed brain. The medical prognosis was that she faced a short life of pain from several weeks to six months. Following detailed discussion, the parents requested termination of her life with lethal injection. Legal regulations were complied with and the doctor was again acquitted. In both cases the courts acquitted on grounds of *force majeure* in an emergency situation.[51]

The difficult case of *Re T*

[11.32] One particular English case stands out from the rest in relation to the weight to be given to parental authority.[52] In *Re T (a minor) (wardship: medical treatment)*[53] the child in question had been born with a life-threatening liver defect for which he underwent an operation at almost one month old. The operation was unsuccessful and caused the child pain and distress. The prognosis was that he would not live beyond two-and-a-half years without a liver transplant. The evidence before the Court was to the effect that, although liver transplantation was complicated surgery, the operation had a

---

49   Judgment of the Groningen District Court in the *Kadijk* case, Parket Nummer: 070093–95, Public Prosecutor's Office, the Hague, Netherlands, 7 November 1995.

50   Verdict of the Amsterdam Court of Appeal in the *Prins* case, Arrest Number 23:002076–95. Public Prosecutor's Office, The Hague, Netherlands, 7 November 1995.

51   See Brownstein, 'Neonatal Euthanasia Case Law in the Netherlands' (1997) 71 Aust LJ 54–58.

52   Freeman refers to this case as 'the nadir of judicial thinking in this area.' See Freeman, 'Whose Life is it Anyway?' (2001) 9 Med L Rev 259 at 273.

53   *Re T (a minor) (wardship: medical treatment)* [1997] 1 All ER 906. This case has generated much academic comment. For example, Fox and McHale, 'In Whose Best Interests?' (1997) 60 MLR 700; Freeman, 'Whose Life is it Anyway?' (2001) 9 Med L Rev 259; Loughrey, 'Medical Treatment – The Status of Parental Opinion' [1998] Fam Law 146.

good chance of success for the child, and if successful, the child would go on to have many years of normal life. The mother refused to give her consent for the surgery on the basis that she did not wish the child to undergo the pain and distress of further surgery.[54] On an application by the local authority at the instigation of the consultants dealing with the care of this child, the trial judge held that the mother's decision was not that of a reasonable parent and directed that the child should have the surgery. On appeal, the Court of Appeal recognised the importance of the mother's support for the surgery especially in terms of the necessary aftercare of the child. The mother's concerns as to the benefits of the surgery, the dangers of failure and the possibility of the need for future transplants, and the effect on the child of these concerns were all factors to be taken into account by the Court. The fact that the mother would be in a position whereby she had to care for the child without the support of the child's father, who lived outside the jurisdiction, and that she would be forced to provide a commitment to the care of her child after surgery which she did not support, all combined to persuade the Court that it would not be in the child's best interests to require him to undergo the surgery.

[11.33] There are a number of aspects of this decision which merit discussion. Until *Re T* all the cases decided by the English courts had shown deference to medical opinion where there was disagreement with parents in relation to the treatment to be provided to their child. The question was always whether the proposed treatment was in the best interests of the child, rather than whether parental wishes should be respected. The other cases involved severely handicapped infants who had little or no prospect of improvement and had little or no interaction with their environment. The child in *Re T* did not fall into that category. The Court in *Re T* held that it had to take into account a range of factors in reaching its decision as to the welfare of the child. These factors included the wishes of the parents, who in this case happened to be health-care professionals themselves, the child's life expectancy, the circumstances of the mother in having to return to the jurisdiction without her partner, and the reluctance of the doctors to perform the surgery in the face of parental opposition. Therefore, the Court took into account other factors apart from the clinical factors. This was unusual in that the medical evidence was unanimously in favour of the surgery on the basis that the prognosis was good. Waite LJ was of the view that one of the distinguishing factors in *Re T* was that the opposition of the parents was not due to dogma or strict principle that may be considered contrary to the principle that the child's best interests should always be paramount, but rather their opposition was due to concerns based on their professional health-care experience and their child's previous surgical experiences. This would seem to be directed at cases such as those involving Jehovah's Witnesses where parents have been opposed, as a matter of religious principle, to the transfusion of blood to their children.[55] In such cases the courts have generally refused to allow religious beliefs to take precedence over the child's best medical interests.[56] However, in *Re T* the Court took a very different view of the rationale behind the parent's opposition, despite stating that the reasonableness of their refusal was not an issue for the Court to decide.

---

[54]   The parents were not married, so only the mother had parental responsibility. Both parents were health-care professionals.

[55]   For discussion of the refusal of treatment by mature minors who are Jehovah's Witnesses, see para **11.105** et seq.

[56]   See *Re S (a minor) (medical treatment)* [1993] 1 FLR.

[11.34] It may be questioned why parental refusal should be accorded more respect in one case rather than the other. 'One distinction may be that the court is prepared to give weight to non-metaphysical factors such as concerns about treatment, but will not consider an assessment of metaphysical factors to be within its competence.'[57] In this case the treatment proposed was unanimously recommended on clinical grounds, it had a relatively minor risk factor that was regarded as well worth taking in light of the fact that it may extend the child's life expectancy considerably. This was not a case where the parents objected to an unusual or experimental treatment that had a poor success rate. It may be argued that parental opposition to treatment should only be relevant where such opposition would jeopardise the chances of success of the treatment, or alternatively where the relationship between the child and its parents would be so adversely affected that it would not be in the child's best interests to proceed with the treatment in question. Butler-Sloss LJ based her decision on the basis that the mother's total commitment to the surgery was essential to its success, and that forcing the mother to take on this commitment where she did not believe that it was the right thing for her son, would not be in the best interests of the child. While the first of these grounds comes within a traditional interpretation of clinical factors to be taken into consideration, the second arguably goes more towards parental interests. This is seen also in the statement of Butler-Sloss LJ where she describes the mother and child as one – 'the welfare of the child depends upon its mother.' In fact, the converse could be said to be true in this particular case, where the interests of the mother and child were in direct conflict. 'The impact of the situation upon the mother may have been severe, but how conscious would the child have been of the difficulties? It may have been preferable from the child's point of view to be in care with a good chance of survival if the mother could not cope.'[58]

[11.35] Another interesting point of distinction here is the aftercare element that played an important role in shaping the attitude of the Court to the mother's refusal. The Court was of the view that this child's problems required major and complicated surgery and many years of aftercare and administration of medication by the mother. However, when one examines the previous cases, such as *Re C* where the parents of a child with Down's syndrome had refused consent to surgery for an intestinal complaint, it is apparent that in some of these other cases the aftercare involved was as onerous if not more so than in *Re T*. Indeed, if anything, when one compares the case of *Re B,* the child in that case was likely to entail an even greater commitment to caring than the child in the present case, given that after the operation the parents in *Re B* were faced with caring for their disabled child for her remaining lifespan, which was estimated to be 20–30 years.[59]

[11.36] On the question of the rights of the child, the Court did not seem to accept any arguments on this basis, saying that this was not an occasion to talk of the rights of the child. Waite LJ said that in cases such as this, the best interests of the child include an expectation that difficult decisions affecting the length and quality of its life will be taken for it by the parent to whom its care has been entrusted. This may seem to be a throwback to common law notions of the natural rights of parents over their children.[60]

---

[57] Loughrey, 'Medical Treatment – The Status of Parental Opinion' [1998] Fam Law 146 at 147.
[58] Bainham, 'Do Babies Have Rights?' (1997) 56(1) CLJ 48.
[59] Fox and McHale, *Health Care Law, Text and Materials* (London: Sweet & Maxwell, 1997) p 703–4.
[60] Bainham, 'Do Babies Have Rights?' (1997) 56(1) CLJ 48.

Freeman criticises the case on the basis that the Court, while stating that the paramountcy principle must be applied, did not do so wisely. Waite LJ's 'unfortunate dismissal' of rights language is not 'calculated to respect the integrity, individuality, or the citizenship of children.'[61] Freeman claims that the Court was:

[O]ver-influenced by parental wishes, taken in by their professional knowledge, over-emphasised the logistic problem of returning the child to the jurisdiction…and too little concerned with the interests of a very sick child…Its decision is a hangover from an era in which the unimpeachable parent held sway, when courts were convinced by the validity of such pseudo-scientific notions as the blood tie and judges could refer to parents' rights (more commonly fathers' rights) as sacrosanct.[62]

[11.37] Many commentators have criticised the Court's emphasis on the parents' status as health-care professionals with experience of paediatric care. 'The Court of Appeal was clearly impressed by their understanding of the situation – so much so that, at times, the mother's views appear to take on the significance of another expert medical opinion.'[63] It is generally considered advisable that medical professionals do not treat members of their own family. The distinction drawn in this case was between 'treatment' and 'caring', which is a distinction fraught with difficulties even apart from the fact that the carers here were health professionals.[64] It is not clear from the judgments why more emphasis was put on the implications for the carers if a decision was made with which they did not agree, than the medical evidence in favour of performing the surgery.

[11.38] *Re T* is best regarded as a problematic case in the line of precedents in the UK on medical treatment of young children. The application of the best interests test here appears to have conflated the interests of the child with those of the parents without recognising the danger of according too much weight to parental views. 'Despite the protestations of all three judges, and despite the court's repeated assurance as to the responsibility and devotion of the parents, an unavoidable impression remains that their interests weighed heavily in the balance at the expense of the paramountcy of those of the child.'[65] The case 'highlights the need for a more sophisticated method of adjudicating in cases where such multi-factored decision-making is at issue.'[66] It has been argued that an alternative would be to adopt the practice of using *amicus curiae* briefs where interested parties can assist in providing expert advice, and help to assess alternative legal arguments and judicial conclusions.[67]

---

[61]   Freeman, 'Whose Life is it Anyway?' (2001) 9 Med L Rev 259 at 263.

[62]   Freeman, 'Whose Life is it Anyway?' (2001) 9 Med L Rev 259 at 258–259.

[63]   Mason and Laurie, *Law and Medical Ethics* (8th edn, OUP, 2010) para 15.62.

[64]   Fox and McHale, *Health Care Law, Text and Materials* (London: Sweet & Maxwell, 1997) p 704.

[65]   Mason and Laurie, *Law and Medical Ethics* (8th edn, OUP, 2010) para 15.63.

[66]   Fox and McHale, *Health Care Law, Text and Materials* (London: Sweet & Maxwell, 1997) p 709.

[67]   Fox and McHale, *Health Care Law, Text and Materials* (London: Sweet & Maxwell, 1997) p 709. For comparative case law see *In the Matter of Baby K* 832 F Supp 1022 (ED Va 1993), affd 16 F 3d 590 (4th Cir, 1994); (contd.../)

Other examples of parental and professional conflict

[11.39] In *Re C (HIV Test)*[68] a local authority applied for an order that a baby born to an HIV positive mother be tested for HIV. The mother had refused medication during the pregnancy and intended to continue to breast feed the child until the child was two years old. The judge found that there was a 20 –25 per cent risk that the baby was infected with HIV and that this risk was increased by breast feeding. Both parents were strongly opposed to the HIV test and to any form of medical intervention. The Court of Appeal concluded that although parental views were an important consideration, the arguments for overriding their wishes in this case were overwhelming. The child had rights in national and international law, such that her interests and welfare must be paramount. The test provided a relatively unintrusive way of determining the child's medical status, enabling those concerned with her future welfare to be better informed as to appropriate avenues of treatment. The Court did not deal with the question of how to treat the child and how to deal with the risks associated with breast feeding at this stage.[69] Whether a court would in fact make an order compelling a woman to refrain from breast feeding her baby is open to question, as it would be highly intrusive of the family's rights and would impossible to police. An alternative would, of course, be to take the child into care, if the child's welfare was deemed to be sufficiently at risk.[70]

[11.40] In Canada, the question of treatment of infants subjected to drug or alcohol abuse in utero has come before the courts by way of application for care orders. In these cases the courts exercised their powers under the *parens patriae* jurisdiction to protect the life and health of the newborn infants.[71] However, the courts have not gone so far as

---

[67] (\...contd) Flannery, 'One Advocate's Viewpoint: Conflicts and Tensions in the *Baby K* Case' (1995) 23 Law Med & Ethics 7; Clayton, 'Commentary: What is Really at Stake in *Baby K?*" (1995) 23 Law Med & Ethics 13. In this case an anencephalic baby was placed on a ventilator but was expected to die within days. Treatment was considered medically and ethically inappropriate. However, the mother insisted on ventilation of the baby despite medical advice to the contrary. The Court decided on the basis of its interpretation of the relevant statute that stabilising measures had to be given for the infant's respiratory distress, rather than on any application of a best interests test. The Court also held that the parents of a child have the Constitutional right to make decisions on behalf of their children, unless the result will be to cause harm to the child. In the Canadian case *Re Superintendent of Family and Child Service and Dawson* [1983] 145 DLR (3d) 610, the Court held that parental refusal to allow replacement of a shunt for the alleviation of hydrocephalus might result in more pain and disability for the child, and therefore the procedure was authorised. See Dickens, 'Withholding Paediatric Medical Care' (1984) Can BR 196.

[68] *Re C (HIV Test)* [1999] 2 FLR 1004.

[69] At the date of the appeal, the Court learned that the couple had disappeared from their home with the baby, and they did not appear at Court for the appeal.

[70] At the trial of this action, Wilson J made no order forbidding the breast-feeding, stating that 'the law could not come between the baby and the breast'. Downie suggests that since there was evidence that breast feeding doubled the risk of the HIV virus being passed from mother to child, it might seem that the threshold criteria for the making of a care order could be established in such circumstances. See Downie, 'Consent to Medical Treatment – Whose View of Welfare?' [1999] Fam Law 818 at 819.

[71] *Re Children's Aid Society of Kenora and JL* [1982] 134 DLR (3d) 249; *Re Superintendent of Family and Child Service and McDonald* [1982] 135 DLR (3d) 330.

to restrict the freedom of a woman to live her life as she wishes while pregnant. In *Winnipeg Child and Family Services v G (DF)*[72] a child welfare agency sought an order requiring that a pregnant woman who was addicted to glue-sniffing be committed to a place of safety and refrain from the use of intoxicants during her pregnancy. The trial judge allowed the agency's application and ordered that the woman be committed to the custody of the director of the agency and detained in a medical centre until the birth of her child, there to follow a course of treatment dictated by the director. One of the bases for the order was the court's *parens patriae* jurisdiction. The order was stayed two days later and set aside on appeal to the Manitoba Court of Appeal. The agency appealed to the Supreme Court of Canada, seeking a restoration of the detention order.

[11.41] The Canadian Supreme Court dismissed the appeal on the basis that the law of tort does not permit an order for the detention and treatment of a pregnant woman for the purpose of preventing harm to the unborn child. The Court held that neither the common law nor the Quebec civil law recognised the unborn child as a legal or juridical person. As the foetus was not a legal person and possessed no legal rights at the time of the application, there was no legal person in whose interests the agency could act or in whose interests a court order could be made. The Court took the view that the proposed order would involve moral choices and would create conflicts between fundamental interests and rights. It would have an immediate and drastic impact on the lives of women as well as men who might find themselves incarcerated and treated against their will for conduct alleged to harm others. Neither did the Court's *parens patriae* power support an order for the detention and treatment of a pregnant woman for the purpose of preventing harm to the unborn child. The Court held that to make orders protecting foetuses would radically impinge on the fundamental liberties of the pregnant woman, both as to lifestyle choices and how and where she chooses to live. 'The court cannot make decisions for the unborn child without inevitably making decisions for the mother herself.'

[11.42] The European Convention on Human Rights Act 2003 is also likely to become of increasing relevance in such disputes. Article 8 of the Convention protects the right to private and family life and thus may protect a parent's right to make decisions for their child. In *Glass v the UK*[73] the European Court of Human Rights held that the United Kingdom was in breach of art 8 in circumstances where the hospital treating Mrs Glass's 14-year-old son, who had physical and intellectual disabilities, placed a Do Not Resuscitate (DNR) order on him without her knowledge or consent. They also administered a pain-relieving drug to him contrary to his mother's wishes, as she believed this would accelerate his death. The Court found this action to be in breach of the boy's right to private life and physical integrity and his mother's right to respect for her family life. The Court said that before a decision was taken to impose a treatment on a child contrary to the wishes of the parents, the matter should be referred to a court for decision. This provides guidance to health-care professionals faced with circumstances in which there is an intractable dispute with parents in relation to treatment of their children, as it appears that under human rights law, all such cases should be referred to a court as final arbiter.

---

[72]   *Winnipeg Child and Family Services v G (DF)* [1997] 2 SCR 925.
[73]   *Glass v the UK* [2004] ECHR 102.

THE IRISH POSITION ON TREATMENT OF INFANTS

[11.43] There have not been any judicial decisions dealing with the non-treatment of neonates in Ireland and very few dealing with parental authority in the treatment of children. The provisions of the Irish Constitution 1937 are important here. Article 41.1.1° provides that 'the State recognises the Family as the natural primary and fundamental unit group of Society, and as a moral institution possessing inalienable and imprescriptible rights, antecedent and superior to all positive law.' Article 41.1.2° provides that the State guarantees 'to protect the Family in its constitution and authority, as the necessary basis of social order'. Article 42.1 provides that the State acknowledges that 'the primary and natural educator of the child is the Family' and goes on to guarantee to respect the right and duty of parents to provide for the education of their children. These principles place the family in a predominant position in terms of its place in society and as regards State intervention.[74]

[11.44] These articles were used as a basis for argument in *Ryan v Attorney General*[75] where the plaintiff claimed that the fluoridation of water violated, inter alia, the Constitutional rights of the family. The Supreme Court held that the allegations made did not come within the meaning of education under the Constitution. 'Education essentially is the teaching and training of a child to make the best possible use of his inherent and potential capacities, physical, mental and moral...To give [a child] water of a nature calculated to minimise the danger of dental caries is in no way to educate him, physically or otherwise, for it does not develop his resources.'[76] However, the Court also stated that one of the duties of parents was to avoid dangers to the health of a child. 'There is nothing in the Constitution which recognises the right of a parent to refuse to allow the provision of measures designed to secure the health of his child when the method of avoiding injury is one which is not fraught with danger to the child.'[77] In *G v An Bord Uchtála*[78] the Supreme Court discussed the personal rights of the child which the Court found would normally be protected by its mother, but equally by the State. These rights included 'the right to be fed and to live, to be reared and educated, to have the opportunity of working and of realising his or her full personality and dignity as a human being.'

[11.45] The Irish courts have, where necessary, applied the provisions of the Child Care Act 1991 to protect vulnerable children from neglect and to vindicate the child's best interests. This is regarded as consistent with Art 42.5, which provides that 'in exceptional cases, where the parents for physical or moral reasons fail in their duty towards their children, the State as guardian of the common good, by appropriate means shall endeavour to supply the place of the parents, but always with due regard for the natural and imprescriptible rights of the child.' The ability and duty of the State to

---

[74] In *In Re Tilson* [1951] IR 1 Gavan Duffy J said that the articles dealing with the family 'exalt the family by proclaiming and adopting in ...the Constitution...the Christian conception of the place of the family in society and in the State.' p 14.
[75] *Ryan v Attorney General* [1965] IR 294.
[76] *Ryan v Attorney General* [1965] IR 294 at 350.
[77] *Ryan v Attorney General* [1965] IR 294 at 350.
[78] *G v An Bord Uchtála* [1980] IR 32.

intervene in family life was considered in *Re Article 26 of the Constitution and the Adoption (No 2) Bill 1987*[79] where Finlay CJ said: 'In the exceptional circumstances envisaged by [Art 42] where a failure in duty has occurred, the State by appropriate means shall endeavour to supply the place of the parents, This must necessarily involve … the parental duty to cater for the personal rights of the child.' Failure by the parents in this context has been held to include not only physical but also psychological damage sustained by a child.[80]

[11.46] In *North Western Health Board v HW and CW*[81] the Supreme Court was asked to decide whether the parents of a 14-month-old child could be required to permit the Health Board to conduct a medical test on the child to ascertain whether the child was suffering from certain biochemical or metabolic disorders. These disorders are treatable if diagnosed at an early stage, but if untreated could have extremely serious consequences for the child, such as severe mental handicap. The test is commonly carried out on newborn babies within a few days of birth. The test, known as the PKU or heel test, is carried out by way of a pinprick to the baby's heel, extracting a small sample of blood, which is then tested for the disorders. The risk to the child involved in taking the blood sample is regarded as minimal. There is no indication of adverse consequences ever having occurred in Ireland as a result of the test since it was introduced in 1966.

[11.47] In this case the parents of the child had no objection to the test being carried out by non-invasive measures, such as through hair or urine samples, but they refused to allow blood samples to be taken, as samples could only be obtained by invasive measures such as puncturing a blood vessel, to which they were opposed. The couple had previous children who had been tested and none of whom had the genetic condition, therefore lowering the familial risk to this particular child. The Health Board claimed that it was in the child's best interests to have the test carried out and that the refusal of his parents to consent to the test was a failure on their part to vindicate his personal rights. They also claimed that using alternative methods of testing would not be reliable or feasible.

[11.48] In the High Court, McCracken J said that while the State had a duty to vindicate the personal rights of citizens, this was not an unlimited or universal obligation. The Court only had a jurisdiction to interfere or provide for children by virtue of the Child Care Act 1991 in exceptional cases where the parents for physical or moral reasons had failed in their duty towards their children. In this case the objective medical evidence clearly indicated that it was in the child's best interests to undergo the test, but the judge also looked at the policy of the State in relation to other facilities such as vaccination against infectious disease, where the decision is left to the parents. McCracken J took the view that the parents in this case, who were regarded as caring and conscientious parents, had made a decision that was contrary to medical opinion but that such a decision could not be said to constitute an exceptional case such that the State could interfere in it. It was not sufficient for the Health Board to claim that the child's welfare was the only factor to be considered, as the 1991 Act also obliges the Health Board to

---

[79]   *Re Article 26 of the Constitution and the Adoption (No 2) Bill 1987* [1989] IR 656.
[80]   *Southern Health Board v Bord Uchtála* [2000] 1 IR 165.
[81]   *North Western Health Board v HW and CW* [2001] IESC 70.

fulfil its statutory functions subject to the Constitutional rights of the parents and the family as a unit. If the State considered that an injustice was being done to the child, then it could provide for compulsory testing by legislation, which would then be tested for its constitutionality. He said:

> If the State were entitled to intervene in every case where professional opinion differed from that of parents, or where the State considered the parents were wrong in a decision, we would be rapidly stepping towards the Brave New World in which the State always knows best. In my view that situation would be totally at variance with both the spirit and the word of the Constitution.

[11.49] McCracken J said that the rights of the family are in a very special position under the Constitution. When seeking to balance parental rights as against a child's rights, where medical opinion was to the effect that it was in the child's best interests to undergo the test, the latter might override parental rights. However, the parents' refusal to consent did not come within the realms of 'exceptional cases' envisaged by the Constitution, as it was within the permissible range of risk that did not affect the very life of the child.[82] It has been argued that McCracken J's approach to the balancing of rights is flawed in not taking account of the child's rights in the case. 'Unfortunately there are no procedures in such cases as this for the appointment of a guardian *ad litem* to represent the views of the child particularly where medical consent is the salient issue and where the application/non-application of the test could have a profound effect on the short or long-term quality of life of the child.'[83] The inclusion in the Constitution of a provision that, in the event of conflict between child rights and parental rights, all decisions should be made taking the child's best interests as the paramount consideration, would resolve any conflict in favour of the child.[84]

[11.50] On appeal to the Supreme Court, it was submitted that the Court had jurisdiction to intervene to protect the interests of a minor where his personal rights were under threat. It was submitted that the welfare of the child must always be the guiding principle for the court in any proceedings concerning the upbringing of a child and that the power of the court to intervene was not limited by Art 42.5 to 'exceptional cases.' It was argued on behalf of the parents that a vast range of decisions are made by parents on a daily basis for their children and that few of those decisions had been overridden by the courts, even where they appeared to be wrong or reckless. It was submitted that there were some decisions that could be overridden, such as refusal of blood transfusions in a life-threatening situation, but that this particular refusal did not come into that category. The Supreme Court upheld the High Court decision by majority of four to one. Keane CJ (dissenting) traced the origins of our democratic system of government back to Locke and Rousseau, who believed that civil government is the result of a contract between the people and their rulers and 'the family existed before that unit and enjoys

---

[82] See discussion by Martin, 'Parental Rights to Withhold Consent to Medical Treatment for Their Child: A Conflict of Rights?' (2001) 7 Irish Law Times 114; and Arthur, '*North Western Health Board v HW and CW* – Reformulating Irish Family Law' (2002) 3 Irish Law Times 39.

[83] Martin, 'Parental Rights to Withhold Consent to Medical Treatment for Their Child: A Conflict of Rights?' (2001) 7 Irish Law Times 114 at 117.

[84] This was suggested by the Whitaker Report on the Constitution in 1996, which recommended amending the Constitution to include explicit rights for children. *Report of the Constitution Review Group* (Government Publications, 1996) p 330.

rights which, in the hierarchy of rights posited by the Constitution, are superior to those which are the result of the positive laws created by the State itself.' Although tensions between the State and the family may exist from time to time, the Constitution 'firmly outlaws any attempt by the State in its laws or its executive actions to usurp the exclusive and privileged role of the family in the social order.'

[11.51] Keane CJ then examined case law from the UK, Canada and Australia in which courts had been asked to override parental decisions in relation to the medical treatment of children. He referred specifically to the non-therapeutic sterilisation cases in those jurisdictions, which he held did not involve the issues at stake in this particular case. He then looked at the English case of *Re C (HIV test)*,[85] discussed above, where the Court had taken the view that a baby born to a HIV positive woman should be tested for HIV despite the parents' refusal of consent, on the basis that the medical case for testing the baby was overwhelming. He also considered *Re T (a minor) (wardship: medical treatment)*,[86] where a mother's refusal of a liver transplant for her young son was upheld by the Court of Appeal on the basis that the trial judge had failed to take into account the weight of the mother's concerns regarding the proposed treatment, as well as the reservations expressed by consultants about coercing the mother into playing a crucial part in the child's care after a treatment to which she was opposed. Keane CJ had no doubt that Waite LJ in *Re T* accurately described the position that also obtained in Ireland when he said:

> All these cases depend on their own facts and render generalisations – tempting though they may be to the legal or social analyst – wholly out of place. It can only be said safely that there is a scale, at one end of which lies the clear case where parental opposition to medical intervention is prompted by scruple or dogma of a kind which is patently irreconcilable with principles of child health and welfare widely accepted by the generality of mankind; and that at the other end lie highly problematic cases where there is genuine scope for difference of view between parent and judge. In both situations it is the duty of the judge to allow the court's own opinion to prevail in the perceived paramount interest of the child concerned, but in cases at the latter end of the scale, there must be a likelihood (though never of course a certainty) that the greater the scope for genuine debate between one view and another the stronger will be the inclination of the court to be influenced by a reflection that in the last analysis the best interests of every child include an expectation that difficult situations affecting the length and quality of its life will be taken for it by the parent to whom its care has been entrusted by nature.

[11.52] Keane CJ adopted this principle while saying that the Constitution does not oblige the State to allow the wishes of parents, no matter how irrational they appear to be, to prevail over the child's best interests. Such an approach would gravely endanger the child's right to a happy and healthy life and his rights as a member of the family. Keane CJ took the view that in this case the parents had refused to protect the child's Constitutional right to be guarded against unnecessary and avoidable dangers to his health, and that the Court should intervene in the child's best interests.

---

[85] *Re C (HIV test)* [1999] 2 FLR 1004, considered above at para **11.39**.
[86] *Re T (a minor) (wardship: medical treatment)* [1997] 1 All ER 906, considered above at para **11.32** et seq.

[11.53] Denham J said that Art 42.5 envisages State intervention in exceptional cases where the parents failed to protect the child's interests. She said that it was clear from that provision that 'the State is the default parent and not the super parent'. Essentially, the issue before the Court was the balance of responsibility between parental rights, the Health Board and the child's rights as a member of a family and as a person. She distinguished *Re C* on the basis that the child in that case was in a life-threatening situation that did not apply here. In trying to find the balance in any case, the threshold would depend on the circumstances, so that if the child's life were in immediate danger, there would be a heavy weight to be put on the child's personal rights as opposed to parental wishes. However, in exceptional cases, such as where the child needed acute medical care, if parents decided that the responsible decision was to refuse such care, that may well come within the range of responsible decisions to be taken by parents. Denham J was concerned that an order in this case in favour of the test would effectively make the test compulsory for all children in the State and that this would turn departmental policy into law, which is a matter more appropriately decided at an executive or legislative level. She said that in the circumstances, she would not interfere with the decision of the parents, as this was not an exceptional case justifying the intervention of the State into the Constitutional rights of the parents. Murphy and Murray JJ took a similar view, although both admitted to being concerned by the possibility that the child would be affected by any of the disorders in question, and to finding the parents' decision unwise and disturbing.

[11.54] Hardiman J regarded this case as seeking to establish a position in which a public authority could compel parents to subject a child to an invasive medical test, which was 'an entirely novel proposition.' He said that lessons to be learned from the compulsory sterilisation cases in the US were that it was 'better to hesitate at the threshold of compulsion, even in its most benevolent form, than to adopt an easy but reductionist utilitarianism whose consequences may be unpredictable.' The principle of voluntarism in respect of medical treatment was plainly established and extended to a person making decisions for himself or for another person for whom he is responsible. The orders sought by the Health Board were directed at denying the right of the parents not to consent to the test, to compel them to consent and to compel them to present their child for the test. Hardiman J concluded that there was a presumption that 'where the constitutional family exists and is discharging its functions as such, and the parents have not for physical or moral reasons failed in their duty towards their children, their decisions should not be overridden by the State and in particular by the Courts in the absence of a jurisdiction conferred by statute...The presumption is not of course conclusive and might be open to displacement by countervailing constitutional considerations as perhaps in the case of an immediate threat to life.' In this case the State could only intervene where the parents failed in their duty towards their child. A conscientious disagreement with the Health Board did not constitute a failure of their duty such as to justify State intervention.

[11.55] It has been argued that this case errs too far in the direction of protection and is, on the whole, unreceptive to the claims of children. It would also 'almost certainly make it impossible to introduce a compulsory vaccination programme for some childhood illnesses.'[87] The case is seen by some as pushing the right of parents too far in the

---

87   Donnelly, *Consent: Bridging the Gap Between Doctor and Patient* (Cork University Press, 2002) at 40.

direction of absolute decision-making power in relation to their children, and identifying child rights only in the context of parental rights.[88] However, it should also be said that the Supreme Court acknowledged that each case of this kind requires a balancing of parental autonomy against the rights and interests of the child. Thus Donnelly states: 'as the consequences of parental refusal become more serious or the grounds for the parents' objections become less serious, the justification for interference with parental autonomy grows. When the threat to the child's welfare becomes too great, it is both ethically desirable and legally justifiable to interfere.'[89] Despite the belief that the court would interfere in cases such as those posited by Donnelly, it may nonetheless be preferable to move towards replacing the language of parental rights with 'parental responsibility', which places the parents, in consultation with their children, in the position of educating and maintaining them, not because of an authority conferred on parents, but in the interests of the child. This would recognise children as persons to whom duties are owed, as opposed to possessions over which power is wielded.[90] Disputes in relation to consent to medical treatment of children are likely to continue to grow in Ireland 'particularly as Irish society becomes more culturally diverse...There may be an increase in the circumstances where medical norms may be challenged by parents from diverse backgrounds concerning their children's health and well-being.'[91]

[11.56] Other cases to have come before Irish courts have granted orders in favour of treatment of children against the wishes of their parents in exceptional circumstances. For example, in a case in 2002 in which a pregnant HIV positive woman initially refused to give birth in hospital, she subsequently agreed during the hearing to facilitate the birth of the child in hospital. Finnegan J directed that the child's welfare demanded that it be made a ward of court on birth, enabling the child to be tested and treated appropriately. The judge also reportedly said that he would have been prepared to consider making more intrusive orders had the woman not agreed to give birth in hospital, and had she intended to breast feed the baby.[92] This could be criticised on the basis that it does not enable the mother to prove her capacity for motherhood before making the child a ward of court. It appears that the judge presumed that by virtue of her decisions in relation to her pregnancy to date, she was to be considered an unfit mother. This appears to follow the line that the reasonableness or otherwise of parental decision-making is not at issue, rather the court must consider as paramount the welfare of the child, which in this instance mandated the testing and treatment if appropriate.

[11.57] In cases involving the refusal of treatment by Jehovah's Witness parents on behalf of their children, the most commonly adopted approach is for the child to be taken into temporary care to facilitate the giving of a blood transfusion in accordance

---

[88] Arthur, '*North Western Health Board v HW and CW* – Reformulating Irish Family Law" (2002) 3 Irish Law Times 39.

[89] Donnelly, *Consent: Bridging the Gap Between Doctor and Patient* (Cork University Press, 2002) at 41.

[90] Bainham, 'The Children Act 1989: Adolescence and Children's Rights' (1990) Fam Law 311.

[91] Martin, 'Parental Rights to Withhold Consent to Medical Treatment for Their Child: A Conflict of Rights?' (2001) 7 Irish Law Times 114 at 119.

[92] See reports in The Irish Times, 20 July 2002.

with the child's best medical interests.[93] In *Temple Street v D and another*,[94] an order allowing for the transfusion of a seriously ill three-month-old baby was made against the wishes of his parents. The baby's haemoglobin was at a level where transfusion was absolutely necessary but the parents, who were Jehovah's Witnesses, were opposed to the treatment. The hospital applied to the High Court for an emergency hearing at which the consultant treating the child gave evidence that the child's life was in immediate danger and that there were no alternatives to a transfusion. The parents refused to grant consent for the procedure but appeared resigned to having their wishes overruled, as this had occurred previously with another of their children. Hogan J granted the emergency order and in his judgment, delivered at a later date, he said that there was no doubting the sincerity of the parents' beliefs and their anxiety for the welfare of their child. He took as his starting point the protection of the free profession and practice of religion under Art 44.2.1° of the Constitution, which provides a vital safeguard for minority religions whose tenets are regarded by some as unconventional. The judge said that most Irish people would express unease about a religious belief that required abstaining from an essential medical treatment, but those who held that faith regard the prohibition of blood as scripturally ordained and as a test of their faith. He also said that the right of a properly informed adult with full capacity to refuse medical treatment, whether for religious or other reasons, is Constitutionally protected.[95] Of course, this case involved not an adult but a very young baby so different considerations arose.

[11.58] Hogan J said that while parents have the right to raise their children in accordance with their own religious views, this is not an absolute right and different considerations have to be taken into account to ensure that children are protected. The State has a vital interest in intervening in exceptional circumstances where there has been a failure on the part of the parents to protect the child's life or welfare. The test of whether the parents had failed in their duty under the Constitution is an objective one, judged by the secular standards of society in general and of the Constitution in particular, irrespective of the subjective and religious views of the parents. He said that the High Court has a jurisdiction and a duty to override the religious objections of parents where those beliefs threaten the life and welfare of their child and it was for this reason that he granted the declaration. Importantly, Hogan J also said that the declaration was limited to the particular clinical events and was not to be construed as

---

[93] For example, a newspaper report in 2000 discusses the case of a young boy who was injured in an accident near his home, and required blood transfusions to save his life. His parents were Jehovah's Witnesses and refused consent for the transfusions. The South Eastern Health Board applied for an order taking the child into temporary care under the Child Care Act, s 12. This enabled the hospital to act in accordance with the child's best medical interests and carry out the transfusion. The child was returned to the custody of his parents within 72 hours. See report in The Irish Times, 3 March 2000. See discussion generally by Bridge, 'Religion, Culture and Conviction – The Medical Treatment of Young Children' (1999) Child and Fam L Q Vol 11 No 1, 1–15, in which she argues that the physical integrity of a young child who is too young to make decisions for himself must be accorded total respect and that parents cannot determine life and death matters, irrespective of their religious convictions.

[94] *Temple Street v D and another* [2011] IEHC 1.

[95] *Fitzpatrick v FK (No 2)* [2008] IEHC 104, [2009] 2 IR 7.

giving clinicians an open-ended entitlement into the future to administer such treatment to the child.

[11.59] This case is important in recognising the Constitutional right to free practice of religion but it also recognises that this, like other Constitutional rights, is not absolute. The Court clearly stated the right of a competent adult to refuse medical treatment for any reason but noted that in circumstances where the patient is a child and therefore not capable of making such a decision, the State must step in where the parents fail in their duty to protect the life and welfare of their child. This is consistent with previous decisions in this context, but the case is significant as the first written High Court judgment on the matter. The restriction of the declaration to the immediate clinical circumstances also ensures that the infringement of parental authority is limited to the extent necessary to safeguard the child's welfare and is not to be taken as providing a *carte blanche* to clinicians in the future care of the child.

THE CASE OF CONJOINED TWINS

[11.60] In recent years the issue of parental authority has been sharply tested in relation to a particular human tragedy involving the separation of conjoined or Siamese twins. While the birth of such babies is still, fortunately, a rare event, it has provoked legal and ethical debate as to whether and how to separate the twins where it is likely to cause the death of one twin. The very nature of conjoined twins has always proved to be a source of fascination for doctors and society in general. The most famous conjoined twins were born in Siam in 1811, thus the description 'Siamese twins' thereafter for such a phenomenon. The twins lived for over 60 years and were exhibited around the world as part of a circus act. Siamese twins continued to be referred to as 'freakish' 'double-headed monsters', well into the 20th century, denying them the routine respect and care given to other infants.[96]

[11.61] Conjoined twins are the result of a single ovum or egg which is fertilised by a single sperm and then attempts to split into two identical twins. For some reason not yet fully understood, whether genetic or environmental or otherwise, the egg fails to split completely, leaving the twins joined, most commonly at the chest and sharing a single heart. In this category it is thought extremely difficult to successfully separate such twins, and even if possible by sacrificing one twin, historically the surviving twin has generally not lived for more than a few months after separation.[97] It is also difficult to keep such twins alive without separation for longer than nine months or so, as the strength of the single heart is generally insufficient to maintain both bodies.[98] Where the

---

[96]   Annas, 'Siamese Twins: Killing One to Save the Other' in *Standard of Care, The Law of American Bioethics* (OUP, 1993) 234.

[97]   Marin-Padilla et al, 'Cardiovascular Abnormalities in Thoracopagus Twins' (1981) 23 Teratology 101–113.

[98]   Annas, 'Siamese Twins: Killing One to Save the Other' in *Standard of Care, The Law of American Bioethics* (OUP, 1993), 234.

twins are joined at another part of the body and do not share vital organs, separation is difficult but sometimes possible.[99]

[11.62] In the US in 1977 conjoined twins were born in circumstances where survival of both twins after separation was impossible, and the survival of one unlikely. The parents were deeply religious Jews and refused to consent to sacrificing one twin so that the other might have a chance to live. Their religious advisors informed them that if one of the twins was 'designated for death' it was acceptable to sacrifice that twin so that the other might live. A family court heard an application by the surgeon to perform the separation and seemed to accept this line of thinking. The procedure was authorised and the separation was successful. However, the surviving twin died a few months later. Similar cases occurred the same year in another part of the US and again 10 years later. In each case it is interesting that the surgeons first sought and received assurances that no criminal prosecution would be brought against them if the procedure were performed.

[11.63] Annas argues that the closest legal precedents deal with the doctrine of necessity, actions taken in response to natural disasters and acts of God. He cites the example of the sinking lifeboat where lots are cast to determine who is thrown overboard in order to save the others from certain death. In these examples, 'having the stronger throw the weaker overboard is not justified by the circumstances.' In the case of conjoined twins if the separation is medically reasonable and the choice of which twin to let die is made fairly, Annas claims that society would probably regard it as justifiable to kill one twin to save the other, although flipping coins would probably be fairer. On this basis it is relevant to examine medical criteria to decide which twin is most likely to survive the separation. This maintains the 'fiction that the decision was an act of God.'

[11.64] The use of a best-interests test in this context is straining its logic. Although separation is in the best interests of the twin chosen to survive, it cannot be in the best interests of the twin 'designated for death' since that twin is alive, is not suffering, and is now about to have its life cut short by deliberate decision. Annas concludes that both law and ethics support reasonable medical attempts to separate conjoined twins on the basis that it is better to intervene to try and save one life rather than to passively watch two lives end.[100] However, it remains an unmet challenge to develop a fair and useful procedure to apply rationale to the decision to be made.

[11.65] The most widely reported and debated case on conjoined twins to date is the English case of *Re A (Conjoined twins: medical treatment)*.[101] The case of the 'Manchester conjoined twins' captured the public imagination worldwide, as the Court was asked to adjudicate on the legitimacy of killing one of the twins in order to save the

---

[99] In April 2010 conjoined twins from Cork, Ireland, Hassan and Hussein Benhaffaf, successfully underwent separation surgery in London. http://www.independent.ie/national-news/surgeon-delighted-as-twins-stable-after-14hour-operation-2131165.html (accessed 5 June 2011).

[100] Sheldon and Wilkinson predicted that in order to avoid the obvious conclusion that separation in these circumstances would be murder, the court would try to find a solution whereby all concerned could feel a comfortable sense of having saved a life. See Sheldon and Wilkinson, 'Conjoined Twins: the Legality and Ethics of Sacrifice' (1997) 5 Med L Rev 149.

[101] *Re A (Conjoined twins: medical treatment)* [2000] 4 All ER 961; [2001] 1 FLR 1.

life of the other. The facts of the case were that the parents of the twins came to Manchester from the Maltese island of Gozo in order to get the best possible medical care for their children.[102] The twins were born in August 2000, their bodies fused from the umbilicus to the sacrum, and the lower ends of their spines and spinal cords were also fused. They shared a common bladder. The smaller twin, known as Mary, had a non-functional heart and lungs and her supply of blood came from her twin, known as Jodie. Mary had severe brain malformations and abnormal neurological responses although she was not vegetative or in a coma, whereas Jodie appeared neurologically normal. The medical evidence was that without separation, Jodie's heart and lungs would slowly become affected by the strain of providing blood for both bodies and both twins would die, or that Mary would die from thrombosis of major vessels, and it would be necessary to perform an emergency separation to save Jodie. It was agreed that any separation would lead to Mary's death and that, although Jodie would have to undergo a series of operations throughout her childhood, she would be able to lead a substantially normal life if separated from Mary. The parents of the twins consistently opposed the separation on religious grounds, preferring that nature take its course.[103] They were of the view that one of their daughters should not be killed in order that the other should live. The hospital sought a declaration from the Court that it would be lawful to perform the separation, thus overriding the parents' wishes. This declaration was granted, and an appeal dismissed. The separation was performed in November 2000, with the result that Mary died. Jodie is expected to enjoy a reasonable quality of life. [104]

[11.66] All of the judges involved in the case, both in the High Court and the Court of Appeal, found in favour of the separation, although for different reasons. The Court of Appeal held that separation was in Jodie's best interests but contrary to Mary's. The difficulty for the Court, then, was in balancing those competing interests. It decided that the balance lay in giving Jodie the chance of life and that such an operation would not violate the criminal law. The complex questions raised by this case include the following: When does a human being become a person? What role can the characteristic of physical separation play in establishing this status? When should considerations of quality of life outweigh the sanctity of life? What is the significance of the distinction between acts and omissions? Who should decide what is in the best interests of a child? What factors should be taken into account in that decision?[105] It is not proposed to address all of these questions here but in summarising the various points made by the

---

[102] See discussion by Harris, 'Human Beings, Persons and Conjoined Twins: An Ethical Analysis of the Judgment in *Re A*' (2001) 9 Med L Rev, 221–236.

[103] Harris points out that although the parents were devout Catholics, it is not clear that Catholicism would demand that the separation not take place. It might in fact be justifiable on the basis of the doctrine of double effect, whereby the act of separation is not intended to cause the death of one, but rather to save the life of the other. Harris, 'Human Beings, Persons and Conjoined Twins: An Ethical Analysis of the Judgment in *Re A*' (2001) 9 Med L Rev, 221–236.

[104] See comments of one of the consultant surgeons in The Times, 18 June 2001, where he said in relation to Jodie that 'she has come on really well, better than expected. Everything works and everything is where it should be, as it is in a normal baby. There are no plans for further surgery and we are confident she will have an excellent quality of life.'

[105] Sheldon and Wilkinson, 'On the Sharpest Horns of a Dilemma: *Re A (Conjoined Twins)*' (2001) 9 Med L Rev 201 at 204.

judges, it is interesting to note that what is abundantly clear from the array of issues dealt with by the judgments is the impossibility of separating the legal issues from the ethical ones, both in use of concepts and language. [106]

[11.67] The academic commentary on this case has been predictably large, with the case drawing sharp criticism for its reasoning, language and failure to justify the overriding of the parents wishes.[107] The Court of Appeal's decision has been 'both attacked as a dangerous breach of the sanctity of life and an unjustifiable erosion of parental authority, and heralded as a triumph of common sense over religious fundamentalism and a creditable act of judicial support for the well intentioned acts of doctors trying to salvage a life from a no-win situation.'[108] One of the criticisms of the Court of Appeal's ruling in *Re A* centres on the implication of the judgments that Mary's death was not murder, even though it was a foreseen, and some would say, intended, consequence of the separation of the twins. Uniacke argues that the Court was confused on some important conceptual matters due, in part, to the legacy of cases dealing with the withdrawal of treatment, which considered these to be omissions as opposed to positive acts.[109] While the judges all agreed that the separation was lawful homicide of Mary, they based their judgments on different reasons.[110]

[11.68] Ward LJ was of the view that the killing was justified on the basis of self-defence or defence of another person, as he perceived that Mary was harming Jodie's chances of life. He said that there was no difference between 'legitimate self-defence and the doctors coming to Jodie's defence and removing the threat of fatal harm to her presented by Mary's draining her life blood.' He argued that as Mary was killing Jodie, to kill Mary in defence of Jodie's life would not violate Mary's right to life. The right to life, for Ward LJ, was not an absolute right not to be killed, but a right not to be killed unjustly. Killing Mary would be legitimate defence of Jodie and therefore would not be murder. However, it has been counter-argued that Mary's relationship with Jodie cannot

---

[106] For arguments as to whether the courts and/or the legislature should have a role in deciding whether to separate conjoined twins, see Excitable, 'Separation of Conjoined Twins: Where Next for English Law?' [2002] Crim L Rev 459–470.

[107] See (2001) 9 Med L Rev, which is entirely devoted to various articles on this case, some of which are mentioned below. Also Bainham, 'Resolving the Unresolvable: The Case of Conjoined Twins' (2001) 60 CLJ 49; Gillon, 'Imposed Separation of Conjoined Twins: Moral Hubris by the English Courts?' (2001) 27 JME 3; McCall Smith, 'The Separating of Conjoined Twins' (2000) 321 BMJ 782; Ratiu and Singer, 'The Ethics and Economics of Heroic Surgery' (March–April 2001) 31 Hastings Center Report 47; Huxtable, 'The Court of Appeal and Conjoined Twins: Condemning the Unworthy Life?' (2000) 162 Bulletin of Medical Ethics 13; Huxtable, 'Logical Separation? Conjoined Twins, Slippery Slopes and Resource Allocation' (2001) 23(4) *J of Social Welfare and Fam Law* 459–471; and Munro, 'Square Pegs and Round Holes: The Dilemma of Conjoined Twins and Individual Rights' (2001) 10 Social and Legal Studies 4.

[108] Sheldon and Wilkinson, 'On the Sharpest Horns of a Dilemma: *Re A (Conjoined Twins)*' (2001) 9 Med L Rev 201 at 207.

[109] Uniacke refers in particular to *Airedale NHS Trust v Bland* [1993] AC 789. See Uniacke, 'Was Mary's Death Murder?' (2001) 9 Med L Rev 208 at 209.

[110] See also the recent similar Australian case of *Queensland v Nolan* [2001] QSC 174, and commentary in [2002] Med L Rev 100–102.

be characterised in terms of her killing Jodie, although her existence certainly constituted a threat to Jodie's life. Mary was an 'entirely passive recipient of oxygenated blood' from Jodie.[111]

[11.69] Brooke LJ argued that the killing was justified on the basis of the defence of necessity or duress of circumstances. Up to *Re A* it was considered that the defence of necessity was not available on a criminal charge and a jury would not have been allowed to consider it. It has been argued that the judges in *Re A*, by allowing necessity as a defence to the killing of Mary, may have made a fundamental change to criminal law doctrine, the effects of which would be profound. For example, a parent could claim that she killed her severely disabled child out of necessity to spare her any further suffering. 'The Court of Appeal has opened the door to lawful acquittal where euthanasia is the reason for a killing, and it can only be a matter of time before such cases are before the courts.'[112] McEwan argues that the means chosen by the Court of Appeal in order to achieve a utilitarian goal of saving at least one life where two are at stake, places the law at risk of having to condone euthanasia by private citizens who raise the defence of necessity.

[11.70] Walker LJ distinguished Mary's death as a foreseen, though not intended, killing. The latter argument is based on the doctrine of double effect, whereby the clamping of the shared artery between Mary and Jodie was intended as a means of saving Jodie's life, and Mary's death was an incidental consequence of that act. However, as Uniacke argues, 'the legal specification of an action's intended effects includes effects that, while incidental to the actor's aim or purpose, are foreseen as virtually certain. This would include Mary's death as the inevitable consequence of the separation surgery.'[113] Similarly, Harris argues that 'the denial that the operation involves the deliberate or intentional killing of Mary is unsustainable.'[114]

[11.71] Another argument that features in this case is the belief that Mary was somehow 'designated for death' and that this justified the deliberate choice to kill her. This idea comes from Annas, quoted above, and is sharply criticised by Harris on the basis that the method by which one would be so designated is unclear and leaves no room for misdiagnosis.[115] To say that someone is 'designated for death', who is going to 'die anyway' is to correlate the value of life with life expectancy, which Harris argues, is profoundly unjust and unethical.[116] Where a person with a short life expectancy has a life to lead and wants to lead it for as much time as is left, 'it would seem inconceivable

---

[111] Uniacke, 'Was Mary's Death Murder?' (2001) 9 Med L Rev 208 at 212.

[112] See discussion by McEwan, 'Murder by Design: The "Feel-Good Factor" and the Criminal Law' (2001) 9 Med L Rev 246–258 at 248.

[113] Uniacke, 'Was Mary's Death Murder?' (2001) 9 Med L Rev 208 at 220.

[114] Harris, 'Human Beings, Persons and Conjoined Twins: An Ethical Analysis of the Judgment in *Re A*' (2001) 9 Med L Rev, 221 at 229.

[115] See discussion in Harris, 'Human Beings, Persons and Conjoined Twins: An Ethical Analysis of the Judgment in *Re A*' (2001) 9 Med L Rev, at 230–232.

[116] See Harris, 'The Concept of the Person and the Value Of Life' (1999) 9 (4) Kennedy Inst of Ethics J, 293–308.

that they would be killed against their will by a decision of the courts.'[117] However, where the quality, as opposed to the duration, of the life available is such that the person could not benefit from its continuation, it may be relevant to take this into account.

[11.72] The nature of personhood is a notoriously difficult concept to define, and different ethicists define it in different ways. Thus, Harris argues that Mary was not a person at the time of the operation, in the sense that he defines persons as individuals with a biographical life and full moral status. He believes that persons are characterised by having the capacity to value existence and that non-persons lack such capacity. Therefore, persons can be harmed by being killed, as they lose something they value, whereas non-persons cannot, by definition, lose something they could be said to value. On this basis non-persons would include embryos, anencephalic infants and individuals in persistent vegetative state. Therefore, at the time of the operation neither Jodie nor Mary were persons on this understanding of personhood. This, for Harris, is the only ethical basis upon which it can be said that the Court's decision was justified. However, he also feels that the Court should have declared the operation lawful but not mandatory, and in that way left the decision to the parents of the twins. He describes the Court's ruling as so confused and inconsistent that it fails to justify the overruling of the parent's wishes.

[11.73] By contrast with Harris, Watt believes that personhood, or being a human moral subject, is synonymous with the biological category of human being, or the living human organism. This means that for her, both Jodie and Mary are persons, as both had separate systems of self-organisation, despite some overlap in various parts. Mary was a member of the human species, even if the interests of the human species were thwarted in her case because of her condition. This did not mean that her existence was worthless,[118] a view also shared by Ward LJ. In short, in this case there were two patients, each of whom had the right to protection from harmful bodily invasions. 'Cutting into Mary in a way which did her serious and permanent harm, was a bad means to the good end of saving her twin sister's life.'[119]

[11.74] Some of the cases considered earlier in this chapter discuss the importance of taking into account the wishes of parents in decision-making for children. As has already been stated, in *Re A*, the parents of the twins were fundamentally opposed to the separation surgery on the basis that one person should not be killed to save the life of another. Some commentators are of the view that when neither law nor ethics can come to a satisfactory way out of such a dilemma, the best solution would be to let the parents take responsibility for the decision.[120] By contrast, Freeman argues that parental autonomy should not be prioritised and that, at least on this ground, the Court of Appeal came to the right decision.[121] He discusses the limits placed on parental authority such that parents cannot, for example, consent to a procedure to be carried out on their child

---

[117] Harris, 'Human Beings, Persons and Conjoined Twins: An Ethical Analysis of the Judgment in *Re A*' (2001) 9 Med L Rev, at 232.

[118] Watt, 'Conjoined Twins: Separation As Mutilation' (2001) 9 Med L Rev, 237–245 at 240.

[119] Watt, 'Conjoined Twins: Separation As Mutilation' (2001) 9 Med L Rev, 237 at 245.

[120] See Hewson, '*A (Children)* – Cruel and Unnatural' (2000) 150 New LJ 1562; and Knowles, 'Hubris in the Court' (2001) 31(1) Hastings Center Report 50.

[121] Freeman, 'Whose Life is it Anyway?' (2001) 9 Med L Rev 259–280.

for the benefit of themselves or the child's sibling. Similarly, parents cannot consent to certain procedures, such as the non-therapeutic sterilisation of a disabled child, and previous judgments have shown that parental decision can be overridden in the best interests of the child.[122] In *Re A* the Court of Appeal specifically recognised the importance of the parents' wishes, especially insofar as they were based on religious convictions[123], but said that the Court could override them, as 'it is the child's best interest that are paramount, not the parents'. Freeman analyses why parents have rights, and finds that they are traditionally based on the fundamental importance of family integrity.[124] He is of the view that those who seek to protect the family from interference derive this argument from a mistaken reliance on classic liberalism, the most obvious source being John Stuart Mill's *On Liberty*, which makes the case that the State should stay out of its citizens' lives out of respect for their moral autonomy and human dignity. But, according to Freeman, 'the paradigmatic family conflict is not between the citizen and the state: it is between two persons. If the state removes itself from concern with this type of conflict…the weak can easily be sacrificed to the strong. There is no moral autonomy or human dignity then for those whose interests can so routinely be trampled upon.'[125]

[11.75] The granting of parental rights has often been seen as based on biology, in the sense that individuals are given rights to their genetic offspring. However, this is not universally true, as is evident both from considerations of the law relating to children born through donation of eggs or sperm, and from the fact that unmarried men have always had a struggle to establish a legal relationship with their biological children. Although the law has, at least in modern times, tended to avoid the ascription of rights on the basis of property interests, towards a more child-centred approach, there is still 'a tendency for the child's best interests to be over-identified with the parents' interests.' Freeman argues that the presumptions that children are best placed with their parents, and that parents know what is in their child's best interests, may not provide empirically sound bases upon which to base legal principle.[126] Other bases for granting rights to parents, such as intention (which may be relevant in relation to assisted reproduction) and marriage, are unpersuasive in relation to parental authority generally. He concludes that the foundations upon which parents are granted rights are shaky and limited, a factor that must be taken into account in deciding whether those rights should be prioritised in the event of conflict.

---

[122] Freeman cites *Re D* [1976] Fam. 185; *Re B* [1981] 1 WLR 1421; *Re B* [1991] 2 FLR 426; and *Re C* [1998] 1 FLR 384.

[123] *per* Walker LJ at 118.

[124] Freeman quotes from Goldstein, Freud, Goldstein and Solnit, *The Best Interests of the Child* (Free Press, 1996): 'The child's need for security within the confines of the family must be met by law through its recognition of family privacy as the barrier to state intrusion upon parental autonomy. These rights – parental autonomy, a child's entitlement to autonomous parents, and privacy – are essential ingredients of family integrity.' This is reminiscent of the Supreme Court's interpretation of the Constitutional protection of the family in *North Western Health Board v HW and CW*, considered above at para **11.46** et seq.

[125] Freeman, 'Whose Life is it Anyway?' (2001) 9 Med L Rev 259 at 270.

[126] Freeman refers to Bartholet, *Family Bonds: Adoption and the Politics of Parenting* (Houghton Mifflin, 1993) at 174–81.

[11.76] In trying to accommodate the judgments in *Re T,* where the wishes of the mother of a child in need of a liver transplant were prioritised over the unanimous medical evidence in favour of the surgery, and *Re A,* where the wishes of the parents were overruled, Freeman says that 'it would be easy to conclude that the judges speak in the rhetoric of children's rights only when they believe the parents' decision is manifestly wrong.' He questions whether the religious and cultural background of the parents influenced the Court's decision and whether, if there objections had been on grounds other than religion, the Court would have been less inclined to overrule them.[127] However, he believes that the Court's decision to separate the twins was ultimately the right decision, albeit for the wrong reasons. The Court was wrong to prioritise Jodie's interests – both were persons with equal rights – but it was in the best interests of both that they should be separated. Mary's life was not worthwhile – if she had been born a single baby, she would have been considered non-viable and would not have been resuscitated. She had a right to life but inherent in the right to life is the right to die with dignity. As treatment would have achieved nothing for Mary on the basis that her body could not sustain life, 'the decision is one which upholds dignity: the right of Jodie to live with dignity, the right of Mary to die with dignity.'

RESPECTING AUTONOMY IN CHILDREN AND MINORS

[11.77] From an ethical perspective, patients have the right to expect appropriate medical care and treatment, to participate in decision-making in relation to their care and, where they lack capacity, that decisions will be taken in their best interests. In the context of the treatment of children it is important that respect for their autonomy be integrated into any medical decision-making in the same way as for adults. This does not mean that the interests and views of parents will be displaced, as in most instances the child's interests will be best represented by its parents, though their interests are not the same. Although parents are generally given wide authority to make decisions on behalf of their children, legal provisions also exist to deal with situations in which parents breach their obligations towards their children. Those who provide medical treatment for children must be careful not to infringe the autonomy and privacy of the family while at the same time acting as an advocate for the child's interests. Walking this tightrope is not an easy task.

[11.78] Whenever a child contracts a chronic or potentially fatal disease, questions arise as to whether to tell the child, how much information to tell them, to what extent should they be told about the risks and benefits of treatment and whether or not they can refuse treatment. If the child, parents and health-care team are all in agreement as to the care plan for the child, the situation is unlikely to cause conflict but often the three interests – that of the child to bodily self-determination, of parents to make decisions for their children and the State to impose decisions in the best interests of the child – do not always coincide.[128]

---

127 Freeman, 'Whose Life is it Anyway?' (2001) 9 Med L Rev 259 at 275.
128 Walker, 'Meaningful Participation of Minors with HIV/AIDS in Decisions Regarding Medical Treatment – Balancing the Rights of Children, Parents, and State' (2002) I J of Law and Psych 25, 271–297.

[11.79] Respect for the autonomy of the child entails the facilitation, wherever possible, of the child's right to make his own decisions. Guidelines on treatment of children generally provide that the child's wishes should be taken into account and, as the child grows towards maturity, given more weight accordingly. Children may have strong views about their own health care and their responses may range from enthusiastic agreement to absolute rejection without clear or obvious reasons for those views. Medical decisions are rarely clear-cut choices between life and death, as statistical chances of success vary between treatments and between particular patients. Decision-making, therefore, involves a balancing of risks and possible benefits, weighing up potential quality of life with dignity and a pain-free existence. In order to participate in decision-making, children should be given the necessary information in a way that they can understand so that they can fully comprehend the consequences of the medical decision, and, as far as possible, given the ability to make such decisions without the influence of parents or doctors.

[11.80] The United Nations Convention of the Rights of the Child[129] requires that 'the child who is capable of forming his or her own views [be accorded] the right to express those views freely in all matters affecting the child, the views of the child being given due weight in accordance with the age and maturity of the child.' Many professional organisations have recommended that decision-making involving the health care of older children and adolescents should include, to the greatest possible degree, the assent of the patient, as well as the participation of the parents and doctors. For example, the Committee on Bioethics of the American Academy of Paediatrics is of the opinion that while paediatricians need not necessarily treat children as rational, autonomous decision-makers, they should give serious consideration to each patient's developing capacities for participating in decision-making, including rationality and autonomy. This would involve helping the patient to achieve an appropriate awareness of the nature of his condition, telling him what he can expect with tests and treatment, making a clinical assessment of his understanding of the situation and how he is responding and soliciting an expression of his willingness to accept the proposed care. Where the patient will have to receive medical care despite his objection, he should not be deceived regarding that fact.[130] 'As children develop, they should gradually become the primary guardians of personal health and the primary partners in medical decision-making, assuming responsibility from their parents.'[131] The difficulties inherent in this process may be exacerbated where the child seeks to make decisions on his own behalf in circumstances where his parents and doctors are of the view that the decision is not in his best interests. This is considered further below.

[11.81] As Donnelly and Kilkelly point out, participation in decision-making is different from autonomous decision-making.[132] In the latter situation, responsibility for the

---

129 General Assembly Resolution 44/25, November 1989, art 12.

130 American Academy of Paediatrics, Committee on Bioethics, 'Informed Consent, Parental Permission, and Assent in Paediatric Practice' (1995) Paediatrics Vol 95(2) 314–317.

131 American Academy of Paediatrics, Committee on Bioethics, 'Informed Consent, Parental Permission, and Assent in Paediatric Practice' (1995) Paediatrics Vol 95(2) 314–317.

132 Donnelly and Kilkelly, 'Child-Friendly Healthcare: Delivering on the Right to Be Heard' (2011) Med Law Review Vol 19, pp 27–54 at 29.

decision lies wholly with the decision-maker whereas in the former situation, the participator is listened to, their views are taken into account, they are involved in the decision-making process and share in the responsibility for the decision. In the context of health-care decisions involving children under the legal age for consent, power is shared between children and adults but if the child's participation is to be meaningful, their views and preferences as to their best interests should be sought and listened to in making this assessment. If the child's preference is overridden, this should be explained to them in language that they can understand.

[11.82] Arguments against children's participation in their own treatment decisions are based on the child's immaturity, the increase of conflict, and the removal of protection from the child.[133] Firstly, in relation to immaturity, it has been argued that the peculiar vulnerability of children and their inability to make critical decisions in an informed manner leads to the conclusion that their Constitutional rights cannot be equated with those of adults.[134] As children are thought to have an incomplete understanding of the finality of death, they should not be considered competent to refuse treatment.[135] Secondly, it has been suggested that giving a child autonomy leads to inevitable and unnecessary conflict.[136] By permitting children to exercise rights of self-determination, parental authority and protection of the child will be seriously damaged. Thirdly, it is argued that where children participate in their own treatment decisions they are conferred with a range of adult burdens and responsibilities, which removes them from 'the protection rights of childhood.'[137]

[11.83] Arguments in favour of children's participation are based on both ethical and pragmatic principles. It has been argued that children, as much as adults, must be treated with dignity, and have their personal decision-making respected.[138] 'Nothing is more fundamental to the experience of being taken seriously than simply having a say and having one's perspective considered – in effect, being part of a conversation about matters of personal significance.'[139] On a practical level, ensuring patient choice enhances compliance and facilitates goal achievement, two elements associated with treatment success.[140] Studies have shown that, as compared to those who have not been involved, minors who have been involved in treatment decisions have had improved and

---

[133] See Hafen and Hafen, 'Abandoning Children to Their Autonomy: The UN Convention on the Rights of the Child' (1996) 37 Harvard I LJ 449.

[134] Per Justice Lewis Powell in the American case *Bellotti v Baird* [1979] 443 US 622 at 634.

[135] See Walker et al, *Children's Rights in the United States: In Search of a National Policy* (Sage Publications Inc, 1998) Ch 7.

[136] Hafen and Hafen, 'Abandoning Children to Their Autonomy: The UN Convention on the Rights of the Child' (1996) 37 Harvard I L J, at 484.

[137] Hafen and Hafen, 'Abandoning Children to Their Autonomy: The UN Convention on the Rights of the Child' (1996) 37 Harvard I L J, at 461.

[138] Walker and Melton, 'The Smallest Democracy' (1998) 2(4) Family Futures 4; Weithorn, 'Youth Participation in Family and Community Decision-Making' (1998) 2 (4) Family Futures 7.

[139] Melton, 'Parents *and* Children' (1998) 2(4) Family Futures 10 at 12.

[140] See Winick, 'Competency to Consent to Treatment: The Distinction Between Assent and Objection' (1991) 28 Houston Law Review 15; Tremper and Kelly, 'The Mental Health Rationale for Policies Fostering Minors' Autonomy' (1987) 10 I J of Law and Psychiatry 111.

more rapid psychological and physical recovery from surgery, increased compliance with recommendations and improved perceptions of the efficacy of treatments.[141] Article 12 of the UN Convention on the Rights of the Child requires State Parties to 'assure to the child who is capable of forming his or her own views the right to express those views freely in all matters affecting the child, the views of the child being given due weight in accordance with the age and maturity of the child.' Article 13 recognises the child's right to freedom of expression, and art 24 recognises the right of the child to the enjoyment of the highest attainable standard of health. 'Thus, state compliance with this most highly ratified instrument in international law requires the development of mechanisms for participation.'[142] The Committee on the Rights of the Child monitors states' reporting obligations under the Convention, including how art 12 is enshrined in legislation. In its Report in 2009, the Committee recommended that in addition to the introduction into law of an age at which children can consent to medical treatment, states should ensure that where a younger child can demonstrate capacity to express an informed view on his or her treatment, this view is given due weight.[143]

[11.84] In Ireland, s 23(1) of the Non-Fatal Offences Against the Person Act 1997 states that a person of more than 16 years can consent to 'surgical, medical or dental treatment'[144] and that the consent of his parent or guardian is not necessary. It is not clear from the Act whether people under 16 may also give a legal consent, as the language used in the section does not appear to be prohibitive of this.[145] The more difficult situation arises in relation to a young person under the age of 16 and the question of whether his competence to consent to or refuse treatment is sufficient to outweigh medical or parental views to the contrary. In England a similar legislative provision was interpreted as meaning that a person aged less than 16 years can give consent provided that he has 'sufficient maturity to understand what is involved.'[146] This means that, in the UK, in a situation where medical treatment is proposed for a young person under the age of 16 years, the medical professional involved must make an assessment of the competence and maturity of the patient. This assessment must look at the patient's understanding of the condition and the proposed treatment, and the consequences of the decision that is made. 'The test for competence is functional – whether somebody has capacity to do something depends on what that something is – and so for all patients the gravity of the decision plays an important part in the

---

[141] Carter and St Lawrence, 'Adolescents' Competency to Make Informed Consent Birth Control and Pregnancy Decisions: An Interface for Psychology and the Law' (1985) 3 Behavioral Sciences and the Law 309.

[142] Donnelly and Kilkelly, 'Child-Friendly Healthcare: Delivering on the Right to Be Heard' (2011) Med Law Review Vol 19, pp 27–54, at 33. The Convention has been ratified by 194 members of the United Nations, with the United States as a notable exception.

[143] Committee on the Rights of the Child, General Comment No 12 (2009) *The Right of the Child to Be Heard,* UN Doc CRC/C/GC/12, para 102.

[144] Defined in the Non-Fatal Offences Against the Person Act 1997, s 23(2) as including 'any procedure undertaken for the purposes of diagnosis' and 'any procedure which is ancillary to any treatment as it applies to that treatment.'

[145] See Donnelly, *Consent: Bridging the Gap Between Doctor and Patient* (Cork University Press, 2002) p 35.

[146] *Gillick v West Norfolk and Wisbech AHA* [1986] AC 112 at 189. This case is considered further at para **11.87**.

assessment of whether consent is valid.'[147] Refusal of treatment is regarded differently, as discussed below.

[11.85] Consent given by a competent person over the age of 16 allows doctors to proceed to treat the patient and it is not necessary to seek parental consent or approval in such cases. The relationship between the doctor and the patient is based on trust and confidentiality, as with any other patient, and therefore the doctor may feel obliged not to disclose to the young person's parents or guardians any information given to him in the course of that relationship. However, the provisions of the Freedom of Information Act 1997–2003 are relevant here in circumstances where the young person is treated without the knowledge of his parents. In *McK v The Information Commissioner*[148] in a challenge to a decision of the Information Commissioner not to direct a hospital to release medical records relating to a girl under the age of 18 years to her father, the Supreme Court held that held that the Commissioner erred in determining that release of the medical information would only be directed where there is tangible evidence that such release would actually serve the best interests of the minor. The court held that as a matter of Constitutional and family law a parent has rights and duties. The 'tangible evidence' test of the Commissioner reversed the onus of proof. The obverse is the correct approach. The presumption is that the release of such medical information would best serve the interests of the minor. However, evidence may be produced that it would not serve her interests, and, in considering the circumstances, her welfare is paramount.

[11.86] The provisions of the European Convention on Human Rights, as incorporated into Irish law by the ECHR Act 2003, are also relevant here. Although the Convention does not explicitly refer to children, the rights contained therein apply to children as well as adults. The European Court of Human Rights has begun in recent years to recognise the importance of the views of children in proceedings that affect them.[149] In *Sabin v Germany*[150]and *Sommerfeld v Germany*[151] the court acknowledged the importance of hearing children's views and taking them into account in family law proceedings, depending on the circumstances of the case and the maturity of the child. Donnelly and Kilkelly suggest that the approach of the court in these cases is in keeping with a concern to ensure that the decision-maker has access to all available information in keeping with the integrity of the process, rather than the specific individual right of the child to be heard but that nonetheless the judgment indicated 'the impact on the ECHR case law of the increasing practice in national courts of hearing children directly.'[152]

---

[147] BMA, *Withholding and Withdrawing Life-Prolonging Medical Treatment: Guidance for Decision-Making* (2nd edn, 2001) para 16.1.

[148] *McK v The Information Commissioner* [2006] IESC 2, considered in Ch 3, para **3.25**.

[149] Donnelly and Kilkelly, 'Child-Friendly Healthcare: Delivering on the Right to Be Heard' (2011) Med Law Review Vol 19, pp 27–54, at 47.

[150] *Sabin v Germany* [GC] (2003) 36 EHRR 765.

[151] *Sommerfeld v Germany* [GC] (2004) 38 EHRR 35.

[152] Donnelly and Kilkelly, 'Child-Friendly Healthcare: Delivering on the Right to Be Heard' (2011) Med Law Review Vol 19, pp 27–54, at 47.

ENGLISH CASE LAW

[11.87] It is worthwhile to examine the case law in the UK in order to look at the kinds of conflicts that have arisen in that jurisdiction before considering how similar issues might be resolved in Ireland. In the leading English case of *Gillick v West Norfolk and Wisbech AHA*[153] a circular had been issued by the Department of Health and Social Security to the effect that if a young girl, under 16, requested contraceptives, a doctor would not be acting unlawfully in providing them in order to protect the girl from the harmful consequences of sexual intercourse. It was also stated that although the doctor should seek to involve the girl's parents, in exceptional circumstances contraceptives could be provided without parental consent. The plaintiff in this case had five daughters under 16 years of age. She sought an assurance from her local Health Authority that her daughters would not be given contraceptives without her prior consent. The Health Authority refused to give such an assurance and the plaintiff sought a declaration from the Court that the advice contained in the circular was unlawful and in breach of her parental rights.

[11.88] By majority decision, the House of Lords found in favour of the Health Authority on the basis that parental rights were limited and that the imposition of a strict age rule failed to take into account the growing understanding of the child. Lord Scarman said that 'the parental right yields to the child's right to make his own decision when he reaches a sufficient understanding and intelligence to be capable of making up his own mind on the matter requiring decision.'[154] He went on to explain that the assessment of the competence of the individual to consent must involve not only an evaluation of whether the patient understands the nature of the advice being given, but also whether the patient has sufficient maturity to understand what is involved.[155] This has been interpreted as imposing such a high standard of understanding that many adults would fail to pass this threshold.[156] In relation to the provision of contraceptive advice or treatment in particular, Lord Scarman said that the girl seeking such treatment must have the maturity to understand that:

> There are moral and family questions, especially her relationship with her parents; long term problems associated with the emotional impact of pregnancy and its termination; and there are the risks to health of sexual intercourse at her age, risks which contraception may diminish but cannot eliminate.[157]

---

[153] *Gillick v West Norfolk and Wisbech AHA* [1986] AC 112.

[154] *Gillick v West Norfolk and Wisbech AHA* [1986] AC 112 at 186.

[155] This approach was also taken in Canada in *Johnston v Wellesley Hospital* [1970] 17 DLR 3d 139, and in Australia in *The Secretary, Dept. of Health and Community Services v JWB and another* [1992] 106 ALR 385.

[156] 'The concept of competence, arguably a more rigorous test of understanding and intelligence than is applicable to adults, was intended to be a major hurdle on the way to autonomous decisions-making.' Bridge, 'Adolescents and Mental Disorder: Who Consents to Treatment?' (1997) 3 Med Law I 51 at 54. Also see Montgomery, 'Children as Property?' (1988) 51 MLR 323.

[157] *Gillick v West Norfolk and Wisbech AHA* [1986] AC 112 at 189.

[11.89] Lord Fraser took the view that there was no distinction to be drawn between consent to medical treatment generally and consent to contraceptive treatment. Therefore, if the argument put forward by the plaintiff were accepted, it would mean that a minor under 16 years of age could not consent to any kind of medical advice, treatment or examination of his or her own body. That proposition was 'so surprising' and 'absurd' that the Court could not accept it. He went on to say that:

[P]rovided the patient, whether a boy or girl, is capable of understanding what is proposed, and of expressing his or her own wishes, I see no good reason for holding that he or she lacks the capacity to express then validly and effectively and to authorise the medical man to make the examination or give the treatment which he advises.

[11.90] Lord Bridge expressly agreed with Lord Fraser and Lord Scarman. Both Lord Brandon and Lord Templeman dissented on the issue of whether a doctor could give contraceptive advice or treatment to a girl under 16 without parental knowledge or consent. Lord Templeman said that 'an unmarried girl under the age of sixteen does not, in my opinion, possess the power in law to decide for herself to practice contraception.' He was of the view, therefore, that the parent had the right to decide on behalf of the minor all matters which the minor was not competent to decide. A doctor should not prescribe contraceptives to such a person on clinical grounds, or on the best interests of the minor because his clinical judgment will be based only on the information provided to him by the minor without a full picture of her family circumstances, the parents will find out the truth at some future time which will rupture good relations in the family and with the doctor and the provision of contraception could encourage participation in sexual activities which may cause her harm.[158] If discretion were given to doctors to provide contraception without parental knowledge simply on the basis that the young person was at risk of becoming pregnant, this 'would enable any girl to obtain contraception on request by threatening to sleep with a man.'

[11.91] Although much public attention was focused on the issue of the provision of contraception to minors as a result of this case, the decision had implications going well beyond that specific matter. It was anticipated that the case would spark new developments in the area of children's rights that would change the way in which disputes involving children had traditionally been decided, on a consideration of children's welfare rather than rights.[159] However, as can be seen from many of the subsequent cases dealing with the refusal of treatment by a minor, the courts seem to have retreated somewhat from such a development. Neither Lord Fraser nor Lord Scarman specifically dealt with the competence of the minor to refuse consent to treatment, although both judgments refute the suggestion that parents have absolute control over children until the age of majority. Both Lord Scarman and Lord Fraser

---

[158] For discussion of the doctor's position in relation to *Gillick,* see Williams, 'The *Gillick* Saga' (1985) 135 NLJ 1156.

[159] At common law a father's authority over his children was regarded as absolute, in the absence of gross misconduct on his part. 'Since Victorian times this has been gradually whittled away, first by conferring equality on the father and mother in relation to custody proceedings, secondly by the recognition of the equally parental authority of the father and mother, and thirdly by the emergence of the child's welfare as the paramount consideration overriding the claims of parents where the child's custody or upbringing is brought before the courts.' Bainham, 'The Balance of Power in Family Decisions' (1986) Camb LJ 262 at 268.

pointed out that the rights accorded to parents only existed for the benefit of the child, and to permit parents to discharge their duties towards their children. While Lord Scarman suggests, obiter, that the minor assumes power both to consent to and refuse treatment once she has reached capacity, Lord Fraser does not go beyond the provision of consent *to* treatment.[160] Thus, the difficult issue of whether a competent minor can refuse medical treatment remained open after *Gillick*. The contexts in which this issue has commonly arisen are considered below.

Adolescents and mental disorder

[11.92] The first case in the UK to consider the concept of the 'mature minor', or the *Gillick* competent minor, was *Re R (a minor) (wardship: consent to medical treatment)*.[161] In this case a 15-year-old girl, R, who was on the local authority's at-risk register, was received into voluntary care and placed in a children's home after a fight with her father. She began to suffer hallucinations and her mental health deteriorated. Her behaviour also became more disturbed and she threatened suicide and attacked her father on one occasion when she had absconded from the home. The local authority obtained place of safety and care orders, and placed her in an adolescent psychiatric unit. Her behaviour remained very disturbed and the unit sought permission to administer anti-psychotic drugs to her. During lucid periods during which R was capable of understanding the nature and effect of the medication, she objected to taking the drugs. The unit was unprepared to continue caring for her without permission to administer the medication[162], and therefore the Local Authority began wardship proceedings seeking permission from the Court to give R the drugs with or without her consent. The Court had to consider whether R was *Gillick* competent and, if so, whether her refusal of the drug treatment could be overridden.

[11.93] Lord Donaldson MR was of the view that *Gillick* did not determine that parental rights to consent terminate with the achievement by the child of competence. Capacity to consent will vary from child to child, and according to the treatment under consideration. If it were the position that when the child was regarded as competent a transfer of rights between parents and child took place, doctors would be faced with 'an intolerable dilemma', particularly when the child was close to 16 years of age and refusing consent. He was of the opinion that a *Gillick* competent child can consent to treatment but if he refuses or declines treatment, consent may be given by someone with parental rights. If all those with power to consent decline or refuse to do so, that creates a veto on treatment. Farquharson LJ said that it was difficult to apply *Gillick* to the facts of this particular case, as R's understanding and capacity was fluctuating from day to day according to the effect of her illness.[163] He said he would 'reject the application of

---

[160] For discussion, see Eekelaar, 'The Emergence of Children's Rights' (1986) 6 Ox J of Legal Studies 161.

[161] *Re R (a minor) (wardship: consent to medical treatment)* [1991] 4 All ER 177.

[162] It may be argued that this is indicative of the manipulation by adults of the acquisition of capacity by children. Bainham, 'The Judge and the Competent Minor' (1992) 108 LQR 194 at 200.

[163] The Court held that R was not competent even in her lucid intervals. 'This is a curious conclusion to reach, since it allows competence to be judged not on the present but on the past or the predicted mental condition of the person.' Elliston, 'If You Know What's Good For You: Refusal of Consent to Medical Treatment by Children' in McLean (ed) *Contemporary Issues in Law, Medicine and Ethics* (Dartmouth Publishing, 1996) 29 at 32.

the *Gillick* test to an on/off situation of that kind.' Whether the Court in this instance approached the question from the point of view of competence, or from the perspective of R's welfare as the paramount consideration, the result would have been the same.

[11.94] The Court held that the *Gillick* test had no application in wardship cases, which had to be determined in accordance with the best interests of the ward. Thus, even if the ward was considered to be *Gillick* competent, her refusal to consent to medical treatment could be overridden by a court in her best interests.[164] 'Hers is a limited autonomy. If she is sixteen her statutory right to authorise treatment cannot be overruled by parents even though their rights co-exist with her own until she is of full age, but if she objects to treatment, the power of parents or the court, can provide the necessary 'flak jacket' and enable lawful treatment.'[165] Lord Donaldson MR introduced the concept of consent providing the key to the therapeutic door and, in the case of the mature minor, there are two keyholders – the minor and the parents. Either keyholder may *enable* treatment to be lawfully given, but this did not *determine* that treatment should be given. This analogy was criticised and later regretted by Lord Donaldson on the basis that keys may lock as well as open doors.

[11.95] It is argued that consent is different to refusal, as the reasons for the refusal may be more 'teenage angst'[166] than principled objection, and the consequences of refusal are usually more serious and potentially dangerous and imply a conflict with profession decision-making.[167] However, if the *Gillick* test is to determine whether a minor has sufficient intelligence and understanding to seek and consent to her own treatment, it may be questioned whether non-application of this principle to refusals of treatment is overly paternalistic.[168] The interpretation of the law as retaining parental power to give consent despite the refusal of a competent minor has been described as 'driving a coach and horses through *Gillick*.'[169] However, the alternative would be to accede to the

---

164 For discussion of parental rights in the context of refusal of consent by a minor, see Thornton, 'Multiple Keyholders – Wardship and Consent to Medical Treatment' [1992] CLJ 34; Bainham, 'The Judge and the Competent Minor' (1992) 108 LQR 194; Grubb, 'Treatment Decisions: Keeping it in the Family' in Grubb (ed) *Choices and Decisions in Health Care* (Wiley, 1993) 60–65.

165 Bridge, 'Adolescents and Mental Disorder: Who Consents to Treatment?' (1997) 3 Med Law I 51 at 55.

166 A minor may refuse treatment for a variety of reasons such as rebellion, resentment of adult control, miscommunication, misunderstanding or fear. Bridge, 'Adolescents and Mental Disorder: Who Consents to Treatment?' (1997) 3 Med Law I 51 at 61.

167 Pearce, 'Consent to Treatment During Childhood: The Assessment of Competence and Avoidance of Conflict' (1994) 165 British Journal of Psychiatry 713.

168 Elliston argues that it is illogical to distinguish between the ability to consent and the ability to refuse, as 'the right to say yes must carry with it the right to say no. If one is able to weigh up the considerations in order to agree to treatment, surely one is equally capable of weighing up the same considerations even though arriving at a different conclusion?' Elliston, 'If You Know What's Good for You: Refusal of Consent to Medical Treatment by Children' in McLean (ed) *Contemporary Issues in Law, Medicine and Ethics* (Dartmouth, 1996) 29 at 34.

169 Kennedy, 'Consent to Treatment: The Capable Person' in Dyer (ed.) *Doctors, Patients and the Law* (Oxford: Scientific Publications, 1992) Ch 3.

minor's wishes when competent and to treat her when incompetent under the mantle of necessity.

[11.96] In *South Glamorgan County Council v W and B*,[170] A was a 15-year-old girl who had suffered psychiatric disturbance following her parents' divorce when she was aged 7. She lived with her father and an older brother in the family home and rarely saw her mother. She had received virtually no schooling for a number of years, and lived as a recluse in a room in her home. She was abusive to her family and threatened harm to herself or others if they did not comply with her wishes as to domestic tasks and privacy. Following the recommendation of a number of child psychiatrists, the local authority began care proceedings and sought Court permission for A to be removed from her home for assessment and treatment. A's father opposed the application.

[11.97] The Court considered the provisions of the Children Act 1989, which provides, inter alia, that local authorities can invoke the inherent jurisdiction of the court where the child could probably suffer significant harm.[171] The Act obliges the court 'to have regard to the ascertainable wishes and feelings of the child concerned (considered in the light of his age and understanding)'[172] and also appears to grant a minor a statutory right to refuse to submit to medical or psychiatric examination or treatment where he has 'sufficient understanding to make an informed decision.'[173] It was argued that where a child exercises this statutory right to refuse, the court has no power to override such refusal. The Court did not accept this argument, saying that the Act had specifically preserved the inherent jurisdiction of the High Court with respect to children. In considering whether the Court should exercise that power the child's welfare had to be the paramount consideration, taking into account also the child's wishes in the matter. Balancing these considerations, the Court gave the Local Authority leave to remove A from her home and take her to a unit for assessment and treatment.

In this case the Court was in the difficult position of deciding to override the wishes of a competent minor.[174] Although she did have a statutory right to refuse treatment, the Court chose to adopt an unsatisfactory route of using its inherent jurisdiction to achieve its intended result.[175] It has been suggested that the judgment 'conveys to children the

---

[170] *South Glamorgan County Council v W and B* [1993] 1 FLR 574.

[171] The Children Act 1989 'severely prunes the local authority's access to the wardship jurisdiction. Wardship cannot be used to place a child in care or under supervision, nor to confer parental responsibility on the local authority.' Brazier and Bridge, 'Coercion or Caring: Analysing Adolescent Autonomy' (1996) Legal Studies 84.

[172] The Children Act 1989, s 1(3)(a).

[173] The Children Act 1989, ss 38(6), 43(8), and 44(7).

[174] Brazier and Bridge suggest that criticism of the case is misplaced and that the Court could not simply wash their hands of A. 'The unfortunate feature of the judgment was to suggest A was capable of autonomous choice, to find her 'not' *Gillick* incompetent.' 'Coercion or Caring: Analysing Adolescent Autonomy' (1996) Legal Studies 84 at 101.

[175] An alternative approach would have been seen if a family member of A's had intervened and made an application for a 'specific issue order' under the Children Act 1989, s 8. This is an order 'giving directions for the purpose of determining a specific question which has arisen, or which may arise, in connection with any aspect of parental responsibility for a child.' In such a case the child is not granted a right of veto over action considered necessary by the courts. (contd.../)

message that they cannot trust that the clearly expressed 'rights' given by Parliament will be safe in the hands of the judges.'[176]

[11.98] While this case deals with conflict between the minor and the medical profession or local authority regarding her care, it does not deal with the situation that may arise where parents and older children or adolescents disagree. In *Re K, W and H (Minors) (Medical Treatment)*[177] three young people, two aged 15 and one nearly 15 years old, were receiving specialist psychiatric treatment in a secure unit at a hospital. Following a number of complaints from children being treated at the unit, the hospital sought court permission to administer emergency medication. The Court held that none of the three patients were *Gillick* competent[178] and, even if they were, their refusal could be overridden on the basis that the patients' parents had all consented in writing to the administration of emergency medication. Thorpe J was of the view if a *Gillick* competent minor refused treatment, consent could be given by someone else with parental rights. Where more than one person has power to consent, only a refusal of all having that power will create a veto. He held that the application in this case was 'misconceived and unnecessary' on the basis that parental consent was in existence and, whether the minor patients were competent or not, their refusal could be overridden. This case 'denies the young person any forum in which to object to medical treatment'[179] and permits compulsory psychiatric treatment based upon parental consent. 'The doctor has his flak jacket. Any ethical concern he may have about whether to proceed against the child's will he must resolve alone.'[180]

Adolescents and eating disorders

[11.99] In the 1990s a number of cases came before the English courts in relation to the forcible feeding of patients suffering from anorexia, bulimia or abstention from eating due to a personality disorder. Despite the refusal of consent to feeding by these patients the courts invariably found ways to allow their detention and feeding under the umbrella of 'best interests.' The first of these cases was *Re W (a minor) (medical treatment: court's jurisdiction)*[181] which provided the Court with the opportunity to consider whether it had the power to sanction medical treatment of a 16-year-old girl against her

---

[175] (\...contd) The Court does not assume parental responsibility as it does in wardship but, more simply, exercises control over a single issue affecting a child. It is thought to be particularly useful to deal with disputes involving medical treatment, for example where parents themselves are in conflict regarding appropriate treatment, or where both parents refuse consent. However, a Local Authority cannot apply for such an order. See Brazier and Bridge, 'Coercion or Caring: Analysing Adolescent Autonomy' (1996) Legal Studies 84 at 100–101.

[176] Lyon, 'What's Happened to the Child's Right to Refuse?' (1994) 6 Journal of Child Law 84 at 87.

[177] *Re K, W and H (Minors) (Medical Treatment)* [1993] 1 FLR 854.

[178] It is unclear where this finding came from since there was no evidence given on this issue. See Bates, 'Children on Secure Psychiatric Units – *Re K, W and H* – Out of Sight, Out of Mind?' (1994) 6 Journal of Child Law 131 at 135.

[179] Fox and McHale, *Health Care Law, Text and Materials* (London: Sweet & Maxwell, 1997).

[180] Brazier and Bridge, 'Coercion or Caring: Analysing Adolescent Autonomy' (1996) Legal Studies 84 at 102.

[181] *Re W (a minor) (medical treatment: court's jurisdiction)* [1992] 4 All ER 627, [1993] 1 FLR 1.

wishes. The facts of *Re W* concerned a 16-year-old girl suffering from anorexia. She was admitted to a specialist residential unit and fed by nasogastric tube. Due to continued deterioration in her condition the Local Authority became concerned that she may begin to reject all treatment. The authority applied for permission to move her to a new unit and to treat her without consent under the inherent jurisdiction of the Court under the Children Act 1989. The Court of Appeal granted the application. It held that competent children do not have an absolute power of veto in relation to their medical treatment – the Court could overrule their views in an appropriate case. The Court confirmed the view taken in *Re R* that all that *Gillick* had decided was that a competent child under 16 could give a valid consent to medical treatment. 'It was *not* to be taken as establishing that such children have a power of veto over treatment, nor was it to be regarded as determining the court's power to sanction or prohibit medical treatment whatever the child's (or parents') views.'[182]

[11.100] Lord Donaldson MR was of the view that 'good parenting involves giving minors as much rope as they can handle without an unacceptable risk that they will hang themselves.' The point at which the court must intervene occurred when the child, refusing treatment, would be facing death or severe permanent injury. He said that anorexia was a condition that could destroy a person's ability to make an informed choice. On the facts of this case the application should be granted to save W from martyring herself. Some commentators regard *Re W* as a pragmatic remedies approach well-suited to the common law tradition.

> It takes a case-by-case approach to individual problems without showing an excessive desire to formulate legal principles. *Gillick*, however, was a rights-based approach where the court advocated a view of rights that was broad and general in terms. That approach has now had its wings clipped. Whether one uses Lord Donaldson MR's 'keyholder analogy' or his 'flak jacket' approach, the effect is the same. It enables the court to prevent… 'permanent disability' or 'unnecessary pain and suffering'.[183]

[11.101] On the other hand the judgment has also been criticised, as it runs directly counter to the *Gillick* principle that was interpreted as meaning that a child who has reached a certain level of intelligence and understanding should be given the right to decide whether to have any proposed medical treatment.[184] Lord Donaldson's view,

---

[182] Lowe and Juss, 'Medical Treatment – Pragmatism and the Search for Principle' (1993) 56 Modern L Rev 865 at 867.

[183] Lowe and Juss, 'Medical Treatment – Pragmatism and the Search for Principle' (1993) 56 Modern L Rev 865 at 871.

[184] Freeman argues that Lord Donaldson may have displayed some understanding of adolescence but little of anorexia, and in *Re W* because W's ability to make her own choices was removed in order to save her life, this was at the price of undermining her identity and integrity. He argues that decisions like *Re W* would create more anorexics and more disturbed adolescents. Freeman, 'Removing Rights from Adolescents' (1993) 17 Adoption & Fostering 14. This is criticised in turn by de Cruz, who says that this argument 'overstates the case for adolescent autonomy and overlooks the life-saving motives for acting in the child's best interests'. De Cruz, 'Adolescent Autonomy, Detention for Medical Treatment and *Re C*' (1999) 62 Mod L Rev 595 at 603. See also Dickenson, 'Children's Informed Consent to Treatment: Is the Law an Ass?' (1994) 20 JME 205; Masson, '*Re W*: Appealing from the Golden Cage' (1993) J Child Law 37.

albeit obiter, that no minor, whatever her age, could, by refusing treatment, override a consent to treatment given by someone with parental authority has been seen as 'a fundamental incursion into the adolescent's right to self-determination.'[185] The case poses difficulties by virtue of the nature of the illness itself, which is characterised by a desire not to be treated. Therefore, if a wish not to be treated is part of the illness, it is difficult to conclude that the refusal is a voluntary exercise of the patient's autonomy, since this has been shaped by the illness. 'However, such a finding should be made only with a great deal of care, since it may be all too easy to subvert the concept of competence in order to hold that a patient's desire not to be treated is a symptom of mental disorder, rather than an expression of their autonomy.'[186] Lord Donaldson used a new analogy in this case, preferring to leave behind the 'keyholder' concept that had been much criticised. In *Re W* he developed the notion of the legal 'flak jacket', which he said:

> [P]rotects the doctor from claims by the litigious whether he acquires it from his patient who may be a minor over the age of sixteen, or a '*Gillick*' competent child under that age or from another person having parental responsibilities which include a right to consent to the treatment of the minor. Anyone who gives him a flak jacket (i.e. consent) may take it back, but the doctor only needs one and as long as he continues to have one he has the legal right to proceed.[187]

Again Lord Donaldson has been subjected to criticism for this analogy, which seems to place more emphasis on protecting doctors from litigation than on patient autonomy. 'Flak jackets conjure up a scenario where health professionals quite sensibly become concerned to grab a jacket, get a signature on the consent form, and then proceed to do what they think best.'[188] Although the courts seem concerned with the ethical principle of autonomy and the respect to be accorded to the wishes of the minor, it may be argued that they are reluctant to import it into legal principle.

[11.102] In *Re C (Detention: medical treatment)*,[189] the Court again dealt with a 16-year-old girl suffering from anorexia nervosa. C's family was described as 'highly dysfunctional' and C had a history of being sexually abused by her brother over a substantial period of time. She suffered from the illness for two years and was on a re-feeding programme, funded by the Local Authority, at a private clinic specialising in the treatment of eating disorders. After her discharge from the clinic, C's health deteriorated rapidly and she was re-admitted. Her behaviour was disturbed, aggressive and sometimes suicidal. She absconded regularly from the clinic and her weight fell to a dangerously low level. The clinic sought an order for her detention on the basis that it believed the treatment would only be successful if she could be forced to stay at the clinic. The Court granted the application on the basis that detention was in C's best

---

[185] Bridgeman, 'Old Enough to Know Best?' (1993) 13 Legal Studies 69; Lewis, 'Feeding Anorexic Patients Who Refuse Food' (Spring 1999) Med Law Rev 7, 21–37.

[186] Elliston, 'If You Know What's Good for You: Refusal of Consent to Medical Treatment by Children' in McLean (ed) *Contemporary Issues in Law, Medicine and Ethics* (Dartmouth, 1996) 29 at 34.

[187] *Re W (a minor) (medical treatment: court's jurisdiction)* [1992] 4 All ER 627 at 635.

[188] Brazier and Bridge, (1996) 'Coercion or Caring: Analysing Adolescent Autonomy' Legal Studies 84 at 87.

[189] *Re C (Detention: medical treatment)* [1997] 2 FLR 180.

interests at this time whether or not she consented to the treatment, and held that she should be detained with reasonable force if necessary, albeit with the least distress and greatest dignity possible.

[11.103] In this case it was held that C was not *Gillick* competent, as she was not capable of evaluating the relevant information concerning her treatment in order to make a balanced choice. Therefore, she could not give a valid consent or refusal of treatment. As in *Re W,* her purported refusal could be overridden in her best interests under the inherent jurisdiction of the Court. Her detention was not solely to deprive her of her liberty but was also justified on the basis that her history demonstrated that she was unable to follow a re-feeding regime outside of the clinic, and since this treatment was in her best interests, detention was also regarded as an essential part of that treatment. Reasonable force was permitted in her detention but not in the feeding since this would be contrary to the ethos of the clinic.

[11.104] *Re C* continues 'the paternalistic line of authority of cases such as *Re W* and negates adolescent autonomy in anorexia cases, but it also enunciates safeguards to protect the child's interests.'[190] It reinforces the message that 'an anorexic adolescent's autonomy ends where her refusal of medical treatment begins to endanger her life – that, in some cases, respecting adolescent autonomy may be simply too high a price to pay.'[191] Although the courts have suggested that the wishes of a child should carry more weight as the child grows more mature, this would appear to be simply paying lip-service to autonomy, since there have been no English cases in which a refusal of medical treatment by a minor has been respected.[192] In all of these cases the courts have relied heavily on the evidence of medical professionals in reaching their decisions. This is probably due to a number of factors, including the traditional deference shown to the profession in medical litigation, the fact that most of these cases are life-threatening and do not allow for lengthy legal research and argument and that the applications are generally brought by institutions with recourse to lawyers and expert witnesses familiar with the issues involved.[193] The result of these cases is that mature and competent minors in the UK can have their decisions respected if, but only if, they know what is good for them and accept the treatment that is offered.[194]

> If society is not prepared to allow adolescents to court unfavourable outcomes in judgments relating to medical treatment, we should say so openly. The law should not pretend to apply

---

[190] De Cruz, 'Adolescent Autonomy, Detention for Medical Treatment and *Re C*' (1999) 62 Mod L Rev 595 at 603.

[191] De Cruz, 'Adolescent Autonomy, Detention for Medical Treatment and *Re C*' (1999) 62 Mod L Rev 595 at 603. See also Lewis, 'Feeding Anorexic Patients Who Refuse Food' (1999) 7 Med L Rev 21–37.

[192] Elliston, 'If You Know What's Good for You: Refusal of Consent to Medical Treatment by Children' in McLean (ed) *Contemporary Issues in Law, Medicine and Ethics* (Dartmouth, 1996) 29 at 39.

[193] Elliston, 'If You Know What's Good for You: Refusal of Consent to Medical Treatment by Children' in McLean (ed) *Contemporary Issues in Law, Medicine and Ethics* (Dartmouth, 1996) p 48.

[194] Elliston 'If You Know What's Good for You: Refusal of Consent to Medical Treatment by Children' in McLean (ed) *Contemporary Issues in Law, Medicine and Ethics* (Dartmouth, 1996) p 52.

a 'functional' test of autonomy to every patient when younger patients are in fact subjected to an 'outcome' test.[195]

Refusal of treatment due to religious beliefs

[11.105] Apart from cases where a young person's refusal of medical treatment is due to mental disturbance or illness, there is also a category of cases where such a refusal is prompted by adherence to strong religious beliefs opposing the medical intervention in question. The problem generated by these 'children of conscience' is how a court should deal with a decision made by a mature, intelligent minor to refuse medical treatment on the basis of religious conviction. Respect for freedom of religion and the right of self-determination would seem to demand that the choice made by a competent minor should be upheld in the same way as if that minor were an adult person making the same choice for the same reasons.

[11.106] In *Re E (A minor) (Wardship: medical treatment)*[196] E, a young man of fifteen and three quarters, was suffering from leukaemia. He and his parents were Jehovah's Witnesses and all three refused consent to the administration of blood and some particular drugs. They gave consent to a different form of drug therapy that had a much lower chance of success. The hospital began wardship proceedings and sought the Court's permission to treat E conventionally if and when his condition became so bad that he would be at risk of death from heart attack or stroke. E's parents were of the view that his decision should be respected, particularly as he was so close to the age of 16, when his consent would be required by statute. However, the judge instead considered whether E was *Gillick* competent, in order for him to be able to refuse treatment.

[11.107] Ward J found that E was a person of sufficient intelligence to be able to take decisions about his own well-being, but that there was a range of decisions that were outside of his ability to fully comprehend. He found that, although E spoke intelligently, calmly and confidently about the consequences of his refusal of treatment, he did not really appreciate the pain, distress and fear that he would face, as well as the implications for his family. Ward J was therefore of the view that E was not *Gillick* competent, but even if he had been, his veto would not have been binding on the basis that the Court would decide the issue on welfare grounds. He was not satisfied that E's decision was truly free of the influence of his religious beliefs and those of his parents. He accepted that forced transfusion would be traumatic for E but found that E would accept the Court's decision. He said that it was 'essential for his well-being to protect him from himself and his parents' and so overrode E's decision.[197]

[11.108] This case raises questions about the level of understanding required of minors and whether a higher standard is expected of them than could be attained even by adult patients. It is not clear from this case why age alone should be a sufficient determinant of competence, as E was evidently intelligent, mature and content in his understanding of the consequences of his decision. The Court seems to have been influenced by the

---

[195] Brazier and Bridge, 'Coercion or Caring: Analysing Adolescent Autonomy' (1996) Legal Studies 84 at 109.

[196] *Re E (A minor) (Wardship: medical treatment)* [1993] 1 FLR 386.

[197] On reaching maturity, E exercised his right to refuse further blood transfusions and subsequently died.

strength of religious belief with which E grew up, E having had these convictions instilled in him throughout his life by his parents. This led to the Court probing whether E's choice was really a free one. E's death two years after the judgment could be regarded as the Court's decision either having prolonged the waiting period in a distressing manner with unwanted treatment being forced on him, or as having given E the opportunity to mature and become even more convinced of the correctness of his decision.

[11.109] Similar issues arose in *Re S (A minor) (medical treatment)*[198] where a young girl aged 15 and a half had suffered from a life-threatening illness since birth. She had endured blood transfusions on a monthly basis and daily injections throughout her life. As a result of irregularity in iron ingestion she did not grow normally and suffered much abuse from her peers in this regard. When S was 10, S's mother converted to the Jehovah's Witness faith and began taking S to meetings with her. S's mother influenced her to stop the treatments and S failed to turn up for transfusions. The Local Authority requested the High Court to exercise its inherent jurisdiction and override S's refusal to have further treatment.

[11.110] Johnson J found that S had only come to this decision recently, was disillusioned with treatment, was influenced by her mother's religious convictions and did not understand the full implications of what would happen to her if she did not receive the transfusions. Her capacity was deemed not to be commensurate with the gravity of the decision to be made. He said that it was not enough that S knew that she would die, although she clearly hoped for a miracle cure. 'For her decision to carry weight she should have a greater understanding of the manner of the death and pain and the distress.' Therefore, Johnson J held that S was not *Gillick* competent and that her decision should be overridden.

[11.111] There are distinctions to be drawn between the facts of *Re E* and *Re S* on grounds of understanding, commitment to religious conviction and influence of others. S was fed up with her debilitating illness and, although she hoped that God might spare her, she felt that she 'might as well die'. She did not display full understanding of why God might want her to refuse transfusions and considered it a possibility that the doctors were wrong in their diagnosis of her illness. E, on the other hand, was committed to his religion from childhood, understood why his religion opposed transfusions and appreciated the fact of his own death, if not the distressing manner of it. Despite the differences between these two young people, both were treated the same by the court and both had their competence questioned and their decisions overruled. This seems to be based, then, not on assessments of competence but on age alone. This ignores the development of the individual and 'flies in the face of evolving autonomy ... Rationality appears to be acquired on a person's eighteenth birthday.'[199]

---

[198] *Re S (A minor) (medical treatment)* [1994] 2 FLR 1065.

[199] Brazier and Bridge, 'Coercion or Caring: Analysing Adolescent Autonomy' (1996) Legal Studies 84 at 107. See also Dickenson and Jones, 'True Wishes: Philosophical and Clinical Approaches to the Developing Case-Law on Consent in Children' (1995) Philosophy, Psychiatry and Psychology 4.

[11.112] In *Re L (Medical treatment: Gillick competency)*[200] again the Court was faced with the question of whether to override the wishes of L, a Jehovah's Witness girl aged 14, in relation to refusal of blood transfusions. L was a firm believer in her faith and had signed a directive that, in the event of an accident, she should not be given blood. She had renewed this directive a short time before an accident in which she sustained very severe burns. Her medical condition demanded at least three operations in order to ensure survival. The anaesthetist was not prepared to proceed with the operation without the availability of blood for the necessary transfusions. The Court was presented with a 'very stark dilemma'. If L received the treatment, her prognosis was very optimistic. If she did not, gangrene was expected to develop and she would, according to the burns consultant, inevitably die a 'horrible death'. The harrowing manner of her death had not been disclosed to L. She was described as 'very religious', 'mature', 'a model of a young person...not attracted by some of the more undisciplined pursuits of youth.' She was clearly a serious, intelligent girl from a sheltered family, immersed in church activities.

[11.113] The hospital authority sought and received permission from the Court, exercising its inherent jurisdiction, to administer blood as necessary during L's treatment. This was on the basis that L's welfare demanded that she be protected against a distressing death, even though this overrode her autonomy. There was no hint of any coercion or that L's community would reject her if she received the transfusions. Her family were supportive of her, irrespective of the Court's decision. However, L's religious convictions, though seriously held, were seen as rigid and inflexible, lacking the constructive formulation that an adult might have. Ultimately, her religious beliefs, understanding and maturity 'were weighed alongside the prospect of an outcome which the majority of the community would deplore.'[201]

[11.114] In this case the Court was influenced by a number of factors, including L's firmly held religious views. The Court seemed to take the view that because L was unquestioning of her religion, this demonstrated an immaturity on her part. However, it has been argued that 'absolute faith or the espousal of views in a very black and white manner is itself a feature of any fundamentalist religious belief. Does this mean therefore that a choice of faith over treatment is the preserve of the adult and that the beliefs of the fourteen or fifteen year old lack the validity of adult faith?'[202] Religious belief itself could be said to defy rationality, as it cannot be based on evidence or established truths. Therefore, if the mature, competent minor is under no coercion, misunderstanding or deception, it may be questioned why her belief should not be respected in the same way as an adult's. The Court also relied on her upbringing within a close family circle founded on religious beliefs, as having sheltered her from external experiences that might have contributed to her understanding of her situation. The fact that she had deliberately not been told, at her family's request, of the nature of her death, meant that the Court was able to find that she could not properly understand her

---

[200] *Re L (Medical treatment: Gillick competency)* [1998] 2 FLR 810.
[201] Bridge, 'Religious Beliefs and Teenage Refusal of Medical Treatment' (1999) 62 Mod L Rev 585 at 587.
[202] Bridge, 'Religious Beliefs and Teenage Refusal of Medical Treatment' (1999) 62 Mod L Rev 585 at 588.

situation and could not make a valid refusal of treatment. Rather than order that L be given the requisite information in order to establish whether her understanding increased, and her decision held steadfast, the Court was content with holding that she was not *Gillick* competent.

[11.115] These decisions on religious convictions in the context of refusal of treatment demonstrate that the court's powers can always be exercised to protect minors' welfare. It seems disingenuous, then, to go through the motions of assessing the competence of a minor when the court's decision will clearly be based on the outcome of the minor's refusal. If mature minors can never refuse treatment, if the consequences are too serious for the court to sanction, it would be more acceptable to enshrine this in the law, rather than have the court go through a pretence of assessing competence, as if an evaluation in the minor's favour would somehow result in the court upholding the right to refuse treatment. Whether the final decision in *Re L* or any of the other cases on adolescent autonomy was correct or not, the judgments demonstrate a pragmatism and determination to reach a desired result rather than a reasoned analysis of the legal issues. It may thus be argued that:

> Judges should not go through the pretence of applying a functional test of capacity when the outcome of the young persons' decision is not one that they, or probably society, would countenance. The law should openly declare that welfare reigns when grave decisions with momentous outcomes are considered and recognise that adolescent autonomy is, inevitably, circumscribed.[203]

REFUSAL OF TREATMENT ON OTHER GROUNDS

[11.116] In *Re M (child: refusal of medical treatment)*[204] M, a girl aged 15 and a half, suffered heart failure. Despite medical treatment, her condition deteriorated and it was concluded that the only course of action to save her life would be a heart transplant. M refused to give her consent for the operation as she did not want to have someone else's heart, and did not want to take medication for the rest of her life. Equally, however, she did not want to die. An emergency application was made to the Court to override M's wishes. The Court held that although M's wishes were important, they were not conclusive. There were risks attached to the surgery, to rejection of both the transplanted heart and continued treatment, and there was also a danger that M might always resent what had been done to her. However, when those risks were matched against the certainty of death, the Court was of the opinion that what was best for M was to give authority for the operation.

[11.117] Johnson J said that in the circumstances of this case, consent could have been given by M herself, by her mother who had parental responsibility for her, or by the Court. Although M's wishes were important, they were not decisive. He felt that M had been overwhelmed by her circumstances and the decision she was being asked to make.

---

[203] Bridge, 'Religious Beliefs and Teenage Refusal of Medical Treatment' (1999) 62 Mod L Rev 585 at 594.
[204] *Re M (child: refusal of medical treatment)* [1999] 2 FCR 577 [1999] Fam Law 753.

'Events have overtaken her so swiftly that she has not been able to come to terms with her situation.' As a result, M was deemed to be incompetent to decide.

[11.118] This case does not provide any new insights into assessment of the competence of adolescents, nor does it deal with the difficulties of balancing the autonomy of minors with judicial and medical perceptions of their welfare.[205] It again displays the apparent inconsistency between the courts' avowed adherence to principles of self-determination for adult patients, irrespective of the consequences, and their unanimous unwillingness to apply those principles to competent minors. It may be distasteful for judges to contemplate any alternative solution than that displayed in the long line of cases discussed above, particularly where life and death issues are at stake. However, there does not seem to be any attempt on the part of the judiciary to admit this inconsistency for what it is, and stand behind their decisions to overrule minors' autonomy on the basis of age, status and outcome. Common sense would suggest that where the life of the minor is at stake, a higher degree of competence should be required, but it should not be set so high that even competent adults would have difficulty attaining that standard.[206] This is an artificial and disingenuous means of avoiding having to justify distinctions between individual patients on the basis of their age alone. The whole area of adolescent autonomy ought to be reconsidered in the light of moves towards greater recognition of children's rights and rights of self-determination in the medical context generally.[207]

> To believe in autonomy is to believe that anyone's autonomy is as morally significant as anyone else's. Nor does autonomy depend on the stage of life that a person has reached …To respect a child's autonomy is to treat that child as a person and as a rights-holder.[208]

---

[205] In a study of children undergoing paediatric orthopaedic surgery, patients, parents and health professionals were asked for their views on when children could decide for themselves whether they wanted surgery or not. Interestingly, the children themselves set the highest threshold age for self-determination at 14 years; the parents put it slightly lower at 13.9 years and the health professionals chose the lowest figure, 10.3 years. See Alderson, *Children's Consent to Surgery* (Open University Press, 1993) at 9. Also Shield J, 'Children's Consent to Treatment' (1994) 308 BMJ 1182–83.

[206] 'It is arguable that a right to consent is meaningless without a corresponding right to refuse and that the Courts have adopted a strict test in determining necessary competence which even those patients for whom competence is assumed (those over 16) are unlikely to satisfy. The British Medical Association (BMA) believes that 'minors who are clearly competent to agree to treatment must be acknowledged as also having an option to refuse treatment if they understand the implications of so doing.' It is accepted that the level of competence necessary to validly refuse life-prolonging treatment is very high but the BMA hopes that the exploration of treatment options and young people's wishes and values will allow agreement to be reached.' BMA, *Withholding and Withdrawing Life-Prolonging Medical Treatment: Guidance for Decision-Making* (2nd edn, 2001) para 16.2. See also BMA *Medical Ethics Today: Its Practice and Philosophy* (1993).

[207] For commentary on *Re M*, see Huxtable '*Re M (Medical Treatment: Consent)* Time to Remove the 'Flak Jacket'?' (2000) 12(1) Child and Family Law Quarterly 83–88.

[208] Freeman, 'Taking Children's Rights More Seriously' in Alston, Parker and Seymour (eds) *Children, Rights and the Law* (OUP, 1992) 52 at 64–5.

THE IRISH POSITION

[11.119] The issues of adolescent autonomy and the 'mature minor' have not yet been judicially considered in Ireland.[209] As discussed at para **11.84**, the Non-Fatal Offences Against the Person Act 1997 states in s 23(1) that a person of more than 16 years can consent to 'surgical, medical or dental treatment' and that the consent of his parent or guardian is not necessary. There are a number of issues in this provision that require clarification. The Act defines the ability to give consent in terms of a person's age and not on his maturity or competence to give consent.[210] It is unclear whether young people under the age of 16 are therefore permitted to give consent, and whether the Irish courts would adopt a principle of individualised assessment of competence similar to *Gillick*. Whether the courts would distinguish between contraceptive treatment/advice and other medical treatment is open to question given the moral and social connotations involved in this issue in the Irish context. It is not clear whether the ability to give consent also implies the ability to refuse treatment, or whether the Irish courts would follow their English counterparts in rejecting the ability of minors to refuse medical treatment.

[11.120] The impact of the Irish Constitution in this context is also a matter for consideration. The personal rights recognised by the Constitution clearly apply equally to children as to adults. As Walsh J said in *G v An Bord Uchtála*[211] 'The child's natural rights spring primarily from the natural right of every individual to life, to be reared and educated, to liberty, to work, to rest and recreation, to the practice of religion, and to follow his or her conscience.'[212] Therefore a child has a right to privacy and to bodily integrity, which might enable an argument to be made that the child has the right to consent to or refuse medical treatment. Whether this would extend to the provision of contraception would have to be viewed in the light of interpretations of the common good and the rights of the parents or family under Arts 41 and 42 of the Constitution.

[11.121] The question of whether respect for the autonomy of the mature minor would interfere with the rights of the family under the Constitution has not been considered in the medical context in any judgment of the Supreme Court to date. Donnelly refers to the case of *Attorney General v Edge*[213] where the Court appeared to envisage some Constitutional difficulty with a rule of law that permitted a boy of 14 to exercise an absolute discretion over where he lived, although Gavan Duffy J was of the view that if the legislature were to pass a statute recognising the common law age of discretion of 14 and its legal consequences, he did not think that this would be ultra vires.[214] In *Ryan v the Attorney General*,[215] the Supreme Court rejected the plaintiff's claim that the State

---

209 For discussion, see Donnelly, 'Capacity of Minors to Consent to Medical and Contraceptive Treatment' (1995) MLJI 18–21; Donnelly, *Consent: Bridging the Gap Between Doctor and Patient* (Cork University Press, 2002) at 35–36.

210 See Rooney, 'The Medico-Legal Impact of Consent to Treatment of Under-Aged Drug Users' (1998) MLJI 74–75.

211 *G v An Bord Uchtála* [1980] IR 32.

212 *G v An Bord Uchtála* [1980] IR 32 at 69.

213 *Attorney General v Edge* [1943] IR 115.

214 Donnelly, 'Capacity of Minors to Consent to Medical and Contraceptive Treatment' (1995) MLJI 18 at 20.

215 *Ryan v the Attorney General* [1965] IR 294.

policy of water fluoridation constituted an unjustifiable attack on the authority of the family and her right to educate her child. The Court was of the view that there was 'nothing in the Constitution which recognises the right of a parent to refuse to allow the provision of measures designed to secure the health of his child.'[216]

[11.122] In *North Western Health Board v HW and CW,*[217] discussed above,[218] the Supreme Court upheld the High Court decision in favour of allowing the parents of a young child to refuse a screening test designed to discover whether the child could have a number of serious metabolic disorders. Keane CJ, dissenting, said that the Constitution does not oblige the State to allow the wishes of parents, no matter how irrational they appear to be, to prevail over the child's best interests. Keane CJ took the view that in this case the parents had refused to protect the child's Constitutional right to be guarded against unnecessary and avoidable dangers to his health, and that the Court should intervene in the child's best interests. Whether this case will have any impact in the context of conflicts between the 'mature minor' and his parents remains open to question. The case of *McK v The Information Commissioner*[219], discussed above, also demonstrates the strong presumption accorded to parental rights under the Constitution which would undoubtedly prove challenging to a young person's attempt to refuse medical treatment against parental wishes.

[11.123] The Guide to Professional Conduct and Ethics published by the Medical Council in 2009[220] provides in para 43.1 that children and young people should be involved as much as possible in discussions about their health care. It advises doctors that when talking to a child or young person, it is important to give them information in an age-appropriate manner, listen to their views and treat them with respect. It goes on to explain that although patients aged 16 years and over are entitled by law to give their own consent to surgical, medical or dental treatment, this entitlement does not apply to other areas such as organ or tissue donation or participation in medical research. It continues:

43.3 A refusal of treatment by a patient between 16 and 18 years, which is against medical advice and parental wishes, is of uncertain legal validity. In this event, you should consider seeking legal advice before acting on such a decision.

43.4 Where the patient is under the age of 16 years, it is usual that the parents will be asked to give their consent to medical treatment on the patient's behalf.

43.5 In exceptional circumstances, a patient under 16 might seek to make a healthcare decision on their own without the knowledge or consent of their parents. In such cases you should encourage the patient to involve their parents in the decision, bearing in mind your paramount responsibility to act in the patient's best interests.

[11.124] The Law Reform Commission (LRC) published proposals in 2009 entitled *Children and the Law: Medical Treatment* in which it suggests a tiered approach to the issue of consent by minors.[221] The Commission suggests that children over the age of 16

---

[216] *Ryan v the Attorney General* [1965] IR 294 at 350.
[217] *North Western Health Board v HW and CW* (November 8 2001, unreported) SC.
[218] At para **11.46**.
[219] *McK v The Information Commissioner* [2006] IESC 2, discussed at para **11.85**.
[220] Medical Council, Guide to Professional Conduct and Ethics (7th edn, 2009).

years should continue to enjoy the presumption of capacity to give consent to their own treatment as is currently the law in Ireland. Between the ages of 14 and 16 years, the Commission proposes that a legislative provision should be introduced by which it would be lawful for a health-care professional to provide treatment to the young person concerned if the health-care professional is satisfied that the patient understands the nature and consequences of the proposed treatment, it is in keeping with the best interests of the patient and that due regard has been taken of any public health concerns. The Commission does not propose that parents must necessarily be informed of such treatment, although the patient may be encouraged to tell his parents. This functional approach is also proposed for patients between 12 and 14 years, but for children in this age group, the Commission recommends that parents must be informed and that their views must be taken into account. For all children, the Commission recommends that health-care professionals should be required to give children the opportunity to express their views, and to give those views due weight according to the child's age and maturity.

[11.125] Donnelly and Kilkelly say that legislation along the lines proposed by the Law Reform Commission would 'raise the profile of children's participation in healthcare decision-making. While clearly not addressing all of the current obstacles to fuller participation, this approach would represent a clear statement of children's rights in the healthcare context.'[222]

---

[221] LRC CP 59, Dublin 2009.

[222] Donnelly and Kilkelly, 'Child-Friendly Healthcare: Delivering on the Right to Be Heard' (2011) Med Law Review Vol 19, pp 27–54, at 53. There has been discussion in Ireland for a number of years about a referendum on children's rights under the Constitution. The current wording proposed by the government at the time of writing would leave the authority of the State to intervene in a family unchanged. The Office of the Minister for Children states that even under a new Constitutional provision, the State could only intervene in a medical context in exceptional circumstances where there is a physical or moral failure in the family. See http:/ /www.omc.gov.ie/documents/legislation/Briefing-note-190207.doc (accessed 4 June 2011).

Chapter 12

Medical Treatment at the End of Life

INTRODUCTION

[12.01] All of us hope for a peaceful, pain-free death and most of us would prefer our death to take place in the comfort of our own homes surrounded by family and friends.[1] The reality is all too often very different, as the success of medical technology in recent years has arguably led to the increasing medicalisation of the dying process, the inexorable rush to hospitalisation of the dying person, the anonymisation of the environment in which the person spends their last days, and the invasiveness of machines, tubing, noise and indignity. The medical treatment of very sick and elderly patients at the end of life brings with it, in addition to concerns about relief of pain and other distressing symptoms, consideration of issues of dignity and self-determination. As life begins to draw to a close, decisions may have to be made in relation to the continuance or discontinuance of life-prolonging treatment, or whether medical intervention is beneficial in the particular patient's circumstances. Some people unfortunately suffer from hopeless conditions of increasing debilitation, accompanied by periods of excruciating pain which is difficult to manage by way of medication. Their deaths may thus come 'not as the peaceful conclusion to a life, but as a violent and cruel destroyer. What it destroys, along with the life in question, is the possibility for release among those left behind. People say that for a long time afterwards, the memory of a painful death-struggle obliterates the much more precious images that they want to preserve.'[2] In order to avoid such circumstances, some people may seek to have control over their deaths and may seek assistance from family, friends or doctors in doing so.

[12.02] The arguments that arise for discussion in the context of end-of-life decision-making focus on the sanctity of life, autonomy, compassion, the slippery slope, fear of being a burden, the impact on the doctor-patient relationship, devaluing disability, respect for human dignity and recognition that assistance with dying is happening anyway.[3] A further underlying issue is the extent to which patients are actually informed about their diagnosis, their fears and anxieties are listened to and their choices about the end of their lives are respected. In some ways this is about communication skills and training, and in other ways it is reflective of the value placed on respect for autonomy. Patient surveys consistently demonstrate dissatisfaction with the amount of information provided to patients by their doctors. In circumstances where communication is poor or

---

1   See Irish Hospice Foundation, *National Audit of End-of-Life Care in Hospitals,* Available at http://www.hospicefriendlyhospitals.net/ (accessed 5 June 2011).
2   Woodman, *Last Rights: The Struggle Over the Right to Die* (Plenum Trade, 1998) at p 25.
3   McLean, *Assisted Dying: Reflections on the Need for Law Reform* (Routledge-Cavendish, 2007) Ch 2.

even absent,[4] as is unfortunately too often the case where the patient is elderly or very ill[5], the scope for misunderstanding may be exacerbated if care and time is not taken to talk and listen to the patient. Such patients may not have a clear picture of their illness, and may not have worked out for themselves what they want to ask or what way they wish to be treated.[6] If elderly, they may be imbued with the notion that the doctor knows best, having grown up with this tradition of not asking questions[7]. However, such an assumption should not be made in the absence of personal knowledge of the patient, their values, beliefs and cultural and religious backgrounds, which may be of huge importance in this context. It should be presumed that all patients are entitled to be told the truth about their medical condition and treated with respect for their dignity.

> In medical decisions near the end of life, and in particular in decisions about life-sustaining treatment, these values if anything strengthen the general case for patients' rights to make treatment decisions. In the debilitated and severely compromised condition of many patients near the end of life, patients often become more concerned with maintaining their comfort, quality of life and dignity than with extending their lives. Patients sometimes reach a point at which they decide that the best life possible for them with life-sustaining treatment is sufficiently poor that it is worse than no further life at all, and so decide to forgo any further life-sustaining treatment. But there is no objectively correct point for all persons at which further treatment and the life it sustains are no longer a benefit, but are instead a burden and without value of meaning. There are only the decisions of different competent patients about that point.[8]

[12.03] Some argue, somewhat controversially, that in some circumstances we may have a duty to die. Although we like to think of modern medicine as 'all triumph with no dark side', medicine also delivers many of us over to chronic illnesses and 'enables us to survive longer than we can take care of ourselves, longer than we know what to do with ourselves, longer than we even are ourselves.'[9] Hardwig bases his argument in favour of a duty to die on what he calls the 'individualistic fantasy', which is the idea that we may

---

4 See Simpson et al, 'Doctor-Patient Communication: The Toronto Consensus Statement' BMJ 303 (1991) 1385. Also Vincent, 'Information in the ICU: Are We Being Honest with Our Patients?' (1998) 24 Intensive Care Medicine 1251, which reports on a survey of doctors from 16 Western European countries in which only 25% responded that they would give complete information to patients, and 75% accepted the right of patients to refuse treatment. For statistics in the Irish context, see *National Patients Perception of the Quality of Healthcare Survey 2002,* available at www.isqh.ie (accessed 11 July 2011) discussed by Donnelly, *Consent: Bridging the Gap Between Doctor and Patient* (Cork University Press, 2002).

5 See Ajaj, Singh and Abdullah, 'Should Elderly Patients Be Told They Have Cancer?' (2001) 323 BMJ 1160.

6 See generally Wilkes, 'Ethics in Terminal Care' in Dunstan and Shinebourne (eds) *Doctors' Decisions, Ethical Conflicts in Medical Practice* (OUP, 1989) p 197–204.

7 However, a survey carried out by Ajaj, Singh and Abdullah shows that 88 per cent of elderly patients living in the community would wish to know the nature of their illness, even if it was cancer. Ajaj, Singh and Abdullah, 'Should Elderly Patients Be Told They Have Cancer?' (2001) 323 BMJ 1160.

8 Brock, 'Medical Decisions at the End of Life' in Kuhse and Singer *A Companion to Bioethics*, (Blackwell Publishing, 1998) 231, p 232–233.

9 Hardwig, 'Is There a Duty to Die?' (1997) *The Hastings Center Report*, Vol 27 pp 34–42 at 35.

like to think that our lives are separate and unconnected and that the way each of us chooses to live is nobody else's business. However, this is 'morally obtuse', as 'we are not a race of hermits'. Most of us are part of a circle of family and friends bound together by legal relationships, obligations, shared living and working spaces, intertwined finances, common projects and shared histories. The fact of deeply interwoven lives 'debars us from making exclusively self-regarding decisions, as the decisions of one member of a family may dramatically affect the lives of all the rest.' Hardwig argues that the lives of our loved ones can be seriously compromised by caring for us, with the burden of providing care 24 hours a day, 7 days a week, sometimes becoming overwhelming. The health, finances, social life and friendships of our loved ones can be destroyed in the process. Hardwig thus describes how a duty to die may develop in such circumstances in order to protect our loved ones from such harm. He does acknowledge that caring for a sick and dying relative may also bring rewards in bringing a family closer, but says that we should not assume that this will be the case. He argues 'if I love my family, I will want to protect them and their lives. I will want not to make choices that compromise their futures…' He also argues that we are so busy trying to postpone death that we do not seek to find meaning in it, with the result that:

> We fear death too much. Our fear of death has led to a massive assault on it. We still crave after virtually any life-prolonging technology that we might conceivably be able to produce. We still too often feel morally impelled to prolong life – virtually any form of life – as long as possible. As if the best death is the one that can be put off longest.[10]

[12.04] Discussions about end of life care generally arise in the context of incurable disease or terminal illness. Terminal illness may be defined as any chronic illness associated with a high chance of dying, and may be seen as beginning when three conditions are satisfied, namely, that diagnosis of the illness has been made and other remedial conditions eliminated, that the advent of death is certain and not too far off and that medical care has turned from the curative to the palliative.[11] Therefore, in relation to the terminally ill patient, death is often not an idea that is unknown to them. If their illness has been protracted, death may have been expected for a period of time. The various component processes involved in dying must be understood as a whole so as to give effect to all the aspects of the patient's quality of life. These aspects include the physical pain involved, the patient's emotional reaction and psychological coping mechanisms, the social impact of the patient's death and the patient's spiritual and intellectual strength. The quality of life of the patient is therefore a measure of the difference between what the patient hoped for his life, and what he is now likely to be able to achieve.[12]

[12.05] One of the primary difficulties in treating terminal illness is the level of uncertainty involved. The doctor may not know whether a particular treatment is going to be effective or whether the patient will respond, when exactly death will occur or

---

[10] Hardwig, 'Is There a Duty to Die?' (1997) *The Hastings Center Report*, Vol 27 pp 34–42 at 35 at 40.

[11] Calman, 'Ethical Implications of Terminal Care' in Freeman (ed) *Medicine, Ethics and Law* (Stevens and Sons, 1988) 103–119, p 104.

[12] Calman, 'Ethical Implications of Terminal Care' in Freeman (ed) *Medicine, Ethics and Law* (Stevens and Sons, 1988) 103–119, p 105.

whether the patient would like to talk about it. Patients and their families may have misconceptions about the facts underlying the illness and may have false expectations of recovery. The fundamental question that patients will usually ask is what length of time they have left, a question that is not always possible to answer with any degree of certainty. The doctor may be reluctant to give bad news if it is felt that this will cause a further setback to the patient, and may in fact have been asked by the relatives not to inform the patient of the bleak prognosis. In such cases, the challenge for the doctor is how to balance the patient's autonomy with beneficence. A paternalistic approach would view compassion and beneficence as taking priority over autonomy in these circumstances and would withhold the information from the patient unless directly asked. This may put other medical professionals, such as the nursing team, in a compromising position where they are complicit in the non-disclosure and are expected to keep up pretences with the patient.[13] A position which prioritises respect for the patient's right to make his own decisions would view truth-telling as more in keeping with the patient's dignity and integrity. This dilemma is something that ought to be addressed if possible at an earlier stage of treatment between the patient and those involved in the patient's care, and an agreement reached as to how to deal with problems that might be expected to arise in this regard.

FUTILE OR NON-PRODUCTIVE MEDICAL TREATMENT

[12.06] Concern has been growing over the last number of years regarding the demographic changes to be expected in Ireland in coming decades. People are living longer, fertility is decreasing and the gap between active life expectancy and death is widening. In other words, although people are living longer, they are increasingly dependant on others in the last years of life and are now using more health-care resources in the last year or months of life. This has led to the difficult, and for some people offensive, question of whether scarce resources are being 'wasted' on the dying, resources that could be spent more productively on other patients.[14] Most people would agree that medical futility should not be used as a method of resource allocation, which would be both ageist and discriminatory. However, it must be acknowledged that in reality a decision not to treat one patient usually frees up resources to treat another. Although decisions on resource allocation may be most appropriately decided on the basis of therapeutic benefit, the danger of arbitrary decision-making is high. 'In view of the practical limitations on the availability of medical resources, some consideration of the appropriate allocation of scarce resources and of cost-effectiveness inevitably must come into the decision-making'.[15]

[12.07] There is also the concern that old and sick patients are being over-treated to comply with the doctor's own compulsion to do something – even half-hearted and ineffective measures that make no medical or ethical sense at all.[16] Doctors, nurses and

---

[13]   Calman, 'Ethical Implications of Terminal Care' in Freeman (ed) *Medicine, Ethics and Law* (Stevens and Sons, 1988) 103–119, p 110.

[14]   Scitovsky and Capron, 'Medical Care at the End of Life: The Interaction of Economics and Ethics' Ann. Rev Public Health (1986) 7:59–75.

[15]   Otlowski, *Voluntary Euthanasia and the Common Law* (OUP, 1997) at 34.

[16]   Hilfiker, 'Allowing the Debilitated to Die: Facing Our Ethical Choices' (1983) New Engl J Med 398:716–19.

other health professionals are trained to protect and preserve life and therefore there is an inevitable medical inclination to prolong life as far as possible. Sometimes, however, a patient may question whether that obligation is right in his particular set of circumstances, in which case the patient may refuse further treatment, request the withdrawal of treatment or seek active assistance in ending his own life. In other situations the health professional may question whether it is right to prolong life in circumstances where treatment may simply delay death for a period of time with no appreciable benefit to the patient. This raises issues of futility or non-beneficial treatment which either has no medical effect or can be seen as being against the patient's best interests. In the last few decades the role of the doctor has evolved in many respects from being a life saver to being a quality of life provider – the goal is no longer solely the prolongation of life but also the achievement of a particular standard or quality of life. With this change in emphasis comes the question of futility. 'Whilst there is widespread agreement that there are limits on the duty of doctors to treat terminally ill patients, the difficulty lies in determining the precise *scope* of that duty and at what point the doctor's duty ceases.'[17] It is no longer a question of whether the patient's life can be saved. It is also now a question of what kind of life the patient will have if it is possible to save him. Difficult questions arise – is there an objective standard against which it can be measured? What is an unacceptable quality of life? Is quantity of life always more important than its quality?

[12.08] The notion of 'medical futility' first appeared in the 1980s and its function was to put a limit to the increasing requests for treatment that patients felt entitled to make to doctors. 'After the 1960s and the 1970s, the principle of patient autonomy was interpreted in a more and more radical way. Besides feeling that they had the right to *refuse* an unwanted medical intervention, with increasing frequency patients (or their family or representatives) were *demanding* specific treatments that doctors had not offered.'[18] There are many definitions of medical futility[19], some of which focus on whether the treatment accomplishes its objectives, some of which examine survival rates and others that look at the quality of benefit to be achieved by the treatment.[20] Some argue that the absence of any universally agreed definition is unexceptional and necessary.[21] If one judges the technique or treatment in terms of its success, this too will be subjective. For some doctors a 10 per cent success rate means the treatment is not futile, while for others it is. Success is not something that can be measured accurately, reliably or consistently and does not have the 'ring of clarity' often associated with decisions in this context.[22] If, on the other hand, one judges futility in terms of quality

---

[17]   Otlowski, *Voluntary Euthanasia and the Common Law* (OUP, 1997) at 34.

[18]   Moratti, 'The Development of "Medical Futility": Towards a Procedural Approach Based on the Role of the Medical Profession' (2009) J Med Ethics 35: 369–372 at 369.

[19]   See Lamb, *Therapy Abatement, Autonomy and Futility: Ethical Decisions at the Edge of Life* (Ashgate Publishing, 1995), Chapter 5.

[20]   Jecker and Pearlman, 'Medical Futility: Who Decides?' (1992) 152 Arch Intern Med 1140; Schneiderman and Jecker, 'Futility in Practice' (1993) 153 Arch Intern Med 437; Cranford and Gostin, 'Futility: A Concept in Search of a Definition' (1992) 20 Law, Med, & Health Care 307.

[21]   Tomlinson and Czlonka, 'Futility and Hospital Care' (1995) Hastings Center Report 31.

[22]   Saunders, 'Medical Futility: CPR' in Morgan and Lee (eds) *Death Rites: Law and Ethics at the End of Life* (Routledge, 1994) p 85.

rather than quantity of life to be obtained as a result of the treatment, this incorporates the patient's own wishes and ambitions in an assessment of whether the treatment would be worthwhile in accomplishing those goals. The use of the term 'futility' may itself be criticised as an emotive term depicting hopelessness, when judgments on such issues ought to be made on clearly rational grounds.[23] The term 'non-productive treatment' is sometimes used as an alternative.

[12.09] The notion of medical futility has been the object of strong criticism since its first appearance. Some saw it as an attempt to reintroduce medical paternalism by allowing doctors to justify a unilateral decision to withhold or withdraw treatment. Thus, it was argued that doctors should not be given the power to impose on their patients their own personal values under the guise of medical expertise. In the 1990s the debate shifted to the issue of whether futility could be measured according to a quantitative and qualitative parameter. Schneiderman and others argued that an intervention could be defined as quantitatively futile if doctors concluded through personal experience, experiences shared with colleagues or consideration of reported empiric data that in the last 100 cases a certain intervention was 'useless',[24] meaning it failed to benefit the person, even if it contributed to the functioning of the organism. A 'qualitatively futile' intervention was described as 'any treatment that merely preserves permanent unconsciousness or that fails to end total dependence on intensive medical care.' Both definitions were criticised on the grounds that the notion of quantitative futility involves value judgment, as it presupposes a certain definition of what a 'person' is. Also the notion of 'qualitative futility' refers only to conditions associated with overwhelming suffering for a predictably short time and excludes patients whose conditions require frequent hospitalisation, or patients who have severe disabilities.[25]

[12.10] Since the mid-1990s, it seems to be accepted that no consensus may be reached on a definition of futile treatment and that a better approach would be to seek to reach consensus about the way in which the decision should be made by those most closely involved. The American Medical Association took the view that such a consensus-driven process should aim to promote communication, minimise conflicts between the various actors (potentially) involved and avoid (where possible) polarisation of conflict and mobilisation of formal legal institutions.[26]

[12.11] In Irish hospitals 'withdrawal of invasive interventions in hopeless cases is not uncommon in intensive care.'[27] A study in 2006 indicates that 69 per cent of deaths in ICU in Ireland occur in association with the limitation of futile life-sustaining treatments.[28] This usually involves withholding CPR (cardio pulmonary resuscitation)

23 Gillon, 'Futility – Too Ambiguous and Pejorative a Term?' (1997) 23 J Med Ethics 339.
24 Schneiderman et al 'Medical Futility: Its Meaning and Ethical Implications' (1990) Ann Intern Med 112: 949.
25 See response to criticisms by Schneiderman et al, 'Medical Futility: Response to Critiques' (1996) Ann Intern Med 125: 669.
26 Report of the Council on Ethical and Judicial Affairs of the American Medical Association, *Medical Futility in End-of-Life Care* (1999) JAMA 281:937–41.
27 Phelan and Kinirons, 'Withdrawal of Futile Interventions in Intensive Care – An Everyday Ethical/Critical Care Issue' (1996) MLJI 49.
28 Collins, Phelan and Carton, 'End of Life in ICU – Care of the Dying or "Pulling the Plug"?' (2006) Irish Medical Journal Vol 99 No 4, p 112.

and stopping inotropic and dialysis treatment. Extubation or stopping ventilation (colloquially known as 'pulling the plug') is less common and usually occurs after other life-sustaining treatments have already been limited.

[12.12] A distinction is sometimes made in discussions about life-prolonging treatment between ordinary and extraordinary treatment, the former being treatment that the patient is obliged or assumed to accept, the latter being a matter of choice for the patient. There are many different ways in which the distinction can be drawn. For example, one could distinguish on grounds of the level of invasiveness involved, the degree to which the treatment is considered common practice, the extent to which the treatment is technology-based, the costs of the treatment and so on. However, these various methods of distinction are not helpful in explaining why some treatments are obligatory and others optional. 'What seems morally important and determines whether any treatment should be employed in particular circumstances with a particular patient is not whether the treatment employs high technology or is simple, but whether the patient judges it to be on balance beneficial.'[29] The distinction between ordinary and extraordinary or heroic measures in Ireland and elsewhere probably emanates from the theology of the Roman Catholic Church where extraordinary treatment is regarded as treatment which is excessively burdensome or without benefit for the patient.[30] It was a distinction mentioned, though not relied upon, in *Re a Ward of Court*, discussed in detail below.[31] It is possible to classify different treatments, such as nutrition and hydration, as always either ordinary or extraordinary, and so as always obligatory or optional. However, this does not take into account the particular patient's condition and wishes and has been increasingly regarded as causing confusion in the debate on end-of-life treatment decisions.[32] It has been argued that "[t]he language of ordinary and extraordinary means of treatment should be discarded because of its imprecision and its tendency to support strong paternalism."[33]

[12.13] There have been a number of judicial decisions in the United States and Canada dealing with futile treatment. The first cases dealt with the right of patients to refuse treatment being offered by a physician on grounds that it was futile. *In re Quinlan* the New Jersey Supreme Court stated in relation to Karen Ann Quinlan's wishes concerning life-sustaining treatment: 'She was said to have firmly evinced her wish, in like circumstances, not to have her life prolonged by the otherwise futile use of extraordinary means.'[34] Other cases have followed suit in emphasising the futility of the life-sustaining treatment as one of the reasons for ordering the withholding or withdrawal of

---

[29] Brock, 'Medical Decisions at the End of Life' in Kuhse and Singer *A Companion to Bioethics*, (Blackwell Publishing, 1998) 231 at 235.

[30] Kelly, 'The Duty to Preserve Life' (1951) Theological Studies 12 550. See Moratti, 'Italy: The Position of the Roman Catholic Church' in Griffiths J et al (eds) *Euthanasia and Law in Europe* (Hart Publishing Company, 2008) 397.

[31] At para. **12.67**.

[32] Kearon argues that whether a medical treatment is ordinary or extraordinary is a judgment that can only be made by the patient or from his perspective. '*Re a Ward of Court:* Ethical Comment' (1995) MLJI 58.

[33] Childress, *Who Should Decide? Paternalism in Healthcare* (OUP, 1982) at p 166.

[34] *In re Quinlan* 70 NJ 10, 355 A 2d 647 (1976) 21.

treatment.[35] The decisions of the courts were principally based on the right to self-determination, but the fact that the treatments in question were considered futile made such decisions easier to make.

[12.14] In the Irish context, there have not been many opportunities for the courts to consider the issue of medical futility.[36] However, in *Re a Ward of Court*[37] the Supreme Court had to consider the question of whether life support, in the form of nutrition and medical treatment, could be withdrawn from a woman in a near persistent vegetative state, at the request of her family. The institution at which the woman was housed was opposed to the withdrawal of treatment and nutrition on ethical grounds. It was accepted that the Court could not make an order which would require a medical institution to contravene its philosophy and code of ethics. The majority held that the right to life under the Constitution necessarily implies the right to let nature take its course and to die a natural and dignified death and, unless the individual chooses otherwise, not to have life artificially maintained by the provision of nourishment which has no curative effect and merely prolongs life. The Constitution provides a right to self-determination in the rights to privacy and bodily integrity, and as part of that right a competent adult has the right to forego or discontinue life-saving medical treatment.

[12.15] Hamilton CJ said: 'There is no doubt but that the ward, if she were mentally competent, had the right, if she so wished, to forego such treatment or at any time, to direct that it be withdrawn, even though such withdrawal would result in her death.' He regarded the provision of nutrition in this case, by way of a surgical tube implanted in the woman's stomach, as an abnormal means of nourishment which constituted an interference with the integrity of her body. He agreed with an opinion expressed by Costello P, writing extra-judicially, in which he said that there were powerful arguments to support the view that the dignity and autonomy of the human person oblige the State to recognise that decisions relating to life and death are ones which competent adults should be free to make without undue interference or restraint by the State.[38] Although there might be circumstances in which the State might have a valid interest in restricting such decisions, such as in the case of contagious diseases, 'in the case of the terminally ill, it is very difficult to see what circumstances would justify the interference with a decision by a competent adult of the right to forego or discontinue life saving treatment'.

[12.16] Although the patient in this case did not have decision-making capacity herself, O'Flaherty J also clearly took the view that a person with decision-making capacity had

---

[35]   *In re Dinnerstein* 6 Mass App 466, 380 NE 2d 134 (Ct App 1978); *Barber v Superior Court* 147 Cal App 3d 1006, 195 Cal Rptr 484 (Ct App 1983); *Bartling v Glendale Adventist Medical Center* 184 Cal App 3d 961, 229 Cal Rptr 360 (Ct App 1986); *In re Westchester County Medical Center* 72 NY 2d 517, 531 N.E. 2d 607 (1988); *Westhart v Mule* 213 Ca App 3d 542, 261 Cal Rptr 640 (Ct App 1989); *In re Greenspan* 137 Ill 2d 1, 558 NE 2d 1194 (1989); *In re Lawrence* 579 NE 2d 32 (Ind. 1991).

[36]   See discussion in Charleton and Bolger, 'The Law at Life's End' (1995) Gazette 29. For discussion of the practical points and medical specialist's perspective, see Phelan and Kinirons, 'Withdrawal of Futile Interventions in Intensive Care – An Everyday Ethical/ Critical Care Issue' (1996) MLJI 49–51.

[37]   *Re a Ward of Court* [1996] 2 IR 79.

[38]   Costello, 'The Terminally Ill – The Law's Concerns' (1986) 21 Ir Jurist 35.

the right to refuse medical treatment even if it leads to death, calling it 'an absolute right' and one which he said was not in dispute in this case. He grounded the right in common law as well as the Constitutional rights of bodily integrity and privacy. Blayney J said 'where a person who is *compos mentis* has a condition which, in the absence of medical intervention, will lead to death, such a person has a right in law to refuse such intervention.' Denham J took the same view, saying that medical treatment given without consent may be a trespass, a battery and a breach of Constitutional rights. She continued:

> The consent which is given by an adult of full capacity is a matter of choice. It is not necessarily a decision based on medical considerations. Thus, medical treatment may be refused for other than medical reasons. Such reasons may not be viewed as good medical reasons, or reasons most citizens would regard as rational, but the person of full age and capacity may make the decision for their own reasons.

[12.17] This case clearly states that a competent adult is entitled to refuse medical treatment for whatever reasons, even though the consequences may be death. This has been further affirmed in *Fitzpatrick and Another v K and Another*[39] discussed in Chapter 9.[40] In relation to the obligation to provide treatment, the Medical Council advises doctors in its most recent Guide to Professional Conduct and Ethics, in 2009, that:

> There is no obligation on you to start or continue a treatment, or artificial nutrition and hydration, that is futile or disproportionately burdensome, even if such treatment may prolong life. You should carefully consider when to start and when to stop attempts to prolong life, while ensuring that patients receive appropriate pain management and relief from distress.[41]

ADVANCE DIRECTIVES

[12.18] There has been discussion in recent years in Ireland and elsewhere about the means by which people can indicate their wishes in relation to medical treatment in advance of illness or incapacity. Such indications of wishes are often referred to as 'advance directives', which may be oral or written statements. They are usually referred to as 'living wills' where they are expressed in writing. The word 'directive' is often criticised, as it implies that the patient is requiring the doctor to treat the patient in a particular way, whereas the ideal situation is that patients and doctors would be partners in discussing the patient's situation and values with a view to coming to an agreement on end-of-life care that both patient and doctor are comfortable with. Acknowledging the validity of these objections and the modern preference for the use of terms such as 'anticipatory decisions' or 'advance healthcare plans', the traditional terminology in legal and ethical discourse still refers to advance directives and for this reason this term is used here.

---

[39] *Fitzpatrick and Another v K and Another* [2008] IEHC 104.
[40] See para **9.19**.
[41] Medical Council, *Guide to Professional Conduct and Ethics* (7th edn, 2009), para 22.2. Available at http://www.medicalcouncil.ie/ (accessed 5 June 2011).

[12.19] As discussed in Chapter 9,[42] where a patient refuses treatment, the courts have generally been supportive of the right to self-determination. However, the facts of such cases often involve contemporaneous as opposed to anticipatory decisions. For example, in *McKay v Bergstadt*[43] a 31-year-old quadriplegic man wanted his life support machine to be turned off. He had been taken care of by his father and had some limited capacities himself, but his father was now dying and he did not want to live without his father to take care of him, or to be looked after by strangers. Although he died naturally before the case was heard, the Court agreed to give a ruling on the issue. The Court looked at the two opposing sets of interests here, the patient's right to self-determination and the State's interest in preserving life, preventing suicide and protecting the integrity of the medical profession. The Court concluded that while the State's interest was fundamental and compelling, it was not an absolute interest and may decrease as the individual's quality of life decreases. The Court concluded that quality of life and the right of self-determination took precedence over the State's interest in such cases.[44]

[12.20] By comparison with a contemporaneous consent or refusal of treatment, an advance directive is a statement made in advance of an illness about the type and extent of treatment one would want, on the assumption that one may be incapable of participating in decision-making about treatment when the need arises.[45] Advance directives are regarded as a means of limiting life-prolonging treatment, rather than as a means by which to request the provision of all possible treatments, as it is generally acknowledged that it would not be ethically defensible to require a doctor to provide treatment which may not be beneficial to the patient. For this reason, although an advance request may be made by a patient, it is not regarded as legally binding.[46]

[12.21] Directives are usually in written form and may either set out specific treatments that are refused in advance, or nominate a person – a health-care surrogate decision-maker – to make decisions on behalf of the author of the directive. The latter allows more flexibility, as the specific circumstances and treatments are not restricted to what has been written in the directive. However, it is also important to recognise that the emotional burden on surrogate decision-makers related to their role in determining a loved one's care can last for months and even years after the treatment choice. It has been noted that the circumstances of decision-making have an impact on how deeply surrogates are affected by stress and guilt in relation to their decision-making, with a

---

[42] See para **9.112**.

[43] *McKay v Bergstadt* (1990) 801 P 2d 617 (Nevada S Ct).

[44] See Canadian decisions *Malette v Shulman* [1990] 72 OR (2d) 417 (CA) in which the Court said that a doctor is obliged to observe the previously stated wishes of a Jehovah's Witness patient to refuse a blood transfusion; and *Nancy B v Hotel Dieu de Quebec* [1992] 86 DLR (4th) 385 where a young woman on a ventilator, suffering from Guillan Barre syndrome, succeeded in her wish to have the machine switched off in order to end her life. The Court in the latter case emphasised that no criminal liability would attach to the doctor who acceded to her request, as death would occur as a result of nature taking its course.

[45] Capron, 'Advance Directives' in Kuhse and Singer, *A Companion to Bioethics*, (Blackwell, 1998) 261–271.

[46] *R (Burke) v GMC* [2005] EWCA Civ 1003 at [31–32].

substantial reduction in situations where the patient has an advance directive that specifies the patient's wishes.[47]

[12.22] Advance directives began as a means of addressing the difficult impasse that may occur when a decision has to be made as to whether to continue with treatment of someone who is unable to communicate his own views. Family members, doctors and nurses often find it extremely difficult to make such decisions where the consequence will be the patient's death. Luis Kutner, a US lawyer involved in a right-to-die organisation, drafted what he termed a 'living will' in 1967 to allow a person to give instructions for medical care at the end of life.[48] It was viewed as having three purposes: first, it relieved the patient's family of the burden of decision-making; second, it enabled the incompetent patient to participate in decision-making despite loss of communicative capacity; and third, it helped to raise public and professional awareness that life-prolonging treatment isn't necessarily always a good thing. However, there are concerns about giving effect to advance directives that, for instance, the person may unwittingly be depriving himself of beneficial advances in medical science that take place after the living will was drafted, and that he may not fully understand the nature of the intervention in question. Others argue from a more philosophical perspective that the person in persistent vegetative state (PVS) is not the same person that made the advance directive and, therefore, that treatment decisions should be made in the best interests of the present patient.[49] Maclean uses Parfit's view of personal identity to explain this as follows:

> If advance directives are predicated on the basis of personal autonomy then…their authority only applies to an individual if he or she is the same moral entity that created the directive. This means that for an advance directive to have the necessary moral force there must be a sufficiently close relationship of psychological connectedness and continuity between the past and present selves…Because the necessary relationships are a matter of degree, it requires a normative judgment to determine whether the past and present selves are identical persons.[50]

[12.23] He goes on to use Parfit's theory to argue that when a person undergoes a catastrophic change that severs the necessary psychological continuity which would otherwise have existed, such as occurs with dementia, head injuries and strokes for example, this might mean that there are some human beings who lack a sufficient connection to their previous self for an advance directive to be morally or legally binding. He acknowledges the problems that the application of such a theory would encounter and suggests that 'although the backward-looking psychological connections may be severed, the asymmetrical prospective relationship, along with the connections maintained by the relationships that the human being exists within, justify the former

47 Wendler and Rid, 'Systematic Review: The Effect on Surrogates of Making Treatment Decisions for Others' (2011) Annals of Internal Medicine, Vol 154, no 5, pp 336–346.

48 Capron, 'Advance Directives' in Kuhse and Singer, *A Companion to Bioethics*, (Blackwell, 1998) p 262.

49 See, for example, Bernat, 'The Living Will: Does an Advance Refusal of Treatment Made with Capacity Always Survive Any Supervening Incapacity?' (1999) Med Law I Vol 4 1–21.

50 Maclean, 'Advance Directives, Future Selves and Decision-Making' (Autumn 2006) Medical Law Review 14, pp 291–320 at 298, quoting Parfit, 'Personal Identity' (1971) 80 The Philosophical Review 3.

competent self having decisional authority.' This authority should not be absolute but should be subject to the limitation that other interested parties may challenge the former self's advance decision.[51]

[12.24] Strict application of agency law, under which one person (the principal) appoints another (the agent) to carry out instructions on his behalf, would generally negate the operation of the living will, as the agency is deemed to be terminated when the principal becomes incompetent. This would mean that 'applied to the medical context, traditional agency law renders instructions in a living will non-binding at the very moment when they are intended to go into effect.'[52] Doctors seeking to justify overriding such instructions frequently used the non-binding nature of advance directives in their reasoning. Legislation began to be introduced following the decision of the New Jersey Supreme Court in *Re Quinlan*,[53] discussed below, although there was no advance directive in that case. The plight of Karen Quinlan and her family reinforced in the public perception the horrific scenario of being maintained by machines indefinitely in a hospital room with doctors controlling the time and means of death. Advance directives are embodied in federal policy by the Patient Self-Determination Act 1990 (PSDA) which requires medical institutions to give patients information about their rights, which include being given written notice upon admission to the health-care facility of their decision-making rights, and policies regarding advance health-care directives in their state and in the institution to which they have been admitted. It also includes the right to have their health-care decisions facilitated, the right to accept or refuse medical treatment and the right to make an advance health-care directive. Facilities must inquire as to the whether the patient already has an advance health-care directive, and make note of this in their medical records.

[12.25] As a result of the PSDA, almost all states in the US provide for living wills, and most states have two statutes, one establishing a living will type directive, the other establishing a proxy or durable power of attorney for health care. Issues have arisen in relation to the precision with which the wording of the directive must be drawn so as to specifically deal with the situation that later arises, and the definition of terms often used such as 'terminal illness' or 'heroic measures'. It has been suggested that a checklist approach would be preferable, which would indicate in much more detail exactly what the patient would or would not want to be done to him. Despite the legislative provisions, in practice it appears that in the United States less than one third of the population have advance directives, many of them don't give them to their doctors and studies indicate that surrogate decision-makers often find it difficult to interpret the wishes of the patient. What's more, 25 per cent of patients receive care inconsistent with their living wills, 29 per cent of patients change their minds about life-sustaining treatment over time and 64 per cent of dying patients' living wills do not cover the clinical realities they face.[54] Rich says that one of the reasons why so few people execute

---

51 Maclean, 'Advance Directives, Future Selves and Decision-Making' (Autumn 2006) Medical Law Review 14, pp 291–320 at 320.

52 Capron, 'Advance Directives' in Kuhse and Singer, *A Companion to Bioethics*, (Blackwell, 1998) p 263.

53 *Re Quinlan* 355 A 2d 647, 97 ALR 3d 205 (S Ct of New Jersey).

54 Fagerlin and Shneider, 'Enough: The Failure of the Living Will' (2004) 34(2) Hastings Center Report, 30–42.

advance directives is due to reluctance to contemplate the prospect of life-threatening illness.

> In addition, people often make two false assumptions. First, they assume that advance directives are unnecessary because those closest to them will know intuitively what should be done in the unlikely event that life-threatening illness should strike. Second, they assume that those persons will be empowered to act as surrogates. Regrettably, nothing could be further from the truth, at least when the action is withdrawing life support and there is a lack of consensus among family members.[55]

[12.26] Outside of the US, legislation on advance directives has been enacted in a number of European jurisdictions, including Austria, the Netherlands, Finland, Denmark and Germany. The European Convention on Human Rights and Biomedicine in 1997 also makes reference to advance directives under art 9, which states that 'the previously expressed wishes relating to a medical intervention by a patient who is not, at the time of the intervention, in a state to express his or her wishes shall be taken into account'. Ireland has not signed this Convention.

[12.27] The English Mental Capacity Act 2005 requires that where an advance directive encompasses a refusal of life-sustaining treatment, it requires a level of formality in order to be considered valid. It must explicitly state that it applies where life is at risk, it must be in writing and executed in the presence of an independent witness.[56] These procedural formalities provide an opportunity to check the patient's capacity and voluntariness and although some argue that such formalities are unduly onerous, they may be seen as a 'reasonable compromise between facilitating the uptake of advance directives and protecting vulnerable patients'.[57] Although there is evidence from the United States that those making advance directives are poorly informed[58], the English legislation only recommends that advance directives are made with medical advice, it does not require it. Maclean explains that this was because the English government took the view that to make this a requirement would be inappropriate and unduly intrusive. However, 'while this approach impacts less on the present person's current autonomy, it makes that person's autonomous choice far more vulnerable at a point when he or she will be incompetent and unable to do anything about it.'[59] Thus, if an individual has not received good medical advice prior to drafting their directive, they may not be able to predict their future medical state and the possible options open to them. This makes their choice inherently vulnerable to being overridden by the court on the grounds that their ignorance meant the person did not fully appreciate the precise circumstances that have now arisen and therefore the directive is not applicable.

---

55 Rich, 'The Ethics of Surrogate Decision Making' (2002) West J Med 176:127–129.
56 Mental Capacity Act 2005, s 25 (5), (6).
57 Maclean, 'Advance Directives and the Rocky Waters of Anticipatory Decision-Making' (Spring 2008) Med Law Review 16, pp 1–22 at 11.
58 Dresser, 'Precommitment: A Misguided Strategy for Securing Death with Dignity' (2003) 81 Texas Law Review 1823, quoted by Maclean, 'Advance Directives and the Rocky Waters of Anticipatory Decision-Making' (Spring 2008) Med Law Review 16, pp 1–22 at 15.
59 Maclean, 'Advance Directives and the Rocky Waters of Anticipatory Decision-Making' (Spring 2008) Med Law Review 16, pp 1–22 at 15.

[12.28] One of the main practical difficulties with advance directives is ensuring that they anticipate the circumstances that may arise in the future. A directive that is drafted in very general terms is unlikely to be upheld if it is considered to lack the degree of specificity deemed necessary by the courts. Section 24 of the English Mental Capacity Act 2005 provides that an advance decision must relate to a 'specified treatment' although this may be phrased in lay language rather than medical terminology. It is unclear how this term will be interpreted, so for example, would it be sufficiently clear for a patient to refuse 'any life-saving treatment'? Maclean says that 'although the restriction will provide a safeguard against the inadvertent exclusion of treatments not anticipated by the decision-maker, it also provides the courts with another means to invalidate decisions with which they are uncomfortable.'[60]

[12.29] In relation to the length of time which may have elapsed between the making of the directive and the circumstances which have now arisen, there is nothing in the case law which indicates that the expiry of a particular length of time should affect its validity. However, in general, the older the directive, the closer the scrutiny it will receive by a court which is trying to ascertain whether it continues to reflect the current wishes of the patient. The Code of Practice for the Mental Capacity Act suggests that anyone who has made an advance directive is advised to regularly review and update it as necessary.[61] Although the setting of a time limit for the validity of an advance directive has sometimes been recommended,[62] it has been seen as preferable to leave the question of applicability of the directive to the relevant health-care professional rather than to set an arbitrary time limit.[63] The professional is protected from liability by s 26 of the Act if he treats a patient in circumstances when he is not satisfied that a valid and applicable advance directive exists. The Act thus gives considerable discretion to the doctor in charge of the patient's care, as his satisfaction as to the validity of the directive is not required to be reasonable. Maclean concludes that the Act provides symbolic support for individual autonomy while providing sufficient scope for interpretation to allow many advance directives to be judged invalid or inapplicable when the likely consequences are contrary to the health-care professional's or judge's view of an appropriate outcome.

[12.30] In the Irish context, the Powers of Attorney Act 1996 provides that a person may appoint another as decision-maker in case of the donor's subsequent mental incapacity. Prior to this, the affairs of a person who lost mental capacity were managed by the wardship procedure,[64] which still applies in the absence of an enduring power of

---

60   Maclean, 'Advance Directives and the Rocky Waters of Anticipatory Decision-Making' (Spring 2008) Med Law Review 16, pp 1–22 at 17.

61   Code of Practice for the Mental Capacity Act 2005, para 9.29.

62   UK Joint Committee on Human Rights. *Fourth Report of 2004* (2005), para 4.22.

63   Maclean, 'Advance Directives and the Rocky Waters of Anticipatory Decision-Making' (Spring 2008) Med Law Review 16, pp 1–22 at 19.

64   This comes from the Lunacy Regulations (Ireland) Act 1871, whereby an adult who has been determined to be an 'idiot, lunatic, or of unsound mind, and incapable of managing himself or his affairs' may be made a ward of court. 'The primary difficulty with the wardship facility is that the procedure is complex, expensive and cumbersome. This means that wardship applications are really only made in practice where the management of property is involved. As a result, most legally incompetent adults have no legally-recognised representative to act on their behalf.' Donnelly, *Consent: Bridging the Gap Between Doctor and Patient* (Cork University Press, 2002).

attorney. Under this procedure the committee of the ward (usually one person) is given limited powers to act in relation to the ward's affairs and may give consent to medical treatment in some instances. However, jurisdiction is given to the High Court to consent to any serious health-care intervention under the ancient *parens patriae* jurisdiction of the Lord Chancellor over 'lunatics and idiots', which obliges the court to act in the best interests of the individual involved. This power, although lost in the UK through legislation, was continued in Ireland.[65] This has been discussed in more detail in Chapter 9.[66]

[12.31] The Powers of Attorney Act 1996 makes provision in relation to the form and registration of an enduring power of attorney and the protection of those relying on it. The attorney is empowered to make personal care decisions on behalf of the donor, including decisions on (a) where the donor should live, (b) with whom the donor should live, (c) whom the donor should see and not see, (d) what training or rehabilitation the donor should get, (e) the donor's diet and dress, (f) inspection of the donor's personal papers, (g) housing, social welfare and other benefits for the donor. There is no provision empowering the attorney to make health-care decisions for the donor.

[12.32] In terms of the likelihood of the advance directive or living will being legally valid in Ireland,[67] it can be surmised from judicial statements that such a decision by a patient would be recognised as legally valid if the patient was competent and informed when the directive was made, and that it was clear and specific to the patient's current situation. As long as the directive was lawful, the courts would uphold its validity. This is consistent with the clear statements of the courts which point to a right to refuse contemporaneous medical treatment. Although in the case of advance directives the choice or refusal of medical treatment is made in anticipation of incapacitating illness rather than contemporaneously, the court would be likely to hold that the same principle applies if the patient's decision was clearly established and applicable in the circumstances in which the patient now presents.[68]

---

[65] The power is currently vested in the President of the High Court by the Courts (Supplemental Provisions) Act 1961, s 9(1).

[66] See para **9.24–9.26**.

[67] It is not known how many people in Ireland have made advance directives, as no case has yet come before the court dealing with them. The Law Reform Commission stated in its Report in 2009, discussed below at para **12.33** that although there is currently no legislative framework for advance care planning in Ireland, many people have prepared written advance care directives, sometimes with the benefit of medical and legal advice, and general hospitals deal on a regular basis with patients who verbally express treatment preferences, including refusals of treatment and 'do not resuscitate' requests. The Commission quotes from a study conducted in 2003 in which 27 per cent of physicians had experience of advance care directives made by Irish patients. (Fennell, Butler, Saaidin and Sheikh, 'Dissatisfaction with Do Not Attempt Resuscitation Orders: A Nationwide Study of Irish Consultant Physician Practices' (2006) 99(7) Irish Medical Journal 208). The Commission also received information during its consultation process that a number of hospitals in Ireland have developed guidelines and protocols to deal with advance care directives, based on best practice models from other states, notably the UK. See also Campbell, 'The Case for Living Wills in Ireland' (2006) *Medico-Legal Journal of Ireland*, 12 (1): 2–18.

[68] Affirmed in the UK by *Re T (Adult: refusal of treatment)* [1992] 4 All ER 649; *Airedale NHS Trust v Bland* [1993] AC 789.

[12.33] The Law Reform Commission (LRC) and the former Irish Council for Bioethics have published opinions on the issue of advance directives. In 2007 the Irish Council for Bioethics published its opinion that 'competent adults should have the right to prepare an advance directive, stemming from their right to self-determination and their related rights to bodily integrity, privacy and dignity.' It took the view that the instrument of the advance directive allows individuals to govern their future medical treatment and care, should they become incapacitated, in a way that reflects their personal values and beliefs[69]. In 2009 the Law Reform Commission published its Report on Advance Directives in which it recognised a growing momentum in Ireland favouring the introduction of a legislative framework for advance care directives.[70] It concluded that 'to the extent that case law in Ireland, notably *In re a Ward of Court (No 2)* and *Fitzpatrick v FK*, has addressed this matter, it is clear that an advance care directive made by a person with full capacity would be upheld.' It recommends that an appropriate legislative framework should be enacted for advance care directives as part of the reform of the law on mental capacity.[71]

[12.34] In the context of psychiatric care, the advance directive poses particular problems. Mental disorder covers many conditions which challenge paternalistic assumptions. The question that arises in this context is whether a competently executed advance directive by a person with a fluctuating mental disorder, made at a time of full competence, can be binding on a health professional. The example of anorexia nervosa is illustrative, where the patient is usually competent but refuses food to the point of death. What is the situation if such a person makes an advance refusal of food and subsequently becomes unconscious due to very low body weight? The strong autonomy argument states that if the patient is competent at any time and states that in the event of future lack of competence, certain treatments are not to be given, then the professional must observe such refusal. The strong paternalism argument takes the view that the advance refusal should be respected until such point as the patient's life is in danger as a result of mental disorder, and it then becomes acceptable to treat the patient in his best interests. The rights-based argument provides that an advance refusal of treatment made by a competent person should be respected except where the person has a mental disorder that requires that they be compulsorily detained for treatment under statutory authority.

[12.35] The English case of *Re C (Refusal of Medical treatment)*[72] is instructive here. In this case a 68-year-old man suffering from paranoid schizophrenia, who had been a long-term patient at a mental institution, developed gangrene in his right foot. Doctors recommended amputation of the leg below the knee in order to save his life. C refused to consent to amputation under any circumstances, now or at any future time. Alternative treatment was provided and the immediate threat to his life receded but there was a chance that it might recur in the future. C was concerned that this might happen at a time

---

[69]   See http://www.bioethics.ie/index.php/reports-and-opinions (accessed 5 June 2011).
[70]   Report on Bioethics: Advance Care Directives (LRC 94–2009) http://www.lawreform.ie/ _fileupload/Reports/Report%20Bioethics.pdf (accessed 5 June 2011).
[71]   For further discussion of the proposed Mental Capacity Bill 2008, see Ch 9 at para **9.45** et seq.
[72]   *Re C (Refusal of Medical treatment)* [1994] 1 FLR 31. See commentary by Grubb, 'Treatment Without Consent: Adult: *Re C (Refusal of Medical Treatment)*' [1994] 2 Med L Rev 92.

when his capacity to refuse consent might be diminished and that the hospital would perform the operation in his 'best interests'. Therefore, he applied to the Court for an injunction restraining the hospital from amputating his foot in the future without his express consent. The High Court granted the injunction relying on *Re T* and *Bland*, discussed above. Thorpe J held that despite the patient's chronic mental illness, there was a rebuttable presumption that an adult has the capacity to decide whether to consent to medical treatment. This presumption had not been displaced in this case. As well as laying down helpful guidelines for the determination of patient competence, the decision clarified that advance refusals were not only directory in nature but were binding as well.

[12.36] If an advance directive exists and is disregarded by the medical team, the most likely form of legal action that could potentially be taken by the patient is an action in negligence.[73] In order to succeed in establishing negligence in the medical context, the patient would have to prove that the doctor owed him a duty of care, which is usually unproblematic; that the doctor breached that duty, which is determined according to the level of skill employed by the doctor as compared to that which might be expected of a reasonable doctor; and that the breach of duty caused harm to the patient. It is this last aspect that may prove difficult for a patient who sues his doctor in negligence for not complying with an advance directive refusing life-saving measures. The harm inflicted in this case is the saving of the patient's life. The courts, on public policy grounds, would most likely be opposed to compensating the patient for being alive when he would rather be dead. An example of this approach can be seen in the American case *Anderson v St Francis-St George Hospital*,[74] where an 82-year-old man was admitted to hospital suffering from cardiac insufficiency. He instructed his doctors that he wanted no extraordinary life-prolonging measures to be taken if his condition got worse,[75] and the doctor entered a Do Not Resuscitate (DNR) order on his chart. Three days later the patient went into ventricular fibrillation and a nurse, who was unaware of the DNR, resuscitated him. Two days later again, the patient suffered a stroke which left him paralysed until his death two years later. His estate sued the hospital for damages for pain and suffering in the last two years of his life and for the medical expenses incurred during that time period. The Ohio Supreme Court accepted that the unauthorised, and indeed specifically refused, medical intervention was a wrongful act, but was not willing to accept that any actual physical harm, such as broken ribs caused by cardio-pulmonary resuscitation (CPR), was inflicted as a result. The Court held that the resuscitation did

---

73   There is also the possibility that a doctor could be prosecuted for assault and battery for 'inflicting' treatment on the patient without consent. However, as the doctor would presumably have acted in good faith, and possibly in emergency circumstances when the imperative was to 'act now and think later', it is unlikely that such a prosecution would be brought, although in the Canadian case *Malette v Shulman* [1990] 72 OR (2d) 417 (CA) the plaintiff, a Jehovah's Witness, was awarded damages in battery for the wrongful administration of a blood transfusion.

74   *Anderson v St. Francis-St. George Hospital* 671 N E 2d 225 (Ohio 1996).

75   Gavaghan, 'Anticipatory Refusals and the Action of Wrongful Living' (2000) Med Law I Vol 5: 67–80 at 74–75. For a challenge to the analogy between these cases and the wrongful life cases see Peters, 'The Illusion of Autonomy at the End of Life: Unconsented Life Support and the Wrongful Life Analogy' (1998) 43 UCLA Rev of Law 673.

not cause the stroke and that all the nurse had done was prolong the patient's life. This was not the sort of harm that the courts were willing to acknowledge and compensate for.[76]

[12.37] By analogy, there have been other circumstances where the plaintiff sued on the basis that he should not have been born, and in which the courts have also traditionally been reluctant to award compensation.[77] These so-called 'wrongful birth' cases deal with situations where the parents of a child born with severe disabilities claim that, due to the negligence of the defendant, they were not given the opportunity to abort the foetus and as a result the child leads an impaired existence, with consequent distress and hardship imposed on the family. 'Wrongful life' cases are those where the *child* sues the doctor for not diagnosing the impairment during pregnancy. An example of such a case is *McKay v Essex Area Health Authority*[78] where the plaintiff had been born deaf and partially blind as a result of her mother's coming into contact with rubella while pregnant. The plaintiff argued that an appalling existence had been thrust upon her as a result of the doctor's negligence in not diagnosing the problem during her mother's pregnancy, thereby denying her mother the opportunity to have an abortion. The Court unanimously agreed that a claim for wrongful life had no place in English law on the grounds that there was no 'damage' caused, it would be contrary to public policy, there was no duty owed to the child to perform an abortion and that damages would not confer any benefit. What is most relevant in the context of arguments relating to non-compliance with advance directives is that the Court found it impossible to accept that life itself could be a harm and that it was impossible to compare existence with non-existence for the purpose of assessing damages.[79]

[12.38] Another strand of cases that may be relevant in the context of the 'harm' of being alive are the 'wrongful conception/pregnancy' cases where the plaintiff claims that, due to the doctor's negligence in performing a sterilisation on her or a vasectomy on her partner, a child was conceived that should not have been conceived. Objections to the award of damages for the unexpected birth of a healthy child again focus on policy grounds that parents cannot be said to be injured by the blessing of a child. For example, in *McFarlane and another v Tayside Health Board*,[80] a married couple sued for damages

---

[76] See similar decision in *Allore v Flower Hospital* 699 NE 2d 560 (Ohio App 6th Dist 1997) where damages for pain and suffering and mental anguish and distress following the unwanted administration of life-saving medical treatment were excluded.

[77] See Donnelly, 'The Injury of Parenthood: The Tort of Wrongful Conception' (1997) Northern Ireland Legal Quarterly, Vol 48, No1, p10.

[78] *McKay v Essex Area Health Authority* [1982] QB 1166.

[79] See Harris's arguments that since such cases are predicated on the argument that the plaintiff has been left with a life that is worse than death, then how could money possibly compensate for this 'wrong'? If money could make the plaintiff's life worth living, then the life is only contingently not worth living (contingent on the plaintiff not receiving compensation). If money could not make the life worth living, then what is the point of the action at all? If the plaintiff's life is indeed worse than death, then the only action that would benefit the patient is euthanasia. Harris, *Wonderwoman and Superman: The Ethics of Human Biotechnology* (OUP, 1992) p 96.

[80] *McFarlane and another v Tayside Health Board* [2000] 2 AC 59, [1999] 4 All ER 961, [2000] 1 FCR 102, [1999] 3 WLR 1301, 52 BMLR 1.

after the wife became pregnant following her husband's vasectomy. The Court held that where medical negligence resulted in an unwanted pregnancy and the birth of a healthy child, the parents were not entitled to recover damages for the costs of rearing that child, but the mother was entitled to recover damages for the pain and distress suffered during the pregnancy and in giving birth, and for financial loss associated with the pregnancy. The object of the vasectomy was to prevent a pregnancy, and accordingly the mother was entitled to claim damages in respect of the physical effects of the pregnancy and the birth. However, damages for the costs of bringing up a healthy child were irrecoverable since it was not fair, just or reasonable to impose liability for such economic losses on a doctor and his employer. To compensate for the life of a child would be almost impossible, as explained by Lord Slynn:

> It may not be impossible to make a rough assessment of the possible costs of feeding, clothing and even housing a child during the likely period of the child's life up to the age of 17 or 18 or 25 or for whatever period a parent is responsible by statute for the support of a child. But even that can only be rough. To reduce the costs by anything resembling a realistic or reliable figure for the benefit to the parents is well nigh impossible unless it is assumed that the benefit of a child must always outweigh the cost which, like many judges in the cases I have referred to, I am not prepared to assume. Of course there should be joy at the birth of a healthy child, at the baby's smile and the teenager's enthusiasms but how can these be put in money terms and trimmed to allow for sleepless nights and teenage disobedience? If the valuation is made early, how can it be known whether the baby will grow up strong or weak, clever or stupid, successful or a failure both personally and careerwise, honest or a crook? It is not impossible to make a stab at finding a figure for the benefits to reduce the costs of rearing a child but the difficulties of finding a reliable figure are sufficient to discourage the acceptance of this approach.

[12.39] In Ireland, foetal impairment is not a precondition for lawful termination of the pregnancy under the Irish Constitution. Therefore, actions for either wrongful birth or wrongful life would not, as a general rule, be available under Irish law. On the other hand, claims for wrongful conception might be successful on the grounds of an ineffectively performed sterilisation procedure. For example, in *Byrne v Ryan*[81] the plaintiff, a mother of five children, voluntarily decided to undergo a tubal ligation, as she did not wish to become pregnant again. In the course of the operation, the consultant mistakenly attached the clips to the tissue beside the plaintiff's fallopian tube, as a result of which the sterilisation turned out to be ineffective. Mrs Byrne subsequently gave birth to two healthy children. The High Court awarded compensation for pain, suffering and inconvenience connected with Mrs Byrne's two pregnancies, which followed the failed tubal ligation. The Court also awarded damages for extra medical expenses involved in having to undergo an additional sterilisation procedure. However, following the reasoning in *McFarlane v Tayside Health Board*, Kelly J rejected the claim for childrearing expenses and declared them as not recoverable. In order to justify such refusal, he invoked the principle that the benefits of a healthy child outweigh any loss incurred in rearing the child, as well as the values protected by the Irish Constitution, including family, dignity and protection of all human beings, which were, in his view, better served by a decision to deny rather than to allow damages of the type claimed.

---

[81]   *Byrne v Ryan* [2007] IEHC 207.

[12.40] In circumstances where an advance refusal of treatment, such as CPR, is disregarded it is unclear whether an Irish court would be prepared to recognise a cause of action by the patient. Michalowski argues that no compelling reasons justify departure from the normal principles of tort law where a patient claims compensation for having had a refusal of life-saving treatment disregarded, and that damages should be available where the cause of action is established and it can be shown that the patient suffered harm as a result.[82] She says the compensable harm should include all physical and mental pain and suffering caused by the unwanted treatment. 'Where a patient wants to live by his/her religious beliefs or wishes to preserve personal dignity, the harm will be mental distress; where the patient wants to prevent life in a painful condition, or medical problems potentially following the administration of life-saving treatment, such as a stroke or the loss of bodily functions, the harm is physical suffering, probably often accompanied by mental suffering.' The compensable harm is not the patient's existence as such, but the suffering caused by the unwanted treatment. She also states that in addition to liability under tort law, there is also the possibility of disciplinary sanctions in case of a violation of the patient's declared wishes. It is noteworthy in this context that the Irish Medical Council's Guide to Professional Conduct and Ethics states that every adult with capacity is entitled to refuse medical treatment and that doctors must respect a patient's decision to refuse treatment, even if they disagree with that decision. It further advises doctors that they should respect a patient's Advance Healthcare Plan or living will.

Do Not Resuscitate orders (DNRs)

[12.41] There has been a growing trend in some countries towards laws dealing with Do Not Resuscitate orders (DNRs) (also called Do Not Attempt Resuscitation or DNARs). A DNR is a doctor's written order not to attempt cardiopulmonary resuscitation (CPR) on a particular patient. It has been described as 'a crucial decision point in the limiting of treatment…a point at which doctors and nurses clarify their therapeutic goals and reconsider the appropriateness of further life-sustaining treatment.'[83] CPR was originally designed to treat unexpected cardiac and respiratory arrests after surgery or accidents[84], but is now commonly used to treat any patient who arrests, on the assumption that all patients would want to receive CPR.[85] It has been argued that in the large majority of cases the procedure is not employed to long-term effect and that, if the patient is expected to die, 'a procedure less dignified and peaceful could hardly be devised'.[86] Routine use of CPR will not always be in the patient's best interests and therefore the practice has developed of making a DNR order to indicate that CPR is inappropriate.

---

[82] Michalowski, 'Trial and Error at the End of Life – No Harm Done?' (2007) Oxford Journal of Legal Studies Vol 27, No 2:257–280 at 270.

[83] Smidira et al, 'Withholding and Withdrawal of Life Support from the Critically Ill' (1990) 322 New England J of Med 309.

[84] Kuowenhoven, Jude and Knickerbocker, 'Closed Chest Cardiac Massage' (1960) 173 JAMA 94.

[85] Florin, 'Do Not Resuscitate Orders: The Need for a Policy' (1993) 27 J of the Royal College of Physicians 135.

[86] Saunders, 'Who's for CPR?' (1992) 26 Journal of the Royal College of Physicians 254.

This does not mean that other medical treatment, such as antibiotics, will not be given. In *Re R (adult: medical treatment)*[87] R was a 23-year-old man who was born with a serious malfunction of the brain and cerebral palsy. He was not in a permanent vegetative state but had minimal awareness, severe epilepsy, was believed to be deaf and blind, and had to be fed through a syringe. In the year leading to the making of the DNR decision, R was hospitalised five times due to recurrent infections, constipation, ulceration, fits, dehydration and under-nutrition. The treating doctor and R's parents agreed that if, in future, R suffered a life-threatening condition, CPR should not be given. Some members of the residential home objected to the DNR decision and an application was brought by way of judicial review to quash it. The judge heard evidence that if CPR was attempted it would be a dangerous operation having regard to R's frailty and might even cause further brain damage. The chances of a successful CPR being performed on someone like R by the staff of a residential care facility were almost nil. The judge was persuaded by the evidence that CPR in this case would be unlikely to be effective or successful and held that it would be lawful for the doctor to withhold such treatment.

[12.42] The decision to record a DNR is influenced by a combination of medical and non-medical factors. If it is possible to consult with the patient, then a refusal of CPR by the patient must be adhered to in this respect. However, as discussed above, an advance refusal of CPR may be disregarded with perhaps few legal repercussions for the doctor, although disciplinary proceedings may be followed. If the patient is not competent to make such a decision then the doctor, following consultation with the medical and nursing team as well as the patient's family, will make the decision in the patient's best interests. If the patient wishes to have CPR performed no matter what the medical likelihood of success, the doctor is not obliged to comply with such wishes in the event that CPR would be futile.[88]

[12.43] In the United States, hospitals began developing policies on DNRs in the 1970s, most of which stipulate that the consent of either the patient or the surrogate decision-maker must be obtained before the order can be issued.[89] However, a few statutes dealing with medical futility in the context of advance directives provide that consent need not be obtained where, in the opinion of the doctor, the procedure cannot benefit the patient. The health-care provider would thus be entitled to decline a particular advance instruction or directive from a patient where it would involve medically ineffective health care or care contrary to generally accepted health-care standards.[90] In New York in 1988 legislation was passed decreeing that consent for CPR was to be presumed (and that it was to be employed, unless medically futile) unless there was a formally obtained

---

[87] *Re R (adult: medical treatment)* [1996] 2 FLR 99.

[88] See detailed discussion in Boozang, 'Death Wish: Resuscitating Self-Determination for the Critically Ill' (1993) 35(1) Arizona Law Review 24.

[89] See discussion in Finucane, 'Thinking About Life-Sustaining Treatment Late in the Life of a Demented Person' (2001) Georgia Law Review Vol 35: 691; Pickering, 'Decisionmaking at the End of Life: Patients with Alzheimer's or other Dementias' (2001) Georgia Law Review Vol 35:539.

[90] The Uniform Health Care Decisions Act, enacted in Maine: Me Rev Stat Tit 18–A, 5–807[f].

and recorded DNR order for a patient.[91] Article 29–B of the Consolidated Laws of the State of New York provides that before giving consent to a DNR, the patient must be given information about his diagnosis and prognosis, the reasonably foreseeable risks and benefits of CPR for him, and the consequences of the DNR order. The patient must consent either in writing or orally, in each case before two witnesses, one of whom must be a hospital doctor. Once consent has been given, the DNR order is recorded in the patient's medical record. Where the patient's doctor is of the opinion that the patient would suffer immediate and severe injury from a discussion of CPR, the doctor may make a DNR without the patient's consent. This must be recorded and seconded by another doctor, and the consent of the patient's surrogate decision-maker must be obtained. The DNR order must be reviewed every week for a hospital patient, and every two months for a nursing home resident. Provision is made in the statute for mediation in instances where the patient and doctor do not agree in relation to the making of a DNR order. It also provides for immunity from prosecution or civil liability for any health professional who complies with a DNR or initiates CPR when unaware of a DNR order in respect of that patient.

[12.44] In *Gilgunn v Massachusetts General Hospital*[92] a jury decided that doctors were not negligent in withdrawing mechanical ventilation and issuing a DNR order despite the objections of the patient's daughter and their apparent belief that the patient herself would have wished to continue treatment. The decision was made on the basis that the treatment was futile. The case was taken after the death of the patient and may well have been decided differently if it had been heard during the patient's lifetime in an application to have treatment withdrawn. This case is seen as problematic because it enables unilateral decision-making to be made by the doctors without taking into account either the patient's own wishes or the wishes of the patient's family.[93]

[12.45] In the UK, guidelines have been drawn up by the British Medical Association (BMA) and the Royal College of Nursing to deal with DNR decisions.[94] These enable doctors and nurses[95] to consider the appropriateness of such a decision where the patient's condition is such that CPR is unlikely to be successful, where CPR is not in accord with the recorded wishes of the patient, and where, if successful, CPR would be

---

91 Hendrick and Brennan, 'Do Not Resuscitate Orders: Guidelines in Practice' (1997) 6(1) Nottingham Law Journal, 25–45 at 26. See also McGinn, 'New York May Point the Way for Irish Law' (2001) St Paul Ireland Newsletter; Sheikh, 'The Status of the 'Do Not Resuscitate' Order (DNR) in Irish Law and Medicine' (2001) St Paul Ireland Newsletter.

92 *Gilgunn v Massachusetts General Hospital* No 922–4820 (Mass. Super Ct Civ Action Suffolk Co April 22 1995).

93 Capron, 'Abandoning a Waning Life' (1995) Hastings Center Report 24 (July-Aug): 24–6.

94 British Medical Association, Resuscitation Council & Royal College of Nursing (2007) *Decisions Relating to Cardiopulmonary Resuscitation*. Available at http://www.resus.org.uk/pages/dnar.htm. (accessed 5 June 2011).

95 The involvement of nurses in decision-making on DNR orders is particularly important, as they may often have a greater insight into the patient's beliefs and wishes, as well as extensive contact with the patient's family. It is also important to note that if the patient goes into cardiac arrest, it is often the nursing staff who have to implement the DNR order by not calling for a crash team to resuscitate the patient. See further, Marchett et al, 'Nurses' Perceptions of the Support of Patient Autonomy in DNR Decisions' (1993) 30 I J of Nursing Studies 37.

likely to be followed by a length and quality of life which would not be acceptable to the patient.[96] The guidelines are reflective of the fact that individual decisions have to be taken in the care of each patient, and that a hospital policy of DNR would be questionable. The consultant in charge of the patient's care will discuss the circumstances with the others in the medical and nursing team, and, if possible, with the patient and the patient's close family.[97]

[12.46] In Ireland, DNR orders are made in hospitals although there is no legislative authority or judicial precedent upholding their legality. The practice appears to be for the medical team to consult with the patient's family and with nursing staff to ensure that such a decision is unanimous and to avoid any possibility that the decision would later be challenged. A study in a large Irish hospital in 2004 found that the majority of DNR orders were clearly documented by senior doctors and had been discussed with the patient or with the relatives.[98] However, it is not clear to what extent the practice in this hospital is reflective of national practice. The Law Reform Commission's Report on Advance Directives recommends that there should be a Code of Practice on advance directives which should also contain guidelines on the process of putting in place a 'Do Not Resuscitate' order (DNR order). The guidelines should provide that before a DNR order is made, there should be a consultative process, documented on the patient's chart, and that the order will be made by the most senior member of the health-care team. The Association of Anaesthetists of Great Britain and Ireland also published guidelines on DNR orders in 2009[99], which state that the management of patients with DNR decisions in the perioperative period should focus on what resuscitative measures *will* be embarked on rather than on what *will not* be done. It advises that a review of the DNR decision by the anaesthetist and surgeon with the patient, proxy decision-maker, other doctor in charge of the patient's care, and relatives or carers, if indicated, is essential before proceeding with surgery and anaesthesia. In an emergency, the doctor must make decisions in the best interests of the patient using whatever information is available.

PATIENTS IN PERSISTENT VEGETATIVE STATE

[12.47] Deprivation of oxygen from the brain through hypoxia can result in varying degrees of intellectual disability, depending on how quickly the brain is oxygenated. The extent of cognitive ability retained depends on the degree of damage to the cortex. The brain stem can continue to function even if the cortex is destroyed, leading to what is known as persistent vegetative state (PVS). The condition is characterised by an irregular but cyclic state of circadian sleeping and waking unaccompanied by any

---

[96]   British Medical Association, Resuscitation Council & Royal College of Nursing (2007) *Decisions Relating to Cardiopulmonary Resuscitation.*

[97]   See discussion of an inherent ageism in the making of DNRs by Ebrahim, 'Do Not Resuscitate Decisions: Flogging Dead Horses or a Dignified Death?' (2000) BMJ 320: 1155–1156, and various letters in reply (2001) BMJ: 322:7278.

[98]   McNamee and O'Keeffe, 'Documentation of Do-Not-Resuscitate Orders in an Irish Hospital' (2004) Ir J Med Sci.;173(2): 99–101.

[99]   Association of Anaesthetists of Great Britain and Ireland 'Do Not Attempt Resuscitation Decisions in the Perioperative Period', (May 2009). Available at http://www.aagbi.org/publications/guidelines/docs/dnar_09.pdf (accessed 5 June 2011).

behaviourally detectable expression of self-awareness, specific recognition of external stimuli, or consistent evidence of attention or inattention or learned responses.[100] Such patients are not immobile and do retain certain reflexes, including those related to auditory and visual stimuli, depending on the degree of damage to the brain. Thus, the patient in PVS is alive, has a beating heart and can breathe but cannot have any contact with the outside world. If well managed, a patient in PVS can live for many years.[101]

[12.48] Ethical and legal difficulties may arise in relation to patients in PVS where it is suggested that treatment should be withdrawn. This raises discussion about medical futility and euthanasia, with the lines between them often indistinct. Decision-making in this context has been based on a number of standards: the subjective, the substituted judgment, and the best-interests test. The subjective test is only applicable in circumstances where the patient has at some time expressed his wishes as to treatment. The substituted judgment test is based on what it is believed the patient would have decided had he been competent to do so, according to his character and stated opinions. The best-interests test is based on the court's interpretation of what is preferable to be done for the patient, in line with good medical practice. Of these tests, the one that most closely adheres to principles of autonomy and self-determination is the subjective, or at the very least, the substituted judgment test which endeavours to treat the patient as he would have wished, rather than according to what others might presume for him.

American case law

[12.49] The volume of cases in the US and the decisions of more than 50 jurisdictions make it unrealistic to expect any uniform or even consistent approach to such a difficult issue. However, it is instructive to examine some of the most important cases, beginning with the classic PVS cases *Re Quinlan*[102] and *Cruzan v Director, Missouri Department of Health*.[103] In *Quinlan* a 22-year-old woman, Karen Ann Quinlan, was in a persistent vegetative state as a result of hypoxia from unknown causes. Her parents sought to remove her from intensive care and sought a declaration that they could give consent on her behalf to the switching off of the life support machine. It was believed that Karen could not survive for very long without the assistance of the respirator, although the exact period of survival could not be estimated. The doctors treating Karen testified that removal of the respirator would be contrary to medical practices, standards and traditions. The Court considered in depth the Constitutional right of privacy. It said that if Karen were herself miraculously lucid for a brief interval, she could decide for herself upon discontinuance of the life-support machine, even if the consequences would be death. There was no compelling external interest of the state to force Karen to endure the unendurable where there was no possibility of returning to any semblance of cognitive life.

---

[100] Multi Society Task Force on PVS, 'Medical Aspects of the Persistent Vegetative State' (1994) 330 NEJM 1499 (Pt 1), 1572 (pt 2).

[101] For further discussion, see McMahan, 'Brain Death, Cortical Death and Persistent Vegetative State', in Kuhse and Singer, *Companion to Bioethics* (Blackwell, 1998) at 250–260.

[102] *Re Quinlan* 355 A 2d 647, 97 ALR 3d 205 (S Ct of New Jersey).

[103] *Cruzan v Director, Missouri Department of Health* 110 S Ct 2841 (1990).

We think that the State's interest …weakens and the individual's right to privacy grows as the degree of bodily invasion increases and the prognosis dims. Ultimately there comes a point at which the individual's rights overcome the state interest. It is for that reason that we believe Karen's choice, if she were competent to make it, would be vindicated by the law.

[12.50] In view of Karen's incompetence to make such a decision herself, the Court held that her right to privacy could be asserted on her behalf by her guardian in consultation with an ethics committee constituted to consider whether any change in Karen's circumstances was possible.[104]

[12.51] In *Cruzan v Director, Missouri Department of Health*[105] the patient was in a similar situation to that of Karen Quinlan, except that she did not require a ventilator. After three years in PVS, her parents requested that feeding and hydration be discontinued, on the basis of their interpretation of her wishes when she was competent. The Missouri court refused permission and the case went to the US Supreme Court on the question of whether states could, under the Constitution, require clear and convincing evidence of a person's expressed wishes while competent, before hydration and nutrition could be withdrawn. The Court agreed with this requirement but also stated that:

> No right is held more sacred, or is more carefully guarded…than the right of every individual to the possession and control of his own person, free from all restraint or interference of other, unless by clear and unquestionable authority of law.

[12.52] Other cases are perhaps not as straightforward as *Quinlan* and *Cruzan*. For example, in *In the matter of Claire Conroy*[106] the Court had to consider the circumstances in which life-sustaining treatments may be withheld or withdrawn from incompetent, institutionalised elderly patients with severe and permanent mental and physical disability, and a limited life expectancy. In this case Ms Conroy was not in a persistent vegetative state but her intellectual capacity was very limited and was unlikely to improve. She suffered from heart disease, hypertension and diabetes. Her leg was gangrenous, she could not control her bowels nor speak nor swallow. On the other hand she did have some limited interaction with her immediate environment in that she had some changes in facial movements in response to various things, her eyes followed individuals in the room, and she moaned sometimes when being fed or having bandages changed.

[12.53] The Court recognised the right of a terminally ill patient to reject medical treatment as that person's right to choose a preferred manner of ending life. The Court also looked at the situation where the person is unable to speak for him or herself, but nonetheless has a right to self-determination. 'The right of an adult who, like Claire Conroy, was once competent, to determine the course of her medical treatment remains intact even when she is no longer able to assert that right or to appreciate its effectuation.' The Court took that view that decision-making for incompetent patients should try to effectuate as far as possible the decision that the patient would have made if competent (ie, the substituted judgment test). In this important sense then the decision

---

[104] Interestingly, Karen lived for nine years after the machine was switched off.
[105] *Cruzan v Director, Missouri Department of Health* 110 S Ct 2841 (1990).
[106] *In the matter of Claire Conroy* (1985) 486 A 2d 1209 (NJ S Ct).

is a subjective one, based on the particular patient's character and wishes as expressed by family members and friends, rather than an examination of what a reasonable person would decide in the circumstances. In the present case, there was insufficient evidence of Ms Conroy's wishes on the matter for the Court to use this test to decide whether she would have wanted the life-sustaining treatment to cease.

[12.54] In *Conroy* and an earlier case, *Superintendent of Belchertown v Saikewicz*,[107] the Court considered the balancing of interests as between the incompetent patient and the state. While the patient had a Constitutional right to privacy which clearly encompassed the right to refuse medical treatment, the state also had interests in maintaining life and protecting innocent third parties or dependents. The state was entitled to maintain policies discouraging suicide and also had to consider the preservation of the integrity of the medical profession. In each of these cases the patient's right outweighed those of the state.

[12.55] More difficult cases have arisen where the patient is not in PVS but is minimally conscious and unlikely to ever improve beyond his current capacity. The courts have been asked to give decisions in relation to whether artificial feeding and hydration should be continued indefinitely in such cases. An illustrative case is *Conservatorship of Wendland*[108] in which a 48-year-old man, Robert Wendland, was left profoundly brain damaged from injuries sustained in a car accident. He emerged from a coma after 16 months, with severe cognitive impairment and paralysis on his right side. He could not swallow, control his bowel or bladder, communicate or act volitionally. He was, however, able to perform simple tasks with repeated prompting, such as catching a ball, or placing a coloured peg in a hole or moving his wheelchair. His family believed that he did not recognise them. The doctors treating him concluded that he had no reasonable chance of further improvement. Wendland's wife and children sought to have the artificial feeding discontinued on the basis that he would not have wanted to exist in this way. Wendland's mother and sister strongly opposed such a move.[109] By the time that the case got to the Supreme Court of California, Wendland had already died of pneumonia, but the ruling of the Court is instructive nonetheless. Case law up to that point had established a right for a competent patient or a surrogate decision-maker to request the withdrawal of artificial feeding. However, the Court recognised that the situation of Wendland fell between PVS and competency, and was therefore unprecedented in California.[110]

---

[107] *Superintendent of Belchertown v Saikewicz* (1977) 370 NE 2d 417 (Mass Sup Jud Ct).

[108] *Conservatorship of Wendland* 26 Cal 4th 519 (2001).

[109] A similar case decided by the Michigan Supreme Court ruled that life support could not be discontinued on the basis that general statements made by the patient before his injuries did not apply, as they did not provide clear and convincing evidence that the patient would have wanted life support to be withdrawn. *In re Martin* 538 NW 2d 399 (Mich, 1995).

[110] *Barber v Superior* Court 147 Cal App 3d 1006 (1983) allowed discontinuance of artificial feeding where the patient was in a coma; *Bartling v Superior Court* 163 Cal App 3d 186 (1984) where a competent patient suffering from an aneurysm and cancer was entitled to request that his ventilator be removed; *Bouvia v Superior Court* 179 Cal App 3d 1127 (1984) where a quadraplegic woman with cerebral palsy was enabled to request doctors to withdraw artificial feeding; (contd.../)

[12.56] The important issue for the Court was the standard of proof required to establish a patient's wishes in relation to life-prolonging treatment. It was held that the law requires 'clear and convincing evidence' of the patient's wishes where the patient is incompetent but conscious. There was a distinction, according to the court, between a decision-maker appointed by the patient himself, such as by advance directive, and a conservator appointed by the court. While the former might be expected to have some special knowledge of the patient's wishes, the latter may not necessarily have the same degree of intimate knowledge. In light of the fact that Wendland had not made an advance directive, the Court had appointed his widow as conservator. The Court held that the law requires clear and convincing evidence of the patient's wishes when a conservator seeks to withdraw life-sustaining treatment from a conscious, incompetent patient who has not left legally cognisable instructions for health care or appointed a surrogate to make health-care decisions. It was not satisfied in this case by statements made by Wendland that he would not want to be kept alive artificially. The case provides a strong incentive for those who want to be able to have their wishes in end-of-life situations followed, to execute an advance directive to that effect.[111]

[12.57] The US cases indicate a judicial unwillingness to decide 'quality of life' issues where these may be avoided by choosing the 'substituted judgment' test. This enables the court to avoid making a decision that it is in the individual's best interests not to be alive. The role of the standard of proof is also important in this context, as it has largely been left to each state to decide whether to adopt the 'clear and convincing evidence' test or the ordinary burden of proof in such cases, thereby leading to considerable variation across the states on this point, depending on what standard is chosen.

English case law

[12.58] The starting point for discussion of the English cases is the important case of *Airedale NHS Trust v Bland*.[112] This case arose out of the tragic incident which took place at the Hillsborough football stadium in 1989 when many fans were crushed during a match. Tony Bland sustained severe anoxic brain damage, as a result of which he was in PVS. While he had a heartbeat and could breathe, there was no chance of his regaining any cognitive function or sensory capacity. After three years without improvement the hospital sought a declaration that it would be lawful to discontinue all life support, and that any further treatment should be given only to enable him to die in dignity.

[12.59] The case eventually came before the House of Lords, which decided that the question should be decided on the best-interests test. As an adult, treatment of Tony

---

[110] (\...contd) *Conservatorship of Drabick* 200 Cal App 3d 185 (1988) where the Court said that a court-appointed conservator could require doctors to withdraw artificial feeding from a patient who had been in PVS for five years following an accident; and *Conservatorship of Morrison* 206 Cal App 3d 304 (1988) where doctors who refused to comply with the request of the conservator of an elderly woman in PVS to withdraw artificial feeding were obliged to transfer the patient to another facility where other doctors would do so.

[111] Eisenberg and Kelso, 'Legal Implications of the Wendland Case for End-Of-Life Decisionmaking' (2002) West J Med 176:124–127; Rich, 'The Ethics of Surrogate Decision Making' 2002 West J Med 176:127–129.

[112] *Airedale NHS Trust v Bland* [1993] 1 All ER 821.

Bland in the absence of his consent was only lawful under the doctrine of necessity. The treatment could only be said to be necessary if it could be shown to be in his best interests. As it was immaterial to the unconscious Tony Bland whether he lived or died, it could not be shown that life-prolonging treatment was in his continued best interests. Essentially, he had no interests at all. Therefore, the House of Lords held that it would be lawful to cease treatment, even though the consequence would be that Tony Bland would die. All of the opinions stressed that it was not a matter of it being in the best interests of Tony Bland to die, but that it was not in his best interests to keep him alive in circumstances where such medical treatment was futile. In making its decision, the Court had to consider whether such conduct would be in conflict with the criminal law, bringing about, as it did, the death of another human being. The Court also had to consider how its judgment fitted in with the duty of the medical profession to care for patients' best interests.

[12.60] The Court recognised that the doctor has a duty to treat his patient in a patient's best interests. However, if it is accepted, as in the present case, that further treatment is futile, then it cannot be in the patient's best interests to receive that treatment. As the proposal in this case was a failure to continue to feed and hydrate rather than an act to cause death, the Court was comfortable in describing this as an omission and not an act. Criminal liability may only be imposed on foot of an omission where there is a duty to act. In this case, as there was an assessment that further treatment would be futile, there was no duty to act imposed on the doctors. This was not, according to the Court, a case of euthanasia, which is a positive act carried out to bring about the death of another.

[12.61] The court in *Bland*, as in many of the other cases on this point, have chosen to classify feeding and hydration as medical treatment, such that it can be withdrawn on medical criteria. Others argue that food and water is not in any way 'medical', that it does not take medical expertise to administer either of these things, and that both are better classified as a basic need of any human being which it would be unethical to deny.[113] Also the distinction drawn in this case between an act and an omission, while necessary in the Court's view to avoid the label of euthanasia, is open to criticism on the grounds of verbal gymnastics. 'Is the physical withdrawal of the feeding tube an "act" or merely a failure to continue to feed? Even if we leave the feeding tube in place until the patient is dead, is the writing–up of the decision in the patient's notes not an "act" from which the negative treatment flows? Which is the morally or legally significant event?'[114] It is said that these cases are not examples of *active* euthanasia but they come within the description of *passive* euthanasia: allowing another to die when a decision is taken that that life should be ended by inaction and when action could sustain the life in question.[115]

[12.62] A year after *Bland* another case came before the English courts dealing with the same issues yet seemed to be decided on less clear and unanimous evidence, thus adding

---

[113] Keown, 'Restoring Moral and Intellectual Shape to the Law After Bland' (1997) 113 LQR 481.

[114] Mason and Laurie, 'Negative Treatment of Vulnerable Patients: Euthanasia by Any Other Name?' (2000) Jur Rev Vol 3, 159–178 at 165.

[115] Mason and Laurie, 'Negative Treatment of Vulnerable Patients: Euthanasia by Any Other Name?' (2000) Jur Rev Vol 3, 159–178, p 165.

to fears of a slippery slope having been created by the House of Lords. *Frenchay Healthcare NHS Trust v S*[116] concerned an application for a declaration that a feeding tube which had become detached from the patient, a 21-year-old man who had been in apparent PVS for two and a half years following a drug overdose, need not be replaced. Due to the short period of time within which this application was made and disposed of by the Court, there was not a great deal of time spent on obtaining independent medical opinion of S's capacity. In granting the application, Bingham MR accepted that the medical evidence was not as emphatic as that in *Bland* but said that he was satisfied that the diagnosis of PVS was correct, that there was no prospect of recovery and that S had no real cognitive function. This was a case that deserved more judicial attention rather than less due to the very fact pointed out by the judge that the medical evidence was less emphatic than in *Bland*. The case is perceived by some as a rubber-stamping exercise whereby the courts agree with the medical evidence provided by the treating doctors, without hearing independent evidence and a properly prepared defence to the application.[117]

[12.63] In the Scottish case, *Law Hospital NHS Trust v Lord Advocate*,[118] a ruling was sought from the Court of Session that it was lawful to remove artificial feeding and hydration from a woman in PVS. Medical experts agreed that her case was hopeless and that there were no further avenues to explore. Her family agreed with the doctors that feeding and hydration should be discontinued, thus allowing her to die. The Court held that where capacity to consent was lacking, the question as to whether it would be lawful to discontinue treatment was a matter not for doctors, but for the courts in the absence of legislation to the contrary. The test to be applied was whether the proposed course of action was in the patient's best interests, and if the treatment could not be of any benefit to her, there were no longer any best interests to be served by continuing it.

[12.64] A more unusual case arose on the facts of *R (Burke) v The General Medical Council*.[119] The patient, Mr Burke, suffered from a degenerative brain condition which would inevitably lead to the need for artificial nutrition and hydration at some point in the future. He argued that the guidelines of the General Medical Council (GMC) on the withdrawal of treatment were inconsistent with his right to medical treatment and respect for his wishes. The guidelines at the time stated that the doctor must make the decision about whether to withhold or withdraw life-prolonging treatment taking into account the views of the patient or those close to the patient. It also stated that 'where death is not imminent, it usually will be appropriate to provide artificial nutrition or hydration. However, circumstances may arise where you judge that a patient's condition is so severe, the prognosis so poor, and that providing artificial nutrition or hydration may cause suffering or to be too burdensome in relation to the possible benefits.' Burke was concerned that doctors may deny him treatment and artificial nutrition and hydration irrespective of his own views. In the High Court, Munby J declared that the guidance was unlawful for a number of reasons, including that it did not recognise the patient's right to require treatment and it did not acknowledge the doctor's duty to go on

---

116   *Healthcare NHS Trust v S* [1994] 2 All ER 403.
117   Unger, 'In Whose Interests?' (1994) Gazette 91/ 29, 18–19.
118   *Law Hospital NHS Trust v Lord Advocate* 1996 SC 301, 1996 SLT 848.
119   *R (Burke) v The General Medical Council* [2005] EWCA Civ 1003.

providing treatment even where he was unwilling to do so, until he could find another doctor to continue treatment. However, the Court of Appeal allowed the appeal by the GMC, stating that the guidelines did not contradict the legal requirement that a doctor take reasonable steps to keep a competent patient alive if that was his expressed wish, nor the obligation to treat an incompetent patient in his best interests. The Court rejected Munby J's rights-based approach and said that a patient cannot insist on treatment above and beyond the doctor's general duty to care for the patient. If a doctor deliberately allows a patient to die contrary to his wishes, there would be a violation of art 2 of the European Convention on Human Rights (ECHR) (right to life) and possibly a charge of murder. Therefore, the law protects the patient to the extent that his wish to remain alive is respected as far as possible.[120] On the subject of withdrawing treatment from incompetent patients (which was not an issue in the present case), the Court of Appeal emphasised that whether or not treatment should be withdrawn is based on a test of 'best interests' only and that intolerability was not the test of best interests, which was to be determined based on the circumstances of each case.[121]

[12.65] As seen in the cases discussed above, the best-interests test is therefore the one that has found most favour with the English courts in the context of PVS, as in other areas of surrogate decision-making. There are, however, some problems with this test. First, it leads to semantic juggling where the question is framed according the result sought to be achieved. In *Bland* the Court was at pains to point out that the question it sought to address was not whether it was in Tony Bland's interests to die, but rather whether it was in his best interest to have his life prolonged by medical treatment. Mason and Laurie question how these two propositions can really be separated? 'How can one avoid the conclusion that to argue that it is in one's best interests to be starved is to say anything other than that it is in one's best interests to die?'[122]

[12.66] The best-interests test may also be criticised on the grounds that it fails to take into account the individual patient. The fundamental importance of consent in this context should not be ignored simply because the patient is incompetent. There must be a way in which the patient's wishes are taken into account in the court's decision as to whether to end that person's life. Admittedly, it is difficult to apply such a framework to a situation in which the patient has never been conscious, or competent to make such wishes clear. However, even where the patient has never expressed his wishes as to preferred treatment, the decision to be made by the courts should take into account the kind of person the patient was and what might have been expected to be his decision in the light of that assessment of his character. This most closely approximates the 'substituted judgment' test described above.

Irish case law

[12.67] The only Irish case to consider the issues raised by PVS is *In re a Ward of Court*[123] in which the facts were quite similar to those in *Bland*. Here the ward was a 45-

---

[120] Gurnham, 'Losing the Wood for the Trees: Burke and the Court of Appeal' (2006) Med Law Review 14(2) 253–263.

[121] See discussion by Coggon, 'Could the Right to Die with Dignity Represent a New Right to Die in English Law?' (2006) Med Law Review 14(2) 219–237.

[122] Mason and Laurie *Law and Medical Ethics* (8th edn, OUP, 2010), para 15.124.

[123] *In re a Ward of Court* [1996] 2 IR 79.

year-old woman who had suffered irreversible brain damage as a result of cardiac arrest during a minor gynaecological operation in 1972. Since then she had been in an almost persistent vegetative state.[124] The trial judge described her condition as follows: 'She is spastic as a result of brain damage. Both arms and hands are contracted. Both legs and feet are extended. Her jaws are clenched and because she had a tendency to bite the insides of her cheeks and her tongue, her back teeth have been capped to prevent the front teeth from fully closing. She cannot swallow. She cannot speak. She is incontinent.'[125]Although she was not fully in PVS and had some minimal cognitive ability to recognise strangers and track people with her eyes, much of this was considered to be reflex from the brain stem, and the judge was of the opinion that 'if such minimal cognition as she has includes an inkling of her catastrophic condition, then I am satisfied that that would be a terrible torment to her and her situation would be worse than if she were fully PVS.' The ward's family requested that the gastrostomy tube used for feeding the woman be withdrawn but the hospital and health-care professionals responsible for her care refused, as it was felt that such action would violate their philosophy and code of ethics. In 1995 the ward's mother, in her capacity as committee of the ward, obtained High Court consent for withdrawal of the feeding tube, Lynch J concluding that the courts should approach such cases from the standpoint of 'a prudent, good and loving parent in deciding what course should be adopted.'[126] The case was appealed to the Supreme Court.

[12.68] As a preliminary issue, the Supreme Court explained the Court's jurisdiction to consent to withdrawal on behalf of the ward, as coming within the ancient *parens patriae* power of the Lord Chancellor of Ireland over those of unsound mind.[127] This power had been transferred to the High Court by various Acts of the English Parliament and the Oireachtas.[128] By a four-to-one majority the Supreme Court held that the High Court was justified in giving consent to withdrawal of the feeding tube on the grounds that this was in the best interests of the ward, it was lawful and in pursuance of the ward's Constitutional rights to life, privacy, self-determination and bodily integrity.[129] In

---

[124] Lynch J in the High Court held that the ward was not terminally ill, in the sense that she would not, in her present condition, die within a few months. As long as her condition was stabilised, she could live for many more years. In the Supreme Court, Hamilton CJ disagreed, stating that the ward was terminally ill since she was kept alive by artificial means which, if withdrawn, would result in her death. Denham J said the classification was irrelevant since the decision to withhold treatment or not would have to be made irrespective of the classification of the illness. Tomkin and McAuley argue that what is important is whether the patient may or may not recover cognition, in '*Re a Ward of Court*: Legal Analysis' (1995) MLJI at 45.

[125] *In re a Ward of Court* [1996] 2 IR 79, per Lynch J.

[126] *In re a Ward of Court* [1995] 2 ILRM 401 at 419. See criticism of this test in Hanafin, 'D(en)ying Narratives: Death, Identity and the Body Politic' (2000) 20 Legal Studies No 3, 393 at 402–403.

[127] For further discussion, see Tomkin and McAuley, '*Re a Ward of Court*: Legal Analysis' (1995) MLJI 45 at 46–47.

[128] Lunacy (Ireland) Act 1901, s 4; Government of Ireland Act 1920; Courts of Justice Act 1924, s 19(1); Courts of Justice Act 1936, s 9(1); and Courts (Supplemental) Provisions Act 1961, s 9(1).

[129] See similar decision in Germany in *OLG Frankfurt, a M,* a decision from 15.7.1998 – 20 W. 224/98, NJW 1998, 2749, discussed in Aziz, 'The Role of Care Assistants in the Withdrawal of Hydration and Nutrition in Germany' (1999) 7 Med L Rev 307–326.

doing so, the Court did not use the 'prudent parent test' applied by Lynch J but came to the same conclusion nonetheless. Egan J, dissenting, decided that the inevitable result of removing the tube would be to kill the ward, which in view of the Constitution's protection of life, would require strong justification not present in this case. All of the majority judgments base their decision on the best interests of the ward, although each one's interpretation of what is meant by that test is slightly different.[130] Hamilton CJ was of the view that the trial judge had decided the matter appropriately, taking into account the ward's condition and its duration, the intrusiveness of the treatment and its futility, the wishes of the ward's mother and the medical evidence. Blayney J seemed to deviate slightly from the language of best interests, saying that the question was whether it was for the 'benefit' of the ward that her life be prolonged. However, as he approved of the High Court decision, which was grounded on best interests, this may have been what he intended. Denham J also seemed to move away from a best-interests test in suggesting that, amongst 15 factors to be taken into account, any wishes expressed by the ward prior to her incapacity should be considered.[131]

[12.69] It is crucial to the decision that in the context of the right to life some of the judges recognise that the right to life is not absolute and necessarily implies the right to die a natural death. Hamilton CJ stated:

> As the process of dying is part, and an ultimate inevitable consequence, of life, the right to life necessarily implies the right to have nature take its course and to die a natural death and, unless the individual concerned so wishes, not to have life artificially maintained by the provision of nourishment by abnormal artificial means, which have no curative effect and which are intended merely to prolong life.[132]

[12.70] He went on to explain that this does not give a right to terminate one's own life or to have death accelerated. It is confined to the natural process of dying. Loss of mental capacity does not result in the diminution of that person's Constitutional rights and in this case the ward's right to life necessarily implies a right to die a natural death. The cause of death would not be the withdrawal of food and nutrition, but the original injuries she sustained during the operation in 1972. O'Flaherty J concurred, saying that the present case was not about euthanasia, which involved the termination of life by a positive act.[133] This case concerned 'the withdrawal of invasive treatment in order to

---

[130] For a general commentary, see Feenan, 'Death, Dying and The Law' (1996) ILT 90–94.

[131] The use of best interests has been criticised by Hanafin, who says that as the patient was unconscious and no longer capable of having interests, this was a 'fictional strategy'. 'D(en)ying Narratives: Death, Identity and the Body Politic' (2000) 20 Legal Studies No 3, 393.

[132] *In re a Ward of Court* [1995] 2 ILRM 401 at 426.

[133] Iglesias argues to the contrary: 'The intent in the deprivation of nourishment is to bring about death, which means to kill. I cannot interpret this but as euthanasia. The issue of whether this mode of death may be chosen by the person themselves, or by their legal representatives, does not alter the facts, nor the fundamental moral and legal question of the euthanasia intent manifested in those facts. And whether intentions to bring about the death of a patient are carried out in what is done (action), or in what is omitted (omission), does not make them less euthanasia intents.' 'Ethics, Brain-Death, and the Medical Concept of the Human Being' (1995) MLJI 51–57 at 57.

allow nature to take its course'.[134] He was of the opinion that the advances of medical technology now resulted in the rendering a patient a prisoner in a ward from which there may be no release for many years without any enjoyment or quality of life, indeed without any life in the proper meaning of the word. He found it impossible to use the substituted judgment test in the circumstances, as the ward had never expressed her wishes on this matter before her injuries, therefore it was necessary to use the best-interests test to decide the matter.[135] On this basis he was satisfied that the trial judge had made the correct decision and that nature should take its course.[136]

[12.71] Denham J also took the view that the right to life under the Constitution is not absolute, no more than life itself is an absolute. She was of the opinion that the sanctity of life was an intrinsically important part of our society, not from a religious perspective, but in terms of the respect granted to all persons' right to life under the Constitution. Respecting death also gives respect to life – life need not be preserved at all costs, as this would not be sanctifying life. 'To care for the dying, to love and cherish them, and to free them from suffering rather than simply to postpone death, is to have fundamental respect for the sanctity of life and its end.'[137] Although the State has an interest in the protection of life in the common good, the State also recognised that respect for the life of an individual also entailed respecting the right to refuse medical treatment for religious or other reasons.

[12.72] Egan J, dissenting, took the view that the right to life is the highest in the hierarchy of rights in the Constitution. It would require a strong and cogent reason to justify the taking of a life, which was, in his view, what was proposed to be done by the removal of a feeding tube. He was concerned about the slippery slope on which the courts might be embarking by accepting the High Court's decision. This was not a case of full PVS, the ward had some minimal cognitive function and Egan J was concerned at the drawing of the line between PVS and cases of minimal consciousness.

> If slightly more cognitive function existed, would a right to withdraw sustenance still be claimed to be permissible? Where would the line be drawn? Cognition in a human being is something which is either present or absent and should, in my opinion, be so recognised and treated. Any effort to measure its value would be dangerous.[138]

---

[134] *In re a Ward of Court* [1995] 2 ILRM 401 at 432.

[135] For arguments as to why the best interests test is inapplicable to patients in PVS, see Harmon, 'Falling Off the Vine: Legal Fictions and the Doctrine of Substituted Judgment' (1990) 110 Yale LJ 1; Minnow, *Making All the Difference: Inclusion, Exclusion and American Law* (1990) at 325.

[136] Brock is of the view that the use of such language as 'letting nature take its course' and 'stopping prolonging the dying process', is part of the court's way of shifting responsibility from the doctor who stops the life support to the fatal disease itself. There is an unease in the courts with equating treatment withdrawal and killing. By distinguishing between the two, the courts are attempting to distance themselves from death's violent nature, and ultimately serve to confuse the issue. See Brock, *Life and Death: Philosophical Essays in Biomedical Ethics* (Cambridge University Press, 1993) p 211.

[137] *In re a Ward of Court* [1995] 2 ILRM 401 at 459.

[138] *In re a Ward of Court* [1995] 2 ILRM 401 at 437.

He was of the view that, notwithstanding the horrendous situation faced by the ward's family, any sympathy for their plight did not justify making the orders sought.

[12.73] The right to privacy was also seen as contributing significantly to the Supreme Court's decision, although the Court did not elaborate on the exact meaning of the right. Hamilton CJ and O'Flaherty J both mentioned privacy as one of the Constitutional rights relevant in this case, and both made the point that such rights were not diminished by the ward's incapacity. In her more detailed judgment, Denham J said that part of the right to privacy is the giving or refusing of consent to medical treatment. 'Merely because medical treatment becomes necessary to sustain life does not mean that the right to privacy is lost, neither is the right lost by a person becoming insentient.' In such cases the exercise of the right may take place through a different process, but the right exists nonetheless. Part of this right is also concerned with the right to die naturally, with dignity and with minimum suffering.

[12.74] Following the judgment of the Supreme Court in this case, the medical profession continued to follow its previous stance on this issue. The Irish Medical Council and the Irish Nursing Board both issued statements to the effect that it was not ethical for a doctor or nurse to withdraw artificial hydration or nutrition from a patient who is not dying, the argument here being that the ward could have lived for many more years in her condition and was not facing imminent death.[139] In the most recent edition of the Guide to Professional Conduct and Ethics, in 2009, the Medical Council states that:

> Nutrition and hydration are basic needs of human beings. All patients are entitled to be provided with nutrition and hydration in a way that meets their needs. If a patient is unable to take sufficient nutrition and hydration orally, you should assess what alternative forms are possible and appropriate in the circumstances. You should bear in mind the burden or risks to the patient, the patient's wishes if known, and the overall benefit to be achieved. Where possible, you should make the patient and/or their primary carer aware of these conclusions.[140]

ASSISTED SUICIDE AND EUTHANASIA

[12.75] At common law, a person who committed suicide was regarded as a self-murderer.[141] Consequently, anyone who instigated or aided another to commit suicide was guilty of murder as an accomplice. In Ireland the Criminal Law (Suicide) Act 1993 was enacted to decriminalise suicide but provides for the criminalisation of assisted suicide in s 2, subs. (2): 'A person who aids, abets, counsels or procures the suicide of another, or an attempt by another to commit suicide, shall be guilty of an offence and shall be liable on conviction on indictment to imprisonment for a term not exceeding

---

139 Irish Medical Council, 'Statement of the Council after Their Statutory Meeting on 4 August 1995' (The Medical Council, 1995) and Irish Nursing Board "Guidance of the Irish Nursing Board of 18 August 1995 (The Nursing Board 1995). Both are extracted in (1995) MLJI p 60.

140 Medical Council, Guide to Professional Conduct and Ethics (7th edn, 2009), para 19.1. Available at http://www.medicalcouncil.ie/ (accessed 5 June 2011).

141 For a discussion of the history of suicide and its prohibition, see Trowell, *The Unfinished Debate on Euthanasia* (SCM Press, 1973) 1–11.

fourteen years.' A prosecution under this section may only be instigated with the consent of the Director of Public Prosecutions. Similar measures exist in the UK,[142] Canada,[143] Australia,[144] New Zealand[145] and in most US states.[146]

[12.76] In England there are similarly worded provisions contained in the Suicide Act 1961. These provisions were interpreted in *Attorney General v Able*[147] where the question for the Court was whether a booklet distributed by the Voluntary Euthanasia Society, called 'A Guide to Self-Deliverance' contravened the Act. The booklet was designed to reduce the incidence of unsuccessful suicides, to discourage hasty and ill-conceived suicides and to overcome people's fear of dying. It also contained information about various methods of suicide. The Court held that for supply of the booklet to amount to an offence under s 2(1) of the Act, it had to be proved that the supplier, whilst intending the booklet to be used by a person actually contemplating suicide and with the object of assisting or otherwise encouraging him, supplied the booklet to such a person who then read it and, except in the case of an attempted offence, was assisted or encouraged by reading it to commit or to attempt to commit suicide. Whilst there might be circumstances in which supply of the booklet would undoubtedly amount to an offence, without proof of the necessary intent it could not be said in advance that any particular supply would be an offence. Accordingly, the Court held that it was for a jury to decide in each case whether the necessary facts had been proved. The Court was particularly concerned about the danger of usurping the jurisdiction of the criminal courts. While recognising the advantages of the application of the law being clear in relation to future conduct, it would only be proper to grant a declaration if it was clearly established that there was no risk of the Court treating conduct as criminal which was not clearly in contravention of the criminal law.

[12.77] Although there is considerable support for the right of competent adults to make autonomous health-care decisions, even where their refusal of treatment will lead to death, concern is commonly expressed when the person expresses a wish or intent to die and seeks assistance in order to do so, usually due to physical impairment which prevents the person being able to take his own life. Some studies show a link between depression and interest in hastened death in patients who are seriously ill, leading to concern over the vulnerability of such patients who actively request assisted dying.[148]

> Depression is a concern in requests for euthanasia or physician-assisted suicide because it is potentially reversible and may affect the patients' competency, particular in the relative

---

[142] Suicide Act 1961, s 2(1).

[143] Criminal Code 1985, s 241.

[144] ACT Crimes (Amendment) Ordinance (No 2) 1990 s 17(1) and (2), NSW Crimes Act 1900 s 31 C (1) and (2), NT Criminal Code 1983 s 168, Qld Criminal Code 1995 s 108, SA Criminal Law Consolidation Act 1935 s 13(a)(5), Tas Criminal Code 1924 s 163, Vic Crimes Act 1958 s 6B(2), WA Criminal Code 1913 s 228.

[145] Crimes Act 1961 s 179.

[146] See New York Task Force on Life and the Law, *When Death Is Sought: Assisted Suicide and Euthanasia in the Medical Context* (1994); Smith, 'What About Legalised Assisted Suicide?' (1993) 8 Issues in Law and Med 505.

[147] *Attorney General v Able* [1984] 1 All ER 277.

[148] Levene and Parker, 'Prevalence of Depression in Granted and Refused Requests for Euthanasia and Assisted Suicide: A Systematic Review' (2011) J Med Ethics 37: 205–211.

weighting they give to positive and negative aspects of their situation and possible future outcomes. Depressed patients can be viewed as a vulnerable population in this context as their request for death may be part of their illness, with the correct response being treatment rather than assistance in dying.[149]

[12.78] In some instances partners, parents or children seek to assist a loved one who requests their help in dying, as they do not have the physical capacity to end their own lives due to disease or disability. The legal position is that a person who intentionally kills another is guilty of murder even though they were motivated by a desire to end the other person's suffering or to give effect to the person's clear wishes. For some people, so-called 'mercy killing' occupies the lower end of the murder spectrum but this does not mean that the courts are willing or able to allow mercy killings to be treated any differently from other murders.[150] Whether the Director of Public Prosecutions would initiate such a criminal charge, or indeed whether a jury would convict a person in such circumstances is open to question and must depend on the facts of the individual case.

[12.79] In *R v Chard*[151] the defendant was prosecuted for providing the deceased person with paracetemol pills at her request, which she used to commit suicide. The defendant said that it had been the deceased's wish to have the option of taking her own life. The judge directed the jury to find the defendant not guilty, as there was no evidence to support the charge of assisting the suicide. He said that providing the deceased with an option of taking her own life was not sufficient to warrant a conviction. Therefore, in England at least, 'it is now clear that assisting a suicide will only be unlawful if conducted on a basis of immediacy and intent – the impersonal distribution of advice or information is hardly likely to attract legal sanction.'[152] Whether this is also the case in Ireland remains to be seen but given the similar wording in both the Irish and English legislation, an Irish court would no doubt take into consideration the judgments of the English courts mentioned above while ensuring that such a similar interpretation in the Irish context fits within our Constitutional framework in relation to the right to life.

[12.80] In January 2002 an American Unitarian Minister, George Exoo, was reported to have assisted a woman to commit suicide in Dublin[153] by apparently being present with her when she took a massive overdose of sleeping pills mixed with alcohol and inhaled helium gas. The Irish government attempted to extradite Exoo from the US to face criminal charges in Ireland but the American court which heard the application on whether or not the extradition treaty between the US and Ireland applied to him, held that although assisting a suicide is a felony under Irish law, there is no equivalent federal law in the US, nor in Exoo's home state of West Virginia. Therefore, his extradition was refused. In 2011 Dr Philip Nitschke, an Australian doctor who advocates on behalf of an

---

[149] Levene and Parker, 'Prevalence of Depression in Granted and Refused Requests for Euthanasia and Assisted Suicide: A Systematic Review' (2011) J Med Ethics 37: 205–211 at 205.
[150] See comprehensive discussion of mercy killing by Huxtable, *Euthanasia, Ethics and The Law: From Conflict to Compromise* (Routledge-Cavendish, 2007) 34–84.
[151] *R v Chard*, The Times, 23 September 1993.
[152] Mason and Laurie *Law and Medical Ethics* (8th edn, OUP, 2010), para 18.53.
[153] See http://www.rte.ie/news/2002/0203/suicide.html (accessed 5 June 2011).

assisted suicide and voluntary euthanasia organisation called Exit International, gave presentations and media interviews in relation to assisted dying.[154]

[12.81] Another issue that has been highlighted in the debate about assisted dying in Ireland relates to death tourism, where people who seek assistance with dying choose to travel, sometimes with their partners or families, to other jurisdictions to avail of such services there. EU citizens are legally entitled to travel abroad to seek access to healthcare services that are unavailable in their own states and this form of tourism has sometimes caught public attention where spouses, parents or children of severely disabled individuals explain their desire to assist their family member to travel, commonly to Switzerland, to avail of assisted suicide procedures available in that country. Similar situations have been highlighted in England and elsewhere where the national laws prohibit assistance with dying. In *A Local Authority v Z*[155] a Local Authority in England applied for an injunction to prevent a man from taking his wife to Switzerland for assisted suicide. She suffered from an incurable condition called cerebellar ataxia, which meant she was unable to look after herself. Hedley J refused the application on the grounds that Mrs Z had been found to be competent and therefore entitled to make her own decisions. Any criminality in the proposed behaviour could be investigated by the appropriate authorities and acted upon as appropriate. This case did not expand on the lawfulness or otherwise of assisted suicide, as the hearing concentrated on the legitimacy of injunctive relief in the circumstances of the case.

[12.82] It had been speculated that when the ECHR was incorporated into English law, there would be a flood of litigation on issues such as assisted suicide. The Human Rights Act 1998 came into force in the UK in October 2000 and was considered in the context of an application for assisted suicide in the case of *R (On the application of Pretty) v DPP*.[156] P, a 42-year-old married woman, was diagnosed with motor neurone disease, which is a progressive neuro-degenerative disease of the central nervous system. The disease causes muscle weakness, difficulty in swallowing and speaking. Death usually occurs as a result of weakness in the breathing muscles, leading to respiratory failure and pneumonia. P's condition had deteriorated rapidly since the diagnosis; she no longer had any movement in her arms or legs and was fed by a tube. 'Essentially she is paralysed from the neck downwards. She has virtually no decipherable speech. The disorder is now at an advanced stage and the prognosis, in particular in relation to her life expectancy, is very poor. Her intellect, however, and her capacity to make decisions are unimpaired.'[157] P sought to be able to control the time and method of her death but, because of the nature of her illness, was unable to take her own life, an action which would not have constituted a criminal offence. She wanted her husband to be able to carry out some of the steps leading to her death, although she stated that the last acts directly leading to her death would be carried out by herself. She sought an undertaking

---

[154] http://www.irishexaminer.com/ireland/kfeyojgbkfql/rss2/#ixzz1Go8EetpD (accessed 5 June 2011).

[155] *A Local Authority v Z* [2005] 1 FLR 740.

[156] *R (On the application of Pretty) v DPP* (2002) 35 EHRR 1, (2002) 66 BMLR 147. See English et al, 'Human Rights and Assisted Suicide' (2002) Journal of Medical Ethics 28(1): 53; Tur, 'Legislative Technique and Human Rights: the Sad Case of Assisted Suicide' (2003) Crim L Rev 3.

[157] *R (On the application of Pretty) v DPP* (2002) 35 EHRR 1, (2002) 66 BMLR, per Tuckey LJ

from the Director of Public Prosecutions (DPP) that her husband would not be prosecuted if he provided such assistance. The DPP refused to give such an undertaking on the basis that it would be improper for him to decline to prosecute in advance of any breach of the criminal law. P sought judicial review of that decision.

[12.83] The Court agreed with the DPP that it was not within his power to give an undertaking regarding future criminal conduct. The Court recognised the conflict that arose here between the right to life and the right to decide what happens to one's own body. The Court was of the view that 'English law curtails a person's right to bodily autonomy in the interest of protecting that person's life even against her own wishes. Thus, deliberate killing, even with consent and in the most pitiable of circumstances, is murder.'[158] Tuckey LJ went on to say that the person's own wishes are not determinative of what can or must be done and that the crucial distinction was between 'killing and letting die'. English law puts helping someone to take their own life on the wrong side of the line because, as Hoffmann LJ said in *Bland*, 'the sanctity of life entails its inviolability by an outsider.'[159] The question for the Court was whether this position was in breach of that person's human rights under the ECHR. In this regard, P based her argument on five articles: art 2 (right to life), art 3 (prohibition of torture and cruel and degrading treatment), art 8 (right to respect for private life), art 9 (right to freedom of thought, conscience and religion) and art 14 (prohibition of discrimination).

[12.84] Article 2 of the ECHR provides that everyone's right to life shall be protected by law and has been interpreted as requiring the State to take adequate measures to safeguard lives from attack. However, it does not require the State to prohibit suicide or force treatment on those who refuse it. Nor does it require the State to prohibit passive euthanasia. The Court concluded that art 2 might permit the State to allow assisted suicide, but could not oblige the State to do so. If the contrary were the case, people attempting suicide could not be saved by medical intervention for fear that they would have a claim for wrongful life, and that outcome was contrary to public policy. Article 3 provides that no one shall be subjected to torture or to inhuman or degrading treatment or punishment. This is an unqualified right which permits of no derogation. As with art 2, the State is obliged not only to refrain from such treatment itself, but also to take reasonable steps to ensure that people are not subjected to such treatment by others.[160] It was argued before the Court that art 3 confers the right to die with dignity. By permitting P to receive the necessary help by which to end her suffering, the State would be protecting her from the degrading effects of her disease. Tuckey LJ did not accept this interpretation of the article. He held that the right to human dignity enshrined in the article was not the right to die with dignity, but the right to live with as much dignity as possible, until life reaches its natural end.[161] 'This may well mean not taking futile and

---

[158] *R (On the application of Pretty) v DPP* (2002) 35 EHRR 1, (2002) 66 BMLR, per Tuckey LJ.
[159] [1993] AC 798 at 831.
[160] *Costello-Roberts v UK* (1995) 19 EHRR 112; *A v UK* (1998) 27 EHRR 611; *Z v UK* E Ct HR 29392/95, 10 May 2001.
[161] He referred here to *D v UK* (1997) 42 BMLR 149, (1997) 24 EHRR 423, where it was held that deporting a person dying of AIDS to a country where he will receive no treatment or proper care amounts to inhuman or degrading treatment. This was the right to live with dignity until natural death.

undignified steps to prolong life beyond its natural death…But that is very different from allowing people to take active steps to bring life to a premature end.'

[12.85] This decision was appealed to the European Court of Human Rights on the basis that the decision of the DPP not to grant immunity from prosecution to the applicant's husband if he assisted her in committing suicide, was contrary to P's rights under arts 2, 3, 8, 9 and 14 of the Convention.[162] The Court was not persuaded by P's argument that the right to life enshrined in art 2 of the Convention also inferred a negative right to end that life. 'Article 2 cannot, without a distortion of language, be interpreted as conferring the diametrically opposite right, namely a right to die; nor can it create a right to self-determination in the sense of conferring on an individual the entitlement to choose death rather than life.' Article 3 was described by the Court as imposing a primarily negative obligation on states to refrain from inflicting serious harm on persons within their jurisdictions, although the article was flexible enough to address other situations that might arise. In this case the State had not inflicted any ill-treatment on P, nor had there been any complaint regarding the medical care that P was receiving. In that sense the case was distinguishable from *D v UK* where the State's act in removing the applicant to a jurisdiction where he would not have received appropriate medical treatment was impugned. P's argument was that by refusing to grant immunity to her husband, the State was failing to protect her from the inevitable suffering she would endure at the end of her illness, and that this constituted inhuman treatment. The Court was of the opinion that this would place a new meaning on the word 'treatment', which was not in accordance with the fundamental objectives of the Convention. An obligation to sanction steps intended to terminate life could therefore not be derived from art 3. The Court, while expressing sympathy for P's situation, similarly dismissed arguments under Articles 8, 9 and 14 of the Convention, taking the view that the prohibition of assisted suicide was not disproportionate to the need to protect vulnerable citizens.

[12.86] The Court's ruling in relation to immunity from prosecution has been criticised on the basis that the legislative provisions in relation to assisted suicide were drafted in such wide terms due to the impossibility of crafting words that would fit only those cases deemed appropriate for prosecution. However, a blanket ban also exposes morally undeserving individuals to prosecution, depending on the view taken by the DPP. Tur says that the legislative technique adopted by the legislation 'privileges justice over certainty because in the absence of any published criteria or policy, the citizen cannot know in advance whether or not morally conscientious and excusable assisted suicide will or will not be prosecuted.[163] Thus, a couple who seeks non-criminal assisted suicide must implement their choice in order to find out whether they are at risk of prosecution. 'There is a peculiar cruelty or inhumanity in the law saying to them that because they respect the law so much they must endure their sad plight.'[164]

---

[162] *Pretty v the United Kingdom*, Application no 2346/02, Strasbourg 29 April 2002.

[163] Tur, 'Legislative Technique and Human Rights: the Sad Case of Assisted Suicide' (2003) Crim L Rev 3, at 10.

[164] Tur, 'Legislative Technique and Human Rights: the Sad Case of Assisted Suicide' (2003) Crim L Rev 3 at 11.

[12.87] The issue of immunity from prosecution was again the subject of judicial ruling in *R (on the application of Debbie Purdy) v DPP*[165] in which Mrs Purdy was concerned about the legal position of her husband if he helped her to travel to another jurisdiction where she could lawfully be assisted to die. She said that the provisions of the Suicide Act engaged her rights under art 8 of the ECHR and that the State's permitted derogation under art 8(2) 'in accordance with the law' could not apply in the absence of a specific public policy as to when the DPP would or would not prosecute in such circumstances. The House of Lords directed the DPP to formulate an offence-specific policy identifying the factors to be considered in deciding whether or not to prosecute.

[12.88] Shortly after the ruling in Purdy, the DPP issued an interim policy for prosecutors, which was finalised after public consultation.[166] One of the factors in particular may be of interest to family members who facilitate travel arrangements for the person intending to commit suicide. Factor 3 against prosecution reads 'the actions of the suspect, although sufficient to come within the definition of the offence, were of only minor encouragement or assistance'.[167] In a case in 2010, the suspect's acts of booking a hotel room in Switzerland for his parents and accompanying them there were described as of minor assistance.[168] Providing medication, setting up a drip or crushing or dissolving tablets for the patient is likely to make prosecution more likely than simply making travel arrangements.[169] Similar guidance is available from the DPP in Northern Ireland[170] but not in the Republic of Ireland.

[12.89] Some jurisdictions, such as Oregon and Washington in the US, impose requirements on legally provided assisted suicide based on the suffering of the patient, in other words, the patient must have had a terminal illness.[171] This would not include patients who are paralysed but not terminally ill. Others, such as Belgium,[172] Luxembourg[173] and the Netherlands[174] state that the patient must be in constant and unbearable suffering which cannot be alleviated.

---

[165] *R (on the application of Debbie Purdy) v DPP* [2008] EWHC 2565 (QB), (2008) 104 BMLR 28.

[166] See discussion by Lewis, 'Informal Legal Change on Assisted Suicide: The Policy for Prosecutors' (2011) Legal Studies Vol 31 No 1 p 119–134.

[167] See http://www.cps.gov.uk/publications/prosecution/assisted_suicide_policy.html (accessed 6 June 2011).

[168] See http://www.cps.gov.uk/news/press_releases/113_10/ (accessed 6 June 2011).

[169] Lewis, 'Informal Legal Change on Assisted Suicide: The Policy for Prosecutors' (2011) Legal Studies Vol 31 No 1, at 121.

[170] See News Release 'PPS Publishes Policy on Assisted Suicide' (25 February 2010), available at http://www.ppsni.gov.uk (accessed 6 June 2011).

[171] Oregon Death with Dignity Act, s 1.01(12); Washington Death with Dignity Act, RCW 70.245.010(13).

[172] Act on Euthanasia, May 28, 2002, s 3(1).

[173] Loi du Mars 2009 sur l'euthanasie et l'assistance au suicide, article 1.

[174] Termination of Life on Request and Assisted Suicide (Review Procedures) Act 2001, s 2(1)(b).

Physician-assisted suicide

[12.90] In some cases a patient may request the assistance of their doctor to provide medication, set up an intravenous drip, or other means to enable the patient to take their own life. As discussed above, Irish law currently provides that any person, including a doctor, who actively assists a patient to commit suicide, will incur criminal liability.[175] A successful prosecution would have to show that the doctor intentionally assisted or encouraged the commission of the act in question or that he was at least ready to assist, if required to do so. An argument could be made, along the lines of *R v Chard*, discussed above,[176] that a doctor who provides medication merely provides the patient with the option of committing suicide, rather than directly assists in the commission of the suicide itself. However, given the stigma attached to such conduct, it is more likely that it would be held to be, at the very least, counselling or procuring suicide. It would most likely be irrelevant that the patient was suffering from a terminal disease, and that death was imminent in any event. The doctor could also face disciplinary proceedings before the Medical Council due to the provisions of the Guide to Professional Conduct and Ethics, which currently provides that doctors must not participate in the deliberate killing of a patient by active means.[177]

[12.91] The distinction between voluntary euthanasia and assisted suicide is based on the level of participation of the person providing the assistance. Thus, if death occurs as a result of an overt deliberate act of the doctor at the request of the patient, this is voluntary euthanasia. If the doctor participates in the events leading up to the suicide, such as by providing the medication by which the patient's death will occur but the patient does the final act himself, this is assisted suicide.[178]

[12.92] Where a doctor complies with a patient's refusal of treatment, resulting in the patient's death, it is possible that an allegation of assisted suicide could be made if the refusal of treatment by the patient was treated as suicide. In older cases such as *John F Kennedy Memorial Hospital v Heston*,[179] the courts drew an analogy between refusals of treatment and suicide, thereby justifying the Court's decision to override the former. 'If the state may interrupt one mode of self-destruction, it may with equal authority interfere with the other...the state's interest in sustaining life in such circumstances is

---

175 Most famously, Dr Jack Kevorkian (widely known as Dr Death) performed, on his own admission, 130 assisted suicides and led a crusade against state laws that prohibited his activities. In November 1998 he recorded one such incident whereby he administered a lethal injection to one of his patients, following which he was charged and convicted of second-degree murder and delivery of a controlled substance. In April 1999 he was sentenced to 10–25 years on the murder charge, and 3–7 on the other charge. He served 8 years in prison and was later paroled in 2007 on the basis that he would not offer suicide advice to any other person.

176 See para **12.79**.

177 Medical Council, *Guide to Professional Conduct and Ethics* (7th edn, 2009), para 22.6. Available at http://www.medicalcouncil.ie/ (accessed 6 June 2011).

178 For comprehensive discussion, see Otlowski, *Voluntary Euthanasia and the Common Law* (OUP, 1997) at 61.

179 *John F Kennedy Memorial Hospital v Heston* 58 NJ 576 (1971).

hardly distinguishable from its interest in the case of suicide.'[180] More recent cases have distinguished between the two as the right to self-determination has taken a stronger foothold. Refusal of treatment is now generally interpreted by the courts as being aimed at the avoidance of unwanted treatment, pain or the violation of religious principles, rather than at causing one's own death.[181] It is also the case that in many refusals of treatment, the courts have taken the view that it is the underlying disease not the withdrawal of life-support that causes the patient's death.

[12.93] Freeman questions the consistency of the law in allowing a person to refuse medical treatment with the consequence that the patient will die, but not allowing a person to have assistance in committing suicide. He says that there are different forms of suicide and different refusals of treatment. Some refusals of treatment are suicidal as opposed to a cry for help. Others demonstrate not so much an intention to put an end to life, as a decision that treatment is no longer worthwhile because it is just putting off the inevitable, or causes more pain than the patient is prepared to endure. The law appears to allow a doctor to withdraw treatment in response to such a refusal but would not require a doctor to respect a request to withhold or withdraw treatment where the patient's intention was suicidal. 'Since the doctor cannot always be certain into which category the patient falls, it may be that the only safe advice to offer him or her is to treat.'[182]

[12.94] In *Bouvia v Superior Court*,[183] the patient was a 28-year-old quadraplegic woman who required permanent hospitalisation, but who was likely to live for a further 20 years. She had expressed the wish to commit suicide and had unsuccessfully sought court permission to starve herself to death. She then applied to the Court for an injunction ordering that the doctors remove the naso-gastric tube with which she was being fed. The California Court of Appeal upheld her claim that she had an absolute right to refuse life-saving treatment, and rejected arguments that the state had an interest here in the prevention of suicide and the preservation of life. The Court held that her refusal of treatment was a decision to let nature take its course, rather than a wish to end her life, thus evading the suicide issue.[184] In any event, the Court was of the view that her motivation was irrelevant, as she had an absolute right to refuse treatment.[185]

[12.95] The doctors and hospital in this case had argued that Ms Bouvia should not be allowed to refuse medical treatment whilst in their care, as it would be tantamount to suicide and that they could accordingly be liable for assisted suicide. The Court held that the patient was not committing suicide but letting nature take its course and therefore no criminal liability attached to the doctors or hospital. The Court held that to establish liability for assisted suicide there must be some affirmative act such as providing a gun, poison, knife or other instrumentality by which a person could inflict upon themselves

---

[180] *John F Kennedy Memorial Hospital v Heston* 58 NJ 576 (1971) pp 581–2.

[181] Otlowski, *Voluntary Euthanasia and the Common Law* (OUP, 1997) at 66.

[182] Freeman, 'Denying Death its Dominion: Thoughts on the Dianne Pretty Case' (2002) Med L Rev 10: 245–270 at 248.

[183] *Bouvia v Superior Court* 225 Cal. Reptr 297 (1986).

[184] See also *B v A NHS Hospital Trust* [2002] EWHC 429.

[185] Fisher, 'The Suicide Trap: *Bouvia v Superior Court* and the Right to Refuse Medical Treatment' (1987) 21 Loy L Rev 219, 237.

an immediate and fatal injury. This was 'far different from the mere presence of a doctor during the exercise of a patient's constitutional rights.'[186]

> On this reasoning, a doctor's compliance with the refusal of treatment by a patient, who has decision-making capacity, would not attract criminal liability for assisting suicide. However, it may be wondered to what extent this reasoning has been influenced by policy considerations and in particular, the natural reluctance of the courts to impose criminal liability on doctors.[187]

[12.96] Two decisions of the US Supreme Court in 1997 dealt with the Constitutional position of state laws which prevented doctors from prescribing medication to hasten death. The Court held that laws which made it a crime to assist a suicide did not violate individual rights guaranteed under the US Constitution. The cases, *Washington v Glucksberg*[188] and *Vacco v Quill*,[189] were brought by terminally ill patients and doctors involved in the care of the terminally ill. The patients were in the final stages of their illnesses and wanted their doctors' help in ending their lives. The doctors testified that, in certain circumstances, it would be consistent with good medical practice to prescribe drugs in order to hasten the death of a mentally competent terminally ill patient. The laws in Washington and New York prohibited them from providing such assistance. In *Glucksberg* it was argued that the due process clause of the Constitution entitled the plaintiffs to a protected liberty interest and that any state law which infringed this fundamental Constitutional right had to be subject to strict scrutiny. The due process clause of the Fourteenth Amendment had been held to protect certain liberties against state interference such as the right to marry, the right to marital privacy, to use contraception and to abortion. However, it was recognised by the Court that to expand the boundaries of the clause would be dangerous, as it would substitute the subjective beliefs of the judiciary for the considered will of the democratic process.[190] Rehnquist CJ, giving the unanimous opinion of the Court, rejected the argument that this case was about the 'right to die' and described it rather as a right to assistance in committing suicide. He concluded that this right did not have any place in American legal tradition, and he distinguished assisted suicide from refusals of medical treatment on the basis of the doctrine of informed consent and the fact that forced medical treatment was a battery. Accordingly, the Court held that the state law prohibiting physician-assisted suicide did not violate the due process clause of the Constitution.

[12.97] In *Quill* it was argued that the New York law prohibiting physician-assisted suicide violated the equal protection clause of the Constitution on the basis that the statute discriminated against terminally ill patients who were not on life support and could not have assistance in dying, as opposed to those patients on life support who had an absolute right to refuse such treatment and thus end their lives. The Court held that there were a number of differences between the two situations: First, in the case of the

---

[186] *Bouvia v Superior Court* 225 Ca Rptr 297 at 306.
[187] Otlowski, *Voluntary Euthanasia and the Common Law* (OUP, 1997) at 78.
[188] *Washington v Glucksberg* 117 S Ct 2258 (1997).
[189] *Vacco v Quill* 117 S Ct 2293 (1997).
[190] See Carolan, 'US Supreme Court Rules: No Constitutional Right to Physician Assisted Suicide' (1997) MLJI 43 at 47; and Carolan, 'US Supreme Court Confronts "Right to Die"' (1998) Medico-Legal Journal Vol 66 Part 2, 65–69.

withdrawal of life-sustaining treatment death was caused by the illness, while in assisted suicide death was caused by the lethal dose of medication. Second, the withdrawal of life support or the administration of high doses of pain relieving medication which might hasten death, was not synonymous with a desire to end life. The patient might want to live, but not with the pain which he suffered. In assisted suicide, the clear intent is to bring about death. The right to decline medical treatment is not based on a right to die, but on a protection of bodily integrity and freedom from non-consensual touching. Accordingly, the New York law protected valid and important public interests and bore a rational relation to the legitimate end pursued by the state.

[12.98] It is perhaps significant that, despite the Court's ruling in these cases, it also expressly acknowledged that the question of physician-assisted suicide will not go away.[191] As Rehnquist CJ said in *Glucksberg* 'Throughout the nation, Americans are engaged in an earnest and profound debate about the morality, legality, and practicality of physician-assisted suicide. Our holding permits this debate to continue, as it should in a democratic society.'

[12.99] There are currently only two US states to approve physician-assisted suicide, namely Oregon and Washington. In Oregon the Death with Dignity Act was introduced in 1997 to legalise physician-assisted suicide. It does not legalise assistance provided by any other party nor does it legalise euthanasia, even where performed by a doctor. The Oregon Health Plan provides for the cost to be borne by the state for low-income people. The Act requires that the patient be an adult who has capacity to make decisions regarding health care, and have an illness that is expected to lead to death within six months. The patient must make one written and two oral requests (at least 15 days apart) to his physician. The patient's primary physician and a consultant are required to confirm the diagnosis of terminal illness and the prognosis, determine that the patient is capable, and refer the patient for counselling if it is felt that the patient's judgment is impaired by depression or other psychiatric or psychological disorder. All feasible alternatives must be made known to the patient and all prescriptions for lethal medications must be reported to the Oregon Health Division. Those who adhere to the requirements of the Act are protected from criminal prosecution. In 2010, 65 patients died after taking medication prescribed by their doctors under these provisions. In Washington, which has had legalised physician-assisted suicide along similar lines to Oregon since 2009, 51 people died after taking legally prescribed medication in 2010.

[12.100] Contrary to fears that had been expressed that, if physician-assisted suicide were legalised, it would be forced upon terminally ill patients who were poor, uneducated or uninsured, no obvious abuses of the law or unintended consequences appear to have occurred so far.[192] Battin also suggests that no evidence exists to support those fears.[193] However, Finlay and George dispute these findings on the basis that Battin's research focused on vulnerability based on race, gender or other socioeconomic

---

[191] For detailed analysis of these cases, see Pratt, 'Too Many Physicians: Physician-Assisted Suicide After *Glucksberg/Quill*' (1999) 9 Alb LJ Sci and Tech 161.

[192] Fraser and Walters, 'Death – Whose Decision? Physician-Assisted Dying and the Terminally Ill' (2002) West J Med 176:120–123.

[193] Battin et al, 'Legal Physician-Assisted Dying in Oregon and the Netherlands: Evidence Concerning the Impact on Patients in "Vulnerable" Groups' J Med Ethics 2007; 33:591–7.

status and did not refer to emotional vulnerability, personality type or the prevalence of depression.[194] The decision to request and use a prescription for lethal medication is most commonly associated with concern about loss of autonomy and dignity, dependency and loss of control of bodily functions, rather than with fear of intractable pain.[195] In both states, the vast majority of patients using the law were white, well-educated, insured, dying of cancer and receiving hospice care.[196] In Montana, the Supreme Court ruled in 2009 that doctors prescribing life-ending medication to patients with terminal illnesses who have requested it and who do the final act themselves, are not subject to homicide statutes.[197] The Court said that although the state's Constitution did not guarantee a right to physician-assisted suicide, there was nothing in case law or statute in Montana indicating that doctor-assisted death is contrary to public policy. The Court said that 'each stage of the physician-patient interaction is private, civil and compassionate … The physician and terminally ill patient work together to create a means by which the patient can be in control of his own mortality. The patient's subsequent private decision whether to take the medicine does not breach public peace or endanger others.'

Active and passive euthanasia

[12.101] While it is generally accepted in most jurisdictions, including Ireland, that doctors must respect their patient's decisions to be allowed to die, killing is regarded as morally and legally different.[198] The most common distinction drawn between killing and allowing someone to die is based on the difference between acts and omissions resulting in death. In other words, a person kills if he does something that causes another to die, who otherwise would not have died. A person allows someone to die if he has the ability and opportunity to prevent someone from dying, but does not act to prevent the death. Another distinction often drawn is that between active and passive euthanasia: 'In active euthanasia, the physician directly and intentionally kills the patient. In passive euthanasia, he does not commence, or else discontinues a particular treatment which is

---

194 It is feared that suicidal ideation or depression will lead people to make erroneous choices motivated by factors which in some cases might be ameliorated. Opponents of assisted suicide therefore argue that depression may make the person incompetent to make such a decision, and also if the person was treated for depression, they might change their mind. However, depression may or may not amount to a negation of competence, as most people who know they will die in the coming months feel some degree of sadness and even depression but this does not negate their competence to make a will or refuse medical treatment. See discussion by McLean, *Assisted Dying: Reflections on the Need for Law Reform* (Routledge-Cavendish, 2007), pp 39–41.

195 Magnusson, *Angels of Death: Exploring the Euthanasia Underground* (Yale University Press, 2002) at p 90.

196 For statistics in Oregon, see http://public.health.oregon.gov/ProviderPartnerResources/ EvaluationResearch/DeathwithDignityAct/Documents/year13.pdf (accessed 13 July 2011). For statistics in Washington, see www.doh.wa.gov/dwda/forms/dwda2010.pdf (accessed 6 June 2011).

197 *Baxter v Montana* MT DA 09–0051, 2009 MT 449.

198 Otlowski argues that this alleged distinction reveals an element of self-deception which may assist doctors in justifying their conduct in permitting patients to die. Otlowski, *Voluntary Euthanasia and the Common Law* (OUP, 1997) at 192.

likely to result in the patient dying, naturally.'[199] Rachels describes the distinction between acts and omissions as follows:

> In the first, Smith stands to gain a large inheritance if anything should happen to his six-year old cousin. One evening, while the child is taking his bath, Smith sneaks into the bathroom and drowns the child, and then arranges things so that it will look like an accident. In the second, Jones also stands to gain if anything happens to his six-year old cousin. Like Smith, Jones sneaks in planning to drown the child in his bath. However, just as he enters the bathroom Jones sees the child slip and hit his head, and fall face down in the water. Jones is delighted; he stands by, ready to push the child's head back under if it is necessary, but it is not necessary. With only a little thrashing about, the child drowns all by himself, 'accidentally,' as Jones watches and does nothing.[200]

[12.102] The question here is whether Smith, who kills, is more culpable than Jones, who allows the child to die. If, as Rachels argues, there is no moral difference between the two, then the fact that one is killing and the other is allowing the child to die, is not a morally important difference. When it comes to medical decision-making at the end of life, the same kind of reasoning may apply. According to this thesis, if, for example, a doctor satisfies his patient's request to switch off the ventilator, he kills his patient just in the same way as if the patient's son, impatient for his inheritance, went into the room and unplugged the machine. When the doctor removes the ventilator he performs an action that causes the patient to die, when otherwise they would have continued to live, in other words, he kills. The intention and effect are the same in both scenarios, although clearly the motivation is different. In the case of the doctor, his actions would probably be held to be justifiable, whereas in the case of the son, they would not. As Brock points out: 'One can kill or allow to die with or without the victim's consent, with a good or bad motive and in or not a social role that authorises such action; these factors determine whether what was done was morally justified, not whether it is a case of killing or allowing to die.'[201] In terms of the law's reaction to the difference between killing and allowing to die, Otlowski neatly summarises the position as follows:

> A doctor may lawfully perform passive euthanasia at the request of a competent patient: that is, he or she may, at the patient's request, deliberately withhold or withdraw treatment with the intention of facilitating the patient's death. This conclusion, in turn, highlights the law's starkly differential treatment of active and passive euthanasia. A doctor who performs active euthanasia will potentially face criminal liability for murder even in circumstances where the acts causing death were performed at the patient's request. Yet, a doctor who withholds or withdraws treatment at the request of a competent patient, intending that the patient's death will result, will not be criminally liable for the patient's death. Thus, even though the object and end result of active and passive euthanasia are the same, the legal consequences are vastly different.[202]

[12.103] On the other side of the argument is the example of the patient with a potentially lethal disease that is prevented from causing the patient's death by the intervention of the doctor's application of life-sustaining treatment. When the treatment

---

[199] Kelleher, 'Euthanasia and Physical Assisted Suicide' (1996) MLJI 77–79 at 77.

[200] Rachels, 'Active and Passive Euthanasia' (1975) New Eng J of Med 292/2, 78–80.

[201] Brock, *Life and Death: Philosophical Essays in Biomedical Ethics* (Cambridge University Press, 1993) p 238.

[202] Otlowski, *Voluntary Euthanasia and the Common Law* (OUP, 1997) at 55.

is withdrawn, even though this involves action by the doctor, the patient is allowed to die, and the doctor's actions are justifiable, because the disease proceeds to kill the patient. However, this would mean that the impatient son in the example above also simply allows his mother to die.[203] Similarly, with the decision not to place the patient on life support in the first place, for example, in the case of a patient who is dying of cancer and who suffers respiratory failure: doing nothing in those circumstances may be acceptable. However, doing nothing is not always justifiable, as where a doctor deliberately lets a patient die who was suffering from a routinely curable disease. In such a case, the doctor's actions are the same, in that he allows the disease to kill the patient, but in the latter case he would be prosecuted.

[12.104] Gillon argues against the *necessary* moral equivalence of killing and letting die though he does acknowledge that there are cases in which they are equivalent.[204] He claims that there is a strong universal prohibition on killing but a much more ambivalent attitude to letting die, and that this arises from the assumption that all of us owe a strong duty to all others not to kill each other, but that we may or may not, depending on the circumstances, owe a duty to each other to preserve each other's lives. Consequentialist arguments may be brought to bear on why the distinction between the two should be maintained, ranging from the public perception of the higher culpability of someone who kills, the costs of keeping people alive as opposed to killing them, the 'harm' inflicted on the patient in killing as opposed to letting die and the respect accorded to the patient's autonomy in each case. By contrast, Otlowski argues from the perspective of patient autonomy, that it is an unjustifiable infringement of liberty to deny active voluntary euthanasia to those who choose it.[205] Harris argues similarly, that it is a form of tyranny, an attempt to control the life of a person who has his own autonomous view about how life should go, and that this constitutes an ultimate denial of respect for persons.[206]

The doctrine of double effect

[12.105] In the treatment of certain illnesses, such as cancer, it sometimes becomes necessary to administer large doses of pain killing drugs to ease the patient's suffering. These drugs may carry higher risks of causing respiratory depression and hastening the

---

[203] For a detailed philosophical perspective on this issue, see Quinn, 'Actions, Intentions and Consequences: The Doctrine of Doing and Allowing' (1989) The Philosophical Review, Vol XCVIII, No 3.

[204] Gillon, 'Euthanasia, Withholding Life-Prolonging Treatment, and Moral Differences Between Killing and Letting Die' (1988) Journal of Medical Ethics, 14:115–117.

[205] It seems ironical that a competent patient who is terminally ill cannot lawfully request medication to induce death, yet an incompetent patient in PVS who has not expressed a wish to die, may have nutrition and hydration withdrawn in his best interests. Otlowski, *Voluntary Euthanasia and the Common Law* (OUP, 1997). Also see Sloss, 'The Right to Choose How to Die: A Constitutional Analysis of State Laws Prohibiting Physician-Assisted Suicide' (1996) 48 Stanford L Rev 937: 'Of course the law must limit the extent to which physicians may act to hasten a patient's death, but should the law define those limits to permit involuntary physician-assisted euthanasia of incompetent, non-terminal patients … while prohibiting voluntary physician-assisted euthanasia for competent, terminally ill patients …?'

[206] Harris, 'Euthanasia and the Value of Life' in Keown, (ed) *Euthanasia Examined: Ethical, Clinical and Legal Perspectives* (Cambridge University Press, 1995) 6 at 19.

patient's death.[207] Most would agree that not to administer such drugs would result in unacceptable pain for the dying patient, and justify the actions of the doctor on the basis of his intention to relieve suffering as opposed to bring on the patient's death.[208] The doctrine of double effect is invoked here to substantiate the argument.[209] The doctrine distinguishes between the consequences a person intends and those that are unintended but foreseen.[210] It holds that an action with a bad consequence, such as the patient's death, is justifiable if that consequence is not intended and is necessary to achieve a proportionately good effect, here, the relief of the patient's pain.[211] Of course, there are cases in which the distinction between foresight and intention are blurred, but in relation to pain control it seems clear that the death of the patient is an unintended but foreseen side-effect and therefore morally permissible.[212] If, however, the doctor gave the patient a lethal injection, this would be a deliberate act causing death, and would be morally prohibited.[213] Some argue that in the latter case, euthanasia, the doctor's intention may also be the relief of suffering, at the request of the patient, and therefore the use of intention in this context is not sufficient to distinguish between permissible and impermissible killing.

[12.106] The doctrine of double effect is thought to have originated with some Roman Catholic theologians such as Thomas Aquinas but has now become part of general moral philosophical doctrine. The doctrine has four conditions. First, the action itself must not be inherently wrong. Secondly, the intention must be solely to produce the good effect. Thirdly, the good effect must not be achieved through the means of the bad effect. Fourthly, there must be a favourable balance between the good and the bad effects of the action. The doctrine may be applied in the area of self-defence where the desired end is to avoid harm, all other effects being unintended, and has traditionally been used in arguments on abortion where the woman's life is endangered by continuation of the pregnancy.[214]

---

[207] The World Health Organisation (WHO) states, 'If shortening of life results from the use of adequate doses of an analgesic drug, this is not the same as intentionally terminating life by overdose'. WHO *Cancer Pain Relief and Palliative Care* (Geneva: 1990).

[208] See comments by Devlin J in *R v Adams* where he noted that the doctrine of double effect permits doctors to relieve pain, even if this incidentally shortens life by hours or even longer. See Palmer, 'Dr. Adams' Trial for Murder' (1957) Crim L Rev 365.

[209] See Dunstan, 'Double Effect' in Dunstan AS, Dunstan GR and Wellbourn (eds) *Dictionary of Medical Ethics* (2nd edn, Darton, Longman and Todd Ltd, 1981) p 145.

[210] Quill, Lo and Brock, 'Palliative Options of Last Resort: A Comparison of Voluntarily Stopping Eating and Drinking, Terminal Sedation, Physician-Assisted Suicide, and Voluntary Active Euthanasia' (1997) 278 JAMA 2099; and Meisel, Snyder and Quill, 'Seven Legal Barriers to End-of-Life Care' (2000) 284 JAMA 2495.

[211] Bole, 'Double Effect: Theoretical Function and Bioethical Implications' (1991) Journal of Medicine and Philosophy, Vol 16: 467–585.

[212] In the same way as surgery is lawful even though there is a chance of death. See Emanuel, 'Why Now?' in Emanuel (ed) *Regulating How We Die: Ethical, Medical and Legal Issues Surrounding Physician Assisted Suicide* (Harvard University Press, 1998).

[213] Brock, *Life and Death: Philosophical Essays in Biomedical Ethics* (Cambridge University Press, 1993), at 239.

[214] For a detailed examination of the doctrine of double effect, see Price, 'Euthanasia, Pain Relief and Double Effect' (1997) 17 (2) Legal Studies 323–342.

[12.107] In *R v Cox*[215] an elderly woman who was terminally ill and in great pain, which was not controlled by drugs, repeatedly asked her consultant Dr Cox, and others, to kill her. Dr Cox administered a lethal injection of potassium chloride, a drug which causes death but has no therapeutic value in this form, and she died almost immediately. Ognall J directed the jury as to the doctrine of double effect in the following terms:

> [I]f he injected her with potassium chloride with the primary purpose of killing her, of hastening her death, he is guilty of the offence charged...If a doctor genuinely believes that a certain course is beneficial to his patient, either therapeutically or analgesically, then even though he recognises that that course carries with it a risk to life, he is fully entitled, nonetheless, to pursue it. If in those circumstances the patient dies, nobody could possibly suggest that in that situation the doctor was guilty of murder of attempted murder.[216]

[12.108] Dr Cox was found guilty of attempted murder[217] because he used death as the means of relieving pain, the charge for murder being problematic due to the body having been cremated and proof of cause of death was therefore difficult. This case was approved in *Bland* although the judges recognised the illogicality of distinguishing between the withdrawal of life-sustaining treatment and taking steps to kill a patient.

[12.109] As an alternative to pain relieving drugs that shorten life, terminal sedation of a patient may be performed[218] to induce a state of decreased consciousness and take away the patient's perception of distressing symptoms. These sedating drugs may be used intermittently or continuously until death, and the depth of the sedation can vary from a lowered state of consciousness to unconsciousness before withdrawal of a ventilator, or to relieve pain where other options have failed.[219] Proponents of terminal sedation who nonetheless seek to distinguish it from euthanasia or assisted suicide say that the intention of the doctor here is to sedate, not to kill, in order to relieve pain. However, this has been criticised as a smokescreen[220] and a fig-leaf for euthanasia.[221] One of the issues in the debate about the ethical acceptability of terminal sedation centres on whether it shortens the patient's life. When the patient's life expectancy is short, for example two weeks, when sedation is started, continuous deep sedation is thought to have no or

---

[215] *R v Cox* (1992) 12 BMLR 38.

[216] *R v Cox* (1992) 12 BMLR 38 at 39.

[217] The jury really had no option in this case due to the drug used by Dr Cox, and many of them were reported to have wept in court as the verdict was delivered. The patient's family considered that the doctor had enabled their relative to die with dignity. Dr Cox was given a suspended sentence and may now practice medicine only under close supervision. The case resulted in much public debate about the issues raised in this case and the difficult role of doctors in similar situations. See further Biggs, 'Euthanasia and Death with Dignity: Still Poised on the Fulcrum of Homicide' (1996) Crim L Rev 878–888.

[218] There seems to be disagreement as to whether this is a common, widely accepted practice or an exceptional event. See Williams, 'The Principle of Double Effect and Terminal Sedation' (2001) 9 Med L Rev 41–53 at 48–49.

[219] Williams, 'The Principle of Double Effect and Terminal Sedation' (2001) 9 Med L Rev 41–53. See also Rietjens et al, 'Continuous Deep Sedation for Patients Nearing Death in the Netherlands: Descriptive Study' (2008) BMJ Vol 336 No 7648.

[220] Clarke, 'What is the Doctrine of Double Effect?' (1997) 93 Nursing Times 15.

[221] Truog, Berde et al, 'Barbituates in the Care of the Terminally Ill' (1991) 327 New Eng J of Med 1678 at 1680.

limited effect on life shortening and thus is said not to be the moral equivalent of euthanasia. When it is used for patients with a longer life expectancy with the intention to hasten death at the patient's request, this practice should be regarded as the moral equivalent of euthanasia. Some argue that the act of inducing unconsciousness crosses the line between making the patient's suffering tolerable and terminating the patient's conscious existence. McLean argues that if one of the reasons why people seek assisted suicide is due to their objection to loss of control over their bodies, terminal sedation merely guarantees that loss and would surely not be a desirable way to end one's life. She also says it is indistinguishable from other assistance in dying, as it requires an act by a doctor and is designed to bring about death.[222]

[12.110] In the context of whether terminal sedation can be justified under the doctrine of double effect, it may be argued that terminal sedation satisfies the requirement that the treatment is beneficial to the patient, and that the doctor does not intend death but the relief of the patient's pain. However, it is also the case that the sedation may precede the withdrawal of nutrition and hydration from the patient, a procedure that is not a method of relieving pain. The British Medical Association (BMA) justifies this on the basis that although the doctor may foresee that withdrawing artificial nutrition and hydration will result in the patient's death, this is 'fundamentally different from action taken with the purpose or objective of ending the patient's life'.[223] However, while the withdrawal of nutrition and hydration may satisfy the doctrine of double effect in that the death is not intended, merely foreseen, it may be argued that it does not satisfy the other prerequisites of the doctrine, namely that the nature of the act must be morally good, such as the relief of pain, and that the bad effect (death) is not a means of achieving the good effect (relief of pain). If the patient does not die from the underlying disease or the medication, he will die from starvation or dehydration.[224] Accordingly, withdrawing food and water from a terminally sedated patient cannot be justified under the principle of double effect. 'It appears, therefore, that any justification for terminal sedation will have to rely on the admittedly "morally and intellectually dubious distinction between acts and omissions"[225] and the notion of the patient's best interests.'[226]

[12.111] Palliative care specialists are some of the strongest opponents of legalised assisted dying and they support their position by claiming that pain can be relieved in almost all cases. However, McLean says that 'we should not permit the legitimate esteem in which they are held to blind us to the paternalism inherent in their approach'.[227] She points to the fact that, apart from pain, there are also other symptoms that can accompany death which are more difficult to treat and may be as terrible for the patient to bear, such as nausea, vomiting, shortness of breath, inability to handle

---

[222] McLean, *Assisted Dying: Reflections on the Need for Law Reform* (Routledge-Cavendish, 2007) at 45.
[223] BMA, *Withholding and Withdrawing Life-Prolonging Medical Treatment. Guidance for Decision-Making* (BMJ Books, 1999) at 50.
[224] Williams, 'The Principle of Double Effect and Terminal Sedation' (2001) 9 Med L Rev, p 52.
[225] Per Mustill J in *Airedale NHS Trust v Bland* [1993] 1 All ER 821 at 399.
[226] Williams, 'The Principle of Double Effect and Terminal Sedation' (2001) 9 Med L Rev, p 53.
[227] McLean, *Assisted Dying: Reflections on the Need for Law Reform* (Routledge-Cavendish, 2007) at 46.

secretions, nightmares and episodic delirium. Given the distress that these symptoms may cause, Davies also challenges the view that the hospice movement's undoubted expertise in dealing with the dying has removed the need for consideration of assisted dying. He says 'even if it were possible to alleviate all of these – and the hospice doctors do not claim that it is – there are still many people who do not want to go on to the bitter end and do not see why that should be required of them.'[228]

[12.112] Terminal sedation was recognised in the US Supreme Court decision *Washington v Glucksberg*[229] as one of the situations in which doctors are already involved in making decisions that hasten the death of terminally ill patients. The American Medical Association decided in 2008 that doctors can offer palliative sedation when symptoms, such as pain, shortness of breath, dyspnea, nausea and vomiting, cannot be diminished through all other means of palliation. It does not accept such sedation to combat emotional distress some terminally ill patients experience at the end of life, and it must never be used to intentionally cause a patient's death.[230] Such measures are also supported by other professional organisations in the US such as the American Academy of Hospice and Palliative Medicine and the American Academy of Pain Medicine. The enactment in the Netherlands of the Termination of Life on Request and Assisted Suicide (Review Procedures) Act in 2002 was followed by a small decrease in rates of euthanasia and an increased application in use of deep sedation, especially for patients with cancer, pulmonary diseases and diseases of the nervous system.[231]

European law and practice on assisted dying

[12.113] In Europe the right to refuse medical treatment is generally recognised, with some jurisdictions, such as Denmark[232] and France[233], enshrining this in statute law. In relation to assisted suicide and euthanasia there is much less unanimity.[234] Germany is unlikely to ever legalise the practice given its legacy of Nazi involuntary euthanasia for racial purification. 'There may be similar sentiments in Scandinavian countries, which have been shaken by recent revelations of state sanctioned sterilisation practices. In southern Europe there is reluctance even to conduct surveys on euthanasia and physician

---

[228] Davies, 'The Case for Legalising Voluntary Euthanasia' Thomasma and Kushner (eds) *Birth to Death: Science And Bioethics* (Cambridge University Press, 1996) 83–85 at 88, cited by McLean, *Assisted Dying: Reflections on the Need for Law Reform* (Routledge-Cavendish, 2007) at 47.

[229] *Washington v Glucksberg* (1997) 138 LEd 2d 772 at 805, per Stevens J.

[230] See http://www.ama-assn.org/resources/doc/code-medical-ethics/2201a.pdf (accessed 6 June 2011).

[231] Euthanasia dropped from 2.6% of all deaths in 2001 to 1.7% in 2005; deep sedation increased from 5.6% to 7.1% in the same period. Rietjens et al, 'Continuous Deep Sedation for Patients Nearing Death in the Netherlands: Descriptive Study' (2008) BMJ Vol 336 No 7648.

[232] Law No 351 of 14 May 1992, s 6.

[233] Law No 94–653 of 29 July 1994, art 3.

[234] See useful analysis in Nys, 'Physician Involvement in a Patient's Death: A Continental European Perspective' (1999) Med L Rev 209.

assisted suicide: convincing a legislature to legalise these interventions seems inconceivable.' [235]

[12.114] In the Netherlands, voluntary euthanasia and physician-assisted suicide have been socially accepted and openly practiced there for many years. When it introduced the Termination of Life on Request and Assisted Suicide (Review Procedures) Act in 2001, it was the first country in the world to legislate for the decriminalisation of voluntary euthanasia, which is defined as behaviour that terminates the life of another at the request of the person concerned. The situation there has been described as having been brought about not so much from the perspective of patient's rights, as from an insistence by doctors that under certain limited circumstances, euthanasia is a legitimate medical procedure.[236] Euthanasia has become somewhat normalised in Dutch medical practice with about 10,000 requests per year, of which about 6,000 are not carried out either because the doctor declines or the patient dies from his illness. The legislation states that doctors must be convinced that the patient's request is voluntary and well considered and that the patient is facing 'unremitting and unbearable suffering'. Doctors must have advised patients of their situation and options and reached the conclusion with the patient that there is no acceptable alternative. One other independent doctor must also be consulted. The law allows for legal recognition of written euthanasia declarations and allows minors aged 12 to 16 to request euthanasia with the consent of their parents.[237]

[12.115] Belgium became the second country in the world to legalise euthanasia in certain circumstances, when in May 2002 legislation was passed which provided that a doctor who carries out a mercy killing will not be guilty of a crime if the patient is terminally ill and has made the decision him or herself. The doctor must be satisfied that the patient is of age and conscious, and that the request is voluntary, fully thought out and consistent.

---

[235] 'Euthanasia: Where the Netherlands Leads Will the World Follow?' Editorial, BMJ 2001:322:1376–1377; de Vries, 'Can a Legal Right to Euthanasia Exist? A Dutch Perspective on a Universal Medico-Ethical Dilemma' Medico-Legal Journal of Ireland Vol 9 No 1 24–35.

[236] Griffiths et al, *Euthanasia and the Law in the Netherlands* (Amsterdam University Press, 1998) at 111.

[237] For discussion, see de Haan, 'The New Dutch Law on Euthanasia' (2002) 10 Med L Rev 57–75.

Chapter 13

Medical Research

INTRODUCTION

[13.01] Progress in medicine cannot occur without research and although sometimes new treatments and techniques can be tested on animals, it is not possible to know with certainty how humans will respond to treatments unless research is carried out with human participants. Until relatively recent times the advances made by medical science, many of which relied heavily on experiments carried out on human beings, were generally accepted as an unqualified and unquestioned good due to the potential benefit to be gained for society.[1] There are numerous historical examples of researchers all across the world who used humans without their knowledge or consent with resulting death, disease and injury in many cases. Until the mid 20th century very few attempts were made to put in place standards for research and, although some researchers saw the need for formal regulation of research, these were the exception rather than the rule. The legacy of unethical experimentation has cast a long shadow over research, which can result in a poor public understanding of the objectives and methodologies employed in biomedical research.

> The term 'research' has a negative meaning to many people; there is an image of a self-serving scientist indulging, in secrecy, in some dubious project, using misappropriated blood or tissue or organs, for personal advancement or gratification. On the other hand, everyone wants to see medicine advance and conquer all the illnesses of mankind and many people feel a duty to help in some way in this advance.[2]

[13.02] In the past, doctors advanced medical care by trying out new therapies on their patients and, in line with prevailing wisdom at that time, little information was sought by or given to patients, as they trusted that their doctors would do the right thing for them. However, 'it was not until the unthinkable happened that it was realised that some doctors could betray that trust.'[3] Contemporary research ethics began as a consequence of disclosure of the unethical experimentation carried out during World War II. As a result of the atrocities carried out during this time, particularly in concentration camps in Germany, which were disclosed during the Nuremberg Trials, the medical profession

---

1   Brazier cites the example of the development of the smallpox vaccine in 'Exploitation and Enrichment: The Paradox of Medical Experimentation' (2008) 34 Journal of Medical Ethics 180–83, in which she describes how the non-therapeutic experiment carried out on an eight-year-old boy has saved the lives of millions of people but would not be sanctioned by a modern research ethics committee.
2   Ó Briain, 'Advancing Medical Knowledge While Protecting Human Research Subjects' (2000) MLJI 79.
3   Ó Briain, 'Advancing Medical Knowledge While Protecting Human Research Subjects' (2000) MLJI 79.

sought to ensure that such horrors could not happen again. International standards for research were developed and have been regularly updated since then to ensure that a proper balance is struck between the protection of the individual research participant[4] and the interests of the common good in finding effective treatments and cures for human diseases. These are discussed in more detail below. Before turning to the specific ethical and legal issues that arise in research, it is important to describe what medical research is, and to set out some relevant distinctions.

Difference between research and clinical audit

[13.03] Research may be described as a structured activity which is intended to be of value to others in similar situations and is therefore intended for dissemination. One of the grey areas in medicine in this context is the difference between research and clinical audit, as there are certain similarities between the two activities but they involve significantly different ethical and legal frameworks. Both research and clinical audit start with a question, both expect the answer to change or influence clinical practice, both require formal data collection on patients, and both depend on using an appropriate method and design to reach sound conclusions. However, by comparison with research, clinical audit is a clinically-led quality improvement process that seeks to improve patient care and outcomes through systematic review of care against explicit criteria, and acts to improve care when standards are not met. The process involves the selection of aspects of the structure, processes and outcomes of care which are then systematically evaluated against explicit criteria. If required, improvements should be implemented at an individual, team or organisation level and then the care re-evaluated to confirm improvements.[5] The major bureaucratic distinction drawn between audit and research may be summarised as follows: research investigates what should be done and why some treatments work better than others, whereas audit investigates whether best practice is being followed, and if not, why not.[6] While not all doctors are actively involved in research activities, all are now expected to participate in clinical audit activities in order to maintain their professional competence and ensure that their practice is in line with national norms.[7]

Research and innovative therapy

[13.04] Another important distinction to draw here is between innovative treatment and research. In general, doctors should only give their patients treatment that has been

---

4   The term 'research subject' is commonly used in texts on this topic but in recent years, the term 'participant' has been considered preferable, as it better symbolises the voluntary and informed nature of the involvement of those who choose to be part of medical research. Therefore, the term 'research participant' will be used in this chapter, except where quoting from other sources.

5   The Commission on Patient Safety and Quality, *Building a Culture of Patient Safety* (2008) at 7.3.1, http://www.dohc.ie/publications/pdf/en_patientsafety.pdf?direct=1 (accessed 6 June 2011).

6   Wade, 'Ethics, Audit and Research: All Shades of Grey' (2005) BMJ 330: 468.

7   Maintenance of professional competence is now mandatory in Ireland under the Medical Practitioners Act 2007. This includes participation in clinical audit. See http://www.medicalcouncil.ie/Professional-Development/Professional-Competence/Info-for-Doctors/ (accessed 6 June 2011).

tested and found to be effective in humans. However, in circumstances where all other possible treatments have been ineffective and the patient's condition is very serious, a doctor may want to give a patient a new treatment which has not yet been tested. The doctor's goal in this instance is not to carry out research on the patient but to provide care for him. The Declaration of Helsinki, discussed in more detail below, states that in the treatment of a patient, where proven interventions do not exist or have been ineffective, the physician, after seeking expert advice, with informed consent from the patient or a legally authorised representative, may use an unproven intervention if in the physician's judgment it offers hope of saving life, re-establishing health or alleviating suffering.[8] This approach was seen in *Simms v Simms*[9] where the parents of an 18-year-old boy and a 16-year-old girl who had variant Creutzfeldt-Jakob disease (the human form of BSE), which is a rare, fatal and incurable neurodegenerative disease, wanted their children to avail of a new treatment which had been tested in mice but not yet in humans. Dame Butler-Sloss P accepted that it was untried treatment and that the legal test for ordinary medical treatment is that it must be accepted as proper by a responsible body of medical opinion. However, she said that if one waited for this test to be satisfied to its fullest extent, no innovative work such as the use of penicillin or performing heart transplant surgery would ever be attempted. She held that 'where there is no alternative treatment available and the disease is progressive and fatal, it seems to me to be reasonable to consider experimental treatment with unknown benefits and risks, but without significant risks of increased suffering to the patient, in cases where there is some chance of benefit to the patient.'

Therapeutic v non-therapeutic research

[13.05] Another important distinction is between therapeutic and non-therapeutic research. Therapeutic research offers potential benefit to the patient-participants and may be regarded as a combination of therapy and research. The goal of therapy is benefit for an individual patient and therefore this must always take precedence in clinical research. Risk of harm or injury is an inevitable factor in any therapy and the patient-participant must be informed of these risks. However, even though risks are included in the research protocol, the protocol for clinical research should never involve a therapy which of itself offers less than standard treatment. Even if a double-blind protocol is employed,[10] the patients in the control group, the group that does not receive the drug or therapy being evaluated, should at least receive a drug or therapy which meets the norms for standard treatment. Non-therapeutic research has an entirely different purpose, as it aims at obtaining knowledge which will be utilised for the health of people in the future. Although ethical principles do allow people to accept a risk of harm even where there is no benefit to themselves, as this is an expression of altruism and a commitment to communitarian welfare, in these cases the participant should be informed clearly that the research protocol is non-therapeutic so that there is no potential for confusion in relation to individual benefit. There may be a danger that

---

[8] World Medical Association, Declaration of Helsinki: Ethical Principles for Medical Research Involving Human Subjects (6th version, adopted in South Korea October 2008), http://www.wma.net/en/30publications/10policies/b3/ (accessed 6 June 2011).

[9] *Simms v Simms* [2002] EWHC 2734.

[10] See discussion at para **13.09**.

researchers might exaggerate the likelihood of a direct benefit to participants in order to avoid the more restrictive rules that govern non-therapeutic research. Noah refers to this as 'benefit creep.'[11] There is also the objection that the purpose of research is to answer the question as to whether the treatment will be effective, so it is difficult to describe a trial as therapeutic if it is unknown in advance whether it will actually provide any medical benefit for the patient.

[13.06] Patients who enrol as participants in clinical trials often mistakenly perceive them as potentially therapeutic even when they have been specifically told that this is not the case. This phenomenon is called 'therapeutic misconception' and is an understandable emotional response based on hope that the trial will prove to be their best chance at recovery from their disease. The terminology used in research ethics guidelines, participant information sheets and consent forms often causes further confusion by blurring the line between research and treatment, obscuring the purposes of the research and exaggerating the potential benefits to participants. The dual role of doctors as researchers may lead to misunderstanding, as patients and families may make trial participation decisions based in part on interactions with their doctors. This poses a challenge for doctors, who may have divided loyalties in attempting to function both as doctor and researcher. As a doctor, the primary obligation is to safeguard his patient's health, whereas as researcher there are additional objectives involved, including the accumulation of knowledge, career advancement and perhaps financial gain. Patients generally find it difficult to recognise and to know how to respond when their doctor has switched hats and is acting primarily as a researcher rather than as a treating doctor focused exclusively on patient benefit.[12] They find it difficult to believe that their doctor would knowingly harm them or use them as a means to his own end. As a result, Annas argues that doctors should not be permitted to play both roles:

> It is unlikely that it will ever be possible…for patients not to indulge in self-deception by imagining that research is really treatment and that they are patients, not research subjects. We cannot separate the subject into two persons. But we can assure that the subject-patient always has a physician whose only obligation is to look out for the best interests of the patient. Thus, we can (and should) prohibit physicians from performing more than minimal risk on their patients, and as a corollary, only permit physician-researchers to recruit the patients of other physicians for their research protocols. In this way, at least the "doubling" of physician and researcher can be physically (and perhaps psychologically) eliminated. [13]

[13.07] Not all phases of the clinical trial process have the same potential for role confusion and therapeutic misconception. It may be argued that the law should go further in regulating this relationship by increasing accountability through tighter supervision of situations where this dual-role is at play and by penalising those who breach their patient's trust.

---

[11] Noah, 'Informed Consent and the Elusive Dichotomy Between Standard and Experimental Therapy' (2002) 28 American Journal of Law and Medicine 361.

[12] Oberman and Frader, 'Dying Children and Medical Research: Access to Clinical Trials as Benefit and Burden' (2003) Am J of Law, Med & Ethics 29:301–317.

[13] Annas, 'Questing for Grails: Duplicity, Betrayal and Self-Deception in Postmodern Medical Research' (1996) 12 J Contemp L & Policy 297 at 322.

Phases of clinical trials

[13.08] The first step in the process towards licensing new medicines for human use involves animal testing. If animal tests show that there is a reasonable likelihood that the new drug will work and that it is unlikely to have unacceptable side-effects, then the trial can commence with human participants.[14] Phase I of the clinical trial will usually involve a small number of healthy volunteers who are given the drug to test its toxicity. Phase I trials are usually non-therapeutic in the sense that the recipients are normally healthy adult volunteers who are not expected to get any clinical benefit from the drug. There are potential risks involved for any such volunteers, as this will be the first application of the drug in humans.[15] Phase II will involve the use of the drug in patients suffering from the condition which the drug aims to treat in order to evaluate its effectiveness and any side-effects. Phase III involves monitoring a larger group of participants who take the drug for a longer period of time under supervision. After this phase, the drug may then be licensed for clinical application but will continue to be monitored in the general population – this may be called Phase IV.

[13.09] In certain clinical trials, participants are randomised or enrolled by chance into various groups within the trial. A researcher might want to evaluate the efficacy of a particular drug when compared with an existing one and in order to ensure that he is not biased to influence the outcome, participants are assigned to different 'arms' of the study to receive either the new drug or the existing treatment. It is usual to also include a 'placebo arm' in the trial, in which participants receive a look-alike drug that has no active ingredient, commonly referred to as a 'sugar pill'. Studies have shown improvement in the condition of some participants after receiving a sugar pill, a phenomenon referred to as 'the placebo effect'.[16] In a double-blind randomised controlled trial, the assignment of participants to the various arms of the trial will be done without the knowledge of either researcher or participants. This may pose ethical problems for researchers who are also the treating doctors of the research participants, as they, as doctors, are obliged to treat in the patient's best interests. Therefore, if a doctor believes that a particular drug is the optimum treatment for his patient's condition, then by enrolling a patient in a research study in which the patient may be randomised to receive a placebo, this may be said to conflict with his ethical duties.[17] However, such a trial is deemed to be ethical as long as the doctor has what is referred to as 'equipoise'. This is a state of uncertainty about the best way to treat a particular

---

[14] Jackson, *Medical Law: Text, Cases and Materials* (OUP, 2010) at 442.

[15] This was seen in England in 2006 when eight men volunteered to take part in a Phase I trial of a drug thought to help in the treatment of arthritis, leukaemia and other conditions. The drug had been tested in primates and it was expected that the dose would be well tolerated in humans but this turned out not to be the case. Six of the men suffered multiple organ failure; the other two had been given a placebo or dummy drug. See findings of an investigation into the incident by Duff *The Expert Group on Phase One Clinical Trials: Final Report* (2006), available at http://www.dh.gov.uk/ (accessed 6 June 2011).

[16] For a useful history and explanation of the placebo effect, see Evans, *Placebo, Mind Over Matter in Modern Medicine* (OUP, 2004) Ch 1.

[17] Jackson, *Medical Law: Text, Cases and Materials* (OUP, 2010) at 445.

condition due to competing information on the topic.[18] The research is thus justified, as it will help to clarify which, if any, treatment is more effective for the condition. Once it becomes clear that one treatment is performing better, then equipoise is lost and the trial should be halted, as there is no longer any justification for continuing research on human participants, and also it would be in the best interests of all participants to receive the effective treatment, not only those who were randomised into this particular group. The principle of equipoise has been criticised on the basis that it would not allow rational individuals to consent to participate in trials that were socially valuable but did not satisfy the requirements of this principle. This attitude has been described as paternalistic interference, in other words, a restriction of a person's liberty on grounds that the restriction will protect or promote the person's welfare.[19]

HISTORICAL CONTEXT OF BIOMEDICAL RESEARCH

[13.10] The major event which shaped modern reactions and ethical responses to medical research is the experimentation carried on in concentration camps in Germany during World War II. During this time, researchers exposed human participants to extreme cold, low-pressure chambers, malaria, typhus and unproved therapies in order to gain information which might prove useful for the treatment of German soldiers and members of the air force.[20] The people used for these experiments were prisoners in the camps who were weak and vulnerable. They suffered horrific injuries and death as part of these experiments and many were deliberately killed in order to obtain biological specimens. In 1947 criminal trials against some of the doctors responsible for these atrocities began in Nuremberg. The doctors argued in their defence that their research was no different from the studies being conducted elsewhere in the world and that there were no internationally agreed standards in place against which they should be measured.[21] They also argued that although initially opposed to these lethal experiments, they became convinced that it made no sense not to risk the lives of a few in order to potentially save the lives of many. One of the best known doctors on trial, Gerhard Rose, illustrated this argument by reference to their attempts to find a vaccine for typhus which had the capacity to save the lives of thousands of people. He said that it was inconsistent of the Allies to fail to acknowledge this point, as they too knowingly risked the lives of soldiers in the war, on the grounds that the sacrifice of a few was necessary to save the lives of many. Most of the doctors were convicted despite their protests.[22]

---

[18] See further London, 'Equipoise and International Human Subjects Research' (2001) 15 Bioethics 312–32.

[19] See further Edwards, Kirchin and Huxtable, 'Research Ethics and Paternalism' Journal of Medical Ethics (2004) 88–91: and Gerrard and Dawson, 'What is the Role of the Research Ethics Committee? Paternalism, Inducements and Harm in Research Ethics' (2005) Journal of Medical Ethics 419–23.

[20] In some instances the object of the experiments was not to find out how to rescue or cure but how to destroy and kill. See Taylor, *Opening Statement of the Prosecution* 9 December 1946, (US Government Printing Office, 1949).

[21] Murphy, *Case Studies in Biomedical Research Ethics* (2004) Mass. Inst. of Technology at 2.

[22] For detailed discussion, see Weindling, 'The Ethical Legacy of Nazi Medical War Crimes: Origins, Human Experiments, and International Justice' In Burley and Harris (eds) *A Companion to Genethics* (Blackwell Publishing, 2004) Ch 5.

[13.11] There were other scandals too in other countries such as Japan and the United States during and after World War II. For example, between 1930 and 1945, Japan conducted extensive trials on biological warfare in China in which it is estimated that over 3,000 people died from deliberate exposure to anthrax, cholera and typhoid as well as being dehydrated, frozen or given transfusions of animal blood. After the war, the United States gave immunity from prosecution to the Japanese researchers in return for sharing of information about their experiments.[23] One of the most infamous examples of unethical research, the memory of which still influences health-care debates in the US, is the Tuskegee Syphilis study. This began in 1932 when the public health service enrolled African-American men in Alabama in a study of the natural history of syphilis. About half of the men had syphilis at the time of enrolment, although they were not told of this fact. Other men contracted syphilis during the course of the study. There was concern at that time that the disease behaved differently according to race as well as the efficacy and safety of certain treatments. The men, who were generally poor and uneducated, were studied at various points during their lives and post-mortem examinations were carried out on them after death to provide definitive data. During the course of the study, effective treatments became available for syphilis but these were not provided to the men, whose names were circulated to doctors in the area to ensure that they did not receive treatment. The study ran from 1932 until 1972 when public attention was drawn to it by the media, and the study was stopped. A formal apology was given by the US President, Bill Clinton, in 1997 to seven participants still living at that time.[24]

[13.12] A final example relates to an article published in 1966 by Beecher who exposed the myth that unethical experimentation was not carried out in a country such as the US when he showed that many studies published in reputable scientific journals at that time were unethical,[25] which shocked many within the research community and led to further calls for tighter regulation. These studies included, for example, one which was designed to learn about the functional anatomy of the urinary tract where doctors inserted catheters into the bladders of healthy newborns, injected radio-opaque dye and performed multiple x-rays to follow the track of the dye. In a second example, doctors suspected that liver injury might result from the administration of an antibiotic so they administered the drug to children in a children's centre including so-called 'mental defectives or juvenile delinquents' who had no disease other than acne. The researchers halted the trial prematurely due to high incidences of significant liver dysfunction. These examples and others led to a demand for international consensus on research ethics standards and governance, which are discussed below.

---

[23] Harris, *Factories of Death: Japanese Biological Warfare 1932–45 and the American Cover-Up* (Routledge, 1994).

[24] Jones, *Bad Blood: The Tuskegee Syphilis Experiment* (Free Press, 1993); Reverby, *Tuskegee's Truths: Rethinking the Tuskegee Syphilis Study* (University of North Carolina Press, 2000).

[25] Beecher, 'Ethics and Clinical Research' (1966) 274 NEJM 1354–60. See also example of cancer immunity study cited by Katz et al in *Experimentation with Human Beings: The Authority of the Investigator, Subject, Professions and State in the Human Experimentations Process* (Russell Sage Foundation, 1972) p 9–65.

INTERNATIONAL CONSENSUS ON RESEARCH ETHICS STANDARDS

[13.13] At the conclusion of the Nuremberg Trials, the Court drew up a set of principles to identify permissible medical experiments, which became known as the Nuremberg Code.[26] These principles stressed that the voluntary consent of the human participants is absolutely essential; the experiment should be such as to yield fruitful results for the good of society; it should be designed and based on the results of animal experimentation and a knowledge of the natural history of the disease or other problem; it should be conducted in such a way as to avoid all unnecessary suffering; no experiment should be conducted where it is likely that death or disabling injury will occur; and the degree of risk to be taken should never exceed that determined by the humanitarian importance of the problem to be solved by the experiment. Although the publication of the Code was symbolically very significant, its impact on the medical profession was limited, as it was assumed to be related to the atrocities carried out in the Nazi concentration camps with very little resonance for the conduct of 'ordinary' research. Thus, the application of the Code to atomic, biological and chemical warfare military research was treated as a state secret in the US and released only in 1975 when the code was declassified. In the 1950s and 1960s the US had additionally begun to put in place a system of research regulation but it was sporadic and not popular with many doctors, who resisted the formalisation of codes which they felt would interfere with the doctor-patient relationship.

[13.14] The publication by the US Department of Health, Education and Welfare of the Belmont Report (entitled Ethical Principles and Guidelines for the Protection of Human Subjects of Research) in 1978 is another important historical document in the field of medical research ethics.[27] The Report identified three main concepts by which to evaluate the ethics of research: respect for persons, beneficence and justice. The first principle, respect for persons, incorporates at least two ethical convictions: firstly, that individuals should be treated as autonomous agents, and secondly that persons with diminished autonomy are entitled to protection. The second principle, beneficence, means that persons are treated in an ethical manner not only by respecting their decisions and protecting them from harm, but also by making efforts to secure their well-being. Two general rules have been formulated as complementary expressions of beneficent actions in this sense: firstly, do no harm and secondly, maximise possible benefits and minimise possible harms. The third principle, justice, means that equals ought to be treated equally. In the specific context of research, the selection of research participants should be scrutinised in order to determine whether some classes (eg, welfare patients, particular racial and ethnic minorities, or persons confined to institutions) are being systematically selected simply because of their easy availability, their compromised position, or their manipulability, rather than for reasons directly related to the problem being studied. Finally, whenever research supported by public funds leads to the development of therapeutic devices and procedures, justice demands

---

[26]　*Trials of War Criminals Before the Nuremberg Military Tribunals Under Control Council Law No10,* Vol 2, 181–2. (US Government Printing Office, 1949).

[27]　The Belmont Report, Ethical Principles and Guidelines for the Protection of Human Subjects of Research (1978), available at http://ohsr.od.nih.gov/guidelines/belmont.html (accessed 6 June 2011).

both that these not provide advantages only to those who can afford them and that such research should not unduly involve persons from groups unlikely to be among the beneficiaries of subsequent applications of the research. This report has been very influential in the development of research ethics in the United States and elsewhere, and it provides the moral framework for understanding regulations in the United States on the use of humans in experimental research.[28]

[13.15] In 1964 the World Medical Association adopted the Declaration of Helsinki, which has been updated on a number of occasions since that time[29], and remains one of the leading reference points in the evaluation of the ethics of research studies. The principles in the Declaration focus on the primacy of the well-being, privacy, autonomy and dignity of human research participants and stress the necessity for studies to be submitted for consideration to an independent research ethics committee prior to commencement. Other international research guidelines include the CIOMS guidelines in 1982, updated most recently in 2002, published by the World Health Organisation (WHO) and the Council for International Organisations of Medical Sciences.[30] These guidelines focus in particular on the application of the Declaration of Helsinki to research carried out in developing countries where different socio-economic, political and cultural factors may otherwise make it easier and cheaper to conduct research without observing restrictive regulations applicable elsewhere. The principle underlying these guidelines is that the research should leave low-resource countries or communities better off than previously or at least no worse off. 'It should be responsive to their health needs and priorities in that any product developed is made reasonably available to them, and as far as possible leave the population in a better position to obtain effective health care and protect its own health.' The participants selected for participation should be the least vulnerable necessary to accomplish the purposes of the research.

[13.16] Further guidance is provided by the International Conference on Harmonisation of Technical Requirements for Registration of Pharmaceuticals for Human Use (ICH) in which the regulatory authorities in Europe, the United States and Japan are participants. The purpose of these guidelines is to strive towards greater harmonisation of regulations in order to reduce duplication in trials of new medicinal products. To do this, there must be mutual acceptance of data generated during clinical trials in these regions which have been conducted following ICH guidelines such as the Guidelines for Good Clinical Practice (GCP).

[13.17] There are certain principles which are common to all these international documents, which include the following:

- the research proposal must be scientifically valid;
- the risks must be proportionate to the benefits;
- it must be approved by an ethics committee;

---

28 For details of the research regulatory system in the US see http://www.hhs.gov/ohrp/ (accessed 6 June 2011).
29 The Declaration of Helsinki. The 8th revision took place in Seoul in 2008. Available at www.wma.net (accessed 6 June 2011).
30 *International Ethical Guidelines for Biomedical Research Involving Human Subjects.* Available at www.cioms.ch/ (accessed 6 June 2011).

- if competent, the research participants must give informed consent;
- if incompetent, there must be sufficient protections in place;
- the research must be halted if there is a risk of injury or death;
- the research must be stopped if equipoise is lost;
- the participants must be free to withdraw at any time;
- the participants should have access to information about the research after it has been concluded;
- research findings should be disseminated, and;
- any participants injured as a result of the trial should be compensated.[31]

Feedback of research results

[13.18] Although there is a good deal of consensus on the principles outlined above, one of the important issues on which there is still some disagreement internationally is whether research data should be fed back to individual research participants. This is perhaps particularly evident in debates about genetic research, where there are a number of competing interests at stake. The Universal Declaration on the Human Genome and Human Rights was adopted by UNESCO in 1997[32] to establish by global consensus broad cross-cultural ethical principles that should inform genetic research and the use of genetic information. Article 5 (c) provides that 'The right of each individual to decide whether or not to be informed of the results of genetic examination and the resulting consequences should be respected.' While researchers do not commonly report individual findings to participants, there is increasing ethical literature stressing the importance of respect for patient autonomy and the requirement to do more than treat participants as a means to an end. Some commentators call for a routine disclosure of research results referring to individual participants, while others restrict the obligation to the communication of general results referring to the sample of participants.[33] Under data protection legislation in Ireland, donors of biological material which has been used for research purposes have the right to make enquiries about personal data relating to them.[34] However, this relates only to personal data and would not necessarily include general study findings. In most studies, researchers accept that they have an ethical duty to disclose general research results to participants and this is generally uncontroversial.

[13.19] It is more problematic to consider the different types of individual data that may be sought by participants and the obligation, if any, on researchers to disclose such information. Apart from identifying information possibly held by researchers (even if coded to respect participants' privacy), genetic mutations may also have been identified

---

[31]   Jackson, *Medical Law: Text, Cases and Materials* (OUP, 2010), at 456.

[32]   The Universal Declaration on the Human Genome and Human Rights (1997). Available at http://www2.ohchr.org/english/law/genome.htm (accessed 6 June 2011).

[33]   See Kollek and Petersen, 'Disclosure of Individual Research Results in Clinico-Genomic Trials: Challenges, Classification and Criteria for Decision-Making' (2011) J Med Ethics 37:271–275; Knoppers et al, 'The Emergence of an Ethical Duty to Disclose Genetic Research Results: International Perspectives' (2006) Eur J Hum Genet;14:1170–8; Ravitsky and Wilfond, 'Disclosing Individual Genetic Results to Research Participants' (2006) Am J Bioeth; 6:8–17; Murphy J et al, 'Public Expectations for Return of Results from Large-Cohort Genetic Research' (2008) Am J Bioeth; 8:36–43; Renegar G et al, 'Returning Genetic Research Results to Individuals: Points to Consider' (2006) Bioethics Vol 20 No 1 pp 24–36.

[34]   Data Protection Acts 1988–2003.

amongst the samples which might have clinical relevance for the individuals concerned. These may, for example, relate to the development of cancer or other diseases and could indicate a need for the individual to follow up with further clinical tests. If the research participants have previously given their consent to receive such information, the question arises as to what information should be fed back and on what basis. If clinical benefit to the participant is to be used as the benchmark for disclosure, then care must be taken to ensure that the quality standards used for detection of the genetic markers are of high clinical validity and consistency. There is no consensus on what constitutes clinical utility in this context and it is likely that the assessment of the clinical utility of genetic data varies widely. It is therefore argued that clinical utility is not sufficient as a criterion to determine whether and in what circumstances individual research results should be disclosed.[35] However, although researchers may argue against disclosure in terms of cost, time and their lack of clinical expertise, Kollek and Petersen argue that taking patient autonomy into account points to the opposite conclusion. They say that the fact that clinical utility cannot be defined in the context of research points instead to a duty to report all individual research findings, irrespective of their character and clinical utility.

[13.20] In addition to feeding back research results to the individual participants, other issues arise in relation to disclosure to genetic relatives of the participants, as the information may have relevance for them also. The potential conflict that may arise where the individual does not consent to wider disclosure of genetic information is considered in Chapter 8.[36] This also points to the need for appropriate counselling of participants both in relation to the significance of the findings for themselves, but also the potential significance for other relatives. There is a danger that the offer of disclosure of genetic data may raise unrealistic expectations or fears and therefore any information disclosed should be made as clear and specific as possible. It may be preferable for the participant to choose a doctor to whom the information may be given and who may be better able to communicate the significance of the findings for the individual, though some may argue that this is a paternalistic approach.

SELECTION OF PARTICIPANTS

[13.21] In the past, researchers commonly conscripted poor, elderly, mentally incapacitated persons and prisoners to their studies, as a result of which they suffered horrific injuries and loss of life. For example, Murphy cites examples of Japanese researchers distributing sweets laced with anthrax to children in China, exposing Chinese civilians to bio weapons and killing people to study the dying process.[37] The unethical experimentation carried out in Germany and the United States has also been discussed above. As a result of these abuses, modern regulations require that the selection of research participants should be scrutinised in order to determine whether some classes of participants are systematically selected simply because of their easy

---

[35] Kollek and Petersen, 'Disclosure of Individual Research Results in Clinico-Genomic Trials: Challenges, Classification and Criteria for Decision-Making' (2011) J Med Ethics 37:271–275 at 272.

[36] See para **8.33** et seq.

[37] Murphy, *Case Studies in Biomedical Research Ethics* (2004) Mass Inst of Technology at 92.

availability, their compromised position or their manipulability. Consent from research participants is now also a fundamental pre-requisite to medical research in all but very exceptional and tightly regulated circumstances. This is discussed further below. The different categories of participants potentially raise different ethical issues and thus will be considered separately.

Older people

[13.22] Pharmaceutical products are rigorously tested for safety and efficacy prior to being licensed for use. During the testing process, the archetypal research participant is a young male and in general, older people are less frequently invited to participate.[38] Two reasons are usually given for the exclusion of older people, one ethical and one physiological. The ethical reason is that there may be a difficulty in obtaining consent from older people due to incapacity. However, it should not be assumed that this is the case, as age is not a pre-determinant of incapacity and all persons should be presumed to have capacity to give consent to participate unless the contrary is established. A second reason relates to the physiology of the older person, as it is thought that they metabolise drugs differently and their participation may therefore distort the research findings. 'The fact that they respond differently to drugs and may manifest adverse reactions at lower doses, does increase the risk that older participants will be injured during drug testing.'[39] Therefore, researchers who recruit younger participants can be more confident that if an adverse reaction is experienced, this is more likely to be as a result of the drug rather than any other medical condition. However, the very fact that they may have different physiological responses to medication means that it is necessary in some cases to include older people in clinical trials in order to test the safety and efficacy of drugs across a broad age spectrum in the community.

Women

[13.23] The non-participation of women in clinical trials is sometimes justified on the basis that women may also metabolise drugs differently and their participation may distort the research findings. However, as with older people, if this is a drug that will be used in the general population, it is necessary to ensure that women are included at the research stage since they may be prescribed these drugs in the future. Therefore, a pharmaceutical company that fails to involve certain groups such as women in a trial for a drug which will ultimately be marketed for those groups may be negligent in not having tested the drugs for safety and efficacy prior to licensing. In *Best v Wellcome Foundation*[40] the defendant pharmaceutical company was sued as a result of injuries caused by its vaccine. One of the issues involved was whether a particular animal testing procedure had been carried out by the company in the development of the vaccine. Although this test would have been part of the manufacturing process rather than the clinical trial stage, it is noteworthy that the Supreme Court held that pharmaceutical companies owe a duty of care in taking all reasonable steps in testing their products.

---

[38]   Ferguson, 'Selecting Participants When Testing New Drugs: The Implications of Age and Gender Discrimination' (2002) Medico-Legal Journal Vol 70 Part 3, 130–134.

[39]   Ferguson, 'Selecting Participants When Testing New Drugs: The Implications of Age and Gender Discrimination' (2002) Medico-Legal Journal Vol 70 Part 3, 130–134 at 131.

[40]   *Best v Wellcome Foundation* [1992] ILRM 609.

Another reason for the exclusion of women from trials is that the drug may have unknown effects on the female reproductive organs, or on any future children. For this reason, women of child-bearing years are commonly excluded to avoid the occurrence of such a risk as the research sponsors try to avoid incurring legal liability to the woman or any children born with a disability as a consequence of the study drug. In the US, federal regulations allow clinical research involving pregnant women as long as earlier studies have been carried out on animals and non-pregnant women, any risks to the foetus are as a result of procedures carried out which offer some benefit to the woman or foetus and other conditions are complied with.[41]

Prisoners

[13.24] The involvement of prisoners in medical research is also ethically difficult due to the historical connotations arising from research carried out during the 1930s and'40s as well as the fact that participants in this group are limited in their choices due to their imprisonment and other social circumstances and may have impaired capacity in terms of the voluntariness of their participation. In the US, federal regulations prohibit such persons being offered advantages such as food, quality of living conditions, etc in return for their participation if they would be such as to affect the person's ability to weigh up the risks involved.[42] It is important not to ban research on this group entirely, however, as very valuable findings may arise from both medical and behavioural research carried out in these settings such as the effect of imprisonment, the social and psychological circumstances of people within this group, alcohol and drug problems and so on.

Children

[13.25] It is necessary to carry out research with children, as they respond differently to drugs and it is impossible to know whether adult-tested drugs will be safe and effective for use with children and in what doses. Children are not miniature versions of adults and thus it is not safe to reduce the adult dosage of a drug by guessing the proportionate weight of the child relative to the adult. As with adults, research with children involves both therapeutic and non-therapeutic components and therefore research will necessarily involve sick children as well as those who can act as healthy controls. There has been considerable debate about the acceptability of children as research participants in biomedical and behavioural research. As far back as the time of the Nuremberg Code and the first Declaration of Helsinki, ethicists have argued that children must not be subjected to medical experimentation. There was a long-running debate in the 1970s in the US between renowned ethicists Ramsay and McCormick on this issue.[43] Ramsay was of the view that, consistent with the Nuremberg Code, children who had not yet achieved some level of intellectual sophistication and emotional maturity could not make autonomous decisions about whether or not to participate in research. This precluded their participation unless the research held out a prospect of providing individual benefit.[44] By contrast, McCormick argued that the wholesale exclusion of

---

[41]   45 Code of Federal Regulation (CFR) 46.204.

[42]   45 CFR 46.306.

[43]   Cited by Oberman and Frader, 'Dying Children and Medical Research: Access to Clinical Trials as Benefit and Burden' (2003) Am J of Law, Med & Ethics 29:301–317.

[44]   Ramsay, *The Patient as Person: Explorations in Medical Ethics* (Yale University Press, 1970) 1–58.

children resulted in disadvantage to the entire paediatric population and that if there were no realistic risks, children *should* participate because their participation would benefit others.[45] The key issues in the debate about children's participation have not fundamentally changed since the 1970s but are perhaps particularly exacerbated in relation to clinical trials. There are a number of difficulties that arise in this context notwithstanding the importance of carrying out such research in the interests of all children, namely the capacity of the child to assent to their own participation and how their best interests should be protected, particularly in non-therapeutic clinical trials. There are a number of international documents and conventions which contain provisions in relation to research with children and which will therefore provide a context for the discussion which follows.

[13.26] The Convention on Human Rights and Biomedicine (1997),[46] commonly known as the Oviedo Convention, provides in art 16 that research on persons may be carried out only if there is no alternative of comparable effectiveness to research on humans; the risks which may be incurred by that person are not disproportionate to the potential benefits of the research; the research project has been approved by the competent body after independent examination of its scientific merit, including assessment of the importance of the aim of the research, and multidisciplinary review of its ethical acceptability; and the persons undergoing research have been informed of their rights and the safeguards prescribed by law for their protection. Article 17 provides that in addition to the conditions set out in art 16, there are further applicable conditions where the person does not have capacity to give consent to their participation in the research, namely that the results of the research have the potential to produce real and direct benefit to their health; research of comparable effectiveness cannot be carried out on individuals capable of giving consent; the necessary authorisation provided for under art 6 has been given specifically and in writing; and the person concerned does not object. It goes on to provide in subs 2 that exceptionally and under the protective conditions prescribed by law, where the research does not have the potential to produce results of direct benefit to the health of the person concerned, such research may be authorised subject to the conditions mentioned above and that the research has the aim of contributing, through significant improvement in the scientific understanding of the individual's condition, disease or disorder, to the ultimate attainment of results capable of conferring benefit to the person concerned or to other persons in the same age category or afflicted with the same disease or disorder or having the same condition, and the research entails only minimal risk and minimal burden for the individual concerned. Ireland has not signed the Oviedo Convention.

[13.27] The European Communities (Clinical Trials on Medicinal Products for Human Use) Regulations, 2004[47] were introduced in Ireland to give effect to Directive 2001/20/EC of the European Parliament, known as the Clinical Trials Directive. Schedule 1 Part

---

[45] McCormick, 'Proxy Consent in Experimental Situations' (1974) 18 Perspectives Biol & Med 2.
[46] http://conventions.coe.int/Treaty/en/Treaties/Word/164.doc (accessed 6 June 2011).
[47] SI 190/2004.
http://www.dohc.ie/legislation/statutory_instruments/pdf/si20040190.pdf?direct=1 (accessed 6 June 2011).

4 of the Regulations sets out the conditions and principles which apply in relation to a minor.[48] They include the following conditions: every person with parental responsibility for the minor must have had an interview with the investigator, or another member of the investigating team, in which he or she has been given the opportunity to understand the nature, objectives, risks and inconveniences of the trial and the conditions under which it is to be conducted; that person's consent has been given in consultation with the registered medical practitioner who has been treating the minor; the minor has received information according to his or her capacity of understanding, from staff with experience with minors, regarding the trial, its risks and its benefits; and the explicit wish of a minor who is capable of forming an opinion and assessing the information referred to in the previous paragraph to refuse participation in, or to be withdrawn from, the clinical trial at any time is considered by the investigator. Under the Regulations, no incentives or financial inducements may be given to the minor or to a person with parental responsibility for that minor, except provision for compensation in the event of injury or loss. The clinical trial must relate directly to a clinical condition from which the minor suffers or is of such a nature that it can only be carried out on minors, and some direct benefit for the group of patients involved in the clinical trial is to be obtained from that trial. It must not be possible to conduct the clinical trial other than by using minors. The principles applicable to all such trials involving minors include the following: that the clinical trial has been designed to minimise pain, discomfort, fear and any other foreseeable risk in relation to the disease and the minor's stage of development; the risk threshold and the degree of distress must be specially defined and constantly monitored; and the interests of the patient must always prevail over those of science and society.

The various stages in the development of children raise different issues in terms of clinical research and will thus be considered separately below.

Foetal research

[13.28] Firstly, we will look at research on foetuses.[49] It is important to carry out research on foetuses and the uterine environment in order to better understand some common diseases affecting children, causes of miscarriage, neurological disabilities and so on. Foetuses may become available for research in Ireland as a result of miscarriage.[50] The distress experienced by a woman who suffers a miscarriage makes it difficult to anticipate how she might be approached in such circumstances to give consent. This issue was briefly addressed in the Report of the Working Group on Post Mortems in 2006,[51] which considered the application of the recommendations of the Madden Report on Post Mortem Practice and Procedure to children who died before birth. Although the

---

[48] The Directive defines an adult as a person who has attained the age of 16. However, although in Ireland the Non-Fatal Offences Against the Person Act 1997 enables an individual over 16 to give consent for surgical, medical or dental treatment, the application of the Act to research is unclear. Therefore, for research purposes, a child is understood to be any person under the age of 18, and the consent of the child's parent(s)/legal guardian is generally required.

[49] Embryo research is controversial in Ireland, as in other countries, due to the differing moral positions in relation to the status of the embryo. This is considered in Ch 6.

[50] In jurisdictions where abortion is permissible, the aborted foetuses may also be available for research purposes with the consent of the woman.

[51] http://www.dohc.ie/publications/pdf/PostMortem.pdf?direct=1 (acessed 6 June 2011).

focus of the report was to look at the area of post-mortem examinations, the possibility of seeking consent from the parents for the use of the foetal remains for teaching and research purposes was also considered.

[13.29] The Report explains that there is no specific statutory regulation of examination of foetal remains in Ireland. It is therefore unclear whether the foetus would come within the definition of a 'person', as it has not achieved independent existence. In *McGeehan v National Maternity Hospital, Stanley and Rafter*[52] the question arose as to whether the Plaintiff was entitled to take an action as a dependent under the Civil Liability Act 1961 on behalf of her child who was stillborn in the National Maternity Hospital in 1991. Section 48(1) of that Act provides that where the death of a person is caused by a wrongful act such that that person, if he had survived, would have been entitled to take an action, then the dependents can bring an action. Section 58 provides that the law relating to wrongs applies to an unborn child for his protection in the same way as if the child were born, provided the child is subsequently born alive. Kearns J held that the only interpretation of the Act is that 'no such wrongful action is deemed in law to take place where the child is not born alive'. However, he also stressed that he was not deciding the issue 'on the basis that the child was not a person and in any way was to be regarded in any way less than any other citizen, whether born alive or, tragically in this case, as a still birth.'

[13.30] The preparation of tissue blocks[53] and slides[54] is an integral and important part of all post-mortem examinations. However, some families may object to the removal and retention of even the smallest amount of tissue. The Report recommends that provided a valid authorisation is given, these blocks and slides may be retained and subsequently used for legitimate educational and research purposes by the hospital.[55] These recommendations have not yet been given statutory force and in the current absence of human tissue legislation in Ireland, it remains a matter of good practice for hospitals to ensure that any research use of foetal remains is subject to consent or authorisation from the parent(s).

Research on newborn infants

[13.31] In relation to some therapeutic clinical trials carried out in this early stage of life, doctors may be hoping to discover which treatment is most effective for premature infants who have breathing difficulties, seizures and other difficulties shortly after birth. Therefore, there are clearly sound and important scientific and ethical justifications for carrying out such research. Research on premature infants is in principle similar to research on children of any age prior to maturity in that the locus of decision-making is with their parents or guardians. However, the context in which such research is carried out raises practical and ethical difficulties in relation to informed consent, as the parents may be distressed following a premature and unexpected delivery of the baby, the

---

[52]   *McGeehan v National Maternity Hospital, Stanley and Rafter* (21 April 2004) HC, Kearns J.

[53]   Small pieces of tissue, usually measuring 2.5 x 2 x 0.75cm, are embedded in paraffin wax and stored in boxes.

[54]   Shavings of tissue blocks about 1/100thmm thick, mounted on glass slides. The glass slides are stained in various ways and placed on the microscope for examination.

[55]   Report of the Working Group on Post Mortem Practice, http://www.dohc.ie/publications/pdf/PostMortem.pdf?direct=1 (acessed 6 June 2011) at 12.

mother may be physically exhausted and in post-partum pain, and the fact that the baby is in neonatal intensive care is likely to be a source of extreme anxiety for both parents. In an English report arising out of complaints by parents of babies who had been enrolled into such a trial, it was acknowledged that there was general recognition and acceptance in society of the need for, and therefore the need to take part in, research of good quality if there are to be advances in medical practice. 'What was totally unacceptable to those interviewed was the apparent lack of adequate explanation, of choice and of consequent properly elicited and recorded consent, and of involvement in later decision making'.[56]

[13.32] Therapeutic research on this category of patients may be justified on the basis that the research has the potential to benefit the child. Therefore, if valid informed consent can be obtained from the parents of the newborn child then, providing the other conditions in relation to minimal risk are satisfied, the research may proceed. However, despite the presence of their signature on a consent form, this will not be sufficient if the parents later complain that their consent was not freely given due to undue influence or pressure from the doctor, particularly where he has a dual role as researcher as well as the person responsible for the treatment of their child.[57] In the face of such an allegation the doctor would have to show that he had adequately explained the gravity of the situation and had taken reasonable steps to ensure that the parent(s) did not overestimate the possible benefits to the child nor underestimated the risks. In light of this it would be best practice, where possible, to have an independent person present during the consent process to provide advice and support to distressed parents, as well as giving information in comprehensible language with as much time as possible in the circumstances for the parents to consider their decision. Details on the consent process involved in such research should be carefully scrutinised by the relevant research ethics committee prior to granting approval for the research.[58]

[13.33] If consent cannot be obtained due, for example, to the absence of the father and the temporary incapacity of the mother due to her medical condition after birth, the situation is very difficult. In an emergency situation where the research drug must be given within a short time after delivery, the mother may be unconscious and the researchers will have to establish that it is in the best interests of the child to be enrolled in the trial.[59] 'But if participation in the trial exposes the child to foreseeable risks which are high or out of proportion to the potential benefits, or participation in the trial deprives the child of the opportunity of receiving alternative treatment which would have been of benefit to her, then inclusion in the trial will be unlawful.'[60] If the mother is

---

56   In addition to research governance failings, there were also allegations that some of the consent forms purportedly signed by the parents were not valid. Report of a Review of the Research Framework in North Staffordshire Hospital NHS Trust, available at http:// www.publications.doh.gov.uk/pdfs/northstaffsexec.pdf (acessed 6 June 2011).

57   See discussion above at para **13.06**.

58   Plomer, 'Participation of Children in Clinical Trials: UK, European and International Legal Perspectives on Consent' (2000) Med Law I Vol 5, 1–24 at 15.

59   Emergency research and the possibility of a waiver of consent are considered below at para **13.49**.

60   Plomer, 'Participation of Children in Clinical Trials: UK, European and International Legal Perspectives on Consent' (2000) Med Law I Vol 5, 1–24 at 13.

not unconscious she may nonetheless be so exhausted, shocked or distressed in the circumstances that this may preclude her ability to understand the necessary medical information to enable her to make a decision as to whether to consent to her child's participation in the trial. The doctor must be extremely cautious in such circumstances before deciding that the mother's psychological condition precludes her capacity to give consent.[61] The test for capacity discussed in Chapter 9[62] requires certain conditions to be satisfied before coming to that conclusion and the doctor should seek a second opinion, preferably from a psychologist or psychiatrist, to ascertain whether the mother has decision-making capacity. Plomer describes the potential legal liability that might arise in such circumstances:

> Clinicians who proceed to include a new born baby in a clinical trial in an emergency without the parent(s) consent on the basis that the parents' mental distress or shock impaired their legal capacity, without independent evidence to support their judgment, are undoubtedly leaving themselves open to an action in battery. If the child has not suffered and even benefitted from inclusion in the trial, liability will still arise in battery if the research procedures involved any form of physical intervention or examination of the child's body, as the tort does not require proof of damage but protects instead the physical integrity of the individual's body: the essence of the tort of battery is the 'unpermitted contact'.[63]

[13.34] The situation is perhaps more difficult in relation to non-therapeutic research with infants. Most guidance documents in the US and England agree that such research is justified in principle in the interests of benefitting other children, although it should not be carried out if the research could be done on adults instead.[64] The guidelines also say that while the consent of the parents or guardians must be obtained, this may not be sufficient if the proposed research involves more than minimal risk to the child, although there is no universal definition of 'minimal risk' in this context. It is thought that the taking of a single blood sample from a child would represent the threshold of minimal risk, though there are different views of the inherent risks of venepuncture for a small child.

Research involving young children and adolescents

[13.35] As discussed in Chapter 11, when the patient is a young child who does not have the legal capacity to make such decisions, someone else, usually a parent, must give consent on his behalf. However, this does not detract from the value and importance of respecting the autonomy of the child and ensuring that they participate as much as possible in decision-making about their own health. Communication to and with

---

[61] Plomer, 'Participation of Children in Clinical Trials: UK, European and International Legal Perspectives on Consent' (2000) Med Law I Vol 5, 1–24 at 13.
[62] See para **9.11** et seq.
[63] Plomer, 'Participation of Children in Clinical Trials: UK, European and International Legal Perspectives on Consent' (2000) Med Law I Vol 5, 1–24 at 14.
[64] For example, the National Institutes of Health in the US *Policy and Guidelines on the Inclusion of Children as Participants in Research Involving Human Subjects* (1998); US Dept of Health and Human Services Code of Federal Regulations, Title 45, part 46 (2005); Royal College of Paediatrics and Child Health: Ethics Advisory Committee 'Guidelines for the Ethical Conduct of Medical Research Involving Children' (2000) 82 Arch Dis Child 177; Medical Research Council *Medical Research Involving Children* (2007).

children, parents or guardians and the medical profession is vital if meaningful collaboration is to take place in making such decisions. Respect for the autonomy of the child entails the facilitation, wherever possible, of the child's right to make his own decisions. Guidelines on treatment of children generally provide that the child's wishes should be taken into account and, as the child grows towards maturity, given more weight accordingly. In order to participate meaningfully in decision-making, children should be given the necessary information in a way that they can understand so that they can fully comprehend the consequences of their decision.

[13.36] The United Nations Convention of the Rights of the Child[65] requires that 'the child who is capable of forming his or her own views [be accorded] the right to express those views freely in all matters affecting the child, the views of the child being given due weight in accordance with the age and maturity of the child.' In 2009, the United Nations Committee on the Rights of the Child stated that '[C]hildren, including young children, should be included in decision-making processes, in a manner consistent with their evolving capacities.'[66] Many professional organisations have thus recommended that decision-making involving the health care of older children and adolescents should include, to the greatest possible degree, the assent of the patient, as well as the participation of the parents and doctors. Participation by the child in medical research raises the same issues about the extent to which the autonomy of the child is respected in enabling the child to make his own decision while at the same time ensuring that the risks of the research do not outweigh any potential harms to the child. These issues have been discussed more fully in the context of medical treatment decisions in Chapter 11.[67]

[13.37] For children under the age of legal maturity, it is important that health-care professionals do not merely pay lip-service to the notion of respecting the child's need for information, but that the child is listened to and provided with sufficient information in a form that is suitable for the child's age to enable him to share the responsibility for the decision-making. This means that the child will not be the only decision-maker but will share this power and responsibility with adults. Difficulties may, of course, arise where there are different views expressed by the child and his parents in this context and ultimately a decision may be made by the adults in the child's best interests to which the child objects. It is argued that if the child's views are to be overruled, the reasons for this should be explained to the child in language that he can understand and efforts should be made to act in a way that most closely accords with the child's wishes where possible.[68]

[13.38] In relation to the provision of information about research, the Child Health Ethics Advisory Committee of the Royal College of Paediatrics states that researchers must discuss a number of issues with families including: the purpose of the research, whether there are any direct benefits for the child, the difference between treatment and research, the meaning of research terms used,[69] the nature of each procedure, how long it will continue, the potential harms, the name of the responsible doctor and how children

---

65   General Assembly Resolution 44/25, November 1989, art 12.

66   Committee on the Rights of the Child, General Comment No 12 *The Right of the Child to Be Heard* (2009) UN Doc CRC/C/GC/12, para 100.

67   See para **11.77** et seq.

68   Donnelly and Kilkelly, 'Child-Friendly Healthcare: Delivering on the Right to Be Heard' (Winter 2011) Med L Rev, 19, pp 27–54 at 31–32.

can withdraw from the project.[70] Consent must also be given freely and without any pressure from the researchers or doctors.

[13.39] It is generally accepted that a decision about a child's competence to give consent should not depend on an arbitrary age limit but rather on an evaluation of the child's ability to understand the nature and purpose of the research and the implications of their decision.[71] This can be influenced by the way in which information is presented to children, and if it is presented in a way that children can understand, such as using age-appropriate language, illustrations and props, then many children will be competent. From a legal perspective, it may be simpler to have a cut-off point for consent and therefore legislation in many countries provides for consent from parents as proxies where the child is under that cut-off point. This usually ranges from 14–16 years of age. Wendler argues that while development varies across individual children, existing data suggests that most children develop this ability by approximately age 14. He argues that it is at this age that most children begin to understand that there are moral reasons to help others, even when doing so is not required, and this may place burdens on them. He suggests that until instruments are developed to assess the assent capacity of individual children, this age should therefore be used as the threshold for assent.[72]

[13.40] In Ireland, s 23 of the Non-Fatal Offences against the Person Act 1997 provides that the legal age of maturity for the purposes of giving consent to medical treatment is 16 years. However, this does not apply to medical research, which therefore means that in this context the legal age for the giving of personal consent is 18 years.

Research involving adults lacking capacity to give consent

[13.41] In the same way as it is necessary to conduct paediatric research in order to provide benefit to children, it is also important to carry out research to ensure the future well-being of incapacitated adults while at the same time ensuring that their rights are not infringed. As Liddell et al point out:

> Not only is research necessary to help identify, understand and manage the unique diseases and conditions which affect people with mental illness, intellectual disability, age-related illness and critical conditions, it is also necessary to address the atypical effects of standard therapies on their bodies. The poor evidence base, the frequency of negative outcomes and the lack of specific therapies suggest that this research should be regarded as a public health priority. To deny incapacitated adults the benefits of medical research through unduly

---

[69] In consent documents, different words are sometimes used to describe the same thing eg 'research project', 'research study', 'research experiment' and 'medical study'. These are considered by researchers as semantically equivalent but parents may rate the risks differently depending on their perception of the description used. See Cico et al, 'Informed Consent Language and Parents' Willingness to Enrol Their Children in Research' (2011) IRB: Ethics & Human Research, Vol 33, No 2.

[70] Royal College of Paediatrics and Child Health: Ethics Advisory Committee: Guidelines for the Ethical Conduct of Medical Research Involving Children (2000). See also van der Pal, Sozanska, Madden, Kosmeda, Debinska, Danielewicz, Boznanski and Detmar: 'Opinions of Children about Participation in Medical Genetic Research' *Public Health Genomics (DOI: 10.1159/000294173).*

[71] Medical Research Council Ethics Guide: Medical Research Involving Children (2004).

[72] Wendler, 'Assent in Paediatric Research: Theoretical and Practical Considerations' (2006) Journal of Medical Ethics 32: 229–234.

cautious research regulation is irresponsible; not kind nor caring. It condemns the population of incapacitated adults to poor quality care.[73]

[13.42] The Clinical Trials Directive makes provision for research involving adults who are incapable of giving informed consent. Article 5 provides that such persons may be included in a trial only if the research meets the general requirements for research participation amongst the general population listed in art 3, as well as nine further specific requirements. The general requirements refer to an assessment that the benefits of the proposed trial outweigh the risks; the necessity to give the participant the opportunity to understand the objectives, risks and inconveniences of the trial; the rights of the participants to physical and mental integrity and privacy; the requirement for written consent; the right to withdraw from the trial at any time; and the provision of insurance to cover the liability of the researcher and sponsor of the trial.

[13.43] The additional requirements that apply to incapacitated adults may be summarised as follows:

(i)   the informed consent of the legal representative must be obtained. This must represent the subject's presumed will and may be revoked at any time;

(ii) the subject must receive information according to his/her capacity about the trial;

(iii) the explicit wish of the subject who is capable of forming an opinion, to refuse participation must be considered by the investigator;

(iv) no financial incentives may be given except compensation;

(v)   such research is essential to validate data obtained in clinical trials on persons able to give informed consent and relates directly to a life-threatening or debilitating clinical condition from which the subject suffers;

(vi) the trial has been designed to minimise pain, discomfort and fear, and is constantly monitored;

(vii) the ethics committee with expertise in the specific disease and the patient population concerned (or having taken advice from such experts) has endorsed the protocol;

(viii) the interests of the patient must always prevail over those of science and society;

(ix) there are grounds for expecting that administering the medicinal product to be tested will produce a benefit to the patient outweighing the risks or produce no risk at all.

[13.44] Liddell et al take issue with many of these requirements on the basis that the wording is unclear, ill-advised or unduly restrictive. For example, they say it fails to recognise any exceptions to the requirement for prior consent, which causes severe problems for research into emergency and critical care. It also fails to define who should be recognised as a legal representative, with the result that Member States have highly disparate definitions with some states such as Austria and Germany imposing a requirement that such a person must be appointed by a judge, whereas in the

---

[73] Liddell et al, 'Medical Research Involving Incapacitated Adults: Implications of the EU Clinical Trials Directive 2001/20/EC' (Autumn 2006) Med Law Review 14, pp 367–417 at 370.

Netherlands a life companion may act as proxy. In England and Northern Ireland any person who by virtue of their relationship with the subject is suitable, available and willing to act as the legal representative will be sufficient. If no such person exists, a doctor primarily responsible for the patient's medical treatment or a person nominated by their doctor may act as long as he is not connected with the trial. Although some pluralism is perhaps justified, it makes international trials cumbersome and unwieldy as well as enabling some member states to define legal representatives in an overly broad way irrespective of whether they are appropriately qualified or subject to potential conflicts of interest.[74] It would have been preferable to define legal representatives on the basis of their personal relationship with the participant so that they may anticipate the way in which the participant may experience the research, and be ready to revoke consent in circumstances where the burdens of the trial become too great.

INFORMED CONSENT

[13.45] The duty imposed upon those engaged in medical research…to those who offer themselves as subjects for experimentation… is at least as great as, if not greater than, the duty owed by the ordinary physician or surgeon to his patient. There can be no exceptions to the ordinary requirements of disclosure in the case of research as there may well be in ordinary medical practice…The subject of medical experimentation is entitled to a full and frank disclosure of all the facts, probabilities and opinions which a reasonable man might be expected to consider before giving his consent.[75]

[13.46] The theory, history and principles of informed consent have been discussed in Chapter 9 in the context of medical treatment.[76] The importance of respecting self-determination is recognised in both ethics and law in most jurisdictions and is now regarded as an essential prerequisite for research with human beings.[77] As discussed above, this was not always so – prior to the 20th century people were used for research without their knowledge and contrary to their wishes in many cases. In modern times it is widely recognised and enshrined in law as well as in ethical guidance documents that participants must be given the opportunity to choose whether to participate based on appropriate information as well as an assessment of their capacity to comprehend the information and make a decision. The kind of information commonly required to be given to potential participants includes the nature of the research, its purposes, risks and benefits, alternatives to participation, who will carry out the research, and whether participants can later change their mind. The amount of information can be overwhelming, and the Belmont Report also rightly points out the importance of ensuring that the research participants understand the data presented to them.

---

[74] Liddell et al, 'Medical Research Involving Incapacitated Adults: Implications of the EU Clinical Trials Directive 2001/20/EC' (Autumn 2006) Med Law Review 14, pp 367–417 at 397.

[75] *Halushka v University of Saskatchewan* 52 WW R 608 (Sask 1965).

[76] See para **9.49** et seq.

[77] However, in some cultures autonomy is not valued in the same way as in Western countries so, for example, husbands may give consent for the involvement of their wives, or the tribal elders may give consent on behalf of those living in their community.

Researchers have a moral responsibility to adapt information so that it is understandable by potential research participants. It should be presented in an organised way in languages…that are understood by potential subjects. The need to ensure comprehension of the study becomes more important as the study's degree of risk increases.[78]

[13.47] The way in which information is presented forms a crucial part of ensuring comprehension, as researchers commonly use a technical vocabulary that acts as a barrier to understanding for those unfamiliar with such terms. However, there is a danger too in over-simplifying information if watered-down, non-technical language is used. The way in which the information is framed may reflect a bias on the part of the researcher which may lead potential participants to focus on the potential benefits without reflecting carefully on the risks. Murphy says that when poorly conducted, the informed consent process may be little more than 'an empty ritual, a piece of paper put in front of a person for a quick signature'.[79] Equally, if the consent process is too lengthy and complicated there is a risk that potential participants may not give close enough attention to their involvement. Therefore, it is difficult for researchers to know what standards of disclosure should be used in this regard and many researchers express frustration with the current informed consent process and find it a confusing area of law.[80] Research is, of course, different from medical treatment in that it is not always possible to know in advance what the potential risks and benefits will be. Thus, some argue that consent can never be fully informed in the same way as perhaps consent to medical treatment can be.

> Despite the extensive laboratory testing of a new drug, the fact remains that a clinical trial is an experiment. The information most useful to a potential volunteer – what will happen? – is unknown. Even the known 'facts' such as toxicology reports and statistics from animal testing are merely interpretations of data. A statistician can easily manipulate such data to imply the desired results. Those with experience in financial accounting may testify to the manipulability of numerical data. [81]

[13.48] In the design of information sheets and consent forms, researchers, doctors and research ethics committees discuss at length how to effectively communicate the risks of participation. As mentioned above, although the readability of these documents must be set at a level that enables participants of all reading abilities to access the information, it is also the case that if the document is overly simple it may not be specific enough to communicate the particular risks and it may necessarily be too long and onerous to expect a layperson to read. Ziker says that 'efficiency demands the standardisation of informed consent documents. However, to effectively communicate health risks, we must resist standardisation and consider the subjective, individual needs of the volunteer. The informed consent document should serve merely as a starting point for the communication.'[82] Further study is required to scrutinise the gap between the ethical

---

[78]   Murphy, *Case Studies in Biomedical Research Ethics* (2004) Mass. Inst. of Technology at 54.
[79]   Murphy, *Case Studies in Biomedical Research Ethics* (2004) Mass. Inst. of Technology at 57.
[80]   Dodds-Smith, 'Clinical Research' in Dyer (ed) *Doctors, Patients and the Law* (Blackwell Publishing, 1992) 140 at 155.
[81]   Ziker, 'Reviving Informed Consent: Using Risk Perception in Clinical Trials' (2003) Duke L & Tech Rev 15.
[82]   Ziker, 'Reviving Informed Consent: Using Risk Perception in Clinical Trials' (2003) Duke L & Tech Rev 15.

ideal of informed consent to research and the reality of the communication between researchers and participants in order to inform the further development of effective policies and informed consent processes in this context. Particular issues relating to informed consent arise in relation to emergency and genetic research, which are considered below.

Emergency research

[13.49] Although it is widely accepted that the consent of the participant is necessary for participation in research, this is usually not possible in emergency research. Such research is very valuable and important in seeking new and more effective treatments for brain trauma, stroke, heart attack and other sudden incapacitating conditions where patients are rushed to hospital for emergency treatment. Typically, treatment for these conditions must commence within hours, preferably as soon as possible. It is often impossible to seek consent within such a tight time frame because the patient is unconscious or unaccompanied. It is necessary to consider how best we should balance the values involved in emergency research, including the crucial need for research to test promising treatments for patients in an emergency setting as weighed against the need to protect individuals from exploitation and harm in the event that the new therapies turn out to be harmful, and respect for autonomy which entails seeking consent from persons prior to their participation in research.[83] Although medical treatment may be given to a person in such circumstances in order to save their lives or prevent serious injury, this does not necessarily apply to research in the same way. Some argue that research in these circumstances is ethically unsound and should simply not take place at all but this would inhibit very valuable research and would be contrary to public health. It may be argued that unless participation in research offers the patient the best chance of saving their life or avoiding serious injury, it may not be ethically justifiable to enrol them in a trial without their consent.[84] However, Brody argues that even when individual autonomy cannot be respected because consent cannot be obtained, the research can still be conducted ethically, as long as other values are sufficiently protected, namely great social need, potential for direct benefit to the participants, and protection of individuals from exploitation and harm.[85]

[13.50] The Council of Europe Convention on Human Rights and Biomedicine (1997), commonly referred to as the Oviedo Convention, provides that consent may be dispensed with only when because of an emergency situation the appropriate consent cannot be obtained (art 8).[86] The purpose of this article is to allow the doctor to act immediately in an emergency without having to wait until the patient or his representative gives consent. This applies to situations such as where the patient is in a coma following an accident and it is necessary to treat in order to protect the patient's life and/or health. Treatments without consent are limited to those which cannot be delayed. The Convention does not explicitly refer to medical research in this context and therefore it is arguable that art 8 does not extend to the participation of patients in emergency research, particularly since the exception given in the article is expressly

---

83   Brody, 'In Case of Emergency: No Need for Consent' (1997) 27 Hastings Centre Rep at 7.

84   Jackson, *Medical Law: Text, Cases and Materials* (OUP, 2010) at 479.

85   Brody, 'In Case of Emergency: No Need for Consent' (1997) 27 Hastings Centre Rep at 7.

86   Ireland is not currently a signatory to the Oviedo Convention.

limited to circumstances where treatment is necessary for 'the benefit of the health of the individual concerned'. Articles 16 and 17 of the Convention refer to the need to obtain specific consent in writing in advance of a clinical trial and there is no mention of an exception for emergency research in either of these two articles. Plomer argues that:

> If the benefit in question was intended by the writers of the Convention to extend to the potential, hypothetical benefits of research rather than the proven benefits of a given treatment then arguably Article 8 would have been drafted differently. In particular, one would have expected the expression 'potential benefit' to have been expressly used to indicate that the emergency provisions contained in Article 8 extend to the conduct of research consistently with Articles 16 and 17 which regulate the conduct of research and refer to the hypothesised benefits of research as 'potential'.[87]

[13.51] In 1996 the European Union adopted guidelines for good clinical practice through the International Conference on Harmonisation of Technical Requirements for Registration of Pharmaceuticals for Human Use (ICH). The objective of the guidelines is to provide a unified standard for the EU, Japan and the US to facilitate the mutual acceptance of clinical data by the regulatory authorities in these jurisdictions. The guidelines are more extensive than the Convention in respect of certain matters such as informed consent, as they require the disclosure of information to the participant in relation to reasonably foreseeable risks and benefits, alternative procedures, rights to compensation in the event of trial-related injury, confidentiality of records and the right to withdraw from the trial at any time. In relation to emergency research the Guidelines allow such research to proceed in the absence of prior consent in the following circumstances:

- the situation is an emergency;
- prior consent of the subject is not possible;
- the subject's legally acceptable representative is not available;
- measures to protect the rights, safety and well-being of the subject have been described in the protocol and/or elsewhere;
- the relevant ethics committee has approved the measures and protocol, and;
- the subject or his/her legally acceptable representative should be informed about the trial as soon as possible and consent to continue should be requested.

[13.52] Plomer explains that there appears to be greater flexibility in the ICH guidelines in this context in that they do not require that the intervention is for the immediate benefit of the individual participant. Therefore, emergency research is not restricted to therapeutic research only and may include non-therapeutic research. 'Such a possibility, however, will undoubtedly give rise to legitimate concerns that the interests of highly vulnerable patients run the danger of being sacrificed in the interest of science. The requirement that the research receive prior approval from an independent research board is undoubtedly an important control. But the requirement that the protocol should contain a description of measures to protect the rights, safety and well-being of the human subject seems too unspecific and weak to import any meaningful limits.'[88]

---

[87] Plomer, 'Participation of Children in Clinical Trials: UK, European and International Legal Perspectives on Consent' (2000) Med Law I Vol 5, 1–24 at 17.

[88] Plomer, 'Participation of Children in Clinical Trials: UK, European and International Legal Perspectives on Consent' (2000) Med Law I Vol 5, 1–24 at 20.

[13.53] In Ireland the European Communities (Clinical Trials on Medicinal Products for Human Use) Regulations 2004[89] do not make any provision for an exception to the requirement for consent in cases of emergency research. The regulations provide that research on adults lacking capacity to give informed consent is only allowed if, inter alia: consent is given by the person's legal representative, the trial relates to a life-threatening or debilitating condition from which the person suffers, it has been approved by a relevant ethics committee and there are grounds for expecting that it will produce a benefit to the patient outweighing the risks or produce no risk at all. This means that, in principle, if no legal representative has previously been appointed in relation to the patient (which, for example, would commonly apply in circumstances involving otherwise healthy adults who have sustained injuries in a road traffic accident), the patient cannot be enrolled in the trial.

[13.54] In the UK, regulations were introduced in 2006 to allow such trials to proceed notwithstanding the absence of consent from a legal representative provided that it is necessary to act as a matter of urgency, it is not practicable to obtain consent from a legal representative, the procedure has been approved by an ethics committee and steps must be taken to seek consent either from the patient himself after recovery of capacity or from a legal representative as soon as practicable after the initial emergency has passed.[90]

[13.55] The responses of Member States to the problems raised by emergency research have been diverse. Some countries adopted a waiver system which allows the research to proceed in the absence of proxy consent if treatment and associated research must commence as a matter of urgency. In most instances, however, it was not a complete waiver but rather a deferral of consent until the patient or his legal representative could be informed and their consent sought to continued participation. The period of time during which consent is waived is usually capped until such time as the emergency circumstances have passed, and as a further protection, notice must be posted at the clinical trial sites notifying the public that such trials are being conducted on patients who are unable to consent.[91]

[13.56] In the absence of explicit statutory provisions in Ireland, non-therapeutic research conducted on patients without consent in accordance with the ICH guidelines on emergencies would probably be unlawful under the terms of the Clinical Trials Regulations. However, it seems that the European legislative bodies never intended to block emergency research and Liddell et al argue that the European Commission takes the view that art 5(a) need not be adhered to literally. Recital 10 of Directive 2005/28 (the Good Clinical Practice Directive) states that the detailed rules adopted in Member States pursuant to the Clinical Trials Directive to protect from abuse those individuals

---

89   SI 190/2004 implementing the European Clinical Trials Directive 2001/20/EC, amended subsequently by SI 878/2004 (charges), SI 374/2006 (investigators brochure and other changes) and most recently in 2009 (SI 1) to add advanced therapy medicinal products.

90   Medicines for Human Use (Clinical Trials) (Amendment No 2) Regulations 2006.

91   Discussed by Liddell *et al*, 'Medical Research Involving Incapacitated Adults: Implications of the EU Clinical Trials Directive 2001/20/EC' (Autumn 2006) Med Law Review 14, pp 367–417 at 404.

who are incapable of giving their informed consent should also cover individuals temporarily incapable of giving their informed consent as in emergency situations. The way in which some countries such as England, Wales and Northern Ireland have interpreted the provisions enables a broad definition of legal representative to be applied so that the patient's doctor or someone appointed by the health service who is unconnected with the trial, can give consent on behalf of the patient if there is no other person suitable or willing to act. This approach would also be consistent with the Helsinki Declaration and the Oviedo Convention, neither of which limit the definition of 'legal representative'.[92]

[13.57] In the United States the Food and Drug Administration (FDA) and the Department of Health and Human Services issued regulations that provide a waiver of informed consent requirements for emergency research under certain conditions.[93] The regulations allow a waiver when the potential subject is in a life-threatening situation, where consent of the subject or a surrogate cannot be obtained, and available treatments are unproven or unsatisfactory. Additional protections for participants are provided by the requirement to publicly disclose the proposed research and consult with the community from which the patients may be drawn. However, Carnahan argues that although in principle a waiver represents a justifiable exception to the requirement of informed consent due to the importance of advancing medical research in emergency care, the wording of this waiver is fraught with ambiguities and may be unethical, as it is not drawn sufficiently narrowly to assure respect for individual autonomy and fails to provide clear guidelines to aid the researcher in complying with the waiver's requirements.[94]

Genetic research

[13.58] When a research study begins, the researcher must have reason to believe, although he does not know for certain, that the intervention will be effective in humans. Research involving genetic material is no different in principle to any other form of research in this regard. Genetic research includes all experimental uses of genetic testing, gene therapy and other forms of gene manipulation in humans.[95] This form of research can be very complicated and sometimes suffers from a negative public perception.[96] In a national study carried out in Ireland in 2005, while those surveyed were generally quite positive about genetic research, there were some reservations

---

92   Liddell, 'Medical Research Involving Incapacitated Adults: Implications of the EU Clinical Trials Directive 2001/20/EC' (Autumn 2006) Med Law Review 14, pp 367–417, at 406.

93   21 CFR 50.24 (1999).

94   Carnahan, 'Promoting Medical Research Without Sacrificing Patient Autonomy: Legal and Ethical Issues Raised by the Waiver of Informed Consent for Emergency Research' (1999) 52 Okla L Rev 565.

95   Holm, 'The Role of Informed Consent in Genetic Experimentation' in Burley and Harris (eds) *A Companion to Genethics* (Blackwell Publishing, 2002) 82–91 at 82.

96   See Medical Research Council's Report in the UK – *Public Perceptions of the Collection of Human Biological Samples* (2000), which showed a wide variation in knowledge and understanding of the goals of genetic research, and a negative association with this type of research where understanding was lacking.

regarding the ethics of such research.[97] O'Neill states that public trust in medicine and science has faltered despite reported successes in this field, increased efforts to respect personal rights, stronger regulations and consideration of environmental concerns than was previously the case.[98]

[13.59] Genetic research challenges the traditional notion that informed consent is adequate to deal with many of the ethical issues that arise in this context and many have argued that informed consent is thus impossible or invalid. Holm questions whether it is in fact possible to inform the average person to such an extent that he is able to give informed consent. He points to the low functional literacy rates even in industrialised societies and says that even for those who do not fall into this category, they may be genetically illiterate in the sense of having no knowledge of modern genetics. In the United States and elsewhere, patients and participants are increasingly given information through pamphlets, videos and computer programmes which aim to convey information more comprehensively and to allow them to make more informed decisions. However, Schwartz says that people interpret data, particularly numerical and graphical information, in different ways and some may give exaggerated importance to small risks or conversely may exhibit optimism bias in exaggerating the chance that they will be in the 'lucky' group that benefits from the trial without suffering any of the potential risks. Whichever group a person falls into depends on the individual's psychology and the way the information is presented, and this can lead to decisions that are not based on reason or facts. As a result, he suggests that more empirical research is necessary to examine the use of quantitative data in decision-making.[99]

[13.60] Genetic research is also actively pursued by pharmaceutical companies in order to investigate the genetics of drugs responsiveness so as to improve the benefit/risk profiles of medicines in the patient populations for whom their products are prescribed. Pharmacogenetics involves the study of DNA variations and their influence on individual differences in drug responses. Research is also ongoing to investigate the effect of polymorphisms[100] in candidate genes known to play a role in a drug's mechanism of action. Research into the genetics of disease characteristics will also help to understand disease susceptibility and biological pathways in order to produce therapies that are better targeted to the disease.[101] Although investment by such

---

[97] For instance, consistent with generally positive attitudes to medical research, over 70% agreed that 'new genetic developments will result in cures for many diseases'. In relation to the ethical question 'Is research on human genetics tampering with nature?', results indicated some concern among the Irish public. A significant proportion (42%) felt that it was tampering with nature. Participants also appeared to be well informed (ie less than 10% reported they had never heard of any of the listed forms of genetic research). Highest approval levels were reported for stem cell research using adult human tissue (49%) and for cloning human cells to combat disease (42%). Cousins, McGee, Ring, Conroy, Kay, Croke, and Tomkin. *Public Perceptions of Biomedical Research: A Survey of the General Population in Ireland*. (Health Research Board: 2005). Psychology Reports. Paper 8.

[98] O'Neill *Autonomy and Trust in Bioethics* (Cambridge University Press, 2002) p 11.

[99] Schwartz, 'Questioning the Quantitative Imperative: Decision Aids, Prevention, and the Ethics of Disclosure,' *Hastings Center Report* 42, No 2 (2011): 30–39.

[100] The presence of genetic variations within a population.

[101] Renegar et al, 'Returning Genetic Research Results to Individuals: Points to Consider' (2006) Bioethics Vol 20, No 1, pp 24–36.

companies in research has produced significant advances in medicine, there is also an associated danger involved in the injection of a profit motive into the system by which new medicines are developed and tested in humans. In particular, there is a concern that doctors who act as researchers acquire financial interests in the drug research they conduct on humans which conflict with their responsibility to protect human participants from unnecessary risk.[102] These issues are considered in the next section.

[13.61] The tragic death of Jesse Gelsinger in 1999 during a gene therapy clinical trial shook the field of clinical research in a similar way to the Tuskegee experiments described earlier. Gelsinger suffered from a rare metabolic disorder that prevents the body from breaking down ammonia. Many people with this disorder die at a young age, but Gelsinger had a mild version and led a fairly normal life through medicine and a special diet. Since a single-gene defect is responsible for OTCD, researchers considered it a prime candidate for gene therapy, a still-experimental treatment that attempts to replace defective genes with normal ones. When he was 18 years old, Gelsinger enrolled in a clinical trial at the University of Pennsylvania as an altruistic measure. He knew he would not benefit from the study himself, but wanted to help those with more severe cases. However, shortly after the researchers injected Gelsinger with the replacement genes his ammonia levels skyrocketed. Within a few days, he suffered brain damage and organ failure, and was in a coma. His family removed him from life support and he died. A Food and Drug Administration (FDA) investigation concluded that the scientists involved in the trial, including the lead researcher, Dr James M. Wilson (University of Pennsylvania), broke several rules of conduct:

- inclusion of Gelsinger as a substitute for another volunteer who dropped out, despite Gelsinger having high ammonia levels that should have led to his exclusion from the trial;
- failure by the university to report that two patients had experienced serious side effects from the gene therapy, and;
- failure to disclose, in the informed-consent documentation, the deaths of monkeys given a similar treatment.

[13.62] The investigation also found that James Wilson did not disclose to the Gelsingers that he was conducting the clinical trial with a private company in which he had a stake, and stood to make a substantial profit if the trial was successful. The FDA sanctioned the researchers and Gelsinger's family sued Wilson and others involved in the study, leading to an out-of-court settlement. It was thought that the revelations, government sanctions and civil lawsuit would lead to widespread reform. However, many argue that this has not come to pass and that things have moved in the opposite direction. More than ever, clinical trials are the lifeblood of the pharmaceutical and biotechnology industries. Their profitability depends upon developing new drugs, which in turn depends upon continued testing on human subjects. Companies can lose substantial sums of money each day that a new drug's approval is held up and demand for quick, easy and plentiful access to human test subjects has therefore become insatiable as companies seek to swiftly move drugs from 'bench to trench'. This

---

102 Gatter, 'Financial Conflicts of Interest in Human Subjects Research; Domestic and International Issues' in Iltis, Johnson and Hinze (eds) *Legal Perspectives in Bioethics* (Routledge, 2008) 29.

situation has led to a number of emerging and proposed research practices which cause concern, including the recruitment of participants from low educational and socio-economic backgrounds and the proliferation of the conduct of clinical trials in the developing world where research ethics governance may not be highly valued.[103] The issue of conflict of interest is discussed further below.

CONFLICT OF INTEREST

[13.63] A number of research 'scandals' in the late 1990s in the US raised issues regarding researchers' and institutional conflicts of interest, the most troubling of which results from a financial interest held by the researcher and/or his institution in the outcome of the clinical trial.[104] The existence of conflicts of interest and their non-disclosure to research participants has led to concerns about the validity of the informed consent process which is a prerequisite for the ethical conduct of clinical trials. The most notable illustration of this problem is that of Jesse Gelsinger, referred to above, where it was alleged that the financial interests of the researcher caused him to take unreasonable risks with Jesse Gelsinger's life that had not been disclosed to Gelsinger, and caused the university's research ethics board to approve both the trial and the fact that a conflict of interest existed.[105] The family argued that informed consent had not been obtained from Jesse due to the non-disclosure of the extent of the financial interests at stake.

[13.64] Financial conflicts of interest may take a number of different forms.[106] Firstly, researchers and research institutions have an interest in obtaining grants from drug companies to conduct future research, as they depend on such grants to help fund substantial portions of their operating expenses. They must compete for these grants with other researchers and institutions and thus offer to conduct the trial in such a way as to encourage the sponsor to choose their particular institution. Secondly, many researchers and institutions have an ownership interest in the material being tested and often establish start-up or spin-off companies to patent their intellectual discoveries. Thirdly, they may own shares in the drug company that is sponsoring the clinical trial. Fourthly, they may have a consulting position within the drug company, arising from the company's desire to benefit from the knowledge of academic expertise. Fifthly, they often receive fees for each participant recruited to the trial. These financial interests may also be supplemented by interests in academic success and promotion, publication interests and other important indirect or non-financial interests. Such financial interests are said to create conflicts because they raise the possibility that researchers will

---

[103] Obasogie, 'Ten Years Later: Jesse Gelsinger's Death and Human Subjects Protection' Bioethics Forum, http://www.geneticsandsociety.org/article.php?id=4955 (accessed 6 June 2011).

[104] Further details of these research scandals are provided by Goldner, 'Regulating Conflicts of Interest in Research: The Paper Tiger Needs Real Teeth' 53 St. Louis U LJ 1211 (2009) at 1229–1231.

[105] *Gelsinger v Trustees of the University of Pennsylvania* (Phila Cnty Ct of CP 2000).

[106] Gatter, 'Financial Conflicts of Interest in Human Subjects Research; Domestic and International Issues' in Iltis, Johnson and Hinze (eds) *Legal Perspectives in Bioethics* (Routledge, 2008), at 31.

conduct clinical trials other than with strict scientific objectivity and may not prioritise the safety and well-being of the human participants in the trials they conduct. This may be evidenced by researchers not observing strict adherence to recruitment criteria, deviating from research protocols, failing to report negative findings of research, failing to inform participants of risks and failing to transfer participants from experimental to standard treatment when their condition has deteriorated.[107]

[13.65] There is also evidence that the involvement of the pharmaceutical industry in research distorts the results.[108] Goldner says that there is a statistically significant relationship between positive findings in studies funded by for-profit entities versus those funded by not-for-profit sources, between industry sponsorship and pro-industry conclusions and between author conflicts of interest and the greater likelihood of reporting a drug to be superior to placebo.[109] He claims that 'industry funding may result in study designs that are more likely to lead to favorable results, such as utilizing protocols that involve placebos or other poor comparators, doses that are inappropriate, carefully constituted experimental populations, inappropriate surrogate endpoints, trials whose lengths are sufficiently short so as to be unlikely to show side effects, and definitions that are unlikely to show activity or not likely to show side effects.' Others too have reported similar findings, for example, Bekelman et al found a 'significant association between industry sponsorship and pro-industry conclusions' in biomedical research, and Lexchin et al showed that studies sponsored by pharmaceutical companies were four times more likely to have outcomes favouring the sponsors' products that studies funded by other sources.[110] Bradley says that 'while there is no evidence that industry funding produces studies of lower methodological quality, it may be that, by setting the research agenda, determining the trial design and suppressing or delaying unfavourable findings, the industry subtly influences the impression of drug therapies under research.'[111] Marcia Angell, former editor of the influential New England Journal of Medicine, states that '[I]t is simply no longer possible to believe much of the clinical research that is published, or to rely on the judgment of trusted physicians or

---

[107] Gatter, 'Financial Conflicts of Interest in Human Subjects Research; Domestic and International Issues' in Iltis, Johnson and Hinze (eds) *Legal Perspectives in Bioethics* (Routledge, 2008), at 34.

[108] Lexchin and O'Donovan state that there is a significant body of empirical sociological evidence of 'corporate bias' in the science of drug testing, bias that has resulted in the pharmaceutical industry being decisive in shaping regulatory policy. Furthermore, they say that recent systematic reviews have shown strong evidence of 'sponsorship bias' in the production of knowledge about pharmaceuticals, evidence that pharmaceutical industry funding of clinical trials significantly enhances the chances of pro-industry results. Lexchin and O'Donovan, 'Prohibiting or "Managing" Conflict of Interest? A Review of Policies and Procedures in Three European Drug Regulation Agencies' Social Science & Medicine 1–5 (2009), doi:10.1016/j.socscimed.2009.09.002.

[109] Goldner, 'Regulating Conflicts of Interest in Research: The Paper Tiger Needs Real Teeth' 53 St. Louis U LJ 1211 (2009) at 1219.

[110] Bekelman, Li and Gross, 'Scope and Impact of Financial Conflicts of Interest in Biomedical Research: A Systematic Review' Journal of the American Medical Association, Vol 289 (2003) pp 454–465; Lexchin et al 'Pharmaceutical Industry Sponsorship and Research Outcome and Quality: Systematic Review' British Medical Journal Vol 326 (2003) pp 1167–1170.

authoritative medical guidelines.' She says that the medical profession needs to wean itself almost entirely from its pervasive dependence on industry money, that conflicts of interest 'corrupt the medical profession, not in a criminal sense, but in the sense of undermining the impartiality that is essential both to medical research and clinical practice'. She argues that:

> There is clearly also a need for the medical profession to wean itself from industry money almost entirely. Although industry–academic collaboration can make important scientific contributions, it is usually in carrying out basic research, not clinical trials, and even here, it is arguable whether it necessitates the personal enrichment of investigators. Members of medical school faculties who conduct clinical trials should not accept any payments from drug companies except research support, and that support should have no strings attached, including control by drug companies over the design, interpretation, and publication of research results.[112]

[13.66] The challenge in this area is to identify policies that will promote greater accountability among research institutions and health-care professionals in relation to their oversight of conflicts of interest. This may, for example, take the form of regulators imposing an absolute prohibition on certain types of conflicts as well as permitting other forms subject to disclosure (for example by way of a public register) and close monitoring.[113] Goldner argues that in order to be effective, an abolitionist position should be enforced with vigour and with meaningful and appropriately severe sanctions for serious violations that would have a significant deterrent effect.[114] He believes that such a policy is unlikely in the United States at least and that a more appropriate response would be to develop new federal conflict of interest committee regulations which would require that institutions develop conflict of interest committees to provide an ethical analysis of the effect of a conflict on research and the appropriate way to remedy it when necessary. A majority of members without institutional ties would be preferable on such a committee. His proposals for reform include recommendations that such regulations should also establish requirements for disclosure of all financial conflicts of interest of any amount to the conflict of interest committee, provide a non-exclusive list of potential management techniques, grant the conflict of interest committee the authority to prohibit research from commencing or continuing until conflict of interest concerns are resolved and require that serious or continuing violations are reported to appropriate governmental agencies. Violations of such regulations, that is the failure of an institution to deal with conflict of interest concerns appropriately and in accordance with the federal guidelines, should result in suspension

---

[111] Bradley, 'The Medical Profession and the Pharmaceutical Industry: Entwined, Entangled or Ensnared?' in O'Donovan and Glavanis-Grantham (eds) *Power, Politics and Pharmaceuticals: Drug Regulation in Ireland in the Global Context* (Cork University Press, 2008) 117–134.

[112] M Angell, 'Drug Companies & Doctors: A Story of Corruption' (January 15, 2009) *New York Review of Books*, http://www.nybooks.com/articles/22237. See also correspondence at http://www.nybooks.com/articles/archives/2009/feb/26/drug-companies-doctors-an-exchange/ [Both accessed 6 June 2006].

[113] See useful discussion of this issue in the US context by Goldner, 'Dealing with Conflicts of Interest in Biomedical Research: IRB Oversight as the Next Best Solution to the Abolitionist Approach' (2000) 28(4) Journal of Law, Med & Ethics 379–404.

[114] Goldner, 'Regulating Conflicts of Interest in Research: The Paper Tiger Needs Real Teeth' 53 St. Louis U LJ 1211 (2009) at 1246–1249.

of federal funding of research for some or all projects at the institution. Researchers who fail to report conflicts or who otherwise violate conflicts of interest regulations should be subject to a range of sanctions, including limitations on participation in research projects, debarment from receiving federal funding and other penalties. He suggests that regulations should also require public disclosure of investigator conflicts of interest, both via a publicly accessible website, and also in informed consent documents provided to participants. Institutions should also be required to mandate training of all investigators in both the ethical norms that underlie appropriate conflict of interest reporting and management prior to the submission of any research protocols for institutional approval.

[13.67] Although there are no legal regulations on this issue in Ireland, there are guidelines in place from the Medical Council as well as the Irish Pharmaceutical Healthcare Association, which represents the pharmaceutical industry in Ireland and which has published a Code of Practice in compliance with advertising regulations for medicinal products.[115] On this point, the Medical Council states in the 7th edition of the Guide to Professional Conduct and Ethics (2009)[116] as follows:

> 53.6 If you are paid, directly or indirectly, by pharmaceutical, medical device or other commercial companies or organisations to conduct medical research, you must make sure that such payment does not influence your study design or interpretation of research data.

> 53.7 If you receive payment, directly or indirectly, from pharmaceutical, medical device or other commercial companies or organisations in connection with medical research, you must address any potential conflict of interest arising from such payment and make an appropriate disclosure in any publication of research results.

LEGAL REGULATION OF BIOMEDICAL RESEARCH IN IRELAND

[13.68] The Control of Clinical Trials Act 1987, as amended in 1990, stipulated that clinical trials had to be approved by the Minister for Health, which would only be forthcoming if the trial had been approved by an authorised ethics committee.[117] The ethics committee were obliged to consider the objectives of the trial, the qualifications of the investigators, the risks to the participants, and the information provided to participants prior to giving consent. No payment to participants was permitted unless this had been specifically approved. If the trial was deemed to be of therapeutic benefit to a person lacking capacity to give consent, a proxy decision-maker could give consent on his behalf. This Act has been replaced by regulations introduced following the European Directive on Clinical Trials in 2001.

---

[115] See http://www.ipha.ie/alist/codes-of-practice.aspx (accessed 6 June 2011).
[116] Medical Council, *Guide to Professional Conduct and Ethics* (7th edn, 2009) available at http://www.medicalcouncil.ie/ (accessed 6 June 2011).
[117] Biomedical research which does not involve a clinical trial on medicinal products is not covered by the Control of Clinical Trials Acts.

[13.69] The European Directive on Clinical Trials 2001[118] was transposed into Irish law by the European Communities (Clinical Trials on Medicinal Products for Human Use) Regulations 2004.[119] These Regulations replace the controls previously applicable to the conduct of clinical trials on medicinal products for human use under the Control of Clinical Trials Acts 1987 and 1990. Therefore, the Regulations do not impact on any other activities traditionally carried out by ethics committees, such as trials not involving medicines. Issues dealt with in the regulations include procedures for obtaining a favourable ethics committee opinion; procedures for obtaining authorisation for the conduct of clinical trials from the Irish Medicines Board;[120] controls that apply to the manufacture, supply and importation of investigational medicinal products; obligations for the reporting of adverse events; obligations for compliance with standards of good clinical practice (GCP) and good manufacturing practice (GMP).

[13.70] Under the Regulations, ethics committees are required to be independent, consisting of health-care professionals and lay members. Schedule 2 of the Regulations provide that the committee must have not more than 21 members, of which at least one-third must be lay members and at least half of those are to be persons who have never been health-care professionals. The committee has responsibility to protect the safety, well-being and rights of participants in a clinical trial. It is also obliged to provide public assurance of that protection in giving their opinion on the study protocol, including in relation to the suitability of the researchers, the facilities, indemnity insurance cover, as well as the adequacy of participant information and informed consent documentation. Such committees are required to be recognised by the Ethics Committee Supervisory Body described in Part 2 of the Regulations.[121]

[13.71] One of the objectives of the Directive was to harmonise provisions across Member States in relation to the conduct of clinical trials, thus making cooperation on such trials easier and more efficient. As part of that objective, the Directive provided that where a trial was being conducted in a number of different sites and in different countries, a single ethics committee opinion from a recognised ethics committee in each Member State would be sufficient. Another important feature of the Directive was that it required that investigational medicinal products should be made available free of charge by the study sponsors. However, it was strenuously argued by academic clinical researchers that this would have significant negative implications for academic research which was not commercially sponsored, as it would impose substantial and perhaps prohibitive cost on the investigator who would be obliged to purchase and make available the study drug or device free of charge to the participants. As a result, an exemption was incorporated into the Regulations for academic researchers whereby the requirement in the Directive will not apply to non-commercial clinical trials conducted by investigator-sponsors, without the participation of the pharmaceutical industry in circumstances where the investigator has no commercial or financial interest in the

---

[118] Directive 2001/20/EC of the European Parliament on the approximation of laws relating to the implementation of good clinical practice in the conduct of clinical trials on medicinal products for human use. (OJ L121 01.05.2001 p. 34–44).

[119] SI 190/2004, which came into force on 1 May 2004.

[120] See http://www.imb.ie/EN/Medicines/Clinical-Trials.aspx (accessed 6 June 2011).

[121] This role has been fulfilled by the Department of Health and Children since 2004.

outcome of the trial insofar as such products have not been obtained free of charge by the investigator-sponsor.

[13.72] The Directive sets out requirements for informed consent which provide that a clinical trial may only be undertaken if the foreseeable risks and inconveniences of the trial have been weighed against the anticipated benefit for the individual trial subject and other present and future patients. The research ethics committee must have come to the conclusion that the anticipated benefits justify those risks. The trial subject (or his legal representative if the person is incapable of giving informed consent) must have had the opportunity, in a prior interview with the investigator (or member of the investigating team), to understand the objectives, risks and inconveniences of the trial, and the conditions under which it is being conducted, and he must have been informed of his right to withdraw from the trial at any time.

[13.73] In relation to the participation of minors, the Directive requires in addition to the foregoing provisions, that the informed consent of the parents or legal guardians must be obtained and that this must represent the minor's presumed will. The minor must have received information according to his capacity to understand the risks and benefits of the trial. Article 4(c) provides that the explicit wish of a competent minor to refuse participation must be 'considered' by the investigator, however it is not specifically stated what the limits of such consideration should be. Article 4 also provides that a clinical trial may only be undertaken on minors if some direct benefit for the group of patients must be obtained from the trial and only where such research is essential to validate data obtained in clinical trials on persons able to give informed consent. Additionally, such research should either relate directly to a clinical condition from which the minor concerned suffers or be of such a nature that it can only be carried out on minors. The ethics committee must have taken advice from paediatric experts prior to endorsing the protocol. Similar conditions are imposed in art 5 of the Directive in relation to clinical trials on incapacitated adults who are incapable of giving informed consent, with the additional pre-requisite in subs (i) that there must be grounds for expecting that administering the medicinal product to be tested will produce a benefit to the patient outweighing the risks or produce no risk at all.

[13.74] It is intended that the functions of the Supervisory Body as set out in the Directive, previously discharged by the Department of Health and Children, will be undertaken by the Health Information and Quality Authority (HIQA). Under the terms of the forthcoming Health Information Bill, it is expected that these functions will include monitoring all approved research ethics committees to see that that they are performing their functions satisfactorily; establishing approved research ethics committees; providing public information in relation to research ethics committees; providing advice, assistance and training to research ethics committees; dealing with complaints; and bringing and prosecuting relevant offences. The specific statutory details of the execution of these functions are not available at the time of writing.

Index